Rates and Limits 20
2018–2019

The following pages contain the Cla the present day, in table form.

Class 1 Contribution Rates 2002–03							
Primary[1]				Secondary[2]			
SR%	RR%	COSR%[5]	COMP%[5]	SR%	RR%	COSR%[3,4]	COMP%[3,4]
10	3.85	8.40	8.40	11.80	11.80	8.30	10.80

1 Primary rates applied only to earnings between the employee's earnings threshold and the UEL.

2 All secondary rates applied only to earnings in excess of the employer's earnings threshold (without limit).

3 The contracted-out rate shown applied only on earnings from the earnings threshold up to the UEL; any balance was subject to the SR (ie not contracted-out rate).

4 In addition, an employer's contracted-out rebate was due on earnings falling between the LEL and the employer's earnings threshold, amounting to 3.5% of such earnings (COSR) or 1.0% of such earnings (COMP).

5 In addition, an employee's contracted-out rebate was due on earnings falling between the LEL and the employee's earnings threshold, amounting to 1.6% of such earnings.

Class 1 Contribution Rates 2003–04, 2004–05, 2005–06 and 2006–07							
Primary[1]				Secondary[2]			
SR%	RR%	COSR%[5]	COMP%[5]	SR%	RR%	COSR%[3, 4]	COMP%[3, 4]
11	4.85	9.40	9.40	12.80	12.80	9.30	11.80
+ 1% on earnings above UEL							

1 Main primary rates applied only to earnings between the employee's earnings threshold and the UEL.

2 All secondary rates applied only to earnings in excess of the employer's earnings threshold (without limit).

3 The contracted-out rate shown applied only on earnings up to the UEL; any balance was subject to the SR (ie not contracted-out rate).

4 In addition, an employer's contracted-out rebate was due on earnings falling between the LEL and the employer's earnings threshold, amounting to 3.5% of such earnings (COSR) or 1.0% of such earnings (COMP).

5 In addition, an employee's contracted-out rebate was due on earnings falling between the LEL and the employee's earnings threshold, amounting to 1.6% of such earnings.

Class 1 Contribution Rates 2007–08 and 2008–09							
Primary[1]				Secondary[2]			
SR%	RR%	COSR%[5]	COMP%[5]	SR%	RR%	COSR%[3, 4]	COMP%[3, 4]
11	4.85	9.40	9.40	12.80	12.80	9.10	11.40
+ 1% on earnings above UEL							

1 Main primary rates applied only to earnings between the employee's earnings threshold and the UEL.

2 All secondary rates applied only to earnings in excess of the employer's earnings threshold (without limit).

3 The contracted-out rate shown applied only on earnings up to the UEL; any balance was subject to the SR (ie not contracted-out rate).

4 In addition, an employer's contracted-out rebate was due on earnings falling between the LEL and the employer's earnings threshold, amounting to 3.7% of such earnings (COSR) or 1.4% of such earnings (COMP).

5 In addition, an employee's contracted-out rebate was due on earnings falling between the LEL and the employee's earnings threshold, amounting to 1.6% of such earnings.

Class 1 Contribution Rates 2009–10 and 2010–11							
Primary[1]				Secondary[2]			
SR%	RR%	COSR%[3, 5]	COMP%[3, 5]	SR%	RR%	COSR%[3, 4]	COMP%[3, 4]
11	4.85	9.40	9.40	12.80	12.80	9.10	11.40
+ 1% on earnings above UEL							

1 Main primary rates applied only to earnings between the employee's earnings threshold and the UEL.

2 All secondary rates applied only to earnings in excess of the employer's earnings threshold (without limit).

3 The contracted-out rate shown applied only on earnings up to the UAP; any balance was subject to the SR (ie not contracted-out rate).

4 In addition, an employer's contracted-out rebate was due on earnings falling between the LEL and the employer's earnings threshold, amounting to 3.7% of such earnings (COSR) or 1.4% of such earnings (COMP).

5 In addition, an employee's contracted-out rebate was due on earnings falling between the LEL and the employee's earnings threshold, amounting to 1.6% of such earnings.

Class 1 Contribution Rates 2011–12							
Primary[1]				Secondary[2]			
SR%	RR%	COSR%[3,5]	COMP%[3,5]	SR%	RR%	COSR%[3,4]	COMP%[3,4]
12	5.85	10.40	10.40	13.80	13.80	10.10	12.40
+ 2% on earnings above UEL							

1 Main primary rates applied only to earnings between the employee's earnings threshold and the UEL.

2 All secondary rates applied only to earnings in excess of the employer's earnings threshold (without limit).

3 The contracted-out rate shown applied only on earnings up to the UAP; any balance was subject to the SR (ie not contracted-out rate).

4 In addition, an employer's contracted-out rebate was due on earnings falling between the LEL and the employer's earnings threshold, amounting to 3.7% of such earnings (COSR) or 1.4% of such earnings (COMP).

5 In addition, an employee's contracted-out rebate was due on earnings falling between the LEL and the employee's earnings threshold, amounting to 1.6% of such earnings.

Class 1 Contribution Rates 2012–13					
Primary[1]			Secondary[2]		
SR%	RR%	COSR%[3,5]	SR%	RR%	COSR%[3,4]
12	5.85	10.60	13.80	13.80	10.40
+ 2% on earnings above UEL					

1 Main primary rates applied only to earnings between the employee's earnings threshold and the UEL.

2 All secondary rates applied only to earnings in excess of the employer's earnings threshold (without limit).

3 The contracted-out rate shown applied only on earnings up to the UAP; any balance was subject to the SR (ie not contracted-out rate).

4 In addition, an employer's contracted-out rebate was due on earnings falling between the LEL and the employer's earnings threshold, amounting to 3.4% of such earnings (COSR only).

5 In addition, an employee's contracted-out rebate was due on earnings falling between the LEL and the employee's earnings threshold, amounting to 1.4% of such earnings.

Class 1 Contribution Rates 2013–14 to 2015–16					
Primary[1]			Secondary[2]		
SR%	RR%	COSR%[3,5]	SR%	RR%	COSR%[3,4]
12	5.85	10.60	13.80[6]	13.80	10.40[6]
+ 2% on earnings above UEL					

1 Main primary rates apply only to earnings between the employee's earnings threshold and the UEL.

2 All secondary rates apply only to earnings in excess of the employer's earnings threshold (without limit).

3 The contracted-out rate shown applies only on earnings up to the UAP; any balance is subject to the SR (ie not contracted-out rate).

4 In addition, an employer's contracted-out rebate is due on earnings falling between the LEL and the employer's earnings threshold, amounting to 3.4% of such earnings (COSR).

5 In addition, an employee's contracted-out rebate is due on earnings falling between the LEL and the employee's earnings threshold, amounting to 1.4%.

6 The secondary rate is reduced from 6 April 2015 to 0% on earnings up to the UST/UEL if the employee is under the age of 21 on the date of payment.

Class 1 Contribution Rates 2016–17 to 2018–19			
Primary[1]		Secondary[2]	
SR%	RR%	SR%	RR%
12	5.85	13.80[3]	13.80
+ 2% on earnings above UEL			

1 Main primary rates apply only to earnings between the employee's earnings threshold and the UEL.

2 All secondary rates apply only to earnings in excess of the employer's earnings threshold (without limit).

3 The secondary rate shown is reduced to 0% for earnings paid to earners under the age of 21 and qualifying apprentices under the age of 25 on earnings up to the UST/AUST (equal to the UEL). The standard rate applies to earnings above these thresholds.

Tolley's National Insurance Contributions 2018–19

Tolley's National Insurance Contributions 2018–19

Edited by

Vince Ashall MSc FCIPP

Tolley®

Members of the LexisNexis Group worldwide

United Kingdom	RELX (UK) Limited trading as LexisNexis, 1–3 Strand, London WC2N 5JR and 9–10 St Andrew Square, Edinburgh EH2 2AF
Australia	Reed International Books Australia Pty Ltd trading as LexisNexis, Chatswood, New South Wales
Austria	LexisNexis Verlag ARD Orac GmbH & Co KG, Vienna
Benelux	LexisNexis Benelux, Amsterdam
Canada	LexisNexis Canada, Markham, Ontario
China	LexisNexis China, Beijing and Shanghai
France	LexisNexis SA, Paris
Germany	LexisNexis GmbH, Dusseldorf
Hong Kong	LexisNexis Hong Kong, Hong Kong
India	LexisNexis India, New Delhi
Italy	Giuffrè Editore, Milan
Japan	LexisNexis Japan, Tokyo
Malaysia	Malayan Law Journal Sdn Bhd, Kuala Lumpur
New Zealand	LexisNexis NZ Ltd, Wellington
Singapore	LexisNexis Singapore, Singapore
South Africa	LexisNexis Butterworths, Durban
USA	LexisNexis, Dayton, Ohio

Published by LexisNexis

This is a Tolley title

A CIP Catalogue record for this book is available from the British Library.

ISBN for this volume: 9780754554912

Printed and bound by CPI Group (UK) Ltd, Croydon, CR0 4YY

Visit LexisNexis at www.lexisnexis.co.uk

Preface

This edition of Tolley's National Insurance Contributions has been fully updated to include relevant tax, employment and National Insurance legislation up to and including Finance Act 2018 and associated NIC regulations. There have been updates across all chapters, dealing with such subjects as earnings, collection and categorisation. Overseas matters are also considered, including the potential impacts of Brexit and the interaction of bilateral treaties. Revised NIC rates, limits and worked examples have been added and updated for 2018–19. Along with general updating, further information on the new 'off-payroll working in the public sector' rules has been included. As well as recent case law developments relating to National Insurance, revised details of National Insurance related forms, leaflets and other relevant guidance has also been added.

The author is Vince Ashall MSc FCIPP, taking over from David Heaton FCA CTA, to whom much thanks for his work in previous years must go.

The book seeks as ever to give comprehensive coverage, but we welcome comments and suggestions for improvement.

Contributor

Vince Ashall MSc FCIPP

Vince Ashall, based in Rochdale, is currently Payroll Manager for Bench Ltd, and also undertakes payroll and pensions training and writes extensively on payroll matters for various publications, including Simon's Taxes, the Payroll Manager Handbook and various payroll magazines. He has over 40 years of payroll and pensions experience, mainly in the NHS. He is a Fellow of the Chartered Institute of Payroll Professionals and has a Master's Degree in Business and Payroll Management.

Contents

Abbreviations and References

For the full names and numbers of statutory instruments which appear in the text, see the Table of Statutory Instruments at the back of the book.

AC	Law Reports, Appeal Cases
A-G	Attorney-General
AER	All England Law Reports
AGM	Annual General Meeting
ALU	Appeals Liaison Unit
AOG	Adjudication Officers' Guide
AUST	Apprentice Upper Secondary Threshold
APP	Appropriate personal pension
Art	Article
BERR	Department for Business, Enterprise and Regulatory Reform
BTC	British Tax Cases
CA	Contributions Agency
cf	Compare
Ch	Law Reports, Chancery Division
CIR	Commissioners of Inland Revenue
cl	Clause
Cm	Command (1986 to date)
Cmnd	Command (1956–1986)
CMLR	Common Market Law Reports
CP	Decision of the Social Security Commissioners (Pension)
c–o	contracted-out
Comm	Community
COMP	Contracted-out money-purchase schemes
COR/cor	contracted-out rate
COSR	Contracted-out salary related
Col	Column

DC	Divisional Court
DEFRA	Department for Environment Food and Rural Affairs
DFEE	Department for Education and Employment (now Skills)
DLR	Dominion Law Reports (Canada)
DoE	Department of Employment
DSS	Department of Social Security (now DWP)
DWP	Department for Work and Pensions
EAT	Employment Appeal Tribunal
E & B	Ellis and Blackburn's Reports
EB	Earnings bracket
E & E	Ellis and Ellis's Reports
EC	European Community
ECJ	European Court of Justice
ECR	European Court Reports
EEA	European Economic Area
EEC	European Economic Community
EEET	Employee's (ie primary) earnings threshold
EFRBS	Employer Financed Retirement Benefit Scheme
EO	Executive Officer
ERET	Employer's (ie secondary) earnings threshold
ESC	Extra-statutory concession
ET	Earnings Threshold
EU	European Union
FA	Finance Act
FICA	Federal Insurance Contributions Act
FTT	First-tier Tribunal
FURBS	Funded Unapproved Retirement Benefit Scheme
GRA	Gender Recognition Act 2004
HCP	House of Commons Paper
HL	House of Lords
HMRC	HM Revenue and Customs
ICAEW	The Institute of Chartered Accountants in England and Wales

ICR	Law Reports, Industrial Cases Reports
ICTA	Income and Corporation Taxes Act
IR	Inland Revenue (now HMRC)
IRLR	Industrial Relations Law Reports
ITA	Income Tax Act 2007
ITEPA	Income Tax (Earnings and Pensions) Act 2003
ITR	Industrial Tax Reports
ITSA	Income Tax Self-Assessment
ITTOIA	Income Tax (Trading and Other Income) Act 2005
J	Mr Justice
JP	Justice of the Peace Reports
JSA	Jobseeker's Act
Kay	Kay's Reports, Chancery
KB	Law Reports, King's Bench Division
KIR	Knight's Industrial Reports
LEL	Lower Earnings Limit
LJ	Lord Justice
MSC	Manpower Services Commission (now Training and Enterprise Councils)
MSCs	Managed Service Companies
NAO	National Audit Office
n-c-o	not contracted-out
NI	National Insurance
NICA	National Insurance Contributions Act
NIC&EO	National Insurance Contributions and Employer Office
NIF	National Insurance Fund
NISPI	National Insurance Services To Pensions Industry
No	Number
O	Order
OTS	Office of Tax Simplification
P	Page
Para	Paragraph
PAYE	Pay As You Earn

PD	Law Reports, Probate, Divorce and Admiralty Division
PDCS	Pension, Disability and Carers Service
PSA	Pensions Schemes Act
PSC	Personal Service Company
Pt	Part
PT	Primary threshold (Class 1 earnings)
QB	Law Reports, Queen's Bench Division
Reg	Regulation
r	Rule
RR/rr	reduced rate
RSC	Rules of the Supreme Court
RTI	Real Time Information
R(P)	Reports of the Social Security Commissioners (Retirement Pension)
R(S)	Reports of the Social Security Commissioners (Sickness Benefits)
R(U)	Reports of the Social Security Commissioners (Unemployment Benefit)
s/Sec	Section
SAP	Statutory Adoption Pay
SC	Court of Session Cases (Scotland)
Sc & Div	Law Reports, Scots and Divorce Appeals
SCD	Special Commissioners' Decision (Simon's Tax Cases)
Sch	Schedule
SEB	Secondary earnings bracket
SEO	Senior Executive Officer
ShPP	Statutory Shared Parental Pay
SI	Statutory Instrument
SLT	Scots Law Times Reports
SMP	Statutory Maternity Pay
Sp C	Special Commissioners Decision
SPP	Statutory Paternity Pay
SR/sr	standard rate

SRT	Statutory Residence Test
SSA	Social Security Act
SSAA	Social Security Administration Act
SSAC	Social Security Advisory Committee
SSCBA	Social Security Contributions and Benefits Act
SSC(TF)A	Social Security Contributions (Transfer of Functions, etc.) Act
SSP	Statutory Sick Pay
SSPA	Social Security Pensions Act
ST	Secondary threshold (Class 1 earnings)
STC	Simon's Tax Cases
STI	Simon's Tax Intelligence
TC	Tax Cases
TC	Tribunal Case
TLR	Times Law Reports
TMA	Taxes Management Act 1970
TPC	Tribunal Procedure Committee
UAP	Upper Accrual Point
UEL	Upper Earnings Limit
UK	United Kingdom
US	United States Supreme Court Reports
UST	Upper Secondary Threshold
UT	Upper Tribunal
UTC	Upper Tribunal Case
Vol	Volume
WLR	Weekly Law Reports
WR	Weekly Reporter
WWR	Western Weekly Reports (Canada)
YT	Youth Training

1

Introduction

Cross-references. See ANTI-AVOIDANCE 8; CLASS 1A CONTRIBUTIONS 16; EARNINGS FROM EMPLOYMENT: EMPLOYMENT-RELATED SECURITIES, READILY CONVERTIBLE ASSETS, ETC 31; EARNINGS LIMITS AND THRESHOLD 33; NATIONAL INSURANCE FUND 48; OVERSEAS MATTERS 51.

The background to this work on National Insurance contributions

[1.1] Just over a century ago, David Lloyd George stood before Parliament and introduced to the honourable members the novel concept of National Insurance. Anticipating a hostile response to the new levy, however, he described his contribution scheme as nothing more than a 'temporary expedient' and he hastened to assure the House that it was something which would 'at no distant date' become 'unnecessary'. Ironically, Lloyd George's 'temporary expedient' has now achieved a permanence even greater than that of income tax (another 'temporary' measure, but one which, unlike National Insurance, requires an annual Finance Act to revive it), and has established itself as, with some regularity, the State's second largest source of income ahead of Value Added Tax. In 2016–17 alone, for example, the yield is expected to exceed, even in post-recessionary times, £124 billion. (See NATIONAL INSURANCE FUND **48**). This includes the portion of the contribution transferred to the NHS.

A neglected area of law

[1.2] It is a curious fact, however, that, despite the size and permanence of this levy, very many people know little about it. Even those who have the task of advising others of their financial responsibilities to the State—accountants, solicitors, business consultants and the like—have (until more recent times) treated it with a disregard that they would not dream of according to any other of Parliament's taxation measures; and they have done so, it seems, in the belief that it cannot 'bite' in the way that other taxes can. (As to whether it is correct to refer to National Insurance contributions as a tax, see **8.1** ANTI-AVOIDANCE.) The increase in the working population's National Insurance contributions by 1% from 6 April 2003 made people far more aware of the existence of this form of taxation, as did the alignment of the Upper Earnings Limit to the income tax higher rate starting point from 6 April 2009. The further universal increase of 1% to both employer and employee contribution rates from 6 April 2011 should also have increased awareness. The government's plan to 'extend the basic rate band' by raising the higher rate tax threshold to £50,000 by the end of this parliament in 2020 will bring with it an extension of the band on which employees (and perhaps the self-employed by then) pay a 12% contribution, with a maximum of £7,000 more (as at 2016–17) in charge at the full rate, rather than the 2% rate, so the tax saving for higher earners will be only 10% net of the extra NIC costs.

Increasing activity

[1.3] Whether or not the hitherto widespread disregard for contribution law has been attributable to the reasons suggested at **1.2** above, developments in this field of law have been such as to bring that disregard to an end. With effect from 6 April 1975, a graduated structure for National Insurance contributions was introduced and, so far as an employer's liability for secondary CLASS 1 CONTRIBUTIONS **15** was concerned, from 6 October 1985 the Upper Earnings Limit (which until then, had provided a contribution ceiling for an employer irrespective of the amount of earnings paid to any particular employee) was removed. (See **33.2** EARNINGS LIMITS AND THRESHOLDS). Those two changes, along with the abolition of the 'entry fee' in April 1999 (until then, when earnings passed the Lower Earnings Limit, all the earnings came into charge, rather than there being a NIC-free band up to that limit) and an increase in employer's and employees' contribution rate by 1% above the Earnings Threshold from 6 April 2003 and a further 1% from 6 April 2011, increased that burden for employers and employees alike. And, since 1991–92, employers have been faced with a further burden—CLASS 1A CONTRIBUTIONS **16**—which, it is estimated, will, before tax relief, cost them, collectively, not much short of £1.35 billion in 2016–17. Faced with all this, and with the increasing vigilance of the authorities in all areas of compliance, the majority of employers and their advisers have now become aware that they have been ignoring a tiger which is by no means as toothless as it once appeared.

The aim of this work on National Insurance contributions

[1.4] Placed in the situation outlined at **1.3** above, many employers and their advisers are now finding themselves in positions of some difficulty. They are asking—or being asked—questions to which they have no ready answers. Is an employee benefit trust still an effective means of avoiding contribution liabilities? Can we split Sally's remuneration among our six subsidiaries so as to take both her and ourselves out of contribution liability? Will Class 1 liabilities be avoided if we pay for Alan's children's school fees instead of giving him a bonus? Are benefits in kind still an effective way of providing Roger's remuneration package?

When things go wrong and one is faced with a demand for contribution arrears or when one is given notice of an adverse decision on a contribution matter, there is a *formal* appeal procedure which is fully considered in APPEALS AND REVIEWS **9**.

Then there are all the problems of a more routine nature. Now that Mrs Jones has received her decree nisi may she still pay reduced rate contributions? Should John pay contributions on his earnings from his school-holiday job? What do we do about Tony's contributions if we send him to the Paris office for twelve months? The new fitter says he wants to be treated as self-employed—what could be the consequences? How do we calculate Alex's contributions if we appoint him director before the end of the tax year? Can we stop paying NIC when an employee works abroad for a short period? What effect does paying NICs have on my state benefits?

The aim of this work is simply to provide a comprehensive reference guide for employers, company secretaries and managers, as well as for accountants, solicitors and other professional advisers, who, in the course of their work, are obliged to answer these and the host of other such questions which arise in the area of contribution law.

Key principles

[1.5] Three particular principles have been adhered to throughout. First, because the statutory source material is extensive (see **1.6** below), the wording of provisions and regulations has been adhered to as closely as possible wherever this has been consistent with the overall principle of clarity. Second, worked examples with, in some cases, forms and standard letters have been provided to illustrate every major point of practical difficulty. Third, because of the increasing mobility of labour throughout the European Union and the rest of the western world, the international aspect of each topic is considered wherever relevant, full reference being made to EU law and, more generally, to bilateral treaties where these bear on the topic in question. No details exist yet on the subject of the UK's cross-border social security coordination agreements and processes once the UK is no longer an EU member state. See 51 OVERSEAS MATTERS.

Sources of contribution law

[1.6] Apart from the relationship created by statute, there is no antecedent relationship between an individual (or company) and the State which could require the payment of contributions. National insurance contributions are, like taxes, creatures of statute, and the main statutes in question are *Social Security Contributions and Benefits Act 1992, Social Security Administration Act 1992* and *Social Security Act 1998*. The first two of these Acts are consolidations of earlier legislation and are largely skeletal. They require the flesh of secondary legislation to make them an effective body of law. The secondary legislation takes the form of regulations and orders made by statutory instrument and there are now scores of these which, either in whole or in part, are of current application in the field of contributions. The main regulations are the *Social Security (Contributions) Regulations 2001, SI 2001/1004*. The increases in contributions of 1% arising from 6 April 2003 and 6 April 2011 had to be committed to the statute book in the form of the *National Insurance Contributions Act 2002* and the *National Insurance Contributions Act 2011*. Both acts are relatively short documents. Further impact on contribution law was made by the Tax Law Rewrite project which threw up the *Income Tax (Earnings and Pensions) Act 2003, The Income Tax (Pay As You Earn) Regulations 2003, SI 2003/2682, Income Tax (Trading and Other Income) Act 2005* and *Income Tax Act 2007*. The *National Insurance Contributions Act 2014* was introduced to create the (then) £2,000 employment allowance for most employers, lay the ground for a new nil rate of contribution for under-21s from April 2015, import the GAAR legislation into NIC law, impose secondary NIC liabilities where the employer is outside the UK, and tackle avoidance by way of a change to the rules governing the status of 'salaried' LLP members with effect from 6 April 2014. The *National Insurance Contributions Act 2015* set out reforms to the basis of liability for, and collection mechanism for, Class 2, imported from *Finance Act 2014* the concept of follower notices and accelerated payment notices in connection with avoidance schemes (somewhat unusually for primary legislation) introduced a targeted anti-avoidance rule into the *Social Security (Categorisation of Earners) Regulations 1978, SI 1978/1689* to buttress the 2014 changes to onshore and offshore employment intermediaries, and laid the ground for the extension, from 6 April 2016, of the nil rate of secondary contributions to apprentices under the age of 25.

And stealthily, in the background, there was passed the *Pensions Act 2014*, which introduced the single-tier state pension from 6 April 2016, in the process introducing a new Class 3A contribution, abolishing contracting out and the State Second Pension (S2P), and undermining the fundamental basis of the Class 1 contribution structure. Now that everyone below state pension age begins to accrue the state pension at the same rate, whether they pay no Class 1 contributions because they earn above the lower earnings limit but below the primary threshold, or pay Class 2 contributions at a cost of £153.40 per year because they are self-employed, or pay Class 1 contributions of over £4,500 per year because they earn above the UEL, questions will have to be asked about the fairness of the new system. Inflation is also posing some questions for the NI scheme: with the 'triple lock' promise on the state pension, the cost of providing the basic state pension will rise by at least 2.5% each year (for existing state pensioners), the basic pension was uprated by 2.9% on 6 April 2016, although inflation was almost 0% and the State Earnings Related Pension Scheme (SERPS) and S2P components of the full state pension were frozen, reflecting the negative CPI index in September 2015. If earnings and the associated contribution levels remain static, the minimum uprating of 2.5% will inevitably impose a huge strain on the finances of the NI Fund. All this comes after the new government, following the 2015 general election promised no rises in main NI rates in the next five years: it seems virtually certain that the base will have to be widened instead, and/or there will have to be a rise in the additional 2% rate. A new social security act and accompanying regulations are expected in 2017, as it will be needed to enact the promised abolition of Class 2 and the conversion of Class 4 to a type of contribution that attracts benefit entitlements from April 2018. The complexity introduced by the apparently simple abolition of Class 2 has been recognised by the postponement of the abolition until April 2019 to 'allow time to engage with interested parties and Parliamentarians with concerns relating to the impact of the abolition of Class 2 NICs on self-employed individuals with low profits'. (*Written statement to Parliament, 2 November 2017, HCWS220.*) But no mention of the benefit entitlements.

Case law

[1.7] There is increasing case law concerning the contribution legislation itself and, where there is, it has been drawn upon fully in this work under the chapter sub-heading *Case Law*, as has case law of more general application where it is relevant to the subject in hand. The concept of 'residence', for example, is a concept common to both tax law and contribution law but until recently defined in neither. As the courts have pronounced very fully on its meaning in its tax law context, however, their pronouncements are a useful guide to its meaning in the context of NIC legislation, which is not based on the new statutory definition for income tax purposes in *Finance Act 2013, Sch 45*. Nor is there any statutory definition of 'contract of service' which lies at the very root of nearly all categorisation questions. Here, case law arising out of employment protection legislation provides an additional useful insight into the judicial mind as it approaches the question of whether a person is truly an employee or not. The number of cases coming before the former Special Commissioners and the courts with regard to IR35 rulings was also quite noticeable a few years ago; this would appear to be a trend that will continue in the future notwithstanding HMRC's efforts regarding clarification of employment status matters. See **40** INTERMEDIARIES. There has even been a case brought before the Special Commissioners where this work has been quoted in the court proceedings. See **29.18** EARNINGS FROM EMPLOYMENT: GENERAL.

Ministers' decisions

[1.8] The old appeal procedure (such as it was) – more commonly known as Secretary of State questions – that applied until 1 April 1999 under contribution law resulted in determinations which were only sometimes published. Those that were published are no longer in print but, where relevant, reference has been made to them in this work. They are of no binding force but will, of course, tend to be followed by the authorities where the circumstances surrounding a current problem are on all fours with the circumstances in a determination case.

Leaflets

[1.9] HM Revenue and Customs and the Department for Work and Pensions used to publish a large number of *leaflets and forms 43* dealing with contribution and benefit matters and the editions of these noted at **43.2** are referred to throughout the text. However, many are now only available on the internet and a number of those produced by HM Revenue and Customs were withdrawn completely in recent years. Although providing a useful insight into departmental views on the meaning of the legislation where they still exist, they do not, however, profess to give an authoritative statement of the law and they have no binding force. The booklet CA47 'Charter for National Insurance contributors' and the Charter itself that it contained were both withdrawn in mid-2004. The charter was replaced for a time by HMRC Code of Practice 1 – leaflet COP 1. That, too, was withdrawn in April 2007 and replaced with a single-sheet factsheet C/FS 'Complaints and putting things right'. A new HMRC Customer Charter then came into effect on 11 November 2009 and has legal recognition, albeit very low profile, little practical importance and nil or negligible impact. [*Finance Act 2009, s 91*.] Tellingly, the complaints guidance (see www.gov.uk/complain-to-hm-revenue-and-customs) makes no reference whatsoever to the Charter. The 2007 factsheet C/FS was replaced in 2015 by a two-sided factsheet, entitled 'Complaints' but containing a section headed 'Putting things right'. This does make reference to the Charter.

Territorial scope of this work

[1.10] This work attempts to give a comprehensive statement of contribution law as it applies in England and Wales. The legislation is generally equally applicable in Scotland, apart from the modifications necessitated by the fact that Scotland possesses separate court and legal systems (eg for 'Court of Appeal' read 'Court of Session' and the *Limitation Act 1980* that applies in England and Wales has a Scottish equivalent with different rules in the *Prescription and Limitation (Scotland) Act 1973*). The work does not apply to Northern Ireland, though contribution law there is virtually identical with that in Great Britain with regular statutory instruments being published in tandem with those applying to England, Scotland and Wales or in some cases in a single combined statutory instrument (see **51.49** OVERSEAS MATTERS). [*Social Security (Contributions) Regulations 2001, SI 2001/1004, Reg 156*]. The future of the Scottish social security system following the announcements about extra devolution of powers after the referendum was settled by the

Smith Commission, which reported under 'Pillar 2' that the five political parties had agreed that National Insurance matters would be reserved to the UK Parliament, and all aspects of the state pension would remain shared across the UK, although certain aspects of non-contributory benefits might be devolved. It is doubtful that anyone involved in writing the earlier policy statements (that had suggested full devolution as an option) had even considered the complexities that would arise if the Scottish NI system diverged for UK citizens resident in Scotland and Scottish residents working in England, Wales or Northern Ireland.

Approach of this work to NICs

[1.11] The remaining chapters in this work are arranged in alphabetical order. This is an ideal arrangement for the person using the work for reference purposes in that each major topic of contribution law has been allotted its own chapter and may thus be found without recourse to the index. It may, however, pose difficulties for the person wishing merely to 'read a book about National Insurance' and it is suggested that any such person should begin with CATEGORISATION 14 and let the cross-referencing system lead him on from there. In addition this work includes Tables of Contents, Statutes, Statutory Instruments, Cases and Published Decisions.

The future of National Insurance contributions

[1.12] It is understood that the question of proceeding with complete harmonisation of income tax with NICs under any of the options contained in the report by the working group under the government's 1993 deregulation initiative is not considered to be viable by Ministers, although the subject is resurrected from time to time by those who can see the superficial attractions of simplification without an appreciation of the necessary complexity of any major reform. In a reply to a question in the House of Commons in February 2003, Dawn Primarolo stated that there were 'no plans for the structural alignment' of tax and NICs but she went on to add that the then Inland Revenue worked with 'employer representatives and others to look for opportunities to align the tax and National Insurance rules at a practical level while having regard to the need to protect the individuals' benefit entitlement'.

However, several positive results of the more general harmonisation process have been seen subsequently: acceptance of Inland Revenue/HM Revenue and Customs dispensations for Class 1 (now consigned to history, with the exemption of deductible expenses introduced with effect from 6 April 2016 by *Finance Act 2015, ss 11–12 (FA 2015)*), the incorporation of some Extra-Statutory Concessions for tax into Class 1 regulations and single compliance visits to employers by Employer Compliance officers who cover both PAYE and NIC matters. Changes to the taxation of earnings are now automatically replicated in NIC law as a matter of course. The more recent suggestion by the Chancellor in his March 2011 Budget that tax and NIC 'operations' should be integrated appeared to have lost momentum, presumably because a detailed examination of the implications for both tax and social security law had led to an acknowledgement that the volume of change needed would cause more upheaval and pain, for HMRC and employers, than could possibly be justified by the minor gains in administration efficiency. Perhaps the recognition that most of the complex calculations are now computerised as a result of the introduction of compulsory RTI reporting led to a recognition that harmonisation is no longer quite as badly needed as it once might have been. It seems that the international issues are also a major stumbling block, and the lack of appetite for adopting an annual assessment system and a single employee and employer NIC threshold at the same level as the single personal allowance means that many of the existing PAYE practices could not be applied. There have been loud calls from some corners for the starting point for Class 1 (£8,424 this year) to be raised to the same level as the single personal allowance (£11,850 this year, and rising towards £12,500 by 2020), so that the lowest earners pay neither PAYE nor NICs. The siren calls have fallen on deaf ears in Westminster – not unsurprisingly, since taking £4,076 of earnings out of charge for around 27m contributors would cut NI Fund income by some £28bn, or around 26%. Rates would have to rise by around 39% to make up the shortfall in state pension funding. Unless the Chancellor merely feels the need to be seen to be 'doing something' about complexity in the tax system, the announcement in Budget 2016 that the Office of Tax Simplification is to consult further on the potential alignment of more aspects of the PAYE and NIC systems, suggests that NIC law is set for a period of upheaval. Not the least problematic simplification that has been proposed is the separation of employer NICs into a separate charge, with a basis that differs from employee NICs. It is a necessary precursor to collecting primary (employee) NICs on a similar basis to PAYE, but it is quite the most remarkable proposition: create two new taxes with different rules, out of one with common rules, in order to (allegedly) simplify NICs and partially align one of the new taxes (ie, except in terms of thresholds, rates and target population) with PAYE. It almost re-defines 'simplification'. Having said that, the introduction of the Apprenticeship Levy, an employer only tax, from April 2017 would appear to be a possible template for any replacement employer NICs charge.

The Taylor Report

[1.13] A report 'Work Incentives; A Report by Martin Taylor', having been commissioned by the incoming government of 1997, was published on 17 March 1998. As regards National Insurance contributions, it recommended:

(1) The Lower Earnings Limit to become an allowance rather than a limit;
(2) The employer's Lower Earnings Limit to be equalised with the single person's tax allowance (then £81 per week);
(3) The employee's Lower Earnings Limit to be equalised with the single person's allowance (then £81 per week);
(4) National Insurance to be charged on all benefits in kind;
(5) Class 2 to be abolished and replaced with a more appropriate Class 4 regime for the self-employed;
(6) The functions of the Contributions Agency to be carried out by the then Inland Revenue.

Items 1, 3 and 4 above were, in fact, amongst the various options set out in the report of September 1993. The then Chancellor of the Exchequer, Gordon Brown, announced on 17 March 1998 that items 1, 2 and 6 would be adopted with effect from April 1999 (see *SSA 1998, s 51; SSC(TF)A, Sch 8 para 4*) and item 3 at a later date once the means had been identified to protect the benefit entitlement of those earning between the Lower Earnings Limit and the Earnings Threshold. The Chancellor would also consider further items 4 and 5. Then, in the economic and fiscal strategy report 'Budget 99' it was stated that:

> From April 2000, the threshold of earnings above which people will pay NICs will increase to £76 per week. A zero rate of NICs will apply on earnings between the previous lower limit and the new threshold, to protect benefit entitlement. The threshold of earnings above which employees will pay no NICs (the Upper Earnings Limit, UEL) will increase to £535 per week.

and in respect of item 4 the report stated:

> From April 2000, employer NICs will be extended to those benefits-in-kind which are already subject to income tax.

Further, although Class 2 was not abolished it was considerably reduced from 6 April 2000, although far outweighed by increases in Class 4 contributions for those with higher profits. With regard to point 5 above, in the debates to the draft *Social Security (Contributions) (Re-rating and National Insurance Funds Payments) Order 2001*, the Paymaster General, Dawn Primarolo MP, stated, with some contrary logic, that:

> Class 2 contributions for self-employed secure access to benefits. The level remains, for the second year, just £2 a week, which is a reduction in real terms. It is available to all self-employed people, and if such a low level — which did not pertain under the previous Government — does not help the self-employed, I am at a loss to know what will.
>
> Hansard Debates, Fourth Standing Committee, 23 January 2001, Col 19.

The Chancellor in the 2015 Budget speech, just before the general election, announced that Class 2 might indeed now be about to be abolished and absorbed into a new Class 4, which would start to count towards benefits (although the measure was not then mentioned in the Queen's speech after the 2015 general election). However, the 2015 Budget came just before the *National Insurance Contributions Act 2015* created a new basis, from 6 April 2015, of measuring earnings (only Class 4 earnings will count) and collecting Class 2 (with Class 4) through the ITSA regime. Much of item 5 has therefore now been adopted too, but the merger of Class 2 into Class 4 has only been deferred until the new system is settled. On 9 December 2015, the government issued a consultation document on the potential abolition of Class 2 and the reformulation of Class 4 so as to introduce a benefit test, starting at the earliest in April 2017 (although this seems very ambitious, in view of the far-reaching amendments to NIC and benefits legislation that will be required). Subsequently, the 2016 Autumn Statement confirmed that abolition of Class 2 would be effective from April 2018, while the 2017 Autumn Budget confirmed that there would a further year's delay, until April 2019. The NICA 2015 changes, under which the former small earnings exception level (renamed the 'small profits threshold') was not harmonised with the lower annual limit for

Class 4, or indeed the Class 1 lower earnings limit, are set to be superseded with a new system that will use the same limits and thresholds as Class 1, and will adopt the Class 1 approach of deeming contributions to have been paid on profits between the LEL and a new Class 4 threshold that mimics the Class 1 primary threshold. The plans will necessitate a new approach to voluntary contributions, since Class 3 currently covers much less than Class 2, but there is no plan to add a secondary contribution to the self-employed rate, despite the fact that benefit entitlements will now be virtually the same for employed and self-employed contributors (with the marginal exception of contributory JSA).

As regards item 4, such a change does no more than raise extra revenue for the government. True harmonisation and co-ordination as regards the tax and National Insurance system would entail ensuring that those items that are subject to PAYE are also subject to Class 1 National Insurance and those that are *not* subject to PAYE are also *not* subject to Class 1 National Insurance contributions but to Class 1A. To impose a Class 1 National Insurance charge where PAYE is not applicable (probably because it has been recognised that either it is not possible to make a deduction from the item in question because of its nature or else it is not possible to quantify the amount at the time that deduction is required) simply because, ultimately, the item is a taxable item does nothing to harmonise the systems from the employer's perspective. It was confirmed that the charge on all benefits in kind subsequently would be achieved by extending the already existing Class 1A charge for cars and fuel. See what is now *Social Security (Contributions) Regulations 2001, SI 2001/1004, Part 3*, Sch 3 and CLASS 1A CONTRIBUTIONS: BENEFITS IN KIND **16**. Even though 6 April 2016 saw the introduction of a new statutory regime for the payrolling of benefits in kind (known by the abbreviation 'PBIK'), only PAYE deductions are included; Class 1A NICs continue to be due after the year-end in respect of non-cash earnings.

The transfer of the Contributions Agency to the then Inland Revenue occurred on 1 April 1999 and confirmed the closer working ties. The *Social Security Contributions (Transfer of Functions, etc) Act 1999* became law in February 1999 and transferred certain functions relating to National Insurance contributions from the Secretary of State to the Commissioners of Inland Revenue.

Prior to the Finance Bill 2005, changes were made to parts of the income tax legislation relating to employment-related securities where securities or securities options are acquired in connection with employment. These changes were intended to counter certain schemes that in the past taxpayers had sought to exploit in order to avoid income tax and NICs. [*ITEPA 2003, ss 420, 424, 429(1A), 431B, 437, 443, 446, 447, 449; FA 2005, s 20* inserting *ITEPA 2003, Part 7 Chapter 4*]. See EARNINGS FROM EMPLOYMENT: EMPLOYMENT-RELATED SECURITIES, READILY CONVERTIBLE ASSETS, ETC **31**.

Also of concern to practitioners and businesses in general are the disclosure rules regarding tax and NICs avoidance. [*FA 2004, s 318*]. In this connection the Paymaster General (in those days a Treasury minister) made a written statement on 2 December 2004, part of which is reproduced below:

> Despite extensive reforms to the tax legislation in 2003, employers and their advisers are continuing to devise more contrived avoidance schemes. One such example of which the Inland Revenue has learnt involves the payment of a bonus to an employee in the form of dividends on shares in a specially constructed company. This avoids tax at 40% and employer and employee NICs.
>
> The Inland Revenue will be challenging such arrangements in the courts where it is appropriate to do so. We cannot, however, await the outcome in the courts before taking action. We intend that from today both tax and NICs legislation should achieve our objective of subjecting the rewards of the employment to the proper amount of tax and NICs, however the rewards are delivered. Taxpayers who contribute their fair share have a right to expect that others will do so. We also want to make it plain that to the extent that legislation may still not achieve our objective in the face of continuing avoidance, we will ensure that it does.
>
> To that end we will be including legislation in FB 05, effective from today, to close down the avoidance schemes that we know about. A technical note explaining what we intend to do in FB 05 will be published today. We will also ensure that NICs is charged on these schemes from today.
>
> However, experience has taught us that we are not always able to anticipate ingenuity and inventiveness of the avoidance industry. Nor should we have to. Our objective is clear and the time has come to close this activity down permanently.
>
> I am therefore giving notice of our intention to deal with any arrangements which attempt to frustrate this intention that employers and employees should pay the proper amount of tax and NICs on the rewards of employment. Where we become aware of arrangements which attempt to frustrate this intention we will introduce legislation to close them down, where necessary from today.

The *National Insurance Contributions Act 2006* provided the power for the issue of regulations to have backdated effect in order to achieve the above aim, such regulations having effect from 6 April 2007 (retrospective liability – see **21** COLLECTION) and 1 May 2007 (disclosure of avoidance schemes – see **8** ANTI-AVOIDANCE). To date, almost inevitably, they have not been used, despite the widespread hysteria among the media and the political classes about tax avoidance. In the Autumn Statement on 25 November 2015, the government stated that it intended to take action against those who have used or continue to use disguised remuneration schemes and who have not yet paid their fair share of tax. The government also stated that it would consider legislating in a future Finance Bill to close down any further new schemes intended to avoid tax on earned income, where necessary, with effect from 25 November 2015. Nothing directly relevant to National Insurance contributions was included in Finance Bill 2016, although the Budget speech promised action against remuneration planning schemes investigated by HMRC that have not been settled by 6 April 2019. New penalties for advisers who promote schemes were added to HMRC's future armoury.

The Mirrlees Review

[1.14] This review was set up in 2006 but did not report until early 2011. The review challenged the validity of the separate PAYE and NIC systems whilst at the same time it questioned whether the contributory principle continued to exist. The review recommended the merger of tax and NIC but recognised that it would bring into charge items which were previously outside NIC liabilities. These included income from savings, most state benefits, tips and gratuities and earnings from those over pension age. To ensure such reliefs continued, some intermediate rate of tax was suggested. Perhaps the most surprising suggestion was to abolish employer NIC altogether and levy a charge only on the individuals (something the Netherlands did in the 1980s, with a corresponding statutory uplift in employee remuneration rates in compensation for the transfer of liability). The report did conclude, however, that a merger of tax and NIC for the individual with a separate employer charge was a more likely possibility. Harmonisation of primary Class 1 contributions with PAYE, taking into account both aggregated earnings from all employments and cumulative calculation would require a new payroll tax to replace secondary Class 1 contributions, and liability to pay SSP, SMP, etc, would have to be reformed (eg, which employer would pay an employee who has more than one job and combined earnings over the threshold?), so any Chancellor is entitled to tread warily in pursuing the proposals, since he or she would, paradoxically, have to introduce a new payroll tax to simplify and harmonise the old one, which would continue to exist alongside the new one as an employee levy. There would be something paradoxical about introducing an additional tax with separate rules, using the excuse that it was a simplification of the old one, which was not being abolished.

Office of Tax Simplification

[1.15] The Office of Tax Simplification is charged, as the name suggests, with making recommendations to Ministers on the simplification of the UK tax system which of course includes NIC. They see the value in merging, or 'aligning', some aspects of the tax and NIC systems but recognise the complexities this would cause. We wait to see how the ideas develop but it was significant that in his March 2011 Budget the Chancellor of the Exchequer mentioned the closer operational integration of tax and NIC but veered away from a complete merger. The NIC legislative changes so far implemented following recommendations from the OTS have been minor in nature, and the payroll-related consultation documents issued in 2014 and legislated in FA 2015 have not focused on any simplification of NIC rules.

However, the Chancellor commissioned another report on the closer alignment of income tax and national insurance contributions, which was published on 7 March 2016, and following that publication announced in his budget speech that the OTS would be commissioned specifically to review the impacts of moving employee NICs to an annual, cumulative and aggregated basis (ACA), and moving employer NICs to a payroll basis (simplification by divergence). In an open letter to the chairman and director of the OTS following the Budget speech, the minister then responsible for HMRC, David Gauke MP, noted that closer alignment is not a straightforward issue, and that there are both benefits and challenges to fundamental reform. Publication of the OTS's report of its further review is expected around the time of the Autumn Statement 2016. See [1.19] for more details.

Investigatory powers

[1.16] Currently HMRC have certain powers to investigate cases of tax evasion using their powers within the current legislation. These were substantially increased by the *Serious Crime Act 2007* and Chapter 3 extended certain investigatory powers of officers of HM Revenue and Customs. This legislation amended the *Regulation of Investigatory Powers Act 2000* to include 'HM Revenue and Customs'. In particular *s 32* covering 'Authorisation of Intrusive Surveillance' now allows HMRC to give each of the senior authorising officers the power to grant authorisations for the carrying out of intrusive surveillance. From 1 December 2007, *Taxes Management Act 1970, ss 20, 20B and 20BB* were superseded, as HMRC can now apply for search warrants under *Police and Criminal Evidence Act 1984*. [*Police and Criminal Evidence Act 1984 (Application and Customs) Order 2007, SI 2007/3175; Civil Evidence Act 1995; FA 2008, s 118, Sch 36 paras 65, 69*]. See **35.2** ENFORCEMENT.

Recent changes in summary

New legislation

[1.17] In its manifesto before the 2015 general election, the Conservative Party undertook (on page 27 of the document) to introduce, if re-elected, and within 100 days of that election, a 'tax lock' that would 'not increase the rates of VAT, income tax or National Insurance in the next parliament'. This was not qualified by reference to which rates might be locked: it was a plain statement of intent.

In a speech, the conservative leader, David Cameron, confirmed that the tax lock also meant that there would not be any extension to the scope of VAT, or an increase in the ceiling set for the main rate of National Insurance contributions by employees (reported in the Financial Times, 29 April 2015). The commitment was also mentioned in the Queen's Speech on 27 May 2015: 'No rises in income tax rates, VAT or National Insurance for the next five years'.

Both the manifesto and the Prime Minister glossed over the fact that Parliament cannot bind itself to refrain from changing the law in the future, but the intention to maintain the status quo on tax and NIC rates was made clear.

However, by the time of the summer budget speech, on 8 July 2015, the Chancellor of the Exchequer announced a slightly different plan, to legislate to 'prohibit any increase in *the main* rates of income tax, National Insurance and VAT for the next five years' (emphasis added, by both the Chancellor and the editor) [HC Deb 8 July 2015 c336]. The income tax and VAT elements were to be included in a summer Finance Bill, and the tax lock duly appeared as Clauses 1 and 2 of *Finance Bill 2015–16* on 14 July 2015.

Statutory provisions on National Insurance cannot be included in the annual Finance Bill, because the Bill's remit specifically excludes any tax that does not raise money for financing central government as a whole. *The National Insurance Contributions (Rate Ceilings) Bill 2015–16* therefore appeared separately at the same time as the parallel provisions in the Finance Bill.

In the event, the *National Insurance Contributions (Rate Ceilings) Act 2015*, passed on 17 December 2015, only applies to the rates of contribution under Classes 1, 1A and 1B. No mention is made of Classes 2, 3 or 4.

- Section 1 limits the main and additional rates of primary Class 1 to 12% and 2% respectively for any tax year from 2016–17 onwards up to and including the tax year that begins immediately before the next general election.
- Section 2, for the same period, limits the secondary rate to 13.8%.
- Section 3 provides that the upper earnings limit during that period shall not exceed the weekly equivalent of the proposed higher rate threshold for each tax year. The proposed higher rate threshold is the sum of the basic rate limit for income tax for the relevant tax year as proposed in the pre-budget proposals for the year (ie, the Autumn Statement as presented to Parliament by the Chancellor of the Exchequer by command of Her Majesty) and the personal allowance for income tax for the relevant year. The weekly equivalent is to be arrived at by dividing the annual threshold by 52 and rounding up or down to the nearest £1. For 2017–18, since the 40% tax threshold has been set at £45,000, the annual Upper Earnings Limit has also been set at £45,000, giving a weekly UEL of £866.

The Act says no more. It makes no reference to Classes 1A and 1B because their rates automatically follow the Class 1 secondary rate (see *SSCBA 1992, ss 10(5) and 10A(6)*), which is dealt with by Section 2. The 2016–17 rates and limits frozen by *NICRCA 2015* are reflected in this edition.

As a general election, held on 8 June 2017, was called on 18 April 2017, *NICRCA 2015* will cease to have effect after 2017–18.

Future legislation

[1.18] The *NIC (Rate Ceilings) Act 2015* makes no reference to Classes 2, 3 or 4. This omission is undoubtedly linked to a further statement in the July 2015 Budget Report: 'Following recommendations by the OTS . . . government will also consult in autumn 2015 on abolishing Class 2 NICs and reforming Class 4 NICs.'

This follows from the announcement in the March 2015 Budget (para 1.109) that the government will 'abolish Class 2 NICs in the next parliament and consult on reforming Class 4 NICs to include a contributory benefit test'. In the House of Commons second reading debates on the 'NIC lock', the junior minister piloting the Bill noted that the OTS had been asked to 'look at Class 2 and Class 4 contributions' and that the consultation would inform the 2016 Budget. [HC Deb 15 September 2015 c926.] In fact, the OTS had been tasked with a much wider review (see further below).

Given the need to rewrite the social security legislation (ie, not just NICs legislation) to realise the Class 4 plan, and the absence of the idea from the Queen's Speech, it was always clear that there would be no change in April 2016, although the OTS proposals were published after Autumn Statement 2015 and the Budget speech in March 2016 included a promise of further consultation on the detail. The earliest possible date for the change is April 2018, although even this might be ambitious given the scale of the necessary changes. We are now in an era where computer system changes determine timescales for new policies, and such changes can only be coded, tested and rolled out once the politicians have laid down a clear and final set of rules. If a concrete proposal is set out in the Autumn Statement 2016, and a new social security act is passed during early 2017, government and private sector systems might just be ready to run under the new rules by April 2018.

Class 4 currently only applies to income from trades, professions and vocations taxed under *ITTOIA 2005, Part 2, Chapter 2*, whereas Class 2 is slightly wider in scope, applying to anyone in 'business', whether or not that amounts to a trade, and open to those who wish to make voluntary contributions despite their ITTOIA income being £nil or falling below the small profits threshold.

The change to Class 2 may also necessitate careful consideration of the UK's treaty obligations. The social security convention with the USA includes, for example, specific references to insurance periods acquired through the payment of 'Class I or II'. All such references will need to be renegotiated with suitable protocols being added to the relevant reciprocal agreements.

The abolition of Class 2 may also mean that the rate of Class 4 has to rise, although nothing has yet been published to outline how that might be achieved. In the Government Actuary's report in January 2016 on the proposed benefits uprating in April 2016, it was estimated that Class 2 contribution receipts in 2016–17 would total around £248 million, while Class 4 would account for around £2.725 billion. The Class 2 figure ought to have been distorted, however, by 2015–16 having been the year in which Class 2 moved from a direct debit or six-monthly payment basis to being included in the self-assessment tax return, so the quoted figure includes hardly anything in respect of 2015–16 itself, since all liabilities for that year will fall due between 6 April 2016 and 31 January 2017. It seems the Government Actuary's estimates for the report were somewhat wide of the mark. The normalised, long-run annual value of Class 2 is around £380 million – there are around 4.5 million registered self-employed traders, but many earn below the small profits threshold, while others have concurrent employment with earnings sufficient to cancel out any Class 2 liabilities.

Taking the true figure into account, the total 'take' from Class 4 may therefore need to rise by around 14% to protect the NI Fund and ensure that there is enough cash coming in to cover benefit expenditure, 97.5% of which is on state retirement pensions. Since the 2% additional rate is unlikely to change (assuming it continues to match the Class 1 additional rate, as fixed by the *NIC (Rate Ceilings) Act 2015*), it must be assumed that the new Class 4 main rate in 2018–19 will be high enough to collect the whole £380 million. This might mean a Class 4 rate of around 11%. The then Chancellor suggested in the 2016 Budget Report that the change would see Class 2 abolished, saving self-employed people a small amount each year, so it remains to be seen what will be decided, especially in view of the strains put on the public finances following the 'Brexit' vote. Such an increase in the Class 4 rate, albeit in two stages, was included in Budget 2017. However following protests by Conservative MPs that this broke a manifesto pledge the proposal was dropped, even though the increase did not contravene the provisions of *NICRCA 2015*.

Taking into account the restructuring of the state pension from April 2016, under which employed and self-employed earners will receive exactly the same entitlements in respect of each qualifying year, except for the right of someone with a satisfactory Class 1 record to claim contributory jobseeker's allowance, it seems there is little justification for any differential in the rates payable to future Class 1 and Class 4 contributors. JSA is estimated to account for just £373 million of NI Fund expenditure in 2016–17, or just 0.4% of the total NI revenue. That might suggest a Class 4 rate of 11.96% compared with the 12% Class 1 rate for employees.

All of this, of course, overlooks the role played by the employer contribution under Class 1, which accounts for 58% of NI Fund revenues. The self-employed currently pay nothing equivalent. The historical justification for this has always been the difference between the state pension entitlements of the two types of contributor: employees have benefitted from an additional SERPS or S2P component to the state pension, but this has been removed from those reaching state pension age on or after 6 April 2016.

Some developed countries require the self-employed to pay the employer contribution in addition to the equivalent of the employee contribution (eg, the USA), while others leave the self-employed free to choose whether or not to contribute to the state scheme, or to most parts of it (eg, Germany) and if they choose not to contribute then they are entitled to no support from the state or state-sponsored funds.

The consultation document on turning Class 4 into a source of benefit entitlement proposed a basis similar to that applied to Class 1 primary contributions. Those with profits above the LEL but below the lower annual limit (set at the same level as the Class 1 primary threshold) would be treated as having earned a qualifying year, with contributions levied at the full rate on earnings between the same limits as Class 1, and the additional rate on profits above the upper limit. The paper had no concrete proposals on dealing with the entitlement of a self-employed woman to maternity allowance, which is automatically problematic where contributions might not be due and payable until after the birth because of the tax return and payment cycle. Nor is the government clear about how those with profits below the LEL might be able to pay voluntarily to protect themselves in benefit terms, since there will be no voluntary Class 2 option (bearing in mind that Class 3 is much more expensive, and it doesn't count for short-term benefits). There are also difficulties to be addressed in relation to special classes of earner, such as examiners, ministers of religion outside Class 1, foster carers, some landlords, share fishermen, volunteer development workers: it seems they are going to have to pay Class 3 instead of Class 2, but that would not solve the problem of protecting entitlement to employment and support allowance and maternity allowance unless the Class 3 rules or the benefit rules are reformed in parallel.

The supposed simplification measure looks like being anything but that by April 2019.

The abolition of Class 2 NICs, inter alia, described above, will require the introduction of a NICs Bill to give effect to the changes. The announcement that this would be delayed to 2019 was made by the Exchequer Secretary to the Treasury in the House of Commons on 2 November 2017. The announcement stated that this would affect the proposed changes to the Class 1A NICs treatment of sporting testimonials.

At the time of writing, no details had been published of the proposed NICs Bill. However, to avoid the somewhat absurd situation of Class 1A NICS not being charged on sporting testimonials in 2017–18, a one-year exemption only [*Social Security (Miscellaneous Amendments) Regulations 2017, SI 2017/307, Reg 3*]; Class 1A being charged in 2018–19 and then exempted from 2019–20 under the proposed NICs Bill, further legislation was introduced to make the exemption apply to years after 2017–18 [*Social Security (Contributions) (Amendment) Regulations 2018, SI 2018/120, Reg 8*].

Further to legislative amendments making Pay As You Earn Settlement Agreements (PSAs) enduring, rather than having to be renewed each year, additional legislation can be expected facilitating digital applications and returns to replace the existing paper processes.

Office of Tax Simplification – tax-NIC alignment

[1.19] The Office of Tax Simplification (OTS) announced in July 2015 that it had agreed with the government to undertake a study into the closer alignment of income tax and National Insurance contributions. The published aim was to build on the OTS's earlier work and recommendations in this area, to understand the different stages of improving the alignment of the taxes.

The OTS published its report ahead of Budget 2016.

The main aim of the project was to explore more fully the steps that would need to be taken to achieve closer alignment of income tax and National Insurance contributions, and the costs, benefits and impacts of each of those steps.

The report considered the evidence already available, including previous OTS work, and undertook further research with stakeholders and taxpayers. The OTS considered in particular:

- the case for change, including the distortions, burdens and costs associated with the current system;
- the changes that could be introduced to bring the two systems closer together in relation to the taxation of earned income (for employers and employees) and the self-employed;
- the costs, benefits and impacts of each step;
- all forms of NIC charge, including employers' NICs;
- how any changes would fit with wider government policy/objectives, including:
  - the system of determining entitlement to contributory benefits;
  - exchequer costs; and
  - burdens for business.

The review was to consider the base of the systems but not the extension of NICs to non-employment income (such as property, dividends and pensions).

In carrying out its work and framing its recommendations, the OTS was instructed to have regard to:

- the effect on taxpayer and business understanding of the system;
- the likely effect on compliance burdens;
- the impact on any distortions to current taxpayer behaviour caused by the current system;
- avoidance risks;
- the principles and design of HMRC's Making Tax Easier reforms, including digital tax accounts, integrated reporting and payment;
- HMRC operational impacts;
- likely revenue implications, both in terms of exchequer impact and the impact on different types of taxpayers;
- administrative costs for government (including the administration of the contributory benefit system); and
- fairness and consistency of treatment of taxpayers.

The OTS is following a path trodden by a number of previous government-sponsored committees and reviews, but the terms of reference suggested that, this time, the Chancellor may be more willing to consider radical reform. The review also took place against a background of the advent of the new single-tier state pension, which is less of an obstacle to reform than the former S2P system, which differentiated in a significant way between employed and self-employed contributors. It also followed the transition of the RTI reporting regime to 'business as usual' for HMRC, which might conceivably make harmonisation simpler because nearly all employers now rely on software to carry out the necessary payroll calculations, and HMRC should have a real-time overview of both the tax and NIC position of every employed taxpayer/contributor that could be used to alleviate some of the problems arising from harmonisation or alignment.

Although superficially both PAYE and NIC are taxes levied on the same sources of earned income, in practice there are wide differences, many of which have been irreconcilable for many years.

Income tax taxes (in principle) all income, but PAYE applies to earnings, with coding adjustments to collect tax on other types of taxable income, and a self-assessment tax return to true-up the tax calculations each year where necessary. In contrast, NICs are charged only on employment earnings and self-employment profits, and not on other forms of income such as savings, pensions or interest and (with the exception of directors) on an earnings period rather than an annual basis. The terms of reference suggested that some of these differences will remain, but this casts doubt on the logic of trying to align. If a PAYE code is used to collect tax on an amount that differs from the earned income for NIC purposes, there will still be two separate calculations using separate rates applied to separate chargeable amounts. Alignment is not feasible unless NICs become chargeable on non-earnings, but that is more easily said than done.

Equally, full alignment cannot happen while NICs are payable only by those between 16 and state pension age while income tax is due at all ages. Could this reasonably be addressed or aligned? The decision to exclude the possibility of making pensions liable to NICs is entirely logical: income tax is constitutionally used for the running of the state, while NICs are ring-fenced in the NI Fund to pay for contributory benefits, which in practice means the state pension. It would make no sense to charge under-16s NICs as, absent a rewriting of the benefits legislation, they would not count for future benefit purposes (and any amounts would almost inevitably be trivial). More importantly, it would make no sense whatsoever to charge state pensioners NICs, of any class, on their state pension since they would then be paying contributions out of the pension they had bought with their earlier contributions. This would amount to a de facto pension cut, which would have the potential to lose elections for the party that introduced it.

The basis of calculation for employment income differs between income tax (assessed on an annual basis across all income sources, but collected weekly or monthly under PAYE) and NICs (on an earnings basis per employment and per pay period for employed earners, and on an annual basis for the self-employed and company directors).

The legal definitions of earnings are different for income tax and employee NICs, with a number of items relating to employment, including benefits in kind and expenses, being treated differently between the two codes for sound historical reasons that have not entirely lost their importance. The lack of a Class 1 charge on payments in kind stems from the inability to deduct a contribution from goods or services provided by the employer. It should not be forgotten that NICs pre-date PAYE, which was bolted on to an annual income tax system when only 20% of the population was liable to make a return. NICs were intended to cover all workers and were never intended to be deducted from payments in kind, which would principally have consisted of free accommodation or items produced or sold by the business (eg, sacks of coal for miners). Unless employee NIC becomes an annual charge, allowing time for employers to evaluate benefits in kind correctly, it must be right that payments in kind (other than in the form of readily convertible assets) remain outside Class 1 liability. The introduction of a statutory basis of payrolling benefits in kind in April 2016 notably did not attempt to levy Class 1 contributions on the benefits that were to be payrolled: Class 1A must still be paid, even though payrolled benefits are no longer reported on form P11D.

If a new primary Class 1A charge was to be invented (ie, using the P11D numbers – or the numbers that would appear on a P11D if a form was needed – as the basis of an annual employee levy), there would also be a need for a mechanism to collect the charge, which would frequently be an amount too large to take from one week's or month's pay. The PAYE system allows for coding adjustments to collect income tax on benefits in kind, so something similar would presumably be required for NIC, but there are several objections to that. The aim of the reform is allegedly simplification rather than revenue raising, but introducing variable NIC codes along the same lines as PAYE codes could not be described as a simplification measure. There would also be the

K-code problem: HMRC cannot require employers to take more than 50% of pay by way of PAYE deduction. Where would the equivalent limit be set for NIC purposes?

Although both income tax and NICs are collected under PAYE, income tax is collected on a cumulative basis; NICs on a pay period basis. NICs could be made cumulative, but there would then be a need for NIC liabilities to be reconciled annually, just as PAYE tax is included in a P800 for non-SA taxpayers. There would also be a need for NIC codes, like PAYE codes, to be issued on a week 1/month 1 basis in the second half of the year, inevitably leading to differences that require a year-end reconciliation. The position would be compounded where a worker has multiple employments, consecutively and/or concurrently. The RTI system struggles to cope now with such cases. The P45 system would have to be extended to include NICs year to date, broken down by the earnings brackets as they are now in the RTI system.

The implications of multiple employments are more than doubled in the case of NICs because, unlike PAYE, there is an employer contribution based on the same earnings as the employee contribution, and employer obligations based on earnings in that employment. How would the employer threshold be shared equitably between employers who might be unaware of each other's existence? Logically, employer NICs must be divorced from employee NICs.

If the worker is to be given a quasi-PAYE code to split NIC thresholds across employments and will carry the history from job to job, why would that not apply to the employer contribution? If that was done, one employer could easily find itself liable for secondary NICs because the annual limit had been used up in a previous job with a different, wholly unrelated employer. Why should Employer 1 be able to pay £8,164 (to take the 2017–18 value by way of example) without liability, but Employer 2 then suffer a 13.8% levy on everything paid to a new recruit? Why would the employer then not prefer to recruit a worker with no previous earnings in that tax year? PAYE can deal with aggregated earnings and multiple employments because it is a collection mechanism with an annual reconciliation process tied to an annual liability decided under separate rules for a single, liable taxpayer. NIC law provides for both liability and collection and currently isolates employments and employers one from another because it is wholly impractical to aggregate and cumulate for both parties.

How would the NIC thresholds be split across concurrent employments? Employees could have the equivalent of a shared PAYE code, but would initially need the NIC equivalent of a BR or 0T PAYE code, and an annual reconciliation process. Employers might also be given a share of the annual secondary threshold, but on hiring a new employee the employer would need the equivalent of the old P46 or new starter declaration, and another (and different) annual reconciliation. How would the split of employer liabilities between unrelated employments be decided? Anyone with a starter or leaver on payroll at some point in the year would want to know that no more than the correct amount of employer NICs had been paid, but each employer would not be entitled to personal data about the employee's earnings that were unrelated to the employment in question. It seems impossible to square that circle as long as employers are to share a single exemption attaching to the employee. It could be solved if each employment was standalone (ie, as it is currently), but that would detach the NIC liability from the PAYE tax liability, which is hardly the object of the 'simplification' exercise. Logically, the employer liability will have to be based on all earnings, not the excess over the secondary threshold, with the rate lowered and the employment allowance increased to compensate for the loss of the nil-rate band up to the secondary threshold for each worker. This seems almost certain to result in a major redistribution of liabilities, which could be politically difficult. The most obvious difference to most observers is that NICs continue to have a contributory link, although some commentators have suggested that this is much weaker than in the past. This may be so, but it is nevertheless still a barrier to alignment.

In the short term, for example, an employer pays SMP based on a woman having worked continuously for the employer and had earnings at the LEL for the 26 weeks leading up to the qualifying week, which is the 15th week before the expected week of childbirth. Entitlement does not depend on having paid NICs, but is instead tied to the NIC LEL, so it might not be too hard to reword the legislation to achieve the same result for employed women without the link to NIC (although the position of self-employed women claiming maternity allowance is much more problematic, given that they report and pay NICs annually).

Contributory jobseeker's allowance is, in contrast, based on having paid (or been treated as paying) Class 1 NICs at a minimum level for the two tax years ended before the calendar year of the JSA claim. State pension entitlement depends on having done so for at least ten years, and the maximum entitlement from April 2016 requires a qualifying contribution record for 35 years, although these contributions can be of Class 1, 2 or 3, or can be credits of earnings or contributions. Widows' pensions and bereavement payments have slightly different rules.

Whatever alignment might involve, it seems unlikely that the government will want to rewrite the social security benefits legislation in order to achieve what is, in effect, a minor simplification in the PAYE system.

The OTS has already noted that the annual starting points for PAYE and NIC, which were once aligned by Gordon Brown as a simplification measure, are now considerably different, and even the employer and employee thresholds for NICs have been different, but have been re-aligned from 2017–18. The government has made it clear that it intends to raise the personal allowance to £12,500 by 2020, and once that level is reached it is intended to rise in line with the national minimum wage earned by a worker paid for 30 hours per week for 52 weeks in the year. It has not yet been clarified whether this will mean the new national living wage for over-25s, which is targeted to reach £9 per hour by 2020, which in turn would imply a personal allowance of £14,040, 32% higher than the 2015–16 allowance when the policy was conceived.

An increase in the 2015–16 primary threshold of £8,060 to match the 2015–16 personal allowance of £10,600 would cost the NI Fund £305 per year per worker, and there are around 30 million workers, some of whom have multiple jobs (HMRC processes around 60 million 'employment' records, including pensioners, each year), so the loss to the NI Fund from aligning the primary contributions threshold might be up to £9 billion per year. The loss of secondary NICs might be around £10 billion on the same basis. Ninety-eight percent of NI Fund income is currently being spent on funding current state pension expenditure, so the loss would have to be made up without delay. The main rates – which have now been locked for five years, while the UEL is to be linked to the 40% tax threshold – would have to rise by around 20% to make up the loss. It is therefore clear that alignment of the starting points for PAYE and Class 1 NICs is not currently part of the plan and is unlikely to feature in the plan in this parliament.

The self-employed pay NICs at a lower rate than employees and under the contributory system, have slightly reduced benefit entitlement, although the planned abolition of Class 2 NICs and transfer into Class 4 would mean that the self-employed will pay a single class of NICs like employees. As already noted, since JSA is the only real employee-only benefit (disregarding the six weeks of higher rate SMP for new mothers), any material differential is hard to justify, and the government (despite its manifesto promise) has avoided locking the rate of self-employed contributions.

Apart from the rates and the treatment of most benefits in kind, employee and employer NICs are largely aligned. Cash and cash-like elements (such as shares and other readily convertible assets) of both are largely aligned and collected through the PAYE system on a pay period basis. Benefits in kind are charged to Class 1A employer NICs only (or Class 1B if they are dealt with through a PAYE Settlement Agreement) and collected at the end of the year in a separate payment, although from 2016 some non-cash elements may be collected voluntarily through the payroll in line with previous OTS recommendations.

In the OTS Small Business Review, differences in the rules and procedures between the income tax and NICs systems were found to be the second highest source of complexity for small businesses.

The OTS report identified that maintaining two separate systems led to a number of anomalies, helping to distort business behaviour. The OTS recommended bringing the two systems close together and, importantly, set out a number of stages that could be taken to implement this while stopping short of a full merger. Each of the stages was expected to yield (unquantified and unquantifiable) simplification dividends.

Following the OTS Small Business Review, in 2011 the government set up a number of stakeholder groups and commissioned external research into attitudes of small employers, and a paper was published summarising the results. It was decided to wait for progress on other changes to the tax system that employers were implementing (for example on Real Time Information and the Scottish Rate of Income Tax) before consulting further on aligning the operation of income tax and NIC.

The OTS's subsequent UK Competitiveness Review and Employment Status report both returned to the issue of IT/NIC alignment. Both reports reiterated the difficulties caused by the differing systems. Closer alignment was seen as a way of improving competitiveness and as the main indirect way of 'solving' employment status problems. The impact of employer NICs was seen a major issue in both cases.

Without all the data and estimates accumulated by the OTS team, it is difficult to rationalise the point about competitiveness. Some commentators find it hard to believe that the UK's competitiveness is really being held back by the fact that the payroll software calculates PAYE on earnings above £11,850 per year and NICs on earnings above £8,424 per year. The burden of employer NICs is a true monetary cost to business, but the OTS is looking for simplification rather than rate cuts.

The Tax/NIC alignment project moved into its next OTS phase with the issue of its 177-page report on closer alignment on 7 March 2016: www.gov.uk/government/publications/closer-alignment-of-income-tax-and-national-insurance-contributions.

It proposed a seven-stage program for bringing the two taxes closer together:

1. moving to an annual, cumulative and aggregate basis for NICs;
2. basing employer NICs on hold payroll costs and renaming the charge;
3. aligning the self-employed NICs more closely with the employees' NICs and benefits;
4. improving transparency for NICs and the contributory principle;
5. aligning the definition of both earnings and expenses for income tax and NICs;
6. bringing taxable benefits in kind into Class 1 NICs; and
7. having a joined up approach for income tax and NIC law and practice.

The report noted that the potential changes it outlined would impact on millions of people: around 7.1 million would pay less NICs but 6.3 million would pay more, albeit with some gain in contributory benefit entitlement (mainly in the longer term, since almost all benefit expenditure from the NI Fund is on the state pension). The OTS strongly recommended that a lot more work needed to be done to consider the impacts of the proposed measures in more detail so that policy options would be better understood.

It will be interesting to see how the OTS project progresses and whether any substantive change emerges. Some people have quite reasonably questioned whether splitting one tax into two, with separate rules, and without full alignment of the employee contributions rules with the PAYE rules, can reasonably be termed 'simplification'. It is also interesting to note that the OTS project is running at the same time as the plan to abolish Class 2 and rework Class 4 in order to attach benefit entitlements. It is not clear whether there are any links between the two programmes, despite the OTS report making explicit reference to reducing the differences between the treatment of the employed and self-employed when designing 'two taxes fit for future working patterns'.

The terms of reference for the future of the tax-NIC alignment project were published in May 2016. The focus is to be narrowed to an annual, cumulative and aggregate basis of calculating NICs (ie, making Class 1 more like PAYE) and divorcing the employer and employee contributions, turning secondary

NICs into a payroll tax. The second is a pre-requisite of the first. A report is due to be published before the Autumn Statement 2016, but the major nature of the upheavals that would follow (in implementation and transition) would mean that there are unlikely to be any legislative or systems changes before 2020.

The Office of Tax Simplification (OTS) review of bringing together Class 1 NICs and PAYE operations that was announced in Budget 2016 resulted in a series of proposals. The then Chancellor asked for further work to be carried out on just two aspects, the potential impacts of:

(a) separating employer and employee NICs, so that they could be calculated separately; and
(b) moving primary contributions onto an 'annualised, cumulative and aggregated' (ACA) basis, so that the PAYE process could be applied.

The brief for the further work explicitly excluded any consideration of changing the exemption from NICs of employer pension contributions, or collecting NICs on payments from registered or state pension schemes, or on investment income such as dividends from both public and private companies.

This further work resulted in a new report, 'Closer Alignment of Income Tax and National Insurance', issued by the OTS on 14 November 2016.

This set out a plan to convert the Class 1 employee threshold into an allowance that would be shared across multiple employments by means of a new NIC code, analogous to a PAYE code, and to convert the Class 1 employer contribution into a separate payroll tax.

The separation of employer and employee contributions would be a prerequisite of the ACA project, as splitting the contribution threshold across multiple employments for which earnings had to be aggregated would result in employers refusing to employ workers with more than one employment because of the increased secondary liability. Given the choice between a worker with one employment and a full secondary threshold available, and a worker whose other employer already takes that secondary threshold into account, the employer would be very likely to choose the former in order to avoid paying 13.8% on the earnings up to the employer threshold in the second employment. Even sharing the threshold would be problematic, so the OTS offered several options for a new basis for an employer payroll tax to support the NI Fund, raising the same amount of money as the current system. This included a simple flat rate of around 10% on all earnings paid, an unchanged rate with an allowance similar to the employment allowance to compensate for the loss of the employer threshold, and several other options for consideration.

With separation of employer and employee systems, primary NICs could be operated on a similar basis to PAYE, sharing a single threshold across employments and aiming to collect the same amount of contributions from different earners with the same level of earnings however many employments they held.

The report made the very valid point that a worker with one employment and total earnings of £15,000, spread over the year, would currently pay much more than a worker with a shorter term employment with the same total earnings (because more would be subject to the 2% additional rate rather than to the 12% main rate), while a worker with three concurrent employments earning £15,000 in total over the same year might pay no NICs and earn no benefit entitlements because the earnings in each job might fall below the LEL.

ACA would result in many low-pay workers paying NICs based on their aggregated earnings, but would equally lead to some with higher pay in multiple employments having to pay less at 12% and more at 2%. Under the current regime, the latter should be able to rely on the existing annual maximum rules to claim a refund of any excessive contributions, but the former would not be given any relief for the extra contributions (beyond earning extra benefit entitlements in marginal cases).

Introducing ACA would involve the introduction into payrolls of a NIC code, necessarily separate from the PAYE code: it would be based broadly on the current level of the primary threshold, not the income tax personal allowance; it would be added to the P45 for job changers; it would not reflect expense deductions, pension contributions or investment income, or indeed income tax underpayments being recouped from later earnings; and it would be based on different rules in the case of cross-border workers. Like PAYE, the NIC code issued late in the year would probably have to be on an emergency or Week 1/Month 1 basis, automatically creating under or overpayments. The move would also require an annual reconciliation, similar to the P800 process, for anyone who changed jobs in the year or had more than one job, paying NICs on the emergency code basis.

It would be hard to describe this fairly as simplification: two tax regimes with necessarily differing rules and separate compliance requirements where formerly there had been one, and with built-in discrepancies and reconciliation.

The government accepted that further work should be done to consider the option of creating a new payroll tax for employer contributions (officials will 'keep this under review', which suggests that any such work will not be a priority), but the idea of moving Class 1 onto an ACA basis has been shelved, according to a letter from the Chancellor to the OTS published with the Autumn Statement 2016. Such a reform 'would be a major upheaval, with consequences for the labour market and a large number of individuals and businesses'. It seems likely that the OTS estimates of 5.5 million losers (ie paying more NICs) and 7.6 million winners (ie paying less NICs) made the likely upheaval and political sensitivity a step too far.

The statutory provisions on National Insurance cannot be included in the annual Finance Bill, because the Bill's remit specifically excludes any tax that does not raise money for financing central government as a whole. The Office of Tax Simplification recommended that NICs legislation should be amended such that future income tax changes apply automatically to NICs (OTS 'Closer alignment of income tax and national insurance: further review', November 2016, Annex B, recommendation 6k).

Should this proposal come to fruition, it would perhaps contrite the minds more of various government departments. For example, the proposed implementation of Class 1A NICs on termination payments over £30,000 has been deferred until 2019 owing to the complexity of abolishing Class 2 NICs/consequent changes to Class 4 NICs, all of which require a NICs Bill. At the time of writing, the NICs Bill had not been published.

Class 3A

[1.20] The window for paying Class 3A contributions to top up existing state pensions (ie, for those state pensioners who will not qualify for the new single-tier state pension because they reached state pension age before 6 April 2016) opened on 12 October 2015 and closed on 5 April 2017. The application process was online or by telephone (0345 600 4270). The background to the contributions is described at **19.11** below.

Apprenticeships

[1.21] *NICA 2015, s 1* introduced a new zero rate of employer contribution to be applied to the earnings of apprentices under the age of 25, which was implemented from 6 April 2016. Details are set out below at **10.2**. The proposed apprenticeship levy, introduced in April 2017, is not a national insurance levy and is not discussed in this work.

Penalties

[1.22] A consultation on penalty reform entitled *HMRC Penalties: a Discussion Document* was issued on 2 February 2015, seeking views on how to change the way that penalties are applied. The consultation period closed on 11 May 2015 and HMRC responded on 17 September 2015.

No detailed proposals for change were advanced, but several principles seem likely to influence any forthcoming reform:

- HMRC will distinguish between 'the vast majority of customers who are generally compliant and those who are not';
- the goal is to charge fewer penalties but counter the activities of careless and intentionally non-compliant 'customers', taking account of their compliance history across all taxes; and
- HMRC will automate and simplify the penalty process as much as possible.

The first priority will be to deal with the large volumes of low-value penalties in relation to late filing with a high incidence of successful appeals, which could easily absorb too much HMRC staff time. HMRC is to explore options for not charging a penalty when:

- no tax is due and where the circumstances for not charging are appropriate;
- the period of lateness is very short;
- there is a first default; or
- the 'customer' otherwise demonstrates a good compliance history across all of the taxes they are involved with.

There may also be increased opportunities for and use of mitigation in recognition of the circumstances surrounding the default and HMRC's desire to encourage future good compliance.

Consideration is also being given to issuing reminders to 'customers' about their return being due (before the due date is reached) and drawing their attention to the default and its consequences for penalty purposes (after the due date has passed). The experience with generic notifications under the RTI regime suggest that this may be problematic unless data quality improves dramatically or there is in-built flexibility to disregard minor delays, such as the three-day easement introduced for the period up to 5 April 2016, which was extended without fanfare to 5 April 2017 by a low-profile change to the online guidance in May 2016.

HMRC is also considering replacing or enhancing penalties for late payment with a penalty interest regime so as to make HMRC's response to non-compliance more proportionate to the offence.

In considering penalties for inaccuracies, HMRC has recognised that the *FA 2007, Sch 24* regime is often too subjective and difficult to operate. The level of penalty for under-declared NICs is currently dependent upon whether the mistake was a simple mistake, a careless error, a deliberate error or a deliberate error that was concealed, and whether the error was disclosed voluntarily or found by HMRC compliance checking. The discounts offered depend on further subjective judgements about how the error is rectified. All of these decisions involve difficult assessments of what caused an inaccuracy and the quality of the assistance offered by the taxpayer and his agent. There is also a question mark (in official minds, at least) over how HMRC should deal with inaccuracies that result from failed attempts at avoidance.

There are numerous factors that will be weighed in designing any new regime. The response document notes that, 'For example, a system that recognises the compliance history of the customer across all taxes, focusing on the number of inaccuracies in a given time period rather than the circumstances of each separate instance of inaccuracy, may be a more objective test of some kinds of behaviour and more suited to automated penalties but risks treating repeated occasions of careless inaccuracy as being more serious than isolated instances of evasion.'

HMRC is to consult further and does not expect to propose new legislation before Finance Bill 2017 (and for NIC purposes, changes will then probably require a further NIC Bill). The only penalty changes made in *Finance Act 2016* relate to the GAAR, frequent tax avoidance and certain offshore activities, although the government has, in August 2016, also announced plans to introduce new penalties for advisers who facilitate the use of avoidance schemes.

European social security coordination

[1.23] *EC Regulations 883/2004* and *987/2009* lay down the rules coordinating social security coverage for migrant workers within the EEA and Switzerland, and some who are posted outside the EEA by an employer in a Member State that it is not their home state.

The regulation determines the identity of the 'competent state', ie, the state that has the right to collect contributions and the obligation to provide social security benefits to migrant workers. Much is made in certain parts of the UK press about the rights of migrants to move freely to the UK and access social security benefits, but the perception of unfairness to locals, and the lack of understanding of the scope of the EC regulations is not limited to the UK, although the UK is the only state to date to have voted to exit the EU based principally on the difficulties with freedom of movement.

It has always been the case that the treaty guarantees freedom of movement within the community or union for the purposes of finding work, and that the regulations are meant to underpin that fundamental freedom, but it has also always been the case that the treaty and the regulations cover only *contributory* benefits, with limits on how migrants may qualify for such benefits in a host Member State. European coordination rules do not and have never been intended to grant rights to '*social assistance*' benefits, ie, non-contributory, means-tested benefits.

The case of *Neukölln v Alimanovic*: C-67/14 (2015) ECLI:EU:C:2015:597, [2015] All ER (D) 73 (Sep) demonstrates the principle in the context of German social security law. The authorities refused subsistence allowances (equivalent broadly to the UK's non-contributory JSA) after paying them for six months to a single-parent family that had come to Germany from Sweden, taking the view that Ms Alimanovic and her eldest daughter were excluded from entitlement to the allowances concerned as foreign jobseekers whose right of residence arose solely out of the search for employment. Consequently, the authority also excluded the other children from entitlement to the allowances pertaining to them.

The Court of Justice of the EU (CJEU) held, in a judgment delivered on 15 September 2015, that denying Union citizens whose right of residence in the territory of a host Member State arises solely out of the search for employment entitlement to certain 'special non-contributory cash benefits', which also constitute 'social assistance', does not contravene the principle of equal treatment, even if nationals of the host Member State in similar circumstances are granted such benefits by domestic legislation.

The CJEU had previously found that the same principle applied to Member State nationals who go to another Member State with no intention of finding employment there. [*Dano v Jobcenter Leipzig*: C-333/13 (2014) ECLI:EU:C:2014:2358, [2015] 1 WLR 2519, [2015] All ER (EC) 1, ECJ.]

The CJEU in *Alimanovic* recorded that, in order to obtain social assistance such as that at issue in the case, an EU citizen can claim equal treatment with nationals of the host Member State only if his residence in the territory of the host Member State complies with the conditions of the 'Free Movement of Citizens' Directive (EC Directive 2004/38/EC). The Court noted that there were two possibilities for the purposes of granting a right of residence to jobseekers such as those in the present case: where an EU citizen who has enjoyed a right of residence as a worker is in involuntary unemployment after having worked for less than a year and has registered as a jobseeker with the relevant employment office, he retains the status of worker and the right of residence for no less than six months. During that period, he can rely on the principle of equal treatment and is entitled to social assistance. Where an EU citizen has not yet worked in the host Member State or where the period of six months has elapsed, a jobseeker cannot be expelled from that Member State for as long as he can provide evidence that he is continuing to seek employment and that he has a genuine chance of being engaged. However, in that case the host Member State may refuse to grant any social assistance.

It should be noted that the rules are not straightforward where the individual has exercised the right of free movement in order to work but has subsequently been unable to work due to childbirth. In *SSWP v SFF*; *ADR v SSWP*; *CS v LB Barnet* [2015] UKUT 502 (AAC), which were lead cases, the Upper Tribunal (Administrative Appeals Chamber) allowed several appeals against the denial by the UK of certain rights to non-contributory benefits on the grounds that the appellants had not established a right of residence. The cases had been stayed pending the outcome of the decision of the Court of Justice of the European Union in *Saint Prix v Secretary of State for Work and Pensions*: C-507/12 (2014) ECLI:EU:C:2014:2007, [2014] All ER (EC) 987, [2015] 1 CMLR 118, ECJ, following a referral to it by the Supreme Court (see [2012] UKSC 49, [2013] 1 All ER 752, [2013] 1 CMLR 1101).

In that case, Ms Saint Prix, a French national, was employed in the UK before giving up work, less than three months before the birth of her child, because of the physical constraints of the late stages of pregnancy and the immediate aftermath of childbirth. She returned to work three months after the birth of her child, without having left the UK during the period of interruption of her professional activity.

She had come to the UK in July 2006 to seek work, mainly as a teaching assistant, and did so from 1 September 2006 until 1 August 2007, paying UK NICs in respect of her earnings. She had then enrolled on a Post-Graduate Certificate in Education course at the University of London, the envisaged period of study being from 17 September 2007 until 27 June 2008. During that period she had become pregnant, with an expected date of childbirth of 2 June 2008.

On 22 January 2008, hoping to find work in secondary schools, Ms Saint Prix had registered with an employment agency and, on 1 February 2008, she had withdrawn from the course that she had been attending at the University of London. As no secondary school work had been available, she had taken agency positions working in nursery schools. On 12 March 2008, when she had been nearly six months pregnant, Ms Saint Prix had stopped that work, however, on the grounds that the demands of caring for nursery school children had become too strenuous for her. She had looked, without success, for work that was more suited to her pregnancy.

On 18 March 2008, ie, 11 weeks before the expected birth, Ms Saint Prix had made a claim for income support. As that claim had been refused by the Secretary of State by decision of 4 May 2008, she had brought an appeal before the First-tier Tribunal.

On 21 August 2008, namely three months after the premature birth of her child, Ms Saint Prix had resumed work.

The CJEU held that the fact that the constraints of maternity require a woman to give up work during the period needed for recovery does not, in principle, deprive her of the status of 'worker' within the meaning of Article 45 of the

TFEU. A woman who gives up work, or seeking work, because of the physical constraints of the late stages of pregnancy and the aftermath of childbirth retains the status of 'worker', within the meaning of that article, provided she returns to work or finds another job within a reasonable period after the birth of her child.

The fact that Ms Saint Prix was not actually available on the UK employment market for a few months did not mean that she had ceased to belong to that market during that period, provided she returned to work or found another job within a reasonable period after childbirth. The DWP had incorrectly denied her income support as a result of misinterpreting her situation in the context of Directive 2004/38/EC.

Travel and subsistence for intermediary workers

[1.24] HMRC has been addressing the loss of tax and NICs from salary sacrifice schemes for some time. On 8 July 2015, HMRC published 'Employment Intermediaries and Tax Relief for Travel and Subsistence', setting out proposals to remove tax and NIC exemption from the expenses of travel between home and work for any employee supplied to a client, to provide personal service to the client, by an intermediary such as an umbrella company or personal service company, while subject to supervision, direction or control ('the SDC condition').

The clear aim of the changes was to remove the tax and NIC advantages available at the time to those who were employed by an intermediary and sent to various clients, being paid the expenses of travel to and from a temporary workplace, which was often combined by 'umbrella' employers with reducing taxable and NICable pay by a similar amount (termed 'salary sacrifice' or the 'payday-by-payday relief model' by HMRC). Such intermediary-supplied workers should then have been placed on an equal footing with directly employed staff who could not be paid tax- and NIC-free expenses for ordinary commuting. The plan was to treat each engagement of the umbrella worker as a separate employment, as was already the case with agency workers on temporary assignments.

In order to avoid collateral damage where employees were supplied to various clients by an ordinary employer that was not an employment business (eg, a firm of accountants seconding a member of staff to a client to cover for a maternity absence), the new rules were not to apply to businesses that were not involved substantially in the supply of labour.

The requirement for there to be supervision, direction or control was similar to, and was to be interpreted in the same way as, the rule introduced in 2014 by amendments to *ITEPA 2003, s 44* and the *Social Security (Categorisation of Earners) Regulations 1978* for bringing otherwise self-employed workers into Class 1 NIC and PAYE liability. HMRC's guidance on SDC is now contained in the Employment Status Manual, principally at ESM2029 onwards.

The consultation document also outlined plans for, in certain circumstances, any liability for the PAYE and NIC debt incurred from the misuse of travel and subsistence tax reliefs to be transferred to the engager. The engager ought to be best placed to be aware whether the worker is subject in any way to supervision, direction or control, and whether the worker is being supplied by an intermediary, but is by no means best placed to deduct PAYE and NIC, so the consultation document was subjected to much criticism.

Any changes were to be introduced by Finance Bill 2016 and parallel NIC regulations. Draft legislation was published shortly after the Autumn Statement 2015, but was changed before it became *Finance Act 2016, s 14*.

As noted above, the new legislation was targeted principally at umbrella companies and personal service companies supplying workers who were effectively operating just like employees of the client business but were being paid tax-free travel expenses instead of taxable wages. The tax relief in question is available generally to those employees travelling to and from a temporary workplace by virtue of *ITEPA 2003, ss 338 and 339*. The change made by *FA 2016* and NIC regulations, with effect from 6 April 2016, deems the target group of workers to have a permanent workplace for each new assignment, which prevents most of the payments from being treated as tax- and NIC-free.

The changes are set out in detail in 30 EARNINGS FROM EMPLOYMENT: EXPENSES.

IR35 reform

[1.25] On 17 July 2015, HMRC published 'Intermediaries Legislation (IR35): discussion document', seeking views on how the IR35 rules for personal service companies (PSCs) might be made more effective. HMRC believes that only 10% of companies within IR35 are compliant, although the document does not explain how this estimate was made. There were estimated to be around 265,000 PSCs in 2012–13, and non-compliance is estimated to cost the Exchequer around £430 million in tax and NICs receipts for 2015–16. The deterrent effect of the IR35 rules was estimated to have 'protected' around £520 million of receipts in 2010–11. Again, no basis for these figures has been published.

The document acknowledged that the area is complex and that 'it is very difficult to create and enforce a system that addresses the problem of disguised employment which doesn't also have some impact on those who are genuinely self-employed and operating through a company for legitimate, commercial reasons.'

HMRC's preferred reform would have seen engagers (clients) required to consider whether, when a worker is engaged through a PSC, IR35 should apply. If it should, the engager would deduct the NIC and PAYE as it would for direct employees. The major advantage for HMRC would be that, if IR35 should have been applied but compliance action establishes that it had not, it would be more likely to be able to assess and collect the deductions from the client, who is more likely to be in existence than a PSC that might have had a life of only a year or two and was then liquidated. The major problem is the impracticality of the proposal. How does an engager know that the worker is supplied by a PSC, especially if the work is arranged through an agency? Even if the engager knows that the worker is being supplied by a company, it might not be a PSC. How does the engager know how much to treat as earnings, especially if there is an agency (or several agencies) involved? How are the necessary information flows to be mandated if any of the parties is outside UK jurisdiction?

To simplify matters for engagers, one option advanced is to align the IR35 test with that used for temporary workers in the agency rules, which is based on supervision, direction or control. Another option could be to look again at some of the suggestions considered by the OTS, such as requiring an engagement to last a certain minimum amount of time to be considered one of employment.

HMRC is clearly concerned to be seen to be cracking down on the abuse of IR35, but the impractical proposals (similar to those considered and rejected when IR35 was first designed in 1999) were unlikely to solve HMRC's problems with its inability to monitor and enforce compliance. The consultation document put no timescale on any potential changes, but a new document was issued in May 2016 proposing to restrict the suggested changes to contracts between personal service companies and public sector.

A revised plan was set out in the document, *'Off-payroll working in the public sector: reform of the intermediaries legislation'*. The government, from April 2017, has imposed an obligation on the entity paying the PSC to deduct PAYE and NIC from the amount paid to the PSC, if the public sector client is not satisfied that the contract falls outside of IR35. If the contract is made directly between the PSC and the client, the public sector client is to operate RTI and account for PAYE and NICs. If an agency is involved (which will almost invariably be the case), the duty falls on the agency paying the PSC. Further details are set out at **40.2** below. It is widely expected that this measure will be extended to the private sector, and Autumn Budget 2017 (para 3.7) stated that the Government will 'carefully consult on how to tackle non-compliance in the private sector, drawing on the experience of the public sector reforms, including through external research already commissioned by the government and due to be published in 2018'.

Travel and subsistence for all workers

[1.26] On 23 September 2015, HM Treasury published a further 'discussion paper' on the general rules on travel and subsistence, in an attempt to find ways of reducing the amount of tax and NIC relief given by simplifying the rules where employees undertake journeys other than those between their normal base and a temporary location.

The case for changed was couched in the following terms:

> 'The physical work environment and patterns of working have evolved since the rules last changed. Better technology enables people to work flexibly across different locations, at their home and while travelling. Many employees do not have a fixed desk at any particular workplace or at a particular geographical location. There has also been an increase in the number of people who have responsibility for a geographical area and, as a result, make regular visits to a number of different sites.
>
> The OTS found that the current system is reasonably well understood by employers and works for the majority of employees – those who attend the same work place

each day and make an occasional business trip. However, the OTS also found that complexities arose for some employees who travel frequently to perform their work duties.

. . . .

The main issues that the OTS review highlighted were:

- a lack of understanding over the level of attendance that constitutes "regular attendance" and how that test fits with the other rules
- confusion around the definitions of permanent and temporary workplaces, particularly as these terms do not take their everyday meaning, making the distinction between them seem contrived and resulting in outcomes that look unfair to some workers (eg those employees who have a series of workplaces which most people would regard as being "temporary" under any ordinary use of the word)
- the fact that the "24 month rule" relies on the employee's intention rather than the amount of time actually spent at the location, making it difficult for an employer to judge when that employee's intention changed
- the fact that the current rules can mean that an employee ends up with more than one permanent workplace, even where their workplaces are a significant distance apart
- confusion around whether or not a journey is "substantively the same" as ordinary commuting or private travel
- confusion around homeworking, and whether or when a home to workplace travel is a workplace to workplace journey rather than ordinary commuting.'

The main suggestions for further discussion were that:

- tax relief should continue to be available for business travel, but not for ordinary commuting;
- any tests should be objective and based on measurable facts as far as possible – they should not rely on the intentions of the employee;
- new rules should not be based on the concepts of 'permanent' and 'temporary' workplaces except and unless these terms carry their everyday meaning;
- employees should not have their journeys to multiple locations or areas which are a significant distance apart all treated as being 'ordinary commuting';
- relief should not be available for subsistence where this is essentially akin to a private expense; and
- any changes should not come at an additional cost to the Exchequer.

The document identified a number of difficulties employers face, such as identifying when a temporary workplace becomes permanent, and dealing with employees who are on 'detached duty' on a regular basis. Potential solutions might involve giving more relief for travel, but balancing the cost by withdrawing all relief for day subsistence rates. International travel rules, the problems with non-statutory industry-specific allowances and the issue of record keeping and evidential requirements to show that expenses have actually been incurred will be brought within the scope of the project in the future.

Consultation meetings took place with various interested bodies but the idea was abandoned without a formal consultation on concrete proposals.

Statutory grandparental leave

[1.27] The then Chancellor announced at the Conservative Party conference in October 2015 a plan to allow working grandparents to take time off and share parental leave and pay to help care for their grandchildren, starting in 2018. This would extend the current system, which allows parents to share leave and statutory parental pay. According to the Chancellor, research has shown two million grandparents have either given up a job, reduced their hours or taken time off work to look after their grandchildren.

Budget 2016 re-announced the proposals, with a consultation document promised for May 2016, but the EU referendum then led to major disruption to the government's plans, and no such details have yet been made available of how the policy might work. The amendments needed to make RTI payroll software and HMRC's systems compatible would mean that introduction would be in April 2019 at the very earliest.

Statutory parental bereavement leave

[1.28] Currently there is no statutory right to bereavement leave and pay, although ACAS has a good practice guide to help employers manage bereavements affecting their employees. A private member's bill that has attracted support from all parties is meandering its way through Parliament.

The Parental Bereavement (Leave and Pay) Bill will provide a day one right to parents who lose a child (under 18) to two weeks of statutory parental bereavement leave. Entitlement to statutory bereavement pay will be dependent on the employee having 26 weeks of continuous service and average weekly earnings at least equal to the lower earnings limit for National Insurance.

Owing to the lead time needed to make HMRC's systems and payroll software compatible, it is unlikely that statutory parental leave and pay will be introduced prior to April 2020.

2

Administration

Cross-references. See **9.4** to **9.23**, APPEALS AND REVIEWS for remedies for dissatisfaction; **35.2** to **35.7** ENFORCEMENT for powers of inspectors; NATIONAL INSURANCE FUND **48**; NATIONAL INSURANCE NUMBER **49** for contribution-recording procedures and inaccuracy of records; **51.20** and **51.41** OVERSEAS MATTERS for derogation of authority to international bodies; **53.1** RATES AND LIMITS for the power to alter contribution rates.

Other Sources. HM Revenue and Customs Departmental Report, 2009 (Cm 7591).

HM Revenue and Customs and the Department for Work and Pensions

[2.1] Until 1 April 1999, the Department for Social Security (DSS) was the Government department responsible for giving effect to parliamentary legislation on matters of social security. The DSS became the Department for Work and Pensions on 8 June 2001, administering the various contributory and non-contributory state benefit schemes throughout Great Britain.

From 1 April 1999 all 8,400 contributions staff at Newcastle and 115 local office locations joined what was then the Inland Revenue, and a new executive office called the National Insurance Contributions Office (NICO) was created. A new department, HM Revenue and Customs, came into being in April 2005 which integrated the Inland Revenue and Customs & Excise departments into one large department. Many employer-related functions were subsequently centralised by HMRC in its Longbenton, Newcastle offices and the department was re-named the NIC & Employer Office, or NIC&EO.

The NIC&EO (which remains a key part of the new HM Revenue and Customs) is responsible for:

- collecting National Insurance contributions, 'with particular emphasis on ensuring full compliance by employers with payment and notification requirements';
- maintaining over 70 million individual records of which around 43 million are active (see **49.6** NATIONAL INSURANCE NUMBER); and
- providing NI-related information to government departments and pension providers to enable benefits to be paid promptly and accurately.

The Social Security Acts grant wide legislative powers and these are exercised by statutory instrument in the making of numerous orders and regulations. Once the drafts of such orders and regulations have been laid before Parliament and approved by a resolution of each House in accordance with the procedures prescribed in *Statutory Instruments Act 1946*, they become law and acquire the force of the enabling statute. [*SSAA 1992, ss 189, 190; SSCBA 1992, ss 175, 176*].

Collection

[2.2] National Insurance administration is dealt with by HM Revenue and Customs following SSC(TF)A 1999. Information obtained for tax purposes may be readily shared across the whole department. The DWP and HM Revenue and Customs are entirely separate departments of Government but, because until 1 April 1999 they had an area of common concern, ie the collection of taxes and contributions levied by Parliament on a common portion of the subject's income, the function of the DSS was, in that area, principally performed by the Inland Revenue. Thus, the then Inland Revenue collected almost all primary and secondary Class 1 contributions and Class 4 contributions due to the then DSS and, from time to time, paid these over to the National Insurance Fund (see **COLLECTION 21**).

Following the two transfers, there remain areas of common interest, including:

- the possibility that HM Revenue and Customs officers may, under arrangements made with the Secretary of State for Work and Pensions, carry out duties under *SSAA 1992, s 110* in connection with benefit matters;
- the operation of NPS, the contribution recording computer, which lies with HM Revenue and Customs following the transfer, although several parts of DWP are major users (NPS – National Insurance and PAYE Service – is the name from summer 2009 for the former National Insurance Recording System, NIRS 2, as this computer now also handles all the merged PAYE records for the whole country);
- the provision of earnings information submitted under the RTI reporting system to DWP (data in respect of taxpayers/contributors in whom DWP has registered an 'interest' with HMRC are transferred four times daily from HMRC to DWP) for the purposes of universal credit assessments;
- the need for liaison if the DWP agencies are to allow a claim for contributory benefit if the required contributions were not paid on time due to misinformation or other error on the part of NIC&EO or one of its predecessors.

Disclosure of information

[2.3] Information held by HM Revenue and Customs in connection with any function of HMRC (including contributions, tax credits, SSP, SMP, SPP, SAP, Statutory Shared Parental Pay (ShPP) and maternity allowance) may be supplied to the DWP in connection with any of its functions. Similarly, information held by DWP in those connections may be disclosed to HM Revenue and Customs for its departmental purposes. [*Welfare Reform Act 2012 (WRA 2012), s 127* from 8 May 2012; *SSAA 1992, ss 121E* and *121F* as inserted by *SSC(TF)A 1999* for earlier periods.] Once information is disclosed to the DWP the Department is as bound as HM Revenue and Customs not to disclose that information further, and vice versa, except with the express authority of the providing department (which may be given for the purpose of, eg, civil or criminal proceedings in relation to contribution law, or in relation to child maintenance payments). [*WRA 2012, s 127(5)* from 8 May 2012; *SSAA 1992, s 122(3)* for earlier periods.]

Inter-departmental disclosure

[2.4] The *Social Security Contributions (Transfer of Functions, etc) Act 1999, Sch 6 para 3 inserted a new SSAA 1992, s 122AA* which lifted the secrecy imposition on what is now HM Revenue and Customs relating to contributions (and also SSP, SMP, SPP and SAP). Disclosure could be made to the Health and Safety Executive, Government Actuary's Department, Office for National Statistics and the Pensions Regulator. The power was extended to include ShPP from 1 December 2014 by *Children and Families Act 2014, Sch 7, para 25(b)*.

> *Example*
>
> The DWP have, following the receipt of information on their fraud hotline, suspicions that individual X has been claiming benefit as a married man and that he is in fact not married, but for the past four years he has been receiving contributions-based jobseeker's allowance relevant to a married person. On investigation by the DWP the marriage certificate is proved to be a forgery and a prosecution is instigated by the DWP. Although the DWP may inform HM Revenue and Customs who may wish to investigate claims for tax credits, neither the DWP nor HMRC can at this stage advise the Registrar General of Births, Deaths and Marriages who would be obliged to undertake proceedings under the *Perjury Act 1911, s 3(1)*.

Specialised groups within HM Revenue and Customs NIC&EO may be contacted as follows

Longbenton, Newcastle upon Tyne, BX9 1AN

Deferment Services	Deferment of Class 1, 2 (now for pre-2015 matters only) and 4 contributions	Tel 0300 056 0631
Self-Employment Services	Class 2 and Class 3 (including direct debit)	Tel 0300 200 3505

Newly Self-Employed Helpline	Advises newly self-employed persons on general HMRC matters and accepts Class 2 registrations by phone	Tel 0300 200 3504
NI Deficiencies	For deficiency (contribution gap) enquiries	Tel 0300 200 3503
NI Registrations	For new NI number registrations	Tel 0345 600 0643/0300 200 3502
Overseas Contributions Helpline ('International Caseworker')		Tel 0300 200 3506 (from overseas +44 191 203 7010)
Overseas Contributions	NI for persons moving overseas	Tel 0300 055 5734
NISPI/Contracted-out Pensions	All aspects of contracted-out employment	Tel 0300 200 3507
General NI enquiries from individuals		Tel 0300 200 3500

Other HMRC contacts (not necessarily based at NIC&EO) are:

Agency workers	Quarterly reporting guidance	Tel 03000 555 995
Agent dedicated lines	PAYE/NIC queries for specific client cases	Tel 0300 200 3311
	Queries about debts and payments for specific clients	Tel 0300 200 3887
Business Payment Support Line	For businesses at risk of not being able to pay NIC on time, where contact is made *before* the due date(s)	Tel 0300 200 3835
Payment Enquiry Line	Debt Management and Banking	Tel 0300 200 3401
Billpay Helpline	Online debit/credit card payments by small employers	Tel 0300 200 3601
CIS Helpline	General queries	Tel 0300 200 3210 (from overseas +44 161 930 8706)
	Payment queries	Tel 0300 200 3401
Employee Share Schemes	General enquiries	Tel 0300 123 1079
	Scheme registration queries	Tel 0300 058 5213 Email shareschemes@hmrc.gsi.gov.uk
Employer Helpline	Queries from long standing employers (inc Statutory Payments and Student Loans)	Tel 0300 200 3200
Employer Helpline	Queries from employers of three years or fewer (inc Statutory Payments and Student Loans)	Tel 0300 200 3211
Employer Helpline	Payment advice (Debt Management)	Tel 0300 200 3401
Welsh Contact Centre for employers	Ganolfan Gyswllt Cymraeg	Tel 0300 200 1900
Employer Orderline	Stationery and booklet requests	Tel 0300 123 1074
Employment Status	Status queries	Tel 0300 123 2326
Incentive Award Unit	Queries on awards made to employees outside the normal pay structure	Tel 0300 057 7340 Fax 01236 783 706

		Email incentive.awards@hmrc.gsi.gov.uk
IR35 Helpline	Dealing with intermediaries legislation	Tel 0300 123 2326
Mariners NIC	HMRC Mariners Unit	Tel 0300 058 2419
	NIC&EO – International Caseworker	Tel 0300 200 3506
NI Avoidance	Advice on reporting and disclosure	Tel 0300 058 8993
Online Services	E-filing helpdesk	Tel 0300 200 3600 Email helpdesk@ir-efile.gov.uk
Payroll Giving		Tel 0300 123 1073
Pension Forecasting	Combined employer issued pension statements	Discontinued April 2016
Pension Forecasting	For individuals – DWP Future Pension Centre	Tel 0345 300 0168 (from overseas +44 191 218 3600)
Pensions Tracing Service	To trace occupational and private pension plans	Tel 0845 600 2537
Welsh Language Contact Centre	NIC, tax and tax credit assistance for Welsh speakers	Tel 0300 200 1900

The Treasury and the Secretary of State for Work and Pensions

The Treasury

[2.5] HM Treasury is the responsibility of the Chancellor of the Exchequer assisted by the Chief Secretary to the Treasury. This post now incorporates the responsibilities undertaken previously by the Paymaster General. The Treasury is responsible for fiscal policy.

HMRC is the direct responsibility of the Financial Secretary to the Treasury and is a non-ministerial department of the UK government responsible for the collection of taxes and social security contributions, the payment of certain state benefits (child benefit and tax credits) and the policing of the National Minimum Wage on behalf of the Department for Business, Energy and Industrial Strategy ('BEIS'), as the Department of Business, Innovation and Skills ('BIS') is now known.

The legislative powers as regards contributions referred to in **2.1** above (but not statutory payments (ie, SSP, SMP, etc)) now lie with HM Revenue and Customs and/or the Treasury, but the concurrence of the Secretary of State for Work and Pensions is still required in certain instances. These are mainly circumstances where the proposed instrument would have an effect on potential contributory benefit entitlement (including statutory payments) for which the Secretary of State retains policy responsibility, notwithstanding the transfer of functions to HMRC on 1 April 1999. BEIS, previously BIS, has policy responsibility for statutory payments.

The Secretary of State

[2.6] At the head of the Department for Work and Pensions (DWP) is the Secretary of State for Work and Pensions. They are a member of the Cabinet and politically responsible to Parliament for the proper administration of the law on matters of social security. For this reason, social security legislation imposes duties on and grants powers to the Secretary of State *per se* and not (as might be expected) to the Department over which he presides, though, in practice, the discharge of such duties and the exercise of such powers is almost invariably delegated to DWP officers who are authorised to act in his name. This is fully in accordance with the common law constitutional principle that powers given to a Secretary of State in a statute may be exercised under his authority by responsible officials of his department unless the common law right to delegate has been negative or confined by express statutory provisions. (*Carltona Ltd v Comr of Works* [1943] 2 All ER 560, CA *per Lord Greene MR at 563*; *R v Secretary of State for the Home Dept ex p Oladehinde* [1991] 1 AC 254, [1990] 2 All ER 367, CA *per Lord Donaldson MR at 381*.)

The Secretary of State is assisted in his task by two non-Cabinet 'Ministers of State': the Minister of State for Employment, and the Minister of State for Disabled People, Health & Work. A third Minister of State had responsibility for pensions, but this was 'downgraded' to an Under-Secretary position in July 2016. A further Parliamentary Under-Secretary has responsibility since July 2016 for Welfare Delivery.

From January 2018, the DWP ministers (relevant) are:

- Secretary of State for Work and Pensions: Esther McVey.
- Minister of State for Employment: Alok Sharma.
- Minister of State for Disabled People, Health & Work: Sarah Newton.
- Parliamentary Under Secretary of State for Pensions and Financial Inclusion: Guy Opperman.
- Parliamentary Under Secretary of State for Work & Pensions (Lords): Baroness Buscombe.

Throughout this work, references to the Secretary of State in relation to actions prior to the transfer to the then Inland Revenue in 1999 are stated as being 'Secretary of State for Social Security', since the current position of Secretary of State for Work and Pensions was not applicable to the time of the historical matters to which those references are made. In earlier incarnations, the role was as Minister of Pensions and National Insurance ('MPNI') or Secretary of State for Health and Social Security (the former 'DHSS').

Headquarters

[2.7] The central offices of HM Revenue and Customs are at 100 Parliament Street, London SW1A 2BQ. The contribution side of the social security scheme is based at the National Insurance Contributions & Employer Office, Benton Park View, Longbenton, Newcastle upon Tyne NE98 1ZZ, at which all PAYE and contribution records are held on computer, and attention is given to specialist matters such as liability for contributions when working abroad (International Caseworker); deferment of contribution liability in multiple employment situations and refund of overpaid contributions (Deferment Services) and questions relating to contracting-out of the state pension scheme (National Insurance Services to the Pensions Industry ('NISPI'), which will continue for several years after the abolition of contracting out).

The DWP headquarters are at Caxton House, Tothill St, London SW1H 9DA. The efficient administration of benefits, the implementation of information technology within the DWP, and the smooth running of reforms is the responsibility of the DWP Departmental Board which is chaired by the DWP Permanent Secretary. Its members are senior DWP officials, plus four non-executive members.

Occupational Pensions

[2.8] There was also an Occupational Pensions Board which ceased in April 1997. Now HM Revenue and Customs NIC&EO is responsible for the contracting out requirements and certification thereof, and currently is working on the results of the abolition of contracting out in April 2016 mandated by *Pensions Act 2014, s 24* and *Sch 14*.

Pensions Regulator

[2.9] The Occupational Pensions Regulatory Authority (OPRA) was superseded by the Pensions Regulator from 6 April 2005 and took over the remaining functions of the Occupational Pensions Board. The Chairman of the Pensions Regulator is Mark Boyle. The address is Napier House, Trafalgar Place, Brighton BN1 4DW Tel: 0345 600 0707. Email: customersupport@tpr.gov.uk. For workplace pensions reform there are separate telephone helplines for employers and advisers (0345 600 1011) and for trustees (0345 600 0707).

Field Operations

[2.10] All contributions work and contributions compliance work which requires a local presence is dealt with by HM Revenue and Customs staff, some of whom will have been Contributions Agency employees before 1 April 1999.

Former CA inspectors became HM Revenue and Customs employer compliance officers and those who remain are now almost exclusively deployed in monitoring and enforcing compliance with contribution and PAYE law. For that reason their powers are necessarily wide and include those of entry, inquiry and examination set under both the tax powers legislation and the social security legislation (see **35.1** to **35.7** enforcement).

Local offices

[2.11] The Local Compliance teams cover all matters relating to tax and NICs in a single review. Under a reorganisation in 2002–03 a new Debt Management and Banking Service was created reducing the number of regions and regional offices and grouping offices into areas. HM Revenue and

Customs also opened customer contact centres in 17 locations. These contact centres deal with PAYE enquiries, NI telephone services and helplines for employers and self-assessment matters. HMRC closed all its local enquiry centres in mid-2014. Record-keeping and centralised NIC operations are based principally in Newcastle, but employer compliance activity is resourced flexibly according to which teams around the country have current capacity. Mail is handled mainly via PO Box addresses in Newcastle, Glasgow, Bootle and Cardiff, from where letters are scanned and distributed to the relevant compliance case workers, who now have non-geographic telephone numbers (beginning 03000) so that they can be mobile. HMRC announced on 12 November 2015 a plan to close 137 local offices and replace them with 13 regional centres over the next 12 years. It remains to be seen how this affects the activities of the compliance teams.

Information

[2.12] The former HM Revenue and Customs publications 'Tax Bulletin' and 'Working Together' contained occasional items of relevance to contributions matters. However, from 1 January 2007 and as mentioned in Tax Bulletin Issue 86, publication was online only. National Insurance has since been covered in a number of 'Revenue & Customs Briefs'. See the library section of the HMRC website at www.gov.uk/government/collections/revenue-and-customs-briefs. The former CA's 'NI News' was not adopted by HMRC but extracts of previous publications which remain of current interest were included in the 2008–09 and previous editions of this work at chapter 61. HMRC Tax Bulletins can be viewed online at http://webarchive.nationalarchives.gov.uk/20130102175236/http://hmrc.gov.uk/thelibrary/briefs.htm. HMRC now publishes Employer Bulletins, focusing on PAYE and NIC matters – see www.gov.uk/government/collections/hm-revenue-and-customs-employer-bulletin.

Explanatory leaflets which are still published may now generally only be downloaded from the HMRC or www.gov.uk website, as all local HM Revenue and Customs enquiry offices have now been closed as a cost-saving measure.

There is an Employer Helpline, the number for which is 0300 200 3200, with calls charged at the local rate. However, a National Audit Office report in 2012 criticised HMRC's customer service, causing HMRC in January 2013 to commit to improvement, as taxpayers and agents were reporting long waiting times on all helplines and frequent disconnections. HMRC's commitment in 2013 included answering 80% of calls within five minutes. The NAO's next report in May 2016 instead depicted a collapse in service quality, with only 71% of calls handled at all, and average call waiting times tripling (and peaking at 47 minutes) in the first seven months of 2015–16. As a result of the NAO's criticisms, HMRC recruited extra staff and moved staff from other work, which led to a reduction to five minutes in call waiting time, but led to a serious increase in unresolved PAYE and NIC discrepancies.

In April 1999 the Inland Revenue launched a 'New Enterprise Support Initiative' (NESI) which included a Helpline for new and small employers and operated in conjunction with their locally based Business Support Teams. This gave advice and support for employers on all aspects of payroll including National Insurance. The service was for a time extended to include an employer 'healthcheck' on the payroll system if required. NESI was abandoned several years ago but the New Employer Helpline number is still available for those who have been employers for less than three years: 0300 200 3211, and newly-registered employers are sent a series of tailored emails to remind them of their obligations and deadlines.

Guidance on HM Revenue and Customs' views on many aspects of National Insurance can be found in the National Insurance Manual, which is available in the library section of the HMRC website, and which is extensively referred to in this work.

Employer Compliance section

[2.13] A special compliance unit of the former Contributions Agency was set up in 1994–95 operating out of Bromley in Kent. The main purpose of the unit was to administer the National Insurance system by way of visits to the major employers who had 2,000–2,500 or more employees. The employer was given six to eight weeks' notice of an impending visit unless there was or it was suspected that there was an NIC mitigation scheme in operation, in which case the visit would be unannounced. It is understood that significant amounts of NICs were being recouped by these visits which involved teams of inspectors spending up to six weeks at the employer's establishment and consequently there was invariably a large amount of arrears payable at the end of the visit. The inspectors were usually satisfied with going back six years but under the *Limitation Act 1980, s 32* in the case of fraud, concealment and mistake this limit could be breached. *Section 37(1)* states that while the *Act* applies to proceedings by or against the Crown it does not apply in the case of recovery of any tax, duty or interest. [*LA 1980, s 37(2)*]. However, National Insurance is not classed as a tax and does not fall under that exception, so any attempts to collect contributions in respect of periods more than six years old are extremely rare.

Large Business Service

[2.14] The activities referred to in **2.13** went on to form part of the Large Employers Group, controlled from Newcastle and, upon transfer to the then Inland Revenue, merged with the latter's Schedule E Compliance section in the Midlands to form what was initially the Large Business Office (LBO) and became the Large Employer Compliance Office (LECO). It was also responsible for employer compliance for PAYE schemes operated by the UK's 3,000 largest employers and public sector bodies. Following the merger with HM Customs and Excise, LBO became part of an extended Large Business Service and now embraces all indirect taxes as well. However, it was reported in 2008 that the Large Business Service suffered a cut in resources and would deal thenceforth only with 750 employers, being those with turnover greater than £600m or assets greater than £2.5 billion. There was also, from 1 September 2005, a Special Civil Investigations unit, which subsequently became Specialist

Investigations, with various project teams set up to focus on particular issues such as intermediary employment schemes and DOTAS-notified remuneration schemes. The HM Revenue and Customs Departmental Report, 2008 (Cm *7402*) stated at page 49:

> During 2007-08 we continued to prioritise our compliance resources to issues of greatest risk – the High Risk Corporate Programme, for example – and working issues more intensely and to faster timescale than was previously the case. This has contributed significantly to resolution of outstanding issues, improved certainty for our customers and also increased our compliance yield.

HMRC has since reorganised its compliance efforts several times in an attempt to become more efficient, especially in the area of avoidance schemes, where a new Counter-Avoidance Directorate was created in mid-2014, with around 800 people moved in from Specialist Investigations, Local Compliance and the old Anti-Avoidance Group to focus on combating avoidance in most areas of tax and NICs, using the GAAR and DOTAS provisions as well as specific anti-avoidance rules, and collecting tax and NICs under the accelerated payment notice regime introduced by *Finance Act 2014*.

3

Age Exception

Cross-references. See 7.4 ANNUAL MAXIMUM; 15.2 CLASS 1 CONTRIBUTIONS; 18.2 CLASS 2 CONTRIBUTIONS; 19.2 CLASS 3 CONTRIBUTIONS; 20.5 CLASS 4 CONTRIBUTIONS.

Other Sources. CWG2 2018 to 2019, HM Revenue and Customs National Insurance Manual NIM 24510, NIM36000–36001.

Persons under 16

Class 1 contributions

[3.1] No liability for either primary or secondary CLASS 1 CONTRIBUTIONS 15 can arise where earnings are paid to an employed earner who has not attained the age of 16. [*SSCBA 1992, s 6(1)*]. Thus the earnings of such school children on work experience schemes, school children working as newspaper delivery boys/girls, etc are entirely exempt from contribution liability. This exception ceases with the sixteenth birthday and any earnings paid to him or for his benefit on or after that date attract a contribution liability in the normal way, even if earned before the relevant date and even if the employed earner is still undergoing full-time education (see also APPRENTICES, TRAINEES AND STUDENTS 10). [*Family Law Reform Act 1969, s 9(1); SSCBA 1992, s 6(1), s 173*].

An employed earner who attains the age of 16 is under no legal obligation to inform his employer of the fact for NI purposes but the employer is legally obliged to discharge any contribution liability which arises on or after that date. Accordingly, any employer who takes into his employment a person who is not yet 16 would be well advised to record the date of the employee's sixteenth birthday on that person's pay record and to request sight of the employee's birth certificate. 16-year-olds may now also be 'non-eligible jobholders' or 'entitled workers' under the auto-enrolment pension rules, unrelated to National Insurance other than in sharing certain thresholds.

Whilst, following EU requirements, Statutory Payments have been extended to under 16s from 1 October 2006, this does not change the contributions position outlined above. Contributions are deemed to have been paid in certain circumstances and are irrelevant to establishing entitlement, since 'employee' is defined for these purposes by reference to earnings for *ITEPA 2003* purposes, rather than the *SSCBA 1992* term 'employed earner'.

Class 2 contributions

[3.2] The 'under 16' exception provision in relation to CLASS 2 CONTRIBUTIONS **18** corresponds to that set out at **3.1** above but, because Class 2 contributions are flat-rated and relate to contribution weeks, a self-employed earner whose sixteenth birthday falls within a contribution week is liable to pay a Class 2 contribution for that week even though he is, for part of it, below the specified age. From 2015–16 onwards, any payment is delayed until the ITSA deadline of 31 January after the end of the tax year. [*SSCBA 1992, s 2(5), s 11(7); Social Security (Contributions) Regulations 2001, SI 2001/1004, Reg 89(2)*.]

A 'contribution week' is a period of seven days beginning with midnight between Saturday and Sunday. [*Social Security (Contributions) Regulations 2001, SI 2001/1004, Reg 1(2)*].

Class 3 contributions

[3.3] No *liability* to pay CLASS 3 CONTRIBUTIONS **19** can ever arise as such contributions are of an entirely voluntary nature. [*SSCBA 1992, s 1(2)*]. The entitlement to pay such contributions is, however, subject to age exception in that payment is prohibited in respect of:

- any week before that in which the sixteenth birthday occurs [*SSCBA 1992, s 13(1), s 173; Family Law Reform Act 1969, s 9(1)*]; and
- the year in which the seventeenth or eighteenth birthday occurs if, in an earlier tax year, Class 1, Class 2 or Class 3 contributions sufficient to yield a qualifying EARNINGS FACTOR **28** for that year have been paid [*Social Security (Contributions) Regulations 2001, SI 2001/1004, Reg 49(1)(f)*].

Class 3A is of no relevance to under-16s (see **19.11** CLASS 3A).

Class 4 contributions

[3.4] In the case of CLASS 4 CONTRIBUTIONS **20**, exception from liability, though available to anyone who at the beginning of the tax year is under the age of 16, will not be obtained unless application is made on form CA2835U. It is unclear how many 16-year-olds are self-employed with profits above the lower annual limit and would therefore need to make this application. HM Revenue and Customs, by issuing a certificate of exception, signifies acceptance that the age condition has been fulfilled. [*SSCBA 1992, s 17(1)(2); Social Security (Contributions) Regulations 2001, SI 2001/1004, Reg 93(2)–(4), (6)*]. As no possible benefit can yet accrue to a contributor from the payment of Class 4 contributions [*SSCBA 1992, s 21(1)(2)*], exception should be claimed whenever it is available. This will change if the government follows through on a proposal in the March 2015, July 2015 and March 2016 Budgets to merge Class 2 and Class 4 in 2018.

Application for Class 4 exception

[3.5] Application is by form CA 2835U which is obtainable from Deferment Services at NIC&EO (see **2.7** ADMINISTRATION) and should be made before the beginning of the tax year for which exception is sought or, if later, before contributions become due and payable. The certificate of exception is issued directly to the HM Revenue and Customs office dealing with the self-assessment tax return and, in accordance therewith, HM Revenue and Customs will not be expecting to receive any Class 4 contributions for which the applicant would otherwise be liable. Box 101 on the SA103F allows the taxpayer to tick to show that he is excepted from Class 4 and instructs the user to 'read the notes'. These are, unfortunately, confusing, as they state that 'You don't have to pay Class 4 NICs if on 6 April 20xx you were . . . under 16' but then go on to say 'Only put an "X" in the box if you're excepted', without explaining the meaning of 'excepted'. The point is not further explained on GOV.UK. It is wholly unclear from the published guidance whether, to comply with the regulation that requires an application for exception before the start of the year or, alternatively, before the contributions become due and payable, a young contributor may simply tick box 101 and rely on HMRC to treat that as an application within the terms of the regulations. The regulations are phrased so as to require the application before the start of the year or at 'the beginning of the year', so switching to a tick box completed after the end of the year would seem to fail to meet the strict requirements for exception to be granted. [*Social Security (Contributions) Regulations 2001, SI 2001/1004, Reg 93(2)–(5).*]

Rectification of erroneous Class 4 assessment

[3.6] If Class 4 contributions are paid for a tax year and a certificate of exception is issued for that year or would have been so issued if application had been made in good time, those contributions must be repaid to the earner, unless (and except to the extent that) they are treated (at HM Revenue and Customs' option) as paid on account of other contributions properly payable under contribution legislation. [*Social Security (Contributions) Regulations 2001, SI 2001/1004, Reg 101, Reg 102(1)*]. Repayment is subject to time limits and application rules (see **55.3** REPAYMENT AND REALLOCATION).

Persons over pensionable age

[3.7] Whilst, following EU requirements, Statutory Payments were extended from 1 October 2006 to those over state pension age, this did not change the contributions position outlined in the remainder of this chapter. Primary contributions may be deemed to have been paid in certain circumstances.

An employed earner who attains pensionable age is excepted from liability for Class 1 primary contributions on any earnings paid to him or for his benefit *after* that date, unless those earnings would normally have fallen to be paid to him or for his benefit *before* that date, in which case the exception is not to apply. [*SSCBA 1992, s 6(3); Social Security (Contributions) Regulations 2001, SI 2001/1004, Reg 29*]. Where a payment of earnings is made to or for the benefit of an employed earner in the tax year in which he attains pensionable age but *before* the date in that tax year on which he reaches that age, and the relevant payment of earnings would normally fall to be made *after* that date, the general rule concerning mis-timed payments applies (see **34.4** EARNINGS PERIODS) so that the earner is to be excepted from liability for Class 1 primary contributions on those earnings also. [*Social Security (Contributions) Regulations 2001, SI 2001/1004, Reg 7(1)(a)*]. That general rule is of no application, however, where the normal payment date and the actual payment date of a mis-timed payment of earnings fall within different tax years. [*Social Security (Contributions) Regulations 2001, SI 2001/1004, Reg 7(3)*]. A special rule has been introduced, therefore, to except a person from liability for primary Class 1 contributions on earnings which, though paid to him before he attains pensionable age, would normally fall to be paid to him in a subsequent tax year. [*Social Security (Contributions) Regulations 2001, SI 2001/1004, Reg 28*].

There was originally some doubt as to whether employees over pensionable age would have to pay the additional 1% in employees primary Class 1 contributions. The *National Insurance Contributions Act 2002* confirmed that they do not. The *National Insurance Contributions Act 2011* confirmed that the further 1% primary NIC from 6 April 2011 is also not payable by those over pension age. From 6 April 2003 Table letters C and W have identified state pensioners so that the Newcastle computer system will not expect primary contributions.

> *Example*
>
> Andrew and Bill each became 65 on 18 March 2016. Each normally received an annual bonus from his employer: Andrew on 31 March and Bill on 30 April. In 2016, however, each received his bonus on 28 February. Although each received his bonus before he reached pensionable age, neither has a primary Class 1 liability as regards that bonus as, in each case, the bonus would normally have fallen to be paid after pensionable age had been attained: in Andrew's case, within the same tax year, and in Bill's case, within a subsequent tax year.

Since 6 April 1978, it has been of no relevance for age exception purposes whether retirement from regular employment actually takes place on the attainment of pensionable age or not.

Example

Gail reaches state pension age on 6 July 2018, as she was born on 6 October 1953 and has a state pension age extended above the age of 60 – see 3.8. She currently works full-time earning £500 per week as a PA to the managing director. Although she will attain state pension age in July 2018 both she and the wages clerk are unsure what the position will be if she goes part-time for three days of the week from that date, earning £300 per week. The managing director is also keen to know whether he will have to pay more Class 1 secondary contributions by employing Jean as his PA for the other two days per week on a wage of £200.

Gail must present her birth certificate to her employer so that the company has proof that age exception is warranted. If it is found that no proof has been obtained then the employer is entirely liable for any underpayment. As an alternative to providing her birth certificate Gail could supply her passport or a certificate of age exception (Form CA 4140 or CF 384) which is issued by the Pension Service (www.gov.uk/employee-reaches-state-pension-age). The certificate will have a validity date on it from which time the wages clerk can stop deducting Class 1 primary contributions but must continue to assess secondary contributions even though she is over pensionable age.

		Class 1			
		*Primary**		*Secondary†*	
	£	%	£	%	£
Gail	500.00	Nil/12	40.56	Nil/13.8	46.64
Gail	300.00	Nil	Nil	Nil/13.8	19.04
Jean	200.00	Nil/12	4.56	Nil/13.8	5.24
	500.00		4.56		24.28
		(* Nil% × £162, 12% × remainder.)		(† Nil% × £162, 13.8% × remainder.)	

Definition – Pensionable age

[3.8] *Pensionable age* is, in the case of a man born before 6 December 1953, 65, and in the case of a woman born before 6 April 1950, 60. For men and women born after 5 April 1960 it is 66, after 5 April 1977 it is 67, and for those born between these dates a sliding scale operates to determine the day on which pensionable age is attained. There is an online calculator at www.gov.uk/calculate-state-pension.

The scale originally set under *Pensions Act 1995* was intended to equalise men and women at a state pension age of 65 by 6 April 2020, increasing the women's state pension date towards age 65, broadly by adding two months to the date every month from 6 May 2010 onwards (ie it was scheduled to take ten years to add five years to the women's pension age).

The *Pensions Act 2011* accelerated the timetable by adding four months instead of two for any woman born between 6 April 1953 and 5 December 1953, so that the state pension age became 65 by 6 November 2018 instead of 6 April 2020.

The rule for those women born between 6 April 1950 and 5 April 1953 is as follows: if the number of tax months or part tax months between 5 April 1950 and the woman's date of birth is an odd number, that number of months is added to the date of the woman's 60th birthday. The day on which she attains pensionable age is deemed to fall on the immediately following 6th of the month. If the number of whole or part tax months falling between 5 April 1950 and her date of birth is an even number, that number of months is added to the date of her 60th birthday, but the day on which she attains pensionable age is deemed to fall on the immediately preceding 6th of the month. A tax month runs from the 6th of one calendar month to the 5th of the next calendar month. Thus, for example, a woman born between 6 August and 5 September 1952 will reach pensionable age on 6 January 2015. See also CWG2 2018 to 2019, para 3.8. [*SSCBA 1992, s 122(1)* and *Pensions Act 1995, Sch 4*].

Example

Imogen was born on 29 March 1952. This fell within the 24th tax month after 5 April 1950. Twenty-four months were therefore added to the date of her 60th birthday, bringing the date to 29 March 2014. As the addition was an even number of months, she reached state pension age on the preceding 6th of the month, ie, on 6 March 2014.

The accelerated process needs a different rule. A woman born between 6 April 1953 and 5 May 1953 will reach state pension age on 6 July 2016. For each extra month after the tax month of April 1953, up to seven, four months are added, so that a woman born on 5 December 1953 will receive her state pension from 6 November 2018, almost one month before her 65th birthday.

Further, under the *Pensions Act 2007*, there were to be subsequent gradual rises in the state pension age for both men and women – from 66 to 67 between 2034 and 2036, and then to 68 in 2044 to 2046. *Pensions Act 2011* advanced that timetable so that any man or woman born between 6 December 1953 and 5 January 1954 will not reach state pension age until 6 March 2019 (ie at, or just above, 65 years and two months). For each tax month after 5 January 1954, two months are added to the state pension age, so that anyone born on or after 6 October 1954 will receive the state pension on his or her 66th birthday.

Age 66 will then apply to anyone born before 6 April 1960, but *Pensions Act 2014* introduced another accelerated timescale for moving all contributors from age 66 to age 67, albeit on a slightly different basis. Rather than starting all state pension entitlements on the 6th of the new month, the increase currently planned will simply see a deferral of state pension age to the same day of the month as the birthday but in a later month. The deferral will be by a number of months determined by the month in which the birthday fell and how many complete tax months had elapsed between 6 April 1960 and the birthday month. So a contributor born on 21 June 1960, with three complete tax months elapsed between 6 April 1960 and his or her birthday, will retire on 21 September 2026, at age 66 years and three months old. A school friend of that contributor born on 21 July 1960 would 'retire' at age 66 years and four months on 21 November 2026.

Anyone born from 6 March 1961 to 5 April 1977 will retire at age 67.

The *Pensions Act 2007* schedule for raising the state pension age to 68 would see it start to increase for those with birthdays from 6 April 1977 to 5 April 1978, by scheduling those born in the April 1977 tax month to retire on 6 May 2044, those born in the May 1977 tax month on 6 July 2044, etc. However, it was announced in the Autumn Statement 2013 that the state pension age would be reviewed again, and *Pensions Act 2014, s 27* provides for a regular review to be undertaken, each report to be published no more than six years after its predecessor. The principle to be adopted is to be based on the proportion of their adult life that people spend in retirement drawing a state pension, which the Chancellor initially targeted as one-third. The first review, undertaken by John Cridland CBE, was published in March 2017. The recommendations, as they relate to this Chapter, are that:

- the state pension age should rise from 67 to 68 over a two-year period starting in 2037 and ending in 2039; and
- the state pension age should not increase more than one year in any ten-year period, assuming there are no exceptional changes in the longevity data.

[*Independent Review of the State Pension Age: Smoothing the Transition; Final Report March 2017*].

In the DWP's report to Parliament, the recommendation to increase state pension age to age 68 over the period 2037 to 2039 was accepted with the reservation that a further review based on more up-to-date life expectancy data would be undertaken before legislating to bring forward the increase.

[*DWP: State Pension age review; July 2017*].

All these deferrals of state pension age will also, of course, increase the number of years for which National Insurance contributions have to be paid, assuming that the contributor continues working, even if not needed to earn a full state pension.

Table – Increased pension ages for women under *Pensions Act 1995*

Date of birth	*(years/months)*	*Pension date*
6 April 1950 to 5 May 1950	60.1 – 60.0	6 May 2010
6 May 1950 to 5 June 1950	60.2 – 60.1	6 July 2010
6 June 1950 to 5 July 1950	60.3 – 60.2	6 September 2010
6 July 1950 to 5 August 1950	60.4 – 60.3	6 November 2010
6 August 1950 to 5 September 1950	60.5 – 60.4	6 January 2011
6 September 1950 to 5 October 1950	60.6 – 60.5	6 March 2011
6 October 1950 to 5 November 1950	60.7 – 60.6	6 May 2011
6 November 1950 to 5 December 1950	60.8 – 60.7	6 July 2011
6 December 1950 to 5 January 1951	60.9 – 60.8	6 September 2011
6 January 1951 to 5 February 1951	60.10 – 60.9	6 November 2011
6 February 1951 to 5 March 1951	60.11 – 60.10	6 January 2012
6 March 1951 to 5 April 1951	61.0 – 60.11	6 March 2012
6 April 1951 to 5 May 1951	61.1 – 61.0	6 May 2012
6 May 1951 to 5 June 1951	61.2 – 61.1	6 July 2012
6 June 1951 to 5 July 1951	61.3 – 61.2	6 September 2012

Date of birth	*(years/months)*	*Pension date*
6 July 1951 to 5 August 1951	61.4 – 61.3	6 November 2012
6 August 1951 to 5 September 1951	61.5 – 61.4	6 January 2013
6 September 1951 to 5 October 1951	61.6 – 61.5	6 March 2013
6 October 1951 to 5 November 1951	61.7 – 61.6	6 May 2013
6 November 1951 to 5 December 1951	61.8 – 61.7	6 July 2013
6 December 1951 to 5 January 1952	61.9 – 61.8	6 September 2013
6 January 1952 to 5 February 1952	61.10 – 61.9	6 November 2013
6 February 1952 to 5 March 1952	61.11 – 61.10	6 January 2014
6 March 1952 to 5 April 1952	62.0 – 61.11	6 March 2014
6 April 1952 to 5 May 1952	62.1 – 62.0	6 May 2014
6 May 1952 to 5 June 1952	62.2 – 62.1	6 July 2014
6 June 1952 to 5 July 1952	62.3 – 62.2	6 September 2014
6 July 1952 to 5 August 1952	62.4 – 62.3	6 November 2014
6 August 1952 to 5 September 1952	62.5 – 62.4	6 January 2015
6 September 1952 to 5 October 1952	62.6 – 62.5	6 March 2015
6 October 1952 to 5 November 1952	62.7 – 62.6	6 May 2015
6 November 1952 to 5 December 1952	62.8 – 62.7	6 July 2015
6 December 1952 to 5 January 1953	62.9 – 62.8	6 September 2015
6 January 1953 to 5 February 1953	62.10 – 62.9	6 November 2015
6 February 1953 to 5 March 1953	62.11 – 62.10	6 January 2016
6 March 1953 to 5 April 1953	63.0 – 62.11	6 March 2016

The *Pensions Act 2011* will cause the woman's state pension age to increase more quickly to age 65 between April 2016 and November 2018 and the state pension for both men and women to increase to age 66, then age 67 as shown below.

Date of birth	*(years/months)*	*Pension date*
For women		
6 April 1953 to 5 May 1953	63.2 – 63.3	6 July 2016
6 May 1953 to 5 June 1953	63.5 – 63.6	6 November 2016
6 June 1953 to 5 July 1953	63.8 – 63.9	6 March 2017
6 July 1953 to 5 August 1953	63.11 – 64.0	6 July 2017
6 August 1953 to 5 September 1953	64.2 – 64.3	6 November 2017
6 September 1953 to 5 October 1953	64.5 – 64.6	6 March 2018
6 October 1953 to 5 November 1953	64.8 – 64.9	6 July 2018
6 November 1953 to 5 December 1953	64.11 – 65.0	6 November 2018
For men and women		
6 December 1953 to 5 January 1954	65.2 – 65.3	6 March 2019
6 January 1954 to 5 February 1954	65.3 – 65.4	6 May 2019
6 February 1954 to 5 March 1954	65.4 – 65.5	6 July 2019
6 March 1954 to 5 April 1954	65.5 – 65.6	6 September 2019
6 April 1954 to 5 May 1954	65.6 – 65.7	6 November 2019
6 May 1954 to 5 June 1954	65.7 – 65.8	6 January 2020
6 June 1954 to 5 July 1954	65.8 – 65.9	6 March 2020
6 July 1954 to 5 August 1954	65.9 – 65.10	6 May 2020
6 August 1954 to 5 September 1954	65.10 – 65.11	6 July 2020
6 September 1954 to 5 October 1954	65.11 – 66	6 September 2020
6 October 1954 to 5 April 1960		66th birthday

Increase from 66 to 67 for men and women

Date of birth	*(years/months)*
6 April 1960 to 5 May 1960	66.1
6 May 1960 to 5 June 1960	66.2
6 June 1960 to 5 July 1960	66.3
6 July 1960 to 5 August 1960	66.4
6 August 1960 to 5 September 1960	66.5
6 September 1960 to 5 October 1960	66.6
6 October 1960 to 5 November 1960	66.7
6 November 1960 to 5 December 1960	66.8
6 December 1960 to 5 January 1961	66.9
6 January 1961 to 5 February 1961	66.10
6 February 1961 to 5 March 1961	66.11
6 March 1961 onwards	67

Class 1 exception pre-6 April 1978

[3.9] Prior to 6 April 1978, exception from contribution liability on the grounds of being over pensionable age was only permitted if the person concerned:

- had actually retired from regular employment; or
- did not qualify for a category A retirement pension; or
- was *deemed* to have retired from regular employment by reason of 5 years having expired from his attaining pensionable age.

[*SSA 1975, s 6 (repealed by SSPA 1975, Sch 5), s 27(5) (repealed by SSA 1989, Sch 1 para 1)*].

Class 1 secondary exclusion

[3.10] An employer's liability to pay secondary CLASS **1** CONTRIBUTIONS (**15.2**) in respect of earnings paid to or for the benefit of an employed earner is unaffected by the employed earner's attainment of pensionable age. [*SSCBA 1992, s 6(2)*.] (CWG2 (2016), para 49.) It should be noted, however, that if the employment was a contracted-out employment (**23.3**), the rate of liability was, until 5 April 2016, changed from the relevant contracted-out rate to the not contracted-out rate upon the employed earner's attainment of pensionable age. [*SSPA 1975, s 30(1)*.] (CWG2 (2015), para 84.) One point to note here is that, before 6 April 2016 when contracting out was abolished, many employers failed to switch from contracted-out to not contracted-out contributions and there resulted an underpayment of NICs despite the fact that the employer was continuing to contribute to the pension scheme. This was a relatively rare problem before age discrimination legislation was introduced in October 2006, as most workers retired at or before state pension age. Since 1 October 2011 there has no longer been a default retirement age when employers can force workers to retire just because they have reached 65. [*Employment Equality (Repeal of Retirement Age Provisions) Regulations 2011, SI 2011/1069, Reg 5.*]

Class 1 extra-statutory procedure

[3.11] An employer is responsible for the payment not only of any secondary contribution liability arising on earnings paid to or for the benefit of an employed earner but also, in the first instance, any primary liability arising in respect of those earnings. [*SSCBA 1992, Sch 1 para 3(1); Social Security (Contributions) Regulations 2001, SI 2001/1004, Reg 67, Reg 68, Reg 69, Sch 4*].

To protect an employer against erroneous non-payment through uncertainty or mistake as to the date on which an employee attains pensionable age, it used to suggest that the employer should continue to calculate primary contributions as normal and to make the appropriate deduction from the employee's earnings until the employee produced a certificate of age exception on either form CA 4140 or CF 384 issued by the Pension Service. However, any employer who did so was making an unlawful deduction from wages if the employee was indeed over state pension age. The safe option for older workers was to insist that they apply for an age exception certificate from NIC&EO, although HMRC's web guidance now instructs employers to rely on sight of a passport or birth certificate because age exception certificates are no longer used (see HMRC's Employer Bulletin 45 (September 2013)).

An employed earner now reaching pensionable age and applying to the Individual Caseworker team in Newcastle for a certificate authorising his employer not to make primary contribution deductions will no longer receive a CA 4140. If the employer has definite evidence (eg sight of a birth certificate) that an employee is, in fact, over pensionable age, as noted above he has no legal right—even in the absence of an exception certificate—to continue to make deductions in respect of primary Class 1 contributions and should cease to do so. (CWG2 2018 to 2019, para 3.8.)

Certificates CA 4140 and CF 384 were HM Revenue and Customs property and had to be returned to HM Revenue and Customs if they had not been given back to an employee when he left his employment. (CWG2 (2015), para 87). A certificate used to be sent to anyone who stated on a retirement pension claim form (BR1) to the Pensions Service at the Department for Work and Pensions that he or she intended to continue in employment. Anyone who did not automatically receive a certificate and who applied for one was formerly asked to complete a form CF 13, but this has now been withdrawn. If it could be verified that the applicant was over retirement age, a certificate would be issued in respect of each employment.

Now, an employer must obtain sight of an employee's birth certificate, passport or other acceptable evidence of the date of birth. Such evidence needs to be scanned or copied and held by the employer as proof that primary Class 1 contributions are not payable. Any existing CA4140 can be copied in the same way and original paper copies destroyed. That clearly removes the need for the certificate to be returned to an employee on leaving or to HMRC if not given to the employee.

In the odd case where an employee is unwilling to produce the birth certificate, perhaps because it contains sensitive information that the employee does not wish to disclose, that employee should be advised to contact HM Revenue and Customs, NIC&EO, BX9 1AN. The employee will then be issued with a letter confirming he has reached State Pension Age.

Rectification of erroneous Class 1 primary deduction

[3.12] Where, in the absence of a certificate of exception and because of the safety first policy described at **3.11** above, an employer has deducted primary Class 1 contributions for which his employee was not liable, rectification may be effected by the employer within the tax year in which the over-deduction occurred (see **21.19** COLLECTION), but not otherwise. [*Social Security (Contributions) Regulations 2001, SI 2001/1004, Sch 4 para 7*]. The overpayment should be refunded to the employee, the pay records should be amended, corrected values should be reported on the next FPS and the next payment to HMRC should reflect the adjustment. (CWG2 2018 to 2019, para 3.8.3.) Over-deductions in other tax years may be rectified only by HMRC, not by the employer. (CWG2 2018 to 2019, para 3.8.3.) This is because, once deduction data have been finalised by the employer's final FPS or EPS at the end of a tax year, contribution records are updated and must, therefore, be directly amended to reflect any subsequent adjustment (see **49.1** NATIONAL INSURANCE NUMBER). In principle, an EYU could (and should) be submitted to correct records for a closed year that was within the RTI regime, but the CWG2 guidance does not refer to this possibility yet, referring only to old P14 and P35 submissions for pre-RTI periods.

Class 2 contributions

[3.13] An exception from liability to pay CLASS 2 CONTRIBUTIONS **18** corresponding to that described at **3.7** above in relation to Class 1 contributions is given in respect of any period after pensionable age is attained. [*SSCBA 1992, s 11(7)*]. If the attainment of state pension age (see **3.8**) occurs during a contribution week (see definition at **3.2** above) and the wording of this provision is strictly construed, no liability can arise for that week as the contribution otherwise payable would, in part, relate to a period after the attainment of pensionable age. This rule was not affected by moving Class 2 into the ITSA regime from 6 April 2015.

Class 3 and 3A contributions

[3.14] Because payment of Class 3 contributions (VOLUNTARY CONTRIBUTIONS: CLASSES 3 AND 3A **19**) is voluntary, no question of exception from liability to pay such contributions can ever arise. There is, however, a form of 'over pensionable age' exception as regards Class 3 contributions in that payment of such contributions in respect of the tax year in which pensionable age is attained (not merely of any part of it falling after the date on which that age is attained) and of any subsequent tax year is prohibited. [*Social Security (Contributions) Regulations 2001, SI 2001/1004, Reg 49(1)(e)*].

The *Social Security (Contributions) (Amendment No 6) Regs 2002, SI 2002/3728* amended *SI 2001/1004, Reg 49* to enable anyone who wishes to pay Class 3 contributions to do so in order to satisfy the contribution conditions for the bereavement benefits introduced in April 2001. See **13.2** BENEFITS CONTRIBUTION REQUIREMENTS. This secured equality of treatment between men and women as regards these particular payments.

As the year in which pensionable age is attained must be disregarded when considering whether or not the contribution conditions for retirement pension have been satisfied, and as payment of Class 3 contributions is to be allowed only with a view to enabling a contributor to satisfy contribution conditions of entitlement to benefit, this age exception from entitlement is entirely necessary. [*SSCBA 1992, s 13(2), s 44(1), Sch 3 para 5* as amended by *Pensions Act 1995, Sch 4 para 4*].

Pensions Act 2014, s 25 and *Sch 15* laid the ground for an additional class of voluntary contribution, Class 3A, which became available from 12 October 2015 to 5 April 2017 (*PA 2014, s 56(1)*). This allowed a new type of contribution by those (of any age) already in receipt of a Category A, B or D state pension, or with deferred entitlement to such at 6 April 2016, and those due to reach state pension age by that date who therefore had prospective entitlement to such a pension (provided they lived long enough). The new single-tier state pension was introduced at that date, and Class 3A enables pensioners to buy additional units of state pension. Only those who would be over state pension age at the 6 April 2016 start date were permitted to pay these contributions, so the remainder of the population is de facto excepted, albeit by virtue of being too young rather than too old. See **19.11** CLASS 3A CONTRIBUTIONS for details of eligibility and exclusions.

Class 4 contributions

[3.15] Automatic exception from liability for CLASS 4 CONTRIBUTIONS **20** is given to any earner who, at the beginning of the tax year, is over pensionable age. [*SSCBA 1992, s 17(1)(2); Social Security (Contributions) Regulations 2001, SI 2001/1004, Reg 91(a)*]. Under *Family Law Reform Act 1969, s 9(1)* and *SSCBA 1992, s 173*, a person is deemed to attain a given age at the commencement of the relevant anniversary of the date of his birth. In law, therefore, a person born on 6 April 1951 will have attained the age of 65 at midnight on 5 April 2016 and, although his sixty-fifth birthday falls on the first day of the tax year 2016–17, he is nevertheless regarded as being over pensionable age at the beginning of that tax year for Class 4 contribution exception purposes. A person who attains pensionable age during the course of a tax year remains liable for Class 4 contributions for the whole of that year.

In the case of *Manning v Revenue and Customs Comrs* [2006] STC (SCD) 588, a contributor argued unsuccessfully that there was discrimination against the self-employed because their liability to Class 4 contributions continued for the remainder of the tax year after the birthday on which they reached state pension age (at the time, age 60 for women, age 65 for men), whereas the primary Class 1 liability of employed earners ceased on that date. The Special Commissioner noted that, at the other end of the working life, Class 1 liability begins on the 16th birthday, whereas Class 4 liability can begin only on 6th April following the 16th birthday if the contributor applies for exception, so there was in fact parity of treatment and no unfair discrimination. [*Social Security (Contributions) Regulations 2001, SI 2001/1004, Reg 93*.]

The following table indicates when Class 4 liability ceases for women during the transitional period as the state pension age increases gradually to 66 (see 3.8).

Date of birth	*Final Class 4 liability*
For women:	
6 April 1950 to 5 October 1950	2010/11
6 October 1950 to 5 April 1951	2011/12
6 April 1951 to 5 October 1951	2012/13
6 October 1951 to 5 April 1952	2013/14
6 April 1952 to 5 October 1952	2014/15
6 October 1952 to 5 April 1953	2015/16
6 April 1953 to 5 July 1953	2016/17
6 July 1953 to 5 October 1953	2017/18
6 October 1953 to 5 January 1954	2018/19
6 January 1954 to 5 July 1954	2019/20
6 July 1954 to 5 April 1955	2020/21
For men:	
6 December 1953 to 5 January 1954	2018/19
6 January 1954 to 5 July 1954	2019/20
6 July 1954 to 5 April 1955	2020/21

Rectification of erroneous Class 4 assessment

[3.16] If Class 4 contributions are erroneously assessed for any tax year at the start of which the earner was over pensionable age, a refund may be obtained by applying to HM Revenue and Customs NIC&EO, Deferment Services, General Administration Section, Longbenton, Newcastle upon Tyne NE98 1ZZ. In the days when tax and NIC administration was handled by different offices, any repayment falling due in respect of contributions wrongly paid by reason of such erroneous assessment would have been made by NIC&EO (as the assessment of tax is not affected) and not by the tax office responsible for the tax return (see 55.3 REPAYMENT AND REALLOCATION). [*Social Security (Contributions) Regulations 2001, SI 2001/1004, Reg 101, Reg 102*].

Persons under 21 — Class 1 secondary contributions

[3.17] *National Insurance Contributions Act 2014, s 9* laid the ground for a nil rate of secondary Class 1 contribution to apply from 6 April 2015 to any earner paid wages on a day when he is at least 16 but not yet 21 years of age. This is the outcome of government plans to promote employment opportunities for younger people. There is no effect on primary contributions, or on Class 1A or Class 1B liabilities. Employers need to hold evidence of their employees' ages if they are to apply the rules correctly, although RTI-compliant software should include dates of birth in every FPS submitted.

The legislation amended *SSCBA 1992, s 9* and inserted a new *s 9A*, creating a new concept of 'age-related secondary percentage', which has initially been set at 0%, applicable to earnings above the earnings threshold and up to a new 'upper secondary threshold' (UST), which has initially been set at the same level as the UEL for the relevant earnings period. Any earnings in excess of the UEL (eg, where a qualifying young person is paid a bonus that exceeds the weekly or monthly UST) will attract the standard secondary liability.

The legislation includes powers for the Treasury to change both the age limits and the percentage rate, although the rate must not exceed the standard rate. It is clear from the choice to define the UST separately from the UEL that there is a plan at some point to see the two thresholds diverge.

Employers' payroll software now uses additional NI tables to apply the 'zero rate' (see **15.8**). Seven new tables were introduced from 6 April 2015 to reflect the new age-related secondary rate of 0% for under-21s in standard, contracted-out (COSR) and deferment tables:

Table letter	Over-20 equivalent	Category of under-21 earner
I	D	COSR
K	L	COSR deferred
M	A	Not-contracted-out standard
P	Q	Mariners' not-contracted-out deferred
V	N	Mariners' COSR
Y	R	Mariners' not-contracted-out standard
Z	C	Not-contracted-out deferred

Tables I, K and V were short-lived, as contracting out was abolished from 6 April 2016.

Apprentices under 25 — Class 1 secondary contributions

[3.18] In the Autumn Statement in December 2014, the Chancellor announced an extension of the new nil rate of secondary Class 1 contribution, to apply from 6 April 2016, to payments of earnings to apprentices under the age of 25. This was subsequently legislated by means of a late amendment to the *National Insurance Contributions Act 2015* during its final stages in the House of Lords in January 2015.

NICA 2015, s 1 inserted a new *s 9B* into *SSCBA 1992* to lay the ground for the 2016 change. The new section follows the same approach as *SSCBA 1992, s 9A*, albeit restricted to 'relevant apprentices', a term that required a new definition. The primary legislation provided for the definition to be set by Treasury regulations. Whilst it may seem obvious to most observers whether a particular trainee is an apprentice, (the person will probably have an 'apprenticeship agreement' or 'contract of apprenticeship' that meets legal requirements such as those set out in *Apprenticeships, Skills, Children and Learning*

Act 2009 for England and Wales), government education and training policy is a matter for the various devolved administrations in the UK, with each setting its own definition of 'apprentice', so further consultations were needed before the definition was fixed for NIC purposes, an area of the law that is not devolved.

After that consultation in late 2015, the *Social Security (Contributions) (Amendment) Regulations 2016, SI 2016/117* added, with effect from 6 April 2016, a new 'Case H' as Reg 154A into the *Contributions Regulations 2001*, creating a new special class of earner, apprentices, with the definition required by *s 9B*.

An 'apprentice' for the purpose of s 9B is a person employed under one of the following:

- an approved English apprenticeship agreement within the meaning of *ASCLA 2009, s A1*;
- an English apprenticeship agreement within the meaning of *ASCLA 2009, s 32* as saved by *Deregulation Act 2015 (Commencement No 1 and Transitional and Saving Provisions) Order 2015, SI 2015/994, Sch 1, para 2*;
- a Welsh apprenticeship agreement within the meaning of *ASCLA 2009, s 32*;
- arrangements made by the Secretary of State or the Scottish Ministers under *Employment and Training Act 1973, s 2*;
- arrangements made by the Secretary of State or the Scottish Ministers under *Enterprise and New Towns (Scotland) Act 1990, s 2*; or
- arrangements made by the Secretary of State or Northern Ireland Ministers under *Employment and Training Act (Northern Ireland) 1950, s 1*.

To qualify, the apprentice must also be training under arrangements in relation to which the Secretary of State has secured the provision of financial resources under *ASCLA 2009*, s 100, or which are set out in a written agreement made between that person, the employer and the training provider containing the following information:

(i) the type of apprenticeship framework or standard being followed;
(ii) the start date of the apprenticeship; and
(iii) the expected completion date of the apprenticeship.

[*Contributions Regulations 2001, Reg 154A(1)–(3)*, as inserted by *Social Security (Contributions) (Amendment) Regulations 2016, SI 2016/117, Reg* 2.]

The definition chosen means that common law apprenticeships of the type that have existed for centuries, and typical professional training contracts, are not recognised for the purposes of the 0% secondary rate. To qualify, there must be a written apprenticeship agreement in place that meets the relevant statutory framework in the part of the UK where the contract is entered into, and that involves an approved training provider.

Earnings paid to an earner employed as a relevant apprentice under the age of 25 are to be subject to a 0% rate of apprentice secondary contribution to the extent that they do not exceed the 'apprentice upper secondary threshold'

(AUST) in the earnings period of payment. The AUST has initially been set at the same level as the UST and UEL, but the mere introduction of the terminology indicates that the government has in mind that it may one day separate the AUST from the UST and the UEL.

Where earnings exceed the AUST, the normal rate (currently 13.8%) of secondary contribution is to apply to the excess.

As is the case with the under-21 rules, there is no impact on primary contributions or Classes 1A or 1B, so the individual apprentices should see no effect on their payslips. Two new NI tables have also been introduced: Table H for under-25 standard rate and Table G for under-25 mariner standard rate. The contracted-out tables available for under-21s in 2015–16 disappeared from 6 April 2016, since contracting out was abolished at the same time as the apprentice 0% rules were introduced.

The Treasury is given the power to modify the AUST, the definition of apprentice, and the age limit applicable, albeit with explicit (ie, affirmative) approval of the House of Commons.

In order to ensure that there is a pecking order in the event that the rules for under-21s and apprentices under 25 diverge, it is specifically provided that the under-21 provisions do not apply if the apprentice rules apply, although at the moment this is of no importance as the rate and thresholds are the same.

Note that the rules for determining according to age the correct national minimum wage for an apprentice are completely separate and different.

Key Points regarding age exceptions and NICs

[3.19] Points to consider are as follows.

- Generally contribution liability under Classes 1 and 2 only arises between the earner's sixteenth birthday and state pension age. Contributions made between 6 April and the date of reaching state pension age do not count for state pension purposes, as they will not be on the earner's record by the time the pension comes into payment, but they are nevertheless payable. For Class 4, under-16s must apply for exception for the year in which they reach age 16, and for those reaching state pension age, liability arises for the full tax year in which the relevant birthday occurs. This class of contribution is likely to replace Class 2 as the basis of benefit entitlement from April 2018.
- A woman's retirement age is gradually changing from April 2010 to December 2018 when it too will become 65 years. Everybody's retirement age will then rise gradually from 65 to 66 and later to 67. Women born after 6 April 1950 will be affected by the changing limit first, and all men and women born after 5 December 1953 will be affected.
- Class 2 liability, if self-employed, begins in the week of the individual's sixteenth birthday.

- Class 3 contributions do not attract benefit entitlement (and therefore cannot be paid) in respect of the year in which state retirement age is reached.
- Class 3A contributions were introduced in October 2015 to allow state pensioners of any age as at 5 April 2016 to top up their state pension.
- Classes 1, 1A and 1B continue to be paid by the secondary contributor in respect of earners even where state retirement age has been reached and primary contribution liability has ceased.
- Since September 2013 HMRC has no longer issued CA4140 age exemption certificates. Employers must now rely on, and retain copies of, other evidence of age such as passports and birth certificates.
- Class 1 secondary liability is 0% in respect of earnings up to the UST paid to under-21s from 6 April 2015.
- Class 1 secondary liability is also 0% from 6 April 2016 in respect of earnings, again up to the AUST, paid to qualifying apprentices under the age of 25 on the date of payment.

4
Agency Workers

Cross-references. See **5.2** and **5.6** AGGREGATION OF EARNINGS for the aggregation rules relating to agency workers; **14.29** CATEGORISATION for categorisation by regulation; CLASS 1 CONTRIBUTIONS **15**; ENTERTAINERS **36**; EXAMINERS **37**; HOMEWORKERS AND OUTWORKERS **38**; INTERMEDIARIES **40**; LABOUR-ONLY CONTRACTORS **41**.

Other Sources. CWG2 (2016), pages 66, 72–76. ESM2000–ESM2380.

Introduction to agency workers and NICs

[4.1] The employment status of agency workers can seem odd. Traditionally, they are hired to fill, temporarily, a role that would normally be taken by an employee who is on holiday or absent through sickness, and they usually work in a very similar way to the employees whose work they carry out. In recent years, with the focus on cutting employment costs by slimming down the permanent staff base of many businesses and dealing with peak demand by using 'temps', there has been much more widespread use of agency workers, to such an extent that their rights as workers have been expanded and protected by the introduction of the *Agency Workers Regulations 2010, SI 2010/95*. There has also been innovation in the way they are engaged and much more widespread use of offshore employment businesses for both avoidance and evasion.

The traditional 'temp' will sign on with a traditional employment agency and that agency will find him or her an assignment with a client of the agency. The engagement starts when the worker arrives at the client's door, and ends when the booked assignment or assignment period is complete, and the worker moves on to the next assignment allocated by the agency. This type of 'temp' works under a contract for services rather than a contract of employment, and is hardly ever an employed earner in employment law terms (which is why the *Agency Workers Regulations 2010* were introduced for the protection of this type of worker), for the reasons outlined below.

In PAYE and NIC terms, however, agencies have for many years been required to treat their typical workers as being in receipt of employment income (in tax law) or as being employed earners (in NIC law), but from 6 April 2014 both sets of rules treat these typical workers as employees, generally of the agency through which they are paid. They are in common law terms not employees, but they usually work alongside and in the same way as employees, so they have generally been treated as earning employment income under *Income Tax (Earnings and Pensions) Act 2003 (ITEPA 2003), s 44* and as employees under the *Social Security (Categorisation of Earners) Regulations 1978, SI 1978/1689*, unless they do not meet the conditions set by the legislation. The earnings of those who are in scope have had to be payrolled, with the agency responsible for deductions and secondary Class 1 liability.

Each engagement is treated as a separate employment, as the agency contract for services typically comes to an end at the conclusion of each assignment. The ability to dispense with a worker's services at short notice without all the constraints created by an employment contract is one of the principal attractions for the clients who source their workers through agencies.

Those who are outside the scope will be self-employed earners for NIC purposes, as they are 'gainfully employed in [the UK] otherwise than in employed earner's employment' (*SSCBA 1992, s 2(1)(b)*).

However, not every temporary worker supplied by an employment agency would be self-employed in the absence of the deeming rules. Occasionally, an agency worker has been able to establish in disputes before a tribunal or court that he has been working under terms and conditions that amount to an implied employment contract (see, eg, *McMeechan v Secretary of State for Employment* [1996] EWCA Civ 1166, [1997] IRLR 353, [1997] ICR 549, a case in which an agency worker succeeded in claiming unpaid earnings from the state in respect of his last assignment when the agency through which he had been working became insolvent).

It is also possible that the terms under which agency workers are engaged do not meet the conditions for the application of the rules deeming pay to be employment income, or (since 2014) deeming the worker to be an employee for PAYE and NIC purposes. Some employment businesses even rely on structuring their business model so as to avoid meeting the conditions and thereby avoid the cost of secondary Class 1 liabilities, which reduces the cost of hiring for their clients. Finance Act 2014 (FA 2014) and revisions to the *Categorisation Regs 1978* reduced (but did not eliminate) the opportunities for this type of structuring as explained below.

'Umbrella' workers

[4.2] There is also a category of 'temps' who are deliberately hired under contracts of employment. Most of the large employment agencies also operate, or source workers from, so called 'umbrella' employment businesses. Workers are given permanent contracts of employment by a company (often in the employment agency's group) and are supplied as temporary workers to a series of the agency's clients. The worker is regarded as having a single 'umbrella' contract of employment that covers without any breaks all the work he carries out for all clients, rather than having a series of separate engagements. HMRC often refers to such contracts as 'overarching' contracts of employment. Until 5 April 2016, there were certain advantages for such umbrella workers and the agencies from being able to pay tax- and NIC-free home-to-work travel expenses for travel to a temporary workplace, instead of higher taxable and NIC-able pay, so savings were made and rates charged to clients could be lower. HMRC referred to this as 'payday-by-payday' relief and claimed it was an ineffective model, although the law has now been changed twice to block its use.

This route to tax- and NIC-free pay was curtailed from 6 April 2016 by two measures.

Firstly, under changes made by *Finance Act 2015, s 11 (FA 2015)* (but not effective until 2016–17) and by *Social Security (Contributions) (Amendment) (No 2) Regulations 2016, SI 2016/352, Reg 4*, when travel expenses would be deductible, they will be exempted, provided they are not paid under a salary sacrifice arrangement (which would encompass the payday-by-payday approach to calculating variable gross pay). If they are paid under such an arrangement on or after 6 April 2016, they will be treated as taxable pay, subject to PAYE and NIC deductions. At the time *FA 2015* was passed, it seemed as if the worker would, after the year-end, need to submit a claim for a deduction under *ITEPA 2003, s 338*. There are now no dispensations for businesses expenses, after 6 April 2016. (See *FA 2015, ss 11, 12*, inserting new *ITEPA 2003, ss 289A–289E* and abolishing *ss 65, 96*.)

Secondly, under changes made by *Finance Act 2016, s 18* also effective from 6 April 2016, even the claim under *ITEPA 2003, s 338* has been blocked for most umbrella workers by the new *s 339A*, which deems workers supplied by an intermediary to be in a separate job for each separate engagement if they are under supervision, direction or control as to the manner of carrying out the work. The equivalent rules for contributions purposes were introduced by *Social Security (Contributions) (Amendment) (No 2) Regulations 2016, SI 2016/352, Reg 5*.

The effect of this change is to deny a claim for relief for travel between home and the main assignment location, although the normal rules about temporary workplaces continue to apply to any travel to a temporary workplace within the context of the assignment (eg, travelling to a meeting held somewhere other than the main assignment location). The changes also do not affect claims under s 336 (expenses incurred wholly exclusively and necessarily in the performance of the duties) or s 337 (travelling appointments, eg, travelling salesmen, meter readers, district nurses, etc) because these claims would be available to any ordinary employee of the client organisation who was doing the same work. Workers providing their services in the client's home are also excluded even if they are supplied by an agency who sources them from an umbrella employment company.

Since umbrella company workers have a formal employment contract, the agency worker deeming rules described above and below are of no relevance to their NIC liabilities: they are already within Class 1, and the umbrella employer must account for PAYE and contributions in respect of their income. This does not mean, however, that the 2014 intermediaries rules are wholly irrelevant, because umbrella company workers might be supplied to an end client under a contract between that client and a different agency or intermediary; see further 4.22 below for the reporting requirements from 6 April 2015.

Personal service company workers

[4.3] Almost the same principle applies to workers who operate through their own personal service company (PSC), which invoices the agency for the services of its employee or officer and is paid gross. Owners of such companies may draw their income by way of dividend rather than salary, attracting neither PAYE nor NIC liability, although the IR35 rules (see INTERMEDIARIES 40) might mean that they have to account for PAYE and NIC at the end of the tax year on a deemed payment of earnings. A one-man personal service company does not fall within the intermediaries reporting rules from 6 April 2015 unless it subcontracts some of its work to another entity or person and thereby itself becomes an intermediary. The April 2016 changes to the expenses rules described above (ie, s 339A) apply equally to PSCs unless they are managed service companies, and if a PSC is within IR35, it is unnecessary to check whether the worker is under supervision, direction or control as to the manner of carrying out the tasks.

Agency workers

[4.4] The rules affecting agency workers typically bring within the category of employed earner for NIC purposes all persons such as secretaries, clerks, teachers, nurses, draughtsmen and computer programmers who, obtaining through agencies temporary employment which is not under a contract of service, in offices, schools, hospitals and nursing homes, etc would otherwise be treated as self-employed earners for social security purposes. But the deeming rules exclude certain categories, and also have a much wider scope than those finding work through recognised employment agencies.

Because the rules were changed fundamentally from 6 April 2014, the positions before and after that date are described separately in what follows.

Categorisation

[4.5] Based on the NIC regulations, rather than the tax rules in *ITEPA 2003*, which were similar in scope but slightly different in detail, it could be said that, before 6 April 2014, a person who, on general principles, would fall to be categorised as a self-employed earner (see **14.18** CATEGORISATION) was nonetheless to be treated as an employed earner if, not being a member of one of the excluded groups described as the modified rule of categorisation at **4.15** below, he:

(a) obtained employment by or through some third party; *and*
(b) rendered, or was under an obligation to render, personal service; *and*
(c) was subject to (or to the right of) supervision, direction and control as to the manner of rendering of such service; *and*
(d) there was a continuing financial relationship between him and the third party (see **4.11** below).

[*Categorisation Regs, Reg 2(1)(2), Sch 1 Part I para 2* (pre-6 April 2014)]. (CWG2 (2013), page 50.)

Exclusions applied for:

- homeworkers;
- those working in premises not under the control or management of the end client (except where that was necessary for the rendering of the service);
- entertainers;
- fashion, photographic or artists' models; and
- employment agencies that merely charged a finder's fee for the recruitment and introduction of workers.

From 6 April 2014, the tests were reformulated with a view to restricting the scope for avoidance. A self-employed worker may now be treated as an employed earner if:

(a) he personally provides services to the end client; and
(b) there is a contract between the end client and an agency under or in consequence of which:
  (i) the services are provided; or
  (ii) the end client pays, or otherwise provides consideration for the services; and
(c) remuneration is receivable by the worker (from any person) in consequence of providing the services.

The exclusion for workers who are not subject to supervision, direction or control as to the manner of rendering the service (a key feature of any employment contract, and therefore equally important in assimilating self-employed 'temps' to employee status) is now approached as a separate rule, grouped together with the continued exclusions for homeworkers, entertainers (now spelt out to include actors, singers, musicians and other entertainers) and the three types of model (fashion, photographic or artist's models). [*Categorisation Regulations 1978, Reg 2(1)(2), Sch 1, Part I, para 2 as substituted by Social Security (Categorisation of Earners) (Amendment) Regulations 2014, SI 2014/635, Reg 2(3)*]. (CWG2 (2015), page 60.)

The key difference is in the area of personal service. Under the pre-2014 rules, the obligation to render personal service was a prerequisite for the application of the Categorisation Regulations to agency workers. This meant that agencies using contracts that explicitly and genuinely permitted the sending of a substitute worker could not fall within these rules and could supply 'agency' workers as self-employed individuals with no secondary Class 1 contribution burden. Under the new rules, the conversion of the worker to employed earner status occurs if there is any actual personal service, irrespective of any right to send a substitute worker.

Case law

[4.6] It has been held that secretarial 'temps', registered at an employment agency on terms which place no obligation on the agency to find the temps work and which place no obligation on the temps to accept work offered, are *in an employment law context*, employed under contracts for services (ie, self-employed), not under contracts of service (*Wickens v Champion Employment* [1984] ICR 365, 134 NLJ 544, EAT). The more recent Court of Appeal case of *Johnson Underwood Ltd v Montgomery* ([2001] EWCA Civ 318, [2001] ICR 819, [2001] IRLR 269) held that a person who was engaged by an employment agency to provide her services as a receptionist/telephonist to a third party was employed (for employment law purposes) neither by the agency nor the third party (HM Revenue and Customs Manual ESM7240).

Perhaps the clearest exposition of the categorisation of typical agency workers may be found in the report of the Court of Appeal decision in *Dacas v Brook Street Bureau (UK) Ltd* [2004] EWCA Civ 217, [2004] ICR 1437, [2004] IRLR 358 (see *Payroll Managers Review*, April 2004, page 14), an employment law case.

Mrs Dacas had been a contract cleaner, provided to the local council on a long-term basis by the agency, and she claimed against the agency for unfair dismissal when her contract was terminated. The court held unanimously that she was not an employee of the agency, although two of the judges thought that, had the point been argued before the Employment Tribunal, they might have been able to find that she had been working under an implied contract of service with the council. Sedley LJ opined that it was 'simply not credible' that Mrs Dacas had been employed by nobody, but he could not find an employment with the council without the point having been argued.

Munby J, however, disagreed with this view and summarised the legal position succinctly: for there to be a contract of service, a certain irreducible minimum of mutual bilateral obligations (ie between employer and employee) must be present, and that could not possibly have happened in the context of a tripartite relationship between worker, agency and end client. He referred to the classic statement of principle by MacKenna J in *Ready Mixed Concrete (South East) Ltd v Minister of Pensions and National Insurance* [1968] 2 QB 497, at p 515:

> A contract of service exists if these three conditions are fulfilled. (i) The servant agrees that, in consideration of a wage or other remuneration, he will provide his own work and skill in the performance of some service for his master. (ii) He agrees, expressly or impliedly, that in the performance of that service he will be subject to the other's control in a sufficient degree to make that other master. (iii) The other provisions of the contract are consistent with its being a contract of service.

While the council gave supervision, direction and control to Mrs Dacas, she was hired by and paid by the agency. There was no contract, express or implied, between the worker and the end client, and the contract between the worker and the agency was clearly not a contract of employment.

It is perhaps worth noting here that an employer is entitled to supervise, direct and control an employee in all manner of ways: when and where to present himself for work, what to do and what not to do, and how to do it. In contrast, the agency rule merely looks to supervision 'as to the manner' of performing the task, which is a more limited test than the test for a full employment contract.

The point was subsequently underlined when the similar case of *James v London Borough of Greenwich* [2008] EWCA Civ 35, [2008] ICR 545, [2008] IRLR 302 considered a similar argument, counsel for the claimant having had the benefit of Sedley LJ's views in *Dacas*. It was decided that there was no implied contract of employment with the end-user despite the worker having been used by the council for five years. The worker was an agency worker, not an employee.

The decision in *McMeechan* that an agency worker was employed by the agency was founded on the fact that a specific engagement which began and ended with the performance of one task was capable of giving rise to a contract of employment, based on the facts, even in the case of a temporary worker for an employment agency who might not be entitled to employee status under his general terms of engagement. In short, he had in effect been a casual employee for the relevant week and was entitled to claim his unpaid wages from the Secretary of State for that single week of employment.

However, all such workers under agency contracts other than those already employed by umbrella employers or their own personal service companies will (if the conditions stated above apply) fall to be treated as *employed earners* in the context of National Insurance law by virtue of the *Categorisation Regs 1978*.

Parallel provisions in *ITEPA 2003, ss 44–47* ensure that such workers were treated before 6 April 2014 as receiving employment income and after that date as employees of the agency for income tax purposes.

The criteria

[4.7] Before 6 April 2014, if HM Revenue and Customs was to succeed in categorising a person as an employed earner for National Insurance contribution purposes merely by virtue of the agency rules, it had to be able to show that the person concerned met all four of the requirements set out at **4.5** above; but, because of the way in which those requirements were set, HMRC sometimes found that task easier than one might imagine. However, because one or two of them were relatively easy to sidestep, and a number of 'payroll companies' exploited this loophole to escape employer NIC liabilities and PAYE, they were reformed into the three tests also set out above.

The 'agency contract' rule

[4.8] The terms set out at 4.5 above, for instance, do not require that employment be obtained through a formal employment agency of some kind. If, because of C's involvement, A obtains employment with B, the terms of this rule are met, whoever or whatever C might be, and whatever C's normal activities happen to be, except where C is in fact a recruitment agent who finds workers for a one-off fee, which in the specific terms of the legislation does not trigger the intermediaries rules. The width of the expression 'by or through' ensures that the terms of this rule also remain satisfied if a second agency, D, is interposed between C and B. The regulations explicitly allow for the third party being a partnership of which the worker supplied is a member. *ITEPA 2003, s 47* specifically defined 'agency contract' for income tax purposes before 6 April 2014, but this was not a feature of the NIC regulations.

Since 6 April 2014, the NIC regulations specifically allow for the agency to be either a UK agency or a foreign agency. This change was specifically aimed at avoidance and evasion techniques involving foreign agencies, which were generally outside the scope of the old rules – see further below.

The 'agency' responsible for compliance with the 2014 rules is the agency that has the contractual relationship with the client. This rule makes that agency responsible for any PAYE and NIC liabilities and any quarterly reporting of gross payments (see 4.22 below), although there will be no liability for PAYE or NIC if some other entity in the supply chain in fact operates PAYE and NIC on the workers' earnings.

The 'personal service' rule

[4.9] The terms set out at 4.5 above did *not* rule out the possibility of A sending a substitute to work for B in his stead. The DSS (now DWP) used to say that, if substitution took place, it would need to establish 'how often, what the actual arrangements [were] and most importantly who [paid] the replacement worker before deciding what effect this might have on the application of the regulations'. (DSS letter 8 December 1987). Occasional substitution, where the substitute worker was paid instead of the worker whose place he took, would, it seems, have been regarded as leaving unaffected the worker's continuing obligation to render personal service.

However, this was clearly an argument that was difficult to sustain, as the regulations were changed on 6 April 2014 to replace the obligation to provide personal service with actual personal service as a precondition of the application of the deeming rules. A number of agencies had begun to focus on this rule as a way of avoiding Class 1 NIC, ensuring that their workers had the contractual right to send substitutes and, in many cases, ensuring that substitution happened in practice so that it could be demonstrated that the right was not a mere sham. While the absence of a personal service obligation is a matter of hypothetical rights and obligations which can be difficult to prove, the presence of actual personal service is much easier to demonstrate and to use as a peg on which to hang a liability.

It is worth observing, however, that this rule does require that the supply by the 'agency' (in the extended sense of the regulations) is the supply of personal *service*. If, instead, the business is supplying a package of some kind, eg some composite arrangement such as a promotional campaign which merely includes the provision of personnel as part of the package, the agency rules do not apply to that third party business. The personnel involved in such a situation may, however, be employees of the 'agency' itself, ie a contract of service may be in existence between the persons concerned and the agency (see **14.5**). The 'agency' may hire self-employed freelancers to fulfil its contract without triggering the agency deeming rules if the workers are working for the 'agency' as part of its service rather than working for the client: the personal service will be rendered to the 'agency'. For example, an accountancy firm may agree with a client to prepare its quarterly VAT returns for a flat quarterly fee. If it is short of staff, the firm may subcontract the work to a suitably skilled and experienced freelance bookkeeper. However the freelance bookkeeper is paid, the personal service is being rendered to the accountancy firm, not a client, so the agency deeming rules will not apply. In contrast, if the client's in-house accountant is absent through prolonged illness, it might ask the accountancy firm to supply somebody to take on that role temporarily. That person is likely to be providing personal service to the client. If the firm sends one of its own employees, it will operate PAYE and NIC deductions in the normal way and the agency rules will be irrelevant, but if the firm sources and pays a freelance bookkeeper, it will be acting as an agent in arranging for the bookkeeper to provide personal services to the client, so the agency rules will apply. Whether PAYE and NIC are then deductible from the payments to the bookkeeper will depend on whether the work is subject to supervision, direction or control as to the manner of its performance.

The 'supervision, direction or control' rule

[4.10] As regards the issue of supervision, direction and control set out at **4.5** above, the then DSS said:

> The rule that the worker must be subject to supervision, direction or control, or right of control, "as to the manner" of the rendering of services generally generates the most arguments. To satisfy this control test, which is more specific than the one in the contract of service rules (see **14.11** categorisation), we need to look not just at what jobs are to be done and when, but at the right to control how the duties are carried out. It matters not whether anyone actually does tell the worker how to go about his work but requires simply to show that someone could. The regulation purposely does not specify who must have that right.
>
> [DSS letter 8 December 1987].

The right may, in other words, lie *either* with the third party who has placed the worker *or* with the person with whom the worker has been placed. In either circumstance, the terms of this test will be met. If it is once established that, at the outset, the person supplied has been told that he or she must perform duties in a particular manner or in accordance with established practices, HMRC can be expected to regard the right of control as to the manner of working as subsisting throughout the engagement.

The views of the former DSS expressed here reflect the judgment in the unreported case of *Staples v Secretary of State for Social Services* (15 March 1985) which concerned an agency relief chef who could be told what food to prepare but not how to prepare it. Two *chefs de cuisine* had been supplied by the same agency, one as head chef and one as a sous chef or banqueting chef. Only the head chef was held to meet the requirement for exclusion from the *Categorisation Regs 1978* as the other roles were by definition subject to the supervision, direction or control of the head chef at the time.

A number of agencies were known to argue that their workers were excluded from the scope of the pre-6 April 2014 regulations not only because the workers were free to send a substitute but also because the agencies engaged only skilled and experienced workers who did not need or accept supervision over the manner of their working. This 'escape route' from re-categorisation still exists under the post-6 April 2014 version of the regulations (so that genuinely self-employed people may still find work through agencies without suffering a PAYE and NIC deduction), so extra safeguards have been built in to the regulations to deter end clients and others from falsely claiming that their temporary workers are unsupervised, by providing for liability to fall on those end clients or others who make the false claims and provide fraudulent documents in support (see further below).

The 'financial relationship' rule

[4.11] So far as the fourth pre-2014 rule set out at **4.5** above is concerned, there was a 'continuing financial relationship' between a person and a third party through whom he obtained employment when either:

- earnings for services such as are described at **4.5** above were paid by, or through, or on the basis of accounts submitted by, that third party, or in accordance with arrangements made with that third party; or
- payments, other than to the person employed, were made by way of fees, commission or other similar payments which related to the continued employment of that person in the employment concerned.

The 6 April 2014 change recast the test and now looks only for remuneration 'receivable by the worker (from any person) in consequence of providing the services'.

[*Categorisation Regs, Sch 1, Part I, para* 2].

There was *no* continuing financial relationship, however, where the only payment to the agency was an introductory fee (Leaflet CA 25 – now withdrawn – and CWG2 (2013), page 50) and the only continuing financial arrangement was one which arose between the person employed and the person to whom the agency had introduced him on the basis of a contract of service entered into as a result of the introduction eg an audit clerk supplied to an accountant through an agency who worked on the premises of the accountant's clients. [*Categorisation Regs, Sch 1, Part I, para* 2]. The fundamental impact of this rule after 6 April 2014 has not been changed by moving the focus onto remuneration paid to the worker as a result of the provision of the services. Under the new rule, the end client must be providing consideration for the services, which will not be the case where there is a simple payment of a one-off recruitment fee.

Foreign agencies

[4.12] The position of foreign agencies had a low profile in the *Categorisation Regs 1978* before 6 April 2014, but they are now dealt with explicitly in consequence of avoidance and evasion of contributions by the use of offshore agencies.

Where the agency that should, according to the agency rules, have been the secondary contributor could not be treated as such because it had no place of business in Great Britain or Northern Ireland and was neither resident nor present here (see **51.9** OVERSEAS MATTERS), the person to whom the person employed was supplied was treated as the secondary contributor instead. [*Categorisation Regs 1978, Reg 5 and Sch 3, Column B, para 2(c)*.] See **4.13** below for further discussion of the agency's position as secondary contributor. Note that there is a separate rule for foreign employers of workers in the UK (*Categorisation Regs 1978, Sch 3, para 9*), as opposed to foreign agencies supplying temporary workers (*Categorisation Regs 1978, Sch 3, para 2*).

Compliance with *para 2(c)* required that the end client be fully aware of payments of wages to the agency workers concerned, but that end client could not comply if, as sometimes occurred, it had no information about when and how much each agency worker was paid. In the context of onshore agencies, PAYE and Class 1 liabilities – and information requirements – could be imposed and enforced, but offshore agencies could not be forced to disclose how much they paid workers or when they paid them, so UK end users had a very reasonable excuse for non-compliance if such information was not provided to them. HMRC was powerless to collect secondary liabilities unless it was able to use mutual assistance arrangements such as those that exist between EU member states. The agencies exploiting this weakness were not based in the EU but in less cooperative offshore jurisdictions.

A new approach was therefore adopted from 6 April 2014 to ensure that a person in the UK could be made liable. In many cases, foreign agencies supply their UK workers via a UK agency or series of agencies, so the last UK agency in the chain has been made liable for the liabilities of the foreign agencies. For example, it is not unknown for a UK agency to have an associated company set up in Poland to recruit staff for UK work. The staff are placed with UK clients by the UK agency, although the workers may have a contract with the Polish agency. The UK agency is responsible for all liabilities and/or reporting.

A foreign agency is defined as 'a person (including a body of persons unincorporate of which the employed person is a member) who does not have a place of business, residence or presence in the UK'. [*Categorisation Regs 1978, Reg 1*.] The regulations treat that agency as the secondary contributor, just like any other UK agency, but if it fails to comply, the liability may now fall on a UK person.

The liability will fall on:

- the UK agency who is party to the contract with the end client;
- the end client, if the end client supplies to the UK agency fraudulent documents purporting to show that there is no supervision, direction or control of the manner of performance of the duties by the worker (and therefore no liability under the agency rules in the *Categorisation Regs 1978*); or
- any other person in a contractual relationship with the UK agency who supplies fraudulent documents in connection with the purported deduction or payment of contributions in connection with the employed person.

[*Categorisation Regs, Reg 5 and Sch 3, para 2.*]

Para 9 lists six circumstances involving a foreign element under which a UK entity is liable to account for contributions, two of which relate to foreign agencies, covering the supply of workers to UK end clients either directly or indirectly via another UK agency or agencies.

Where there is a direct contract between a foreign agency and an end client in the UK (defined as 'a person (including any connected person within the meaning given by *section 993* of the *Income Tax Act 2007*) who has a place of business, residence or presence in the UK and to whom the worker personally provides services' (*Reg 1*) for the worker to provide services to that end client, the end client is deemed to be the secondary contributor. This new rule would appear to leave HMRC in no better position than the old rule when faced with an uncooperative offshore entity that refuses to tell the end client how much the temporary worker has been paid.

As already noted, where a foreign agency supplies a worker to a UK agency to perform work for an end client under a contract between the end client and the UK agency, the UK agency with the contractual relationship with the end client is the deemed secondary contributor and will bear the liability if the foreign agency fails to withhold an account for deductions. The same practical problem with non-disclosure of information would seem to arise here as it has in the past.

Secondary contributor

[4.13] The third person by whom, or through whose agency, the person employed is supplied will normally fall to be treated as the secondary contributor as regards Class 1 contribution liability on the earnings of the person supplied (see **14.32** CATEGORISATION). If, however, the 'third person' is a partnership subject to English law and the person supplied is himself one of its members, the other members of the partnership will be treated as the secondary contributor. [*SSCBA 1992, s 7(2); Categorisation Regs, Reg 5 and Sch 3 para 2(a)*]. A similar rule applies if the person employed is a member of an unincorporated association other than a partnership, when the secondary contributor is the remaining members.

As noted above, where the person who should, according to these rules, have been the secondary contributor could not be treated as such because he had no place of business in Great Britain or Northern Ireland and was neither resident nor present here (see **51.9** OVERSEAS MATTERS), the person to whom the person employed was supplied was treated as the secondary contributor instead under *Reg 5* and *Sch 3 para 2(c)* as they applied before 6 April 2014.

For some years there was uncertainty as to whether this rule could be applied in situations where a person was sent by a foreign employer to work for someone in GB while remaining under a contract of service with that foreign employer. This uncertainty was not limited to employment businesses, but extended to any businesses seconding workers to UK associated companies. It was thought that the foreign employer supplying the worker to the UK employer might in effect be classed as an agency, because *Reg 2* did not explicitly exclude workers who were already working under a contract of employment (although this exclusion arguably ought to have been inferred from the wording of the regulation). Having sought information from a number of companies in the UK who were host to such seconded employees, the then DSS issued an undated and unreferenced note early in 1993, the text of which is reproduced in extract below:

Workers seconded from abroad
—Liability for national insurance contributions (NICs)

1. This Note announces the conclusions of a DSS review of the liability for employers' secondary NICs for certain overseas workers (in the main, those from countries outside the EEC or with which there is no bi-lateral agreement) seconded to the UK by a foreign employer to work temporarily for a subsidiary or independent company.
2. Generally, under the provisions of the Social Security (Contributions) Regulations 1979 SI No 591, NICs do not become payable until such workers have been resident in GB for a period of 52 weeks. Thereafter, liability for primary (employee) Class 1 NICs arises but, where the worker remains under a contract of service only with the foreign employer, and that employer has no place of business in GB, the Contributions Regulations do not impose secondary (employer) liability on the UK company or organisation to which the worker is seconded.
3. Against a background of increasing numbers of such workers and doubts raised in individual cases, the DSS has been reviewing the position in regard to provisions within the Social Security (Categorisation of Earners) Regulations 1978 SI 1689, which, inter alia, provide for certain persons to be treated as secondary Class 1 contributors. Following full and detailed consideration, however, it has now been accepted that those provisions are not appropriate in these cases. Secondary liability, therefore, will continue currently to be based solely on the considerations described in paragraph 2 above.
4. It should be noted, however, that it is the policy of the DSS that, in the interests of equity, a primary Class 1 liability should normally be matched by a secondary NIC liability. Accordingly, the DSS will be considering bringing forward amending Social Security legislation, at some future date, to put the matter beyond doubt.
5. It is expected that, in the majority of past and current cases, primary Class 1 NICs only are being paid or will have been paid. In other cases, however, it may be that secondary NICs are being or have been paid where, in the light of this Note, no liability existed. In such cases, refunds may be appropriate, subject to satisfactory confirmation that the conditions are met.

The amending legislation referred to in paragraph 4 of that note was contained in *Categorisation Amendment Regs 1994, Reg 2, Reg 4*, and is described at **51.9** OVERSEAS MATTERS. In addition, the *Social Security (Contributions) Amendment (No 4) Regulations 1994, SI 1994/2299* which came into force on 30 September 1994 brought into effect for NIC purposes similar provisions to those for PAYE that were introduced by the *Finance Act 1994* in respect of seconded workers, imposing a liability on the UK 'host' employer of any secondee.

Where an employee works for another person who is not his employer then that person ('the principal employer' in terms of the regulations, but generally referred to as the 'host employer') is deemed to be the employer for the collection purposes of *Social Security (Contributions) Regulations 2001, SI 2001/1004, Sch 4*. This means that the principal employer is responsible for the payment of Class 1 contributions of the seconded employee and can deduct an amount equal to the employee's contributions from the payments to the immediate employer (ie the legal employer who holds the contract of employment overseas). This rule will only apply where HM Revenue and Customs has issued a direction under *ITEPA 2003, s 691* that payments should be deducted from any payments made. [*Social Security (Contributions) Regulations 2001, SI 2001/1004, Sch 4 para 3*].

Where a member of a partnership obtains temporary employment through an agency (other than the partnership itself) in such a way as to bring about his categorisation as an employed earner under the rules described at **4.5** above, the basic rules stated above as regards the identification of the secondary contributor apply in their entirety; in other words, the agency will be treated as the secondary contributor. Where, however, a director or employee of a limited company obtains temporary employment through an agency in the manner described, the company and not the agency will be treated as the secondary contributor, *unless* the employee or director obtains his temporary employment *independently* of the company, in which case the normal rules will apply. (Leaflet CA 25 – now withdrawn).

It appears, however, that the 1994 changes to the legislation may not have been as effective as the Contributions Agency and (later) HMRC believed. In late 2012 it came to light that large numbers of teachers employed in the UK had an employer in Sark in the Channel Islands. As this employer had no place of business in the UK it was not paying secondary NIC. The purpose of the 1994 legislation was to impose the secondary liability on the end user of such employees but HMRC acknowledged that it might not be possible to enforce such a liability, for the reasons outlined above. On 30 May 2013 HMRC issued a consultative document entitled *Offshore Employment Intermediaries* in which it set out proposals to levy the secondary liability on the end user client if the offshore employer and then any intermediary employer did not pay the secondary NIC.

As noted above in the context of foreign agencies, the legislation was indeed changed from 6 April 2014 in an attempt to impose liabilities more effectively in these circumstances. Most of the staff supplied by the Sark businesses were procured via a UK agency, rather than directly, so the obvious way to block the avoidance was to make that UK agency liable as the secondary contributor.

The initial liability therefore now falls on that UK agency. [*Categorisation Regs 1978, Sch 3, para 2, column B*.] As noted above, the end client might become the secondary contributor in the event that it issues fraudulent documents purporting to show that the worker is not under supervision as to the manner of performing the work. Any third party in a contractual relationship with the UK agency who issues fraudulent documents purporting to show that NICs have already been accounted for may also become the secondary contributor. Similar rules apply from 6 April 2016 to those issuing fraudulent documents in support of a claimed absence of supervision, direction and control for the purposes of the intermediary travel and subsistence rules introduced from that date.

It was originally planned that the offshore employer would be regarded as the secondary contributor in the first instance and such entities would have all the usual employer obligations which were currently undertaken by a UK-based employer. If the offshore employer did not meet these obligations the responsibility would revert to the first intermediary in the chain and if that entity defaulted, responsibility would pass to the end user. However, after consultation, the powers granted by *NICA 2014* merely changed the rules in respect of oil and gas workers in the UK North Sea, while the position of those working for host employers was changed by amendments to the *Categorisation Regs 1978*.

The identification of the default secondary contributor is most easily represented by the following table, in which it is assumed that the worker (W) is supplied to provide services personally by a foreign employer (FE) or foreign agency (FA) to a UK business.

	Circumstances	**Secondary contributor**
(a)	FE supplies W to a host employer under a contract between FE and the host	Host employer
(b)	FA supplies W to a UK end client under a contract between FA and the end client	End client
(c)	FE supplies W to a UK end client under a contract between the end client and a UK agency	The UK agency that has the contractual relationship with the end client*
(d)	FA supplies W to a UK end client under a contract between the end client and a UK agency	The UK agency that has the contractual relationship with the end client*
(e)	UK employer supplies W to a business outside the UK under a contract between the non-UK business and a UK agency, where W is eligible to pay UK NICs in relation to that employment	The UK employer or UK agency that has the contractual relationship with the non-UK business

	Circumstances	Secondary contributor
(f)	FE supplies W to a non-UK business under a contract between the non-UK business and a UK agency, where W is eligible to pay UK NICs in relation to that employment	The UK agency that has the contractual relationship with the non-UK business

* If the end client provides any fraudulent documents in connection with the supervision, direction or control test to the UK agency under (c) or (d) above, the end client will become the secondary contributor and will become liable for any arrears and penalties. If any UK resident person other than the end client who is in a contractual relationship with the UK agency provides to that agency any fraudulent documents purporting to show that contributions have already been deducted and accounted for, that person will become the secondary contributor and will become liable for any arrears and penalties. It remains to be seen how easy it will be for HMRC to prove fraud: fraud is a well-established concept and requires intent, rather than mere recklessness or carelessness. Any agency supplying workers and paying them gross on the basis that they are not subject to supervision, direction or control will only escape liability, and transfer that liability to their client, if intent to defraud can be established. In other words, the problem lies with the agency, not HMRC. The potential difficulties are clear.

The effect of the changes is intended to be the imposition of a UK primary and secondary liability in cases where workers would trigger such a liability if they were employed by a UK employer, even if they are in fact employed by a non-UK entity beyond the reach of UK law. The use of agencies and umbrella employers sending workers both into and out of the UK has thus become more expensive because certain types of avoidance and evasion have been forestalled.

Guidance in booklet CWG2 (2014) stated (on page 50) that, in addition to the exclusions noted below, an agency was not responsible for the operation of PAYE and the payment of NIC when the worker was legitimately providing his services in a self-employed capacity. The agency simply had to obtain and keep evidence to prove that this was the case. In the 2015 edition, the advice was changed and is at times incorrect: 'In this guide, "employee" means anyone who is gainfully employed in the UK and is: . . . engaged through an agency or some other third party . . . ' (page 4). The guidance in Chapter 4 (page 52) was better in that it admitted that the agency 'may' be responsible for operating PAYE and paying NICs, then listed the conditions for the agency to be treated as the secondary contributor. It also noted (page 53) that an employment business is 'usually' responsible for operating PAYE and NIC deductions but gave no indication of what might be unusual. The guidance was repeated in CWG2 (2016), page 66 and CWG2 (2017), para 4.2 – note that CWG2 (2017) is only available in HTML format.

Further changes were also made on 6 April 2014 by *NICA 2014, s 12* and the *Social Security (Contributions) (Amendment No 2) Regulations 2014, SI 2014/572* to impose a secondary contribution liability on the employers of oil and gas workers supplied to operators in the UK North Sea (see OIL RIG WORKERS, DIVERS, ETC 50).

Aggregation of earnings

[4.14] A special aggregation rule operates so as to ensure that where earnings in respect of different employments are paid by different persons and some other person is, in accordance with the rule stated at **4.13** above, treated as the secondary contributor, all earnings paid in a given earnings period are treated as a single payment of earnings in respect of a single employment (see EARNINGS PERIODS 34 as well as sections 5.2, 5.6 AGGREGATION OF EARNINGS).

Exceptions to the agency rule

[4.15] The modified rule of categorisation described at **4.5** above does not apply to:

- anyone who, although falling to be categorised under the modified rule, does so under some other regulation (see **39.1** HUSBAND AND WIFE, AND CIVIL PARTNERS; **41.19** LABOUR-ONLY CONTRACTORS and **46.1** MINISTERS OF RELIGION);
- anyone who, although satisfying the conditions set out at **4.5** above, renders his services in his own home or on other premises not under the control or management of the person to whom he is supplied eg an audit clerk supplied to an accountant through an agency who works on the premises of the accountant's clients (see **38.2** and **38.3** HOMEWORKERS AND OUTWORKERS); or
- anyone who is employed as an actor, singer, musician or other entertainer or as a fashion, photographic or artist's model, though some such persons will fall to be categorised as an employed earner by virtue of the nature of their activities alone (see **36.1** ENTERTAINERS and CWG2 (2016), page 66). Following on from a consultation document entitled *National Insurance and self-employed entertainers* issued on 15 May 2013, the Government repealed from 6 April 2014 the relevant part of the *Social Security (Categorisation of Earners) Regulations 1978 (SI 1978/1689)* so that entertainers now have their employment status determined in the same way as any other individual.

[*Categorisation Regs, Sch 1 Part I para 2, 5A*].

As noted above, HMRC guidance (CWG2 (2014), page 50) used to state that 'legitimate' self-employed workers are also outside the scope of the rules, although this is difficult to reconcile with the plain words of the legislation. Logically, self-employed subcontractors whose services are used as part of a composite supply by a business supplying goods or services are excluded (eg where an electrical contractor uses subcontract labour to carry out a wiring installation), but it will sometimes be debatable whether the subcontractor is 'legitimately' self-employed and providing his services to the main contractor, or rather has questionable self-employed status and is in practice supplying personal service, via the main contractor, to the end client. There is nothing in the regulations to prevent the main contractor being classed as an agency. The retention in the 2014 rules of the absence of a right of supervision, direction or control as an escape route from PAYE and NIC deductions should ensure that skilled and experienced workers are less often deemed to be employed by the agency's client but, if they are in fact supervised, directed or controlled as to how they work, it will be irrelevant whether they are otherwise genuinely self-employed: the agency rules will apply. Even if they escape PAYE and NIC deductions, the fact that they have been paid gross for agency work will now usually have to be reported quarterly by the agency.

Specific types of agency

[4.16] Many employment agencies specialise in particular kinds of placement and some such types of agency warrant special comment.

It should be noted that where there is an ongoing relationship this is strictly called an 'employment business', whereas an introduction agency is called an 'employment agency'. [*Employment Agencies Act 1973, s 13(2)(3).*]

Nursing and home-care agencies

[4.17] Nurses and others supplied to hospitals, institutions, old people's homes etc by a nursing agency will, if the agency has a continuing financial relationship with the nurses, usually fall to be treated as employees of the agency according to the rules described in this chapter, because a matron or some other senior person will have the right to direct how the nurses should perform their duties. Special considerations apply, however, where nurses or other types of helper or carer are supplied to disabled, elderly, or incapacitated people in their own homes. In such cases, HMRC will look closely at the position regarding the right of control over how duties are performed. Normally, such a right will be possessed by the person who is being cared for, or by another member of that person's household; but if the person lives alone and is so incapacitated as to be wholly reliant upon the carer or virtually so, the right of control may, effectively, be non-existent or may have been totally abrogated, and in such a case, if the agency itself exercises no control, the agency rules will not apply. It is worth noting that the then DSS never considered that medical guidance given by the GP, consultant or hospital responsible for the patient's health, amounted to supervision, direction or control of the nurse or carer – see Employment Status Manual, para ESM4251. See also *Bhadra v Ellam* 019880 TC 466. Nursing 'banks' are known to cause particular difficulties because of the AGGREGATION OF EARNINGS (5.2) rules. See ESM4251 onwards.

Agricultural agencies

[4.18] Some agencies specialise in the supply of agricultural workers to farms, including herd managers and farm managers. The then DSS accepted that, so far as many such placements are concerned, the right of supervision, direction or control may be entirely lacking (eg where the farm owner is absent) and that, where it is lacking, the agency rules do not apply. However, many agricultural workers are supervised, directed and paid by gangmasters, who will be responsible for PAYE and NIC deductions. Such arrangements will often come under scrutiny from the Gangmasters Licensing Authority as well as HMRC's Fraud Investigation Service – Labour Providers teams.

Promotional agencies

[4.19] Demonstrators and merchandisers are often agency-supplied workers who are placed in stores and supermarkets or at shows, exhibitions, sports grounds, race tracks etc and given the task of promoting and/or shelf-stocking the products of the agency's client, ie the product manufacturer. The question whether the agency rules apply in such situations often, again, resolves itself into the question whether the demonstrators and merchandisers concerned are subject to the right of control over how they carry out their duties. The fact that such persons are unsupervised at the time they carry out their task does not mean that the right to control is lacking; and, indeed, if it can be established that preliminary instructions are issued to the persons concerned or that initial training is supplied, HMRC will maintain that a right of control is proved to exist. See ESM2068 and ESM4025.

One of the triggers for the April 2014 changes to the *Categorisation Regs 1978* was HMRC's loss of the *Talentcore* case (*Talentcore Limited (t/a Team Spirits)* [2011] UKUT 423 (TCC)) which involved demonstrators and merchandisers in airport duty-free shops. They were allowed and even required to send a substitute if they could not fulfil a shift commitment, so there was a demonstrable absence of an obligation to provide personal service and therefore, held both the First-tier Tribunal and Upper Tribunal, no liability under the agency rules for either PAYE or NICs. The decision of both tribunals was that there was a right of supervision as to the manner of carrying out the work, so the company in question will have been affected by the April 2014 changes.

Professional services agencies

[4.20] Many agencies supply professionally qualified personnel to their clients, eg draughtsmen, architects, management consultants, engineers, computer programmers, chefs, and quantity surveyors. Often, such people have businesses of their own and use agency work to supplement their income. Again, the test of whether the agency rules apply will come down to the question of the right of control. If the person's expertise in his or her particular field is such that all the agency's client can do is to recognise the professional's independence and to give him or her a free hand to produce in his or her own way the result which the client requires, the agency rules are unlikely to apply. But if, while carrying out his or her assignment for the agency, the professional has to work under the same constraints as employees of the client, the agency rules will serve to give him or her deemed employed earner status in relation to the agency work. See ESM2014 and ESM 2057.

Construction industry workers

[4.21] Since the status reviews of subcontractors that had to be performed by 6 April 1997 (see **41.9** LABOUR-ONLY CONTRACTORS), the incidence of agency-supplied subcontractors had increased, indicating that many who had failed the status review had subsequently been taken on by agencies. This trend towards the employment of agency-supplied subcontractors had been evident in some large construction projects and had enabled construction companies to relieve themselves of the administrative tax burden of deducting tax at basic rate and accounting for the tax and NIC to HMRC.

Many agency subcontractors in construction were given contracts by 'CIS payroll contractors' that explicitly allowed substitution so as to prevent the application of the pre-April 2014 agency rules. HMRC is known to have challenged such arrangements but had little success. The Impact Notice issued with the 2013 consultation on the changes indicated that some 200,000 construction industry subcontractors were expected to be reclassified with effect from 6 April 2014 (alongside some 50,000 in other industries). Many of those potentially affected may well feel that they are experienced craftsmen who can and do work unsupervised, so that they will be able to argue that there is no right of supervision as to the manner of their working, but HMRC can be expected to examine any such claims very closely and very sceptically.

Guidance notes with frequently asked questions and case studies illustrating the working of the new rules were issued by HMRC. These indicate amongst other things how a construction industry worker might be able to demonstrate freedom from supervision in carrying out joinery work (in being given a drawing of a door which he then makes in his own workshop and hangs), and how some of his co-workers might not be able to do so (by being asked to work alongside employed joiners and move from task to task as they do so), but the examples used are at opposite ends of the spectrum of possible (and likely) contractual arrangements: they seem likely to prove to be of little practical use in the real world where most cases fall into a grey area. See ESM2060.

Reporting of gross payments

[4.22] In order to track those cases where agencies continue to pay workers gross on a self-employed basis, the PAYE and NIC regulations were amended with effect from 6 April 2015 by the *Income Tax (Pay As You Earn) (Amendment No 2) Regulations 2015 (SI 2015/171)* to require those agencies with a contract with a client for the supply of a worker (called 'specified intermediaries') to make quarterly reports of such payments to HMRC. The first reports are expected by 5 August 2015 covering the quarter to 6 July 2015. The reporting system covers both onshore and offshore intermediary payments (although not workers who carry out their duties or provide their services wholly offshore on the UK Continental Shelf).

The specified intermediaries are obliged to continue to submit reports for four consecutive tax quarters after they have ceased to satisfy the conditions that create the obligation to report in *Regs 84E(b)–84E(d)* of the *Income Tax (Pay As You Earn) Regulations 2003 (SI 2003/2682)*, ie:

- that more than one individual has been supplied to one or more clients by the intermediary in the quarter;
- the services were not provided exclusively on the Continental Shelf; and
- the employment intermediary has made one or more payments that are not liable to PAYE deduction (whether or not such deduction was made) or was not required to include a payment in an RTI return because the individual was not an employee or treated as an employee under *SI 2003/2682, Reg 10*.

Alternatively, where the intermediary ceases trading as such, HMRC may be notified and any reporting requirements cease from the point. [*SI 2003/2682, Reg 84F(5)*].

Where there is a chain of intermediaries, only the intermediary that has a contract with the end client is responsible for sending HMRC the reports. In a typical situation where an agency contracts with an end client to supply a number of workers and then sources those workers under a contract with an umbrella business, the agency that contracts with the end client is responsible for PAYE and NIC (if applicable) and reporting (if there is no PAYE and NIC liability), even if it has no direct relationship with, or knowledge of, the workers concerned. This means that the other intermediaries in the chain must be contractually bound by the final intermediary to supply the information required for the quarterly reports, and agree in contract with the workers that their data may be passed on. Without such contractual obligations, data protection issues may arise.

It may not always be easy to identify the last intermediary in the chain because it is not always easy to identify the end of the chain, but every intermediary in that chain will need to know whether it is at the end if it is to meet its obligations.

Example

A large construction project: a major utility is building a new power station, and it appoints a main contractor (MC) who is responsible for letting and supervising contracts for each element of the construction process. At the far end of the chain is a quantity surveyor (QS) with his own personal service company (PSC). One of MC's sub-contracts is for the provision of concrete for the project, and the concrete contractor subcontracts the quantity surveying work to an appropriately skilled surveyors' practice. However, the practice is busy and subcontracts the work to the PSC, which sends QS to work on site for the concrete contractor. A tiny part of the contract payments made by the utility will find its way via a number of contracts to the PSC.

It is likely that QS will be a skilled and independent professional who is not subject to supervision direction or control – his PSC would not have been offered the contract if that had not been the case. There is no PAYE or NIC obligation on the practice, but it is open to question whether it must make a quarterly report of the gross payments to the PSC. The practice is supplying a service to the concrete contractor, but the concrete contractor is also supplying materials and services to MC. It is a moot point whether the practice is the last intermediary in the chain and the concrete contractor is the client, on the basis that the contractor is not supplying QS's personal services to MC: it is supplying concrete, manufactured and delivered to specification. QS's services are a tiny part of the large project, but it is not clear whether the end client is the utility, MC, the concrete contractor or, indeed, the surveyor's practice, which itself is providing a service rather than merely providing labour. Further guidance on how to identify the end client is awaited from HMRC, but it had not emerged by mid-2016.

The employment intermediary, as defined in *ITEPA 2003, s 716B(2)*, specified in *SI 2003/2682, reg 84E*, and identified by those involved in the supply chain, is required to provide to HMRC specified information within 30 days after the end of the quarter, in prescribed form (ie, online, using HMRC's report template, via a new portal designated the Employment Intermediaries Service, and with a declaration that the information is correct).

There are penalties for late, incomplete or incorrect returns. For the first failure to report, the penalty is £250, while the penalty for the second offence is £500 and any further offences will attract a penalty of £1,000. HMRC has yet to decide or announce how penalties for incomplete returns will be imposed. The maximum penalty permitted by *Taxes Management Act 1970, s 98(4F)*, as amended by *FA 2014, s 18*, and commenced from 6 April 2015 by *FA 2014, s 18(2)–(4) (Appointed Day) Order 2015, SI 2015/931*, is £3,000 for the initial failure and £600 per day of continued failure after the imposition of the first penalty. It remains to be seen how HMRC will try to use the penalty provisions, as they are not automatic.

The intermediary will be allowed to amend the quarterly return up to 30 days after the end of the tax quarter following the tax quarter to which the return relates. The information specified by *SI 2003/2682, reg 84G* is as follows.

Information about the specified employment intermediary:

- its name;
- its address and postcode;
- its employer's PAYE reference where it is required to have one (it may, for example, be an LLP with no employees and no requirement for a PAYE reference);

Information about each individual worker providing the relevant services:

- the worker's full name and address with postcode;
- either the worker's date of birth and gender or, if one has been allocated, the worker's NI number;
- the worker's UTR if self-employed or a member of a partnership; and
- the dates on which the worker began and ceased to provide the relevant services.

In addition, where the intermediary has paid somebody for the services of a worker who falls outside the deeming rules (eg, a PSC or umbrella company), the intermediary must report:

- the recipient person's (ie, typically the umbrella business's) full name (company name or partnership trading name) and address;
- in the case of a company its company registration number;
- the total of all payments made to the recipient in the quarter;
- the currency in which payment has been made (which must be converted to £ or € only);

- the reason why no deductions have been made from the payments; and
- whether the payments included VAT.

The official online reporting template is in either Comma Separated Value (CSV) or Open Document Spreadsheet (ODS) format and includes a cell giving the reason for non-deduction. The reporting intermediary must indicate whether the non-deduction of PAYE was because:

(A) the worker was self-employed;
(B) the worker was member of a partnership;
(C) the worker was member of an LLP;
(D) the worker was employed by a limited company (including personal service companies);
(E) the engagement was carried out outside the UK; or
(F) another party operated PAYE on the payments to the worker.

If more than one reason applies, the intermediary is instructed to select the option that comes first on the list. The guidance and design of the template have been questioned because in a typical case where umbrella company employees are supplied to an end client, PAYE will have been applied to all of the earnings of the worker, but reason (F) will never be reached because the worker is employed by a limited company and covered by reason (D).

There is also an additional record-keeping requirement, imposed because the existing rules only apply to PAYE and NIC payments. The intermediary must keep otherwise irrelevant non-PAYE records for at least three complete tax years. The records may be kept in electronic form. [*SI 2003/2682, reg 84H.*] It is open to question why HMRC cannot rely on the normal requirement to keep records relevant for tax purposes under the self-assessment rules for both corporate and non-corporate taxpayers.

The electronic reporting system was in the process of being designed as the relevant regulations were passed in February 2015 but was live in advance of the first reporting deadline of 5 July 2015. The templates are available for download at www.gov.uk/government/publications/employment-intermediaries-report-template.

It is understood that HMRC received far fewer returns at the end of the second quarter of operation of the 2015 rules than at the end of the first quarter. It then set up some special teams in the Fraud Investigation Service – Labour Providers unit to focus on those cases where no second-quarter return had been received and others where gross payment was being reported where deduction of PAYE was expected.

Targeted Anti-Avoidance Rule (TAAR)

[4.23] The changes to the onshore and offshore intermediary rules from 6 April 2014 clearly did not achieve the full intended outcome for HMRC, because *National Insurance Contributions Act 2015, s 6* created an additional targeted anti-avoidance rule. It added *Reg 5A* into the *Social Security (Categorisation of Earners) Regulations 1978* on 12 February 2015 but the change was backdated to 6 April 2014.

A worker will be treated as falling within the category of employed earner if three conditions apply:

- the worker has an employment in which he personally provides services to a person who is resident or present or has a place of business in the UK;
- a third person enters into 'relevant avoidance arrangements'; and
- the earner would not otherwise be, or be treated as falling, within the employed earner category in relation to the employment.

[*Regulation 5A(1)*.]

Note that 'employment' encompasses both employed and self-employed activity under the definitions in the legislation.

The definition of 'relevant avoidance arrangements' is arrangements the main purpose, or one of the main purposes, of which is to avoid the rule that deems the worker to be an employee or to avoid the rule that deems the agency or end client to be the secondary contributor. [*Regulation 5A(3)*.] As might be expected, 'arrangements' is widely defined to include any scheme, transaction or series of transactions, agreement or understanding, whether or not legally enforceable, and any associated operations. [*Regulation 5A(7)*.]

If the agency or end client who would be liable for the secondary contributions is resident or present or has a place of business in the UK, it is to be treated as the secondary contributor where it has entered into arrangements to avoid that liability and there is no other person in the UK fulfilling those conditions who would be, or be deemed to be, the secondary contributor in respect of the payments of earnings in question. [*Regulation 5A(4)(5)*.]

Public sector procurement

[4.24] The government and HMRC consulted (with a document entitled *Intermediaries Legislation (IR35): discussion document*, published on 17 July 2015) on the possibility of making IR35 more effective by transferring to the client (or to the agency supplying the PSC's owner's services) the obligation to assess whether IR35 might apply to a contract undertaken by a PSC worker, since the client is generally the only person in a position to know whether the worker is subject to supervision, direction or control and is in disguised employment. After a significant number of responses was received (over 160 separate submissions), many of which pointed out the impracticability of the proposals, and qualitative research was undertaken outside HMRC, the plans were scaled back.

The next plan appeared on 26 May 2016 in a document entitled *Off-payroll working in the public sector: reform of the intermediaries legislation*, indicating that a revised version of the original proposals might be adopted, but only for public sector clients. The new rules from April 2017 are aimed at off-payroll engagements through third parties such as employment agencies, outsourcing companies and consultancy firms who supply workers.

Although there are many reasons why personal service companies are created, including the fact that work will not be forthcoming unless the worker is already employed by another entity, such as their own PSC, HMRC is determined to deal with alleged IR35 non-compliance. After abandoning proposals in 2015 to simply transfer all IR35 liabilities to the end-user, which would not have worked (and had been an option discarded in 1999 when IR35 was being designed), it has now been decided to apply the same arguably impractical changes, but only to public sector bodies who engage workers through personal service companies. Public sector bodies are those listed in the Freedom of Information Act 2000 and the Freedom of Information (Scotland) Act 2002.

Where workers are engaged through a PSC, responsibility for applying the intermediaries rules will fall to the public sector body, agency or other third party paying the workers' company. The public sector body, agency or other third party will be liable to pay any associated income tax and NICs. Public procurement policy note 08/15 already requires that for any individuals engaged for more than six months and paid more than £220 per day, departments and their arm's-length bodies must include a contractual provision that allows the department to seek assurance that the worker is paying the correct amount of tax and NICs and to terminate the contract if assurance is not provided. The note also specifies that, regardless of their tax arrangements, board-level officials and those with significant financial responsibility must be on the payroll of the department or employing body.

It was confirmed in the Autumn Statement 2016 that the new restrictions are scheduled to take effect in April 2017, although HMRC has left little time for public sector bodies, agencies and HMRC itself to rewrite systems to deal with compliance and the problems this seems likely to create.

In outline, the public sector end-user is seen as the only person or entity that is able to determine whether the contract falls within IR35, because it knows whether the work is subject to close supervision, direction and control in the same way as for an employee. If the end-user contracts directly with a PSC, and it determines that the contract is a IR35 contract, it will be obliged to operate PAYE and NIC on 100% of the invoice value excluding materials and VAT. It was originally proposed that the PAYE charge should be based on just 95%, to match the 5% expense allowance in the IR35 rules, but this was changed as a response to feedback during the consultation, allegedly to recognise that workers will no longer have to bear the administrative burden of deciding whether the IR35 rules apply. Given that HMRC has previously claimed that there is 90% non-compliance with the IR35 rules, the expected yield from this change that is listed in Table 2.1 of the Statement, at just £115 million over five years, seems somewhat low.

If the PSC supplies its worker through an agency, the agency that pays the PSC will have the obligation to account for the PAYE and NIC if the public sector client informs it that the contract is within IR35.

Accordingly, the public sector body will need to apply the IR35 rules in circumstances where:

(a) an individual (the 'worker') personally performs, or is under an obligation personally to perform, services for another person (the 'client');
(b) the client is a public authority;

(c) the services are provided not under a contract directly between the client and the worker but under arrangements involving a third party (the 'intermediary'); and
(d) the circumstances are such that:
   (i) if the services were provided under a contract directly between the client and the worker, the worker would be regarded for the purposes of Parts I to V of the Social Security Contributions and Benefits Act 1992 as employed in employed earner's employment by the client; or
   (ii) the worker is an office holder who holds that office under the client and the services relate to that office.

The worker is treated as having earnings from employment if one of the following conditions is met [*Social Security Contributions (Intermediaries) Regulations 2000, SI 2000/727, Part 2, Reg 14(9)–(11) inserted by Social Security (Miscellaneous Amendments No 2) Regulations 2017, SI 2017/373, Reg 2(13)*]:

- Condition A [*Reg 14(9)*]:
   (a) the intermediary is a company; and
   (b) the conditions in *Reg 15* are met in relation to the intermediary.
- Condition B [*Reg 14(10)*]:
   (a) the intermediary is a partnership;
   (b) the worker is a member of the partnership;
   (c) the provision of the services is by the worker as a member of the partnership; and
   (d) the condition in *Reg 16* is met in relation to the intermediary.
- Condition C [*Reg 14(11)*]:
   (a) The intermediary is an individual.

The further conditions in *Reg 15* in respect of Condition A are as follows:

(1) The conditions mentioned in *Reg 14(9)(b)* are that:
   (a) the intermediary is not an associated company of the client that falls within sub-para (2); and
   (b) the worker has a material interest in the intermediary.
(2) An associated company of the client falls within this paragraph if it is such a company by reason of the intermediary and the client being under the control:
   (a) of the worker; or
   (b) of the worker and other persons.
(3) The worker is treated as having a material interest in the intermediary if:
   (a) the worker, alone or with one or more associates of the worker; or
   (b) an associate of the worker, with or without other associates of the worker, has a material interest in the intermediary.
(4) For this purpose 'material interest' has the meaning given by section 51(4) and (5) of ITEPA 2003.
(5) In this regulation 'associated company' has the meaning given by section 449 of CTA 2010.

The condition in *Reg 16* in respect of Condition B is:

(1) The condition mentioned in *Reg 14(10)(d)* is:
- (a) that the worker, alone or with one or more relatives, is entitled to 60% or more of the profits of the partnership; or
- (b) that most of the profits of the partnership derive from the provision of services under engagements to which one or other of this Part and Part 1 applies:
  - (i) to a single client; or
  - (ii) to a single client together with associates of that client, or
- (c) that under the profit sharing arrangements the income of any of the partners is based on the amount of income generated by that partner by the provision of services under engagements to which one or other of this Part and Part 1 applies.

(2) In sub-para (1)(a), 'relative' means spouse or civil partner, parent or child or remoter relation in the direct line, or brother or sister.

(3) For the purposes of this regulation s 61(4) and (5) of ITEPA 2003 apply as they apply for the purposes of Chapter 8 of that Act.

The earnings from the employment, the 'deemed direct earnings' from which the income tax and NICs should be deducted, are calculated in four steps as follows:

- Step 1: identify the amount or value of the chain payment made by the person who is treated as making the deemed direct earnings, and deduct from that amount so much of it (if any) as is in respect of value added tax.
- Step 2: deduct, from the amount resulting from Step 1, so much of that amount as represents the direct cost to the intermediary of materials used, or to be used, in the performance of the services.
- Step 3: deduct, at the option of the person treated as making the deemed direct earnings, from the amount resulting from Step 2, so much of that amount as represents expenses met by the intermediary that under ITEPA 2003 would have been deductible from the taxable earnings of the employment under s 10 of ITEPA 2003, in accordance with s 327(3)–(5) of that Act, if:
  - (a) the worker had been employed by the client; and
  - (b) the expenses had been met by the worker out of those earnings.
- Step 4: if the amount resulting from the preceding Steps is nil or negative, there are no deemed direct earnings. Otherwise, that amount is the amount of the deemed direct earnings.

[*Social Security Contributions (Intermediaries) Regulations 2000, SI 2000/727, Part 2, Reg 17(1) inserted by Social Security (Miscellaneous Amendments No 2) Regulations 2017, SI 2017/373, Reg 2(13)*.]

The liability to deduct income tax and NICs from the deemed direct earnings applies to payments made on or after 6 April 2017, even though the services may have been rendered, or the contract entered into, before that date.

The legislation take the policy a step further by strengthening responsibility for accounting correctly for the tax of contract workers taken on through an intermediary. Where an individual provides services to a public sector engager through an intermediary and is doing a similar job in a similar manner to an employee, both engager and worker should be required to pay broadly the same tax and NICs as would have been due if the worker had been taken on as an employee. The liable engager or liable agency, if the agency is paying the intermediary, will use the RTI system in the same way as it does for its own direct employees.

HMRC has provided a new interactive online tool (Employment Status Service (ESS)) to give a real-time and definitive HMRC view on whether or not the rules apply to a particular engagement. The service is available at www.tax.service.gov.uk/check-employment-status-for-tax/setup. The service is anonymous and doesn't store any information entered or the result given. The results can be printed, and it is recommended that they are printed, as a record of the status returned from the inputs made.

HMRC has stated that it will 'stand by the result given unless a compliance check finds the information provided isn't accurate'. However, results achieved through contrived arrangements designed to get a particular outcome from the service will be treated as evidence of deliberate non-compliance with its associated higher penalties.

Provisions have been made to prevent double taxation (what will become new *Reg 61W, Chapter 10 of Part 2 of ITEPA 2003*), and a similar prevention of a double National Insurance liability arising has been included in the equivalent Social Security regulations. [*Social Security Contributions (Intermediaries) Regulations 2000, SI 2000/727, Part 2, Reg 23 inserted by Social Security (Miscellaneous Amendments No 2) Regulations 2017, SI 2017/373, Reg 2(13)*.] The RTI system seems unlikely to be able to cope with the same income being paid out twice on separate employer references. To avoid the double taxation and NICs liabilities, the payment by the PSC of the net 'deemed direct earnings' will need to be included in the PSC's FPS as a payment not subject to tax and NI. Whether the increase in such payments will raise questions within HMRC remains to be seen. Given that this will require changes in HMRC systems, the proposals scheduled to take effect in April 2017 may have to be introduced with very light touch regulatory action.

No equivalent action is proposed, yet, for private sector contracts. Given the new danger for public sector bodies that they may be held liable for any missed deductions if their assessment of the contracts is incorrect, it may be presumed that most will take a safety first approach to the new regime and require most contractors to go onto the public sector body's, or the contractor's agent's, payroll unless they can credibly certify that their business and the contract in question are outside IR35.

The plan recognises that most contract workers in the public sector are supplied via agencies, and that sometimes more than one agency is involved in a supply chain. The legislation is intended to apply to the agency that contracts directly with the PSC since this has the closest commercial relationship with the PSC and is best placed to deduct the tax and NICs and deliver the personal details of the worker needed to operate the payroll. With little regard for practicality, the plan simply says that, in complex contractual chains, where the agency may be a subcontractor with no immediate relationship with the engager, it will need to put in place systems with its clients to ensure it can accurately assess the tax and NIC obligations.

Where the agency, or one of the agencies in the chain, is resident outside the UK, the liability will fall on the last party in the chain which is resident in the UK. This may be a second agency, or maybe the public sector engager. The document does not address potential problems with data flows and overseas equivalents of the UK's Data Protection Act that might prevent personal information being supplied back to the UK.

The May 2016 document recognises explicitly that the changes proposed will require major systems amendments for both public sector organisations, agencies and intermediaries, who will have to join up systems such as purchase ledger and payroll that have to date been separate. Since the final specification for the changes and the draft legislation are unlikely to appear before the autumn statement, it seems highly unlikely that the necessary systems changes can be put in place for the planned implementation date of April 2017.

[*Social Security Contributions (Intermediaries) Regulations 2000, SI 2000/727, Part 2, inserted by Social Security (Miscellaneous Amendments No 2) Regulations 2017, SI 2017/373, Reg 2(13)*.]

The legislation appears to create a different sort of employee (a second class employee?). The contractor is an employee in all but name, yet seems not to be entitled to the statutory payments and other rights accruing to employees. HMRC's technical note (www.gov.uk/government/publications/off-payroll-working-in-the-public-sector-reform-of-the-intermediaries-legislation-technical-note/off-payroll-working-in-the-public-sector-reform-of-the-intermediaries-legislation-technical-note) states that 'statutory payments and other employment rights are unaffected by the new legislation', ie these rights are available through the PSC rather than the public sector body. This includes not having to apply the employer duties in respect of workers under the pension auto-enrolment regulations. However, while this may be the intention, there does not appear to be anything in the legislation that specifically precludes the worker from claiming these statutory rights from the public sector body.

Key Points concerning agency workers and NICs

[4.25] Points to consider are as follows.

- Any person(s) may come within the 'agency rule' where they arrange the supply of another person's services to a third party even in cases of secondment of staff.
- The company to which the individual provides his services may in certain circumstances become liable to secondary contributions.
- If a non-UK employer or agency posts an employee to work for a business in the UK then that UK business is the secondary contributor and liable for secondary contributions on the UK duties (subject to the worker falling within the definition of 'employed earner' and not being excluded by the residence and presence requirements in *Social Security (Contributions) Regulations 2001, Reg 145*).

- If the intermediary holding the contract to supply the workers pays a worker gross because he is not caught by the deemed employment provisions, or pays somebody else for the worker's services (be that an umbrella company, a personal service company or an LLP), the intermediary must report the payments with associated specified details every quarter, with the first report due for the quarter to 5 July 2015, and failure to do so will attract escalating penalties.
- Agencies acting as intermediaries between public bodies and PSCs that supply the services of their owner-directors will face new obligations from April 2017 to withhold PAYE and NICs from the contract payments made to the PSCs.

5

Aggregation of Earnings

Cross-references. See AGENCY WORKERS **4**; CLASS **1** CONTRIBUTIONS **15**; **18.4** CLASS **2** CONTRIBUTIONS for small earnings exception; CLASS **4** CONTRIBUTIONS **20**; **29** EARNINGS FROM EMPLOYMENT: GENERAL; **52.7** PARTNERS.

Other Sources. Simon's Taxes, Volume 2, para A8.240; Tolley's National Insurance Brief, March 1996, page 19, April 1997, pages 25–28 and June 1999, pages 42 and 43; CWG2 2018 to 2019, E24 (2014), HM Revenue and Customs National Insurance Manual NIM10000.

Introduction to the aggregation of earnings

[5.1] A fundamental tenet of the contribution scheme is that, where earnings are paid to or for the benefit of an earner in respect of any one of his employments as an employed earner, primary and secondary Class 1 contributions are to be paid without regard to any other earnings in respect of any other employment. [*SSCBA 1992, s 6(1)(4)*.] The basis for this rule lies in practicality, as employers have no way of knowing what each is paying in any particular earnings period, and even if they did know, would have no fair and straightforward way to split the employer's secondary threshold between them, or to split the 12% and 2% allocations across unrelated employments.

However, because there are certain situations in which this rule would (or could be made to) work to a contributor's advantage, aggregation rules which become operative in such situations have been introduced into the legislation.

Subject to certain modifications in the case of an earner who has been, but is no longer, a director of a company (see **5.8** below) and subject also, in some instances, to a test of practicability (see **5.7** below), the legislation provides that *all* earnings paid to an earner in a given earnings period (see **EARNINGS PERIODS 34**) in respect of one or more related employed earner's employments must be aggregated and treated as a single payment of earnings as detailed in **5.2** below.

It was announced at Budget 2016 that the Office of Tax Simplification has been tasked by the government with considering and reporting on the possibility of converting Class 1 NICs to an annual, cumulative and aggregated system, much like PAYE income tax. The aim appears to be to make the NIC scheme fairer, so that earners with similar levels of aggregate earnings pay similar levels of contributions and accrue similar levels of benefit entitlement, but it is a radical departure for the OTS, as it will (if it goes ahead) provide the opposite of simplicity. Firstly, the employer's NIC charge will have to become a completely separate payroll levy, so the simplification of NIC will involve creating an extra tax. Secondly, HMRC will need to introduce a system of NIC codes and coding notices similar to, but necessarily different from, PAYE codes, with all that this entails, including an expanded P45, an additional annual reconciliation process similar to the P800 for anybody who changes jobs during the course of the year, and amendments to the RTI system to facilitate the necessary information flows. And this will affect anyone with multiple employments, not just those whose earnings from related employments must be treated as if they came from a single course.

Given that the OTS estimated in Chapter 9 of its report *The closer alignment of income tax and national insurance* in March 2016 that the proposed change might lead to 6.3 million earners paying more NICs, and 7.1 million paying less (these latter supposedly being more likely to be lower earners), it seems that any major reform will be politically unacceptable ahead of a general election, and may prove completely unacceptable once fully explored.

The aggregation rules

[5.2] Until any OTS proposals come to fruition, employments must be aggregated and treated as a single payment of earnings in respect of one such employment if the earnings are:

(a) in respect of employments under the same employer (see **5.3** Rule 1 below) [*SSCBA 1992, Sch 1 para 1(1)(a); Social Security (Contributions) Regulations 2001, SI 2001/1004, Reg 14*]; or
(b) in respect of different employments and are paid by different secondary contributors (see **14.33**) who, in respect of those employments, carry on business in association with each other (see **5.4** Rule 2 below and

Samuels & Samuels Ltd v Richardson [2005] STC SCD 1 Sp C 431) [*SSCBA 1992, Sch 1 para (1)(b); Social Security (Contributions) Regulations 2001, SI 2001/1004, Reg 15(1)(a)*]; or

(c) in respect of different employments and are paid by different employers of whom one is, by regulation, treated as the secondary contributor (see **14.32** CATEGORISATION) in respect of each employment (see **5.5** Rule 3 below) [*SSCBA 1992, Sch 1 para 1(b); Social Security (Contributions) Regulations 2001, SI 2001/1004, Reg 15(1)(b)*]; or

(d) in respect of different employments and are paid by different persons in respect of work performed for those persons by the earner in those employments, and, in respect of those earnings, some other person is, by regulation, treated as the secondary contributor (see **4.13** and **5.6** Rule 4 below) [*SSCBA 1992, Sch 1 para 1(b); Social Security (Contributions) Regulations 2001, SI 2001/1004, Reg 15(1)(c)*].

A payment of earnings made at an irregular interval (see **34.4** EARNINGS PERIODS) is, however, not to be aggregated with any other earnings except where it and the other earnings would, if paid at the normal time, have been paid within the same earnings period. [*Social Security (Contributions) Regulations 2001, SI 2001/1004, Reg 7(4)(5)*]. Nor is a payment of earnings made to an earner in the tax year in which he attains pensionable age but before he attains that age to be aggregated with other earnings if that payment of earnings would, under normal circumstances, fall to be paid in a later tax year (see **3.7** AGE EXCEPTION). [*Social Security (Contributions) Regulations 2001, SI 2001/1004, Reg 16*].

Rule 1—employments under the same employer

[5.3] The first aggregation rule (see **5.2**(a) above) is of dual effect. *First*, it ensures that, where earnings in respect of an employed earner's employment are of different parts, those parts will, whether paid at the same or at different pay intervals, be aggregated and treated as a single amount of earnings, insofar as they are paid within the same EARNINGS PERIOD **34**.

Example

Arnold is employed by Bauble Bros as a part-time sales representative. He receives a weekly wage, quarterly commission and an annual bonus. Under the earnings period rules, his earnings period is a week (unless HM Revenue and Customs has directed otherwise). In the week ended 15 July 2018, A receives:

	£
Wages for the week ended 15 July 2018	100
Commission for the quarter ended 30 June 2018	387
Bonus for the year ended 31 December 2017	3,300
	£3,787

By virtue of *SSCBA 1992, Sch 1 para 1(1)(a)*, the contribution liabilities of A and of B for that week will be assessed by reference to a single amount of earnings of £3,787.

Secondly, it precludes the avoidance or reduction of Class 1 contribution liabilities which might otherwise be attained through the fragmentation of an earner's earnings over two or more separate employments within the same company, firm or organisation. Although the operation of this rule is not dependent on the amount of earnings in at least one of the employments being below the current Earnings Thresholds, the rule is of no anti-avoidance effect unless that is so.

Example

Throughout 2018–19, Cyril is employed by the Dainty Dish Restaurant under two separate contracts of service. As barman, he is paid earnings of £150 per week and, as wine waiter, he is paid earnings of £200 per week. If each amount of earnings were to be viewed in isolation from the other amount of earnings and contribution liabilities were to be assessed on that basis in accordance with *SSCBA 1992, s 6(4)*, no liability for either primary or secondary contributions would arise as regards C's earnings as barman (those earnings being below the 2018–19 Primary Threshold of £162 per week) and a Class 1 liability of only £4.56 primary (ie (£162 × Nil) + (£38 × 12%)) and £5.24 (ie £200 – £162 × 13.8%) secondary would arise as regards C's earnings as wine waiter. Because C's two employments are under the same employer, however, the provisions of *SSCBA 1992, Sch 1 para 1(1)(a)* take effect and override s 6(4) by requiring that all his earnings in respect of those employments be aggregated and treated as a single weekly payment of £350 in respect of a single employment. Instead of a total liability of only £9.80, therefore, a liability of £48.50 per week arises, viz.

Class 1			£
Primary	£162	@ Nil	Nil
	188	@ 12%	22.56
	£350		22.56
Secondary	£162	@ Nil	Nil
	£188	@ 13.8%	25.94
	£350		£48.50

The expression 'under the same employer' is not defined in the legislation, nor has it been subjected to judicial interpretation, nor was it explained in the article on this subject in CA National Insurance News, Issue 2, page 3. In May 1985, however, the ICAEW asked the DSS to give its interpretation of the term and to say, in particular, whether it considered that (*a*) different divisions of the same company and (*b*) wholly owned subsidiaries and their parent company constituted 'the same employer'. The DSS replied on 7 August 1985 in the following terms:

> Firstly, as regards divisions of the same company we assume that they are in fact sections of that company and not separate legal entities like subsidiary companies. If this is so, then even though a person has more than one job within the company concerned, his contracts will lie with the company. Earnings from each job will normally be aggregated and national insurance contributions levied on the total. If however, aggregation is not reasonably practicable because the earnings in the respective jobs are separately calculated, contribution liability may be assessed on each separate payment.

> Turning to your point about subsidiaries and the parent company, the fact that they are wholly owned subsidiaries does not cause them to be regarded as "the same employer". What determines whether one company is liable (as the secondary contributor) to pay contributions on all the earnings or whether various companies are each liable to do so in respect of the earnings they pay depends on the answer to the question—in respect of which contract of service or directorship (as an office holder) is/are the payment(s) made?

The *impracticability* exception referred to in the first paragraph of this reply is discussed at 5.7 below. Further, although a parent company and a subsidiary will not be considered to be the same employer, if they are carrying on business in association Rule 2 (see 5.4 below) will operate and have the same arithmetical effect.

Rule 2—different employments, but secondary contributors in association

[5.4] The second aggregation rule (see 5.2(b) above) is more complex than the first and contains four terms which frequently give rise to difficulty and which, therefore, require elaboration.

- The rule relates to earnings in respect of different employments paid by different secondary contributors. A secondary contributor is the person who, in respect of earnings from an employed earner's employment is—or but for the operation of the Earnings Threshold would be (see **33.2** to **33.4** EARNINGS LIMITS AND THRESHOLDS)—liable to pay a secondary contribution under *SSCBA 1992, s 6* and *Social Security (Contributions) Regulations 2001, SI 2001/1004, Reg 1(2)* and will not necessarily, therefore, be the employed earner's employer (see **14.32** CATEGORISATION).
- The secondary contributors who pay the earnings must carry on business in association. Although the term 'association' has acquired a precise legal meaning in tax law (see *CTA 2010, s 449*) and employment law (see *the Employments Rights Act 1996, s 218*), it remains undefined in social security legislation (and the proposed apprenticeship levy rules for 2017 opt for 'member of a company unit' to define an associated employer). The question whether or not particular secondary contributors 'carry on business in association' is, therefore, purely a question of fact and cannot be decided merely by reference to any 'associated' status which those secondary contributors possess under other branches of law. HMRC takes the view, for social security purposes, that the expression means that the businesses 'serve a common purpose, and to a significant degree they share such things as accommodation, personnel, equipment or customers'. (CWG2 (2016), para 65). Some light was shed on the meaning of these words in a letter from the DSS dated 30 November 1983 in which it was stated that:

  > for the purpose of the Contribution Regulations, what is considered is the actual relationship between the companies. What we therefore look for is some degree of common purpose, substantiated by, for example, the sharing of facilities, personnel, accommodation, customers etc. Basically, the greater the interdependence the greater the likelihood of our treating the companies

> as being in association. Companies in association would normally share profits or losses and, to a significant degree, resources. When I say 'sharing profits or losses' I mean that one would expect the companies' relationship to be such that the fortunes of one would be reflected in those of the other(s). So, for example, where two companies share expenses—say for staff or premises—this would tend to affect the profits or losses of both.

The stress is on the nature of the *trading* relationship between two businesses, not on their *constitutional* links. This was made plain in an earlier letter dated 25 October 1982, in which the DSS said:

> The Department's intention is that the phrase should be used in a restricted sense as the principle [set out at **5.1** above] of contributions liability arising in each separate employment is one of the central features of the Act . . . We are obliged to ensure that in any circumstances where the provision may be invoked we are satisfied that the secondary contributors . . . are acting in concert to a common goal . . . For instance, the fact that two companies associate together for mutual aid or that one company has one or more directors common to each does not of itself cause these two companies to be carrying on business in association. If however, two companies agree together to undertake together a definite business project, say, one to manufacture goods and the other to sell them, both companies sharing in agreed proportions the overall costs and profits, the two companies should be regarded as carrying on business in association. Alternatively the companies could also be regarded as carrying on business in association if they constitute a group. Conversely if one company manufactures goods and sells them to another company which in turn markets them, each charging and making its own profits, one can hardly say that the "businesses are carried on in association". This would also apply where two or more companies were set up to carry on different facets of the same enterprise and were linked through a holding company.

It should be noted, however, that more recent activity by the authorities suggests that greater importance is now being attached to constitutional links alone although it is arguable that this is not justified by the wording of the regulation. Conversely, the guidance now stresses that the sharing of facilities must be 'to a significant degree'; a small amount of sharing is not sufficient to cause two employers to be carrying on business in association. This was covered at the October 1997 Contributions Conference where it was stated that it is not sufficient that two employers occupy the same premises and have the same directors. 'There are many aspects that we would need to look at to arrive at a decision on trading in association, such as: whether or not they are sharing resources; whether or not they are sharing staff; if they are involved in contracts where they would both share etc;'
Further information was given in Inland Revenue Tax Bulletin, August 2000.

- The carrying on of a business in association is to be in respect of those employments to which the earnings relate. Where, therefore, two or more companies etc carry on business in association but also engage in other unassociated activities, the earnings of a person employed by two or more of those companies etc in the unassociated aspects of their businesses will not be aggregable under the rule.

Example

Throughout 2018–19, Edward is paid earnings of £157 per week in respect of his employment with Fabrications Ltd; £167 per week in respect of his employment with Gudroofs; £88 per week in respect of his employment with Homemakers Ltd and £103 per week with Interiors Ltd. H is in voluntary liquidation under John, a liquidator, but is continuing to play its part in a joint project with F, G and I involving the development of a residential building site. E is employed by G, H and I in connection with that joint project but his employment with F is in connection with unassociated activities in which that company is involved. There are four secondary contributors who pay earnings to E: F, G, John (as liquidator of H—see **14.32**) and I, but of these only F, G and I are carrying on business in association (John, as liquidator, is not), and of these only G and I are doing so in respect of E's employments. Accordingly, only the earnings E receives from G and I fall to be aggregated under *Social Security (Contributions) Regulations 2001, SI 2001/1004, Reg 15(1)(a)*, with contribution liabilities arising as follows.

		Class 1			
		*Primary**		*Secondary†*	
	£	%	£	%	£
F	157.00	Nil/12	0.00	Nil/13.8	0.00
G	167.00				
I	103.00				
G+I	270.00	Nil/12	12.96	Nil/13.8	14.90
H	88.00	Nil	Nil	Nil	Nil
		(* Nil% × £162, 12% × remainder.)		(† Nil% × £162, 13.8% × remainder.)	

On 24 October 2011 HMRC published a discussion document on PAYE pooling. The proposal was that closely connected employers might be given the option of being treated as a single entity for PAYE reporting purposes. It seemed fairly obvious that any group of employers opting for PAYE pooling would not then have been able to consider the employments separately for NIC purposes. Where the employers had previously decided that the businesses were not operating in association, the extra NIC threshold on the separate employments would have been lost. In the event, the result of the review, announced in August 2012, was that no action would be taken on the idea until the RTI system has bedded down, but employers operating informal pooling would be allowed to continue with the practice.

Rule 3—different employments, different employers one of whom is secondary contributor

[5.5] The third aggregation rule (see 5.2(*c*) above) is of limited application as there are presently only six circumstances in which a person who is an employed earner's employer will also fall to be treated as a secondary contributor under the *Categorisation Regs, Sch 3* as regards earnings paid to that earner in respect of other employed earner's employments (see **14.32** CATEGORISATION). Such circumstances will arise where an earner is employed:

- by a head of chambers and also as a barrister's clerk by one or more barristers in those chambers; or
- by a liquidator and also as an employee of one or more companies in voluntary liquidation but carrying on business under that liquidator; or
- by the Church Commissioners for England and also as a minister of the Church of England; or
- by the person responsible for the administration of a fund from which a minister of religion is remunerated and also as a minister of religion remunerated from that fund; or
- by an agency and also as an office cleaner or other type of agency worker remunerated through that agency; or
- by a UK employer and also as a secondee from a foreign employer providing personal service to the UK 'host' employer or a UK agency supplying to a UK host employer.

Example

From 6 April 2018, Keith is employed part-time by the Lively Lazarites Central Fund as an accountant at a salary of £167 per week. He is also remunerated by that fund at the rate of £159 per week as minister of the LL Free Church in Lincoln. Under the provisions of *SSCBA 1992, s 6(4)* (which require the earnings from each employment to be viewed in isolation from the other) Class 1 contribution liabilities of £0.60 primary and £0.69 secondary would arise on the earnings of £167 per week as those earnings exceed the Earnings Threshold (see EARNINGS LIMITS AND THRESHOLDS **33**) and attract a main primary contribution rate of 12%, and also a secondary contribution rate of 13.8%. On the earnings of £159 per week, no Class 1 contribution liabilities would arise as those earnings do not exceed the Earnings Thresholds. As the fund is not only K's employer, however, but also the secondary contributor as regards the earnings paid to him as a minister of religion (see **46.5** MINISTERS OF RELIGION), his earnings must, by virtue of *Social Security (Contributions) Regulations 2001, SI 2001/1004, Reg 15(1)(b)*, be aggregated and, in consequence, Class 1 contributions of £19.68 primary and £22.63 secondary will be payable on the combined earnings of £326 as these attract a main primary contribution rate of 12% on the combined earnings over £162, and for secondary contribution purposes amounts also over £162 attract a contribution rate of 13.8% on combined earnings.

Rule 4—different employments, secondary contributor other than one of the employers

[5.6] The fourth aggregation rule (see 5.2(*d*) above) currently relates only to persons who have a continuing financial relationship with agencies through which they are employed by other persons (see AGENCY WORKERS **4**).

Example

In 2018–19, Marveltipe Agencies obtain temporary part-time engagements for Norma, a secretary, with Oliver Ltd, Petersco and Quill Ltd. Through M, Norma is paid weekly earnings of £98 from O, £108 from P and £78 from Q. Although the earnings are in respect of different deemed employments and are paid by different persons, M (though not itself one of N's employers in law) is the secondary contributor as regards those earnings (see **4.13** AGENCY WORKERS) and, accordingly, by virtue of *Social Security (Contributions) Regulations 2001, SI 2001/1004, Reg 15(1)(c)*, the earnings must be aggregated. Contributions will, in consequence, be payable on earnings of £284 per week. Were it not for *Social Security (Contributions) Regulations 2001, SI 2001/1004, Reg 15(1)(c)*, all of N's earnings would, under *SSCBA 1992, s 6(4)*, have escaped liability as each amount falls below the 2018–19 weekly Primary and Secondary Thresholds of £162.

M also obtains work for Jean with O, P and Q. Through M, Jean is paid monthly earnings of £2,500, £1,900 and £1,100 respectively. But for the agency rules, J would pay 12% contributions on the earnings (less £702 primary threshold) from each source – subject to the ANNUAL MAXIMUM 7. However, the agency rules will result in a single calculation on the combined earnings so that only 2% is deducted on earnings of £1,637 (total earnings £5,500 less UEL £3,863).

Impracticability exception

[5.7] Aggregation under the first or second of the aggregation rules (see 5.3 and 5.4 above) is *not* to take place if such aggregation is not reasonably practicable. [*Social Security (Contributions) Regulations 2001, SI 2001/1004, Reg 14, Reg 15(1)*]. The term 'reasonably practicable' has created difficulties for employers and the then DSS once looked at an option whereby the employer could agree non-aggregation before the event (see CA Consultation Panel and CA Specialist Conference written response, 20 February 1996) but this was never implemented.

As regards the first aggregation rule, however, the exception is, in law, confined to situations in which the earnings in the respective employments are separately calculated. [*Social Security (Contributions) Regulations 2001, SI 2001/1004, Reg 15(1)*]. The matter is described in published guidance as follows.

> If the earnings from each job are separately calculated, you do not have to add the earnings from the separate jobs together if it is not reasonably practicable to do so. For example, it might not be practicable to do so if you operate a computerised payroll system which is unable to perform the calculation and you would then have to do it manually. In such cases, you may be required to show why it has not been reasonably practicable to add the earnings together from each job. There is no definition of the phrase 'not reasonably practicable' in National Insurance law. We rely upon the ordinary dictionary meaning and any relevant court decisions. The onus is on you as the employer to show that aggregation is not reasonably practicable. You will need to take into account costs, resources, and the effects on running the business. We consider the following points if we review your decision:
>
> - Is it a fact that your payroll software cannot aggregate earnings?
> - Is your payroll software provided by an external supplier or provided by an internal IT section?
> - Does the provider of an outside IT package give an update service that includes aggregation?
> - If the work has to be carried out manually, what are the costs?
> - How many employees are potentially affected?
> - Has there been a material change in the labour force since the decision not to aggregate was taken?
>
> . . . Please refer to section 10009 of the National Insurance Manual . . . .

(CWG2 2018 to 2019, para 3.4.3.)

It is understood that the inclusion of a person in different PAYE schemes had, on occasions, been regarded by the DSS as rendering the aggregation of that person's earnings impracticable, but that is not an exclusive test. The DSS said:

> In the Department's view, the question practicable/impracticable can only be determined by examination of the specific circumstances of each individual case taking into consideration such factors as the physical/geographical position of the business concerned, the location of pay points and associated payroll documentation, the variety and range of pay practices operated, and the percentage of the workforce affected. We do not accept that, simply because separate PAYE schemes exist, it will necessarily be impracticable to aggregate earnings.
>
> (Letter 11 July 1988).

The term 'reasonably practicable' is not defined in the legislation, but it is one which has received judicial interpretation in other contexts. It is 'a narrower term than "physically possible"' and implies that the potential loss which might result from failure to do the thing called for (here, presumably, the contribution loss to the NI Fund as a result of non-aggregation) must be balanced against the costs of doing the thing called for (here, aggregation of earnings)—not only in terms of money but in terms of time and trouble also. Where there is a 'gross disproportion' between the two, the doing of the thing called for will not be 'reasonably practicable'. (*Edwards v National Coal Board* [1949] 1 KB 704, [1949] 1 All ER 743, CA at 747 per Asquith LJ). The 'disproportionately costly in terms of time, trouble and expense' test was approved by Lord Oaksey in *Marshall v Gotham Co Ltd* [1954] AC 360, [1954] 1 AER 937, HL at 939 and, more recently, by Lord Goff in *Mailer v Austin Rover Group plc* [1989] 2 All ER 1087, HL. In the Inland Revenue Tax Bulletin of August 2000 it was stated with regard to the above cases:

> The cases consider the balance between risk on one hand and the sacrifices necessary for averting the risk on the other hand. Basically, an employer needs to balance his employee's interests against his own costs. It is very important that the consequences for the primary contributor are considered, especially the low paid, because of the potential loss of benefits and pension rights.

Clearly, therefore, the loss of benefit rights by the primary contributor is seen by HM Revenue and Customs as being an important factor to take into account and this may sway the decision in favour of aggregation whether or not this proves difficult for the secondary contributor. See Inland Revenue Tax Bulletin, August 2000; Tolley's Practical NIC Service, November 2000, page 84 and www.hmrc.gov.uk/thelibrary/briefs.htm

Exclusion of earnings relating to periods of former directorship

[5.8] Where an earner who was, but is no longer, a director of a company (see COMPANY DIRECTORS 22) receives earnings in any tax year after that in which he ceased to be a director, those earnings, insofar as they are paid in respect of any period during which he was a director, are *not* to be aggregated with any other earnings with which they would otherwise fall to be aggregated. [*Social Security (Contributions) Regulations 2001, SI 2001/1004, Reg 8(5)(a)*].

The qualification contained in this regulation is of time only and it is, therefore, irrelevant whether the earnings actually relate to the former directorship or relate to other non-directorial activities performed during the earlier period in question.

Example

Throughout 2018–19, Richard is employed by Stiffs Ltd as an embalmer at a salary of £2,000 per month. Until 31 December 2017 he had been a director of the company but had, on that date, resigned because of worsening health. In September 2018, the board votes him a bonus of £7,000 in respect of his services as director during the year ended 31 December 2016 and a further £5,000 in respect of his services as embalmer during the same period. Were it not for *Social Security (Contributions) Regulations 2001, SI 2001/1004, Reg 8(5)(a)*, Richard's earnings of £2,000 (salary) and £12,000 (bonuses) in September 2018 would fall to be aggregated as the amounts are derived from different employments under the same employer, and, in consequence of that and the earnings period rules (see EARNINGS PERIODS 34), contribution liabilities would arise as follows.

		Class 1			
		Primary		*Secondary*	
Salary		%	£	%	£
£702	Primary Threshold	Nil			
£702	Secondary Threshold			Nil	
£3,161	Primary balance to UEL	12	379.32		
£3,161	Secondary balance to UEL			13.8	436.22
£10,137		2	202.74	13.8	1,398.91
£14,000			582.06		1,835.13

As illustrated above, were the earnings of £12,000 to be added to the regular salary of £2,000, virtually the whole of the £12,000 bonuses would escape the primary charge at 12% but be chargeable only to the 2% over the monthly UEL of £3,863. Because both elements of the £12,000 are in respect of a period during which R was a director of the company, however, *Social Security (Contributions) Regulations 2001, SI 2001/1004, Reg 8(5)(a)* prohibits aggregation of the £12,000 with R's other earnings and, because *Social Security (Contributions) Regulations 2001, SI 2001/1004, Reg 8(5)(b)* imposes an annual earnings period on the earnings relating to the period when R was a director, contribution liabilities will, in fact, be as follows.

	Class 1			
	Primary		*Secondary*	
Salary	%	£	%	£
£702	Nil		Nil	
£1,298/£1,298	12	155.76	13.8	179.12
£2,000				

		Class 1			
		Primary		*Secondary*	
Salary		%	£	%	£
	(less than *monthly* UEL for primary contribution purposes £3,863)				
Bonuses					
£8,424/8,424		Nil		Nil	
£3,576/3,576		12	429.12	13.8	493.49
£12,000					
	(less than *annual* UEL for primary contribution purposes £46,350)				
£14,000			584.88		672.61

It should be noted that whilst the effect of the disaggregation rules has been to increase Richard's own contributions, his employer has benefited due to a second (and annual) earnings threshold.

Exclusion of SSP, SMP, SPP, SAP and ShPP paid by HM Revenue and Customs

[5.9] Where Statutory Maternity Pay, Statutory Paternity Pay, Statutory Adoption Pay or Statutory Shared Parental Pay is paid by HM Revenue and Customs rather than by an employer under the *Statutory Maternity Pay General Regulations 1986, Reg 7*, *Statutory Paternity Pay and Adoption Pay (General) Regulations 2002, SI 2002/2822, Reg 43* or *Statutory Shared Parental Pay (General) Regulations 2014, SI 2014/3051, Reg 45* (eg where an employer has become insolvent and – for example – a maternity pay period has not expired), that payment is not to be aggregated with any other earnings for contribution purposes. [*Social Security (Contributions) Regulations 2001, SI 2001/1004, Reg 9(2)(2A)* as amended by *Social Security (Contributions) (Amendment) Regulations 2003, SI 2003/193, Regs 2, 4* and *Social Security and Tax Credits (Miscellaneous Amendments) Regulations 2015, SI 2015/175, Regs 2, 3*].

The same applies in respect of Statutory Sick Pay. [*Social Security (Contributions) Regulations 2001, SI 2001/1004, Reg 9(3)*].

Aggregation of earnings where related earnings periods are of different lengths

[5.10] The treatment of earnings paid at different intervals in respect of a single employment has been discussed at **5.3** above. Where, however, earnings in respect of two or more employed earner's employments fall to be aggregated under any of the rules described above, the earnings period (see EARNINGS PERIODS **34**) relative to the earnings derived from each employment is first to be determined under the normal earnings period rules or, as the case may be, under the director's earnings period rules. [*Social Security (Contributions) Regulations 2001, SI 2001/1004, Reg 2*].

Should the earnings periods so determined for the employments in question then be found to be of different lengths, a common earnings period is to be determined by application of the following rules.

- Where at least one of the earnings periods in question has been determined under the director's earnings period rules (see **34.12 EARNINGS PERIODS**), the common earnings period is to be the longer earnings period (or, if there is more than one, the *longest* earnings period) so determined. [*Social Security (Contributions) Regulations 2001, SI 2001/1004, Reg 8(4)*.]
- Where none of the earnings periods has been determined under the directors' earnings period rules and the earnings are all derived from the same types of employment, the common earnings period is to be the shorter or shortest earnings period derived from such employments. [*Social Security (Contributions) Regulations 2001, SI 2001/1004, Reg 6(3)(d)*.]

Before 6 April 2016, when contracting out via a salary-related (COSR) scheme was still relevant, where none of the earnings periods were determined under the directors' earnings period rules but the earnings were derived from different types of employment, eg contracted-out and not contracted-out, the common earnings period was to be the earnings period (or, if there was more than one, the shorter or shortest earnings period) derived from the contracted-out employment(s).

Prior to 2012–13, the position would have been different had there been an Approved Personal Pension or a COMPS arrangement. See earlier editions of this work to see how the earnings period would have been determined.

Example

Throughout 2015–16, Terry was employed by Upholstery Ltd and by Veneer Ltd. The two companies were jointly engaged in producing and marketing a new range of office furniture and T's employments both related to the associated operations. His employment by U was not contracted-out and he was paid £2,000 per month. His employment by V was contracted-out (through a COSR scheme) and he received earnings of £750 per week. On 1 February 2016 he was appointed a director of that company.

In accordance with *Social Security (Contributions) Regulations 2001, SI 2001/1004, Reg 15(1)(a)*, T's earnings from his two employments fell to be aggregated (unless it was impracticable to do so—see 5.7 above) but, because the earnings in each employment were paid at different intervals and thus gave rise to different earnings periods, a common earnings period had to be determined. As T did not become a director of V until 1 February 2016, the common earnings period as regards earnings paid before that date fell to be determined in accordance with *Social Security (Contributions) Regulations 2001, SI 2001/1004, Reg 6(3)* and, as there was a 'mixture' of employments, was to be the earnings period relating to the COSR employment, ie a week. The common earnings period as regards earnings paid after that date fell to be determined under *Reg 8(4)* in consequence of T's appointment as director of V and, as that directorship will have attracted an earnings period of nine weeks, was to be nine weeks.

It follows, therefore, that, in the month of June 2015, for example, contribution liabilities will have fallen to be determined by reference to earnings of £750 for each of the weeks ended 3, 10 and 17 June but by reference to earnings of £2,750 (ie £750 + £2,000) for the week ended 24 June. This basis will have continued to 31 January 2016. The period from 1 February 2016 to 5 April 2016 then formed a single earnings period, however, and contribution liabilities will have fallen to be determined by reference to earnings of £10,750 (ie [9 × £750] + [2 × £2,000]).

From 1 February 2016, for as long as Terry remains a director, the annual earnings period should apply to all aggregated earnings. The abolition of contracting out from 6 April 2016 will mean that, in 2016–17, the first rule stated above will always apply.

Calculation of contributions on aggregated earnings

[5.11] Where earnings from different employments fall to be aggregated, calculation of the Class 1 contribution liabilities gives rise to no particular difficulty. This was not the case before 6 April 2016 when contracting out might have been relevant to an employment. Where the employments were mixed, a question of precedence arose and, unless this was resolved in accordance with certain rules, Class 1 contribution liabilities would have been incorrectly calculated. The position was more complex still before 6 April 2012 when contracting out via money purchase pension schemes was abolished, as the rules of precedence involved taking into account not only NCO and COSR employments, but also COMP scheme employment and Appropriate Personal Pensions (see earlier editions for detailed coverage of this point).

The position was complicated by the introduction of the Upper Accrual Point (UAP) from 6 April 2009. The UAP was a threshold for the calculation of both State Second Pension and contracted-out rebates and affected the calculation of certain NIC deductions and rebates. The UAP was permanently fixed at £770 per week for all years up to 5 April 2016, when it was abolished. For State Second Pension and rebate calculations, it replaced the Upper Earnings Limit (UEL). It meant that there were effectively four thresholds (the Lower Earnings Limit, Earnings Threshold, Upper Accrual Point and the Upper Earnings Limit) to take into account in certain situations.

The arrangements for 2012–13 to 2015–16 were much simpler than in earlier periods in that there were no longer APP or COMPS rebates to take into account. When looking at an aggregation calculation for these four years where there was a mixture of contracted-out and not contracted-out earnings, the contracted-out took priority. The following method should be used to establish aggregated liabilities when looking back at any earnings periods in the four-year period:

(a) Add together for the earnings period arrived at under **5.10** above all the aggregable earnings paid in that earnings period. If the total earnings thus ascertained are below the Lower Earnings Limit (LEL) appropriate to the earnings period concerned (see **33.4** EARNINGS LIMITS AND THRESHOLDS), go no further: no contributions are due. The earnings will nevertheless have needed to be shown on a FPS on or before the date of payment.

(b) If the total earnings arrived at in (*a*) equal or exceed the relevant LEL, divide the total earnings into

(i) earnings from not contracted-out employments ('*NCO earnings*'), and
(ii) earnings from contracted-out employments ('*COSR earnings*').

Notes:

LEL = Lower Earnings Limit.
PT = Primary Threshold.
ST = Secondary Threshold.
UAP = Upper Accrual Point.
UEL = Upper Earnings Limit.

All rates shown below are standard rates for 2015–16, the last year to which these rules applied (Table A for NCO, Table D for CO; for married women with reduced rate elections, Table B or E would have been used; for under-21s no secondary contributions would have been due (in 2015–16 only) and Table M for NCO, Table I for CO would have applied).

(c) If COSR earnings alone reach the UEL for the relevant earnings period, the total primary Class 1 contribution liability on total earnings for the earnings period is:
 (i) [UAP – PT] × contracted-out rate (10.6%), plus
 (ii) [UEL – UAP] × not contracted-out rate (12%), plus
 (iii) [total earnings – UEL] × additional rate (2%);
 and the total secondary Class 1 contribution liability on total earnings for the earnings period is:
 (i) [UAP – ST] × contracted-out rate (10.4%), plus
 (ii) [UEL – UAP] × not contracted-out rate (13.8%), plus
 (iii) [total earnings – UEL] × not contracted-out rate (13.8%),
 and both employee's and employer's contracted-out rebates are due in respect of earnings between the LEL and the PT or ST.

(d) If COSR earnings alone do not reach the UEL but total earnings do, then:
 (i) If COSR earnings reach the UAP, the total primary Class 1 contribution liability on total earnings for the earnings period is:
  (A) [UAP – PT] × contracted-out rate (10.6%), plus
  (B) [UEL – UAP] × not contracted-out rate (12%), plus
  (C) [total earnings – UEL] × additional rate (2%);
  and the total secondary Class 1 contribution liability on total earnings for the earnings period is:
  (A) [UAP – ST] × contracted-out rate (10.4%), plus
  (B) [UEL – UAP] × not contracted-out rate (13.8%), plus
  (C) [total earnings – UEL] × not contracted-out rate (13.8%),
  and both employee's and employer's contracted-out rebates are due in respect of earnings between the LEL and the PT or ST.
 (ii) If COSR earnings reach the PT but not the UAP, the total primary Class 1 contribution liability on total earnings for the earnings period is:
  (A) [COSR earnings – PT] × contracted-out rate (10.6%), plus

(B) [UAP – COSR earnings] × not contracted-out rate (12%), plus
(C) [UEL – UAP] × not contracted-out rate (12%), plus
(D) [total earnings – UEL] × additional rate (2%);

and the total secondary Class 1 contribution liability on total earnings for the earnings period is:

(A) [COSR earnings – ST] × contracted-out rate (10.4%), plus
(B) [UAP – COSR earnings] × not contracted-out rate (13.8%), plus
(C) [UEL – UAP] × not contracted-out rate (13.8%), plus
(D) [total earnings – UEL] × not contracted-out rate (13.8%),

and both employee's and employer's contracted-out rebates are due in respect of earnings between the LEL and the PT or ST.

(iii) If COSR earnings reach the LEL but not the PT, the total primary Class 1 contributions liability on total earnings for the earnings period is:

(A) [UEL – PT] × not contracted-out rate (12%), plus
(B) [total earnings – UEL] × additional rate (2%);

and the total secondary Class 1 contribution liability on total earnings for the earnings period is:

[total earnings – ST] × not contracted-out rate (13.8%).

and the employer's contracted-out rebate is due in respect of the excess of COSR earnings over the LEL. The employee's contracted-out rebate is also available in respect of the excess of COSR earnings over the LEL, but it will be treated in accordance with the rules in **23.5**.

(iv) If COSR earnings do not reach the appropriate LEL, the total primary Class 1 contributions liability on total earnings for the earnings period is:

(A) [UEL – PT] × not contracted-out rate (12%), plus
(B) [total earnings – UEL] × additional rate (2%);

and the total secondary Class 1 contribution liability on total earnings for the earnings period is:

[total earnings – ST] × not contracted-out rate (13.8%),

and no contracted-out rebates are due.

(e) If neither COSR earnings alone nor total earnings reach the UEL, then:

(i) If COSR earnings reach the UAP, the total primary Class 1 contribution liability on total earnings for the earnings period is:

(A) [UAP – PT] × contracted-out rate (10.6%), plus
(B) [COSR earnings – UAP] × not contracted-out rate (12%), and
(C) NCO earnings × not contracted-out rate (12%),

the total secondary Class 1 contribution liability on total earnings for the earnings period is:

(A) [UAP – ST] × contracted-out rate (10.4%), plus
(B) [total earnings – UAP] × not contracted-out rate (13.8%),

and both employee's and employer's contracted-out rebates are due in respect of earnings between the LEL and the PT or ST.

(ii) If COSR earnings reach the PT but not the UAP, the total primary Class 1 contribution liability on total earnings for the earnings period is:
(A) [COSR earnings – PT] × contracted-out rate (10.6%), plus
(B) [total earnings – COSR earnings] × not contracted-out rate (12%),
the total secondary Class 1 contribution liability on total earnings for the earnings period is:
(A) [COSR earnings – ST] × contracted-out rate (10.4%), plus
(B) [total earnings – COSR earnings] × not contracted-out rate (13.8%),
and the employer's contracted-out rebate is due in respect of earnings between the LEL and the ST. The employee's contracted-out rebate is also available in respect of the earnings between the LEL and the PT, but it will be treated in accordance with the rules in **23.5** CONTRACTED-OUT EMPLOYMENT.

(iii) If COSR earnings reach the LEL but not the PT, the total primary Class 1 contribution liability on total earnings for the earnings period is:
[total earnings – PT] × not contracted-out rate (12%),
and the total secondary Class 1 contribution liability on total earnings for the earnings period is:
[total earnings – ST] × not contracted-out rate (13.8%),
and the employer's contracted-out rebate is due in respect of the excess of COSR earnings over the LEL. The employee's contracted-out rebate is also available in respect of the excess of COSR earnings over the LEL, but it will be treated in accordance with the rules in **23.5** CONTRACTED-OUT EMPLOYMENT.

(iv) If COSR earnings do not reach the LEL, the total primary Class 1 contribution liability on total earnings for the earnings period is:
[total earnings – PT] × main not contracted-out rate (12%);
and the total secondary Class 1 contribution liability on total earnings for the earnings period is:
[total earnings– ST] × not contracted-out rate (13.8%),
and no contracted-out rebates are due.

Example

Throughout 2015–16, Wendy was employed by X-Press Printers Ltd both as a part-time cashier and as part-time safety officer. Her employment as cashier was a contracted-out (COSR) employment and carried a salary of £757 per month. Her employment as safety officer was not contracted-out and carried a wage of £58 per week.

Because W's salary and wage were earnings in respect of employments under the same employer, they had to be aggregated in accordance with the provisions of *SSCBA 1992, Sch 1 para 1(1)(a)* (see **5.3** above). The common earnings period had to be a month (see **5.10** above) and the aggregated earnings will, accordingly, have been £989 in most months (ie £757 + (4 × £58)) which, since it exceeded the relevant monthly Earnings Thresholds of £672 and £676 and since the employments were a mix of contracted-out and not contracted-out, brought the provisions of SSCBA 1992, Sch 1 para 1(2)–(6) into effect. These dictated that, as the total amount of earnings from the contracted-out employments (£757 per month) did not exceed the then-current Upper Accrual Point of £3,337, contributions had first to be calculated on those earnings at rates attributable to contracted-out employments, then on the balance of earnings from the not contracted-out employment using the not contracted-out rates.

		Class 1			
		Primary		*Secondary*	
		%	£	%	£
486.00	(monthly LEL)	Nil	0.00	Nil	0.00
186.00/190.00	(c-o rebate on PT/ST–LEL)	Nil	(2.60)	Nil	(6.46)
672.00/676.00	(monthly PT/ST)				
85.00/81.00	(balance of c-o earnings)	10.6	9.01	10.4	8.42
757.00					
232.00	(n-c-o earnings)	12	27.84	13.8	30.02
989.00	(aggregated earnings)		34.25		33.98

The employer's contracted-out rebate was £9.21 ie [£757 – £486] × 3.4% and the employee's contracted-out rebate was £3.79 ie [£757 – £486] × 1.4%. The £3.79 could be deducted from the employee's liability of £38.04 [£989 – £672] × 12% leaving a reduced overall employee's National Insurance deduction of £34.25, which included contracted-out contributions of £9.01. See **23.5** CONTRACTED-OUT EMPLOYMENT.

For the interaction of COSR, COMP, APP and NCO employments in periods before 6 April 2012, please refer to earlier editions of this work.

The abolition of the rules on aggregation of mixed employments was effected by *Social Security (Contributions) (Amendment) (No 2) Regulations 2016, SI 2016/352, Part 2, para 9*, which amended *Contributions Regulations 2001, Reg 6(3)* to refer to the designated earnings period simply as the shorter or shortest of the earnings periods derived from the multiple employments.

Aggregation of earnings with gratuities etc paid separately

[5.12] In certain circumstances (essentially, where the employer is involved in some way in allocating them to staff), tips, gratuities and service charges are earnings for contribution purposes (see **29.37** EARNINGS FROM EMPLOYMENT: GENERAL).

Where that is so, but where the allocation of gratuities is not physically carried out by the person who is the secondary contributor as regards the ordinary earnings of the employed earner to whom such gratuities etc are allocated, the secondary contributor must aggregate with ordinary earnings the amount of the gratuities etc allocated and account for Class 1 contributions on the aggregated amount. (E24 (2014).) See also Tolley's Practical NIC Newsletter,

March 2003 pages 17, 18 and 19, Tolley's Practical NIC Newsletter, February 2004 pages 12 and 13, Tolley's Practical NIC Newsletter, March 2004 page 19, Tolley's Practical NIC Newsletter, March 2005 pages 17 and 18, March 2006 page 22 and Taxation Magazine, 3 March 2005 page 536.

Example

Anthony runs a small hotel in which he employs Bonnie and Clyde as waiters. For the week ending 25 June 2018, B's earnings are £146 and C's earnings are £192. On the face of it, no contribution liabilities arise as regards B's earnings as they fall below the primary threshold of £162, and liability for primary and secondary Class 1 contributions as regards C's earnings are at only 12% primary and 13.8% secondary on the earnings over £162. In the week concerned, however, guests have asked for tips of £50 to be added to their bills and A has passed those tips to David, the hall porter, instructing him that B is to receive £25 and C is to receive £25. In those circumstances, contribution liabilities for which A is accountable are as follows:

		£		£
B	Class 1 primary:	162	@ Nil%	0.00
		9	@ 12%	1.08
		171		1.08
	Class 1 secondary:	162	@ Nil%	0.00
		9	@ 13.8%	1.24
		171		1.24

		£		£
C	Class 1 primary:	162	@ Nil%	0.00
		55	@ 12%	6.60
		217		6.60
	Class 1 secondary:	162	@ Nil%	0.00
		55	@ 13.8%	7.59
		217		7.59

Apportionment of secondary contributions on aggregated earnings

[5.13] Where earnings fall to be aggregated under the aggregation rules described at 5.4 above, liability for Class 1 secondary contributions payable in respect of those earnings is to be apportioned among the secondary contributors in such proportions as they agree among themselves or, in the absence of any such agreement, in the proportions which the earnings paid by each bear to the aggregated earnings. [*Social Security (Contributions) Regulations 2001, SI 2001/1004, Reg 15(2)*].

Primary contributions payable by an employed earner in respect of aggregated earnings may be deducted either wholly from one of the two or more aggregated payments or partly from the other or any one or more of the others (see **21.19** COLLECTION). [*Social Security (Contributions) Regulations 2001, SI 2001/1004, Sch 4 para 7*].

Records of aggregation of earnings

[5.14] Where earnings fall to be aggregated under any of the aggregation rules described above, the relevant employments will now all be not contracted-out. Separate records need not be kept for each employment and contributions should be entered on a single payroll record using the shortest earnings period, with the 'aggregated earnings indicator' (field 49) set in the FPS. [CWG2 2018 to 2019, para 3.5.]

However, it is also possible that a young earner might hold two employments with the same organisation, one of which is an apprenticeship that qualifies for the 0% rate of secondary contribution on earnings up to the AUST. An earner under the age of 21 would qualify the employer for the 0% rate up to the UST in both jobs, but a mix of apprentice and non-apprentice wages for an earner who is over 20 but under 25 creates a need for an order of priority.

HMRC instructs employers to calculate NICs in the order, albeit without authority in the regulations:

- Z: Under-21 employer-only contributions in deferment cases;
- M or H: Under-21 standard or under-25 apprentice standard;
- J: Standard employer-only contributions in deferment cases;
- B: Married woman or widow's reduced rate;
- A: Standard rate contributions;
- C: Employer-only contributions (eg, a state pensioner in employment).

HMRC posits in CWG2 2018 to 2019, para 3.5.1 two examples, one of an earner aged under 21 with two jobs, both of which entitle the employer to the 0% rate on the whole amount of the earnings they pay, and another of an earner aged 23 who holds an apprenticeship agreement with one part of the organisation, on one payroll reference (Table H applies), and another role that is under a standard employment contract, on a different payroll (Table A applies).

The employer must aggregate the earnings from the two jobs. For the under-21 earner, the calculations are straightforward, as no employer contributions are due. There would be added complexity if the earnings exceeded the UST in an earnings period.

Initially, each payroll treats the wages as from a standalone employment, applying the correct category of A or H, deducting appropriate employee NICs and flagging the fact that there are aggregated earnings in both FPSs. The employer must then choose the payroll in which to show the aggregated earnings, updating the record in the chosen payroll to show the employer NICs due for the period, adding in any extra employee NICs due as a result of aggregation and correcting the year-to-date figures to show the correct cumulative and aggregate values. It is a matter for the employer which part of the organisation bears the cost of any secondary contributions arising on earnings that exceed the UST. Where two separate employers are involved, they must also agree between themselves how to split the secondary liability, and in default of agreement the apportionment is pro rata to the earnings paid by each. [*Contributions Regulations 2001, Reg 15(2)*.]

Before 2016–17, the position was potentially more complex, as the multiple employments could have been either:

(a) all not contracted-out; or
(b) all contracted-out under the same occupational pension scheme; or
(c) all contracted-out but under different occupational pension schemes; or
(d) not contracted-out and contracted-out under the same occupational pension scheme; or
(e) not contracted-out and contracted-out but under different occupational pension schemes.

In cases falling within (a) or (b) above, separate records need not have been kept for each employment and contributions should have been entered on a single payroll record using the shortest earnings period. [CWG2 (2015), paras 68, 69.]

In cases falling within (c) above, the same approach of working out NICs on one total amount applied, but separate records had to be kept for each employment showing the earnings between the LEL and the UAP in that employment. [CWG2 (2015), para 70.]

In cases falling within (d) above, separate records (as in (c) above) and separate payroll IDs had to be maintained: one for the contracted-out employment(s) and one for the not contracted-out employments. However, contributions liability had to be worked out based on total earnings and the shorter or shortest earnings period for contracted-out employment, taking the contracted out earnings (Table D or E) as the lowest tranche as outlined above. [CWG2 (2015), para 71.]

In cases falling within (e) above, separate records had to be kept for each COSR employment (as in (c) above) and for the not contracted-out employments. No more than *two* payroll records ought to have been maintained, however: one for the COSR employment(s) and one for the not contracted-out employments.

In *all* cases, a single amount of contributions had to be entered on each deductions working sheet in the past, and the regulations stipulated the recording of a single figure in the payroll records. [*Social Security (Contributions) Regulations 2001, SI 2001/1004, Sch 4 para 7(14)*.] However the RTI guidance stated that reporting depended on how many payroll IDs the employee had.

If the employee had one payroll ID, the employer had to add together all the payments made in one earnings period and calculate NICs due on the total amount, reporting on one FPS (assuming payment on the same day from both jobs).

Reporting became complex under RTI if there was more than one payroll ID for the employee. CWG2 2018 to 2019, para 3.5.1 states:

'If an employee receives payments under two different payroll identities, you must use the following procedure:

- Every time you pay the employee, record and report the pay and employee NICs in this pay period for each job in the usual way.
- In addition, on one of the payroll records, you must also:
  - Step 1 add together the earnings from each job (the total is the 'aggregated earnings')
  - Step 2 calculate and record the employer NICs due on the aggregated earnings for the pay period
  - Step 3 calculate and record the employee NICs due on the aggregated earnings, and so find out any additional employee NICs due (over and above what's already been recorded for the two jobs separately for earnings paid in the same earnings period)
  - Step 4 pay HMRC all the employee and employer NICs due on the aggregated earnings
  - Step 5 update the year-to-date NICs figures on the payroll record for the employee, to reflect the NICs data for the aggregated earnings
  - Step 6 set the Aggregated Earnings Indicator on the payroll record
  - Step 7 report the payroll information to HMRC.

  You will need to decide under which Payroll ID you want to record the data for the aggregated earnings.

  This reference will be the one under which HMRC will expect payment for both the employer NICs and employee NICs to be made.
- For the other job or jobs, update the employee's payroll record:
  - Step 1 put '0.00' for the year-to-date NICs fields
  - Step 2 put '0.00' for the employer NICs in this period
  - Step 3 set the Aggregated Earnings Indicator.'

On the first occasion when, in cases falling within (d) or (e) above, *two or more* payroll records were opened in respect of one employee, HMRC will have been notified by the Aggregated Earnings Indicator in the FPS. If, for PAYE purposes, all earnings were recorded on only one of the payroll records, the payroll record on which COSR contributions were to be recorded should have been used. The other(s) should have had 'NI' entered in the tax code box.

In cases falling within (b), (c), (d) or (e) above, records should have been retained throughout the period of the employment concerned and for three years after it ended.

Computer payroll systems are now in use for almost all payrolls. Under the pre-RTI regime, if a system was programmed to prevent two deduction records being maintained for the same employee, both contributions might, exceptionally, in cases falling within (d) or (e) above, be recorded on one document but each had to be identified by its appropriate contribution table letter (see **15.9** CLASS **1** CONTRIBUTIONS) and separate details had to be shown in the pay records. Para 71 of the CWG2 (2015) guidance set out extensive guidance on the correct procedures to be followed for multiple aggregated jobs under RTI. The guidance was updated in CWG 2018 to 2019, para 3.5 for the abolition of COSR employments and the introduction of the 0% rates for under-21s and under-25 apprentices, as outlined above.

Beneficial use of aggregation rules

[5.15] Although the aggregation rules are an anti-avoidance device, it is possible, in certain circumstances, for a primary contributor to turn the rules to his advantage. If, for instance, an earner was being paid earnings in respect of two or more employments and those earnings *together* exceeded the Upper Earnings Limit but *separately* did not, the application of the aggregation rules (if that could be brought about) would ensure that less primary Class 1 contributions would be paid than would otherwise be the case, because some of the earnings would be subject to the additional rate rather than the main rate of primary contribution.

In practice, the employee can obtain a very similar result through normal use of his personalised ANNUAL MAXIMUM 7, and by obtaining deferment where possible or a refund after the end of the tax year otherwise.

If aggregation does not take place where it seems that it may be appropriate, employers should have clear evidence for their reasons for not aggregating. The former CA found that local authorities, for example, often gave reasons why aggregation *did* not take place but not why it *could not* take place (CA Annual Conference 11 October 1994). See also Inland Revenue Tax Bulletin, August 2000 and the comments above.

Aggregation for Class 2 small earnings exception purposes

[5.16] A self-employed earner could be excepted from liability to pay Class 2 contributions (18.3) in respect of any period before 6 April 2015 in which his earnings from such employment were, or were treated as being, less than a specified amount. [*SSCBA 1992, s 11(4)*]. For this purpose, 'earnings' were defined by *Social Security (Contributions) Regulations 2001, SI 2001/1004, Reg 45(2) (revoked by Social Security (Miscellaneous Amendments No 2) Regulations 2015, SI 2015/478, Reg 24 from 6 April 2015)* as 'net earnings from employment as a self-employed earner' and, though the term 'net earnings' was not further defined in the legislation, it was taken to mean earnings such as would be shown in a profit and loss account prepared in accordance with proper accounting principles. As a person has but a single 'self' by whom to be employed, the term had to be taken to embrace all self-employed activities in which a person was engaged, and, accordingly, the net earnings from each activity had to be aggregated and any net loss set against those aggregated profits. However, a surplus of loss(es) in any year could not be carried forward for Class 2 purposes.

The earnings in question related to tax years and, accordingly, in strict law, time apportionment will have been a prerequisite to aggregation unless the accounting periods already ran from 6 April in one year to 5 April in the next. [*Social Security (Contributions) Regulations 2001, SI 2001/1004, Reg 1(2), Reg 45(1), now revoked*].

Example

Esmeralda had been self-employed as a dressmaker and also as a hairdresser for many years. Her accounts revealed the following trading results

Year ended	*Trade*		£
31 December 2014	Dressmaker	Loss	(2,000)
31 December 2015	Dressmaker	Profit	6,000
30 September 2014	Hairdresser	Profit	5,000
30 September 2015	Hairdresser	Profit	7,000

Her 2014–15 earnings for Class 2 exception purposes were

	£
9/12 × £(2,000)	(1,500)
3/12 × £6,000	1,500
6/12 × £5,000	2,500
6/12 × £7,000	3,500
	£6,000

and thus exception was not available to Esmeralda.

It used to be the practice of the former DSS to accept an account ending in a tax year as being coterminous with the tax year. Thus, in the case of Esmeralda above, it would have been expected that the DSS would have regarded her earnings as being £5,000 – £2,000 (loss), ie £3,000, for 2014–15 but this practice was discontinued during 1990–91.

From 6 April 2015, Class 2 contributions are self-assessed in arrears, in the same way as Class 4, so there is no longer a need for an advance exception or estimated aggregation of profits.

Aggregation for Class 4 purposes

[5.17] CLASS 4 CONTRIBUTIONS 20 are payable in respect of all profits immediately derived from the carrying on or exercise of one or more trades, professions or vocations, and are profits chargeable to income tax under the *Income Tax (Trading and Other Income) Act 2005, Chapter 2, Part 2*. [*SSCBA 1992, s 15(1)*, as amended by *Income Tax (Trading and Other Income) Act 2005, Schedule 1, Part 2*; *Income Tax Act 2007*]. The Class 4 contribution for any tax year is to be an amount equal to a prescribed percentage of so much of those profits or gains as exceeds a prescribed lower annual limit and does not exceed a prescribed upper annual limit, together with 2% on all profits exceeding the upper limit. [*Sec 15(3)*]. Clearly, therefore, profits must be aggregated for Class 4 purposes but, because social security legislation has, in this instance, adopted the basis of assessment applied for the purposes of income tax, no question of time-apportionment arises and aggregation is simply a matter of totalling the adjusted profits assessable to tax in a particular tax year. In the case of a partner, it will be his share of the adjusted profits. [*SSCBA 1992, Sch 2 para 4(1)*]. (See further **52.7** PARTNERS.)

Example

Francis owns two businesses, an interior decorating business and a furniture renovation workshop. He is also an equal partner in a firm that supplies fitted kitchens. His interior decorating business was established several years ago with a 31 October accounting date but the furniture renovating business commenced on 1 May 2011 with a 30 April accounting date. The fitted kitchen partnership is long-established (with a 31 December accounting date) and F's share of profits one-half. Trading results adjusted in accordance with the tax and Class 4 rules are

Year ended	*Trade*	
31 October 2013	Interior decorator	£10,000
31 October 2014	Interior decorator	£12,500
31 October 2015	Interior decorator	£13,500
31 October 2016	Interior decorator	£14,500
30 April 2013	Furniture renovator	£1,200
30 April 2014	Furniture renovator	£1,350
30 April 2015	Furniture renovator	£1,550
30 April 2016	Furniture renovator	£1,950
31 December 2013	Fitted kitchens	£28,500
31 December 2014	Fitted kitchens	£29,000
31 December 2015	Fitted kitchens	£32,000
31 December 2016	Fitted kitchens	£34,000

Income tax assessments under *Income Tax (Trading and Other Income) Act 2005, Chapter 2, Part 2* for 2013–14 will have been as follows

	£
Interior decorator (current year basis)	10,000
Furniture renovator (current year basis)	1,200
Fitted kitchens (current year basis split according to profit share in 2013–14: ½ × £28,500)	14,250
	£25,450

Income tax assessments under *Income Tax (Trading and Other Income) Act 2005, Chapter 2, Part 2* for 2014–15 will have been as follows

	£
Interior decorator (current year basis)	12,500
Furniture renovator (current year basis)	1,350

Fitted kitchens (current year basis split according to profit share in 2014–15:½ × £29,000)	14,500
	£28,350

Income tax assessments under *Income Tax (Trading and Other Income) Act 2005, Chapter 2, Part 2* for 2015–16 will have been as follows

	£
Interior decorator (current year basis)	13,500
Furniture renovator (current year basis)	1,550
Fitted kitchens (current year basis split according to profit share in 2015–16:½ × £32,000)	16,000
	£31,050

Income tax assessments under *Income Tax (Trading and Other Income) Act 2005, Chapter 2, Part 2* for 2016–17 will be as follows

	£
Interior decorator (current year basis)	14,500
Furniture renovator (current year basis)	1,950
Fitted kitchens (current year basis split according to profit share in 2016–17:½ × £34,000)	17,000
	£33,450

Losses (arising from activities the profits of which would be brought into computation for Class 4 contribution purposes) are available for relief against the aggregated profits arrived at on the principles outlined above (see **32.7** EARNINGS FROM SELF-EMPLOYMENT: GENERAL). [*SSCBA 1992, Sch 2 para 3(1)*; *ITA 2007, Sch 1 para 293*].

Key Points concerning the aggregation of earnings

[5.18] Points to consider are as follows.

- Where all employments of the employee before 6 April 2016 were contracted-out then normal aggregation rules will have applied.
- Where such employments of the employee were not all of the same category ie, contracted-out and not contracted-out, then the employee's earnings from each were calculated separately. This approach continues where an under-25 apprentice also has a non-apprenticeship employment with an employer carrying on business in association with the employer training the apprentice.
- Contracted-out earnings took precedence when working out the NICs liability.

- An employer had to keep separate details of the not contracted-out earnings compared to the contracted-out earnings and follow HMRC guidance in the CWG2 on reporting payments in all FPSs.

6

Airmen

Cross-references. See ARMED FORCES **11** for members of the regular air forces of the Crown; CLASS **1** CONTRIBUTIONS **15**; OVERSEAS MATTERS **51** for domicile, residence and EC/EEA and reciprocal agreements.

Other Sources. Simon's Taxes, Volume 2, para A8.719; HM Revenue and Customs Booklet 490 (2015), HM Revenue and Customs Manual NIM27000.

Introduction to airmen and NICs

[6.1] The social security system is, like the tax system, subject to territorial limitations, but in a different way (see **51.3** OVERSEAS MATTERS). Where an insured person works outside the UK, he ceases to be 'gainfully employed in Great Britain or Northern Ireland', with the result that he can be neither an 'employed earner' nor a 'self-employed earner' for contributions purposes (see **14.2** and **14.18** CATEGORISATION). This implies that there is no liability to pay National Insurance contributions. In the absence of special rules to change the position, those UK residents employed in international transport would often cease to be compulsorily insured when they left the UK and might have to rely on Class 2 or 3 voluntary contributions to maintain their entitlement to the basic State pension and other contributory benefits.

In the absence of a social security agreement the system copes with any temporary overseas absences for those normally within Class 1 liability by deeming the individuals concerned to continue to be 'employed earners' for 52 weeks after departure. There is a corresponding 52-week period of non-liability for those sent to work only temporarily in the UK by non-UK employers (see **51.9** OVERSEAS MATTERS). [*Social Security (Contributions) Regulations 2001, SI 2001/1004, Reg 145(1), Reg 146(2)(a)*].

Workers in international transport, however, do not fit neatly into that framework. Because of the brevity of their stays in many different jurisdictions and the length of time they spend outside national jurisdictions, they may not qualify for the protection of any state's social security system. To provide such protection for essentially UK-based workers in international air transport, the *Social Security (Contributions) Regulations 2001, SI 2001/1004, Regs 111–113* include provisions governing the UK National Insurance liabilities of 'airmen'. These provisions broadly limit liability to those domiciled in the UK or having a place of residence in the UK, subject to the provisions of reciprocal agreements and EC regulations.

Definitions related to airmen

[6.2] An *airman* is any person, other than a serving member of the ARMED FORCES **11**, who is, or has been, employed under a contract of service (see **14.5** CATEGORISATION) and falls into one of two categories:

- a pilot, commander, navigator or other member of crew (eg stewards and stewardesses) of any aircraft, wherever the contract of service is entered into; or
- in any other capacity on board any aircraft for the purposes of the aircraft, its crew, or any passengers or cargo or mails carried thereby, where the contract of service is entered into in the UK with a view to its performance, wholly or partly, while the aircraft is in flight.

[*Social Security (Contributions) Regulations 2001, SI 2001/1004, Reg 111*].

It should be noted that the definition does not extend to self-employed earners working under a contract for services (see **14.5** CATEGORISATION). Their liability to CLASS **2** CONTRIBUTIONS **18** therefore depends on the normal rules and, in particular, the ordinary residence test prescribed by *Social Security (Contributions) Regulations 2001, SI 2001/1004, Reg 145(1)(d)*.

A *place of residence* is a factual matter and is to be distinguished from the status of residence. The latter is a qualitative attribute which a person may or may not possess whether he has a place of residence or not (see **51.5** OVERSEAS MATTERS). Many non-UK airmen who fly regularly into the UK rent a flat near the airport, but a caravan may also be a place of residence, as may a yacht anchored in territorial waters. (*Makins v Elson (Inspector of Taxes)* [1977] 1 All ER 572, [1977] 1 WLR 221; *Brown v Burt (Surveyor of Taxes)* (1911) 5 TC 667, 81 LJKB 17, CA). For the meaning of *place of business* see **51.8** OVERSEAS MATTERS.

A *British aircraft* is an aircraft which 'belongs to Her Majesty' (ie is owned by the Crown) or is registered in the UK with an owner, or managing owner if there is more than one owner, who resides or has his principal place of business (see **51.5, 51.8** OVERSEAS MATTERS) in the United Kingdom. For this purpose, a charterer or sub-charterer entitled as hirer for the time being to possession and control of the aircraft is to be taken to be the owner. [*Social Security (Contributions) Regulations 2001, SI 2001/1004, Reg 111*].

Example

Peter is a UK national, UK domiciled, and works as a pilot for British Airways. He flies out of the UK as and when his shift pattern dictates. He commutes from France where he has a residence. Half way through 2016–17 he reaches the age of retirement for British Airways and joins Singapore Airlines on a yearly renewable contract through a Jersey-based agency which regularly contracts pilots to the head office of Singapore Airlines in the Far East. In terms of *Social Security (Contributions) Regulations 2001, SI 2001/1004, Reg 112(1)* (see above) where does the NICs burden fall?

As an employee of British Airways within *SSCBA 1992, s 2(1)(a)* he meets the following points:

(a) he is employed as an airman on board an aircraft; and

(b) his employer, or

  (i) the person paying his earnings in respect of that employment (whether as agent for the employer or not), or

  (ii) the person under whose directions the terms of his employment and the amount of his earnings are determined,

 where the aircraft is British, has a place of business in Great Britain or Northern Ireland.

However, when he joins Singapore Airlines, even though he is employed through an agency based in Jersey and *(a)* above applies, the aircraft is not British. The deeming provision applies only if the person referred to in *(b)* has his principal place of business in Great Britain or Northern Ireland. In this case his employer does not have its principal place of business in Great Britain or Northern Ireland. Therefore under these rules he is *treated* as being employed in employed earner's employment only for the part of the year he is employed by British Airways. Thereafter he is not within the terms of *Social Security (Contributions) Regulations 2001, SI 2001/1004, Reg 112(1)*. The offshore employment intermediary rules introduced into the *Social Security (Categorisation of Earners) Regulations 1978, SI 1978/1689*, Sch 3 by SI 2014/635 are irrelevant, as the provisions on airmen in Regs 111–113 explicitly apply 'whether or not the person making the payment [of earnings] is acting as agent for the employer'.

The amenability rule in contribution legislation

[6.3] The primary factor linking an employed airman to the UK social security system is a UK base. Contributions are payable by or in respect of an airman only if he is either domiciled (see **51.6** OVERSEAS MATTERS) or has a place of residence in the UK. [*Social Security (Contributions) Regulations 2001, SI 2001/1004, Reg 112(2)*]. This is subject to contrary provisions in reciprocal agreements and EC Regulations. [*Social Security (Contributions) Regulations 2001, SI 2001/1004, Reg 112(3)*].

However, a UK-domiciled airman and non-domiciled airman with a UK place of residence can spend significant periods overseas and, as mentioned above, under the general rules of categorisation a person must be gainfully employed in Great Britain or Northern Ireland (see **51.3** OVERSEAS MATTERS for definition of Great Britain) if he is to fall within the category of employed earner. [*SSCBA 1992, s 2(1)(a)*]. He must then fulfil certain conditions of residence or presence (see **51.9** OVERSEAS MATTERS) if he is to be liable to pay CLASS **1** CONTRIBUTIONS **15**.

Although an airman may fail to meet these requirements by the very nature of his employment, he is, nevertheless, to be *treated* as being employed in employed earner's employment and as present in Great Britain or Northern Ireland if he fulfils two conditions:

(a) he is employed as an airman on board an aircraft; and

(b) his employer, or
  (i) the person paying his earnings in respect of that employment (whether as agent for the employer or not), or
  (ii) the person under whose directions the terms of his employment and the amount of his earnings are determined,

where the aircraft is British (see Example in **6.2**), has a place of business in Great Britain or Northern Ireland.

Where the aircraft is not British, the deeming provision applies only if the person referred to in (*b*) has his principal place of business in Great Britain or Northern Ireland.

[*Social Security (Contributions) Regulations 2001, SI 2001/1004, Reg 112(1)*].

This amenability rule is, however, subject to any different rule arising under reciprocal agreements given effect in Great Britain or Northern Ireland by Order in Council (see **6.4** below) or under EC Regulations (see **6.5** below). [*Social Security (Contributions) Regulations 2001, SI 2001/1004, Reg 112(3); European Communities Act 1972, ss 2, 3*].

Example

Pedro is a Moroccan national, with Moroccan domicile, but works as a pilot for British Airways and flies out of the UK as and when his shift pattern dictates. He commutes from Morocco where he continues to live.

As an employee of British Airways within *SSCBA 1992, s 2(1)(a)* he meets the following points:

(a) he is employed as an airman on board an aircraft; and
(b) his employer, or
  (i) the person paying his earnings in respect of that employment (whether as agent for the employer or not), or
  (ii) the person under whose directions the terms of his employment and the amount of his earnings are determined,

where the aircraft is British, has a place of business in Great Britain or Northern Ireland.

However, as he is not UK domiciled and has no place of residence in the UK, there is no UK liability for either employer or employee. [*Social Security (Contributions) Regulations 2001, SI 2001/1004, Reg 112(2)*.] See NIM27008 and 33021.

Reciprocal agreement rules

[6.4] Where an airman falls within the scope of a reciprocal agreement which has effect in the United Kingdom, the general amenability rule (see **6.3** above) will usually be superseded by rules contained in the agreement. The provisions of reciprocal agreements as regards travelling personnel of an undertaking engaged in the transport of passengers or goods by air tend to imitate the terms of the now withdrawn *EC Reg 1408/71, Art 14(2)(a)* which dealt with 'travelling or flying personnel' in EC Member States (see **6.5** below). Such provisions are generally that:

(a) subject to (b) and (c) below, where a person is employed by an undertaking which has its principal place of business in the territory of one of the parties to the reciprocal agreement, the legislation of that party is to apply to him, even if he is employed in the territory of the other party;

(b) subject to (c) below, where the undertaking has a branch or agency in the territory of one of the parties to the reciprocal agreement and a person is employed by that branch or agency, the legislation of that party is to apply to him;

(c) where a person is ordinarily resident (see **51.5** OVERSEAS MATTERS) in the territory of one of the parties to a reciprocal agreement and is employed wholly or mainly in that territory, the legislation of that party is to apply to him, even if the undertaking which employs him does not have its principal place of business or a branch or an agency in that territory.

The provision made for determining the relevant contribution legislation as regards airmen in agreements originating prior to 1973 may differ considerably from the provision set out above and reference to the appropriate agreement will be necessary in every case. (See **51.52** OVERSEAS MATTERS for a complete list of reciprocal agreements currently in force.) Although those with EC/EEA countries are of little application from 1 June 2003 (except for Manxmen and, in some cases, Channel Islanders), the agreements between the UK and Austria, Barbados, Belgium, Bermuda, Chile, Cyprus, Denmark, Finland, France, Germany, Guernsey, Italy, Jamaica, Japan, Jersey, Luxembourg, Mauritius, the Netherlands, Norway, the Philippines, Portugal, Republic of Korea, Spain, Sweden, Switzerland, Turkey and former Yugoslavia all contain special provisions regarding airmen. Included in this group is the relatively recent agreement between the Republic of Korea and the UK which, for instance, states at Article 6:

> A person who, but for the provisions of this Convention, would be subject to the legislation of both Parties in respect of employment as an officer or member of a crew on a ship or aircraft shall, in respect of that employment, be subject only to the legislation of the Party in whose territory he ordinarily resides.

Taking a different line, the 2015 double contributions convention with Chile (*SI 2015/828*) states:

> 'Aircraft crew who perform work in the territories of both Parties and who would otherwise be covered under the laws of both Parties shall, with respect to that work, be subject to the laws of only the Party in the territory of which the employer has its main office. However, if such employees are ordinarily resident of [sic] the other Party, they shall be subject to the laws of only that Party.' [*Article 7(2)*.]

The term 'ordinarily resident', which is not used in the usual UK contribution provisions for airmen, is to be 'given its natural and ordinary meaning in the context of its legislation' in the UK. [*Article 1(1)(i)*.]

EC Social Security Regulations

[6.5] For the provisions of EC Social Security Regulations concerning travelling or flying personnel engaged in international transport of goods or passengers by air, see **51.27** OVERSEAS MATTERS. New EC Social Security

Regulations came into force on 1 May 2010 (*EC Reg 883/2004* and *EC Reg 987/2009*), which by and large superseded *EC Regs 1408/71* and *574/72*. Unlike *EC Regulation 1408/71*, which made – under *Article 14.2(a)* – specific provision for 'International Transport Workers', there were no specific provisions in *EC Reg 883/2004*; rather, the new, all-embracing *Article 13* covered all persons who normally worked in two or more member states, although that was found to be problematic and was quickly changed – see below. *EC Regs 1408/71* and *574/72* will still apply to third country nationals, and to anyone covered under UK law before 1 May 2010 who would fall under a different member state's social security scheme as a result of the 2010 changes, unless they opt to be covered by *EC Reg 883/2004*. Movement between Switzerland, Iceland, Norway and Liechtenstein and the EEA countries was subject to *EC Regs 1408/71* and *574/72* until 1 April 2012 for Switzerland and from 1 June 2012 for the others. From these dates they adopted *EC Regs 883/2004* and *987/2009*.

Applications for form A1 should be made to HM Revenue & Customs NIC&EO International Caseworker on application form CA8421i, which makes specific reference to its relevance to 'flight crew or cabin crew performing air passenger or freight services whose home base is in the UK'.

The provisions in *EC Reg 883/04* were amended so that contribution liabilities are now linked to the country in which members of the flight crew have their home base. These changes were introduced on 28 June 2012, delayed primarily because a number of countries were not convinced the proposed changes would be effective. 'Home base' is already defined in EU civil aviation legislation and is a concept with which entities employing aircrew will be familiar. The general rule for multi-state workers, that contributions will be payable in the country of residence if at least 25% of the duties are performed in that country, is to be disregarded. This means that the country in which contributions are to be paid will have changed in 2012 for many aircrew. Transitional rules apply to enable existing contribution liabilities to continue after the 2012 change of rules. [*EC Reg 465/2012, substituting a new Art 13 into EC Reg 883/2004*.]

Unless individual EC/EEA member states elect otherwise, these Regulations supersede any reciprocal agreements between such States, and no elections are currently in force relating to airmen. See also *Civil Aviation Act 1982* and *Air Navigation Orders*.

Example

Tommy takes up a position with a UK-based airline on 2 July 2016. He will have a working pattern of six days on followed by eight days off, flying routes out of Paris Charles de Gaulle airport. He catches a late night flight to Paris and he then flies in and out of Paris for six days when he then catches a flight back to the UK. Tommy is a passenger on the flights to and from Paris. As his home base is Paris he and his employer are liable to pay contributions under French social security laws.

> *Example*
>
> If the only change to the facts in the above example was that Tommy had taken up his employment before 28 June 2012, a different result would have been obtained. Tommy would have been habitually resident in the UK and so UK NIC would have been payable. Under the transitional rules such NIC liabilities could have continued until the earlier of a material change in circumstances or ten years.

Time limits

[6.6] Where an airman is outside Great Britain or Northern Ireland by reason of his employment as an airman and is, in consequence, unable to comply at or within the allotted time with a requirement of the contributions legislation, he is to be deemed to have complied if he meets the requirement as soon thereafter as is reasonably practicable. [*Social Security (Contributions) Regulations 2001, SI 2001/1004, Reg 113*].

Travel expenses

[6.7] Expenses of travelling between home and airport may sometimes qualify for deduction for tax purposes under *ITEPA 2003, ss 328-330, 341, 342, 369–372, 376* (see *Nolder (Inspector of Taxes) v Walters*, (1930) 15 TC 380, 9 ATC 251 and **30.13** earnings from employment: expenses). Where an airman is within Class 1 liability but is not taxable on payments of, or contributions towards, expenses which are deductible for tax purposes under those provisions because they relate to duties performed wholly or partly outside the UK, such payments are excluded from earnings for contribution purposes. [*Social Security (Contributions) Regulations 2001, SI 2001/1004, Sch 3 Part VIII para 4*]. The cost of travel to an airport other than the normal base should also be excluded from earnings by virtue of the normal business expenses rule (see **30.13** EARNINGS FROM EMPLOYMENT: EXPENSES and HMRC Booklet 490, Chapter 7). Pilots working through an intermediary crewing agency may, from 6 April 2016, find that their UK travel expenses from home to airport are, subject to the exact circumstances, no longer tax deductible because of *ITEPA 2003, s 339A* (introduced by *FA 2016*) and the matching changes to *Contributions Regulations 2001, Sch 3, Part VIII, para 3ZB*, headed 'Travel for necessary attendance: employment intermediaries', although these rules should not affect travel to a foreign location.

Furthermore, if the employer books and pays for the transport, the normal rule for payments in kind (see **29.28** EARNINGS FROM EMPLOYMENT: GENERAL) should apply to exclude the cost from the airman's earnings for Class 1 purposes. In many cases union representatives for BALPA will have negotiated a fixed tax free allowance with HM Revenue and Customs and this is claimed on the tax return at Box 18 (see SA102 (2016), page E1).

The report of the decision of the Supreme Court in *British Airways plc v Williams* [2012] UKSC 43, a dispute about holiday pay and how it should be calculated, revealed that the airline had an agreement with the pilots' union, BALPA, to pay a 'Time Away From Base' (TAFB) allowance, which had been introduced to cover meal allowances, sundries and a Gatwick Duty Allowance and which had been challenged by HMRC. It had been agreed between the airline and HMRC that 18% of the allowance did not represent genuine business expenses and should be treated as pay. Whether any of the pay was taxable was irrelevant, however, to the question of whether the allowance was a component of the worker's total remuneration under the *Working Time Regulations 1998, SI 1998/1833* and EU law, which look merely to the intention of the allowance, not the detail of its estimation (see also *Wood v Hertel (UK) Limited* ET Case No 2603803/2012, in which the Employment Tribunal expressly rejected treating the taxable part of a travel allowance as pay for holiday pay calculation purposes because it was an allowance paid only if the employee was travelling to and from work to compensate for that expense).

Airmen born abroad

[6.8] An airman born outside Great Britain or Northern Ireland who is not covered by EC Regulations or a reciprocal agreement is not liable for payment of Class 1 contributions unless he has a UK place of residence or is domiciled in Great Britain or Northern Ireland. If there is no primary (employee's) liability, there can be no secondary liability either [*Social Security (Contributions) Regulations 2001, SI 2001/1004, Reg 112(2)*]. Such an airman may write to International Caseworker, NIC&EO, BP1301, Benton Park View, Newcastle upon Tyne, NE98 1ZZ seeking a ruling to confirm non-liability, although this option is no longer mentioned in the NI Manual.

Key Points regarding airmen and NICs

[6.9] Points to consider are as follows.

- Where a reciprocal agreement is in point, the actual agreement must be checked for specific terms regarding airmen.
- The 'time away from base' (TAFB) allowance for meal costs paid by many airlines is largely or wholly tax and NICs-free depending on how the allowance has been calculated and paid, and any agreement with HMRC. However, this allowance is subject to review by HMRC at least once every five years, and receipts must be provided if requested to substantiate the meal allowances for TAFB.
- E101 or A1 certificates or other certificates of coverage should be obtained to give certainty as to where contribution liabilities arise.
- From 28 June 2012, contribution liabilities for EEA flight crew and their employer have arisen in the country in which the home base is situated. Transitional rules may apply where the member of the aircrew was in that employment before 28 June 2012. See

51.31 OVERSEAS MATTERS.

7

Annual Maximum

Cross-references. See CLASS 1 CONTRIBUTIONS **15**; CLASS 2 CONTRIBUTIONS **18**; CLASS 3 CONTRIBUTIONS **19**; CLASS 4 CONTRIBUTIONS **20**; **47.1** MULTIPLE EMPLOYMENTS for circumstances in which excessive contributions may be paid; DEFERMENT OF PAYMENT **27** for circumstances in which excess payment of contributions may be prevented; **55.6** REPAYMENT AND REALLOCATION for repayment of excess contributions.

Other Sources. Simon's Taxes, Volume 2, para A8.266.

Introduction to the annual maximum

[7.1] This chapter is mainly concerned with the specific statutory rules in *regulation 21* of the *Social Security (Contributions) Regulations 2001, SI 2001/1004* which apply so as to limit the amount of contributions payable where a person has multiple employments, possibly including self-employment. Since the origin of the NI scheme was the provision of a flat-rate benefit in exchange for flat-rate contributions, and main rate contributions are still capped (as a contributor's S2P entitlement was before the single-tier pension regime was introduced on 6 April 2016), it is logical that there is a limit on how much any individual should pay for his social security cover. It remains to be seen how the contributions structure will be reformed now that those with earnings between the LEL and the primary threshold 'earn' entitlement, while paying no contributions, to the same level of single state pension as those who pay NICs on remuneration of £46,350, paying around £4,500, and the self-employed earn the same by paying just £153.40 in Class 2 contributions and 9% on profits between the lower and upper annual limits. The promised abolition of Class 2 and attachment of benefit entitlement to Class 4 in 2019 may lead to a wholesale re-think of the link between contributions and benefits. Some consideration of this link may have given rise to the Spring Budget 2017 announcement of proposed increases in the rate of Class 4 contributions, although the proposed increases were subsequently withdrawn on the grounds that the proposed increase broke a 2015 election manifesto pledge.

Regulation 52A of the *Contributions Regulations* applies in the case of the annual maxima for those with more than one employment, setting out an order of precedence for refunds of the different types of contribution that might be made. This has been much simplified by the abolition on 6 April 2016 of contracting out.

Since 6 April 2003 there has no longer been a single, fixed maximum amount of contributions payable for any tax year because the additional rate (currently 2%) payable on earnings over the Upper Earnings Limit came into effect at that time. This 'notional maximum' for earnings at the UEL in a single employment is £4,642.80 (see calculation below at **7.4**) for 2018–19.

There is a simple, logical basis for all annual maximum calculations: standard rate Class 1 contributions on 53 weeks' earnings at the UEL should be the maximum anyone should pay for their benefits. This rule dates from the time when NIC stamps were stuck on cards weekly and allows for a 53rd payday in a year. If the first weekly payday of the tax year falls on 6 April, or 7 April in a year preceding a leap year, the final, 53rd, payday will fall on 5 April, meaning the employee is paid 53 times (see further **7.2** below).

If the employer operates a lunar payroll (ie, payday falls every four weeks), it is also possible to have 56 weeks' pay included in one tax year if the first payday falls on 6 April (7 April for leap years). In a lunar payroll, pay may never exceed the four-weekly UEL, but contributions may nevertheless be payable at 12% on more than 53 times the weekly UEL. Any extra earnings or profits above the maximum should be subject to contributions at the additional rate (2%), which does not count towards benefits and is simply a tax. However, even this applies only to the extent that, in each employment, earnings exceed the earnings threshold or, in the case of Class 4, the lower annual limit.

It is a quirk of the system that a person with more than one job will often pay less NICs than another person with the same total earnings from a single job. This is because, for each separate job with earnings over the Earnings Threshold of £8,424 for 2018–19, a separate Earnings Threshold is given. This does not apply in the case of 'associated employments' where earnings fall to be aggregated. [*Social Security (Contributions) (Amendment) Regulations 2003, SI 2003/193, Reg 6*].

Liability for Class 1 contributions is imposed where 'in any tax week' earnings are paid to or for the benefit of an earner. [*SSCBA 1992, s 6(1)*].

It is worth noting that the annual maximum rule in Reg 21 is only relevant to earners with more than one employment (using the *Social Security Contributions and Benefits Act 1992, s 122 (SCCBA 1992)* sense of the word, ie, two or more jobs or a job and a self-employed activity). Because it is technically possible for an earner with a single employment to pay more than 53 weeks' contributions (eg, in a lunar payroll), it is also possible to pay more than the 53-week limit at 12% and not be subject to the annual maximum, but only if the job with lunar pay is the only job.

It is perhaps also worth noting that Class 3 is of no relevance in the consideration of the annual maximum. Class 3 contributions may only be paid if the record shows insufficient qualifying weeks, which will never be the case if other contributions have reached the maximum. Any Class 3 contributions paid early (eg, where an expatriate is paying by direct debit, before returning to UK employment in mid-year), that do not enhance benefit entitlements, will be repaid.

Definitions

[7.2] A 'tax week' is 'one of the successive periods in a tax year beginning with the first day of that year and every 7th day thereafter; the last day of the tax year (or, in the case of a tax year ending in a leap year eg 2015–16, the last 2 days) to be treated accordingly as a separate tax week'. A 'tax year' is 'the 12 months beginning with 6th April in any year'. [*SSCBA 1992, s 122(1)*]. It is because some years have 53 paydays falling within the tax year (eg, with the last payday of the year falling on 5 April) that the annual maximum is based on earnings over 53 rather than 52 weeks.

Multiple employments

[7.3] *Section 6(4)* imposes liability 'without regard to any other payment of earnings . . . in respect of any other employment', so it does not limit the earner's *combined* liabilities. In the case of an earner with two or more employments, the special liability-limiting provision supplied by *SSCBA 1992, s 19* and *SI 2001/1004, Reg 21* amended by *Social Security Contributions (Amendment) Regulations 2003, SI 2003/193, Reg 6* (see **7.4** below) comes into play. Where an earner has more than one employment and/or self-employment then specific statutory provisions and regulations serve to limit contributions payable as described below. However, the insertion of *Reg 52A(6)* prevents the refund of Class 1 primary contributions to an individual in cases where the *Social Security (Additional Pension) (Contributions Paid in Error) Regulations 1996, SI 1996/1245, Reg 3* applied for years up to 5 April 2016.

The limitations on contributions

Class 1 and Class 2 limitation

[7.4] Where an earner is employed in more than one employment (irrespective of whether the employments are employed earner's employments or self-employment), liability in any tax year for:

- primary Class 1 contributions; or
- where both Class 1 and Class 2 contributions are payable, both primary Class 1 and Class 2 contributions,

is not to exceed an amount equal to 53 primary Class 1 contributions at the main primary percentage payable on earnings at the Upper Earnings Limit together with, from 6 April 2003, such other liabilities which arise at the additional rate. [*Social Security (Contributions) Regulations 2001, SI 2001/1004, Reg 21 as substituted by Social Security (Contributions) (Amendment) Regulations 2003, SI 2003/193, Reg 5*].

The maximum for the 2018–19 year is £4,642.80 plus additional rate liabilities on earnings above the threshold in other employments ie 53 × (£892 – £162) × 12% plus 2% on other earnings or profits. The effect of this is that for 2003–04 onwards each person has – in effect – their own 'personalised maximum' (see example below).

If the contributor was in contracted-out employment before 6 April 2016 when S2P was abolished for new state pensioners, or had and continues to have a reduced rate election, the rebated or reduced rate contributions in a refund claim are grossed up to the standard rate for comparison with the maximum, then netted down again for the purposes of paying refunds, so that workers only receive the excess of what they have actually paid over the limit.

This annual maximum is, in the case of VOLUNTEER DEVELOPMENT WORKERS **59** (but not in the case of SHARE FISHERMEN **56**) to be reduced by the amount of any special Class 2 contributions which have been paid in respect of the year in question. [*Social Security (Contributions) Regulations 2001, SI 2001/1004, Reg 152(c)*]. The effect of this is to ensure that, where a volunteer development worker pays contributions in excess of the maximum in a year, any repayment obtained by him will consist entirely of contributions other than any special Class 2 contributions which he may have paid in respect of that year (see **55.8** REPAYMENT AND REALLOCATION).

There are no provisions enabling the annual maximum to be reduced if the contributor attains pensionable age during the year, thereby ceasing to be liable to primary Class 1 and Class 2 contributions, so very high earners may well pay the maximum at the 12% rate in two or more jobs in the weeks between 6 April and the date they reach state pension age, but there is no time-apportioned cap; unless the contributions paid amount in total to more than 53 weeks' earnings at the UEL at 12%, the annual maximum is likely to be irrelevant (see **3.7** and **3.13** AGE EXCEPTION).

Since refund claims based on the annual maximum may, for 2015–16 and earlier years, relate to periods before the abolition of contracting out, the following examples include (unless made clear) the implications of contracting out, which complicate the computations. For contributions paid in 2016–17 and future years, the calculations will be simpler, without contracting out, and from 2019–20 onwards, without Class 2.

The personalised annual maximum for 2015–16 was 53 × [£815 – £155] × 12% = £4,197.60, plus 2% of any 'excess' earnings (ie, after allowing for the Class 4 lower annual limit and the Class 1 primary threshold in separate employments).

Example

For the whole of 2015–16, Chaffinch was employed by Dunnock in a contracted-out employment at a salary of £3,375 per month. From 6 October 2015 to 5 April 2016, she was also employed by Egret in a not contracted-out employment at a salary of £1,510 per month; and from 1 January 2016, she was also self-employed. The Class 1 primary contributions paid on her earnings from her employed earner's employments were as follows:

	£			£	£
Dunnock	486.00	(monthly LEL)	@ Nil%	0.00 × 12 =	0.00
	186	(balance to PT)	@ –1.4%	(2.60) × 12 =	(31.20)
	2,665.00	(balance to UAP)	@ 10.6%	282.49 × 12 =	3,389.88
	38.00	(excess over UAP)	@ 12%	4.56 × 12 =	54.72
	3,375.00				3,413.40
Egret	672.00	(monthly PT)	@ Nil%	0.00 × 6 =	0.00
	838.00		@ 12%	100.56 × 6 =	603.36
	1,510.00				603.36
Total Class 1 paid:					4,016.76
Chaffinch also paid:					
Class 2 contributions				£2.80 × 14 =	39.20
					4,055.96

On the face of it, Chaffinch will not have paid excessive contributions since the notional annual maximum for 2015–16 was £4,197.60. Such a judgement is premature, however. Before the question of any excess can be decided, the primary Class 1 contributions paid at less than standard rate (ie £3,389.88 – 31.20 = £3,358.68 must be converted to contributions at the appropriate standard rate (ie £3,358.68 × 12/10.6 = £3,802.28) and a fresh total must be arrived at (ie £4,499.56). As this fresh total exceeds £4,197.60, excess contributions appear to have been paid. It is therefore necessary to consider Chaffinch's personalised maximum following the numbered steps set out in new *Reg 21* as follows:

Step		£	£
1.	Calculate 53 × (UEL – PT), ie 53 × (£815 – £155)		34,980.00
2.	12% thereof		4,197.60
3.	Earnings from each employment that fell between PT and Upper Earnings Limit: [£2,665 + £38] × 12 = £32,436 £838 × 6 = £5,028	37,464	
4.	Deduct figure in step 1. from 3. (£37,464 – £34,980)	2,484	
5.	If the line above was a positive figure, multiply by 2%		49.68
6.	Earnings from each employment which exceeds UEL	Nil	
7.	Multiply step 6 result by 2%		Nil
8.	Add steps 2, 5, 7 – this gives the personalised annual maximum		4,247.28

The grossed-up contributions paid did exceed this personalised maximum and, provided the necessary conditions are met, the excess, suitably adjusted, will be repayable (see 55.3 and 55.8 REPAYMENT AND REALLOCATION).

It is important to recognise that the earnings to be included at Step 3 are those which fell between the threshold and the Upper Earnings Limit on a pay-period by pay-period basis, ie the annual total of those earnings which bore full rate liability (or contracted-out or other equivalents, as the case may have been). NIC&EO will in the past have ascertained this from Box 1c on the Forms P14/P60 but it will now extract it from the final RTI returns for the year.

Example

For the whole of 2018–19, Finch was employed by Grebe in a not contracted-out employment at a salary of £3,100 per month, and was paid an annual bonus in March of £8,000. She was also employed by Heron in another not contracted-out employment at a salary of £1,875 per month. Neither employment was a directorship. The Class 1 primary contributions paid on her earnings from her employed earner's employments were as follows:

	£			£	£
Grebe	702.00	(monthly ET)	@ Nil%	0.00 × 11 =	0.00
(First 11 months)	2,398.00		@ 12%	287.76 × 11 =	3,165.36
	3,100.00				3,165.36
(March)	702.00	(monthly ET)	@ Nil%	0.00 × 1 =	0.00
	3,161.00		@ 12%	379.32 × 1 =	379.32
	3,863.00	(monthly UEL)			
	7,237.00		@ 2%	144.74 × 1 =	144.74
	11,100.00				524.06
(Total)					3,689.42
Heron	702.00	(monthly ET)	@ Nil%	0.00 × 12 =	0.00
	1,173.00		@ 12%	140.76 × 12 =	1,689.12
	1,875.00				1,689.12
Total Class 1 paid:					5,378.54

Finch's personalised maximum following the numbered steps set out in *Reg 21* is as follows:

Step	£	£
1. Calculate 53 × (UEL – PT), ie 53 × (£892 – £162)		38,690.00
2. 12% thereof		4,642.80
3. Earnings from each employment that fell between PT and Upper Earnings Limit: £2,398 × 11 = £26,378 £3,161 × 1 = £3,161 £1,173 × 12 = £14,076	43,615	
4. Deduct figure in step 1 from 3. (£43,615 – £38,690)	4,925	
5. If the line above is a positive figure, multiply by 2%		98.50
6. Earnings from each employment which exceeded UEL	7,237	
7. Multiply step 6 result by 2%		144.74

Step	£	£
8. Add steps 2, 5, 7 – this gives the personalised annual maximum		4,886.04

The contributions paid exceeded this personalised maximum and, provided the necessary conditions were met, the excess will be repayable (see **55.3** and **55.8** repayment and reallocation).

Class 4 limitation

[7.5] *Social Security (Contributions) Regulations 2001, SI 2001/1004, Reg 21* effectively ensures that an earner's liability for primary Class 1 contributions and Class 2 contributions is limited to a personalised annual maximum amount which he would pay were he employed in a single employed earner's employment with earnings at the Upper Earnings Limit (see **7.4** above). However, that regulation does nothing to limit liability for Class 4 contributions which the earner may also have paid or be due to pay. Class 4 limitation is, however, provided by *Social Security (Contributions) Regulations 2001, SI 2001/1004, Reg 100(1)*, as follows. Before April 2003 where such contributions were payable *in addition to*:

- primary Class 1 contributions; or
- Class 2 contributions; or
- both primary Class 1 contributions and Class 2 contributions,

the liability of the earner for Class 4 contributions for that year was not to exceed such amount as, *when added to the amount of primary Class 1 contributions and Class 2 contributions ultimately payable* by him for the year (ie after applying the Class 1 and Class 2 annual maximum rule described at **7.2** above) *equalled* in value *the sum of*

(a) the amount of Class 4 contributions which would have been payable by that earner on profits or gains equal to the upper annual limit (see **33.6** EARNINGS LIMITS AND THRESHOLDS); and
(b) 53 times the amount of a Class 2 contribution payable for the year.

For 2003–04 onwards, further adjustment is made for the additional rate of 1% or 2%.

For 2018–19, the sum of items (a) and (b) will normally be £3,569.69, to which must be added amounts payable at 2% on profits above £46,350. Class 4 calculations were not directly affected by contracting out.

		£	
£46,350 – £8,424 @ 9%	=	3,413.34	(Class 4)
£2.95 × 53	=	156.35	(Class 2)
		£3,569.69	

For years up to 5 April 2015, Class 2 contributions were paid during the year, so this calculation will have been made in checking whether a refund was due. Since Class 2 collection was moved from 2015–16 to the self-assessment regime, the calculation is now a check to be carried out before the ITSA return is filed and before the 31 January payment is made.

It should be noted, however, that where Class 2 contributions are, by reason of their late payment, payable at a rate other than the rate set for the tax year, that other rate is the rate which must be used for the purposes of the calculation shown above. [*Social Security (Contributions) Regulations 2001, SI 2001/1004, Reg 100(1)*]. Were it not for this provision, the penal effect of the late-paid contribution rules (see **42.8** LATE-PAID CONTRIBUTIONS) might, in some circumstances, be frustrated. Similarly, in the case of SHARE FISHERMEN **56** who pay a special higher rate of Class 2 contributions, the higher rate must be used for the purposes of the calculation. [*Social Security (Contributions) Regulations 2001, SI 2001/1004, Reg 125(d)*].

Because the Class 4 limiting amount, calculated as explained above, is invariably less than the Class 1 and Class 2 personalised annual maximum described at **7.4** above (ie at least £4,642.80 for 2018–19), it is clear that no liability for Class 4 contributions can possibly arise at the full 9% rate where liabilities have already been limited by reference to the Class 1 and Class 2 personalised annual maximum. In such cases Class 4 contributions will be due at the additional rate (currently 2%) on the entire profits above the lower annual profit limit. Note that the Class 4 lower annual limit still applies even though the earner has had the benefit of a primary threshold in the Class 1 employment.

The regulation also affords relief from Class 4 liability, however, in some situations where earnings are too low for the Class 1 and Class 2 annual maximum to be of any effect.

Contracting out may have an influence on such calculations for years up to 5 April 2016, and a reduced rate election may apply to a married woman with multiple jobs. Therefore, for the purpose of determining the extent of an earner's liability for Class 4 contributions under *Social Security (Contributions) Regulations 2001, SI 2001/1004, Reg 100(1)* for any year where either non-standard rate is or was relevant, the amount of any primary Class 1 contributions paid at a rate less than the standard rate is to be converted into its standard rate equivalent. [*Social Security (Contributions) Regulations 2001, SI 2001/1004, Reg 100(4)* as inserted by *Social Security (Contributions)(Amendment) Regulations 2003, SI 2003/193, Reg 14*].

Example

Iris is a self-employed dressmaker with profits assessable to income tax under the self-assessment basis for 2018–19 (and requiring no further adjustment) of £19,250. She is liable for Class 2 contributions for the year but, intermittently, when business is poor, she supplements her income by taking employment with Jeans Ltd. Her earnings from Jeans Ltd during the year were 32 weeks at £625. Contributions are calculated and paid as follows:

		£
Class 1 primary	£162 × Nil% × 32	0.00
	£463 × 12% × 32	1,777.92
Class 2	£2.95 × 52	153.40
		1,931.32

The total earnings are well below the personalised annual maximum, so the Class 2 contributions will be payable by 31 January 2020. In the absence of a relieving provision, Class 4 contributions of £974.34 (ie [£19,250 – £8,424] @ 9%) would also be payable. Under the terms of *Social Security (Contributions) Regulations 2001, SI 2001/1004, Reg 100(1)*, however, the Class 4 liability is not to exceed the amount determined following the numbered steps in the legislation as follows:

Step		£	£
1.	Subtract the 2018–19 Class 4 lower profits limit from upper profits limit ie £46,350 – £8,424		37,926.00
2.	9% thereof	3,413.34	
3.	Add 53 times the weekly rate of Class 2 ie 53 × £2.95	156.35	3,569.69
4.	Subtract from Step 3 the amount of Class 2 paid and Class 1 paid at the main percentage rate (ie other than 2%)		
	Class 1	1,777.92	
	Class 2 – £2.95 × 52	153.40	1,931.32
	This produces a positive result which must be compared with Class 1 and Class 4 – payable at the main 9% rate – and Class 2:		1,638.37
	Class 1	1,777.92	
	Class 2	153.40	
	Class 4 (£19,250 – £8,424) × 9%	974.34	
	As £1,638.37 is less than these potential liabilities, this is the figure of Class 4 payable at the main rate (ie 9%) – a 'Case 2' situation as defined in *Reg 100*.	2,905.66	
5.	Multiply the result of Step 4 (ie, £1,638.37) by 100/9	18,204.11	
6.	Subtract the lower profits limit from the lesser of the upper profits limit and the amount of assessable profits	10,826	
7.	Subtract the answer in 5 from the answer in 6. (If negative, treat as nil.)	Nil	
8.	Multiply the above by 2%		Nil
9.	Multiply the profits less the upper profits limit by 2%		Nil
	CLASS 4 CONTRIBUTIONS ('Case 2', so add 4, 8 and 9)		£1,638.37

In consequence, Iris's liability is limited to that of someone deriving equivalent total earnings exclusively from self-employment.

Where an earner has higher Class 1 earnings and contributions, it may be unnecessary to pay either Class 2 or Class 4, or to pay a smaller amount of Class 2 without Class 4, or for years before 6 April 2015 it may be necessary to make a refund claim.

Example

Jan is a self-employed printer with profits assessable to income tax on the self-assessment basis for 2018–19 (and requiring no further adjustment) of £48,000. She is expecting to have to pay Class 2 contributions, but throughout the year she was also a director of Jan's Jeans Ltd. Her earnings from J during the year were £47,350. Contributions were paid or are estimated as follows:

		£
Class 1 primary	£8,424 × Nil%	0.00
	£37,926 (£46,350 – £8,424) × 12%	4,551.12
	£1,000 (£47,350 – £46,350) × 2%	20.00
Class 2	£2.95 × 52 normally due	153.40
		4,724.52

Her Class 4 liability for 2018–19 is not to exceed the amount determined following the numbered steps in the legislation as follows:

Step	£	£
1. Subtract the Class 4 lower profits limit from upper profits limit ie £46,350 – £8,424		37,926.00
2. 9% thereof	3,413.34	
3. Add 53 times the weekly rate of Class 2 ie 53 × £2.95	156.35	3,569.69
4. Subtract from Step 3 the amount of Class 2 potentially payable and Class 1 paid at the main percentage rate (ie other than 2%)		
Class 1	4,551.12	
Class 2 – £2.95 × 52	153.40	4,704.52
		(1,134.83)
This produces a negative result, called 'Case 3' in the legislation – see Step 9 also. No Class 4 contributions are payable at the main (9%) rate.		
The consequence is that the result of this Step 4 is treated as nil.		Nil
5. Multiply the result of Step 4 by $^{100}/_{9}$	Nil	
6. Subtract the lower profits limit from the lesser of the upper profits limit and the amount of assessable profits	37,926	
7. Subtract the answer in 5 from the answer in 6. (If negative, treat as nil.)	37,926	
8. Multiply the above by 2%		758.52
9. Multiply the profits less the upper profits limit by 2% ie £48,000 – £46,350 × 2%		33.00
CLASS 4 CONTRIBUTIONS ('Case 3', so add 4, 8 and 9)		£791.52

Example

Kate is a self-employed artist with profits assessable to income tax under the self-assessment basis for 2018–19 (and requiring no further adjustment) of £15,500. Class 2 contributions were potentially due for the year. Throughout 2018–19 she is also a director of Kate's Krafts Ltd. Her earnings from K during the year were £13,450. Contributions are paid as follows:

		£
Class 1 primary	£8,424 × Nil%	0.00
	£5,026 (£13,450 – £8,424) × 12%	603.12
Class 2	£2.95 × 52 normally due	153.40
		756.52

Her 2018–19 Class 4 liability is not to exceed the amount determined following the numbered steps in the legislation as follows:

Step	£	£
1. Subtract the Class 4 lower profits limit from upper profits limit ie £46,350 – £8,424		37,926.00
2. 9% thereof	3,413.34	
3. Add 53 times the weekly rate of Class 2 ie 53 × £2.95	156.35	3,569.69
4. Subtract from Step 3 the amount of Class 2 potentially due and Class 1 paid at the main percentage rate (ie other than 2%)		
Class 1	603.12	
Class 2 – £2.95 × 52	153.40	756.52
		2,813.17
This produces a positive result which must be compared with Class 1 and Class 4 – payable at the main rate – and potential Class 2:		
Class 1	603.12	
Class 2	153.40	
Class 4 (£15,500 – £8,424) × 9%	636.84	636.84
	1,393.36	
As £2,813.17 is more than these potential liabilities, the figure of Class 4 payable at the main rate (ie, 9%) is the figure calculated above (ie £636.84). This is a 'Case 1' situation and no further steps are necessary, because there is no liability at the additional rate of 2%.		
CLASS 4 CONTRIBUTIONS ('Case 1', so equal to Step 4)		636.84

Secondary contributors

[7.6] Because secondary Class 1 contributions have no insurance content whatsoever, the considerations which give rise to a limitation of contribution liability to an annual maximum in the case of a primary Class 1 contributor are of no relevance in the case of a secondary contributor. Accordingly, no provision is made to limit the amount of secondary contributions payable by an employer or other secondary contributor in respect of any particular employed earner. The same is true of Class 1A and Class 1B contributions, which are paid only by secondary contributors.

Key Points regarding the annual maximum

[7.7] Points to consider are as follows.

- Since 6 April 2003 there has been no fixed annual maximum amount of contributions in an employment or self-employment. However, where the individual is employed in more than one job, and they are separate employments, and the remuneration from one or more of them exceeds the UEL, a maximum will generally apply to limit the amount of NICs payable.
- An employee may apply for deferment of NICs at the main primary rate where contributions in respect of one or more of the jobs are expected to exceed the maximum at the main primary rate (see 27.2).
- The employer in a job for which deferment is granted is notified on form CA2700, but if this form is not received until after the start of the tax year the employer may refund overpaid contributions provided that the month of the refund is still in the same tax year. The report to HMRC will simply involve an adjustment to the cumulative figures on the next FPS.
- Class 4 liability may be reduced where an earner also pays Class 1 primary contributions.
- The maximum Class 1 liability is based on 53 weeks, so even if an earner who is both employed and self-employed has paid maximum Class 1 contributions for 52 weeks, there may still be a small liability for Class 2 contributions. At 2018–19 rates, 29 weeks of Class 2 contribution would almost equal the standard rate Class 1 contributions on earnings at the UEL for one week.
- The annual maximum has for many years been used in arrears to calculate refunds, and this continues to be the case for those with two or more unconnected employments. Now that Class 2 has been moved into the ITSA regime, it is necessary in cases involving self-employed earners to carry out the calculations before filing the SA return so that the correct Class 2 and/or Class 4 contributions are paid.

8

Anti-Avoidance

Cross-references. See AGGREGATION OF EARNINGS **5** for circumstances in which aggregation of fragmented earnings may be enforced; CATEGORISATION **14** for criteria to be applied in determining an earner's status; EARNINGS FROM EMPLOYMENT: READILY CONVERTIBLE ASSETS, ETC **31**; **34.3** and **34.12** EARNINGS PERIODS for *Reg 3(2B)* direction and for anti-avoidance rules for company directors.

Other Sources. Tolley's Tax Planning 2016–17.

Introduction to anti-avoidance

[8.1] Attempts at avoidance of contribution liability generally centre on making payments that are not treated as earnings or, where that is not possible, reducing the contribution liability by adopting self-employed rather than employed status (which avoids the secondary Class 1 liability) or strategies that ensure that every possible relief is utilised. Arrangements typically involve either:

(a) the removal of factors which would point towards the existence of a 'master/servant' relationship, and the exposure or creation of factors which would suggest that the 'servant' is, in fact, an independent contractor who may properly be categorised as a self-employed earner (from 6 April 2000, this includes avoidance of correct operation of the intermediaries (IR35) rules and from 6 April 2007 avoidance of correct operation of the rules for managed service companies (MSCs)) – see **40** INTERMEDIARIES; or

(b) the fragmentation of a single employment into multiple concurrent employments, one or more of which give rise to earnings at a level below the relevant Earnings Thresholds (see **33.1** to **33.5** EARNINGS LIMITS AND THRESHOLDS); or

(c) the creation of a pay structure which features two or more regular pay intervals of different lengths (see **34.3** EARNINGS PERIODS) and such a division of earnings between those pay intervals as ensures that earnings paid at the longer intervals are subject to, and exceed for primary contribution purposes, the Upper Earnings Limit (see **33.5** EARNINGS LIMITS AND THRESHOLDS) applicable to the shortest interval; or

(d) the substitution of payments disregarded in arriving at EARNINGS FROM EMPLOYMENT: GENERAL **29** for contribution purposes for payments which may not so be disregarded, although where this involves payment in kind rather than cash such action is likely in most cases to result in a Class 1A charge on the employer instead.

Arrangements involving intermediaries are now also widespread, structured so as to avoid the worker being classified as a deemed employed earner under the *Social Security (Categorisation of Earners) Regulations 1978* (see **4.5**).

Some businesses may attempt to conceal evidence of factors that point towards a master/servant relationship, or the existence of supervision, direction or control over a worker, but that could constitute (criminal) evasion rather than (lawful) avoidance.

Where avoidance activity of the kind described at (a) above is encountered, it may be remedied by re-categorisation grounded on the various judicial tests whereby the existence of a contract of service may be revealed (see **14.5** to **14.15** CATEGORISATION).

Where avoidance of contribution liability takes the form described at (b) above, the application of the aggregation rules (see **5.2** to **5.7** AGGREGATION OF EARNINGS) will, wherever possible, be enforced.

Where avoidance of liability has been achieved through a pay structure of the kind described at (c) above and the greater part of earnings has been paid at intervals of greater length than the shortest, future avoidance by those means will be prevented by notifying the persons concerned that the normal earnings period rule is thereafter to be reversed (*Reg 3(2B)*) direction, see **34.3** EARNINGS PERIODS).

Further counteraction of the activity described at (c) above is possible under *Social Security (Contributions) Regulations 2001, SI 2001/1004, Reg 30, Reg 31*, considered at **8.10** below.

As regards activities described under (d) above, until 1999 the then DSS showed little enthusiasm for seeking the application to contribution avoidance schemes of the anti-avoidance principles enunciated by the courts in the tax cases of *W T Ramsay Ltd v IRC* [1982] AC 300, [1981] 1 AER 865, HL and *Furniss (Inspector of Taxes) v Dawson* [1984] AC 474, [1984] 1 All ER 530, HL, though it seems clear that the judiciary could always have extended into an area such as that of National Insurance contributions the 'abuse of rights' doctrine which lies at the heart of those principles, should it see fit to do so. Until then, however, the courts had mainly confined themselves to applying the doctrine only where clearly identifiable *taxes* had been avoided. That attitude has now changed completely, and artificiality in rewarding employees will often be challenged by HMRC and disregarded by the tribunals and courts, as in *PA Holdings Ltd v HM Revenue and Customs Comrs* [2011] EWCA Civ 1414, where a plan to convert taxable earnings into dividends from a special purpose company in order to avoid PAYE and Class 1 NIC liability was held to have been ineffective.

The changes made to the intermediary rules in 2014 and 2015 in an attempt to block the avoidance through artificially self-employed agency work are detailed in **4** AGENCY WORKERS. The 2016 changes to block the use of 'payday-by-payday' salary sacrifice to reduce tax and NIC liabilities in respect of home-to-work travel expenses of intermediary workers are discussed in **30** EARNINGS FROM EMPLOYMENT: EXPENSES.

Case law

[8.2] The courts have now moved towards the view that National Insurance contributions are, in reality, a tax. In *Westwood v Secretary of State for Employment* [1985] AC 20, [1984] 1 AER 874, HL Lord Bridge stated that 'the payments which sustain the [National Insurance] fund, by whatever name called, are made by way of compulsory levies on citizens in different circumstances, and to some extent on the general body of taxpayers, so that *they may properly be regarded as much more closely analogous to a tax than to a contractual premium under an insurance policy*' and, in the case of *Minister of Housing and National Insurance and Another v Smith [1990] PC*, the Privy Council decided that '*the contributions of employed persons, employers and self-employed persons* [payable under the Bahamian National Insurance Act 1972] *are properly to be regarded as taxes . . . they are a tax on employment*'. Given that the Bahamian contribution scheme was closely modelled on the UK contribution scheme, that decision must potentially have great persuasive authority, should the issue of whether or not UK contributions are a tax for this purpose ever be taken before the English or Scottish courts. Early in 1999, a number of Secretary of State's decisions (see 9 APPEALS AND REVIEWS) cited the case of *WT Ramsay Ltd v IRC* [1982] AC 300, [1981] 1 All ER 865, HL in concluding that National Insurance contributions were payable in a number of avoidance schemes. It is believed that such decisions were made in the cases of gold jewellery, insurance policies and platinum sponge. One such decision in respect of platinum sponge was appealed to the High Court but the appeal was dismissed in May 2000 (*NMB Holdings Ltd v Secretary of State for Social Security*) (*CO/357/2000*).

However, in the tax case of *DTE Financial Services Ltd v Wilson (Inspector of Taxes)* [2001] STC 777, 74 TC 14, CA an avoidance scheme involving reversionary interests in offshore trusts and which therefore also had tradeable assets implications for NICs expanded on the *Ramsay* principle. The Special Commissioner in that case gave the following view:

> I am happy to accept the analysis of *Ramsay* provided by my learned colleagues in the *Dunstall* case (see [1999] STC (SCD) 26 at 39–41, paras 65 to 70). In particular, to repeat para 68 of that case (at 40):
>
> "The principles were further developed by Lord Oliver of Aylmerton in *Craven (Inspector of Taxes) v White* [1988] STC 476 at 507, [1989] AC 398 at 514 in the following way: "as the law currently stands, the essentials emerging from *Furniss (Inspector of Taxes) v Dawson* [1984] STC 153, [1984] AC 474 appear to me to be four in number: (1) that the series of transactions was, at the time when the intermediate transaction was entered into, pre-ordained in order to produce a given result; (2) that the transaction had no other purpose than tax mitigation; (3) that there was at that time no practical likelihood that the pre-planned events would not take place in the order ordained, so that the intermediate transaction was not even contemplated practically as having an independent life; and (4) that the pre-ordained events did in fact take place. In these circumstances the court can be justified in linking the beginning with the end so as to make a single composite whole to which the fiscal results of the single composite whole are applied."
>
> I have no hesitation in finding that all these four essentials are to be found in the present case. The series of transactions was pre-ordained in order to produce the result that Mr MacDonald received £40,000; the intermediate transactions had no other purpose than tax mitigation; there was no practical likelihood (despite what I say in para 15 above) that the pre-planned events would not take place in the order ordained; those events did in fact so take place.
>
> Mr Thornhill QC for the company contends that *WT Ramsay Ltd v IRC* [1982] AC 300, [1981] 1 All ER 865, HL cannot apply in this case unless one postulates an independent life for one of the transactions which, on *Ramsay* principles, cannot be regarded as having been contemplated as having that independent life. It would be odd if *Ramsay* could be circumvented by planning the intermediate transactions in this particular way. The company decided that Mr MacDonald should have a £40,000 bonus; Mr MacDonald got a bonus; that is—in both senses—the beginning and end of the matter. £40,000 started off in the company's bank account; it ended up in Mr MacDonald's bank account. The £40,000 appears in the company's accounts as a bonus paid and in Mr MacDonald's return as an emolument received; those entries reflect the reality of the situation which is that, in effect, the company paid Mr MacDonald a bonus of £40,000. How the company should have deducted tax from the sum is a question which, as in *Paul Dunstall Organisation Ltd v*

> *Hedges (Inspector of Taxes)* [1999] STC (SCD) 26, I find it unnecessary to address; the essential point is that the company should have accounted for that tax.
>
> It might perhaps be argued that, while it is permissible to use *Ramsay* to bring something within a charging section, it is less clearly permissible to use it to bring something within a pure machinery section, which is what s 203 [*Income and Corporation Taxes Act 1988 (ICTA 1988)*] is. I should not be convinced by such an argument. Section 203 is an exceedingly important section in its own right; the machinery which it provides applies to a majority of the taxpayers in this country and is essential for the regular flow of money to the Exchequer. Even if the main object of the present scheme was the avoidance of national insurance contributions, a further and by no means negligible object was the avoidance, by deferral, of PAYE—by keeping the Exchequer out of its money for a year or more. I see no reason why *Ramsay* should not be used to counter such a scheme; in the present case I find that, in accordance with *Ramsay* principles, the company is to be treated as having made a payment within s 203. The appeal is accordingly dismissed.

The dicta in the judgment suggest that the *Ramsay* principle, even following the dismissal of the appeal in the Court of Appeal, may be less applicable in some other similar cases where the outcome for the employee is less certain. In the dismissal of the case in the Court of Appeal the judges stated:

> It was plainly legitimate to apply the *Ramsay* approach to the concept of "payment" in the context of the PAYE system. The concept of payment was a practical, commercial concept and for the purposes of the PAYE system "payment" meant actual payment, namely a transfer of cash or its equivalent. Accordingly applying the *Ramsay* approach to the composite transaction in the instant case, the employer had decided that the directors would receive cash bonus and that was what the directors had received. It followed that the cash payment received by the directors was a payment of assessable income within the meaning of s 203(1) of the 1988 Act.

It may therefore follow that where the PAYE liability is found to be due following the determination that a scheme is an avoidance vehicle for PAYE purposes then a Class 1 NICs liability will also be appropriate alongside the outstanding tax.

Social Security (Contributions) Regulations 2001, SI 2001/1004, Sch 3 Part III para 3 includes vouchers exchangeable for any asset referred to in *Social Security (Contributions) Regulations 2001, SI 2001/1004, Sch 3 Part III paras 1–2*. See also 'Taxation', 7 November 2002, page 141.

In *Dextra Accessories Ltd and others v Macdonald* [2002] STC SCD 413 Sp C 331; Ch D [2003] STC 749; CA [2004] STC 339; *Macdonald v Dextra Securities Ltd & Ors* HL [2005] HKHL 47 the Commissioners found that there was no tax or NICs liability at the time that contributions were made to an employment benefit trust (EBT). The Commissioners also found that a corporation tax deduction was due at the time of the payment of the contribution, notwithstanding the nine-month rule in *Finance Act 1989, s 43*. The arguments of the former Inland Revenue revolved around the *Ramsay* principle contending that:

> . . . contributions by the appellant companies to the EBT are "potential emoluments" within s 43(11) since they are held by the trustee of the EBT, who is conceded to be an intermediary, with a view to their becoming relevant emoluments,

> defined as emoluments for a period after 5 April 1989 in respect of a particular office or employment. This provides symmetry between deductibility by the companies and taxability of the employees . . .

In applying the *Ramsay* approach in their decision the Commissioners found that

> ... applying a commercial approach to the relevant statutory concepts, in this case there was no payment of emoluments or earnings by reason of these particular arrangements involving the EBT. If it is necessary for us to decide it we do not categorise the EBT as an artificial avoidance scheme.

The case went on appeal to the Chancery Division and on 16 April 2003 the appeal by the Inland Revenue was dismissed. However, on further appeal, the Court of Appeal held that the contributions to the EBT were potential emoluments. The fact that the EBT empowered the trustee to apply funds subject to the EBT otherwise than in the provision of emoluments did not have the effect of taking contributions to the EBT outside the definition of 'potential emoluments' within *FA 1989, s 43(11)(a)*. The former Inland Revenue's appeal was therefore allowed. The companies appealed, contending that the payments should not be treated as 'potential emoluments' within *s 43(11)*. The House of Lords unanimously rejected this contention and dismissed the companies' appeals. Lord Hoffmann held that:

> In the ordinary use of language, the whole of the funds were potential emoluments. They could be used to pay emoluments.

He observed, quoting Jonathan Parker LJ in the Court of Appeal, that this was:

> the result of an arrangement into which the taxpayers have chosen to enter. Any untoward consequences can be avoided by segregating the funds held on trust to pay emoluments from funds held to benefit employees in other ways.

See also *Sempra Metals Ltd v Revenue and Customs Comrs* [2008] STC (SCD) 1062.

The *Dextra* case may now only be directly relevant for tax purposes to past periods, since the deductibility rules for EBT contributions were changed by *FA 2003, Sch 24*, but HMRC issued a statement on 19 August 2005 stating that, having obtained legal advice, it would pursue recovery of the NICs also alleged to be due for up to six years within *Limitation Act 1980*. Their method of doing this was to issue protective claims through the County Court to the relevant employers they considered had unpaid NICs liability in this context. See Tolley's Practical NIC, September 2005 p 58 and October 2005 p 68.

In practice, HMRC was granting corporation tax relief – notwithstanding the Court of Appeal and House of Lords judgments – provided that Class 1 NIC was paid in a settlement offer. In the Pre-Budget Report Statement on 27 November 2002, subsequently legislated in *FA 2003*, the Chancellor had reversed the practical benefit of the decision by denying a deduction for contributions to an EBT or other relevant intermediary unless and until 'qualifying benefits' were provided that were taxable as what are now known as general earnings and liable to NICs. Now, where an employer makes a contribution to an EBT, a deduction for the current period will only be allowed to the extent that qualifying benefits are provided within nine months of the end of the period. These anti-avoidance rules do not apply to retirement benefit schemes, personal pension schemes, share incentive plans, or approved employee share schemes, to which different rules apply. [*Social Security (Contributions) (Amendment No 5) Regulations 2002, SI 2002/2929*].

The decisions of the First-tier and Upper Tribunals in *Murray Group Holdings Ltd v Revenue and Customs Comrs* [2012] UKFTT 692 and [2014] UKUT 0292 examined a situation similar to that in *Dextra* where, despite the *Dextra* decision, HMRC had argued that payment to an EBT, or appointments from an EBT into discretionary sub-trusts which included the employees as discretionary objects should have been subject to PAYE and NIC.

In brief, HMRC had spent over five years arguing with the employer in *Dextra*, eventually convincing the House of Lords, that the money paid into the trust was not a payment of emoluments, so it did not qualify for a corporation tax deduction. When it came to *Murray Group Holdings*, where there were so many corporate tax losses available that any denial of a corporation tax deduction would have been fruitless in terms of immediate tax yield, HMRC chose to argue instead that the EBT payments were indeed earnings, and therefore should have generated a PAYE and NIC liability.

Murray owned Glasgow Rangers FC and had used an EBT to make loans to a number of employees of the club via numerous sub-trusts. The loans had been reported on P11D as employment-related and the beneficiaries had been taxed on that basis. However, HMRC argued that the loans were nothing but remuneration and sought to charge PAYE and NIC on the payments made to the sub-trusts: when payment was made by the main EBT to a particular sub-trust that would primarily or exclusively benefit a named employee or his family, argued HMRC, the money was unreservedly put at the disposal of the employee concerned as remuneration rather than a loan.

The First-tier Tribunal noted the contradiction in HMRC's arguments in *Dextra* and in this case, and found against HMRC. The loans were indeed loans, not remuneration, and there was detailed tax legislation to deal with levying income tax on the benefit of the loans advanced by the trustees of the 108 trusts involved. Class 1A liability should have arisen on the deemed benefit of the taxable loans, but HMRC had been arguing for Class 1 liability, which would have been due if the payments in question had been found to be earnings.

HMRC's appeal to the Upper Tribunal was unsuccessful in July 2014 because, in its judgment, the First-tier Tribunal had considered the relevant facts and applied the relevant law in a way that was not open to challenge. Only one minor point on termination payments was remitted to the First-tier Tribunal. HMRC sought leave to appeal to the Court of Session, but the case stalled when the last appellant company was put into compulsory liquidation in January 2015.

When the liquidator and HMRC took the appeal from the Upper Tribunal decision to the Inner House of the Court of Session in late 2015 (*Advocate General for Scotland v Murray Group Holdings Ltd* [2015] CSIH 77, [2016] STC 468, 2015 Scot (D) 2/11), HMRC changed tack and introduced a new argument. Instead of the payment to the sub-trust constituting a payment of earnings, HMRC argued, and the court agreed, that the relevant payment of emoluments or earnings was that made by the employer to the trustee of the principal trust.

In what is arguably something of a non sequitur, the court found that the critical feature of earnings is that they represent consideration for services provided under a contract of employment, and such consideration is ultimately provided by the employer, so the payment to the principal trust must have been a payment of earnings subject to income tax at that point. It is unclear how the holding and lending of cash by a properly constituted trust, which continues to own the loan value as an asset, and for which there is adequate provision in the employment tax legislation, as noted by the lower tribunals, can be characterised as the making of a payment of earnings.

For the court, the critical point when it can be said that earnings have been paid is when the employer makes a payment either directly to the employee or in a manner that has been requested or at least acquiesced in by the employee. The court had no difficulty in identifying the point when funds left the employer, and in identifying that they were made to an entity that had been selected by the employee, or at least acquiesced in by the employee, and therefore found that there had simply been a 'redirection of earnings'.

Confusingly for those employers who have adopted similar structures to the Murray Group's EBT and loan arrangements, it is wholly unclear how the decision of the Court of Session is compatible with the decision of the Supreme Court in *Forde and McHugh Ltd v Revenue and Customs Comrs* [2014] UKSC 14, [2014] 2 All ER 356, [2014] 1 WLR 810. The court found it readily distinguishable on the basis that it was concerned primarily with liability to NICs on 'earnings' as defined for SSCBA 1992 purposes rather than income tax as defined for *Income Tax (Earnings and Pensions) Act 2003 (ITEPA 2003)* purposes, without explaining how the fact that there was no unconditional entitlement to the cash (the *ratio* in both *Dextra* – a tax case – and *Forde & McHugh* – a NIC case) could be reconciled with the decision in *Murray*. Despite having used this distinction to justify disregarding the NIC case in arriving at the decision, the court went on to find that both PAYE and NICs were due on the payment to the principal trust, which seems rather illogical.

Permission was granted for an appeal to the Supreme Court, so the decision is not likely to be final until sometime in 2017.

Another avoidance scheme that attracted considerable media attention involved soft currency loans. Under the scheme, instead of part of an employee's remuneration, such as a bonus, being in cash, there was a loan to the employee in a soft currency such as the Turkish lira that was expected to depreciate substantially against sterling. The employee was then expected to realise a non-taxable exchange gain in sterling terms when the loan was repaid in full in the soft currency years later. This represented his or her 'bonus', while the employer made an equivalent deductible exchange loss. The tax and NICs treatment of payments made in this way will depend upon the precise contractual arrangements between employer and employee. A detailed investigation of all the facts surrounding the payment will be required in every case to determine the precise contractual arrangements. The scheme was effectively closed with the November 2002 changes regarding employee benefit trusts, since an EBT was invariably a part of the scheme to ensure that the employer obtained tax relief for what might otherwise be transactions within the capital gains regime or else not for the benefit of the trade. See IR Tax Bulletin 63, February 2003.

However, a similar loan scheme for contractors was eventually litigated by HMRC. The First-tier Tribunal found in *Philip Boyle* TC03103 [2013] UKFTT 723 (TC) that the soft currency loan was no more than a device to disguise a payment of remuneration and it held that it should take a realistic view of the facts. The case did not involve any National Insurance contribution decisions, but the principles being adopted by the tribunals were summarised by the judges as follows:

> 'In reaching the . . . conclusions and deciding this appeal we have borne in mind Parliament's intention which is to render liable to tax income which in substance and reality is employment income. We find that the monies which were ostensibly paid over to Mr Boyle as loans were in substance and reality income from his employment, bearing in mind in particular that Mr Boyle had no need for a loan, there was an entirely artificial exchange rate; the reality is that there was no borrowing by Mr Boyle and he never believed that the "loans" were other than a means of receiving his income without suffering tax on that income'.

In practice, HMRC's approach to settling enquiries into contractor loan schemes appears to involve treating payments as taxable under the *ICTA 1988, s 739* 'transfer of assets abroad' legislation, which was an alternative argument advanced by HMRC and explicitly accepted by the tribunal in the *Boyle* case. Section 739 has no NIC consequences as it does not deem a payment to be 'earnings', even for tax purposes.

The *Boyle* and *Murray*-type schemes were blocked by legislation in *Finance Act 2011, Sch 2 (FA 2011)* that deemed loans made via third parties to be taxable as disguised remuneration by inserting the new *Pt 7A* into *ITEPA 2003* and inserting *Reg 22B* into the *Contributions Regulations 2001* (see **29.69** EMPLOYMENT INCOME PROVIDED THROUGH THIRD PARTIES). Having successfully litigated these two types of EBT-and-loan scheme to combat avoidance that took place before the 2011 changes, HMRC decided to tidy up all the unresolved disputes in this area by legislating again rather than pursuing all the remaining schemes through the tribunals. It was announced in Budget 2016 that several measures were planned, some being minor technical changes and others actually raising more revenue (approximately £2.5 billion over five years):

- A new targeted anti-avoidance rule was to be inserted into the disguised remuneration legislation with effect from 16 March 2016 to prevent relief for the giving of consideration in relation to an asset transfer that constitutes a relevant step. This was achieved by adding a condition related to the existence of a tax avoidance arrangement linked to a payment into *ITEPA 2003, s 554Z8(5)*.

- It was to be made clear that the payment of an accelerated payment or a payment on account does not constitute a payment of tax for the purposes of the relief from tax on later payments in *FA 2011, Sch 2, para 59*.
- *Part 7A* was to be extended by *Finance Act 2016, s 18 (FA 2016)* to bring into charge to income tax any income and gains of an offshore employee benefit trust that, to date, had been disregarded by means of a transitional relief on investment returns where there was an agreement between the taxpayer employer and HMRC under *FA 2011, Sch 2, para 59*. The tax charge accepted by the employer in respect of the payments is matched, where there is such an agreement, by a relief on later payments of the funds from the trust, even if those funds include investment returns in addition to the employer's contributions to the trust. The relief was intended to be used with the EBT settlement opportunity which closed on 31 July 2015 in an attempt to offer an incentive to employers to settle early. The change in *FA 2016* is that anyone who has not settled with HMRC on or before 31 March 2017 will not be able to qualify for the relief, leading to an additional tax charge when the funds are extracted at a later date. Since the NIC charge on deemed earnings depends directly on any tax charge under the *FA 2011* provisions, this change automatically creates NIC liabilities when there are tax charges in respect of scheme payments or loans made out of these accrued income funds that arise on or after 1 April 2017.
- A technical consultation on further changes to the legislation which will include a new charge on loans paid through disguised remuneration schemes which have not been taxed and are still outstanding on 5 April 2019. The restriction to the benefits of making a *para 59* agreement on or after 1 April 2017 is clearly not expected to induce all those who have used loan schemes to settle. The Budget Report indicated that any loans still outstanding at the end of 2018–19 will simply be deemed to be taxable income. Legislation was included in *Finance Act 2017, s 15, Sch 6*, which made the necessary amendments to *ITEPA 2003, Part 7A*. Separate NIC legislation may also be expected, given that the 2019 charge is likely to create liabilities in respect of loans taken before *FA 2011* and still outstanding, which arguably constitutes retrospective legislation affecting a period more than six years old for which enforcement by HMRC would ordinarily be impossible because of the *Limitation Act 1980*. It is unclear how the new charge on loans is justified when HMRC has just spent several years trying to convince the tribunals and the courts that loans were in fact earnings and not really loans.

EDI Services Ltd v Revenue and Customs Comrs [2006] STC (SCD) 60 foreshadowed an anti-avoidance lead case in so much as part of the administrative procedures was to join together a number of other cases where similar bonus schemes were operated. This ensured that *Special Commissioners (Jurisdiction and Procedure) Regs 1994, SI 1994/1811, Reg 7* did not prevent parties being joined in a lead case. After the earlier directions case, the judgment in *EDI Services Ltd v Revenue and Customs Comrs* [2006] STC

(SCD) 392 was handed down on 26 April 2006. It was held that for 1995/96 onwards the provision of bonuses by way of demonetised French gold coins followed invariably by sale back by the employee to the original vendor – even though various other options were open to the recipient of the bonus – constituted 'trading arrangements' as defined. Further for 1994-95, applying the *Ramsay* principles in the light of the *Westmoreland Investments Ltd v Macniven (Inspector of Taxes)* [1997] STC (SCD) 69 decision, the Special Commissioners reviewed the evidence in detail and dismissed the companies' appeals, holding that the arrangements were a 'mechanism to deliver cash' and the payments were not 'payments in kind' within the meaning of the *Social Security (Contributions) Regulations*. No appeal was pursued, but it was commented that the issue under the EDI appeal had been decided under the then Department of Social Security appeals procedure during the 1990s – in favour of the employer. The right of HMRC to re-litigate matters which had already been dealt with in a proper way by another government department, just because HMRC had taken over responsibility for particular aspects of the former department's responsibilities, was very much open to question. (Taxation magazine, 6 July 2006 page 372.)

Some affected parties with 'protective writs' will also have been dismayed by a separate decision just three days later – see *Hyde Industrial Holdings Ltd* below.

In *Spectrum Computer Supplies Ltd & Kirkstall Timber Ltd v HMRC Commissioners* [2006] STC (SCD) 668 the employers' transfer of trade debts by way of directors' bonuses was not successful in avoiding National Insurance contributions. Citing the *EDI Services* case (see above), it was held that the transfer was not a payment in kind as, like the French gold coins, there was never any intention that the asset be 'enjoyed' by the recipient. It was accepted here that the asset was different in that the employer had not bought it specifically for transfer, but the purposive approach to the legislation (as stated by the House of Lords in *Barclays Mercantile Business Finance Ltd v Mawson (Inspector of Taxes)* [2004] UKHL 51, [2005] 1 AC 684, [2005] 1 All ER 97 and *IR Commissioners v Scottish Provident Institution* [2003] STC 1035) produced the same result nonetheless. In the case of *Kirkstall* there was a very small amount of bad debts amongst the 940 individual debts transferred but this did not affect the Commissioners' decision. It was incidentally held that there were no 'trading arrangements' in force for this particular type of asset. Again, this type of arrangement had previously been decided by the Secretary of State in favour of the employer.

Hyde Industrial Holdings had used an avoidance scheme in the 1990s and, after long years of dispute over the NIC liability, the then Inland Revenue issued a protective writ in 2002. Over a period of about two years, the district judge made various orders against the Inland Revenue with which it did not comply. In early 2004, of his own motion, the district judge ordered the claim to be struck out. Again the Inland Revenue did not respond, but in 2005 its application to another judge to have the application reinstated was rejected. In *Revenue and Customs Comrs v Hyde Industrial Holdings Ltd* [2006] EWCA Civ 502, [2006] SWTI 1439, [2006] All ER (D) 281 (Apr), in the Court of Appeal the HMRC appeal was allowed and the action was reinstated in the county court. The successful HMRC argument was that *Social Security*

Administration Act 1992 (SSAA 1992), s 117A requires that, where there is an open appeal to the tax tribunals, 'the [county] court shall adjourn the proceedings until such time as the final decision is known; and that decision shall be conclusive for the purposes of the proceedings.' Accordingly, the district judge may have been entitled to monitor the progress of the case but had no jurisdiction to throw the case out, no matter how offended he was by the then Inland Revenue's disregard of his court. See **appeals and reviews 9**. The introduction of Accelerated Payment Notices (APNs) and Follower Notices (FNs) (see 8.13 below) brought with them the introduction of an explicit exception to SSAA 1992, s 117A, which is understandable when the aim of the APN and FN regime is to force taxpayers and contributors to pay the amount claimed by HMRC to be due, whether or not it is at that point definitively due in law. Amounts found not to be due should be refunded, but *s 117A* would have frustrated HMRC's purpose if no exception had been made. Note that the exception applies to the amounts due under an APN or a FN, not (in the context of NICs) under the original notice of decision, in respect of which the appeal continues and collection remains stayed.

A Scottish employer entered into a tax avoidance scheme, devised by an accountancy firm and described as a 'discounted options scheme', with the aim of providing additional remuneration to seven of its employees without incurring liability to PAYE or NIC. The scheme involved payments into an employee benefit trust, which acquired 15 Isle of Man companies, and which purported to settle nominal sums on family benefit trusts for the relevant employees and to grant each of the family benefit trusts share options in one of the Isle of Man companies. The intention of the scheme was that there would be no UK tax charge on the cash held in the Isle of Man company until the cash was brought back to the UK (for example, by dividend or liquidation). HMRC issued determinations under *Income Tax (PAYE) Regulations 2003 (SI 2003/2682), reg 80*. The company appealed, contending inter alia that none of the seven employees had ever become contractually entitled to payment of, or on account of, any earnings. The First-Tier Tribunal reviewed the evidence in detail, rejected this contention, and dismissed the appeal in principle (subject to agreement as to figures). Applying the principles laid down by Ribeiro PJ in *Hong Kong Collector of Stamp Revenue v Arrowtown Assets Ltd*, 'the ultimate question is whether the relevant statutory provisions, construed purposively, were intended to apply to the transaction, viewed realistically'. On the evidence, there was 'a composite transaction consisting of a series of steps which began with the establishment of, and transfer of money into, the EBT and ended with the transfer of the shares to the employees'. The cash in the Isle of Man companies was 'unreservedly at the disposal of the employee as sole shareholder' and there had been 'a form of payment which the statutory provisions in question, construed purposively, were plainly designed to catch'. The shares were 'a profit which is taxable', and were subject to PAYE and National Insurance contributions, since 'the receipt by an employee of valuable shares is an asset which can be turned to pecuniary account or disposed of to his advantage'. *Aberdeen Asset Management plc v HMRC* FTT [2010] UKFTT 524 (TC), TC00779, [2013] CSIH 84.

In a NIC avoidance case that should stand as a warning to every employer to ensure that it always follows procedures and executes documents at the right times and in the right order, a company (Uniplex Ltd) failed to account for PAYE and NIC on the amounts which it paid to its employees. HMRC issued determinations under *Income Tax (PAYE) Regulations 2003 (SI 2003/2682), reg 80*, and Uniplex appealed, contending that it had entered into an arrangement whereby the employees had agreed to receive only the national minimum wage as their earnings, and that the bulk of the payments represented dividends paid to them as shareholders. The First-Tier Tribunal reviewed the evidence in detail, rejected this contention, and dismissed the appeal. Judge Barlow observed that the promoter of the scheme had produced a brochure explaining it, and commented that 'it is very surprising that the appellant is unable to produce the brochure'. It appeared that the employees had been persuaded to give up the bulk of their wages or salary 'on the basis of a promise that they would potentially benefit from a discretionary trust, the source of income for which was not stated'. However, on the evidence, 'no discretionary trust was ever set up'. The employees 'who had agreed to have their wages and salary reduced to the minimum wage rates were in fact paid exactly the same amount as they would have received had they not made that election'. Uniplex had failed to show that the employees had been issued with any shares, and the payments which the employees received did not appear to arise from the ownership of any shares. On the evidence, the payments which the employees received arose from their employment and were taxable and subject to Class 1 contributions accordingly. *Uniplex (UK) Ltd v HMRC* FTT [2010] UKFTT 422 (TC), TC00698.

Avoidance counter-measures

[8.3] In January 2003 the then Inland Revenue Chairman, Nick Montagu, pledged vigilance against artificial tax avoidance schemes stating:

> We will scrutinise artificial schemes very carefully to see whether they involve dishonesty and warrant prosecution.

A later HMRC Permanent Secretary, Dave Hartnett, is known to have referred to film investment schemes as 'scams for scumbags' (see *R (Ingenious Media Holdings plc) v HMRC [2015] EWCA Civ 173*), so the attitude of senior management at HMRC to tax planning has clearly become less gentlemanly.

'Disclosure of tax avoidance schemes' rules were introduced in *Finance Act 2004 (FA 2004)* (usually referred to as DOTAS) which imposed upon those scheme providers the requirement to reveal the intricacies of income tax/PAYE avoidance schemes to HM Revenue and Customs for approval. Many of these would involve NICs too. [*FA 2004, s 318*]. However, to accommodate avoidance schemes where NIC is in point but neither tax nor PAYE, NIC-only avoidance schemes were also brought within DOTAS regulations made under *NICA 2006, s 7*. See **8.5** below.

In the 2004 Pre-Budget Report (*Cm 6408*) at page 109, point 5.89 it was stated:

> The Government is taking action in this Pre-Budget Report to remove the ability to avoid Pay As You Earn (PAYE) and national insurance contributions (NICs) liability

> on certain remuneration arrangements. This follows action by the Government in recent years against a variety of schemes, particularly ones designed to avoid tax and NICs on bonuses received by higher paid employees. To prevent exploitation of similar loopholes, the Government has also announced in a statement issued alongside the Pre-Budget Report that it is prepared to bring forward legislation to counter any schemes of this type which are developed in the future. If necessary, such legislation would be effective from today.

As a result of the above and the former Paymaster General Dawn Primarolo MP's written statement on 2 December 2004 (see below), HM Revenue and Customs published on 3 February 2005 anti-avoidance measures that involve employment-related securities. See **31** EARNINGS FROM EMPLOYMENT: READILY CONVERTIBLE ASSETS, ETC. The effect of this draft clause and schedule prior to the *Finance Act 2005* was to prevent employers using employment-related securities to avoid paying tax and NICs from 2 December 2004. The legislation extended the definition of securities to include certain insurance contracts, tightened the rules relating to securities that have restrictions and rights of conversion placed on them, and expanded the anti-avoidance provisions relating to benefits from employment-related securities. [*ITEPA 2003, Part 7*].

From the perspective of *Human Rights Act 1998, Sch 1*, retrospective anti-avoidance legislation has already been deemed to be in line with the European Convention on Human Rights in *Woolwich Building Society v CIR* [1992] BTC 470. In the ECtHR it was held that retrospective legislation was appropriate in the particular circumstances to ensure that building societies did not benefit from windfalls arising out of the implementation of a new tax payment regime. See *National & Provincial Building Society v United Kingdom (Application 21319/93)* (1997) 25 EHRR 127, [1997] STC 1466, ECtHR. Similarly, in other Council of Europe countries where retrospective legislation has been questioned in the courts it was confirmed that Article 1 of the First Protocol of the European Convention on Human Rights did not prevent retrospective legislation from applying where a fair balance must be met between the particular taxpayers affected by the legislation and the population at large. See *MA and 34 others v Finland (Application 27793/95)*. This would perhaps be the reason why the Paymaster General's statement on 2 December 2004 was worded as it was, ie, 'Taxpayers who contribute their fair share have a right to expect that others will also do so.'

The full text of Dawn Primarolo MP's written statement of 2 December 2004 is as follows:

> This Government are determined to ensure that all employers and employees pay the proper amount of tax and NICs on the rewards of employment, however those rewards are delivered. Despite the efforts of successive Governments of all persuasions over several years, we continue to be presented with ever more complex and contrived attempts to avoid paying tax and NICs on rewards from employment, particularly in relation to bonuses in the City. In the most recent year for which we have figures, well-rewarded individuals receiving bonuses of at least £1.5 billion in total sought to avoid paying their fair share of tax and NICs.
>
> The disclosure rules in *Finance Act 2004* have revealed that this kind of avoidance is still rife. Without prompt and decisive action we think there could be up to £2

billion paid this year in bonuses on which the amount of tax and NICs properly due is at risk, as a result of increasing ingenuity and inventiveness of the tax avoidance industry.

We cannot allow avoidance on this scale to continue. It is only right that everyone who should pay tax and NICs, does pay and that they pay their fair share when it is due. The overwhelming majority of employers and employees do pay their fair share. But for too long some employers and employees with the benefit of sophisticated tax advice have sought to avoid their responsibilities and to pass more of a burden onto the rest of us.

Early attempts at avoidance in this area took the form of paying bonuses and salaries in gold bullion, diamonds and fine wines. When these routes were closed, employers started to pay bonuses through shares and share options to reduce the amount of NICs they had to pay, avoid their obligation to operate PAYE, and reduce employees' tax bills. When, in 1998, assets readily convertible into cash were brought within PAYE, and NICs, avoidance schemes moved on to more complex arrangements.

Despite extensive reforms to the tax legislation in 2003, employers and their advisers are continuing to devise and operate ever more contrived avoidance schemes. One such example of which Inland Revenue has learnt involves payment of a bonus to an employee in the form of dividends on shares in a specially constructed company. This avoids tax at 40% and employer and employee NICs.

The Inland Revenue will be challenging such arrangements in the courts where it is appropriate to do so. We cannot however await the outcome in the courts before taking action. We intend that from today both tax and NICs legislation should achieve our objective of subjecting the rewards of employment to the proper amount of tax and NICs, however the rewards are delivered. Taxpayers who contribute their fair share have a right to expect that others will also do so. We also want to make it plain that to the extent that legislation may still not achieve our objective in the face of continuing avoidance, we will ensure it does.

To that end we will be including legislation in FB 05, effective from today, to close down the avoidance schemes we know about. A technical note explaining what we intend to do in FB 05 will be published today. We will also ensure that NICs is charged on these schemes with effect from today.

However, experience has taught us that we are not always able to anticipate the ingenuity and inventiveness of the avoidance industry. Nor should we have to. Our objective is clear and the time has come to close this activity down permanently.

I am therefore giving notice of our intention to deal with any arrangements that emerge in future designed to frustrate our intention that employers and employees should pay the proper amount of tax and NICs on the rewards of employment. Where we become aware of arrangements which attempt to frustrate this intention we will introduce legislation to close them down, where necessary from today.

This action will not affect employers and employees who organise their affairs in a straightforward and ordinary way—the vast majority. In particular, genuine employee share schemes and share option plans will not be affected. We continue to believe these make an important contribution to the Government's productivity agenda.

In the 2006 Pre-Budget Report (Press Release PN 03) further anti-avoidance measures were announced and detailed in the *Finance Act 2007 (FA 2007)* at *s 25* specifically in respect of Managed Service Companies (MSCs) so that these companies were obliged to operate PAYE from 6 April 2007 and deduct Class 1 NICs for the relevant workers from 6 August 2007. In addition, there are transfer of debt provisions to enable HM Revenue and Customs to recover such monies due where, inter alia, the MSC has ceased business with no funds remaining. Also, the treatment of travel expenses of employees of MSCs was placed on the same footing as other companies with permanent employees. See consultation document *Tackling Managed Service Companies* issued on 6 December 2006 and **40** INTERMEDIARIES.

The same approach to transfer of debts arising from failed avoidance schemes was adopted with the advent of the new agency worker rules in 2014 and the new intermediary worker travel and subsistence rules in 2016 (see *ITEPA 2003, ss 688A–688B*, and *Income Tax (PAYE) Regulations 2003, Regs 97ZA–97ZM*). However, these have not been extended to NICs: the personal liability notice regime in *SSAA 1992, s 121C* only applies to the directors and officers of the failed organisation itself, rather than to a third party who has contributed to the failure to pay the NIC liability.

Retrospective action

[8.4] The *National Insurance Contributions Act 2006* was introduced on 30 March 2006, providing in *ss 1–4* the vires for regulations that enable HMRC to apply a NIC liability retrospectively. The power was first used in relation to those additional employment-related securities within the charge to tax under *F(No 2)A 2005, Sch* 2 backdated to 2 December 2004. See **8.3** and **21.3** Collection. *NICA 2006* also provided for the payment and collection of NICs in these circumstances and the disallowance of joint elections between employer and employee to transfer part or all of the liability in respect of securities options to the employee where the liability arises retrospectively. [*NICA 2006, ss 5–6*.] See EARNINGS FROM EMPLOYMENT: READILY CONVERTIBLE ASSETS, ETC **31**. The Act also provided powers to introduce regulations that apply the income tax avoidance disclosure rules to NICs avoidance schemes [*NICA 2006, s 7*]. See **8.5**. In response to retrospective anti-avoidance legislation put in place from 2 December 2004 and further expanded in the March 2006 Budget Statement, the meaning of 'securities' was amended at *ITEPA 2003, s 420* to include the proviso that a right or opportunity to acquire securities or an interest in securities shall not apply where the main (or one of the main purposes) was to avoid tax or NICs. See EARNINGS FROM EMPLOYMENT: READILY CONVERTIBLE ASSETS, ETC **31**.

It was announced in Budget 2016 that all old loans from EBTs that had not been taxed as income by 5 April 2019 will be treated as income under the disguised remuneration rules, but the announcement was vague about the scope of the charge. This will effectively constitute retrospective legislation, as it will catch loans made before the introduction of *ITEPA 2003, Pt 7A* in 2011. HMRC has challenged contractor loan schemes in two ways: either the money paid to the EBT was alleged to be redirected earnings (see above re *Murray Group Holdings*) subject to PAYE and NIC, or there was a charge under the provisions in *Income and Corporation Taxes Act 1970, s 739* (now *Income Tax Act 2007, s 720 (ITA 2007)*) on the transfer of assets abroad, both of which were supported by the First-tier Tribunal in *Philip Boyle* [2013] UKFTT 723. If the former argument succeeds, NICs will be due, but any newly-deemed earnings will have been paid more than six years before the change in the law (pre-*FA 2011* loans will become chargeable in 2019), so there may be a problem of enforcement of NIC liabilities because of the six-year time limit in *Limitation Act 1980*, unless the point is specifically addressed when the new law is made. If the charge is to arise under *ITA 2007, s 720*, there may be no NIC consequences as there is no equivalent in contributions law.

Having won the *Philip Boyle* [2013] UKFTT 723 case on contractor loans, and launched the related settlement opportunity, HMRC is still facing a backlog of tens of thousands of cases, so the legislation is to be amended in several ways. FA 2016, s 18 had already limited the effect of agreements made under *FA 2011, Sch 2, para 59* to prevent the sweeping up of offshore income and gains if the settlement is not reached before 1 April 2017. In addition, there is to be a one-off charge on 5 April 2019 on any loans outstanding that have not been subject to PAYE or NIC. The legislation has been included in Finance Act 2017 (*Finance Act 2017, s 15, Sch 6*, which made the necessary amendments to *ITEPA 2003, Part 7A*).

The proposals were set out in the consultation document. They go much wider than was suggested in Budget 2016. Some of the measures appear to be aimed at saving HMRC the trouble of litigating, since they merely make it easier to impose a charge on something that is already liable to tax, but others are punitive.

HMRC's concern is apparently to stay ahead of the scheme providers, who refuse to accept that their product does not succeed in saving tax.

In particular, HMRC proposed to deny a corporation tax deduction to any employer who used a disguised remuneration scheme, even if the amount paid represented otherwise deductible remuneration. The Autumn Statement announced a toned-down version of this idea, stating that a deduction would be denied if the remuneration was not subject to tax and NICs 'within a specified period' (albeit not actually specified in the announcement). This proposal was dropped from *Finance Act 2017* owing to the calling of the 2017 General Election, but it is expected to be included in a future Finance Bill.

There will also be power to transfer liability to the contractor or director personally where the employer who is liable does not pay, for whatever reason. This includes allowing HMRC not to pursue the UK user of the worker's services even when *ITEPA 2003, s 689* is in point, because it is easier to pursue the individual who has benefited rather than the business that is already liable (often a public body) under current legislation.

Remarkably, the proposals blatantly undermine HMRC's long-standing view that payments made through disguised remuneration schemes are already subject to PAYE and NIC liability, a proposition that has been used to pursue employers for tax and NICs for a number of years and that is to be tested in the Supreme Court in 2017 in an appeal against the Court of Session decision in favour of HMRC in *Murray Group Holdings Ltd* [2015] CSIH 77.

In the *Philip Boyle* case, HMRC argued successfully in the First-tier Tribunal that the loans made to the taxpayer by the offshore EBT were not real loans and were in fact earnings when paid. The Department also went to great lengths to establish in the Court of Session in *Murray* that the First-tier and Upper Tribunals had been incorrect in holding that the loans made by the offshore EBT were genuine and should be taxed under the existing legislation for employer-sponsored or employer-provided loans. The judgement supported HMRC's view that the payments made were simply redirected earnings of the individuals. It is simply extraordinary that HMRC has now introduced new legislation that acknowledges that the payments are indeed loans and that additional legislation is needed to treat the money as earnings.

Registration of avoidance schemes and counteraction

[8.5] From the date of Royal Assent to *FA 2004* on 22 July 2004, it has been necessary for promoters and users of tax avoidance schemes to register and disclose these to HM Revenue and Customs. [*FA 2004, ss 306–319*]. At first this requirement did not extend to schemes where only National Insurance contributions were avoided. However, most such schemes do also involve the avoidance of tax (even if only the timing difference that the absence of PAYE deduction affords) and so would fall to be registered/disclosed for that reason. The first sign of government response to reports made under these new provisions was the issuing of draft clauses and schedules prior to the Finance Bill 2005 in connection with employment-related securities. These were issued in advance and were later incorporated into *Finance Act 2005*. [*FA 2005, s 20 inserting ITEPA 2003, Part 7 Ch 4A*]. See **8.1** above.

The tightening of the disclosure rules and a series of successful tribunal and court challenges by HMRC to artificial avoidance arrangements has seen the number of new schemes registered drop to an insignificant level (just seven NIC schemes were registered in the year to 31 March 2014, and none in the half-year to 30 September 2014 (see www.gov.uk/government/statistics/tax-avoidance-and-disclosure-statistics). Updated statistics were due to be published on 1 May 2015, but nothing has been released.

Those employers who have used NIC avoidance schemes over the last ten years will now also be faced with having to pay any disputed NIC liabilities on account under the accelerated payment notice (APN) and follower notice (FN) regimes introduced by *Finance Act 2014 (FA 2014), Pt 4 (ss 199–233)* and *NICA 2015, ss 4–5* and *Sch 2*. Those promoters of avoidance schemes within *FA 2014, Pt 5* are also made subject to equivalent rules for NICs by virtue of *NICA 2015, Sch 2, Pt 2*.

The NIC rules on APNs and FNs follow the tax rules very closely, albeit commencing on 12 April 2015, two months after Royal Assent to *NICA 2015* rather than at the same time as the tax rules, except for certain regulation-making powers in respect of promoters that came into force with Royal Assent. [*NICA 2015, Sch 4, para 33*.]

The provisions of the APN and FN rules applicable to NICs are discussed further at **8.11** below.

Disclosure rules

[8.6] *NICA 2006, s 7* provided the power for regulations to introduce a similar registration and notification scheme as regards NIC – to the extent that any such scheme, by also avoiding tax and/or PAYE, was not already required to be disclosed. The practical application of the tax disclosure rules mentioned above was extended from 1 August 2006 – and the 'filters' replaced with 'hallmarks'. Consultation on draft regulations under *NICA 2006* closed in November 2006 and the *National Insurance Contributions (Application of Part 7 of the FA 2004) Regulations 2007, SI 2007/785* finally came into force on 1 May 2007. They required disclosure of an arrangement where:

- it will, or might be expected to, enable any person to obtain a National Insurance contribution advantage;
- that advantage was, or might be expected to be, the main benefit or one of the main benefits of the arrangement; and
- it was a National Insurance contribution arrangement that fell within any description (the 'hallmarks' – see below) prescribed in the relevant regulations.

However, disclosure of a National Insurance contribution arrangement was not required when either of the following circumstances applied:

- the obligation to disclose the arrangement fell before 1 May 2007; or
- the obligation to disclose the arrangement fell after 30 April 2007, the arrangement was the same or substantially the same as a tax arrangement that had been notified to HM Revenue and Customs in compliance with the disclosure of tax avoidance scheme rules, and the liability for disclosing that tax arrangement (but not necessarily the due date for doing so) fell before 1 May 2007.

The 2007 Regulations and subsequent amendments were consolidated and rationalised in *National Insurance Contributions (Application of Part 7 of the Finance Act 2004) Regulations 2012, SI 2012/1868* with effect from 1 September 2012. The 2012 Regulations list (in *Reg 5*) the tax provisions in *FA 2004, Pt 7* and make appropriate provision for each of *FA 2004, ss 306–316* to be replicated in the NIC regulations.

The duty to make disclosure of a National Insurance contribution scheme is the same as for income tax, corporation tax and capital gains tax and normally falls on the scheme promoter. [*SI 2012/1868, Reg 8*.] Special rules apply where:

- a non-UK based promoter fails to comply with any disclosure obligation. In this case the client of the promoter is required to disclose the scheme;
- the promoter is a lawyer and legal and professional privilege prevents him from providing all or part of the prescribed information to HM Revenue and Customs. In this case the lawyer's client must disclose the scheme;
- there is no promoter (ie the scheme is devised 'in-house' for use within that entity or a corporate group to which it belongs). In this circumstance the scheme must be disclosed by the scheme user, which in the case of a National Insurance contribution scheme will be the employer.

Broadly, where the scheme 'promoter' is required to make the disclosure it must be made within five days of the earlier of the date on which the promoter:

- makes the scheme available for implementation by another person; or
- becomes aware that the scheme has been implemented by a transaction taking place that forms part of it.

Where the scheme user is required to make the disclosure as a result of the scheme being marketed by an offshore promoter or by a lawyer who is unable to make a disclosure because of legal professional privilege it must be made within five days of entering into the first transaction forming part of the scheme.

Where there is no promoter, such as with 'in-house' schemes, the scheme user must disclose within 30 days of entering into the first transaction forming part of the scheme.

HMRC issues promoters with a scheme reference number (SRN) that must be given to scheme users and, in employment scheme cases, their employees (see below).

Since 16 April 2015, employers have been required to provide information annually to HMRC about employees where as a result of notifiable arrangements either:

- the employees might expect to receive a tax (including NIC) advantage; or
- the employer might expect to receive an advantage in relation to the employment of those employees.

This information must be provided by 19 April after the end of each tax year in which a tax advantage is expected to arise (so the deadline for the first report due was 19 April 2016).

For each SRN received from a promoter, and for each relevant person, the employer must supply to HMRC the following:

- the name, address and tax reference number of the employer;
- the name and any national insurance number of the employee;
- the SRN of the scheme;
- the tax year the employee obtained or expects to obtain the advantage;
- if the tax advantage is only expected to be obtained by a person other than the employee, confirmation that there is no tax advantage for the employee; and
- the name and address of the promoter, and the name given to the notifiable arrangement, if any.

[*FA 2004, s 313ZC*, inserted by *FA 2015, s 117, Sch 17; Tax Avoidance Schemes (Information) Regulations 2012, SI 2012/1836, Reg 13B* as amended by *Tax Avoidance Schemes (Information) (Amendment) Regulations 2015, SI 2015/948*.]

Where an employer expects to receive an advantage from an arrangement in relation to the employment or former employment of one or more of its employees, the employer must, within the prescribed period, provide to each employee prescribed information relating to the SRN. This is currently limited to the employer's name and address, the SRN and a brief description or name of the scheme. The official notification form, AAG 7, includes various warnings to employees about HMRC enquiring into their affairs and the potential effect on their reputation. [*FA 2004, s 312A*, inserted by *FA 2015, Sch 17, para 5; Tax Avoidance Schemes (Information) Regulations 2012, SI 2012/1836, Reg 13B* as amended by *Tax Avoidance Schemes (Information) (Amendment) Regulations 2015, SI 2015/948*.]

The DOTAS procedures are managed by HMRC's Counter Avoidance Directorate (formerly known as Anti-Avoidance Group or AAG).

The forms to use, required by law, are:

- AAG 1 – Notification of scheme by promoter;
- AAG 2 – Notification of scheme by user where the promoter is off-shore;
- AAG 3 – Notification of scheme by user in other circumstances (eg where legal privilege applies or the scheme is devised for use 'in-house');
- AAG 5 – Continuation sheet;
- AAG 7 – Employers providing a SRN to an employee [ie, notice to employee of SRN]; and
- AAG 8 – Disclosure of details about employees in relation to avoidance schemes.

Form AAG 4 will be used in ordinary circumstances by a scheme user. Form AAG 6 relates only to SDLT.

These can be obtained from the HMRC orderline: 03000 588993. Alternatively, the forms can be downloaded from www.gov.uk/forms-to-disclose-tax-avoidance-schemes and there is also provision there for disclosure to be made online.

The information to be disclosed about schemes is:

- the name and address of the promoter or other person required to make the disclosure;
- details of the provisions that make the scheme disclosable;
- a summary of the proposal/arrangements and the name by which it/they are known;
- information explaining the elements and how the expected National Insurance contribution advantage arises; and
- the statutory provisions on which that advantage is based.

Queries may be put by structured email via a link at www.gov.uk/government/organisations/hm-revenue-customs/contact/tax-avoidance or by telephone (03000 588993).

Tests and hallmarks

[8.7] The term 'arrangements' is widely defined in the primary legislation to include any scheme, transaction or series of transactions. [*SSAA 1992, s 132A(7)*].

'National Insurance contribution advantage' means:

- the avoidance or reduction of a liability for such a contribution, or
- the deferral of the payment of that contribution.

[*SSAA 1992, s 132A(7)*].

This definition potentially applies to all classes of National Insurance contribution. However, in practice, HM Revenue and Customs acknowledges that it is likely that disclosable schemes will only arise in respect of Class 1 primary (employees) and secondary (employers), and Class 1A contributions.

With regard to whether the advantage is a main benefit of the arrangements or whether there is a promoter, the tax guidance dated 4 February 2014 (www.gov.uk/disclosure-of-tax-avoidance-schemes-overview) applies.

When there is a promoter of the arrangement, it is a hallmarked scheme when any one of the following hallmarks applies, subject to appropriate modification to the tax definition for compatibility with the NIC rules made by *SI 2012/1868, Reg 5*:

- Hallmark 1(a): Confidentiality from other promoters [*Tax Avoidance Schemes (Prescribed Descriptions of Arrangements) Regulations 2006, SI 2006/1543, Reg 6*].
- Hallmark 1(b): Confidentiality from HM Revenue and Customs [*Tax Avoidance Schemes (Prescribed Descriptions of Arrangements) Regulations 2006, SI 2006/1543, Reg 6*].
- Hallmark 3: Premium fee [*Tax Avoidance Schemes (Prescribed Descriptions of Arrangements) Regulations 2006, SI 2006/1543, Reg 8*].
- Hallmark 4: Off-market terms [*Tax Avoidance Schemes (Prescribed Descriptions of Arrangements) Regulations 2006, SI 2006/1543, Reg 9*].
- Hallmark 5: Standardised national insurance contributions product [*Tax Avoidance Schemes (Prescribed Descriptions of Arrangements) Regulations 2006, SI 2006/1543, Regs 10, 11*].

Specifically excepted from Hallmark 5 are:

- arrangements which consist solely of one or more plant or machinery leases;
- an enterprise investment scheme (*ICTA 1988, Chapter 3, Part 7, ITA 2007, Pt 5 Ch 1* and *TCGA 1992, Schs 5B, 5BA,*);
- arrangements using a venture capital trust (*ICTA 1988, s 842AA, Sch 15B, ITA 2007, Pt 6* and *TCGA 1992, Sch 5C*);
- arrangements qualifying under the corporate venturing scheme (*FA 2000, Schedule 15*);
- arrangements qualifying for community investment tax relief (*FA 2002, Schs 16, 17*);
- an account which satisfies the conditions in the *Individual Savings Account Regulations 1998, SI 1998/1870*;
- Schedule 2 share incentive plan (*ITEPA 2003, Chapter 6, Part 7, Sch 2*);
- Schedule 3 SAYE share option scheme (*ITEPA 2003, Chapter 7, Part 7, Sch 3*);
- Schedule 4 CSOP scheme (*ITEPA 2003, Chapter 8, Part 7, Sch 4*)

- the grant of one or more qualifying options which meet the requirements of *ITEPA 2003, Sch 5* (enterprise management incentives):
  - (a) together only with such other steps as are reasonably necessary in all the circumstances for the purposes of facilitating it, or
  - (b) which fall to be notified to HM Revenue and Customs in accordance with Part 7 of that Schedule;
- a registered pension scheme (*FA 2004, s 150(2)*);
- an overseas pension scheme in respect of which tax relief is granted in the United Kingdom under *ITEPA 2003, s 647 et seq* (exemption from tax for superannuation payments in respect of persons not resident in the United Kingdom or in respect of trades carried on wholly or partly outside the United Kingdom);
- a pension scheme which is a relevant non-UK pension scheme within the meaning given by *FA 2004, Sch 34, para 1(5)*;
- a scheme to which *ITTOIA 2005, s 731* applies (periodical payments of personal injury damages).

It will be noted in particular that the key tax hallmarks in respect of loss schemes and leasing of plant and machinery do not apply in the case of the National Insurance regime.

If an arrangement is devised 'in-house', it is only necessary to consider whether it is a hallmarked scheme (and disclose it to HM Revenue and Customs) if the person intended to obtain the advantage is a business that is not a small or medium-sized enterprise. 'Businesses' are companies, partnerships and any other person whose profits are charged to income tax as trading or property income. Guidance on whether a business is a small or medium-sized enterprise for the purposes of the 2003 EC Recommendation tests is at Corporate Intangibles Research and Development Manual, CIRD91400 and in particular the flow chart at CIRD92850. When the arrangement is designed 'in-house', it is a hallmarked scheme when either of the following hallmarks apply:

- Hallmark 2: Confidentiality from HMRC [*Tax Avoidance Schemes (Prescribed Descriptions of Arrangements) Regulations 2006, SI 2006/1543, Reg 7*].
- Hallmark 3: Premium fee [*Tax Avoidance Schemes (Prescribed Descriptions of Arrangements) Regulations 2006, SI 2006/1543, Reg 8*].

Disclosure and subsequent issue of scheme reference numbers

[8.8] A single arrangement may provide both a National Insurance contribution advantage and a tax advantage. In such cases each advantage is legally subject to its own disclosure considerations. Where both advantages are required to be disclosed, HM Revenue and Customs expects that the timing rules will always require them to be disclosed at the same time. For administrative ease, HM Revenue and Customs will accept combined disclosure. However, the scheme description must make it clear that there is both a National Insurance contribution advantage and a tax advantage and explain how each of those advantages arises. Only one scheme reference number will be issued.

The Counter Avoidance Directorate in HM Revenue and Customs will issue a unique scheme reference number for each disclosure of a National Insurance contribution scheme it receives. The number is issued within 30 days of the CAD receiving the disclosure.

The reference numbers are eight digits in length and are issued to either scheme promoters or, where he has the liability to make disclosure, the scheme user.

Promoters are required to provide the reference numbers allocated by the CAD to clients who use their schemes. [*National Insurance Contributions (Application of Part 7 of the Finance Act 2004) Regulations 2012, SI 2012/1868, Reg 13*.] Promoters may find it more convenient to issue the number to their clients when it is received although there is no strict statutory requirement for this. Promoters should ensure that they inform their clients of their obligation to include the reference number on form AAG 4 (see below).

Clients who are notified by a promoter of a scheme reference number are also required, unless HMRC directs otherwise, to pass on the relevant information to any other person who the client might reasonably be expected to know is, or is likely to be, a party to the arrangements or proposed arrangements, and who might reasonably be expected to gain an advantage by reason of the arrangements or proposed arrangements. [*National Insurance Contributions (Application of Part 7 of the Finance Act 2004) Regulations 2012, SI 2012/1868, Reg 14*.]

With effect from 4 November 2013, a duty was also imposed on clients to provide prescribed information about themselves to any promoter who has provided them with a scheme reference number, and the promoter may pass that information to HMRC. [*National Insurance Contributions (Application of Part 7 of the Finance Act 2004) Regulations 2012, SI 2012/1868, Reg 14A, as inserted by SI 2013/2600, Regs 2, 4*.]

Employers using NI contribution schemes are required to notify HMRC that they have used or are using it. *National Insurance Contributions (Application of Part 7 of the Finance Act 2004) Regulations 2007, SI 2012/1868, Reg 15*. As it is most likely that users of these schemes will be employers, the employer should make a disclosure on form AAG 4 within the following time limits:

Pre-RTI years

- arrangements relating to Class 1 contributions – by the filing date of the PAYE return that relates to the earnings period in which the advantage is first expected to arise (ie by 19 May);
- arrangements relating to Class 1A contributions – by the filing date of the P11D(b) return that relates to the tax year in which the advantage is first expected to arise (ie by 6 July).

Under RTI

- arrangements relating to Class 1 contributions subject to the RTI provisions – by 14 days after the end of the final tax period of the tax year in which the employer first enters into a transaction forming part of the notifiable contribution arrangements and by 14 days after the end of each subsequent tax year until the contributions advantage ceases to apply to any person;

- arrangements relating to Class 1 contributions in respect of employers exempt from RTI reporting – by 19 May following the end of the tax year; and
- arrangements relating solely to Class 1A contributions with no equivalent tax advantage – by the P11D(b) deadline for the year in which the employer first enters into a transaction forming part of the notifiable contribution arrangements and for each subsequent year until the advantage ceases to apply to any person.

If a scheme involves both Class 1 and 1A contributions, the employer now should submit the disclosure by 19 April, although for pre-RTI years the deadline was 19 May. Employees are not required to disclose use of NIC schemes where this is done by the employer. The *National Insurance Contributions (Application of Part 7 of the Finance Act 2004) (Amendment) (No 2) Regulations 2009, SI 2009/621* made changes to the 2007 disclosure rules by ensuring that the Commissioners for HM Revenue and Customs must be advised, in the prescribed manner, of the number, earnings period and Unique Tax Reference number any time before the date prescribed in *Social Security (Contributions) Regulations 2001, SI 2001/1004, Sch 4 para 22(1) and ibid Reg 80(1)*. This rule is now found in *National Insurance Contributions (Application of Part 7 of the Finance Act 2004) Regulations 2012, SI 2012/1868, Reg 26.*

The disclosure rules were tightened further by *National Insurance Contributions (Application of Part 7 of the Finance Act 2004) (Amendment) Regulations 2015, SI 2015/531* with effect from 12 April 2015, the day on which the NICA 2015 changes generally (and the APN and FN provisions in particular) came into force. The changes in essence mirror changes made by *FA 2014, ss 275, 284* to the DOTAS regime for income tax purposes. The changes amended the *National Insurance Contributions (Application of Part 7 of the Finance Act 2004) Regulations 2012, SI 2012/1868*, the consolidated 'NICs Disclosure Regulations'.

Changes made to *FA 2004, s 310A* (duty to provide further information requested by HMRC) and s 310B (failure to provide information under *s 310A*: Application to the Tribunal) were mirrored in new *Regs 11A and 11B* respectively in the NICs Disclosure Regulations. In addition to defining 'working day' in order to make clearer the time limits for providing information or documents to HMRC, it is provided that, where a person has made a disclosure in compliance, or purported compliance, with the NICs Disclosure Regulations, HMRC may require the person to provide documents or more information about the avoidance scheme. [*Regulation 11A.*] Where a person has failed to provide information or documents required by HMRC, the tribunal may be asked for an order requiring their provision, which must be in the manner and form specified by HMRC. [*Regulations 11B, 21.*]

Penalties

[8.9] Promoters are liable to a penalty if they fail to comply with their obligations. (*National Insurance Contributions (Application of Part 7 of the Finance Act 2004) Regulations 2012, SI 2012/1868, Regs 22, 23.*) The penalties are as set out in *Taxes Management Act 1970 (TMA 1970), s 98C(1).*

A penalty may be charged where a promoter fails, without reasonable excuse, to:

- make a disclosure to the Counter Avoidance Directorate in HMRC when required to do so; or
- advise the scheme user of the reference number issued by the CAD when required to do so.

In both instances there is an initial penalty and a daily penalty. The maximum initial penalty for failing to disclose when required to do so is either:

- £600 per day during the initial period, for failure in the duty of a promoter in relation to notifiable contribution proposals and arrangements, for failure in the duty of a person dealing with a promoter outside the UK, and for failure in the duty of parties to notifiable contribution arrangements; or
- £5,000 for each failure in other cases (ie, failure to supply or notify reference numbers, failure by the promoter to provide details of clients, respond to enquiries or give details of persons who have provided information, or failure of employers to supply information to employees).

If the failure continues after the initial penalty has been imposed then an additional penalty of up to £600 per day after the imposition of the initial penalty can be imposed. The First-tier Tribunals are responsible for imposing any initial penalty and there is a right of appeal. HM Revenue and Customs can impose the further daily penalty or penalties where the promoter fails to comply after an initial penalty has been imposed.

Scheme users may be liable to a penalty where, without reasonable excuse, they fail to:

- disclose a scheme when required to do so (ie when a non-UK based promoter fails to comply with any disclosure obligation; the promoter is a lawyer and legal and professional privilege prevents him from providing all or part of the prescribed information to HMRC; or the scheme is devised for use 'in-house'); or
- declare on their tax return the scheme reference number.

[*National Insurance Contributions (Application of Part 7 of the Finance Act 2004) Regulations 2012, SI 2012/1868, Regs 22, 23*.]

These are as set out in *section 98C(3), Taxes Management Act 1970*.

The penalty for failure to disclose a scheme is the same as that for promoters – ie an initial penalty of £600 per day or £5,000, and daily penalties of £600 per day for continued failure.

The penalty for each failure to declare a scheme reference number will increase as follows:

- first failure penalty £100;
- second failure penalty £500;
- third and subsequent failure penalty £1,000.

[*National Insurance Contributions (Application of Part 7 of the Finance Act 2004) Regulations 2012, SI 2012/1868, Reg 22(11)(12)*.]

There is a right of appeal against the penalty to the First-tier Tribunal and onwards; see 9 APPEALS AND REVIEWS.

[*National Insurance Contributions (Application of Part 7 of the Finance Act 2004) Regulations 2012, SI 2012/1868, Reg 24.*]

No penalty will be charged where the promoter or user (as the case may be) has a reasonable excuse and the failure to comply is remedied within a reasonable time after the excuse ceased. Consideration of reasonable excuse will include whether the promoter or user has clearly followed current guidance or has otherwise made a reasonable judgement in determining whether or not a disclosure is required. [*National Insurance Contributions (Application of Part 7 of the Finance Act 2004) Regulations 2012, SI 2012/1868, Reg 23.*]

No penalty will be charged for a failure to disclose a NI contribution arrangement if the arrangement, or substantially the same arrangement, is also a disclosable tax arrangement and a penalty has been imposed for failing to disclose the tax arrangement. [*National Insurance Contributions (Application of Part 7 of the Finance Act 2004) Regulations 2012, SI 2012/1868, Reg 22(14).*]

The same principle applies for failures to declare a scheme reference number.

Following the *Tax Avoidance Schemes (Information) (Amendment) Regulations 2007, SI 2007/2153* new obligations were imposed from 1 September 2007 on promoters of avoidance schemes to provide information and documents.

The *National Insurance Contributions (Application of Part 7 of the Finance Act 2004) (Amendment) Regulations 2008, SI 2008/2678* and *National Insurance Contributions (Application of Part 7 of the Finance Act 2004) (Amendment) (No 2) Regulations 2009, SI 2009/621* made further changes in line with those made to the scheme disclosure rules made by *FA 2007* and *Finance Act 2008*. The *FA 2007* powers for the Commissioners for HM Revenue and Customs to require by notice scheme promoters to explain why a scheme is not notifiable and to apply to the Tax Tribunal for orders to provide information or for orders that a scheme is or is not notifiable were all extended to NIC from 1 November 2008. The *Finance Act 2008* changes in regard to 'Scheme Reference Numbers' (SRNs) were also extended to NIC from 1 November 2008 – the co-promoter rule having been amended to ensure that all promoters receive a SRN, that they are required to pass them to clients and that clients are required to pass those SRNs to other users of the scheme in question. In appropriate circumstances form AAG6 will be used.

As outlined above, the NICs Disclosure Regulations of 2012 (*SI 2012/1868*) provide for penalties where a person has failed to provide information or documents. [*Regulation 22.*] These penalties were extended from 12 April 2015 to encompass a failure to provide further information or documents required under the new *Reg 11A*. This corresponds with changes made to *TMA 1970, s 98C* by *FA 2014, s 284*. In addition, a new *Reg 22(10A)* was added to limit the ability of employers making a disclosure to claim a reasonable excuse for a failure to comply with *Reg 10 or 11*. They may not now rely on legal advice given to them or obtained by a monitored promoter as justification for any failure.

In the same vein, new *Reg 22(10B)* was also added at the same so that a monitored promoter may only argue that it has a reasonable excuse under *Reg 23* for a failure to comply with any of the obligations if the advice was based on a full and accurate description of the facts *and* the conclusions in the advice were reasonable. This corresponds with changes made to *TMA 1970, s 98C* by *FA 2014, s 275*.

High risk tax avoidance schemes

[8.10] Despite the raft of legislation in place to prevent the use of avoidance schemes, or to ensure they are reported to HMRC at an early stage, HMRC have major concerns about a small number of promoters and employers who are still willing to use high risk tax and NIC avoidance schemes. In doing so they seek to gain a financial advantage in that they enjoy the use of underpaid tax or NIC until such time as any dispute is resolved in favour of HMRC and that can take a number of years. HMRC issued a consultative document on 31 May 2011 entitled *High Risk Tax Avoidance Schemes* on their proposals to levy an additional charge on any tax or NIC underpaid at a level which would negate any cash flow advantage emanating from the use of the scheme. In the event, what we now have is the extension by *NICA 2015*, with effect from 12 April 2015, of the accelerated payment notice and follower notice regime to NICs as already mentioned.

APNs, FNs and high-risk promoters

[8.11] One of the greatest problems faced by HMRC in challenging avoidance schemes, and in collecting tax and NICs allegedly due, has been that litigation is very slow and, in the context of tens of thousands of schemes, almost overwhelming, given the limited resources available within HMRC for such challenges. Numerous avoidance schemes have been devised over many years, and each has a number of variants, with features added during the evolution of each scheme in order to counter arguments advanced by the Inland Revenue, DSS and HMRC from time to time. It has therefore been very difficult for HMRC to challenge many of the schemes before the tribunals because of the volume of detailed and careful work needed to investigate and prepare each case to litigation standard. The existence of scheme variants and slightly different fact patterns has been an obstacle to the effective use of lead cases to challenge schemes.

Before *FA 2014*, there was no incentive for taxpayers and scheme promoters to expedite cases because HMRC could not collect the claimed amounts while they were subject to appeal. In particular, *SSAA 1992, s 117A* specifically instructs county courts to adjourn NIC arrears cases automatically where an appeal against a notice of decision is unresolved, meaning that HMRC could only collect the arrears once it had litigated the case successfully and any tribunal or higher court appeal had been settled. Some scheme promoters have been known to use HMRC's inability to litigate quickly as a selling point for their product, with the worst outcome purportedly expected to be that the taxpayer might have to pay the tax due many years in the future, perhaps with some statutory interest charges.

FA 2014, Pt 4 took steps to address this state of affairs for tax purposes by instituting a new regime of follower notices (FNs) and accelerated payment notices (APNs). In summary, where a taxpayer has used an avoidance scheme that has been defeated in the courts, or that is a DOTAS-registered scheme subject to an enquiry or appeal, HMRC now has the power to require payment of the disputed amounts irrespective of whether the enquiry has been concluded or the appeal decided. In effect, the taxpayer has to deposit the disputed tax with HMRC while the dispute is pursued, which provides a serious financial disincentive to taxpayers who to date have simply paid nothing while deferring any arguments as HMRC slowly built its case against the scheme or schemes in question.

While most of these new rules began to take effect from Royal Assent to *FA 2014*, equivalent rules for NIC purposes, suitably adjusted to reflect the differences between the tax and NIC regimes, required separate primary legislation, which eventually followed in *NICA 2015* on 12 February 2015, although apart from the regulation-making powers the relevant sections only took effect two months later on 12 April 2015.

It should be noted that the new rules affect all outstanding disputes, whether or not the scheme or schemes in question predated the DOTAS regime introduced by *FA 2004*. It has been claimed by some that the new rules constitute retrospective legislation and as such are unlawful, but it is clear that the intention of the legislature is to clear the backlog of many tens of thousands of scheme disputes, some of which are well over ten years old.

Follower notices (FNs)

[8.12] In outline, HMRC is now empowered to issue a FN in respect of schemes where the application of a judicial ruling in favour of HMRC in another taxpayer's case would deny the tax advantage claimed by the taxpayer in his return. A FN can be issued to taxpayers where:

- there is an open tax enquiry or tax appeal in relation to a relevant tax;
- a tax advantage arises from the tax arrangement;
- there is, in HMRC's opinion, a relevant judicial ruling in favour of HMRC in another taxpayer's case that has become final; and
- no previous FN has been given to the taxpayer by reference to the same tax advantage.

[*FA 2014, s 204*].

Whether a judicial ruling is relevant is determined by *FA 2014 s 205*, and the content of a FN is set by *FA 2014, s 206*. It is not yet clear how tightly or loosely HMRC will attempt to compare schemes in dispute with schemes that have been examined by the tribunals and higher courts. HMRC has claimed success in 80% of court challenges to schemes in recent years, although this does not necessarily mean that 80% of schemes have been defeated, since many of them involve the use of employee benefit trusts and HMRC has been defeated in several of its challenges to common structures (see, eg, *Murray Group Holdings Ltd v Revenue and Customs Comrs* [2014] All ER (D) 109 (Jul), [2014] UKUT 0292 (TCC), which involved a widely-used structure of paying money to an EBT which was then lent to employees rather than paid to them as remuneration). As EBTs come in various shapes and sizes, it remains to be seen whether follower notices will be of wide relevance.

Where a decision thought to be final is in fact reopened because the taxpayer in question is granted leave to appeal out of time, HMRC must suspend any FN issued pending a final outcome. If the original case on which the FN is based is decided on a basis that shows it not to be relevant to the current case, the FN ceases to have effect once the suspension ends. [*FA 2014, s 216*].

The taxpayer is permitted, within 90 days of the issue of the FN, to make written representations to HMRC objecting to the notice, but while HMRC must consider any such representations it is entitled to reject them and there is no further right of appeal. The only grounds for objection are that the conditions of issue under *FA 2014, s 204* were not met, that the judicial ruling specified in the notice was not relevant to the arrangements in question (such as where the scheme under challenge was a variant of a scheme that has been litigated), or that the notice was not given in time (ie, within 12 months of the date of the judicial ruling on which HMRC seeks to rely or, if later, the day the return or claim in dispute was received by HMRC, or the day the tax appeal was made). [*FA 2014, s 207*]. Where a notice is based on a judicial ruling made before 17 July 2014, the date of Royal Assent to *FA 2014*, HMRC's window for issuing the notice is 24 months from Royal Assent or, if later, 12 months from the date of submission of the relevant disputed return or claim. [*FA 2014, s 217*].

The taxpayer is required to take 'corrective action' by amending the relevant return or claim to counteract the denied tax advantage, or to enter into a written agreement with HMRC to relinquish the denied advantage. These actions must be taken within 90 days of the issue of the FN or, if representations are made about the validity or accuracy of the notice, within the same 90 day period or, if later, within 30 days from the date on which the taxpayer is notified of HMRC's determination in response to the representations. The taxpayer is liable to pay a penalty if the necessary corrective action is not taken. [*FA 2014, s 208*].

The penalty is 50% of the value of the denied advantage as calculated under the provisions of *FA 2014, Sch 30* [*FA 2014, s 209*]. The size of the penalty is clearly intended as a serious deterrent to those taxpayers who might consider fighting on.

Any penalty may be reduced to a minimum of 10% to reflect the taxpayer's cooperation with HMRC. As is the case with inaccuracy penalties under *FA 2007, Sch 24*, the reduction will reflect the quality of the cooperation in terms of its timing, nature and extent. [*FA 2014, s 210*].

Further provisions on assessing, calculating, altering and appealing against tax-based penalties are set out in *FA 2014, ss 211–214*. The application of the provisions on FNs to partners and partnerships is dealt with by *FA 2014, s 215* and *Sch 31*.

Accelerated payment notices (APNs)

[8.13] While a FN can now be used to enforce the amendment of a return to show the correct liability, it does not alone enforce payment by a taxpayer of a disputed amount, especially if there is an outstanding appeal against an assessment or amended self-assessment. HMRC has therefore also been empowered to serve accelerated payment notices (APNs) on many avoidance scheme users, requiring them to pay any disputed amounts, generally within 90 days of the issue of the notice. Tax collected is regarded as a payment on account of the ultimate liability and is refundable if the scheme user, or a user of the same scheme, establishes in court that the scheme succeeded. A court challenge to HMRC's original assessments is not ruled out, but the taxpayer is required to pay any disputed taxes on account until those assessments are withdrawn or finalised.

The APN and FN elements to the anti-avoidance regime are separate but related. APNs apply to schemes required to be registered under DOTAS (the Disclosure of Tax Avoidance Schemes) rules and can be issued if:

- there is an open enquiry or an open appeal;
- there is a tax advantage arising from the particular tax arrangement; and
- either:
  - HMRC has issued a FN;
  - the arrangement was registered under DOTAS, in which case the taxpayer should have included a Scheme Reference Number (SRN) on the tax return or will have otherwise notified HMRC of a SRN; or
  - a GAAR counteraction notice has been given in respect of the arrangement.

[*FA 2014, s 219*].

Under the original proposals, APNs were also to be issued to taxpayers who had implemented schemes which *should* have been registered under DOTAS but which were not, but this was omitted from the legislation (although the FN rules might still apply if there is a relevant judicial ruling). No GAAR referrals had been made to the GAAR Panel by mid-2016, meaning no counteraction notices can have been issued, so APNs currently relate solely to schemes with valid DOTAS numbers or in respect of which FNs have been issued.

Shortly after Royal Assent to *FA 2014* in July 2014, HMRC published a list of DOTAS-registered schemes that may trigger an APN, although the list included only the relevant scheme reference numbers rather than the marketing names given to schemes by promoters, each of which came with variants and often with a range of SRNs (see www.gov.uk/government/uploads/system/uploads/attachment_data/file/326655/Reviewed_Tax_Avoidance_Scheme_Ref__Numbers_July_2014.pdf).

The content of an APN is specified by *FA 2014, ss 220-221*, with slightly different mechanisms applying according to whether the early payment is due in relation to open enquiries into returns claims, or in relation to appeals which have not been finally determined.

In a sign of the government's hardening and increasingly authoritarian attitude towards perceived tax avoidance, no right of appeal against an APN is available to taxpayers. HMRC will contact the taxpayer before an APN is issued and the taxpayer may, within 90 days of issue, make written representations to argue that the conditions for issuing the APN were not met, or dispute the amount of the payment demanded, but while HMRC must 'consider' any such representations, it can reject them. [*FA 2014, s 222*].

Where the APN is issued while a tax enquiry is open, the taxpayer must pay on account the disputed tax specified in the notice, within 90 days of the date of issue or, if the taxpayer has made representations to challenge the validity or accuracy of the notice, 30 days after the issue of HMRC's determination in response to the representations, if that is later than the original 90 day deadline. [*FA 2014, s 223*].

TMA 1970, s 55 was amended by *FA 2014, s 224* to deal with tax subject to an APN that has already been postponed pending the hearing of an appeal. In summary, HMRC is empowered in the context of APNs to bring such postponed amounts back into charge and to reject further postponement applications, even in respect of old cases. The effect is to make the disputed tax due and payable.

Where a taxpayer makes a successful appeal in an avoidance case, but HMRC appeals to a higher tribunal or court, any tax paid by the taxpayer before the first appeal would normally be repaid after the first decision in his favour has been made. In the APN context, HMRC is now empowered to seek to protect itself by applying to the court or tribunal to prevent repayment of all or part of any amount apparently due, or to require the provision of adequate security before repayment is made. [*FA 2014, s 225*]. This provision was extended to NICs by an amendment to *Social Security Contributions (Decisions and Appeals) Regulations 1999, Reg 12* made with effect from 12 April 2015 by *Social Security Contributions (Amendments in Consequence of Part 4 of the Finance Act 2014) Regulations 2015, SI 2015/521, Reg 2*.

Penalties will be applied for failure to comply with an APN: initially, 5% of the tax due if the amount levied by the APN is not paid within 90 days of its issue or, if later, 30 days after HMRC's determination of the taxpayer's representations challenging the accuracy of the figure. A further 5% penalty will be added if the amount remains unpaid after five months, and an additional 5% penalty for failure to pay within eleven months. [*FA 2014, s 226*].

Provisions on the withdrawal, modification or suspension of APNs and on their application to partners and partnerships are contained in *FA 2014, ss 227-228* and *Sch 32* respectively.

A judicial review of the APN rules in mid-2015 was reported as *R (on the application of Rowe) v Revenue and Customs Comrs* [2015] EWHC 2293 (Admin), [2015] All ER (D) 12 (Aug), which was a lead case for a group of investors who had participated in a film production arrangement that had not yet reached the First-tier Tribunal. As noted above, there is no right of appeal against an APN that meets the stated conditions and is correctly calculated, so the only legal challenge open to affected taxpayers is by way of judicial review proceedings, which could result in HMRC actions or the law being struck down in the event of a breach of natural justice, ultra vires actions, a breach of legitimate expectation, irrational official actions or incompatibility with human rights, including retrospection and proportionality. The High Court dismissed the appeal on all grounds.

In January 2016, it was reported that HMRC had withdrawn some 2,000 APNs issued in March 2015 because the conditions for their issue had not been satisfied. The case in question involved IR35 Manx partnerships dating as far back as 2004 that had not needed to be notified under the DOTAS regime but had been so notified as a precautionary measure by promoters who were concerned about the potential penalties for failure to notify. HMRC apologised for its technically incorrect actions. The fact that the scheme had been notified and that a SRN had been issued was insufficient to meet one of the conditions for the use by HMRC of an APN. [*Tax Journal, Issue 1293, 22.*]

In June 2016 it was also reported that HMRC had decided to withdraw hundreds more APNs issued to taxpayers involved in EBT arrangements that were technically not notifiable schemes, rather than await the outcome of a further judicial review application. [*Tax Journal, Issue 1311, 2.*]

It is also known that HMRC's rush to issue APNs led it to overlook the conditions in a number of other cases. For example, it has been reported that a taxpayer first discovered that the arrangement he had been using had been challenged when he was visited by a debt collector seeking to enforce an APN. The APN was withdrawn by HMRC when it was pointed out that the taxpayer had not received a notice of assessment before the time of issue of the APN, so there could have been no open appeal that would fulfil one of the preconditions for the issue.

Implementation for NIC purposes

[8.14] Alignment of the NIC rules with the tax rules arrived with *NICA 2015, ss 4-5*. Regulation-making powers were granted by *s 5*, while the substantive provisions were applied by *s 4* and laid out in *Sch 2*. The provisions of *NICA 2015 Sch 2, Part 1* on FNs and APNs came into force two months after Royal Assent to *NICA 2015* on 12 April 2015. [*Para 32(1)*].

Part 1 applies *FA 2014, Part 4* on both follower notices and accelerated payment notices to Class 1, Class 1A, Class 1B and certain Class 2 contributions. In simple terms, references from the tax legislation are translated to fit NIC legislation as follows.

Tax reference in Part 4	Includes for NIC purposes	Para no
tax or relevant tax	relevant contributions	2
a charge to tax	a liability to pay relevant contributions	3
chargeable to tax	liable to pay NICs	3
tax charged	NICs charged	3
assessment to tax	NICs decision	4
tax enquiry	relevant contributions dispute	5
tax appeal	NICs appeal	9

There are also certain related problems of terminology which require further definitions.

For example, since there is no concept in NIC legislation of 'enquiry', *NICA 2015, Sch 2* has to define 'relevant contributions dispute' as the written notification by HMRC to a person of its belief that there is a liability to pay an amount of relevant contributions and that person notifies HMRC in writing that he disputes the liability for some or all of the contributions. [*NICA 2015, Sch 2, para 6*].

The dispute begins with that notification by the contributor and ends with the payment in full of the disputed contributions, the settlement in writing of the dispute involving payment by the contributor of an agreed sum of disputed contributions, the issue by an officer of Revenue and Customs of a formal NICs decision or HMRC's withdrawal in writing from the dispute. [*NICA 2015, Sch 2, para 7*].

Any reference to a return into which a tax enquiry is in progress includes a notification of dispute in relation to which the relevant contributions dispute is in progress. [*NICA 2015, Sch 2, para 8*].

The term 'NICs appeal' means, as might be expected, an appeal under *SSC(TF)A 1999, s 11* or its Northern Ireland equivalent against a NIC decision relating to relevant contributions, or an appeal against a tribunal or lower court decision. [*NICA 2015, Sch 2, para 10*].

Any reference to a 'DOTAS provision' in the context of *FA 2004, Part 7* is deemed to include that DOTAS provision as applied by NIC regulations under *SSAA 1992, s 132A*, with any provision of regulations under that section deemed to correspond to that DOTAS provision, whenever the regulations are made, although further NIC regulations made under those same powers made the supply or modify the effect of this deeming rule. [*NICA 2015, Sch 2, para 11*].

NICs are deemed to be included in the list of relevant taxes in *FA 2014, s 200*. [*NICA 2015, Sch 2, para 12*].

As noted above, one of the conditions to be satisfied before HMRC may issue a FN is that a return, claim or appeal asserts a 'tax' advantage from particular 'tax' arrangements. This condition is deemed to be met if a person disputes liability for relevant contributions on the basis that he asserts a NIC advantage from the chosen arrangements. [*NICA 2015, Sch 2, para 13*].

FA 2014, s 208 sets out how tax penalties will apply if the taxpayer does not take necessary corrective action in response to the issue of a follower notice. Various steps are set out by means of which the taxpayer may take acceptable corrective action to avoid incurring a penalty, including the amendment of return or claim. This is clearly incompatible with the structure of NICs, so in a FN case where there is merely the NIC equivalent of an open enquiry, the only possible corrective actions are for the contributor to pay HMRC the disputed amount and notify HMRC to that effect, or for the contributor to take all necessary action to enter into a written settlement agreement with HMRC. [*NICA 2015, Sch 2, para 14*].

It was also necessary to modify for NIC purposes the provisions of *FA 2014, s 212* that cap aggregate penalties where two or more tax-geared penalties are incurred by the same person in respect of the same matter. There could, for example, be a penalty in respect of a follower notice under *FA 2014, s 208* and another penalty under *FA 2007, Sch 24* (inaccuracy), *FA 2008, Sch 41* (failure to notify), or *Finance Act 2009 (FA 2009), Sch 55* (failure to make a return). Those penalties all extend to some extent to NIC legislation by virtue of regulations intended to harmonise income tax and NIC powers and sanctions, so the provisions of that legislation are also covered by the limitations imposed by *FA 2014, s 212*. [*NICA 2015, Sch 2, para 15*.] To ensure that the Contributions Regulations 2001 match the change in primary legislation, *Social Security (Contributions) Regulations 2001, SI 2001/1004, Reg 1(3)* was amended by *Security Contributions (Amendments in Consequence of Part 4 of the Finance Act 2014) Regulations 2015, SI 2015/521, Reg 3* from 12 April 2015 to ensure that references to *FA 2007, Sch 24* and *FA 2009, Sch 55* are read for the purposes of NICs as amended by *FA 2014, Sch 33, paras 3, 5*. These amendments effectively exclude penalties where corrective action has not been taken after the issue of a follower notice from the scope of the term 'any other penalty', ie, the normal rule against double counting of penalties is set aside and FN-related penalties do not reduce a penalty for which the taxpayer is otherwise liable.

As with follower notices, where a person disputes liability for relevant contributions on the basis that a particular NIC advantage results from particular arrangements, the second condition for the issue of an APN is deemed to be satisfied, ie, it is assumed that a return or claim has been made asserting an advantage from the arrangements in question. [*NICA 2015, Sch 2, para 16*].

One major difference between the tax and NIC versions of the APN regime is that, to the extent that an accelerated payment represents understated contributions, it is not treated as a payment on account but as a payment of those understated contributions. The payment deadline for NIC purposes is the end of the 'payment period', which is the same as outlined above for tax purposes (ie, generally 90 days from the issue of the notice, with a potential extension if the taxpayer or contributor makes representations about the notice – this is also the case where a NIC appeal is open (see *NICA 2015, Sch 2, para 18*)).

As also noted above, *SSAA 1992, s 117A* could frustrate the purposes of the APN regime if no specific provision was made, because it would prevent HMRC taking any enforcement action through the County Court for any claimed NIC arrears for as long as there was an outstanding NIC appeal. For this reason, that provision is specifically disapplied in connection with proceedings for the recovery of any amount of the accelerated payment that is unpaid at the end of the payment period. If an officer of Revenue and Customs certifies the unpaid APN debt under *CRCA 2005, s 25A*, the certificate is to be treated by any court as conclusive evidence that the amount is unpaid. [*NICA 2015, Sch 2, paras 17, 18*].

A further difference between the two regimes derives from the fundamental difference between tax and NICs: the latter are paid to create entitlements to state benefit or statutory payments (eg, SMP). It is therefore possible that payments under the APN regime will create an entitlement because they are deemed to be a payment of contributions rather than a payment on account. To deal with the possibility that the amount paid under an APN becomes repayable when the contributor wins his case, it is provided that contributions repaid are to be treated for future benefit and statutory payment purposes only as not having been paid, although any payments of benefit made to a person before the repayment are left to stand. [*NICA 2015, Sch 2, para 17*].

The rule deeming NICs paid under an APN to be actual contributions rather than a payment on account appears to be potentially problematic, as the APN legislation makes no provision for refunds. Class 1 contributions may generally only be repaid if they exceed the annual maximum (irrelevant to secondary contributions) or if they have been paid 'in error'. [*SSCBA 1992, Sch 1, para 8(1)(m)*; *Social Security (Contributions) Regulations 2001, SI 2001/1004, Reg 52*]. The rule would ordinarily cover, eg, miscategorisation of a worker as an employee when he was in fact already known to be a self-employed earner (see 55.3 REPAYMENT AND REALLOCATION). The provision deeming a payment under an APN to be an actual payment of contributions rather than a payment on account means that, when paid, those contributions cannot have been paid 'in error', so there would appear to be no right of refund if the contributor wins the argument in due course. HMRC could, of course, in the interests of fairness and justice be expected to find a way to make the necessary repayment.

The failure to provide in *NICA 2015* for refunds in the event that HMRC does not prove its case against a particular avoidance scheme perhaps betrays a belief within HMRC that it will not lose any avoidance cases in the courts. As with the tax provisions in *FA 2014, s 226(7)* applicable to failure to make an accelerated payment, the penalty is applied, separately from but on the equivalent basis to the tax penalty. [*NICA 2015, Sch 2, para 19*]. Any penalty under *FA 2014, ss 208* or *226* may be recovered as if it were an amount of relevant contributions which is due and payable, and again the limitations imposed by *SSAA 1992, s 117A* are excluded in relation to proceedings before a court to recover such penalties. [*NICA 2015, Sch 2, para 20*].

The provisions of *FA 2014, s 227* in connection with the withdrawal, modification or suspension of APN's are also replicated in the NIC legislation. [*NICA 2015, Sch 2, para 21*].

Promoters of NIC avoidance schemes

[8.15] *FA 2014, Part 5* sets out to tackle the problem known by HMRC as 'high-risk promoters'. The provisions are extended to NICs by *NICA 2015, Schedule 2, Part 2*, although the NIC rules are unlikely to be used separately from the tax rules in practice because there are now few (if any) schemes which offer only NIC avoidance.

For the purpose of making regulations, the relevant provisions of *NICA 2015, Sch 2, Part 2* came into force at Royal Assent, but the substantive provisions came into force two months later on 12 April 2015. [*NICA 2015, Sch 2, para 32(2)*]. *FA 2014, ss 234–283* set out to target promoters of tax avoidance schemes who, in the main, are perceived by HMRC as constituting a higher risk than average, principally because they often fail to comply with their duties under the DOTAS regime. The new provisions attempt to discourage the supply of tax avoidance schemes by identifying promoters who meet certain threshold conditions, and providing for them to be issued with a conduct notice. The new conditions will apply if:

- the promoter's name has been published in a list of deliberate tax defaulters;
- the promoter has breached the code of practice on taxation for banks by promoting the scheme;
- the promoter has been given a conduct notice for dishonest conduct as a tax agent;
- the promoter has failed to comply with certain provisions under the DOTAS legislation;
- the promoter has been charged with a relevant criminal offence in relation to taxation;
- the promoter has been a promoter of arrangements that the GAAR Panel considers unreasonable;
- the promoter has been found guilty of misconduct by a professional body;
- the promoter has failed to comply with information notices served under certain provisions of *FA 2008, Sch 36*;
- the promoter has required a client to keep information confidential from HMRC or contribute to a fighting fund; or
- the promoter has continued to promote arrangements after being served with a stop notice.

If any of the above conditions are met, HMRC may consider the promoter to be high-risk. Breaches of the provisions of the regime may be subject to a penalty, which is £5,000 in most cases, and £10,000 under *FA 2014, s 261*, although for certain breaches (eg, failure to comply with the duty to publicise a monitoring notice (*FA 2014 s 249(3)*), to include that information in correspondence (*FA 2014 s 249(10)*) or failure to provide information documents under *FA 2014 ss 255, 257* and *258*, the maximum is increased to £1 million. Continued failure to comply after penalty has been imposed triggers daily penalties of up to £600 (where the initial penalty is £5,000) or £10,000 (where the initial penalty is £1 million).

In broader terms, the *FA 2014, Part 5* high-risk promoter rules read across into the NIC legislation with the substitution of relevant contributions for any mention of tax, and any references to tax advantages including the avoidance or reduction of liability to pay relevant contributions. [*NICA 2015, Schedule 2, paras 24, 25*]. Any reference to a DOTAS provision in *FA 2004, Part 7* is to include a reference to the DOTAS provisions as applied to NICs whenever the relevant regulations are or were made. [*NICA 2015, Sch 2, para 26*].

As might be expected, certain provisions of the tax legislation make no sense in the context of the NIC legislation, such as where reference is made to tax returns. In *FA 2014, s 253* there is, for example, a requirement that anyone notified of a promoter reference number under *FA 2014, ss 250, 251 or 252* must report to HMRC if he expects to obtain a tax advantage from relevant arrangements that a monitored promoter was promoting and he must report the scheme reference number in each of his tax returns for a period that is or includes a period during which he will be expecting to obtain the tax advantage. This clearly cannot apply to NICs, but references in *FA 2014, s 253* to a tax return are nevertheless deemed to include a return relating to relevant contributions that is required by or under an enactment. [*NICA 2015, Sch 2, para 27*].

NIC avoidance schemes almost exclusively target savings of secondary Class 1 contributions, which now are only ever reported to HMRC under the RTI regime, or Class 1A contributions which are reported on a form P11D(b). Neither the RTI schema nor the P11D(b) makes any provision whatsoever for the inclusion of a scheme reference number in a return, so the rule in *NICA 2015, Sch 2, para 27* seems obtuse in the extreme, since a contributor can never comply.

Further provisions seem rather less impractical: the power for HMRC to obtain information and documents (*FA 2014, s 255*) is extended by making references to a person's tax position to include the person's position as regards deductions or repayments of relevant contributions, or of sums representing relevant contributions, that the person is required to make by or under an enactment. [*NICA 2015, Sch 2, para 28*]. The definition of 'tax' in *FA 2014, s 283(1)* is quite sensibly extended to have effect as if relevant contributions were included in the list. [*NICA 2015, Sch 2, para 29*].

As is the case with FNs and APNs, the definition of 'relevant contributions' for the purpose of the high-risk promoter provisions extends to Classes 1, 1A and 1B, plus Class 2 contributions which must be paid (ie, they exclude Class 2 contributions that are now optional under the April 2015 reform of Class 2). [*NICA 2015, Sch 2, para 30*].

Class 4

[8.16] From 12 April 2015, *NICA 2015, Schedule 2, Part 3* extended the FN, APN and high-risk promoter regimes to Class 4 contributions by adding the provisions of *FA 2014, Parts 4* and *5* explicitly to the list of the provisions of the Income Tax Acts in *SSCBA 1992, s 16(1)* that are to apply in relation to Class 4 contributions as if those contributions were income tax chargeable under *ITTOIA 2005, Part 2, Chapter 2* in respect of the profits of a trade, profession or vocation which is not carried on wholly outside the UK. [Paras 31, 32].

Negation of abnormal pay practices

[8.17] An officer of HM Revenue and Customs is given powers with a view to securing that liability for the payment of CLASS 1 CONTRIBUTIONS **15** is not avoided or reduced by a secondary contributor (see **14.16** CATEGORISATION) following any practice in the payment of earnings which is abnormal for the employment in respect of which the earnings are paid. Such an officer may, if he thinks fit, determine any question relating to a person's Class 1 contributions where any such practice has been or is being followed, as if the secondary contributor concerned had not followed any abnormal pay practice, but had followed a practice or practices normal for the employment in question. See also *Goldman Sachs International v HMRC (No 2)* [2010] UKFTT 205, TC00507. [*Social Security (Contributions) Regulations 2001, SI 2001/1004, Reg 30(2)* as amended by *Social Security Contributions (Amendment No 3) Regulations 2002, SI 2002/2366*].

These powers formerly rested with the Secretary of State for Social Security but, following the transfer of the CA on 1 April 1999, are now exercisable by the Commissioners for HM Revenue and Customs. [*SSC(TF)A 1999, s 1(2), Sch 2*].

With effect from 8 October 2002, not only may an officer of HM Revenue and Customs decide any such question of his own volition, but he must do so if so requested either by the earner or by the secondary contributor. [*Social Security (Contributions) Regulations 2001, SI 2001/1004, Reg 30(2)* as amended by *Social Security Contributions (Amendment No 3) Regulations 2002, SI 2002/2366, Reg 5*].

Retrospective effect

[8.18] *Social Security (Contributions) Regulations 2001, SI 2001/1004, Reg 30(2)* may be of limited retrospective effect, it being stated that its provisions are *not* to apply insofar as the decision relates to contributions based on payments made more than one year before the beginning of the year in which that decision is given. [*Social Security (Contributions) Regulations 2001, SI 2001/1004, Reg 30(3)*, as amended by *Social Security (Contributions) (Amendment No 3) Regulations 2002, SI 2002/2366, Reg 5*]. 'Year' does, as usual, mean 'tax year'. [*Social Security (Contributions) Regulations 2001, SI 2001/1004, Reg 1(2)*]. Although this retrospective limitation was no doubt introduced to *favour* the contributor (in that it will usually be at least two years before a decision is reached on any dispute concerning contribution liability), its introduction may well have rendered the regulation *ultra vires*. That is because the primary legislation under which *Social Security (Contributions) Regulations 2001, SI 2001/1004, Reg 30* is made (*SSCBA 1992 Sch 1 para 4(c)*) does not itself authorise the retrospective creation of contribution liabilities and the application of *Reg 30* in a retrospective manner would, therefore, be an attempt on the part of an authorised officer of HM Revenue and Customs or, previously, the Secretary of State for Social Security to levy money for the use of the Crown without the authority of Parliament. Such action contravenes the *Bill of Rights 1688* and has in the past been declared unlawful by the courts (see *Congreve v Home Office* [1976] QB 629, [1976] 1 All ER 697, CA).

Whilst *NICA 2006* provides the power for regulations to impose a retrospective NIC liability, this power only extends to provisions that run parallel to anti-avoidance measures included in a Finance Act for income tax purposes, and so cannot extend to *Reg 30*.

The meaning of abnormal

[8.19] The legislation provides no definition of 'abnormal for the employment'. On 7 August 1985, however, in response to a request by the ICAEW for a note of the DSS's view on the meaning of the expression, the DSS stated that any "abnormality" must be tested against normal procedures in the employment in question' and that 'the abnormality has to be in the act of making payments and not in the payments themselves'.

It is understood that, in practice, a compliance officer will look at past pay practices within the organisation itself, within the particular sector of industry or commerce in which the organisation operates, and within other similar organisations in the locality but, given that the employment to which *Reg 30* relates is the 'employment in respect of which the earnings are paid', that approach is surely incorrect. How other employees in the same organisation, industrial sector or locality are paid would seem to be irrelevant. The only legitimate comparison would seem to be a comparison between the contractually correct payment procedure (as established by any written contract of service or by past practice) as regards the individual concerned and the payment procedure which is in fact being followed. See HM Revenue and Customs National Insurance Manual NIM09600 which, as well as confirming the above view, states that *Reg 30* directives are therefore very rare.

The DSS took the view that, as dividends and payments in kind are not EARNINGS FROM EMPLOYMENT: GENERAL 29 for contribution purposes, the substitution of dividends or payments in kind for remuneration which would be earnings for contribution purposes cannot be regarded as an abnormal pay practice for the purposes of *Social Security (Contributions) Regulations 2001, SI 2001/1004, Reg 30*. This is consistent with more recent announcements in respect of payments by intermediaries, where HMRC has taken the view that payment of dividends by a one-man personal service company is not classed as payment of remuneration.

Appeal and review

[8.20] It would seem that, if an appeal against a decision on the question of whether or not a particular pay practice was abnormal for the employment in respect of which earnings had been paid were to be taken before the Tribunal, the Tribunal would ask itself whether, in the light of such evidence as had been offered of normal procedures in the employment in question, any reasonable person could have come to the conclusion arrived at by HM Revenue and Customs, or an officer of HM Revenue and Customs whether by that officer's own volition or on application by the employer or employee. An affirmative answer would then conclude the matter. Accordingly, there would seem to be little scope for challenging a decision of this kind. See APPEALS AND REVIEWS 9.

Liability for additional contributions

[8.21] *Social Security (Contributions) Regulations 2001, SI 2001/1004, Reg 30* is silent on the question of who is to bear any additional contribution burden which arises as a result of a determination under those powers. Where, however, the under-deduction can be shown to have occurred by reason of an error made in good faith, there would appear to be no grounds on which to prohibit recovery of primary contributions from the employed earner to whom they relate, provided the recovery rules are properly observed (see **21.19** COLLECTION). [*SI 2001/1004, Sch 4 para 7*]. The April 1981 version of DSS Leaflet NI 35 (now superseded) bore this out by stating that, in the application of what is now *Reg 30* to abnormal pay practices concerning company directors, 'in many cases' (ie not all) 'the company will not be entitled to deduct from the director's earnings his share of arrears to be paid' (page 5). Alternatively, HMRC might make direct collection arrangements with the employee.

Irregular or unequal payments

[8.22] In addition to any anti-avoidance action which may be taken under *Reg 30*, HM Revenue and Customs (or an officer of HM Revenue and Customs) may, where it or he is satisfied as to the existence of any practice in respect of the payment of earnings whereby the incidence of Class 1 contributions is *avoided or reduced by means of irregular or unequal payments*, give directions for securing that such contributions are payable as if that practice were not followed. [*Social Security (Contributions) Regulations 2001, SI 2001/1004, Reg 31*, as amended by *Social Security Contributions (Amendment No 3) Regulations 2002, SI 2002/2366, Reg 6*].

Reg 31 directions are often made in situations where employees are remunerated largely by means of irregular or unequal commission payments and basic remuneration (if any) is at only a low level.

These powers now exercisable by HM Revenue and Customs, or an officer of HM Revenue and Customs, were previously the remit of the Secretary of State for Social Security. [*SSC(TF)A 1999, s 1(2), Sch 2*].

With effect from 8 October 2002, not only may an officer of HM Revenue and Customs decide any such question of his own volition, but he must do so if so requested either by the earner or by the secondary contributor. [*Social Security (Contributions) Regulations 2001, SI 2001/1004, Reg 30(2)*, as amended by *Social Security Contributions (Amendment No 3) Regulations 2002, SI 2002/2366, Reg 6*].

Lack of intent to avoid of no relevance

[8.23] *Reg 31* is of extremely wide application in that, in order to justify the giving of a direction, HM Revenue and Customs (or an officer of HM Revenue and Customs) needs merely to demonstrate that earnings amenable to payment at regular intervals or in equal amounts would, in the latter case, have attracted a greater contribution liability than they did, in fact, attract. The motive for the irregularity or inequality of the payments is of no consequence and, even where it is unrelated to the consequential reduction or avoidance of contributions, will be disregarded.

Non-retrospective effect

[8.24] The tenses of the verbs formerly used in *Reg 31* suggested that a direction made under its provisions was of only current and future effect and this was specifically confirmed by the April 1981 version of DSS Leaflet NI 35 (now superseded) which stated that a direction under what is now *Reg 31* 'cannot be applied retrospectively' (page 5). The matter was unequivocally confirmed by new *Reg 31(2)(a), as inserted by Social Security (Contributions) (Amendment No 3) Regulations 2002, SI 2002/2366, Reg 6*, with effect from 8 October 2002.

Application

[8.25] Despite the fact that *Reg 31* (negation of practices avoiding liability) may not be applied with retrospective effect, it is nevertheless of far greater use for anti-avoidance purposes than is *Reg 30* (negation of abnormal pay practices). This is not due merely to the fact that the area of avoidance activity which will justify its use is far wider than that of *Reg 30* but to the fact that the power it grants is that of a 'direction' rather than a 'determination of a question'. Administratively, the former merely requires the writing of a letter, whereas the latter will normally require a formal inquiry at which the parties involved may make representations, call witnesses etc and a formal decision. It is interesting that the 2001 consolidated form of *Reg 31* inserted for the first time the following sentence at the conclusion of *Reg 31* that states:

> The provision of this regulation does not limit the operation of regulation 30.

A typical letter that might be received is as follows:

Example Letter

Dear . . .

At a recent visit to you, an officer found that your pay practice in respect of (a)/(b). . . . . is one which results in liability for National Insurance contributions (NICs) being reduced or avoided by means of irregular or unequal payments.

Although NICs are being paid in accordance with Social Security legislation, where such a pay practice exists HM Revenue and Customs may direct what the earnings period shall be. The purpose of this letter is to notify you that, in order to ensure liability for NICs is commensurate with the total earnings paid, it is our intention to invoke the provisions of Regulation 31 of the Social Security (Contributions) Regulations 2001. This would mean that, with effect from (c) . . . . NICs for (a)/(b). . . . . should be calculated using a (d). . . . . earnings period.

You will receive formal notification of this in 28 days. In the meantime, if you think there are reasons why the earnings period should not be changed, please let me know within 28 days of the date of this letter. If I do not hear from you within that period I will take it that you accept our proposal and the Direction will be issued.

A similar letter has been sent to (a)/(b). . . . .

Notes	Explanation
(a)	insert name of employee
(b)	use 'the employees on the enclosed list', if more than one employee is involved
(c)	insert date 28 days from date of letter
(d)	insert period-monthly, quarterly etc

It will be noted that *Reg 31* contains no *de minimis* amount which avoided contribution liability must exceed before a direction may be made. HM Revenue and Customs National Insurance Manual NIM09650 states that such a directive will not normally be issued where the current pay practice gives a shortfall of contributions of less than £250 per year. See also HM Revenue and Customs National Insurance Manual NIM09653–NIM09680.

A direction under *Reg 31* almost inevitably takes the form of an earnings period rule designed to frustrate the particular avoidance arrangement which gave rise to the direction (see EARNINGS PERIODS 34). Invariably, although not inevitably, the direction is to apply an annual earnings period.

Appeals

[8.26] *Reg 31* itself contains no provision for appeal against a direction made within its terms but, as such a direction must necessarily 'relate to a person's contributions', any question arising in connection with it must inevitably be capable of being the subject of an appealable decision (see 9 APPEALS AND REVIEWS). From 8 October 2002 the matter was put beyond doubt by new *Reg 155A (2)(c)* inserted by the *Social Security (Contributions) (Amendment No 3) Regulations 2002, Reg 18*.

General Anti-Abuse Rule (GAAR)

[8.27] *Finance Act 2013, ss 206-207* enabled a panel of appointed experts (comprising tax experts, not necessarily lawyers and excluding representatives of HMRC) to decide whether arrangements entered into with a view to obtaining a tax advantage are 'abusive', ie, if the arrangements 'cannot reasonably be regarded as a reasonable course of action in relation to the relevant tax provisions, having regard to all the circumstances' (this is known as the 'double reasonableness test'). If arrangements are found to be 'abusive' as above defined, any tax advantage which would otherwise result therefrom may be counteracted by 'just and reasonable' adjustments (*Finance Act 2013, s 209*).

National Insurance Contributions Act 2014, ss 10–11 extended the operation of the GAAR mutatis mutandis to 'abusive' arrangements intended to achieve a National Insurance contributions advantage ('abusive' as defined above), and counteraction is again by way of just and reasonable adjustment. The Treasury may modify the application of the GAAR in relation to National Insurance contributions by regulations. These provisions apply from 13 March 2014.

The government issued a discussion document on 29 January 2015 entitled 'Strengthening sanctions for tax avoidance', asking whether and how to introduce specific penalties for cases where the GAAR applies. When the GAAR was in genesis, GAAR-specific penalties were mooted but the possibility was deferred because it was accepted that taxpayers would need time to familiarise themselves with the GAAR. Given that there has, at the time of writing (2016–17 Annual), been not a single referral to the GAAR Panel, and therefore no counteraction notices, the discussion of penalties seems premature to many.

Nevertheless, a further consultation on possible penalties in respect of GAAR adjustments having been published on 22 July 2015, *FA 2016* has indeed introduced new penalty provisions. The new rules in *Finance Act 2013, Pt 5, s 212A (FA 2013)* levy a penalty at the rate of 60% of the 'counteracted advantage' (defined in a new *FA 2013, Sch 43C*), so as to deter taxpayers from adopting aggressive tax and NICs avoidance arrangements. *Finance Act 2016*, in accordance with convention, did not make equivalent changes to NIC legislation.

The first opinion of the GAAR panel was issued on 18 July 2017. It concerned the case where a company wished to reward two of its key employees, Mr X and Mrs Y who were also the only directors of the company, in gold bullion. The arrangement also involved the use of an Employee Benefit Trust (EBT). The reward was structured in the following way: a purchase of gold for the employees was funded by the company; that gold was immediately sold by the employees; the company's liability to pay the third-party gold supplier was settled by the employees in return for a director's loan account credit in favour of the employees; in connection with the purchase of the gold a long-term obligation was created under which the employees were required in the future to pay to the trustees of the EBT an amount at least equal to the purchase price of the gold (plus indexation). The panel found that the entering into and carrying out of the tax arrangements was not a 'reasonable course of action in relation to the relevant tax provisions'. Mr X and Mrs Y will subsequently be denied the tax and NICs advantages that they were seeking, and the company denied a corporation tax deduction.

Since this first opinion, several more have followed in fairly quick succession given the elapsed time to the publication of the first opinion.

The second opinion issued on 9 November 2017 concerned a very similar arrangement to that in the first opinion. Unsurprisingly, the outcome was the same.

A third opinion was issued on 26 January 2018 regarding employee rewards using multiple tripartite arrangements outlined as follows:

> '3.1. ABC Ltd acknowledges the arrangements are put in place to "motivate and incentivise employees".
>
> 3.2. On 8 November 2013 ABC Ltd enters into two deeds of covenant with Trustee under each of which ABC Ltd covenants to pay about £100,000 to Trustee to be held on trust for ABC Ltd.
>
> 3.3. On 11 November 2013 the EFRB is established.
>
> 3.4. On 12 November 2013 an initial sub-fund and a subsequent sub-fund are created within the EFRB. The beneficiaries of the subsequent sub-fund are Mr D and Mr E and their respective relatives and dependents.
>
> 3.5. On 26 November 2013 the benefit of the two 8 November covenants, together with £2,000 from ABC Ltd, is contributed to the EFRB's initial sub-fund and subsequent sub-fund in the ratio of 1:99.
>
> 3.6. On 27 November 2013 ABC Ltd determines the quantum of employee awards and allocates about £100,000 to each of Mr D and Mr E.

3.7. On 28 November 2013 a first tripartite deed is entered into under which:

a) ABC Ltd undertakes to pay Accommodation Party about £100,000;
b) Accommodation Party undertakes to pay Mr D about £100,000; and
c) Mr D undertakes to pay ABC Ltd about £100,000.

3.8. On 2 December 2013 a second tripartite deed is entered into under which:

a) Accommodation Party is released from its obligation to pay Mr D about £100,000;
b) ABC Ltd is released from its obligation to pay Accommodation Party about £100,000; and
c) ABC Ltd is obliged to pay Mr D about £100,000.

3.9. On 3 December 2013 a third tripartite deed is entered into under which:

a) ABC Ltd is released from its obligation to pay Trustee about £100,000 under the 8 November deed of covenant;
b) Mr D's obligation to pay about £100,000 to ABC Ltd under the first tripartite deed is satisfied by Mr D procuring ABC Ltd's release from its obligation to pay Trustee under the 8 November deed of covenant; and
c) Mr D is obligated to pay Trustee (in its capacity as trustee of the EFRB) about £100,000.

3.10. As at 3 December 2013 ABC Ltd owes Mr D about £100,000, this amount is credited to Mr D's loan account with ABC Ltd.

3.11. In the case of each of the steps in 3.7 to 3.10 above relating to Mr D, there are mirror arrangements in relation to Mr E.

3.12. On 6 December 2013 under an instrument of transposition the assets of the sub-funds are organised so the initial sub-fund holds £2,000 cash and the subsequent sub-fund the obligations owed by Mr D and Mr E.

3.13. As at 6 December 2013 Mr D and Mr E each owe the EFRB about £100,000. The debts are due in 2033 (with a right for the debtor to pay early) and carry no interest (but with the EFRB trustee having the right to impose an obligation to pay interest at the higher of a commercial rate or the official rate).'

Although there is nothing abnormal in setting up an EFRB, the panel found that it was:

> 'abnormal and contrived for an employer to arrange long term funding of an employee trust and the provision of money to employees through the mechanism of the deeds of covenant, assignment of the benefit of these covenants and the three sets of tripartite deeds adopted in this case.'

The fourth (and so far last) opinion was issued on 28 February 2018. This has very similar arrangements to those in the third opinion viz.

> '3.1. BCD Ltd adopted the arrangements as an incentivisation and reward arrangement for its key employees.
>
> 3.2. On 8 July 2013 the EFRB is established with an initial £100 contribution from BCD Ltd.
>
> 3.3. On 8 July 2013 an Initial Sub Fund and a Conventional Sub Fund are created within the EFRB and £5 is appointed to each.
>
> 3.4. On 8 July 2013 BCD Ltd signs two deeds of covenant that provide for a series of several BCD Ltd covenants relating to accounting periods 2013 to 2022. Each

deed of covenant provides for BCD Ltd to make a payment to the EFRB trustee in respect of the relevant accounting period of an unspecified percentage of up to 100 per cent of the estimated profits for that accounting period. As far as we can see, even at the time estimated profits for a relevant accounting period are determined, the amount of the payment is not capable of being calculated under the terms of the deeds of covenant. The trustee is to hold each payment it receives on trust for the Initial Sub Fund and Conventional Sub Fund in the ratio 0.5:99.5 (the "Sub Fund Trusts").

3.5. On 8 July 2013 BCD Ltd and Trustee sign a deed of agreement with each of Mr J and Mr K. Each agreement provides that:

a) BCD Ltd makes an interest free loan repayable on demand to Mr J and Mr K respectively shortly before the end of each of the accounting periods 2013 to 2022. The loan amount for the relevant accounting period is an unspecified percentage of up to 100 per cent of the estimated profits for that accounting period. As far as we can see, even at the time estimated profits for a relevant accounting period are determined, the amount of the loan is not capable of being calculated under the terms of the deeds of agreement;
b) BCD Ltd enters into future deeds of covenant under which it covenants to pay an amount equal to each loan once made to the Trustee, the Trustee to hold the benefit of the covenant for BCD Ltd;
c) BCD Ltd assigns to the EFRB trustee its beneficial interest in the future deeds of covenant, the benefit to be held on the Sub Fund Trusts;
d) BCD Ltd, Trustee and Mr J and Mr K respectively, and for each accounting period, enter into future tripartite deeds the future result of those deeds is intended to be that Mr J and Mr K incur obligations to the EFRB trustee equivalent to their obligations under the loans at a), Mr J's and Mr K's loans at a) are treated as repaid, and BCD Ltd's obligations under b) are released.

3.6. On 30 September 2013 BCD Ltd enters into a loan agreement with Mr J under which it agrees to advance about £120,000. The loan is in part drawn down on 1 October 2013, the balance relating primarily to an amount already owing on Mr J's company loan account. The loan is interest free and repayable on demand.

3.7. On 30 September 2013 BCD Ltd enters into a loan agreement with Mr K under which it agrees to advance about £100,000. The loan is drawn down on 1 October 2013. The loan is interest free and repayable on demand.

3.8. On 11 November 2013 BCD Ltd enters into two deeds of covenant under one of which BCD Ltd covenants to pay about £120,000 and under the other about £100,000 to Trustee, to be held on trust for BCD Ltd.

3.9. On 12 November 2013 the benefit of the two 11 November covenants is contributed by BCD Ltd to Trustee as trustee of the Sub Fund Trusts.

3.10. On 22 January 2014 two tripartite deeds are entered under which:

a) Mr J's obligation to pay about £120,000 to BCD Ltd under his loan agreement is treated as having been satisfied in full;
b) Mr J undertakes an equivalent obligation to the EFRB trustee;
c) Mr K's obligation to pay about £100,000 to BCD Ltd under his loan agreement is treated as having been satisfied in full;
d) Mr K undertakes an equivalent obligation to the EFRB trustee;
e) the EFRB trustee holds the debt claims for the Sub Fund Trusts; and
f) BCD Ltd is released from its obligation to pay about £220,000 under the two 11 November deeds of covenant.'

Accordingly, the panel found that the entering into and carrying out of the tax arrangements was not a 'reasonable course of action in relation to the relevant tax provisions'.

Key Points regarding anti-avoidance

[8.28] Points to consider are as follows.

- Self-employed labour may be used by a company instead of employees thereby avoiding secondary Class 1 contributions but, as in the construction industry, re-categorisation may be imposed leading to imposition of Class 1 NICs, interest and penalties. Companies that dispense with staff and then rehire them under the guise of 'self-employment' will increasingly have to justify their actions as being a non-avoidance measure.
- Where payments in kind are manipulated so that they represent a quid pro quo for salary payments to the employee as a means of NICs avoidance, HMRC will attack.
- Whilst personal service companies and managed service companies are affected by the measures in *FA 2007, Sch 3* other companies can still pay dividends instead of earnings thereby avoiding NICs (but see *HM Revenue and Customs v P A Holdings Ltd* [2011] EWCA Civ 1414, 30 November 2011, CA. and 29 EARNINGS FROM EMPLOYMENT-GENERAL.
- Back-dated anti-avoidance provisions applying to employment-related securities are limited to just that form of income and cannot be used to combat other schemes (ie not involving securities) that may arise.
- The GAAR created by *Finance Act 2013* to counter tax abuses was extended to NIC arrangements by *NICA 2014* with effect from 13 March 2014, but the new 60% GAAR penalty introduced by *FA 2016* does not extend to NICs that are the subject of a counteraction notice.

9

Appeals and Reviews

Cross-references. See **2.4** ADMINISTRATION in earlier editions for administrative (rather than judicial) status also enjoyed by the Secretary of State for Work and Pensions.

Other Sources. Tolley's National Insurance Brief, January 1997, page 7; Tolley's Practical NIC, May 1999, page 33; HMRC *Appeals reviews and tribunals guidance* (ARTG) manual and *Decisions and Appeals for National Insurance Contributions and Statutory Payments* (DANSP) manual; Leaflet 'Tax Appeals' (Department of Constitutional Affairs).

Introduction to appeals and reviews

[9.1] In pre-1999 editions of this work it had been necessary to explain that there was, in the Social Security Acts, no provision for appeals in connection with contribution matters and that the appellate bodies which operated in connection with State benefits had no jurisdiction so far as the contribution side of the State scheme was concerned. Although there was *effectively* an appeal procedure in connection with contributions it was not widely known or understood and, if described under its correct title, would not immediately have been recognised as such. (Indeed, only 1,500 or so persons a year employed the procedure, including the courts and insurance officers.)

However, with the transfer of the former Contributions Agency to the then Inland Revenue with effect from 1 April 1999 and the transfer of contributions policy functions from the then Department of Social Security to the Treasury from the same date, the opportunity was taken to modernise the appeals system, such as it was. It is now brought almost entirely into line with those procedures encountered in dealing with other imposts (and indeed statutory payment matters related to SSP, SMP, etc) for which HM Revenue and Customs is responsible. Prior to 1 April 2009, NIC appeals were generally heard by the General and Special Commissioners. From 1 April 2009, the Tax Tribunals hear NIC appeals, although disagreements about child benefit or maternity allowance, administered by HMRC, fall under the ambit of the Social Entitlement Chamber of the Tribunals Service.

Until 1 April 2009 appeals in respect of Home Responsibilities Protection (now carer's credit) and also contracting-out decisions were also heard through the social security appeals route instead. For details of the latter, and also the pre-1999 system of NIC appeals, see the 2008–09 and earlier editions of this work. From November 2008, such appeals under the social security appeals route are heard by the Social Entitlement Chamber of the First-Tier Tribunal. Such appeals are governed by *The Tribunal Procedure (First-tier Tribunal) (Social Entitlement Chamber) Rules 2008, SI 2008/2685* rather than *The Tribunal Procedure (First-tier Tribunal) (Tax Chamber) Rules 2009, SI 2009/273* so whilst many of the procedures set out in this chapter in relation to mainstream HMRC decisions are identical or similar, there are certainly some minor differences.

The fact that there remain some small differences, and the previous absence of a formal appeal system in relation to contributions, is explained by the fact that the Social Security Acts (unlike the Taxes Acts) make no provision for formal assessments of their levies—other than CLASS 4 CONTRIBUTIONS **20**, for appeals against which see **9.23** below. The liability is either self-assessed at a fixed rate or employer-assessed by reference to earnings paid (see CLASS 1 CONTRIBUTIONS **15**, CLASS 2 CONTRIBUTIONS **18**) or by reference in the case of Class 1A to cars, fuel and other benefits in kind made available to employees (see CLASS 1A CONTRIBUTIONS **16**).

The new system has operated from 1 April 1999 and is largely regulated by *Social Security Contributions (Transfer of Functions, etc) Act 1999* and *Social Security Contributions (Decisions and Appeals) Regulations 1999 (SI 1999/1027)*, in a process now founded on the *Tribunals, Courts and Enforcement Act 2007*.

First-tier and Upper Tribunals

[9.2] From 1 April 2009 appeal reforms came into effect covering both direct and indirect taxes. NICs are categorised as direct taxes under the auspices of the *TCEA 2007*. This enabling Act is supplemented by various rules and regulations, including principally the *Tribunal Procedure (First-tier Tribunal) (Tax Chamber) Rules 2009, SI 2009/273* and the *Tribunal Procedure (Upper Tribunal) Rules 2008, SI 2008/2698*. The General Commissioners were abolished with effect from 1 April 2009 – *Tribunals, Courts and Enforcement*

Act 2007, Schedule 23, Part 1; *Tribunals, Courts and Enforcement Act 2007 (Commencement No 6 and Transitional Provisions) Order 2008, SI 2008/2696*. Time limits which had already started will continue to run and all appeals made on and after 1 April 2009 will be to the Tribunals Service (see below). Cases remitted by a court on or after 1 April 2009 will also be remitted to the Tribunals Service.

From 1 April 2009, the Tax Chamber of the Tribunals Service is headed by a Senior President and has its own judiciary, Rules of Procedure and its own location for processing direct tax appeals. The Tribunals Service (an agency of the Ministry of Justice), which merged with HM Courts Service (HMCS) on 1 April 2011 to form HM Courts and Tribunal Service, is independent of HM Revenue and Customs, who previously controlled listing and other aspects of case management in the former General Commissioners system, which many outside observers always doubted was sufficiently distanced from HM Revenue and Customs. This new Central Processing Centre (CPC) for direct tax appeals is now situated at Tribunals Service, Tax, 4th Floor, 54 Hagley Rd, Birmingham B16 6TZ (tel: 0300 123 1024, email: taxappeals@hmcts.gsi.gov.uk, mail should be addressed to PO Box 16972 at the above address), where specialist tax/NIC appeals work is dealt with by dedicated tax appeals staff. There is a network of 130 hearing centres across the country and the facility for additional private hearings. In cases of complex hearings (see **9.13**) there are limited locations for hearings (the major centres are in Birmingham, London, Manchester, Belfast and Edinburgh).

Appeal notices must now be sent directly to the Tribunals Service by the appellant rather than to HM Revenue and Customs. There are four procedural tracks depending on the complexity of the appeal (see **9.13**) and there is a costs regime that did not apply in the days of the General Commissioners.

Members of the judiciary will work at the CPC in order to give judicial direction where required and manage cases appropriately. There are also full-time, tax-dedicated registrars at the CPC, who carry out quasi-judicial functions, eg categorise cases received at the CPC into tracks, identify tax cases which are complex (and therefore eligible to enter the costs regime) and bring these to the attention of the judiciary for a decision and establish liaison with the Upper Tribunal regarding those rare cases which start at that court, or when there is an appeal to it from the First-tier Tax Tribunal.

The route of appeal from the First-tier Tax Tribunal is to the Upper Tribunal, which is a superior court of record akin to the High Court. Appeal to the Upper Tribunal is on a point of law only, and with permission of the First-tier Tax Tribunal or the Upper Tribunal. The exception to this will be those extremely rare cases which start in the Upper Tribunal, where onward appeals will be to the Court of Appeal or the Court of Session in Scotland. Any of the tribunals or courts might currently make a referral when appropriate to the Court of Justice of the European Union. The ultimate court of appeal is now the Supreme Court (which may also refer a matter to the CJEU for clarification of the interpretation of relevant EU law for as long as the UK remains a signatory to the relevant *Treaty on the Functioning of the European Union*).

Composition of Tribunals

[9.3] In all there are six Chambers in the First-tier Tribunal, as follows:

- Social Entitlement;
- Health, Education and Social Care;
- War Pensions and Armed Forces Compensation;
- Tax and Chancery (formerly Taxation);
- Land, Property and Housing; and
- General Regulatory.

The Social Entitlement Chamber handles appeals about state benefits, tax credits and related matters.

There are three Upper Tribunal Chambers, as follows:

- Administrative Appeals;
- Lands; and
- Tax and Chancery (formerly Finance and Tax).

The remainder of this chapter deals with:

- Current procedure for appeals to the Tax Chamber of the Tribunals Service (**9.9** to **9.22**).
- Disputes concerning Class 4 contributions (**9.23**).

Decisions of officers of HM Revenue and Customs

[9.4] Where a contributor or his employer is faced with a demand for payment which is considered to be wrong or excessive the matter will first be considered informally. If the dispute cannot be resolved in this way, it will then be for an officer of HM Revenue and Customs to issue a formal 'decision' under *Social Security Contributions (Transfer of Functions, etc) Act 1999 (SSC(TF)A 1999), s 8*.

The formal decision is then appealable (see **9.9** below) in much the same way as an old style tax assessment or an amendment to a self-assessment, and is made to the office that issued the decision. See *Siwek v IRC* [2004] STC (SCD) 493; *Siwek Ltd v IRC (No 2)* [2005] STC (SCD) 163. A decision as to the availability or amount of an employment allowance is also appealable.

The Tribunal Procedure Committee (TPC) has set out a number of rules that govern the operation of the Tribunal system as well as specific rules for the area of taxation. Most appeals including NICs appeals against HMRC decisions, will be, in the first instance, to the First-tier Tax Tribunal. The initial appeal against a decision by HMRC will have been received by them within 30 days of their decision and if the appellant and HMRC have failed to agree or no review has been requested or offered (*The Tribunal Procedure (First-tier Tribunal) (Tax Chamber) Rules 2009, SI 2009/273, rules 25 and 26*) – see **9.9** and **9.10**). Any HMRC internal review will be conducted by someone else in the HMRC's Business Unit apart from the initial caseworker. A decision will normally be made, after considering representations, within 45 days or some longer period as may be agreed between the parties. In cases where the appeal was made before 1 April 2009 and the review option was exercised before 1 April 2010 then the review period was 90 days and not 45 days subject to a longer period by agreement. If, having exhausted these options, an appeal is being made against the decision by HMRC it must be notified in writing to the Tax Tribunal situated in Birmingham within 30 days of receiving the reviewing officer's decision letter. The Tax Tribunal will then manage the case by discussing it with the parties to the dispute. See Appeal to First-tier Tax Tribunal form in **9.10** below.

The subject matter of a decision

[9.5] An officer may decide:

(a) whether a person is or was an earner and, if he is or was, in which category of earners he should be included (see CATEGORISATION **14**);

(b) whether a person is or was employed in employed earner's employment for industrial injuries purposes (*Social Security Contributions and Benefits Act 1992 (SSCBA 1992), Part V*);

(c) whether a person is or was liable to pay any contributions of any class and the amount of the liability;

(d) whether a person is or was entitled to pay contributions, notwithstanding that there is no liability to pay, eg, payment of voluntary contributions (see CLASS 3 CONTRIBUTIONS **19**);

(e) whether contributions of a particular class have been paid for any period;

(f) from 6 April 2014, whether a person is or was entitled to claim an employment allowance under *National Insurance Contributions Act 2014 (NICA 2014), s 4*;

(g) from the same date, whether a person is or was entitled to a repayment under the employment allowance rules, and if so, the amount of the repayment;

(h) on any issue in connection with statutory payments, including decisions that fall to be made under regulations under *Employment Act 2002, s 7*;

Note: the shorthand term used here of 'statutory payments', in the context of the regulations on decisions and appeals (*SI 1999/1027*), has included statutory sick pay (SSP) and statutory maternity pay (SMP) from the introduction of the regulations in 1999. Statutory adoption pay (SAP) and statutory paternity pay (SPP) were added when the benefits were introduced on 7 January 2003 (by *SI 2002/3120*). References to SPP were amended to refer to ordinary SPP (OSPP) and additional SPP (ASPP) from 14 November 2010 (by *SI 2010/2451*), when a mother was first allowed to transfer part of her maternity leave and pay to the father. With the introduction of statutory shared parental pay (ShPP) by *Children and Families Act 2014, s 119*, that right was extended, with fathers becoming entitled to SPP or ShPP. The concept of ShPP was brought into the list of topics upon which decisions might be made with effect from 5 March 2015, while the references to OSPP and ASPP reverted to the simple SPP from 5 April

2015 [*SI 2015/174, Reg 2*], except in relation to decisions and appeals about OSPP and ASPP entitlement already in process at the date of change [*SI 2015/174, Reg 3*.]

(i) on matters concerning the issue or content of any notice under *Social Security Administration Act 1992 (SSAA 1992), s 121C* (notices of company officer's personal liability for unpaid contributions);

(j) any issue arising under *Jobseekers Act 1995, s 27* (Back To Work schemes for long-term unemployed);

(k) whether to give or withdraw approval or wording for the transfer to the employee of the employer's Class 1 liability in respect of certain unapproved share options;

(l) whether a person is liable to a penalty;

(m) the amount of penalty;

(n) other issues as may be prescribed by regulations made by the Commissioners for HM Revenue and Customs.

[*Social Security Contributions (Transfer of Functions, etc) Act 1999, s 8(1)*; as amended by *Employment Act 2002, s 9*, brought into effect by *SI 2005/2286, NICA 2014, s 6(1)* and *Children and Families Act 2014, s 26, Sch 7*, commenced by *SI 2014/1640, Art 5*.]

Following the transfer from 6 April 2015 of Class 2 into the income tax self-assessment regime alongside Class 4, it is now specifically provided that no decision on compulsory Class 2 contributions under *SSCBA 1992, s 11(2)* may be made under categories (c) or (e) above if the contributor concerned has appealed under *Taxes Management Act 1970 (TMA 1970), Part 5* in relation to the issue, or still has the right to such an appeal, or might be able to make such an appeal in the future.

[*Social Security Contributions (Transfer of Functions, etc) Act 1999, s 8(1A)*; as inserted by *National Insurance Contributions Act 2015 (NICA 2015), Sch 1*, para 25.]

Categories (c) and (e) above have since 1999 excluded decisions relating to Class 4 contributions which have, because they are invariably collected along with income tax, always been dealt with under tax appeal procedures. The addition of Class 2 to the exclusions in April 2015 follows logically the Class 4 treatment.

[*Social Security Contributions (Transfer of Functions, etc) Act 1999, s 8(2)*.]

Issues under (l) above have been prescribed from 8 October 2002 (except where stated to the contrary), as follows:

(o) whether a notice should be given under *Reg 3(2B)* and if so the terms of such notice;

(p) whether a notice given under *Reg 3(2B)* should cease to have effect;

(q) whether a direction should be given under *Reg 31* and if so the terms of the direction;

(r) whether the condition in *Reg 50(2)* is satisfied;

(s) whether late applications under *Reg 52(8)*, *Reg 54(3)* or *Reg 55(3)* for the refund of (respectively) contributions generally, Class 1 contributions paid at the wrong rate or Class 1A contributions should be admitted;

(t) whether, where a secondary contributor has failed to pay primary contributions that failure was with the consent or connivance of the primary contributor, as is mentioned in *Reg 60*;
(u) whether the condition in *Reg 61(2)* is satisfied;
(v) whether in the case of Class 2 contributions remaining unpaid at the due date, the reason for non-payment is the contributor's ignorance or error, and if so whether that is due to failure to exercise due care and diligence (*Reg 65(2)*);
(w) whether the reason for non-payment of Class 3 within the prescribed period is the contributor's ignorance or error, and if so whether that is due to failure to exercise due care and diligence (*Reg 65(3)*);
(x) whether the reason for non-payment of Class 3 within two years of the end of the year to which the contributions relate is the contributor's ignorance or error, and if so whether that is due to failure to exercise due care and diligence (*Reg 65(4)*);
(y) whether a late application under *Reg 110(3)* for the return of a special Class 4 contribution should be admitted;
(z) whether a contribution (other than a Class 4 contribution) has been paid in error (*Reg 52(1)(a)*);
(aa) whether there has been a payment of contributions in excess of the amount specified in *Reg 21* (*Reg 52(1)(b)*);
(ab) whether certain delays mentioned in the now superseded *National Insurance (Contributions) Regulations 1969* were reasonable, etc;
(ac) whether the delay in making payment of primary Class 1 contributions was with neither with the consent nor the connivance of the primary contributor (*Social Security (Crediting and Treatment of Contributions, and National Insurance Numbers) Regulations 2001, Reg 5*);
(ad) whether in the case of a contribution paid after the due date, the failure was due to ignorance or error and not failure to exercise due care and diligence (*Social Security (Crediting and Treatment of Contributions, and National Insurance Numbers) Regulations 2001, Reg 6*);
(ae) with effect from 6 August 2007, whether the circumstances are such that the managed service company provisions (see **40.20** INTERMEDIARIES) apply.

[*Contributions Regs, Reg 155A*, inserted by *Social Security (Contributions) (Amendment No 3) Regulations 2002, SI 2002/2366, Reg 18*, and amended by *Social Security Contributions (Managed Service Companies) Regs 2007, SI 2007/2070, Reg 3(6)*].

Items (c) and (e) above do not include decisions relating to Class 4 contributions which have, because they are invariably collected along with income tax, always been dealt with under tax appeal procedures. [*SSC(TF)A 1999, s 8(2)*].

Item (f) does not extend to any decision as to the making of subordinate legislation since policy for statutory payments (ie, SSP, SMP, SAP, SPP or ShPP) remains with the Secretary of State for Work and Pensions, even though it is now administered by HM Revenue and Customs. Nor does it extend to any decision as to whether the liability to make a statutory payment is that of HM Revenue and Customs or the employer. [*SSC(TF)A 1999, s 8(3)*, as amended for the introduction of ShPP by *Children and Families Act 2014, s 126, Sch 7*, commenced by *SI 2014/1640, Art 5*.]

HM Revenue and Customs may make regulations with regard to the making of decisions and officers may direct that they shall have the assistance of an 'expert' where it appears that a question of fact requires special expertise. [*SSC(TF)A 1999, s 9(1)(2)*].

'Expert' means a person appearing to the officer of HM Revenue and Customs to have knowledge or experience which would be relevant in determining the question of fact. [*SSC(TF)A 1999, s 9(3)*].

HM Revenue and Customs may make regulations enabling decisions under *section 8* to be varied or superseded. [*SSC(TF)A 1999, s 10*].

The principal regulations made are the *Social Security Contributions (Decisions and Appeals) Regulations 1999, SI 1999/1027*, to which reference is made below.

A decision must be made to the best of the officer's information and belief and must state the name of every person in respect of whom it is made, and:

- the date from which it has effect, or
- the period for which it has effect.

[*SI 1999/1027, Reg 3(1)*.]

[*Social Security Contributions (Decisions and Appeals) Regulations 1999, Reg 3(1)*].

In *Netherlane Ltd v York* [2005] STC SCD 305, an IR35 case, a notice of appeal was not sent to a company (NPI) that was named in the decision and therefore the decision was tantamount to being invalid. The Special Commissioner found that the reference to persons named in *Reg 3(1)* had to be construed as persons affected by the notice who were named in it. Whilst the company NPI, which was the customer for whom the IT services were provided, might have been affected by the decision if regulations applied legally, NPI was in the same position whether or not it was advised of the decision.

An officer may entrust responsibility for completing procedures to some other officer, whether by means involving the use of a computer or not, including the responsibility for serving the notice on any person named in it. [*SI 1999/1027, Reg 3(2)*.]

Any decision of an officer of the board under *SSC(TF)A 1999, s 8* (initial decisions) or *s 10(1)(b) or (c)* (variation of decisions) in respect of statutory payments that may be taken to a tribunal brings with it the right for both the employee and employer concerned to appeal separately. In the case of other decisions, the person in respect of whom the decision is made and such other person as may be prescribed in regulations have the right of appeal. It is, however, explicitly provided that appeals against personal liability notices issued under *SSAA 1992, s 121C* may only be dealt with under the rules set out in *s 121D*. [*Social Security Contributions (Transfer of Functions, etc) Act 1999, s 11*.] In the case of such a decision, other than one which relates to a person's entitlement to a statutory payment, each person named in the decision has a right to appeal to the First-tier Tribunal. [*SI 1999/1027, Reg 3(3)*, as amended by *Social Security Contributions (Decisions and Appeals) (Amendment) Regulations 2015, SI 2015/174*.]

Giving notice of the decision

[9.6] Notice of a decision must be given to every person named in it or, in the case of a decision relating to entitlement to SSP, SMP, SPP, SAP or ShPP, to the employee and employer concerned. [*SI 1999/1027, Reg 4(1)*, as amended by *Social Security Contributions (Decisions and Appeals) (Amendment) Regulations 2002, SI 2002/3120* and *Social Security Contributions (Decisions and Appeals) (Amendment) Regulations 2015, SI 2015/174*.]

In the case of Class 1 contributions the former Inland Revenue stated in 1999 that the notice would name the employer and each affected employee. Where the number of employees exceeds six, HM Revenue and Customs will seek to agree a representative sample of employees with the employer or the agent and will name only those selected employees (as well as the employer) in the Notice. This is an extra-statutory arrangement, there being no legal basis for the selection of six employees as the number beyond which not to name each case individually.

Where the dispute relates to Class 1A contributions, only the employer is affected as no employee contribution arises. However, whilst there is therefore no obligation on the part of HM Revenue and Customs to name employees in the notice, it will usually do so where the decision concerns the provision of particular cars, fuel or other benefits. Presumably, similar procedures will also apply in the case of disputed Class 1B liability.

In the case of Class 2, Class 3 or Class 4 decisions (the first and last now (after *NICA 2015* reformed Class 2 to treat it in the same way as Class 4) relating only to cases where Classes 2 and 4 are not collected through the self-assessment Tax Return), there will invariably be only one person named in the notice.

Case law

[9.7] In *Westek Ltd v HMRC Commissioners* [2008] STC SCD 169 Sp C 629, a notice of decision sent to the employer had merely referred to 'earnings of employees' without naming the employees in question. W, inter alia, challenged the validity of the notices. The Special Commissioner upheld the view of HMRC that the decisions had been made under *Social Security Contributions (Transfer of Functions, Etc) Act 1999, s 8(1)(c)* and it was only the employer that in the first instance was liable to pay both the primary and the secondary contributions. Accordingly, the notice needed only to name the employer, as it did, and it was therefore only the employer who had to be sent a copy of the decision notice (*Social Security Contributions (Decisions and Appeals) Regs 1999, SI 1999/1027, Reg 4*). It is therefore clear that the undertaking given in 1999 as set out above can no longer be expected to be applied consistently.

In *Lewis (t/a MAL Scaffolding) and Others v HMRC* [2006] STC SCD 253 Sp C 527, the Special Commissioner (Dr Williams, known to have particular expertise in social security and National Insurance matters) himself raised the point that because the National Insurance charge on employed earners is essentially a weekly one, *s 8* notices should perhaps be issued on a weekly basis rather than the annual basis that HM Revenue and Customs does in fact use. The matter did not need to be addressed, because it was held that the individuals in the case were self-employed, but it is a matter that may yet need to be tested in the future.

Parade Park Hotel and Anor v Revenue and Customs Commissioners [2007] STC SCD 430 SpC 599 essentially concerned the employment status of a worker. However, another issue addressed was the technicality of the notice of decision which was made out in the name of the hotel rather than the partners' names being shown. It was held that this did not invalidate the notice – indeed in the case of very large partnerships it would be impossible to list every partner's name on such a document.

Administrative rules

[9.8] The notice must state the date on which it is issued and may be served by post addressed to any person at his usual or last known place of residence or his place of business or employment. Notice to a company may be addressed to its registered office or its principal place of business. [*SI 1999/1027, Reg 4(2)(3).*]

A decision may be varied by an officer of HM Revenue and Customs if he has reason to believe that it was incorrect at the time it was made. Notice of such variation must be given to the same persons and in the same manner as the original decision. [*SI 1999/1027, Reg 5(1)(2).*]

If a decision is under appeal, it may be varied at any time before the Tribunal determines the appeal. [*SI 1999/1027, Reg 5(4)* as amended by the *Transfer of Tribunal Functions and Revenue and Customs Appeals Order 2009, SI 2009/56, Sch 2, para 61.*]

A decision may be made superseding an earlier decision, including a varied decision, which has become inappropriate *for any reason.* A superseding decision will have effect from the date of the change in circumstances which rendered the previous decision (or varied decision) inappropriate. The previous decision ceases to have effect immediately the superseding decision comes into effect. [*SI 1999/1027, Reg 6(1)(2).*]

Decisions are issued on Form DAA1(A) which tells the recipient to let his professional adviser or agent, if he has one, see it. Copies will be issued direct to agents, if known to HMRC to be acting as such. Where copies have to be sent to more than one person, the notes on the face of the notice will be adjusted on each copy to reflect the differing effects of the decision on different categories of people affected, eg where copies are sent to employers and one or more employees. The Notice of Decision also includes a payslip for making payment of the National Insurance contributions in question and will be sent with a letter of explanation which will, in practice, usually be a summary of what has been established in previous correspondence. A personalised guidance note, DAA2 'A Guide to Your Notice of Decision', will also be sent to every recipient.

Example Notice of Decision

HM REVENUE AND CUSTOMS	*NOTICE OF DECISION*
L Ltd	HM Revenue and
10 Any Road	[Address and telephone number of issuing office]
Any Town	
Any County	
AN10 2YZ	

Date of Issue	1 April 2016	*Reference* AB123456C (employee) or 037/X23456 (employer) *Please use this reference if you write or call it will help avoid delay*

National Insurance contributions and statutory payments

My decision is as follows:

1. That L Ltd is liable to pay primary and secondary Class 1 contributions for the period 6 April 2010 to 5 April 2014 in respect of the earnings of Mrs F Smith.
2. The amount that L Ltd is liable to pay in respect of those earnings is £5,490.
3. The amount that L Ltd has paid in respect of those earnings is £4,270.
4. The difference is due to Class 1 contributions on school fees.

A N Other
Officer of HM Revenue and Customs

Notes

General

This Notice of Decision is addressed to you personally as required by law. If you have a professional adviser or agent Please let them see this notice at once.

This notice contains my formal decision. You will find details of how the decision has been reached and additional information in the accompanying letter and/or *DAA2 Guide*, 'A Guide to your Notice of Decision'.

Appeals

If you do not accept this decision please appeal telling us why you think the decision is wrong. The appeal must be made in writing to me within 30 days of the date of issue shown above.

If agreement cannot be reached we will arrange for your appeal and any other appeal to be heard by [an independent tribunal]. See page 4 of the *DAA2 Guide*.

Payment If you accept this decision please pay any outstanding amount of National Insurance contributions due from you using the enclosed payslip. Pay any Statutory Sick Pay or Statutory Maternity Pay to the employee.	**Variation of decision** *A decision is varied when agreement has been reached or the decision is incorrect. See page 6 of the DAA2 Guide.*
	Interest charges on late payment *Interest may be charged on National Insurance Contributions paid late. See page 6 of the DAA2 Guide.*
DAA1(A)	

Appeals against officer's decisions

[9.9] Any person named in a notice of decision, which in the case of decisions relating to entitlement to statutory payments or to liability to Class 1 contributions will usually – see *Westek Ltd v HMRC Commissioners* (9.7) – be both the employee and the employer, has the right of appeal to the tribunals. The same right also extends to personal liability notices issued to company officers in respect of company contribution debts. [*SSC(TF)A 1999, s 11(1)(2)(4); SSAA 1992, s 121D* as inserted by *SSA 1998, s 64*].

Ordinarily, an appeal will be made first to HM Revenue and Customs who should always offer an internal review or who may be asked to undertake a review. The appeal may not be notified to the tribunal while an internal review is under way.

Manner of making an appeal

[9.10] An appeal must be made in writing within 30 days after the date on which the notice of decision was issued, or the result of the internal review was given. The Guide DAA2 contains a tear-off appeal form (DAA3) which may be used if appealing to HM Revenue and Customs but an appeal made in any format in writing and within the specified 30 days is legally valid.

The notice of appeal must specify the grounds of appeal but on hearing by the tribunal it may allow additional grounds, not stated in the notice of appeal, to be put forward if satisfied that the omission was neither wilful nor unreasonable. [*SSC(TF)A 1999, s 12(3)*]. An appeal made direct to the tribunal or notified following an unsuccessful review will be made to the Tribunals Service using the T240 Notice of Appeal (confusingly headed TS TaxAp1) and thereafter all administration is undertaken by the Tribunals Service. See form below. Forms may be downloaded from the Tribunals Service website at hmctsformfinder.justice.gov.uk/HMCTS/GetForm.do?court_forms_id=3015.

The statutory internal review procedure mentioned above was introduced from 1 April 2009 and is a statutory right for appellants, but not compulsory. This internal review by HM Revenue and Customs will, in NIC cases, usually be carried out by someone in the Regional Appeals Unit but the reviewing officer cannot be the advocate at the appeal hearing on the same case. Even if outside the Regional Appeals Unit, the review will always be carried out by someone outside the direct line management of the case-worker or decision-maker.

Where the appellant requests a review, HM Revenue and Customs must issue a letter within 30 days which then constitutes the start of the review period. Where HM Revenue and Customs itself offers a review, the appellant has 30 days to either accept the review offer or notify the appeal to the tribunal. The appellant's letter accepting the review offer constitutes the start of the review period.

Except in 2009 transitional cases, the review period is 45 days unless HM Revenue and Customs requests a longer period. If HM Revenue and Customs requests a longer period and the appellant is minded not to allow a longer period, the original decision stands and must be either accepted or the appeal notified to the tribunal.

Thus, the notifying of an appeal to the tribunal can be summarised as follows:

- within 30 days of the appeal being notified to HM Revenue and Customs provided a review has not been requested nor has an offer from HM Revenue and Customs of a review been accepted;
- within 30 days of the conclusion of a review (*TMA 1970, s 49G(5)(a)*);
- within 30 days of the time by which HM Revenue and Customs should have given notice of the conclusion of their review, but they have not done so (*TMA 1970, s 49G(5)(b)*); or
- within 30 days of the day on which HM Revenue and Customs notified the offer of a review, where the offer is not being accepted (*TMA 1970, s 49H*).

[*TMA 1970, ss 49A-49I* as inserted by *Transfer of Tribunal Functions and Revenue and Customs Appeal Order 2009, SI 2009/56, Sch 1, para 30*.]

T240

Notice of appeal

Reference (office use only)

Ask a judge from the First-tier Tribunal (Tax Chamber) to decide a dispute with HM Revenue & Customs (HMRC), UK Border Force (UKBF) or the National Crime Agency (NCA). All references below to HMRC include the UKBF and the NCA.

gov.uk/tax-tribunals

1. Your details

Please complete all questions in turn unless directed to move ahead to another question.

Company or organisation name (if applicable)

Your name

The tax tribunal will send correspondence to your representative and not to you directly.

Address

You must enter an email address if you want the tribunal to use email as a preferred way of contact.

Postcode

Email

Phone

2. How would you like the tax tribunal to contact you?

The tribunal will only contact you by your preferred choice.

☐ Email (you must include an email address in questions 1 or 4)

or

☐ Post

3. Do you have someone to represent you?

☐ Practising solicitor or barrister in England, Wales or Northern Ireland

☐ Practising solicitor or advocate in Scotland

☐ Other (such as tax agent, accountant, friend or family member)

☐ I do not have a representative

Unless the representative is a practising solicitor, barrister or advocate, you must sign the declaration in question 20 before your representative receives correspondence.

4. Your representative's details

Company or organisation name (if applicable)

Representative's name

Address

Postcode

Email

Phone

If you provide us with details of somebody who is representing you, you should ensure they agree for their details to be put down on the form.

If you nominate a representative all correspondence and documents, including hearing date notifications, will be sent to them and not directly to you.

If you want the tribunal to use email as a preferred way of contact, you must enter an email address.

If you change your representative, please inform us immediately in writing so that we can ensure that no further correspondence is sent to your previous representative and we can liaise directly with your new representative.

Page 2

5. What is your appeal about? (Tick all that apply)

A – Direct Tax

☐ Income Tax – including tax paid via self assessment and pay as you earn (PAYE)

☐ Capital Gains Tax ☐ Corporation Tax

☐ National Insurance (NI) contributions ☐ Penalties related to direct tax

☐ Other (please write details below)

Check the guide for a full list of types of direct and indirect tax disputes, and other areas where the tax tribunal has jurisdiction.

→ go to question 6

B – Indirect tax

☐ Value Added Tax (VAT) ☐ Excise Duty

☐ Penalties related to indirect tax ☐ Customs Duty

☐ Other (please write details below)

→ go to question 8

C – Other

☐ Information notice **→ go to question 6**

☐ Restoration of seized goods **→ go to question 8**

6. Did you appeal the original decision to HMRC?

For direct tax or information notices, you must appeal to HMRC before you can appeal to the tax tribunal.

☐ Yes **→ go to question 7**

☐ No

Page 3

7. What happened after you appealed to HMRC?

- ☐ I accepted the offer of a review → **go to question 9**
- ☐ I declined the offer of a review → **go to question 10**
- ☐ I am appealing direct to the tribunal before receiving a response from HMRC → **go to question 10**
- ☐ My appeal to HMRC was late. I am applying to be allowed to make a late appeal to HMRC → **go to question 17**

If HMRC reject your appeal for being late, you can apply to the tax tribunal to be allowed to make a late appeal to HMRC.

8. Did you have a review of the original decision?

- ☐ Yes → **go to question 9**
- ☐ No → **go to question 10** (for restoration of seized goods)
- ☐ No. I am applying to be able to request a late review (for restoration of seized goods) → **go to question 17**

For the restoration of seized goods, you must ask HMRC for a review before appealing to the tribunal. If your request is rejected for being late, you can apply to the tribunal to request a late review.

9. Has the review finished?

- ☐ Yes. I have a review conclusion letter → **go to question 10**
- ☐ No. I have been waiting over 45 days → **go to question 10**
- ☐ No. I have been waiting 44 days or less **STOP** - see side note →

You can only appeal to the tax tribunal when you receive a review conclusion letter or **wait 45 days or more** without receiving the conclusion letter.

10. What is your dispute about? (enter details for all that apply)

- ☐ The amount HMRC claim I owe
  £ ______ → **go to question 11** (indirect tax) → **go to question 15** (direct tax)
- ☐ I want HMRC to repay
  £ ______ → **go to question 15**
- ☐ Penalty or surcharge of
  £ ______ → **go to question 15**
- ☐ Other (please write details below)
  ______ → **go to question 15**

Check the original notice or review conclusion letter for details of your dispute.

Page 4

11. Have you paid the amount HMRC claim you owe?
(indirect taxes only)

☐ Yes → **go to question 15**

☐ No → **go to question 12**

12. Did you ask HMRC if you could appeal without paying the amount first?

☐ Yes → **go to question 13**

☐ No **STOP – you must ask HMRC before proceeding**

13. Did HMRC allow you to defer paying because of financial hardship?

☐ Yes → **go to question 15**

☐ Awaiting decision → **go to question 15**

☐ No → **go to question 14**

14. Why will paying the tax under dispute cause you financial hardship?

For indirect taxes, you must normally pay any amount HMRC claim you owe before you appeal. However, you may be excused for reasons of financial hardship.

You do not have to pay a penalty or surcharge before you can appeal.

If payment of the tax will cause financial hardship, **you must ask HMRC if you can defer paying** before your appeal is allowed to proceed.

If HMRC doesn't allow you to defer, fill in question 14 (or give reasons in a document). The judge will decide whether your appeal can go ahead without paying the amount first.

If you are awaiting a decision, and HMRC later refuse, you may apply to the tribunal to consider your case for financial hardship at that point.

Page 5

15. Are you in time to appeal to the tax tribunal?

- ☐ Yes. I am in time → **go to question 17**
- ☐ No. I am late → **go to question 16**
- ☐ I am not sure → **go to question 16**

You have **30 calendar days** from the date of the original decision or review conclusion letter (or expiry of the 45-day period for review if you didn't receive a review conclusion letter).

16. Why are you late or might be late, with your appeal to the tax tribunal?

The judge will consider your reasons and any response from HMRC. There may be a hearing to decide if your appeal can go ahead. If you are not allowed to appeal late, you will be told why.

You can enclose a document if you need more space to write.

Page 6

17. Grounds for appeal

Clearly explain why you are appealing, giving reasons for each decision you dispute. The judge will want to hear things from your side.

You can write reasons here or enclose a supporting document if you need more space.

Page 7

Form: *First-tier Tribunal (Tax Chamber) Notice of Appeal*

Once the appeal has been notified to the Tax Tribunal it will be allocated to one of four case categories (*Tribunal Procedure (First-tier Tribunal) (Tax Chamber) Rules 2009, SI 2009/273, rule 23*) ie default paper, basic, standard or complex. For instance, Construction Industry (CIS) late return penalties and Class 2 notification penalties will be classed as within the default paper category. See **41.4** LABOUR-ONLY CONTRACTORS. The category allocation will be notified to the appellant who is entitled to question it. If the appellant has a representative, the Tribunals Service will correspond only with the representative. Once allocated by the Birmingham office, most standard and all complex cases are administered by one of the Tribunals Service's other offices in London, Manchester or Edinburgh.

The category of case will be decided on written evidence submitted and HMRC's statement of case. An oral hearing may be requested by either HM Revenue and Customs or by the appellant (*Tribunal Procedure (First-tier Tribunal) (Tax Chamber) Rules 2009, SI 2009/273, rules 25(3) and 26 (3)(c)*), and any decision may be listed for hearing if the decision is not agreed. Detailed information on the default paper process is available in the Appeals Reviews and Tribunals Guidance at ARTG8370.

Basic appeals

[9.11] A basic appeal will include, amongst other things, CIS gross payment decisions and penalties for incorrect returns. See **21.31** COLLECTION and **41.9** LABOUR ONLY CONTRACTORS. There is a limited exchange of papers in this category and the notification will be made at the hearing and notified in writing. Detailed information on the basic process is available in the Appeals Reviews and Tribunals Guidance at ARTG8350.

Either party to the appeal can appoint a representative to attend the hearing and that person does not need to be legally qualified (*Tribunal Procedure (First-tier Tribunal) (Tax Chamber) Rules 2009, SI 2009/273, rule 11*).

Standard appeals

[9.12] A standard appeal will cover most contentious appeal cases that do not come within the default and basic categories. It is likely that a majority of NICs appeals will come into this category. HMRC will provide a statement of case (see ARTG8395) within 60 days of being notified by the tribunal. At this stage the parties have 42 days to provide a list of documents which will be relied upon at the hearing. Guidance on the preparation needed for a standard appeal is available at ARTG8390. The parties may be invited to a case management hearing (see ARTG8500) and are expected to attend the hearing in person or by representative but if they do not, the case may proceed in their absence if it is in the interests of justice to do so. Decisions will normally be made in writing to the parties but may be made on the day of the hearing.

Complex cases

[9.13] Complex cases may proceed like standard cases but usually involve lengthy and involved issues or large amounts of tax/NICs and are likely to be heard in the first instance by the Upper Tribunal. HMRC will provide a statement of case within 60 days of being notified by the tribunal. At this stage the parties then have 42 days to provide a list of documents which will be relied upon at the hearing (*Tribunal Procedure (First-tier Tribunal) (Tax Chamber) Rules 2009, SI 2009/273, rules 25 and 27*). Decisions will normally be given in writing to the parties but may be made on the day of the hearing.

Private hearings

[9.14] All hearings are held in public except in the rare instances where the tribunal directs that all or part of the proceedings are to be heard in private where justified:

- in the interest of public order or national security;
- to protect the appellant's or another person's right to privacy;
- to preserve the confidentiality of sensitive information; or
- in the interests of justice.

Striking out

[9.15] Where the appellant fails to comply with certain directions of the tribunal, or fails to cooperate with the tribunal or the tribunal concludes that there is no realistic prospect of the case succeeding then the case may be struck out. The same obligations fall upon HM Revenue and Customs also, but in this instance the case will not be struck out but will be heard without HM Revenue and Customs taking any further part in the proceedings.

Power to make regulations

[9.16] HM Revenue and Customs has the power to make regulations, with the concurrence of the Lord Chancellor and the Secretary of State for Scotland, in respect of contributions or statutory payment appeals and may also make regulations regarding matters arising pending a decision of an officer under *s 8*, pending the determination by the tribunal, out of the variation of a decision or out of the superseding of a decision. [*SSC(TF)A 1999, s 13* as amended by *Revenue and Customs Appeals Order 2009, SI 2009/777, Reg 3; SSC(TF)A 1999, s 14* and modified by *Transfer of Functions (Lord Advocate and Secretary of State) Order 1999, SI 1999/678*].

Place of hearing of appeal

[9.17] There is a network of hearing centres across the country and the facility for additional private hearings. See also *TMA 1970, ss 49A–49I* inserted by *Transfer of Tribunal Functions and Revenue and Customs Appeals Order 2009, SI 2009/56, Sch 1, para 30* as well as *Social Security Contributions (Decisions and Appeals) Regulations 1999, SI 1999/1027, Reg 7* as amended by *Transfer of Tribunal Functions and Revenue and Customs Appeals Order 2009, SI 2009/56, Sch 2, para 62.*

Cases within the complex category will usually be heard in London, Manchester or Edinburgh but might also be heard in other venues.

Multiple appeals and lead cases

[9.18] Where more than one appeal is made in respect of the same decision (eg, both employer and employee, or more than one affected employee), all such appeals must be heard at the same time.

In *EDI Services Ltd v HMRC* [2006] STC SCD 60 Sp C 515 a number of companies had entered into arrangements, devised by an accountancy firm, whereby bonuses were paid to directors or employees in the form of antique gold coins situated outside the UK, with the aim of making payments in kind which were excluded from Class 1 NIC liability. All the coins in question were purchased from the same broker. The companies did not account for Class 1 NIC on the bonuses. HMRC issued rulings that NICs were due, and the companies appealed. HMRC and the companies' accountants made a joint application for one of the appeals to be designated as the 'lead case' under the then current *Special Commissioners (Jurisdiction and Procedure) Regulations 1994, SI 1994/1811, Reg 7A*. The Commissioner granted the application. After the earlier directions case, the judgment in *EDI Services Ltd v HMRC (and related appeals) (No 2)* [2006] STC SCD 392 Sp C 539 was handed down on 26 April 2006 (8.2 ANTI-AVOIDANCE). The Special Commissioner made a similar direction concerning a number of appeals relating to Class 1 NIC arising out of the provision of bonuses by way of the assignment of trade debts. *Spectrum Computer Supplies Ltd v HMRC* [2006] STC SCD 668 Sp C 559 (8.2 ANTI-AVOIDANCE). See also **31** EARNINGS FROM EMPLOYMENT: READILY CONVERTIBLE ASSETS, ETC.

Late appeals

[9.19] Late appeals may be admitted if the officer of HM Revenue and Customs is satisfied that there was a reasonable excuse for not bringing the appeal within the normal time limit, provided that application is made without undue delay thereafter. See *Gurney v Spence Ch D*, [2002] STC 758 and also *PA Holdings Ltd v HMRC* [2008] STC SCD 1185 Sp C 707 where a joint PAYE and NICs hearing did not prejudice the taxpayer company. [*Social Security Contributions (Decisions and Appeals) Regulations 1999, SI 1999/1027, Reg 9, applying the provisions of TMA 1970, s 49*, as amended by *Transfer of Tribunal Functions and Revenue and Customs Appeals Order 2009, SI 2009/56, Sch 2, para 64*].

If HMRC declines a late appeal (which it may do if there is no 'reasonable excuse'), the potential appellant may apply to the tribunal to make a late appeal and the tribunal may consider factors beyond those that constitute a 'reasonable excuse' to HMRC.

An employer (C) failed to account for PAYE and NIC to HMRC, which issued determinations under the *Income Tax (PAYE) Regulations 2003, SI 2003/2682*. C did not appeal, and HMRC lodged a statutory demand and issued a bankruptcy petition. C then lodged a late appeal, which HMRC referred to the General Commissioners under *TMA 1970, s 49*. The Commissioners rejected the application, holding that there was no reasonable excuse for the delay in lodging the appeal. C applied for judicial review of the Commissioners' decision. At an initial hearing, Burton J granted the application.

The Commissioners re-heard the case and again held that the conditions of *TMA 1970, s 49(1)* had not been complied with. C again applied for judicial review. Dyson LJ rejected his application, holding that public interest required 'the achievement of finality in the proceedings' and 'the observance of the strict time limits for lodging appeals against assessments made by the Revenue'. *R (on the application of Cook) v General Commissioners of Income Tax* [2009] EWHC 590 (Admin), [2009] SWTI 683, [2009] All ER (D) 12 (Mar).

The hearing and determination by First-tier Tax Tribunal

[9.20] A notice giving the time, date and place of hearing will be sent to the appellant(s) and any agent or professional adviser, normally at least 14 days before the hearing. For standard and complex cases the Tribunals Service will ask in advance about dates which may be inconvenient to the parties. The case may last a number of days. In basic cases the parties are required to attend at either 10am or 2pm. Less than 14 days' notice may be given where all parties agree or in urgent or exceptional circumstances.

It is normally down to the parties to arrange for witnesses to attend and give evidence. If a witness is reluctant to attend, the tribunal has the power to compel attendance by way of a witness summons. Where the evidence of a witness is unlikely to be challenged by the other party it can be provided by way of a witness statement – this must be in writing and be signed and dated by the witness himself.

In standard and complex cases witnesses usually give evidence on oath or affirmation.

Normally, the appellant (on whose shoulders falls the burden of proof) will present his case first. The HMRC representative will then present his case and the appellant will then make a concluding statement.

The tribunal may decide that the decision shall be varied in any manner or that it shall stand good. The tribunal may examine the appellant on oath or affirmation or take other evidence. [*Social Security Contributions (Decisions and Appeals) Regulations 1999, SI 1999/1027, Reg 10*, as amended by *Transfer of Tribunal Functions and Revenue and Customs Appeals Order 2009, SI 2009/56, Sch 2, para 65*.]

The tribunal may give an oral decision at the conclusion of the hearing. In any event, the decision must be notified in writing to the parties within 28 days (although that can be extended by the tribunal in complex cases (eg, in *Commissioners for HMRC v Murray Group Holdings Ltd* [2014] UKUT 0292, involving an alleged PAYE and NIC avoidance scheme, a hearing on 3–7 March 2014 led to a decision promulgated only on 8 July 2014). That notice must also set out remaining appeal rights. Except where all parties to the appeal agree that it is not required, the notification must either include a summary of the findings of fact and reasons for the decision or a separate attachment setting out the full findings of fact and reasons for the decision. Where no reasons or findings are set out – or only a summary of findings included – either party to the appeal may apply for full written findings and reasons to be provided. This must be done within 28 days of the date that the notice of the tribunal decision was sent, and be in writing. The tribunal must send the full findings and reasons within 28 days or 'as soon as practicable thereafter'. [*Tribunal Procedure (First-tier Tribunal) (Tax Chamber) Rules 2009, SI 2009/273, rule 35*].

A copy of the full, written reasons must be included in any application to appeal the decision further. [*Tribunal Procedure (First-tier Tribunal) (Tax Chamber) Rules 2009, SI 2009/273, rule 36*].

As regards costs, there will be no awards in the First-tier Tribunal except where:

- either side has acted unreasonably;
- wasted costs have been incurred through the improper, unreasonable or negligent conduct of one of the parties' representatives;
- pre-1 April 2009 appeals are involved (in certain instances); or
- the case is a complex one.

Costs can be awarded in complex cases though the appellant (not HMRC) can opt out of this before the hearing. [*Tribunal Procedure (First-tier Tribunal) (Tax Chamber) Rules 2009, SI 2009/273, rule 10*]. In contrast the Upper Tribunal has a full costs regime (see 9.21).

Settling appeals by agreement

[9.21] Appellants may, before an appeal is heard by the First-tier Tax Tribunal, come to an agreement with an officer of HM Revenue and Customs that the decision under appeal should be treated as:

- upheld without variation, or
- varied in a particular manner, or
- superseded by a further decision,

and the same consequences will then ensue as would have ensued if the officer had made a decision in the same terms as that under appeal, had varied the decision or made a superseding decision, as the case may be.

In any of these circumstances, all appeals against the original decision lapse and notice of the agreement must be given by the officer of HM Revenue and Customs to all persons named in the decision who did not appeal against it. [*Social Security Contributions (Decisions and Appeals) Regulations 1999, SI 1999/1027, Reg 11(1)(2)(3)*, as amended by *Transfer of Tribunal Functions and Revenue and Customs Appeals Order 2009, SI 2009/56, Sch 2, para 66*].

If such an agreement is not made in writing it is necessary for the officer to confirm by written notice to every appellant the fact that an agreement was come to and details of its terms. [*SI 1999/1027, Reg 11(4).*]

An appellant may, before an appeal is heard by the tribunal, notify the officer of HM Revenue and Customs and every other person named in the decision, either orally or in writing, that he does not wish to proceed with the appeal. Unless, within 30 days, any person to whom that notice is given indicates that he is unwilling that the appeal should be treated as withdrawn then the appellant, the officer and every person named in the decision are treated as having reached an agreement that the decision should be upheld without variation. [*SI 1999/1027, Reg 11(5)*, as amended by *Transfer of Tribunal Functions and Revenue and Customs Appeals Order 2009, SI 2009/56, Sch 2, para* 66.]

Where an appeal is to be settled by agreement in any manner mentioned above, the agreement may be made with any person acting on behalf of an appellant or any other person named in the decision and notices may be validly given to such persons. [*SI 1999/1027, Reg 11(6)*.]

'Other persons named in the decision' includes both the employer and the employee in cases concerned with statutory payments. [*SI 1999/1027, Reg 11(7)*, inserted by *Security Contributions (Decisions and Appeals) Regulations 2002, SI 2002/3120*.]

Dissatisfaction with First-tier Tax Tribunal's determination

[9.22] If HM Revenue and Customs, the appellant or another party to the proceedings thinks that the First-tier Tribunal's decision is wrong on a point of law, then an appeal may be made to the Tax and Chancery Chamber of the Upper Tribunal (the Finance and Tax Chamber was re-named with effect from 1 September 2009 by the *First-tier Tribunal and Upper Tribunal (Chambers) (Amendment No 3) Order 2009, SI 2009/1590*). Permission to appeal a First-tier Tribunal decision must be requested from the tribunal that made the decision within 56 days of the date on the decision letter. No appeal may lie if it is classed as an excluded decision either on the face of the Act or in any order made by the Lord Chancellor. [*Tribunals, Courts and Enforcement Act 2007, s 11(1)*].

The address of the Upper Tribunal Office for England and Wales is: Tax and Chancery Chamber, Fifth Floor, Rolls Building, Fetter Lane, London EC4A 1NL, tel: 020 7612 9730, email: uttc@hmcts.gsi.gov.uk. If the First-tier appeal was heard in Scotland or the contributor lives in Scotland, an Edinburgh address is available: George House, 126 George St, Edinburgh EH2 4HH.

At this stage, the contributions in dispute must, if that is not already the case, be paid. If the appellant is successful, the amount will be repaid. If the hearing is with regard to statutory payments, employers do not have to pay SSP, SMP, SAP, SPP or ShPP until the appeal is finally settled.

The First-tier Tribunal may initially review its own decision on receipt of an application of appeal to the Upper Tribunal (*The Tribunal Procedure (First-tier Tribunal) (Tax Chamber) Rules 2009, SI 2009/273, rule 41* and the *Tribunals, Courts and Enforcement Act 2007, s 9*). The form for First-tier Application for Permission to Appeal to Upper Tribunal, T247, is available online at s3-eu-west-1.amazonaws.com/hmctsformfinder/t247-eng.pdf. A refusal of appeal by the First-tier Tribunal must be accompanied by an explanation why and a notification of the option to have the rejection reviewed by the Upper Tribunal. Further, appeals against the Upper Tribunal decisions will be heard by the Court of Appeal in England and Wales or Court of Session in Scotland. Complex cases follow the same procedures as those for standard cases but with more directions for the appeal and ending with a special directions hearing (*Tribunal Procedure (First-tier Tribunal) (Tax Chamber) Rules 2009, SI 2009/273, rule 27*). Costs may be awarded to the other party to the appeal where it is considered that one party has acted 'unreasonably' or the case was 'complex' (*Tribunal Procedure (First-tier Tribunal) (Tax Chamber) Rules 2009, SI 2009/273, rule 10*). A party may opt out of the costs within 28 days of the case being categorised (*Tribunal Procedure (First-tier Tribunal) (Tax Chamber) Rules 2009, SI 2009/273, rule 10 para 1*). Therefore most cases that are default paper, basic or standard will have no costs ruling attaching. In certain cases, there can be a 'striking out' where the party has acted unconscionably or where the tribunal cannot deal with the case fairly and justly and in such a case the respondent (normally, but not always, HMRC) will be barred from taking part in any further proceedings. In such cases the tribunal may summarily determine the issues not withstanding that the respondent has been barred (TPC rule 8 para 8).

[*SI 1999/1027, Reg 12* as amended by *Transfer of Tribunal Functions and Revenue and Customs Appeals Order 2009, SI 2009/56, Sch 2, para 67* and *Revenue and Customs Appeals Order 2009, SI 2009/777, Reg 6*.]

An application for permission to appeal must first be made to the First-tier Tribunal, in writing, and within 56 days of the latest of the following dates:

- receipt of the fully reasoned decision;
- receipt of notification of amended reasons for the decision following a review (or corrected decision); and
- receipt of notification that an application for the decision to be set aside has been declined.

[*Tribunal Procedure (First-tier Tribunal) (Tax Chamber) Rules 2009, SI 2009/273, rule 39(2)*].

The First-tier Tribunal must first consider whether to review its decision. [*Tribunal Procedure (First-tier Tribunal) (Tax Chamber) Rules 2009, SI 2009/273, rule 40*]. It can only do so where it is satisfied that there was an error of law and having given all parties the opportunity to make representations. [*Tribunal Procedure (First-tier Tribunal) (Tax Chamber) Rules 2009, SI 2009/273, rule 41(1)(b)*]. If the First-tier Tribunal decides not to review its decision, then it must go on to give consideration to the request for permission to appeal.

If that permission is refused, a written request may be made for an oral hearing by the Upper Tribunal. [*Tribunal Procedure (Upper Tribunal) Rules 2008, SI 2008/2698, rule 22(3)-(5)*]. If the Upper Tribunal also refuses permission, the appellant may then appeal to the Court of Appeal (or Court of Session) for permission for the appeal to be heard. [*Tribunal Procedure (Upper Tribunal) Rules 2008, SI 2008/2698, rule 45(4)(b)*].

Once permission is granted, written notice of the appeal must be received by the Upper Tribunal within one month after notice of permission to appeal was sent to the appellant. However, if it was the Upper Tribunal itself that granted the permission the application for permission is itself treated as notice of appeal and a copy will be sent to the respondents by the Upper Tribunal. [*Tribunal Procedure (Upper Tribunal) Rules 2008, SI 2008/2698, rule 22(2)(b)*]. The respondents have one month to lodge any response to the Upper Tribunal and to indicate whether or not they require a full hearing. [*Tribunal Procedure (Upper Tribunal) Rules 2008, SI 2008/2698, rule 24*]. The appellant has one month to reply to that response. [*Tribunal Procedure (Upper Tribunal) Rules 2008, SI 2008/2698, rule 25*].

If the Upper Tribunal makes a decision without an oral hearing, it must obtain the views of both parties to the appeal and take them into consideration. [*Tribunal Procedure (Upper Tribunal) Rules 2008, SI 2008/2698, rule 34*].

The Upper Tribunal may set aside the First-tier Tribunal decision and either remit it back or give a new decision itself.

The Upper Tribunal may give an oral decision at the conclusion of the hearing. [*Tribunal Procedure (Upper Tribunal) Rules 2008, SI 2008/2698, rule 40*]. A written decision, also containing reasons and information on appeal rights, must be sent to all parties as soon as is 'reasonably practical' (undefined) after the making of the decision. [*Tribunal Procedure (Upper Tribunal) Rules 2008, SI 2008/2698, rule 40(2)*].

Upper Tribunal appeal hearings will generally be held at London, Manchester, Birmingham, Belfast or Edinburgh.

Class 2 and class 4 questions

[9.23] Because Class 4 contributions (see CLASS 4 CONTRIBUTIONS 20) are payable in accordance with assessments made under the Income Tax Acts, the provisions of *Taxes Management Act 1970, Pt V* have always applied with necessary modifications in relation to such contributions as they apply in relation to income tax. [*SSCBA 1992, s 15(1)(2)(5), Sch 2 para 8*.] Class 2 contributions (see CLASS 2 CONTRIBUTIONS 18) were brought within the same regime on 6 April 2015 by *NICA 2015, Sch 1*, which moved Class 2 into the income tax self-assessment regime and introduced a new *SSCBA 1992, s 11A* to apply the *TMA 1970, Pt V* management provisions to Class 2 contributions. The effect of this is that an appeal against a Class 2 or Class 4 assessment must be made in writing within 30 days of the issue of the notice of assessment, must state the grounds on which it is based and must be made direct to the First-tier Tribunal. An appeal may be brought out of time if there is a reasonable excuse for the delay. An appeal against the decision of the tribunal may be made to the Upper Tribunal. (See, for example, *Martin v O'Sullivan* [1982] STC 416.) [*TMA 1970, s 31(1)(4)(5), s 49(1), s 56*].

Under 'self-assessment' from 6 April 1996, there are few assessments issued now. However, in the case of a dispute, whether for income tax, Class 2 or Class 4 contributions or both, it will be necessary for HM Revenue and Customs, exceptionally, to issue an assessment or an amendment to the self-assessment in order to enable an appeal to be made by the taxpayer/contributor.

The only questions concerning Class 4 contributions which were excluded from this jurisdiction were:

- whether by regulations made under *SSCBA 1992, s 17(1)* a person was excepted from Class 4 liability or his liability was deferred; and/or
- whether he was liable for Class 4 contributions that may be collected directly under *SSCBA 1992, s 17(3)–(6), s 18*.

[Former *SSAA 1992, s 17(2), Sch 2 para 8*].

These two matters previously fell within the Secretary of State's remit (see the 2008–09 and previous editions of this work). However, from 1 April 1999, they became matters for a decision of an officer of HM Revenue and Customs under *SSC(TF)A 1999, s 8* (see **9.4** to **9.21** above) and then, only by those means, will the matter now fall to be put before the tribunal.

Key Points regarding appeals and reviews

[9.24] Points to consider are as follows.

- Where a decision is disputed and an appeal made to it, HM Revenue and Customs may offer a review. If not the contributor may require a statutory independent review.
- If still dissatisfied after any review, the contributor must separately notify the appeal direct to the Tribunals Service.
- An appeal may not be notified to the Tribunals Service after a review has been accepted or requested until after it has concluded.
- No costs are awarded in the First-tier Tribunal except in complex cases and even then the appellant (but not HM Revenue and Customs) may opt out in advance. Costs may exceptionally be awarded in the case of unreasonable conduct by either party.

10

Apprentices, Trainees and Students

Cross-references. See **3.1** to **3.4** AGE EXCEPTION for those under 16; **14.5** to **14.7** CATEGORISATION for contract of service; CLASS **1** CONTRIBUTIONS **15**; **24.4** to **24.8** CREDITS for contributions awarded in early years and during and after training etc; **30.25** for certain training costs; NATIONAL INSURANCE NUMBER **49** for entry into the social security scheme; **51.4** and **51.5** OVERSEAS MATTERS for meaning of present, resident and ordinarily resident.

Other Sources. Simon's Taxes, Volume 2, para A8.229B; Section 4, Chapter 14 and Section 8, Chapter 46; Tolley's National Insurance Brief, February 1997, page 15; Tolley's Practical NIC, December 1999, page 95.

Age limitations

[10.1] No liability for either primary or secondary CLASS **1** CONTRIBUTIONS **15** or for CLASS **2** CONTRIBUTIONS **18** can arise in respect of a person who has not yet attained the age of 16, and exception from CLASS **4** CONTRIBUTIONS **20** may be claimed by anyonc who is not over that age at the beginning of a tax year (see **3.1** to **3.6** AGE EXCEPTION).

This remains the case after 1 October 2006 despite the extension from that date of eligibility to Statutory Payments to those aged under 16. Primary contributions may be deemed to have been paid in appropriate cases.

From 6 April 2015, a nil rate of age-related secondary Class 1 contributions applies to earnings paid to an earner aged under 21 on the date of payment, to the extent that such earnings do not exceed the upper secondary threshold or

'UST' for the relevant earnings period. The UST has initially been set at the same level as the normal UEL, but the legislation has been deliberately framed to keep the definitions separate so that both the UST and age-related secondary rate may be amended independently in future. [*Social Security Contributions and Benefits Act 1992 (SSCBA 1992), s 9A, as inserted by National Insurance Contributions Act 2014 (NICA 2014), s 9.*]

From 6 April 2016, a similar nil rate applies to apprentices under the age of 25 (see below).

Apprentices

[10.2] A person who is gainfully employed in Great Britain or Northern Ireland under a contract of service (see **14.5** CATEGORISATION) is an employed earner for contribution purposes, and a contract of service includes a contract of apprenticeship. [*SSCBA 1992, s 2(1)(a), s 122(1)*].

A 'contract of apprenticeship' is a contract by which a person is bound to and *serves* another for the purpose of learning something which the other is to teach him. (*St Pancras Parish v Clapham Parish* (1860) 2 E & E 742, *per Lord Cockburn CJ at p 750*). Where, however, the primary purpose of a contract is not service but is teaching or learning, the contract is neither a contract of apprenticeship nor a contract of service. (*Wiltshire Police Authority v Wynn* [1981] QB 95, [1980] 3 WLR 445, CA, but note that the decision on the status of police cadets in that case was later overruled by *Police Act 1996, s 28*: for the purposes of any enactment relating to the functions of employers, the police authority that maintains a police force is treated as the employer of any police cadets undergoing training with the force.) A person engaged under a training contract which is neither a contract of service nor a contract of apprenticeship is not an employed earner for contribution purposes, and any allowances paid to him will, therefore, attract no contribution liability. That such a possibility exists is borne out by *Employment Rights Act 1996, s 171*, which makes specific and separate provision for protecting workers in employments that are not under contracts of service or apprenticeship.

The DSS (now DWP) regarded apprentice jockeys and stable boys who receive board and lodgings as employed earners (see **14.2** CATEGORISATION).

See Tolley's Practical NIC, December 1999, page 95.

From 6 April 2016, *SSCBA 1992, s 9B* applies a nil rate of secondary Class 1 contributions to the earnings of apprentices to the extent that they do not exceed an Apprentice Upper Secondary Threshold (AUST) in the relevant earnings period. The AUST has initially been set at the same level as the under-21 UST (above) and the normal UEL, but *s 9B* has been deliberately framed to keep the definitions separate so that the AUST, UST and UEL and the age-related secondary rate may be changed independently in future. [*Social Security Contributions and Benefits Act 1992, s 9B, as inserted by NICA 2015, s 1.*]

The AUST (like the UEL) was set for 2016–17 at £827 per week. If an apprentice receives a bonus in a particular week that takes the total earnings in that week above the AUST, secondary contributions at the normal rate are due on the excess. The age-related secondary rate has no effect on the apprentice's own primary liability. (Note for 2018–19 the AUST, UST and UEL are all set at £892 per week.)

The introduction of the nil rate led to the introduction of two new contributions tables for under 25 apprentices, H (standard rate) and G (apprentice mariners standard rate), from 6 April 2016.

The definition of 'apprentice' is prescribed in regulations by the Treasury. [*Section 9B(9)*.] Education and training are devolved responsibilities, so the word may in general law terms have slightly different meanings in England and Wales, Scotland and Northern Ireland, which means that a common definition is required for contributions purposes.

HMRC issued a consultation on 24 July 2015 on the definition to be used, together with a first draft of the proposed regulations. A new *reg 154A* was then added to the *Social Security (Contributions) Regulations 2001* by *Social Security (Contributions) (Amendment) Regulations 2016, SI 2016/117, reg 2*. An apprentice is defined for the purposes of *s 9B* as a person employed under:

- an approved English apprenticeship agreement within the meaning of *Apprenticeships, Skills, Children and Learning Act 2009, s A1*;
- an English apprenticeship agreement within the meaning of *ASCLA 2009, s 32*;
- a Welsh apprenticeship agreement within the meaning of *ASCLA 2009, s 32*;
- arrangements made by the Secretary of State or the Scottish Ministers under *Employment and Training Act 1973, s 2*;
- arrangements made by the Secretary of State or the Scottish Ministers under *Enterprise and New Towns (Scotland) Act 1990, s 2*; or
- arrangements made by the Department for Employment and Learning under *Employment and Training Act (Northern Ireland) 1950, s 1*.

Any such apprentice must have entered into a written agreement with the employer and the training provider that sets out the type of apprenticeship framework or standard being followed, the start date of the apprenticeship and the expected completion date of the apprenticeship.

No allowance is to be made for common law apprenticeships because they do not follow government-approved frameworks, so it seems possible that employers who offer such apprenticeships will amend their training programmes to fit within the frameworks and ensure that they operate through approved training providers so as to qualify for the nil rate of secondary NIC. They may thereby also benefit from extra government funding.

Guidance on what evidence an employer must hold in order to satisfy HMRC that it may qualify for the apprentice nil rate was published on GOV.UK on 2 February 2016. This can be either the written agreement between the employer, the apprentice and a training provider, or, in England and Wales, evidence that the apprenticeship receives government funding. If the training provider has not signed the written agreement, it will have to provide the employer with a document that shows that it is an approved or recognised training provider and summarising the training the apprentice is undertaking, and any training already done. An employer can also be a trainer if it has been approved by the Skills Funding Agency in England, or holds a contract for the delivery of Apprenticeships in Wales.

[10.3] Further stimulation for the growth of training by apprenticeship is likely to come from the government's introduction of an apprenticeship levy in April 2017. *Finance Act 2016, Part 6 (ss 87–110)* set the levy rate at 0.5% of NICable pay in any pay period, on all 'large' employers.

The base of NICable pay was chosen in order to make the calculation of the levy simple, since it is a number that employers' payroll software will already have determined. Every employer will be a secondary contributor when paying earnings to employees, and the 'pay bill' will be the total of all such earnings, even if the earnings of any particular worker attract no secondary NICs because they fall below the secondary threshold. [*Finance Act 2016, s 89*.]

The limitation to 'large' employers is to be achieved by imposing the levy on all employers while giving each a 'levy allowance' of £15,000 per year, so that only businesses with an annual pay bill of £3 million should be liable. The levy allowance is to be shared around a group in proportions nominated by the employer at the start of the year, but connected companies and connected charities are to be entitled to only one such allowance per year, using the connection rules applicable to employment allowance under *NICA 2014*. [*Finance Act 2016, s 90(4)*.]

The proposed mechanics of the levy involve bolting it on to the RTI system so that it is collected monthly with the PAYE and NIC deductions. The funds are to be distributed to employers of all sizes by means of an electronic voucher redeemable against all or part of apprenticeship course fees. The ICAEW in its TAXREP 50/15 questioned whether the levy is not merely a hypothecated tax on larger employers, even where those employers are in industries where apprenticeships are not available, to fund apprenticeships for all businesses.

The Department for Business, Innovation and Skills (BIS) (now BEIS) consulted from 29 July to 19 August 2015 on protecting the term 'apprenticeship' and announced on 21 September that a clause would be included in the government's Enterprise Bill to protect the term 'apprenticeship' from misuse by unauthorised training providers. Under what became *Enterprise Act 2016, s 25*, effective from 5 May 2016, a provision was introduced into *Apprenticeships, Skills, Children and Learning Act 2009, s A11 (ASCLA 2009)* to ensure that, in England, only statutory apprenticeships may be described by training providers as 'apprenticeships'. It is therefore an offence for a person, in the course of business, to provide or offer a course or training as an apprenticeship if it is not a statutory apprenticeship, although an employer providing training itself may continue to use the term without committing an offence. The penalty will be a fine on summary conviction. Enforcement of the provision rests with local weights and measures authorities in England.

Participants in government training schemes

[10.4] Where a participant in Youth Training received only the basic allowance, no contribution liability arose as the amount of such allowances fell below the earnings threshold. Where, however, the allowance was topped-up by the 'managing agent' (ie the employer who had charge of the participant) to a level which equalled or exceeded the Lower Earnings Limit, the contribution position depended on whether, in the particular circumstances of his case, the participant was, in law, under a contract of service, a contract of apprenticeship or a training contract. A managing agent had considerable freedom in the arrangements he entered into with the participant, and he might, with the participant's consent, have written into the training agreement a declaration that the agreement was not intended to establish a contractual relationship between himself and a participant. The Youth Training Scheme has long since disappeared, but historically it illustrates the possible status of payments and trainees.

EIM10500 still states that 'There is no charge to tax on payments made to young people taking part in government or other work experience schemes if they hold the status of trainee and not employee', which underlines the principle. However, the manual also makes clear that the source of funding for particular training schemes has no special significance for tax purposes. The taxation treatment of allowances paid to participants will still depend on whether they are trainees or employees.

Case law—contracts

[10.5] Such a declaration as mentioned in **10.4** will result in a contract which is binding only in honour (*Rose & Frank Crompton Co v J R Crompton & Bros Ltd* [1923] 2 KB 261) and which, therefore, it seems, precludes the participant from falling into the category of employed earner for contribution purposes. If, on the other hand, the training agreement expressly states that the participant is to be regarded as an employee, the training agreement will, it seems, bring the participant within the category of employed earner for contribution purposes and contribution liabilities will ensue. In the absence of such an express statement, a participant will not be an employee (*Daley v Allied Suppliers Ltd* [1983] IRLR 14), but he may be a trainee or an apprentice and, in order to decide which, the tests outlined at **10.2** above must be applied. If the primary purpose of the training agreement is merely to formalise an arrangement under which the participant may be taught certain skills, the contract is a training contract, not a contract of service or apprenticeship, and, because it does not bring the participant into the category of employed earners, no contribution liabilities can arise. If, however, the primary purpose of the training agreement is to formalise an arrangement under which the participant is to serve the managing agent in order to learn a trade, the contract may be construed as a contract of apprenticeship and contribution liabilities will arise if the earnings paid are sufficiently great, but the nil rate of secondary contribution will only apply if the apprenticeship meets the statutory conditions outlined above. It is thought that a clause within the agreement which guarantees the participant employment at the end of the training period will be strongly indicative of a common law apprenticeship.

Statutory deeming

[10.6] The *Health and Safety (Training for Employment) Regs 1990, SI 1990/1380* provided that, for the purposes of health and safety legislation, trainees were to be *treated as* employees. By implication, their status as trainees meant that they would not otherwise qualify as employees and the deeming regulation was required to bring them under the cover of health and safety law. This has been perpetuated under the *Employment Rights Act 1996* and, more recently, the *Apprenticeships, Skills, Children and Learning Act 2009*, which by *s 1(6)* encompasses 'working otherwise than for reward' and by *s 35* provides that an 'apprenticeship agreement' will not be treated as a contract of apprenticeship but as a contract of service, for the purposes of any enactment or rule of law, so that any trainee signing up to an apprenticeship agreement under the *ASCLA 2009* will for all purposes be treated as employed. Note, however, that *ASCLA 2009* applies only in England and Wales.

The training schemes

[10.7] The Training Agreement held by the participant under earlier law indicated whether the participating young person had employee status or not. A further indication was the position on paid overtime which could not be worked by a person with trainee-only status.

Where a participant had employed earner status, Class 1 contributions had to be calculated by reference to the total pay the participant received, *including* the training allowance.

Training premiums paid to participants in Employment Training (which commenced on 5 September 1988 and replaced various other employment and training programmes for those aged 18 or over) attracted neither primary nor secondary Class 1 contribution liability nor Class 2 contribution liability if the participant was in receipt of a training premium under *Employment and Training Act 1973, s 2* (effective 5 September 1988) or *Enterprise and New Towns (Scotland) Act 1990, s 2* (effective 1 April 1991). [*Employment Training Payments Order 1988, Art 2* as amended].

With effect from 1 October 1991, any payment made to a person using the facilities provided under the Employment Action Programme was not to be treated as a payment of earnings for contribution purposes. [*Employment Action (Miscellaneous Provisions) Order 1991, Reg 3*].

New deal for young people

[10.8] Under the 'New Deal for Young People' for 18–24 year olds (introduced from April 1998) there were the following options:

- full-time education and training;
- self-employment option;
- environment task force and voluntary sector work.

In the case of subsidised employment the actual wage paid by the employer was liable to NIC in the usual way, regardless of subsidy received, but the training allowance was not subject to NIC (CA National Consultation Panel,

14 January 1998 and CWG2 (2011) page 32 para 47. Of course, usually the training allowance would not find itself reaching the hands of the employee so NIC liability or otherwise would not be in point. See also *Social Security (New Deal Pilot) Regulations 1999, SI 1999/3156*.

Despite this, it seems that it was not usual to pay NIC in respect of people working in the Environmental Task Force or the voluntary sector options prior to 6 April 2000 (see Inland Revenue Employer's Bulletin, Issue 5, April 2000).

New Deal 50-plus

[10.9] This contrasts with payments under the 'New Deal 50-Plus' training programme to those aged 50 or more going back into work. They did not pay tax or NICs on the payments they received through the scheme. The employment credit payment and the training grant should not have been chargeable to NICs as earnings from employment (Class 1) or assessable for self employment (Class 2). See HM Revenue and Customs National Insurance Manual NIM02395.

[*Social Security (Contributions) (Amendment No 5) Regulations 1999, SI 1999/2736* and *Social Security (Contributions) Regulations 2001, SI 2001/1004, Sch 3 Part VII paras 4, 5*].

Training or occupational centre attenders

[10.10] Some local authorities and other organisations provide work, training or occupational centres directed to the welfare and rehabilitation of persons who are physically or mentally handicapped. The question whether a person attending such a centre is or is not gainfully employed is determined by the arrangements and conditions applying at the centre. (R(U)2/67). The Department for Work and Pensions (formerly DSS) normally accepted that an attender was not in gainful employment, if:

- the main object of any work performed was therapeutic, not commercial;
- arrangements for attendance were elastic and informal; and
- payments did not depend on output but were in the nature of pocket money given as an incident of rehabilitation.

Students

[10.11] In accordance with the principle stated at 10.2 above, students who are required to undertake practical work as part of their education do not thereby become party to a contract of service, even if they receive a maintenance allowance or fees for the work they perform. (*M7 (1950); M16 (1951); M19 (1951)*). A person who, *while under a contract of service* with an employer, enters upon a course of study (either full-time or as part of a sandwich course) does not, however, cease thereby to be under a contract of service and is, accordingly, liable as an employed earner for contributions on pay or financial assistance which constitutes earnings received from his employer, even if received during the periods of education.

In the 2005 Budget, a change was announced to income tax Statement of Practice 4/86 concerning payments made by employers to employees who are required to be in full-time attendance at universities and technical colleges. The main change for tax purposes was that the financial limit for exemption rose to £15,000 per academic year with effect from 1 September 2005 (the start of the 2005–06 academic year). It then rose to £15,480 per annum from 1 September 2007. *The Social Security (Contributions) (Amendment No 2) Regulations 2005, SI 2005/728* replicated the Statement of Practice as far as possible, including the date the change took effect. Previously, such amounts would have been exempt from Class 1 contributions if the payments had been made under a training contract, but would otherwise have been liable if paid under an employment contract. The *Regulations* provided amendments to *Social Security (Contributions) Regulations 2001, Reg 40* and *Schedule 3, Part VII, para 12*. In particular, the educational establishment must be one as defined in *ITTOIA 2005, s 776(1)* and not one run by the employer; the course must last for at least one academic year; and the amount paid to the employee for attendance must not exceed £15,480 per annum inclusive of lodging, travel and subsistence allowances (but excluding tuition fees). The exemption does not – for the avoidance of doubt – apply to payments for actual work done, whether during holidays or otherwise.

[*Social Security (Contributions) (Amendment No 7) Regulations 2007, SI 2007/2401; NIM02402*].

Until 5 April 2013, HMRC allowed students working during a vacation (but not during term time) to sign a P38(S) certificate, certifying that their earnings for the tax year would not exceed the personal allowance, and permitting the employer holding the certificate to operate a PAYE code of NT (no tax) without first requesting the code from HMRC. With the introduction of RTI reporting, which should have enabled HMRC to issue a relevant code accurately and quickly to any employer of a student, the P38(S) was withdrawn. It should be noted that the P38(S) had no relevance to NIC liabilities. Although the employer holding the P38(S) was entitled to pay the working student without deduction of PAYE, NICs were still due as for any employed earner.

Post-graduate students and researchers

[10.12] The position of post-graduate students and researchers will be determined by application of the tests relating to the existence or otherwise of a contract of service (see **14.5** to **14.7** CATEGORISATION). A person who is remunerated for teaching, demonstrating or assisting in research will, however, normally be regarded as either an employed earner (*Vandyk v Minister of Pensions and National Insurance* [1955] 1 QB 29, [1954] 2 All ER 723), or a self-employed earner (*M39 (1954)*). However, training in research has been held to be education not employment, as has research supervised by teaching staff, and beyond the control of the person paying a grant towards that research. (*M56 (1956); M6 (1950)*).

Case law—MBA course

[10.13] In the case of *Silva v Charnock* [2002] STC SCD 426 Sp C 332 the taxpayer commenced an MBA course but entered into an agreement with a consultancy firm that she would commence working for the firm after the course and they would provide a 'signing on' bonus equal to the amount of the MBA fees. The taxpayer agreed that in the event of her leaving the firm within 12 months of joining she would reimburse the signing on fee. The Inspector of Taxes considered that the £18,000 signing on bonus would be part of the individual's taxable income and subject to tax, and the company paid the sum under deduction of PAYE, which the taxpayer reclaimed under *ICTA 1988, s 200B* (now *ITEPA 2003, s 250* etc). Although not discussed in the judgment, relevant NICs would also have been due if the Inland Revenue had succeeded.

The Special Commissioner found that the payment was a reimbursement of training expenses as correspondence showed that had there been no training costs there would have been no signing on fee.

The then Inland Revenue issued on 17 April 2003 an interpretation regarding employers who reimbursed the cost of an employee's work-related training. This interpretation of the terms to exclude payments by the employer from tax and NICs for work-related training expenses depended on a demonstrable link between the individual's undertaking the training and the particular employment he subsequently obtained and the reimbursement of the pre-employment training costs was outside the exemption where this link was not evident.

Under *ITEPA 2003, s 251* the criteria that the trainee/employee must 'hold', or have a serious opportunity of holding, or can realistically expect to have a serious opportunity of holding, a job with that employer or person connected may not be met in similar circumstances, so it is not automatic that no tax or NICs will be due. If the statutory tax exemption for work-related training is indeed available, then there is a matching NIC exemption. This exemption is necessary because, without it, any payment by the employer cannot be characterised for NIC purposes as an expense incurred in carrying out the employment unless the employee is hired before the training starts. See IR Tax Bulletin, April 2003 page 1022. [*Income Tax (Earnings and Pensions) Act 2003, s 250 formerly ICTA 1988, s 200B*; *Social Security (Contributions) Regulations 2001, SI 2001/1004, Sch 3, Part VII, para* 2].

Vacation studentships

[10.14] Various government departments and large corporates award vacation studentships to university students whom they wish to recruit into their service at the end of the university course. Such students usually receive travelling expenses and an allowance but, as their activity does not constitute gainful employment, the allowances attract no contribution liability.

Registered seafarers and cadets

[10.15] Training allowances paid to a registered seafarer or cadet who is undergoing approved training do not attract contribution liabilities unless the seafarer's agreement or the cadet's indentures continue throughout the period of training.

Articled clerks, etc

[10.16] A *solicitor's* articled clerk will normally occupy the dual position of being concurrently under both a training contract (which is not a contract of service) with his principal *and* a contract of employment (which is a contract of service) with the firm of which his principal is a member. (*Oliver v J P Malnick & Co* [1983] 3 All ER 795, [1983] ICR 708, EAT).

The position of an *accountant's* trainee is somewhat different, however. Under the Education and Training Regulations of the Institute of Chartered Accountants in England and Wales, training contracts are, from 1 January 1983, between a firm and a student and not, as formerly, between an authorised principal and a student. Thus, a trainee chartered accountant will be under two contracts (one of training and one of service) but both will be with the firm concerned. Note also the position for income tax where a trainee accountant (P) claimed a deduction for the cost of studying for an ACCA qualification. HMRC rejected the claim and the Special Commissioner dismissed P's appeal, holding that the expenses were not 'incurred wholly, exclusively and necessarily in the performance of the duties of his employment'. *D W Perrin v HMRC* [2008] STC SCD 672 Sp C 671. See also **30.28** EARNINGS FROM EMPLOYMENT: EXPENSES.

The Secretary of State for Social Security has, in the past, formally determined that the articled clerks of both accountants and auctioneers are, quite apart from their training contracts, under contracts of service with the firms to which their principals belong. (*M29 (1953); M53 (1956)*).

Barristers' pupils

[10.17] Before a barrister can practise unsupervised in England and Wales he or she is required first to complete at least twelve months pupillage. The DSS regarded the whole of the first twelve months of any period of pupillage as a period of training and not of gainful occupation, even though work might be done for a fee under the guidance of the pupil master after the first six months' pupillage had been completed. In the decision *Edmonds v Lawson* [2000] QB 501, [2000] 2 WLR 1091, CA in the Court of Appeal the Judge commented on the remuneration a pupil receives as follows:

> . . . it cannot be conclusive that pupils are not now generally paid. This is true even of funded pupils since, as we understand, chambers grants are treated as professional earnings for tax purposes only in part. But the fact that the generality of barrister pupils have been unpaid, not just in the distant past but also in modern times, is in our view of significance in determining whether a relationship of or equivalent to apprenticeship exists. For although trade apprentices have always received reduced wages, reflecting both the value of the practical training they receive and their reduced productivity, they have always in modern times received some wages and in earlier times board and lodging . . . The freedom of a pupil who has obtained a provisional practising certificate to practise during the second six months of pupillage, not for the benefit of the chambers or the pupil master but for his own sole benefit and reward, would be highly anomalous if this were anything approaching an orthodox employment or apprentice relationship. While a small point in itself it is in our view another pointer against such a relationship.

If a period of pupillage extends beyond twelve months, the DSS (now DWP) had regard to the frequency of paid briefs in deciding whether the extended pupillage constituted training or gainful occupation. If training was minimal and paid briefs accepted regularly, the DSS regarded the barrister as a self-employed earner (see **14.18** CATEGORISATION).

A barrister who has completed his or her pupillage but cannot find a full tenancy in chambers may become a 'squatter' in chambers. The DSS regarded a squatter as a self-employed earner (see **14.18** CATEGORISATION).

In Scotland, an advocate's pupillage lasts for between nine and twelve months (depending on admission dates) during which time no paid legal work may be undertaken. The DSS regarded the whole period of pupillage as one of training.

See Tolley's Practical NIC, December 1999, page 95.

Students and apprentices not ordinarily resident in Great Britain

[10.18] Until 5 April 2012 where, provided he was not ordinarily resident in Great Britain or Northern Ireland (see **51.5** OVERSEAS MATTERS):

- a full-time student, other than a national of another EEA Member State, who was following a course of studies outside the United Kingdom undertook, during his vacation, temporary employment of a nature similar or related to his course of studies as an employed earner in Great Britain or Northern Ireland; or
- a person who had a relationship with someone outside the UK comparable with the relationship which exists between an apprentice and his master in Great Britain or Northern Ireland commenced, before he attained the age of 25, a period of employment in Great Britain or Northern Ireland which was of a nature similar or related to his employment under the relationship outside the UK,

liability for contributions was not to arise until the student or apprentice had been resident in Great Britain or Northern Ireland for a *continuous* period of 52 contribution weeks beginning with the contribution week following the date of his *last* entry into Great Britain or Northern Ireland. [*Social Security (Contributions) Regulations 2001, SI 2001/1004, Reg 145(2), (3)(a)(b)*]. A contribution week is a period of seven days beginning with midnight between Saturday and Sunday. [*Social Security (Contributions) Regulations 2001, SI 2001/1004, Reg 1(2)*]. This 52–week exemption was abolished from 6 April 2012. [*Social Security (Contributions) (Amendment No 2) Regs 2012, SI 2012/817, Reg 7(3)*.]

UK and France reciprocal agreement

[10.19] The 1958 reciprocal agreement between the UK and France provided that students and apprentices who, having been insured under the French contribution scheme, were temporarily employed in the UK were to be insured under the UK contribution scheme from the outset unless they were French or British nationals seconded for no more than six months by an employer in the other state. Thus the provisions of *Social Security (Contributions) Regulations 2001, SI 2001/1004, Reg 145* described above and applicable up to 5 April 2012 were *not* to apply. [*National Insurance (France) Order 1958, Arts 4(2), 6(1)*]. That agreement was superseded by the EC regulations so far as EEA nationals are concerned, but it now applies only to non-EEA nationals coming from France to the UK. The parallel reciprocal agreement provision for students moving from the UK to France covered only UK nationals, who are now exclusively within the EC regulations instead.

Benefit entitlements

[10.20] Credits may be awarded to:

- new entrants to the contribution scheme;
- persons undergoing a course of full-time approved training (special rules apply to disabled people who can only attend a course part-time);
- persons who have reached the end of a course of full-time education, a course of approved training, or an apprenticeship,

so as to enable them to fulfil the *second* contribution condition for certain benefits (see **13.5** BENEFITS: CONTRIBUTION REQUIREMENTS and **24.4** to **24.8** CREDITS).

If the last tax year before the benefit year in which a person's claim for State benefit arises is the tax year in which or before which his liability to pay contributions first arises, that person may, for the purpose of enabling the contribution condition for bereavement (formerly widow's) payment to be met (see **13.5** BENEFITS: CONTRIBUTION REQUIREMENTS):

- aggregate all EARNINGS FACTORS 28 derived from the aggregate of earnings on which he has paid or has been treated as having paid primary Class 1 contributions and from Class 2 contributions he has actually paid before the date of claim, and
- treat that aggregate sum as his earnings factor for the last complete year before the beginning of the benefit year in which a claim arises.

[*SSCBA 1992, Sch 3 para 7*].

Key Points regarding apprentices, trainees and students and NICs

[10.21] Points to consider are as follows.

- True trainees who are not working under a contract of service or apprenticeship, or an apprenticeship agreement, have no National Insurance liability.
- Students from abroad working in the UK were subject to particular rules until 5 April 2012.

- Apprentices are deemed to be employed earners but, if under the age of 25, will attract the nil rate of secondary contribution on earnings up to the Apprentice Upper Secondary Threshold if they meet the conditions of holding a formal, written apprenticeship agreement under one of the statutory frameworks in the relevant part of the UK, and working with a recognised training provider.

11

Armed Forces

Cross-references. See CLASS **1** CONTRIBUTIONS **15**; CROWN SERVANTS AND STATUTORY EMPLOYEES **25**; **51.4** and **51.5** OVERSEAS MATTERS for meaning of resident, ordinarily resident and present.

Other Sources. HM Revenue and Customs National Insurance Manual NIM32000–NIM32007.

Introduction to the armed forces and NICs

[11.1] A serving member of the forces is any person who, being over the age of 16 and not absent on desertion, is a member (giving full pay service) of any establishment or organisation listed in **11.2**, subject to the exceptions stated below. See HM Revenue and Customs National Insurance Manual NIM32003. [*Social Security (Contributions) Regulations 2001, SI 2001/1004, Reg 1(2), 140 and Sch 6*].

None of the following is within the term 'serving member of the forces':

- a serving member of any naval force of HM forces who locally entered that force at an overseas base and who had not previously been insured under the UK scheme;
- a serving member of any military force of HM forces who entered that force, or was recruited for that force, outside the UK and the depot of whose unit is situated outside the UK; and
- a serving member of any air force of HM forces who entered that force, or was recruited for that force, outside the UK and is liable under the terms of his engagement to serve only in a specified part of the world outside the UK. See HM Revenue and Customs National Insurance Manual NIM32004.

[*Social Security (Contributions) Regulations 2001, SI 2001/1004, Sch 6 para 10*].

Prescribed organisation

[11.2] Prescribed establishments and organisations that form the Armed Forces are:

(a) any of the regular naval, military or air forces of the Crown;
(b) Royal Fleet Reserve;
(c) Royal Naval Reserves (including Women's Royal Naval Reserve and Queen Alexandra's Royal Naval Nursing Service Reserve);
(d) Royal Marines Reserve;
(e) Army Reserves (including Regular Army Reserve of Officers, Regular Reserves, Long Term Reserves and Army Pensioners);
(f) Territorial Army;
(g) Royal Air Force Reserves (including Royal Air Force Reserve of Officers, Women's Royal Air Force Reserve of Officers, Royal Air Force Volunteer Reserve, Women's Royal Air Force Volunteer Reserve, Class E Reserve of Airmen, Princess Mary's Royal Air Force Nursing Service Reserve, Officers on the Retired List of the Royal Air Force, Royal Air Force Pensioners and University Air Squadron);
(h) Royal Auxiliary Air Force (including Women's Royal Auxiliary Air Force);
(i) Princess Mary's Royal Air Force Nursing Service Reserve; and
(j) The Royal Irish Regiment to the extent that its members are not members of any force within (a) above.

[*Social Security (Contributions) Regulations 2001, SI 2001/1004, Reg 140 and Sch 6 paras 1–9*].

Categorisation of armed forces for NICs

[11.3] A serving member of the forces is treated as an employed earner in respect of his membership of those forces and as present in Great Britain even if he is, in fact, serving overseas. [*SSCBA 1992, s 116; Social Security (Contributions) Regulations 2001, SI 2001/1004, Reg 141*]. This accords with EC rules which provide that, irrespective of his presence in another State, a person called up or recalled for service in the armed forces of a Member State is to be subject to the social security legislation of that State. [*EC Reg 883/2004, Art 11(3)(d)*].

Members of the forces were excepted from the provisions of *Arts 6 and 9* of the agreement between the United Kingdom and Cyprus which stated that the Cypriot scheme was to apply to all persons employed in the British Sovereign Base areas of Akrotiri and Dhekelia. [*Social Security (Cyprus) Order 1983, Art 8* as amended by *Social Security (Cyprus) Order 1994*]. This ceased to be of practical effect from 1 May 2004 when Cyprus was admitted to the European Union.

Earnings

[11.4] The earnings from employment of serving members of the forces are, for contribution purposes, to exclude:

- Emergency Service grants [*Social Security (Contributions) Regulations 2001, SI 2001/1004, Reg 143(1)(a)*];
- payments in lieu of food and drink certified by the Treasury under *Income Tax (Earnings and Pensions) Act 2003 (ITEPA 2003), s 297(1)* [*Social Security (Contributions) Regulations 2001, SI 2001/1004, Reg 143(1)(b)*];
- contributions to mess expenses certified by the Treasury under *ITEPA 2003, s 297(2)* [*Social Security (Contributions) Regulations 2001, SI 2001/1004, Reg 143(1)(b)*];
- payments of reserve and auxiliary forces' training allowances under *ITEPA 2003, s 298* [*Social Security (Contributions) Regulations 2001, SI 2001/1004, Reg 143(1)(b)*];
- bounties in recognition of liability for immediate call-up in times of emergency [*Social Security (Contributions) Regulations 2001, SI 2001/1004, Reg 143(1)(c)*];
- with effect from November 2006, operational allowance paid to soldiers in respect of service in an operational area specified by the Secretary of State for Defence [*Social Security (Contributions) Regulations 2001, SI 2001/1004, Sch 3 Part VIII para 12A*, inserted by *Social Security (Contributions) (Amendment No 6) Regulations 2006, SI 2006/2924; ITEPA 2003, s 297A*]. From 6 April 2012, the allowance is designated under a Royal Warrant made under the *Armed Forces Act 1986*. [*Social Security (Contributions) (Amendment No 2) Regulations 2012, SI 2012/817, Reg 9*];
- with effect from 1 April 2008, Council Tax Relief payments designated by the Secretary of State for Defence to members of the armed forces. This is an operational welfare package that will give relief on 25% of council tax whilst Forces personnel are on operations. [*Social Security (Contributions) Regulations 2001, SI 2001/1004, Sch 3 Part VIII para 12B*, inserted by *Social Security (Contributions) (Amendment No 2) Regulations 2008, SI 2008/607, Reg 3; ITEPA 2003, s 297B*, inserted by *FA 2008, s 51*]. From 6 April 2012, the Relief is designated under a Royal Warrant made under the *Armed Forces Act 1986*. [*Social Security (Contributions) (Amendment No 2) Regulations 2012, SI 2012/817, Reg 9*];
- with effect from 6 April 2012, Continuity of Education Allowance designated under a Royal Warrant made under *s 333* of the *Armed Forces Act 2006*; and
- with effect from 6 April 2013, Early Departure Payments made to qualifying service personnel who leave the armed forces between the age of 40 and the relevant pension age for MOD personnel specified in the Armed Forces Pension Scheme [*Social Security (Contributions) Regulations 2001, SI 2001/1004, Sch 3, Part VI, para 10A*, inserted by *Social Security (Contributions) (Amendment and Application of Schedule 38 to the Finance Act 2012) Regulations 2013, SI 2013/622, Reg 40(b)*]. Note that the income tax exemption inserted by *Finance Act*

2015, s 15 into *ITEPA 2003, s 640A for lump sums paid under the Armed Forces Early Departure Payments Scheme Regulations 2014 (SI 2014/2328)* was matched by an addition to Sch 3, Part VI, para 10A by *Social Security (Miscellaneous Amendments No 2) Regulations 2015, SI 2015/478, regs 2, 21*, with effect from 1 April 2015.

The 2013 disregard for AFEDPS payment was backdated to 6 April 2005 by the *National Insurance Act 2014, s 16*, but, as noted, the 2015 change was not backdated to the same date as the income tax change.

See HM Revenue and Customs National Insurance Manual NIM32006 and EARNINGS FROM EMPLOYMENT: GENERAL 29.

Earnings period

[11.5] The earnings period (see HM Revenue and Customs National Insurance Manual NIM32007 and EARNINGS PERIODS **34**) of a serving member of the forces is:

- in the case of a member of the regular forces, the accounting period under the Naval Pay Regulations, Army Pay Warrant, Queen's Regulations or the Air Council Instructions, as appropriate; or
- in the case of a person undergoing training in any of the prescribed establishments in (b) to (j) at **11.2** above, a month.

[*Social Security (Contributions) Regulations 2001, SI 2001/1004, Reg 143(2)*].

Contribution rates

[11.6] Although a serving member of the forces is eligible for only a restricted range of State benefits [*Members of the Forces Benefits Regs 1975; The Naval, Military and Air Forces Etc (Disablement and Death) Service Pensions Amendment Order 2003, SI 2003/434; The Naval, Military and Air Forces Etc (Disablement and Death) Service Pensions (Amendment) Order 2005, SI 2005/851*], no allowance has been made since 6 April 1996 for this factor in determining the rates of Class 1 contributions by, and in respect of, such a person.

Contributions are to be calculated in accordance with the normal rules (see CLASS 1 CONTRIBUTIONS 15) and paid into the NATIONAL INSURANCE FUND 48.

Late-paid contributions

[11.7] For the purpose of any entitlement to BENEFITS **13**, any Class 1 contributions paid after the due date in respect of earnings paid to or for the benefit of a person in respect of his employment as a member of the forces are to be treated as paid on the due date (see **21.5** COLLECTION). [*Social Security (Contributions) Regulations 2001, SI 2001/1004, Reg 142*].

Non-compliance with time limits

[11.8] Where a serving member of the forces is unable to comply with a time limit laid down in the legislation by reason of being at sea or outside Great Britain because of his employment, he will be deemed to have complied if he does whatever is required of him as soon as is reasonably practicable. [*Social Security (Contributions) Regulations 2001, SI 2001/1004, Reg 144*].

As far as employers and share option scheme providers are concerned income tax Extra-Statutory Concession ESC A103 – effective from 7 January 2003 – generally has the desired NIC effect also. Where an Armed Forces Reservist is absent from the employer on active service this period of armed service can be treated as continuing employment with the grantor employer for the purpose of Enterprise Management Incentives, Company Share Option Plans, Share Incentive Plans and SAYE schemes. Further, some actions can be taken late so as not to disadvantage the Reservist merely by virtue of his absence. Such actions will not compromise the scheme's tax advantaged status and appropriate NIC exemptions can therefore be maintained. (Inland Revenue Press Release 70/03).

Employment in or by visiting forces

[11.9] Employment as a member of the naval, military or air forces of a country to which *Visiting Forces Act 1952* applies is entirely disregarded for contribution purposes, and this applies equally to any civilian employed by such a force unless he is ordinarily resident in the United Kingdom (see **51.5** OVERSEAS MATTERS). [*Categorisation Regs, Reg 2(4), Sch 1 Part III para 11*, as amended by *Categorisation Amendment Regs 1980, Reg 2; ITA 2007, s 833(1)(3)*].

Employment as a member of international headquarters or defence organisations

[11.10] Employment as a member of any international headquarters or defence organisation designated under *International Headquarters and Defence Organisations Act 1964, s 1* is entirely disregarded for contribution purposes unless the person so employed is:

- a serving member of Her Majesty's regular forces raised in the UK or having its depot or headquarters in the UK; or
- a civilian ordinarily resident in the United Kingdom (see **51.5** OVERSEAS MATTERS) who is not a member of any scheme which the headquarters or organisation has established for the provision of pensions, lump sums, gratuities or like benefits to persons who cease to be in its employment.

[*Categorisation Regs, Reg 2(4), Sch 1 Part III para 12*, as amended by *Categorisation Amendment Regs 1980, Reg 2, Categorisation Amendment Regs 1984, Reg 3* and *Categorisation Amendment Regs 2006, SI 2006/1530, Reg 2(2)*].

British Forces in Germany

[11.11] In the case of members of the UK forces (and the civilian component of such forces) stationed in Germany, *Social Security (Contributions) Regulations 2001, SI 2001/1004, Reg 141* and *EC Reg 883/2004, Art 11(3)(d)* are overridden in appropriate cases by *Reciprocal Agreement (SI 1961/1202)—Germany, Arts 7(5)* and *7(6)* and *Reciprocal Agreement (SI 1961/1513)—Germany, Arts 5(5)* and *5(6). [EC Reg 883/2004, Annex II GERMANY – UNITED KINGDOM.*]

A NATO Status of Forces Agreement was concluded in 1951 to regulate relations between Germany as the host country and the US, UK and French forces permanently stationed there. This was followed by a Supplementary Agreement in 1959 which included provisions on social security as follows:

(1) Except where expressly provided otherwise, international agreements or other provisions in force in the Federal territory concerning social security, including social and medical assistance, shall not apply to members of a force or of a civilian component or to dependents. However, rights and obligations of such persons in the field of social security which have arisen during previous presence in the Federal territory remain unaffected. Furthermore, the fact that a person belongs to one of the categories referred to in the preceding sentences shall not preclude the possibility of his paying contributions to the German social security (soziale Kranken- und Rentenversicherung) for the purpose of continuing insurance on a voluntary basis (Weiterversicherung) nor the possibility of his acquiring and asserting rights deriving from existing insurance.

(2) Nothing in this Article shall affect the obligations of a member of a force or of a civilian component or of a dependent in the capacity of an employer.

Serving members of the BAOR (now British Forces Germany) therefore remained within UK Class 1 liability when stationed in Germany even before EC regulations began to apply in 1973. Serving members of BFG remain subject to UK NIC legislation under *EC Reg 883/2004*, as do UK civil servants [*Art 3(b)(d)*.]

As a result of a carve-out in *Annex II* to *EC Reg 883/2004* civilians remain UK-insured, as if they were employed in the UK, under the terms of the UK-Germany reciprocal agreements of 1961 (the Annex refers to two bilateral agreements made in Bonn on 20 April 1960, but they were legislated by separate SIs in the UK in 1961) if they are employed in Germany by BFG or by an organisation serving those forces and they are not ordinarily resident in Germany. The British and German authorities have agreed a list of the ancillary organisations to which these provisions apply (see below).

This is of less importance now that fewer HM Forces are regularly stationed in Germany and will cease to be relevant once the Rhine Army leaves Germany permanently.

Designated organisations serving the armed forces

[11.12] A list of the designated organisations referred to above was set out in the now superseded DSS Leaflet FB5. In addition to the Ministry of Defence and the NAAFI, a number of religious and welfare-related organisations were specified in the April 1998 edition of FB5 as follows:

- Malcolm Clubs;
- Services Sound and Vision Corporation;
- SSAFA/Forces Help;
- Order of St John of Jerusalem and the British Red Cross Society Joint Committee Service Hospitals Welfare Department (SHWD);
- St Andrew's Ambulance Association;
- CVWW (Council for Voluntary Welfare Work) and the following organisations which are attached to it:
  (a) Catholic Women's League;
  (b) Church Army;
  (c) Church of England Soldiers', Sailors' and Airmen's Clubs;
  (d) Methodist Church Forces' Board;
  (e) Mission to Military Garrisons;
  (f) Royal Sailors' Rest;
  (g) Salvation Army Red Shield Services;
  (h) Sandes Soldiers' and Airmen's Centres;
  (i) Soldiers' and Airmen's Scripture Readers Association;
  (j) Toc H;
  (k) WRVS (Women's Royal Voluntary Service);
  (l) YMCA (Young Men's Christian Association);
  (m) YWCA (Young Women's Christian Association).

Under the terms of the EC regulations and the reciprocal agreement, civilian dependants of British forces personnel working for non-designated organisations or for German employers are usually subject to the German social security system. This is particularly true of German nationals married to UK forces personnel who have never been ordinarily resident in the UK.

Brigade of Gurkhas

[11.13] Until 5 July 2006, employment (other than as a member of any designated international headquarters or defence organisation (see **11.10** above)) as a Queen's Gurkha officer or as any other member of the Brigade of Gurkhas of a person who was recruited for that Brigade in Nepal was disregarded. [*Categorisation Regs, Reg 2(4), Sch 1 Part III para 13*]. This provision had originally been introduced with effect from 6 April 1994 (by *Categorisation of Earners (Amendment) Regs 1994, Reg 3*) at the same time as provisions which imposed a secondary Class 1 liability on 'host employers' using the services in the UK of employees supplied by a 'foreign employer' (see **51.14** OVERSEAS MATTERS).

However, as the Gurkhas were, after public pressure, given entitlement to earn a full UK state pension on the same basis as the UK military, that special categorisation was removed by *Social Security (Categorisation of Earners) (Amendment) Regulations 2006, SI 2006/1530* from 5 July 2006. There was also a consequential change in *Categorisation Regs, Sch 1 Part III* para 12 as regards the qualification it contained regarding naval, military and air forces of the Crown.

The earnings of members of the Brigade of Gurkhas also became taxable, but from the slightly earlier date of 13 June 2006.

The Ministry of Defence made up NIC records by paying contributions on behalf of Brigade members in respect of the period from 1 July 1997 to 30 April 2006. Some such members received incorrect NIC demands from HM Revenue and Customs in respect of 2005–06 but these were subsequently withdrawn following MOD liaison with HM Revenue and Customs.

Key Points regarding the armed forces and NICs

[11.14] Points to consider are as follows.

- Most British service personnel have UK National Insurance liability even when outside the UK.
- There are no longer reduced contributions rates for the armed forces.
- The British forces and their civilian component still in Germany generally have UK liability by virtue of the 1961 reciprocal agreements.
- The special exception for Gurkhas ceased in 2006.

12

Arrears of Contributions

Cross-references. See CLASS **1** CONTRIBUTIONS **15** for liability; CLASS **1**A CONTRIBUTIONS **16** for liability; CLASS **2** CONTRIBUTIONS **18** for liability; CLASS **4** CONTRIBUTIONS **20** for liability and assessment; **21.5**, **21.31** and **21.46** COLLECTION for dates when contributions fall due; **35.13** ENFORCEMENT for prosecution procedure; **51.20** OVERSEAS MATTERS for recovery of foreign contribution arrears.

Introduction to arrears of contributions

[12.1] Contribution arrears will frequently be associated with arrears of income tax. Where they are, they will invariably be recovered under the extensive powers enjoyed by HM Revenue and Customs generally (see **12.3**, **12.4** and **12.14** below). Where they are not so associated, or the association is disregarded, they may be recovered either as a debt due to the Crown or, exceptionally, by means of prosecution under powers contained in *Social Security Administration Act 1992 (SSAA 1992)* (see **12.6** below). Additionally, where the person prosecuted is a limited company, arrears can, in certain circumstances, be recovered from the company's directors as a civil debt. One of the reasons cited for the original abolition of this provision in 1984 was that it discouraged the appointment of non-executive directors and was a disincentive to new entrepreneurs to take over an ailing business with a view to attempting to secure its recovery, but the rule was reinstated in 1999 in the form of a power to issue a personal liability notice to culpable officers of the company. [*SSAA 1992, s 121C*.] The 2014 changes to the agency worker deeming rules and the 2016 travel and subsistence rules for 'intermediary workers' (ie, employees of umbrella companies and personal services companies) added extra 'transfer of debt' provisions so that directors of intermediaries can be pursued if the legal employer and the agency fail to pay PAYE due.

Methods of recovery vary as to the time within which, and the amount for which, an action may be brought. Clearly, HM Revenue and Customs will be influenced by such factors in arriving at its decision as to how to proceed in any particular case.

Following consultation in 2007 and 2008, steps were taken to harmonise collection of the various taxes and duties for which HM Revenue and Customs is responsible (including National Insurance contributions) as well as providing means to set an overpayment of one duty against an underpayment of another. [*FA 2008, s 127* (taking control of goods), *s 130* (set-off).]

'Phoenix' companies

[12.2] The creation of personal liability notices was prompted by the phenomenon of 'phoenix' companies, where directors incur large debts through non-payment of creditors, then liquidate the company, relying on its limited liability status to protect themselves. Such businesses then re-appear in a new company, free of debt, but typically with the same directors and staff. The former CA successfully prosecuted such a director under *s 115(1)* of the *SSAA 1992* (see **12.6** below and **22.14** COMPANY DIRECTORS). In the case in question the director was fined £2,400, ordered to pay costs of £500 and National Insurance arrears of over £50,000. At the time, the CA indicated that it would bring similar prosecutions in the future (CA Press Release 95/14, 27 September 1995. See also Department of Trade and Industry press notice P/96/848 on 12 November 1996 and notice P/99/79 on 28 January 1999). The change of 1984 was reversed with the introduction of *Social Security Act 1998, s 64 (*introducing new *SSAA 1992, s 121C)*, effective from 6 April 1999. [*Social Security Act 1998 (Commencement No 4) Order 1999, Reg* 2]. This enables any failed company's unpaid National Insurance contributions to be recharged to any one or more directors and/or to the company secretary by way of a 'personal liability notice' where the failure of the company to pay appears to HM Revenue and Customs to be attributable to fraud or neglect on the part of such persons. See **22.14**.

Similar – but wider – transfer of debt provisions came into force in August 2007 in respect of unpaid tax and National Insurance contributions debts of managed service companies (see **40.18** INTERMEDIARIES) and, as noted above, in 2014 and 2016 in respect of PAYE liabilities arising on the earnings of agency workers and intermediary travel and subsistence expenses respectively.

Contribution arrears recoverable as income tax

[12.3] Any primary or secondary Class 1 contributions which an employer is liable to pay to HMRC for any income tax month (see **21.5** COLLECTION) may be recovered by application of the recovery provisions contained in income tax legislation and PAYE regulations *as if those contributions were tax* due under *ITEPA 2003, s 684* (formerly *ICTA 1988, s 203*) and the related PAYE regulations. [*Social Security (Contributions) Regulations 2001, SI 2001/1004, Sch 4 para 16* amended by *Social Security (Contributions) (Amendment No 3) Regulations 2012, SI 2012/821*].

The recovery provisions referred to include the following:

- *distraint* in relation to goods and chattels of the person by whom the unpaid amount is due;
- *summary proceedings* commenced in the name of a 'collector' (in practice by the Debt Management and Banking Service) for recovery of the unpaid amount as a civil debt;
- *county court proceedings* commenced in the name of a 'collector' (in practice by the Debt Management and Banking Service) for recovery of the unpaid amount as a debt due to the Crown;
- *High Court proceedings* subject to the *Civil Procedure Rules* for recovery of the unpaid amount as a debt due to the Crown.

[*TMA 1970, ss 61–68; Crown Proceedings Act 1947, ss 13, 15 and 17(2); The Distraint by Collectors (Fees, Costs and Charges) (Amendment) Regulations 1995*].

Proceedings may, in the first instance, be brought by the Debt Management and Banking Service (see DMBM525110 and DMBM650000). This service is responsible for pursuing debts in respect of outstanding taxes and NICs. Arrears may be paid by instalment option. See Working Together Bulletin Issue 19, November 2004, page 5. Collection through the magistrates' courts may be made where the amount due (or any instalment) is less than £2,000 (from 1 July 1999) and less than 12 months old. [*TMA 1970, ss 65(1), 66(1); FA 1984, s 57; County Courts Act 1984, s 16; Recovery of Tax in Summary Proceedings (Financial Limits) Order 1991 (SI 1991/1625); Finance Act 1994, Sch 19 para 19(1)*]. In applying this provision, the tax elements and the contribution element in a debt which includes both elements are statutorily each to be viewed *without regard to the other*, ie an action for recovery of a debt of £5,999.97, being £1,999.99 PAYE, £1,999.99 CIS deductions and £1,999.99 contributions, is within the limit for proceedings in a magistrates' court. Furthermore, earnings-related contributions, Class 1A contributions and Class 1B contributions may each be treated as separate debts for these purposes. [*Social Security (Contributions) Regulations 2001, SI 2001/1004, Sch 4 para 16(5)*]. However, DMBM660060 instructs enforcement staff not to take multiple actions for recovery, ie, not to split a debt up into its constituent parts in order to take separate actions.

With effect from 6 April 2008 HM Revenue and Customs has been able to specify a total amount of combined PAYE/NIC debt without specifying the component elements [*Social Security (Contributions) (Amendment No 3) Regs 2008, SI 2008/636* and *Income Tax (Pay As You Earn) (Amendment) Regs 2008, SI 2008/783, Regs 8–16*].

Class 4 contribution arrears

[12.4] Class 4 contributions which become payable in accordance with assessments (including self–assessments) made under income tax legislation *are* (not merely may be) recoverable as if they were income tax chargeable under *Income Tax (Trading and Other Income) Act 2005 (ITTOIA 2005), Part 2 Chapter 2*. [*SSCBA 1992, s 16(1)*]. Only special CLASS **4** CONTRIBUTIONS (**20.5**) are collected using a different process. [*SSCBA 1992, s 18(2)*.] Such ordinary Class 4 contributions as, following upon the issue of a certificate of deferment, are separately calculated at NIC&EO, cannot be recovered through tax assessments (see **27.8** to **27.9** DEFERMENT OF PAYMENT). [*SSCBA 1992, s 16(2), s 18(2); Social Security (Contributions) Regulations 2001, SI 2001/1004, Reg 99(1)(b)*].

It follows that the recovery provisions summarised at **12.3** above must be applied in relation to arrears of the latter kind.

Furthermore, the penalty provisions of *Taxes Management Act 1970 (TMA 1970), Part X* apply in relation to Class 4 contributions assessable by HM Revenue and Customs as did the interest provisions of the now repealed *TMA 1970, s 88(1)(4)(5)(a)(b)* in relation to tax recovered to make good loss due to a taxpayer's fault. The interest provisions of *TMA 1970, s 86* in relation to amounts overdue did not, however, apply to arrears of Class 4 contributions until 19 April 1993. [*SSCBA 1992, s 16(1)(2), Sch 2 para 6; SSCPA 1992 Appointed Day Order 1993 (SI 1993/1025)*]. From 1 April 2011, the *Social Security Contributions and Benefits Act 1992 (SSCBA 1992), s 16* provisions were amended, albeit incoherently, in an attempt to apply the provisions of *Finance Act 2009 (FA 2009), Schs 55* and *56* on failure to make a return of, and failure to pay, Class 4 liabilities. From 1 April 2013, these were supplemented by importing the new penalty rules on dishonest conduct in *FA 2012, Sch 38*. [*The Finance Act 2012, Schedule 38 (Tax Agents: Dishonest Conduct) (Appointed Day and Savings) Order 2013, SI 2013/279*.]

Class 2 contribution arrears post-6 April 2015

[12.5] Before the changes made by *National Insurance Contributions Act 2015 (NICA 2015), Sch 1* from 6 April 2015, Class 2 arrears were dealt with solely under the NIC legislation (see 21.47). Class 2 contributions which become payable under *SSCBA 1992, s 11(2)* (ie, compulsory contributions due by a self-employed earner under self-assessment) for 2015–16 and later years *are* now recoverable as if they were income tax chargeable under *ITTOIA 2005, Part 2, Chapter 2*, and the collection and recovery provisions of *TMA 1970, Part 6* now apply. [*SSCBA 1992, s 11A*, as inserted by *NICA 2015, Sch 1, para 12*].

Whereas Class 2 contributions were previously included in the regulation-making powers of *SSCBA 1992, Sch 1, paras 6, 7BZA* (powers to combine the collection of contributions with tax), *Social Security Contributions (Transfer of Functions, etc) Act 1999 (SSC(TF)A 1999), s 4* applied the recovery provisions of *SSC(TF)A 1999, Sch 4* to Class 2 contributions where such regulations did not apply. From 6 April 2015, *s 4* was amended so that *Sch 4* is excluded where Class 2 contributions are subject to regulations under neither *paras 6, 7BZA* nor *TMA 1970, Part 6*. In effect, compulsory Class 2 liabilities are now collectible and enforceable in the same way as Class 4 contributions, rather than under the NI enforcement regime.

Prosecution for non-payment of contributions

[12.6] Where contribution arrears are not associated with arrears of tax (or where any such association is disregarded), HM Revenue and Customs can, by High Court writ, proceed for the recovery of the arrears as a debt due to the Crown. Such a course of action has the advantage of being without monetary limits (see **12.3** above and **12.10** below), but is costly, subject to delay and, above all, where the debtor is a limited company, confined to the company itself. Summary proceedings have none of these detriments and unless a time or monetary limit presents an insurmountable obstacle, the magistrates' court recovery route will usually be taken instead. From 6 April 1999, recovery may be made more easily by distraint under *SSAA 1992, s 121A* in England and Wales or under *s 121B* containing similar recovery provisions under Scottish law, both sections inserted by *Social Security Act 1999, s 63* with effect from 6 April 1999. See DMBM655000. [*The Social Security Act 1998 (Commencement No 4) Order 1999, SI 1999/526, Reg 2*]. Otherwise, recovery as a debt due to the Crown by proceedings in a County Court may be commenced in the name of an authorised officer of HM Revenue and Customs. Such person is empowered to conduct any such proceedings whether or not he is legally qualified. See DMBM665000. [*SSC(TF)A 1999, Sch 4 para 3*].

It is no defence against an action for non-payment of contributions to show that there had been no intent to avoid payment, nor is it a defence to have paid the amount outstanding by the time of the court appearance. (*R v Highbury Corner Stipendiary Magistrate, ex p DHSS*, The Times, 4 February 1987). However, with the move of most enforcement into the civil regime since HMRC's takeover of the Contributions Agency in 1999, prosecution for failure to pay is now a rare occurrence.

If a person failed to pay, at or within the time prescribed for the purpose, any contribution which he was liable to pay, he was liable on summary conviction to a fine of not more than £1,000. [*Former SSAA 1992, s 114(1), Criminal Justice Act 1982, s 37(2), Criminal Justice Act 1991, s 17*]. If the contribution remained unpaid at the date of the conviction, he was liable to pay a sum equal to the amount which he failed to pay. [*Sec 119(1)*]. These offences were decriminalised from 6 April 1999 (*Social Security Act 1998 (Commencement No 4) Order 1999, SI 1999/526, Reg 2*) but some of the replacement civil offences have yet to carry any penalties as the introduction of various measures has been deferred.

Fraudulent evasion

[12.7] The *Social Security Act 1998, s 61* introduced with effect from 6 April 1999 a new *criminal* offence of fraudulent evasion and being knowingly involved in fraudulent evasion of contributions. [*The Social Security Act 1998 (Commencement No 4) Order 1999, Reg 2* introducing *SSAA 1992, s 114*]. The offence is brought to trial summarily or on indictment. In summary proceedings the maximum fine is expressed to be at level 5 on the standard scale. This was originally £5,000 with the possibility of increases at some future date by an order made under the *Legal Aid, Sentencing and Punishment of Offenders Act 2012 (LASPOA 2012)*, but in the event, the limit was removed completely (in England and Wales) by *LASPOA 2012, s 85*, effected by *Legal Aid, Sentencing and Punishment of Offenders Act 2012 (Commencement No 11) Order 2015, SI 2015/504, Reg 2*, with effect from 12 March 2015. On indictment the maximum penalty is seven years' imprisonment and/or an unlimited fine. [*SSAA 1992, s 114(1)(2)* as amended by *Social Security Act 1998, s 61*].

Where the offence of non-payment has been committed by a body corporate and is proved to have been committed with the consent or connivance of, or to be attributable to any neglect on the part of, a director, manager, secretary or other similar officer of the body corporate, that person, as well as the body corporate, is guilty of the offence and is liable to be proceeded against accordingly. If the affairs of a body corporate are managed by its members, this provision applies to any member who acts or defaults in the manner described in connection with his managerial functions as if he were a director of the body corporate. [*SSAA 1992, s 115*]. In practice, these provisions have been, from April 1999, short-circuited by involving the new offence under *s 114(1)* and *(2)*, mentioned above and/or *s 121C* (see **12.2** above).

See **42.4** LATE-PAID CONTRIBUTIONS for the meaning of 'connivance'.

In *Dean v Hiesler* [1942] 2 All ER 340, 40 LGR 262, DC it was held that the word 'director', if unqualified, means only a person who has been validly appointed a director in accordance with the provisions of the Companies Acts and does not extend to a person whose appointment is defective (eg, by his failure to take up qualification shares as required by the company's articles of association or by the failure of the board of directors properly to convene the meeting at which he is appointed), even though that person may act as a director, describe himself as such, and even give proper notice of his appointment to the registrar of companies. See also *Gemma Ltd v Davies* [2008] EWHC 546 (Ch), [2009] Bus LR D4, [2008] 2 BCLC 281 for five separate factors that determine whether a person is a *de facto* director.

Provisions originally intended to be used only against 'phoenix companies' in *SSAA 1992, s 121C* may also be relevant (see **12.2** above and **22.14**).

Social Security Fraud Act

[12.8] The *Social Security Fraud Act 2001, s 15* may result in further cases being uncovered of collusion and connivance by employers and their staff to evade tax and NICs. Further, the *Social Security Fraud Act 2001 (Commence-*

ment No 6) Order 2003, SI 2003/273 resulted in the possibility of exchange of information with overseas authorities from 14 February 2003. In addition, the *Insolvency Act 2000* also provided the mechanism for a new procedure for directors' disqualification. Notwithstanding that the employer will be subject to the full force of these acts it is necessary for the information to be passed on to the other relevant departments.

For a detailed description of *prosecution procedure* see **35.13** to **35.19** ENFORCEMENT.

Evidence of non-payment

[12.9] Where the contributions in question (however recoverable) are contributions which fall to be paid in the same way as income tax under the PAYE scheme (see **21.3** COLLECTION), a certificate of an authorised officer that any amount of contributions which a person is liable to pay for any period has not been paid either to the officer or, to the best of his knowledge or belief, to any other person to whom it might lawfully be paid, is, until the contrary is proved, sufficient evidence in any proceedings before a court that the sum stated in the certificate is unpaid and due. [*CRCA 2005, s 25A*]. A document purporting to be such a certificate is to be treated as being so until the contrary is proved. From 6 April 2008, the amount specified may be solely contributions or may be a combined amount including also PAYE, student loan deductions or both. With the introduction of RTI for PAYE and Class 1 NIC reporting, HMRC's computer system has taken over the 'certification' of amounts due. Where an employer has failed to submit an FPS or nil payment EPS for a period, the computer estimates the amount due for PAYE, NICs and student loans and applies it as a 'specified charge' to the employer's tax account. Once it has been shown on the account for seven days, any amount still unpaid is treated as an amount of, or an amount including, Class 1 contributions, that the employer was liable to pay for that period and HMRC may certify it as unpaid. The specified charge will only be removed from the account and cease to be payable when the employer has submitted the relevant FPS, EPS or EYU showing the correct cumulative amount due.

[*Social Security (Contributions) Regulations 2001, SI 2001/1004, Sch 4 para 15(2)(4)*, as amended by *Social Security (Contributions) (Amendment No 3) Regs 2008, SI 2008/636, Reg 4*].

Where non-payment of any contribution, interest or penalty is contested, a certificate of an authorised officer that the searches specified in the declaration for a record of a particular contribution have been made, and that the record in question has not been found, is admissible in any proceedings for an offence as evidence of the facts stated in the declaration *unless*:

- oral evidence to like effect would not have been admissible; or
- a copy of the declaration has not been served on the person charged with the offence seven days or more before the hearing or trial [*SSAA 1992, s 118(6)(a)*]; or

- the person charged with the offence gives notice to the prosecutor, not later than three days before the hearing or trial or within such further time as the court may in special circumstances allow, requiring the person who made the declaration to attend the trial; [*SSAA 1992, s 118(6)(b)*];
- the contrary is proved. [*CRCA 2005, s 25A(3)*].

Time limits on the recovery of arrears

[12.10] Where proceedings for the recovery of unpaid contributions are commenced under the recovery provisions relating to income tax (see **12.3** and 12.4 above), the time limits are as follows.

- *Distraint*. The date on which the person concerned closes his accounts for the year in which the unpaid contributions became due. (*Elliott v Yates* [1900] CA 2 QB 370).
- *Summary proceedings*. In the case of Class 4 contributions, the time limit used to be six months from the date when the contributions became due irrespective of when the demand was made. (*Mann v Cleaver* (1930) 15 TC 367). In the case of Class 1, 1A, 2 and 4 contributions, the limit is now one year from the time the matter complained of first arose. [*Magistrates' Courts Act 1980, s 127(1); TMA 1970, s 65(3)*; DMBM660040].
- *County Court and High Court proceedings*. The *Limitation Act 1980*, which applies a general six-year bar on action to recover statutorily imposed debts, is of no application to proceedings by the Crown for the recovery of any tax or duty [*Limitation Act 1980, s 9(1), s 37(2)(a)*]. However, it is accepted by HMRC (see DMBM527120) that National Insurance contributions (other than Class 4 and, with effect from 6 April 2015, compulsory Class 2 contributions) are not within the scope of 'tax or duty', so the *Limitation Act 1980* restricts the time allowed for HMRC to enforce payment of arrears by civil proceedings to six years from when the debt arose. The position of Class 2 changed in 2015 as a result of *NICA 2015, Sch 1*, inserting a new *s 11A* into *SSCBA 1992*, as a Class 2 liability is to be treated as if it were income tax, in the same way as Class 4 liabilities, and be covered by the same assessment, collection, appeal and penalty rules of *TMA 1970*.

Effect of Limitation Act 1980

[12.11] Because all the provisions of the Taxes Acts, including those relating to collection and recovery are to apply in relation to Class 4 contributions and compulsory Class 2 liabilities from 6 April 2015, the Crown exception to the Limitation Act in respect of tax or duty applies to such unpaid contributions which may therefore be recovered in respect of periods ending more than six years before (eg, under the discovery provisions). [*Limitation Act 1980, s 37(2)(a), SSCBA 1992, ss 11A(1), 16(2)*].

As the payment of Class 2 contributions under *SSCBA 1992, s 11(6)* and Class 3 contributions is voluntary, no question of enforcing their payment can arise.

Where earnings are paid to an employed earner, Class 1 contributions are payable by the employer for the first time on the 19th of the following tax month. The six-year limitation period therefore runs from the following day and expires on the 19th of the same month, six years later (see DMBM527120), although HMRC may claim that reporting the earnings and deductions on the P14 and P35 at the end of the year in pre-RTI years amounted to an acknowledgement of the debt that extends the time limit (see DMBM527130).

This is because, although *LA 1980, s 9(1)* prevents an action to recover any sum recoverable by virtue of any enactment from being brought after the expiration of six years from the date on which the cause of action accrued, *s 29(5)* of that Act treats the cause of action as having accrued on the date that any person liable for a debt, or his authorised agent, acknowledges it in a signed document or makes any payment in respect of it (provided the acknowledgement or part-payment occurs within the original six-year period).

Acknowledgement of a smaller sum than that demanded is an acknowledgement only of that smaller sum (*Surrendra Overseas Ltd v Government of Sri Lanka* [1977] 2 All ER 481, [1977] 1 WLR 565), whereas a general admission of debt will be regarded as an acknowledgement of the whole of the debt if the precise amount can be ascertained by extrinsic evidence (*Dungate v Dungate* [1965] 3 All ER 818, [1965] 1 WLR 1477, CA). Acknowledgement of the debt can be made electronically. In the Court of Appeal case, *Good Challenger Navegante SA v Metal export import SA* [2003] EWHC 10 (Comm), [2003] 1 Lloyd's Rep 471, [2003] ArbLR 20, a telex with typed signature was sent and was held to comply with the requirements of *Limitation Act 1980*. It was intended as a signature and the court said that it must look to the function and not its form. An electronic signature is 'anything in electronic form that is incorporated into or otherwise logically associated with any electronic communication or electronic data' [*Electronic Communications Act 2000, s 7*]. The *Limitation Act 1980* does not apply in Scotland where equivalent legislation provides instead a twenty-year time limit. [*Prescription and Limitation (Scotland) Act 1973, s 6(1)*; DMBM527120]. The Northern Ireland process falls under the *Limitation (Northern Ireland) Order 1989, SO 1989/1339 (NI 11)* for employers in Northern Ireland.

Since the *Limitation Act 1980, s 9(1)* does not extinguish the right to a debt over six years' old, but merely deprives the creditor of a remedy of action for its enforcement, the authorities are entitled to apply any payment that is less than the amount demanded and which does not identify the debts that it is to settle, to the statute-barred debts first. The former CA acknowledged that it was bound by the *Limitation Act* to the six-year time limit but it would still send a 'request for payment' for the whole amount in the first instance (CA Consultation Panel, 11 December 1995). It is evident that HM Revenue and Customs is continuing to apply this practice in respect of contributions in some, although an ever decreasing number of, cases (mainly Class 2 debts originating in NIC&EO, Newcastle and those caused by contracting-out errors) following the transfer of the CA in April 1999. The Tax Faculty of the Institute of Chartered Accountants in England and Wales was informed in Autumn 2009 that new instructions (not seen) have been issued to staff stressing that where arrears of National Insurance cannot be enforced through the courts then they should not be requested in the first place. However, further instances have arisen since that time, notwithstanding the new internal guidance. If such a request is made, any acknowledgement of contributions alleged to be due will, if within the six-year limit, revive HMRC's enforcement powers.

It should also be noted that changes to time limits for various taxes (including PAYE) in *Finance Act 2008 (FA 2008), s 118, Sch 39* are not replicated for National Insurance, which continues to be governed by the six-year limit in the *Limitation Act 1980* (subject to the observations made above about Class 4 and post-6 April 2015 Class 2 liabilities).

When NIC debts are approaching six years old (ie, six years from the cause of action), HMRC may commence distraint to recover the debt within the time limit or, alternatively, lodge a protective claim in the county court, which prevents the limit from applying while any dispute over liability is resolved.

The expression 'cause of action' means the factual situation stated by a plaintiff which (if substantiated) entitles the plaintiff to a remedy at law against the defendant (*Letang v Cooper* [1965] 1 QB 232, [1964] 2 All ER 929, CA). In the case of a National Insurance contribution, it is simply the date on which the payment of the contribution first becomes overdue. (See **21.27** and **21.42** COLLECTION for due dates). An action is 'brought' in the High Court when a claim or originating summons is issued and in a county court when a summons or originating application is issued, and time continues to run until that date. It follows, therefore, that a mere request or even a demand for payment of outstanding contributions not yet six years overdue will be of no consequence if they are more than six years overdue by the time a claim or summons is issued.

Limitation Act 1980, s 32 merits careful attention, however. It provides that where any fact relevant to the plaintiff's right of action has been deliberately concealed from him by the defendant, the period of limitation does not begin to run until the plaintiff has discovered the concealment or could with reasonable diligence have discovered it. That section then goes on to provide that, for this purpose, deliberate commission of a breach of duty in circumstances in which it is unlikely to be discovered for some time amounts to deliberate concealment of the facts involved in that breach of duty. In the majority of cases where HMRC seeks to recover arrears of contributions, those arrears will have arisen through ignorance and there will have been no deliberate concealment of liability or deliberate commission of a breach of duty by the contributor. If, however, HMRC can show that in any particular case there *was* deliberate concealment of liability or deliberate commission of a breach of duty by the contributor *and* that HMRC could not with reasonable diligence have discovered it, time will run not from the due date of the contributions in question but from the date of discovery by HMRC. From correspondence, it appears that the former DSS equated any ignorance or misunderstanding of the law, giving rise to a potential contributor's failure to make contributions (or to claim exception therefrom), with a *deliberate* breach of duty by that individual. This interpretation of *Limitation Act 1980, s 32*, which effectively denies that the commission of an offence can be an honest blunder (see *King v Victor Parsons & Co* [1973] 1 WLR 29) is unsupportable and, were it correct, would prevent that section applying to any situation in which there has been a failure to make proper contributions.

In December 1999 the then Inland Revenue served a statutory demand relating to a judgment debt, comprising unpaid income tax, which was more than six years old. The debtor applied to have the demand set aside, on the grounds that the judgment debt was time-barred under *Limitation Act 1980, s 24*. The registrar dismissed the application and authorised the Inland Revenue to present a bankruptcy petition, but the Ch D allowed the debtor's appeal. Hart J held that presenting a bankruptcy petition based on a judgment debt was within *Limitation Act 1980, s 24*, and that in the case in question, it was not permissible to present a bankruptcy petition in respect of the debt. *Re A Debtor (No 647 of 1999)* [2000] All ER (D) 266.

It should also be noted that any action in the courts to recover contributions claimed to be due must be adjourned (ie, there is no discretion) if a decision by HMRC is still subject to an open appeal. Only once that appeal has been finally determined by a tribunal or court may the county court or High Court hear the debt action. [*SSAA 1992, s 117A*.] In practice the final determination of the tribunal appeal as to the liability will usually lead to cancellation or confirmation of the liability, so the other court where the action has been adjourned is unlikely to be troubled for a second time by the adjourned case.

The only exception to this rule arises where HMRC has issued an accelerated payment notice (APN) or follower notice (FN) in respect of an avoidance scheme. *NICA 2015, ss 4, 5, Sch 2* extended the APN and FN regime that had been introduced into tax legislation by *Finance Act 2014, Parts 4, 5* to encompass contributions under Classes 1, 1A, 1B, compulsory Class 2 and Class 4 with effect from 12 April 2015 (two months after Royal Assent to *NICA 2015*). It is specifically provided that *SSAA 1992, s 117A* does not apply to proceedings before a court for recovery of the disputed contributions. [*NICA 2015, Sch 2, para 18(3)*]. Where any proceedings to enforce a notice of decision under *SSC(TF)A 1999, s 8* have been adjourned because of an appeal to the tribunals, the issue of an APN or FN automatically lifts the stay on proceedings with effect from the due date for payment under the APN or FN. [*NICA 2015, Sch 2, para 18(4)*].

Case law—Benchdollar

[12.12] In the *Benchdollar* case HMRC issued determinations that Class 1 NIC was chargeable on remuneration paid as benefits in kind in 1994–95 in an attempt to avoid NICs. The employers appealed. However, several of these appeals took a very long time to resolve, and HMRC became concerned that they might be unable to collect the contributions because of the six-year time limit laid down by *Limitation Act 1980, s 9*. HMRC also wished to avoid the cost of beginning county court proceedings to recover the contributions, knowing that the recovery proceedings would have to be adjourned pending the outcome of the employers' appeals. HMRC therefore asked the employers to give a formal acknowledgement of HMRC's claims, albeit without making any admission of liability. Unsurprisingly, however, in August 2001, HMRC received legal advice that this procedure did not have the desired effect of circumventing the statutory time limit laid down by *Limitation Act 1980, s 9*, because a denial of liability cannot act as an acknowledgement. The substantive appeals were subsequently determined in favour of HMRC, but the employers declined to pay the contributions, and HMRC began proceedings in the county court. The employers defended the proceedings, contending that the effect of *Limitation Act 1980, s 9* was that they had been begun outside the statutory time limit. The county court referred the case to the Chancery Division for rulings on the interpretation of *Limitation Act 1980, s 9*. Briggs J reviewed the relevant correspondence in detail and held that 'the combination of a detrimental reliance by HMRC, coupled with the obtaining by the relevant employers of the expected benefit of HMRC's reliance upon the shared assumption, were sufficient to render it unfair and unjust for those employers now to advance a limitation defence in relation to NICs arising out of the 1994–95 tax year. In short, in relation to NICs for that tax year, the employers were estopped by convention from asserting the ineffectiveness of the acknowledgements or part payments.' However, HMRC had demonstrably become aware of the ineffectiveness of their proposed procedure by August 2001. Therefore, with regard to claims that became time-barred after September 2001, HMRC should have taken alternative steps to protect its position. By failing to do so, HMRC was 'the author of its own misfortune' and employers facing such claims were entitled to 'assert a limitation defence to those claims, arising out of HMRC's decision not to protect them once aware of the true legal position'. See *HMRC v Benchdollar Ltd & Others* Ch D [2009] EWHC 1310 (Ch); Ch D [2010] All ER 174.

Practice regarding prosecution

[12.13] For the sake of clarity, it must be stated that a separate offence is committed each time an employer fails to pay a contribution in respect of one of his employees and each time a self-employed earner fails to pay a Class 2 contribution that he is liable to pay.

> *Example*
>
> Cliff had 100 monthly-paid employees. In paying their wages for the month ended 31 August 2014 he deducted primary Class 1 contributions but by 22 September had failed to make a remittance to HMRC. He also failed to pay a Class 2 contribution for himself for each week in August. C had committed 104 separate offences!

The introduction of quarterly and half-yearly billing for Class 2 contributions and the abolition of the requirement to pay weekly with effect from 6 April 1993 reduced the opportunity for an offence to be committed, and the 2015 reform of Class 2 has now moved compulsory contributions into the self-assessment system for income tax, so the offence of failure to pay will be dealt with under *FA 2009, Sch 56*.

Since 6 April 1999 distraint procedures are followed (*SSAA 1992, s 121A* — England and Wales — or *SSAA 1992, s 121B* – Scotland). Debt Management and Banking pursues, collects and allocates pre-2015 Class 2 arrears. Contact is made by telephone to secure settlement with instalment options available. However, if payment is not forthcoming cases are transferred to an office of Debt Management and Banking based in Scotland to undertake legal proceedings through the civil courts.

From 1 September 2004, the previous thirty-day time limits in *ss 121A* and *121B* were amended by *National Insurance Contributions and Statutory Payments Act 2004, s 5* to 7 days and 14 days respectively. [*National Insurance Contributions and Statutory Payments Act 2004 (Commencement Order) 2004, SI 2004/1943*]. Often, where National Insurance arrears exist there are also arrears of income tax or other taxes. The standard debt collection procedures for tax in HM Revenue and Customs provide for a series of stages where the debt(s) can be challenged and, if necessary, appealed against before the issue of a notice of distraint. There is no statutory requirement in tax legislation to provide notice of distraint, but HM Revenue and Customs guidance specifies that debtors should then be given a seven-day period of notice of distraint action (except in Scotland – see **12.15**). This change in NIC legislation therefore enables both tax and contribution debts to be recovered in a single action and as a result debtors will not face separate actions for recovery and the attendant duplication of costs. It was confirmed in the Explanatory Notes to the 2004 *Act* the Government had no intention of disturbing the provisions at *SSAA 1992, s 117A*, whereby if a person had appealed against a notice of decision on liability for contributions, no action to recover the debt could be taken until the appeal had been decided by the tribunal. See *HMRC v Hyde Industrial Holdings Ltd* [2006] EWCA Civ 502 where the Court of Appeal held that once a *s 117A* application had been made there did not seem to be any circumstances in which the court could refuse a stay unless the proceedings were issued outside the limitation period. This was subject to the taxpayer seeking dismissal as opposed to an adjournment of the case. See 12.10 above for how *s 117A* has in fact been changed, as a result of a change in policy to combat avoidance and bring in revenue earlier.

Arrears recoverable as a penalty

[12.14] Any sum which a person is liable to pay on conviction for non-payment of contributions is recoverable from him as a penalty. [*SSAA 1992, s 121(4)*]. This does not mean that the sum is a penalty: it is not; and the sum cannot, therefore, be mitigated, for example, under *Magistrates' Court Act 1980, s 34(1)*, in the way that a penalty can be mitigated. (*Leach v Litchfield* [1960] 3 All ER 739, [1960] 1 WLR 1392, DC). Nor do the words 'liable to pay' import any discretion. They are equivalent in meaning to 'shall be ordered to pay' and magistrates cannot, therefore, decline to make an order for payment of arrears where such arrears have been proved. (*Shilvock v Booth* [1956] 1 All ER 382, [1956] 1 WLR 135, DC per Lord Goddard CJ at p 384; *R v Melksham Justices, ex p Williams*, (1983) 147 JP 283). Once an order has been made, it is not appropriate for the prosecution to be requested to commence civil proceedings for recovery (see **12.3** above). (*Morgan v Quality Tools and Engineering (Stourbridge) Ltd* [1972] 1 AER 744).

A sum ordered to be paid after summary proceedings, is not enforceable against the defendant as a civil debt. (*R v Marlow (Bucks) JJ, ex p Schiller* [1957] 2 AER 783). A defendant who fails to comply with an order is, therefore, liable to be committed to prison under *Magistrates' Courts Act 1980, Sch 4* for up to 90 days.

The *Social Security Act 1998*, inserting *SSAA 1994, ss 121A, 121B*, provided for distraint action to be taken in England and Wales where a person served with a certificate confirming his debt, failed to make payment within the required time. A magistrate's warrant was required for forced entry to premises and, where necessary, the assistance of a constable might also be secured. Any goods distrained would be held for a five-day period and then sold at public auction. See Working Together Issue 19, November 2004 page 6. After recovery of the debt the balance of the proceeds, if any, was to be paid to the debtor. [*SSAA 1992, s 121A* inserted by *Social Security Act 1998, s 63*]. 'Premises' did not include a private dwelling house unless an authorised officer had reasonable grounds to believe that a trade or business was being carried on from those premises. [*SSAA 1992, s 121A(10)*].

Social Security Administration Act 1992, s 121B was repealed by *FA 2008, s 129, Sch 43, para 14* with effect from 23 November 2009, and the repeal of *s 121A* followed, by virtue of *FA 2008, s 129, Sch 43, para 2*, albeit with effect only from 6 April 2014. [*FA 2008, s 127 and Part 1 of Sch 43 (Appointed Day) Order 2014, SI 2014/906, art 2*].

DISTRESS WARRANT

SO No 2/06

Derby & South Derbyshire Magistrates' Court (Code)

Date	*6 May 2010*
Debtor	*A Smith T/A Racing Services*
Address	*1–5 Epsom Road, Derby*
Amount ordered	
To be paid	*£867.00*
Costs	*£16.50* (including the fee paid by the complainant for the minute of the order)

The debtor was on 20 . . . at Magistrates' Court ordered to pay the sums specified above [by . . .] [immediately]. The debtor has been served with a copy of a minute of the order and default has been made in the payment.

Total amount still outstanding	*£883.50*
Costs of issuing this warrant	*£6.50*
Amount now payable	*£890.00*
Direction:	

> You [the Constables of   Police Force] are required immediately to make distress of the money and goods of the debtor (except the clothing and bedding of the debtor and the debtor's family and the tools and implements of the debtor's trade; and if the amount shown as now payable, together with the costs and charges of taking and keeping the distress, is not paid, then not earlier than the sixth day after the making of the distress, unless the debtor consents in writing to an earlier sale, to sell the goods and pay the proceeds of the distress to the Clerk of the Magistrates' Court and if [no] [insufficient] distress can be found, to certify the same to that Magistrates' Court.
>
> Magistrate/Justice of the Peace
> [By order of the Court/Clerk of the Court]

Poinding

[12.15] In Scotland, *poinding* proceedings under *Debtors (Scotland) Act 1987, Sch 5* could be instituted where a person had been served with a certificate confirming the debt (*CRCA 2005, s 25A*) but failed to make payment within 14 days. A sheriff's summary warrant was required for recovery and sale by way of poinding. Applications had to be accompanied by the certificate of debt and a certificate stating that it (the certificate of debt) was served on the person in question and the debt remained unpaid. [*SSAA 1992, s 121B* inserted by *Social Security Act 1998, s 63* as amended by *NICSPA 2004, s 5(2)*, repealed by *FA 2008, s 129, Sch 43, para 14* with effect from 23 November 2009].

'Class 6' settlements

[12.16] If, as a result of a PAYE inspection during which income tax underpayments are discovered, an employer is invited to make a voluntary offer in consideration of HM Revenue and Customs' agreeing not to take formal proceedings to recover tax, interest and penalties (referred to in the past by HMRC as a 'Class 6 settlement'), it is HM Revenue and Customs' practice to augment the figure for lost income tax by (currently) 13.8% to represent a hypothetical secondary Class 1 liability on the tax borne by the employer on the grounds that he is meeting what should have been the employee's liability if PAYE had been operated correctly. Under the rule in *Hartland v Diggines* [1926] 10 TC 247 the discharge of employees' tax liabilities is equivalent to cash payments to those employees. From 6 April 2011, the figure of 13.8% is used even for years where the employer's rate was different, since the calculation must be performed at the time of the payment of the alleged liability, not when that liability is claimed to have arisen.

The statutory authority for this practice is weak because a Class 1 liability can only arise where in any tax week earnings are paid to or for the benefit of an earner in respect of any one employment of his which is employed earner's employment (*SSCBA 1992, s 6(1)*). In the case of such a settlement the payment is made in order that HM Revenue and Customs will waive its right to recover the tax lost by assessment; the payment is not earnings paid to or for the benefit of an earner and so there are no grounds for levying Class 1 contributions. The DSS always rejected this interpretation, as does HMRC, on the grounds that the voluntary nature of the offer means that the contract, of which it forms part, is merely an administrative easement which cannot be allowed to remove a legal liability for contributions. (Letter from DSS dated 2 September 1993). It is, however, unclear how a valid contract can be entered into other than voluntarily. A second objection is that the settlement figure is rarely calculated precisely enough to establish the exact amount attributable to each employee so that the requirements of *s 6(1)* are satisfied.

Where a Class 1 liability arises on cash payments to employees which should have been payrolled, that liability is not subject to the same objections and may be due at 12.8% up to 5 April 2011 and 13.8% thereafter. A primary contribution may also be collected.

The introduction of legislation concerning PAYE settlement agreements (PSAs) (previously known as Annual Voluntary Settlements), which enables HM Revenue and Customs to exact the tax liability from the employer without recourse to the employee, impacts on NICs treatment in a more regulated environment. [*ITEPA 2003, ss 703–707*]. See 17 CLASS 1B CONTRIBUTIONS. In settlement cases, however, HM Revenue and Customs practice of charging NIC on the tax settlement still remains questionable. Further, it was held in *IRC v Nuttall* [1990] STC 194 CA and *IRC v Wollen* [1992] STC 944 CA that payments made under such an agreement are in consideration of no further recovery proceedings being taken against the employer, and that the original sums lose their identity as tax. It therefore appears that there is no pecuniary liability of the employee which the employer can be regarded as having settled. See *Tolley's Practical NIC Newsletter* Vol 2, pp 78-80, October 1983.

There was originally no provision to deny tax relief for interest on late-paid contributions but the Chancellor announced in the 2003 Budget that new legislation to take effect for accounting periods ended after 9 April 2003 would correct what the authorities saw as an anomaly. *FA 2003, s 147(2)* inserted *SSCBA 1992, Sch 1, para 6(4B)*. However, the vires for this change are questionable as legislation that states what is and is not taxable or allowable ought to appear in the Taxes Acts and not SSCBA 1992.

Bankruptcy, liquidation and receivership

[12.17] In the winding-up of a company and in the distribution of a bankrupt's estate, certain unpaid National Insurance contributions were formerly preferential debts and ranked equally with, and fell to be paid along with, other preferential debts in priority to all other debts. However, the *Enterprise Act 2002* changed that in November 2002. Provisions affecting the Crown's preferential charge came into effect on 15 September 2003 so that its status as a preferential creditor was abolished as regards amounts due to what is now HM Revenue and Customs in respect of income tax and National Insurance contributions in the 12 months prior to the relevant date. This means that the Crown is often far stricter in seeking prompt payment of tax, due to the abolition of its preferential creditor status. [*Insolvency Act 1986, s 175, s 328(1), Sch 6 paras 6 and 7* as amended by *Insolvency Act 2000; Enterprise Act 2002, s 251(1)*].

Definition—Relevant date

[12.18] In relation to a company, the *relevant date* is:

(a) in the case of a company being wound up by the court where the winding-up order was made immediately upon the discharge of the administration order, the date of the making of the administration order;
(b) in a case not falling within (a) above where a company being wound up by the court had not commenced to be wound up voluntarily before the date of the making of the winding-up order, the date of the appointment (or first appointment) of a provisional liquidator, or, if no such appointment has been made, the date of the winding-up order, and
(c) in any other case, the date of the passing of the resolution for the winding-up of the company.

[*Insolvency Act 1986, s 387(3)* as amended by *Insolvency Act 2000*].

In relation to a bankrupt, the *relevant date* is:

- where at the time the bankruptcy order was made, there was an interim receiver of the debtor's estate appointed under *Insolvency Act 1986, s 286*, the date on which the interim receiver was first appointed after the presentation of the bankruptcy petition; and
- in any other case, the date of the making of the bankruptcy order.

[*Insolvency Act 1986, s 387(6)* as amended by *Insolvency Act 2000*].

Where there is a voluntary winding up arrangement it will be managed by HM Revenue and Customs through the Voluntary Arrangement Service (VAS) situated at Worthing.

Set-off of Crown debts

[12.19] Under *Insolvency Act 1986, s 323* (in the case of the distribution of a bankrupt's estate) and *Insolvency Rules 1986, Rule 4.90* (in the case of the distribution of the property of a company which is being wound up), sums due from and to parties involved in mutual dealings are to be set off against each other, and this applies to Crown debts such as VAT, income tax and social security contributions. (*Re Cushla Ltd* [1979] STC 615). The set-off rules were formerly contained in *Bankruptcy Act 1914, s 31* (now repealed) which, by virtue of *Companies Act 1985, s 612* (also repealed) applied also in the case of the winding-up of an insolvent company. Thus, in *R A Cullen Ltd v Nottingham Health Authority*, (1986) 2 BCC 99, 368, CA it was held that where a health authority obtained services and materials from an outside supplier did so as an agent of the Crown and the supplier of such services and materials could, under *Bankruptcy Act 1914, s 31* as applied by *Companies Act 1985, s 612*, set money due to it from the health authority in that respect against its arrears of National Insurance contributions. See also *Companies Act 2006, s 754(3)*.

Where a company is in receivership the *Civil Procedure Rules 1998, SI 1998/3132, Order 42*, prevents the setting off by the receiver of any debts due from the Crown against liabilities for other taxes, duties or penalties (these include National Insurance contributions).

In the case of *CIR v Lawrence & Another*, Ch D 10 February 2000 All ER (D) 157 administration orders were made in respect of a number of associated companies. One of the companies continued to trade and to pay its employees. The administrators failed to pay PAYE and NIC deductions to what is now HM Revenue and Customs. HM Revenue and Customs applied to the Ch D, which held that the administrators were required to pay these sums. The effect of *Insolvency Act 1986, s 19(5)* was that PAYE and primary Class 1 National Insurance contributions enjoyed special priority over the general expenses of the administrators, since 'administrators should not be encouraged to fund an administration with PAYE or NIC deductions they have made or will make from the salary roll'. However, the Ch D held that this special priority did *not* extend to secondary Class 1 NICs.

From Royal Assent to the *FA 2008* (21 July 2008), HM Revenue and Customs has the power to act on its own volition to set an overpayment of one duty for which it is responsible against an underpayment of another. Previously, this could happen only at the request of, or with the consent of, the individual or body concerned. The set-off applies to all duties for which HM Revenue and Customs is responsible and therefore includes National Insurance contributions. This provision has been used as the basis of allowing employers to claim the employment allowance, since no specific provision was made for the allowance in *Social Security (Contributions) Regulations 2001, SI 2001/1004, Sch 4*. [*ITA 2007, s 429; FA 2008, s 130*.]

Waiver of arrears

[12.20] Standing instructions (unpublished) provide for officials to waive proceedings for arrears where, for example, a person would have been entitled to exception from contribution liability had he claimed it, or where it would not be practicable to recover the arrears because of a person's financial circumstances. (Hansard 24 February 1978 Vol 944 No 67 Col 836). There is no limit to the amount which may be so waived and authority for granting waivers was, from April 1983, delegated to local office management, although those decisions will now be made centrally. The guidance of the former DSS to its local offices suggested that, in deciding whether a waiver should be granted, they should take account of such factors as whether there was a genuine and reasonable doubt about the class of contribution payable, whether the DSS or another Government Department may have misdirected the employer on National Insurance contribution liability, and the size of the arrears. In combination with one or more of those factors, local offices may take into account the assets of the employer (Hansard 20 July 1988 Vol 137 Col 683). It is understood, for example, that individuals will not normally be pursued for arrears of contributions if they are in receipt of income support (or income-based jobseeker's allowance) and unlikely to be able to pay any sums demanded.

Payment of arrears by instalments

[12.21] Rather than take proceedings against a defaulting contributor, NIC&EO will, wherever possible, make an arrangement which will enable him to discharge his liabilities over a period of time. However, interest is a statutory charge and cannot be waived or frozen. The arrangement will normally involve the contributor's agreement to pay by instalments an agreed amount of contribution arrears (possibly a lesser amount than the actual contribution debt—see **12.20** above) over a period of 12 months or longer. The arrangements will be set down in writing on a form CA 5719 (for a company or other business) or form CA 5721 (self-employed contributor) which must be signed by the contributor and will contain, in addition to the instalment terms, both an admission of liability and a declaration of inability to pay in full. Failure to adhere to the arrangement will, of course, result in the proceedings being taken against the contributor and, in that event, the admission of liability on the form CA 5719 or CA 5721 will be evidence of the unpaid debt. In Working Together Issue 19, November 2004 page 5, the Debt Management and Banking Service confirm that:

> Whilst payments due from employers mainly represent deductions from employees we do not preclude helping such businesses overcome temporary difficulties but we would look for such debts to be cleared within a maximum of 12 months with payment of current deductions, and submission of any returns, being an absolute condition.
>
> Where agreeing to a payment plan which extends for more than three months we will seek and record comprehensive details of income, expenditure and assets to enable us to agree a repayment figure. Arrangements are always confirmed in writing and are subject to periodic review.

In the 2008 Pre Budget Report, the Chancellor announced that HM Revenue and Customs had that day introduced a new, dedicated Business Payment Support Service designed to meet the needs of businesses affected by the current economic conditions. The service reaches across all HMRC imposts including National Insurance contributions. Anyone concerned about being able to meet tax, National Insurance or other payments owed to HMRC or who expects that payments coming due will cause problems, may get in touch to discuss payment options to ease temporary cashflow difficulties.

The Business Payment Support Service is available on 0300 200 3835 (Mondays to Fridays 8.00am to 8.00pm, Saturday and Sunday 8.00am to 4.00pm) to any individual or business who has not yet received a payment demand. However, HMRC stresses that the BPSS is intended for new enquiries only. When contacted, HMRC staff will review the business circumstances and discuss temporary options tailored to the business needs, such as arranging for payments to be made over a longer period. They will not charge additional late payment surcharges on payments included in the arrangement, although interest will continue to be payable in those cases where it applies.

Where the date for paying Class 2 and Class 4 contributions has already passed, the Self-Assessment Payment Helpline is the appropriate contact point: 0300 200 3822, with the same availability as the BPSS, except for Sundays, when it is closed.

Tax relief for Class 1, Class 1A and Class 1B contributions

[12.22] No tax relief may be obtained in respect of any primary element of Class 1 contribution arrears which are paid by an employer. [*ITTOIA 2005, ss 53, 272, 868* and *ITEPA 2003, s 360A; ITA 2007, Sch 1, para 507*]. This is so despite the fact that the employer may be debarred from recovering the primary contributions from the employee to whose earnings they relate. (See **15.20** CLASS 1 CONTRIBUTIONS, **14.25** CATEGORISATION and **21.19** COLLECTION). Relief may be obtained in respect of the secondary element of the arrears, however, but difficulties may be encountered with HM Revenue and Customs in this respect. Officers of H M Revenue and Customs have been known to cite *James Spencer and Co v IRC* (1950) 32 TC 111 as authority for the proposition that secondary Class 1 contribution arrears paid must be allowed as a deduction from trading profits in the year in which they are paid rather than in the years to which they relate. The case cited establishes no such principle. The liabilities there in question were contingent liabilities, not matured liabilities. By contrast, Class 1 arrears comprise liabilities which have fully matured in earlier years and it is, therefore, in those earlier years that relief should be given (*Simpson v Jones* (1968) 44 TC 599). The machinery for obtaining relief in years for which tax assessments have become final is the former 'error or mistake' claim, now overpayment relief claim, provided for by *TMA 1970, s 33, Sch 1AB* and by *FA 1998, Sch 18, para 51*.

The *FA 1997, s 65* change to this original provision in *ICTA 1988* gave statutory effect to the former ESC B48 so that Class 1A National Insurance contributions may be allowed as a deduction in arriving at profits or gains. *FA 1997, s 65(3)* first provided for the deduction of Class 1A contributions from profits and gains where the contributions were paid on or after 26 November 1996. In practice, relief was given on an extra-statutory basis for earlier payments. Further amendment was made by *FA 1999, s 61* so as to permit tax relief on Class 1B contributions paid by employers. See now *Corporation Tax Act 2009, ss 1302, 1306*.

Where an employer settles liabilities claimed by HMRC in respect of avoidance schemes using employee benefit trusts (EBTs) or employer-financed retirement benefits schemes (EFRBS), HMRC practice is to permit the employer contributions claimed to be deducted from the total payments made to the trust before calculating any PAYE and primary contributions. The total settlement paid by the employer (including any amounts representing employee income tax and primary NICs) usually includes an allowance for corporation tax or income tax relief for the employer that would have been due if the original payments to the trust had been treated at the outset as remuneration of employees.

Key Points regarding arrears of contributions

[12.23] Points to consider are as follows.

- Company officers can be pursued personally for unpaid company NIC debts.
- Persons can face a criminal prosecution where contributions have been fraudulently evaded.
- The six-year time limit in England and Wales stems from the *Limitation Act 1980*, though it is important not to revive the six-year period by acknowledging the debt or making any payment.
- That six-year limit is not affected by recent changes to various tax time limits, but the transfer of Class 2 into the Class 4 management regime means that it is now subject to the enforcement rules for income tax rather than NICs.

13

Benefits: Contribution Requirements

Cross-references. See CONTRACTED-OUT EMPLOYMENT 23; CREDITS 24 for circumstances in which contributions will be awarded rather than paid; 26.4 DEATH OF CONTRIBUTOR for widow's right to make good her deceased husband's contribution record; EARNINGS FACTORS 28 for calculation of factors; NATIONAL INSURANCE NUMBER 49 for contribution records.

Other Sources. Tolley's Practical NIC, August 2001 page 60; Tolley's Practical NIC, June 2005 page 44.

Introduction to benfits: contribution requirements

[13.1] Contributions payable under the provisions and regulations described in this work are levied with the primary objective of providing funds for the payment of contributory benefits, 97% of all funds being spent on paying state pensions (see NATIONAL INSURANCE FUND 48). [*SSCBA 1992, s 1(1)*]. Non-contributory benefits (with the exception of guardian's allowance) are paid by the Exchequer. Some are means-tested (or 'income-related') while others are payable without regard to means. They include the following:

- attendance allowance;
- carer's allowance (formerly invalid care allowance);
- category D retirement pensions and age addition;
- child benefit;
- child tax credit;
- council tax benefit;
- guardian's allowance;
- housing benefit;
- income support;

- income-related jobseeker's allowance (JSA(IR));
- income-related employment & support allowance (ESA(IR) / incapacity benefit);
- industrial injuries disablement benefit;
- pension credit;
- personal independence payment (being phased in);
- severe disablement allowance;
- social fund payments (maternity, funeral, cold weather);
- universal credit;
- war widow's pension;
- winter fuel payment; and
- working tax credit.

[*SSCBA 1992, ss 63–150*; *Welfare Reform Act 2012*.]

Contributory benefits

[13.2] Non-contributory benefits are of no further concern in this work. Contributory benefits and the particular class of contribution that buys entitlement are of concern, however, and include

		Class
(*a*)	contribution-based jobseeker's allowance (JSA(C));	1
(*b*)	Statutory Sick Pay (SSP)†;	1
(*c*)	Statutory Maternity Pay (SMP)†;	1
(*d*)	Statutory Paternity Pay (SPP)†;	1
(*e*)	Statutory Adoption Pay (SAP)†;	1
(*f*)	Statutory Shared Parental Pay (ShPP)†;	1 and 2§
(*g*)	incapacity benefit (IB) or contribution-based employment and support allowance (ESA(C));	1 and 2
(*h*)	maternity allowance;	1 and 2
(*i*)	bereavement (formerly widow's) payment;	1, 2 and 3
(*j*)	widowed parent's (formerly widowed mother's) allowance;	1, 2 and 3
(*k*)	bereavement allowance (formerly widow's pension);	1, 2 and 3
(*l*)	category A and B retirement pensions.	1, 2 and 3
(*m*)	single-tier state pension under *Pensions Act 2014*	1, 2 and 3
(*n*)	state pension top-up to 1975 scheme state pensions	3A

† Strictly, no contribution is necessary but the receipt of SSP, SMP, SPP and SAP is compromised for an employee with *average* earnings below the NIC LEL. This remains the applicable earnings limit notwithstanding that, from 6 April 2000, employees do not pay contributions until earnings reach the (primary) Earnings Threshold.
§ The mother must be an employee eligible for SMP or SAP, but the father can claim if eligible for SPP when the mother is eligible for SMP, MA or SAP. MA is the only relevant benefit that applies to Class 2 contributors.

Social Security

Benefit Rates for 2018–19

	Weekly rate
Attendance Allowance	
Higher rate	£85.60
Lower rate	£57.30
Bereavement Benefits*	
Bereavement payment (lump sum)	£2,000.00
Widowed parent's allowance	£117.10
Bereavement allowance/Widow's pension (standard)	£117.10
Widower's pension (standard rate)	£117.10
(Lower amounts may be due depending on age.)	
Carer's Allowance	£64.60
Child Benefit	
First or only child	£20.70
Each subsequent child	£13.70
Disability Living Allowance	
Care component	
– highest	£85.60
– middle	£57.30
– lowest	£22.65
Mobility component	
– higher	£59.75
– lower	£22.65
Earnings rules	
Carer's Allowance weekly limit	£120.00
Employment and support allowance (replaced Incapacity benefit for new claims from 27 October 2008)	
Single, basic allowance	
– under 25	£57.90
– 25 or over	£73.10
Components	
– work related activity group	£29.05
– support group	£37.65
Guardian's Allowance	£17.20
Incapacity Benefit* – see ESA	
Invalidity allowance (transitional) – applies to claims before 13 April 1995	
– higher rate	£11.60
– middle rate	£6.45
– lower rate	£6.45

	Weekly rate
Income Support	
Single/lone parent	
– up to 24	£57.90
– 25 or over	£73.10
Couple	
– both under 18	£57.90
– both over 18	£114.85
Industrial Death Benefit	
Widow's/widower's pension	
– higher rate	£125.95
– lower rate	£37.79
Industrial Injuries Disablement Pension	
100% disability	£174.80
20% disability	£34.96
Jobseeker's Allowance (Contribution-based)*	
Single 25 or over	£73.10
Single under 25	£57.90
Maternity Allowance*	
Standard rate	£145.18
Threshold	£30.00
Pension Credit	
Standard minimum guarantee (single)	£163.00
Standard minimum guarantee (couple)	£248.80
Personal independence payment	
Living — enhanced	£85.60
Living — standard	£57.30
Mobility — enhanced	£59.75
Mobility — standard	£22.65
Retirement Pension*	
Pre-2016: Category A or B (maximum)	£125.95
Category B (lower)	
– spouse or civil partner's contribution	£75.50
Category C or D	
– non-contributory	£75.50
Addition at age 80	£0.25
After 2016: New state pension (maximum for 35 years' contributions)	£164.35
Severe Disablement Allowance	
Basic rate	£77.65
Age related addition	
– higher rate	£11.60
– middle rate	£6.45
– lower rate	£6.45

	Weekly rate
Statutory Adoption, Maternity, Paternity and Shared Parental Pay*	
Earnings threshold	£116.00
Standard rate	£145.18
Statutory Sick Pay*	
Earnings threshold	£116.00
Standard rate	£92.05

[*SSCBA 1992, s 20(1)*].

The weekly rates of the major benefits shown above apply from 9 April 2018. [*Social Security Benefits Up-rating Order 2018, SI 2018/281*].

Retirement pensions

[13.3] Pensions under the 1975 state pension scheme that applies to all those who reached state pension age before 6 April 2016 were awarded under four categories: A, B, C and D. Category C is now obsolete as it covered those who had reached state pension age under the pre-1948 scheme rules. Anyone reaching state pension age on or after 6 April 2016 falls under the rules for the 'new state pension' in *Pensions Act 2014*, which is variously referred to as the single-tier state pension or the flat-rate state pension, since it comprises a single weekly amount rather than one made up of a basic component with graduated or earnings-related additions.

A category A pension is a retirement pension claimed on a person's own contribution record whereas a category B pension (see above) is a retirement pension claimed on the record of a spouse, former spouse or deceased spouse or civil partner. Category D pensions are, however, non-contributory retirement pensions payable to people aged 80 or over whose contribution record is so inadequate that they receive no category A pension or one which is very small. For a person to become entitled to any of these benefits, he must have reached state pension age before 6 April 2016 and satisfied not only any circumstantial conditions attaching to the benefit concerned but also various contribution conditions. See *TJ Beamish v HMRC* [2009] UKFTT 271, TC00217.

From April 2005 men over 65 and women over 60 were able to defer their State pension and receive an increased weekly amount at a higher rate previously, or, after at least twelve months' deferral, a taxable lump sum with interest (thus the first lump sums under this new arrangement could not be paid earlier than 6 April 2006). See Tolley's Practical NIC, June 2005 page 44.

When the single-tier state pension was introduced on 6 April 2016, existing pensions continued to be payable on the existing basis, but those who reach state pension age on or after that date will receive a state pension based solely on their own contributions, with the exception of women who chose to rely on their husband's contributions and made a reduced rate election before 11 May 1977 that is still valid. As with the old rules, the new state pension can also be deferred by virtue of simply not claiming it. For every nine weeks of deferral after state pension age, the state pension increases by 1%, which represents just under 5.8% for each full year. [*State Pension Regulations 2015, SI 2015/173, Reg 10*].

Gender Recognition Act

[13.4] Under the *Gender Recognition Act 2004, Sch 5* those contributors whose gender has been reassigned are legally entitled to change their recorded gender. This can affect their benefit entitlement arising out of the NICs paid prior to issue of the Gender Recognition Certificate. The Act came into effect on 4 April 2005 and affects the treatment of contributory and non-contributory benefits where a full Gender Recognition Certificate has been issued to the individual. The nature of the adjustment will depend on the allowance or benefit being claimed. See *Richards v Secretary of State for Work and Pensions* C-423/04, [2006] ECR I-3585, [2006] All ER (EC) 895, ECJ. [*Gender Recognition Act 2004, Sch 5, s 13*].

In a recent case affecting NICs, an individual (M) was born in 1942 with 'the physical characteristics of a male'. He subsequently lived as a male and married a female. In 2004 he decided to live as a female, and in October 2004 he divorced his wife. In December 2005 he underwent gender reassignment surgery. In December 2006 the Gender Recognition Panel, established under the *Gender Recognition Act 2004*, recognised M as a female. Having been recognised as a female and having reached the age of 60, M was thus no longer required to pay National Insurance contributions. HMRC issued a ruling that this change of status could not be backdated, and that M was still required to pay contributions until the issue of the certificate. M appealed, contending that her change of gender should be backdated to June 2004. The First-Tier Tribunal rejected this contention and dismissed M's appeal. Judge Paines held that M 'was required to continue paying NICs until the issue to her of a gender recognition certificate under the *Gender Recognition Act 2004*'. *M v HMRC* [2010] UKFTT 356, TC00638.

Contribution conditions

[13.5] All references below to the payment of Class 1 contributions includes, from 6 April 2000, receipt of earnings subject to Class 1 equal to or exceeding the Lower Earnings Limit (LEL) but on which no contributions have actually been paid due to the earnings not exceeding the primary Earnings Threshold. [*SSCBA 1992, s 6A(1)(2)* inserted by *Welfare Reform and Pensions Act 1999, Sch 9 para 3*, and *The Social Security Contributions (Notional Payment of Primary Class 1 Contributions) Regulations 2000, SI 2000/747*].

First contribution condition

[13.6] Most contributory benefits have two contribution conditions attached. The first contribution condition for:

- *contribution-based jobseeker's allowance* (JSA(C)), payable for up to 26 weeks without means-testing, is that, before the day in respect of which benefit is claimed, the claimant has actually paid primary Class

1 contributions on earnings of at least the LEL in 26 weeks (which need not be consecutive) in one of the last two complete tax years before the benefit year (ie, the first Sunday in January to the Saturday before the equivalent Sunday in the next year) in which the beginning of the period of interruption of employment falls. Before 1 November 2010, the EARNINGS FACTORS 28 derived from earnings on which primary Class 1 contributions had been paid or treated as paid had to be not less than *25 times* that year's weekly LEL in one of the two years. With higher earnings this condition could have been met in rather less than 25 weeks (see *SSCBA 1992, s 21, Sch 3 para 1; JSA 1995, s 2; Welfare Reform Act 2009 (Commencement No 3) Order 2010, SI 2010/2377* and *Social Security (Contribution Conditions for Jobseeker's Allowance and Employment and Support Allowance) Regulations 2010, SI 2010/2446*; EARNINGS LIMITS AND THRESHOLDS 33). From 1 January 2012, certain spouses and civil partners who accompany a member of HM forces on a posting outside the UK will be treated as satisfying the first contribution condition on their return to the UK provided they have satisfied the condition in any previous tax year. [Social Security (Contribution Conditions for Jobseekers Allowance and Employment and Support Allowance) Regulations 2011, SI 2011/2862];

- *contribution-based employment and support allowance* (ESA(C)), payable for up to one year without means-testing, is that, before the day in respect of which benefit is claimed, the claimant has actually paid or been treated as paying primary Class 1 contributions or Class 2 contributions in respect of weeks in one of the last *two* completed tax years on earnings at the LEL for the year. Before 1 November 2010, the period was *three* years, and the EARNINGS FACTOR 28 derived from earnings on which primary Class 1 contributions had been paid or treated as paid or from Class 2 contributions had to be not less than *25 times* that year's weekly LEL. With higher earnings this condition could have been met in rather less than 25 weeks. (See *SSCBA 1992, s 21, Sch 3 para 2; Welfare Reform Act 2009 (Commencement No 3) Order 2010, SI 2010/2377* and *Social Security (Contribution Conditions for Jobseeker's Allowance and Employment and Support Allowance) Regulations 2010, SI 2010/2446*; EARNINGS LIMITS AND THRESHOLDS 33). From 1 January 2012, certain spouses and civil partners who accompany a member of HM forces on a posting outside the UK will be treated as satisfying the first contribution condition on their return to the UK provided they have satisfied the condition in any previous tax year. [*Social Security (Contribution Conditions for Jobseekers Allowance and Employment and Support Allowance) Regulations 2011, SI 2011/2862*];
- *maternity allowance*, payable for up to 39 weeks, is that the claimant has actually been self-employed or employed and earning at least £30 per week for any 13-week period in the 66 weeks before the baby's expected date of birth, but is not eligible for SMP from any employer, or self-employed paying Class 2 contributions (or before 6 April 2015 holding a small earnings exception) in respect of at least 26 weeks in the 66 weeks immediately preceding the week before the baby is due (see *SSCBA 1992, s 35(1), Sch 3 para 3*). From 6 April

2015, when Class 2 collection was reformed by NICA 2015 so that it occurs in arrears after the end of the tax year, a self-employed woman intending to give birth or adopt a child must consider whether to pay Class 2 contributions voluntarily during the year so as to ensure that she can meet the contributions test of having paid the relevant contributions for 13 weeks;

- *bereavement (formerly widow's) payment* is that the contributor concerned (ie the claimant, the claimant's spouse, or the claimant's former spouse, or civil partner, etc) has actually paid primary Class 1 contributions or Class 2 contributions or Class 3 contributions in respect of any tax year ending before the date on which the contributor concerned attained pensionable age or died under that age, and that the EARNINGS FACTOR 28 derived from earnings on which primary Class 1 contributions have been paid or treated as paid and from any Class 2 contributions or Class 3 contributions is not less than *25 times* that year's weekly LEL (see *SSCBA 1992, Sch 3 para 4, para 7*; EARNINGS LIMITS AND THRESHOLDS 33);
- *widowed parent's (formerly widowed mother's) allowance, bereavement allowance (formerly widow's pension), category A and B retirement pensions* is that the contributor concerned (ie the claimant, the claimant's spouse, or civil partner, or the claimant's former spouse, etc) has actually paid primary Class 1 contributions or Class 2 contributions or Class 3 contributions in respect of any one tax year ending before the date on which the contributor concerned attained pensionable age or died under that age, and that the EARNINGS FACTOR 28 derived from earnings on which primary Class 1 contributions have been paid or treated as paid and from any Class 2 contributions or Class 3 contributions is not less than *52 times* that year's weekly LEL (see *SSCBA 1992, Sch 3 para 5*; EARNINGS LIMITS AND THRESHOLDS 33);
- *new state pension* is that the contributor concerned (note: *not* the spouse or civil partner) has the same level of earnings factor as required for category A pensions under the 1975 regime, ie, 52 qualifying weeks made up of Class 1, Class 2 and/or Class 3 for a qualifying year (see *Pensions Act 2014, s 2*).

[*SSCBA 1992, s 21(1)(2), Sch 3 paras 1, 2, 3, 4, 5*].

There is no first contribution condition in respect of long-term incapacity benefit because that benefit rests on eligibility for, and is in continuation of, short-term incapacity benefit, Statutory Sick Pay or, previously, sickness benefit. New claimants under the ESA regime, which replaced the incapacity benefit regime in 2008 (see below), will receive ESA based on the contribution conditions above (and other circumstantial conditions).

Second contribution condition – short-term benefits

[13.7] The second contribution condition for:

- *contribution-based jobseeker's allowance* (JSA(C)) is that, in respect of the last two complete tax years before the beginning of the benefit year in which the beginning of the period of interruption of employment falls, the claimant has paid (or is treated as having paid) primary Class 1 contributions on earnings, or has been credited with earnings, from which he has derived an EARNINGS FACTOR 28 of not less than *50 times* the year's weekly LEL in each of those years (see EARNINGS LIMITS AND THRESHOLDS 33). From 1 November 2010 this changed to the requirement to have paid Class 1 NICs on, or been treated as having paid them, or credited with earnings of, at least 50 times the LEL within the last two complete tax years before the beginning of the relevant benefit year, but any earnings in a period in of excess of the LEL are to be disregarded;

- *contribution-based employment and support allowance* is that, in respect of the last two complete tax years before the beginning of the benefit year in which the beginning of the period of interruption of employment falls, the claimant has either paid or been credited with Class 2 contributions, or has paid (or is treated as having paid) primary Class 1 contributions on earnings, or been credited with earnings, from which he has derived an EARNINGS FACTOR 28 of not less than *50 times* the year's weekly LEL in each of those years (see EARNINGS LIMITS AND THRESHOLDS 33). From 1 November 2010 this changed to the requirement to have paid (or be treated as having paid) Class 1 or Class 2 NICs or been credited with earnings of at least 50 times the LEL within the last two tax years before the beginning of the relevant benefit year, with earnings above the LEL in any earnings period disregarded;

Second contribution condition – long-term benefits

[13.8] The second contribution condition for long-term benefits, for:

- *widowed parent's (formerly widowed mother's) allowance, bereavement allowance (formerly widow's pension), category A and B retirement pensions* is that, in respect of each of the requisite number of tax years of his working life, the contributor concerned has either paid or been credited with Class 2 or Class 3 contributions, or has paid (or is treated as having paid) primary Class 1 contributions on earnings, or been credited with earnings, from which he has derived an EARNINGS FACTOR 28 of not less than *52 times* the year's weekly LEL in each of those years (see EARNINGS LIMITS AND THRESHOLDS 33).
- *new state pension* is that the contributor has a qualifying record for at least the minimum number of years, which has been set at ten years and not more than 35 years.

[*SSCBA 1992, s 21(1)(2), Sch 3 paras 1, 2, 3, 4, 5; PA 2014, ss 2(3), 3; State Pension Regulations 2015, SI 2015/173, Reg 13*].

There is no second contribution condition for maternity allowance or bereavement (formerly widow's) payment.

Incapacity benefit

[13.9] Incapacity benefit (and income support) was replaced for new claimants from 27 October 2008 by an employment and support allowance (ESA) which has neither age nor dependency additions and, like jobseeker's allowance, has both contributory (ESA(C)) and non-contributory or income-related (ESA(IR)) elements. The employment and support allowance was at first only paid to new claimants – those already in receipt of short-term incapacity benefit before the change moved over to the new benefit during a phased changeover, with long-term IB claimants migrating over a period intended to last until April 2014, although well-publicised problems with the work capability assessments pushed the timetable back.

[*Welfare Reform Act 2007, ss 1, 70(2)*].

[13.10] The requisite number of tax years in respect of each of which the second contribution condition must have been satisfied in connection with a claim for category A or B retirement pension where the individual reached state pension age (see CHAPTER 3) on or after 6 April 2010 but before 6 April 2016 was 30 years. This changed to 35 years for individuals reaching state pension age on or after 6 April 2016 under *Pensions Act 2014* reforms.

The requisite number of tax years in respect of each of which the *second* contribution condition must have been satisfied in connection with a claim for category A or B retirement pension where the recipient reached state pension age (see CHAPTER 3) before 6 April 2010 or (regardless of age) a claim for widowed parent's (formerly widowed mother's) allowance, or bereavement allowance (formerly widow's pension) was made depended on the duration of the working life of the contributor concerned. A person's 'working life' was the period between (inclusive) the tax year in which he attained the age of 16 and (exclusive) the tax year in which he attained pensionable age or died under that age.

Not paying contributions for a number of years reduces the number of qualifying years for the purposes of the second condition under both the old and new regimes. However, minor gaps could be disregarded, so that, for example, a man with a potential working life of 49 years under the old regime could achieve a full basic state pension with only 44 qualifying years, and a woman with a potential working life of 44 years needed just 39 qualifying years. For an example of how missing years could affect a claimant, see *PL Rose v HMRC* [2007] STC SCD 129 Sp C 574B where the Commissioner accepted HMRC's evidence that, between 1956 and 1964, Rose had been informed of the potential consequences of not paying voluntary contributions. However, Rose had chosen not 'to exercise due care and diligence in protecting his contribution record'. [*SSCBA 1992, Sch 3 para 5(8), Pensions Act 2007, s 1*].

A minimum of ten qualifying years was needed before any entitlement to basic pension arose at retirement age, although this did not apply to the additional component of the SERPS or S2P pension. A minimum of ten qualifying years is also required for entitlement to the single-tier state pension at a reduced rate. [*The State Pension Regulations 2015, SI 2015/173, Reg 13*].

The pre-April 2010 calculation may be summarised as follows:

Duration of 'working life'	*'Requisite number of years' = the number of actual years of the working life minus*
10 years or less	1
20 years or less (but more than 10)	2
30 years or less (but more than 20)	3
40 years or less (but more than 30)	4
more than 40 years	5

[*SSCBA 1992, Sch 3 para 5(5)*].

For those reaching state pension age from April 2010, the unisex target for meeting the second condition in full became 30 years, and if the number of qualifying years on the record was less, the pension became payable on a straight pro rata basis (eg, a person with ten qualifying years would be entitled to one-third of a full basic pension). The minimum of ten years' contributions was abolished.

From April 2016, the minimum number of qualifying years before any pension is payable will be ten. The rule will apply to pensions calculated under both the new rules and the transitional rules that protect SERPS/S2P entitlements with a foundation amount that is higher than the pension calculated under the new rules. [*Pensions Act 2014, s 2(3); State Pension Regulations 2015, SI 2015/173, Reg 13*].

Additional pensions

[13.11] Insofar as the contribution conditions described at **13.5** above relate to bereavement allowance (formerly widow's pension), parent's (formerly widowed mother's) allowance and category A or B retirement pension, they relate only to the *basic* pension and allowance. An *additional* pension or allowance is payable also if the contributor concerned was not in CONTRACTED-OUT EMPLOYMENT **23** paying a rebated rate of contributions. [*SSCBA 1992, s 33(3), s 39(1)(2), s 41(4)(5), s 44(3)(4), s 48B(3)(4), s 51(2)* amended by *Pensions Act 1995, Sch 4*]. The S2P pension was abolished for new claimants with effect from 6 April 2016 under reforms in *Pensions Act 2014*.

Prior to the *Pensions Act 2007* provisions as regards earnings-related pension taking effect the position was as follows. This calculation is still potentially relevant, as the new single-tier pension from April 2016 protects any existing entitlements to an additional pension from the old regime to the extent that they lead to a pension value, measured at April 2016, in excess of the new single-tier pension value. In summary, contributors who had not reached state pension age at 6 April 2016 will have their entitlements assessed as at that date as if they had reached state pension age, using both the old and the new rules and their contribution record at that date. The higher value gives a 'foundation amount' for the new state pension. If the 'old' calculation (including SERPS and S2P additions to the basic pension, and having deducted any contracted-out reductions) results in a foundation amount above the 'new' single-tier pension rate, the excess becomes a protected (ie, indexed) addition to the new state pension in perpetuity (or until the next change in pensions policy). This ensures that those who paid into SERPS and S2P for many years and who might reach state pension age in the years shortly after the transition to the new rules, with a maximum 'old rules' state pension of around £270 per week (compared to the maximum flat-rate new state pension amount of £155.65 per week) are not unduly disadvantaged by the changes.

Category A pension

[13.12] The additional Category A pension is the weekly equivalent of a specified percentage applied to the amount of the surpluses (if any) in the pensioner's EARNINGS FACTORS 28 in tax years beginning with the year 1978–79 and up to and including 2001–02. The percentage rate and the surpluses to which it is to be applied are determined by reference to the tax year in which the pensioner attains pensionable age, viz:

(a) *1998–99 or earlier*—1¼% of the surplus in 1978–79 and each subsequent year.
(b) *2008–09 or earlier but after 1998–99*—25/N% of the surplus in 1978–79 and each subsequent year up to and including 1987–88, plus (20 + X)/N% of the surplus in 1988–89 and each subsequent year, where N is the number of tax years in the pensioner's working life and X is 0.5 for each tax year by which the tax year in which the pensioner attains pensionable age precedes the tax year 2008–09.
(c) *2009–10 to 2011–12*—25/N% of the surplus in 1978–79 and each subsequent year up to and including 1987–88, plus 20/N% of the surplus in 1988–89 and each subsequent year, where N is the number of tax years in the pensioner's working life.
(d) *2012–13 to 2015–16*—the specified percentage became a flat weekly amount (£1.80 for 2015–16) representing earnings up to the Low Earnings Threshold (LET – see below) for the year, and any earnings above the LET up to the UAP attracted an accrual at 10%.

[*SSCBA 1992, s 45(1)*].

With the phased movement of the pensionable age for women from 60 to 65 over the period 2010–2018, the calculation in (c) will vary between women over the eight-year period from 2010 (see **3.7** AGE EXCEPTION).

From 6 April 2002, the old additional pension (often known as 'State earnings-related pensions scheme' – SERPS) was replaced by the State Second Pension (S2P). It operates in a similar way to the former SERPS but entitlement is skewed to favour lower earners in that those earning less than the 'Low Earnings Threshold' (LET), originally £10,800 but by now uprated to £15,300 (2015–16) will be deemed to have an entitlement that is better than *pro rata* to their contributions. Until April 2012, they were simply deemed to have earnings equal to the LET for S2P purposes, provided that they had earnings equalling or exceeding the LEL (now £5,824 for 2015–16). From 2012–13 until 2015–16 (when S2P was abolished), earnings at or above the LEL gave, instead, an entitlement to a flat-rate addition to pension instead of a percentage of the surplus deemed earnings. Those earning at least at the LEL in not contracted-out employment during 2015–16 will have £93.60 (£1.80 pw) added to their annual notional S2P entitlement.

A lower accrual rate will then operate on earnings above the LET.

Originally, the band of earnings between the LEL and the UEL was split into three equal tranches. The lowest, up to the LET, was covered by the rule just described. The so-called surplus earnings in that band accrued S2P pension at a rate of 40%. In the middle band, the accrual rate on actual earnings in the band was 10%, and on the top the rate became 20%. For those earning in the top band, the effective accrual was 20% overall, equal to the previous SERPS accrual.

This three-way split of surplus earnings with differential accrual rates had the effect of skewing entitlement towards the lower paid, although every earner except those with earnings at or above the starting point for the top band was better off in terms of the overall average rate of accrual: those in the bottom band accrued at 40%, then in the mid-band the average rate slowly fell to 20% at the top of the band as earnings rose.

The three-band split was proving too expensive, so the 10% accrual rate was extended from 6 April 2010 to the whole of the earnings above the LET, thereby reducing the S2P entitlement of higher earners. This followed the introduction on 6 April 2009 of an Upper Accrual Point (UAP), capping earnings attracting S2P at £770 per week (£40,040 pa), although the UEL continued to rise thereafter, so higher earners were paying more NICs without earning more state pension. The 10% accrual on earnings above the LET still applied, on top of the flat-rate addition for earnings between the LEL and LET.

These accrual rates will have determined the additional pension for anyone retiring before 6 April 2016 with a history of paying not contracted-out contributions. They will also be taken into account when calculating the foundation amount for all earners at the changeover date to the new regime, and if they produce a higher state pension under the old rules than would arise under the new rules, as noted above, the difference will become a protected addition to the new single-tier pension.

See also **53.16** RATES AND LIMITS.

[*Social Security Pensions (Low Earnings Threshold) Order 2015, SI 2015/186*; *Social Security Pensions (Flat Rate Accrual Amount) Order 2015, SI 2015/3185*.]

Category B pension

[13.13] Where the surviving spouse (or civil partner since 6 April 2010) has an inadequate contribution record, a Category B pension may be payable based on the deceased spouse or partner's record. The additional Category B pension for a widower is to be calculated as above except that references to the pensioner are to be taken as references to his wife. [*SSCBA 1992, s 51(2)*].

The additional Category B pension for a widow's pension, widowed parent's (formerly widowed mother's) allowance, bereavement allowance (formerly widow's pension) or invalidity pension for widowers in a case where the deceased spouse died under pensionable age is calculated as above except that N is calculated under a complex formula set out in *SSCBA 1992, s 46(2)* (as amended).

Similarly, until 5 April 1995, the additional invalidity pension for persons under pensionable age was to be calculated as above except that N was the lesser of 49 (where the person entitled to the pension was male) or 44 (where the person entitled to the pension was female) and the number of tax years beginning with 1978–79 and ending with the tax year preceding the first day of entitlement to the additional pension in the period of interruption of employment in which that day falls. [*SSCBA 1992, s 46(1)*].

There is a surplus in an earnings factor of a contributor concerned for a relevant year if that factor, revalued under the *Revaluation of Earnings Factors Orders 1979 to date* exceeds the qualifying earnings factor (see **28.7** EARNINGS FACTORS) for the tax year immediately preceding the tax year in which pensionable age is attained. A contributor's earnings factor for these purposes is the aggregate of his earnings factors from earnings upon which primary Class 1 contributions were paid or treated as paid in respect of that year and earnings factors derived from Class 2 and Class 3 contributions actually paid by him in respect of a year. [*SSCBA 1992, s 44(5)–(7); Social Security Revaluation of Earnings Factors Orders 2011, SI 2011/475*].

It was expected that once the *Pensions Act 2007* provisions regarding earnings-related state pensions started to take effect and over a subsequent period of just over twenty years the earnings-related elements of state pension would start to be phased out and be replaced by a higher but flat-rate state pension. Instead, *Pensions Act 2014 has* now introduced a single-tier state pension to replace basic pension and SERPS/S2P additional pension with effect from 6 April 2016. If, at that date, a contributor would have been entitled to a combined state pension under the current rules that is better than the new single-tier entitlement, that 'old' entitlement will be protected as a 'foundation amount', as already outlined. This is likely to be relevant only to older contributors who have already built up significant SERPS/S2P entitlements over many years.

New state pension and spouses

[13.14] The new regime includes no equivalent to the category B pension: a spouse or civil partner reaching state pension age on or after 6 April 2016 can no longer rely on his or her partner's contribution record, and there is no 'married couple's rate' equivalent to 160% of the basic pension under the new rules. The only exception is for married women with a reduced rate election in place since before May 1977. Such women have been allowed ever since then to rely on their husband's contribution record, and they would have received no entitlement under the new regime without special rules to protect their position.

A woman who, on reaching state pension age under the new regime, can show that she had a valid reduced rate election in place at some point in the last 35 complete tax years before the tax year in which state pension age is reached will not need a minimum of ten qualifying years and should receive a pension that is based on the pre-2016 lower rate basic pension (now £75.50 per week) if she is married or in a civil partnership and her partner has reached state pension age, or the full pre-2016 basic pension (now £125.95 per week) if she is a widow or divorcee, or her civil partnership has been dissolved. Any SERPS/S2P additions for years of standard-rate contributions after a reduced rate election ceased should also be added. A widow should also inherit part or all of her late husband's SERPS pension if the spouse died or reached state pension age under the old regime before 6 April 2016.

European law

[13.15] *EC Reg 883/2004* co-ordinates benefit entitlement for migrant workers within the EEA and it applies to the UK until the UK officially ceases to be a member of the EU. If the result of the 'Brexit' negotiations is that the UK becomes, instead, a member of the European Economic Area, or puts itself into the same position as Switzerland by virtue of a similar association agreement that keeps the Single Market open to the UK, the regulation will continue to apply.

The detailed rules are beyond the scope of this work, but one example of co-ordination may be found in *Arts 17-22*. Where UK legislation makes the acquisition, retention or recovery of the right to sickness and maternity benefits conditional upon the completion of periods of insurance, employment or residence, the Department for Work and Pensions must (to the extent necessary) take account of periods of insurance, employment or residence completed under the legislation of any other Member State as if they were periods completed under UK legislation. The rule was not relevant to UK state pensions from 6 April 2010 to 5 April 2016, as any UK qualifying year gave rise to a proportionate entitlement in the UK. However, looking forward, this rule means that qualifying years in other Member States may count towards reaching the minimum ten years required from 6 April 2016 before any UK state pension is payable, although only actual years of entitlement will be reflected in the amount due. For example, an EEA migrant worker might have eight qualifying years in the UK and reach UK state pension age in 2020. He or she will be entitled to 8/35ths of a UK pension, despite not having ten UK qualifying years on the record, because years contributing in other EEA states must be respected in the calculation so as to avoid discrimination against migrant workers. On the assumption that neither the UK nor the EEA Member States will wish to upset this particular existing arrangement, since it mirrors the pension totalisation rules in most of the reciprocal agreements that the UK has with non-EEA states, this position may be expected to survive any 'Brexit' changes.

See *Iurlalo v Istituto Nazionale della Previdenza Sociale (INPS)* C-322/95 [1997] ECR I-4881, [1998] All ER (EC) 366, ECJ for treatment of unemployment periods in one Member State extending the reference period in another Member State in respect of invalidity benefit. See also *Gottardo v Istituto Nazionale della Previdenza Sociale (INPS)* C-55/00 [2002] All ER (D) 30 (Jan) for an example of the interaction of the provisions of *EC Regulation 1408/71* (now replaced by *Regulation 883/2004*) on recognition of contribution periods with the provisions of similar reciprocal agreements with non-EU states.

Case law

[13.16] European Regulations will not always hold sway, even while the UK is still a member. This may be amply demonstrated by *Art 48, EC Reg 1408/71* and the case of *Graf v Filzmoser Maschinenbau GmbH* C-190/98, [2000] ECR I-493, [2000] All ER (EC) 170, ECJ where a German national terminated his contract of employment in Austria to commence new employment in Germany and claimed compensation (two months' salary). The Advocate General concluded that

> . . . Art 48 of the Treaty does not preclude national provisions which deny a worker entitlement to compensation on termination of the employment if he terminates his contract of employment in another member state, when those provisions grant him entitlement to such compensation if the contract ends without termination being at his own initiative or attributable to him.

A further example was the Northern Irish Court of Appeal case regarding full pay for maternity leave, known as the *Gillespie* case, referred to the ECJ (*Gillespie v Northern Health and Social Services Board* C-342/93 [1996] ECR I-475, [1996] All ER (EC) 284, ECJ. In the judgment on 13 February 1996 the Court stated that account must be taken of any backdated pay rises where a woman's maternity pay is calculated without taking account of pay increases during maternity leave. Regulations effective from June 1996 redressed the balance. See also *Curr v Marks and Spencer plc* [2002] EWCA Civ 1852, [2003] ICR 443, [2003] IRLR 74 *January 2003*. (The position in respect of Statutory Maternity Pay was further affected by *Alabaster v Woolwich* C-147/02 [2004] ECR I-3101, [2005] All ER (EC) 490, ECJ.) See **15.19** CLASS 1 CONTRIBUTIONS: EMPLOYED EARNERS). Also, in the case of Statutory Paternity Pay (SPP) and Statutory Adoption Pay (SAP), introduced from April 2003, the European Regulations pertaining in the EEA have now had to be introduced into the legislation in the United Kingdom. It is too early to say how these rules might be affected by 'Brexit' and the UK's freedom to adopt its own employment rights laws without reference to EU legislation.

Statutory Paternity Pay, Statutory Adoption Pay and Statutory Shared Parental Pay (ShPP) operate in the same way as Statutory Maternity Pay previously, with the employer being reimbursed wholly or partly by the state. From 1 April 2018, SMP payment has been six weeks at 90% of average weekly earnings and then 33 weeks at £145.18 or 90% of average weekly earnings (AWE) whichever is the lesser. The payments under SPP will be payable for up to two weeks at 90% of AWE or £145.18, whichever is the lesser. SAP is payable at the same rates as SMP. ShPP is payable at the same rates as SPP and is recovered at the same rate [*Statutory Shared Parental Pay (General) Regulations 2014, SI 2014/3051, Reg 40*; *Welfare Benefits Up-rating Order 2015, SI 2015/30, Arts 3, 4, 5*].

In *R (on the application of Wilkinson) v IRC* [2005] UKHL 30, [2006] 1 All ER 529, [2005] 1 WLR 1718 a taxpayer who was a widower claimed under *The Human Rights Act 1998 s 6* that he should have been entitled to a bereavement allowance for income tax similar to that which widows receive on the death of their spouse. It was argued that having to pay tax in such a manner affected his peaceful enjoyment of his possessions within Article 1, First Protocol, European Convention on Human Rights. The House of Lords dismissed the appeal and ruled that legislation in the form of *TMA 1970 s 1* gave the former Inland Revenue discretion to formulate policy to deal with anomalies and shortcomings in legislation but it did not allow the granting of an allowance for widowers to ensure equity between men and women. See also *R (on the application of Hooper) v Secretary of State for Work and Pensions* [2005] UKHL 29, [2006] 1 All ER 487, [2005] 1 WLR 1681 and ECHR case of *Hobbs v United Kingdom* (Applications 63469/00, 63475/00, 63484/00, 63684/00) (2006) 44 EHRR 1113, [2008] STC 1469, ECtHR.

More recently in *Carson v United Kingdom* (Application No 42184/05) (2008) 48 EHRR 941, (2008) Times, 20 November, ECtHR the exclusion of certain pensioners living abroad from the index-linked uprating scheme applicable to all pensioners in the UK was not in breach of Human Rights Act 1998, Art 14. The ECtHR agreed with the British Government that it did not exceed its very broad discretion (or 'margin of appreciation') on matters of macroeconomic policy by entering into different reciprocal agreements with certain countries and not others. In addition, the British Government had taken steps to forewarn citizens, in a series of leaflets which referred to the implications of moving abroad and the absence of index-linking for pensions in certain countries. [*Social Security Benefits Up-rating Order 2001, SI 2001/910*]. See also **43.2** LEAFLETS AND FORMS and OVERSEAS MATTERS **51**. Note that these decisions based on human rights claims should be unaffected by 'Brexit', which relates to disengagement from the EU, not from the European Convention on Human Rights, which is unconnected with the EU and was not the subject of the 2016 referendum.

Key Points regarding benfits: contribution requirements

[13.17] Points to consider are as follows.

- Both contributory and non-contributory benefits are generally uprated each April.
- Those who reached state pension age between 6 April 2010 and 6 April 2016 needed only 30 'qualifying years' to attain full-rate basic state pension. This has increased to 35 years from 6 April 2016.
- For those contributors reaching state pension age on or after 6 April 2016, a minimum of ten qualifying years are required before any state pension is paid (except for EEA migrant workers, who are currently entitled to count years of contribution in other Member States towards reaching the ten-year threshold, although their UK entitlement is then only pro rata to their UK contribution years).
- The 90% of working life requirement still applies to all persons as regards entitlement to bereavement benefits.

- Bereavement benefits are to be reformed in April 2017, but the detail is not yet known.

14
Categorisation

Cross-references. See AGENCY WORKERS 4; AIRMEN 6; APPEALS AND REVIEWS 9 for means of contesting categorisation decisions; APPRENTICES, TRAINEES AND STUDENTS 10; ARMED FORCES 11; COMPANY DIRECTORS 22; CROWN SERVANTS AND STATUTORY EMPLOYEES 25; ENTERTAINERS 36; EXAMINERS 37; HOMEWORKERS AND OUTWORKERS 38; HUSBAND AND WIFE, AND CIVIL PARTNERS 39; INTERMEDIARIES 40; LABOUR-ONLY CONTRACTORS 41; LECTURERS, TEACHERS AND INSTRUCTORS 44; MARINERS 45; MINISTERS OF RELIGION 46; OIL-RIG WORKERS, DIVERS, ETC 50; PARTNERS 52; SHARE FISHERMEN 56; SUBPOSTMASTERS 57; VOLUNTEER DEVELOPMENT WORKERS 59.

Other Sources. Tolley's National Insurance Contributions Brief, July 1996, pages 53–55 and August 1996, pages 57–60; www.gov.uk/employment-status/overview; former HM Revenue and Customs factsheets ES/FS2 and CIS 349 (2007); Taxation Magazine, 26 October 2017, page 7.

Introduction to categorisation for NICs

[14.1] Whether an individual is employed or self-employed will depend upon the nature of the relationship with the person for whom the services are provided. In most cases it is clear whether someone is an employee or self-employed. However, there will be many cases where it will not be so easy to decide and consequently regulations provide for a determination. The operation of the regulations is not, however, confined to doubtful cases. For instance, where two individuals are engaged by a company to carry out similar work, it is possible for one to be self-employed and the other to be an employee because they have been taken on under contracts with different terms and conditions. Also in certain circumstances the Secretary of State for Social Security *had*, and now the Treasury *has*, the power to determine that certain groups of workers should be treated as Class 1 (employed) or Class 2 (self-employed) contributors. See **14.3** below. This is an area of NICs that is littered with case law. See **14.6, 14.10, 14.12, 14.15, 14.20** and **14.28** below.

Earners in employment

[14.2] In order to establish whether a person is liable to pay contributions and, if so, of which class (or classes), it is necessary to ascertain whether or not, for NIC purposes, he falls within either or both of the two categories of earner around which the contribution legislation has been framed. Those categories are:

- *employed* earners; and
- *self-employed* earners.

[*SSCBA 1992, s 2(1)*].

Somewhat confusingly, both statuses are referred to in the legislation as 'employment' – see *SSCBA 1992, s 122* – so care must be taken whenever this word is read in a social security act or regulation to avoid confusion about the meaning.

It should also be noted that the common law and employment law statutes now recognise at least six statuses:

- *employees* under a contract of employment (*Employment Rights Act 1996, s 230(1)*);
- *workers* who are not under a contract of employment but have committed to providing personal service without that occurring in the ordinary course of a business they run (*ERA 1996, s 230(3)(b)*);
- *employee-shareholders*, a subset of the first category, who have signed away certain employment rights (eg, the right to redundancy payments and the right not to be unfairly dismissed) in exchange for tax-advantaged share awards (*ERA 1996, s 205A* as inserted by the *Growth and Infrastructure Act 2013, s 31*);

- *office holders*, who are not employees, but deemed to be employees for certain purposes (*ERA 1996, s 171*);
- *apprentices*, who are deemed to be employees for all purposes if they are not so in common law (*Apprenticeships, Skills, Children and Learning Act 2009, s 35* in England and Wales); and
- *self-employed* earners.

All are 'employed earners' for NIC purposes except for 'workers' and the 'truly' self-employed.

Note that, for NIC purposes, there are territorial restrictions on both: a person will only fall within either category if they are 'gainfully employed' (ie, earning income from work) in the UK. See **51.9** and **51.16**.

Determination by regulation

[14.3] If a person falls within the employed earner category, contributions will, in normal circumstances, be payable not only by that person himself but also by some other person (usually his employer) who is known as the *secondary contributor*. Though they are not specifically referred to as such by the legislation it is useful to regard secondary contributors as forming a third, separate category of person for contribution purposes and they are so regarded in this chapter. The application of the regulations is independent of other areas of law as outlined above and is not restricted to doubtful cases.

A fourth type of person to which the contribution legislation applies is the person who, whether already belonging to one of the categories mentioned or not, wishes to pay contributions on a voluntary basis in order to provide or make up his entitlement to benefit. Although forming a group of sorts, such persons attract no categorisation problems of any kind and are, accordingly, afforded no separate treatment in this chapter (but see CLASS **3** CONTRIBUTIONS **19**).

It should also be noted that the Secretary of State for Social Security had the power to determine by Statutory Instrument that certain particular groups of workers should be treated as Class 1 (employed) or Class 2 (self-employed) contributors, or disregarded altogether. The former DSS made use of these powers for certain groups as evidenced by the *Categorisation Regs* and the NIC&EO will apply the regulations whenever it is appropriate:

- Electoral workers (generally exempt from NIC).
- Examiners, moderators, etc of certain examining bodies (generally treated as self-employed, see HM Revenue and Customs Employment Status Manual, paras ESM4150 to ESM4153 and **37** EXAMINERS).
- Domestic employment by close relatives (generally exempt from NIC) see **41.18** LABOUR-ONLY CONTRACTORS.
- Ministers of religion (generally treated as employees) see **46** MINISTERS OF RELIGION.
- Office cleaners (generally treated as employees).
- Employment of a person for business purposes by his or her spouse or civil partner (generally treated as an employee) see **39** HUSBAND AND WIFE, AND CIVIL PARTNERS.

- Until 6 April 2014, certain actors, musicians and other performers (generally treated as employees) see HM Revenue and Customs Employment Status Manual, para ESM4121 and **36** ENTERTAINERS (although the part of the regulations concerning such entertainers was repealed with effect from 6 April 2014).

These deeming rules are contained in *Social Security (Categorisation of Earners) Regulations 1978, SI 1978/1689*, which were also extensively amended from 6 April 2014 to deem many agency workers to be employed earners and the associated agencies to be their employers. See **14.31** below and **4** AGENCY WORKERS.

Where these regulations do apply it can mean that National Insurance treatment differs from the income tax and/or PAYE treatment. [*SSCBA 1992, s 2(2)*].

The power to make further regulations now lies with the Treasury (*SSCBA 1992, s 2(2A)* inserted by *SSC(TF)A 1999, s 2, Sch 3 para* 2).

Definitions in categorisation of earners for NICs

[14.4] An 'earner' at **14.2** is anyone who derives remuneration or profit from an employment and an 'employment' includes any trade, business, profession, office or vocation and the exercise of the powers and duties of a public or local authority. [*SSCBA 1992, ss 3(1), 122(1)*].

'Business', according to Lord Diplock, is 'a wider concept than a trade' (*American Leaf Blending Co Sdn Bhd v Director-General of Inland Revenue* [1978] STC 561) and has been held by Rowlatt J to mean 'an active occupation . . . continuously carried on' (*CIR v Marine Steam Turbine Co* (1920) 12 TC 174) and by Widgery J to mean 'a serious undertaking earnestly pursued'. (*Rael-Brook Ltd v Minister of Housing and Local Government* [1967] 2 QB 65, [1967] 1 All ER 262). (See **14.18** below for the significance of these judicial comments.) It was held by the Upper Tribunal in *Personal representatives of Nicolette Pawson v HMRC* [2013] UKUT 050 (TCC) that, for the purposes of inheritance tax business property relief, the active management of rental property was a business. This decision appears to be equally valid for NIC purposes.

An 'employed earner' is any person who is gainfully employed in Great Britain either:

- under a *contract of service*, or
- in an *office* (including elective office) from which he derives earnings.

[*SSCBA 1992, s 2(1)(a)*]. Confusingly, as already noted, both categories of earner are referred to in a National Insurance context as being in 'employment'. The distinction is drawn between 'employed earner's employment' (under a contract of service) and 'self-employment' (under a contract for services).

Any contribution liability which arises as a result of a person's categorisation as an employed earner is a liability under Class 1 (see **15** CLASS **1** CONTRIBUTIONS) and is, therefore, wholly earnings-related. [*SSCBA 1992, s 1(2)*]. It follows that no liability can possibly arise unless an employed earner is 'gainfully' employed and that, in the context of this definition (though not in the definition of a self-employed earner before 6 April 2015 – see **14.18** below), the qualification is otiose. Under the earlier legislation from which the phrase was borrowed, however, Class 1 contributions were flat-rated and 'gainfully' was held by the courts to mean 'for the purposes of gain'. (*Vandyk v Minister of Pensions and National Insurance* [1955] 1 QB 29, [1954] 2 All ER 723). The phrase thus once served, in certain circumstances, to permit contributions to be collected where no true earnings actually arose from an employment. (*Benjamin v Minister of Pensions and National Insurance* [1960] 3 WLR 430; *J B Griffiths Quinn & Co, Re, Quinn v Heron* (1968) 112 Sol Jo 563).

An employment must be regarded as 'gainful' if a person is engaged in it with a desire, hope and intention of obtaining remuneration or profit in return for services or efforts. (*CP 7/49*). Thus, a person will be regarded as gainfully employed throughout any period for which he is under a contract of service whether or not he actually works during that period. (*R(U) 4/60, R(U) 5/83*). However, where work *is* done, the absence of any hope or intention to profit from it will not prevent the employment being gainful if the person doing the work is in fact paid for doing it. (*CP 7/49, R(P) 1/65*). (See AOG Vol 6 paras 50055–50059).

An important observation by the then DSS on the wording of *SSCBA 1992, s 2(1)(a)* was that:

> The words "in Great Britain" qualify the words "gainfully employed", not the following words "under a contract of service". When read together with the definitions of "employed" and "employment" to be found in [Sec 122(1)(2)] of the Act, the words "gainfully employed in Great Britain" clearly require no more than that the person concerned should undertake in Great Britain, with a view to gain, activities in the course of, inter alia, some trade, business, office, profession or vocation.
>
> (DSS Letter, 10 October 1986).

Example

The wages clerk at Benevolent Ltd wrote to the NIC&EO asking for their determination on the employment status of the managing director's wife who was to provide consultancy services to the company for the period 29 October 2014 to 16 April 2015. The NIC&EO replied to the wages officer as follows:

"Dear Sir,

Under the provisions of Section 2(1)(a) of the Social Security Contributions and Benefits Act 1992 ('the 1992 Act') the distinction between employed earner's employment and self-employment depends mainly on the existence of a contract of service.

Where there is a contract of service, then in general, the person is regarded as an employee.

A contract of service need not be in writing. Section 122 of the 1992 Act provides that it can also be an oral agreement and can be an expressed one or one implied from the working arrangements.

There is however no precise legal definition of what constitutes a contract of service, ie what makes the relationship in law between the two parties that of employer and employee.

The National Insurance Contributions & Employer Office relies on principles established from the case law of the Courts over many years and applies these to the facts of the individual case concerned.

Some of the facts which the Courts consider important are:

(1) is the person in business on his own account;

(2) must the person personally render services for which he is paid;

(3) can the 'employer' control what the person does, when he does it and how he does it, even if the right of control is not exercised;

(4) is the person part and parcel of the 'employer's' business or organisation;

(5) does the person supply tools, equipment and materials and, if so, to what extent;

(6) who makes a profit or loss from the work;

(7) is the person paid for the job or for the hours or days he works;

(8) can the 'employer' select, suspend or dismiss the person; and

(9) is self-employment the intention of both parties?

The National Insurance Contributions & Employer Office weighs all the factors in a working relationship, including those mentioned above, before deciding if a contract of service exists.

A person may say that he is self-employed or work on a casual basis but this does not alter the fact that if the work is carried out under conditions which amount to a contract of service the person is an employed earner under the 1992 Act.

Our ruling

In this case, Jane Smith,

I consider the weight of evidence of these factors in the working relationship between

29 October 2014 and 16 April 2015 shows that there is a contract of service.

National Insurance contributions and income tax may be payable on different basis.

Keep this letter safe in a case you have to show it to other officers of HM Revenue and Customs.

Further information

If you think this decision or ruling is incorrect, please let us know, in writing within 28 days. Please include:

- reasons why you think it is wrong and
- any further information and/or documentation which you think is relevant."

[Letter continues]

The meaning of 'contract of service'

[14.5] A 'contract of service' is any contract of service or apprenticeship, whether written or oral and whether expressed or implied and is, therefore, synonymous with a contract of employment. [*SSCBA 1992, s 122(1); Employment Rights Act 1996, s 230(2)*].

Case law—'contract of service'

[14.6] Whether or not such a contract exists is a question to be determined only after looking at the totality of the evidence. (*Argent v Minister of Social Security* [1968] 3 All ER 208, [1968] 1 WLR 1749, *per Roskill J*). That determination will be a conclusion of law and will depend both on the rights conferred and the duties imposed by the contract. If the rights conferred and the duties imposed are such that the relationship created is one of master and servant, it is irrelevant that the parties may have declared it to be something else. (*Ready Mixed Concrete (South East) Ltd v Minister of Pensions and National Insurance* [1968] 2 QB 497, [1968] 1 All ER 433, *per MacKenna J*). The parties cannot alter the truth of their relationship by putting a different label on it. (*Massey v Crown Life Insurance Co* [1978] 2 All ER 576, [1978] 1 WLR 676, CA, *per Lord Denning*). It is equally irrelevant that a statutory authority such as HM Revenue and Customs may have accepted the relationship as being other than what it, in fact, is: a convenient arrangement for tax or National Insurance purposes is not determinative. (*Tyne & Clyde Warehouses Ltd v Hamerton* [1978] ICR 661; *Young & Woods Ltd v West* [1980] IRLR 201; *Warner Holidays Ltd v Secretary of State for Social Services* [1983] ICR 440). However, unless there are obvious indicators that a person's employment status is other than that claimed by him, HM Revenue and Customs usually accepts without query the status claimed. This would also include persuasive authority in connection with, say, *Employment Rights Act 1996, Part X* and *Equality Act 2010, Part 5*. (See *Carver v Saudi Arabian Airlines*, Times Law Reports, 24 March 1999).

It is not necessary that bad faith should be proved before a written contract may be disregarded. (*Reade v Brearley* (1933) 17 TC 687). It is merely necessary that the contract is inconsistent with the realities of the relationship. (*Global Plant Ltd v Secretary of State for Health and Social Security* [1972] 1 QB 139, [1971] 3 All ER 385). If, however, the parties' relationship is ambiguous, any agreement between them then becomes the best material from which to gather the true legal relationship between them. (*Massey v Crown Life Insurance Co* [1978] 2 All ER 576, [1978] 1 WLR 676, CA, *per Lord Denning; BSM (1257) Ltd v Secretary of State for Social Services* [1978] ICR 894). In construing a written agreement one must look at all the circumstances at the time the agreement was entered into and the intention of the parties must be determined from the words of the agreement in the light of those circumstances. (*Plumb Brothers v Dolmac (Agriculture) Ltd*, (1984) 271 Estates Gazette 373, CA, *per Lord Justice May*). The parties' *subjective* intentions are of no relevance. (*Ibid, per Lord Justice Purchas*). If the agreed terms accurately reflect the parties' intentions and are given practical effect, the status of the parties is that to which the agreed terms point. (*McMenamin v Diggles* [1991] STC 419).

If the true relationship between parties to an agreement of the kind envisaged is not that of master and servant, it will usually be that of engager and independent contractor and, because such a contract (which is known as a 'contract for services') is indicative of self-employment rather than employment, the distinction between the one and the other has assumed great importance and has led to the evolution of various tests by which the true nature of a contract may be decided. It is a question of law as to what are the right tests to be applied in determining whether a contract falls into the one or the other class. (*Construction Industry Training Board v Labour Force Ltd* [1970] 3 All ER 220, 114 Sol Jo 704, DC, *per Fisher J*).

In the more recent case of *Talentcore*, a company (T) provided temporary staff for companies which sold cosmetics at duty-free shops at airports. It did not account for PAYE or NICs on the amounts paid to the staff, which it referred to as 'consultants'. HMRC issued assessments totalling more than £3,600,000, on the basis that the effect of *ITEPA 2003, ss 44-47* and the *Categorisation Regs 1978* was that T should have accounted for tax and NICs. T appealed. The First-Tier Tribunal allowed the appeal, finding that there was 'no framework contract' between T and the consultants, and that there were no written contracts between T and the cosmetics companies. The Tribunal found that the consultants had 'an unfettered right of substitution', that there was no 'contract of service', and that there was 'no obligation to render (or provide) personal service(s) within the legislation'. *Talentcore Ltd (t/a Team Spirits) v HMRC* [2010] UKFTT 148, TC 000454. HMRC's appeal was dismissed by the Upper Tribunal at [2011] UKUT 423 (TCC). HMRC regarded the shop workers as being in 'false self-employment', as they worked in a very similar way to regular employees, so having conceded defeat in this case, HMRC changed the law from 6 April 2014 by amending *ITEPA 2003, s 44* and the *Categorisation Regs 1978* to make actual personal service, rather than an obligation to provide personal service, a trigger for PAYE and NIC liability (see AGENCY WORKERS 4).

Another recent case involving Weight Watchers provided the opposite result to that of *Talentcore*, although the arguments here were not centred on the agency worker provisions. W had not deducted Class 1 NICs or PAYE from those individuals who were leaders at Weight Watchers classes. Such individuals were regarded by the parties to the contract as self-employed and had been for a long period of years. The Tribunal accepted that the contract in place gave leaders absolute discretion in the conduct of their classes and there was an agreement they would be responsible for their own tax and NIC. There was, however, further evidence in the form of two handbooks setting out how the leaders had to conduct meetings and controlling the leaders' performance. This was inconsistent with the existence of any contract for services. In addition, premises were booked by the leaders in the name of Weight Watchers and if a leader did not personally lead a class he was not paid. On balance, the Tribunal decided there were contracts of employment in place and Class 1 NICs and PAYE were due. (*Weight Watchers (UK) Ltd (and others) v HMRC* [2010] UKFTT 54 (TC).)

'Contract of service' through separate limited company

[14.7] It is sometimes the case that a person who is about to perform work for another will arrange to provide his services through the medium of a limited company which he owns and of which he is the sole director. Underlying such arrangements is the mistaken belief that what might otherwise be a contract *of* service between *the worker* and the person for whom he is to work is thereby turned automatically into a contract *for* services between the *limited company* and that person. This is not necessarily so. Anyone adopting this way of working must ensure that appropriately drafted written contracts are put in place so that it is clear that the individual is bound to supply his services only to his company under a contract of employment, and only the company is contracting to provide a service to the client under a wholly separate contract for services. If, in the absence of correct documentation, the truth of the arrangement is that the worker is obliged to render services in person, is subject to personal control as to the manner of doing his work (see **14.11**) and is not, as a matter of economic reality, in business on his own account (see **14.14**), it has always been, and still is, open to HM Revenue and Customs and others to attempt to draw aside the corporate veil and to have regard to any implied direct contract of service which the veil is intended to conceal.

The argument for HMRC is, though, challenging: it is only generally permissible to imply terms where they are necessary to make the contract make sense or remedy a defect (see, eg, *Trollope & Colls Ltd v North West Metropolitan Regional Hospital Board* [1973] 2 All ER 260).

It is equally not permissible to imply a contract of employment between the worker and a business to which he is providing his services just because the worker, HMRC, or the court would like to do so. The Court of Appeal held, for example, in *Smith v Carillion (JM) Ltd* [2015] EWCA Civ 209, [2015] IRLR 467 that:

- the onus is on the claimant (eg, a self-employed worker trying to claim unfair dismissal) to establish that a contract should be implied;
- a contract can be implied only if it is necessary to do so;
- no implication is warranted simply because the conduct of the parties was more consistent with an intention to contract than with an intention not to contract;
- the focus must be on the facts of the case; and
- in an agency situation, if the arrangements which actually operate between the worker and the end user no longer reflect how the agency arrangements were intended to operate, it may be appropriate to infer that they are only consistent with a separate contract between the worker and the contractor.

It was no surprise, therefore, that the government tackled the problem of indirect employment by introducing the IR35 and, later, the managed service company rules (see **40** INTERMEDIARIES).

The five tests

Is there a binding contract?

[14.8] The first hurdle for any claimant to overcome in proving that there is a contract of employment or a contract for services is to prove that there is a contract of any kind. For a contract of any kind to exist and be binding, certain minimum requirements must be met: there must be offer and acceptance, there must be consensus, there must be sufficient consideration, and there must be an intention to create legal relations. This last point has been important in a number of employment status cases, particularly in relation to 46 MINISTERS OF RELIGION, who often believe that they answer to a higher authority than the body that heads their particular denomination. It may also be a relevant consideration when HMRC argues that volunteer drivers are in receipt of taxable income when their motor expenses are reimbursed.

Once it has been established that there is indeed a binding contract, four further tests are required to establish whether it is a contract of service or a contract for services.

The mutual obligations test

[14.9] It is intrinsic to any contract that the parties to it incur obligations towards each other; and a contract of service is no exception. Where, therefore, a situation arises in which no obligations exist, there can be neither a contract of service nor a contract for services—even though one party might be found to be performing a service for the other and the other might be found to be remunerating the first party in some way. Accordingly, a fundamental task of any tribunal which is addressing itself to the question whether a person is an employed earner or a self-employed earner is to ascertain whether or not a certain irreducible minimum of obligation lics on the person receiving services and on the person providing services and, if such obligations exist, whether they are more compatible with employment or with self-employment.

Case law—the mutual obligations test

[14.10] For a contract of service to exist, the minimum obligation required of the alleged employee is that he accepts and performs some reasonable amount of work for the alleged employer (*Nethermere (St Neots) Ltd v Gardiner* [1984] ICR 612, *per Kerr LJ*), that he makes himself available to the alleged employer and that he refrains from seeking or accepting employment from another employer during the continuance of his relationship with the alleged employer. (*Hellyer Brothers Ltd v McLeod*, [1986] ICR 122, *per Slade LJ*). See HM Revenue and Customs Employment Status Manual, para ESM0514. So far as the alleged employer is concerned, that minimum obligation is that he offers continuing employment to the alleged employee. (the *Hellyer* case). Thus, where a person *may*, but *need not*, be asked to perform a service and, if asked, is free to decline to provide the service asked for, there exists no mutuality of obligation consistent with a contract of service, even though the person's services may frequently be requested and those services may frequently be supplied. (*Mailway (Southern) Ltd v Willsher* [1978] IRLR 322; *O'Kelly v Trusthouse Forte plc* [1984] QB 90, [1983] 3 All ER 456, CA).

It may however be the case that, despite the initial absence of mutual obligations, the regular giving and taking of work over a period of a year or more may give rise to expectations which harden into such obligations and such obligations may, in turn, give rise to an enforceable contract of service. (*Nethermere (St Neots) Ltd v Gardiner* [1984] ICR 615, *per Stephenson LJ*). In other words, the conduct of the parties to a relationship may, over a substantial period of time, turn that relationship into a contract of service by creating mutual obligations between the parties. (*Airfix Footwear Ltd v Cope*

[1978] ICR 1210). Mutuality of obligation may also, in some instances, be inferred from the economic dependence of each party on the other, eg if a situation exists where, should work offered to an alleged employee be refused, further work would be withheld and where, should further work not be offered, the alleged employee would look elsewhere (*Four Seasons (Inn on the Park) Ltd v Hamarat*, 17 April 1985, EAT 369/84). Furthermore, where evidence discloses what, on the face of it, is a series of contracts for services entered into between the same parties and covering a substantial period of time, it might be open to a tribunal properly to infer from the parties' conduct, notwithstanding the absence of any evidence as to any express agreement of that nature, the existence of a continuing overriding arrangement which governs the whole of their relationship and itself amounts to a contract of service, ie a 'global' or 'umbrella' contract. (The *Hellyer* case). In such cases, it will be the gaps between each period of service that become significant. Does the alleged employee have an obligation to make himself available to the alleged employer during those intervening periods and must he, during those periods, refrain from seeking or accepting other employment? Does the alleged employer have an ongoing obligation to offer the alleged employee any employment which is available throughout those intervening periods? If the answer is affirmative, a global contract of employment will probably exist. (*Boyd Line Ltd v Pitts* [1986] ICR 244). If not, each may be a separate employment or engagement with no continuing mutual obligations in the gaps between working periods (*Reed Employment plc and others v Revenue and Customs Comrs* [2014] UKUT 0160). The NIC&EO attitude where there is a series of short-term assignments carried out by a person, with no obligation to offer or accept further such assignments at any point, appears to be that there is no continuous contract of employment, but when each assignment is carried out there may very well exist a short-term contract. The terms of each short-term assignment will determine whether the contract is one 'of service' or 'for services'. In the 'IR35' case, *R (on the application of Professional Contractors Group Ltd) v IRC* [2001] EWHC Admin 236, [2001] STC 629, 74 TC 393, the judgment criticised the then Employment Services Manual in concluding at para ESM 0514 (in the version as it existed at that time) that the mutuality of obligation test is not a relevant issue, adding that it was a 'central piece of guidance in the analysis of whether there is an employment or self-employment'. See further at 40 INTERMEDIARIES. See also *Carmichael and Another v National Power Plc* (1999) 1 WLR 2042.

The control test

[14.11] Having established that there exists a contract which gives rise to mutual obligations, for however short a period, the next step is to determine whether or not that contract is a contract of service. The principal test to be applied is whether a person who has agreed, in consideration of a wage or other remuneration, to provide his *own* work and skill in the performance of some service for some other person, has also agreed, expressly or impliedly, to be 'subject to that other person's control in a sufficient degree to make that other person master'. If he has, and if other provisions of the contract between them are not sufficiently inconsistent with its being a contract of service to outweigh the control factor, the contract is a contract of service. (*Ready Mixed Concrete (South East) Ltd v Minister of Pensions and National Insurance* [1968] 2 QB 497, [1968] 1 All ER 433, *per MacKenna J at pp 439 to 440*).

Case law—the control test

[14.12] The reference to the provision of *personal* service and the reference to the method of remuneration are both important. A person's obligation to do work himself rather than hiring someone else to do it on his behalf is a strong indication that the contract is a contract *of service* rather than a contract *for services* (*Pauley v Kenaldo Ltd* [1953] 1 WLR 187). (former IR leaflet IR 56). Conversely, an arrangement under which payment is to be of a specified amount for the whole of the work to which the contract relates, rather than by weekly or monthly wage or salary, is a strong indicator that the contract is a contract for services. (*Writers Guild of Great Britain v BBC* [1974] ICR 234). The working of set hours, or of a given number of hours a week or month, and payment by the hour, the week, or the month is indicative of employed earner status, as is the ability to earn overtime pay. (*Short v J and W Henderson Ltd* (1946) 62 TLR 427). (Leaflet IR 56). See HM Revenue and Customs Employment Status Manual, para ESM0509.

The control question will always have to be considered. (*Market Investigations Ltd v Minister of Social Security* [1969] 2 QB 173, [1968] 3 All ER 732, *per Cooke J*). However, the emphasis has shifted over the years so that it can be said that control need no longer be the decisive factor, but it remains of very great importance. (*Argent v Minister of Social Security* [1968] 3 All ER 208, [1968] 1 WLR 1749, *per Roskill J*). In 1984, the Privy Council held that, in most cases, the decisive criterion for determining the relationship between the parties to a contract is the extent to which the person, whose status as an employee or independent contractor is in issue, is under the direction and control of the other party to the contract with regard to the manner in which he does his work under it. (*Narich Pty Ltd v Commissioner of Pay-roll Tax* [1984] ICR 286).

In a 1995 case, Mr Justice Lightman said 'The lack of "control" . . . does not have the significance today that it once may have had as the litmus test for a contract of employment. It is certainly not a universal litmus test, and its importance (and indeed relevance) must depend in particular on the role to be played by the "employee" in the "employer's" business'. (*Horner v Hasted* [1995] 67 TC 439).

In *Littlewood (t/a Window and Door Services) v Revenue and Customs Comrs* [2009] STC (SCD) 243, the Special Commissioner said that it was unnecessary in an individual assignment to show that there was an obligation to provide work and an obligation to perform it. In this case there were subcontractors led by a charge hand – the latter provided the liaison with the employing partnership but the subcontractors were not under the control of the partnership. Further, the completion of time sheets and the provision of training were neutral factors in relation to the control test.

In practice, of course, many employees have considerable independence. Accordingly, when applying the control test to assess whether a contract of service is in place, HM Revenue and Customs has regard to any *right* of control which exists – even if it is seldom or never exercised – and to whether that control extends beyond the duties imposed to the method and performance of those duties. This is as it should be, for 'a servant is a person subject to the command of his master as to the manner in which he shall do his work' and the ultimate question is not what specific orders, or whether any specific orders, were given, but who is entitled to give the orders as to how the work should be done. Reference should be made to *Express and Echo Publications Ltd v Tanton* [1999] ICR 693, [1999] IRLR 367, CA. See also (*Yewens v Noakes* (1880) 6 QBD 530; *Simmons v Heath Laundry Co* [1910] 1 KB 543; *Mersey Docks and Harbour Board v Coggins and Griffith (Liverpool) Ltd* [1947] AC 1, [1946] 2 All ER 345, HL). In *Real Time Civil Engineering Ltd v Callaghan* [2006] All ER (D) 222 (Jan), EAT, December 2005, it was held that the right of substitution in a contract may only be disregarded if it is a 'sham' – the latter means a clause in the context which the parties to it do not intend to be truthful. HM Revenue and Customs considers that, in general, if a person can be told 'where to work, when to work, how to work or what to do' he is under a contract of service (*Ferguson v John Dawson & Partners (Contractors) Ltd* [1976] 3 AER 817). (Leaflet EC/FS2). Where a right to suspend or dismiss exists, this too is indicative that the contract is a contract of service. (*Willard v Whiteley Ltd* [1938] 3 All ER 779, 82 Sol Jo 711, CA; *Morren v Swinton and Pendlebury Borough Council* [1965] 1 WLR 576).

In *R (on the application of Professional Contractors Group Ltd) v IRC* [2001] EWHC Admin 236, [2001] STC 629, 74 TC 393, the judge queried whether the then Inland Revenue was correct to reject substitution clauses which were dependent on obtaining the client's permission, referring to *Express and Echo Publications Ltd v Tanton* (1999) All ER (D) 256. In this latter case there was a contract between the parties which stated '. . . in the event that the contractor is unable or unwilling to perform the services personally he shall arrange at his own expense for another suitable person to perform the services' and therefore as the contract did not require Mr Tanton to perform any services personally the contract could not be held to be a contract of service. Mr Tanton also paid for his substitute himself and it might be preferable to concrete such a clause occasionally to send a substitute in these circumstances. Specifically, Peter Gibson LJ said in the Tanton case:

> . . . it is necessary for a contract of employment to contain an obligation on the part of the employee to provide his services personally. Without such an irreducible minimum of obligation, it cannot be said that the contract is one of service . . . it is established on the authorities that, where, as here, a person who works for another is not required to perform his services personally, then as a matter of law the relationship between the worker and the person for whom he works is not that of employee and employer.

In the case of *McFarlane v Glasgow City Council* [2001] IRLR 7, [2000] All ER (D) 1048 the Tribunal distinguished the case from Tanton because the Council paid the substitutes, whereas in the case of Tanton he paid them himself. See also *Ready Mixed Concrete (South East) Ltd v Minister of Pensions and National Insurance* [1968] 2 QB 497, [1968] 1 All ER 433 where any substitute sent by the lorry driver (held to be self-employed) was to be paid by himself.

In the Employment Status Manual, para ESM0537:

> Disproving a claimed right of substitution can be difficult. Unless there is reason to doubt a claimed right of substitution it may normally be accepted at face value . . . Enquiries are more likely to be appropriate where other alleged terms are found to be false or a claimed right of substitution does not seem to make sense in relation to the contract. For example, an engager is unlikely to want to accept a substitute when engaging a person with specialist skills etc personal to them (for example, a well-known actor, footballer, designer, etc)
>
> - where a high quality job is required and a particular individual is deliberately chosen because of his/her own abilities (for example, an 'ace' carpenter chosen to construct a particularly difficult film set)
> - where the work involves a complex task worked on a team basis and is likely to take some time to complete and where ongoing work relies on a knowledge of the whole system being worked on (for example, in some computer programming situations).
>
> Also, if a worker is hourly paid, an engager may be slow to accept a substitute where a known, helpful and highly productive individual is engaged. For example, an engager hires a fit 22 year old man as a removal operative on a long term contract at a weekly wage, perhaps paying above the going rate for their particular experience, etc. Is it likely a substitute would be accepted who might be 'suitable' but perhaps not nearly as productive and useful as the originally contracted worker?
>
> The above list is not exhaustive – and the examples are not set in stone. Each situation needs to be considered on its own merits.

The Manual continues (at para ESM 1055) as follows:

> . . . it is the right of substitution that is important. The fact that substitution has not actually occurred during a contract is not necessarily relevant. Workers with such a right are of course entirely free to carry out the work themselves if they wish. We may want to consider claims that there is a right of substitution critically if substitution does not occur over a long period of time. However, we should not automatically assume, in such cases, that this means that there is no real right of substitution.

It should be noted that the control test in the context of distinguishing between employment and self-employment is subtly different from the question of control in the context of the **4 AGENCY WORKERS** provisions. An agency worker will rarely be able to show that he is an employee of the client or the agency because the bilateral mutual obligations outlined above are split three ways when the agency enters the arrangement. For the rule that deems an agency worker to be an employee of the agency, the crucial control factor is limited to the *manner* of carrying out the work, ie, the 'how', not the full control over whether, where and when to carry out the work described here.

The integration test

[14.13] Another test (which increasingly is seen as but part of the economic reality test—see **14.14**) involves a consideration of the relationship between the services a person performs and the business of the person for whom he performs them. If the services are performed as an integral part of the business rather than being merely accessory to it, the contract under which those services are performed is more likely to be a contract of service. (*Stevenson, Jordan and Harrison Ltd v MacDonald and Evans* (1952) 69 RPC 10, [1952] 1 TLR 101, CA, *per Lord Denning*.) This is because the person will be 'part and parcel' of the business, whether the services he renders are subject to control or not. (*Bank Voor Handel en Scheepvaart NV v Slatford* [1953] 1 QB 248, [1952] 2 All ER 956, CA). Thus, though a hospital board may be in no position to tell its surgeons what to do or how to do it, those surgeons may well be under contracts of service with the board as the operations they perform are an integral part of the hospital's activity. This can be crucial in determining liability for torts as well as liability for Class 1 contributions. (*Cassidy v Minister of Health* [1951] 2 KB 343, [1951] 1 All ER 574, CA; see also *Amalgamated Engineering Union v Minister of Pensions and National Insurance* [1963] 1 All ER 864, [1963] 1 WLR 441).

The economic reality test

[14.14] The economic reality test approaches matters from yet another direction. (It originated in the United States and Canada—see *US v Silk* (1946) 331 US 704 and *Montreal Locomotive Works Ltd v Montreal and Attorney-General for Canada* (1947) 1 DLR 161.) Rather than looking at the facts and deciding whether there is a contract of service, and finding self-employment only if no such contract can be made out, the economic reality test asks whether a person who has engaged himself to perform services is performing them as a person 'in business on his own account' (*Market Investigations Ltd v Minister of Social Security* [1969] 2 QB 173, [1968] 3 All ER 732, *per Cooke J*) or, to put the question into the vernacular, is the person 'his own boss'. (*Withers v Flackwell Heath Football Supporters' Club* [1981] IRLR 307). If the answer is negative, the person is a party to a contract of service.

Among the relevant factors which will need to be considered in applying the economic reality test are whether (and to what degree) a person performing services:

(a) provides his own equipment,
(b) hires his own helpers,
(c) takes financial risk,
(d) takes responsibility for investment and management, and
(e) has an opportunity of profiting from sound management in the performance of his task.

(*Market Investigations Ltd v Minister of Social Security* [1969] 3 AER 732). See also IR Tax Bulletin, February 2000, page 716, Tax Bulletin, February 2001 and HM Revenue and Customs Employment Status Manual, paras ESM0511, ESM0512.

As far as (a) is concerned, HM Revenue and Customs points out that it is the provision of *major* items of equipment that is of relevance—many employees provide the small tools which are needed for them to perform their tasks. (former Leaflet EC/FS2). IR Tax Bulletin, February 2000, page 716 stated:

> . . . a self-employed contractor generally provides whatever equipment is needed to do the job (though in many trades, such as carpentry, it is common for employees, as well as self-employed workers, to provide their own hand tools). The provision of significant equipment (and/or materials) which are fundamental to the engagement is of particular importance.

Indeed, leaflet CIS 349 stated:

> It is becoming increasingly common for both skilled and semi-skilled workers within the construction industry, to supply power tools such as drills, saws, nail guns, angle grinders, planes, routers, and so on. The provision and use of power tools is usually the personal preference of an individual worker to provide such tools irrespective of whether they are self-employed or employed.

In *Ready Mixed Concrete (South East) Ltd v Minister of Pensions and National Insurance* [1968] 2 QB 497, [1968] 1 All ER 433, the lorry driver held to be self-employed provided his own lorry. The fact that its level of maintenance had to meet certain requirements specified in the contract was insufficient to render it a contract of service.

As far as (b) is concerned, HM Revenue and Customs suggested a distinction between being free to hire people on terms of one's own choice to do the work which one has taken on, paying them out of one's own pocket, and merely being authorised to delegate work or to engage others on behalf of one's employer (former Leaflet EC/FS2). Delegation is now contrasted with substitution at ESM7220 in a discussion of the *MacFarlane v Glasgow City Council* and *Express & Echo Publications Ltd v Tanton* cases.

As far as (c) is concerned, HMRC asked: 'Does the worker risk their own money? Do they have to correct unsatisfactory work in their own time and at their own expense?' (former Leaflet EC/FS2). IR Tax Bulletin, February 2000, page 716 stated:

> . . . A person who has the freedom to choose whether to do the job himself or hire somebody else to provide substantial help is probably self-employed.

The method of remuneration (see **14.11** above) is also an important consideration in relation to this test. If a person is paid by way of a fixed wage or salary, financial risk will be virtually non-existent, whereas remuneration by commission only may indicate that a person is risking his own money in carrying out a contract. The issue in 1995 of now-withdrawn leaflet IR 148/CA 69 for the construction industry 'Are your workers employed or self-employed?' went some way towards clarifying the position. The leaflet reiterated the standard tests of control, mutual obligation and integration from the point of view of subcontractors. Whilst this view clarifies a number of matters by setting out indicators, each case will be viewed according to its own particular circumstances (see **41.9** LABOUR-ONLY CONTRACTORS). Similarly in the more recently issued leaflet CIS 349 'Are your workers employed or self-employed? – Advice for contractors' it is stated: 'Each case must be viewed on its own merits'.

Case law—the economic reality test

[14.15] In *Hall v Lorimer* [1994] STC 23, the Court of Appeal rejected a checklist approach to categorisation, but added to the tests summarised by Cooke J in *Market Investigations*. In particular, it is important to determine whether a person has set up a business-like organisation of his own and whether there is a degree of continuity in the relationship between the person performing the services and the person for whom they are performed. In *Lorimer*, the taxpayer, a vision mixer, regularly worked for over twenty different clients and took on over 500 separate engagements over four years, the longest lasting two weeks and most only a day or less. Although the taxpayer provided none of his own equipment, the engagements he undertook were merely incidents in his professional career. He ran the risk of bad debts, which an employee would not face, and he incurred significant expenditure on obtaining more engagements. His expenses were different in nature and scale from those incurred by employees. The then Inland Revenue argued that the taxpayer could not be treated as self-employed as had no capital tied up in the productions on which he was working, but the Special Commissioner, quoted approvingly by Nolan LJ in the Court of Appeal, noted that the production company was not Lorimer's business. *His* business was to exploit his undoubted skills as a vision mixer, controlling his own costs and profiting from being successful, thereby attracting more work as his reputation grew. In both the High Court and the Court of Appeal, the dictum of Vinelott J in *Walls v Sinnett* CA [1986] 60 TC 150 was quoted with approval –

> The facts as a whole must be looked at, and what may be compelling in one case in the light of all the facts may not be compelling in the context of another case.

In *R (on the application of Professional Contractors Group Ltd) v IRC* [2001] EWHC Admin 236, [2001] STC 629, 74 TC 393, the judge said — in the context of IT workers — that the 'in business on own account' test 'is and must be a central consideration' involving 'The question of whether the service contractor himself has, prior to that engagement, performed or is, simultaneously with that engagement, performing (an important contrast to the duty of fidelity ordinarily owed by an employee), or will subsequently, after the termination of that engagement, perform services for others'. See further INTERMEDIARIES 40.

Contracts of apprenticeship

[14.16] See 10.2 APPRENTICES, TRAINEES AND STUDENTS.

The meaning of 'office'

[14.17] An 'office' is a post which can be recognised as existing, whether it be occupied for the time being or vacant, and which, if occupied, does not owe its existence in any way to the identity of the incumbent or his appointment to the post. (*Edwards (Inspector of Taxes) v Clinch* [1981] Ch 1, [1980] 3 All ER 278, CA, *per Buckley LJ*). A company director occupies an office though he may also be under a contract of service (see **22.4** company directors and *McMillan v Guest (Inspector of Taxes)* [1942] AC 561, [1942] 1 All ER 606,

HL, *per Lord Atkin*). So do a member of Parliament, a minister of the Crown and a judge. (Hansard 16 December 1975 Vol 902 No 20 Col 578). A bishop of the Church of England is an office-holder (DSS Leaflet NP 21, long since out of print) as is a member of the Church of England clergy, a NHS consultant, a stipendiary reader in the Church of England, a police officer, a justice of the peace, a trustee or executor, a company auditor, a local land charges registrar, a student union president, a club secretary, a trade union officer, a company registrar and a superintendent registrar of births, deaths and marriages. (*Re Employment of Church of England Curates* [1912] 2 Ch 563; *Mitchell and Edon (Inspector of Taxes) v Ross* [1962] AC 813, [1961] 3 All ER 49, HL; *Barthorpe v Exeter Diocesan Board* [1979] ICR 900; *Ridge v Baldwin* [1964] AC 40; *Knight v A-G* [1979] ICR 194; *Dale v IRC* [1951] Ch 893, [1951] 2 All ER 517; *Ellis (Inspector of Taxes) v Lucas* [1967] Ch 858, [1966] 2 All ER 935; *Ministry of Housing and Local Government v Sharp* [1969] 3 All ER 225, [1969] 3 WLR 1020; *Oleskar v Sunderland Polytechnic Students' Union EAT 482/79; 102 Social Club & Institute v Bickerton* [1977] ICR 911; *Stevenson v United Road Transport Union* [1977] ICR 893; *IRC v Brander and Cruickshank* [1971] 1 All ER 36, [1971] 1 WLR 212, HL; *Miles v Wakefield Metropolitan District Council* [1985] IRLR 108). This list is not exhaustive and it is clear that elected members of local authorities, CROWN SERVANTS 25 and the like are all officers within the terms of the definition.

The holding of an office is not in itself sufficient to place a person in the category of employed earners. The office has to have an entitlement to earnings. [*SSCBA 1992, s 2(1)(a)*]. (From 6 April 2003 to 5 April 2014, the reference was to 'general earnings' as defined in *ITEPA 2003, s 7(3)*, a misguided attempt at harmonisation of income tax and NIC rules when *ITEPA 2003* came into force that was incompatible with many other social security provisions and was finally corrected by *NICA 2014, s 15*.) 'General earnings' for *ITEPA 2003* purposes includes all salaries, fees, wages, perquisites and profits whatsoever, including anything else that constitutes earnings from employment. [*ITEPA 2003, s 62(2)*]. For earnings to be chargeable to income tax as general earnings in respect of an office, they must be earnings *therefrom*. This means that a payment is not chargeable to tax as general earnings unless it has been made to a person 'in return for acting as or being an employee' (or, as the case may be, an office-holder). (*Hochstrasser (Inspector of Taxes) v Mayes* [1960] AC 376, [1959] 3 All ER 817, HL, *per Lord Radcliffe*.) 'Chargeable' is not, of course, the same thing as 'charged'. HM Revenue and Customs may fail to charge to tax as general earnings payments made to an office holder which should be so charged, or may charge to tax as general earnings payments made to an office holder which should not be so charged. In the first event the office was nonetheless an office with earnings chargeable to tax as general earnings for the purpose of *SSCBA 1992, s 2(1)(a)* while in the latter event it was not. This problem has now been resolved by the reinstatement of the pre-*ITEPA 2003* definition from 6 April 2014: 'earnings' is now once again defined as including 'any remuneration or profit derived from an employment. [*SSCBA 1992, s 3(1)(a)*.] Bearing in mind that 'employment' encompasses 'office' (*SSCBA 1992, s 122(1)*), it should now be clear that office holders fall within Class 1 liability. The term 'general earnings' was also corrected to 'earnings' by *Social Security (Miscellaneous Amendments No 2) Regulations 2015, 2015/478, Regs 7, 22, 23*.

If, as is frequently the case, a partnership holds the office of auditor of a limited company, each of the partners is (if the partnership is subject to English, rather than Scottish, law) jointly and severally responsible for the discharge of the duties attaching to that office. (*Saddler v Whiteman* [1910] 1 KB 868, *per Farwell LJ at p 889*). As the auditor's remuneration or fee is clearly chargeable to income tax as general earnings, each partner of the firm falls within the category of employed earner by reason of the office and is, in law, liable for Class 1 contributions on the earnings received. HMRC practice is, however, to allow such earnings to be included in the profits of the partnership chargeable to income tax under *ITTOIA 2005*, and the former DSS always followed suit, effectively collecting CLASS 4 CONTRIBUTIONS 20 on the earnings.

Self-employed earners

Definition—a 'self-employed earner'

[14.18] A 'self-employed earner' is any person who is gainfully employed in Great Britain otherwise than in employed earner's employment (whether or not he is also employed in such employment). [*SSCBA 1992, s 2(1)(b)*].

Because this definition is largely negative and because categorisation as a self-employed earner will result in liability for contributions being determined under the Class 2 (ie earnings-*un*related) contribution rules (see CLASS 2 CONTRIBUTIONS 18), much depends on the meaning of the words 'gainfully employed'. This phrase differs slightly from the pre-1975 phrase 'gainfully occupied in employment' but not, it is thought, sufficiently to alter the test to which those original words gave rise, ie 'whether or not a person holds himself out as being anxious to become employed for the purposes of gain', not whether or not he has in fact received some net profit from his activities as a self-employed person. (*Vandyk v Minister of Pensions and National Insurance* [1955] 1 QB 29, [1954] 2 All ER 723).

A person's business or occupation must, of course, have actually *begun* before that person can be regarded as 'gainfully employed' as a self-employed earner. Pre-commencement preparatory activity, eg finding premises, obtaining finance, researching the likely market etc, does not constitute gainful employment as a self-employed earner. But, once the business or occupation has begun, its profitability or otherwise becomes irrelevant to the determination of status for National Insurance purposes. The motive of gain is there, whatever the trading results might be, and self-employed earner status will continue until the business or occupation is actually discontinued. In deciding whether or not a person is gainfully employed as a self-employed earner for any week, the test to be applied is, therefore: Has he begun to run a business or practise a profession or engage in an occupation on his own account and is that business, profession or occupation continuing—even if dormant and inactive—or has it been discontinued, temporarily or permanently? A person does not cease to be gainfully employed as a self-employed earner merely because, for a time, no work is actually done.

Active involvement in enterprise

[14.19] Thus, the Secretary of State for Social Security did, for instance, formally determine that a theatrical producer who specialised in summer shows and Christmas pantomimes but who held himself out as available to put on productions at other times of the year was consequently self-employed during his periods of inactivity. (*M37 (1953)*). The Secretary of State for Social Security similarly determined that the proprietor of a boarding house is a self-employed earner throughout a year even though the greater part of the year is spent in cleaning and decorating in preparation for the holiday season during which actual gain arises. (*M36 (1953)*).

It should be noted that this may also be true of a person deriving profits or gains from the commercial letting of furnished holiday accommodation. Although such an activity is not a trade but is merely treated as such for taxation purposes (see *ITTOIA 2005, Part 2; ICTA 1988, s 504A*), it may well constitute a 'business' (see 14.2 above and Vinelott J's comments in *Griffiths v Jackson* [1983] STC 184) and, if it does, the presence of a profit-motive will render the person letting the accommodation liable to categorisation as a self-employed earner (although, since the Class 2 reform from 6 April 2015, any Class 2 contributions will be voluntary unless the business amounts to a trade).

The DSS, as it then was, stated its policy as being that a person who has furnished holiday lettings must be self-employed because the activity of taking bookings, dealing with payments, keeping accounts, cleaning etc constitutes business activity. (Letter, 29 January 1993). However, in subsequent correspondence it acknowledged that where very little time is spent working (ie collecting rents, taking bookings, etc) then the question whether a business is being carried on for these purposes may be disregarded. The words 'very little time', were originally supposed to have been representative of a limit of 8 hours per week. However, the CA wrote to point out that it is not possible to define a set number of hours that may be taken to be inconsiderable. Its view was that it is necessary to look at the facts present in each case. It went on to state that if Inspectors were in doubt about the level of activity they should *not* treat it as inconsiderable and in those circumstances it relied on the level of earnings to decide whether or not liability existed. (Letter from CA, 16 October 1995). If, though, the person carried on other business and was therefore self-employed in another capacity then if, taking the two businesses together, the individual would be classed as self-employed with regard to the two combined incomes under self-employment activities, then it would not be possible to disregard the furnished holiday lettings element. In order to resolve the matter, a question was put to the Secretary of State for Social Security for his determination and the results of an enquiry held on 8 June 1994 decided that in the particular circumstances mentioned above there was no gainful employment as a self-employed earner for the purposes of *SSA 1975* and *SSCBA 1992*. In contrast, in a determination by the Secretary of State for Social Security in a more recent case, the fact that an individual with lettings had responsibilities which required him to be on call 24 hours a day with no pattern to his working hours did not preclude self-employed status. In fact, it was stated that although the business was not as active as he would have wished he continued to be engaged in it and the position was analogous to that of a shopkeeper who remains open for business but has few customers.

Case law—the motive tests

[14.20] The mere receipt of rents from property is, however, to raise no *presumption* in law that a business is being carried on. (*American Leaf Blending Co Sdn Bhd v Director-General of Inland Revenue* [1978] STC 561, *per Lord Diplock*).

In a written reply the CA stated that it is not possible to define what constitutes 'trivial' but in the circumstances noted above, ie collecting rents, furnishing and maintaining the property, repairing/contracting for repairs, then the person letting the property will be considered gainfully employed as a self-employed earner and therefore (under the pre-2015 rules) liable to Class 2 contributions (CA Specialist Conference written response, 20 February 1996). Yet in contrast, in *Rashid v Garcia (Status Inspector)* [2003] STC (SCD) 36 it was held that the receipt of rents in that case did not constitute self-employment and Rashid was not therefore entitled to pay voluntary Class 2 contributions and subsequently receive State benefits on the basis of such contributions. In a case unrelated to NIC, but considering the question of whether a taxpayer was running a 'business', using the term in its natural way, the Upper Tribunal decided that the letting of ten flats in a single property amounted to a business. The taxpayer had transferred the property to a limited company and claimed incorporation relief under *TCGA 1992, s 162*. HMRC had denied the relief and assessed a chargeable gain on the transfer of the property. The First-tier Tribunal had dismissed the taxpayer's appeal on the grounds that the claimed business did not produce income from a trade or business under what was then Schedule D. The Upper Tribunal overturned that decision, as this approach was flawed. It was instead necessary to look at the degree of activity as a whole to determine whether the taxpayer had a business or merely an investment, and on the facts the level of activity outweighed what might normally be expected to be carried out by a mere passive investor. [*Ramsay v R & C Comrs* [2013] UKUT 226.]

Although, under this test, the motive of gain is, alone, sufficient to place a person within the category of self-employed earners, the absence of the motive of gain is not sufficient to remove him from that category where actual gain has in fact arisen. (*Benjamin v Minister of Pensions and National Insurance* [1960] 3 WLR 430). Thus, for instance, the former DSS took the view that fee-earning foster parents who receive a separate or distinct 'reward element' are self-employed earners for contribution purposes. (See also the website of the National Fostering Agency at www.nfa.co.uk/fostering/financial-support, which states clearly that HMRC regards foster carers as self-employed, which means they may be eligible for tax credits (ie, WTC and CTC), although a normal fostering allowance is generally exempt from income tax.) In Summer 2003 the then Inland Revenue posted a note on its website stating that the new tax legislation in *Finance Act 2003* (including the alternative method of profits calculation, where adopted) would be applied for Class 2 and Class 4 National Insurance purposes. The same note seemed to accept that all foster carers are to be treated as self-employed. If, however, both motive and actual gain become absent, a person will cease to be within the category of self-employed earners, as, for instance, a cricket umpire and an ice-cream salesman, each of whom was, according to the formal determinations of the Secretary of State for Social Security, non-employed during the winter months. *(M38 (1954); M45 (1954))*.

The National Insurance Commissioners held that a sleeping partner in a business is not a self-employed earner so long as he rendered no services to the business. (*R(S)10/79, CP 5/75*). He might have a motive of gain but, as there was no employment of any kind, he could not be said to be 'gainfully employed'. See also Tax Bulletin, February 2001. HMRC unexpectedly decided in 2013 to take a different view – see PARTNERS **52** – but has now resolved the muddle it thereby created by reforming Class 2 from 6 April 2015 so that it is charged on the same basis as Class 4. [*NICA 2015, s 2* and *Sch 1*.]

Definition—ordinarily employed

[14.21] Unfortunately, interpretative problems do not end with the 'gainfully' test for even if, by application of that test, a person is seen to be within the category of self-employed earners, he will be removed from that category and his earnings from that self-employed earner's employment disregarded for contribution purposes if he is not *ordinarily* employed in such employment. [*Categorisation Regs, Reg 2(4), Sch 1 Part III para 9*].

Although the meaning of 'ordinarily' has never been considered by the courts in the context of employment, it has been so considered in the context of residence and has been held to mean habitually, regularly, normally, with a settled purpose, not extraordinarily (see **51.5** overseas matters). (*Lysaght v CIR HL* (1928) 13 TC 511). It is submitted that, in order to be able to judge whether or not these qualities are attached to an employment, it is necessary to consider a person's activities over a period of time, and that the period of time should be a whole year or, if the nature of the activity is seasonal, that season within a year. If, then, within the selected period, a person is gainfully employed in a self-employed earner's employment on a regular basis for more than 50% of the time (disregarding holidays and days of incapacity), he should be regarded as being ordinarily self-employed.

The only published statement by the former DSS of its views on the meaning of the word 'ordinarily' in this context was contained in an early version of the long-obsolete leaflet NI 192 which informed non-NHS nurses and midwives that if their only self-employment is occasional home nursing at long and irregular intervals, eg less than once a fortnight, they might be regarded as not ordinarily self-employed.

A test of what constitutes ordinary, gainful self-employed earner's employment was formerly applied where (but only where) the earner in question was also employed in an employed earner's employment from which he derived substantial earnings. The test asked whether the earnings from the spare-time self-employment exceeded an amount set annually, ie £250 for 1977–78 and 1978–79, £400 for 1979–80 and 1980–81, £800 for 1981–82 to 2001–02 and £1,300 for 2002–03 to 2009–10. If the answer was negative, the employment was disregarded. (obsolete Leaflet CA 02). This test had no actual basis in law, however, and for that reason and in the light of the House of Lords decision in *R v IRC, ex parte Wilkinson* [2005] UKHL 30 the concession was withdrawn during 2009.

Under regulations revoked in 1978, self-employment was to be disregarded if it occupied the person concerned for less than eight hours a week. Until more recent times, some officers continued to apply that test (extra-statutorily) to determine whether a person should be regarded as 'ordinarily' self-employed, but the DSS subsequently disclaimed the validity of such an approach. The DSS did admit, however, that 'if a person's self-employment only involves a couple of hours per week then we deem it to be "inconsiderable" and do not enforce payment of a self-employed contribution'. (Letter, 29 January 1993). But see Secretary of State's determination regarding an individual who was 'on-call' 24 hours a day but was not as active as desired due to the property industry depression (see above).

However, the CA confirmed in writing (16 October 1995) that 'The Agency's view is that we need to look at the facts present in each case. Inspectors may still disregard self-employment as *inconsiderable* but that is a matter for individual judgement depending on the nature of employment. They are specifically told it is not possible to define a set number of hours that may be treated as inconsiderable. Inspectors are also instructed that if they are in doubt about the level of activity they should not treat it as inconsiderable. In those circumstances the Agency relies on the level of earnings to decide whether or not liability exists.' Part of the reason for this is that it may be possible for some businesses to generate enough income to attract NICs without investing a great deal of effort. If an arbitrary limit was imposed on the time invested then a clear route to being excused NIC has been created. Another contributor may do similar work, earn the same amount, but do longer hours and therefore have a NIC liability. This is perceived by NIC&EO as being unfair so it prefers to rely on the level of earnings to decide liability in the majority of cases.

Categorisation as a self-employed earner will not have been of significance where earnings from the self-employed earner's employment did not exceed the small earnings exception level and small earnings exception was claimed for years before 6 April 2015, and will be of equal insignificance for self-employed earners with trading profits below the small profits threshold for 2015–16 onwards (see **29.66** EARNINGS FROM EMPLOYMENT: GENERAL; **18.4** CLASS 2 CONTRIBUTIONS and **53.9** RATES AND LIMITS).

The relevance of tax treatment

[14.22] The intention of Parliament in redefining the categories of employed earner and self-employed earner was to align CLASS 1 CONTRIBUTIONS **15** with income tax on employment income and CLASS 2 CONTRIBUTIONS **18** with what was then Schedule D. (See 847 House of Commons Debates 5th Series Col 124). It must be expected, therefore, that where HM Revenue and Customs brings a person's earnings within the charge to tax as earnings rather than profits, it will also seek to categorise that person as an employed earner for

NICs. Prior to 1 April 1999, there was never any obligation on either the then Inland Revenue or the then DSS to follow the rulings of the other and the cautious attitude which the DSS generally maintained is well illustrated by the Secretary of State's confirmation at one time that possession of a subcontractor's tax exemption certificate was *normally* accepted as evidence of self-employment *unless* investigation revealed that a contract of service was in existence. (Hansard 13 November 1981 Vol 12 No 8 Pt II Col 188). DSS practice was, apparently, to proceed on the basis that, unless suitable evidence to the contrary was produced, the Inland Revenue had issued a subcontractor's certificate without full enquiry into the applicant's circumstances. The DSS would therefore make its own decision on employment status and inform the then Inland Revenue of that decision.

The courts have indicated that, where they make a decision as to the employment status of an individual, they expect HM Revenue and Customs to give full effect to it, even though the decision may have been made in some connection other than income tax or social security contributions. (*Young and Woods Ltd v West* [1980] IRLR 201). The courts consider such consistency necessary if an individual is to be discouraged from asserting (as he otherwise might) that he had one employment status for, say, tax and National Insurance purposes, but a different status for, say, redundancy and unfair dismissal purposes. That is not to say that the courts themselves will always feel bound take into account status decisions made by HMRC. In *Autoclenz Ltd v Belcher* [2011] UKSC 41, a group of car valets had been found to be self-employed by an HMRC status inspector. Several years later, in a dispute over National Minimum Wage and working time entitlements (started by the workers, not HMRC minimum wage inspectors), two tribunals held that the men were 'workers' because they were providing personal service, but the Court of Appeal and the Supreme Court went further and found them to be employees under a contract of service. The contract under which they were working, which had included a free substitution clause so as to ensure that the men would be treated as self-employed (see above), had in the Supreme Court's view been foisted on them by an employer who held all the bargaining power, so the court felt free to decide what the true terms of the contract had been. Since the substitution right was illusory rather than real, it was simply disregarded. It is not known whether HMRC subsequently revised its decision that the men had been self-employed.

The *Social Security Contributions (Transfer of Functions, etc) Act 1999, ss 8–19, Sch 7* provides HM Revenue and Customs with the right for their staff to take decisions on matters that were in the past administered by the CA. Similar or identical issues such as whether a person is employed or self-employed will now be determined by HMRC staff and appeals against such decisions lie to the Tax Tribunal. See APPEALS AND REVIEWS 9.

However, the tax and NICs treatment of a person can sometimes differ, as indicated in the following case.

Case law—Big Bad Wolff Ltd

[14.23] In the case of *Big Bad Wolff Ltd v HMRC* [2017] UKFTT 729 (TC), [2018] SFTD 468, Big Bad Wolff Ltd (BBW) was the personal company of an actor, Mr G and his wife. Mr G provided his services directly to clients. He was a director of BBW and received employment income and dividends in respect of his acting services.

At issue was the correct statutory construction of *SSCBA 1992, s 4A* and the *Social Security Contributions (Intermediaries) Regulations 2000 (SI 2000/727), reg 6*, and the application of the *Social Security (Categorisation of Earners) Regulations 1978 (SI 1978/1689)*.

The First-tier Tax Tribunal observed that the clear intention of Parliament in enacting *s 4A* had been to prevent the avoidance of NICs by the introduction of intermediary or personal service companies. Prior to the introduction of *s 4A*, a worker, who would otherwise be in employment, would avoid NICs by using an intermediary company to supply his services to the client. Mr G would, as a matter of general law, be a self-employed actor. However, if he contracted directly with a client and was paid a salary (with the result that he was not within the *Social Security (Categorisation of Earners) Regulations 1978 (SI 1978/1689)* exclusion in *Sch 1, Part 1 Column (B)*) he would be treated as being in employed earner's employment for NIC purposes. So, although Mr G would be a self-employed person as a matter of general law, he was treated as being in employment by the *Social Security (Categorisation of Earners) Regulations 1978 (SI 1978/1689)*. This was therefore a case where someone who would otherwise be treated as being in employment had sought, by using an intermediary company, to reduce his liability to NICs. The Tribunal concluded that providing his services via a personal service company did not prevent Mr G from being employed by his clients for NIC purposes.

There appears to be no dispute regarding the tax position, ie IR35 did not apply; only the NICs position was being contested. At paragraph 95 of the decision, the tribunal judge stated:

> 'Finally, I do not consider that the difference in treatment between NIC legislation and income tax legislation can affect the position. Whilst the two statutory codes work closely together there are divergences, of which this is one.'

This is a test case and there are several other cases, particularly concerning actors, awaiting its outcome. Given the interaction between the provisions on intermediary companies (*SSCBA 1992, s 4A* and the *Social Security Contributions (Intermediaries) Regulations 2000 (SI 2000/727), reg 6*) and the *Social Security (Categorisation of Earners) Regulations 1978 (SI 1978/1689)*, this case confirms that, in most cases, the use of a personal services company will not achieve an NIC saving. (See Taxation Magazine 26 October 2017, page 7.)

Mr G has appealed to the Upper Tribunal and a hearing date is awaited.

Determination of doubtful cases

[14.24] Official advice used to be that, where there was any doubt as to the category or categories in which a person belongs, the local Status Inspector or Status Officer at the local office should be consulted. Now that there are no local offices, this is no longer an option. There was often a reluctance to heed this advice as it was thought that the local office would always err in favour of employed earner status. It should be borne in mind, however, that no decision given by officers is final and that a question as to whether a person is an earner and, if he is, as to the category of earners in which he is to be included, can be made the subject of an appeal to the tribunals (and beyond). [*SSC(TF)A 1999, s 11*]. (See APPEALS AND REVIEWS 9).

HM Revenue and Customs has also encouraged, since 2005, the use of the Employment Status Indicator tool on its website – tools.hmrc.gov.uk/esi (see also former factsheet EC/FS2). The tool gives no more than an indication of the position, though in practice HM Revenue and Customs will generally accept the result that the tool gives where all information has been accurately provided. Further, HMRC stated in late 2007 that it would be bound (provided the answers given to the ESI questions accurately reflected the terms and conditions under which the services were provided at the relevant time) by the ESI outcome where the engager or his authorised representative provided copies of the printer-friendly version of the ESI Result screen, bearing the 14 digit ESI reference number, and the Enquiry Details screen. The user was also to retain a copy of the written contract (if available) in relation to the engagement to which the print-out referred along with any other documentation relied upon when completing the ESI (Leaflet EC/FS2).

The instructions for the use of the ESI now state almost the same:

> 'When you have answered all the questions, the ESI tool will provide it's [*sic*] indication of the worker's employment status. You can rely on the ESI outcome as evidence of a worker's status for tax/NICs/VAT purposes if both of the following apply:
>
> - your answers to the ESI questions accurately reflect the terms and conditions under which the worker provides their services
> - the ESI has been completed by an engager or their authorised representative (if the tool has been completed by or on behalf of a worker the result is only indicative)
>
> However, you should download and print or save the PDF bearing the 14 digit ESI reference number from the summary of outcome screen. If the worker's employment status is questioned in the future, HMRC will only be bound by the ESI outcome if this document can be produced.'

With the changes introduced by *Finance Act 2017* concerning workers' services provided to public sector [sic] through intermediaries (often referred to as 'off-payroll working' in the public sector), the ESI has been renamed as the 'Employment Status Service' (ESS) and enhanced to cater for the changes to the intermediaries legislation.

In outline, the public sector end-user is seen as the only person or entity that is able to determine whether the contract falls within IR35, because it knows whether the work is subject to close supervision, direction and control in the same way as for an employee. If the end-user contracts directly with a PSC, and it determines that the contract is a IR35 contract, it will be obliged to operate PAYE and NIC on 100% of the invoice value excluding materials. It was originally proposed that the PAYE charge should be based on just 95%, to match the 5% expense allowance in the IR35 rules, but this was changed as a response to feedback during the consultation, allegedly to recognise that workers will no longer have to bear the administrative burden of deciding whether the IR35 rules apply. Given that HMRC has previously claimed that there is 90% non-compliance with the IR35 rules, the expected yield from this change that is listed in Table 2.1 of the Statement, at just £115 million over five years, seems somewhat low.

If the PSC supplies its worker through an agency, the agency that pays the PSC will have the obligation to account for the PAYE and NIC if the public sector client informs it that the contract is within IR35.

Whether it is the client or the agency that is liable to account for deductions, it must do so under RTI. HMRC has not yet explained how double taxation will be avoided and it seems little thought may have been given to this beyond the need to make some provision along these lines. If the client or agency deducts PAYE and accounts for it under RTI, it will pay employer National Insurance contributions, and when the PSC itself pays out the net money as wages, it will also be liable to account for PAYE and NIC, unless provision is made for the income to be streamed and excluded from liability under both regimes. The RTI system seems unlikely to be able to cope with the same income being paid out twice on separate employer references. Given that this will require changes in HMRC systems, the proposals scheduled to take effect in April 2017 may have to be introduced with very light touch regulatory action.

No equivalent action is proposed, yet, for private sector contracts. Given the new danger for public sector bodies that they may be held liable for any missed deductions if their assessment of the contracts is incorrect, it may be presumed that most will take a safety first approach to the new regime and require most contractors to go onto their, or their agents', payroll unless they can credibly certify that their business and the contract in question are outside IR35.

[*ITEPA 2003, Pt 2, Ch 10* inserted by *FA 2017, s 6, Sch 1*].

For cross-references to the various categorisation determinations made by the Secretary of State for Social Security and noted in this work, see the Table of Published Decisions.

Retrospective effect of a categorisation decision

[14.25] HM Revenue and Customs will invariably take steps to remedy any case of mis-categorisation which comes to its knowledge, but the extent to which corrective action will be retrospective will depend on the nature of the mis-categorisation.

If it is found that a person who has been treated as an employed earner properly belongs in the category of self-employed earners, its decision to that effect will normally relate only to the present and future, thus ensuring that re-categorisation will be effective only from the date of the decision and that no question of repayment of excess contributions arises. (But see **41.15** LABOUR-ONLY CONTRACTORS for an exception in the case of film and TV industry workers.) If, therefore, a person wishes to obtain a repayment of contributions in such circumstances, it will be necessary to obtain the authorities' agreement that during the past period for which the repayment is sought, he properly belonged in the category of self-employed earners (see REPAYMENT AND REALLOCATION 55). This may not easily be obtained but, should HM Revenue and Customs decline to give a ruling on the matter, a formal decision may be requested and, if necessary, insisted upon (see APPEALS AND REVIEWS 9) [*SSC(TF)A 1999, s 8*].

Reallocation as Class 1 primary NICs

[14.26] If, on the other hand, it is found that a person who has been treated as a self-employed earner properly belongs in the category of employed earners, the date from which HM Revenue and Customs will re-categorise the earner concerned will depend on the circumstances of the case. Guidance has, for many years, been as follows. The 'Department' is the then Department of Social Security, the NIC functions of which are now combined with the then Inland Revenue in HM Revenue and Customs.

> Each case has to be considered on its merits. If after investigation it is decided that a person should be reclassified as an employed earner for national insurance purposes the Department's main responsibility is to ensure that the correct contributions are being paid *currently*. The date of change of classification could however be effective from an earlier date. In those circumstances any Class 2 contributions which the contributor has paid erroneously as a result of the change of status from self-employed to employed earner are reallocated as primary Class 1 contributions. Any balance of primary contributions due and any arrears of secondary contributions are generally requested from the employer. If the erroneous Class 2 contributions amount to more than the primary Class 1 contributions due the excess is refundable. The Inland Revenue deals with Class 4 contributions overpaid as a result of a change of status.
>
> (Hansard 27 February 1984 Vol 55 No 108 Cols 62–63).

Four points must be made concerning that Parliamentary answer.

(a) There are grounds for supposing that the date of re-categorisation *will* (not 'may') be effective from a date earlier than the date the mis-categorisation is discovered—particularly if HM Revenue and Customs was not asked to give a ruling when the contractual relationship in question was entered into (see **14.24** CATEGORISATION) and if there are grounds for supposing that the mis-categorisation was deliberate rather than accidental. The then DSS partially confirmed that this is the case by stating that 'the normal practice is to assess earlier liability under Class 1 when a person previously paying Class 2 contributions is re-categorised as an employee. However, full account is taken of all the circumstances before a decision is made to require payment by the employer of any amounts due'. (Hansard 6 March 1986 Vol 93 Col 243). In practice now, HM Revenue and Customs usually restricts the period of re-categorisation to six years. Whilst the former DSS had historically taken the view that it can recover arrears without time limit, latterly the CA generally accepted that the provisions of the *Limitation Act 1980* apply and HM Revenue and Customs currently follows the same approach (see **12.10** ARREARS OF CONTRIBUTIONS).

(b) Erroneously paid Class 2 contributions *may* be reallocated as primary Class 1 contributions, but no legal obligation to reallocate is imposed. The matter is within the discretion of HM Revenue and Customs. [*Social Security (Contributions) Regulations 2001, SI 2001/1004, Reg 51*]. See HM Revenue and Customs National Insurance Manual para NIM37019. In addition, following the merger in 1999 with the then Inland Revenue, it has increasingly been the practice to give credit for Class 4 also – though such credit is by no means automatic.

(c) Any balance of primary and secondary Class 1 contributions which remains outstanding after any erroneously-paid Class 2 contributions have been reallocated is *invariably demanded* (not 'generally requested') from the secondary contributor concerned.

(d) The secondary contributor may recover from his employee only such part (if any) of the contributions demanded from him as are *primary* contributions which should have been deducted from his employee's earnings in the *current* tax year and, with practical effect from 6 April 2005, the previous tax year, but which he did not deduct *by reason of an error* which he made in good faith. [*Social Security (Contributions) Regulations 2001, SI 2001/1004, Sch 4 para 7(3)*, as amended by *Social Security (Contributions, Categorisation of Earners and Intermediaries) (Amendment) Regulations 2004, SI 2004/770*]. In addition, the amount of arrears which can be deducted in any earnings period is limited to the amount that equals the correct deduction for that earnings period itself. [*Social Security (Contributions) Regulations 2001, SI 2001/1004, Sch 4 para 7(5)*]. Any other recovery from the employee is unlawful within the terms of the NI legislation, although employers may find a court claim in restitution will be available (see *McCarthy v McCarthy & Stone plc* [2008] 1 AER 221).

The restriction in (*d*) above was lifted from 10 June 2003 but only in the cases of payments of shares, options and from employee benefit trusts (*Social Security (Contributions) Regulations 2001, SI 2001/1004, Sch 4 paras 5A, 5B*, inserted by *Social Security (Contributions) (Amendment No 4) Regs 2003*).

Example

In mid-2003, Algernon began to undertake television maintenance work for Bloggs TV Rentals Ltd. It was agreed between A and B that A would be treated as self-employed and would discharge his own tax and National Insurance liabilities. A's earnings from B taking into account the downturn from 2009, and the contributions he paid, were as follows

Year ended 5 April	*Earnings* £	*Class 2* £	*Class 4* £
2004	43,000	106.00	2,226.60
2005	44,000	106.60	2,280.80
2006	46,000	109.20	2,361.60
2007	47,000	109.20	2,415.00
2008	50,000	114.40	2,520.80
2009	53,000	119.60	2,898.00
2010	44,000	124.80	3,054.05

2011	42,000	124.80	2,902.80
2012	40,000	130.00	2,949.75
2013	38,000	137.80	2,735.55
2014	36,000	140.40	2,542.05
2015	40,000	143.00	2,883.96
		£1,465.80	£31,770.96

In August 2015, an employer compliance officer called on B to make a routine inspection of the wages records and, in the course of that examination, saw a note in the wages book reading 'Algernon—£770 per week from 6 April 2015'. The officer inquired further into the matter and decided that A had properly belonged in the category of employed earners since the engagement began. He computed the Class 1 liabilities to be

Year ended 5 April	*Primary*	*Secondary*	*Total*
	£	£	£
2004	3,016.35	4,913.28	7,929.63
2005	3,090.05	5,024.64	8,114.69
2006	3,197.55	5,261.44	8,458.99
2007	3,270.15	5,371.52	8,641.67
2008	3,409.25	5,731.20	9,140.45
2009	3,936.15	6,088.32	10,024.47
2010	4,198.85	4,900.48	9,099.33
2011	4,198.85	4,900.48	9,099.33
2012	3,933.00	4,544.06	8,477.06
2013	3,647.40	4,210.66	7,858.06
2014	3,389.40	3,905.95	7,295.35
2015	3,844.80	4,421.52	8,266.32
	£43,131.80	£59,273.55	£102,405.35

Even assuming HM Revenue and Customs permits the set-off of Class 2 contributions and Class 4 contributions already paid by A, it may request an amount due from B (but see **12.9** ARREARS OF CONTRIBUTIONS as regards its enforceability) of £69,168.59 (ie £102,405.35 – £1,465.80 – £31,770.96) and only a small part of this amount relating to 2014–15 may be recoverable from A. If, however, A had misled B the position might alter. See **21.30** COLLECTION. Note that A or B may argue that the reduction in payments in the years from 6 April 2011 to 6 April 2014 indicates that there is risk of financial loss that would be a factor in indicating A was self-employed. However, this merely acknowledges that a change in contract terms has been invoked to take account of the recession as many employers have done in similar circumstances and any association with point 5 below in the letter is spurious.

"Dear Mr Bloggs,

As you are aware I have been considering the employment status of [Algernon] in respect of [his] engagement with you for the period from 06/04/2003 to date.

I have enclosed guidance at Annex A describing how HMRC decides employment status.

In this case I consider Algernon to be and have always been an employee of Bloggs TV Rentals Ltd due to factors contained in the Annex to this letter.

A contract of service need not be in writing and therefore the absence of a written agreement is not a definitive factor. It can also be an oral agreement and can be express or implied from the working arrangements.

There is however no precise legal definition of what constitutes a contract of service, ie what makes the relationship in law between the two parties that of employer and employee. This opinion applies for the purposes of tax and National Insurance contributions. It does not apply for other purposes for example, National Minimum Wage and employment protection legislation.

Further Information

If you disagree with the contents of this letter you should tell me as soon as possible why you think it is wrong and provide any further information and/or documentation which you think is relevant. I will consider what you have told me and advise you accordingly.

Yours

A Compliance Officer

Annex A

How we decide employment status

A person's tax and National Insurance contributions liabilities are determined in accordance with the person's employment status. An employee is a person who works under a contract of service, also referred to sometimes as a contract of employment. A person who works under a contract for services is self-employed.

Tax and National Insurance legislation does not define 'contract of service' and we have to seek guidance from the employment status case law handed down by the Courts over the years. The Courts have identified factors that help to determine if a particular contract amounts to employment or self-employment. A contract does not have to be in writing. It can be written, oral, implied or a combination of all three.

Relevant factors include:

(1) whether there is an ultimate right of control on the part of the engager over what tasks have to be done, where the services have to be performed, when they have to be performed and how they have to be performed;
(2) whether personal service is required;
(3) whether the worker has the right to provide a substitute or engage a helper;
(4) who has to provide the equipment and/or materials;
(5) whether the worker has a real risk of financial loss;
(6) whether the worker has the opportunity to profit from sound management for example, by reducing overheads and organising work effectively;
(7) the basis of payment;
(8) whether there are 'employee type' benefits, for example, sick pay, pensions, holiday pay, etc;
(9) whether the worker works exclusively for the engager;
(10) whether the worker is part and parcel of the engager's business or organisation;
(11) whether there is a right of dismissal by giving notice of a specific length;
(12) factors personal to the worker, for example, number of engagements and business organisation;
(13) the intention of the engager and worker as regards employment status.

When all the facts have been established the approach endorsed by the Courts is to stand back and look at the picture as a whole. It can then be seen whether the overall effect is that of a person in business on his/her own account or a person working as an employee in somebody else's business."

Effect of Limitation Act

[14.27] One point to take into account in the above example is the effect of the *Limitation Act 1980* on 'demands' for payment of contributions. In an interview with Payroll Manager's Review in April 1996 the former Chief Executive of the then CA, Mrs Faith Boardman, stated 'If there is no response to the request then we will issue a demand warning that legal action will be taken in the event of non-payment. But when we issue that demand the arrears are restricted to six years, in accordance with the *Limitation Act 1980*. I'm certainly not aware of demands, as such, being issued for periods up to twenty years ago, in part because, frankly, it would be quite unusual for us to query the payments made by an employer as far back as that!'

The effect of this is that Bloggs TV Rentals Ltd should pay only £50,095.45 (£100,894.96 *less* the total Class 1 liabilities for the years ended 5 April 2004 to 5 April 2009 inclusive, and it may be further reduced by the Class 2 and Class 4 paid from 6 April 2009 onwards). Assuming it concedes or loses the status argument, the company should, when making the payment, make clear that the payment being made relates to 2009–10 to 2014–15 inclusive. Otherwise, the NIC&EO is entitled to, and will, allocate the payment as part-payment against the total amount it has computed, ie, including the out-of-date years. It can then pursue the outstanding amount due for 'in-date' years. HM Revenue and Customs at NIC&EO, Newcastle sometimes still requests payments for more than six years (eg where arrears of Class 2 contributions are due). However, this is now rare.

In fact, even the payment for only six years mentioned above can potentially be reduced a little further as the six-year limit runs from the date that the NIC was due for payment, ie on the 19th or 22nd of each month. Thus, in early August 2015, the monthly amounts for 2009–10 that were due for payment by 19 May, 19 June and 19 July 2009 are also time-barred.

It should be noted that whilst from 1 April 2010 arrears of PAYE can only be demanded for four years (six years where there has been careless inaccuracy and 20 years where a deliberate inaccuracy has been discovered), the operation of the *Limitation Act 1980* is not affected by the 'harmonisation' of tax time limits. [*FA 2008, Sch 39*]. Note, though, that Class 4 and, from 6 April 2015, Class 2 contributions are subject to the Taxes Management Act 1970 collection provisions, so HMRC should apply the tax time limits (ie, four years for refunds, and four, six or twenty years for arrears of payment).

Where a person is re-categorised in consequence of, previously, a formal determination by the Secretary of State for Social Security or, now, on appeal to the tribunal and then, later, the decision is reversed on review or overturned by the High Court on appeal, there are certain discretionary powers. These are to prevent the new decision becoming retrospective in its effect by directing that the person in question is, up to the date of the decision on review or appeal, to be treated as though he properly belonged in the category of earners corresponding to the contributions which are now seen to have been incorrectly paid. The right to exercise this power is conditional upon it appearing that it would be in the interest of the person by or in respect of whom such contributions have been paid, or of any claimant or beneficiary by virtue of that person's contributions. [*Categorisation Regs, Reg 4*]. In practice, this power is only exercised where a self-employed earner has been re-categorised as an employed earner, has paid Class 1 contributions, and has then had his re-categorisation reversed (ie back to self-employed earner) on review or appeal.

Case law—the *Demibourne Ltd* case

[14.28] In *Demibourne Ltd v Revenue and Customs Comrs* [2005] STC (SCD) 667 a company operated a hotel. It had employed a maintenance worker (B), who retired at the age of 65. Following his retirement, B continued to do regular maintenance work at the hotel, but the company treated him as self-employed because its HR policies would not permit his employment as an employee. HMRC issued a ruling that he was an 'employed earner', within the charge to Class 1 National Insurance contributions. The Special Commissioner upheld HMRC's ruling and dismissed the company's appeal, holding that the changes which took place when B reached the age of 65 were not 'sufficient to replace the relationship of employer and employee with one between client and independent contractor'.

This created a problem of double taxation. The company had to settle the PAYE (and secondary NIC liability – he was over 65, so there was no primary liability), but B had already paid his tax under Schedule D. Because the dispute had taken so long to reach the Special Commissioners, B was out of time to make a repayment claim for the incorrectly paid Schedule D tax. The company pleaded this as part of its case, but the Special Commissioner could not make an order that was contrary to the law, even if justice demanded it.

HMRC might have reached a contract settlement with the employer, allowing set-off of the incorrect Schedule D tax, but that would have closed the case only against the employer, and B could, if the time frame had been shorter, have made a refund claim for his tax that the employer had already set off against its liability. HMRC was therefore reluctant to use contract settlements involving a set-off of employee taxes against employer liabilities.

In the Autumn of 2006 a working party met with HMRC to discuss the change in tax policy on PAYE settlement cases arising from the *Demibourne* case. HMRC sought the opinion of Tax Counsel on an interim solution to resolve outstanding and any new settlements in employment status cases prior to any change in legislation, as well as the possibility of changing the legislation. After some delay the *Income Tax (Pay As You Earn) Regulations 2003, SI 2003/2682, Regs 72E, 72F* inserted by *Income Tax (Pay As You Earn) (Amendment) Regs 2008, SI 2008/782, Reg 7* broadly restored the income tax set-off position to what the informal practice had been prior to the *Demibourne* case.

In notes published by HM Revenue and Customs, no action was proposed on National Insurance but the wording made clear that – now that the department deals with both income tax and National Insurance – HM Revenue and Customs is often in a position to set off the recategorised employee's Class 4 liability against the Class 1 liability (see HM Revenue and Customs National Insurance Manual NIM37019). This is an obvious improvement on the 1984 Hansard statement quoted earlier and affected businesses should therefore press for complete set-off of both Class 2 contributions and Class 4 contributions in all cases.

The *Social Security Act 1998* contains provisions (*section 54*) where an individual has been treated as an employed earner but is subsequently recategorised as self-employed. In respect of Class 1 and Class 1A contributions for tax years 1998–99 onwards, contributions will be refunded only for the current tax year and the most recently closed tax year. The provision also applies to Class 1B contributions from 6 April 1999.

This draconian measure was partially eased with effect from 6 April 2000 by *The Social Security (Contributions) (Amendment No 3) Regulations 2000, SI 2000/736*. The rule will not apply where either an appeal has been lodged by the end of 'year 2' or, within the same time scale, a written request has been made that the Commissioners for HM Revenue and Customs decide the categorisation question. [*Social Security (Contributions) Regulations 2001, SI 2001/1004, Reg 59*].

Categorisation by regulation

[14.29] In order to enable difficult or inconvenient categorisation questions to be resolved in an administratively convenient manner, regulations may be made to provide:

- for employment of any prescribed description to be disregarded in relation to the liability for contributions which would otherwise arise from employment of that description; and
- for a person in employment of any prescribed description to be treated as falling within a category of earner *other than that in which he would otherwise fall.*

[*SSCBA 1992, s 2(2)*. See also *Social Security (Categorisation of Earners) Regulations 1978, SI 1978/1689*].

Employment disregards

[14.30] In accordance with regulations which have been made under these provisions, the following employments are *disregarded* entirely.

- Certain employments by close relatives in domestic roles (see **41.18** LABOUR-ONLY CONTRACTORS).
- Certain employments of a person by his or her spouse or civil partner (but not 'common law' spouse) other than in business roles (see **39.2** HUSBAND AND WIFE, AND CIVIL PARTNERS).

- Extraordinary employment as a self-employed earner (see **14.14** above).
- Employments on or after 6 April 1978 as a returning (or acting returning) officer or as counting officer for the purpose of any parliamentary or local government election or referendum authorised by Act of Parliament; or employments by any such officers for such purposes. [*Categorisation Regs, Sch 1 Part III Para 10*].
- Certain employments in a visiting force or as a member of an international headquarters or defence organisation (see **11.9**, **11.10** and **11.13** ARMED FORCES).
- Until 5 July 2006, certain employments as a Queen's Gurkha officer or as a member of the Brigade of Gurkhas (see **11.13** ARMED FORCES).

Categorisation as employed

[14.31] Also, as stated in **14.2** above, in accordance with such regulations, earners in respect of employments of the following kinds are treated as falling within the category of *employed earner*.

- Employment as an office cleaner (see **41.19** LABOUR-ONLY CONTRACTORS).
- Employment as a cleaner of telephone apparatus and associated fixtures (see **41.21** LABOUR-ONLY CONTRACTORS).
- Certain employments through the agency of others (see **4.5** AGENCY WORKERS).
- Certain employments of a person by his or her spouse or civil partner for business purposes (see **39.2** HUSBAND AND WIFE, AND CIVIL PARTNERS).
- Certain employments as MINISTERS OF RELIGION (**46.1**).
- Until 6 April 2012, certain employments as LECTURERS, TEACHERS, OR INSTRUCTORS **44**
- Until 5 April 2014, certain employments as actors, musicians and other performers (see **36** ENTERTAINERS).

Certain earners gainfully employed as EXAMINERS (**37.1**) are, on the other hand, to be treated by regulation as falling within the category of self-employed earner.

VOLUNTEER DEVELOPMENT WORKERS **59** working outside Great Britain are categorised as self-employed earners, provided they do not derive from their employment earnings in respect of which Class 1 contributions are payable. [*Social Security (Contributions) Regulations 2001, SI 2001/1004, Reg 150*].

Rent officers and deputy rent officers appointed under a rent registration scheme are regarded as employed under a contract of service and are thus to be treated as employed earners for contribution purposes. [*Rent Act 1977, s 63(3)*]. Likewise, magistrates' clerks are regarded as employed under a contract of service with the magistrate's court committee in the area in which they are based. [*Justices of the Peace Act 1997, s 44*].

Secondary contributors

[14.32] A secondary contributor can only exist in relation to any payment of earnings to, or for the benefit of, an employed earner. [*SSCBA 1992, s 7(1)*]. Subject to certain exceptions listed below, the secondary contributor will be:

- in the case of an earner employed under a contract of service (see **14.5** to **14.11** above), his employer;
- in the case of an earner employed in an office with earnings chargeable to income tax as general earnings (see **14.17** above),
  - (a) any person who is prescribed in relation to that office under, for example, the charter, statute, declaration of trust or other instrument creating the office or, if no such person is prescribed,
  - (b) the government department, public authority or body of persons responsible for paying the general earnings of the office.

[*SSCBA 1992, s 7(1)*].

Note that the payer of earnings need not actually pay any secondary contributions to be a secondary contributor within this definition: it is the payment of earnings rather than contributions that counts. If all employees of the employer earn below the earnings thresholds, the employer will have no liability to deduct or pay any contributions, but will nevertheless be the secondary contributor in relation to those earnings and be obliged to undertake the duties of the secondary contributor in reporting the earnings to HMRC.

Modifications to the secondary contributor rule

[14.33] The *exceptions* are as follows.

(a) Where a person works under the general control and management of a person other than his immediate employer, that person rather than the immediate employer is treated as the secondary contributor [*SSCBA 1992, s 7(2)(b); Categorisation Regs, Reg 5, Sch 3 para 2*]; or

(b) Where a person falls to be treated as an employed earner by application of the regulations described at **14.29** above, the person prescribed by those regulations is treated as the secondary contributor (see **4.13** AGENCY WORKERS, **36** ENTERTAINERS, **39.2** HUSBAND AND WIFE, AND CIVIL PARTNERS, **41.19** and **41.21** LABOUR-ONLY CONTRACTORS and **46.5** MINISTERS OF RELIGION) [*SSCBA 1992, s 7(2); Categorisation Regs, Reg 5, Sch 3 paras 1, 2, 3, 7, 8* as amended by *Categorisation Amendment Regs 1990, Reg 3(1)*]; or

(c) Where a person is employed by a company in voluntary liquidation which is carrying on business under a liquidator, the liquidator is treated as the secondary contributor [*Categorisation Regs, Reg 5, Sch 3 para 4*]; or

(d) Where a person is in employed earner's employment as a barrister's clerk, the head of chambers is treated as the secondary contributor [*Categorisation Regs, Reg 5, Sch 3 para 5*]; or

(e) Where a person is employed by a foreign employer and, in pursuance of that employment, his personal service is first made available to a host employer on or after 6 April 1994 and is rendered for the purposes of the host employer's business, the host employer to whom the personal service is made available is treated as the secondary Class 1 contributor was liable until 6 April 2014. Thereafter, where liability falls depends on the exact circumstances: it might be on the host employer, on the end client if there is no UK agency involved, on the UK agency that supplies the worker's services to the end client or, in a case involving the production of fraudulent documents for use as evidence in avoiding the categorisation of a worker as an employee, on the producer of those documents. (See **4.13** AGENCY WORKERS and **51.14** OVERSEAS MATTERS) [*Categorisation Regs, Reg 5, Sch 3 para 9* as inserted by *Categorisation Amendment Regs 1994, Reg 4*]. For this purpose, a 'foreign employer' is a person who does not fulfil the conditions as to residence or presence in Great Britain and who, if he did fulfil those conditions, would be the secondary contributor in relation to any payment of earnings to or for the benefit of the person employed; and a 'host employer' is a person who has a place of business in Great Britain. [*Categorisation Regs, Reg 1(2)* as amended by *Categorisation Amendment Regs 1994, Reg 2*]. It should be noted that the word 'employer' in this context does not import any of the common law considerations such as mutual obligations, control and economic reality into the identification of the employer. It is important to note that the 1993 change to the regulations only applied to secondments taking place on or after 6 April 1994. In view of the operation of the '52-week rule' (see **51.12** OVERSEAS MATTERS) the first actual liability for secondary contributions could not have arisen in respect of such employees until at least 5 April 1995.

(f) Where a person is employed as a mariner (see **45.10** MARINERS) and his employer does not satisfy conditions of residence and presence (see **51.4** and **51.5** OVERSEAS MATTERS), the person who pays his earnings is treated as the secondary contributor but only if that person satisfies the residence and presence conditions. However, where an employee is employed by a foreign employer, and his services are made available, after 6 April 1994, to a person with a place of business in the UK then the UK employer is liable for payment of Class 1 contributions only if the mariner's employment duties are wholly or mainly in Category A, B, C and D waters under *Merchant Shipping (Categorisation of Waters) Regulations 1992*. [*Social Security (Contributions) Regulations 2001, SI 2001/1004, Reg 122; Categorisation Regs, Reg 5, Sch 3 para 9* as amended by *Social Security (Categorisation of Earners) (Amendment No 2) Regulations 2003, SI 2003/2420, Reg 5*].

(g) Where a person was employed as an entertainer, the person who had engaged the entertainer under that contract of services was treated as the secondary contributor up to and including 5 April 2003 but thereafter until 5 April 2014 it was the producer of the entertainment in question. [*Categorisation Regs, Reg 5, Sch 3 para 10* as amended by *Categorisation Amendment Regs 1998, Reg 4 and Social Security (Categorisation of Earners) Amendment Regulations 2003, SI 2003/736, Reg 4*].

(h) Where a person is employed by a foreign employer and supplied to perform work in the UK sector of the North Sea on an oil or gas installation, the UK agency or onshore associate of the employer or, in default of that, the licensee of the oilfield (see OIL RIG WORKERS **50**). [*Social Security (Contributions) Regulations 2001, SI 2001/1004, Reg114(4)* as inserted by *Social Security (Contributions) (Amendment No 2) Regulations 2014, SI 2014/572.*]

In rule (a) above, an outsourcing company that paid the wages of workers which were supplied by another company could not account for PAYE and NICs under its own tax reference but should have done so under the tax reference of the labour provider. The outsourcing company is therefore an intermediary which merely discharges the liability of the other company which is the employer notwithstanding the commercial arrangement between the two companies. See *Regina (Oriel Support Ltd) v HMRC* [2008] EWHC 1304 (Admin); CA [2009] Times Law Reports 25 March 2009. The rule in (c) above was necessitated by a determination by the Secretary of State (see **14.24** above) that, in law, the appointment of a liquidator or receiver does not terminate a contract of service under which a person working for a company supplies his services and that, in consequence, the company and not the liquidator is liable as secondary contributor for contributions on earnings paid after the date of the appointment. (*M30 (1953)*). Likewise, the rule in (d) above was necessitated by a determination by the Secretary of State for Social Security that, in law, a barrister's clerk (if employed rather than self-employed—see *McMenamin v Diggles* [1991] STC 419) is employed under a separate contract of service between himself and each of the barristers occupying the chambers in which he works. (*M49 (1956)*). In (g) the entertainer's employment was to be treated as employed earner's employment *unless* his remuneration did not include any payment by way of salary. For these purposes salary meant payments made for services rendered, paid under a contract for services, where there was more than one payment (payable at a specific period or intervals) and computed by reference to the amount of time for which the work has been performed. [*Social Security (Categorisation of Earners) Regulations 1978, SI 1978/1689, Sch 1 para 5A as substituted by Social Security (Categorisation of Earners) Amendment Regulations 2003, SI 2003/736, Reg 3*]. See *ITV Services Ltd v HMRC* [2012] UKUT 47 (TCC), 7 February 2012. See also **36** ENTERTAINERS

A local authority is regarded as the secondary contributor in relation to earnings paid to rent officers and clerks to the justices (and their staff) based in its area. [*Rent Act 1977, s 63(3); Justices of the Peace Act 1979, ss 5, 57, 58*].

A person who would otherwise fall to be treated as a secondary contributor according to the rules stated will not be so treated if he fails to satisfy conditions of residence or presence in Great Britain (see **51.14** OVERSEAS MATTERS).

Under the *Apprenticeships, Skills, Children and Learning Act 2009, s 35*, an apprenticeship agreement is, in England and Wales, deemed to be a contract of service for all purposes. *ASCLA 2009, s 39(3)* defines the employer by reference to *s 32*, which makes the person for whom the apprentice undertakes to work the employer for the purposes of the Act. Since that person will be the other party to the deemed contract of service, that person will be the secondary contributor in relation to earnings paid to the apprentice under the agreement.

Illegal contracts of service

[14.34] It has been explained at **14.3** and **14.18** that for a person other than an office holder to be an *employed earner* for contribution purposes he must be gainfully employed in Great Britain *under a contract of service*; and that anyone gainfully employed in Great Britain otherwise than in employed earner's employment will be a *self-employed earner*. It follows, therefore, that anyone who enters into a contract of service which, in law, is or becomes void will, for contribution purposes, fall to be categorised as a self-employed earner rather than an employed earner and that his employer under the contract will not be a secondary contributor (See **14.11** above).

Certain contracts of service are void by statute. Examples are as follows.

- A contract under which a person works for a bookmaker, commission agent or turf accountant and whose duties involve taking bets
  - (a) employment as a tout or street betting runner;
  - (b) employment at a racecourse — unless he is 18 or over and has written and registered authority and the bookmaker has a current permit issued by the Betting Licensing Authority (see Example (4) below); or
  - (c) employment at a betting shop — unless he is 18 or over.

  [*Gambling Act 2005*].
- A contract under which a non-patrial within the terms of *Immigration Act 1971, s 2* was employed contrary to restrictions placed on his freedom to work under Sec 3 of that Act as amended by the *Nationality, Immigration and Asylum Act 2002* and *Immigration, Asylum and Nationality Act 2006*. (See *Rastegarnia v Richmond Designs Ltd 19 May 1978 IT Case Number 11141/78/A*). The same principles apply under current immigration legislation which makes such employment an offence.

Other contracts of service may be void at common law. These are contracts of service which require the commission of crimes or torts or the perpetration of fraud; contracts of service which are for sexually immoral purposes or are prejudicial to public safety or to the administration of justice; and contracts of service tending to corruption in public life. However in *IRC v Aken* (1990) 63 TC 395 the earnings of a prostitute were held to represent the profits of a trade and, as such, are at least potentially liable to Class 2 and Class 4 contributions.

> *Example (1)*
>
> Arthur is engaged by Knight Hotels Ltd as a concierge. At his interview he was told that he would have to procure prostitutes for hotel guests should he be asked to do so. That makes his contract of service void as the contract has a sexually immoral purpose, and Arthur is, for contribution purposes, a self-employed earner. Neither Knight Hotels nor Arthur will have any Class 1 liabilities as regards the earnings paid to Arthur.

Example (2)

Guinevere is engaged by Lancelot Enterprises Ltd as a sales representative. At her interview she is told that she will receive two-thirds of her agreed salary as declared gross pay but that the other third will be paid to her as expenses so as to evade tax and National Insurance. That makes her contract void as one of its objects is to defraud HM Revenue and Customs, and she is, therefore, a self-employed earner for contribution purposes (as well as a criminal conspirator, which is much more serious). (See *Napier v National Business Agency Ltd* [1951] 2 All ER 264, 30 ATC 180, CA).

Example (3)

Galahad, who is in the UK on a non-work tourist visa from South Africa, is engaged by Camelot Mediaeval Banquets Ltd as a court jester. The *Immigration, Asylum and Nationality Act 2006, s 15* makes it a civil offence to employ a person of 16 or over who is subject to immigration control unless he has current and valid authority and that authority does not restrict his applying for the position in question or the person comes into a category where employment is allowed. The contract is void for illegality, so Galahad is a self-employed earner for NIC purposes (as well as having committed an offence by working illegally).

Example (4)

Bill 'the bet' Hill, an authorised bookmaker, is an on-course bookmaker with a 'pitch' at Sandown Park racecourse as well as his own independent bookmakers in Wallington, Surrey. The 'pitch' at Sandown has a number of employees who also work at the business in Wallington where he conducts his business other than on race days at Sandown Park. Bill employs a young man aged 17 years who works at the bookmakers shop in Wallington and Sandown for the business on race days. However, Bill is in breach of the *Gambling Act 2005, ss 45, 51* which state that he is not allowed to employ a person to provide facilities for commercial gambling who is under the age of 18 years.

Intermediaries

[14.35] The basic status rules are overridden in many cases involving the provision of workers via intermediaries. See INTERMEDIARIES 40 and 14.24 above.

Employment Status

[14.36] The Employment Tribunal decision in the case of *Aslam v Uber BV* [2017] IRLR 4 and others in October 2016 illustrated a key difference between employment status arguments for NIC purposes and those for employment law and certain pension purposes.

The claimants were at the time or had been drivers for Uber who made tribunal claims alleging failure to pay the national minimum wage and to provide paid leave under the Working Time Regulations 1998. Some press reports misleadingly stated that Uber had been treating the drivers as self-employed but that the tribunal had found them not to be self-employed. It would have been more accurate to state that the drivers were found to be 'workers' rather than 'not self-employed', since the latter led some commentators to suggest that the drivers had established an entitlement to sick pay and other employee benefits.

It seems there was no question that the workers were indeed self-employed for tax and NIC purposes. There are only two statuses for these purposes, and the workers were clearly not employees: they provided and ran the car, a significant capital investment, they paid Uber a commission for finding them their customers and collecting their fares, and were free to turn off the Uber 'app' at any time and make themselves unavailable, provided they had not accepted a fare.

Separate rules apply for employment law, minimum wage, working time and auto-enrolment purposes: there is a third status of 'worker', which applies to even genuinely self-employed workers who commit to providing personal services under the contract for services into which they enter and are not, by virtue of the contract, suppliers to a client or customer of any profession or business undertaking carried on by the worker (see for example the *Employment Rights Act 1996, s 230(3)*). The drivers were found to fall into this category and were therefore entitled to be paid at least the national minimum wage and to take paid holiday leave. Auto-enrolment rights were not mentioned in the case, but their status as workers should have meant that the drivers were eligible jobholders. They nevertheless remain self-employed for tax and NIC purposes.

A similar decision was made in the case of *Dewhurst v City Sprint UK Ltd* Case No 220512/2016 in November 2016.

Key Points regarding the categorisation of earners for NICs

[14.37] Points to consider are as follows.

- Those engaging workers in activities covered by the *Categorisation Regulations* must not overlook (as is common) the Class 1 liability – even though those persons will often be correctly treated as self-employed for tax, employment law and other purposes. By the same token, a 'worker' who is entitled to be paid the National Minimum Wage and holiday pay but is not under a contract of service should nevertheless not be paid subject to deduction of Class 1 contributions as he or she will usually be self-employed.
- A deemed employer – either under the *Categorisation Regulations* or generally – will be liable for Class 1 contributions, interest and penalties notwithstanding that the employee purported to be a self-employed earner and is recategorised by HMRC.

- Consultancy roles in whatever capacity may be challenged as coming within the ambit of office holder or an employee.

15

Class 1 Contributions: Employed Earners

Cross-references. See AGE EXCEPTION 3 for age limitations on liability; AGGREGATION OF EARNINGS 5; ANTI-AVOIDANCE 8; APPEALS AND REVIEWS 9 for remedies for dissatisfaction with amounts assessed; ARREARS OF CONTRIBUTIONS 12 for recovery provisions; CATEGORISATION 14; COLLECTION 21; COMPANY DIRECTORS 22; CONTRACTED-OUT EMPLOYMENT 23; CREDITS 24 for circumstances in which Class 1 contributions are awarded; DEATH OF CONTRIBUTOR 26 for non-liability on earnings paid thereafter; DEFERMENT OF PAYMENT 27; EARNINGS FROM EMPLOYMENT: GENERAL 29; EARNINGS LIMITS AND THRESHOLDS 33; EARNINGS PERIODS 34; ENFORCEMENT 35; MARINERS 45; MULTIPLE EMPLOYMENTS 47; NATIONAL INSURANCE NUMBER 49; OVERSEAS MATTERS 51; RATES AND LIMITS 53; REDUCED LIABILITY ELECTIONS 54; REPAYMENT AND REALLOCATION 55.

Other Sources. Tolley's Tax Planning 2016–17; Leaflets CWG2 (2016). 2013 editions of E14, E15, E16, E19 (all now converted to web-only guidance); National Insurance Fund Accounts (Great Britain) 2016–17.

Introduction to class 1 contributions: employed earners

[15.1] Class 1 contributions account for over 96% of the National Insurance Fund's contribution income. In monetary terms, this amounted to some £92 billion in the year 2016–17. A further £23.4 billion was diverted directly to the National Health Service – and this element included the entire revenue from the 1% rate increase of 6 April 2003. The further 1% increase from 6 April 2011 does not go to the NHS.

Liability

[15.2] The following terms are relevant to Class 1 liability. For the sake of brevity, the abbreviations here will be used throughout the chapter:

- LEL = Lower Earnings Limit: a measure now only relevant to benefits and, up to April 2016, contracted-out NICs, but formerly the starting point for liability for employees and employers.
- ET = Earnings Threshold: the starting point for liability.
- PT = Primary Earnings Threshold: the starting point for employee contribution liability.
- ST = Secondary Earnings Threshold: the starting point for employer contribution liability.
- UAP = Upper Accrual Point: the maximum level of earnings counted for S2P and contracting-out rebates up to April 2016.
- UEL = Upper Earnings Limit: the maximum level of earnings liable at the main Class 1 primary rate.
- UST = Upper Secondary Threshold (relevant from 6 April 2015 to under-21s).
- AUST = Apprentice Upper Secondary Threshold (relevant from 6 April 2016 to apprentices under the age of 25).

Subject to the qualification stated below, both a primary (ie employed earner's) and a secondary (ie employer's) Class 1 contribution are payable where, in any tax week, EARNINGS FROM EMPLOYMENT: GENERAL **29** are *paid* (see **15.4** below) to or for the benefit of an earner in respect of any one employment of his and:

- he is categorised as an employed earner in relation to that employment (see **14.2** to **14.17** CATEGORISATION); and
- he is over the age of 16 (but see **3.1** AGE EXCEPTION); and
- as regards primary contributions, the amount paid exceeds the current PT – or, up to 5 April 2000, LEL – (scaled-up as appropriate in either case if his earnings periods 34 are longer than a week; see **33.2** to **33.4** EARNINGS LIMITS AND THRESHOLDS) and as regards secondary contributions, the amount paid exceeds the current ST — or, up to 5 April 1999, LEL (scaled-up as appropriate in either case if his EARNINGS PERIODS **34** are longer than a week; see **33.2** to **33.4** EARNINGS LIMITS AND THRESHOLDS). From 2001–02 to 2010–11 inclusive, the PT and ST were the same as one another, then they diverged until 6 April 2014, when they were

re-harmonised for a year until they diverged again. From 2017–18, on the recommendation of the Office of Tax Simplification (OTS), the PT and ST have again been re-harmonised.

[*SSCBA 1992, s 6(1)* as amended by *Social Security Act 1998, s 51(2)*].

If, however, the earnings relate to a period after the earner has attained pensionable age, only a secondary contribution is payable in respect of those earnings (see 3.7 AGE EXCEPTION). *[SSCBA 1992, s 6(3)*.] This remains the case after 5 April 2003, ie pensioners do not pay the 1% or 2% additional rate.

Young earners and apprentices

[15.3] From 6 April 2015, employers began to benefit from a new age-related Class 1 (but not Class 1A or Class 1B) secondary contribution rate, initially set at 0%, on earnings of employees and office-holders under the age of 21 on the date of payment of the earnings. The legislation in *SSCBA 1992, s 9A*, introduced by *NICA 2014*, s 9, explicitly treats the employer as liable to pay a secondary contribution, albeit at the 0% rate. [*SSCBA 1992, s 9A(6)*.] The 0% rate applies on all earnings up to a new Upper Secondary Threshold (UST), initially set at the same level as the UEL. Earnings above the UST in any earnings period attract the normal rate of employer contribution. The new legislation was deliberately structured so that the government may amend either the rate or the threshold without having to re-write the legislation, and specific provision was made for nominating other age groups in future.

From 6 April 2016, employers of apprentices under the age of 25 also began to benefit from a 0% rate of Class 1 secondary contribution on all earnings up to a new Apprentice Upper Secondary Threshold (AUST), again with the full rate applying above the AUST. [*SSCBA 1992, ss 9(1A)(aa), 9B*, introduced by *NICA 2015*, s 1.] Again, the legislation has been constructed as a stand-alone relief so that it may be amended easily without disturbing other similar legislation; the Apprentice UST (AUST) is defined separately from the UST and UEL, although all will have the same value at the outset. To resolve the obvious conflict between relief under *s 9A* (all under-21s) and *s 9B* (apprentices who might also be under 21) if the rates and threshold diverge, it is specifically provided that the apprentice rules will take precedence. [*SSCBA 1992, s 9A(1A)*, as inserted by *NICA 2015, s 1(3)*.]

The exact scope of the 2016 change required the term 'apprentice' to be defined. Education and training are responsibilities devolved to the regional administrations in the UK, and each defines the term in its own way. The definition for the purposes of the age-related secondary rate was eventually set by the Treasury by statutory instrument once it had been agreed by all the departments concerned. [*SSCBA 1992, s 9B(9)* as inserted by *NICA 2015, s 1*.]

A new *Regulation 154A* was added to the *Social Security (Contributions) Regulations 2001*. An apprentice is now defined for NIC purposes as a person employed under:

- an approved English apprenticeship agreement within the meaning of *Apprenticeships, Skills, Children and Learning Act 2009, s A1 (ASCLA 2009)*;

- an English apprenticeship agreement within the meaning of *ASCLA 2009, s 32*;
- a Welsh apprenticeship agreement within the meaning of *ASCLA 2009, s 32*;
- arrangements made by the Secretary of State or the Scottish Ministers under *Employment and Training Act 1973, s 2*;
- arrangements made by the Secretary of State or the Scottish Ministers under *Enterprise and New Towns (Scotland) Act 1990, s 2*; or
- arrangements made by the Department for Employment and Learning under *Employment and Training Act (Northern Ireland) 1950, s 1*.

Any such apprentice must have entered into a written agreement with the employer and the training provider that sets out the type of statutory apprenticeship framework or standard being followed, the start date of the apprenticeship and the expected completion date of the apprenticeship.

No allowance is to be made for common law apprenticeships because they do not follow government-approved frameworks, so it seems possible that employers who offer such apprenticeships will amend their training programmes to fit within the frameworks and ensure that they operate through approved training providers so as to qualify for the zero rate of secondary NIC and apprenticeship funding from the Skills Funding Agency and its regional equivalents.

In order to apply the 0% rate, the employer must hold evidence of the apprenticeship, which may be either the written agreement between the employer, apprentice and approved training provider or some other evidence that the apprenticeship receives government funding, such as the declaration to receive apprenticeship incentive payments, or the employer payment schedule to the training provider. If the training provider has not signed the written agreement, it must provide the employer with a document that shows that it is an approved training provider and the training that the apprentices are undertaking or have already done. Employers may also be training providers for their own apprentices if they have been approved by the Skills Funding Agency in England, or hold a contract for the delivery of Apprenticeships in Wales. (See www.gov.uk/government/publications/national-insurance-contributions-for-under-25s-employer-guide/paying-employer-national-insurance-contributions-for-apprentices-under-25.)

Note that the primary contributor is wholly unaffected by the 0% rate afforded to the employer (other than indirectly by the obvious incentive effect targeted by the new policy of persuading employers to take on and train younger workers). The apprentice sees no effect on net pay and may not even be aware of the employer's nil rate of contribution.

For the meaning of 'secondary contributor' see **14.32** CATEGORISATION.

In thus determining liability, no regard need be given to any other payment of earnings to, or for the benefit of, the earner in respect of any other employment unless one or other of the AGGREGATION OF EARNINGS **5** rules applies. [*SSCBA 1992, s 6(1)*].

The meaning of 'paid'

[15.4] Class 1 contribution liability arises in relation to earnings *paid*, not earnings earned. Unlike income tax—which is an annual charge—Class 1 contributions are due on earnings paid in an EARNINGS PERIOD **34**. It is of considerable importance, therefore, to determine precisely when, in law, payment of earnings takes place. The general rule is that payment of earnings takes place when a sum equivalent to those earnings is placed unreservedly at the disposal of the earner. (*Garforth (Inspector of Taxes) v Newsmith Stainless Ltd* [1979] 2 All ER 73, [1979] 1 WLR 409). It is sufficient, therefore, that they are placed to the credit of an account (whether with the employer or with a bank or some other third party) on which the earner is free to draw, whether he does, in fact, draw on the account or not. It is suggested, however, that a mere book entry is not sufficient to constitute a payment of earnings and that, for example, a credit to a director's current account with his company is *not* a payment of earnings unless the company places an equivalent monetary resource at the director's disposal. Insofar as the *Garforth* case purports to state otherwise it is thought to be bad law. An absence of funds to support a credit entry in a director's current account with his company will necessarily impose a restriction on his right to draw on the sum placed to his credit, and any restriction on the right to draw a sum placed to an earner's credit will prevent payment from taking place until the restriction is removed. It was important that an employer kept these principles in mind if he decided to pay to an employee a bonus in kind rather than in cash so as to avoid Class 1 contribution liabilities (see **29.28** EARNINGS FROM EMPLOYMENT: GENERAL). If the bonus was voted to the employee unconditionally, payment (in the form of a credit against which the employee was thereupon free to draw) was deemed to be made at the time of voting and Class 1 liabilities then arose. The form in which drawings were later made was, accordingly, quite irrelevant. Contribution liabilities were avoided only if the bonus etc was voted subject to the condition that it was paid and received in the specified non-cash form selected by the employer and not otherwise. Since there is a Class 1A charge on all taxable benefits in kind from 6 April 2000, such arrangements are now unlikely to be entered into in practice.

It is interesting to note in connection with the above comments on restrictions on the right to draw remuneration the provisions of *FA 1989, s 45(2)* inserting *ICTA 1988, s 203A* and now to be found at *ITEPA 2003, s 686* which provide that, for PAYE purposes, any 'fetter' on the right to draw sums credited to a director's account with a company is to be disregarded in determining when those sums are paid. The then Inland Revenue confirmed in relation to income tax (Press Release, 28 July 1989) that earnings voted subject to a condition being fulfilled are not 'fettered'—entitlement to those earnings does not arise until the condition is fulfilled, at which point it is possible that income tax under PAYE and Class 1 liability arise.

Where a loan or advance is made in anticipation of earnings, payment of earnings will normally take place only when the obligation to repay is released. (*Clayton (Inspector of Taxes) v Gothorp* [1971] 2 All ER 1311, [1971] 1 WLR 999). (But it should be noted that the mere writing-off – ie, a bookkeeping entry, as opposed to the execution of a legal release document – by an employer of a loan made to an employee does not release the employee from the obligation to repay and consequently does *not* constitute a payment of earnings—contrary to what HM Revenue and Customs says. (See EARNINGS FROM EMPLOYMENT: GENERAL **29**). In the case of COMPANY DIRECTORS (**22.4**) only, this general rule is reversed so that a loan or advance in anticipation of earnings is earnings at the time of the advance itself. Though not always the case, it is now accepted that where an employee uses a company credit card or company charge card to purchase goods or services for business purposes, the amount is not earnings so long as the employee had prior authority to make the purchase and the employee explained to the supplier in advance of the contract being made, and the supplier accepted, that the purchase was being made on the employer's behalf. See CWG2 2018 to 2019, para 5.1 ('Type of payment: Credit cards, charge cards-employees use your card to purchase goods or services bought on your behalf') and HM Revenue and Customs National Insurance Manual NIM02090.

The position of loans made under avoidance schemes is somewhat different. HMRC's Spotlight 26 is entitled *Contractor loan schemes – too good to be true*. Under such schemes, workers sign up to an employment contract with a company, typically offshore, that pays them a minimum wage through payroll and routes the balance of their earnings through an employee benefit trust that lends the money to the workers. The loans are claimed to be non-taxable because they do not form part of the worker's income, but HMRC believes the loans are not intended to be repaid and the money is used by the worker as if it was his or her income. It appears the long-term plan is for the loan to remain outstanding until the worker's death, at which point the trustees will write it off without an income tax charge. HMRC argues that the scheme does not work and that the loans are in fact payments of employment income to the workers. In the only case to have reached the tribunals so far, *Philip Boyle* [2013] UKFTT 723 (TC), the judges agreed with HMRC's view on the basis that it was Parliament's intention to render liable to tax income which, in substance and reality, is employment income and that the monies ostensibly paid over to the worker as loans were, in substance and reality, income from his employment, bearing in mind in particular that the worker had no need for a loan. Interestingly, the judges also found that the monies placed at the worker's disposal were not 'unreservedly' so placed, and the benefit to the worker was the subsequent release or waiver of repayment of a large part of the amount lent. He had no legal entitlement to a release or waiver, and therefore for the purposes of the legislation there was no payment. The judges accepted instead an alternative argument that the workers entering an employment contract with the provider constituted a transfer of his assets abroad. National insurance contribution liability was apparently not assessed and did not form part of the case.

Where an employed earner's regular remuneration is, as a term of his employment, paid in advance, the amounts paid are, because of the earner's unfettered right to them, treated as earnings arising at the time of payment.

Certain irregular payments of earnings made in respect of regular periods have, by regulation, a deemed date of payment (see **34.4** EARNINGS PERIODS).

Payment need not be to the earner himself for it to be liable to Class 1 contributions: it is sufficient that it is for his benefit. [*SSCBA 1992, s 6(1)*]. (Though it is arguable that no primary Class 1 contribution is collectible—see

21.2 COLLECTION.) Therefore, the discharge of an earner's pecuniary obligation by his employer will be (if the payment is made in return for the earner's acting as or being an employee and for no other reason—see **29.49** earnings from employment: general) a payment of earnings. (*Hartland v Diggines* (1926) 10 TC 247). Thus, for example, the amount paid by an employer in settlement of *private* telephone charges made to one of his employees is, if the employee himself is the telephone subscriber, earnings for contribution purposes (see **30.12** EARNINGS FROM EMPLOYMENT: EXPENSES).

The question then arises whether, if an employer declines to recover primary Class 1 contributions from an employee, the same principle applies. Has the employer effectively discharged his employee's indebtedness and do the primary contributions themselves become earnings on which further contributions are due? Although the DSS (now DWP) never took the point (see **21.5** COLLECTION), the answer may be 'yes'. The liability for primary Class 1 contributions is clearly the liability of the earner [*SSCBA 1992, s 6(4)(a)*] and, even though the employer is obliged by law to discharge that liability [*Sch 1 para 3*], the employee normally has no choice but to 'pay' by suffering a deduction from his earnings equivalent to the amount which the employer has discharged. If the employer declines to make the deduction, the employee is relieved of the liability to finance that deduction, which is arguably equivalent to an additional payment of earnings equivalent to the amount which ought to have been deducted.

Rates

[15.5] The amount of a primary Class 1 contribution for which liability arises as described at **15.2** above, is, from 6 April 2003, the main primary percentage of so much of the earnings paid in the tax week as exceeds the current PT but does not exceed the current UEL *and* the additional primary percentage of so much of those earnings as exceeds the current UEL (or the prescribed equivalent). Since 2012–13 this has been 12% for the former and 2% for the additional primary percentage. The PT, ST and the UEL are scaled up as appropriate if the EARNINGS PERIODS **34** is longer than a week; see **33.2** to **33.4** EARNINGS LIMITS AND THRESHOLDS. [*SSCBA 1992, s 8(1)* as amended by *National Insurance Contributions Act 2002, s 1*].

Earnings in excess of the UEL were ignored for primary Class 1 contribution purposes until 6 April 2003.

Example

Kevin employed Glenn at a rate of £900 per week from 25 March to 7 April 2018, making payment on Saturday each week. Primary contributions due are:

Week ended 31 March 2018	157	×	Nil%	Nil
	709	×	12%	85.08
	34	×	2%	0.68
				£85.76

Week ended 7 April 2018	162	×	Nil%	Nil
	730	×	12%	87.60
	8	×	2%	0.16
				£87.76

The amount of a secondary Class 1 contribution for which liability arises as described at **15.2** above, is, from 6 April 1999, the secondary percentage of so much of the earnings paid in the tax week as exceeds the current ST. This is 13.8% for 2017–18, unless the earner is under the age of 21 on the date of payment, or a qualifying apprentice under the age of 25, in which case it is 0% up to the UST or AUST respectively. *[SSCBA 1992, ss 9(2), 9A, 9B* as amended.]

Example

Following the previous example, Kevin's secondary contributions in respect of Glenn's employment are:

Week ended 31 March 2018	157	×	Nil%	Nil
	743	×	13.8%	102.53
				£102.53
Week ended 7 April 2018	162	×	Nil%	Nil
	738	×	13.8%	101.84
				£101.84

From 6 April 2015, as already noted, *NICA 2014, s 9* introduced a new age-related secondary contribution rate of 0% that applies to payments to any earner under the age of 21 on the date of payment, unless the earnings payment exceeds the relevant UEL for the earnings period, in which case the standard employer rate applies to any earnings above the UEL. The primary contribution rate is unaffected, as are the Class 1A and Class 1B rates. This was extended to relevant apprentices under the age of 25 from 6 April 2016, with the apprenticeship rules taking precedence in the case of apprentices under the age of 21.

The new age-related rate has initially been set at 0%, and the maximum level of earnings eligible for the 0% rate is designated an 'upper secondary threshold', or 'apprentice upper secondary threshold' but this will initially be in line with the UEL. See also **15.8** below in respect of new contributions tables and **3.17** AGE EXCEPTION.

If, in the above example, Kevin had been an apprentice aged 23 when both payments were made, the payment for the week ended 31 March 2018 would have attracted a secondary contribution of £4.69, while the earnings paid in the following week, would have attracted a secondary liability of £1.10, saving Glenn £198.58. Only the £34 of earnings above the AUST (UEL) of £866 in 2017–18 and the £8 of earnings above the AUST (UEL) of £892 in 2018–19 would have been liable at the full secondary rate of 13.8%.

Standard rate exceptions

[15.6] The above rates will not always be appropriate, however (see **53.3** RATES AND LIMITS). Certain married women and widows (but not their secondary contributors) are entitled to contribute at a *reduced* rate (see **REDUCED LIABILITY ELECTIONS 54**) and, where an employed earner's earnings were derived from a CONTRACTED-OUT EMPLOYMENT **23**, both the employed earner and his secondary contributor were, until the State Second Pension (S2P) was abolished on 6 April 2016, to pay contributions at a special *contracted-out* rate on earnings falling between the LEL and UAP (see **33.2** EARNINGS LIMITS AND THRESHOLDS and **53.2** to **53.6** RATES AND LIMITS) when the earner was a member of a contracted-out salary-related (COSR) occupational pension scheme. From 6 April 2009 until 5 April 2016, there was a UAP fixed at £770 per week which impacted on the way that contracted-out rates applied up to the UEL – see **23.5** CONTRACTED-OUT EMPLOYMENT. The full standard rate applied to earnings between the UAP and the UEL. Before 2009, contracted-out rebates applied between the LEL and the UEL. It is no longer possible for a pension scheme to be contracted out.

For 2018–19, the reduced rate remains at 5.85% on earnings between the PT and the UEL but there was no contracted-out rate for any earner. In the case of married women with a reduced rate election, the additional rate of 2% is due on all earnings above the UEL.

In the case of contracted-out employments before 6 April 2016, the same 2% rule used to apply. A contracted-out rebate was due on earnings between the LEL and the ET for both employer and employee, reducing the liabilities payable to HMRC.

An alternative way of seeing the contracted out rate was as follows:

- a charge at 12% on earnings from PT to UEL, less
- a rebate of 1.4% employee and 3.4% employer on earnings from LEL to UAP, plus
- a 2% additional rate employee charge on earnings above the UEL.

The secondary contracted-out rates for 2015–16 were:

On weekly earnings		*Rate*
From	*To*	
£0.00	£112.00	Nil
£112.01	£156.00	3.4% rebate
£156.01	£770.00	10.4%
Over £770.00		13.8%

See also **23.5** CONTRACTED-OUT EMPLOYMENT.

The earnings of under-21s who were members of a COSR scheme attracted the 0% rate of standard secondary contributions for that age group, but the employer was nevertheless entitled to recover the contracting out rebate of 3.4% on all earnings between LEL and UAP in 2015–16 (but not after 5 April 2016).

[*Social Security (Contributions) Regulations 2001, SI 2001/1004, Reg 131; Pensions Schemes Act 1993, ss 41(1A)(1B), 42A; Social Security (Reduced Rates of Class 1 Contributions) (Salary Related Contracted-out Schemes) Order 2001, SI 2001/1356; Social Security (Reduced Rates of Class 1 Contributions, Rebates and Minimum Contributions) Order 2011, SI 2011/1036*].

Further standard rate reductions

[15.7] Certain of these rates are reduced (or further reduced) where the employed earner in question is a mariner (primary and secondary, standard and contracted-out rates, with a further secondary reduction where the earnings relate to employment on a foreign-going ship—see **45.11** to **45.13** MARINERS).

If it is considered necessary, the Treasury (subject to Parliamentary approval) may, at any time, make an order altering:

- the main primary percentage; and/or
- the secondary percentage

provided that neither the main primary percentage nor the secondary percentage is increased to a rate more than 0.25% higher than the relevant rate applicable for the preceding tax year.

These powers were vested in the Secretary of State for Social Security prior to 1 April 1999.

[*SSAA 1992, s 143, s 145(1)–(3)* as amended by *SSC(TF)A 1999, Sch 3 paras 46–49* and *National Insurance Contributions Act 2002, Sch 1, paras 17, 18*.]

The legislation introducing the reliefs for all earners under 21 (from April 2015) and apprentices under 25 (from April 2016) provides for the Treasury to amend the upper thresholds (UST and AUST) and the age limits by order. There is also a power to reduce (but not increase) the age-related secondary rate, but this seems unlikely to be used, given that the initial rate has been set at 0%. [*SSCBA 1992, s 9A(4)(a)*.]

Changes which overstep these restrictions must be brought about by statute and it should be noted in particular that any change (whether increase or decrease) to the amount of the additional rate introduced with effect from 6 April 2003 and the 2% rate from 6 April 2011 cannot be made by mere order but would require a further Act of Parliament.

Calculation

[15.8] Class 1 contributions may be calculated by one of two methods. The first is the 'exact percentage method' and is mainly used in connection with computerised payrolls or the calculation of contributions payable on the earnings of COMPANY DIRECTORS (**22.4**). It is also the method adopted in all worked examples, unless clearly to the contrary, in this work. Under this method primary and secondary contributions are each to be calculated separately at each of whichever rates apply and each such calculation is to be to the nearest penny with any amount of a halfpenny or less being disregarded. [*Social Security (Contributions) Regulations 2001, SI 2001/1004, Reg 12(1)(a)(b)*].

The alternative (and usual) method of calculation is in accordance with scales and a contributions calculator prepared by HM Revenue and Customs. [*Social Security (Contributions) Regulations 2001, SI 2001/1004, Reg 12(2)*]. These take the form of tables lettered A to Z. Volumes containing selections of these tables appropriate to the needs of different types of employer are available from HM Revenue and Customs' website. These volumes are or were as follows:

CA 38	—	standard rate contributions (Tables A, H, J, M, Z).
CA 39	—	until 5 April 2016 only: contracted-out contributions for employers (Tables D, E, L, I, K).
CA 40	—	employees with no secondary contributor (Tables A, B, H, M).
CA 41	—	standard rate contributions for employers (Tables B and C).
CA 42	—	mariners with foreign-going rebate (Tables G, P, Q, R, T, W, Y. Tables N, O and V used to relate to contracted-out employment and were withdrawn from 6 April 2016).

Seven new tables were introduced from 6 April 2015 to reflect the new age-related secondary rate of 0% for under-21s:

Table	Over-20 equivalent	Category of under-21 earner
I	D	contracted-out salary-related standard rate contributions – withdrawn 6 April 2016
K	L	contracted-out salary-related deferred rate contributions – withdrawn 6 April 2016
M	A	not-contracted-out standard rate contributions
P	Q	mariners' not-contracted-out deferred rate contributions
V	N	mariners' contracted-out salary-related contributions – withdrawn 6 April 2016
Y	R	mariners' not-contracted-out standard rate contributions
Z	C	not-contracted-out deferred rate contributions

RTI-compliant software will already include the employee's date of birth in every FPS, so implementation of the new tables should have been automatic for any employer using up-to-date payroll software or HMRC's Basic PAYE Tools.

Tables D, E, I, K, L, N and V were withdrawn from 6 April 2016 with the abolition of contracting out. Tables H (standard under-25) and G (mariner under-25) with 0% secondary contributions on earnings up to the AUST, were introduced to encompass relevant apprentices at the same time.

'Simplified Deduction Scheme' tables

[15.9] Until 5 April 2013 and the mandation of RTI reporting, there were also 'Simplified Deduction Scheme' tables (CA37) for employers of low paid persons, without pension schemes, containing Table letters A, B, C and J. Although described as 'simplified' they were simply shorter than the CA38 tables and could only be used for earnings up to (in 2013–14) £342 per week or £1,485 per month. These were generally used only by householders employing domestic staff (potentially including lower paid nannies) at a fixed wage – the PAYE / NIC remittances were made quarterly and they were referred to at HMRC as 'DOME' schemes (ie, domestic).

The tables most commonly in use (and included in several of the volumes described) are or were the following.

	Over-20	Under-21		
Table A	A	M	—	not contracted-out standard rate contributions.
Table B	B	n/a	—	not contracted-out reduced rate contributions.
Table C	C	n/a	—	not contracted-out employer-only contributions (eg, pensioners and, prior to 6 April 2003 COSR contributions for employers).
Table J	J	Z	—	not contracted-out employer-only contributions: deferral cases only.
Table D	D	I	—	contracted-out standard rate contributions in COSR schemes before 6 April 2016.
Table E	E	n/a	—	contracted-out reduced rate contributions on COSR schemes before 6 April 2016.
Table L	L	K	—	contracted-out employer only contributions before 6 April 2016: deferral cases only.

When the NIC&EO speaks of a person's table letter, it is the letter indicated above to which it refers. Other table letters were used before 6 April 2012 when COMP (contracted-out money purchase) schemes and their different payroll rebates were abolished. Employers of incoming expatriate secondees who are exempt from UK NICs because they hold a certificate of coverage from an EEA or treaty state used to use Table X in their payroll records before RTI was introduced, signifying no NICs due, but in the RTI FPS the NI category and value fields are now left blank, although HMRC continues to accept Table Letter X. This may be because many payroll systems insist on a table letter being present on an employee's or pensioner's payroll record.

The tables cater for EARNINGS PERIODS 34 of one week or one month only, so that, where the earnings period is a multiple of a week or a month, the earnings in question must be divided as necessary and the contributions shown by the tables as appropriate to the result must then be multiplied by the divisor. In the case of weekly earnings periods, the tables are banded in earnings steps of £1 and, in the case of monthly earnings periods, in earnings steps of £4 except where earnings reach the Earnings Threshold or Upper Earnings Limit. Where the amount of earnings on which contributions are to be calculated does not appear in the tables, the next lower figure on the scale is to be used. [*Social Security (Contributions) Regulations 2001, SI 2001/1004, Reg 12(3)(4)*].

Tables method v exact percentage method

[15.10] The contribution liability revealed by use of the tables has been calculated on the mid-point of each table band except at the LEL and UEL where it has been calculated on the limit itself. The following examples illustrate the process for 2015–16, before the abolition of contracting out. The process in 2016–17 and after is simpler because there is no longer a need to separate earnings at the Upper Accrual Point.

Example

Alistair was aged 30 and in a contracted-out employment. His earnings for the quarter ended 30 June 2015 were £11,257 and, in accordance with the normal procedures of the company by which he is employed were paid to him on 3 July 2015. Class 1 contributions could be calculated by either the exact percentage method or the tables method (see CA39), as follows.

Exact percentage method
LEL = £5,824 ÷ 12 × 3 = £1,456.00
PT = £8,060 ÷ 12 × 3 = £2,015.00
ST = £8,112 ÷ 12 × 3 = £2,028.00
Employee's UAP = £3,337 × 3 = £10,011.00
Employee's UEL = £42,385 ÷ 12 × 3 = £10,596.00

	£				£
Primary:	559.00	×	-1.4%	=	(7.83)
	2,015.00	×	Nil%	=	0.00
	7,996.00	×	10.6%	=	847.58
	585.00	×	12%	=	70.20
	661.00	×	2%	=	13.22
	£11,257.00				£923.17
Secondary:	572.00	×	-3.4%	=	(19.45)

2,028.00	×	Nil%	=	0.00
7,983.00	×	10.4%	=	830.23
585.00	×	13.8%	=	80.73
661.00	×	13.8%	=	91.22
£11,257.00				£982.73

Tables method

Tables CA 39 (2015), either:

Weekly Table D

£11,257.00/13 = £865.92

Table entry £815.00

Primary: £69.99 × 13 =	£909.87
† (per calculator at end of Table – on £50) £1.00 × 13 =	£13.00
	£922.87
Secondary: £68.58 × 13 =	£891.54
† (per calculator at end of Table – on £50) £6.90 × 13 =	89.70
	£981.24

Or:

Monthly Table D

£11,257.00/3 = £3,752.33

Table entry £3,532.00

Primary: £303.29 × 3 =	£909.87
† (per calculator at end of Tables – on £220) £4.40 × 3 =	£13.20
	£923.07
Secondary: £297.19 × 3 =	£891.57
† (per calculator at end of Tables – on £220) £30.36 × 3 =	91.08
	£982.65

Two notes need to be made about the above example. First, from the total contributions calculated on the exact percentage method employers had to deduct the employee's and employer's contracted-out rebate on earnings falling between the respective LEL and ET. This rebate is considered further in **23** CONTRACTED-OUT EMPLOYMENT, but accounts for the wider variation in the results under that computation method. Secondly, the table calculations (whilst in accordance with HMRC instructions) are not strictly correct since the PT and ST, as well as being expressed in terms of a weekly amount, are also expressed in terms of monthly or annual amounts. [*Social Security (Contributions) Regulations 2001, SI 2001/1004, Regs 10, 11* as amended by *Social Security (Contributions) (Amendment) Regulations 2007, SI 2007/118, Regs 3, 4* and *Social Security (Contributions) (Limits and Thresholds) (Amendment) Regulations 2014, SI 2014/569*.] The PT/ST is not to be multiplied in the conventional way where the earnings period is a multiple of either a week or a month and, in this example, the PT should strictly be £8,060 ÷ 12 × 3 = £2,015. This happens to give a whole number, but in other years, the number may be rounded. However, it is impossible for standard tables to accommodate this and the instructions for use of the tables have not been amended since the introduction of the PT and ST. [*Social Security (Contributions) Regulations 2001, SI 2001/1004, Reg 11(3)*].

Using the example of Alistair, now with quarterly earnings of £12,000, to illustrate the simplified calculation following the abolition of contracting-out, the contributions due under the exact percentage and tables' method using the 2018–19 thresholds will be:

Exact percentage method
LEL = £6,032 ÷ 12 × 3 = £1,508.00
PT = £8,424 ÷ 12 × 3 = £2,106.00
ST = £8,424 ÷ 12 × 3 = £2,106.00
Employee's UEL = £46,350 ÷ 12 × 3 = £11,589.00

	£				£
Primary:	2,106.00	×	Nil%	=	0.00
	9,483.00	×	12%	=	1,137.96
	411.00	×	2%	=	8.22
	£12,000.00				£1,146.18
Secondary:	2,106.00	×	Nil%	=	0.00
	9,483.00	×	13.8%	=	1,308.65
	411.00	×	13.8%	=	56.72
	£12,000.00				£1,365.37

Tables method
Tables CA38 (2018), either:
Weekly Table A
£12,000.00/13 = £923.08
Table entry £892.00

Primary: £87.60 × 13 =	£1,138.80
† (per calculator at end of Table – on £31) £0.62 × 13 =	£8.06
	£1,146.86
Secondary: £100.74 × 13 =	£1,309.62
† (per calculator at end of Table – on £31) £4.28 × 13 =	55.64
	£1,365.26

Or:
Monthly Table A
£12,000.00/3 = £4,000.00
Table entry £3,863.00

Primary: £379.32 × 3 =	£1,137.96
† (per calculator at end of Tables – on £137) £2.74 × 3 =	£8.22
	£1,146.18
Secondary: £436.22 × 3 =	£1,308.66
† (per calculator at end of Tables – on £137) £18.91 × 3 =	56.73
	£1,365.39

Although either method may be used, all the contributions payable in a particular tax year as regards the earnings paid to or for the benefit of an employed earner in respect of his employed earner's employment (or employments, if he has more than one and they fall to be aggregated) must, unless HM Revenue and Customs agrees to the contrary, be calculated wholly in accordance with one method or the other. [*Social Security (Contributions) Regulations 2001, SI 2001/1004, Reg 12(5)*]. Permission to change from one method to the other is not required, however, where the change is attributable to a change in payroll procedure (eg, payroll computerisation) or to an employed earner's being transferred from an 'exact percentage' payroll to a 'tables' payroll, or vice versa. (CWG2 2018 to 2019, para 3.3.)

Special calculation rules were applied where an earner's earnings in respect of different employed earner's employments had to be aggregated and those employments included both contracted-out and not contracted-out employments (see **5.11** AGGREGATION OF EARNINGS).

Special calculation rules applied also for 1989–90 in the case of company directors who held office and received payments of earnings during periods which straddled 5 October 1989, when a mid-year rule change was made (see COMPANY DIRECTORS **22**).

Collection

[15.11] Where earnings are paid to an employed earner and a liability for a primary and a secondary Class 1 contribution arises in respect of the payment, the secondary contributor is liable not only for his own secondary contribution but, in the first instance, to pay the earner's primary contribution also. [*SSCBA 1992, Sch 1 para 3(1)*]. This is so *unless*:

- he is a person against whom the contribution legislation cannot be enforced (because he is, for example, an employer who is neither resident nor present in Great Britain (or, from 6 April 2010, in the European Union) and who has no place of business here—see **51.14** OVERSEAS MATTERS); or
- for a year up to and including 2002–03, the earner has agreed (under, for example, a deferment of CONTRIBUTIONS **27** arrangement) that he himself will pay any primary contributions payable in respect of his earnings. (From 6 April 2003, even where there is deferment in operation, some primary contributions will be due once the Earnings Threshold is exceeded – currently at 2%.)

The machinery for the discharge of these liabilities and for the recovery of primary contributions from the earnings to which they relate was created by the DSS (now DWP) and lies in the PAYE system which, with the concurrence of what is now HM Revenue and Customs, has been adapted and extended so as to be suitable for use in such a way. See also *The Income Tax (Pay As You Earn) Regulations 2003, SI 2003/2682, Regs 68, 81*.

For a detailed explanation of collection procedures see **21.2** to **21.30** COLLECTION and, for a description of the powers of recovery available where normal collection procedures are ineffective, see ARREARS OF CONTRIBUTIONS **12**.

Compensation for secondary contributions paid on SSP, SMP, SPP, SAP and SHPP

[15.12] With the introduction of Statutory Sick Pay (SSP) and Statutory Maternity Pay (SMP), employers became responsible for paying what used to be a state benefit to employees. However, both SSP and SMP have always been treated as pay (see **29.24** EARNINGS FROM EMPLOYMENT: GENERAL), so employers must account for Class 1 contributions on any SSP or SMP payments. Under RTI, they are included in the payroll and the FPS with each relevant employee's earnings as each amount is paid. Employers therefore pay secondary contributions in respect of what used to be state benefits. Until 5 April 1991, employers were entitled under *Statutory Sick Pay Compensation Regulations 1983, Reg 2* to recover by deduction from payments due to the then Collector of Taxes in respect of contributions, or under *Reg 3* to have refunded by the Secretary of State for Social Security, all SSP paid, together with an amount by way of compensation for secondary Class 1 contributions which they were deemed to have accounted for on such SSP. The recovery of statutory payments by employers, where allowed, is dealt with under RTI by the submission of a monthly EPS, which in effect reconciles the total contributions due according to all the FPSs submitted with the net contributions actually paid over.

Before RTI, each employee's statutory payments were identified separately on the deductions working sheet (P11) in columns 1g to 1k, and summarised on the employee's P14. Then the totals of all statutory payments for the year and the compensation amounts used to appear in their own boxes (12–22) as reconciling items on the annual P35 submitted by the employer.

SSP

[15.13] From 6 April 1991, for most employers the recovery of SSP was restricted to 80% of SSP paid.

A replacement Percentage Threshold Scheme (PTS) took effect from 6 April 1995 until 6 April 2014, when it was abolished. Employers had to calculate each month the ratio of SSP paid (NB paid, not due) to Class 1 contributions liability in the month. If SSP exceeded 13% of the contributions liability, the employer recovered the excess from the monthly remittance to HMRC as detailed in *The Income Tax (Pay As You Earn) Regulations 2003, SI 2003/2682, Regs 68(2), 70(2)*. The effect was to help employers with a large proportion of the workforce sick at any time. This calculation had to be performed monthly, even if the employer paid PAYE / NIC over on a quarterly basis for any reason. Before RTI, the employer had to record on forms P14/P60, and with RTI on the payroll records, the SSP in respect of each employee for which recovery had been made in each income tax month and year. See Employer's Help Book E14 (2013) page 31. [*Statutory Sick Pay Percentage Threshold Order 1995* and *Statutory Sick Pay Percentage Threshold Order 1995 (Consequential) Regulations 1995; Social Security (Contributions) Regulations 2001, SI 2001/1004, Sch 4 paras 22(3) and 25*] amended by the *Social Security (Contributions) (Amendment No 3) Regulations 2012, SI 2012/821*]. The requirement to supply information in this way did not apply where the employer (an 'RTI' employer) was obliged to operate Real Time Information because the numbers were included by the software.

The PTS was abolished on 6 April 2014.

Example

Sickly Limited had few employees in 2013–14 and a total monthly liability for primary and secondary contributions of £698.40. The PTS threshold was therefore £90.79 (ie £698.40 × 13% rounded down). If one employee became entitled to SSP of £86.70 (ie one week's absence following the waiting days), no recovery was possible, as the SSP paid was below the limit. However, if two employees became entitled to SSP of £86.70 each in the month, Sickly could recover (£173.40 – £90.79) = £82.61 from the normal remittance of £698.40.

Since 6 April 1997, where the employer had provided contractual remuneration (wages or occupational sick pay) that equalled or exceeded the rate of SSP there was no longer the requirement to maintain records of the calculation of SSP. The change in legislation arose from the *Statutory Sick Pay (General) Regulations 1996, Reg 2* and it entitled the employer voluntarily to apply the easement arrangements. The regulations provided that payment of contractual remuneration equal to or exceeding the amount of SSP payable in respect of a day of incapacity would not be regarded as a payment of SSP for the purposes of record keeping requirements of *Statutory Sick Pay (General) Regulations 1982, Reg 13*. Once the easement arrangements had been undertaken, and it was not necessary to give any notification of this, the following procedures could be effected by the employer:

- the easement could apply to some or all of the employees;
- the contractual sick pay arrangements could vary according to the length of incapacity;
- informal or discretionary arrangements for sick pay also allowed easement entitlement where contractual pay was at least as good as SSP; and
- recovery of SSP costs under the percentage threshold scheme (PTS) still applied until 5 April 2014 as long as the amount the employer would have paid in SSP for pay-days falling between the sixth of the month and the following fifth exceeded the then-current threshold of 13% of NICs for the month.

In these cases where the employer opted out of the SSP rules the payment effectively became occupational sick pay when paid to the employee. Any employer who wished to take advantage of the easement was obliged formally to advise his/her employees by reason of *Employment Rights Act 1996, s 1(4)(d)(ii)*, in writing, in the case of new employees, of the terms and conditions relating to incapacity for work due to sickness or injury. Existing employees did not have to be advised in writing as they still retained an underlying right to SSP anyway but it was probably appropriate to advise them or their representatives of the new arrangements. The record-keeping rules remain unchanged despite the abolition of any SSP recovery.

Example

Death's Door Ltd has decided that it will take advantage of the SSP easement arrangement for all its employees (from 6 April 2015). However, although there is no requirement to advise the existing employees of the change, new employees must be advised within two months of the date when the employee's employment begins. Death's Door Ltd's personnel department took the opportunity to advise existing employees by way of a revised notice to their Staff Handbook rather than a personalised letter. New and recently joined employees received a similar notice incorporated within their Staff Handbook along the same lines as what follows:

To: Ivor Binov
From: Personnel Department, Death's Door Ltd.
Date:
I attach a revised page . . . , Appendix . . . and index which should be inserted into your Staff Handbook. We believe that our obligations under the Employment Rights Act 1996, sections 1(4)(d)(ii) and 2(2) have been fulfilled. Your co-operation with this change would be appreciated.
Sickness Absence
In accordance with statutory regulations, if you are absent from work due to sickness, the company will pay Company Sick Pay (full basic pay including Statutory Sick Pay) for up to 28 weeks after which period any payments of employment and support allowance, which follows SSP in cases of long-term sickness, will be made by the DWP.
Company Sick Pay, which is the full basic pay being not less than the SSP equivalent, is payable, dependent on length of continuous company service as follows:

Period of service at the date of commencement of illness	*Period during which payment will be made*	
	Full basic salary	*Followed by ½ basic salary*
Up to 6 months	4 weeks	4 weeks
6 months–2 years	8 weeks	8 weeks
2–5 years	13 weeks	13 weeks
5–10 years	26 weeks	26 weeks
Over 10 years	52 weeks	—

For the purposes of calculating Company Sick Pay, periods of sickness separated from each other by 12 months or less will be added together.

Please note the following in relation to **Sickness Absence.**

1. The payment of Company Sick Pay will be withheld unless a signed Statement of Reasons for Absence (SRA form) is received.
2. A medical certificate must be produced on request.
3. The Company reserves the right to require you to be examined by a Doctor of its own choosing.
4. The Board will take into consideration special circumstances, which might warrant extending the period of Company Sick Pay.
5. Unexplained absences could lead to pay being withheld.
6. The Company reserves the right to request the return of a Company car if this is required for operational reasons.

Your attention is also drawn to the notification procedure in Section . . . , the Grievance procedure in section . . . and Appendix . . .

Agency workers with contracts of less than three months are eligible for SSP within those first three months of their contract. This change came into effect on 27 October 2008 following the Court of Appeal case of *Revenue and Customs Comrs v Thorn Baker Ltd* [2007] EWCA Civ 626, 79 TC 1, [2008] ICR 46. See former Employer Helpbook E14 (2013), page 37.

SMP

[15.14] In order to pay for improvements to maternity benefits required under the EC's Pregnant Workers Directive from 16 October 1994, the government reduced the SMP recovery rate to 92% for most employers in respect of SMP paid on or after 4 September 1994. For 'small' employers (defined as those with a £45,000 limit of National Insurance contributions paid in the preceding year), recovery continued in 1994–95 at the rate of 104.5%, including compensation. [*Statutory Maternity Pay Compensation Amendment Regs 1994*]. It is now 103% — see the following table for recovery rates in earlier years.

The same arrangements as for SMP have also applied in respect of Statutory Paternity Pay (SPP) and Statutory Adoption Pay (SAP) since their introduction in 2003, and also to Statutory Shared Parental Pay (ShPP) when it was introduced in April 2015.

In the case of SMP 'small' employers need to check their gross Class 1 contributions liability for the 'qualifying year' (QY). The QY is the last complete tax year before each employee's qualifying week (QW). The QW is the 15th week before the expected week of childbirth or adoption. For a birth or adoption expected in the week before Sunday, 22 July 2018, the QW would fall in 2017–18, so the QY would be 2016–17. SMP for a baby due a week later would have a QW in 2018–19 and the QY would be 2017–18. It is the first day of the QW week that determines in which tax year the QW falls. [*Statutory Maternity Pay (Compensation of Employers) and Miscellaneous Amendment Regs 1994, SI 1994/1882, Reg 1(4)*.]

Where the employer is not 'small', recovery of only 92% of the gross (ie, NIC exclusive) amount of SMP currently remains available, although the government is reportedly considering transferring some or all of the cost onto employers.

From 6 April 2003 to 5 April 2011, a small employer could recover 104.5% of SMP, SAP or SPP paid. Since that date, the compensatory rate has been set at 103%. The compensation is recovered by inclusion in an Employer Payment Summary at the end of the tax month of payment, with deduction from the associated remittance of monthly PAYE and NICs.

[*Statutory Sick Pay Additional Compensation Regs 1985, Reg 3; Statutory Maternity Pay Compensation Regs 1987, Reg 3; Statutory Maternity Pay (Compensation of Employers) Amendment Regs 2003, SI 2003/672, Reg 2*].

SPP

[15.15] For pay weeks that begin on or after 5 April 2015, Statutory Paternity Pay (SPP) is payable at the flat current (2018–19) rate of £145.18 per week, or 90% of average earnings if less, for a period of either one or two weeks taken in the first eight weeks after the birth. SPP is available to the biological father or the mother's husband, partner (male or female) or civil partner. The employee is required to give 28 days' notice for taking leave. The amount of compensation that the employer receives follows exactly the SMP arrangements and will therefore depend on the total gross employer's and employees' Class 1 contributions liability. Where this is always more than £45,000 the employer will be entitled to:

- recover 92% of the SPP, and
- will have to fund the remaining 8% himself.

If the annual liability for NICs in the qualifying year is £45,000 or less, then 100% of the SPP will be refunded. In addition, there will also, as with SMP, be a compensation rate payable of 3% claimed via the monthly EPS. See **15.14**.

Additional statutory paternity leave (ASPL) and pay (ASPP) were introduced for babies due or children matched for adoption on or after 3 April 2011. The original SPP was renamed 'ordinary SPP' (OSPP). Under the then new ASPL rules, a mother could return to work early and transfer the balance of her statutory maternity leave and SMP entitlement, converted into ASPP, to the father. The father then became entitled to the weekly payments, which were at the same standard rate as OSPP and SMP, and were recoverable by employers in the same way. OSPP and ASPP rules applied for any babies expected up to, or babies adopted by, 4 April 2015 (see **15.16** below). Entitlements to OSPP or ASPP continued to be payable in 2015–16 even though the rules changed for parents of babies due or adopted on or after 5 April 2015, to whom Statutory Shared Parental Leave and Pay will apply.

SAP

[15.16] Statutory adoption pay (SAP) and adoption leave also came into effect on 6 April 2003. For pay weeks that began on or after 6 April 2014, SAP is available for 39 weeks (26 weeks prior to April 2007) and from 5 April 2015 is payable at the following rates (matching SMP):

- 90% of average earnings for the first six weeks; followed by
- up to 33 weeks at the current (2018–19) standard rate of £145.18 or 90% of average earnings, whichever is less.

The employee is required to give 28 days' notice of the intended leave period. The amount the employer receives depends on whether the total annual gross NICs figure of £45,000 is exceeded as stated in **15.14** in connection with SMP. [*Social Security, Statutory Maternity Pay and Statutory Sick Pay (Miscellaneous Amendment) Regulations 2002, SI 2002/2690; Social Security (Paternity and Adoption) Amendment Regulations 2002, SI 2002/2689*]. Prior to 5 April 2015, SAP was payable at the lower of 90% of average earnings and the flat rate.

Statutory shared parental pay (ShPP)

[15.17] For births due and adoption matching occurring from 5 April 2015 onwards, new rules apply under the *Children And Families Act 2014* which allow parents more flexibility to share entitlement to maternity and paternity leave and pay, although the standard rates of statutory payment will continue to apply, and the rules on recovery by employers remain the same as for SMP and SPP. The rules for OSPP and ASPP will have applied only to those whose entitlement was triggered before the changeover, and in due course ceased to apply as entitlements expired.

Shared parental pay (ShPP) may become payable to each parent in phases, as the scheme introduced flexibility into the taking of shared parental leave (SPL), so that the mother can return to work as early as two weeks after the birth or adoption (four weeks for factory workers) and the father may then take leave and ShPP for a period, before the mother takes another period of statutory leave and the father returns to work. It is also possible for both parents to take ShPL at the same time and for both to have returned to work for a period before a further tranche of single or joint leave is then taken. ShPP may therefore be payable in two or three discontinuous periods. Each parent may take leave in up to three tranches, with the couple entitled in aggregate to up to 52 weeks' leave and 39 weeks' statutory payments, although each must give the employer eight weeks' notice of eligibility and all leave must have been taken before the newborn child's first birthday or the anniversary of the adoption. Employers began to see notices of eligibility as early as February 2015, and parents of babies due on or after 5 April 2015 but born prematurely before that date will have been able to claim ShPL and ShPP under the new regime from the outset. The ShPP legislation may be found principally in *Statutory Shared Parental Pay (General) Regulations 2014, SI 2014/3051*, while the provisions on statutory leave were created in *Shared Parental Leave Regulations 2014, SI 2014/3050*, both made on 1 December 2014 (to cope with premature babies).

Employer compensation

[15.18] An employer may compensate himself to the extent of his entitlement to the various recoveries due for SMP, SAP, SPP and ShPP by deducting the amount due to him from his contribution payments to HMRC except where and insofar as:

- the contribution payments relate to earnings paid before the beginning of the income tax month in which the payment of SMP was made;
- the contribution payments are made by him later than six years after the end of the tax year in which the payment of SMP was made;
- the amount has already been paid to him by the Secretary of State for Social Security or by HM Revenue and Customs in the circumstances described below; or
- he has made a written request for direct payment of the compensation and has not, or not yet, received notification that the request is refused.

Where the contribution payments due to HMRC are insufficient to enable full compensation and recovery to be made, an employer is entitled to claim advance funding which can be done by completing the relevant 'structured form' online (via www.gov.uk rather than HMRC's website) or by contacting the relevant Accounts Office by fax only (Cumbernauld: 03000 583998; Shipley: 03000 518344), including all the details specified in the web guidance at www.gov.uk/recover-statutory-payments/if-you-cant-afford-to-make-payments. HMRC does not yet routinely use standard email due to security concerns. Employers have, however, been known to complain that a mail backlog at HMRC has resulted in funding being delayed by several months.

Example

In the month ended 5 June 2018, Brandon paid £178.70 SSP and £422.94 SMP to employees.

His payments due to HMRC for that month, before recoveries, were £102.85 contributions and £122.60 PAYE. He is entitled to SMP recovery as a 'small employer'.

He may recover:

SSP	NIL
SMP £422.94 × 103%	435.63
	£435.63

This amount is first set off against Class 1 contributions leaving a difference of £332.78. This may be set off against the PAYE of £122.60 leaving nothing payable to HMRC for that month and a surplus of £210.18 unrecovered. This may be carried forward to the following month or as indicated above, an employer can make written claim for advance funding by contacting the Accounts Office, see www.gov.uk/recover-statutory-payments/reclaiming. In any event it is recommended that a nil payment EPS be sent in covering that month so that HMRC does not send a reminder or apply a spurious specified charge (ie, estimated unpaid liability) to the employer's account.

[*Statutory Sick Pay Percentage Threshold Order 1995, Reg 3; Statutory Maternity Pay Compensation Amendment Regs 1994, Reg 5*].

Case law

[15.19] As a result of the Sally Brown (Child Poverty Action Group sponsored) case any individual who is employed on a series of contracts with the same employer, linked by a period of not more than eight weeks, where the period in employment exceeds 13 weeks, will be regarded as being in continuous employment for SSP purposes. The person's contract should be regarded as being for an indefinite period and therefore cannot be terminated without seven days' notice. See CA National Insurance News, Summer 1997 page 6. From 1 October 2002, the length of contract is irrelevant and all short-term contract workers will receive SSP provided that all other conditions are met.

Two European Court of Justice (ECJ) cases affect the maternity pay position of UK workers and their employers. See *MK Alabaster v (1) Woolwich Plc (2) Secretary of State for Social Security* Case C-147/02 [2004] All ER (D) 558 (Mar) and *Ms Merino Gómez v Continental Industrias del Caucho SA* C-342/01 [2004] ECR I-2605, [2004] 2 CMLR 38, ECJ. These follow on from the ECJ case of *Gillespie and others v Northern Ireland Health and Social Security* C-342/93 [1996] All ER (EC) 284, after which the *Statutory Maternity Pay (General) Regs 1986* had to be amended in 1996 to ensure that any employer's backdated pay rise which would have applied in the 'relevant period' of maternity is in fact taken into account in calculating SMP. The more recent cases also affect SMP and holiday entitlement respectively, the former case requiring SMP to be recalculated to take into account all pay rises from the start of the 'set period' to the end of both ordinary and, if taken, additional maternity leave; and the latter ensuring that holiday periods that clash with maternity leave are not forgone. See former Employer Helpbook E15 (2013).

Tax relief

[15.20] In no circumstances may tax relief be given or a tax deduction allowed in respect of *primary* Class 1 contributions. [*ITTOIA 2005, ss 53, 272, 868* and *ITEPA 2003, s 360A*]. Accordingly, no relief is available even to an employer who has accounted for primary Class 1 contributions in circumstances which preclude his recovery of such contributions from the employed earner concerned (see **14.25** CATEGORISATION and **21.19** COLLECTION). Class 1 *secondary* contributions, Class 1A contributions and Class 1B contributions paid by a secondary contributor are allowable as a deduction in computing his profits and gains, however, provided those secondary contributions have been wholly and exclusively laid out or expended for the purposes of his trade, profession or vocation or, in the case of an investment company, insurance company or the owner of mineral rights, have been disbursed as expenses of management. [*ITTOIA 2005, ss 53, 272, 868* as amended by *ITA 2007, Sch 1, para 507* and *ITEPA 2003, s 360A*]. This proviso will operate so as to preclude a deduction from profits for tax purposes in respect of secondary Class 1 contributions on earnings which are themselves disallowed, eg where the earnings are considered excessive as in *Copeman v William Flood & Sons Ltd* (1940) 24 TC 53. Until 25 November 1996 relief applied only to secondary Class 1 contributions paid by employers. Previously, relief for Class 1A contributions had been allowed by reason of Extra–Statutory Concession (B48) but this was subsequently statutorily provided for by *FA 1997, s 65(3)*. Class 1A (or for that matter secondary Class 1) contributions are now allowable as a deduction in computing profits or gains where these are claimed as a deduction under *ITEPA 2003, s 336* (relief for necessary expenses) or *ITEPA 2003, s 359* (performance of duties as a clergyman or minister) in order to cover the situation where office holders, and ministers of religion engage assistance in connection with their work.

The relief was further amended by *FA 1999, s 61* so as to give tax relief for the payment of Class 1B contributions.

There had in the past been no provision, as there is for interest on overdue tax, to disallow in the employer's own computation of taxable profits any interest on late paid contributions. In the 2003 Budget, the Chancellor announced that this would be remedied for accounting periods ending on or after 9 April 2003. This was enacted by *Finance Act 2003, s 147*, inserting *SSCBA 1992, Sch 1, para 6(4B)*.

NIC holiday

[15.21] On 22 June 2010, the Chancellor announced a NIC holiday scheme available until 5 September 2013, which provided for new businesses to escape liability for a limited amount of employer NICs for the first year of their operation. Although the scheme started on 6 September 2010 in respect of new businesses that commenced on and after 22 June 2010 the legislation – contained in National Insurance Contributions Bill 2010 printed on 14 October 2010 – was only presented in the House of Commons in October 2010 and was enacted on 22 March 2011.

Clearly a business commencing after 6 September 2012 will have had less chance of maximising the relief due as no Holiday was available in respect of earnings paid after 5 September 2013. The key features of the scheme were as follows.

- Relief for up to £5,000 of employer Class 1 contributions in the first year of employment per employee (up to a maximum of ten employees) taken on in the first year of a new business's life. Class 1A and/or Class 1B contributions were unaffected. Note that as the relief was in respect of payments made in the first twelve months of the employment, in practice the relief was in most cases have been only on the first month's salary (part of a normal month's payment) and then the next eleven months' full salary.
- The scheme applied to the whole of the United Kingdom except three excluded regions (which were not as badly affected as the rest of the country by unemployment) as follows:
  - (a) Greater London;
  - (b) The Eastern Region, comprising:
    - (i) the counties of Bedford, Cambridgeshire, Central Bedfordshire, Essex, Hertfordshire, Norfolk and Suffolk;
    - (ii) the non-metropolitan districts of Luton, Peterborough, Southend-on-Sea and Thurrock;
  - (c) the South East Region, comprising:
    - (i) the counties of Buckinghamshire, East Sussex, Hampshire, the Isle of Wight, Kent, Oxfordshire, Surrey and West Sussex; and
    - (ii) the non-metropolitan districts of Bracknell Forest, Brighton and Hove, Medway, Milton Keynes, Portsmouth, Reading, Slough, Southampton, West Berkshire, Windsor and Maidenhead and Wokingham.
- Where a business commenced before 6 September 2010 (but after 21 June 2010) the 12 months' relief for any employee commenced on 6 September 2010, but the first ten qualifying employees had to be taken on within 12 months of the actual start date.
- Investment and property business were potentially eligible.
- The Holiday was administered as 'de minimis' State Aid for which there was an overall entitlement of €200,000 over three years. Any new business which was getting other such State Aid will have had its NIC Holiday cap reduced, if necessary, to ensure that the €200,000 limit was

not exceeded. For the same reason, the coal industry was completely excluded. Lower de minimis State Aid limits applied to the agriculture (€7,500), fisheries and aquaculture (€30,000) and road transport (€100,000) sectors.

- Managed service companies could not benefit and nor could IR35 companies as regards 'deemed payments'. Any regular salary paid month by month by an IR35 company would however have been eligible for the Holiday.
- Where – very unusually for a new business – National Insurance contributions were due at the contracted-out rate, the Holiday entitlement was to be valued as a reduction of the full, not contracted-out contributions that would have been due on the same earnings. This reflected the employer's liability to make 'minimum payments' to a pension scheme under the COMP rules.
- Qualifying employees included directors – paid or unpaid – as well as any employees earning below the earnings threshold (in which case the Holiday for that employee was zero, and could not be replaced by a – higher-earning – eleventh employee). If on the first day that any employee was taken on at least another ten were also taken on, then the business could choose which ten would be covered by the Holiday. This required careful assessment of likely future bonuses, commissions, etc to optimise relief.
- If an employee left, his replacement would not qualify if ten employees had already been recruited. If the employee was re-employed (whether or not ten employees were already in place by then) the Holiday for that employee continued up to the original end-date or until the £5,000 maximum relief had been obtained for that employee.
- There were anti-avoidance rules as to the meaning of a new business, and a business already claiming the Holiday that was taken over or sold would cease to be eligible immediately. An existing business taken over by a new owner was not considered a new business for the purposes of the scheme. A business was not a new business if at any time within the previous six months the person applying for the Holiday had carried on another business consisting of most of the activities of the 'new' business. Rules also prevented relief where there were arrangements between the potential Holiday claimant and the previous owner and / or where there were arrangements between the potential Holiday claimant and the previous owner and / or where there were arrangements whereby after a new business had started it took over other activities which would not have been eligible for the Holiday if those activities had started at the same time as the new business itself. In addition, there was an overriding anti-avoidance provision in *s 10* of the *National Insurance Contributions Act 2011*.

[*National Insurance Contributions Act 2011, ss 4–11*.]

If the new business was based in two places, one in an excluded region and the other in a qualifying region, then the NIC holiday was only available if the greater part of the business was not carried on in an excluded region when it was started. The new business needed to demonstrate that the principal place where, for example, the business records were kept and from which the business was administered was not in any of the excluded regions. If the greater part of the new business was not carried on in the excluded regions then the NIC holiday was available to all of the employees including those working for the business situated in the excluded region. If the greater part of the business was carried on in the excluded regions the new business was not eligible for the NIC holiday, not even in respect of employees working outside the excluded areas. The onus was on the new business to demonstrate that the principal place at which its business was carried on when it was started was not in any of the excluded regions.

The Government is understood to have briefly considered extending the scheme to all very small businesses, but decided against doing so because the scheme failed badly: initially the government forecast that the NIC Holiday would cost £940m in total over its three-year lifespan, and it was estimated at launch that 400,000 new businesses would benefit from the scheme. In fact, only 26,000 applied, of which 600 were unsuccessful, and the cost of the relief was put at around £60m (Hansard, HC Deb 31 October 2013 c534W). The Government therefore opted instead to introduce the employment allowance, to provide capped relief for all non-public sector or domestic employers across the UK from secondary Class 1 liability.

Example (1)

A new business (sole trader) was started up by Ben on the Hampshire / Dorset border providing the Bournemouth and Southampton areas with gardening services. He was looking for premises out of which to provide his work and wanted to employ seven workers based in Hampshire and Dorset to service the particular areas. If he had taken premises in Hampshire it would have been in an excluded region, whereas if he had opted for Dorset only a few miles away he would, subject to following the correct procedures, have been entitled to the NIC Holiday in respect of his business. It did not matter that a greater proportion of the work was actually carried out in Hampshire. The principal place at which the new business was carried out when it started up was not in an excluded region. The Holiday was available up to the first ten employees engaged during the initial period. The initial period was one year from when the business started or, if earlier, one year from the first date on which an earner was employed for the purposes of the new business.

Example (2)

Harry and Michael commenced, in partnership, a new business on 2 August 2010 based in Edinburgh. The first employee was however taken on two weeks earlier on 19 July. Another (part-time) employee commenced on 2 August 2010 and after interest and trade had been built up a third employee started on 4 July 2011. The business could claim NIC Holiday in respect of up to the first ten employees taken on from 19 July 2010 to 18 July 2011 inclusive. No relief was due before the scheme start date of 6 September 2010, but it could then be claimed for up to the first twelve months from that date in respect of existing employees. Recoveries of employer NIC will have been due as follows:

Month	*NIC due re 1st employee*	*NIC due re 2nd employee*	*NIC due re 3rd employee*	*NIC recoverable*	*Notes*
2010					
September	600	100	–	700	
October	600	100	–	700	
November	600	100	–	700	
December	600	100	–	700	
2011					
January	600	100	–	700	
February	600	100	–	700	
March	600	100	–	700	
April	600	100	–	700	(1)
May	600	100	–	300	(2)
June	600	100	–	100	
July	600	100	500	600	(3)
August	600	100	500	500	(4)
September	600	100	500	500	

Notes:

(1) The scheme ran continuously across the tax year-end.

(2) For the first employee, relief of £4,800 had been received in previous months; only £200 therefore remained eligible for relief (maximum £5,000 per employee).

(3) Relief was not available in respect of any further employees taken on from 18 July 2011. But relief was due for the third employee (hired within the first 12 months of the first employee being taken on). Relief for the third employee stopped after 12 months' employment or when the relief for that employee reached £5,000 (so in this case there was no relief after April 2012).

(4) Final month of eligibility for second employee – 12 months of post-6 September 2010 employment completed.

Relief was not automatic and businesses needed to apply. Most businesses could apply online. Employers who had received or were applying for other de minimis State Aid or who were in the agriculture, fisheries, aquaculture and road transport sectors needed to apply on paper. Holiday relief could not be taken until HMRC had approved the application. All normal payroll documentation needed to be kept in the usual way and the year-end Forms P14 and P35 reflected the full National Insurance contributions and separate paper-only returns were made for the amounts not remitted as a result of claiming the Holiday.

Employers needed to keep records of the employees who were the subject of Holiday relief, specifically the:

- name;

- National Insurance number;
- date employment commenced;
- date the Holiday period for the employee ended (may be less than twelve months);
- amount of Holiday claimed in each tax year; and
- amount (where applicable) of the Holiday claimed in the previous tax year, together with a note of the date on which the business started.

A very useful interactive pdf Form E89 was available from HMRC's website, although records could be kept in any format of the employer's choosing.

A separate (ie additional) NIC Holiday end-of-year return needed to be made as at each 5 April. This enabled HMRC to avoid picking up the Holiday relief obtained as what would otherwise have appeared to be an underpayment on the P35. An E89 was needed for each eligible employee and a summary was needed for all employees for the tax year on an E92. Neither form was included in the RTI specification as the Holiday was always a temporary measure.

Employment allowance

[15.22] From 6 April 2014 under the *National Insurance Contributions Act 2014* a secondary contributor is entitled to an 'employment allowance' for a tax year in which he pays earnings to, or for the benefit of, one or more employees, in respect of which he is liable to pay secondary Class 1 National Insurance contributions. From 6 April 2016, no allowance is due to one-man companies (see below).

The allowance was originally the lower of £2,000 and such of those secondary liabilities as are not excluded liabilities. The £2,000 limit was increased to £3,000 from 6 April 2016. The eligible employer simply does not pay any secondary Class 1 liabilities to HMRC until his liability exceeds £3,000 in a tax year, and then pays only on the excess over £3,000. The reduction is claimed via the monthly EPS, by ticking a single box.

The announcement of the allowance in Budget 2013 included an estimate of 450,000 small businesses that would no longer have to pay secondary contributions, and of 1.25 million businesses that might benefit to some extent (ie, all private sector employers). Statistics published for the first six months of the regime showed that 856,000 employers had claimed the allowance, around 68% of the employer population. Take-up was lowest among the large employer group (ie, those with 250 or more employees), for whom a £2,000 allowance was probably immaterial. The rate among small and micro-businesses (ie, 1 to 9 employees) was also only at 68%, but many of the population will have been small companies with an annual scheme who would not claim the allowance until March 2015. The statistics for the first full year later showed an 89% take-up (1.18 million employers), with 94% of small and micro-employers having claimed. The rate for large employers remained low at 40%.

In the July 2015 Budget speech, the Chancellor announced a plan to increase the employment allowance to £3,000 with effect from 6 April 2016, taking some 90,000 further employers out of liability at a cost to the NI Fund of around £700 million per year. This was duly introduced by *Employment Allowance (Increase of Maximum Amount) Regulations 2016, SI 2016/63*, which simply changed the value of the allowance in *National Insurance Contributions Act 2014, s 1(2)(a)* to £3,000.

Exceptions

[15.23] The employment allowance is not available:

(a) to public authorities (as defined, which includes private sector employers to which an authority's statutory functions have been outsourced) which are not charities;
(b) where the employee in question, subject now to one exception, is employed wholly or partly for purposes connected with the employer's personal, family or household affairs (eg domestic cleaners, nannies);
(c) in respect of notional payments (but real salary is not excluded) under the IR35 rules where the employee's services are supplied by a service company; and
(d) from 6 April 2016, to companies whose only paid employee is the sole director.

[*NICA 2014, ss 1(3), 2(1)–(4A)*].

The exception in respect of domestic employees relates to 'care and support' employees in the home. From 6 April 2015, the rules were changed to permit a claim for employment allowance where the employee in question meets specified criteria. The secondary NIC liabilities in respect of domestic employees are from that date not 'excluded liabilities' if *all* the duties of the employed earner's employment which relate to the employer's personal, family or household affairs are performed for an individual who needs those duties to be performed because of the individual's:

(a) old age,
(b) mental or physical disability,
(c) past or present dependence on alcohol or drugs,
(d) past or present illness, or
(e) past or present mental disorder.

[*Employment Allowance (Care and Support Workers) Regulations 2015, SI 2015/578*.]

In the July 2015 Budget speech, the Chancellor announced that the employment allowance entitlement would be withdrawn with effect from 6 April 2016 from companies with a sole director (ie, the target was clearly personal service companies), since the aim of the allowance was to foster employment. The *Employment Allowance (Excluded Companies) Regulations 2016, SI 2016/344* added with effect from 6 April 2016 the planned exclusion as *NICA 2014, s 2(4A)*.

A company cannot, for 2016–17 onwards, qualify for an employment allowance for a tax year if all the payments of earnings in relation to which the company is the secondary contributor in that year are paid to, or for the benefit of, the same employed earner, and when each of those payments is made, that employed earner is a director of the company.

In its Employer Bulletin, issue 59 in April 2016, HMRC misinterpreted the change in rules by stating that 'if you are a limited company where the director is the only employee who is paid earnings *above the secondary threshold* [emphasis added], you will no longer be eligible to claim the employment allowance'. The legislation plainly makes no reference to the secondary threshold, so a payment of £1 to a second earner is enough to ensure that the company continues to qualify for the allowance, despite HMRC's statement to the contrary.

An employer is a secondary contributor in relation to *any* payment of earnings to an employee even if the payment results in no secondary contribution liability. [*SSCBA 1992, s 7*]. An employer would otherwise have no employer duties as a secondary contributor where it paid its employees below the secondary threshold, which would plainly be absurd since earnings above £116 per week must be reflected in the computer record as they count for benefit purposes, so they must be reported, and the report is the duty of the secondary contributor. HMRC's view cannot be what the legislation intended.

HMRC's explanation for the misinterpretation of the rules is based on a misreading of *NICA 2014, s 1(1)*, which sets the basic qualification criteria for the allowance. A company qualifies if, in the tax year, it is the secondary contributor in relation to payments of earnings to, or for the benefit of, one or more employed earners, and in consequence, incurs liabilities to pay secondary Class 1 contributions under *SSCBA 1992*. HMRC incorrectly assumes that the allowance removes any such liability in a one-person company which therefore disqualifies the company from claiming it because it no longer meets the terms of *s 1(1)*. This is a circular argument that is clearly invalid. If the new *s 2(4A)* does not apply because there is a second paid earner (with or without a secondary contribution liability), the secondary contributor clearly is not paying earnings to only one earner, so the disqualification cannot apply, which means that the secondary contribution liability in respect of the sole director's earnings is sufficient by itself to attract the employment allowance. It is hoped that the guidance will be amended to reflect the legislation in due course. The legislative change was expected to save the NI Fund around £70 million per year, but since each and every one-person company can preserve its entitlement by employing and paying a casual worker for just one shift (or appointing and paying a second director), it seems unlikely that the savings will materialise.

A one-person corporate employer wishing to protect its entitlement to the allowance without provoking an argument with HMRC over its incorrect interpretation of the law may do so by employing a casual worker for just one shift for which earnings of at least £162.08 are paid, since this will result in a secondary contribution liability of 1p, meeting HMRC's stated requirement of having a secondary liability in respect of earnings paid to the second earner. More likely will be the appointment of a second director, who is paid at least once in the year above the pro rata secondary threshold so as to create a secondary liability in the year.

Where a one-man company is no longer eligible to claim the allowance as a result of the new legislation, the RTI system will require the submission of an Employer Payment Summary confirming that the allowance is no longer being claimed.

Note that a one-person unincorporated business is wholly unaffected by the 2016 change, which applies only to companies with a sole paid director.

If a business (or part thereof) is transferred in a tax year, liabilities to pay secondary Class 1 contributions incurred by the transferee in the tax year in respect of an employee who is employed wholly or partly for purposes connected with the transferred business or part are disregarded for employment allowance purposes. [*NICA 2014, ss 1(3), 2(5)-(6)*.] For this purpose, a business or part of a business is transferred in a tax year if, in that year, another person (the transferor) is carrying on that business or part, and, in consequence of arrangements involving the transferor and the transferee, the transferee begins to carry on the business or part when or after the transferor ceases to do so. 'Business' here includes a trade, profession or vocation, and a property business, and any charitable, non-profit-making or similar undertaking, and 'arrangements' includes any agreement, understanding, scheme, transaction or series of transactions (whether or not legally enforceable). [*NICA 2014, s 2(7)-(9)*.]

A person cannot qualify for an employment allowance if his entitlement would arise by virtue of anti-avoidance arrangements, ie 'arrangements' a main purpose of which is to secure that a person benefits, or benefits further, from the application of the employment allowance provisions. [*NICA 2014, s 1(2), (3), (10), (12)*.] In a case not covered by this provision, liabilities to pay secondary Class 1 contributions are excluded liabilities for employment allowance purposes if they are incurred by the employer or incurred by him in a particular tax year rather than another as a result of anti-avoidance arrangements (as defined above). [*NICA 2014, ss 1(3), 2(11)*.] HMRC might be expected to try to apply these anti-avoidance rules to sole director companies that engage casual workers for a single shift if it can be shown that this was done solely in order to qualify for the employment allowance. However, the effort involved in proving such motives would be wholly disproportionate in the context of such small businesses.

On 29 June 2015, HMRC published its avoidance 'Spotlight 24' highlighting an arrangement uncovered by the BBC, and reported widely on 29 May 2015, that was, in HMRC's view, caught by this anti-avoidance rule and was therefore ineffective. An alleged promoter was offering workers the opportunity to work for a small company that would supply their services to other businesses. It had created many such companies, none of which would have employer NIC liabilities in a year that would exceed £2,000. However, it seems the promoters had overlooked the question of control: all the companies were effectively controlled by one business, so only one £2,000 employment allowance was available to share among them – see further below. HMRC noted that the scheme should have been notified under the DOTAS rules.

Connected persons

[15.24] If, at the beginning of a tax year, two or more companies which are not charities are connected, and two or more of those companies would otherwise qualify for an employment allowance for that tax year, only one such company may so qualify. [*NICA 2014, ss 1(3), 3(1), (3)*]. Separate, but corresponding, provision is made for charities by *s 3(2)*. The choice of which is to receive the allowance lies with the companies or charities concerned (*s 3(4)*). 'Charity' has the meaning given by the *Small Charitable Donations Act 2012, s 18(1)*, but if a charity ('A') as so defined controls a company ('B') which would not otherwise be a charity, that company is nevertheless treated as such for these purposes (including this provision) and A and B are treated as connected. [*NICA 2014, s 3(7)*]. 'Company' has the meaning given in the *Corporation Tax Act 2010, s 1121(1)* and includes a limited liability partnership. [*NICA 2014, s 3(7)*].

For these purposes, two companies are 'connected' if:

(a) one has control over the other; or
(b) both are under the control of the same person or persons.

[*NICA 2014, Sch 1, para 2(1).*]

'Control' has the meaning given by the *Corporation Tax Act 2010, ss 450, 451*, and a Limited Liability Partnership is treated as a company for the purposes of employment allowance; but for these purposes, where under *CTA 2010, s 450* 'C' is a limited liability partnership, *s 450(3)* has effect as if the following additional paragraph were inserted before *s 450(3)(a)*: '(za) rights to a share of more than half the assets, or of more than half the income, of C'. [*NICA 2014, Sch 1, para 2(1)-(3).*]

Where the relationship between two companies is via a connected person of the person who controls it and it is not one of substantial commercial interdependence, then in the application of *Corporation Tax Act 2010, s 451* for the purposes of determining whether the companies are connected, any person to whom rights and duties fall to be treated under *s 451(4),(5)* is treated, for the purposes of those provisions, as having no associates. [*NICA 2014, Sch 1, para 3(1),(2).*] In determining whether two companies have a relationship of substantial commercial interdependence for this purpose, the following factors must be taken into account:

(a) the degree of financial interdependence;
(b) the degree of economic interdependence; and
(c) the degree of organisational interdependence.

For this purpose, two companies are 'financially interdependent' if (in particular) (i) one gives financial support (directly or indirectly) to the other, or (ii) each has (directly or indirectly) a financial interest in the other's affairs. Two companies are 'economically interdependent' if (in particular) they seek to realise the same economic objective, the activities of one benefit the other, or their activities involve common customers; and two companies are 'organisationally interdependent' if (in particular) they have common management, common employees, common premises or common equipment.

[*NICA 2014, Sch 1, para 3(2)-(6).*]

In determining for these purposes whether one company is under the control of another, fixed-rate preference shares held by a company are ignored if that company is not a close company, takes no part in the management or conduct of the company which issued the shares or of that company's business, and subscribed for the shares in the ordinary course of a business which includes the provision of finance. [*NICA 2014, Sch 1, para 4(1).*]. 'Fixed-rate preference shares' here means shares which were issued wholly for new consideration (as defined in *CTA 2010, s 1115*) which do not carry any right either to conversion into shares or securities of any other description or to the acquisition of any additional shares or securities, and which do not carry any right to dividends other than those which (a) are of a fixed amount or at a fixed rate per cent of the nominal value of the shares, and (b) together with any sum paid on redemption, represent no more than a reasonable commercial return on the consideration for which the shares are issued. [*NICA 2014, Sch 1, para 4(2),(3)*]. 'Close company' must be read in accordance with *CTA 2010, Pt 10, Ch 2* (see, in particular, *s 439*). [*NICA 2014, Sch 1, para 4(4).*]

A company ('A') is not under the control of another company ('B') for these purposes if the only connection between the two is that B is a loan creditor of A, and either the loan creditor is not a close company (as above defined) or B's relationship to A as a loan creditor arose in the ordinary course of a business which B carries on. [*NICA 2014, Sch 1, para 5(1).*]

If two companies ('A' and 'B') are under the control of the same person who is a loan creditor of each of them, there is no other connection between them, and either the loan creditor is a company which is not a close company, or the loan creditor's relationship to each of A and B as a loan creditor arose in the ordinary course of a business which the loan creditor carries on, then in determining for these purposes whether A and B are connected, rights which the loan creditor has as such in A or B are ignored. [*NICA 2014, Sch 1, para 5(2),(3).*] 'Loan creditor' is to be read in accordance with the *CTA 2010, s 453* and for the above purposes 'connection' includes a past as well as a present connection, and references to a connection between two companies include any dealings between them. [*NICA 2014, Sch 1, para 5(5).*]

If two companies ('A' and 'B') are under the control of the same person by virtue of rights or powers (or both) held in trust by that person, and there is no other connection between A and B, then in determining for these purposes whether A and B are connected with one another, those rights and powers are to be disregarded. For the above purposes 'connection' includes a past as well as a present connection, and references to a connection between two companies include any dealings between them. [*NICA 2014, Sch 1, para 6.*]

If a company ('A') is connected (see *NICA 2014, Sch 1, paras 2-7*) with another company ('B'), and B is connected (by virtue of *Sch 1, paras 2-6* above) with another company ('C'), A and C are also connected with one another (if that would not otherwise be the case). [*NICA 2014, Sch 1, para 7.*]

Two charities are connected with each other for the purposes of *Sch 1, para 3* above if they are so connected by virtue of *ITA 2007, s 993* and their purposes and activities are the same or substantially similar. [*NICA 2014, Sch 1, para 8(1).*]. In applying *ITA 2007, s 993* for the purposes of the above provision, for the purposes of *s 993(1)(a)* (as well as this provision) a charity which is a trust is to be treated as if it were a company and, accordingly, a person; a charity which is a trust has 'control' of another person if the trustees (in their capacity as such) have, or any of them has, control of the person; and a person (other than a charity regulator) has control of a charity which is a trust if (i) that person is a trustee of the charity and some or all of the powers of the trustees of the charity could be exercised by the person acting alone or acting together with any other such trustees who are connected with that person, (ii) that person, alone or together with other persons, has power to appoint or remove a trustee of the charity, or (iii) that person, alone or together with other persons, has any power of approval or direction in relation to the carrying out by the trustees of their functions. [*NICA 2014, Sch 1, para 8(2)*.]

A charity which is a trust is also connected with another charity for these purposes which is a trust if at least half of the trustees of one of the charities are trustees of the other, or are connected with such trustees, or a combination of both, and the charities' purposes and activities are the same or substantially similar. [*NICA 2014, Sch 1, para 8(2),(3)*.] In determining for the above purposes whether a person who is a trustee is connected with another person, *ITA 2007, s 993* must be applied with the omission of *s 993(3)* and without the modifications in *NICA 2014, Sch 1, para 8(2)* (see *Sch 1, para 8(4)*).

If a charity ('A') is connected (by virtue of *Sch 1, para 8 or 9*) with another charity ('B'), and B is connected by virtue of *Sch 1, para 8* with another charity, A and C are also connected for these purposes (if that would not otherwise be the case). [*NICA 2014, Sch 1, para 9*.]

Obtaining the employment allowance

[15.25] The employment allowance is claimed by deducting the amount due from secondary Class 1 contributions for the tax year which are not excluded liabilities (see above), referred to in the legislation as 'qualifying payments'. The deduction must be made in priority to any other deduction which the employer is entitled to make from the qualifying payments. If the full amount has not been deducted by 30 April following the end of the tax year, repayment of the balance may be claimed from HMRC before the end of the fourth tax year following that in which the allowance was due. Any such repayment must be made out of the National Insurance Fund. Employment allowance may not be given in any other way. Repayment interest may be due on delayed repayments of employment allowance, and the repayment interest start date is the date on which HMRC received the application for repayment. In practice, employers will claim the employment allowance by deducting it from the first available secondary contributions for the year on the monthly EPS. If total secondary contributions for the year do not reach £3,000 (£2,000 for 2014–15 and 2015–16), any unused balance is lost.

HMRC must, from time to time, make such arrangements as it considers appropriate for the making of such deductions. Such arrangements may deny a deduction in specified circumstances, and may place limits on the amounts to be deducted. They may also provide for the keeping and maintenance of records. An application for repayment of the allowance must be made in such form and manner, and contain such information, as HMRC may require.

The Treasury is given extensive powers to amend the employment allowance provisions by statutory instrument.

If a deduction or repayment is denied, this constitutes a decision against which an appeal lies. [*NICA 2014, ss 4-8*; *Social Security (Transfer of Functions, etc) Act 1999, s 8(1)*; *Finance Act 2009, s 102*.]

Examples

Gary and Alan own and run a number of businesses, all run separately and with their own staff and payrolls: two companies (offering corporate hospitality arrangements at Premier League and Championship matches respectively), two LLPs (one running a nursing home and the other offering refuse collection services to the local authority), and a 50:50 general partnership (running a local pharmacy). Alan has also set up two sole trader business selling World Cup memorabilia and all-inclusive tours to Scotland's away matches. Alan employs Morag part-time in the tour business and part-time as his housekeeper. Alan's wife also owns two trading companies, wholly unconnected with any of Alan's businesses and in different lines of business from each other.

Who can claim the employment allowance, and how much can they claim?

The LLPs are treated as companies, so the four 'corporate' entities are all connected, and G and A must therefore nominate which of the four is to claim the allowance. If none of the four has an employer NIC liability (Class 1 only) that reaches £3,000, some of the allowance will be wasted, as it cannot be partially transferred, or carried forward, or set against PAYE liabilities.

The LLP undertaking refuse collection for the local council cannot make the claim as it is fulfilling the statutory duty of the local council in emptying bins, so it is subject to the exclusion for public authorities.

The other LLP running a nursing home will need to assess where the majority of its income arises: if the residents are predominantly paid for by the local authority under its statutory duty to provide such care home places, then the LLP will also be disqualified under the public authority rule. If, however, there are few such patients and the majority are privately-funded, the LLP will not be disqualified.

The general partnership is not connected with the company, because the connection rules only apply between companies and LLPs, not between companies / LLPs and unincorporated businesses owned and controlled by the same people. However, the business is a pharmacy, so it could be argued to be fulfilling the statutory duties of the NHS in dispensing prescription medicines. In fact, any private pharmacy is likely to be able to fulfil that statutory duty only through the person of the licensed pharmacist, while the rest of the staff are selling off-the-shelf non-prescription drugs, as well as baby milk, nappies, cosmetics, etc, so most pharmacies will qualify for the allowance as the business will not consist predominantly of the NHS work (the measures used for assessing what the business mainly does can be staff time, or business turnover, or some other factor that is relevant).

The sole trader businesses are not 'connected' with the general partnership (the connection rules explicitly connect only companies and LLPs, not two unincorporated businesses under different control), so Alan can claim up to £3,000 in those businesses, and the general partnership can also claim up to £3,000.

Because Alan is the only employer in the two sole trades, he can split the allowance between the two payrolls, so if the employer liability in the tour business is only £1,000, he can claim that through the payroll there and set the remaining £2,000 against the employer liability in the memorabilia business by making a claim at the year-end.

Alan cannot claim any allowance in respect of Morag's wages, because some of her work is for Alan's domestic rather than business purposes.

Alan's wife controls two separate companies that are not interdependent, but only one of the companies may claim the allowance, because she alone owns and controls both.

If Alan and his wife (ie, a connected person) had jointly owned and controlled two companies, only one allowance would be due between them, as there is direct common control of both entities by the two acting together.

However, Alan's wife's companies and Alan's companies have no substantial commercial interdependence between them (rather than the owners), so both companies may claim the allowance.

Key Points regarding class 1 contributions: employed earners

[15.26] Points to consider are as follows.

- The main rate for primary Class 1 contributions is now only reduced in the case of married women with a certificate of reduced rate election or certain mariners. Contracting-out rebates no longer apply to reduce contribution rates from 6 April 2016.
- There is a multiplicity of contribution tables covering the various rates.
- Contributions can be calculated using either the tables or the exact percentage method. The fact that software is used to make the calculations does not necessarily mean that the exact percentage method is in use as much software imports the HMRC-produced tables.
- Where an employer becomes insolvent or bankrupt then HMRC may be liable to pay SMP, SSP, SAP, SPP and ShPP but such payments are not aggregated with other payments.
- From April 2011 a woman is able to transfer her maternity leave entitlement to the father of her newborn child. The six-month period of leave may be wholly transferred to the father or shared between them and, if taken during the mother's 39-week maternity pay period, it may be paid leave that is transferred and the father may claim Additional SPP. For babies due or adopted on or after 5 April 2015, this was extended to allow couples to share parental leave and statutory pay entitlements.
- From 6 April 2014, most employers were entitled to make a deduction of up to £2,000 from secondary Class 1 contributions payable to HMRC (the 'employment allowance'). This was increased to £3,000 from 6 April 2016.
- From 6 April 2015, secondary Class 1 contributions are not payable in respect of earnings paid to employees under the age of 21, and the same applies to qualifying apprentices under the age of 25 with effect from 6 April 2016.

- From 6 April 2016, companies employing a sole director and no other paid staff at any time in the tax year are ineligible for the employment allowance, but the appointment of a second paid director or the employment of a single casual worker will protect the entitlement to the allowance.

16

Class 1A Contributions: Benefits in kind

Cross-references. See APPEALS AND REVIEWS **9** for remedies for dissatisfaction; ARREARS OF CONTRIBUTIONS **12** for recovery provisions; CATEGORISATION **14** for meaning of secondary contributor; COLLECTION **21**; EARNINGS FROM EMPLOYMENT: GENERAL **29** for payments in kind; EARNINGS FROM EMPLOYMENT: READILY CONVERTIBLE ASSETS, ETC **31**; ENFORCEMENT **35**.

Other Sources. Tolley's Income Tax 2017–18; Leaflets CWG5 (2018) and former CA33 (2015). See also HMRC Leaflet 480 (2018). See Tolley's Practical NIC Service, 1999, page 56 and HM Revenue and Customs National Insurance Manual NIM13000–NIM13190, NIM14001–NIM14610, NIM15001–NIM15750, NIM16001–NIM16650, NIM17000–NIM17560. HMRC Employer Bulletin October 2017.

Introduction to class 1A contributions: benefits in kind

[16.1] Class 1A contributions were initially introduced by *Social Security (Contributions) Act 1991* with effect from 6 April 1991 'to fill . . . an important gap in the National Insurance contributions system, as a result of which employers did not make contributions to the National Insurance fund if they paid their employees in cars rather than in cash' (Hansard 9 May 1991 col 849). The first such contributions were payable in respect of the year 1991–92. Until 5 April 2000, Class 1A contributions were charged only on the provision by employers of cars and fuel for private use in company cars but Class 1A liability was extended to most taxable benefits in kind after that date and, together with CLASS 1B CONTRIBUTIONS **17** they produced estimated income to the NATIONAL INSURANCE FUND **48** and NHS combined of around £1.4bn for 2017–18.

The principal HMRC guidance is in booklet CWG5 (and in the past in booklet CA33), available online. All references below are to the 2018 online edition of this guidance unless otherwise stated.

From 6 April 2000 employer National Insurance contributions are charged on all taxable benefits in kind. This was achieved by way of an extension to the original Class 1A structure (which until that time covered only cars and car fuel), rather than the creation of any new charge. These procedures are explained in more detail in this section and at **16.9** below.

Since 6 April 2000, the remuneration of employees paid by means of most benefits in kind are therefore captured within the revised Class 1A NICs net, in those cases where a Class 1 liability does not already arise.

Since 6 April 2015, earnings of employees under the age of 21 have attracted a nil rate of Class 1 secondary contribution, and from 6 April 2016 the same has applied to the earnings of apprentices under the age of 25. Note that this nil rate does **not** extend to Class 1A payable in respect of benefits in kind provided to under-21s or under-25 apprentices.

The Class 1A liability was, until 6 April 2016, limited to benefits in kind provided to P11D employees and directors, but it now applies in principle to almost all taxable benefits since the abolition from that date of the distinction between P9D (lower paid) and P11D (higher paid) employees by *FA 2015, s 13*. The former P9D 'lower paid' rules were retained by updated express statutory provisions in *Income Tax (Earnings and Pensions) Act 2003, ss 290–290G (ITEPA 2003)* for certain benefits provided for ministers of religion, and in *ITEPA 2003, s 306A* for benefits provided in connection with accommodation for live-in carers. These are now the only exceptions from Class 1A liability based on low earnings.

Reporting requirements

[16.2] The Class 1A return P11D(b) and existing P11D reports continue to be submitted to the usual PAYE offices but payment is now made to the employer's existing PAYE/NICs reference at the Accounts Office using a special payslip P30B(Class 1A) sent to employers each April, or online. The returns and payment under these arrangements are due on 19 July annually. If payment is made electronically, the time limit is extended to 22 July. There is no compulsion to pay Class 1A contributions electronically – even where the employer is of such size that Class 1 contributions (and PAYE, etc) do have to be so paid compulsorily (see **21.5** COLLECTION).

A Class 1A return is still required where the employer has elected to payroll benefits in kind from 6 April 2016, following the introduction of statutory 'PBIK' provisions by *Income Tax (Pay As You Earn) (Amendment No 4) Regulations 2015, SI 2015/1927*. The benefits should automatically have been removed from employees' PAYE codes by HMRC and should not be reported on Form P11D by the employer. However, the PBIK rules are purely a creature of tax statute: employers deduct PAYE in respect of the tax on the benefits but are not required to account for Class 1 contributions instead of Class 1A. Despite the fact that the benefits are removed from the P11D, they must still be included in accounting for the Class 1A liability on the P11D(b) at the end of the year. Software providers and HMRC are rewriting their software so that it is able to submit or accept a P11D(b) by 6 July 2017 without submitting or receiving corresponding P11Ds, which are no longer needed if all benefits are payrolled.

Exclusions from Class 1A

[16.3] Class 1A NICs do not apply to benefits in kind which are:

(a) not required to be reported via the P11D return arrangements because they are exempt from income tax [*SSCBA 1992, s 10(1)(a)*]; or
(b) covered by Class 1 NICs [*SSCBA 1992, s 10(1)(c)*] eg 'readily convertible assets'; or

(c) included in a PAYE Settlement Agreement (PSA) [*SSCBA 1992, s 10(6)*]; or
(d) exempt from Class 1 NICs [*Social Security (Contributions) Regulations 2001, SI 2001/1004, Reg 40(2), Sch 3*]; or
(e) earnings (previously 'emoluments') excluded from a person's earnings by virtue of *Sch 3, Part VII, para 3* (qualifying travelling expenses) or which are specific and distinct expenses of the employment as specified in *Sch 3, Part VIII, para 9* [*Social Security (Contributions) Regulations 2001, SI 2001/1004, Reg 40(3)*]; or
(f) removal expenses in respect of a qualifying move which occurred before 6 April 1988 which are not eligible removal expenses under *ITEPA 2003, ss 271–287* [*Social Security (Contributions) Regulations 2001, SI 2001/1004, Reg 40(4)*]; or
(g) specifically exempt from Class 1A NICs (*Reg 40(5)*). The only such item was child care (but not school fees) in respect of a child not exceeding the age of 16 but this exemption ceased with effect from 6 April 2005, in line with the tax changes introduced in *ITEPA 2003, s 318* and *Finance Act 2004, s 78, Sch 13*); or
(h) benefits under the various types of retirement benefit schemes covered by *ITEPA 2003, ss 386, 387, 389, 390, 590, 591* [*Social Security (Contributions) Regulations 2001, SI 2001/1004, Reg 40(6)(a)–(c)*]; or
(i) covered by those HM Revenue and Customs Extra-Statutory Concessions listed in *Reg 40(7)*; or
(j) provided for business use but where insignificant private use is allowed (*ITEPA 2003, s 316*) thereby bringing (a) above into play.

Until 2015–16 ended, no Class 1A liability arose in respect of benefits in kind provided for employees earning less than £8,500 per year, but this became irrelevant once the £8,500 limit for bringing employees into the benefits code was removed. [*SSCBA 1992, s 10(1)(b)*]. Benefits that were covered by a dispensation used to fall automatically under (a) above [*former ITEPA 2003, ss 65, 96, Sch 7, para 15*]. Dispensations were abolished on 5 April 2016 by *FA 2015, s 12*, but the payments to which they would have related (ie, payments that would have been deductible) were at the same time made exempt from tax, provided they were not made under relevant salary sacrifice arrangements and were not the home-to-work travel expenses of intermediary workers. Either of these types of payment will now constitute a payment of earnings that should be payrolled, so Class 1 should be payable instead of Class 1A.

All employees are now within the scope of the benefits code, but certain exemptions are provided for specific categories of income or employee so that, where no tax charge arises on a benefit, there is equally no Class 1A liability.

Note that the application of *ITEPA 2003, s 316(5)* will result in Class 1A being due in full where a motor vehicle (other than, from 6 April 2005, a van), boat, aircraft or an improvement to living accommodation is provided whether the private use is 'insignificant' or more extensive as these are 'excluded benefits'. In *Antique Buildings Ltd v HMRC* a company carried on a business of restoring old buildings. It owned a helicopter, which its controlling director used for private flying as well as for the company's business. The business use of the helicopter varied from 59% (in 2005–06) to 87% (in 2004–05). HMRC issued a ruling that the company was required to pay Class 1A national insurance contributions in respect of the helicopter. The company appealed, contending that it should be allowed a deduction under *ITEPA 2003, s 365* in respect of the business use of the helicopter. The First-Tier Tribunal accepted this contention and allowed the appeal. Judge Avery Jones observed that *SSCBA 1992, s 10(7)*, as amended by *ITEPA 2003* and as in force for 2003–04 to 2005–06, disallowed deductions under *ITEPA 2003, Part 5, Chs 2 and 5*. However it did not disallow a deduction under *ITEPA 2003, Part 5, Ch 3*, which was what the company was claiming here. *SSCBA 1992, s 10* was subsequently amended by *SI 2007/799* with effect from 6 April 2006 to add *ITEPA 2003, s 365* to the list of 'excluded provisions'. [2010] UKFTT 97, TC00408, so the apportionment allowed in this case is now precluded.

Note also that there can be no charge to Class 1A NIC if there is no tax charge. In *Willett Ltd v HMRC* (2012) TC02301, directors of the company paid the full cost of benefits provided to them by the company, thereby eliminating any charge to tax thereon by virtue of *ITEPA 2003, s 203(2)*. On the ground that there is no specific provision in the NIC legislation that a Class 1A charge shall be eliminated by full reimbursement, HMRC attempted to impose such a charge, a contention rejected by the Tribunal. See *TAXline*, the magazine of the ICAEW's Tax Faculty, December 2012, p 19.

A similar situation arose in *Revenue and Customs Comrs v Apollo Fuels Ltd* [2016] EWCA Civ 157, 166 NLJ 7693, [2016] All ER (D) 170 (Mar), in which HMRC had assessed a number of employees to tax on the cash equivalent of the benefit of a company car, and the employer to Class 1A on the same amount. The company had bought second-hand cars and leased them to employees at a market rate (ie, reflecting the reduced capital value of a second-hand vehicle in the leasing rentals). HMRC took the view, incorrectly, that a benefit arose under *ITEPA 2003, Part 3, Ch 6* applying the usual CO_2-based formula to the full list price, with a deduction allowed for the contribution made by the employees towards the private use. The company countered by arguing that, since the employees had paid open market value under a fair bargain with the company, and therefore had enjoyed no economic benefit from the arrangement, there could be no taxable benefit, a proposition with which both tribunals and the Court of Appeal agreed.

The case resulted in the government changing the law in *FA 2016, s 7* by inserting into *ITEPA 2003, s 114* (with backdated effect from 6 April 2016) a provision to the effect that the making available of a car or van should be taxed on the basis of the formula in *ITEPA 2003* irrespective of whether the terms on which it is made available to an employee constitute a fair bargain. Similar provision was made for living accommodation (*ITEPA 2003, s 97*) and beneficial loans (*ITEPA 2003, s 173*), albeit preserving the existing exception in the latter for public rate loans.

Paragraphs **16.12** to **16.32** below relate only to the provision of cars and fuel by employers for private use.

Pensions advice, generally speaking, has a tax exemption and therefore no Class 1A liability arises. However, there are various types of pensions advice that have different conditions attached to the tax exemption.

In respect of pensions advice provided, or the reimbursement of the cost of such advice, pertaining to conversions and transfers of pension benefits, no income tax liability (and thus no Class 1A liability) arises provided that three conditions are met:

(A) the provision, payment or reimbursement is required by regulations under *Pension Schemes Act 2015, s 49 or 52*;
(B) the provision, payment or reimbursement is not pursuant to relevant salary sacrifice arrangements; and
(C) such other requirements as may be specified in regulations made by the Treasury are satisfied in relation to the provision, payment or reimbursement.

No limit has been placed on the cost of this type of advice.

[*ITEPA 2003, s 308B; Social Security (Contributions) Regulations, SI 2001/1004, Sch 3, Part VI, para 12*].

A more limited exemption of up to £500 in a tax year is available in respect of:

- the provision of relevant pensions advice to an employee or former or prospective employee; or
- the payment or reimbursement of costs incurred, by or in respect of an employee or former or prospective employee, in obtaining relevant pensions advice.

Two conditions need to be met to obtain the exemption.

Condition A is that the relevant pensions advice, or payment or reimbursement, is provided under a scheme that is open:

(a) to the employer's employees generally; or
(b) generally to the employer's employees at a particular location.

Condition B is that the relevant pensions advice, or payment or reimbursement, is provided under a scheme that is open generally to the employer's employees, or generally to those of the employer's employees at a particular location, who:

(a) have reached the minimum qualifying age; or
(b) meet the ill-health condition.

[*ITEPA 2003, s 308C; Social Security (Contributions) Regulations, SI 2001/1004, Sch 3, Part VI, para 13*].

This type of advice can be provided under salary sacrifice arrangements, and is exempt from the OpRA regime, see **16.50**.

To complete the picture (although this does not impact on Class 1A or income tax), individuals can use up to £500 from their pension pot to pay for retirement financial advice. This facility can only be used once in any financial year, and no more than three times in total. The maximum amount that can be taken from the pension pot is thus £1,500. This can be used in conjunction with the £500 employer provided advice above, giving an employee a £1,000 allowance in a tax year.

Liability of the employer

[16.4] A Class 1A contribution is payable, by the employer only, for any tax year in respect of an earner (ie certain directors, employees and members of the family or household of an employee) to whom benefits are made available if:

- for that tax year, the earner is chargeable to income tax under *ITEPA 2003* (formerly Schedule E) on an amount of general earnings received by him from any employment; and
- the employment by reason of which the benefit is made available is both employed earner's employment (see **14.2** CATEGORISATION) and employment, other than an excluded employment, within the meaning of the benefits code (*ITEPA 2003, Chapter 2, Part 3*); and
- the whole or a part of the general earnings (previously, 'emoluments') falls, for the purpose of Class 1 contributions, to be left out of account in the computation of the earnings paid to or for the benefit of the earner.

[*SSCBA 1992, s 10(1)*, as amended by *ITEPA 2003, Schedule 6, paras 169, 174*].

As noted above, the benefits code applied until 5 April 2016 to directors and to those earning at a rate of £8,500 or more, but it now applies to all employees. The reform means that even benefits in kind with a low value provided to those who would previously have been P9D employees will now have to be reported on P11D and give rise to a Class 1A liability for the employer. The exception will be those non-contractual trivial benefits that are exempted from tax by *ITEPA 2003, ss 323A–323C*, introduced by *FA 2016, s 13*, which means that there can be no associated Class 1A liability for the employer.

The £8,500 limit (abolished April 2016)

[16.5] As already noted, Class 1A NICs were, until 5 April 2016, not payable on benefits provided to employees earning at a rate of less than £8,500 a year (often referred to as 'P9D employees'). [*SSCBA 1992, s 10(1)(b)*]. However the government issued a consultation paper in June 2014 proposing the abolition of the £8,500 limit for tax purposes as a simplification measure and this was legislated in *FA 2015*, albeit with a commencement date of 6 April 2016. All benefits in kind (with the exception of certain benefits provided to ministers of religion and live-in carers) will therefore be dealt with under the *ITEPA 2003* benefits code from 6 April 2016, but for 2015–16 for the last time there was no Class 1A liability in respect of benefits in kind provided to P9D employees.

The Class 1A charge now extends to 'returnable benefits' for all employees and directors. Before 6 April 2016, where a 'car' (see below) was made available (without transfer of title) only to an employed earner (or to members of his family or household) who was a 'company director' (see below) or who had 'general earnings' (see below) of £8,500 a year or more, and it was so available by reason of his employment and it was available for his (or their) travel other than 'business travel' (see below). In *GR Solutions Ltd v Revenue and Customs Comrs* [2012] UKFTT 234 (TC), it was held that a car in which the director in question had a 10% share, and towards the running costs of which he made a 10% contribution, was nevertheless 'made available' to him during the period he had use of it, and Class 1A NICs were due accordingly. In *S Barnard Ltd v Revenue and Customs Comrs* (TC00491) [2010] UKFTT 187(TC), the employer tried to take advantage of the £8,500 limit to provide an expensive car to the wife of the managing director as the whole of her remuneration for the occasional work she carried out for the company. Since the formula value of the benefit was below £8,500, she was a P9D employee, so the company did not report the benefit on a P11D. HMRC argued successfully that the car was in fact provided by reason of the husband's employment so that he owed income tax and the company owed Class 1A NICs. The tribunal felt able to side with HMRC because the employer produced no evidence to support its argument that it was normal for a small business to reward a part-time company secretary like Mrs B carrying out only light duties, so HMRC's views could not be displaced. Under the new rules from 6 April 2016, Mrs Barnard would automatically have a P11D benefit and the company a Class 1A liability.

From 6 April 2007 to 5 April 2016, those employees earning less than £8,500 who received a company car/fuel allowance and used their employer's credit card or vouchers were no longer subject to double counting for the purposes of computing benefits relevant to the £8,500 limit. [*ITEPA 2003, ss 7(5), 114, 120, 216–220; FA 2007, s 62*]. This replaced ESC A104 which came into effect in July 2004.

Definitions – general

[16.6] A *returnable benefit* (see **16.9** *et seq* below), is a benefit that is not excluded by reason of (a) to (j) above in 16.3 and is reportable on form P11D in respect of company directors and employees. Class 1A therefore now covers most true benefits in kind and the Table at **16.11** details the differing NICs treatment as between Class 1 and Class 1A. See CWG5 Appendix 1.

A '*company director*', in this context, is:

- in relation to a company whose affairs are managed by a board of directors or a similar body, a member of that body;
- in relation to a company whose affairs are managed by a single director or a similar person, that person;
- in relation to a company whose affairs are managed by the members themselves, a member of the company; or
- anyone (other than a professional adviser acting as such) in accordance with whose instructions the directors (as defined above) are accustomed to act (eg a controlling shareholder),

unless, either on his own or in conjunction with his associates and relatives, he does not own or control more than 5% of the company's ordinary share capital nor is entitled to receive more than 5% of the capital on winding up, and:

- he is required to devote substantially the whole of his time to the service of the company in a managerial or technical capacity; or

- the company
  - (a) does not carry on a trade and its functions do not consist wholly or mainly in the holding of investments or other property (this is referred to in the legislation as a 'non-profit-making' company), or
  - (b) is established for charitable purposes only.

[*ITEPA 2003, ss 67, 68, 216(3)*].

It is important to note that although certain full-time working directors etc may fall to be treated as being outside the scope of *ITEPA 2003* etc under the definition of 'company director' given above, those same directors may fall to be treated as within the scope of the charge by reason of the quantum of their 'general earnings'.

'*General earnings*' (previously, '*emoluments*'), in this context, includes all salaries, fees, pay, wages, overtime pay, leave pay, bonuses, commissions, perquisites, tips, gratuities, benefits in kind (whether provided to the employee himself or to members of his household or family), expense payments and allowances, before the deduction of any expenses allowable for tax purposes other than:

- contributions to a registered pension scheme in respect of which the individual is entitled to tax relief as an expense; and
- contributions under an approved payroll giving scheme;

and, for the purpose of deciding whether the general earnings amount to £8,500 or more, general earnings derived from two or more offices or employments with the same employer or from a number of offices or employments with inter-connected companies used to be treated as if they were general earnings derived from a single office or employment.
[*ITEPA 2003, ss 216–220*].

'*Business travel*', in this context, is travelling which a person is necessarily obliged to do in the performance of the duties of his employment. [*ITEPA 2003, ss 118(2), 171(1)*]. It does *not* include home-to-business travel.

Secondees abroad

[16.7] An area where the tax and NIC rules diverge is where an inbound expatriate employee remains under contract to his home country employer outside the UK and continues to pay contributions to his home country social security scheme; if, in such cases, no UK NIC is paid by the secondee, then there is no liability to Class 1A. See CWG5, para 27. Also, where no contributions treaty exists (eg Australia, New Zealand, etc) there is no Class 1 liability until the employee has been resident in the UK for 52 weeks and only then will Class 1A liability arise. (Tolley's Practical NIC, Vol 3, number 12, p 90).

A similar complication arises for outbound expatriate employees. When an employee leaves the UK for full-time work abroad for a foreign employer, NIC liability ceases even if tax liability does not (ie, because the worker does not break residence). If the employee is, in contrast, seconded by his UK employer for a period of full-time work abroad that spans a whole tax year, he will usually continue to be subject to UK social security law for at least 52 weeks, but he will generally cease to be UK tax-resident immediately on departure (tax residence will now depend on the statutory residence test and split-year rules introduced by *Finance Act 2013*, but that legislation is not directly relevant to Class 1A liability). His benefits in kind, even if provided in the UK (eg, medical insurance or company car for the family) will then be provided in respect of non-UK duties, the remuneration from which is generally not taxable in the UK, and they will not appear on his P11D or, in consequence, be liable to Class 1A contributions.

The person liable

[16.8] The charge to income tax as general earnings which arises by virtue of *ITEPA 2003, s 201* where a benefit is made available to an employee or director for his private use is on the employee or director himself; but the Class 1A contribution is payable by:

(a) the person who is liable to pay the secondary Class 1 contribution relating to the last (or only) 'relevant payment of earnings' in the tax year in relation to which there is a liability to pay such a contribution (see **14.32** CATEGORISATION); or
(b) if no such contribution is payable in relation to a relevant payment of earnings in the tax year, the person who, if the benefit in respect of which the Class 1A contribution is payable were earnings in respect of which Class 1 contributions would be payable, would be liable to pay those secondary Class 1 contributions; or
(c) the third party provider of non-cash incentives and benefits can be liable for Class 1A contributions from 6 April 2000 rather than the employer and is, in any event, so liable without exception from 6 April 2001.

See also CWG5, para 6.

[*SSCBA 1992, s 10(2)* as amended by *Social Security Act 1998, s 52; Child Support, Pensions and Social Security Act 2000; ITEPA 2003, Schedule 6, para 174; SSCBA 1992, s 10ZA, s 10ZB* as amended by *Child Support, Pensions and Social Security Act 2000, s 76(1)*].

The above item (b) would, for instance, apply in circumstances where a retired director still receives the use of a company car but has no other source of general earnings from the company. See CWG5, para 47. Prior to the change on 8 September 1998, no Class 1A charge could have arisen because there were no earnings (even below the Lower Earnings Limit) subject to Class 1.

For these purposes, a '*relevant payment of earnings*' is defined as 'a payment of earnings . . . made to or for the benefit of an earner in respect of the relevant employment'. [*SSCBA 1992, s 10(3)*].

Where, in relation to his employment, an earner is paid by one person but has benefits made available to him by another, the effect of these provisions is to impose a Class 1A charge on the person paying the earner, not on the person who makes the benefits available.

> *Example*
>
> Aston is a sales representative. Throughout 2018–19, his contract of service is with Beetle and they pay Aston his salary and commission. He is provided with a car and private medical insurance; but the car he uses is owned and made available to him by Caddy, Beetle's parent company, which also pays the medical insurance premium. Because Aston has been provided with benefits and private use of the car, he is chargeable to income tax on an amount arrived at under *ITEPA 2003, ss 201–203*, and, in consequence, a Class 1A contribution is payable for 2018–19 in respect of Aston and the benefits provided to him. But, because the secondary Class 1 contribution on the last payment of earnings made to Aston in 2018–19 is paid by Beetle, Beetle must pay the Class 1A contribution even though Caddy, not Beetle, is the person who owns the car and paid for the medical insurance.

Where a person works successively for two or more employers in a tax year and is provided with benefits in respect of each employment for private use, *SSCBA 1992, s 10(1)(2)* ensures that a Class 1A contribution will be payable in respect of each employment.

> *Example*
>
> Herald works for Integra until 5 January 2019 when he changes jobs and takes up employment with Jetta. He is provided with a car (which is available for his private use) in each job. A tax charge will arise in respect of each car for 2018–19 so a Class 1A contribution will be payable in respect of each car for that year. Integra will pay secondary Class 1 contributions in relation to Herald's last earnings in his employment with Integra so Integra will be liable to pay a Class 1A contribution in respect of the car provided in that job, while Jetta will pay secondary Class 1 contributions in relation to Herald's last earnings in the tax year so Jetta will be liable to pay a Class 1A contribution in respect of the car provided in the second job.

In such circumstances, each Class 1A charge will reflect the length of time for which the car has been made available.

Where a person succeeds to a business and pays general earnings to a person who was an employee in the business before the succession took place, the successor employer will be liable for the whole of any Class 1A contribution which is payable in respect of the employee for the tax year of change as the successor employer will be the person making the last 'relevant payment of earnings' to the earner in the tax year.

> *Example*
>
> Octavia works for Panda by whom she is provided with a car which is available for her private use. In October 2018, Panda sells his business to Qashqai and Qashqai continues to employ Octavia and to allow her the private use of the car. As Qashqai will pay a secondary Class 1 contribution in relation to Octavia's last payment of earnings in 2018–19 in respect of the employment by reason of which the car is made available, he (to the exclusion of Panda) will be liable to pay the entire Class 1A contribution for the year in respect of the car – and any other benefits in kind – provided throughout the year.

If, of course, Octavia had left Panda's employment before the change took place, the Class 1A liability in respect of the car provided to her from 6 April 2018 to the date of her leaving would, for the same reason, rest with Panda.

Returnable benefits and computation

[16.9] Where a liability to pay a Class 1A contribution arises, the amount of that contribution is the 'Class 1A percentage' of the amounts which fall under *ITEPA 2003* to be treated as general earnings and which are left out of account in the computation of earnings for Class 1 purposes. [*SSCBA 1992, s 10(4)*, as amended by *ITEPA 2003, Sch 6, para 174*].

The '*Class 1A percentage*' is a rate equivalent to the secondary Class 1 percentage rate appropriate for the tax year in question, ie 13.8% for 2017–18 and 2018–19. See RATES AND LIMITS 53. [SSCBA 1992, s 10(5)]. It is not reduced to nil% for employees under the age of 21 or apprentices under the age of 25, since the age-related secondary percentage applies only to Class 1 secondary contributions.

Business and private expenses

[16.10] In the case of most benefits where there is a mixture of both business use and private use, the full amount of the benefit will be chargeable to Class 1A NICs. However, where the private element is insignificant then there is a relaxation. 'Insignificant' is not defined in legislation nor in CWG5, para 7 nor are 'on premises' benefits or those provided off the work premises. In the latter case CWG5 goes on to give two examples regarding a fax machine and a telephone. CWG5, para 7 states that ' . . . no Class 1A NICs are payable when you provide benefits off your premises, as long as your sole purpose in providing the benefit is so that the employee can carry out his or her duties . . . If this exemption does not apply (for instance, if the private use is *not insignificant*, or the benefit is a motor vehicle, boat, aeroplane or an improvement to living accommodation) Class 1A NICs will be due'. This therefore would seem to preclude the use of tools by the individual over the weekend but would apply if the individual returned home directly from a job and used the tool that evening only. The distinction is obviously very fine and one can imagine the regular use of an employer's laptop computer used at home over the weekend by the individual to surf the Internet might not be considered 'insignificant', in the absence of the separate relief (until 6 April 2006) for employer-provided computers.

HMRC's table of expenses

[16.11] CWG5 Appendix 1 contains a helpful table of expenses and their treatment distinguishing between the Class 1 and Class 1A NICs charge. However, the table is not comprehensive and even CWG5 states that it has no legal force. The table can be obtained from www.gov.uk/government/publications/cwg5-class-1a-national-insurance-contributions-on-benefits-in-kind/2016-class-1a-national-insurance-contributions-on-benefits-in-kind#app1.

The HM Revenue and Customs list and notes in CWG5 should be read in conjunction with the P11D (2017 to 2018) and P11D(b) expenses, benefits and Class 1A NICs returns 2017–18. In a majority of benefit cases, Class 1A contributions will be due on the full amount of the benefit where there is a mixture of private use but see above for where private use is insignificant. Further commentary on vans, works buses, childcare, telephones and mobiles, computers, relocation expenses, loans, medical benefits, holiday homes abroad and credit cards can be found at **16.33–16.49** below. Also note that from 6 April 2011 if an employer sets up a salary sacrifice arrangement either before or after the employment commences where the employee gives up any earnings in return for free or subsidised meals then the exemption in the table explicitly will not apply. The provisions relate to 'relevant salary sacrifice arrangements' ie the forgoing of general or specific earnings from that employer, or 'relevant flexible remuneration arrangements' ie forgoing some other description of employment income and this could apply to performance related bonuses. [*FA 2010, s 62*]. HMRC launched in August 2016 a consultation on tightening the rules on salary sacrifice arrangements in order to deny tax and NIC advantages, albeit with no proposals to restrict such arrangements in relation to pension contributions, childcare or employee health-related benefits such as cycle-to-work schemes. Following the consultation, restrictions were placed on the tax and NICs advantages arising when benefits in kind are provided under salary sacrifice and other, such as 'flex schemes', arrangements. See **16.50** Salary sacrifice/Optional remuneration arrangements below.

Cars, vans and fuel

Definition — cars

[16.12] Following the April 2000 changes to the Class 1A system, such liability continues to arise in respect of the provision of company cars and also fuel for company cars.

A '*car*' is any mechanically propelled road vehicle other than:

- a vehicle of a construction primarily suited for the conveyance of goods or burden of any description, eg a lorry or pickup truck;
- a vehicle of a type not commonly used, and not suitable to be used, as a private vehicle, eg a Grand Prix racing car. (In *Gurney v Richards* (1989) 62 TC 287, it was held that an official car, fitted with a flashing light, which a deputy fire officer was required to use when on call, was unsuitable for use as a private vehicle.) As to emergency vehicles, see further below;
- a motor cycle or an invalid carriage (within the terms of *Road Traffic Act 1988, s 185(1)*).

See *ITEPA 2003, s 115(1)* and former leaflet CA33 (2015), para 12.

Fuel is provided for this purpose if:

- any liability in respect of the provision of fuel for the car is discharged;
- a non-cash voucher or a credit-token is used to obtain fuel for the car or money which is spent on such fuel;
- any sum is paid in respect of expenses incurred in providing fuel for the car;

but no charge is imposed in respect of such fuel if the fuel is made available *only* for business travel. [*ITEPA 2003, ss 151(3), 721(1)*].

HMRC considers '*price*' to be the manufacturer's, importer's or distributor's list price on the day before it was first registered and delivery charges, taxes (but not road tax nor the car registration fee) are included. Also included are accessories and the cost of fitting them. As well as the invoice, specialist lists such as Glass's Guide or GAP Nationwide Motor Research Limited can also be used (CA National Insurance News, Issue 4, page 4). Some questions have been raised as to the meaning of 'distributor' for the purposes of gauging the list price. HM Revenue and Customs remains of the opinion that the list price that matters is the manufacturer's, importer's or distributor's published list price (see also former leaflet CA33 (2015), paras **20**, **21**, **29**).

CO_2 emissions charge

[16.13] From 6 April 2002, a percentage charge based on carbon dioxide emissions is applied to the list price of the car as per the Table below. 'List price' is defined as the inclusive price, including any accessories, published by the car's manufacturer, importer or distributor, in respect of a single UK retail sale in the open market, on the day before the car's first registration. It includes delivery costs and car tax. No account can be taken of bulk purchase terms or other favourable discounts. [*ITEPA 2003, ss 122–123*].

CO_2 emissions tables

[16.14] The following CO_2 emissions tables are taken from booklet 480 (2018), Appendix 2, and the Budget 2016 announcements (legislated in *FA 2016, ss 8–10*), and are for petrol cars. Diesel cars until at least 5 April 2021 incur a 3% surcharge on the figures shown below, but the maximum percentage will always be as shown in the table. Note that the 3% diesel surcharge was increased to 4% from April 2018 for those diesel vehicles that do not meet the Real Driving Emissions 2 (RDE2) standard.

CO_2 band	2016–17	2017–18	2018–19	2019–20
Zero	7%	9%	13%	16%
1–50	7%	9%	13%	16%
51–75	11%	13%	16%	19%
76–94	15%	17%	19%	22%
95	16%	18%	20%	23%
100	17%	19%	21%	24%
105	18%	20%	22%	25%
110	19%	21%	23%	26%
115	20%	22%	24%	27%
120	21%	23%	25%	28%
125	22%	24%	26%	29%
130	23%	25%	27%	30%
135	24%	26%	28%	31%
140	25%	27%	29%	32%
145	26%	28%	30%	33%
150	27%	29%	31%	34%

CO_2 band	2016–17	2017–18	2018–19	2019–20
155	28%	30%	32%	35%
160	29%	31%	33%	36%
165	30%	32%	34%	37%
170	31%	33%	35%	37%
175	32%	34%	36%	37%
180	33%	35%	37%	37%
185	34%	36%	37%	37%
190	35%	37%	37%	37%
195	36%	37%	37%	37%
200+	37%	37%	37%	37%

From 6 April 2016 the emissions-based percentage rose by 2% at all levels, except that the maximum remained at 37%. Further increases are scheduled for all years up to 5 April 2020 as indicated. The 3% diesel surcharge was scheduled to cease to apply from 6 April 2016, so that the sole focus of the scale would become the carbon dioxide emissions of the vehicle, but this legislation was repealed by *FA 2016, s 10* in order to raise £1.3bn in extra taxes.

The diesel surcharge was increased to 4% from 6 April 2018 for those diesel cars that do not meet the Real Driving Emissions 2 (RDE2) standard. Where cars are certified to the RDE2 standard, then the diesel surcharge will be removed completely. [*Finance Act 2018, s 9*].

See earlier editions of this work for appropriate percentages for years before 6 April 2016. In particular, from 6 April 2006 until 5 April 2011, the emissions-based percentage was discounted by:

- for diesels meeting Euro IV standards, 3% (in other words, the 3% diesel supplement was waived) if the car was registered before 1 January 2006;
- for petrol/battery hybrids, 3%;
- for cars running on gas and petrol bi-fuel, 2%.

From 6 April 1998, any premium on the price of a car which is manufactured to run on road fuel gases has been disregarded when calculating the car's price. Road fuel gas means any substance which is gaseous at a temperature of 15°C and under pressure of 1013.25 millibars, and which is for use as fuel in road vehicles. Currently, the two types of fuel in use which fall within this definition are compressed natural gas and liquid petroleum gas. [*ITEPA 2003, ss 146, 171*]. (See also former leaflet CA33 paras 18, 24).

From 6 April 2008 until 5 April 2011, there was a 2% discount for cars capable of being run on E85 fuel (fuel which consists of at least 85% bio-ethanol, the balance unleaded petrol). In 2010–11 and subsequent tax years the lower threshold of grams of carbon dioxide emissions per kilometre was reduced from 135 g/km to 130 g/km and to 125 g/km for 2011–12. Also, from 6 April 2010 for a five-year period the charge for all electric cars (ie, zero tailpipe emissions) was zero. [*ITEPA 2003, s 139* as amended by *FA 2009, Sch 28 paras 6, 9*; *FA 2009, Sch 28 para 6; FA 2010, s 60*].

From 6 April 2011 there are no discounts but the temporary reduction in respect of electric vehicles to 0% until 2014–15 continued to be given by secondary legislation. [*ITEPA 2003, ss 139, 140(3)(a)* as amended by *FA 2009, Sch 28 paras 6, 7, 9, 10*; *FA 2009, Sch 28 paras 6, 7; FA 2010, s 60*].

There was a '10%' band (13% for diesel) from 6 April 2008 for cars with a CO2 emissions figure of exactly 120 g/km or lower as the normal rounding did not apply to this band. Such cars were called 'qualifying low emissions cars' in the legislation, QUALECs for short. Apart from diesel, no other reduction which is available on other cars applied to QUALECs (from 2012–13 the special rules for QUALECs were no longer required). As a result, the only possible figures for the appropriate percentage for QUALECs were 13%—cars to which the diesel supplement applied, and 10%—all other cars. This was also the case for electric-only cars which therefore retained their net appropriate percentage of 9% in all cases until 6 April 2010, and 0% on and after that date.

Prior to April 2006, the emissions based percentage (15% or more) was discounted by:

- for cars running on electricity only, 6% (ie to 9%, as emissions were zero);
- for petrol/battery hybrids registered on or after 1 January 1998, 1% plus a further 1% for each 20g/km by which the emissions were less than the minimum charge;
- for diesels meeting Euro IV standards, 3% (in other words, the 3% diesel supplement was waived). However, as the Euro IV standards became compulsory EC Directives required that financial incentives such as the waiver were withdrawn and so from 6 April 2006 the 3% waiver was no longer applicable for cars registered from 1 January 2006. Cars registered before 1 January 2006 continued to benefit from the waiver;
- for cars registered on or after 1 January 1998 and running on gas, 1%, plus a further 1% for each 20g/km by which the emissions were less than the minimum charge;
- for gas/petrol hybrids the discount varied but it was as for cars running on gas alone if the car was built after 31 December 1999 to run on both petrol and gas.

For cars costing more than £80,000, the price was – prior to 6 April 2011 – restricted to £80,000, but the cap was then removed, increasing the taxable benefit and associated Class 1A charge significantly for luxury cars and 'supercars'.

[*The Income Tax (Car Benefits) (Reduction of Value of Appropriate Percentage) Regs 2001, SI 2001/1123* as amended by *The Income Tax (Car Benefits) (Reduction of Value of Appropriate Percentage) (Amendment) Regs 2005, SI 2005/2209, Reg 2; Income Tax (Car Benefits) (Reduction of Value of Appropriate Percentage) (Revocation) Regs 2001, SI 2010/659*].

Further tightening of the screws on manufacturers of fleet cars, by lowering the starting point of the CO_2 scale or raising the maximum percentage of the list price, may be expected, as it encourages more efficient engine design, thereby cutting emissions, and raises more tax and Class 1A contributions. The Budget 2015 announcement of increases in the carbon dioxide percentages in future periods was stated to raise around £1.49bn in extra tax and Class 1A NIC, and the Budget 2016 report forecast extra revenues of around £2bn from the reform of the taxation of company cars and vans over five years.

From tax year 2020–21, changes will come into effect for ultra-low emission vehicles (ULEVs) that reflect their 'electric range', ie the number of miles that can be driven in electric mode without recharging the battery. The CO_2 and electric range are detailed in the table below:

Car	Appropriate Percentage
Car with CO_2 emissions figure of 0	2%
Car with CO_2 emissions figure of 1–50 and with	
• electric range figure of 130 miles or more	2%
• electric rangc figurc of 70–129 miles	5%
• electric range figure of 40–69 miles	8%
• electric range figure of 30–39 miles	12%
• electric range figure of under 30 miles	14%
Car with CO_2 emissions figure of 51–54	15%
Car with CO_2 emissions figure of 55–59	16%
Car with CO_2 emissions figure of 60–64	17%
Car with CO_2 emissions figure of 65–69	18%
Car with CO_2 emissions figure of 70–74	19%

Note the reduction in the CO_2 emission level for vehicles considered to be 'low emission' from '75g/km or less' to 'under 75g/km'.

At the same time, the 'appropriate percentage' will become 20% and will apply to cars with an emissions figure of 75g/km and which then increases by 1% for each 5g/km by which the CO_2 emissions figure exceeds 75 (up to a maximum of 37%). The percentages (for petrol driven cars) from 2020–21 are detailed below together with the 2019–20 percentages for comparison.

2019–20		2020–21	
CO_2 band	% Charge	CO_2 band	% Charge
Zero	16%	Zero	See table above
1–50	16%	1–50	See table above
51–75	19%	51–74	See table above
76–94	22%	75–79	20%
76–94	22%	80–84	21%
76–94	22%	85–89	22%
76–94	22%	90–94	23%
95	23%	95	24%
100	24%	100	25%
105	25%	105	26%
110	26%	110	27%
115	27%	115	28%

2019–20		2020–21	
CO_2 band	% Charge	CO_2 band	% Charge
120	28%	120	29%
125	29%	125	30%
130	30%	130	31%
135	31%	135	32%
140	32%	140	33%
145	33%	145	34%
150	34%	150	35%
155	35%	155	36%
160	36%	160	37%
165+	37%	165+	37%

[*Finance (No 2) Act 2017, s 2(2)*].

CO_2 emissions table – cars registered prior to 1998 or no CO_2 rating

[16.15] The appropriate percentage for cars first registered before 1 January 1998 and cars registered after that date with no approved CO_2 emissions figure is based on the car's engine size as follows:

Engine Size	*Registered after 1997 with no approved CO_2 emissions figure*				
	2016–17	2017–18	2018–19	2019–20	2020–21
0–1,400cc	16	18	20	23	24
1,401cc –2,000cc	27	29	31	34	35
over 2,000cc	37	37	37	37	37
Rotary engine	37	37	37	37	37

Engine Size	*Registered before 1 January 1998 (%)*				
	2016–17	2017–18	2018–19	2019–20	2020–21
0–1,400cc	16	18	20	23	24
1,401cc –2,000cc	27	29	31	34	35
over 2,000cc	37	37	37	37	37
Rotary engine	37	37	37	37	37

[*Finance (No 2) Act 2017, s 2(3), (4)*].

If the engine can under no circumstances emit CO_2, the percentage was reduced to nil for 2010–15, was set at 5% for 2015–16, 7% from 6 April 2016 and then 9% from 6 April 2017, 13% from 6 April 2018 and 16% from 6 April 2019.

Disabled drivers

[16.16] Certain accessories needed by disabled persons who qualify for a 'blue badge' to enable them to drive the car may be disregarded, with effect from 6 April 1995, in calculating the list price. This not only includes accessories specifically designed for disabled drivers such as special steering wheels but also features which are of particular assistance to disabled drivers such as electric windows and automatic transmission, provided they are not standard accessories. If, under *sections 122–124*, the price of the automatic car is more than it would have been if the automatic car had been an equivalent manual car, the price of the automatic car is to be the price of an equivalent manual car. [*ITEPA 2003, ss 124A, 125; FA 2009, s 54.*] (See also former leaflet CA33 para 33).

Second-hand cars

[16.17] The list price of second-hand cars is more difficult to determine but the former Contributions Agency stated that they would accept the reported price agreed for tax purposes. The price paid by the employer is irrelevant to the formula-based calculation of the cash equivalent. As noted above, in *Apollo Fuels Ltd*, the company's employees avoided a car and fuel benefit by paying the full market rate leasing rental that was based on the second-hand value when the employer bought the cars, and the company argued successfully in the Court of Appeal that a fair bargain between employer and employee, with no economic benefit to the employee, could not reasonably give rise to a taxable benefit. However, *FA 2016* has now changed the rules so that fair bargains are disregarded, with only the formula-based cash equivalent applying to calculate whether the employee should pay tax (even if full market value is paid as the employee's contribution) and whether the employer should pay Class 1A NICs, on the provision of a company car.

For cars which are more than 15 years old, which have a market value of at least £15,000, and which have appreciated in value since they were first purchased (referred to as classic cars in the legislation), the cash equivalent is the market value on the last day in the tax year that the car was available to the employee. [*ITEPA 2003, s 147*]. Values of classic cars may be determined by recent valuations for insurance purposes, prices in the 'market' or published prices. The value was – prior to 6 April 2011 – restricted to £80,000. (See also leaflet CA33 paras 36–39).

Optional accessories

[16.18] The list price is increased by the cost of optional accessories, excluding mobile telephones. If an accessory costing more than £100 is added after the car is first made available, then the cost of that accessory is added to the list price of the car for each year during any part of which it is available provided that the accessory was first made available after 31 July 1993. [*ITEPA 2003, ss 126, 127*]. Certain accessories for disabled drivers may be disregarded from 6 April 1995 as well as, from 6 April 1998, equipment which enables the car to run on road fuel gas. From 6 April 2012 certain accessories intended to improve the safety of the employee are disregarded. [*ITEPA 2003, ss 125, 125A* (as amended by the *Finance Act 2012, s 14*),*146, 172*]. (See also leaflet CA33 paras 26–31).

If an employee makes a capital contribution towards the provision of the car or accessories, that contribution, limited to a maximum of £5,000, is deducted from the list price in the year that the contribution is made, and in all subsequent years. [*ITEPA 2003, s 132*]. (See also former leaflet CA33 paras 34–35).

Note that a 'personalised plate' or 'cherished number' transferred onto a company car is not an accessory for these purposes: the two pieces of plastic cost less than £100. The benefit to the employee is the right to use the number in question on his company car, which is already covered by the scale charge. If the right to a personalised number is made available to an employee for use on his own car, not within the scale charge rules, the income tax charge is based on 20% of the market value when first made available as a benefit, and the Class 1A liability is based on that taxable value.

Leased or owned personally

[16.19] Where cars are owned or leased personally by employees under a group scheme arranged by the employer (ie, the employee contracts personally with the leasing company, but on terms negotiated by the employer) and provided the scheme was properly set up there are no car benefit or fuel benefit charges as the car is not being provided by the employer. See HM Revenue and Customs National Insurance Manual NIM05770.

In the case *Vasili v Christensen (Inspector of Taxes)*, [2003] STC (SCD) 428, V – a company director – entered into joint ownership of a car with his employer, with V owning 5% and the employer 95%. The Special Commissioners held that car benefit and fuel scale charges could not be applied because there had been some transfer of ownership. However, this decision was overturned on the Revenue's appeal to the High Court (Chancery Division). Had the mixed ownership been successful then V would have been assessable to tax on only 20% charge of the annual value and there would have been no Class 1A National Insurance contributions until the general charge on all benefits was introduced in 2000. However, from that time the Class 1A charge would have been on the whole 20% charge without any reduction for business use due to the mixed use rule in *SSCBA 1992, s 10(7A)*.

In a more recent case a company (S) arranged for a leasing company (D) to lease two Mercedes motor vehicles to its directors. S failed to account for Class 1A NICs. HMRC issued a notice under *SSCTFA 1999, s 8* charging Class 1A contributions. S appealed against the notice, contending that it had acted as a nominee for the directors and should not be required to account for contributions. The First-Tier Tribunal rejected this contention and dismissed the appeals, finding that the directors 'had not made any attempt to execute any agency or nominee arrangement'. The relevant contract had been signed between S and D, and S would have been liable to D if it had defaulted on the payments. Furthermore, 'even if there had been such an agreement, the legislation was not concerned with agency or any other law. It stipulated the correct tax treatment to be used when an employer provides a car for its employees. The contract was in the name of the company, the legislation was satisfied and so a benefit arose.' (The Tribunal also dismissed appeals by the directors against closure notices charging income tax.) *Stanford Management Services Ltd v HMRC (and related appeals)* [2010] UKFTT98, TC00409. See also *A Whitby v HMRC (and related appeal)* [2009] UKFTT 311, TC00255.

As already noted above, *Apollo Fuels v Revenue and Customs Comrs* [2013] UKFTT 350, [2014] UKUT 0095 and [2016] EWCA Civ 157 concerned car leasing arrangements, where the employee leased a car from the employer, who had bought it second-hand and owned it, for the market lease rate (ie, the employer had benchmarked the rental it charged against open market rates for a car of that value). HMRC argued unsuccessfully that, where the lease charges paid by the employee were less than the CO_2-based scale charge, then there should be a liability to the scale charge (and Class 1A liability). The tribunals found that the benefits code charge could not be in point where there was no economic benefit to the employee, who was required to pay the full market rate to lease the car from the employer. There was also an alternative argument about whether, because the employee was free to lease the car on to a third party, the provision of the car represented money's worth and was therefore taken outside the scope of the benefits code by *ITEPA 2003, s 114(3)*. The tribunals upheld the company's contention, but that subsection was deleted by *FA 2014, s 23* with effect from 6 April 2014. See also an article by Oliver Marre, junior counsel for the taxpayer in *Apollo*, in *Taxation*, 6 June 2013. The fact that the employer won the case with an argument that there was no economic benefit, and therefore no possible taxable benefit, to the employees, led to a second change in the law from 6 April 2016 by *FA 2016, s 7* to ensure that, even where an employee pays the employer the full market rate for the provision of a benefit, as happened in *Apollo Fuels*, the statutory formula for calculating the benefit nevertheless still applies. The new (tax-raising) principle also applies to two other formula-based benefits in kind: the provision of living accommodation and cheap loans, with specified exceptions, so that the tax and Class 1A charges cannot be avoided.

Cash conversion

[16.20] In some instances where the benefit of a car was freely convertible into cash, the benefit of providing a car would have been taxable under the general income tax rules rather than the special provisions for company cars and would thus have fallen outside the pre-2000 Class 1A net. This led many employers to offer a cash alternative that was £5 higher than the formula- or table-based benefit of the car, to ensure that the cash alternative overrode the formula or table value. These cash alternative schemes meant that some employers avoided their Class 1A NIC liability because the early Class 1A rules relied on there being a cash equivalent based on the table or formula rather than a simple earnings charge based on the cash alternative. In order to rectify this loophole, where a cash alternative was offered, the employer had to pay Class 1A NICs if the employee had the benefit of the car or Class 1 NICs if the employee took the cash alternative. Employers were so liable from 6 April 1995 onwards. (CA National Insurance News, Issue 2, page 1 and *ITEPA 2003, s 119*.)

Car fuel provided for private use

[16.21] Fuel is provided for the purpose of this charge if:

- any liability in respect of the provision of private use fuel for the car is discharged;
- a non-cash voucher or a credit-token is used to obtain fuel for the car or money which is spent on such fuel;
- any sum is paid in respect of expenses incurred in providing fuel for the car;

but no charge is imposed in respect of such fuel if the fuel is made available *only* for business travel. [*ITEPA 2003, ss 151(3), 721(1)*].

From 2003–04 onwards, the cash equivalent of the benefit of fuel supplied for private use is ascertained by reference to the CO_2 emissions of the employee's company car so that, like the car benefit charge in **16.12** above, the amount the employee is penalised will depend largely on the type of car he/she is driving. The percentage derived from the table above is charged on a fixed figure which has been specified as £23,400 for 2018–19 (£22,600 for 2017–18). [*Van Benefit and Car and Van Fuel Benefit Order 2017, SI 2017/1176*].

Also, from 2003–04 onwards the annual fuel charge may be time-apportioned where fuel ceases to be provided for private use – even though the car itself may still be provided – unless such provision is resumed before the end of the same tax year. Previously, the fuel charge was not removed by the mere cessation of provision of private fuel part way through a tax year, unless the car itself was changed or no car at all was then provided. [*The Car Benefit Order 2008, SI 2008/511; Car and Van Fuel Benefit Order 2010, SI 2010/406*]. (See also former leaflet CA33 para 59).

In respect of fuel provided for private use there was originally a possibility that both Class 1A and Class 1 NICs could arise at the same time. However, the Contributions Agency never intended such a dual liability and did not pursue the Class 1 NICs which arose. (See CA National Insurance News, Issue 4, page 8. Also, CA Press Release 96/1, 15 March 1996.) This practice was given the force of law from 6 April 2001 with the insertion of *Social Security (Contributions) Regulations 2001, SI 2001/1004, Sch 3 Part VIII para 7*.

Car used for business purposes

[16.22] From 6 April 2002 there is no discount for business mileage driven and the current system is based only on a percentage of the car's list price graduated according to the carbon dioxide emissions of that particular car.

Additional cars

[16.23] From 6 April 2002 there is no additional charge, as there once was, where two or more cars are provided for the private use of an employee.

There may in the past have been occasions where a car was provided to a family member earning less than £8,500 pa where it was not normal for the employment for a car to be provided and it will therefore have fallen to be taxed an another family member. As already noted, this was the outcome in *S Barnard Ltd v HMRC*, [2010] UKFTT 187 (TC), TC00491. A family company carried on a plumbing business and provided its company secretary (who was the wife of the controlling director) with a BMW car, costing about £32,000. The company failed to account for Class 1A National Insurance contributions in respect of the car. HMRC issued a ruling that the company was required to pay Class 1A contributions. The company appealed, contending that the provision of the car was 'normal commercial practice', within *ITEPA 2003, s 169(4)*. The First-Tier Tribunal rejected this contention and dismissed the appeal, finding that the company had provided insufficient evidence to support its claim.

Cars more than four years old

[16.24] From 6 April 2002 there has been no discount, as there once was, for the age of the car. The current system is based merely on a percentage of the car's list price graduated according to the carbon dioxide emissions of that particular car (except for the very small number of pre-1998 cars still in use as company cars, for which engine size and type are relevant). See **16.13** above.

Reduction for periods when car not available for use

[16.25] If, for any part of any relevant tax year, the car in question is 'unavailable' for at least 30 days, the car benefits as described at **16.12** above are, for *tax* purposes, to be *reduced* by multiplying them by the fraction

$$\frac{365 - \textit{number of days of unavailability}}{365}$$

From 2003–04 (which was itself a leap year) the actual number of days (ie 366 days in a leap year) is to be used in the above formula and this therefore also affected 2007–08, 2011–12 and 2015–16. [*ITEPA 2003, s 143(3)*]. Previously, the figure of 365 in the equation was always used, even if the year was a leap year.

A car is to be treated as 'unavailable' for a particular day if:

(a) it was not made available to the employee until after that day; or
(b) it had ceased to be available to him before that day; or
(c) it was incapable of being used at all throughout a period of not less than 30 consecutive days of which that day was one.

[*ITEPA 2003, s 143* and see also CA33, para 60].

The former Contributions Agency confirmed that the car would not be regarded as unavailable for use when the employee/director is disqualified from driving, nor when he is on an overseas business trip lasting more than 30 days, unless the car is in fact no longer available to the employee/director or his family. (*Letter from CA to local General Practitioners Group*).

> *Example*
>
> Kadett takes up employment by Legend on 2 June 2017 and a fleet car, a petrol driven, 1,800 cc car, with CO_2 emissions of 125 grams per kilometre with an original list price of £15,000 is made available for his business and private use.

Petrol is also provided. On 15 June, Kadett is involved in an accident and the car is off the road until 8 July. On 21 September, Kadett is involved in another accident and this time the car is off the road until 29 October. On 2 November, Kadett is moved into a clerical post within the company where he no longer has the use of a company car. The cash equivalent of the car and fuel benefits for 2017–18 are £3,600 (£15,000 × 24%) and £5,424 (£22,600 × 24%) respectively, but the car is unavailable for 57 days at the start of the tax year, for 37 days in September/October, and for 155 days at the end of the tax year. The period of repair in June/July does not count as unavailability because it lasted for only 22 consecutive days. The cash equivalents of £3,600 and £5,424 are, therefore, reduced by 249/365 to £1,144 and £1,724.

The same rules apply for Class 1A purposes except that a car is *not* to be regarded as unavailable for a day under (iii) above unless the person liable to pay the Class 1A contribution has information to show that the condition specified at (c) above is satisfied as regards the day in question. [former *SSCBA 1992, s 10(6)(a)*]. The nature of the information required by this provision is discussed at **16.12** above.

A specimen letter is shown below:

Specimen Letter

Legend Ltd

Kadett

. . . .

. . . .

Dear K,

Provision of company car and fuel

The company has decided that, with immediate effect, it shall no longer provide you with a company vehicle for either business and/or private use.

You are required to return the vehicle . . . . [make, model] . . . . [Reg no.] . . . . to . . . . [Name] . . . . at . . . . [Location] . . . . by . . . . [Time] . . . . on . . . . [Date] . . . . along with all sets of ignition and related keys. You will wish to remove all personal possessions before doing so.

On return from . . . . [Country] /the end of your disqualification/the company will consider whether to make available the same, or another, company vehicle, which may or may not extend to permission to use such vehicle for non-business travel.

Reduction for employee paying for use of car and/or fuel

[16.26] If, in the relevant tax year, an employee is required, as a condition of the car being available for his private use, to pay any amount of money (whether by deduction from his earnings or otherwise) for that use, the car benefit for the car described at **16.12** above is to be reduced (or if already reduced under the rules described at **16.25** above, further reduced) by the amount so paid in, or (for years before 2014–15 only) in respect of, that year.

[*ITEPA 2003, s 144*]. Before *Finance Act 2014, s 25 (FA 2014)* changed the rule in *ITEPA 2003, s 144* (car) and *s 158* (fuel), a payment made after the end of the relevant tax year could also qualify as making good the car and fuel benefit under this rule. The change was made as a result of the taxpayer in *Peter Marshall* [2013] UKFTT 046 trying to make good the car benefit charge many years after the fact and only after he had been challenged by Employer Compliance officers over the value of the benefit of the company car he used. In practice HMRC will permit making good up to the P11D deadline on 6 July after the end of the tax year, despite the new statutory deadline. (Letter from Treasury minister to ICAEW, June 2014.)

The statutory deadline for making good to offset the private use car and/or car fuel benefit charge(s) has now been set at 6 July following the end of the tax year. This was effective from the 2017–18 tax year, so its first practical impact, as far as the Class 1A charge is concerned, is that made good payments for 2017–18 must be made by 6 July 2018. [*Finance (No 2) Act 2017, s 1*].

Note that where the car and/or fuel benefit is being payrolled, any made good payments need to be made before the end of the tax year. [*Income Tax (PAYE) Regulations 2003, SI 2003/2682, Regs 61E, 61F*]. Recognising some of the practical difficulties in assessing private mileage before the end of the tax year, employees have until 31 May following the end of the tax year to make the making good payment in respect of car or van fuel. [*Income Tax (PAYE) Regulations 2003, SI 2003/2682, Reg 61L(2)*].

Failure to make making good payments in payrolling benefit cases by the end of the tax year/31 May, results in the shortfall, ie the difference between agreed making good amounts and any amounts actually made good, being added to the benefit-in-kind value for the following tax year. Further, making good payments cannot be taken into account in assessing the cash equivalent for that following year. [*Income Tax (PAYE) Regulations 2003, SI 2003/2682, Regs 61K, 61L*].

Example

Ford has a company car available for private use, and car fuel is provided. The car has a 105 CO_2 emission level giving a car fuel benefit for 2017/18 of £4,520 (20% × £22,600). She agrees to make good the cost of private fuel and has £350 deducted from her net pay each month to offset the final bill. However, she fails to make the final making good payment of £320 by the due date.

The car fuel benefit, instead of being reduced to nil for 2017–18 is now £320. This needs to be added to the 2018–19 car fuel benefit of £5,148 (22% × £23,400) giving a total car fuel payrolled benefit for 2018–19 of £5,468. Other points to note here are that:

- any amounts made good in 2018–19 cannot be taken into account in determining the payrolled fuel benefit value;
- payrolled benefits are apportioned equally over the number of pay periods in the tax year. For a benefit payrolled since the start of the tax year, this would usually be 12 for monthly paid employees. In this example, because the due date is 31 May, the benefit value is apportioned over ten periods (months 03 to 12 inclusive). This in turn results in a higher than normal

monthly tax charge, some £547 as opposed to £456 assuming a basic rate taxpayer.

Class 1A contributions are not (yet) paid in real time in respect of payrolled benefits. The value of such payrolled benefits needs to be recorded, and added to the value of any non-payrolled benefits, to facilitate the return of Form P11D(b) and the subsequent calculation of Class 1A contributions. With the expected imposition of Class 1A NICs in real time on termination payments from April 2019, surely it will not be long before it is extended to payrolled benefits, with the potential impact on employers' cash flow that that will entail.

Paying Class 1A in real time would appear to be a disincentive to payrolling. However, with HMRC moving towards all things digital, it would appear to be the logical extension of payrolling benefits. The mandating of payrolling benefits is also a logical extension of 'making tax digital' and cannot be far behind.

If, in the relevant tax year, an employee is required to make good to the person providing the fuel the *whole* of the expense incurred by the fuel-provider in, or in connection with, the provision of fuel for the employee's private use and the employee does so, the cash equivalent shown by the Table at **16.14** above is reduced to nil. This provision was amended with effect from 6 April 2003 so that time apportionment is possible where fuel ceases to be provided (unless provision recommences later in the same tax year, in which case a full year's charge still applies). [*ITEPA 2003 s 152*]. (See also leaflet CA33 para 62).

The rates set out in **30.21** may also be used in making calculations where employees are required to reimburse the cost of private fuel paid for by the employer. Even in circumstances where the cost of fuel to be reimbursed by the employee should arguably be higher HM Revenue and Customs will not so argue for cars of 3,000cc or less. This gives some certainty to employers who keep to the guidelines in that they can now expect that their agreed reimbursements from the employee will not be overturned. See IR Press Release, 21 February 2002.

In respect of such re-imbursement, a company provided two of its employees with cars, and allowed the employees to use them for private motoring. The employees submitted expenses claims for fuel, which the company paid. HMRC discovered that the employees had reclaimed some fuel for private motoring as well as that for business mileage, and issued assessments charging tax on this and Notices of Decision in respect of Class 1A National Insurance contributions. In 2005 the company asked the employees to repay the amounts which they had claimed for private motoring in 2002–03 and 2003–04. The employees did so, and the company and employees appealed against the assessments and Notices, contending that the effect of *ITEPA 2003, s 151* was that the assessments should be withdrawn. The Special Commissioner dismissed the appeals, observing that *s 151* required that the employee should repay the cost of providing the fuel 'in the tax year in question'. The employees here had not reimbursed the cost of the fuel until after the end of the tax year in question, so there were no grounds for discharging the assessments. See *Impact Foiling Ltd v HMRC (and related appeals)* [2006] STC SCD 764 Sp C

562. Note that there were until 6 April 2014 some circumstances in which it was permissible for repayment to be made after the end of the tax year to which it related – see HM Revenue and Customs Employment Income Manual EIM25650.

The impracticality of imposing a 'making good' deadline of the last day of the tax year for some benefits in kind was pointed out to HMRC by many respondents to its draft legislative change that was subsequently enacted in *FA 2014*, but all objections were simply brushed aside. With the experience of the first two annual P11D cycles following the change having exposed the validity of the objections, HMRC issued a consultation document on 9 August 2016, entitled 'Alignment of dates for 'making good' on benefits in kind', that proposed allowing employers until 1 June after the end of the tax year to catch up with payments from employees in respect of car fuel and non-cash vouchers or credit tokens, but leaving the deadline for car benefit payments at the current statutory deadline of 5 April, on the basis that car benefits are predictable, whereas company credit and fuel card statements for March will often not arrive until April, and employees then need time to calculate amounts due to be repaid. Given payroll deadlines in large businesses, it is clear that the 5 April deadline is still wholly impracticable, so 1 June may yet be adopted across the board when the legislation is amended in April 2017. These proposals were subsequently dropped from Finance Bill 2017 when the 2017 general election was called.

Where BIKs are not subjected to tax through the payroll, there were several dates by which an amount made good could be paid, and in respect of some BIKs no date was specified at all. A made good date of 6 July following the end of the tax year in which the tax liability arises now applies to the following BIKs:

- non-cash vouchers and credit tokens;
- living accommodation;
- payments for private use of a car;
- payments to offset the car fuel benefit charge;
- payments for private use of a van;
- payments to offset the van fuel benefit charge; and
- BIKs treated as earnings.

This change is effective from the 2017–18 tax year. Thus the first practical effect is that amounts made good will have to be made by 6 July 2018 at the latest. [*Finance (No 2) Act 2017, s 1*].

Benefits made available by reason of more than one employment

[16.27] Where a benefit is made available to an employee by reason of two or more employments of his, whether under the same or different employers, the amount of any Class 1A contribution which would be payable for the year in accordance with the rules described in the foregoing paragraphs is to be reduced for each employer in accordance with the following rules. [*Social Security (Contributions) Regulations 2001, SI 2001/1004, Reg 36*]. In the case of cars the amount (= 'Y') for 2002–03 or any subsequent year is then to be reduced (or further reduced) by deducting from it an amount equal to

$$Y \times \frac{X-1}{X}$$

where 'X' is the number of employments in question. [*Social Security (Contributions) Regulations 2001, SI 2001/1004, Reg 36*].

> *Example*
>
> Robin works for Senator, Trevi and Uno and, by reason of those three employments, is provided with a petrol driven car costing £22,500 and with CO_2 emissions of 116 g/km. This is available for his private use but fuel is not provided. In 2018–19, the car benefit of £5,400 (24% × £22,500) is reduced under *Social Security (Contributions) Regulations 2001, SI 2001/1004, Reg 36* by deducting from it:
>
> $$£5,400 \times \frac{3-1}{3} = £3,600$$

In other words, each employer will be liable for a Class 1A contribution on £1,800 and the aggregate of those reduced scale amounts (3 × £1,800) is £5,400, ie, the scale amount on which a single employer of Robin would have been liable for a Class 1A contribution.

Cars and fuel for severely disabled employees

[16.28] In addition to the *FA 1995* rules excluding certain accessories from the list price of the car, no tax charge is made by HM Revenue and Customs where a specially adapted car is made available to a severely and permanently disabled employee only for home to work travel and business travel or where fuel is provided only for such travel. (ESC A59 until 5 April 2003; *ITEPA 2003, ss 246, 247* thereafter). For Class 1A purposes, the following rules apply in respect of a car made available by reason of his employment and on account of his disability to an employed earner who is disabled for purposes of (or for purposes which include) assisting, on account of his disability, his travelling between his home and place of employment. [*Social Security (Contributions) Regulations 2001, SI 2001/1004, Reg 38(1)(a), former Reg 37(1)*].

- Where the terms on which the car is made available to the employed earner prohibit private use other than use by that employed earner in travelling between his home and place of employment, and no prohibited private use of the car has been made in the tax year, the person who would otherwise be liable to pay a Class 1A contribution for the year in respect of that employed earner and that car is to be excepted from that liability. [*Social Security (Contributions) Regulations 2001, SI 2001/1004, Reg 38*].
- the employed earner's travelling between his home and place of employment is to be regarded as business travel. [former *Social Security (Contributions) Regulations 2001, SI 2001/1004, Reg 37*].

> *Example*
>
> Viva is so disabled as not to be able to use public transport but is able to drive an adapted car costing £22,000, made available to her by her employer Windsor, and with CO_2 emissions of 124 g/km. This is available for home to work travel but no other private use is permitted. In 2018–19, Viva travels 2,000 miles on business and 5,000 miles between her home and her place of employment. The 5,000 miles of home to work travel are simply not treated as private travel and there is no Class 1A charge.

Pooled cars

[16.29] For *tax* purposes, a car is treated as *not* having been available for the private use of any of the employees to whom it was made available if, in the relevant tax year, it was included in a car pool and:

- it was made available to and used by more than one employee and was not ordinarily used by any one employee to the exclusion of the others;
- any private use of it by any employee was merely incidental to (see HMRC leaflet 480 (2018) para 15.2) its business use; and
- it was not normally kept overnight at or near the residence of any of the employees unless it was kept on premises occupied by the provider of the car.

[*ITEPA 2003, s 167*]. See also former CA33, paras 66–71.

If a car is recognised as a pooled car by HM Revenue and Customs (which in practice outside national and local government is hard to achieve), no tax charge will arise in respect of that car under *ITEPA 2003* and it follows, therefore, no Class 1A liability will arise either (see **16.3** above). [*SSCBA 1992, s 10(1)*].

HMRC issued a ruling that a company was required to pay Class 1A National Insurance contributions in respect of two cars. The company appealed, contending that the cars were 'pooled cars', within *ITEPA 2003, s 167*. The First-Tier Tribunal accepted this contention and allowed the appeal. The Tribunal found that 'the cars were from time to time taken home overnight by employees particularly where they required these to start the next working day making a journey which would make more sense to start from their home rather than from the parking area for the cars'. However the Tribunal held that this did not prevent the cars from qualifying as 'pooled cars', since they were normally kept at the company's premises and 'met the condition that pooled cars are not normally kept overnight on or near the residence of any of their employees'. *Industrial Doors (Scotland) Ltd v HMRC* [2010] UKFTT 282, TC00571.

Where a car has been incorrectly treated as a pooled car, the taxpayer will face a benefit charge for the car and any free fuel, whether or not that benefit charge is economically sound, and the employer will have to pay arrears of Class 1A liability (plus a penalty of 5%, 10% or 15%, depending on how late the payment is). See, eg, *Prince Erediauwa* TC00869, where an employee mistakenly believed he was driving a pooled car that was very old but had an original list price of £51,000 and a 35% CO_2 rating. The income tax charge for car and fuel upheld by the tribunal for just one of the years assessed was approximately £9,000 (plus Class 1A liability for the employer), £3,000 more than the car's then-current market value.

Shared cars

[16.30] HM Revenue and Customs apportions among the users of a shared car the cash equivalent of the benefit of that car. (ESC A71 until 5 April 2003, *ITEPA 2003, ss 148, 169* thereafter). So far as Class 1A contribution liability is concerned, where a car is made available for private use to two or more employed earners concurrently by reason of their respective employments under the same employer, the amount of any Class 1A contribution which would be payable for the year in accordance with the rules described in the foregoing paragraphs is to be reduced as follows. The amount (= 'Y') for 2002–03 or any subsequent year is then to be further reduced (or reduced) by deducting from it an amount equal to

$$Y \times \frac{X-1}{X}$$

where 'X' is the number of employments in question. [former *Social Security (Contributions) Regulations 2001, SI 2001/1004, Reg 36*].

> *Example*
>
> Accord, Bacara and Clio work for Dedra and, by reason of their employments, are concurrently provided with one petrol hybrid car costing £20,000 and with CO_2 emissions of 92 g/km. This is available for private use but fuel is not provided. For 2018–19, the scale charge in each case is £3,800 (£20,000 × 19%) but these three amounts are then each reduced under Social Security (Contributions) Regulations 2001, SI 2001/1004, Reg 36 by deducting
>
> $$£3{,}800 \times \frac{3-1}{3} = £2{,}533$$
>
> In other words, Dedra will be liable for three Class 1A contributions on £1,267 and the aggregate of those reduced scale amounts (3 × £1,267) is £3,801, ie, the car benefit on which he would have been liable for a Class 1A contribution if he had made the car available to just one employee throughout the year (£1 difference owing to rounding).

There is also relief under *ITEPA 2003, s 248* (Extra-Statutory Concession ESC A66 prior to 6 April 2003) that lifts the tax and NICs charge on payments that are used to provide alternative travel arrangements when employees cannot use their usual car sharing scheme where, for instance, an employee has to go home early because of a domestic emergency and the employer pays the cost of that journey home. This relief applies to a maximum of 60 journeys in one tax year.

Cars made available to relatives of an employee

[16.31] Where a person and a relative of his both work for the same employer and a car is made available for the private use of the relative, that car is, for *tax* purposes, deemed to be made available to the relative by reason not only of his own employment but also of the employment of the employee to whom he is related. [*ITEPA 2003, ss 117, 118*]. That being so, a dual liability might be seen to arise for tax purposes: once on the relative and once on the employee to whom he is related; or, for periods before 6 April 2016, even if no dual liability arose because the relative was not a director and earned below £8,500 a year, a liability might still have arisen in law on the employee to whom he was related. Now, it is irrelevant whether the relative earns £8,500 as all employees fall into the benefits code.

Under *ITEPA 2003, ss 148, 169* (Extra-Statutory Concession ESC A71 prior to 6 April 2003), however, for tax purposes, a director or employee will not be taxed on the benefit of a car made available for the private use of a member of his family or household if:

- the relative etc is himself charged to tax on the benefit; or
- the relative etc is *not* himself charged to tax on the benefit but he receives the car in his own right as an employee, and:
  - (a) it can be shown that equivalent cars are made available on the same terms to employees in similar employment with the same employer who are unrelated to directors or employees earning £8,500 a year or more, or
  - (b) the provision of an equivalent car is in accordance with normal commercial practice for the employment concerned.

The terms of this former concession were paralleled for Class 1A purposes by *Social Security (Contributions) Regulations 2001, SI 2001/1004, Reg 33* which provides that the person who, in the circumstances described above, would be liable to pay a Class 1A contribution in respect of the employee to whom the relative is related is to be excepted from liability if:

- a Class 1A contribution is payable in respect of the relative and the car; or
- no Class 1A contribution is payable in respect of the relative and the car because the relative is not chargeable to tax (by reason of not being a director and not having earnings of £8,500 or more a year) and:
  - (a) cars equivalent to that made available to the relative are made available on the same terms to other employed earners who are in similar employment with the same employer and who are not related to other employed earners under that employer; or
  - (b) the making available for private use of a car equivalent to that made available to the relative is in accordance with normal commercial practice for employment of the type concerned.

[Former *Social Security (Contributions) Regulations 2001, SI 2001/1004, Reg 33(1)–(3)*].

For these purposes, a 'relative' is a spouse, a parent or remoter forebear, a child or remoter issue, a brother or sister, or a spouse of any of these. [*Social Security (Contributions) Regulations 2001, SI 2001/1004, Reg 33(4)*].

Reg 33 is no longer of any practical application as the old ESC has the force of (tax) law from 6 April 2003 and accordingly it was omitted from the 2001 Regulations with effect from 6 April 2004. The same practical effect continues to ensue through application of National Insurance law to the amounts arrived at under the tax statutes. [*Social Security (Contributions, Categorisation of Earners and Intermediaries) (Amendment) Regulations 2004, Reg 6*].

Cars in the motor industry

[16.32] If, as part of his normal duties, a car salesman or demonstrator has to take a demonstration, test or experimental car home for the purpose of calling on a prospective customer, it is HM Revenue and Customs practice not to regard the car, on that account alone, as being available for private use; but if such cars are otherwise available for the employee's private use, they attract a tax charge, and will therefore attract a Class 1A charge, in the normal way. In practice, HM Revenue and Customs is prepared to agree an estimated benefit with a motor industry employer and the then DSS generally accepted the figures agreed also. In practice an averaged CO_2 figure (rather than an averaged percentage) will be agreed. See HMRC leaflet 480, paras 11.23–11.24 and HM Revenue and Customs Employment Income Manual EIM23765.

Nonetheless, this had in the past still led to slightly different applications in procedures from one area of the country to another. For that reason, HM Revenue and Customs introduced a standard method of calculation for the trade with effect from 6 April 2009 and slightly varied it from 6 April 2010. Any arrangements previously agreed as described above on a local basis were no longer valid from that date. Broadly, it is now necessary to group cars together and apply average prices and CO_2 emissions, there being nine price bands up to and including 5 April 2010 and ten thereafter – see HM Revenue and Customs Employment Income Manual EIM23450. The arrangements put in place for 2009–10 and subsequent years apply to:

- test and experimental cars;
- demonstrator and courtesy cars; and
- employees with frequent changes of car.

[HM Revenue and Customs Employment Income Manual EIM23490].

Vans and similar vehicles

[16.33] Following the Budget 2002 announcement on the determination of the taxing requirements of employer-provided vans informal discussions took place, which focused on the simplification of the rules on shared vans and on the scope for encouraging the use of environmentally friendly vans. From 6 April 2005 a nil charge now applies to an employee who has to take his employer-provided van home and is not allowed other private usage. Where other private use is insignificant, eg taking rubbish to a tip once or twice a year or regularly making a slight detour to stop at a newsagent on the way to work, then no tax or Class 1A will be due in respect of the company van used in this way. See Working Together Issue 19, November 2004 and Employer Bulletin Issue 19, February 2005.

Where the private usage is unrestricted the previous £500 or £350 scale charges continued to apply until 6 April 2007. From 6 April 2007 until 5 April 2014, a van with unrestricted private use had a flat benefit rate of £3,000 regardless of the age of the van. It was then raised to £3,090, then for 2015–16 to £3,150, for 2016–17 to £3,170, for 2017–18 to £3,230 and for 2018–19 it is set at £3,350. If the employer provides fuel for unrestricted private use an additional fuel charge also applies. This was at the annual rate of £500 up to and including the tax year 2009–10, but was raised to £550 for 2010–11 to 2012–13, £564 for 2013–14, £581 for 2014–15, £594 for 2015–16, £598 for 2016–17, £610 for 2017–18 and £633 for 2018–19, and the government announced that it will continue to uprate both the van and fuel numbers for inflation each year. Where fuel for a van is provided or it is in the form of a non-cash voucher then it is disregarded for the purposes of primary Class 1 liability.

From 6 April 2010 for a five-year period all *electric* vans had a 0% private use charge, but it was announced at Budget 2014 that they would be gradually aligned with normal vans over the five years to April 2020 (albeit without a fuel charge for any electricity paid for by the employer). The private use electric van charge for 2015–16 was therefore set at 20% of the standard van benefit, ie, £630. The percentage was due to rise to 40% for 2016–17, 60% for 2017–18, 80% for 2018–19, 90% for 2019–20, with full alignment achieved from 6 April 2020. [*ITEPA 2003, ss 155–170*, as amended by *FA 2015, 10; Social Security (Contributions) Regulations 2001, SI 2001/1004, Sch 3* as amended by *Social Security (Contributions) (Amendment No 2) Regulations 2008, SI 2008/607, Reg 3; FA 2008, s 48*]. However, Budget 2016 announced that the rises had been deferred (the change was described by the government as extending 'van benefit charge support' – para 2.162 of the Budget Report), and *FA 2016, s 11* set a new schedule in *ITEPA 2003*, s 155 for the increases:

2016–17 and 2017–18	20% of the normal charge
2018–19	40%
2019–20	60%
2020–21	80%
2021–22	90%
2022–23	100%

The impact of the 'incentive' is to be reviewed at Budget 2018.

See also Leaflet 480 (2018), Chapter 14.

Distinction between a car and a van

[16.34] The distinction between a car and a van is sometimes difficult to determine. As a temporary measure for 2002–03 and 2003–04 (as a new regime for company vans had originally been expected to come into force from 6 April 2004), the then Inland Revenue stated in summer 2002 that when deciding whether double-cab pick-ups counted as cars or vans, they would interpret *ITEPA 2003, s 115(1)* in line with the definitions used by Customs & Excise for VAT purposes. Customs practice is that 'vehicles which can legally carry a payload of 1 tonne or more are not treated as cars for VAT purposes.

The practical effect of this was to change the VAT status of dual purpose vehicles such as some "double cab" pick-ups . . . It should be noted that some dual purpose vehicles carry a payload of less than 1 tonne and will remain cars'. The then Inland Revenue announced in March 2004 that this temporary interpretation could now be regarded as permanent. The 1 tonne payload capacity is now held in practice, and purely as a rule of thumb, to point towards the vehicle having been designed primarily for carrying 'goods or burden'.

Under a separate agreement between Customs and the Society of Motor Manufacturers and Traders, a hard top consisting of metal, fibre glass or similar material, with or without windows is accorded a generic weight of 45kg. Therefore the inclusion of a hard top on a double cab with an ex-works payload capacity of 1010kg will convert the vehicle into a car since the payload is then reduced to 965kg. The weight of all other optional accessories is disregarded. The former Inland Revenue also adopted this same treatment. See EIM23150.

See Tolley's Practical NIC Newsletter, October 2005.

See also *County Pharmacy Ltd v HMRC*; *Morris v HMRC* [2005] STC SCD 729 Sp C 495 where a company purchased a motorhome for the use of its managing director. HMRC issued an amendment to his self-assessment, requiring him to pay income tax on the car and car fuel benefit. They also issued a ruling that the company was required to pay Class 1A National Insurance contributions. The director and the company appealed, contending that the motorhome was not a 'car' for the purposes of the legislation. The Special Commissioner rejected this contention and dismissed the appeals. The director appealed to the Chancery Division, which upheld the Commissioner's decision.

Table of van benefit charge

[16.35] Van benefit charges are as follows:

Usage	*2013–14*	*2014–15*	*2015–16*	*2016–17*	*2017–18*	*2018–19*
Electric vans						
Business/private use	£0	£0	£630	£634	£646	£1,292
Conventionally-fuelled vans						
Business use only (ie, van kept on employer's premises) – van and any fuel	£0	£0	£0	£0	£0	£0
Business use and work to home only (ie, van kept at or near employee's home) – van and any fuel	£0	£0	£0	£0	£0	£0

Usage	*2013–14*	*2014–15*	*2015–16*	*2016–17*	*2017–18*	*2018–19*
Business and full private use – van only	£3,000	£3,090	£3,150	£3,170	£3,230	£3,350
Business and full private use – van and fuel	£3,564	£3,671	£3,744	£3,768	£3,840	£3,983

Emergency service workers in the fire, police and ambulance services are often required to take their vehicles home at night so that they can respond quickly to emergencies. The tax and NICs charges that might have applied when this occurs were removed from 6 April 2004.

Works buses etc

[16.36] Since 6 April 1999, the tax and NICs charge has been lifted for employers who set up 'Green Transport Plans' which offer employees free or subsidised works buses, a subsidy to public bus services, bicycles and safety equipment (eg helmets made available to employees), workplace parking for bicycles and motorcycles. There is no requirement for the employer or employees to report these 'green' benefits to HM Revenue and Customs provided the necessary requirements are adhered to. For instance, a works bus is any bus or coach that seats nine or more passengers that is provided by the employer and is available to the employees generally and used to transport them to and from work. However, the works bus may also be used occasionally for, say, shopping trips without it affecting the exemption. From 2003–04 where an employer subsidises a public bus service that entitles employees to transport by way of a non-cash voucher within *ITEPA 2003, s 243* the tax and NICs treatment is now aligned. [*Social Security (Contributions) Regulations 2001, SI 2001/1004, Sch 3, Part V, para 5A* inserted by *Social Security (Contributions) (Amendment No 7) Regulations 2003, SI 2003/2958, Reg 5*].

From 19 December 2009 HMRC changed its interpretation of the qualifying rules for bus passes being used in conjunction with new salary sacrifice arrangements that are aimed at providing employees with a travel subsidy. Therefore any renewal after 18 December 2009 of the old bus pass agreement for a new bus pass or to extend the period of the existing bus pass will have been treated as a new arrangement. The new arrangement will only have been treated as exempt if the conditions of the exemption were fully satisfied and therefore any arrangements that relied on area bus passes as opposed to travel on a specific supported bus route will not have qualified for exemption. Where the conditions for the exemption of the provision of public bus services were not satisfied and were not treated as satisfied for an interim period (ie that the agreement related to a bus pass that lasted for no more than 12 months entered into before 19 December 2009), the employer was then responsible for including details of the taxable benefit on form P11D for each affected employee and for accounting for employer's Class 1A NIC liability. See **16.42** below.

Childcare

[16.37] An in-house nursery or crèche constitutes a payment in kind but is tax- and NIC-free.

The position up to and including 2004–05 regarding childcare provided under an employer's contract with an external care provider was that there was no Class 1A liability even if a tax charge arose because the provision was 'outside' the workplace. The government then restricted the NIC relief but gave a limited tax relief to match. Following consultation that commenced in February 2003, costs incurred under an *employer's* contract for registered childcare, including approved home childcare, exceeding £55 per week (originally £50 per week until April 2006), became subject to Class 1A contributions in line with the changes under the new tax regime from 6 April 2005. (See Inland Revenue Press Release IR 99/03, 11 December 2003 and Employers Bulletin Issue 19, February 2005). Thus the tax relief was extended, but the Class 1A relief curtailed — and only at the time up to expenditure of £50 per week per employee (not per child), but it was then increased further to £55 per week or £243 per month from 6 April 2006. This relief is not due if, instead, childcare vouchers are provided and tax/NIC relief is given on their provision (see 29.30). [*ITEPA 2003, 318* as amended by *FA 2004, s 78, Sch 13; Social Security (Contributions) (Amendment No 3) Regs 2006, SI 2006/883; FA 2006, s 63*]. See Inland Revenue Tax Bulletin Issue 75, February 2005. See also former leaflet E18 'How to help your employees with childcare'; CHILD CARE VOUCHERS **29.32**.

Telephones

[16.38] If the employer is the subscriber, ie, the contract is between the employer and the telephone company, payments by the employer are not earnings for Class 1 contribution purposes because such payments are payments in kind. From 6 April 2000 however, provision in this manner will almost certainly attract a Class 1A charge. Although unusual, prior to 2000 a number of employers changed the way that they paid for employees' telephone bills in order to avoid the Class 1 contributions that would arise on the rental and private calls element (see **30.12**) by having the employee cancel his existing contract with the telephone line supplier and putting in place a contract with the employer. It was said that British Telecom would continue to charge such lines at domestic charge rates where the premises were clearly residential.

Where such arrangements are still in place they may not, since 2000, provide a financially effective way of dealing with such expenditure as, unless the private usage is not significant, the employer will incur a Class 1A contribution on the *full* cost of the telephone service. Depending on whether the employee's earnings are above or below the Upper Earnings Limit and the precise extent of private use it may incur less National Insurance cost if an employee contract for the line were to be reinstated.
See **30.12**.

Mobile phones

[16.39] From the introduction of the extended Class 1A charge to all benefits in kind (6 April 2000), there was no taxable benefit in kind up to 5 April 2006 on any number of mobile telephones provided by the *employer* even if for the sole purpose of non-business use. As some businesses were providing mobiles for employees' children, etc, this 'loophole' was closed with effect from 6 April 2006. The exemption is now restricted to one mobile phone per employee unless the mobiles are provided entirely for business use or private use is insignificant or unless the mobile was or mobiles were first provided before 6 April 2006. [*ITEPA 2003, s 319, FA 2006, s 60(3)*]. Also, providing only *one* mobile phone is made available to the employee through salary sacrifice, or if a voucher is used as a means of making the phone available to the employee, then neither tax nor NICs will arise. If, however, the employer reimburses an employee for the cost of a mobile purchased by the employee, or the employee's monthly bills, then Class 1 liability will continue to be, as it always has been, in point. Where top-up vouchers are provided, Class 1 liability will arise on a non-business use as such items are 'non-cash vouchers'. Note that Booklet 480 at para 22.2 states that handsets with two SIM cards with different numbers represent two mobile phones, not one, which accords with *ITEPA 2003, s 319(3)*. See HMRC leaflet 480, Chapter 22 and Table at **16.11** CLASS **1**A CONTRIBUTIONS: BENEFITS IN KIND. [*ITEPA 2003, ss 316, 319; FA 2006, s 60*].

A 'Blackberry' or any similar PDA device was for several years considered to be a computer rather than a mobile phone, but the evolution of digital technology has seen PDAs transformed into smartphones, and HMRC now accepts that a smartphone that is a telephone but also has the capabilities of a PDA will be classed as a mobile telephone. Laptops and tablets that are primarily computers but can be used for voice messaging with the relevant apps will not be classed as mobile phones, as they are not designed or adapted for the primary purpose of transmitting or receiving spoken messages. (See HM Revenue and Customs Employment Income Manual EIM21701 and EIM21778 and 480, para 22.5).

Computers and bicycles

[16.40] Bicycles for business use loaned to an employee by his employer are exempt from tax and NICs (see the Table at **16.11** above). Where an employee is allowed to buy the asset sometime later at an undervalue, a charge arises to both tax and Class 1A NICs. Where the asset has been used or depreciated, the charge is generally by reference to market value. Various commercial schemes are offered for the purchase/lease of bicycles that take advantage of the above relaxation in rules.

Employers sometimes choose to provide the benefit of a loaned cycle in conjunction with salary sacrifice arrangements. From 19 December 2009 if an employer excludes some employees from the salary sacrifice arrangements, the exemption will only apply if the employer still extends availability of loaned cycles to those employees that are barred from entering into the salary sacrifice arrangements. [*ITEPA 2003, s 244*]. This means that the availability condition can still be satisfied if employees who enter into salary sacrifice arrangements are offered the use of more expensive cycles than those offered to employees outside salary sacrifice arrangements. In some salary sacrifice arrangements employees are offered the opportunity to buy the cycle after the end of the loan/salary sacrifice period. Where this happens, market value must be ascertained in the normal way. If a cycle is transferred to an employee at a nominal value (say 5 to 10% of the original retail price), then if the market value is higher, the employee will be taxable on the difference (see HM Revenue and Customs Employment Income Manual EIM21664).

A similar relief applied up to and including 5 April 2006 as regards computers up to an annual value of £500. [*ITEPA 2003, s 320; FA 2006, s 61*]. Where a computer is still loaned after 5 April 2006 but was first so provided before 6 April 2006 the exemption continues to apply until that particular computer is replaced (see HM Revenue and Customs Employment Income Manual EIM21701). See **16.39** regarding the treatment of a 'Blackberry', etc as a computer and not as a mobile phone.

There is an alternative basis of valuation where ownership of an asset is transferred to an employee after being used as an employee benefit. The taxable value on transfer is the higher of (a) market value at date of transfer or (b) the value of the asset when first used as a benefit, less the total cost of the benefit during the loan period. In the case of computers (see below) and bicycles, which are exempt from a taxable benefit during the period of the loan, the amount that would have been taxable each year is taken into account.

In order to remove any uncertainty the position was simplified so that no tax or Class 1A charge will arise from 6 April 2005 if the employee pays the full market value at the time of transfer. This only applies to computers (up to and including 5 April 2006) and bicycles. [*ITEPA 2003, ss 201, 206, 244, 320; FA 2005, s 17; FA 2006, s 61*]. See also HM Revenue and Customs Press Release, 20 February 2005.

Removal expenses

[16.41] Where an employer helps towards the cost of moving an employee, the first £8,000 of *qualifying* removal expenses and benefits is exempt from tax and, from 6 April 2000, from Class 1A National Insurance contributions. See IR Press Release, 20 November 2000. Also added in March 2001 but not incorporated in the list in **16.11** above are certain travel and subsistence benefits provided to employees seconded in the UK or abroad and certain personal security items which an employer provides to employees. [*Social Security Contributions and Benefits Act 1992 (Modification of Section 10(7)) Regulations 2001, SI 2001/966, Reg 2*.]

The treatment of removal expenses where the amount exceeds £8,000 is unusual in that the charge on the excess is always to Class 1A even if there are items included which are personally contracted expenses reimbursed to the employee. But for the fact that these relate to removal, such reimbursed expenses would, of course, ordinarily attract a Class 1 liability.

See **30.4**.

Loans

[16.42] Under a change in the *Finance Act 2000* which took effect from 6 April 2000, loans where the interest would qualify for full tax relief are exempted from the beneficial loans charge and need not be reported on the P11D. No Class 1A liability arises.

Other loans, including those which partly qualify for tax relief, continue to be reportable in the usual way. The official rate of interest is 2.5% per annum for the year 2018–19. See *SSCBA 1992, s 10(7A)* as amended by *ITEPA 2003, Sch 6, para 174, ITEPA 2003, s 181(1)*. See also Table in **16.11** above.

The actual official rate of interest since the introduction of Class 1A liability on, inter alia, beneficial loans where the loan is denominated in sterling or any other currency apart from those stated below has been as follows in the last six years.

Year	*Average official rate (%)*
2017–18	2.50
2016–17	3.00
2015–16	3.00
2014–15	3.25
2013–14	4.00
2012–13	4.00

The rates applicable to loans in stated currencies have been as follows since 1994:

- Japanese yen: 3.9%
- Swiss franc: 5.5%

Neither now represents market rate but no change has been indicated.

[*ITEPA 2003, s 181*]

Medical benefits

[16.43] Ordinarily, medical insurance benefits are just that – benefits in kind, liable to Class 1A – as the provision is made through a group policy organised by the employer.

Occasionally, however, an employer may meet directly the renewal premium of a medical insurance policy that the employee (a newly recruited employee, for instance) has himself arranged. Alternatively, since it is understood that some providers will not enter into a group scheme for fewer than five employees, it may be that in very small companies one or two employees have personal policies (albeit arranged and administered by the company) because that is the only way that the company can, in practice, obtain the required cover. Whatever the reason for the policy being a personal one if, as a matter of fact, such premiums are met by the employer then the National Insurance liability is to Class 1 contributions, not Class 1A, as the employer is merely meeting the employee's pecuniary liability rather than providing a benefit in kind.

In the Autumn Statement 2013, the Chancellor announced an intention to exempt from tax and NIC the provision of 'recommended' medical treatment. The medical treatment exempted is capped at £500 per employee per year and must be treatment provided in accordance with a recommendation from an occupational health service in order to help an employee return to work after a period of absence due to ill-health or injury.

The exemption was eventually legislated with effect from 1 January 2015, for income tax purposes by *Income Tax (Recommended Medical Treatment) Regulations 2014, SI 2014/3227* and for NIC purposes by the *Social Security (Contributions) (Amendment No 6) Regulations 2014, SI 2014/3228*. The latter inserted into *Pt 5* of *Sch 3* to the *Contributions Regulations 2001* a disregard for non-cash vouchers for qualifying medical treatment exempt from tax under *ITEPA 2003, s 320C*, and into *Pt 8* of *Sch 3*, a new *paragraph 14A* that excludes from earnings that are paid on or reimbursement to which no liability to income tax arises by virtue of that same section.

ITEPA 2003, s 320C was created by *FA 2014, s 12* and implemented by *SI 2014/3227*. When the government decided to abolish the SSP Percentage Threshold Scheme with effect from 6 April 2014 in order to fund a new Health & Work Service from 2015, it decided to try to encourage employers to fund occupational health treatment for their employees by granting this new tax exemption.

The exemption applies only to medical treatment which is in accordance with a recommendation made to the employee as part of occupational health services provided to the employee by a service provided under *s 2* of the *Employment and Training Act 1973* or by, or in accordance with arrangements made by, the employer, for the purposes of assisting the employee to return to work after a period of absence due to injury or ill-health.

The income tax regulations further stipulate that a recommendation for medical treatment can only be given after the employee has been assessed by a 'healthcare professional' as unfit for work for at least 28 consecutive days or absent from work due to injury or ill-health for such a period. A qualifying healthcare professional is a registered medical practitioner, a registered nurse, or an occupational therapist, physiotherapist or psychologist registered with the regulatory body under *s 60* of the *Health Act 1999*. The recommendation must be in writing to both employer and employee and specify the medical treatment that is recommended. Somewhat oddly, the consultations with the new Health and Work Service are conducted by telephone rather than face to face, but qualifying treatment can nevertheless be recommended. Owing to low referral rates, the Fit for Work assessment service in England and Wales closed to new referrals on 15 December 2017 and ended on 31 March 2018, the equivalent service in Scotland on 31 May 2018. The websites and telephone advice services continue to operate.

No liability to tax arises in respect of the provision to an employee of 'recommended' medical treatment, or the payment, to or in respect of an employee, of the cost of such treatment, up to a value of £500 in a year, provided no relevant salary sacrifice arrangements or relevant flexible remuneration arrangements are in place. It was always intended that the tax exemption would be matched by a disregard for Class 1 NIC purposes.

Holiday homes abroad

[16.44] A very welcome change announced in the 2007 Budget was that directors would no longer face a benefit in kind charge (many might not have realised that technically they did) where they owned a home abroad (not in the UK) through the medium of a company of which they were directors or 'shadow' directors. The resultant tax legislation now excludes from tax liability any situation where the property is owned by a company that is owned by individuals, the company's only activities are ones that are incidental to its ownership of the property (eg letting when not in use by the owner and/or family members), the property is the company's only or main asset and the property is not funded directly or indirectly by a connected company. [*ITEPA 2003, ss 100A, 100B* as inserted by *FA 2008, s 45*]. HM Revenue and Customs said that it would not seek tax prior to the legislation taking effect and this is confirmed in *Finance Act 2008, s 45(2)*. Due to the structure of the Class 1A system the change in tax legislation will flow through automatically for Class 1A purposes.

The exemption was extended from that in the draft legislation issued in summer 2007 to include cases where the company that owns the property is in turn owned by a holding company which does no more than own the shares in its subsidiary. The definition of the latter is as in *ITA 2007, s 992* being any body corporate or an unincorporated association other than a partnership, a local authority or a local authority association. It is therefore sufficiently wide to include bodies such as a Société Civile Immobilière (SCI) in France and a Limited Liability Company (LLC) in the USA. In addition, the exemption will not be prejudiced where the property is rented out to third parties when not being used by members and friends of the family.

The provisions are considered by HM Revenue and Customs to include time-shares owned through a company.

The tax and related Class 1A charges will still apply where the property was acquired from a connected company at undervalue, a connected company directly or indirectly incurs expenditure on the property or directly or indirectly lends money after the property is acquired, or the accommodation is provided in pursuance of an arrangement the main purpose (or one of the main purposes) of which is the avoidance of tax or National Insurance.

It is believed that only a tiny number of companies have been required actually to pay Class 1A (or income tax) in respect of such 'benefits' previously, though arguably the law – certainly following *R v Dimsey* and *R v Allen* (74 TC 263) – was unequivocal.

Indeed, there may still be an issue in some cases. Due to the nature of the law of property in certain countries the ownership of the holiday home may be through a trust, or the shares in the company owning the property may be held in one or more trusts. No relief is offered in these situations and whilst the past inactivity was welcome it must be assumed that from now on HM Revenue and Customs officers will enforce liability that falls outside the *FA 2008* parameters.

See HM Revenue and Customs Employment Income Manual EIM11371-11374.

Credit cards

[16.45] Where a company credit card has been used the treatment varies. Liability depends on whether an individual is acting in his own right or is acting as a representative of his employer when he uses the card. It is a difficult distinction and the use of the credit card to obtain money, goods or services for personal benefit is treated as payment of earnings and subject to Class 1 NICs. Business expenses are disregarded. Two exceptions arise in respect of the credit card so that no Class 1 NICs are due, as follows.

- Private fuel purchased by means of a company credit card where a Class 1A contribution liability already exists on the provision of free private fuel. See **16.8** and **16.36** above.
- Any purchase made using a company credit card which can be regarded as motoring expense associated with a car liable to Class 1A contributions.

Collection

[16.46] See 21.43 COLLECTION for details.

Repayment

[16.47] See 21.44 COLLECTION for details.

Penalties and interest

[16.48] See 21.45 COLLECTION for more details.

Appeals related to class 1A contributions: benefits in kind

[16.49] The procedure for an appeal (see **9.9** APPEALS AND REVIEWS) is extended to cover a question about whether a Class 1A contribution is payable or otherwise relating to a Class 1A contribution.

Salary sacrifice/optional remuneration arrangements

[16.50] The Government has expressed concern over the last few years about the losses to the Exchequer caused by the growth of salary sacrifice and flexible benefits arrangements. A consultation document was issued on 10 August 2016 setting out proposals to curb these losses by changing the basis of valuing most benefits provided under salary sacrifice arrangements.

By far the most widespread use of salary sacrifice relates to pension contributions, where the tax and NIC rules differ: employer contributions are both tax- and NIC-free, but employee contributions must be made out of pay after the deduction of primary NICs. This is avoided if the employee salary is reduced and the employer pension contribution increased accordingly. HMRC currently accepts that this kind of arrangement is not aggressive tax avoidance and the consultation document specifically excluded any intention to change this position.

Also excluded from the proposals are employer-supported childcare, employer-provided pension advice based on the recommendations of the Financial Advice Market Review, the provision of cycles and cyclists' safety equipment which meet the statutory conditions, and arrangements for the provision of ultra-low emission vehicles. The first of these is known to have a significant cost to the Exchequer, but the typical childcare voucher arrangement is already set to be replaced by the tax-free childcare scheme in stages from April 2017 onwards, so it was perhaps felt unnecessary to attempt to change the basis now. The others have a limited impact on Exchequer revenues.

However, other benefits provided under salary sacrifice arrangements from April 2017 will be subject to new rules on the valuation of the benefits provided. The professed aim of the change is to ensure that 'employees swapping salary for benefits pay the same tax as the vast majority of individuals who buy them out of their post-tax income' (*Autumn Statement 2016, para 4.13*), but the change is in fact likely to result in two employees with effectively the same package being taxed on different bases.

Most benefits in kind are currently subject to tax and Class 1A NICs based on either the cost to the employer of providing the benefit or a formula provided in *ITEPA 2003*. Some benefits are tax-free, eg parking at or near the workplace and a single mobile phone for personal use. Others are taxed on a discounted basis because the marginal cost to the employer of providing the benefit is lower than the market value of the goods or services provided. There is therefore a clear advantage to the employer and employee in providing a benefit rather than paying cash remuneration, since PAYE and Class 1 NICs are likely to be saved.

Any benefit obtained by sacrificing an amount of salary will become taxable and subject to Class 1A NICs after April 2017 based on the higher of the amount of salary forgone or the normal value of the benefit. The effect of this will be to tax and levy NICs on a higher cash equivalent in many cases. Even benefits that are ordinarily tax- and NIC-free under the current regime will become liable if provided under salary sacrifice arrangements.

Note that the new arrangements do nothing to stop the reduction in Class 1 NICs that the employee enjoys by entering into a salary sacrifice/optional remuneration arrangement. It will depend on the difference between the higher of value and the benefit's normal value as to whether the primary Class 1 saving is sufficient to offset the additional income tax that will be charged.

[*ITEPA 2003, Pt 3, ss 69A, 69B, 87A, 94A, 103A, 120A, 121A, 121B, 132A, 147A, 149A, 154A, 158A, 160A, 175A, 203A; Pt 4, s 228A* inserted by *FA 2017, s 7, Sch* 2].

Arrangements in place before 6 April 2017 will be protected until 6 April 2018, and arrangements for cars, living accommodation and school fees, which are typically made under longer term agreements, will be protected until April 2021. Note that this does not mean that schemes offering a choice of a company car or cash allowance may continue unchanged until April 2021; any change in the arrangement, such as a new sacrifice amount or a new lease, is likely to be treated as a new arrangement if it occurs on or after 6 April 2017.

The removal of the tax and NIC advantages of salary sacrifice is expected to raise around £1 billion over the next five years (*Autumn Statement 2016*, Table 2.1).

> *Example*
>
> Jeremy has a choice between a company car with a taxable value, calculated in accordance with 16.12 to 16.18 above, of £3,780 or a car allowance of £5,000. Should he choose the car allowance, a cash payment, this will be treated as earnings and subject to Class 1 NICs. However, should he opt for the company car, the taxable value to be reported on Form P11D will be £5,000 – the higher of value.

Optional remuneration arrangements – car benefit

[16.51] Salary sacrifice arrangements for cars quite often reflect the value of the total benefits package. Thus elements of the salary sacrifice may be in respect of, say, private use, insurance and other running costs.

HMRC Policy has now confirmed that in these circumstances, the amount foregone that is to be compared with the normal car benefit value is that portion of the salary sacrifice that refers to the car itself. Further confirmation of this is contained in HMRC's October 2017 Employer Bulletin which states on page 2 under 'P46 (Car)':

> 'The P46 (Car) data you submit will have a new field "cash forgone". This is *the cash foregone for the car only* [emphasis added] (excluding fuel, maintenance or any other attributable service).'

ITEPA 2003, s 69B deals with situations where a salary sacrifice is made in connection with a number of different benefits. The legislation provides that where 'necessary', for example where the value of the salary sacrifice relating to individual benefits is not transparent, there is provision for a just and reasonable apportionment. The legislation relating to the taxation of the provision of a car is at *ITEPA 2003, ss 120 and 120A* and the tax consequences of the provision of 'other payments and benefits' such as insurance and maintenance is dealt with at *ITEPA 2003, s 239*. The legislation provides that the salary foregone should relate to the provision of the benefit ie the salary sacrifice for the car, so at this point we do not need to consider the salary foregone in relation to insurance, maintenance, etc.

The changes brought in under OpRA introduced specific legislation at *ITEPA 2003, s 228A* that stops certain exemptions applying to a benefit where it is provided in conjunction with an OpRA. An example would be a salary sacrifice mobile phone which was previously an exempt benefit. *Section 228A* stops the relevant exemption applying so it is now taxable by reference to the higher of zero (as it would have been exempt) and the salary foregone. The exemption relating to 'payments and benefits provided in connection with a taxable vehicle' is protected as *s 228A(5)(a)* lists *s 239* as an excluded exemption – *s 239* being the legislation that provides that pensions, childcare and low emission vehicles are unaffected by OpRA.

Optional remuneration arrangements – car benefit ultra-low emission vehicles (ULEVs)

[16.52] Under OpRA, cars with CO_2 emissions of 75g/km or less are excluded from the 'higher of' rules. The taxable value is that produced under the normal car benefit calculation rules.

It is worth pointing out that there is a potential mismatch between the 75g/km or less exception mentioned above and what constitutes a ULEV, especially when the ULEV percentages change in 2020–21, which could catch an unwary employer out. See **16.14**.

From 2020–21, low emission vehicles are those with CO_2 emissions of *less than* 75g/km.

It would seem somewhat anomalous if the OpRA rules were not amended in the near future to bring them into line with the ULEV definition contained in *Finance (No 2) Act 2017, s 2(2)*, which will come into effect from 2020–21.

Key Points regarding class 1A contributions: benefits in kind

[16.53] Points to consider are

- A Class 1A liability cannot arise where there is no tax liability (see **16.3** above).
- Class 1A contributions in respect of employees are payable by employers or '*others*' only. Others include the person who is liable for the Class 1 secondary contributions on the final or the relevant payment of earnings in the tax year so will not necessarily be the person making the benefit available.
- Internationally mobile employees who are subject to a continuing contribution liability overseas may not be within the scope of Class 1A even though they have taxable benefits that are reported on Form P11D by the UK company. Certificates of coverage or EEA 'portable documents' or 'attestations' (ie, forms A1) should be held where appropriate.
- P11D dispensations could be sought by an employer for periods before 6 April 2016 in respect of employees regarding particular common benefits stipulated, but in order to secure a dispensation all previous P11Ds had to be up to date and have been audited by

HMRC. Dispensations have been abolished with effect from 6 April 2016. Any benefits provided by an employer will now be taxable or exempt. Round-sum allowances might constitute taxable benefits but will ordinarily attract Class 1 liability unless they are the subject of a bespoke rate agreement with HMRC.

- Company assets such as boats and cars made available for private use, or improvements to living accommodation, attract a full Class 1A charge on the annual benefit and running costs, even if there is part business usage.
- For cars costing more than £80,000, the list price since 6 April 2011 has been unlimited. This change means that high-end prestige company cars will have incurred a substantial increase in the benefit charge from 2011–12 onwards.
- For drivers whose private mileage is only average or lower, the income tax and Class 1A costs of having the benefit for free fuel of private motoring in a company car generally mean that savings can be made by giving up the right to free fuel and claiming a mileage allowance at the authorised rate for business mileage instead.
- From 6 April 2017 the reportable value of benefits in kind will be the higher of the amount of salary foregone or the normal value of the benefit. Exclusions from this are employer-supported childcare, employer-provided pension advice based on the recommendations of the Financial Advice Market Review, the provision of cycles and cyclists' safety equipment which meet the statutory conditions, and arrangements for the provision of ultra-low emission vehicles.

17

Class 1B Contributions: PAYE settlement agreements

Cross-reference. See APPEALS AND REVIEWS 9 for remedies for dissatisfaction.

Other Sources. Simon's Taxes, Volume 2, para A8.280; CWG2 (2018–19), page 89; HM Revenue and Customs National Insurance Manual NIM18001–NIM19000.

Introduction to class 1B contributions: PAYE settlement agreements

[17.1] PAYE settlement agreements (PSAs) enable HMRC to collect the tax liability on minor or irregular benefits from the employer without recourse to the employee. [*ITEPA 2003, ss 703–707*]. PSAs came into being from 6 April 1996 to formally replace more informal Annual Voluntary Settlements that some employers were able to agree with their tax districts. Under the Tax Law Rewrite, consolidated employer regulations have resulted in the *Income Tax (Pay As You Earn) Regulations 2003, SI 2003/2682, Regs 105–117* which cover the making and effect of PSAs. At first, the NIC position of PSAs was unclear, but it was formalised from April 1999.

PAYE settlement agreements

[17.2] A PAYE Settlement Agreement (PSA) is a voluntary arrangement between an employer and HMRC, the precise details of which are set out on Form P626 on a case by case basis, whereby the employer agrees to pay the tax and contributions that are due on certain expenses and/or benefits in kind. Having entered into a PSA in respect of particular items, those items do not then appear on the Forms P11D or on the employee's self-assessment tax return. The agreement lasts only for one year, so if the procedure is required by the employer to be repeated, a fresh application must be made for each succeeding year.

It was confirmed by the *Social Security Act 1998 (Commencement No 1) Order 1998, Reg 2* that PSAs and NICs alignment would apply from 6 April 1999 onwards with the introduction of a new class of contribution, Class 1B. See HM Revenue and Customs Manual NIM18010.

Class 1B arises at the same rate that applies to employer's standard Class 1 when the employer has entered into a PSA with HM Revenue and Customs. No employee contribution is due under the Class 1B system. Class 1A and Class 1B contributions are no longer accounted for separately in the National Insurance Fund Accounts, but Class 1B would be expected to yield only around £25-30 million per annum. Part of this is diverted to the National Health Service.

The PAYE settlement agreement (PSA) process is being simplified such that the PSA will no longer need to be agreed in advance with HMRC. The PAYE Regulations have been amended from 2018–19 so that PSAs will no longer have to be agreed annually. PSAs, once set up, will continue for subsequent years until varied or cancelled either by the employer or HMRC.

[*Income Tax (Pay As You Earn) (Amendment) Regulations 2018, SI 2018/267, Regs 7–16*].

The amendment paves the way for automated agreements with HMRC, who will look to develop a digital return to replace the current paper-based PSA returns. Further changes will be needed to the Income Tax Regulations.

Where a PSA is already in place, HMRC have been writing to affected employees advising them of the new arrangements and inviting them to renew for 2018–19 and subsequent years under the new basis.

Class 1B

[17.3] The *Social Security Act 1998* introduced the power to make regulations in respect of Class 1B contributions, to be paid where a PSA has been agreed for income tax purposes. Class 1B may therefore be payable for example, instead of Class 1 or Class 1A, on cash vouchers where the provision of those vouchers has been included in a PSA between HMRC and the employer.

Since 6 April 1999, Class 1B NICs have also been due on all the tax payable under the PSA, whether that tax relates to items otherwise liable to NICs or not. [*SSCBA 1992, s 10A* as inserted by *Social Security Act 1998, s 53*]. Under the rule in *Hartland v Diggines* [1926] 10 TC 247 the discharge of employees' tax liabilities is equivalent to cash payments to those employees. The then CA always alleged that the payment of tax under an old annual voluntary settlement constituted such a personal discharge even though no individual personal liability was ever calculated. The income tax legislation creating PSAs specifically provides that the tax due under a PSA is, for the avoidance of doubt, deemed to be the employer's liability. Hence, there cannot be a Class 1 charge on the tax, even if the particular item itself falls to be treated as earnings so that Class 1 would ordinarily be due.

Rates and collection

[17.4] Class 1B is payable by 19 October following the end of the year to which it relates (ie at the same time as the tax due under the PSA) so that the payment will be due by 19 October 2016 for 2015–16 at a rate of 13.8% or by 22 October 2016 if paid electronically. [*Social Security (Contributions) Regulations 2001, SI 2001/1004, Sch 4 Reg 13(1); Social Security (Categorisation of Earners and Intermediaries) (Amendment) Regs 2004, SI 2004/770, Reg 32; The Income Tax (Pay As You Earn) Regulations 2003, SI 2003/2682, Reg 109*]. This is an employer-only charge similar to Class 1A and, like Class 1A, does not generate any benefit entitlement in return for the payment. *The Welfare Reform and Pensions Act 1999, ss 77, 78* provided that, as with Class 1A, the rate of Class 1B contributions is tied to the Class 1 secondary rate. See HM Revenue and Customs Manual NIM18060.

In respect of the liability for 2010–11 onwards, employers who are late with their PSA payments beyond the due date will be subject to a late payment penalty as detailed in **42** LATE PAID CONTRIBUTIONS.

Exclusions

[17.5] Employers are allowed under the regulations to exclude from their calculations amounts in respect of employees normally excluded by reason of a social security agreement and where the EC rules, reciprocal agreement or standard residence and presence conditions result in there being no Class 1 liability at all. Class 1B is a replacement for Class 1 or Class 1A contributions, so if there is no UK liability in those classes, there should equally be none under Class 1B. However, one of the purposes of a PSA is to dispense with the need to keep detailed records and calculations of small amounts for every individual employee. Employers will therefore be allowed to pay Class 1B in these cases if they want to. This approach will be favourable in many cases as it reduces the administrative requirements and the amounts involved are likely to be fairly small. See HM Revenue and Customs Manual NIM18120. [*Social Security (Contributions) Regulations 2001, SI 2001/1004, Reg 42*].

Example

Benevolent Ltd has 500 employees and it has agreed with its workers that all are provided with late night taxis each year prior to Christmas when a large, regular and anticipated order is placed by an overseas customer that is time-sensitive, necessitating late working. The taxi fares amount to an average of £50 per employee during the year ended 5 April 2017. In view of the rules on the provision of late night taxis for staff who work late (see **30.14** EARNINGS FROM EMPLOYMENT: EXPENSES), the fact that the trivial benefits exemption in ITEPA 2003, s 323A (introduced by FA 2016, s 13) cannot apply because the benefit is a reward for extra overtime, and Benevolent Ltd's wish to avoid having to submit P11Ds for the employees as well as the administrative burden of advising employees of the necessity to notify HM Revenue and Customs of the benefit under the self-assessment legislation, a PSA has been sought. Of the employees affected, 400 are basic rate taxpayers and the other 100 are higher rate taxpayers. Also, 100 employees receive expenses amounting to £2,000 in total relating to home to work travel (all higher rate taxpayers). In addition, accounting for the

Class 1 contributions on the £2,000 of expenses is not without its practical difficulties. See *The Income Tax (Pay As You Earn) Regulations 2003, SI 2003/2682, Regs 107(5), 117*. The PSA calculation might be as follows:

Tax for 2017–18 due under PSA	£	£
Value of benefits provided to basic rate taxpayers		
(400 × £50)	20,000	
Tax thereon @ 20%	4,000	
$£4{,}000 \times \frac{100}{100-20}$		
Gross up tax		5,000
Value of benefits provided to higher rate taxpayers		
(100 × £50)	5,000	
Value of expenses provided to higher rate taxpayers	2,000	
	7,000	
Tax thereon @ 40%	2,800	
$£2,800 \times \frac{100}{100-40}$		
Gross up tax		£4,667
Total tax		£9,667.00
NICs for 2017–18 due under PSA		
Value of expenses otherwise liable for Class 1 NICs	2,000	
Class 1B NICs due @ 13.8% on £2,000		276
Value of benefits otherwise liable to Class 1A NICs	25,000	
Class 1B NICs due @ 13.8% on £25,000		3,450
Tax paid by employer liable to Class 1B charge	9,667	
Class 1B NICs due re tax paid by employer @ 13.8%		1,334
Total NICs and tax payable by Benevolent Ltd		£14,727

The tax and Class 1B are payable to HM Revenue and Customs on or before 19 October 2018 (22 October 2018 if paid electronically).

Scottish taxpayers example

As the rUK (rest of the UK) tax rates have not changed, a direct comparison can be made between the above example and this example, which assumes that all employees are Scottish taxpayers. Adapting the employee split to reflect the Scottish rates, 300 are Scottish basic rate (20%) taxpayers, 100 are Scottish intermediate rate (21%) taxpayers. There is no change in the number of higher rate taxpayers (Scottish higher rate 41%).

Tax for 2018–19 due under PSA	£	£
Value of benefits provided to basic rate taxpayers		
(300 × £50)	15,000	
Tax thereon @ 20%	3,000	
$£3,000 \times \frac{100}{(100-20)}$		
Gross up tax		3,750

Value of benefits provided to intermediate rate taxpayers		
100 × £50	5,000	
Tax thereon @ 21%	1,050	
$£1,050 \times \frac{100}{(100-21)}$		
Gross up tax		1,329
Value of benefits provided to higher rate taxpayers		
(100 × £50)	5,000	
Value of expenses provided to higher rate taxpayers	2,000	
	7,000	
Tax thereon @ 41%	2,870	
$£2,870 \times \frac{100}{(100-41)}$		
Gross up tax		£4,864
Total tax		£9,943.00
NICs for 2018–19 due under PSA		
Value of expenses otherwise liable for Class 1 NICs	2,000	
Class 1B NICs due @ 13.8% on £2,000		276
Value of benefits otherwise liable to Class 1A NICs	25,000	
Class 1B NICs due @ 13.8% on £25,000		3,450
Tax paid by employer liable to Class 1B charge	9,943	
Class 1B NICs due re tax paid by employer @ 13.8%		1,372
Total NICs and tax payable by Benevolent Ltd		£15,041

The tax and Class 1B will be payable to HM Revenue and Customs on or before 19 October 2019 (22 October 2019 if paid electronically) as this example is for 2018–19.

PSAs involving Scottish taxpayers could be more complex since the above example does not take into account either the Scottish starter rate (19%) or the Scottish top rate (46%).

Incorrect payments

[17.6] Provision is included for rounding of contributions and recovery of unpaid contributions. [*Social Security (Contributions) Regulations 2001, SI 2001/1004, Reg 41*]. Interest will be charged on unpaid amounts from 20 October following the year to which the payment relates at the same rate as applies to underpayments of Class 1 and Class 1A. See HM Revenue and Customs Manual NIM18130. [*Social Security (Contributions) Regulations 2001, SI 2001/1004, Reg 67, Sch 4 paras 17, 18; The Income Tax (Pay As You Earn) Regulations 2003, SI 2003/2682, Reg 115*].

Recording requirements

[17.7] No new records are required to be kept over and above those needed for tax purposes and to distinguish between items which would or would not otherwise have been liable to NICs. Such records must be kept for at least three years.

Note that from 2018–19 details will need to be kept of those employees covered by the PSA who are Scottish taxpayers. This is down to the introduction from 2018–19 of additional tax rates and bands by the Scottish government. These Scottish tax rates are to be used to assess the tax due which will then impact on the Class 1B NICs due – see the example at **17.6**.

However, where an employee fails to qualify for SSP, SMP, SPP, SAP or, since 1 December 2014, Statutory Shared Parental Pay only because the average weekly earnings fall below the specified limit, it is a requirement that if any amounts included in the PSA relate to that employee and would otherwise have been liable to Class 1 contributions, the relevant value must be treated as earnings and included in average earnings calculations, if falling in the relevant weeks, so payments included in the PSA must be tracked. [*Statutory Maternity Pay (General) Regs 1986, Reg 20(2) and Statutory Sick Pay (General) Regs 1982, Reg 17(2)* as amended by *The Social Security Contributions Statutory Maternity Pay and Statutory Sick Pay (Miscellaneous Amendments) Regs 1999, Regs 12, Reg 13; Statutory Paternity Pay and Adoption Pay (General) Regulations 2002, Reg 39*; *Statutory Shared Parental Pay (General) Regulations 2014, Reg 32(7)(b)*.] See HM Revenue and Customs Manual NIM18120 and NIM18160.

Timing of PSA

[17.8] Class 1B only applies once a PSA is entered into. So if this is done in mid-tax year, or even after the end of it, then Class 1, rather than Class 1B, applies to relevant payments made before the PSA is agreed.

Class 1B will be due on all tax paid under PSAs regardless of the time at which the PSA is entered into. This is also the case even if there are no payments at all included in the PSA which would otherwise have been liable to Class 1/Class 1A. [*SSCBA 1992, s 10A(5)* as inserted by *Social Security Act 1998, s 53; The Income Tax (Pay As You Earn) Regulations 2003, SI 2003/2682, Regs 112–114*]. See HM Revenue and Customs Manual NIM18110.

Penalties and interest

[17.9] See 21.45 COLLECTION.

Key Points regarding class 1B contributions: PAYE settlement agreements

[17.10] Points to consider are as follows.

- For *income tax* purposes a PSA agreement may be entered into at any time prior to the 6 July following the end of the tax year. This contrasts with the need to enter into the agreement at the start of the relevant tax year if the agreement is intended to render minor earnings liable to Class 1B rather than Class 1 NICs.
- If an employee is tax resident in the UK but not working in the UK, such that Class 1 and Class 1A are not applicable, then Class 1B cannot be relevant and may, at the employer's option, be excluded from the calculations. The same applies to individuals working in the UK but not subject to Class 1 or Class 1A because of the provisions of EC regulations or a social security agreement.
- PSA calculations need to take account of Scottish taxpayers separately owing to the additional tax bands and different tax rates.

18

Class 2 Contributions: Self-employed Earners

Cross-references. See AGE EXCEPTION 3 for age limitations on liability; 5.16 AGGREGATION OF EARNINGS for small earnings exception; APPEALS AND REVIEWS 9; ARREARS OF CONTRIBUTIONS 12 for recovery powers and procedures; CATEGORISATION 14; COLLECTION 21; CREDITS 24 for circumstances in which Class 2 contributions may be awarded; DEFERMENT OF PAYMENT 27; EARNINGS FROM EMPLOYMENT: GENERAL 29; ENFORCEMENT 35; LATE-PAID CONTRIBUTIONS 42; MULTIPLE EMPLOYMENTS 47; NATIONAL INSURANCE NUMBER 49; OVERSEAS MATTERS 51; PARTNERS 52; RATES AND LIMITS 53; REDUCED LIABILITY ELECTIONS 54; REPAYMENT AND REALLOCATION 55; SHARE FISHERMEN 56; SUBPOSTMASTERS 57; VOLUNTEER DEVELOPMENT WORKERS 59.

Other Sources. Simon's Taxes, Volume 2, para A8.3; HM Revenue and Customs National Insurance Manual NIM20000, NIM21000, NIM22000, NIM23000 and NIM23500.

Introduction to class 2 contributions: self-employed earners

[18.1] Class 2 contributions are paid by around 2.65 million self-employed earners and, in the year 2016–17, produced some £400 million of National Insurance Fund income (see 48.4 national insurance fund).

This is significantly more than the £191 million collected in 2015–16 (originally forecast to be £381 million), for which no explanation was given in the Government Actuary's report on the April 2016 NIC changes. The increase may be attributable to the change of collection regime when Class 2 was transferred into the ITSA process with effect from April 2015, with the first Class 2 falling due for 2015–16 being expected by 31 January 2017 rather than month-by-month in the year in question. Given the publication date and lead time for the report's preparation, it seems clear that the 2015–16 'outturn' is in fact merely an estimate, and that it overlooked the change in basis. HMRC could hardly have reported mid-year receipts figures for Class 2 in 2015 on which the estimate might have been based, since it was no longer collecting any such contributions, so both the 2015–16 and 2016–17 estimates must be treated with a certain degree of caution.

According to the ONS's 'Trends in self-employment in the UK: 2001 – 2015', published in July 2016, around 4.6 million people were self-employed in 2015, accounting for 15% of those in work, which was the highest percentage at any point in the past four decades, since data were first collected. Around 4.3% of the 15% were in part-time self-employment, suggesting that they might not earn enough to be compulsory Class 2 contributors, but the figures imply a much more significant proportion is not liable to pay Class 2. The NI Fund accounts for 2014–15, published in October 2015, stated that some 2.3 million 'customers' had profits below the small earnings exception limit, and HMRC had failed to collect some Class 2 balances due, which had increased from £1.048 million in April 2014 to £1.126 million in April 2015.

There were also an additional 350,000 employees who had a second job in which they were self-employed. The difference between the number in self-employment and the number paying contributions as such seems likely to be attributable principally to three factors: (1) many people in self-employment, according to the ONS, have fairly low profits and are therefore likely from 6 April 2015 to have profits falling below the small profits threshold – see below) – median income among the self-employed has been estimated at approximately £10,760 per annum, so there will be significant numbers with profits below the SPT threshold; (2) 468,000 of the population are aged over 65 and therefore exempt from Class 2 liability; and (3) those for whom self-employment is a secondary activity may qualify for SPT or, because they already pay maximum Class 1 contributions, exemption from Class 2.

When compared with total contributions from employed earners (£48 billion) and their secondary contributors (£71 billion), however, the amount is small and represents around 0.2% of total fund income from contributions. The total amount of Class 2 receivable by the Fund reduced from 2000–01 onwards due to a substantial reduction in the weekly rate for political reasons. Of the total amount collected, 15.5% is diverted to the National Health Service. In a report by the Social Security Advisory Committee published in September 2014, serious questions were posed about why the self-employed appear to make such a minimal contribution to the NI Fund when they make up 15% of the working population. To date, the major difference between employed and self-employed earners has been the entitlement of those who pay Class 1 contributions to the state earnings-related pension (SERPS) or state second pension (S2P), so this question of inequality will come even more sharply into focus now that everybody earns the same single-tier state pension entitlement from 6 April 2016. The only real difference now is the entitlement of Class 1 contributors to contributions-based jobseeker's allowance, which is currently a maximum of £73.10 per week for 26 weeks, and costs the NI Fund just £265 million in 2016–17, which is a tiny element of the NI regime that does not justify the differential between the levels of contribution.

In a consultation document '*Improving the collection of National Insurance Contributions from the self-employed*' issued on Budget Day, 12 March 2008, HM Revenue and Customs proposed to streamline Class 2 collection where payment was not made by direct debit. One idea was simply to add Class 2 information to self-assessment (SA) statements when there were Class 2 arrears. Another was to adjust the Class 2 due dates to the last days of January, April, July and October so that two of them coincided with the SA due dates. Alternatively, there could have been two due dates to match the SA due dates, and from April 2011 such arrangements were put in place, and any opportunity to pay following a quarterly invoice from Newcastle was no longer an option. Those self-employed individuals who paid monthly by direct debit continued to do so until the last payment for 2014–15 liabilities, albeit from 11 April 2011 contributions were collected four months in arrears. There was also an option to pay on a six-monthly basis which aligned collection with the self-assessment arrangements. For those not due to make a SA payment in July, the SA statement would show only the Class 2 due.

Further changes were proposed when, on 18 July 2013, HMRC published a consultation document, 'Simplifying the National Insurance Processes for the Self-Employed'. This proposed moving Class 2 collection into the self-assessment regime and collecting contributions six-monthly. In Budget 2014, it was announced that the government would collect Class 2 NICs through self-assessment from April 2015, with detail in a new NIC Bill, now the *National Insurance Contributions Act 2015 (NICA 2015)*. The reform introduced by NICA 2015 is described at 18.13 below and it prevented spurious debt balances being generated from the 2.3 million 'customers' whose profits were below the threshold. No new applications to pay by direct debit were to be accepted, according to the information at www.gov.uk/pay-class-2-national-insurance/direct-debit, although the option has in fact continued for voluntary contributors or those who are outside self-assessment, such as those resident and working abroad in the short term with a continuing UK NIC liability.

A revised penalty regime was introduced from 6 April 2009 – see **21.47** – but that was again changed by *NICA 2015*, which moved Class 2 collection into the ITSA regime, including applying the income tax penalty and interest regime that applies to Class 4 instead of the specific provisions for Class 2.

HMRC's actions to collect Class 2 more effectively were summarised in the NI Fund accounts for 2014–15:

- The Department continued to collect Class 2 debt through the PAYE tax code, and customers (in employed earner's employment) with debts above £32 were included within the annual coding exercise.
- Class 2 debt not suitable for coding was being transferred to debt collection agencies.
- A large-scale campaign using bespoke letters and SMS messages was launched.

- The amount of debt was reduced by 'stripping out debt not actually due because the customer [had], for example, ceased self-employment'.
- Time-barred debt was removed from the insolvency process, which was to be automated from April 2016.

The accounts also revealed that the reported Class 2 debt figure included spurious amounts generated in respect of customers who had ceased self-employment but not told HMRC.

The next development is likely to be the abolition in April 2018 (since postponed until April 2019) of Class 2, with its function as a qualifier for state benefits being transferred to Class 4. This was announced in broad terms in the March 2015 Budget and reiterated in the July 2015 Budget after the general election. It was then subject to consultation in mid-to-late 2015, and confirmed (again in broad terms) in the March 2016 Budget. The latest plan suggests that there is to be a further consultation on detailed proposals in late 2016, followed by a Social Security Bill in 2017, and the abolition will be effected on 5 April 2018. No detail has yet been released of how the abolition of the class of contribution and the transfer of contributory effect are to be implemented. The detail will principally involve determining how Class 4 contributions will convert into benefit entitlements rather than how collection of Class 2, now in the ITSA regime, will cease. There will inevitably be some transitional provisions to deal with liabilities arising before abolition that remain uncollected by the normal payment date for 2018–19, ie, 31 January 2020, and it is hoped that the changes will tidy up some of the anomalies of the Class 2 regime around people in business without trading profits, women entitled to maternity allowance based on recent contributions (in a system that only requires payment nine and one-half months after the end of the tax year), and special rates for share fishermen and volunteer development workers.

In a written statement to the House of Commons on 2 November 2017, the Government announced that the National Insurance Contributions Bill, required for the abolition of Class 2 NICs, would be introduced 'in 2018' and that the 'measures it will implement will now take effect one year later, from April 2019'. The delay was justified as allowing more time to deal with the concerns highlighted in the previous paragraph.

The history of Class 2 and how the Class 2 regime will operate for 2016–17 to 2018–19 are described below.

Liability

[18.2] Until 5 April 2015, every 'self-employed earner' was, if he was over the age of 16 and under pensionable age, liable to pay Class 2 contributions at a prescribed weekly rate (see **14.18** CATEGORISATION; **3.2**, **3.13** AGE EXCEPTION; **53.8** RATES AND LIMITS). See HM Revenue and Customs National Insurance Manual NIM20000. [*Social Security Contributions and Benefits Act 1992 (SSCBA 1992), s 11(1)(2).*] From 6 April 2015, this liability has applied only to earners with relevant profits from a trade, profession or vocation of, or exceeding, a small profits threshold (SPT), set initially at £5,965 for 2015–16 and unchanged for 2016–17. [*New SSCBA 1992, s 11(2) as inserted by NICA 2015,*

Sch 1, para 3.] The SPT for 2018–19 is set at £6,205. In addition to changing the basis of liability, the reform has also moved the payment date: liability is now only established once profits for the year are known, and payment is now due in the same manner that Class 4 contributions in respect of relevant profits are, or would be, payable. [*Social Security Contributions and Benefits Act 1992, s 11(5)*.] Contributions are therefore now payable with the annual tax return final payment rather than by monthly direct debit or six-monthly bill.

In view of the reform from 6 April 2015, it is worthwhile considering briefly the term 'self-employed earner'. As explained in **14.4** CATEGORISATION, an 'earner' is anyone who derives remuneration or profit from an 'employment', a term which includes any trade, business, profession, office or vocation [*Social Security Contributions and Benefits Act 1992, ss 3(1), 122(1)*.] The effect of this definition is to draw into the scope of the term 'self-employed earner' anyone carrying on a 'business' activity, even if it is an investment activity (eg, letting property) rather than a trade or profession.

Before 6 April 2015, this was enough to create a Class 2 liability in respect of any unincorporated business (subject to a claim for small earnings exception), but from that date liability is limited to cases where there is income ('relevant income') at least equal to the new SPT from a trade, profession or vocation taxable under *Income Tax (Trading and Other Income) Act 2005 (ITTOIA 2005), Pt 2, Ch 2*, ie, the same basic definition of the source as is used for Class 4, albeit with a different starting threshold.

Those classed as self-employed earners who do not have trading, etc profits now have no *liability* to pay Class 2 contributions: *s 11(2)* is now limited to those with 'relevant profits' above the SPT. They do, however, have the *right* to do so in order to protect their benefit entitlements: *s 11(6)* now provides that the earner may pay the same level of Class 2 contribution as a trader (with sufficient annual profits to create a compulsory liability) in respect of any week in the relevant tax year in which the earner is in the 'employment'. This enables both traders with low profits or losses and non-traders with business income to maintain their entitlement to the state pension and contributory short-term employment and support allowance.

Liability will always be measured in complete weeks as a person is to be treated as a self-employed earner in respect of any week during any part of which he is such an earner. [*SSCBA 1992, s 2(5)*]. Liability will, furthermore, continue unless and until a person is no longer ordinarily gainfully employed in his self-employed earner's employment. [*Categorisation Regs, Reg 3, Sch 2*]. The effect of this latter regulation is to impose a liability even for weeks of holiday, weeks of inactivity and weeks where there are no earnings from the self-employment, provided the self-employment has not ceased or become so irregular and exceptional and non-gainful as to be disregarded under *Categorisation Regs, Reg 2(4), Sch 1 Part III Para 9* (see **14.18** CATEGORISATION).

Where a Class 2 contribution is paid late it will, in certain circumstances, be payable at a rate other than the rate at which it would have been payable had it been paid on or by its due date (see **42.8** LATE-PAID CONTRIBUTIONS). Before 6 April 2015, this rule applied to all Class 2 contributions, but from that date late payment of compulsory contributions (*new SSCBA 1992, s 11(2) as* *amended by NICA 2015, Sch 1, para 3*) has been dealt with under the rules applicable to Class 4 contributions. [*Social Security Contributions and Benefits Act 1992, s 11A, as inserted by NICA 2015, Sch 1, para 3*.] The traditional Class 2 late payment provisions are now reserved for voluntary contributions (under *new s 11(6)*).

Case law

[18.3] Once a person ceases to be ordinarily self-employed, however, his liability will cease, on 'doctrine of source' principles. (*National Provident Institution v Brown* (1921) 8 TC 57). This is so even if his self-employed activities were such that they will continue to produce earnings for him into the future (eg book royalties from ceased self-employed authorship).

In *Rashid v Garcia (Status Inspector)* [2003] STC (SCD) 36 an individual (R) had carried on business as a taxi driver, and paid Class 2 National Insurance contributions. He also received income from the letting of four properties of mixed commercial and residential nature. In June 1997 he suffered a heart attack and ceased to work as a taxi driver. He continued to pay Class 2 contributions, in order to qualify for invalidity benefit. HM Revenue and Customs issued a ruling that he was not a 'self-employed earner' within *SSCBA 1992, s 2(1)(b)*. The Special Commissioner dismissed R's appeal, holding on the evidence that his property income represented an investment rather than a business. This decision appears to conflict with the HMRC announcements in 2013 on the position of sleeping and inactive partners – see **18.16**. Under the post-April 2015 regime, Mr Rashid would have had no liability, as he had no Class 4 income, and the same question about whether he was in business would have arisen in determining whether he was entitled to make a Class 2 contribution.

The case of *Ramsay v Revenue and Customs Comrs* [2013] UKUT 226 (TCC), [2013] SWTI 1902, [2013] All ER (D) 290 (May) provides an interesting alternative view of what constitutes a 'business' when a taxpayer is letting property, albeit in the context of different legislation. The taxpayer incorporated her letting activities, which consisted of ten flats in one property, and claimed relief under TCGA 1992, s 162 on the basis that her activities amounted to a business for the purposes of that section – the word is not specifically defined, so it is reasonable to assume that it means the same as the word used in the social security legislation, ie, its ordinary English meaning. While the First-tier Tribunal held that she was not trading and disallowed her appeal against a CGT assessment on the gain she 'realised' on exchanging her business for an issue of shares, the Upper Tribunal decided that the use of the word 'business' in s 162 did not connote trading, and that she was indeed in business and entitled to claim the incorporation relief.

Exception from liability on grounds of small income

[18.4] An earner who would otherwise be liable for Class 2 contributions in respect of his employment as a self-employed earner was for many years until 6 April 2015 open to exception from such liability in respect of any period in which his earnings from self-employment (**32.2**) from such employment were, or were treated as being, less than a specified amount (see **53.9** RATES AND LIMITS). [*SSCBA 1992, s 11(4)*]. For 2014–15 the prescribed amount was £5,885. See HM Revenue and Customs National Insurance Manuals NIM21001. [SSCBA 1992, s 11(4) as amended by *Social Security (Contributions) (Re-rating) Order 2013, SI 2013/597, Reg 2(b)*.] The Autumn Statement 2014 announced the 2015–16 equivalent as £5,965, but as noted above the limit is now known as the small profits threshold (SPT) and the basis of its use has been changed. Whereas traditionally an earner has been able to apply in advance for exception in the expectation of low profits, *NICA 2015* recast the rules, moving liability for 2015–16 to 31 January 2017, the ITSA deadline after the end of the tax year, and removing liability altogether if profits do not reach the SPT.

Exception under the pre-2015 provisions was not granted automatically, but had to be on the earner's own application. [*Social Security Contributions and Benefits Act 1992, old s 11(5)*.] In contrast, under the 2015 provisions, an earner is exempt if profits do not reach the SPT, so no application is now needed. If granted, the former exception might, at HM Revenue and Customs' discretion and as was considered appropriate to the circumstances of the case, commence on a date earlier than the date of application, but not more than 13 weeks earlier. [*Social Security (Contributions) Regulations 2001, SI 2001/1004, Reg 44(5)(b), revoked by Social Security (Miscellaneous Amendments No 2) Regulations 2015, SI 2015, 478, Reg 24*.] If exception was granted to someone paying contributions by direct debit, it was normally effective from the Sunday after the date of application and a refund would be made in respect of contributions paid after that date – HM Revenue and Customs National Insurance Manual NIM21043.

Where Class 2 contributions had not been paid but small earnings exception would have been available had an application been made within the time limit prescribed, waiver of the Class 2 liabilities might be granted by concession for years up to 5 April 2015 (see **12.20** ARREARS OF CONTRIBUTIONS).

Where Class 2 contributions had been paid but small earnings exception would have been available had an application been made within the time limit prescribed, a repayment of those contributions might, under certain conditions, be obtained (see **55.10** REPAYMENT AND REALLOCATION).

Under the pre-2015 rules, the earnings for any particular tax year were to be treated as less than the specified amount for that year (see **53.9** RATES AND LIMITS) if it was shown to the satisfaction of HM Revenue and Customs that:

- in the tax year preceding the particular tax year concerned, the applicant's earnings from self-employment (**32.2**) had been less than the amount specified for the preceding tax year and that there had since been no material change of circumstances; or
- in the particular tax year concerned, the applicant's earnings from self-employment (**32.2**) were expected to be less than the specified amount.

[*Social Security (Contributions) Regulations 2001, SI 2001/1004, Reg 45(1), revoked by Social Security (Miscellaneous Amendments No 2) Regulations 2015, SI 2015, 478, Reg 24*.]

Example

Ambrose is a florist. His accounts (prepared in October 2014) showed that his net profits for the year ended 5 April 2014 were only £2,800. As trade was continually worsening and as he was already behind with his Class 2 payments, he decided to apply for 2014–15 Class 2 exception and did so on 5 November 2014. As his earnings in 2013–14 were less than £5,725 (the specified amount for 2013–14) and as things were changing only for the worse, exception will have been granted—but only from (and including) the week beginning 3 August 2014. Ambrose should, of course, have applied for 2014–15 Class 2 exception *before* 6 April 2014 on the grounds that he expected his net profits for the year ended 5 April 2015 to be less than £5,885 (the specified amount for 2014–15).

Under the 2015 regime, Ambrose would need no advance application. When he prepares his ITSA tax return for 2015–16 (and subsequent years), he will already know his profit figure for the year and will know whether he has a liability for Class 2 contributions for the year. If his profits turn out to be below the small profits threshold of £5,965 for the year, he may choose whether to pay Class 2 contributions with his tax liability.

Application for Class 2 exception on the grounds of small income had to be made to HM Revenue and Customs in a form approved by it. In practical terms, this involved completing and signing a form CF10 (available from HM Revenue and Customs website – see CHAPTER 41 – or from Self Employment Services) and lodging it with HM Revenue and Customs NIC&EO, Self-Employment Services. The application was to be supported by such information and evidence as might be required and until 27 May 1996 this usually took the form of accounts, tax assessments or records of receipts and payments. (Leaflet CA 02, now withdrawn). Renewals were made on either the personalised CF17 invitation issued by HM Revenue and Customs shortly before the existing exemption certificate expired, or, failing that, on a fresh form CF10. [*Social Security (Contributions) Regulations 2001, SI 2001/1004, Reg 44(1)–(3), revoked by Social Security (Miscellaneous Amendments No 2) Regulations 2015, SI 2015, 478, Reg 24.*]

After 27 May 1996 evidence of earnings was no longer needed in support of the declaration of earnings on Form CF10 (CA notice CA6813, June 1996) whether the applicant was newly self-employed or not but *Social Security (Contributions) Regulations 2001, SI 2001/1004, Reg 44(3)* (revoked from 6 April 2015) stated that the applicant should give such '. . . *evidence relating to his earnings as the Board may require on the making of an application and at any subsequent time*'.

If the application was approved, HM Revenue and Customs issued to the applicant a 'certificate of exception' which stated the period for which the exception was to apply. This period was normally three years unless a shorter period was thought to be appropriate (eg in the case of a new business) and ended on a Saturday immediately following a 5 April (or 5 April itself, if that was a Saturday). If the conditions attaching to a certificate of exception ceased to be fulfilled, the certificate automatically ceased to be in force and HM Revenue and Customs had to be notified. [*Social Security (Contributions) Regulations 2001, SI 2001/1004, Reg 44(4), (5)(a), revoked by Social Security (Miscellaneous Amendments No 2) Regulations 2015, SI 2015, 478, Reg 24.*]

It should be noted that the increase of earnings to a level in excess of the small earnings exception limit was *not* a breach of the conditions attaching to a certificate and did *not* automatically terminate any exception which had been granted. Indeed, the former DSS was usually content to let a certificate of exception run to its expiry in such circumstances, even when made aware that earnings were above the limit. If, however, the holder of a certificate wished to cancel it for that or any reason he could do so by completing the back page of the certificate and then returning it to the NIC&EO. If self-employment ceased, the same procedure was followed. Cancellation of a certificate took place from such date as HM Revenue and Customs determined. [*Social Security (Contributions) Regulations 2001, SI 2001/1004, Reg 44(6)(b), revoked by Social Security (Miscellaneous Amendments No 2) Regulations 2015, SI 2015, 478, Reg 24.*]

Anyone holding a certificate of exception was obliged to produce it for inspection if required to do so. [*Social Security (Contributions) Regulations 2001, SI 2001/1004, Reg 44(6)(a), revoked by Social Security (Miscellaneous Amendments No 2) Regulations 2015, SI 2015, 478, Reg 24.*]

Although a certificate of exception excepted the holder from liability to pay a Class 2 contribution for any contribution week during the whole of which it was in force, the holder was nonetheless entitled to pay a contribution if he so wished. [*Social Security (Contributions) Regulations 2001, SI 2001/1004, Reg 46, revoked by Social Security (Miscellaneous Amendments No 2) Regulations 2015, SI 2015, 478, Reg 24.*] The reverse of the exemption certificate had to be completed accordingly. He might have wished to do so to protect his benefit entitlement (see BENEFITS: CONTRIBUTION REQUIREMENTS **13**) as no CREDITS **24** are awarded for periods of exception on grounds of small income. Under the 2015 regime, entitlement to pay voluntarily is granted formally by *SSCBA 1992, s 11(6) as amended by NICA 2015, Sch 1, para 3*. The situation was therefore reversed with the new rules: instead of having a liability unless and until exception was granted, the current rules automatically except any earner with profits below the SPT and an earner must actively choose (via the ITSA return or by lodging a form) to pay voluntarily.

See **57.6** SUBPOSTMASTERS for the application of these rules to a subpostmaster who carries on an ancillary business as a self-employed earner.

Under the *NICA 2015* reforms, from 6 April 2015, the SEE procedures are redundant and of historical relevance only, as liability is now assessed in arrears, and contributors should know actual profit figures before making any payment.

Exception from liability on other grounds

[18.5] A self-employed earner is to be excepted from liability for Class 2 for any contribution week if, as regards that week, he satisfies any of the following conditions. See also HM Revenue and Customs Manual NIM20775.

- He is, in respect of the whole of the week, in receipt of incapacity benefit or employment and support allowance. [*Social Security (Contributions) Regulations 2001, SI 2001/1004, Reg 43(1)(a)(ab)*].

From 13 April 1995, incapacity benefit replaced the previous invalidity and sickness benefits which were not taxable, but most elements of incapacity benefit are taxable. See also Inland Revenue Press Release 22 March 1995 and DWP Press Release 18 November 2002. It is a common misconception that the self-employed are not entitled to state benefits whilst sick. This is not the case.

- He is, throughout the whole of the week, incapable of work. Incapacity for work is the primary test of eligibility for employment and support allowance and for Statutory Sick Pay and, that being so, the words will, it is submitted, be accorded no wider meaning here than they are accorded in their benefit context. [*Social Security (Contributions) Regulations 2001, SI 2001/1004, Reg 43(1)(b)*].
- She is, in respect of the week, in receipt of maternity allowance. [*Social Security (Contributions) Regulations 2001, SI 2001/1004, Reg 43(1)(c)*].
- He is, throughout the whole of the week, undergoing imprisonment or detention in legal custody. [*Social Security (Contributions) Regulations 2001, SI 2001/1004, Reg 43(1)(d)*]. Legal custody covers detention by reason of a legal proceeding or as the result of a court proceeding whether the detention has a punitive or corrective purpose or not. (*R v National Insurance Commissioner, Ex p Timmis* [1955] 1 QB 139, [1954] 3 All ER 292). It thus includes detention in a mental hospital or a similar institution following a court order (*R(S) 20/53*, and numerous other reported decisions of the National Insurance Commissioners in the sickness benefit series) but, as in that decision, the Commissioners have made it clear that the related proceedings must be criminal proceedings or be grounded on a criminal act. A detainee allowed out of a mental hospital to work under daily licence is nonetheless under detention. (*R(S) 23/54*). Whether, or when, a person will cease to be 'ordinarily self-employed' by reason of a period of imprisonment or detention in legal custody will presumably depend largely on the length of the period for which actual self-employment is suspended (see **14.18** CATEGORISATION).
- He is, in respect of any part of the week, in receipt of carer's allowance (formerly invalid care allowance) or unemployability supplement (an addition to a war pension). [*Social Security (Contributions) Regulations 2001, SI 2001/1004, Reg 43(1)(e)*].

A volunteer development worker (VDW) (see VOLUNTEER DEVELOPMENT WORKER **59**) was, until 5 April 2015, also excepted, but since such a worker has no trading, etc income within the scope of Class 4, no liability now arises, so no exception provisions are necessary. [*Social Security (Contributions) Regulations 2001, SI 2001/1004, Reg 151(a) revoked by Social Security (Miscellaneous Amendments No 2) Regulations 2015, SI 2015/478, Reg 19.*] A VDW can now, as before, still choose to pay voluntarily.

A whole week for these purposes is a period of seven days beginning with midnight between Saturday and Sunday but excluding Sunday or some religiously acceptable alternative day. [*Social Security (Contributions) Regulations 2001, SI 2001/1004, Reg 1(2), Reg 43(2)(a)(b)*].

A self-employed earner who is excepted from Class 2 liability in accordance with these regulations, and volunteer development workers, remain entitled to pay a contribution for any week, should they wish to do so. [*Social Security (Contributions) Regulations 2001, SI 2001/1004, Reg 43(3), Reg 151(b)*].

Certain married women and widows are effectively excepted from liability by reason of a reduced rate election (see **18.7** below).

Rates

[18.6] Class 2 liability arises at a specified flat rate for each contribution week in the tax year that the earner is in the employment. [*Social Security Contributions and Benefits Act 1992, s 11(1)(2).*] Provision is made for the imposition of liability at a higher flat rate than normal in the case of earners who, by virtue of the *Categorisation Regulations* are moved from the category of employed earner to that of self-employed earner. [Pre-2015: *Sec 11(3); post-2015: Sec 11(8).*] However, to date, this power has not been exercised. The only group of earners who could currently be affected, were that to be so, are certain EXAMINERS **37**. The Autumn Statement 2014 announced a rate of £2.80 per week for 2015–16, which was duly set by *NICA 2015, Sch 1, para 12* and the same level was maintained for 2016–17. (See **53.9** RATES AND LIMITS for earlier years.) The rate is set at £2.95 for 2018–19.

If it is considered necessary, the Treasury (previously the Secretary of State for Social Security) but subject to Parliamentary approval may, at any time, make an order altering the weekly rate of Class 2 contribution. [*SSAA 1992, ss 143(1), 144(1), 189(9)* as amended by *Social Security Contributions (Transfer of Functions, etc) Act 1999 (SSC(TF)A 1999), Sch 3 para 46, para 49 and NICA 2015, Sch 1, para 21*].

A *special higher rate* of Class 2 contributions is imposed under *Sec 117(1)* in respect of share fishermen (**56.3**) because, though self-employed earners, such persons are eligible for jobseeker's allowance. The Autumn Statement 2014 announced a rate of £3.45 for 2015–16, which was duly introduced and maintained for 2016–17. [*Social Security (Contributions) Regulations 2001, SI 2001/1004, Reg 125(c) as amended by NICA 2015, Sch 1, para 33.*] The rate for 2018–19 is £3.60. The rate at which VOLUNTEER DEVELOPMENT WORKERS **59** are entitled to pay a Class 2 contribution, should they wished to do so was £5.60 for 2015–16 and 2016–17. [*Social Security (Contributions) Regulations 2001, SI 2001/1004, Reg 152(b) as amended by Social Security (Miscellaneous Amendments No 2) Regulations 2015, SI 2015/478, Reg 20.*] The rate is £5.80 for 2018–19.

Married women

[18.7] Certain married women and widows who would, were they employed earners, be entitled to pay primary Class 1 contributions at a reduced rate are, if they are self-employed earners, under *no liability* to pay Class 2 contributions. [*Social Security (Contributions) Regulations 2001, SI 2001/1004, Reg 127(1)(b)*]. The enabling provision under which this regulation was made,

SSCBA 1992, s 19(4)(b), permits, as an alternative to nil liability, the imposition of a reduced liability, but no such reduced Class 2 liability has ever been imposed (see REDUCED LIABILITY ELECTIONS **54**).

Collection

[18.8] For many years until April 1993, Class 2 was collected by buying contribution stamps and affixing them to a card, which was sent in to the DHSS Longbenton office each year. The 'stamp' was replaced by a quarterly billing regime in April 1993, with an option to pay by monthly direct debit instead. The quarterly bill later became a six-monthly bill, but for most contributors, a Class 2 contribution liability for years before 6 April 2015 would be discharged by direct debit of a bank account (see **21.47** COLLECTION). Where the collection method was ineffective, recovery proceedings could be taken (see ARREARS OF CONTRIBUTIONS **12**). (CA Press Release 25 March 1993). A consultation document was issued on 12 March 2008 proposing changes to collection methods. From April 2014 HMRC may collect outstanding arrears of Class 2 NIC by adjusting the tax codes of individual contributors who have employment income. [*Social Security (Contributions) (Amendment and Application of Schedule 38 to the Finance Act 2012) Regulations 2013, SI 2013/622, Reg 38*]. This introduced a new *regulation 63A to the Social Security (Contributions) Regulations 2001, SI 2001/1004*.

Since April 2013 HMRC have been sending payment requests to individuals who owe Class 2 NIC. The request makes clear that if the debt is not settled HMRC may collect the debt through the PAYE code or pass the debt to a private debt collection agency. Those individuals who have not paid or made arrangements to settle the debt and who are within the PAYE system are likely to have received a Coding Notice between January and March 2014 and this will have shown the Class 2 NIC debt to be collected from April 2014. See the HMRC announcement in 'What's New' dated 11 December 2013.

The DWP then introduced the *Social Security (Crediting and Treatment of Contributions and National Insurance Numbers) (Amendment) Regulations 2013, SI 2013/3165*, which for benefit purposes will treat any contributions collected via the PAYE system as having been paid on 5 April at the end of the tax year in which they are paid. This will significantly reduce the period for which such contributions can provide entitlement to short-term social security benefits. For the purposes of any benefit claim, any such contributions collected via PAYE are treated as not having been paid before that date, which could penalise recalcitrant contributors who claim.

In their review of small business in 2012 the Office for Tax Simplification recommended that the Government review the NIC processes for the self-employed and, in particular, that Class 2 contributions should be collected through the self-assessment process. As noted above, the Government agreed and announced in the 2014 Budget that it would bring Class 2 collection into the self-assessment payment regime from April 2015, which was duly implemented by NICA 2015, Sch 1 and *Social Security (Miscellaneous Amendments No 2) Regulations 2015, SI 2015/478*.

The government's response to the 2013 consultation suggested that the monthly direct debit payment system was expected to remain available for those who wished to spread the Class 2 liability across the year and for those self-employed and voluntary contributors who are not in the self-assessment regime (eg, because they are non-resident although still within the UK social security system). In the event, no new direct debit applications are to be accepted, according to the HMRC guidance at www.gov.uk/pay-class-2-national-insurance. The web guidance on voluntary Class 2 contributions indicates that, while no new direct debits will be set up, HMRC will continue to take payments by that method if the contributor has previously set one up. Where no direct debit mandate is in place, HMRC offers the usual routes of payment: online or telephone banking, CHAPS (unlikely in practice), via a bank, building society or Post Office counter, BACS or cheque.

National Insurance Contributions Act 2015, Schedule 1 rewrote SSCBA 1992, s 11 to redefine liability and entitlement to pay Class 2 contributions. *Section 11(5)* now provides that compulsory Class 2 contributions under s *11(2)* are to be payable in the same manner that Class 4 contributions in respect of relevant profits are, or would be, payable, subject to certain exceptions contained in a *new section 11A*.

Section 11A applies a series of provisions of the Income Tax Acts to Class 2 contributions payable under s 11(2). In particular, *TMA 1970 Part 5A* (payment of tax) and *Part 6* (collection and recovery) are applied so as to deal with Class 2 in the same way as Class 4 through the self-assessment system. The major difference is that *TMA 1970, s 59A*, which mandates six monthly payments on account of income tax and Class 4 contributions by 31 January and 31 July each year, is not to apply to Class 2 liability. [*Social Security Contributions and Benefits Act 1992, s 11A(2)*.] The liability for the previous tax year will therefore fall due by 31 January and can be paid with the income tax and Class 4 liability in the usual ways. As is the case with income tax and Class 4 contributions, a taxpayer whose tax affairs are up-to-date may agree a 'budget payment plan' with HMRC to make regular payments in advance – see www.gov.uk/pay-self-assessment-tax-bill/budget-payment-plan. If the total paid during the year does not cover the whole amount due, the balance must be paid by the normal 31 January deadline.

Tax relief

[18.9] No tax relief may be given or a tax deduction allowed in respect of any Class 2 contribution paid. [*ITTOIA 2005, ss 53, 272, 868* as amended by *ITA 2007, Sch 1, para 507* and *ITEPA 2003, s 360A*].

Voluntary Class 2 contributions

[18.10] In limited circumstances, Class 2 contributions may be paid voluntarily in order to protect entitlement to short-term benefits (other than jobseeker's allowance) and basic retirement pension and bereavement benefits.

Under the pre-2015 regime, this was generally found only during absence from the UK (see OVERSEAS MATTERS **51.9**). See HM Revenue and Customs National Insurance Manual NIM33500. See Tolley's Practical NIC Newsletter, October 2002, pages 79 and 80.

Under the reformed Class 2 regime from 6 April 2015, Class 2 *liability* will arise only for self-employed earners with profits within the Class 4 definition in excess of the small profits threshold each year, so there are now more potential voluntary contributors:

- traders with small profits;
- those contributors in a non-trading business (eg, landlords) who no longer have a liability despite being self-employed earners within the definition outlined above;
- examiners, moderators, invigilators and people who set exam questions who are deemed to be self-employed but have no trading income; and
- ministers of religion who do not receive a salary or stipend.

The time limit for paying voluntary Class 2 contributions is normally six years from the end of the relevant tax year, but for the years 2006/07 to 2015/16 for those who retire on or after 6 April 2017 the limits have been extended on account of the single-tier state pension scheme being introduced from April 2016. [*Social Security (Contributions) (Amendment and Application of Schedule 38 to the Finance Act 2012) Regulations 2013, SI 2013/622, Reg 37*].

A man born after 5 April 1951 (ie, not yet 66 years old on 6 April 2017) is permitted until 5 April 2019 to pay Class 2 contributions voluntarily for 2006–07 to 2010–11 inclusive at the rate of £2.65 per week, and for 2011–12 to 2015–16 at the rate for the year to which the contribution relates.

The same rule applies to a woman born after 5 April 1953 (ie, not yet 64 on 6 April 2017).

The extended deadline of 5 April 2019 gives three years after the changeover to the new single-tier state pension scheme for contributors to check their entitlements with the DWP and make arrangements to pay voluntarily to fill any holes in the contribution record.

Disputed Class 2 payable voluntarily

[18.11] On 5 June 2013 HMRC announced via a 'What's New?' item that their long-held view that 'sleeping partners' and other 'inactive limited partners' were outside the scope of Class 2 NIC had been incorrect. The revised view, also shared by the DWP, was that such individuals were gainfully employed on a self-employed basis and fell within the scope of *SSCBA 1992, s 2(1)(b)*. HMRC considered that the reference to 'business' in *SSCBA 1992, s 122* coupled with the definition in *Partnership Act 1890, s 1(1)* brought such individuals into Class 2 liability because they must have been carrying on a business in common with a view to a profit, and any 'business' activity would constitute an 'employment' for contribution purposes, even without the partner being active in the business. The original view was that if there was no activity there could be no liability, but they concluded that *SSCBA 1992, s 2(1)(b)* imposes no requirement for partners to be active in the business. The new view was subsequently reflected in NIM24521-24524.

Such a conclusion was questionable (many limited partners are no more than investors, and the HMRC view cannot be correct in relation to investment-only partnerships, since there will be no earned income and possibly even no 'business' – see, eg, *Rashid v Garcia* SpC 348, [2003] STC (SCD) 36) – and whilst any Class 2 contributions would not impose any real financial burden the same cannot be said for Class 4 contributions. For that reason the matter seemed likely to be challenged until the law was changed as a result of the project to simplify the NI processes for the self-employed referred to above.

HMRC said its revised view would apply from 6 April 2013 only, and no action would be taken to collect arrears for earlier periods but, equally, no refunds would be given where contributions had been paid contrary to the advice given by HMRC at the time those contributions were paid. HMRC undertook to offer the opportunity for some individuals to pay Class 2 NIC voluntarily for past periods when they were inactive and thereby improve their entitlement to retirement pension. HMRC undertook in June 2013 to issue details on how this might be done by the end of summer 2013, but in the event nothing new was published and new procedures were still awaited at April 2015.

As outlined above, *NICA 2015* changed the basis of liability for Class 2, in the process sidestepping the problem described above. While those 'in business' will still be in 'employment' within the terms of *SSCBA 1992, s 122*, there will only be a liability to pay contributions (under new *SSCBA 1992, s 11(2)*) if their income falls to be taxed under *Chapter 2* of *Part 2*, *ITTOIA 2005*, ie, the Class 4 basis of assessment. This means that only trading income will attract compulsory contributions. However, because those with other types of business income are still in 'employment' (in the sense of self-employment), they have the right, under new *SSCBA 1992, s 11(6)* to pay voluntarily.

The right to make voluntary contributions is also extended to women who expect to take maternity leave and claim maternity allowance. Entitlement to claim maternity allowance depends on the woman having been self-employed for at least 26 weeks in the 66 weeks before the week the baby is due or the adoption certificate is issued, and having paid Class 2 contributions (or, under the pre-2015 rules, having held an SEE certificate). Under the new *NICA 2015* regime with contributions payable ten months after the end of the tax year, a woman might not pay a Class 2 liability until well after the date of birth or adoption, so it is now provided that she may pay Class 2 contributions voluntarily under *SSCBA 1992, s 11(6)* so as to ensure that, by paying early, she qualifies for the allowance. If her profits prove to be above the SPT in due course, those contributions will be converted into compulsory contributions under *s 11(2)*.

Members of Limited Liability Partnerships

[18.12] *Section 14* of the *National Insurance Contributions Act 2014* disapplies *s 4(4)* of the *Limited Liability Partnerships Act 2000* for the purposes of regulations to be made under a new *s 4AA* of *SSCBA 1992*. *LLPA 2000, s 4(4)* provides that a member of an LLP cannot be regarded as being employed by the LLP for any purpose unless he would have been so treated had the LLP been a partnership. In the past, this ensured that all LLP members were treated as self-employed, and a number of non-NIC cases have supported the view that LLP members cannot be employees of the LLP (see, eg, *Tiffin v Lester Aldridge LLP* [2012] EWCA Civ 35, in which a fixed-share member was held to be self-employed).

To counteract avoidance of Class 1 employer contributions by businesses that allegedly made many of their junior employees salaried members of an LLP, *NICA 2014, s 14* granted regulation-making powers with a view to deeming such 'salaried members' to be employed by the LLP for NIC purposes. *Finance Act 2014, s 74* and *Sch 17* made parallel provision for income tax.

Following the changes, which were given retroactive effect to 6 April 2014 after Royal Assent to *Finance Act 2014*, a 'salaried member', as now defined in *ITTOIA 2005, s 863A*, is treated as being employed by the LLP for income tax. *The Social Security Contributions (Limited Liability Partnership) Regulations 2014, SI 2014/3159* mirror this status for contributions purposes, which means that no Class 2 (or Class 4) contributions can be payable by the salaried member for 2014–15 or later years.

This means that only qualifying members within an LLP (those with an acceptably variable share of profits, or material amounts of capital invested, or real influence in the running of the LLP) will retain their self-employed status and have a Class 2 liability (or be entitled to pay voluntarily if profits are low). See PARTNERS 52.

In addition to the salaried member being treated as employed in employed earner's employment by the LLP, any amount that is treated by virtue of *ITTOIA 2005, s 863A* (or *s 863G(4)*, the targeted anti-avoidance rule for those who attempt to sidestep *s 863A*) as employment income (except benefits in kind taxed under the benefits code of *ITEPA 2003*) is treated as an amount of earnings paid to for the benefit of the salaried member, in respect of the salaried member's employed earner's employment with the LLP, and the LLP is deemed to be the secondary contributor.

[*SSCBA 1992, s 4AA* as inserted by the *National Insurance Contributions Act 2014*.]

Despite it having taken until 5 December 2014 to implement the April 2014 LLP changes in NIC regulations (*SI 2014/3159*), the regulations were, shortly thereafter, nevertheless found to be incomplete, and had to be corrected with effect from 6 April 2015 by *Social Security Contributions (Limited Liability Partnership) (Amendment) Regulations 2015, SI 2015/607*.

As described above, *SSCBA 1992, s 122* provides a definition of employment which includes any trade or business, profession, office or vocation, and a person will be a self-employed earner, according to *SSCBA 1992, s 2(1)*, if he is gainfully employed in the UK otherwise than in employed earner's employment. Technically, any trade or profession carried on by an LLP is not carried on by the members: the LLP is a separate legal entity. This distinction explains why *SSCBA 1992, s 15(3A)* was introduced in April 2001 to charge Class 4 contributions on the profit share of a member of a trading LLP 'if they would be payable were the trade or profession carried on in partnership by the members'.

Following the December 2014 changes, HMRC apparently realised that inactive members of LLPs would have no Class 2 liability, because they are not 'employed' or, as is the case with Class 4, deemed self-employed, even if they make a gain. So as to ensure that inactive members of LLPs will be liable to pay Class 2 contributions in the same way as sleeping partners and inactive limited partners, which should mean that liability to pay Class 2 contributions is not a determining factor in the decision of whether individuals operate through an LLP or a partnership, *SI 2015/607* inserted two new provisions with effect from 6 April 2015.

For the purposes of *SSCBA 1992, Part 1* and *Part 6* (to the extent that it relates to contributions), *Reg 2A* first deems 'employment' to include membership of an LLP which carries on a trade, profession or business with a view to profit. *Regulation 2B* then deems a person in employment as a member of an LLP that carries on a trade, profession or business with a view to profit to be a self-employed earner for the purposes of *SSCBA 1992*. *Regulation 2C* makes equivalent provision for Northern Ireland.

It seems that, in crafting the provisions deeming salaried members to be employed in employed earner's employment by the LLP, HMRC spotted that, on basic principles, they were not in fact in scope for contributions purposes at all. Salaried members have now been treated as employees since 6 April 2014, while other members are now, since 6 April 2015, treated as being self-employed for contributions purposes. If HMRC's current view is sound, it is open to question whether either type of LLP member should have had a Class 2 liability between 6 April 2001 and 5 April 2014. Class 4 liability is not in question: *SSCBA 1992, s 15(3A)* dealt with that adequately from the introduction of LLPs into UK law. It is of course doubtful that anybody would feel it worthwhile challenging the validity of any Class 2 payments made in the 13 years now in question.

Reform from April 2015 – summary

[18.13] *National Insurance Contributions Act 2015, Sch 1* introduced a reform of Class 2 with effect from 6 April 2015. In summary, the government decided to turn Class 2 into an adjunct of Class 4 rather than a weekly liability, although the Class 2 liability included in the annual self-assessment is still based on the number of weeks or part-weeks of self-employment in the relevant year.

Class 2 has not been extended to earners under the age of 16 or over state pension age.

From 6 April 2015 collection is moved onto almost the same basis as Class 4 (ie, by reporting and payments through the self-assessment system). Class 2 has adopted all the mechanisms applicable to Class 4 for returns, assessment and claims, appeals, payment, collection and recovery, and penalties in *TMA 1970*, penalties for in accuracies in *FA 2007, Sch 24*, interest and penalties in *FA 2009, ss 101–102*, and *Schedules 55-56*, and follower notices and accelerated payments in FA 2014. The only exception is that the requirement for half yearly payments on account under *TMA 1970, s 59* does not apply to Class 2 liabilities, although contributors are able to enter into a voluntary payment plan which will, in effect, allow them to pay self-assessed income tax and National Insurance contributions, now including Class 2, in monthly instalments in advance.

Earnings measurement under the new rules is on the same basis as Class 4 (ie, only taking into account profits chargeable to tax under *ITTOIA 2005, Part 2, Chapter 2*). This should, for example, make it clear that income from renting property is not subject to Class 2 liability even if the property rental activity amounts to a 'business'. However, those who make a living from letting property can ensure that they preserve benefit entitlements because the new *SSCBA 1992, s 11(6)* permits them to pay voluntarily.

Earners who leave the UK to take up employment or self-employment abroad also fall within the scope of this new section. If they move within the EEA (until 'Brexit' actually happens) or to a reciprocal agreement country in the course of their trade, they may remain subject to UK social security rules despite becoming non-resident for tax purposes. In such cases, they may not have an obligation to file a self-assessment tax return but are still required to pay Class 2 contributions. Non-trading contributors and migrant employees who meet the eligibility criteria are able to make voluntary contributions, even if they otherwise have no UK tax liability because they have become non-resident. Arrangements will be made for annual Class 2 collection to take place, with HMRC issuing a bill in the autumn if direct debit is not in place. Web guidance suggests that HMRC will send out an annual statement in April each year.

As noted above, in order to simplify the Class 2 processes for low earners, the SEE has been converted into a 'small profits threshold', with earners able to decide in arrears whether they would like to pay Class 2 contributions in years where their profits dip below the threshold in order to secure future benefit entitlement. It is not proposed to align the small profits threshold with the employed earner's lower earnings limit, although the two numbers are similar. This may form part of the promised 2018 reform instead. The new structure should simplify the administration of Class 2 for low earners because they no longer need to consider applying for exception or refunds, and staff at NIC&EO in Newcastle who in the past have had to deal with six-monthly billing, exception certificates and refunds should be able to be redeployed to more productive tasks.

To ensure that earners within Class 2 do not automatically lose maternity allowance (MA) entitlement because they have not paid contributions before the relevant date, *NICA 2015* provides a power for regulations to allow payment to be taken into account provided such payment is made before a prescribed date.

- Women continue to be eligible for the standard rate of MA where they have a record of Class 2 NICs paid through SA or have made voluntary contributions before they have filed their SA return (and so before their liability to pay Class 2 contributions has been established).

- Self-employed women who choose not to make an early payment of Class 2 receive the lower rate of MA, unless they have an SA record which demonstrates that they have made the requisite number of Class 2 contributions.
- Women who are neither employed nor self-employed but who participate in the business of their spouse or civil partner can receive the lower rate of MA for 14 weeks if their spouse or civil partner has paid Class 2 NICs for 26 weeks, voluntarily or as evidenced by their SA return. Those spouses or civil partners who have not had the opportunity to file an SA return and pay Class 2 NICs are also able to pay Class 2 contributions early.
- Women with profits falling below the small profits threshold who choose not to pay Class 2 contributions voluntarily are still able to receive the lower rate of MA.

The Act also makes provision for those Class 2 contributions that are paid early to be given their correct classification (either liable contributions or voluntary contributions) when the woman has filed her SA return and her actual Class 2 position has been established. [*Social Security Contributions and Benefits Act 1992, Sch 1, para 7BB as inserted by NICA 2015, Sch 1, para 9.*]

The established late payment provisions which apply a higher weekly rate if Class 2 contributions are paid more than a year after the relevant tax year now apply only to voluntary contributions under the new *SSCBA 1992, s 11(6)*. Late paid contributions under the new *s 11(2)* (ie, compulsory contributions in respect of profits exceeding the small profits threshold) are subject to the same interest and penalty rules as Class 4.

The Act also deals with incompatibilities between Class 2 and Class 4 procedures. For example, Class 4 liabilities would normally be determined by a tax assessment, while unpaid and disputed Class 2 liabilities would be collected by means of a notice of decision under *Social Security Contributions (Transfer of Functions, etc) Act 1999, s 8*, so the Act provides that only one appeal can be heard on any matter covered by both provisions. [*Social Security Contributions (Transfer of Functions, etc) Act 1999, s 8 as amended by NICA 2015, Sch 1, para 25.*] *Social Security Contributions (Transfer of Functions, etc) Act 1999* now covers Class 2 recovery only where *TMA 1970, Part 6* collection provisions do not apply. [*Social Security Contributions (Transfer of Functions, etc) Act 1999, s 4 as amended by NICA 2015, Sch 1, para 24.*]

A further example of the resolution of an incompatibility is found in the treatment of married women with a reduced rate election. The election to reduce contributions payments and relinquish benefit rights has never applied to Class 4 (which already carried no benefit entitlement), so simply moving Class 2 liability into the Class 4 framework could have meant, in the absence of special provision, that liability would have arisen despite a valid election still subsisting. For the few hundreds of women potentially affected, the validity of the election for Class 2 has been protected. [*Social Security (Contributions) Regulations 2001, SI 2001/1004, Reg 127(3)(b) as amended by NICA 2015,Sch 1, para 34.*]

Planned further reform

[18.14] As already noted in the introduction, in the Budget speech in March 2015, the Chancellor announced plans to consider merging Class 2 into Class 4, combined with converting Class 4 into the basis of contributory benefit entitlements for self-employed earners. It was thought that, in order to protect the income of the NI Fund, Class 4 rates would need to be increased to compensate for the loss of (as it was then) £381 million of Class 2 contributions, and the question of non-trading voluntary contributors would need to be addressed, since they would have no liability to Class 4 contributions.

The measure did not appear in the list of proposed bills in the Queen's Speech following the general election in May 2015 but the July 2015 and March 2016 Budgets confirmed that Class 2 will be abolished from April 2018. Surprisingly, there is to be no increase in Class 4 rates to protect the NI Fund (despite Class 4 not being covered by the 'NIC lock' provisions of the *National Insurance Contributions (Rate Ceilings) Act 2015*), but the endowment of Class 4 records with benefit entitlements is likely to lead to complications with voluntary contributions. Voluntary Class 2 contributions currently cost £2.95 per week, compared to Class 3 contributions at £14.65 per week, and they provide better state benefit coverage. As noted above, they can also be paid in advance to protect maternity allowance entitlements, so the Class 4 reform will need to address these complications in some way that has not yet been found.

On 8 March, the March 2016 Budget did propose a one percentage point increase in the Class 4 rate from April 2018 and April 2019 (to 10% and 11% respectively). However, on 15 March in a statement in the House of Commons, the Chancellor announced that these increases would not be going ahead. As noted above, although Class 4 NICs were not covered by the NIC lock provisions, the backtracking was on the political grounds that such increases were not in keeping with the spirit of a manifesto pledge not to increase the rate of National Insurance.

Abolition of Class 2 in 2019

[18.15] It was also confirmed in the *Autumn Statement 2016*, at para 4.8, that the plan to abolish Class 2 and attach benefit entitlements to Class 4 is to go ahead in April 2018. No details were provided. The abolition has since been deferred to April 2019.

Class 3 is also to be reformed so that it can be used instead of voluntary Class 2 contributions, which are currently payable by those who are self-employed without trading profits (or without trading profits subject to UK NICs), or with profits below the small profits threshold. Rather than only giving entitlement to state pension and bereavement benefits, Class 3 will be used by the self-employed and deemed self-employed to buy entitlement to certain short-term benefits such as contributory employment and support allowance when profits are below the 'small profits limit' or do not arise from trading. This is likely to affect:

- examiners, exam moderators, invigilators or persons who set exam questions;

- those running a business involving land or property without trading;
- ministers of religion who do not receive a salary or stipend that would bring them within Class 1;
- those living abroad and currently paying voluntary Class 2 contributions as expatriates with no Class 1 liability;
- persons who makes investments other than as a business and without receiving a fee or commission; and
- non-UK residents who are self-employed in the UK (Class 4 does not apply to such traders).

This 'small profits limit' appears to be a new term, replacing the 'small profits threshold' (SPT) currently used for Class 2. The consultation document after the Autumn Statement 2015 proposed to align the level of Class 4 profits at which state benefits begin to accrue for the self-employed with the Class 1 LEL, which is currently lower than the SPT for Class 2. This level of income seems to have been entitled 'small profits limit'.

Self-employed earners are to earn benefit entitlement under Class 4, which is to be levied, as now, on profits above the lower annual limit, at a main rate up to the upper annual limit, and an additional rate thereafter. These limits are, respectively, at the same levels as the Class 1 LEL and UEL. As with Class 1, earnings (ie profits) above the small profits limit but below the lower annual limit will earn benefit entitlement without requiring any contributions.

Class 2 has always extended to anyone 'in business', which includes property letting businesses, even if they do not have trading profits. Until NICA 2015, those in business with profits above the small earnings exception limit had a liability, but that Act attached Class 2 liability only to Class 4 (ie trading) profits above the SPT, making contributions voluntary for non-traders and those with low earnings or no Class 4 liability from 6 April 2015.

One problem with the 2015 reform, which moved Class 2 payment to the ITSA filing date, on 31 January after the end of the year rather than in-year, is that self-employed women expecting a baby can only qualify for full maternity allowance if they have paid sufficient contributions (ie for 13 weeks) in a 66-week window before the expected date of birth or adoption. If 2015–16 Class 2 contributions are not paid until 31 January 2017, it is quite possible for a woman to fail the contributions test for a birth in 2016 or January 2017. The new legislation anticipated this and provided that such women could make voluntary Class 2 contributions in-year in order to create the entitlement to maternity allowance.

The procedure devised to enable this involves the woman making a claim for maternity allowance to the DWP (on form MA1) so that payment can commence 11 weeks before the expected week of childbirth. If the claimant's NIC record is deficient, the DWP will advise HMRC to issue a Class 2 bill to the claimant so that the necessary voluntary contributions may be paid. If their profits subsequently prove to exceed the SPT, the voluntary contributions are treated automatically as compulsory contributions. The abolition of Class 2 in 2018 will therefore necessitate an alternative arrangement for pregnant self-employed women.

The Autumn Statement announced that all self-employed women will continue to be able to access the standard rate of maternity allowance and that there will be provision to support self-employed individuals with low profits during the transition period, although no details were provided.

In order for all of this to be implemented from April 2019, a Social Security Bill is to be introduced in 2018.

Key Points regarding class 2 contributions: self-employed earners

[18.16] Points to consider are as follows.

- The payment of Class 2 contributions is currently the only contributory element of the package of compulsory contributions paid by the self-employed.
- Class 2 contributions paid by the self-employed cannot be deferred or cancelled because of holiday, seasonal drop in income or if the self-employed business becomes inactive unless the business is being wound up, but liabilities are now assessed only in arrears, so those with low profits have the opportunity to decide whether to pay voluntarily.
- Individuals who started self-employment on or after 10 April 2011 could pay Class 2 contributions either monthly, in which case they would be collected four months in arrears, or six-monthly at the same time as their income tax fell due. This option ceased after the final direct debit payments for 2014–15 were collected, although direct debit payments from existing voluntary contributors should still be accepted.
- From April 2014 HMRC can recover arrears of Class 2 contributions by making adjustments to PAYE codes.
- From April 2013 HMRC expect sleeping partners and other non-active individuals to pay Class 2 contributions as self-employed earners, and Class 4 contributions on any share of profits they may receive from 'the business'. From April 2015, any such individuals who are in business but not trading will be able to pay voluntarily but will have no liability.
- Class 2 contributions are collected through the self-assessment process after April 2015.
- LLP members who are not classed as 'salaried members' now have their liability on a firmer footing: if the LLP has profits from a trade or profession the member is deemed to be self-employed.
- Class 2 is likely to be abolished on 6 April 2019. Details of the changes to Class 4 to make this possible are awaited from the Chancellor.

19

Voluntary Contributions: Classes 3 and 3A

Cross-references. See AGE EXCEPTION **3** for age limitations on entitlement to pay; APPEALS AND REVIEWS **9** for procedure for questioning a decision on entitlement to pay; BENEFITS **13** for relevance of Class 3 contributions to benefit entitlement; **21.48** COLLECTION for payment procedure; DEATH OF CONTRIBUTOR **26**; EARNINGS FACTORS **28** for relationship of factors with entitlement to pay Class 3 contributions; LATE-PAID CONTRIBUTIONS **42**; NATIONAL INSURANCE NUMBER **49** for contribution records; RATES AND LIMITS **53**.

Other Sources. Simon's Taxes, Volume 2, para A8.4; HM Revenue and Customs National Insurance Manual NIM25000–25112.

Introduction to voluntary contributions: classes 3 and 3A

[19.1] As may be expected, Class 3 contributions, being entirely voluntary in nature, account for only a minute proportion of the National Insurance Fund's (NIF) contribution income (see **48.4** NATIONAL INSURANCE FUND). The figure paid to the National Insurance Fund in 2016–17 was some £12.8 million, down from £29.8 million in 2015–16. This fall from earlier years' values of around £60 million probably reflects contributors' uncertainty over the future of the state pension created by the announcement in 2013 of a plan to move to a single-tier state pension from April 2017, a date which was later advanced to April 2016. Class 3 receipts fell to £28 million in 2014–15 and as noted just £26 million in 2015–16. This was the final year before the new single-tier state pension was introduced, the value of which may be increased by having had a full contribution record as at 6 April 2016, so it might have been expected that contributors would pay more, rather than less. The explanation may lie in the extended time limits for paying voluntary contributions (see below) or in simple ignorance of the impact of the change in 2016.

The amount allocated to the NHS is currently 15.5% of the Class 3 contributions collected each year, although the payment of contributions is not a prerequisite of treatment by the NHS. This proportion was extended to Class 3A contributions from 12 October 2015. [*Social Security Administration Act 1992, s 162(5)(ea) inserted by the Pensions Act 2014, s 25, Sch 15, Pt 1, para 13(1), (2)*.]

Class 3 contributions can serve no purpose but that of enabling a person to satisfy the contribution conditions for entitlement to basic category A or B retirement pension, bereavement payment, basic widowed parent's allowance and basic bereavement allowance (see BENEFITS **13**). [*SSCBA 1992, s 13(2); Social Security (Contributions) Regulations 2001, SI 2001/1004, Reg 48(1), Reg 49(2)* as amended by *Social Security (Contributions)(Amendment No 6) Regs 2001, SI 2001/3728, Reg 2*]. This being so, however, the entitlement to pay Class 3 contributions may be of particular importance to persons who are excluded by regulation from both the category of employed earners and the category of self-employed earners and who cannot, therefore, create such an entitlement by normal means (see **14.29** CATEGORISATION). See HM Revenue and Customs National Insurance Manual NIM25001. It is also of use both to those who, though paying Class 1 or Class 2 contributions, fail to do so in a particular year or years at a sufficiently high level and, in some instances, those working abroad, see OVERSEAS MATTERS **51**.

Class 3A is a temporary measure (available only from 12 October 2015 to 5 April 2017) introduced by *Pensions Act 2014, Sch 15* to enable existing state pensioners at 6 April 2016 to enhance their old-regime state pension by up to £25 per week, but it is very different in nature and cost to Class 3. The position is described at **19.11** onwards. Somewhat surprisingly, 15.5% of any contributions collected will be directed to the NHS: no other class of contribution is payable by state pensioners, so they ordinarily do not pay through the NI system towards the NHS.

The Government Actuary forecast (based on DWP estimates) Class 3A receipts of £433 million in 2015–16, and exactly the same amount again in 2016–17. These estimates seem a little odd. Firstly, the window for payment did not open until 12 October 2015, so the first year's receipts actually represent only six months. Secondly, the rate is determined by the age of the contributor at the date of payment, not at 6 April 2016, so it is in every contributor's interest to wait until after the last birthday before 6 April 2017 to make the payment, as it will be cheaper and will cost only tiny amounts of forgone extra pension. Based on the NIF accounts for 2015–16 the GAD forecast would appear to be an overestimate. The accounts show Class 3A receipts of £58.2 million, implying gross Class 3A contributions of £68.8 million for six months. The 2016–17 accounts show receipts of £98.8 million for Class 3A contributions. Allowing for the NHS allocation, this implies gross Class 3A receipts of some £116.9 million.

Entitlement to contribute: Class 3

[19.2] Payment of Class 3 contributions is allowed only with a view to enabling a person to satisfy conditions of entitlement to BENEFITS: CONTRIBUTION REQUIREMENTS **13**. To be eligible, a contributor must be over 16, or not working and therefore not paying Class 1 or Class 2 contributions, or not liable to pay such contributions. A married woman with a reduced rate election is not permitted to contribute unless she revokes the election in the year in question. Class 3 (unlike Classes 1 and 2) contributions cannot be paid for the tax year in which the contributor reaches state pension age, because that part-year of contribution does not count in assessing state pension entitlement. For the same reason, Class 3 contributions cannot be paid *for* later years, although in some cases they may be paid *in* later years in respect of deficient contribution records in years before the year in which state retirement age was reached. See **19.3** below for the detailed exclusions.

A contributor wishing to make up his or her contribution record must comply with time limits for making the payments and must meet residence and presence conditions (see **51.17** OVERSEAS MATTERS). [*SSCBA 1992, s 13(2); Social Security (Contributions) Regulations 2001, SI 2001/1004, Regs 48(1), 145.*] Entitlement to pay a Class 3 contribution does not, therefore, (as it does in the case of Class 1 or Class 2 contributions) rest on a person's CATEGORISATION **14** but merely on the level of Class 1, Class 2 or Class 3 contribution or credit, if any, which has already been attained with regard to a particular tax year. This level is quantified in terms of EARNINGS FACTORS **28**, and only where a person's earnings factor (or the aggregate of his earnings factors) for a tax year has neither equalled nor exceeded the qualifying earnings factor for that year may a Class 3 contribution be paid (subject to the prohibitions described below). [*SSCBA 1992, s 14(1)*].

A *qualifying earnings factor* in relation to a tax year means an earnings factor equal to the weekly Lower Earnings Limit for that year multiplied by 52 (see EARNINGS LIMITS AND THRESHOLDS **33**). [*Social Security (Crediting and Treatment of Contributions, and National Insurance Numbers) Regulations 2001, SI 2001/769, Reg 3*].

A number of cases have been decided in connection with the entitlement to contribute and the time limits for doing so.

In *Kearney v HMRC* a British citizen (K) was born in 1929. In 1948 he began working for the Kenyan police. He continued to work in Kenya until 1975. While he was in Kenya, he did not pay any National Insurance contributions until 1971, when he was permitted to pay backdated contributions for the previous six years. He subsequently applied to pay backdated Class 3 NICs to cover the period from 1948 to 1965, in order to qualify for a full UK pension.

HMRC rejected the claim on the basis that his failure to pay these contributions was attributable to his 'failure to exercise due care and diligence', within *Social Security (Contributions) Regulations 2001, SI 2001/1004, Reg 50*. K appealed.

The General Commissioners allowed his appeal and the CA upheld their decision as one of fact. Arden LJ observed that 'the facts of this case are unusual', since K had left the UK at the age of 19, and that 'in 1948 the NIC scheme was a novel and unfamiliar concept'. CA [2010] EWCA Civ 288. See also *WB Langthorne v HMRC*, [2010] UKFTT 171 (TC), TC00475 and *JA Garland v HMRC* [2011] UK FTT 273 (TC), TC01135.

In the case of *D Ashworth v HMRC* [2011] UKFTT 796(TC), TC01632, HMRC agreed that D or his employer could pay back-dated contributions for the period from 1974 to 1979 when D was out of the country. D's former employer indicated it was willing to pay the contributions but went into receivership without doing so. D appealed contending that he should be credited with the contributions without actually paying them. The FTT rejected this contention on the grounds that it had no jurisdiction to make such an order.

In April 2010, the basis of qualification for the basic state pension was changed. All contributors would after that date need only 30 qualifying years in order to receive a full entitlement, instead of the previous threshold of 44 years for men and 39 years for women. This change also led to a number of cases where individuals realised after they had made voluntary contributions that those payments had been unnecessary, and they tried to claim a refund: while they had been entitled to pay at the time, they subsequently became aware that the payment of Class 3 contributions had in fact been pointless because their existing record would have satisfied the new rule.

In *HMRC v Fenton* an individual (F), who had paid Class 3 contributions from 2003 to 2006 in order to reach the previous 44-year limit, submitted a repayment claim under *Social Security (Contributions) Regulations 2001, SI 2001/1004 Reg 52*. HMRC rejected the claim on the basis that the contributions had not been 'paid in error'. The Ch D upheld HMRC's rejection of the claim. David Richards J held that the only circumstances in which refunds could be given were either where contributions had been made in error or where precluded contributions had been made. There was no other basis for entitlement to a refund. On the evidence, the relevant contributions had not been made in error, so that F was not entitled to a refund. Ch D [2010] unreported 17 June 2010.

The First-Tier Tribunal heard thirteen appeals against similar decisions, reviewed the evidence in detail and allowed two of the appeals, finding that the relevant payments had been made after the publication of the Government's proposal and holding that those payments had been made 'in error'. However the Tribunal dismissed the other eleven appeals, finding that the relevant payments had been made before the publication of the Government White Paper. Judge Berner held that a payment made in ignorance of 'a prospective change in law about which nobody outside the policy-making body itself is aware' could not be regarded as a payment made 'in error'.

HMRC appealed to the Upper Tribunal in one of the cases where the First-Tier Tribunal had allowed the appeal, and six of the unsuccessful appellants also appealed to the Upper Tribunal. The Upper Tribunal upheld the First-Tier Tribunal decision in all seven cases. *C Bonner v HMRC (and related appeals)* UT [2010] UKUT 450 (TCC).

Exclusion from Class 3 contributions

[19.3] Even if the condition described above has been met, a person is *not* entitled to pay a Class 3 contribution in respect of a year if:

(a) he would, but for the payment of a Class 3 contribution, be entitled to be credited with a contribution (see CREDITS **24**) *Social Security (Contributions) Regulations 2001, SI 2001/1004, Reg 49(1)(a)* as amended by *Social Security (Contributions)(Amendment) Regulations 2003, SI 2003/193, Reg 7*; or

(b) the aggregate of his earnings factors derived from earnings upon which primary Class 1 contributions payable at the main primary percentage rate have been paid, credited earnings, or Class 2 or Class 3 contributions paid or credited (see EARNINGS FACTORS **28**) is less than the qualifying earnings factor and
   (i) the period has passed within which any Class 3 contributions may be treated as paid for that year (see **42.6** LATE-PAID CONTRIBUTIONS); or
   (ii) he has previously applied for the return of any Class 3 contributions paid in respect of that year (see **55.7** REPAYMENT AND REALLOCATION)

   [*Social Security (Contributions) Regulations 2001, SI 2001/1004, Reg 49(1)(b)(c); Social Security (Crediting and Treatment of Contributions, and National Insurance Numbers) Regulations 2001, SI 2001/769, Reg 2, Reg 3* as amended by *Social Security (Contributions)(Amendment) Regulations 2003, SI 2003/193, Reg 7*]; or

(c) it would cause the aggregate of his earnings factors derived from earnings upon which primary Class 1 contributions payable at the main primary percentage rate have been paid, credited earnings, or Class 2 or Class 3 contributions paid or credited to exceed the qualifying earnings factor by an amount which is half or more than half that year's weekly Lower Earnings Limit. [*Social Security (Contributions) Regulations 2001, SI 2001/1004, Reg 49(1)(d)* as amended by *Social Security (Contributions)(Amendment) Regulations 2003, SI 2003/193, Reg 7*]; or

(d) he is subject to the age limitation rules (see **3.3** and **3.14** AGE EXCEPTION) *Social Security (Contributions) Regulations 2001, SI 2001/1004, Reg 49(2A)*, as amended by *Social Security (Contributions) (Amendment No 3) Regulations 2005, SI 2005/778, Reg 6*). A person aged from the female state pension age up to 64 who acquires male gender under the *Gender Recognition Act 2004*, which came into effect on 4 April 2005, will be permitted to pay Class 3 contributions not just from that time but right back to age 60 with no 'penalty rate' being applied. [*Social*

Security (Contributions) Regulations 2001, SI 2001/1004, Reg 49(2B), Reg 49(2C), as inserted by *Social Security (Contributions) (Amendment No 3) Regulations 2005, SI 2005/778, Reg 6*]; or

(e) she has made a reduced rate election and that election is in force (see REDUCED LIABILITY ELECTIONS **54**) [*Social Security (Contributions) Regulations 2001, SI 2001/1004, Reg 132*];

(f) he attains the age of 17 or 18 and he has in an earlier year satisfied the contribution condition for retirement pension or bereavement allowance or widowed parent's allowance [*Social Security (Contributions) Regulations 2001, SI 2001/1004, Reg 49(1)(f)*];

[*Social Security (Contributions) Regulations 2001, SI 2001/1004, Reg 49, Reg 132*].

(g) he satisfies the residence test in *Social Security (Contributions) Regulations 2001, SI 2001/1004, Reg 147* by virtue of residence in another EU Member State and has not previously been subject to compulsory Class 1 or 2 contribution liabilities.

[*Article 14.4* of *EC Regulation 883/04*]

Disregards for Class 3

[19.4] Prohibitions (a) and (b) above (but *not* prohibitions (c) (d) (e) (f) and (g)) may, however, be disregarded if the payment of a Class 3 contribution in respect of a year would enable a person to satisfy:

- the first contribution condition for retirement pension or bereavement allowance or widowed mother's allowance or widowed parent's allowance if that condition has not been satisfied at the beginning of that year (see **13.5** BENEFITS); or
- the contribution condition for bereavement allowance if that condition has not been satisfied at the beginning of that year (see **13.5** BENEFITS).

[*Social Security (Contributions) Regulations 2001, SI 2001/1004, Reg 49(2)(a)(b)* as amended by *Social Security (Contributions)(Amendment No 6) Regulations 2001, SI 2001/3728*].

In the foregoing description of prohibited Class 3 contributions, 'credited' means credited for the purpose of retirement pension, widowed parent's allowance and bereavement allowance, and, therefore, *excludes* primary Class 1 starting credits or credits in relation to the termination of training or education (see CREDITS **24**). [*Social Security (Contributions) Regulations 2001, SI 2001/1004, Reg 49(3)*]. See also HM Revenue and Customs National Insurance Manual NIM25006.

Benefit entitlements from Class 3

[19.5] The *Social Security (Contributions) (Amendment No 6) Regs 2002, SI 2002/3728* amended *SI 2001/1004, Reg 49* to enable anyone who so wishes to pay Class 3 contributions in order to satisfy the contribution conditions for the bereavement benefits introduced in April 2001. See **13.2** BENEFITS: CONTRIBUTION REQUIREMENTS. This secured equality of treatment between men and women as regards these particular payments.

It should be borne in mind that under the *Pensions Act 2007*, for those reaching state pension age from 6 April 2010 to 5 April 2016, only 30 qualifying years were required for retirement pension purposes. This may therefore affect considerations on the payment of Class 3 contributions for recent years. However, the position has not changed for the relevant bereavement benefits where contributions are still required in 90% of the deceased's working life. The single-tier pension introduced from April 2016 raises the number of qualifying years from 30 to 35, with a minimum requirement of ten years of contributions on the record. Any decision in 2015–16 relating to the payment of voluntary contributions should have taken this known change into account.

Class 3 currently creates no entitlement to any short-term benefits. For years up to 5 April 2016, it counted for basic pension and bereavement purposes but not for SERPS or S2P. It currently counts towards creating a qualifying year for the new single-tier state pension. At some point in the future, possibly from April 2018 according to a consultation document in December 2015 and an announcement in Budget 2016, it may become possible for certain groups to use Class 3 towards short-term benefits because Class 2 is to be abolished and Class 4 is to form the basis of contribution records for the self-employed (see 20.12). This is part of the Government's simplification agenda.

Class 3 payment

[19.6] From 6 April 2009 to 5 April 2015, anyone who wished to pay, or to cease to pay, Class 3 contributions had to notify HMRC immediately in writing or by means of approved electronic communication of the relevant date of commencement or cessation. For these purposes 'relevant date' was taken as the date the person commenced or ceased paying Class 3 contributions. In certain circumstances HMRC might extend this time limit as they thought fit. As Class 3 contributions are voluntary there is, however, no penalty for failure to adhere to this requirement. [*Social Security (Contributions) Regulations 2001, SI 2001/1004, Regs 87, 87A* as inserted by *Social Security (Contributions) (Amendment No 3) Regulations 2009, SI 2009/600, Reg 5* and amended by *Social Security (Miscellaneous Amendments No 2) Regulations 2015, SI 2015/478, Reg 10*.]

The detailed notification rules were amended with effect from 6 April 2015 because of the transfer of Class 2 liability into the Class 4 regime, because the old rules applied to both Class 2 and Class 3. Under the new regime, the new Class 3 rules are not significantly different from their predecessors: a person who, on or after 6 April 2015, is entitled to pay a Class 3 contribution and either wishes to do so or cease doing so, must immediately notify the relevant date to HMRC in writing or by such means of electronic communication as may be approved. The relevant date is the date on which the contributor wishes to commence or cease paying Class 3 contributions. The word 'immediately' is undefined, but the regulations permit HMRC to allow 'further time' for notification, and application form CA5603 makes no reference to any short-term time limits for payment. [*Social Security (Contributions) Regulations 2001, SI 2001/1004, Reg 87AA*, inserted by *Social Security (Miscellaneous Amendments No 2) Regulations 2015, SI 2015/478, Reg 11*.]

In practice payment after the end of the year in a lump sum is perfectly acceptable and, indeed, is actively encouraged by HM Revenue and Customs where it issues a shortfall letter (see **28.8**). Direct debit is available to those who know they will be paying as they go along (eg, because they know they will not be working), but one-off payments must be made by online or telephone banking, BACS or CHAPS, via a bank or building society or the Post Office (HMRC provides a payslip), or by cheque through the post.

A new tool on GOV.UK (www.gov.uk/check-national-insurance-record) launched after 6 April 2016 allows contributors to obtain a statement to check for gaps in the contribution record and establish if voluntary contributions can be paid to fill those gaps, and how much to pay. For those with no internet access, the same may be obtained by writing to NIC&EO, HMRC, BX9 1AN or calling the NI helpline (0300 200 3500, or +44 191 203 7010 from abroad).

Appropriation of Class 3 contributions

[19.7] Class 3 contributions paid in one year may be appropriated to the earnings factor of another year if such contributions may be paid for that other year according to the entitlement conditions described at **19.2** above. Such appropriation may be made either at the contributor's request or by HM Revenue and Customs with the contributor's consent. [*Social Security (Crediting and Treatment of Contributions, and National Insurance Numbers) Regulations 2001, SI 2001/769, Reg 2*].

Rate

[19.8] A Class 3 contribution is of a specified fixed amount (set out in **53.10** RATES AND LIMITS). For 2018–19, this has been set at £14.65. [*SSCBA 1992, s 13(1),* as amended by *Social Security (Contributions) (Rates, Limits and Thresholds Amendments and National Insurance Funds Payments) Regulations 2018, SI 2018/337, Reg 4*.]

If it is considered necessary, the Treasury (previously the Secretary of State for Social Security) but subject to Parliamentary approval may, at any time, make an order altering the amount of a Class 3 contribution. [*SSAA 1992, ss 143(1), 144(1), 189(9)* as amended by *SSC(TF)A 1999, Sch 3 para 46, para 49*].

Where a Class 3 contribution is paid after the end of the contribution year to which it relates, it may be payable at a rate other than that applicable for the contribution year to which it relates (see **42.8** LATE-PAID CONTRIBUTIONS).

There is ordinarily a six-year time limit for paying voluntary Class 3 contributions. [*Social Security (Contributions) Regulations 2001, SI 2001/1004, Reg 48(3)(b)(i)*.] The *Pensions Act 2014*, laying the ground for the new single-tier state pension in April 2016, which depends equally heavily on the number of qualifying years on a contributor's record, was passed on 14 May 2014. Because of extensive changes needed to the DWP IT systems to effect the changes they were no longer able to provide state pension statements before April 2016. These are generally required before voluntary Class 3 contributions are paid. In order that individuals retiring on or after 6 April

2016 are not disadvantaged, the time limits for the payment of voluntary contributions for the years 2006–07 to 2015–16 have been extended to 5 April 2023. In addition, the higher rate provisions have been disapplied with the 2012–13 rate applying until 5 April 2019 in respect of Class 3 contributions from 2006–07 to 2009–10 and Class 2 for 2006–07 to 2010–11. For the remaining years to 2015–16 no higher rate provisions will be applied until 6 April 2019. These changes were enacted by introducing new *regs 50C* and *61B* into *Social Security (Contributions) Regulations 2001, SI 2001/1004* by virtue of the *Social Security (Contributions) (Amendment and Application of Schedule 38 to the Finance Act 2012) Regulations 2013, SI 2013/622, Regs 35* and *37*.

The single-tier pension proposals were originally planned to arrive in 2017, then brought forward to April 2016 and *Regs 50C* and *61B* were amended so that any reference to pensionable age in 2017 should now read 2016. [*Social Security (Contributions) (Amendment) Regulations 2013, SI 2013/718*.] Whether there will be further changes to the tax years covered by the relaxation remains to be seen.

Collection: Class 3

[19.9] A Class 3 contribution planned in advance may be made by either paying a quarterly bill or by direct debit of a bank account. In practice, it is also possible to pay by cheque or otherwise through a bank in a lump sum during or after the tax year in question, subject only to the proviso as to the rate of contribution that may then be payable (see **19.8** above and **42.8** LATE-PAID CONTRIBUTIONS). See HM Revenue and Customs National Insurance Manual NIM25021.

In any event, where a contributor knows in advance that he or she wishes to pay Class 3 voluntarily, such as when an overseas job results in no Class 1 contributions being paid for several years, application will need to be made on form CA5603 'Application to pay Class 3 NI contributions'. The 2015 version of the application form warned contributors that, before deciding to pay voluntary Class 3 contributions, they should obtain information about their state pension entitlement, including the number of qualifying years already on the record. The warning has been removed from the 2016 version and has been substituted with a cross-reference to 'the easiest way to check how much state pension you might receive' on GOV.UK. The information will be provided by the Pension Service of the DWP on a pension statement, or now online for those who can pass online identity checks, but based on the pre-2016 state pension system. Contributors were warned in 2015 that, if they reach state pension age after April 2016, they should wait until pension statements for the new post-2016 pension became available before deciding whether to pay voluntary contributions. Contributions for the final years of the pre-2016 regime may be paid up to 5 April 2023.

Contributors who contact NIC&EO (address: NIC&EO, HMRC, BX9 1AN) in 2016–17 to arrange to pay voluntary Class 3 contributions for past years should be sent a letter or statement setting out in detail where there are deficient years, how much is needed to make up the deficiency for each year if paid by 5 April 2019, and the final deadline for payment of 5 April 2023 (payments after 5 April 2019 are likely to be at a higher rate than those paid before that date). The deficiency letter will be accompanied by a payslip and instructions on how to pay electronically. Contributors may choose which years' deficiencies are to be made up so as to minimise the cost of creating the higher state pension entitlement from adding extra years to the record.

Example

Helga has lived and worked in the UK since 1980 and will reach state pension age in mid-2019. Taking into account years of employment (some of it contracted out) and years spent looking after children who qualified for child benefit, which entitles her to home responsibilities protection and carer's credits, she had 27 qualifying years as at 5 April 2015, and the last year in which she paid contributions was 2008–09.

She contacted the DWP Pension Service for a pension forecast. Under the pre-2016 rules, her state pension was predicted to be £107.21 per week (27/30ths of the basic pension plus a small amount of S2P for not contracted-out years). Under the post-2016 rules, her entitlement was predicted to be £76.65 per week (27/35ths of the flat rate pension less a contracted-out deduction to reflect her lower contributions while working as a member of a final salary pension scheme). The starting point for her entitlement from 6 April 2016 would therefore be £107.21 per week, the higher of the two possible pension rights, which became her 'foundation amount' under the new rules.

She could increase this by £3.87 per week (£115.95 ÷ 30) under the pre-2016 rules by paying Class 3 contributions to create another qualifying year. The maximum pension she could create under the pre-2016 rules was based on having 30 qualifying years on the record, so she ought to have considered paying Class 3 contributions for three years.

Provided she pays before 5 April 2019, making three further years qualify will cost:

	£	
2010–11	626.60	(52 × £12.05)
2011–12	655.20	(52 × £12.60)
2012–13	689.00	(52 × £13.25)
Total cost	1,970.80	

She can therefore increase her state pension entitlement as at 5 April 2016 by £603.72 per year (£3.87 × 52 × 3), 'triple-lock' protected for life, for a total one-off cost of £1,970.80.

Whether she should increase the pension further under the post-2016 rules, now that the maximum pension is based on 35 qualifying years, will depend on the rate of Class 3 contributions between 6 April 2016 and 5 April 2019 and the amount of extra pension that extra contributions for 2013–14 to 2018–19 might generate, which the DWP could not forecast before 6 April 2016. It is possible that extra contributions under the new regime will not increase the state pension above the 2016 foundation amount, so paying such contributions would make no sense.

In principle, paying 52 × £14.10 (ie, £733.20) for 2016–17 should add a year under the new regime to her record, which would increase her entitlement by 1/35th of the single-tier pension rate, ie, £4.45 per week or £231.40 per year, index-linked (or better, under the triple-lock mechanism for uprating) for life, so the payback period is short for someone so close to state pension age. She should be able to do the same for 2017–18 and 2018–19, but she will not be able to contribute for any weeks falling after 5 April 2019, as they will fall in the year in which she reaches state pension age, but she will be able to pay Class 3 contributions up to 5 April 2023 for earlier periods. HMRC will provide a statement of a contributor's NI account for all years up to the start of the previous tax year (ie, in 2016–17, the latest available period is 2014–15) to identify gaps where Class 3 can be paid, and the Future Pension Centre will provide a pension statement if it cannot be obtained online.

It will be possible for pensioners slightly older than Helga, who reached state pension age before 6 April 2016, to pay both Class 3 and Class 3A contributions to improve their pension, with Class 3 taking priority because it is cheaper.

Tax relief

[19.10] No tax relief may be given or a tax deduction allowed in respect of any Class 3 contribution paid. [*ITTOIA 2005, ss 53, 272, 868* as amended by *ITA 2007, Sch 1 para 507* and *ITEPA 2003, s 360A*].

Class 3A contributions

[19.11] In the 2013 Autumn Statement it was announced that a new Class 3A contribution was to be introduced from 12 October 2015. The intention was that individuals who had reached or would reach pension age before 6 April 2016 (and would therefore not qualify for the higher single-tier pension that applies to those who reach state pension age on or after that date) might enhance their existing state pension by buying an entitlement to additional state pension (equivalent to a SERPS addition) from the commencement of the new regime in April 2016. The opportunity to pay Class 3A contributions was available until 5 April 2017.

The ground was laid for Class 3A by the *Pensions Act 2014, Sch 15* introducing new *SSCBA 1992, ss 14A-14C*, which provided that an eligible person is entitled to pay a Class 3A contribution in return for a unit of additional pension.

The official publicity material refers to the new regime as 'State Pension Top Up' ('SPTU' below).

Eligibility

[19.12] Eligibility depends on entitlement to a Category A, Category B or Category D retirement pension or graduated retirement benefit, or a deferred entitlement to a Category A or Category B retirement pension or graduated retirement benefit before 6 April 2016. Prospective entitlement to any of these benefits that would crystallise before 6 April 2016 sufficed to permit payment from 12 October 2015 onwards. [*PA 2014, Sch 15, para 4*].

Perhaps the simplest way of considering eligibility is by looking at the individual's date of birth: Class 3A is open to those entitled to a UK contributory state pension who are men born before 6 April 1951 and women born before 6 April 1953.

Category A is the single person's basic pension under the 1975 regime, Category B is the 60% addition for a spouse or civil partner (to give a couple's pension where the spouse or civil partner's own entitlement is lower), and Category D is the 25p per week addition for state pensioners over the age of 80. (There was once a Category C, but it became obsolete some years ago when the last pensioners who were entitled – those who were already over state pension age in 1948 – died.)

Eligibility is personal to each contributor, so either spouse or civil partner or both spouses and partners may choose to contribute and buy an amount of SPTU.

Eligibility is also not restricted by reference to the class of contributions paid during the working life, so it is open to anyone, even if they have never made a SERPS contribution as an employee.

Rates

[19.13] The rates of Class 3A contributions have been set (by *Social Security Class 3A Contributions (Units of Additional Pension) Regulations 2014 (SI 2014/3240)*) using unisex actuarial principles, in consultation with the Government Actuary. The result is that older pensioners pay less than younger pensioners, because they will on average not live as long and therefore receive less in return. Eligible persons have been able, from 12 October 2015, to buy extra units (ie, £1 per week – *SI 2014/3240, reg 4*) of pension to add to their state pension. They may make more than one application and payment (*SSCBA 1992, s 14A(5)*) but may not acquire more than the maximum number of units, which has been set at 25 (*SI 2014/3240, reg 3*), which means that they can increase their state pension by up to £25 per week, or £1,300 per year.

The first announcement of the likely rate suggested that a 65-year-old would have to contribute £890 to add £1 per week to his or her state pension (ie £22,250 as a lump sum to add £25 per week to the state pension entitlement already held – an implicit annuity rate of 5.84%). In contrast, a 90-year-old pensioner would have to pay £270 to add £1 per week to his or her pension for the rest of his or her life. *SI 2014/3240* in fact set the rates as originally announced. The full range of rates is set out in the table below.

Age of person on the date of payment	Class 3A cost per £1 unit of additional weekly pension
62 (women only)	£956
63 (women only)	£934
64 (women only)	£913
65	£890
66	£871

Age of person on the date of payment	Class 3A cost per £1 unit of additional weekly pension
67	£847
68	£827
69	£801
70	£779
71	£761
72	£738
73	£719
74	£694
75	£674
76	£646
77	£625
78	£596
79	£574
80	£544
81	£514
82	£484
83	£454
84	£424
85	£394
86	£366
87	£339
88	£314
89	£291
90	£270
91	£251
92	£232
93	£216
94	£200
95	£185
96	£172
97	£159
98	£148
99	£137
100 and over	£127

HMRC provides an online calculator at www.gov.uk/state-pension-topup to show the lump sum contribution needed to increase pension income by between £1 and £25 per week.

The DWP also points out in its publicity material that contributors should consider whether paying Class 2 or Class 3 voluntary contributions might be a better investment, but there is no reason why they may not be paid in addition to Class 3A.

Where Class 2 and Class 3 are a possibility, they will certainly be a cheaper way to add extra pension, although the time limits will restrict their use to recently 'retired' pensioners. As the new state pension was initially set at £155.65 per week, each added year would be worth £4.45 (ie, 1/35th) per week in additional pension. For 2017–18 with the flat rate pension set at £159.55, each added year should be worth £4.56. Paying Class 3 contributions in 2017–18 at £14.25 per week would cost £741.00, or £162.50 per extra £1 of weekly pension, for life; a slight decrease from the 2016–17 cost of £164.76. Class 2 paid voluntarily, where this is possible, would be significantly cheaper. Whether any such contributions would be a sensible choice will depend on personal circumstances, as the additional pension will impact on other income related benefits such as pension credit, which may be withdrawn as pension income is increased by the top up. Pension credit is not available to pensioners who reach state pension age under the post-2016 regime.

Timing

[19.14] The opportunity to pay the new Class 3A contribution is to be time-limited, available from 12 October 2015 until 5 April 2017 (or if later, 30 days from the date on which a contributor is sent information about Class 3A contributions by HMRC in response to a request made before 6 April 2017), as it is a transitional measure to ensure that existing pensioners have the opportunity to benefit from a higher state pension after April 2016. Note that, despite it always having been the policy intention, the original version of *SSCBA 1992, s 14A* as created by *Pensions Act 2014* did not refer to such a cut-off date, and that this was inserted by later regulations. [*Social Security Class 3A Contributions (Amendment) Regulations 2014, SI 2014/2746, reg* 2].

Refunds and 'cooling off'

[19.15] A new *reg 56A* has been added to the *Contributions Regulations 2001* to deal with repayment of Class 3A contributions if the contributor dies within 90 days of making the payment or changes his mind and makes an application for a refund within those 90 days. If any increased state pension has been paid in the meantime, the extra amounts purchased with the contributions will be deducted from the repayment. Refunds in respect of deceased Class 3A contributors may be made to the surviving spouse or civil partner. [*Social Security Class 3A Contributions (Amendment) Regulations 2014, SI 2014/2746, reg 4*.]

If the contributor dies more than 90 days after making the payment, the contribution will only be refunded if the state pension has been deferred [www.gov.uk/statepensiontopup]. This entitlement is not, however, reflected in the regulations or statute. A contributor who reached state pension age before 6 April 2016 but who has deferred entitlement to the Category A or B state pension is still eligible to pay a Class 3A contribution despite the pension not being in payment. [*SSCBA 1992, s 14A*.]

Inheritance

[19.16] The SPTU will be equivalent to a SERPS addition to the basic pension, which means that some or all of it can be inherited by a surviving spouse or civil partner. SERPS pensions were earned before April 2002, when S2P was introduced as a less expensive replacement. Whereas the maximum amount of S2P pension that may be inherited has always been set at 50% of the deceased's earnings-related pension, the change from the SERPS rule to the S2P rule was graduated to ease pensioners into the new regime over time. Inheritance of SERPS is on a sliding scale dependent on the deceased's date of birth. This scale will be applied to the SPTU.

Man's date of birth	Age at 6 April 2016	Woman's date of birth	Age at 6 April 2016	Maximum SPTU% inheritable
5 10 37 or before	78y 6m	5 10 42 or before	73y 6m+	100%
6 10 37 to 5 10 39	76y 6m	6 10 42 to 5 10 44	71y 6m	90%
6 10 39 to 5 10 41	74y 6m	6 10 44 to 5 10 46	69y 6m	80%
6 10 41 to 5 10 43	72y 6m	6 10 46 to 5 10 48	67y 6m	70%
6 10 43 to 5 10 45	70y 6m	6 10 48 to 5 7 50	65y 9m	60%
6 10 45 and after	Below 70y 6m	6 7 50 and after	Below 65y 9m	50%

The inherited SPTU will be payable immediately if the survivor is already receiving the state pension when widowed. If he or she is below state pension age at the date of death and is entitled to widowed parent's allowance, the SPTU will be paid as part of that allowance. It should be payable in any event when the survivor reaches state pension age.

SPTU entitlement, unlike SERPS additions, should be inherited in full by the survivor, even if the survivor also buys an entitlement to SPTU. Whereas the maximum inheritance of SERPS is capped when both partners have additional state pension, the inherited percentage of SPTU should not be taken into account when assessing the maximum level of additional state pension payable.

SPTU will not be inheritable if the survivor is under state pension age at the date of death and remarries or forms a new civil partnership before reaching state pension age. A state pensioner who marries or enters into a civil partnership on or after 6 April 2016 with a spouse or civil partner under state pension age at 6 April 2016 will also not be able to pass on any entitlement on death.

Couples should therefore consider carefully which of them might be better placed in terms of life expectancy to buy the additional pension income.

International aspects

[19.17] There are no residence or presence criteria attached to the option to pay Class 3A contributions: eligibility is determined, as noted above, purely by age and entitlement to a UK state pension. This means that those UK state pensioners who live overseas can choose to buy the SPTU, although the same rules will apply as already apply to the ordinary state pension, namely that annual indexation increases will only be applied to pensioners resident in an EEA state or state with which the UK has a reciprocal social security agreement. Depending on age and life expectancy, the lack of indexation for those retiring to non-treaty territories (eg, Australia, South Africa) may not be a handicap in view of the generous annuity rate assumed in setting the level of the Class 3A contribution, but contributors will probably be best advised to take expert financial advice, especially if they already qualify in that territory for a means-tested benefit that would be reduced if their UK pension increased.

Further considerations

[19.18] The implicit annuity rate offered by the Class 3A provisions has been assessed by some experts as much better than any equivalent commercial annuity could offer to a typical pensioner. However, the decision about whether to invest in a higher state pension by means of a Class 3A contribution will depend on personal circumstances, such as personalised life expectancy, rather than on any 'typical' assumptions.

Other considerations are as follows:

- The additional pension purchased with Class 3A NICs will be treated like a SERPS additional component, so it will increase in line with CPI inflation.
- SPTU will be taxable. Couples should therefore consider carefully which of the pair would benefit most from an additional pension income, since typically one may be a taxpayer while the other is not, or one may be a higher rate taxpayer.
- The additional pension will be reckonable in any assessment of means-tested benefits, including pension credit, housing benefit and council tax benefit, so the marginal 'tax' rate may be higher than expected once loss of income-related benefits is factored into the calculations. However, the *Pensions Act 2014 (Consequential Amendments) (Units of Additional Pension) Order 2014, SI 2014/3213* introduced provisions to prevent an individual suffering a reduction in their state pension or disablement pension as a result of buying extra units under the Class 3A rules.
- The rates on which it is based are unisex, so they are more favourable to women than men, in view of their greater life expectancy.
- The details of how to apply and make a contribution were not available when the SPTU opened on 12 October 2015. Eligible contributors could register their interest and obtain more information by emailing p

aid.caxtonhouse@dwp.gsi.gov.uk or calling 0345 600 4270. The application process eventually launched via an online portal at www.gov.uk/statepensiontopup. Applicants need to be able to provide proof of identity (eg, P60, or last four digits of the number of the bank account into which their state pension is paid) and their NI number. Applications are also accepted over the telephone on the number given above (0300 200 1900 for pensioners who prefer to speak Welsh).

Key Points concerning voluntary contributions: classes 3 and 3A

[19.19] Points to consider are as follows.

- The payment of the weekly Class 3 voluntary contributions which is currently £14.65 would, for pensioners under the pre-2016 regime, entitle the payer to Category A pension of £125.95 per week if there are at least 30 years' contributions on the record. Any year of deficiency will have reduced the pension by £4.20 per week. From 6 April 2018, the standard rate of state pension is £164.35 per week, but 35 years of contributions are required to qualify for the full amount, so each year of deficiency reduces the state pension for those who reach state pension age under the new regime by £4.70 per week.
- Class 3 may not be paid where other contributions and/or credits are sufficient to create a 'qualifying year', although they may be paid in addition to Class 3A contributions where the contributor is eligible to pay both.
- If some contributions have been paid or credited then only a reduced numbers of weeks' voluntary contributions will need to be paid.
- In practice payment of Class 3 can be made in a lump sum shortly after the end of the tax year, and in many cases up to six years after the end of the year. Some people have until April 2023 to pay for years back to 6 April 2006.
- State pensioners as at 6 April 2016 should assess whether they ought to invest savings in enhancing their future state pension by paying a Class 3A contribution by 5 April 2017. The scheme is attractive to the self-employed, who will typically have had no SERPS/S2P entitlement, and to women, who will on average benefit more than men of the same age. Those with reduced life expectancy may not find the opportunity attractive.
- An online tool (via www.gov.uk/voluntary-national-insurance-contributions/why-pay-voluntary-contributions) offers most contributors a speedy overview of their contribution record and any gaps in it, and a link to a form to request a statement of voluntary

contributions that may be paid.

20

Class 4 Contributions: On Profits of a Trade etc

Cross-references. See AGE EXCEPTION **3** for age limitations on liability; **5.17** AGGREGATION OF EARNINGS; **7.5** ANNUAL MAXIMUM for Class 4 limiting maximum; APPEALS AND REVIEWS **9**; **12.4** ARREARS OF CONTRIBUTIONS for recovery provisions; **21.49** to **21.53** COLLECTION; DEFERMENT OF PAYMENT **27**; **32.5** to **32.13** EARNINGS FROM SELF-EMPLOYMENT; **33.6** EARNINGS LIMITS; **50.8** OIL-RIG WORKERS, DIVERS, ETC; **51.19** OVERSEAS MATTERS; PARTNERS **52**; **53.8** RATES AND LIMITS; REPAYMENT AND REALLOCATION **55**; SUBPOSTMASTERS **57**

Other Sources. HM Revenue and Customs Collection Manual; HM Revenue and Customs National Insurance Manual NIM24000–24715; HM Revenue and Customs Business Income Manual.

Introduction to class 4 contributions: on profits of a trade etc

[20.1] Class 4 contributions account for around 1.3% of the National Insurance Fund's contribution income (see **48.4** NATIONAL INSURANCE FUND). In monetary terms, this is expected to amount to some £2,725 million in 2016–17. Of this, some £771 million is diverted to the National Health Service.

This class of contribution was created in 1975 and, because liability for contributions within it cannot (except in special circumstances—see **20.8** below) arise without an income tax assessment under *Chapter 2* of *Part 2* of *Income Tax (Trading and Other Income) Act 2005 (ITTOIA 2005)* (what was Schedule D Case I or II) and can neither create nor augment a benefit entitlement for the contributor, has been seen by self-employed earners as a thinly-disguised additional tax on a specific range of their profits. Strong feelings have, therefore, brought even the validity of the imposing provisions under attack, but without success. (*Martin v O'Sullivan (Inspector of Taxes)* [1984] STC 258, 57 TC 709, CA). See **18.1** CLASS **2** CONTRIBUTIONS in relation to government discussion documents and Reports on the National Insurance position of the self-employed. See HM Revenue and Customs National Insurance Manual NIM24001.

The Chancellor announced in his pre-election March 2015 Budget Report (para 2.74) a plan to reform Class 4, involving the abolition of Class 2 NICs in the next Parliament, and the introduction of a new contributory benefit test for Class 4. The government was to consult on the detail and timing of these reforms 'later in 2015', but the Queens' Speech and the associated list of legislative proposals after the subsequent general election made no mention of this proposal. It did, however, include a commitment that tax and NIC rates would not rise throughout the Parliament (the so called 'tax lock'), and that the upper earnings limit (which presumably encompasses the Class 4 upper annual limit) would not rise above the higher rate tax threshold.

A consultation document entitled 'The abolition of Class 2 National Insurance: Introducing a benefit test into Class 4 National Insurance for the self-employed' was eventually issued on 9 December 2015, and the consultation closed on 24 February 2016. The paper explicitly recognised that any change will be complex and noted that it had been decided that no timetable would be set.

The headline outcome of the consultation emerged with Budget 2016: Class 2 is to be abolished from April 2018 and, it seems, will not be replaced by an increase in the rate of Class 4, as the Red Book referred to a plan to 'cut National Insurance contributions for 3.4 million self-employed people by abolishing Class 2', and the cost to the NI Fund is expected to be £1.075 billion between April 2018 and April 2021. The government confirmed that it intends to reform Class 4 so that it creates entitlement to the state pension and other contributory benefits following the abolition of Class 2, although no details were revealed as the outcome of the consultation was still being considered. A NICs Bill will be required in order to amend the various provisions of social security law in a number of different Acts affected by the proposals. The NICs Bill is being introduced in 2018, resulting in the abolition of Class 2 being deferred until April 2019.

Since every penny of contributions income is required by the NI Fund to cover expenditure on contributory benefits, it was expected that the Class 4 rate would have to be increased in order to raise the £360 million raised from Class 2 each year, but it seems that instead the Treasury grant to the NI Fund will have to be increased. It is also remains to be seen whether the basis of a revised Class 4 might not have to change to recognise the single-tier state pension implemented in April 2016, since employed and self-employed contributors now buy entitlements to exactly the same benefits, with the exception of a relatively small amount of contributory jobseeker's allowance to which Class 1 contributors may be entitled. The aggregate of the Class 4 main rate and the Class 2 flat rate have typically been roughly in line with the contracted-out rate of Class 1 for many years, but the removal of S2P arguably removes the justification for the lower rate of contributions for self-employed earners.

Given the lack of information about the future structure of Class 4, and the uncertainties in the proposals set out in the December 2015 consultation document, the text that follows focuses solely on the current regime unless otherwise made clear.

Liability

[20.2] Although Class 4 contributions are effectively payable by self-employed earners, liability is not solely dependent on such CATEGORISATION **14** as it is in the case of Class 2 contributions. Instead, Class 4 contributions are payable in respect of profits 'immediately derived' from the carrying on or exercise of one or more trades, professions or vocations, being profits or gains *chargeable to income tax under ITTOIA 2005, Part 2, Chapter 2* for any tax year of assessment beginning on or after 6 April 1975. [*SSCBA 1992, s 15(1))*, as amended by *ITTOIA 2005, Sch 1, Part 2, para 420*]. (See HM Revenue and Customs National Insurance Manual NIM24001). Note that the profits of separate trades and any shares of trading profits from partnerships and LLPs are aggregated for Class 4 purposes, so that only one liability calculation is needed each year.

For these purposes, profits chargeable to income tax under *ITTOIA 2005, Part 2, Chapter 2* have in the past been deemed to include profits consisting of payments of Business Start-Up Allowance (formerly Enterprise Allowance) made from March 1986 under *Employment and Training Act 1973, s 2(2)(d)* or *Enterprise and New Towns (Scotland) Act 1990, s 2(4)(c)* and chargeable to income tax as trading income under *ITTOIA 2005, s 207*. Later payments of government support under the New Deal (from 1998) and the Flexible New Deal (from October 2009 to September 2011) (also under the *ETA 1973*) were also chargeable to Class 4 as business earnings (although they were classed as unemployability supplement for the purposes of *Reg 44* of the *Contributions Regs 2001* and therefore were not earnings for Class 2 purposes and did not prevent a claim for small earnings exception). New Deal 50-Plus payments were exempt from income tax and NICs for all purposes. (*Contributions Regs 2001, Reg 45(2)(b)(ii)*).

The New Enterprise Allowance from April 2011, also made under *ETA 1973, s 2*, is exempt from income tax and Class 4, and until the Class 2 reform from 6 April 2015, it was disregarded from earnings for Class 2 purposes. [BIM40401].

The definition of earnings for Class 2 is now the same as the Class 4 definition as a result of *NICA 2015, Sch 1*. The exclusions from Class 2 earnings in *Regs 44* and *45* were therefore removed (as redundant) by their revocation from 6 April 2015 by *Social Security (Miscellaneous Amendments No 2) Regulations 2015, SI 2015/478, Reg 24*.

Profits immediately derived from the carrying on of a trade etc and chargeable to tax under *ITTOIA 2005, Part 2, Chapter 2* are subject to various adjustments before they become earnings for Class 4 contribution purposes. Class 4 contributions at 9% are then payable only on so much of earnings as falls between a lower and an upper annual limit and at 2% on the remainder above the upper annual limit without restriction. [*SSCBA 1992, s 15(3)(3ZA)* as amended by *National Insurance Contributions Act 2011, s 3(1)* and *ITTOIA 2005, Schedule 1, Part 2, para 420*] (see **32.4** to **32.13** EARNINGS FROM SELF-EMPLOYMENT and **33.6** EARNINGS LIMITS AND THRESHOLDS). Until 6 April 2003, no Class 4 liability of any kind existed on profits in excess of the upper annual limit. From 6 April 2003 to 5 April 2011 amounts above the upper annual limit attracted a contribution rate of 1% but this increased to 2% from 6 April 2011.

Until 6 April 2014, all members of limited liability partnerships were also subject to Class 4 contributions on their profits if they would have been chargeable in the same way on the same profits as members of a general partnership carrying on the same business (*s 15(3A), SSCBA 1992* inserted by *s 13, Limited Liability Partnerships Act 2000* from 6 April 2001 following *Limited Liability Partnerships Act 2000 (Commencement) Order 2000, SI 2000/3316* and *ITTOIA 2005, Schedule 1, Part 2, para 420*). See also *Limited Liability Partnerships Act 2000, s 10.*

From 6 April 2014, *Finance Act 2014* created the status of 'salaried member', liable to Class 1 instead of Class 4, and introduced measures against profit diversion as anti-avoidance provisions. These were reflected in *NICA 2014, ss 13-14,* and *s 14* overrides any rule in the *LLPA 2000* treating any member as self-employed.

NICA 2014, s 13 provides for the profits of a corporate member of an LLP to be treated as belonging to an individual member, thereby making them liable in that individual member's hands to income tax and Class 4 NICs rather than corporation tax.

Under the *Social Security Contributions (Limited Liability Partnership) Regulations 2014*, a member will be a 'salaried member' if he, either directly or through an intermediary, meets three conditions now set out in *ITTOIA 2005, ss 863A-863G*:

(1) It is reasonable to expect that at least 80% of the total amount payable by the LLP for the member's services will be fixed or, if variable, variable without reference to, or in practice unaffected by, the overall profits or losses of the LLP (ie, the member is seen to be entitled to disguised salary).
(2) The member has no significant influence over the affairs of the LLP.
(3) The member's capital contribution to the LLP is less than 25% of the disguised salary likely to be paid by the LLP in the relevant tax year.

Where a member is classed as a salaried member, he is treated for NICs purposes as employed in employed earner's employment by the LLP, liable to pay Class 1 primary contributions (and eligible for SSP, SMP, etc), and the LLP is classed as the secondary contributor in respect of any payment of earnings. As a deemed employed earner, the member cannot be liable to pay Class 4 contributions on his profit share. Note that the deeming applies only for income tax and NICs: the salaried member is not otherwise treated as an employee.

Where a member does not meet one or two of the conditions (eg, his capital contribution to the LLP exceeds 25% of his likely salary), he remains a self-employed earner and is subject to Classes 2 and 4 rather than Class 1. Where his circumstances change and he ceases to meet one of the conditions (eg, by increasing his capital contribution), his position may be reassessed and he will fall outside the deeming provisions and will once more become subject to Class 2 and 4 instead of Class 1. [*ITTOIA 2005, s 863B(1)(b)*.]

Before the changes to the treatment of LLP members, HMRC announced on 5 June 2013 that all sleeping partners and other inactive limited partners would be subject to Class 2 and Class 4 liabilities from 6 April 2013. The change in view was not to have retrospective effect. The blanket policy change was clearly wrong in the case of investment partnerships, since Class 4 can only apply to trading profits chargeable under *Chapter 2* of *Part 2* of *ITTOIA 2005*, not to property or other investment income. It is also questionable whether the profit share of a limited partner, who has no right to be involved in the business other than as an investor, fits within the scope of Class 4, which is based on profits immediately derived from carrying on a trade. It was hoped that the review of Classes 2 and 4 under the project heading 'Simplifying the National Insurance Processes for the Self-Employed', launched in July 2013, would result in due course in the issue of some clarifications by HMRC. This duly came about with the Class 2 reform by *NICA 2015* – see **18.2** – but at the same time HMRC also spotted a problem with Class 2 and membership of LLPs, which are technically corporate bodies. While profit shares from trading LLPs have from the introduction of LLPs in the UK been deemed to be within the scope of Class 4 (above), there was no equivalent deeming provision for Class 2 earnings. Members were members of a corporate body to which the profits accrued, and in the absence of deeming provisions their drawings should not have been treated as earnings from self-employment. This has now been addressed as part of the Class 2 reform, although there should be no impact on Class 4 liabilities – see **18.11**.

Section 13 of the *National Insurance Contributions Act 2014* inserted a new *s 18A* into *SSCBA 1992*. This allows regulations to be made to modify the way in which Class 4 contribution liabilities are determined for partners. It covers the deeming of salaried members' earnings to fall within Class 1 (and benefits in kind within Class 1A). The *Social Security Contributions (Limited Liability Partnership) Regulations 2014*, made only after Royal Assent to *FA 2014* which introduced the parallel tax provisions, were retrospective to 6 April 2014.

For the effect of trading etc losses set against other income see **32.7** EARNINGS FROM SELF-EMPLOYMENT.

As Class 4 NICs are calculated on 'profits' above the Lower Profits Limit, it is worth noting recent legislation that impacts on the calculation of profits. From 6 April 2017, the calculation of the profits of unincorporated businesses using the cash basis is to be simplified by amending the rules surrounding capital expenditure. The general disallowance of capital expenditure is replaced with a more limited disallowance of capital expenditure in relation to assets which are not used up in the business over a limited period.

Unincorporated property businesses will now be allowed to use a version of the cash basis for calculating their profits. The property cash basis can be used by unincorporated property businesses whose receipts do not exceed £150,000 (subject to certain exclusions).

[*Finance (No 2) Act 2017, s 16*].

Furnished holiday accommodation

[20.3] There is no deeming provision with regard to profits derived from the commercial letting of furnished holiday accommodation (on basic principles, not normally chargeable to income tax as income from a trade) and, accordingly, no Class 4 liability can arise in respect of such profits. (See *Gittos v Barclay* [1982] STC 390; *Griffiths v Jackson* [1983] STC 184, and *ICTA 1988, s 504A*, formerly *ICTA 1988, s 503(1)* repealed in part by *ITTOIA 2005, Sch 1 para 197* and *ITA 2007, ss 127, 836, Sch 1 para 473*). (See **14.18** CATEGORISATION for the Class 2 implications of commercially letting such accommodation.) HMRC have confirmed no Class 4 liabilities arise in these circumstances.

Case law

[20.4] The wording of *SSCBA 1992, s 15(1)* is borrowed largely from what was *ICTA 1988, s 833(4)(c)* which would indicate that, though not bound to do so, the former DSS would follow established case law in deciding what are, and what are not, profits 'immediately derived' from the carrying on of a trade etc. If that is so, a person will not be liable for Class 4 contributions on profits in the creation of which he has had no direct involvement. Thus, a pension to a retired partner under a partnership deed will not be an immediately derived profit or gain. (*Pegler v Abell* (1972) 48 TC 564; *Lawrence v Hayman* [1976] STC 227). Neither will a consultancy share of profits paid to a retired partner where the services are minimal, nor a sleeping partner's share in partnership profits. (*Hale v Shea* (1964) 42 TC 260). The HMRC announcement on sleeping partners (above) evidences HMRC's view that *Hale v Shea* is not relevant to this question, but it is not certain that HMRC's view was tenable before the 6 April 2015 changes outlined at **18.11**.

Exception from liability

[20.5] Exception from liability for Class 4 contributions will be granted to:

- anyone who, at the beginning of a tax year, is over pensionable age (see **3.15** AGE EXCEPTION and HM Revenue and Customs National Insurance Manual NIM24510, point 2) [*Social Security (Contributions) Regulations 2001, SI 2001/1004, Reg 91(a)*];
- anyone who, at the beginning of a tax year is under the age of 16 and applies for exception (see **3.4** to **3.6** AGE EXCEPTION and HM Revenue and Customs National Insurance Manual NIM24510, point 1) [*Social Security (Contributions) Regulations 2001, SI 2001/1004, Reg 93*];
- anyone who is non-resident for tax purposes (see **51.19** OVERSEAS MATTERS and HM Revenue and Customs National Insurance Manual NIM24515, and note that, uniquely in the context of NICs, residence

is determined for this purpose alone under the *income tax* rules, ie, the statutory residence test, rather than the rules that apply to Classes 1, 2 and 3 under *Reg 145*) [*Social Security (Contributions) Regulations 2001, SI 2001/1004, Reg 91(b)*];

- anyone who, though deriving profits or gains from a trade, profession or vocation, does not *immediately* so derive them (see **20.2** above);
- any trustee, guardian, tutor, curator, or committee of an incapacitated person who would otherwise be assessable and chargeable to Class 4 contributions under *TMA 1970, s 72* [*SSCBA 1992, Sch 2 para 5(a)*];
- any trustee who would otherwise be liable for Class 4 contributions under *ITTOIA 2005, Part 2, Chapter 2* which imposes a charge to tax under what was Schedule D on persons entitled to or receiving profits [*SSCBA 1992, Sch 2 para 5(b)*, as amended by *ITTOIA 2005, Schedule 1, Part 2, para 422*];
- certain divers and diving supervisors who, though working as employees in the North Sea are charged to tax under what was Schedule D on their earnings (see **50.8** OIL-RIG WORKERS, DIVERS, ETC – they pay Class 1 NICs despite their taxable earnings being deemed to be from self-employment) [*Social Security (Contributions) Regulations 2001, SI 2001/1004, Reg 92*];
- certain Class 1 contributors whose earnings are chargeable to income tax under what was Schedule D (see **20.6** below) [*Social Security (Contributions) Regulations 2001, SI 2001/1004, Regs 94, 94A*]; and
- certain salaried members of LLPs as defined whose earnings will be treated as falling within Class 1 liability as the earnings of an employed earner (see **20.2** above) [*Social Security Contributions (Limited Liability Partnership) Regulations 2014, Reg 2*].

Exception of Class 1 contributors in respect of earnings chargeable to tax under Chapter 2 of Part 2 of ITTOIA 2005

[20.6] It is often the case that persons employed as self-employed earners in certain trades, professions or vocations receive some earnings, for example, fees from offices held and salaries under contracts of service, which, though assessable to income tax under *ITTOIA 2005, Part 2 Chapter 2* as part of their trading profits, attract (or are, for precautionary reasons (see **14.25** CATEGORISATION), treated by persons for whom they provide services as attracting) a liability for Class 1 contributions. Examples of such people are solicitors, accountants, ENTERTAINERS **36** (until 5 April 2014), film technicians and (possibly) SUBPOSTMASTERS **57**. See HM Revenue and Customs National Insurance Manual NIM24620. Any such person (and any person treated as an employed earner for contribution purposes but assessed to tax under *ITTOIA 2005, Part 2, Chapter 2* as a self-employed earner — see **14.29** CATEGORISATION) may apply for exception from any Class 4 liability which would otherwise arise. [*Social Security (Contributions) Regulations 2001, SI 2001/1004, Reg 94*].

In some cases, notably those of subpostmasters, the taxable profits may include amounts that have suffered Class 1 contributions that, whilst charged for convenience under what was Schedule D, are strictly chargeable as employment income (general earnings). Given the additional rate charge without limit on both the self-employed and employees from 6 April 2003, this would have left affected contributors with a liability (originally at 1%, now 2%) on the same income under both Class 1 and Class 4. Accordingly, relief is afforded from 2003–04 onwards [*Reg 94A*, inserted by *Social Security (Contributions) (Amendment) No 7 Regs 2003, Reg 4*].

Example

Ariadne is a practising solicitor and also the company secretary of Web Ltd. Her accounting year ends on 30 June and her 2017–18 assessable profits for Class 4 purposes (based on her accounts to 30 June 2017 under *ITTOIA 2005, ss 198(1), 200(3), 201(1)*) are £33,000. During 2017–18, she is paid secretarial fees (under deduction of standard rate primary Class 1 contributions, on a quarterly basis as follows.

	Gross fees	*Class 1 primary*	
	£	£	
June 2017	500.00	—	(below PT)
September 2017	500.00	—	(below PT)
December 2017	2,100.00	Nil	(Nil% on PT [£8,164 ÷ 4 = £2,041])
		7.08	(12% on remainder [£2,100 – £2,041 = £59])
March 2018	14,000.00	Nil	(Nil% on PT [£8,164 ÷ 4 = £2,041])
		1,105.08	(12% on remainder up to the UEL [£45,000 ÷ 4 = £11,250] less £2,041)
		55.00	(2% on the remainder up to £14,000 = £2,750)
	£17,100.00	£1,167.16	

As these fees are included gross in Ariadne's accounts (the Class 1 contributions being correctly debited to drawings), the amount of £17,100 is therefore deducted from the profits on which Class 4 contributions would be payable. The position for 2017–18 would, for example, be

	£
Profits as stated	33,000
Less: Class 4 exception	17,100
	15,900
Less: lower annual limit	8,164
	£7,736

Total Class 4 liability	£
£7,736 × 9% =	£696.24

Application for exception

[20.7] Where the earnings that have suffered Class 1 contributions are properly chargeable under *ITTOIA 2005, Part 2, Chapter 2* then exception from Class 4 liability is – strictly, but see below – conditional upon an application being made by the earner to HM Revenue and Customs before the beginning of the year to which the exception relates or before such later date as HM Revenue and Customs allows. [*Social Security (Contributions) Regulations 2001, SI 2001/1004, Reg 94(2)*]. The application is to be made in such manner as HM Revenue and Customs directs and must be supported by such information and evidence as is required for the purpose of confirming the earner's entitlement to exception. [*Social Security (Contributions) Regulations 2001, SI 2001/1004, Reg 94(3)*]. A successful application will result in the issue of a certificate of exception. In that eventuality Box 101 on the SA103F tax return should be ticked. Box 100 used to be used only if the taxpayer was exempt from Class 4, eg, below the age of 16, or over pension age at the start of the year, or not resident during the year, or a diver or diving instructor. The 2015–16 return, the first since the Class 2 reform, changed its purpose to signify an election by those with profits below the small profits threshold for Class 2 to pay such contributions voluntarily to protect benefit entitlements.

If, however, relevant information has been withheld or the information supplied was erroneous, the exception certificate may be revoked by HM Revenue and Customs and thereupon the earner will become liable to pay all Class 4 contributions which, but for the certificate, would have been due.

Where, for 2003–04 onwards, the earnings are strictly taxable under ITEPA as 'general earnings' but included in the accounts for convenience no application for exception is required. [*Social Security (Contributions) Regulations 2001, SI 2001/1004, Reg 94A*]. The Class 4 entries on the tax return are adjusted to take account of this and for years up to 5 April 2015 Box 100 should not have been ticked as there is no deferment certificate. The SA103F Notes instruct taxpayers whose profit includes employment earnings to enter those earnings in Box 102 on the SA103F, entitled 'Adjustment to profits chargeable to Class 4 NICs'.

The practical difficulty intrinsic to these exception provisions is that the total amount of earnings liable to Class 1 contributions received during a tax year cannot be ascertained until after the year has ended, by which time the first self-assessment payment on account of Class 4 contributions for that year of assessment will have fallen due (see **21.49** COLLECTION). Accordingly, an application for exception which is made (as it should be) *before* the beginning of a tax year is treated as an application for Class 4 DEFERMENT OF PAYMENT (**27.8**) [*Social Security (Contributions) Regulations 2001, SI 2001/1004, Reg 94(4)*], while an application made *after* the end of the tax year is treated as an application for repayment of contributions (see **55.7** REPAYMENT AND REALLOCATION).

Special Class 4 contributions

[20.8] Special Class 4 contributions are payable by any earner who is, by regulation, treated as being self-employed (see **14.29** CATEGORISATION) and who has, in any tax year, earnings from that self-employment which:

- would otherwise be Class 1 earnings; and
- are chargeable to tax as general earnings; and
- exceed the special Class 4 lower annual limit.

[*SSCBA 1992, s 18(1); Social Security (Contributions) Regulations 2001, SI 2001/1004, Reg 103* as amended by *Social Security (Contributions) (Amendment) Regulations 2003, SI 2003/193, Reg 15*].

Such earnings are to be calculated as if they were employed earner's earnings and the total is to be rounded *down* to the nearest pound (see EARNINGS FROM EMPLOYMENT: GENERAL **29** and HM Revenue and Customs National Insurance Manual NIM24002). [*Social Security (Contributions) Regulations 2001, SI 2001/1004, Reg 105(b)*].

Where both ordinary and special Class 4 contributions are payable for any year, the amount of special Class 4 contributions at the main rate is not to exceed the difference (if any) between the ordinary Class 4 contributions payable and the amount of Class 4 contributions which would be payable at the main rate on profits or gains equal to the upper annual limit for the year. [*Social Security (Contributions) Regulations 2001, SI 2001/1004, Reg 108(1)(2)*].

The only group of earners to whom these provisions currently relate are certain EXAMINERS **37** and some SHARE FISHERMEN **56.** See also HM Revenue and Customs National Insurance Manual NIM24000.

Rate

[20.9] Class 4 ordinary and special contributions are payable at a prescribed main percentage rate on so much of Class 4 earnings as exceeds the lower annual limit but does not exceed the upper annual limit and at an additional rate on those earnings that exceed the upper annual limit (see **32.5–32.13** EARNINGS FROM SELF-EMPLOYMENT and **53.11–53.13** RATES AND LIMITS). [*SSCBA 1992, ss 15(3)(3ZA), 18(1)(1A)*].

For 2018–19, the lower annual limit and the upper annual limit are, respectively, £8,424 and £46,350. The main rate is 9% and the additional rate is 2%. [*SSCBA 1992, ss 15(3), 18(1)*, as amended by *Social Security (Contributions) (Limits and Thresholds Amendments and National Insurance Fund Payments) Regulations 2018, SI 2018/337, Reg 5* and *National Insurance Contributions Act 2011, s 2(1)*].

The main rate may at any time be changed by order of the Treasury (previously the Secretary of State for Social Security) provided the new rate does not exceed 9.25%. [*SSAA 1992, s 143(1)–(4)* as amended by *SSC(TF)A 1999, Sch 3 para 46, para 49* and *National Insurance Contributions Act 2011, s 2(2)*]. Any greater increase must be effected by statute but the *National Insurance Contributions Act 2002, s 3* nonetheless increased the rate from 7% to 8% with effect from 6 April 2003. Although, therefore arguably an unnecessary inclusion in that Act, it did institute at the same time the additional Class 4 percentage, with effect from 6 April 2003, of 1% on so much of the profits or gains as exceeded the upper annual limit. [*SSCBA 1992, ss 15(3ZA), 18(1A)* as inserted by *National Insurance Contributions Act 2002, s 3*, as amended by *Social Security (Contributions) (Re-rating and National Insurance Fund Payments) Order 2014, SI 2014/475, Reg 4*]. The *National Insurance Contributions Act 2011* increased the main rate up to the upper annual limit to 9% and the additional rate to 2% on other profits of gains. [*National Insurance Contributions Act 2011, s 2.*]

Assessment and collection

[20.10] Class 4 contributions are normally collected by HM Revenue and Customs along with income tax as part of the self-assessment instalment process (see **21.49, 21.51** COLLECTION). This came into effect for 1996–97 and subsequent years, resulting in interim payments being required on 31 January and 31 July along with the income tax, but with the exception that, where the tax and Class 4 NICs liability is less than £1,000 from 2009–10 (previously £500), it will be deferred until the following 31 January. [*FA 1996, s 147; Income Tax (Payments on Account) (Amendment) Regulations 2008, SI 2008/838.*] Class 2 liability is added only to the 31 January income tax and Class 4 liability for 2015–16 and later years following the *NICA 2015* reforms outlined at **18** CLASS 2 CONTRIBUTIONS. The Class 2 liability is not split across the two six monthly payments on account.

From November 2008 deferment of payment of tax and Class 4 has been available via the Business Payment Support Service in justified cases of hardship. See www.gov.uk/government/organisations/hm-revenue-customs/contact/business-payment-support-service and **21.49** COLLECTION.

Where an assessment (including a self-assessment) has become final and conclusive for income tax purposes, it is final and conclusive for Class 4 contribution purposes also and no subsequent adjustment is permissible except in relation to relief for interest, annuities or other annual payments made in the tax year (see **32.10** EARNINGS FROM SELF-EMPLOYMENT). [*SSCBA 1992, Sch 2 para 3(5)*].

Tax relief

[20.11] Since 1996–97, no tax relief has been available in respect of any part of Class 4 contributions. At one time, half of the Class 4 liability was deductible against income tax due, but this was abandoned because of the complexity of calculation that it caused. [*ITTOIA 2005, ss 53, 272, 868* as amended by *ITA 2007, Sch 1 para 507*; *ITEPA 2003, s 360A*].

Future changes

[20.12] The Government has announced several times that it proposes, following a recommendation from the Office of Tax Simplification, to abolish Class 2 contributions and make Class 4 the basis of future benefit claims instead. It issued a consultation document on 9 December 2015 entitled 'The abolition of Class 2 National Insurance: introducing a benefit test into Class 4 National Insurance for the self-employed'.

In outline, the document suggested that Class 4 would become broadly similar to Class 1 in terms of calculating liability, with the same approach:

- deeming Class 1 contributions to have been paid on profits between the Class 1 lower earnings limit and the Class 4 lower annual limit, set at the same level as the Class 1 primary threshold;
- charging full rate contributions on annual profits up to the upper annual limit (UAL), set at the same level as the Class 1 upper earnings limit; and
- charging additional rate contributions on profits above the UAL.

It became clear from the Budget 2016 papers that any changes would be delayed until April 2018, and Class 2 would simply be abolished, offering a tax cut to the self-employed. No mention was made of increasing the Class 4 rate to plug the resultant gap in the NI Fund.

Introducing a contributory benefit test into Class 4 will, however, be complicated, particularly for short-term benefits, and in particular for maternity allowance, which currently look for 26 weeks' worth of Class 2 contributions having been paid in the 66 weeks leading up to the birth or adoption. Since Class 4 is calculated on an annual basis, and then only once accounting profits for the period have been established, a new method of providing cover for short-term benefits will have to be devised.

It seems likely, therefore, that entitlement will have to be based on estimated earnings (which could be done now without a major Class 4 reform) or Class 3 contributions will also have to be reformed in order to accommodate the changes to Class 4. At the moment, Class 3 is relevant only to state pension entitlement, and the self-employed need to pay Class 2 contributions to earn short-term benefit cover. The Government's stated aim is to protect the self-employed and to simplify the system. This may mean that a number of rules in the benefits system have to be changed, extending Class 3 cover to short-term benefits and requiring a much smaller number of Class 3 contributions so that the monetary value remains similar to the current Class 2 cost.

Since a single Class 3 contribution is currently worth the same in terms of earnings factors as a single Class 2 contribution (ie, a week's contribution of either is deemed to be equivalent of Class 1 earnings equal to the lower earnings limit), any such reform is bound to introduce added complexity. Where a contributor currently pays 52 × £2.85 = £148.20 to earn a qualifying year, this amounts to 10.40 weeks' worth of Class 3 contributions. A reform of Class 3 to accommodate this differential will add yet more complexity as part of the alleged simplification process.

The unusual groups who pay special Class 2 contributions, namely share fishermen and volunteer development workers (VDWs), will also need special provisions. The plan is to allow share fishermen to use Class 4 instead of special Class 2 to earn their entitlements, and to abolish their right to contributory JSA when not working, which is currently why they pay a higher rate of Class 2. They would then be left to rely on means-tested JSA if their assets were low enough to qualify. VDWs would begin to pay Class 3 contributions instead of special Class 2, increasing their contribution costs from (currently) £5.80 per week to £14.65 per week. No conclusions had been reached on how to protect rights to contributory employment & support allowance and maternity entitlements that might be lost by paying Class 3 contributions instead of Class 2/4.

Another large group for whom special arrangements need to be considered are those who work abroad (both employed and self-employed may currently use Class 2 to protect their entitlements while away) and those who work as mariners on foreign-flagged vessels. Where the self-employed have no UK taxable profits, they currently have no Class 4 liability, so would need a new Class 3 arrangement to replace the Class 2 that they may currently pay.

Other groups who are treated as self-employed for NICs, such as examiners, ministers of religion not paid mainly by stipend, foster carers and some landlords, will also need to be considered, as will the very small number of self-employed older women who have a reduced rate election and are currently exempt from Class 2 and cannot pay Class 3. These groups may all need a special category of Class 4 or Class 3, or a new credit regime (eg, for foster carers), or may just be told to pay Class 3 (£761.80 per year currently) instead.

A new social security act will be needed to introduce any such changes to Classes 2, 3 and 4, and there will have to be numerous systems changes, alongside the digitisation of the personal tax system that has been promised, so April 2018 may be a very optimistic target date for the introduction of the reforms. This has proved to be the case with the abolition of Class 2 contributions now deferred until April 2019.

Key Points concerning class 4 contributions: on profits of a trade etc

[20.13] Points to consider are as follows.

- Class 4 liability rests on there being profits from a trade, profession or vocation within the charge to UK tax and taxed under *ITTOIA 2005*, *Part 2*, *Chapter 2*.
- Class 4 contributions will not be due on profits where there is a Class 1 liability on the same income.
- Members of an LLP other than full equity partners may be subject to Class 1 rather than Class 4 liabilities from 6 April 2014.
- The Class 4 rules on determining earnings and on collection, enforcement and payment also apply to Class 2 with effect from 6 April 2015.
- Class 4 currently does not count for contributory benefit purposes, but the Government has proposed the abolition of Class 2 from April 2019, with Class 4 becoming the basis of future benefit claims for the self-employed instead, together with a reform of Class 3 to protect certain groups of contributor who currently rely

on Class 2 and have no Class 4 liability.

21
Collection

Cross-references. See ARREARS OF CONTRIBUTIONS **12** for overdue contributions recovery provisions; CLASS 1 CONTRIBUTIONS **15**; CLASS 1A CONTRIBUTIONS **16**; CLASS 1B CONTRIBUTIONS **17**; CLASS 2 CONTRIBUTIONS **18**; CLASS 3 CONTRIBUTIONS **19**; CLASS 4 CONTRIBUTIONS **20**; DEFERMENT OF PAYMENT **27**; ENFORCEMENT **35** for offences and penalties and powers of inspectors; NATIONAL INSURANCE NUMBER **49** for recording of contributions.

Other Sources. Employer's Help Book E10(2013) (now withdrawn); Tolley's Practical NIC, December 2001 page 96.

Introduction to collection

[21.1] Social security legislation contains no provision for formal assessment or determination of Class 1 liability, other than where such liability, or its amount, is in dispute. Instead, rules are laid down in relation to the kind of employment in which Class 1 liabilities will arise, the kind of EARNINGS FROM EMPLOYMENT: GENERAL **29** to which such liability will relate, the basis period by reference to which the liability must be computed, the extent to which earnings in such a period may be disregarded, and the rate at which calculation must take place. The task of assessment and discharge of liability is then left to any person who, finding he is liable to contribute under these rules, is directed by the legislation to perform that task (see CATEGORISATION 14, EARNINGS LIMITS AND THRESHOLDS 33, EARNINGS PERIODS 34, RATES AND LIMITS 53).

Class 1 contributions

[21.2] Normally, the person liable to contribute will be the *secondary contributor* (see 14.32 CATEGORISATION). This is because where earnings are paid to an employed earner and a liability for primary and secondary CLASS 1 CONTRIBUTIONS 15 arises in respect of that payment, the secondary contributor, as well as being liable for his own secondary contribution, is liable in the first instance to pay the earner's primary contribution also, on behalf of and to the exclusion of the earner. [*SSCBA 1992, s 6(4)* and *Sch 1 para 3(1) as amended by National Insurance Contributions Act 2002, Sch 1 para 13(3)*]. He is, however, entitled to recover such primary contributions or a prescribed part of the earner's primary contribution from the earner's earnings (and, for all practical purposes, *must* in fact do so) as the primary contribution is the liability of the earner.

It is arguable that, where earnings are paid not *to* the earner but to someone else *for the benefit of* the earner (eg when an employer discharges an employee's personal debt to a third party), any primary Class 1 liability imposed by *SSCBA 1992, s 6* becomes uncollectible in law. This is because *s 6(4)* requires the primary liability imposed on the earner to be discharged in the manner provided for in *Sch 1 para 3*, but *Sch 1 para 3* addresses itself only to the situation where earnings are paid *to* an earner and makes no mention of the situation where earnings are paid *for the benefit of* an earner. It follows that, where a payment is made to someone other than the earner (even though for his benefit) no primary Class 1 contribution becomes due from the employer and, in consequence, the collection machinery of *Social Security (Contributions) Regulations 2001, SI 2001/1004, Sch 4* can be applied only to the secondary Class 1 contribution which is due. It might be thought that the authorities could have resort to direct collection procedures in order to obtain payment of the primary Class 1 contribution which is due, but such procedures are available only in deferment situations and situations where the employer is outside the jurisdiction of Parliament. [*Social Security (Contributions) Regulations 2001, SI 2001/1004, Reg 68, Reg 84, Sch 4 para 30*].

Collection as income tax

[21.3] PAYE was introduced in 1944 as a tax collection mechanism for income tax only. At the time, employer and employee National Insurance contributions were collected by requiring employers to buy flat-rate contributions stamps, stick them on cards (which were given to employees to take to a new employer when they changed jobs, or to the 'labour exchange' when they were 'signing on' as unemployed), and send them to the Ministry of Pensions and National Insurance annually, from which contribution records for benefit purposes were constructed. Class 1 NICs became fully earnings-related only with *SSA 1975*. The principle on which the imposition of the new Class 1 contribution liability was based was broadly the same as that which underlay the collection of tax on earnings chargeable to tax as 'Schedule E emoluments' (referred to in tax legislation since the introduction of *ITEPA 2003* as 'general earnings') (see **21.2** above). It follows, therefore, that, as the objective of the CATEGORISATION **14** rules was to align Class 1 with income tax liability on earnings, and as an elaborate and developed PAYE system already enabled such tax on earnings to be collected in accordance with the principle enunciated, the PAYE system incorporated in what is now the *Income Tax (Pay As You Earn) Regulations 2003, SI 2003/2682* was the most appropriate means of collecting Class 1 contributions.

Accordingly, it has been provided since 1975 that, subject to any alternative arrangements which might be made, Class 1 contributions are to be *paid, accounted for and recovered in like manner as income tax* deducted from the emoluments or general earnings of an office or employment by virtue of PAYE arrangements under *ITEPA 2003, s 684*, and that extended and modified PAYE regulations are to apply to, and for the purpose of, such contributions. However, HM Revenue and Customs may authorise arrangements whereby earnings related contributions are paid in a different manner from those prescribed under *Contributions Reg 67*, by reason of *Reg 68*. [*SSCBA 1992, s 6(1); Contributions Regs, Reg 67; Contributions Regs, Reg 68*].

Alignment of PAYE and NICs

[21.4] The PAYE regulations, adapted as necessary (eg, NICs were to be collected weekly on a non-cumulative basis and without the equivalent of a tax code, just like the earlier stamps), were incorporated almost wholesale as the new collection mechanism into the *Social Security (Contributions) Regulations 1975, SI 1975/492*, which were consolidated, after the introduction of contracting out in 1978, into the *Social Security (Contributions) Regulations 1979, SI 1979/591, Sch 1*. Having been modified on multiple occasions each year since, in their latest incarnation they appear in social security legislation as *Social Security (Contributions) Regulations 2001, SI 2001/1004, Sch 4*.

ITEPA 2003, s 686 defines 'payment' for PAYE purposes. *Social Security (Contributions) Regulations 2001, SI 2001/1004, Reg 67, Sch 4* does not, however, import into contribution law principles of income tax law, rather it simply borrows the collection and recovery machinery of the PAYE system. The definition of 'payment' for income tax purposes is therefore not applicable for contribution purposes. As a result of this a disparity sometimes exists between the rules for collection and recovery of PAYE tax and NICs. In order to eliminate some of these disparities the *National Insurance Contributions and Statutory Payments Act 2004* sought to reduce technical differences between tax and NICs in certain areas such as shares (*sections 1–4*), distraint (*sections 5 and 6*), inspection powers (*sections 7 and 8*) and applying civil penalties for non-compliance in relation to SSP and SMP rather than criminal penalties (*sections 9 and 10*). [*National Insurance Contributions and Statutory Payments Act 2004 (Commencement) Order 2004, SI 2004/1943* and *Social Security (Contributions) (Amendment No 4) Regulations 2004, SI*

2004/2096]. The *National Insurance Contributions Act 2006* did likewise by providing for the first time the power to make regulations that imposed National Insurance liability on a retrospective basis. The power is, however, confined to cases where a retrospective tax liability has also been imposed through a Finance Act – see **21.42** and **31.2** EARNINGS FROM EMPLOYMENT: READILY CONVERTIBLE ASSETS, ETC. [*National Insurance Contributions Act 2006, ss 1-4*]. Following the HMRC powers review, the *FA 2008* and *FA 2009* changes to the penalty and inspection regime for income taxes were also imported into NIC legislation (see, eg, *FA 2008, Sch 36, para 84*).

By the time HMRC decided to move payroll taxes reporting onto a Real Time Information (RTI) basis between April 2012 and October 2013, it was entirely logical that the RTI changes introduced for PAYE enforcement should be matched, as far as possible (differences remain inevitable because of certain NIC-only rules), in the NIC regulations.

In theory, only the reporting system has changed. Logically, therefore, it might be expected that, since the collection timetable has not technically changed – remittances are still due monthly or quarterly, as in the pre-RTI days – there should be few differences between the old and new regimes.

One of HMRC's reasons for wanting to introduce RTI was to improve collection of PAYE and NICs in-year, because under the old annual reporting regime employers could underpay, carefully, throughout the first eleven months of the tax year without HMRC knowing about it or taking any action. Once employers were obliged to report every payment as it was made, HMRC would know whether the remittance of deductions was understated. In effect, HMRC's guesswork about how much should have been remitted monthly or quarterly should disappear, and employers could be pursued promptly if they did not pay over the full amount due.

What follows attempts to describe both the current (RTI) rules (involving reporting of every payment and deduction almost in real time) and the former pre-RTI rules (involving payment to HMRC monthly or quarterly but reporting mostly annually).

Liability of a secondary contributor

[21.5] Where earnings are paid to an employed earner and, in respect of that payment, liability arises for primary and secondary Class 1 contributions, the secondary contributor is, except where a special alternative arrangement has been made, to discharge the *whole* liability (see **21.1** above). This is done by paying to HMRC, within 14 days of the end of every income tax month (or, where quarterly remittances are permitted, the income tax quarter—see below) during which the earnings were paid, the amount of those contributions less any amount which the secondary contributor has deducted from such contributions by way of recovery of payments of Statutory Maternity Pay, Statutory Paternity Pay, Statutory Adoption Pay and Statutory Shared Parental Pay or by way of compensation for secondary Class 1 contributions paid on payments of SMP, SAP, SPP and ShPP (see **15.12** CLASS 1 CONTRIBUTIONS). CIS deductions may also be set off by subcontractor companies (note: companies, not unincorporated traders) with net payment status. Payment need not be made until 17 days after the end of the period if made electronically (ie, cleared funds must be in HMRC's account by that date). [*Social Security (Contributions) Regulations 2001, SI 2001/1004, Sch 4 para 1*]. Where appropriate, the monthly payment also includes student loan repayments deducted from employees and/or (until 31 March 2006) it was sometimes reduced by tax credits recoverable.

The amount to be paid to HMRC in accordance with the foregoing paragraph is not to include any amount which could have been, but was not, deducted from a payment of earnings which fell to be aggregated with another payment of earnings (see **5.13** AGGREGATION). A secondary contributor will, however, be deemed to have deducted from the last of any payments of earnings which fell to be aggregated any Class 1 contributions deductible but not in fact deducted from those payments, and will, accordingly, be obliged to include in his payment to HMRC the amount of the deemed deduction. [*Social Security (Contributions) Regulations 2001, SI 2001/1004, Sch 4 para 10(2)(3A)* amended by *Social Security (Contributions) (Amendment No 3) Regulations 2012, SI 2012/821*].

Where an officer of HM Revenue and Customs has authorised a secondary contributor to deduct tax from each payment of earnings which he makes to an earner who is in receipt of a fixed salary or wage by reference only to the amount of that payment, payment of Class 1 contributions related to those earnings is to be made to HMRC quarterly, ie payment of such contributions for the three months ended 5 July 2016 will not, in such circumstances, be due for payment until 19 July 2016 (or 22 July 2016 if payment is made electronically).

Likewise, where an employer has reasonable grounds for believing that, for income tax months falling within the current tax year, the average monthly total amount to be paid to HMRC will be less than the currently specified amount of £1,500 per month in respect of the net total of deductions less recoveries (PAYE, Class 1 contributions, less SSP, SMP, SAP, SPP and ShPP plus deductions made from payments made to subcontractors under the CIS and student loan repayments, *less* (for company subcontractors only) CIS recoveries, and liabilities that have been transferred from secondary contributors to employed earners) Class 1 contributions need only be paid over to HMRC quarterly. [*Social Security (Contributions) Regulations 2001, SI 2001/1004, Sch 4 para 11(1)(a) and (4); The Income Tax (Pay As You Earn) Regulations 2003, SI 2003/2682, Reg 70; Income Tax (Construction Industry Scheme) (Amendment) Regulations 2010, SI 2010/717*].

Methods of payment

[21.6] With effect from 6 April 1996, a payment made by cheque to an officer of HM Revenue and Customs will be treated for PAYE and NIC purposes under *Taxes Management Act 1970* (*TMA 1970*) as made on the day on which the cheque was received by HMRC, provided the cheque is paid on its first presentation to the bank on which it is drawn. Where the due date is at the weekend, a cheque received on the following Monday is treated as received on time. However, HMRC has the power to make regulations to treat the payment by cheque as made at the time the funds clear and not as made on the day on which the cheque is received, but these have so far only been made in relation to VAT and corporation tax. Such regulations, when eventually introduced by HMRC, will bring cheque payments into line with electronic payments as the former payment method gives a cashflow advantage to the payer of a few days over those paying electronically. Whilst such powers have been exercised in relation to VAT payments from April 2010, no equivalent change has yet been made in respect of PAYE/NIC monthly and quarterly remittances. [*TMA 1970, s 70A* inserted by virtue of *FA 1994, Sch 19 para 22; Income Tax (Employments) (Amendment No 2) Regs 1996, Regs 3–5* and *Social Security (Contributions) Regulations 2001, SI 2001/1004, Sch 4 para 29; FA 2007, s 95; Income and Corporation Taxes (Electronic Communications) (Amendment) Regulations 2009, SI 2009/3218; Debt Management and Banking Manual DMBM201020*]. See also IR Press Release 1 April 1996 regarding cheques received on or after 19 April 1996 whereby interest is charged from different dates for Class 1 and 1A depending on the payment method.

Receipts for remittances will be issued only if requested. [*Social Security (Contributions) Regulations 2001, SI 2001/1004, Sch 4 para 12(1)*].

Since 2004, employers of 250 or more people in any one PAYE scheme ('large employers' within *Reg 198A* of the *Income Tax (Pay As You Earn) Regulations 2003, SI 2003/2682* have been obliged to pay over their monthly remittance electronically, other than in cases where retrospective legislation is enacted. [*Social Security (Contributions) Regulations 2001, SI 2001/1004, Reg 90H.*] See further **21.17** below

For other employers, HM Revenue and Customs accepts payment of NICs in Euros (notes, not coins) and states that it will not pass on its administrative costs of collection and conversion. It will not, however, meet the cost of currency value fluctuations and overpayments will be repaid/set off in sterling. HMRC will now accept credit card-supported payments in relation to tax and NICs although a surcharge is imposed. From 13 January 2018, the recharging of associated fees back to customers can no longer be made under the EU Payment Services Directive 2. This has resulted in HMRC not accepting payments by personal credit card from that date. Corporate, business and commercial credit cards are not affected by this change and HMRC will continue to accept personal and commercial debit cards.

HMRC used to accept payments made at the Post Office using the 'Transcash' service. This facility was withdrawn from 15 December 2017.

Any person wishing to make payment of up to £99,999.99 can go direct to the HMRC's payment page at www.tax.service.gov.uk/pay-online/epaye. HMRC does not accept American Express or Diners Club cards. Full bank details for making e-payment by BACS, CHAPS or Faster Payment of ordinary Class 1 National Insurance liabilities are provided at www.gov.uk/pay-paye-tax/bank-details.

Where a secondary contributor has made a deduction from a contributions payment by way of recovery of payments of SSP, SMP, SAP, SPP and ShPP made by him or by way of compensation for secondary Class 1 contributions paid on such statutory payments (before 6 April 1991, only SSP was relevant, from 6 April 2014, SSP is no longer recoverable), the deemed date of payment of the contributions represented by that deduction is:

- if the deduction by way of recovery or compensation does not wholly extinguish the contributions payment, the first date on which any part of the remainder is paid, or
- if the deduction by way of recovery and/or compensation wholly extinguishes the contributions payment, the fourteenth day after the end of the income tax month during which there were paid the earnings in respect of which the contributions payment was payable.

[*Statutory Sick Pay Compensation Regulations 1983, Reg 4; Statutory Maternity Pay Compensation Regulations 1987, Reg 6; Statutory Shared Parental Pay (Administration) Regulations 2014, SI 2014/2929, Reg 5.*]

Compliance documentation

[21.7] From the start of the 2008–09 year, HM Revenue and Customs redesigned its payslips for employers and only a single total for tax and NICs can now be shown, the split of the various elements being decided by HM Revenue and Customs where necessary using the RTI information submitted on FPS and EPS. Before RTI was introduced, HMRC waited until the P35 was submitted at the end of the year. In these contexts, from 6 April 2000 'tax' means PAYE income tax, *plus* student loan repayments and subcontractors' payments *less* (until 31 March 2006) tax credits. [*ICTA 1988, s 559; Tax Credits (Payments by Employers) Regulations 1999, Reg 6(2), Reg 7(2)(3); Education (Student Loans) (Repayment) Regulations 2000, Reg 39(1); Income Tax (Sub-contractors in the Construction Industry and Employments) (Amendment) Regulations 2003, SI 2003/536, Regs 4, 8*]. The reason why a separate figure used to be required for NIC and was then estimated during the year by HM Revenue and Customs in advance of receipt of the fully detailed P35 was that, although all amounts paid to HMRC are paid into the HMRC account, HMRC accounts for and pays to the National Insurance Fund (when directed to do so by the Treasury) sums which it estimates have been paid to it as contributions. It is suggested that, where an insufficient amount is paid to satisfy both tax and contributions which are due, the secondary contributor may, because both debts are due to a single creditor (ie the Crown), appropriate the payment he makes to either the tax debt or the contribution debt or partly to each. The creditor must accept the nomination by the debtor of the reason for the payment – see below.

For 'Real Time Information' returns see the *Social Security (Contributions) Regulations 2001, SI 2001/1004, Sch 4, paras 21A-21F* (added by the *Social Security (Contributions) (Amendment No 3) Regulations 2012, SI 2012/821*).

Company's unpaid debts

[21.8] HM Revenue and Customs has, in the case of contributions but not tax (except in the case of – from August 2007 – a managed service company or a composite company), the power of proceeding against the directors of a limited company for certain of the company's unpaid debts (see **12** ARREARS OF

CONTRIBUTIONS). Thus, prudence dictates that the directors of a company which is encountering difficulties should ensure that sums paid to HM Revenue and Customs are expressly appropriated to contribution debts rather than to debts for tax under the PAYE scheme. It is an established maxim of law that, when money is paid, it is to be applied according to the will of the payer not of the receiver, and, if the party to whom the money is offered does not agree to apply it according to the expressed will of the party offering it, he must refuse it. (*Croft v Lumley* (1855) 5 E & B 648, 25 LJQB 73, 223, Ex Ch, *per Lord Campbell*). Non-return of a cheque sent to HM Revenue and Customs, therefore, signifies acceptance of any expressed application by the payer – the fact that the cheque value is posted to a suspense account by the Accounts Office does not constitute rejection of the payment. Where HMRC agrees to accept a payment which is less than an employer's full tax and Class 1 contribution liability, it was in the past instructed to agree with the employer how the payment is to be apportioned. (Hansard 22 February 1984 Vol 54 No 104 Cols 543–544). Clearly, from 2008–09 onwards the 'combined' payslips make identification of payment more difficult, but if in really exceptional circumstances such identification was required, a letter enclosing a cheque and making the sender's requirements clear would be necessary or alternatively, if paying electronically, two separate monthly payments could be made denoting each with the appropriate prefix at the start of the collection reference number, viz 'N' (NICs) or 'P' (PAYE tax), for example for PAYE payments, P123PA00012345 and for National Insurance contributions, N123PA00012345. Since most incoming cheque handling in HMRC is automated, the latter option is perhaps more reliable.

In *Williams v Glover & Pearson (re GP Aviation Group International Ltd)* [2013] EWHC 1447 (CH) two former directors of a company in liquidation, from whom unpaid corporation tax had been sought by the liquidator, were refused permission to have the company's right of appeal against the corporation tax assessments assigned to them.

Error in good faith

[21.9] Where, by reason of an error made by the secondary contributor in good faith or as a result of a change from not contracted-out to CONTRACTED-OUT EMPLOYMENT 23 or because a refund has been made under *Social Security (Refunds) (Repayment of Contractual Maternity Pay) Regs 1990, Reg 2*, an overpayment of contributions is made to HMRC, the amount overpaid may be deducted in arriving at any amount subsequently remitted to HMRC *within the same tax year*. This is so provided that, if there was a corresponding over-deduction from any payment of earnings to an employed earner, the employed earner has been reimbursed. Regulations may also provide for repayment of contributions paid by reference to earnings which have become repayable. The relevant FPS cumulative totals should be corrected so that the RTI computer recognises that a lesser amount is due than might otherwise be expected. [*SSCBA 1992, Sch 1 para 8(1)(h)*].

P60

[21.10] A secondary contributor is required to give the employee a certificate of tax deducted showing primary Class 1 contributions paid during the tax year (P60). Despite the pre-RTI requirement for most employers to send Forms P14 to HM Revenue and Customs by electronic means, the P60 for many years nevertheless had to be provided on paper and through no other medium. However, in respect of certificates P60 relating to 2010–11 and later years the form may be provided electronically. In the case of an employee leaving during the tax year, the employer must not provide a form P60. [*Social Security (Contributions) Regulations 2001, SI 2001/1004, Sch 4 para 9* amended by the *Social Security (Contributions) (Amendment No 3) Regulations 2012, SI 2012/821; The Income Tax (Pay As You Earn) Regulations 2003, SI 2003/2682, Reg 67; Income Tax (Pay As You Earn) (Amendment) Regulations 2010, SI 2010/668, Reg 13*]. Instead, a form P45 is appropriate.

Death of secondary contributor

[21.11] If a secondary contributor dies, anything which he would have been liable to do under the *Contribution Regs* is to be done by his personal representative or, if he paid earnings only as an agent, the person succeeding him or, if there is no successor, his principal. [*Social Security (Contributions) Regulations 2001, SI 2001/1004, Sch 4 para 27; The Income Tax (Pay As You Earn) Regulations 2003, SI 2003/2682, Regs 101–104*].

Succession of secondary contributor

[21.12] Similarly, but to a more restricted degree, a person who becomes a secondary contributor by succeeding to a trade or business is to do under the *Contributions Regs* anything which the former secondary contributor would have been liable to do, except that he is not to be liable for contributions which were deductible from earnings paid to an employed earner before the succession took place but are no longer so deductible. [*Social Security (Contributions) Regulations 2001, SI 2001/1004, Sch 4 para 28* and see also *Transfer of Undertakings (Protection of Employment) Regulations 1981*].

Example

Clips Hair Salon employs a number of assistants to assist the stylists, who are self-employed and 'rent a chair', with washing and preparation prior to cut. The owner has decided to sell the business and retire to Spain. It transpires that he has not deducted tax or NICs in respect of the assistants' wages, all of whom earned over £153 per week including tips during 2015–16. The owner sold the business to one of the existing stylists and contracts were exchanged on 9 April 2016.

The total tax and NICs unpaid by the previous owner for 2015–16 amounted to £1,207.80 (tax), £1,131.35 (primary contributions) and £1,316.48 (secondary contributions). In most circumstances, the previous owner will continue to bear the total liability of £3,655.63. However, the question may arise whether the employees knew and/or colluded with the underpayment of PAYE and NICs. If they did so, then HMRC may direct that recovery of the arrears be made from the employees because HMRC is of the opinion that they knew of the 'wilful failure' to pay tax and NICs. It is necessary that the employees actually knew of the failure and not just that they ought to have known or even suspected the failure by the employer to pay PAYE and NICs.

Also, an appropriate 'final submission' return should have been made on FPS or EPS by 19 April 2016 in respect of tax and NICs. If the deadline of 19 April 2016 for payment of outstanding tax and NICs, ie the amount of £3,655.63, is missed, then interest will run from 20 April 2016, unless payment is in due course made electronically – in which case interest will be due from 23 April 2016. Any late payments in respect of 2016–17 will attract monthly interest charges, but that is within the new owner's control. [*The Income Tax (Pay As You Earn) Regulations 2003, SI 2003/2682, Reg 102(4)*.]

Depending on the drafting of the Deed of Taxation Indemnity there may also be a potential liability on the vendor to pay the outstanding PAYE and NICs liability if the relevant clause is appropriately worded, eg:

"All income tax under the PAYE system and payments due in respect of employees' contributions to National Insurance have been deducted from all payments made or treated as made by [Clips Hair Salon Ltd] (the Company) and (together with an employer's contribution) have been duly paid by the Company to HM Revenue and Customs in the appropriate manner and the Company has complied with all its reporting obligations in connection with the benefits provided for employees and Directors of the Company."

However, Clips Hair Salon's vendor protection provision in the purchase and sale agreement may include the clause below extricating the vendor from the liability and effectively passing this on to the purchaser.

"The Vendors shall not be liable in respect of all and any claims made by the Purchaser under the Warranties or under the Tax Deed unless and until the aggregate cumulative liability of the Vendors in respect of all and any such claims (ignoring for these purposes all and any claims in respect of which the Vendors do not have any liability pursuant to the provisions of clause [. . .]) exceeds £5,000 in which event the Vendors shall be liable for [the entire amount of such liability or the excess of such liability over £ . . .]."

Clearly, in a case of tax evasion it might be preferable for the purchaser to enter into a net asset sale agreement or withdraw from the purchase altogether. In this case it is not clear whether the vendor of the business will actually co-operate or be available to co-operate with any investigation, especially as his subsequent residence is intended to be Spain. In such a case HMRC may attempt to look to the purchaser or the current employees to resolve the underpayment of PAYE and NICs to the satisfaction of the Crown, despite the liability clearly resting with the vendor.

If the business had been Clips Hair Salon Ltd, and the purchaser had bought shares, the liability for arrears would have remained with the company, although similar warranties and indemnities might have been sought at the time of sale.

International aspect

[21.13] A secondary contributor against whom, by reason of some international treaty or convention, liability to pay and account for contributions cannot be enforced may pay and account for contributions on a voluntary basis. [*Social Security (Contributions) Regulations 2001, SI 2001/1004, Reg 86(2)*]. In cases where a secondary contributor neither chooses, nor can be made, to pay and account for contributions, a direct collection arrangement for primary contributions only will be made with the primary contributor concerned (see **21.30** below). Since 1 May 2010, when *EC Reg 883/2004* took effect, employers with a place of business in any EEA state are liable to fulfil any obligations that would have been laid upon them if they had been UK-based, so they must register as an employer in the UK if they have any employees subject to UK NICs (see **51.45**). It remains to be seen how the law on this point will change, if at all, once the UK leaves the EU and is no longer subject to the EC regulations: numerous other countries have a special regime for employers who have no presence within their jurisdiction, and there is no reason why the UK should not adopt one of those models.

Case law

[21.14] No *quantum meruit* for work which compliance with the regulations necessitates may be deducted from the amount which a secondary contributor is liable to pay, and the failure of the regulations to provide for such remuneration does not render them *ultra vires*. (*Meredith v Hazell* (1964) 42 TC 435).

Where funds which have been set aside by a secondary contributor to meet his liabilities are stolen, the liabilities cannot on those grounds be treated as discharged. (*A-G v Antoine* [1949] 2 All ER 1000, 31 TC 213.) However, the facts may serve as a valid reasonable excuse in any discussion with HMRC about penalties for late remittance of the deductions.

'Net of tax' pay and grossing up

[21.15] If a secondary contributor agrees to pay earnings without any deductions or taxes, the agreement must be treated as being to pay such earnings as, after deductions, would leave the specified amount. (*Jaworski v Institution of Polish Engineers in Great Britain Ltd* [1951] 1 KB 768, [1950] 2 All ER 1191, CA). It seems that, in practice, the authorities have not strictly applied this rule in the past but have been content to recover from the employer Class 1 contributions calculated on an amount which, after the deduction of tax calculated in accordance with the PAYE code issued in respect of the employee in question, is reduced to the agreed free-of-tax pay.

Example

Zebedee agreed to pay Dougal £600 per month throughout 2016–17, free of all tax and National Insurance. D has been issued with a BR tax code, ie he has no surplus allowances and is liable to tax at 20%. Free-of-tax pay of £600 is equivalent to £750.00 gross of tax at 20% and HM Revenue and Customs will, therefore, require Z to account to it for a deemed tax deduction of £150.00 each month on a FPS. But the HM Revenue and Customs requirement will not end there. The primary Class 1 liability on earnings of £750.00 is £9.36 (ie Nil% × £672.00 + 12% × £78.00) and as Z has agreed to discharge that primary Class

1 liability also, HM Revenue and Customs will require Z to account for tax of £2.34, being tax on the gross equivalent of £9.36, ie £11.70. The position will then be as follows:

	£	£
Gross pay = £750.00 + £11.70 =		761.70
Deemed tax deduction therefrom @ 20%		152.34
		609.36
Deemed primary Class 1 deduction		9.36
Net pay		£600.00
PAYE payable by Z to HM Revenue and Customs		152.34
NIC payable by Z to HM Revenue and Customs:		
Class 1 primary	11.70	
Class 1 secondary 13.8% × (£761.70 – £676.00)	11.83	23.53
		£175.87

It is understood that this position has been accepted as being correct by HM Revenue and Customs as it was, previously, by the then DSS even though, as will have been noted, the authorities are collecting the wrong amount of primary contributions. They are collecting £11.70 primary and £11.83 secondary Class 1 contributions on £761.70, whereas they should be collecting £10.76 primary (ie £672 × Nil% + £89.70 × 12%) and £11.83 secondary (ie £676 × Nil% + £85.70 × 13.8%). For the authorities to insist on absolute mathematical accuracy, however, would be to create an endless spiral. Revision of the contribution liability would necessitate a revision of the true gross pay which, in turn, would necessitate a revision of the contribution liability which, in turn . . . The correct answer can of course be reached using algebra, but this requirement seems unlikely to be imposed because of the impracticality of requiring it from a large population of small businesses. Nonetheless, this matter has been reviewed internally by HM Revenue and Customs – see the meeting of the Joint Forum on Expatriate Tax and NICs on 30 Aug 2007 (webarchive.nationalarchives.gov.uk/20140109143644/http://www.hmrc.gov.uk/consultations/expat-mins300807.htm). It is submitted that the legal position is quite clear — contributions should be due on the higher amount of £761.70 in the above example — but the practicalities of the required calculations is quite a separate matter. Perhaps for that reason a subsequent meeting (webarchive.nationalarchives.gov.uk/20140109143644/http://www.hmrc.gov.uk/consultations/expat-mins051207.htm) confirmed at section 4 of the minutes that calculations on the above basis would be accepted:

> Currently HMRC had not indicated a definitive approach which employers must follow. This meant that employers were free to use the Tolley's version of the grossing formula for NIC reporting. However, where HMRC identified additional unreported liabilities, they would calculate the additional NIC arising in respect of these earnings by reference to the HMRC formula. In these circumstances, HMRC would not seek to recalculate the previously reported NIC by reference to the HMRC formula.

The HM Revenue and Customs formula takes full account of grossing up for both tax and NIC.

It should be pointed out that, in fact, the 'Tolley's version of the grossing formula' is nothing more than that adopted by the former DSS and Contributions Agency.

Other HM Revenue and Customs guidance is to be found in web archive copies of HM Revenue and Customs Leaflet FOT 1, P11 (FOT) and FOT Tax Tables (Tables G).

Recovery from employee – securities

[21.16] The liability for secondary contributions – but only in respect of the exercise of unapproved securities options – may, from 19 May 2000, be recovered from the employee where the two parties have either made an agreement (*SSCBA 1992, Sch 1 para 3A*) or made an election (*SSCBA 1992, Sch 1 para 3B*) to that effect. In the latter situation only, duties placed on employers are extended to affected employees [*Social Security (Contributions) Regulations 2001, SI 2001/1004, Sch 4 para 21*]. *SSCBA 1992, Sch 1, paras 3A* and *3B* are extended by *National Insurance Contributions and Statutory Payments Act 2004, s 3* to include the wider range of securities liable to income tax under *ITEPA 2003, 2003, Part 7* the original legislation having referred to only share options. Where a retrospective liability (see **21.42**) arises through the exercise of powers in the *National Insurance Contributions Act 2006*, any such agreements do not apply to the retrospective liability that arises. [*National Insurance Contributions Act 2006, ss 5-6, Social Security Contributions (Consequential Provisions) Regs 2007, SI 2007/1056, Reg 2*]. New elections are required to include a clause within the election itself to that effect. [*Social Security (Contributions) (Amendment No 3) Regs 2007, SI 2007/1175, Reg 2*].

Large employer electronic payments

[21.17] As noted briefly above, large employers (those with 250 or more employees in the previous tax year) must make payments of PAYE and Class 1 (but not Class 1A and/or Class 1B) contributions by approved electronic means in respect of payments for 2004–05 and later years. From 2010–11 onwards such employers have no longer been specifically notified by HM Revenue and Customs of this obligation, but retain that obligation nonetheless. Electronic funds may be transferred through the employer's bank's internet service, BACS Direct Credit, telephone banking, Billpay or CHAPS. The BACS Direct Credit payment for tax and NICs can be made in one single amount each month from May 2005 onwards. The monthly/quarterly return payment will now be split between tax and NICs according to FPS returns under the relevant payroll reference, whereas before RTI it was allocated provisionally by HM Revenue and Customs and the accurate allocation made at the end of the year once the P35s and P14s had been received. If an accurate record of the split was required by the employer before the year end then separate payments could be made. [*Social Security (Contributions) Regulations 2001, Reg 90H*, inserted by *Social Security (Contributions, Categorisation of Earners and Intermediaries) (Amendment) Regulations 2004, SI 2004/770, Reg 23* and amended by *Social Security (Contributions) (Amendment No 4) Regs 2010, SI 2010/721, Reg 5*]. Such payments are presumed to have been made if they have been recorded on an official computer system and are presumed not to have been made if they are not so recorded unless in either case the contrary is proved and the time of payment is as recorded on an official computer system. The allocation of payments under RTI has proven to be a widespread problem, with Debt Management and Banking staff pursuing employers for phantom liabilities due to the fact that amounts have been posted to the wrong account, or posted in the wrong month, or made-up specified charges in respect of allegedly unfiled FPS and EPS returns have confused both HMRC and employers. Experience suggests that, inexplicably, even the inclusion in the payslip or electronic banking payment instruction of a full HMRC-specified payment reference number will not always guarantee the correct allocation of a payment to the employer's appropriate tax accounts, which shows that the allocation is not automatic but is subject to human intervention. [*Social Security (Contributions) Regulations 2001, Reg 90F*, inserted by *Social Security (Contributions, Categorisation of Earners and Intermediaries) (Amendment) Regulations 2004, SI 2004/770, Reg 23; Income Tax (Pay As You Earn) (Amendment) Regulations 2010, SI 2010/668*].

Modified PAYE Schemes

[21.18] HM Revenue & Customs changed from 6 April 2006 the arrangements for Modified PAYE Schemes where employees going out of the country or coming in are tax equalised. These are now found in the HMRC PAYE Manual at PAYE82002.

There are associated NIC arrangements which extend and replace the previous 'P350 procedure'. The standard agreements for so called EP Appendix 6 agreements (formerly found in the Employment Procedures manual, whence the name came) were updated for the introduction of RTI.

The revised Modified PAYE arrangements for tax equalised employees coming from abroad are the only type of arrangement that can apply from 6 April 2013. Employers who wished to use the new arrangements for 2013–14 had to apply before then. Equivalent time limits apply in subsequent years. Most worldwide 'general earnings' must be included but things such as termination payments and gains from the exercise of unapproved securities options need not be included. Estimated tax payments are then made monthly (or quarterly if there are five or fewer employees in the Modified PAYE Scheme) with FPS submissions of best estimate numbers being dealt with in normal timescales. Residual tax liability must be settled by 31 January following the end of the tax year along with the submission of Forms P11D and any NSR (NIC settlement return – see below) for the related NIC EP Appendix 7a agreement.

This is due where an employee has come from abroad and is included in a (new-style) Modified PAYE Scheme as described above, and application is made for a similar arrangement to apply for Class 1 and Class 1A National Insurance contributions. Details are now found at PAYE82003.

Application needed to be made by 6 April 2013 in respect of the 2013–14 tax year. It can be made before the start of the first affected tax month if this is later. Equivalent time limits apply in subsequent years. In addition to being within a new Modified PAYE Scheme, employees to be covered must be:

- assigned from abroad to work in the UK and have an employer or a host employer in the UK liable for secondary National Insurance contributions; and
- pay National Insurance contributions on earnings above the annual Upper Earnings Limit for the year, or above the Upper Earnings Limit in each earnings period within the year (in the case of employees joining/leaving or whose tour of duty is beginning/ending).

Estimated NIC is paid along the same lines as described for PAYE above. As with PAYE, the employer must carry out an in-year review between December and 5 April to take account of any material changes and in particular to include any year-end bonuses (PAYE and NIC) and NIC on awards from securities options or awards at undervalue of securities. Class 1A is paid at the normal time on a best estimate with a final P11D(b) due by 31 March after the end of the year.

Any residual NIC (Class 1 and/or Class 1A) still owed must be settled by 31 March after the end of the tax year (this is later than the tax – which is effectively settled through Self-Assessment) and is done using a 'NIC Settlement Return'.

A similar arrangement was introduced for employees who are sent abroad to work, and is in lieu of the former P350 procedure. In this case there is no requirement for an EP Appendix 6 agreement.

The arrangement can apply to employees who:

- are seconded abroad for a complete tax year or more, and
- have an ongoing liability to UK Class 1 NIC, and
- are not resident and ordinarily resident and not liable to pay tax in the UK, and
- earn above the Upper Earnings Limit, and
- are paid part of their earnings from abroad.

The new rules operate in a very similar way to those for employees coming to the UK as described earlier and also apply from 6 April 2006 onwards, with modifications to suit RTI reporting.

In this circumstance, however, Class 1A National Insurance contributions will not ordinarily arise, but may do so if the employee returns to the UK sooner than expected such that his general earnings from the employment become chargeable to UK income tax. In that case, the employee in question will no longer fall within the scheme and his Class 1 and Class 1A liabilities must be dealt with in the conventional manner.

In all cases involving Appendix 6, Appendix 7A and Appendix 7B agreements, interest and penalties will not be charged on the residual amounts of tax and NIC due, provided the original estimates used for the monthly or quarterly payments were properly prepared under the terms of the respective arrangements. Interest will be charged automatically on the best estimate instalments if they are paid late and late payment penalties under *FA 2009, Sch 56* may also be charged.

Recovery by a secondary contributor of primary contributions paid

[21.19] Except in certain circumstances involving earnings in the form of securities or securities options (see **21.16**), a secondary contributor may not make, from earnings paid by him, any deduction in respect of his own or any other person's secondary contributions or otherwise recover such contributions from any earner to whom he pays earnings, even if he has contracted with the earner that he will do so. [*SSCBA 1992, Sch 1, para 3A* and *Social Security (Contributions) Regulations 2001, SI 2001/1004, Sch 4 para 6(2), (3)*].

A secondary contributor is, however, entitled to recover from an earner the amount of any primary contribution paid, or to be paid, by him on behalf of the earner, but recovery must be made by deduction from the earner's earnings in accordance with the rules set out below *and not in any other way*. [*SSCBA 1992, Sch 1 para 3(3); Social Security (Contributions) Regulations 2001, SI 2001/1004, Sch 4 para 6(1)(b)*]. The amount of primary contributions which a secondary contributor is entitled to deduct from an earner's earnings is the amount of the primary contributions based on those earnings, except that, where two or more payments of earnings fall to be aggregated (see AGGREGATION OF EARNINGS 5), the secondary contributor may deduct the primary contributions based on those earnings either wholly from one such payment or partly from one and partly from the other or any one or more others. [*Social Security (Contributions) Regulations 2001, SI 2001/1004, Sch 4 para 7(1)(2)*].

Where a secondary contributor has not deducted from an earner's earnings the full amount of primary contributions which he was entitled to deduct, he may (subject to the limitations set out below) recover the under-deduction by deduction from any subsequent payment of earnings to that earner *during the same tax year* (or from 6 April 2004 in cases (a) and (f) the following year also) if, but only if, the under-deduction occurred:

(a) by reason of an error made by the secondary contributor in good faith; or
(b) in respect of payments made under employment protection legislation and treated as earnings by virtue of *SSCBA 1992, s 112* (see **29.13** EARNINGS FROM EMPLOYMENT: GENERAL); or
(c) as a result of the cancellation, variation or surrender of a contracting-out certificate issued in respect of the employment in respect of which the payment of earnings was made except where the cancellation is of a *further* contracting-out certificate under *PSA 1993, s 36(3) (formerly SSPA 1975, s 51A(5))* and recovery is prohibited by *Contracting-Out (Recovery of Class 1 Contributions) Regs 1982, Reg 2* (see CONTRACTED-OUT EMPLOYMENT 23); or
(d) in respect of a sickness payment treated as earnings under *SSCBA 1992, s 4(1)* and paid by a person other than the secondary contributor; or
(e) in respect of a payment that the employer is treated as having made himself that was made by an intermediary (such as an employee benefit trust); or
(f) in respect of a payment made to a person whose place of employment is outside the UK and where there is no tax liability, but there is a Class 1 liability.

[*Social Security (Contributions) Regulations 2001, SI 2001/1004, Sch 4 para 7(4)*, as amended by *Social Security (Contributions) (Amendment No 5) Regulations 2002, SI 2002/2929* and *Social Security (Contributions, Categorisation of Earners and Intermediaries) (Amendment) Regulations 2004, SI 2004/770*].

In respect of underpayments arising under items (*a*) or (*f*) above with effect from 6 April 2004, the underpayment may be recovered in either the current tax year (as previously) or the following year. HM Revenue and Customs has interpreted this as meaning that the extension first applies to under-recoveries that arise on and after 6 April 2004 so that the first 'recoveries more than one year later' did not arise until 6 April 2005. This interpretation is not, however, free from doubt.

Where a deduction falls to be made from earnings which must be aggregated with other earnings (see AGGREGATION OF EARNINGS 5, the employer may make the deduction either wholly from those earnings or from earnings which are so aggregated, or partly from one and partly from the other. However, while such a deduction will, of course, be additional to the deduction otherwise made from those earnings in respect of primary contributions, the amount of that addition cannot exceed the total amount of the latter. [*Social Security (Contributions) Regulations 2001, SI 2001/1004, Sch 4 para 7(3)–(5)* as amended by *Social Security (Contributions, Categorisation of Earners and Intermediaries) (Amendment) Regulations 2004, SI 2004/770 para 31*].

Example

Anne works for Boleyn Ltd and is paid £179.75 per week. When preparing the wages for 25 March 2017, B realises that an incorrect amount of primary contributions has been deducted from Anne's wage for each of the previous three weeks, thus

Pay day	*Gross pay*	*Primary contribution due*	*Primary contribution deducted*
	£	£	£
4 March	179.75	2.97	0.70
11 March	179.75	2.97	0.70
18 March	179.75	2.97	0.70

The correct normal deduction on 25 March is £2.97 and an additional £2.97 may, therefore, be deducted on that date as a partial recovery of the £6.81 under-deduction. Similarly, a further £2.97 may be recovered by way of an additional deduction on 2 April 2017. If the equivalent error had occurred in 2003–04 the balance of £0.87 would not, however, have been *recoverable* as the next payday was not in the same year as that in which the under-deduction occurred. Given the change effective from 6 April 2004, however, Boleyn can now make the further and final arrears deduction of £0.87 subsequently in the first week of 2017–18.

An earlier change took effect from 10 June 2003 but only in respect of share-based payments and payments out of employee benefit trusts (*Social Security (Contributions) (Amendment No 4) Regs 2003, SI 2003/1337*). *The*

National Insurance Contributions and Statutory Payments Act 2004, ss 1, 2 subsequently further extend the rules on the employer's recovering primary contributions from the employee with regard to Class 1 primary contributions of the employees or ex-employees who benefit from security based securities. This change took effect on 1 September 2004. In the debates, the then Paymaster General, Dawn Primarolo, stated:

> We are enabling employers, with the written agreement of the employee, to withhold an amount of shares equal to the value of the primary contributions paid on their behalf for current employees, as well as those who have ceased to work for them.
> Standing Committee Debate D, 13 January 2004, Col 6.

The restriction to mainly securities-based remuneration of wider recovery provisions and the extension for good faith errors could cause difficulty where other non-cash payments were made which attracted Class 1 liability. Such instances included non-cash vouchers, the payment of an employee's personal telephone bill or – if the HM Revenue and Customs assertion of liability up to 5 April 2006 had been correct (see **29.19**) – FURBS contributions. The recovery difficulty is exacerbated by the fact that whereas until April 2003 this difficulty would only have affected employees below the Upper Earnings Limit, it now affects all such payments as there will always be a liability at least at the additional rate (currently 2%). It might be thought that the standard recovery rules will be of some help, albeit that recovery is then restricted to the same amount of arrears as the normal deduction for the earnings period. However, this applies, *inter alia*, only if there has been an error and in such instances there is no 'error' – it is the nature of the earnings that prevents deduction therefrom. Where non-monetary earnings of this kind are paid, the primary Class 1 contribution may nevertheless be deducted from future monetary earnings in the same tax year or, in the case of an employee who leaves, the following tax year [*Social Security (Contributions) Regulations 2001, SI 2001/1004, Sch 4 para 7(6)–(8)*]. Even with this provision there may very well still be a problem where payments of earnings of the kind mentioned occur late in the tax year.

Following the decision in *McCarthy v McCarthy & Stone plc* [2007] All ER D (55) Jul, [2007] EWCA Civ 664, it seems clear that employers who cannot recover significant amounts of primary contributions under the NIC regulations may bring a claim in 'restitution', since in general, anybody who has under compulsion of law made a payment whereby he has discharged the primary liability of another is entitled to be reimbursed by that other. This extends to PAYE and primary contributions liabilities.

Records

[21.20] The record-keeping requirements changed radically with the advent of RTI, which was piloted by a small number of employers during 2012–13 and mandated for all but a few employers (ie, those of care and support workers in domestic situations and those who refuse to use computers on religious grounds – see below) for 2013–14 onwards. The bulk of SME employers switched to RTI at 6 April 2013. New employers registered in 2012–13 were expected to file under RTI immediately, although some were allowed to defer to 6 April 2013 if they needed time to acquire or upgrade software. Certain large employers (with over 5,000 staff), who typically had custom-built payroll software integrated into their accounting systems, which needed more time to convert to the new record-keeping and reporting requirements, were staged into the new regime, and given until October 2013 to start RTI reporting.

Two of those types of employer who were not forced into RTI at all had a statutory excuse: domestic-only 'care and support' employers (known as 'CAS employers') and those with religious objections to using computers (eg, Plymouth Brethren). Before RTI, CAS employers typically used to use a simplified deduction scheme for domestic staff known as 'DOME', completing a P12 working sheet rather than the normal P11 deductions working sheet. That scheme closed in April 2014. From that date, CAS employers were able to choose to e-file in the same way as nearly all other employers, or file quarterly using a new paper return and an RT11 working sheet.

For these two types of employer, and for a small number of others who have significant difficulty using online channels or who cannot use them, and therefore have a reasonable excuse for not using RTI, the alternative paper method is being made available until April 2017. The necessary paper returns are available only from the HMRC Orderline (0300 123 1074) as downloading could obviously not be an option.

Certain other returns remain paper-based because they are used by small numbers and the HMRC system has not yet been upgraded to cope with their peculiarities (eg, the NSR for expatriates referred to at **21.18** above). 'Electoral' and 'Exam' schemes, special arrangements for around 450 employers of examiners and around 50 employers of electoral staff were excused from RTI for the first year, but were all instructed to use the scheme from 6 April 2014.

All employers except those indicated above must now use RTI procedures for reporting and record-keeping.

RTI periods

[21.21] The records needed under RTI appear at first sight to be far more extensive than under the previous paper-based regime, but in reality the only thing that has changed is how much of the information already held by the employer is reported to HMRC regularly. Because RTI requires the use of payroll software (or at the very least HMRC's own Basic PAYE Tools package), all records kept for payroll purposes can easily be copied to HMRC at the press of a key. It is beyond the scope of this work to examine the detailed specification for payroll software used to report contribution records in real time, but in summary the full payment submission (FPS), employer payment summary (EPS) and earlier year update (EYU) will need to include so far as relevant in the circumstances all the information set out at www.gov.uk/what-payroll-information-to-report-to-hmrc.

This involves identifying the employer by various reference numbers, and the employee by NINO, title and full name(s), date of birth, gender, full address and postcode (even if non-UK), payroll ID and any changes, and passport number if a foreign employee has no NINO. The record must flag any irregular payment pattern.

In respect of each employment or pension, start and end dates, details from the starter declaration (formerly P46 information), an indication of whether student loan deductions are required, and if the employee is a secondee from abroad, a series of data items about his residence, nationality and relevant type of PAYE scheme. There is a list of required data items relevant only to pensioner payrolls which are beyond the scope of this work.

The payroll information required for each payment to each employee is extensive, but will generally be no more than is already entered in order to generate a payslip and payment. There follows a condensed list of the data to be recorded and reported as required under *Social Security (Contributions) Regulations 2001, SI 2001/1004, Reg 67(3), Sch 4, paras 21A–21F, Schs 4A & 4B* with effect from 6 April 2012 for those employers who voluntarily adopted RTI early or from 6 April 2013 for those directed to use RTI from the start of mandatory RTI filing.

- Taxable pay to date
- Total tax to date
- Total Student Loan repayment recovered to date
- Pay frequency
- Payment date
- Tax week number
- Tax month number
- Number of earnings periods covered by payment
- Aggregated Earnings Indicator
- Number of normal hours worked
- Tax code
- Week 1 / Month 1 indicator
- BACS hash code – for matching remittances to FPS reports

From April 2014, a new field was added allowing employers to notify simply a reason for their FPS being late (ie, after the payment date). The entries for this field are as follows (in the order of importance attached by HMRC):

Then comes the pay and deductions data for the period:

G	Reasonable excuse (see www.gov.uk/tax-appeals/reasonable-excuses).
H	Correction of earlier FPS.
F	Employee worked for less than a week or was paid below the LEL (ie, free to report within seven days of payment).
D	Benefit in kind subject to Class 1 NICs through payroll but not PAYE (ie, free to report within 14 days of the end of the tax month).
E	Existing small employer, fewer than ten employees, exempt from reporting every time they are paid (ie, eligible to report on or before the last payday in the month). This reason cannot be used for 2016–17 and subsequent years.
A	Overseas employer paying an expatriate, or paying the employee through a third party (ie, eligible to pay by the 19th of the tax month following the date of payment).
B	Pay in shares below market value (HMRC notes under www.gov.uk/what-payroll-information-to-report-to-HMRC that reporting is 'usually by the 19th of the tax month of giving them the shares', which is incorrect; HMRC means the 19th of the next following tax month, which is the only feasible approach).
C	Other non-cash payments, eg, vouchers (reporting due by the 19th of the tax month after making the payment).

- Taxable pay in this period
- Benefits taxed via payroll
- Tax deducted or refunded
- Student Loan deduction recovered this period
- Pay after statutory deductions
- Employee pension contributions
- Deductions from net pay
- Non-tax or NIC payment
- Items subject to Class 1 NIC
- Employee pension contributions not paid under a 'net pay arrangement'
- Statutory Maternity Pay (SMP) year to date
- Statutory Paternity Pay (SPP) year to date
- Statutory Adoption Pay (SAP) year to date
- Shared Parental Pay (ShPP) year to date
- Partner name and NINO data where ShPP paid
- Benefits taxed via payroll year to date (identifying separately items subject to Class 1 NICs only and the benefits taxed in the current period)
- Employee pension contributions paid under 'net pay arrangements' year to date
- Employee pension contributions not paid under a 'net pay arrangement' year to date
- On strike
- Unpaid absence (not yet required)

The following NIC data are required:

- NI category letter
- Gross earnings for NICs in this period
- Gross earnings for NICs year to date
- Earnings at the LEL year to date
- Earnings above LEL up to and including the PT year to date
- Earnings above the PT, up to and including the UAP year to date
- Earnings above the UAP, up to and including the UEL year to date
- Scheme contracted-out number (SCON) - mandatory from April 2014 to April 2016
- Total of employer's contributions payable in this pay period
- Total of employer's contributions payable year to date
- Employee contributions payable this period
- Employee contributions payable year to date

And if the record is for a director:

- Director's NIC calculation method
- Week of director's appointment

For an EPS, the following must be recorded and reported where relevant:

- No payment for period
- No payment dates from and to
- Period of inactivity from and to

- Separate year-to-date figures for recovered amounts of SSP (to 5 April 2014 only, as then abolished); SMP; OSPP; SAP; ASPP (or, for 2015–16 onwards, ShPP); and NIC compensation on SMP; OSPP; SAP; ASPP and ShPP
- CIS deductions suffered year to date
- NICs holiday (removed from the EPS from 6 April 2014 as the scheme ended in 2013)
- Full bank or building society account details for any repayment due
- Employment allowance indicator

New fields were added to the RTI specification in 2016 to reflect the changes to allow flexi-access pensions. Since pensions paid by registered schemes do not constitute earnings for NIC purposes, none of these field changes affect the NIC elements of the records.

At the year-end, just as under the pre-RTI P35 regime, various statements and a declaration are required. However, after the switch to RTI, but not until early 2015, HMRC announced that it would no longer require employers to answer the six annual questions that had formerly been included in the P35. Sadly, the policy change was announced at such a late stage in the year that software houses could not remove the questions from their year-end routines and many employers had to answer the questions simply in order to reach the stage where their payroll software would allow them to make the final submission. Ironically, HMRC's own Basic PAYE Tools package for small employers fell into the same category, requiring answers that were no longer needed and would not be used by HMRC. The questions included in final submissions and still required for 2014–15 onwards are as follows:

- Scheme ceased indicator
- Date scheme ceased
- Final submission for year

The questions no longer required from April 2015 were as follows:

- Free of tax payments – no longer
- Expenses and benefits
- Employees out of UK
- Employees pay to third party
- Forms P11D and P11D(b) are due?
- Service company – only if the employer is an IR35 company and has operated the IR35 rules

Paper filers now complete a new kind of deductions working sheet, a form RT11, and file a quarterly return, the last of which each year is the 'final submission'.

Pre-RTI periods

[21.22] If, during any year before RTI was mandated (6 April 2013) or piloted (some point in 2012–13 when an existing employer joined the RTI pilot or a new employer was registered for the first time), a secondary contributor made to an employed earner any payment of earnings in respect of which Class 1 contributions were payable or there was — even where no contributions were payable — a payment of earnings equal to or exceeding the Lower Earnings Limit, he was obliged to prepare and maintain a deductions working sheet P11 for that earner. [*SSCBA 1992, Sch 1 para 6(1); Social Security (Contributions) Regulations 2001, SI 2001/1004, Sch 4 para 6(1)(a); The Income Tax (Pay As You Earn) Regulations 2003, SI 2003/2682, Reg 66*].

On the deductions working sheet (P11) he had to record (see Employer's Help Book E11 (2013), page 3):

- the tax year to which the deductions working sheet related;
- the name and NATIONAL INSURANCE NUMBER **49** of the employed earner;
- the employed earner's category letter (see **15.8** CLASS **1** CONTRIBUTIONS); and
- in relation to each payment of earnings which he made to the employed earner
  - (a) the date of payment;
  - (b) the amount of earnings up to the Lower Earnings Limit, if that limit was equalled or exceeded;
  - (c) the amount of earnings falling between the Lower Earnings Limit and the Earnings Threshold;
  - (d) the amount of earnings falling between the Earnings Threshold up to and including the Upper Accrual Point (from 6 April 2009 to 5 April 2016);
  - (e) the amount of earnings falling between the Upper Accrual Point (from 6 April 2009 to 5 April 2016) up to and including the Upper Earnings Limit;
  - (f) the amount of all the Class 1 contributions payable on the earnings;
  - (g) the amount of primary contributions included in (e);
  - (h) the amount of any Statutory Maternity Pay, Statutory Paternity Pay and Statutory Adoption Pay;
  - (i) the amount of any Statutory Sick Pay (optional from 6 April 1996 unless recovery was made under the Percentage Threshold Scheme—see **15.12** CLASS **1** CONTRIBUTIONS).

[*Social Security (Contributions) Regulations 2001, SI 2001/1004, Sch 4 para 7(13)(14)* as amended by *Social Security (Contributions) (Amendment) Regulations 2003, SI 2003/193 Reg 16* and *Social Security (Contributions) (Amendment) Regulations 2009, SI 2009/111, Reg 4*].

All years

[21.23] The employer must retain for the three succeeding tax years a record of the date and amount of earnings paid in a tax year. [*Social Security (Contributions) Regulations 2001, SI 2001/1004, Sch 4 para 7(15)*]. The requirement to record the earnings at the Lower Earnings Limit from 6 April 1999 onwards was a result of the government's policy to treat employees not paying contributions (because their earnings fell between the LEL and the earnings threshold) as having paid contributions nonetheless provided that they would have done so under the Class 1 structure prior to the changes in

April 1999 and April 2000. The reason put forward for the recording of other bands of earnings included the same factor but it is submitted that these supposed reasons were, in fact, superfluous.

See **5.14** AGGREGATION OF EARNINGS for recording of aggregated earnings and contributions thereon. Under RTI, one of the employers must record and report all the aggregated earnings and NIC deductions from the aggregated sum for the earnings period, and pay the deductions to HMRC. This employer flags the fact that the record includes aggregated earnings in the relevant payroll record, which will flow through into the FPS. The other employer(s) must then set all 'this period' and 'year-to-date' figures for NIC to zero (NB not blank or empty fields) and also set the aggregated earnings indicator. The same rules apply in principle where an employee is on two separate payrolls with different payroll IDs with a single employer.

A secondary contributor pre-RTI was obliged to render to HMRC an end-of-year return not later than 44 days after the end of a tax year ie 19 May (see Employer's Help Book E10 (2013), page 2). This was form P14 (see Employer's Help Book E10 (2013), pages 7-11) (or such other form as HM Revenue and Customs approved or prescribed) and had to be submitted in respect of each employed earner in respect of whom the secondary contributor was required, at *any* time during the year, to prepare or maintain a deductions working sheet, summarising that employed earner's deductions working sheet and showing:

(a) particulars identifying the employed earner;
(b) the year to which the return related;
(c) under each category letter:
    (i) the amount of earnings up to and including the Lower Earnings Limit, but only if that limit was reached or exceeded;
    (ii) the amount of earnings between the Lower Earnings Limit and the Earnings Threshold;
    (iii) the amount of earnings between the Earnings Threshold up to and including the Upper Accrual Point (from 6 April 2009);
    (iv) the amount of earnings falling between the Upper Accrual Point (from 6 April 2009) up to and including the Upper Earnings Limit;
    (v) the total amount of all Class 1 contributions payable on earnings;
    (vi) the total amount of primary contributions included in (v); and
(d) where contracted-out contributions were payable by virtue of a money purchase scheme (applicable only up to April 2012), a scheme contracted-out number ('SCON');
(e) the total amount of Statutory Maternity Pay, Statutory Paternity Pay, and Statutory Adoption Pay paid during the year;
(f) the total amount of Statutory Sick Pay paid during the year (optional from 6 April 1996 unless recovery is made under the Percentage Threshold Scheme—see **15.12** CLASS 1 CONTRIBUTIONS: EMPLOYED EARNERS and also below);

(g) the amount of any Class 1A contribution payable in respect of the year preceding the year to which the return related if that preceding year was 1999–2000 or earlier;

(h) where Class 1A contributions for 1999–2000 or earlier were payable other than on 19 July due to a cessation of, or succession to, a business, the amount of any such Class 1A contribution payable in respect of the year to which the return related.

[*Social Security (Contributions) Regulations 2001, SI 2001/1004, Sch 4 para 22(1)* as amended by *Social Security (Contributions) (Amendment) Regulations 2003, SI 2003/193 Reg 16, Social Security (Contributions) (Amendment) Regulations 2009, SI 2009/111 Reg 4(4)* and *Social Security (Contributions) (Amendment No 3) Regulations 2012, SI 2012/821*].

The deadline under RTI for making the equivalent final submission with the old P35 questions answered was advanced to 19 April, just two weeks after the end of the last earnings period, until the questions were abandoned as indicated above.

As regards (f) above, it was only necessary to record, from 6 April 1996, Statutory Sick Pay where a recovery was made under the Percentage Threshold Scheme. This is now irrelevant following the abolition of the PTS from 6 April 2014 by *Statutory Sick Pay Percentage Threshold (Revocations, Transitional and Saving Provisions) (Great Britain and Northern Ireland) Order 2014, SI 2014/897*, and the reporting element of the regulations was also revoked, albeit with retrospective effect, from that date by *Social Security (Contributions) (Amendment No 4) Regulations 2014, SI 2014/2397*. Employers still have the *option* to record all Statutory Sick Pay paid, whether recovered or not, if they wish, or some other meaningful figure between the amount actually recovered and the total amount paid, again if they wish. The intention of the changes is to reduce the burden of record keeping and prescribe the *minimum* requirement rather than the precise manner in which all employers *must* keep records (CA Specialist Conference, 20 February 1996).

Pre-RTI, not later than 44 days after the end of a tax year ie 19 May, a secondary contributor was obliged to render to HM Revenue and Customs an annual statement and declaration (P35 or such other form as HM Revenue and Customs approved or prescribed) summarising those end-of-year returns and showing:

- the total amount of all Class 1 contributions payable by him in respect of each employee during the year;
- the total amount of all Class 1 contributions payable by him in respect of all employees during the year;
- in relation to any employment contracted-out by virtue of a salary-related scheme, the employer's number recorded on his contracting-out certificate issued by the Occupational Pensions Board (in practice, this is known as the 'ECON' or employer's contracting-out number);
- the total amount of all Statutory Maternity Pay, all Statutory Paternity Pay and all Statutory Adoption Pay paid by him to each employee during the year;

- the total amount of all Statutory Maternity Pay, Statutory Paternity Pay and Statutory Adoption Pay paid by him to all employees during the year;
- the total amount deducted, in respect of Statutory Maternity Pay, Statutory Paternity Pay and Statutory Adoption Pay paid by him during the year, as compensation for secondary Class 1 contributions paid on such Statutory Maternity Pay, Statutory Paternity Pay and Statutory Adoption Pay (see **15.12** CLASS 1 CONTRIBUTIONS: EMPLOYED EARNERS);
- the total amount of all Statutory Sick Pay paid by him to each employee during the year but, from 6 April 1996, only to the extent that such amounts had been recovered under the Percentage Threshold Scheme (see **15.12** CLASS 1 CONTRIBUTIONS: EMPLOYED EARNERS and also above);
- the total amount of all Statutory Sick Pay paid by him to all employees during the year but, from 6 April 1996, only to the extent that such amounts had been recovered under the Percentage Threshold Scheme (see **15.12** CLASS 1 CONTRIBUTIONS: EMPLOYED EARNERS and also above);

[*Social Security (Contributions) Regulations 2001, SI 2001/1004, Sch 4 para 22(2)* amended by *Social Security (Contributions) (Amendment No 3) Regulations 2012, SI 2012/821*].

All this information is now effectively reported in every FPS submitted (with the obvious exception of contracting out information from 6 April 2016), and in the monthly EPS where there is a difference between the aggregate deductions reported on all FPSs for the period and the remittance at the end of the period, so there is no longer a requirement to submit a year-end P14 or RTI equivalent.

In the case of a corporate body, the pre-RTI declaration had to be signed by a director or the company secretary. HM Revenue and Customs could require the end-of-year returns to be in some form other than that prescribed for tax purposes and, if so required, the return was to be made in accordance with the conditions prescribed. [*Social Security (Contributions) Regulations 2001, SI 2001/1004, Sch 4 para 22(4)*]. This requirement has now disappeared under RTI.

Common errors

Pre-RTI

[21.24] See Employer Bulletin, Issue 22, February 2006 for details of the most common errors arising from the preparation of Form P35 and Forms P14. In the Employer's Help Book E10 (2012) at page 5 'Quality Checks', there were listed the strict procedures for submitting end-of-year forms which indicated that such forms would be returned if not completed on the correct documents or even if there was a smudge of the carbon ink. These strict requirements gave an enormous potential for errors for employers who would then face a penalty if they had not returned the corrected forms by the appropriate date, ie 19 May after the end of the tax year.

Under RTI

RTI is a complex system and the first four years of its operation have identified numerous problem areas as both HMRC and employers have learned how the system works.

The most common problem seems to be the creation of duplicate employments, because the RTI computer system interprets data submitted very strictly in accordance with the programmed rules and cannot make the intelligent decisions that a human tax officer could make. When payroll data submitted in respect of an employee differs in some way from the previous submission, the computer assumes that a new employee record has been created because the record cannot be matched exactly, so it creates a new employment record unnecessarily. This leads to the system estimating tax and NICs due by the employer in respect of non-existent employees, and to HMRC trying to collect it. It also leads to the incorrect issue of multiple tax codes to employees with only one employment, and feeds corrupt data to the Universal Credit system, which picks up RTI information from HMRC four times daily. Correcting the problem created can sometimes be difficult, because commercial software, built to HMRC's specification, has no facility for making submissions that fix HMRC's false assumptions. Employers frequently choose to use HMRC's Basic PAYE Tools to make corrective submissions (ie, to bring HMRC's data into line with the employer's data) so that their own systems are not corrupted by data they know to be incorrect.

It is therefore crucial that the first submission of an FPS for an employee contains the correct personal data, so that it does not require later correction that might be interpreted incorrectly as opening a new employee record. If a single FPS updates more than one of the name, date of birth and gender fields in the record, a duplicate will arise. There have also been problems around payroll ID changes and there is a specific procedure to be followed to notify a change that will be registered. Problems also arise where an employer changes payroll provider in mid-year, because HMRC's system often assumes that both providers should be submitting returns, and sometimes issues a second tax code to the employees for the phantom second job. Duplicate employee records are also frequently created where an employee changes job and is paid, with a correct FPS submission, by the new employer before the old employer has submitted a final FPS in respect of the old job (eg, because overtime, bonuses or commissions cannot be calculated until some point after the cessation of the employment). Although the employee only ever has one job, the RTI system sees the old job as still live when the new job is created, so it treats it automatically as a second job and issues an incorrect tax code to the employee.

Where an employee leaves and is re-employed later in the year, a new payroll ID must be used, and the year-to-date information must be set to zero.

The start date for a new employee, and the end date for a leaver, must generally also only appear on one FPS. A second submission could be interpreted as the start or end of a different employment. If the information originally submitted about an employee's date of birth is found to be incorrect, HMRC prefers the employer to alter the date in the payroll record without including it in a correction FPS, but some payroll software will not allow this. If a payment made after leaving needs correction, the same leaving date must be used on the FPS for the correction or further payment.

Where data for an earlier period need correction, there is now a flag in the specification for signalling this as a late reporting reason. It is the cumulative values on the latest returns, rather than the 'this period' amounts, that HMRC Debt Management teams will use to check against payments made by the employer.

Where a correction is required after 19 April to data for the tax year just ended, no FPS for the old year will be recognised, so the employer must use an Earlier Year Update (EYU). However, there is a fault in the specification in that any EYU (if indeed the software package in question includes this facility – it was an afterthought when the system was designed) that does not change any of the monetary values, the EYU will not be actioned. This might occur, eg, where the final figures for the year were on the final FPS, but the employer forgot to signal that no payment was due on that final FPS, making the year-end declaration on an EPS showing nil due. The employer cannot signal that no payment was due in respect of that final FPS after 19 April by submitting an EYU. Because of the poor design of the system, it is necessary to file an EYU with a fictitious 1p correction to one of the figures, so that it will be processed. HMRC then needs the employer to file a second EYU with an equal and opposite correction to put the numbers back to the correct totals. Such unnecessary workarounds suggest that the RTI system was mandated for use before it had been fully tested. Instead of introducing a system that effectively made employers act as HMRC input clerks without adequate safeguards as to the integrity of the data, it would arguably have made more sense to spend more time on systems design and testing. The problem with duplicate employments has necessitated extra work for employers and HMRC staff, and the design of new software filters and processes so that HMRC traps the problem cases before they corrupt the database. To date, the problems with these cases have centred on multiple tax codes and phantom underpayments, but only time will tell how many NI records have also been corrupted with a consequent impact on benefit entitlements, possibly decades in the future.

It is also not always clear how to populate certain fields in the FPS. One particular problem noted relates to the field showing the 'annual amount of occupational pension'. For non-pensioners, this must be blank rather than £0.00: if the employer mistakenly puts £0.00, because no pension is in payment, the system will assume that there is indeed a pension in payment but that no pension has been paid for the period. It will then create another spurious employee record for the phantom pensioner who is actually just an ordinary employee.

A further problem worthy of mention is the use of the annual payment indicator for one-man companies where the sole director declares a bonus once per year. An annual scheme must have only employees who are paid annually, within the same single tax month, and the employer must pay HMRC only once per year. If the annual indicator is set, HMRC will expect only one FPS and EPS in a nominated month: no nil EPS will be required in the other eleven months. If the employer pays employees more than once, or does indeed submit an EPS when none is required, the system automatically cancels the annual reporting status and expects monthly submissions. Employers should be notified of this by letter, but many have missed the notification and have found HMRC pursuing them for estimated liabilities for months when HMRC has guessed at the amount paid and put a 'specified charge' in the employer's online tax account, which is legally payable by the employer until he submits an FPS with the correct figures for that period.

Employers who are not registered as having an annual scheme but do not make any payment in a particular period must submit a monthly EPS return showing nil due, or the same process of phantom debt creation and pursuit will be triggered. Before October 2014, the EPS was not specific to any pay period and was processed as the latest information at the time of receipt. From 6 October 2014, HMRC changed the specification so that an EPS should indicate the month to which it relates. HMRC also created a window, from the start of the tax month to the normal remittance date for that month, within which each EPS should be submitted. For example, for October 2014, the EPS could be submitted on any date between 6 October and 19 November (inclusive). The EPS for the tax month of November could in similar fashion be submitted between 6 November and 19 December. The Basic PAYE Tools package now allows EPS submissions for any past period in the current year.

A correction for an earlier period must therefore be recorded on a FPS or, for an earlier RTI year, on an EYU, as noted above (bearing in mind that a correction such as substituting the correct NI number will not be recognised unless some monetary value is also changed).

Electronic filing pre-RTI

[21.25] Electronic filing was largely compulsory for the year 2009–10 (ie May 2010 filing date) until RTI was introduced, when one annual electronic return was replaced by numerous returns. There were a few exceptions – see below. There had been a small financial incentive in earlier years to persuade small employers to move to e-filing, but that ceased to be payable from 2008 and it should be noted that the announcement on Budget day 2007 of the deferral of requirements to submit Forms P45 and P46 electronically extended only to those particular proposals and not to the P35/P14 e-filing plans. For employers employing between 50 and 249 employees the first compulsory filing year had been 2005–06 (ie May 2006) and employers with over 249 employees had had to file electronically for 2004–05 (ie May 2005). [*Social Security (Contributions) Regulations 2001, Reg 90N*, inserted by *Social Security (Contributions, Categorisation of Earners and Intermediaries) (Amendment) Regulations 2004, SI 2004/770, Reg 23* and amended by *Social Security (Contributions) (Amendment No 4) Regs 2010, SI 2010/721, Reg 8*]. There was a separate penalty of up to £3,000 per annum per PAYE scheme where an employer was required to 'e-file' but failed to do so either at all or otherwise than electronically and this was in *addition* the pre-existing late filing penalty. [*Social Security (Contributions) Regulations 2001, Reg 90P*, inserted by *Social Security (Contributions, Categorisation of Earners and Intermediaries) (Amendment) Regulations 2004, SI 2004/770, Reg 23* and amended by *Social Security (Contributions) (Amendment No 4) Regs 2010, SI*

2010/721, Reg 9]. See IR Press Release IR 90/03, 3 November 2003 and Working Together, Issue 12 page 4, Issue 22 page 1. The late filing penalty under RTI is to be introduced from October 2014.

The electronic filing requirement did apply to any PAYE scheme which ceased to pay any employees during 2009–10 if the return was filed on paper before 6 April 2010. Beyond this, the following employers could claim exemption from the requirement to file online, just as they can now under RTI:

- religious groups whose beliefs are incompatible with using electronic communications; and
- care and support employers.

The last group covers an individual who employs a person to provide domestic or personal services at the employer's home where:

- the employee's services are provided to the employer or a member of the employer's family; and
- the person receiving the services suffers from a physical or mental disability, or is elderly or infirm.

Domestic PAYE schemes seeking exemption from electronic filing that had received an e-filing incentive ceased to be exempt; the same applied to care and support employers seeking exemption from electronic filing, and they should not have received an e-filing incentive in the previous three years (thus making the stipulation redundant in respect of returns for 2011–12 onwards). [*Social Security (Contributions) Regulations 2001, Reg 90NA*, inserted by *Social Security (Contributions) (Amendment No 4) Regs 2010, SI 2010/721, Reg 8, Social Security (Contributions) (Amendment No 4) Regulations 2009, SI 2009/2028* and *Income Tax (Pay As You Earn) (Amendment No 2) Regulations 2009, SI 2009/2029* and amended by *Social Security (Contributions) (Amendment and Application of Schedule 38 to the Finance Act 2012) Regulations 2013, SI 2013/622*].

All electronic returns had to meet a Quality Standard (QS) and HM Revenue and Customs strongly recommended that QS be built into day to day payroll software. [*Social Security (Contributions) Regulations 2001,Reg 90O*, inserted by *Social Security (Contributions, Categorisation of Earners and Intermediaries) (Amendment) Regulations 2004, SI 2004/770, Reg 23*]. The exacting standards were set out on the website. Commercially marketed software with the *Payroll Standard* accreditation will have met the QS requirements. The *Finance Act 2007* added further powers to the e-filing requirements of large businesses in the form of extending *FA 2003, s 204* to require the making of payments electronically across all HMRC taxes and duties in due course. [*FA 2003, s 204 as amended by FA 2007, s 94*].

Computerised payrolls

[21.26] Where a computerised payroll system is in use, the system must be capable of producing the detailed records described above, and computer records must be retained for three years (or, in the case of CONTRACTED-OUT EMPLOYMENT 23 where separate records are required, see **5.12** AGGREGATION OF EARNINGS, for the period of the employment concerned and for three years after that employment ends) as in the case of manual records. Employers can design and operate their own computer program or use a recognised payroll software house. Relevant guidance notes are available from www.gov.uk/government/collections/paye-online-support-for-software-developers, which leads to detailed technical specifications for PAYE, NIC, statutory payments and the collection of student loans. Guidance is also available from HMRC's Software Developers Support Team, who will help test software for internet and EDI filing and award 'PAYE Recognition' to packages that meet the specification. A listing of HMRC-tested and -recognised software is listed at www.gov.uk/payroll-software/paid-for-software. HMRC's own Basic PAYE Tools may be used.

The records may be retained merely on the computer system – they do not need to be in paper form.

Enforcement

[21.27] The following provisions apply in case of default.

Before an employer became subject to RTI

[21.28] If, within 17 days of the end of any income tax month, a secondary contributor had:

- paid no Class 1 contributions to HMRC for that month, and HMRC was unaware of the amount if any which the secondary contributor was liable to pay; or
- had paid an amount, but HMRC was not satisfied that it was the *full* amount which the secondary contributor was liable to pay,

HMRC could give notice to the secondary contributor requiring him to render a return within 14 days informing HMRC of the amount of Class 1 contributions which he, the secondary contributor, was liable to pay for that month or for that and earlier months. See Employer's Help Book E13 (2013), pages 15-18. [*Social Security (Contributions) Regulations 2001, SI 2001/1004, Sch 4 para 14(1); The Income Tax (Pay As You Earn) Regulations 2003, SI 2003/2682, Reg 147*].

Where the employer had paid no amount of Class 1A for 2000–01 onwards HMRC could take the same steps to issue a notice requiring a return. [*Social Security (Contributions) Regulations 2001, SI 2001/1004, Reg 74*].

If no return was made by the secondary contributor, HMRC had two alternatives.

(a) It could require the secondary contributor to produce for inspection at the 'specified place' all (or such as might be specified) of the wages sheets, deductions working sheets, and other documents and records relating to the calculation of earnings or of Class 1 contributions payable for such tax years or income tax months as might be specified; and, by reference to information obtained from the inspection, could prepare a certificate showing the amount of Class 1 contributions which the secondary contributor appeared to be liable to pay. From 1 April

2009 such other documents as might be required to be produced in accordance with the tax provisions at *FA 2008, Sch 36* might also be used to support any necessary computations.

The 'specified place' was:

(i) such place in Great Britain or Northern Ireland as the employer and HMRC might agree upon; or

(ii) in default of such agreement, the place in Great Britain or Northern Ireland at which the documents and records referred to were normally kept; or

(iii) in default of such agreement, and if there was no such place in Great Britain or Northern Ireland, the employer's principal place of business in Great Britain.

The provision also specifically allowed HMRC to take copies of, or make extracts from, any documents produced to it for inspection and, if it appears to it to be necessary to do so, at a reasonable time and for a reasonable period, to remove any such document, giving the employer a receipt for the same. If such documents were reasonably required for the proper conduct of the business, HMRC was obliged to provide a copy, at no charge, to the person by whom it was produced (*Income Tax (Sub-contractors in the Construction Industry and Employments) (Amendment) Regulations 2003, SI 2003/536, Reg 7; The Income Tax (Pay As You Earn) Regulations 2003, SI 2003/2682, Reg 97(4)*).

(b) HMRC could, upon consideration of the secondary contributor's record of past payments, specify, to the best of its judgment, the amount of Class 1 or Class 1B contributions which it considered the secondary contributor was liable to pay and give notice to him of that amount.

If the amount or any part of the amount specified in the notice remained unpaid seven days after the date specified in the notice, HMRC could certify the amount due, which would be treated as unpaid earnings-related contributions or Class 1B contributions as appropriate. The certificate was sufficient evidence of the debt for HMRC to initiate proceedings against the employer.

From 2008–09 onwards, HM Revenue and Customs needed only specify a single 'combined amount' – which could include any or all of PAYE, CIS deductions, National Insurance contributions and student loan deductions.

[*Social Security (Contributions) Regulations 2001, SI 2001/1004, Sch 4 para 26, para 26A* as inserted by *Social Security (Contributions) (Amendment No 3) Regulations 2009, SI 2009/600, Reg 8(4)*; *Social Security (Contributions) Regulations 2001, SI 2001/1004, Reg 67, 75, Sch 4 para 15*, as amended by *Social Security (Contributions) (Amendment No 3) Regulations 2008, SI 2008/636, Reg 4, Social Security (Contributions) (Amendment No 3) Regulations 2012, SI 2012/821; The Income Tax (Pay As You Earn) Regulations 2003, SI 2003/2682, Reg 97*].

If HMRC took course (b) above and the secondary contributor failed, within the seven days allowed by the notice, either:

- to pay the full amount specified by the notice – whether an amount of contributions or a 'combined amount'; or
- to pay the amount of Class 1 or Class 1B contributions *actually* due for the income tax period or periods concerned; or

- to satisfy HMRC that no amount of Class 1/Class 1B contributions (or, if applicable, 'combined amount') was due for the income tax period or periods concerned,

HMRC could then certify the amount of contributions or 'combined amount' as if it was an amount arrived at by taking course (a) above. [*Social Security (Contributions) Regulations 2001, SI 2001/1004, Reg 75, Sch 4, para 15*, as amended by *Social Security (Contributions) (Amendment No 3) Regulations 2008, SI 2008/636, Reg 4*].

The procedure under course (b) above was not confined to situations where there had been *no* payment of Class 1 or Class 1B contributions by a secondary contributor within the relevant time limit, but could be followed by HMRC where, after seeking the secondary contributor's explanation as to an amount of Class 1/Class 1B contributions which had been paid, they were not satisfied that the amount was the full amount which the secondary contributor was liable to pay for that period. [*Social Security (Contributions) Regulations 2001, SI 2001/1004, Reg 75, Sch 4 para 13, para 15(6)*]. If, however, during that seven days allowed by the notice, the secondary contributor claimed, but did not satisfy HMRC, that the payment of Class 1 or Class 1B contributions which he had made was the full amount of Class 1 or Class 1B contributions for which he was liable, the secondary contributor could require HMRC to follow the procedure laid down as course (a) above as if HMRC had required the production of documents etc. [*Social Security (Contributions) Regulations 2001, SI 2001/1004, Reg 75(2), Sch 4 para 15(7)*, as amended by *Social Security (Contributions) (Amendment No 3) Regulations 2008, SI 2008/636, Reg 4*].

Any excess of Class 1 or Class 1B contributions paid as the result of a secondary contributor's compliance with an HMRC notice under course (b) could be set off against any amount which the secondary contributor was liable to pay to HMRC for any subsequent income tax period, and if any such excess (verified by reference to the end-of-year returns etc) remained unrecovered by the end of the tax year, it would be repaid. [*Social Security (Contributions) Regulations 2001, SI 2001/1004, Sch 4 para 15(9)*].

After the employer became subject to RTI

[21.29] The reporting and enforcement regulations were amended from 6 April 2012 to cover the RTI regime that became available to pilot employers who tested the system for HMRC and any newly registered employers who were put into RTI immediately. [*Social Security (Contributions) (Amendment No 3) Regulations 2012, SI 2012/821*.] The remainder of the employer population (other than exempt employers, such as qualifying care and support employers) was originally mandated by the same regulations in 2012 to join RTI from 6 April 2013, when all employers were to become 'Real Time Information employers (see *Social Security (Contributions) Regulations 2001, SI 2001/1004, Sch 4, para 1(4)*). In the event, larger employers were excused compliance until 6 October 2013, at which point the re-cast regulations began to apply to all but the exempt.

In principle, the information set out above should been retained by the employer and reported to HMRC on or before the date of payment, except where the employer cannot comply or is permitted to report at the end of the month. HMRC should then know how much to expect to receive by the 19th (or 22nd of the following month, the same due date as under the pre-RTI regime for both monthly and quarterly payers. [*Social Security (Contributions) Regulations 2001, SI 2001/1004, Sch 4, para 10(1), 11(1).*]

The employer must remit the total amount of Class 1 NICs due in respect of payments of earnings in the period and reported under *Sch 4, para 21A* (nearly all employers) or *para 21D* (RTI-exempt paper filers), net of recoveries of statutory payments. [*Social Security (Contributions) Regulations 2001, SI 2001/1004, Sch 4, paras 10(2), 11(2).*]

To cope with the switch from annual to monthly reporting, RTI requires employers to report corrections to past deductions by the submission of updated figures on a FPS under *Sch 4, para 21E*. The corrected FPS should include the corrected cumulative totals of deductions. HMRC will expect the difference between the latest reported cumulative totals at the end of the period, and the equivalent numbers at the end of the previous period, to be remitted at the end of the month or quarter by the due date. If the difference is a negative number (ie, an over-payment has been made), the employer may recover it from other deductions or by refund claim, provided any overpaid primary contributions have been refunded to the employee concerned. [*Social Security (Contributions) Regulations 2001, SI 2001/1004, Sch 4, para 11ZA.*]

Where regulations have been changed with retrospective effect to counter avoidance, the employer is required to remit the contributions due by the due date for the month following the month in which the new retrospective regulations come into effect. [*Social Security (Contributions) Regulations 2001, SI 2001/1004, Sch 4, para 11A.*]

If the amount due for any period is not paid by the due date, HMRC may consider the employer's payment history and to the best of its judgment specify the amount considered to be due (for PAYE, NIC, CIS and student loans deductions). The specified charge will in practice be added to the employer's tax account and will be visible through its business tax dashboard (or 'liabilities and payments viewer'). The amount estimated and specified by HMRC is treated, if still unpaid after seven days, as a real liability and is enforceable, unless and until the employer files a return that displaces it. [*Social Security (Contributions) Regulations 2001, SI 2001/1004, Sch 4, para 15(2).*] Experience suggests that the algorithm for estimating the unpaid sums does not always produce a number that a human officer would regard as falling within the scope of the term 'best judgment', such as amounts added to the tax account of a company with a pattern of making no payments to employees and reporting that fact on EPS every month.

Because of the problems created by employers' and HMRC staff's lack of familiarity with the new system, there have been numerous occasions when Debt Management and Banking staff have pursued employers for phantom amounts of incorrectly estimated contributions under this rule. This has even occurred, not just with duplicate employment records, but with employers who no longer have employees or liability for any period, but who have omitted to close their scheme or notify inactivity. This has resulted in a visit by bailiffs to collect specified charges that have been estimated based on information from long past periods. These specified charges can usually be removed most efficiently by the submission of a corrective FPS (or EYU, if for a period in the previous year), but it is arguable that the charges are invalid in any case because HMRC's algorithm cannot be said to have estimated the charge to the best of HMRC's judgment as required by the regulations. Employers whose software does not include a facility for submitting an EYU may use HMRC's Basic PAYE Tools, even if they have more than nine employees, which is a restriction only for regular payroll records (see guidance at www.gov.uk/payroll-errors#3).

Where HMRC needs to take recovery action for Class 1 or Class 1B, the process under RTI is the same (see *Sch 4, Para 16*) as set out above for earlier periods.

Direct collection of primary contributions

[21.30] An employed earner will himself be liable to pay and account for primary Class 1 contributions in respect of his earnings from an employed earner's employment in the following circumstances.

(a) Where under a DEFERMENT OF PAYMENT (**27.2**) arrangement authorised by HM Revenue and Customs, the earner has agreed that he himself will pay part of any such contributions on such earnings. The 1% (from 6 April 2003) or 2% (from 6 April 2011) liability at the additional rate will still be collected through the employer payroll even where deferment is granted.

(b) Where such contributions should have, but have not, been paid by a secondary contributor and the failure to pay is due to an *act or default of the earner* and not to any negligence on the part of the secondary contributor.

(c) Where the secondary contributor is a person against whom, by reason of an international treaty or convention (see **25.11** CROWN SERVANTS AND STATUTORY EMPLOYEES), the collection provisions are *not enforceable* and who is not willing to comply with those provisions on a voluntary basis.

(d) Where the earner's employer who would otherwise fall to be treated as the secondary contributor cannot be so treated by reason of his *failure to fulfil prescribed conditions as to residence and presence* in Great Britain or the EC and no 'host employer' can be specified to be the secondary contributor in accordance with *Categorisation Regs, Reg 1(2)* as amended by *Categorisation Regs 1994, Reg 2* (see **51.14** OVERSEAS MATTERS).

[*Social Security (Contributions) Regulations 2001, SI 2001/1004, Reg 60, Reg 84, Reg 86*].

In a case falling within (b) to (d) above, the employed earner himself will be subject to all the regulations (suitably modified) as to payment, recording and enforcement of primary Class 1 contributions, as described at **21.16**, **21.20** and **21.27** above. This is generally known as a Direct Payment NI scheme, or

'DPNI'. The RTI process must, from 6 April 2014, be followed by any such earner, standing in the shoes of the employer in dealing with the primary liability. Such employers were free to do so voluntarily from April 2013.

DPNI is typically applied to Roman Catholic priests, clergy of the Church of Ireland, registrars who, as office holders, receive their income mainly from the public, and certain employees of foreign governments (eg, British chauffeurs on the staff of an exempt foreign embassy). It may also apply to mariners under offshore manning arrangements where there is no liable UK employer.

In a case falling within (a) above, where an amount has been deferred in excess of the contribution liability which is ultimately excepted, HM Revenue and Customs NIC&EO will inform the earner of the amount of primary Class 1 contributions yet to be paid.

It is arguable that *Social Security (Contributions) Regulations 2001, SI 2001/1004, Sch 4 para 30* (which covers the circumstance described at (*d*) above) is *ultra vires* for the following reasons. Whenever a payment of earnings is made to an earner, the secondary contributor in relation to that payment of earnings is the employer of the employee concerned irrespective of who makes the payment. [*SSCBA 1992, s 7(1)(a)*]. That employer is liable for the secondary contribution on the payment and the employee is liable for the primary contribution but the *manner* in which those liabilities fall to be discharged is governed entirely by *SSCBA 1992, Sch 1 para 3*. The terms of *Sch 1 para 3* are mandatory, not merely permissive, and provide that where earnings are paid to an employed earner and in respect of that payment liability arises for primary and secondary Class 1 contributions, the secondary contributor *shall* (except in prescribed circumstances), as well as being liable for his own secondary contribution, be liable in the first instance to pay also the earner's primary contribution, on behalf of and to the exclusion of the earner. 'Prescribed' means 'prescribed by regulations' [*s 122(1)*] and the *only* regulation which does in fact prescribe circumstances in which the secondary contributor shall *not* be liable to pay an earner's primary contributions is *Social Security (Contributions) Regulations 2001, SI 2001/1004, Reg 68*. This provides that HM Revenue and Customs may, if thought fit, *authorise* a direct collection arrangement, but, as *SI 2001/1004, Reg 84* as amended by *Social Security (Contributions) (Amendment) Regulations 2003, SI 2003/193, Reg 8* makes clear, the provisions of *SSCBA 1992, Sch 1 para 3* are only set aside by such an arrangement if the earner himself has *agreed* to pay the primary contribution.

If there is no such agreement by the employee, liability for both primary and secondary contributions lies with the secondary contributor and it would seem that that incidence of liability cannot be altered or varied by anything in *SI 2001/1004, Sch 4*. That Schedule (which applies the PAYE regulations to Class 1 contributions) is brought into operation only by, and for the purposes of, *SI 2001/1004, Reg 67* (as *Reg 67* itself and the side note to the Schedule make plain) and, insofar as *SI 2001/1004, Sch 4 para 30* purports to impose a direct collection procedure on the employee where the person paying general earnings is beyond the jurisdiction of Parliament, it would seem to go beyond the enabling power. *SI 2001/1004, Sch 4 para 30* is not made under *SSCBA 1992, Sch 1 para 3* which it would need to be in order to alter the incidence of liability for which *Sch 1 para 3* provides. The 2014 changes to the rules around offshore employment intermediaries (see AGENCY WORKERS 4 and OIL RIG WORKERS ETC 50) made no change to this position, as they impose liability only on a UK employer, a UK agency, or an oilfield licensee on the UK continental shelf.

Even if *SI 2001/1004, Sch 4 para 30* is *intra vires*, however, it may not be of any effect in situations where payments to a UK employee are made by someone who is not his contractual employer or deemed secondary contributor and who does not fulfil prescribed conditions as to residence and presence in GB or Northern Ireland or the EC. 'Employer' means, for the purpose of *SI 2001/1004, Sch 4*, (broadly) the employer [*SI 2001/1004, Sch 4 para 1(2)*], and *SI 2001/1004, Sch 4 para 3(1)* provides that where an employee works under the general control and management of a person who is not his 'immediate employer', that person is to be deemed to be the employer for the purpose of *SI 2001/1004, Sch 4*. In other words, although an overseas third party pays the employee and would thus, in the absence of *SI 2001/1004, Sch 4 para 3(1)* be the 'employer' who, under *SI 2001/1004, Sch 4*, would have to pay and account for contributions, the UK employer is, instead, deemed to be 'the employer' for the purpose of *SI 2001/1004, Sch 4* as amended by *Social Security (Contributions) (Amendment No 4) Regulations 2002, SI 2002/2924, Regs 6, 7* generally *and* for the purpose of *SI 2001/1004, Sch 4 para 30* in particular. But *SI 2001/1004, Sch 4 para 30* is of effect only where 'the employer' (ie the UK employer, not the overseas payer of earnings) is non-resident etc, which is not the case in the situation referred to here. The consequences are as follows:

- The employee has no obligation to pay and account for his own primary contributions because only *SI 2001/1004, Sch 4 para 30* imposes such an obligation.
- The UK employer or deemed secondary contributor has an obligation to pay and account for primary and secondary contributions under *SI 2001/1004, Sch 4 para 10* (amended by *Social Security (Contributions) (Amendment No 3) Regulations 2012, SI 2012/821*), but that obligation extends only to the total amount of earnings-related contributions *due* in respect of the general earnings paid by the overseas payer but which the UK employer is (under *SI 2001/1004, Sch 4 para 3(1)*) deemed to have paid.

The use of the term 'contributions due' presupposes that the liability for contributions can be quantified, but, in the circumstances being considered here, where the earnings are paid by someone other than the person who, under the deeming provisions of *SI 2001/1004, Sch 4 para 3(1)*, is liable to pay the contributions, the person liable can know what the liability is only if the person actually paying the earnings informs the deemed employer (the UK employer) of the necessary particulars. *SI 2001/1004, Sch 4 para 3(1)* recognises this by purporting to require the person paying the earnings to provide just such information ('such particulars . . . as may be necessary'), but it seems that, in law, such a requirement is *ultra vires* where the person paying the earnings is outside EEA jurisdiction (before 1 May 2010, outside UK jurisdiction). (*Colquhoun v Heddon* (1890) 2 TC 621).

It is now, of course, possible to request the relevant information from elsewhere in HM Revenue and Customs under *SSAA 1992, s 122(1)* (on the assumption that the employee concerned will make a return under self–assessment of his income from the overseas source). But, even were the information to be obtained by such means, the information would be of no use because HM Revenue and Customs is prohibited from passing it on to anyone, including the UK employer. It would seem, therefore, that, in the situation where an employee receives a payment of earnings from someone who is not his contractual employer and who is outside the jurisdiction of Parliament, the employee cannot be required to pay or account for his primary contributions and the UK employer cannot be required to pay or account for either primary or secondary contributions unless the overseas payer of the earnings informs the UK employer directly, on a voluntary basis, of the payment made to the employee concerned. Arguably, this remains the case even though, since 6 April 1994, *Categorisation Regs 1978, Sch 3 para 9* has deemed a 'host employer' to be the secondary contributor in respect of an employee sent to work for the host employer by a 'foreign employer'. Accounting for any contributions requires knowledge of the amount and date of any payment of earnings, but these facts may not be known to the UK host employer. A similar problem affects the operation of PAYE under *ITEPA 2003, s 689*. See *Agassi v Robinson (Inspector of Taxes)* [2004] EWCA Civ 1518, [2005] 1 WLR 1090, [2005] STC 303 and **51.9** OVERSEAS MATTERS. It is precisely this problem that led HMRC to impose the new deeming rules on UK agencies supplying, and UK employers using the services of, workers employed by an employer outside the UK with no UK place of business (see AGENCY WORKERS **4**).

Penalties

[21.31] Penalties are intended to deter 'non-compliant' behaviour. This generally means not making a return or not making it on time, making an inaccurate return, and / or not paying over what is due. Late payment penalties are dealt with at **21.36** below.

There are currently five penalty regimes that could apply to periods that are still open to challenge by HMRC:

- *TMA 1970, s 98A* for late and inaccurate filing;
- *FA 2007, Sch 24* for inaccuracies in returns;
- *FA 2009, Sch 55* for failure to file a return;
- *FA 2009, Sch 56* for failure to pay on time (see **21.36**); and
- RTI changes introduced into *Social Security (Contributions) Regulations 2001, SI 2001/1004, Sch 4*.

Section 98A

[21.32] In response to poor levels of compliance with PAYE regulations, *FA 1989, ss 164, 165* introduced substantial changes to the previous penalty regime for PAYE returns and payments, which were imported into the *Social Security (Contributions) Regulations 1979, SI 1979/591, Sch 1, para 30(7)* from 22 October 1990. This schedule was where the PAYE collection mechanisms had been adopted and adapted to Class 1 NICs. This link was maintained in the consolidated *Social Security (Contributions) Regulations 2001, SI 2001/1004, Sch 4, para 22(7)*. All references below to '*Sch 4*' are to these regulations.

FA 1989 applied a new *TMA 1970, s 98A* to the late submission of employers' year-end returns (eg P14 and P35) and to the fraudulent or negligent completion of incorrect year-end returns by virtue of what later became the current *Income Tax (Pay As You Earn) Regulations 2003, SI 2003/2682, Reg 73(10)* and *SI 2001/1004, Sch 4, para 22(7)*. There was, however, no penalty or surcharge for simple late payment beyond the interest charged under *SSCBA 1992, Sch 1, para 6(2)* and *SI 2001/1004, Sch 4, para 17*, which meant that there was little deterrent for employers who perceived that they could borrow more cheaply from HMRC than from the bank by not paying over the due sums.

The *TMA 1970, s 98A* regime for inaccurate returns was largely superseded when *Finance Act 2007* introduced a new framework of tax-geared penalties relating to PAYE reporting, extended to Class 1 NICs liabilities. These first applied to return periods commencing on or after 1 April 2008, where the return was filed on or after 1 April 2009, and are detailed below. [*FA 2007, s 97, Sch 24*; *Social Security (Contributions) Regulations 2001, SI 2001/1004, Sch 4, para 22(7)*.]

Until in effect April 2009, the penalty for the submission of an incorrect PAYE return made fraudulently or negligently was an amount up to the difference between the amount paid for the tax year to which the return related and the amount which would have been payable had the return been correct. [*TMA 1970, s 98A(4)*.]

The penalty regime for *late* returns, which did not cease in 2009, was geared to the number of employees covered by the P35. This was achieved by relating the penalty to a 'relevant monthly amount', which was set at £100 per 50 employees or part thereof. A late return for 51 employees would therefore attract a relevant monthly amount of £200, as the number of employees was rounded up to the nearest 50. If a return was 32 days late (ie, it had stretched into the second month, it was classed as two months late, so such an instance for 51 employees would have resulted in a £400 automatic penalty. [*TMA 1970, s 98A(2)(a),(3)*; *Social Security (Contributions) Regulations 2001, SI 2001/1004, Sch 4, para 22(7)*.]

If the failure continued beyond twelve months, in addition to any penalties under *TMA 1970, s 98A(2)(a)*, the employer faced a penalty of up to the amount unpaid as at 19 April after the end of the tax year to which the return related (ie the last date by which month 12 remittances should have been paid). [*TMA 1970, s 98A(2)(b)*.]

The above penalties for late, fraudulent and negligent returns for tax purposes also applied in relation to the 'contributions returns' described at **20.5** and the provisions of *TMA 1970, ss 100–100D, ss 102–104* applied in relation to such penalties. [*SSCBA 1992, Sch 1 para 6(7), 7*; *Social Security (Contributions) Regulations 2001, SI 2001/1004, Sch 4 para 22(7), para 31(8)*.]

For contributions purposes, the penalty provisions were modified as follows.

- Where a person had failed to render a tax return for a particular tax year within the time prescribed and was thus liable for a penalty for a default in the first twelve months, he was not liable for a similar penalty in respect of the associated contributions return (which was effectively constituted by the same piece of paper or electronic return). [*SSCBA 1992, Sch 1 para 7(3)*.]
- Where a person had failed to render a tax return and associated contributions return for a particular tax year and the failure had continued beyond twelve months, a single penalty could apply of up to the sum of any tax and contributions remaining unpaid at the end of 19 April following the end of the tax year to which the return related (22 April if payment is made electronically). An authorised officer of HM Revenue and Customs had to determine that a penalty was to be imposed in respect of both returns. [*SSCBA 1992, Sch 1, para 7(4)(5)*.]
- Where a person had fraudulently or negligently made an incorrect tax return and an associated contributions return for a particular tax year, a single penalty could apply of up to the sum of any tax and contributions remaining unpaid at the end of 19 April following the end of the tax year to which the return related (22 April if payment was made electronically). Again, an authorised officer of HM Revenue and Customs had to determine that a penalty was to be imposed in respect of both returns. [*SSCBA 1992, Sch 1, para 7(4)(5)*.]

Any contributions-related penalties collected by HM Revenue and Customs under the foregoing rules were, net of collection costs, paid to the National Insurance Fund. [*SSCBA 1992, Sch 1 para 7(6), (8)* as amended by *SSC(TF)A 1999, Sch 3 para 36*.]

The starting point for pre-*FA 2007* penalties for errors (only later renamed 'inaccuracies') was 100% of any under-declaration. This figure was then discounted for three factors based on how the process of correcting the error had progressed.

Factor	*Maximum discount*
Disclosure	20%–30%
Co-operation	40%
Size and gravity	40%

These penalties may still be encountered in 'discovery' cases in relation to tax matters, which can look back up to twenty years, but the six-year time limit on enforcement of NIC arrears under *Limitation Act 1980* should mean that they will now rarely be encountered in a review of past contributions.

FA 2007, Sch 24

[21.33] When a review of HMRC's powers was carried out after the merger of the Inland Revenue and Customs & Excise in 2005, one of the first matters addressed was the penalty for making inaccurate returns. The new regime was applied to PAYE and NICs for tax periods starting on or after 1 April 2008 where the return was due on or after 1 April 2009. In effect, it first applied to the P14 and P35 returns filed by 19 May 2009. [*SI 2001/1004, Sch 4,* *para 22(7)* as amended by *SI 2008/636, Regs 2, 7A*]. It was extended, for returns filed on or after 1 April 2010 for periods beginning on or after 1 April 2009, to third parties who deliberately supply false information or deliberately withhold information from the taxpayer with the intention of making any taxpayer return inaccurate. [*FA 2007, Sch 24, para 1A*, automatically read across into *SI 2001/1004, Sch 4, para 22(7)*.]

Instead of starting with a 100% of the 'potential lost revenue' as a penalty in every case, a scale of penalties was introduced that depended on the behaviour of the taxpayer and whether the disclosure of the inaccuracy was prompted or unprompted (ie, whether HMRC identified the inaccuracy or the employer volunteered the information before HMRC asked any questions). The penalties above 100% for inaccuracies involving an offshore matter do not apply to NICs.

Four 'behaviours' were specified, and the level of penalty set in the following ranges.

Behaviour	*Range of penalties* *Unprompted disclosure*	*Prompted disclosure*
Mistake without carelessness	0%	0%
Failure to take due care	0%–30%	15%–30%
Deliberate error	20%–70%	35%–70%
Deliberate error with concealment	30%–100%	50%–100%

The penalties in the table above may be reduced for the quality of the taxpayer's disclosure: up to 30% may be given for 'telling' HMRC about the inaccuracy, 40% for 'helping' HMRC to repair it, and 30% for giving HMRC 'access' to the relevant information. [*FA 2007, Sch 24, para 9*.]

The penalty for a simple timing difference (ie, where an amount is under-declared in one period and over-declared in the next) that automatically reverses itself, or would reverse itself but for earlier HMRC intervention, is different: 5% pa, pro-rated to the period concerned. So if £1,000 is omitted from a return but automatically corrected in the next, the penalty would be £1,000 × 5% × 1/12 = £4.17. [*FA 2007, Sch 24, para 8*.]

These provisions now apply to Class 1 inaccuracies, but are separate from the late filing and late payment penalties introduced by *FA 2009, Schs 55* and *56* and adapted for RTI.

FA 2009, Sch 55

[21.34] *Finance Act 2009* prospectively changed the rules on failure to make a return (*FA 2009, Sch 55*) and introduced, on top of the existing *Sch 55, para 17* late payment interest charge, a new surcharge for failure to pay on time (*FA 2009, Sch 56* – see **21.36** below), but these were not implemented immediately for PAYE and NICs.

The *Schedule 55* penalties were not commenced for PAYE and NIC purposes in 2010 at the same time as the late payment penalties in *Sch 56*. The penalties for late returns continued as described above for all years up to and including 2013–14.

The harmonised failure-to-file penalty was intended, for occasional and annual returns, to be an initial £100 for returns that were at least three months late, with £10 per day added for failures lasting up to 90 further days. For failures lasting over six months, a 5% penalty (or £300 if greater) was to be added. For failures lasting over a year, another 5% (or £300 if greater) was to be added, unless there was an aggravating factor. If there was deliberate withholding of information, the addition was to be 70% (or £300 if greater), and if there was deliberate withholding and concealment, 100% (or £300 if greater). [*FA 2009, Sch 55, paras 2–6*.] The penalty for delay of over 12 months was to be subject to discounts, as outlined for *FA 2007, Sch 24* penalties above, and any special reduction agreed by HMRC because of 'specific circumstances' other than inability to pay or errors by associated taxpayers that cancel each other out. [*FA 2009, Sch 55, paras 14–16*.] If the *Schedule 55* penalty overlapped with any other tax-geared penalty on the same sum, it was to be capped at 100%. [*FA 2009, Sch 55, para 17*.] Any penalty under the schedule was to be assessed and notified by HMRC rather than being automatic, and be subject to an appeal right.

Although *FA 2009, Sch 55, para 1* specifically included PAYE returns in the table of returns covered, the new structure did not really make any more sense than the original *TMA 1970, s 98A* penalties outlined above, and were not commenced for PAYE or applied to NIC.

RTI changes

[21.35] With the introduction of RTI in the planning stages, a new penalty regime for failure to file was needed: *TMA 1970, s 98A* worked, and *Schedule 55* might have been made to work, for annual returns, but made no sense at all in the context of returns required every time any employee was paid, especially when some employers might be making a return on 364 days a year. The potential for a bureaucratic quagmire was foreseen and, while *Schedule 55* was applied to ITSA returns, it was not applied to payroll taxes.

When RTI was inserted into *SI 2001/1004* from April 2012 by *SI 2012/821*, to legitimise the RTI pilot activity, *Reg 21A(8)* continued to apply *FA 2007, Sch 24* to inaccuracies in reports of pay, while *Reg 21F(12)* applied it to statutory payments. *Reg 22* continued to apply *TMA 1970, s 98A* to late filing for non-RTI reporting years, even for pilot employers. In effect, a penalty for late filing would only apply if returns were outstanding at 20 May after the end of the tax year. HMRC recognised that its systems and staff, and the employer population, would not cope well with the new regime initially.

In practice, the 'penalty' for an employer who failed to file an FPS or nil EPS under RTI or, to be more accurate, was assumed by HMRC's system to have failed to file the returns, was the addition of a 'specified charge' to the employer's tax account for the month. As noted above, HMRC is empowered to estimate a liability in the absence of a known figure, and that amount is enforceable as a contributions debt unless a return is filed. The charge is removed from the account by the submission of an FPS or EPS, but the extra work involved for employers in working out why a charge has been levied can itself be a practical disincentive to failing to file on time.

From 6 April 2013, the *Social Security (Contributions) (Amendment and Application of Schedule 38 to the Finance Act 2012) Regulations 2013, SI 2013/622* inserted *Reg 21EA* into *Schedule 4*. This originally provided that, where an employer did not make an FPS return as required by *Reg 21A* (online) or *Reg 21D* (paper), it had to provide the missing information in the next return under either of those regulations (ie, when the next payment was made), or at the latest by 20 May after the end of the tax year. The return had to be made as soon as reasonably practicable after the discovery of the failure to make a return, and the penalty for failure to make a return was still to be based on *TMA 1970, s 98A*, which only applied from 20 May after the tax year-end.

In effect, if an employer did not report the final payment made to employees for 2013–14 before 20 May 2014, there would have been a late filing penalty based on £100 per 50 employees per month of delay beyond that date. If returns remained outstanding for four months, a penalty warning letter or secure message should have arrived in late September 2014, and further such letters should have followed in January 2015 and May 2015 if returns still remained outstanding.

It was originally intended that in-year late filing penalties would be applied from April 2014, but the implementation was initially deferred until 6 October 2014 once it became clear that HMRC's system was not correctly identifying all FPS submissions and would generate too many 'false positives' and inaccurate penalty charges. Doubts were expressed widely about how often incorrect penalties would be charged because the HMRC record was often incorrect.

From 6 October 2014, HMRC planned to apply a late-filing or non-filing penalty where an FPS had not been filed on or before the date an employee was paid or, where the employer had not ticked the appropriate 'late reporting reason' on the FPS in question. HMRC also intended to issue an automatic penalty where it had not received the expected number of FPS from the employer. Experience of RTI operation to date suggested that this was likely to prove problematic due to inaccuracies in HMRC's records and the algorithms it was using to estimate what it expected to be filed. It has not been unknown for an employer who has transferred all the employees onto a new payroll reference to be pursued for amounts estimated to be due under the old reference by HMRC's automated processes, merely because the employer has omitted to tick the 'no payment due' box on the EPS return for the month for the old reference and has not notified HMRC that the payroll reference should be closed. If the computer system could not recognise that all employees had been transferred to a new reference, it was likely to create spurious records and associated spurious late-filing penalties, and unnecessary work for HMRC and the employer concerned, from October 2014. If RTI worked properly, the system would not need the employer to submit an EPS to notify that it had no employees for the period.

In the face of evidence of problems with numerous employers, HMRC announced on 8 September 2014 that it would defer the planned introduction of auto-penalties for employers who had no more than 49 employees on payroll. *Social Security (Contributions) (Amendment No 4) Regulations 2014, SI 2014/2397* disapplied *Reg 21EA* for 2014–15 and subsequent years, substituting new *Reg 21G* into *Schedule 4* instead. This applied new *Income Tax (Pay As You Earn) Regulations 2003, SI 2003/2682, Regs 67I–61K*, but with the proviso that only one penalty should apply in respect of the failure covering both PAYE and NICs. As originally introduced, *Reg 21G* did not permit the charging of an extended failure penalty, ie, the RTI penalty for filing more than three months late under *FA 2009, Sch 55, para 6D*. However, this was remedied by *Social Security (Contributions) (Amendment) (No 2) Regulations 2016, SI 2016/352, Reg 7* with effect from 6 April 2016 which inserted a new *Reg 21G(2A)* to remove the bar on such a penalty where an employer is liable to a penalty for failing to file a return under the *PAYE Regulations 2003, Reg 67B or 67D*.

The revised PAYE regulations applied the new scale of penalties from 6 October 2014 to so called 'large existing RTI employers', ie, those with 50 or more employees on payroll, but deferred the penalties for smaller employers and those who registered from that date as new employers until 6 March 2015. Since only a few thousands of employers have 50 or more employees on payroll, this effectively deferred the RTI late filing regime until the end of 2014–15 for nearly all employers, saving HMRC resources that might have been spent on correcting unwarranted penalty notices.

HMRC took another step backwards from the planned penalty regime with an announcement on 17 February 2015 in a press release that reminded employers that the filing deadlines were unchanged, and that employers with 50 or fewer employees would fall within the late filing regime from 6 March 2015. The release did not state explicitly that HMRC was struggling to ensure that the volume of automatic penalties would not be alarmingly high, or that the volume of appeals expected against such penalties would be unmanageable, but there was a widespread assumption outside HMRC that this was the case. HMRC has not disclosed publicly the number of warning notices issued to employers under its generic notification service (GNS) since 2014, but it is widely understood to have been in the order of hundreds of thousands, which would have translated into unmanageable volumes of work if they had been allowed to convert into automatic penalties that mainly resulted in appeals.

The release focused on how HMRC was reviewing the penalty regime generally, looking for 'potential improvements' to the use of late filing and late payment penalties so as to differentiate between those who 'deliberately and persistently fail to meet statutory deadlines or to pay what they should on time, and those who make occasional and genuine errors for which other responses might be more appropriate'.

It would continue to risk assess late payment penalties rather than issue them electronically. This was undoubtedly due to an undisclosed number of continuing errors in employers' tax accounts, some of which remained unreconciled after several years, so that HMRC had no confidence in the integrity of the figures on which any such penalties might be based, although this was also not mentioned in the release. One example of a problem reported by an ICAEW Tax Faculty member on its website in June 2015 stemmed from the issue of an unjustified penalty. The employer's next PAYE remittance had been applied by HMRC to clearing the penalty before the balance was set against the current month's PAYE debt, and before the employer was even aware of the spurious penalty. The resulting apparent underpayment for that month led to the issue of another spurious penalty, with similar misallocation of remittances, and the cycle repeated itself. Other members reported having received no reply to letters querying penalties, and others having received penalties for non-submission of past returns by dormant companies which had recommenced their activities but had had nothing to report in the periods to which the penalties related.

The 17 February release ended with this announcement: 'Any employer that has received an in-year late filing penalty for the period 6 October 2014 to 5 January 2015 and was 3 days late or less, should appeal online by completing the "Other" box and add "Return filed within 3 days".' This easement, which HMRC later stated would run until 5 April 2016 and would be applied retrospectively to penalties due since 6 October 2014, was clearly intended to remove from the disputes and appeals process the majority of minor infringements of the 'on or before payment date' filing rule. The use of the three-day easement was extended to 6 April 2017, without an official HMRC announcement, by a change to the information on penalties on the gov.uk website on 23 May 2016 (see www.gov.uk/guidance/what-happens-if-you-dont-report-payroll-information-on-time). It was confirmed in the Employer Bulletin, issue 60 in June 2016, which also stated that HMRC would 'continue to review [the] approach to PAYE late filing penalties beyond 6 April 2017' (page 2). However, the scope of the easement has been narrowed: it will not be afforded to employers who persistently file late, as it is intended to relieve the burdens on employers who make occasional mistakes rather than being an extension of the statutory filing date.

An employer who had received a late filing penalty was advised to appeal using the online Penalty and Appeals Service (PAS) and, if the post-October 2014 FPS in question had been filed no more than three days late, to tick 'other' as the reason and give some narrative to the effect that the return had been fewer than three days late. In a later, separate announcement in the Employer Bulletin of 18 June 2015 the advice was changed to use new 'reason code A' on the appeal submission, a category added to the PAS specifically for this purpose. Where attempts to file within three days had been thwarted by software difficulties, the appeal was to be made on the grounds of 'reasonable excuse'. The penalty rules apply to each PAYE scheme separately. One penalty will be charged for each tax month that the employer fails to file on time once within the new regime, so weekly and monthly filers will receive the same, single penalty if several returns are late in a month. Employers with nine or fewer employees at 6 April 2014 were permitted to file a single monthly FPS return, for 2014–15 and 2015–16 only, on or before the last payday in each month, rather than on or before the date of each payment, but guidance instructed them to include late reporting code 'E' in the FPS so that no penalties were registered. In contrast, new employers registered after 6 April 2014 have been required to file an FPS on or before payment. *[SI 2001/1004,*

Sch 4, para 21A, as amended by *Social Security (Contributions) (Amendment) Regulations 2014, SI 2014/608, Reg 7*.] All should be equally affected by the new rules on late filing according to the new timetable.

Once the penalty regime has been fully introduced, the first month of failure will be penalty-free, although the employer should receive an electronic warning message from HMRC under its so called 'GNS' (Generic Notification Service). The GNS messages for late filing commenced in May 2014 but were suspended temporarily when it became clear that too many phantom errors were being created by the system (hundreds of thousands each month). New employers are allowed 30 days from making their first payment of earnings to file a FPS (this gives HMRC enough time to register the employer and the employer to set up the online access required). The deferral of the late filing regime for small employers to 6 March 2015, rather than 6 April 2015, was intended to permit the charging of a penalty for both small and new employers, and annual schemes, as new *Reg 67K* of the *Income Tax (Pay As You Earn) Regulations 2003, SI 2003/2682* (inserted by *Income Tax (Pay As You Earn) (Amendment No 3) Regulations 2014, SI 2014/2396*) disapplied the rule allowing one penalty-free error. This was only logical: if an employer with an annual scheme, making one FPS/EPS return per year, could disregard its first late filing of the tax year, that employer could never receive a late filing penalty, which would effectively neuter the penalty rules.

For 'large existing RTI employers' from October 2014, and for the remainder from 6 March 2015, no penalty should be charged provided an EPS showing no FPS due is filed by the 19th of the month after the month for which HMRC is expecting a return.

The size of the late-filing penalty depends on the number of employees within the PAYE scheme, according to HMRC's latest information:

No of employees	*Amount of the monthly filing penalty per PAYE scheme*
1 to 9	£100
10 to 49	£200
50 to 249	£300
250 or more	£400

Penalty notices (showing a unique ID for each) should be issued quarterly in July, October, January and April, for the quarter ended on 5 July, 5 October etc, indicating the months in which the defaults arose.

If a return remains outstanding for more than three months and the missing information has not already been included in a later return, an additional 5% penalty may be charged. HMRC has indicated that it will use this penalty for the most serious and persistent failures.

All penalties are open to a claim that there was a reasonable excuse for the failure (eg, death or serious illness of the responsible person or a close relative or partner, or system failure due to fire, flood or IT problems) and an appeal to the First-tier Tribunal. From October 2014, an online appeal system became available (the PAS to which reference was made above), which may either handle the submission of the appeal or permit HMRC to accept and settle the matter automatically. Appeals will also be accepted in writing to Customer Operations Employer Office, BP4102, Chillingham House, Benton Park View, Newcastle-upon-Tyne NE98 1ZZ., quoting the unique ID.

In another sign of a system not working wholly as expected, HMRC announced in the 17 February 2015 release that one of the problems seemed to be around 15,000 PAYE schemes that had not made a PAYE report since April 2013. HMRC announced that it would deal with this by unilaterally closing such schemes, as they appeared to have ceased operation without having informed HMRC. As noted above, any large existing RTI employers who had received an in-year late-filing penalty for the first penalty quarter (6 October 2014 to 5 January 2015) in respect of filing that had been late by no more than three days were advised to appeal online against the penalty, using the 'Penalty & Appeals Service' (PAS), ticking the box for an 'other' reason and annotating it with 'Return filed within three days'.

HMRC subsequently confirmed that the new three-day rule would apply until 5 April 2016 (and later extended it by another year as outlined above). GNS warnings were issued for January and February 2015 (ie, before the decision to change the policy) but were suppressed for March 2015 for large existing RTI employers and, if the three-day rule applied, no GNS warnings or penalties were to be issued from 6 March 2015 onwards, saving employers the need to appeal. Any penalties issued in May 2015 for 6 January to 5 April 2015 to large employers could be appealed in the same way as the October to December batch. If the tolerance was applicable, HMRC's intention was that no warnings should be issued or penalties issued for small employers for month 12 only.

The automatic penalty regime was effectively put on ice for the foreseeable future during 2015, pending the improvement of the systems software that generated the warnings and notices, which was plainly not working as intended. Penalties now seem to be issued only in cases that are specifically identified by Employer Compliance staff. The post-2007 penalty regime was also made subject to a formal review, and a consultation document was issued on 2 February 2015, before the three-day relaxation was introduced. The document expressed concerns about penalties in general, and automated penalties in particular. It recognised that automation plays a key role in a simple, cost-effective digital tax system, but that the large-scale issue of penalties could be counter-productive if it undermined people's natural motivation to comply with what the tax system asks them to do. Tellingly, it also noted that automated penalties tend to be small and therefore more costly and resource-intensive for HMRC to pursue because a substantial amount of 'customer' contact is required. The consultation document was expected to lead to specific proposals which themselves would require further consultation, but apart from the issue of a summary of responses on 17 September 2015, there have to date been no further developments. The responses document stated that the earliest possible opportunity for legislation would be Finance Bill 2017, but also suggested obliquely that the penalties project had been subsumed into the planning for Making Tax Digital, which will require a major restructuring of HMRC's administration and policing powers and a rewriting of *TMA 1970*. The Budget Report 2016 made no mention of the RTI penalties consultations.

Late payment penalty

[21.36] Before 6 April 2010, when *FA 2009, Sch 56* introduced a surcharge regime, there was no general penalty for an employer who chose to pay over the PAYE and NIC remittance late.

However, monthly remittance was required to be made electronically by any 'large' employer (ie, one with 250 or more employees, as set out in the *Income Tax (Pay As You Earn) Regulations 2003, SI 2003/2682, reg 198A*) in respect of the years 2004–05 to 2009–10 inclusive except for any contributions arising from deemed retrospective earnings under anti-avoidance provisions. If that monthly payment was not made to HM Revenue and Customs on time (by the 22nd of the month), or in full, then the employer was in default unless it could show a reasonable excuse. [*Social Security (Contributions) Regulations 2001, Regs 90H-90I*, inserted by *Social Security (Contributions, Categorisation of Earners and Intermediaries) (Amendment) Regulations 2004, SI 2004/770, Reg 23*.]

HMRC was obliged to issue a default notice. The only ground for appeal against such a notice was that there was no default and contact had to be made with the Receivables Employer Unit to deal with the appeal. [*Social Security (Contributions) Regulations 2001, Reg 90J*, inserted by *Social Security (Contributions, Categorisation of Earners and Intermediaries) (Amendment) Regulations 2004, SI 2004/770, Reg 23*].

A surcharge was imposed for defaults on an increasing scale, potentially reaching 10% of the annual amount due after twelve defaults in a review period. The surcharge stopped accumulating only when there had been no defaults for a whole tax year. [*Social Security (Contributions) Regulations 2001, Reg 90K, 90L*, inserted by *Social Security (Contributions, Categorisation of Earners and Intermediaries) (Amendment) Regulations 2004, SI 2004/770, Reg 23*].

All the above provisions were repealed by *Social Security (Contributions) (Amendment No 4) Regs 2010, SI 2010/721, Reg 6* with effect from 6 April 2010.

FA 2009, Sch 56

[21.37] As a result of the HMRC powers review mentioned above in connection with inaccuracy penalties under *FA 2007, Sch 24*, from 6 April 2010 employers and contractors of any size and whatever the method of payment who were late with their PAYE / NIC remittances became subject to a late payment penalty as detailed in the table below. The *Social Security (Contributions) Regulations 2001, SI 2001/1004, Reg 67A* (inserted by *The Social Security (Contributions) (Amendment No 4) Regulations 2010, SI*

2010/721) applied the *FA 2009, Sch 56* penalties to Class 1 remittances with effect from 6 April 2010. At the same time, new *SI 2001/1004, Reg 67B* applied the *Sch 56* regime to the annual contributions made under Classes 1A and 1B.

New late-payment penalty charges were introduced to cover a number of circumstances as follows:

- monthly or quarterly PAYE;
- Construction Industry Scheme (CIS) payments;
- collection of student loans;
- Class 1 NICs;
- annual payments of Class 1A NICs;
- annual PSA payments; and
- PAYE determinations or charges raised by HMRC.

The surcharge for late remittance of monthly PAYE and Class 1 deductions replaced the 'large employer' regime outlined above, which was repealed as indicated. It was also extended to quarterly payers.

The design of the *FA 2009* regime also differed in that it ran for one tax year at a time and the employer started each new tax year with a clean slate. In summary, the total number of default in the year determined the level of the surcharge for the whole year, and the surcharge was levied only after the end of the year on all amounts that had been paid late during the year. Numerous appeals against these new penalties reached the First-tier Tribunal in 2012 and 2013, mainly from employers who had simply not been aware of the new rules and had carried on as before (ie, borrowing from HMRC rather than the bank), but also from employers for whom the penalty was wholly disproportionate.

The potential disproportionality stemmed from the surcharge's design, and the fact that HMRC did not send warning letters until the penalty had already accumulated to the maximum level and had already fallen due. An employer who paid a day late on eleven occasions would have cost the Exchequer virtually nothing in lost interest, but the surcharge would have been 4% of all of those eleven payments.

No of late payments in the year	*Penalty*
1	No penalty if < 6 months late
2 to 4	1%
5 to 7	2%
8 to 10	3%
11 or 12	4%

Example

Mervyn Ltd had cash flow problems for several years from 2008 onwards, and his main customer, George, always paid late. In 2010–11, until Mervyn Ltd was alerted to the new surcharge by its accountants in late November, it regularly paid its PAYE and NIC deductions over on the last day of the month, because that was when funds were available. Its regular monthly remittance was £20,000.

HMRC raised a penalty assessment for the year based on the deductions for April to October inclusive all having been remitted after the due date. There were seven defaults, of which six counted for the surcharge. In the relevant six months, Mervyn had paid £120,000 late, so the penalty at 2% was £2,400.

If any single payment (including the first) was made over six months late, a 5% surcharge was applied. Any payment that remained outstanding for more than 12 months attracted a further 5% penalty.

[*Social Security (Contributions) Regulations 2001, SI 2001/1004, Reg 67A; Social Security (Contributions) (Amendment No 4) Regulations 2010, SI 2010/721, Reg 3; FA 2009, Sch 56*].

For annual payments, such as Class 1A and Class 1B contributions, a surcharge of 5% was applied if they remained unpaid 30 days after the due date. Six months after the due date, the surcharge on unpaid liabilities increased by a further 5%, and after twelve months a further 5% was added.

It is worth noting that other annual payments, such as the IR35 correction to the deemed payment, due by 31 January after the end of the tax year, and the NIC Settlement Return payment under an EP Appendix 7a or 7b scheme did not carry late-payment penalty risk, provided the required payments were made at the due time. This has not changed.

From April 2014

[21.38] This approach to Class 1A and Class 1B defaults has not changed, but the disproportionality of some of the penalties that were taken to appeal before the tribunals led to a reform of the surcharge structure for PAYE and Class 1 NICs from 6 April 2014.

While the same bandings apply, the penalty rate now applies (ie, if risk assessment by HMRC results in the issue of a penalty) on the escalating scale to each default in order, so the first three chargeable defaults (ie, disregarding the first late payment) will result in a charge of 1% of the amounts paid late, the next three in a charge of 2% of those amounts paid late, etc. The rate will not be revised upwards retrospectively based on the annual cumulative number of defaults if there are later defaults in the same year. It was expected that charges would be levied quarterly and added automatically to the employer's account, but the introduction of automatic late payment penalties was deferred for the same reasons that underlay the relaxation of the reporting penalties outlined above.

Example

Carney Ltd runs into cash flow problems in mid-2016 because it has tried to support too many projects. It too relies on George as its main customer, and George still insists on paying late. From June to November 2016, Carney pays its PAYE and NIC deductions over on the last day of the month, because that is when funds are available. Its regular monthly remittance is £30,000.

HMRC raises a penalty assessment for Quarter 1 based on the deductions for May being paid remitted after 22 June, and those for June being paid over after 22 July. The first default is disregarded, but the payment for June is late and incurs a 1% penalty of £300.

The next three payments are also remitted after the due date. The first two of those in Quarter 2 also attract a 1% penalty, the third is penalised at 2% as it is the fourth reckonable default. The penalty for Quarter 2 is therefore £1,200 (£300 + £300 + £600).

The liabilities for October and November fall in Quarter 3 and when paid late are the fifth and sixth reckonable defaults, also attracting a 2% penalty, in total £1,200.

Up to three further defaults for 2016–17 will attract a 3% penalty, whether occurring in Quarter 3 or Quarter 4, and if Carney Ltd remits every remaining month's deductions late, it will reach a penalty rate of 4% in respect of its final payment.

Again, there is a reasonable excuse defence to any surcharge. Penalties will not be charged during an agreed time-to-pay arrangement (unless the taxpayer defaults or 'misuses' the arrangement). Appeals against late payment penalties will be in writing, addressed to HMRC Southend Debt Management, 6th Floor, Alexander House, 21 Victoria Ave, Southend on Sea, SS99 1AA quoting the unique ID to identify the penalty subject to appeal. Appeals have been possible via an online facility from April 2015.

For 2014–15, HMRC originally said that it would issue late-payment penalties 'on a risk-assessed basis' (ie, if it caught an employer due to ordinary checks, rather than on an automated basis), and the penalty would only be used against the most serious and persistent failures. On 17 February 2015, it was announced that late payment penalties would continue to be issued on that basis beyond April 2015 and would be reviewed by 5 April 2016, following the consultation on HMRC's use of penalties more generally from April 2015.

From April 2015

[21.39] From 6 April 2015, HMRC originally proposed to issue late payment penalties automatically using information from the RTI system (which, was expected – over-optimistically as it turned out – by then to be sufficiently reliable as a basis). The first penalty notices to employers, which should have identified the alleged defaults so that they could be checked and challenged, were scheduled to be issued in July 2015, then quarterly thereafter. That is not now likely to happen before the penalties review project and the Making Tax Digital project have reached firm conclusions. HMRC announced on 17 February 2015 that late payment penalties would continue to be reviewed on a risk-assessed basis, without putting a revised date on the introduction of automated penalties. As noted above, the review is to continue 'beyond 5 April 2017'. It seems clear that problems with Debt Management & Banking's link to the RTI system, leading to widely reported demands for non-existent PAYE debts, had forced a recognition of the potential problems caused to employers and HMRC by issuing automatic penalties based on inadequate data.

Once penalties are charged, amounts charged will be added to the employer's tax account. In advance of the introduction of the new late payment penalty, the main risk for employers is expected to be the practice of HMRC allocating employer payments to incorrect months or references without the agreement of the employer, resulting in phantom underpayments and spurious penalty warnings, which is presumably the problem that underlays the deferral of the late payment penalty regime.

HMRC attempted to restrict the possibilities for defaults under 'time to pay' arrangements by imposing a requirement that the taxpayer sign a direct debit mandate before HMRC would agree to the arrangements. This new requirement, announced in an agent update on 14 July 2015, applied to new TTP arrangements only and from 3 August 2015 onwards.

Interest on late payments

[21.40] Until 6 April 2014, interest on Class 1 liabilities was only charged on payments not made by the last date for remitting Class 1, ie, 19 or 22 May each year, and on Class 1A by fourteen days after the P11D(b) deadline, ie, 19 or 22 July. The *FA 2009* late-payment penalties discussed above were intended to deter employers from paying late, while the interest provisions were intended to compensate the NI Fund and ensure fairness between taxpayers who were compliant and those who paid late, but they were an annual event because, until the advent of universal RTI, reporting of contributions due was annual and, without carrying out a detailed inspection, HMRC could not really tell whether an employer was paying over the true amounts due each period.

Interest on late-paid Class 1 and Class 1A contributions and on refunds of such contributions was introduced from 19 April 1993 by the *Social Security (Contributions) Regulations 2001, SI 2001/1004, Sch 4 paras 17–21* and also applied immediately upon the introduction of Class 1B contributions (see **42.11** LATE-PAID CONTRIBUTIONS, **55.12** REPAYMENT AND REALLOCATION and NI News, Issue 7, page 12). The last old-style interest charge in respect of Class 1 will have applied to any payment for 2013–14 not made before 19 or 22 April 2014, calculated from that date to the date of payment.

The Class 1A rule has not changed, but from 6 April 2014, when all but exempt employers were brought into the RTI system, HMRC has, in theory, had the data in real time to enable it to identify when an employer has not remitted the correct amount of Class 1 contributions. It has therefore now started to charge monthly interest in-year, adding it automatically to the employer's tax account for the first time in May 2014. Interest now runs from each periodical due date of payment (monthly or quarterly) to the date of actual payment. Interest will also apply to any penalties not paid within 30 days of issue. Overpayments will benefit from repayment interest (albeit at just 0.5%).

Where an employer identifies a mistake in an earlier period and a new FPS is submitted to correct the error, it is unclear whether and how, if at all, HMRC could identify a late payment and charge interest. The system compares (a) the cumulative total amount due to HMRC for a month according to the last FPS for the month sent before the 19th of the following month with (b) the equivalent for the previous month. Any corrections after the 19th are reflected in the later period when they are submitted. It is this amount that the system will regard as due by the payment deadline, and interest will run if the amount has not been paid.

If an error in an RTI return for one tax year is spotted by the employer in the next tax year, the employer must submit an EYU. If there was an underpayment for 2013–14, it will carry interest only from 19 or 22 April 2014 until payment was or is made, in accordance with the pre-RTI rules.

Tax relief for interest

[21.41] There was originally no provision to deny tax relief for interest on late-paid contributions but new legislation for accounting periods ended after 9 April 2003 corrected what the authorities saw as an anomaly. [*FA 2003, s 147(2)* inserting *SSCBA 1992, Sch 1, para 6(4b)*]. However, the vires for this change were questionable as legislation that states what is and is not taxable or allowable ought to appear in the Taxes Acts and not *SSCBA 1992*.

Retrospective liability

[21.42] *National Insurance Contributions Act 2006* provided the power, by inserting *SSCBA 1992, s 4B*, to make regulations in respect of retrospective National Insurance liability where a Finance Act has similarly imposed retrospective tax liability in respect of what the government sees as abusive schemes involving employment income taxable under *ITEPA 2003*. In practice, the powers were aimed at employment-related security schemes.

Various Regulations came into force on 6 April 2007 with effect from 2 December 2004 but the powers have not been used since. HMRC's Anti-Avoidance Group, now renamed the Counter Avoidance Directorate, has focused instead on using the DOTAS regime to identify avoidance schemes and block them by changes in legislation and, from late 2014, making employers pay disputed amounts on account by means of an accelerated payment notice under *NICA 2015, s 4*, or pursuing litigation to prove that schemes undertaken many years ago (some undertaken before the *NICA 2006* changes were made) were always ineffective.

The *2001 Regulations* were amended to mirror changes made by the *Income Tax (Pay As You Earn)) (Amendment) Regulations 2007, SI 2007/1077*. The latter introduced the concept of a special return P35(RL) to cover retrospective tax and National Insurance liability. Those returns could not be made electronically and payment by large employers could not be made electronically in the case of closed tax years. In case it might have applied, there was also provision to exclude the tax and National Insurance on retrospective payments being counted when determining whether the employer was small enough to qualify for quarterly remittances to HMRC (see **21.5**). Payment of the retrospective National Insurance was due 14 days after the end of the tax month following the tax month in which the relevant contributions regulations came into force. The first such payments under *SI 2007/1057* (see below) were therefore due by 19 June 2007. The first P35(RL) returns were due by 19 May 2008.

[*SSCBA 1992, Sch 1, para 3* and various provisions of the *Social Security (Contributions) Regulations 2001, SI 2001/1004* as amended by the *Social Security Contributions (Consequential Provisions) Regulations 2007, SI 2007/1056*].

Retrospective National Insurance contribution liability applied to employment income arising by virtue of *F(No 2)A 2005, Sch 2* from 2 December 2004 and before 20 July 2005 and to similar income arising by virtue of *FA 2006, s 92* from 2 December 2004 and before 19 July 2006.

[*Contributions Regs 2001, Reg 22(9)(10) inserted by the Social Security (Contributions) (Amendment No 2) Regs 2007, SI 2007/1057*].

Further regulations ensured that the retrospective earnings were taken into account for Statutory Payments, maternity allowance and other benefit purposes and enabled occupational pension contributions to be deducted from the retrospective earnings.

[*Social Security, Occupational Pension Schemes and Statutory Payments (Consequential Provisions) Regulations 2007, SI 2007/1154*].

The good faith error rules (see **21.9** above) were replicated by *SI 2007/1154* so employers could well have faced situations where the employee liability on retrospective earnings could not be recovered from the employee. This is theoretically still a possibility, although thought to be unlikely.

ESC B46 (see **21.31** above) did apply to the submission of Forms P35(RL) and associated P14s, to allow for postal delays, but the concession was withdrawn in March 2011 because all but a few employers had been compelled to e-file their year-end returns. Nothing has changed in this respect with the advent of RTI filing: in theory there is still a paper return under these retrospective liability rules, and there is no RTI obligation. The question of whether postal delays affecting retrospective paper returns might still arise seems unlikely ever to be asked.

The rules remain in the legislation, so they might one day be applied.

Employers do not have to recompute student loan deductions where retrospective liability applies as *Education (Student Loans) (Repayments) Regulations 2000, SI 2000/944, Reg 39* already states that no recalculation is required where NIC-able earnings increase for any reason.

As regards calculation of the retrospective National Insurance due the rates, limits and thresholds applicable to the tax year in which the payment or payments were originally made (ie, when it was thought that the payments were not 'earnings' for National Insurance purposes) should be used. In addition, it is necessary to look at the particular earnings period in which the payments were made.

Payment for closed years must be made by cheque, sent with a letter stating the name and address of the employer, the Accounts Office reference, the years to which the payment relates and for each year a breakdown between the PAYE and NIC. The address for payment is HM Revenue and Customs, Section 10 (RPL), Accounts Office, Bradford BD98 1YY, but this is hidden on the HMRC website and only now available via an external search engine. The hidden guidance still refers to amending the P11 deductions working sheet and submitting forms P14, which all no longer exist, suggesting that the system is unlikely to be revived.

Returns (P35(RL) for closed years and continuation sheets (P35(RL) Continuation Sheet) – where there were more than eight P14s to summarise and enclose – appeared to be available only on the Internet, but they are now hidden and available only via an external search engine. Completed forms had to be signed, dated and sent along with the accompanying forms P14 to Customer Operations Employer Office, BP4009. Chillingham House, Benton Park View, Newcastle Upon Tyne, NE98 1ZZ.

Class 1A collection

[21.43] The statutory collection arrangements are as follows in respect of Class 1A liability.

- The contribution is to be paid to HMRC not later than 19 July in the tax year immediately following the end of the tax year in respect of which that contribution is payable. Payment need not be made until 22 July if it is made electronically and cleared funds are received by this date. This is notwithstanding the submission of the P11D(b) together with P11Ds by 6 July. Where an employer of 250 or more persons is compelled to make payment of PAYE and Class 1 NIC by electronic means that compulsion does not extend to Class 1A, but in practice such employers may naturally be inclined to do so in any event. See Employer's Help Book E10 (2013), page 2. [*Social Security (Contributions) Regulations 2001, SI 2001/1004, Reg 71*, as amended by *Social Security (Contributions, Categorisation of Earners and Intermediaries) (Amendment) Regulations 2004, SI 2004/770, Reg 16*];
- Where there is a change in the employer who is liable to pay earnings to or for the benefit of all the persons who are employed in a business in respect of their employment in the business (ie, a succession) and one or more employees have ceased to be employed in the business before the change of employer occurs, the employer before the change must, not later than 14 days after the end of the final income tax month in which he pays earnings pay the Class 1A contribution due to HMRC and, if the final income tax month is that beginning on 6 April, 6 May or 6 June, pay also any Class 1A contribution in respect of the tax year immediately preceding the tax year in which the final income tax month occurs. The required time is extended to 17 days after the end of the relevant tax month if the payment is made electronically. [*Social Security (Contributions) Regulations 2001, SI 2001/1004, Reg 72*, as amended by *Social Security (Contributions, Categorisation of Earners and Intermediaries) (Amendment) Regulations 2004, SI 2004/770, Reg 17*].

Example

On 28 April 2016, Egg sells his business to Chicken. Yolk, one of Egg's employees to whom Egg had made a car available for private use throughout his employment, left Egg's employment on 21 April 2016. Egg made his final payment of earnings to the remaining employees on 30 May. By 19 June 2016 (or 22 June 2016 if payment is made electronically), Egg must pay to HMRC the

Class 1A contribution for 2016–17 and the Class 1A contribution due in respect of Yolk for 2015–16.

- Where an employer ceases to carry on business and upon that cessation no other person becomes liable to pay general earnings to or for the benefit of any employee in respect of his employment in that business (ie there is no succession), the employer must, not later than 14 days after the end of the final income tax month in which he pays general earnings, pay the Class 1A contribution to HMRC and, if the final income tax month is that beginning on 6 April, 6 May or 6 June, pay also any Class 1A contribution in respect of the tax year immediately preceding the tax year in which the final income tax month occurs. The required time is extended to 17 days after the end of the relevant tax month if the payment is made electronically. [*Social Security (Contributions) Regulations 2001, SI 2001/1004, Reg 73*].
- An employer who pays to HMRC an amount in respect of Class 1A contributions which he was not liable to pay may deduct the overpayment from any payment of secondary Class 1 contributions which he is liable to pay subsequently for any income tax period in the same tax year. [*Social Security (Contributions) Regulations 2001, SI 2001/1004, Reg 83*]. It is unclear how this set-off might be effected under the RTI regime as the software specification includes no data field for setting off Class 1A overpayments against a Class 1 liability. This is clearly an oversight by HMRC, as the regulations permit the set-off.
- If an employer has paid no Class 1A contribution by the due date, or has paid an amount which HMRC is not satisfied is the full amount due, and HMRC is unaware of the full extent (if any) of the employer's liability, HMRC may give notice to the employer requiring him to make a return within 14 days showing the extent of his liability. [*Social Security (Contributions) Regulations 2001, SI 2001/1004, Reg 74(1)*].
- If, after 14 days following the due date mentioned the employer has paid no amount of Class 1A contributions to HMRC in respect of the year in question and there is reason to believe that the employer has a liability to pay, HMRC may specify the amount due to the best of his judgment and give the employer seven days' notice to pay after which HMRC may, in the absence of payment, certify the amount for recovery purposes. [*Social Security (Contributions) Regulations 2001, SI 2001/1004, Reg 75*].
- With effect from 6 April 1999, in calculating Class 1A contributions, employers are to round fractional amounts to the nearest whole penny, with £0.05 or less being disregarded. [*Social Security (Contributions) Regulations 2001, SI 2001/1004, Reg 39*].
- With effect from 6 April 2012, when the provisions for requiring security for payment of PAYE and NICs were introduced as *SI 2001/1004, Sch 4, paras 29M to 29X*, they encompassed both Class 1 and Class 1A, with appropriate modifications to the terminology and cross-references. [*Social Security (Contributions) Regulations 2001, SI 2001/1004, Reg 83A*, added by *Social Security (Contributions) (Amendment No 3) Regulations 2012, SI 2012/821*.]

Disclosure of liability is on the forms P11D and P11D(b) that are completed for tax purposes, the P11D being colour-coded so that it can be used as a basis for identifying those items which attract Class 1A liability. The P11D(b) is then used to calculate the Class 1A liability, with any adjustments to the liability (eg, for expatriates who have P11D benefits but no Class 1A liability) dealt with on the reverse of the form.

In the first week of April each year a special payslip (P30B Class 1A) used to be issued to all employers identified by HM Revenue and Customs systems as being potentially liable to Class 1A NIC. Payment was then made to the employer's usual accounts office at either Shipley or Cumbernauld. HMRC now encourages employers only to use electronic payment (direct debit, Billpay using a debit or credit card, BACS, CHAPS or Faster Payment) but for those who wish to pay by putting a cheque in the post, a payslip can be printed off. This payslip cannot be used at a bank or post office.

With the increasing reliance on employers doing HMRC's clerical work, it is crucial that any electronic payment includes the correct reference number so that the correct account is credited and the payment is identified as a Class 1A remittance. Employers should therefore quote their 13 character Accounts Office reference, followed by the year, and 'month 13'. To make a payment in July 2016, for the year 2015–16 (the previous year), the employer would add '1613' to its Accounts Office reference, to give, eg, 123PA000123451613. By using '13' as the final two digits, the employer flags that the payment is intended for Class 1A NIC. '13' should not be used as the final two digits for paying any other employer/contractor liabilities, even if there are, because of the incidence of payroll payment dates, thirteen pay periods in a year.

If the tax year and month number are not included, the payment will not be posted to the correct year and the employer and HMRC will then waste time finding the payment and correcting the records.

Class 1A repayment

[21.44] The provision for repayment of wrongly paid Class 1A contributions is very restrictive and applies only where a person has paid a Class 1A contribution in respect of a particular employee, and, in calculating the cash equivalent of the benefit for the purposes of ascertaining the amount of the Class 1A contribution:

- he used information that later proved to be inaccurate or incomplete; or
- the employee who received the general earnings in respect of which the Class 1A contribution was payable is later found to have not resided in the United Kingdom for the purposes of income tax at the time of receipt of those general earnings.

[*Social Security (Contributions) Regulations 2001, SI 2001/1004, Reg 55*, as amended by *Social Security (Contributions, Categorisation of Earners and Intermediaries) (Amendment) Regulations 2004, SI 2004/770, Reg 13*].

In such circumstances, the person who has paid the Class 1A contribution may apply for repayment of the overpaid element of the contribution and, if HMRC is satisfied in the light of the information provided that the overpayment has occurred, repayment will be made unless it does not exceed 50 pence. [*Social Security (Contributions) Regulations 2001, SI 2001/1004, Reg 55(1)*]. The application must be in writing and must be made within six years of the end of the tax year in which the contribution was paid, or, where there has been a good cause for delay, within such longer period as may be allowed. [*Social Security (Contributions) Regulations 2001, SI 2001/1004, Reg 55(3)*].

It seems that strictly there is no provision under which a repayment of Class 1A contributions may be made in other circumstances, eg where a person who has complete and accurate information simply miscalculates the contribution. However, where the overpaid amount cannot have been due in the first place, because it was never a valid Class 1A contribution, it cannot fall within the restriction on repayment that applies to such contributions, so HMRC has no right to refuse a refund.

Class 1A penalties and interest

[21.45] The penalty provisions for late, fraudulent or negligent returns made to HMRC are extended to returns required in connection with Class 1A contributions. [*SSCBA 1992, Sch 1 para 7(11)(a)*].

From 19 April 1993 interest has been chargeable on Class 1A contributions which are paid late. [*Social Security (Contributions) Regulations 2001, SI 2001/1004, Reg 76*]. (See **42.11** LATE-PAID CONTRIBUTIONS.)

HM Revenue and Customs is given the power to require a return to be rendered and, in the event of non-payment, to specify an amount which it estimates is properly due. Such an estimated amount can then be recovered as though it were actual Class 1A National Insurance contributions. [*Social Security (Contributions) Regulations 2001, SI 2001/1004, Regs 74, 75, 81(6)*].

Interest is charged on an overdue payment at the rate applicable under *SSCBA 1992, Sch 1 para 6(3)*[*Social Security (Contributions) Regulations 2001, SI 2001/1004, Reg 76(5)*] from the reckonable date ie 19 July until payment. If payment is made electronically, the relevant date is 22 July. See CWG5 (2016), page 20.

Provision has been made to permit the payment of interest on a refund of overpaid Class 1A contributions from the relevant date, ie, the fourteenth day after the end of the year or, if later, the date on which the contribution was paid until the date of repayment (*Social Security (Contributions) Regulations 2001, SI 2001/1004, Reg 77*); the repayment of overpaid interest (*Social Security (Contributions) Regulations 2001, SI 2001/1004, Reg 78*); the set off of repayable Class 1A contributions against earnings related contributions (*Social Security (Contributions) Regulations 2001, SI 2001/1004, Reg 83*) and the remission of interest in the case of official error (*Social Security (Contributions) Regulations 2001, SI 2001/1004, Reg 79*).

Where a return:

(a) is made incorrectly due to careless or deliberate conduct, a penalty may be charged following the rules under *FA 2007, Sch 24* since 6 April 2010. The calculation of the penalty bands determined by behaviour, and the discounts determined by the quality of disclosure, are outlined above. [*Social Security (Contributions) Regulations 2001, SI 2001/1004, Reg 81(1)*, as amended by *Social Security (Contributions) (Amendment No 4) Regulations 2010, SI 2010/721, Regs 2, 4*.];

(b) is not made, then the following penalties may be imposed:
   (i) where the number of earners is 50 or less then the penalty is £100 for each of the first twelve months, or, where the number is greater than 50 then £100 for each such 50 thereafter and an additional £100 where the number is not a multiple of 50; and
   (ii) if the failure extends beyond twelve months, a further penalty not exceeding the amount of contributions unpaid. [*Social Security (Contributions) Regulations 2001, SI 2001/1004, Reg 81(2), (3), (4)*].

The total penalty under (b)(ii) above may not exceed the Class 1A contributions due [*Social Security (Contributions) Regulations 2001, SI 2001/1004, Reg 81(5)*].

These penalties may be recovered as if they were Class 1A contributions due. [*Social Security (Contributions) Regulations 2001, SI 2001/1004, Reg 81(6)*].

Finance Act 2009, Sch 56 sets the framework for a new harmonised regime of penalties across all HM Revenue and Customs areas of business. In respect of the 2010–11 liability onwards there are penalties of 5% on unpaid Class 1A contributions after 30 days and a further 5% (each time) as at six and twelve months after the due date. [*Social Security (Contributions) Regulations 2001, SI 2001/1004, Reg 67B*, as inserted by *Social Security (Contributions) (Amendment) Regulations 2010, SI 2010/721, Reg 3*]. Note that as the July 2010 payment related to an earlier year these new 5% penalties did not apply to that payment.

As the specified date for the payment of Class 1A contributions (unless paid electronically or on a business transfer) is, under *Reg 71*, 19th July (or 22 July for e-payment) after the end of the year in which the benefits in kind were provided, it appears that no penalty can arise in such a case if payment is made on or before 18th or 21st August.

The due date for payment of a penalty under these provisions is 30 days from the date of issue (including that day) of the penalty notice. [*Social Security (Contributions) Regulations 2001, SI 2001/1004, Reg 81(7)*].

HM Revenue and Customs may mitigate or remit any penalty at its discretion and this extends to allowing further time. [*Social Security (Contributions) Regulations 2001, SI 2001/1004, Reg 81(8)*].

Provisions similar to *TMA 1970, s 100, s 104 and s 105* apply to the determination of any penalty under *Social Security (Contributions) Regulations 2001, SI 2001/1004, Reg 81*.

Where a Modified PAYE Scheme applies (the employer having made an application under EP Appendix 7A in respect of foreign employees sent to work in the UK, the deadline for sending the form P11D(b) has been extended from the usual 6 July to the following 31 January. This is the same as the extended return date for the return of forms P11D for such workers and reflects the extra time that it can take to assemble the full details for P11Ds in this sort of case. The usual penalty arrangements will apply from the normal due date of 6 July if the return is not made by the following 31 January and a P11D(b) by 31 March along with any balancing payment. Further, this extension does not extend to the due date for payment, so interest will run as normal from 19th July (or 22nd July if payment is made electronically). Employers are therefore recommended to make a payment based on a best estimate in order to mitigate interest charges.

Class 1B penalties and interest

[21.46] Class 1B contributions are payable by 19 October following the end of the year to which they relate (ie at the same time as the tax due under the PSA) so that the payment will be due by 19 October 2016 for 2015–16 at a rate of 13.8%. [*Social Security (Contributions) Regulations 2001, SI 2001/1004, Sch 4 Reg 13(1)*, as amended by *Social Security (Contributions, Categorisation of Earners and Intermediaries) (Amendment) Regulations 2004, SI 2004/770, Reg 32*]. Alternatively, if payment is made electronically, the due date is 22 October. This is an employer-only charge in the same way as Class 1A and, like Class 1A, not generating any benefit entitlement in return for the payment. Interest is charged on late payments. [*Sch 4, para 17*, as amended by *Social Security (Contributions) (Amendment No 3) Regulations 2008, SI 2008/636, Reg 6*]. Interest that is not properly due is repayable. Interest will be added to repayments of overpaid Class 1B at the same rate as applicable to Class 1/Class 1A and will run from the 20 October date (23 October, if paid electronically) or, if later, the actual date of payment. Class 1B contributions overpaid may also be treated as contributions paid on account of secondary Class 1, and also Class 1A and Class 2 may be offset against Class 1B. [*Social Security (Contributions) Regulations 2001, SI 2001/1004, Sch 4, paras 18, 19*].

The penalties referred to in **21.31** as regards Class 1 contributions apply also to Class 1B. Further, as mentioned in that paragraph, *Finance Act 2009, Sch 56* sets the framework for a new harmonised regime of late-payment penalties across all HM Revenue and Customs areas of business. In respect of the 2010–11 liability onwards there are penalties of 5% on unpaid Class 1B contributions after 30 days and a further 5% (each time) as at six and twelve months after the due date. [*Social Security (Contributions) Regulations 2001, SI 2001/1004, Reg 67B*, as inserted by *Social Security (Contributions) (Amendment) Regulations 2010, SI 2010/721, Reg 3*]. Note that as the October 2010 payment related to an earlier year these new 5% penalties did not apply to that payment.

Class 2 contributions

[21.47] The treatment of Class 2 contributions was changed from 6 April 2015 by *NICA 2015, ss 2, 3, and Sch 1*. Irrespective of contributions of other classes which may be payable, under the pre-2015 rules a single Class 2 contribution was to be paid in respect of every contribution week during any part of which an earner was ordinarily employed in one or more self-employed earner's employments unless the earner had been excepted from liability for that week (eg by advance application for small earnings exception, by reason of receipt of incapacity benefit, incapability for work, receipt of maternity allowance or detention in legal custody) or his liability had been deferred or she had a valid reduced rate election (see **18.4** and **18.5** CLASS 2 CONTRIBUTIONS, **27.8** DEFERMENT OF PAYMENT and **54** REDUCED LIABILITY ELECTIONS). From April 2015, no compulsory liability arises if profits do not exceed the small profits threshold, although contributions may be paid voluntarily to maintain benefit entitlements. Voluntary contributions may still be paid. The charge is now an annual charge collected under the ITSA system. It is still based on weeks of ordinary self-employment in the tax year being reported, but the advance small earnings exception has been replaced by a retrospective small profits threshold, so the earner should know whether he or she has a compulsory liability before paying the contribution with the balancing income tax payment for the year. The rules on incapacity, maternity and legal detention have not changed, so the payment due by 31 January might not in fact represent 52 weeks of flat-rate contributions. Collection mechanisms, appeals and penalties are now dealt with under the same rules as Class 4.

From 6 April 2011 such contributions were payable for the first bi-annual contribution period no later than 31 January following the end of that period and by the 31 July following the end of the second bi-annual period.

From 6 April 2015, collection moved onto the same basis as Class 4 contributions, ie, the income tax self-assessment system, except that the mid-year payment on account rule was not applied to the Class 2 liability, so payments of compulsory contributions are due annually by 31 January following the relevant tax year-end. Voluntary contributions are subject to a similar time limit, although it is possible to pay in advance under a payment plan.

A Class 2 contribution liability could be discharged until 6 April 2015 by:

(a) making a payment to HM Revenue and Customs of the amount of contributions specified in a written notice no later than 31 January or 31 July following the bi-annual contribution period; or
(b) making payment by *direct debit* of a bank or Girobank account under an arrangement authorised by HM Revenue and Customs.

[*Social Security (Contributions) Regulations 2001, SI 2001/1004, Reg 89(1)(2)(3), Reg 90*].

The payment date specified in (a) above could be delayed until 28 days after the date specified as the date of notification in the payment notice in the following circumstances:

(a) when a notice had been issued, but the recipient had informed HM Revenue and Customs immediately that the notice he received had since been lost, destroyed or defaced and the notice was re-issued; or
(b) when a notice had been issued, but the recipient informed HM Revenue and Customs immediately that he disputed the amount of contributions shown in the notice and the notice was re-issued; or

(c) when the contributor had notified HM Revenue and Customs within 28 days after the end of the quarter that he had not received a notice and one was subsequently issued; or
(d) when the contributor had, after more than fourteen days from the end of the quarter had elapsed, not received a written notice in respect of any week or weeks in that contribution quarter and he notified HM Revenue and Customs accordingly. [*Social Security (Contributions) Regulations 2001, SI 2001/1004, Reg 89(4)(5)(6)* as amended by *Social Security Contributions (Amendment No 3) Regulations 2011, SI 2011/797*].

A bi-annual contribution period was one of the two periods of not less than 26 weeks beginning on the first and twenty-seventh Sundays of any tax year. [*Social Security (Contributions) Regulations 2001, SI 2001/1004, Reg 89(7)* as amended by *Social Security Contributions (Amendment No 3) Regulations 2011, SI 2011/797*].

From 6 April 2014 arrears of Class 2 contributions that are overdue may be collected, in appropriate cases, by an adjustment to an employed contributor's notice of coding ('coded out'). [*Social Security (Contributions) Regulations 2001, SI 2001/1004, Reg 63A* inserted by the *Social Security (Contributions) (Amendment and Application of Schedule 38 to the Finance Act 2012) Regulations 2013, SI 2013/622, Reg 38*.] For the purposes of assessing resulting state benefit entitlement, any such collection is deemed to be a payment on 5 April of the tax year in which the payment is collected. [*Social Security (Crediting and Treatment of Contributions, and National Insurance Numbers) (Amendment) Regulations 2013, SI 2013/3165*.]

Because of the use of PAYE codes for the first time in 2014–15, the Class 2 contributions may appear as a reconciling item in the P800 process from May 2015 onwards.

All arrears from 'suitable cases' from 2008–09 to 2011–12 were considered for collection by coding out. [DMBM618640.] Coding will not be suggested if the debtor is insolvent, deceased, abroad, or of state pension age within the tax year or the next following year, or has no current address known to HMRC (classed as 'taxpayer gone unknown (RLS)'). It will also not be used if the debt is so old that it is about to become time-barred.

HMRC's Debt Management and Banking operates a unit in Newcastle known as Debt Technical Office, which supports a Debt Management and Telephone Centre (DMTC) and a Debt Collection Agency Referral Unit (DCARU) and handles all letters and queries at its office in Room BP3201, Warkworth House, Benton Park View, Newcastle, NE98 1YX. It decides whether the contributor in arrears will be required to pay by referral to a Debt Collection Agency or by PAYE coding adjustment. The first step is a payment request, followed by a 'first opportunity letter'. [DMBM618621.] Where recovery through PAYE coding is not possible, county court proceedings may be taken.

Any legal proceedings or administrative act authorised or done under *Sch 4* commenced by one officer of HMRC or HMRC may be continued by another officer. [*Social Security (Contributions) Regulations 2001, SI 2001/1004, Sch 4, para 5*.] HMRC Enforcement Office in Worthing (Durrington Bridge House,

Barrington Road, Worthing BN12 4SE) may commence bankruptcy process against the debtor with a statutory demand. This provides a period of 21 days during which the debt must be paid or HM Revenue and Customs can file a bankruptcy petition. There are 18 days in which to make an application to the court to set aside the demand.

See **12.9** ARREARS OF CONTRIBUTIONS.

From April 2015, under the reform introduced by *National Insurance Contributions Act 2015, s 2* and *Sch 1*, Class 2 contributions for 2015–16 onwards will now be collected through the self-assessment system in the same way and subject to the same processes as Class 4 contributions. As noted, they became an annual charge rather than a weekly charge (ie, payable annually in respect of the relevant number of weeks of self-employment), although payment on account by monthly direct debit remains a possibility under what is described as a budget payment plan, albeit only for those who do not have to file a self-assessment tax return or who pay voluntarily because their profits are below the small profits threshold each year.

A question as to whether payment of contributions has been properly made within the terms of (d) above will be a matter for a decision of an officer of HM Revenue and Customs and not one which the magistrates may decide (see APPEALS AND REVIEWS **9**). (*Department of Health and Social Security v Walker Dean Walker Ltd* [1970] 2 QB 74, [1970] 1 All ER 757).

Under the pre-April 2015 regime, if a contributor wished to discharge his liability by direct debit, he completed and sent to HM Revenue and Customs NIC&EO a form CA5601 (which was available from the HMRC website). The form was transmitted to the bankers concerned who then made contribution payments from the contributor's account monthly in arrears, normally on the second Friday in each calendar month. Each debit covered four or five contributions depending on the number of Sundays in the preceding tax month, but did not include contributions for weeks of proven incapacity. If the authority necessary for a bank to make such payments was withdrawn or ceased, any payment made thereafter by the bank would not be accepted as a payment of contributions. [*Social Security (Contributions) Regulations 2001, SI 2001/1004, Reg 90(6)*].

For the purpose of summary proceedings under *SSAA 1992, s 114 as substituted by Social Security Act 1998, s 61* (see **12.6** ARREARS OF CONTRIBUTIONS) or of proceedings in the High Court or a county court (see **12.1** ARREARS OF CONTRIBUTIONS), the amount of each Class 2 contribution which a contributor is to be treated as having failed to pay is the amount he would have paid under the rules for late-paid Class 2 contributions (see **18.6** CLASS 2 CONTRIBUTIONS) if he had paid the outstanding contributions on the date the proceedings commenced. [*SSCBA 1992, s 12(5)*]. Summary proceedings commence on the date an information is laid (see **35.14** ENFORCEMENT) and proceedings in the High Court or a county court commence when an action commences. [*SSCBA 1992, s 12(7)*].

Such a contribution is, unless an alternative arrangement has been approved (see below), due for payment by the date specified in the notice. [*Social Security (Contributions) Regulations 2001, SI 2001/1004, Reg 89* as amended by *Social Security Contributions (Amendment No 3) Regulations 2011, SI 2011/797*].

For Class 2 purposes, a contribution week which falls partly in one tax year and partly in another is treated as falling wholly in the tax year in which it begins. [*Social Security (Contributions) Regulations 2001, SI 2001/1004, Reg 155*].

Under the pre-April 2015 regime no penalty could be imposed for late payment (except in prosecution cases). A penalty could be imposed in respect of late notification of liability, and if payment was made sufficiently late, the payment might have been due at a higher rate (see **42.8** LATE-PAID CONTRIBUTIONS). The *Social Security Act 1998* enabled regulations to be made to also impose the penalty in such circumstances and introduced it from 6 April 2009. A penalty would be payable for a failure to notify HMRC by 31 January following the end of the year in which the Class 2 contributions should have been paid. The penalty regime expressed as a percentage of the outstanding contributions would depend on whether the failure to notify was as a result of 'deliberate and concealed' action (100% penalty), or 'deliberate but not concealed' action (70% penalty) or any other case where the penalty would be 30%. [*Social Security (Contributions) Regulations 2001, SI 2001/1004, Reg 87A–87D* as inserted by *Social Security (Contributions) (Amendment No 3) Regulations 2009, SI 2009/600, Regs 1–5*.]

In certain cases, a penalty will not have been charged where the outstanding contributions due were in excess of six years in arrears or where any amount was excepted from liability on account of the small earnings exception. See **18.4**. In addition, no penalty arose where the person satisfied HMRC or the Tax Tribunal (see **9** APPEALS AND REVIEWS) on appeal that there was a 'reasonable excuse' for the failure to notify. Reasonable excuse in these circumstances did not include cases of insufficiency of funds, reliance on another person to notify HMRC or where there was a reasonable excuse but HMRC had not been notified until after an unreasonable delay. [*Reg 87B, paras 5–8*.] Where the failure to notify HMRC of Class 2 liability was by someone acting on the contributor's behalf, such as an agent, then if HMRC considered that the person liable for the contributions had taken reasonable care to avoid the failure to notify notwithstanding the agent's conduct then this might have been considered to be a reasonable excuse on the contributor's part. [*Reg 87B, para 8*.] See also **35.11** ENFORCEMENT for reductions in penalties in certain circumstances.

Prior to 6 April 2009, anyone who was liable to pay a Class 2 contribution or who, being entitled though not liable to pay such a contribution, wished to do so, was liable to notify HM Revenue and Customs immediately in writing of the date upon which he commenced or ceased to be a self-employed earner, or of the date upon which he wished to commence or cease paying Class 2 contributions as appropriate. The deadline was three complete calendar months. However, this was tempered with the introduction from January 2001 of a £100 penalty for failure to notify unless the business estimated trading profits would be below the NICs small earnings exception even if, in the event, the exception was not actually claimed. See IR Press Releases 17 October 2000; 3/01, 10 January 2001 and 21/01, 23 February 2001. [*Social Security (Contributions) Regulations 2001, SI 2001/1004, Reg 87*.] (See also **18.1** CLASS 2 CONTRIBUTIONS.)

From 6 April 2015, the old regime was replaced, at least for compulsory contributions payable under the revised *SSCBA 1992, s 11(2)*, by the same rules as apply for Class 4: the *FA 2007, Sch 24* penalties for inaccuracies, the *FA 2009, ss 101-102* interest charges, and the *FA 2009, Schs 55, 56* penalties for failure to make returns or payments on time. [*SSCBA 1992, s 11A*, as inserted by *NICA 2015, Sch 1, Para 3*]. Voluntary contributions under the revised *SSCBA 1992, s 11(6)* remain within the scope of *SSCBA 1992, s 12*.

A Class 2 contributor, whether paying compulsorily or voluntarily, must notify HM Revenue and Customs in writing of any change of his address. [*Social Security (Contributions) Regulations 2001, SI 2001/1004, Reg 88*].

SSC(TF)A 1999, Sch 4 paras 1–3 enables the recovery of contributions, interest and penalties summarily as a civil debt in proceedings commenced in the name of an authorised officer on application to a Magistrates' Court. 'Authorised officer' means an officer of HM Revenue and Customs authorised by them for that purpose.

Nonetheless, separate penalties for non–notification of liability were introduced in January 2001 — see above and **18.1** CLASS 2 CONTRIBUTIONS.

Class 3 and Class 3A contributions

[21.48] Where a person wishes, and is permitted, to pay CLASS 3 CONTRIBUTIONS **19**, he may do so, since 6 April 1993, by the method described at the start of **21.47** above or by making a remittance at, or after, the end of the tax year to which they are to relate. The 'due date' for payment of a Class 3 contribution is not later than 42 days after the end of the tax year in respect of which it is paid but, since payment of Class 3 contributions cannot be enforced and since late paid contributions may, in certain circumstances, be admitted and will, if paid within the two tax years next following the tax year to which they relate, be payable at the rate at which they would have been payable had they been paid within the tax year to which they relate, the requirement is of little significance (see **42.6** and **42.8** LATE-PAID CONTRIBUTIONS). [*Social Security (Contributions) Regulations 2001, SI 2001/1004, Regs 87, 87A* as inserted by *Social Security (Contributions) (Amendment No 3) Regulations 2009, SI 2009/600, Regs 1–5*.] Furthermore, where a contributor shows to the satisfaction of HM Revenue and Customs that the late payment has been made through ignorance or error rather than through failure to exercise due care and diligence, the two-year time limit may be extended so that the contributor may pay the contributions at the original rate rather than a higher rate (see **42.8** LATE-PAID CONTRIBUTIONS). It was held in *Adojutelegan v Clark* (SpC) 430) [2004] SWTI 2241 that exercising due diligence involves the positive step of making enquiries (either personally or through an agent). In deciding whether due care and diligence has been exercised for this purpose, the NIC&EO will also take into account:

(a) the contributor's age and state of health;
(b) the contributor's level of education;
(c) what steps the contributor has made to establish pension entitlement; and
(d) what questions the contributor asked and what information he was given.

If it can be established that the contributor made an earlier enquiry, when he could have been given more information but was not, the exercise of due care and diligence may be accepted as at the date of the earlier enquiry (*Revenue and Customs Comrs v Kearney* [2008] EWHC 842 (Ch) per Lawson J, and National Insurance Manual NIM25031).

There is an established procedure whereby employers may make *annual* payments to NIC&EO in respect of the Class 3 contributions of their employees overseas.

The mechanisms for paying Class 3A contributions have not been published. The gov.uk website instructs those who wish to apply to pay Class 3A contributions to apply online (at www.gov.uk/statepensiontopup) or by telephone (0345 600 4270 or +44 191 218 2076), after which the DWP will post out a form explaining how to pay, which may be by one-off direct debit, 'direct payment' (undefined), at a bank or post office, or by putting a cheque in the post. The commencement date for *Pensions Act 2014*, *s 25* and *Sch 15*, *paras 1–10* and *12–14*, the basis of Class 3A provision, was set as 12 October 2015 by *Pensions Act 2014 (Commencement No 5) Order 2015*, *SI 2015/1475*, *art 3*, which was not made until 6 July 2015.

Class 4 contributions

[21.49] Class 4 contributions are payable in the same manner as any income tax which is, or would be, chargeable in respect of the profits which form the basis of assessment or self-assessment (whether or not income tax in fact falls to be paid) and are payable by the person on whom the income tax is (or would be) charged in accordance with an assessment or self-assessment made under the *Income Tax Acts* (see **20.10** CLASS 4 CONTRIBUTIONS). [*SSCBA 1992, s 15(1)(2)(5)*]. Except where liability for such contributions has been deferred or the contributions are special Class 4 contributions (see **20.8** CLASS 4 CONTRIBUTIONS), the provisions of those Acts as to collection and recovery apply, with necessary modifications, in relation to Class 4 contributions. Contributions are subject to the collection and recovery provisions of the Income Tax Acts *as if they were income tax* chargeable under *ITTOIA 2005, Part 2 Chapter 2*. It should be noted particularly that the former penalty provisions of *TMA 1970, Part X* applied to Class 4 contributions separately from the associated income tax liability. Therefore, a penalty for, eg failure to render a return, might have been levied twice by some HMRC officers, who treated the failure as two separate contraventions in respect of income tax and contributions, despite the fact that only one return would, in fact, have been made. (See **27.8** DEFERMENT OF PAYMENT and **21.52**, **21.53** below). [*SSCBA 1992, s 16(1)(2)*].

Under self-assessment for income tax, interim payments are due on 31 January in the year to which payment relates, 31 July after the end of the year; and a balancing payment on 31 January following the end of the year. See CLASS 4 CONTRIBUTIONS **20**.

For 2017–18, under self-assessment, the Class 4 (and tax) demands will, in principle, be based on the following dates:

31 January 2018	50% of the total income tax and Class 4 liability for 2016–17 as finally computed, plus the Class 2 liability for that year
31 July 2018	50% of the total income tax and Class 4 liability for 2016–17 as finally computed
31 January 2019	Balancing payment of tax and Class 4 for 2017–18, plus the Class 2 liability for that year

For effective dates of payment see **21.6** above.

All sums received by HMRC are initially paid into HM Revenue and Customs account but then, when directed to do so by the Treasury, HM Revenue and Customs accounts for, and pay over to, the National Insurance Fund, sums estimated to have been collected in respect of Class 4 contributions. [*Commissioners for Revenue and Customs Act 2005, s 44*].

Where, under the provisions of *FA 2004, Part 3, Chapter 3*, a contractor deducts from a payment made to a subcontractor under a contract relating to construction operations a sum equal to 20% (but see **41.9** LABOUR-ONLY CONTRACTORS) of so much of the payment as does not represent the direct cost of materials to be used in the construction operations and pays that sum over to HM Revenue and Customs, the excess (if any) of that sum over the subcontractor's liability to income tax in respect of his profits or gains is treated (to the extent of the subcontractor's liability, if any, for Class 4 contributions) as Class 4 contributions paid in respect of his profits or gains. [*FA 2004, s 62(2)*.] (See also **41.9** LABOUR-ONLY CONTRACTORS). Where a return of deductions on form P35 (and, previously, SC35) was delayed and there was a claim that the failure to comply was 'minor and technical' any reason to expect that the obligations would not be complied with on a timely basis would preclude relief. (*T & C Hill (Haulage) (a firm) v Gleig (Inspector of Taxes)* [2000] STC (SCD) 64).

Example

Chris has for some years been a labour-only subcontractor and he is a registered subcontractor under the CIS. He suffers deductions under the CIS at the rate for 2016–17 of 20%. His accounts for the year ended 30 June 2016 under the self-assessment rules show assessable profits of £15,000 for 2016–17. In the tax year 2016–17 he receives subcontract payments from which £1,600 has been deducted at source. He already has a small pension against which £3,000 of his personal allowance is allocated. The position for 2016–17 is:

	£	£
Trading profit	15,000	
Less: adjusted personal allowances	8,000	
Taxable income	7,000	
Tax liability:		
£7,000 @ 20%		1,400.00
Class 4 profit	15,000	
Less: lower annual limit	8,060	
	6,940	
Class 4 liability: £6,940 at 9%		624.60
Class 2 liability: 52 × £2.80		145.60
		2,170.20
2016–17 deductions at source		1,600.00
Class 4 payable		£570.20

Note: the timing of the payment of £570.20 will be influenced by the size of the previous year's total liability and the interim payments resulting.

Assessments

[21.50] Class 4 contributions must be paid by the person from whom the corresponding income tax is (or, if there were any, would be) due. [*SSCBA 1992, s 15(1)(2)(3A)(5)*].

Special Class 4 contributions

[21.51] Where a person is liable to pay special Class 4 contributions, the responsibility for collection of those contributions lies with HM Revenue and Customs NIC&EO (see **20.8** CLASS 4 CONTRIBUTIONS). [*SSCBA 1992, s 18*].

HM Revenue and Customs NIC&EO must notify the earner of the special Class 4 contribution due from him for the tax year concerned unless some other arrangement is made with the earner concerned. The earner must, unless he appeals against a decision of an officer of HM Revenue and Customs, pay that contribution to HM Revenue and Customs within 28 days from the receipt of the notice (see APPEALS AND REVIEWS **9** as well as **21.52** below). [*Social Security (Contributions) Regulations 2001, SI 2001/1004, Reg 106*].

Collection of deferred contributions

[21.52] The assessment of an earner's profits (and the earner's right of appeal against such an assessment) is unaffected by the issue of a certificate of deferment CA2703 (see **27.11** DEFERMENT OF PAYMENT). However, the notice of assessment or, as applicable, the self-assessment showed no figure representing Class 4 contributions payable at the main rate and the collection provisions of the *Income Tax Acts* were *not* to apply prior to 6 April 2003. They will, however, apply thereafter to collect (initially) 1% and (from 5 April 2011) 2%

on the deferred profits, as well as on those profits above the upper annual limit. Responsibility for the calculation, administration and recovery of Class 4 contributions ultimately payable at the main rate in respect of the profits or gains assessed for the tax year to which the certificate of deferment relates lies with HM Revenue and Customs NIC&EO. [*Social Security (Contributions) Regulations 2001, SI 2001/1004, Reg 99(1)* as amended by *Social Security (Contributions) (Amendment) Regulations 2003, SI 2003/193, Reg 13(2)*].

For the purpose of enabling the NIC&EO to make the necessary calculations, NIC&EO may obtain from elsewhere in HM Revenue and Customs the amount of the earner's profits or gains (as adjusted for Class 4 purposes) (see **33.6** EARNINGS LIMITS). [*Social Security (Contributions) Regulations 2001, SI 2001/1004, Reg 99(3)(4)* as amended by *Social Security (Contributions) (Amendment) Regulations 2003, SI 2003/193, Reg 13(3)(4)*].

Any exception from Class 4 contribution liability available by reason of Class 1 contributions being paid on earnings chargeable to income tax under *ITTOIA 2005, Part 2 Chapter 2* is to be recognised in calculating an earner's Class 4 liability (see **20.6** CLASS 4 CONTRIBUTIONS). [*Social Security (Contributions) Regulations 2001, SI 2001/1004, Reg 99(2)*].

When the NIC&EO has made its calculation of the earner's liability for Class 4 contributions deferred but payable it must give the earner notice of the amount. [*Social Security (Contributions) Regulations 2001, SI 2001/1004, Reg 99(5)*]. The earner must then, within 28 days of receipt of the notice, pay the stated amount before the expiry of that period, unless:

- he disputes a decision of an officer of HM Revenue and Customs by lodging an appeal (see APPEALS AND REVIEWS **9** as well as **21.53** below); or
- he has made some claim or late appeal which affects the certified profits or gains, and has notified the NIC&EO that he has done so.

[*Social Security (Contributions) Regulations 2001, SI 2001/1004, Reg 99(6)*].

If HM Revenue and Customs makes any amendment to an assessment and that amendment affects the amount of profits or gains computed for Class 4 contribution purposes, notice of the altered amount must be supplied forthwith to the earner and to NIC&EO. [*Social Security (Contributions) Regulations 2001, SI 2001/1004, Reg 99(7)*].

Collection of deferred or special Class 4 contributions after appeal

[21.53] Following claims or appeals, the earner will receive notice to pay the Class 4 contributions owing. The collection procedure is set out below.

Following:

(a) a claim or appeal in connection with an assessment of deferred Class 4 contributions made by NICO (see **21.49** above); or
(b) an appeal in connection with special Class 4 contributions (see **21.51** above)

HM Revenue and Customs NIC&EO must, after the time stated below, give the earner notice (or revised notice) of such Class 4 contributions as are due from the earner, having regard to the outcome of the appeal, claim or determination. The earner must, within 28 days of receipt of that notice pay the amount specified. [*Social Security (Contributions) Regulations 2001, SI 2001/1004, Reg 107(1)(2)*].

The time after which notice or revised notice may be given is:

- in the case of an altered amount of profits or gains being certified by HM Revenue and Customs, the date on which they are certified;
- in the case of a late appeal (other than one resulting in (a) above), the date of the determination of the appeal;
- in the case of a claim or appeal against a decision on a claim made under the *Income Tax Acts* (other than one resulting in (a) above), the date on which the time for appealing against the decision on the claim expires, or, if later, the date of the determination of the appeal;
- in the case of a decision under *SSC(TF)A 1999, s 8* by an officer of HM Revenue and Customs, the date on which the time for appealing expires, or, if later, the date of the determination of the appeal.

[*Social Security (Contributions) Regulations 2001, SI 2001/1004, Reg 107(3)*].

For the means of recovery available to HM Revenue and Customs where normal methods of collection fail, see ARREARS OF CONTRIBUTIONS **12** and ENFORCEMENT **35**.

Interest can be charged under *FA 2009, s 101* (previously *TMA 1970, s 86*) on overdue Class 4 contributions in just the same way as it is charged on overdue tax when the contribution is included in an assessment issued on or after 19 April 1993. From 19 April 1993, overpaid Class 4 contributions attracted a repayment supplement under *ITTOIA 2005, s 749* upon repayment (now under *FA 2009, s 102* since 31 October 2011). HM Revenue and Customs has the same powers in relation to the remission of interest on Class 4 contributions as it has in relation to the remission of interest on tax. [*SSCBA 1992, Sch 2 para 6(1)*].

Before *FA 2009* reformed the system, interest could also be charged on unpaid Class 4 contributions where the liability for those contributions arose as a result of a *tax* assessment being made to recover for the Crown a loss of tax wholly or partly attributable to the taxpayer's fault. Then, the related Class 4 contributions attracted an interest charge just as the tax did, and the tax provisions relating to the discretionary mitigation of interest, the staying or compounding of proceedings for its recovery, and the determination of the date from which it was to run, applied as regarded the interest on Class 4 contributions also. [*SSCBA 1992, Sch 2 para 6* and *Taxes (Interest Rate) (Amendment No 3) Regulations 2001, SI 2001/3860*].

The provisions of *TMA 1970, Part X* in relation to penalties for failure to make a return or for making a return fraudulently or negligently specifically applied as regarded Class 4 contributions. The provision applying *Part X* was updated, albeit incoherently, when *FA 2009, Schs 55* and *56* were introduced with effect from 1 April 2011 so as to ensure that the new penalty regime applies to Class 4. [*SSCBA 1992, s 16(1)(2)*.] See **42.11** LATE-PAID CONTRIBUTIONS and **21.31**.)

Key Points regarding collection

[21.54] Points to consider are as follows.

- National Insurance is a self-assessed system.
- There are strict rules for the recovery by employers of under-deducted employee contributions – extended for contributions relating to securities-based remuneration. Where employee contributions cannot be recovered they must be borne by the employer.
- There are three extra days for making payment of Class 1, Class 1A and Class 1B contributions where payment is made by electronic means.
- In respect of 2010–11 liabilities onwards there are potential penalties where monthly Class 1 payments made during the year are made late.
- From April 2015, Class 2 collection was reformed by *NICA 2015* so that it is subject to almost all the same rules as Class 4.

22

Company Directors

Cross-references. See AGE EXCEPTION **3**; **4.16** AGENCY WORKERS for position where director obtains temporary employment through an agency; AGGREGATION OF EARNINGS **5**; **12.6** ARREARS OF CONTRIBUTIONS for personal liability of directors for company contribution arrears; CATEGORISATION **14**; CLASS **1** CONTRIBUTIONS **15**; EARNINGS FROM EMPLOYMENT: GENERAL **29**; **34.12** EARNINGS PERIODS; **40** INTERMEDIARIES; **47.2** MULTIPLE EMPLOYMENTS; **51.4** OVERSEAS MATTERS for position of non-resident director of a UK company.

Other Sources. Simon's Taxes, Volume 2, para A8.290; Tolley's National Insurance Brief, September 1996, pages 65–66; Leaflet CA44 (2018); HM Revenue and Customs National Insurance Manual NIM12000–12034.

Introduction to company directors and NICs

[22.1] Because pre-1975 National Insurance legislation did not bring office-holders within its definition of an employed earner, company directors who were *not* under contracts of service were, until 6 April 1975, regarded as self-employed earners (see CATEGORISATION **14** and *M4 (1950)* and *M10 (1950)*). This is the view still taken by many foreign tax and social security authorities (eg, Belgium). The operation of *SSA 1975, s 2(1)(a)* (which re-defined an employed earner) brought this to an end in the UK, however, and, from 6 April 1975, *all* company directors who derive at least part of their remuneration from their office were (and continue to be) categorised as *employed earners*.

Such categorisation meant that all company directors became liable for Class 1 contributions on their earnings in accordance with the normal rules but that they alone among employed earners were in a position to exploit those rules by carefully contrived arrangements of salaries, bonuses and pay intervals. Attempts in 1980 by the then DSS to render many such arrangements ineffective by a strict application of a court ruling on the meaning of 'payment' in relation to the voting of remuneration were largely unsuccessful (see **15.5** CLASS **1** CONTRIBUTIONS). Pressured by the Public Accounts Committee of the House of Commons in 1981 to bring to an end the avoidance by company directors, the Secretary of State for Social Security introduced new regulations which came into effect on 6 April 1983. These changed the basis on which the Class 1 liability of a director thereafter arises (see **22.4** and **22.8** below).

On 31 January 1996 proposals were announced which would have, if implemented, eased from 6 April 1997 the administration procedures necessary to operate that special basis for directors. However, in the event no change was made until the *Social Security Act 1998* which enabled, from 6 April 1999, contributions to be paid on account in the case of a company director provided they were 'trued up' by the end of the year. These provisions placed on a legal footing at least some of the practices adopted by employers in the intervening years. See **22.7** below.

[*Social Security (Contributions) Regulations 2001, SI 2001/1004, Reg 8*].

Note that, in the international context, careful attention must be paid to the status of company directors. Directors of non-UK companies may not be treated as employees under their domestic law. However, if they join the board of a UK company and are remunerated by that UK company, they will be classed in UK tax and NIC law as employees, although treaties and EC regulations may mean that they have no UK NIC liability in respect of such earnings.

It should be noted that not all payments of directors' fees do, in fact, attract a Class 1 liability, even if all the work is carried out in the UK. While directors are always classed as employed earners, certain situations lead to their fees being excluded from liability – see **22.8** below.

The meaning of 'company director'

[22.2] With effect from 6 April 1997 a director is defined for social security purposes as:

(a) where a company is managed by a board of directors or a similar body, a member of that board or body;
(b) where a company is managed by a single director or person, that person;
(c) any person in accordance with whose directions or instructions the directors are accustomed to act.

In the case of (c), this will not apply if the other person's instructions are limited to professional advice eg a solicitor. See HM Revenue and Customs National Insurance Manual NIM12002. [*Social Security (Contributions)*

Regulations 2001, SI 2001/1004, Reg 1(2)]. The definition here is probably wide enough to encompass 'shadow directors' without amendment to reflect the definition of that term in *CA 2006, s 251(2)*, although the exclusion for professional advisers is likely to be extended by HMRC to a person giving instructions or directions in the exercise of a statutory function and to Ministers of the Crown issuing guidance or advice, as these are about to be specifically excluded for company law purposes by *Small Business, Enterprise and Employment Act 2015, s 90*.

The definition in *SI 2001/1004, Reg 1(2)* bears a close resemblance to that in *Income Tax (Earnings and Pensions) Act 2003, s 18(3)(4) (ITEPA 2003)*.

Based on the legislation, it is arguable that a director is *not* a company director for social security contribution purposes if the company in relation to which he is a director is *neither*:

- a company within the meaning of *Companies Act 2006, s 1* (formerly *Companies Act 1985, s 735(1)*); *nor*
- a body corporate to which, by virtue of *CA 2006, s 1173*, any provision of *CA 2006* applies.

However, it is known that HM Revenue and Customs does not accept that this is so.

Certainly, a director of an unincorporated association is, therefore, outside the definition of company director. So, too, is the director of a building society within the meaning of *Building Societies Act 1986* unless of course, the society has de-mutualised. (Leaflet CA 44, Para 4). But see **22.11** below for an exception to this rule.

The definition as it has stood for many years is in fact wide enough to encompass corporate directors. Such directors cannot, though, be subject to contribution liability in their own right as they are not natural persons. Under changes made by *SBEEA 2015, s 87* to *CA 2006, ss 156–156C*, companies will in future no longer be permitted to act as company directors and will be required to replace existing corporate directors with human beings within twelve months of the commencement by order of the provision (ie, it is expected to come into force on 1 October 2016, according to www.gov.uk/government/news/the-small-business-enterprise-and-employment-bill-is-coming. However, the commencement order has not yet been made. All company directors, with the exception of special cases nominated by the Secretary of State for Business, will therefore be natural persons and accordingly potentially within the scope of the social security legislation (ie, if they fulfil residence and presence conditions – without treaty exception – and have liable earnings).

Case law

[22.3] In *Re Lo-Line Electric Motors Ltd* [1988] Ch 477, [1988] 2 All ER 692 it was confirmed that the word 'director' when used without qualification or definition is capable of including *de facto* directors, but whether it does so or not in any specific instance depends on the context. Similarly, whilst under

Companies Act 2006, effective from 1 October 2009, the minimum age for a company director in England is 16, a person purportedly appointed as a director who is under that age might be considered a director for some purposes. If the context is penal, a strict construction might be necessary (and that would exclude *de facto* directors); but where the context is non-penal, the word 'director' probably includes a person validly appointed a director, a person invalidly appointed a director, and a person merely *de facto* acting as director. Thus, in relation to the penal provisions described at **12.6** arrears of contributions a narrow construction of the word is, arguably, to be preferred.

Every UK company director is, *ipso facto*, an office-holder. (*McMillan v Guest (Inspector of Taxes)* [1942] AC 561, [1942] 1 All ER 606, HL, *per Lord Atkin*). But that leaves open the question whether he derives his remuneration from his office or from a contract of service or even a contract for services with the company concerned. In *Allen v Minister of National Insurance* (1956) QBD reported as M59 (1958), for instance, it was held that although Mr Allen was chairman and director of a company called Woodcrafts (Leigh-on-Sea) Ltd in which he held all but one of the shares, he derived his remuneration not from his office but from a contract with the company for his services as a self-employed woodworker. More frequently, an executive director of a company will be found to derive his remuneration from a contract of service with the company in which he also holds office. (*Lee v Lee's Air Farming Ltd* [1961] AC 12, [1960] 3 All ER 420, PC; *Ferguson v Telford Greir Mackay & Co Ltd* (1967) 2 ITR 387; *Eaton v Robert Eaton Ltd* [1988] ICR 302).

Definition of company directors' earnings

[22.4] If a company director derives all his remuneration from a contract *for services*, he is a *self-employed earner* for contribution purposes because he is not 'gainfully employed . . . under a contract of service or in an office . . . with earnings' (see **14.2** CATEGORISATION). [*SSCBA 1992, s 2(1)(a)*.] And, if that is so, the special rules which, from 6 April 1983, govern the calculation of earnings for contribution purposes (see below), are, it seems, of no application. Note that, from 2003–04 until 13 May 2014, the definition used the term 'general earnings', ie, the *ITEPA 2003* definition, which is not congruent with the definition of earnings for National Insurance purposes, but that mistake (a result of the tax law rewrite and attempted harmonisation project) was eventually rectified by *National Insurance Contributions Act 2014, s 15 (NICA 2014)*.

The treatment of the earnings of company directors who derive all their earnings from their office, or derive it partly from their office and partly from a contract of service, varied for a time but from 6 April 1983, any payment made by a company to or for the benefit of any of its directors has been treated as remuneration derived from employed earner's employment if that payment would not otherwise have been earnings for contribution purposes but has been made on account of, or by way of an advance on, a sum which would have been earnings for contribution purposes. [*SSCBA 1992, s 4(5); Social*

Security (Contributions) Regulations 2001, SI 2001/1004, Reg 22(2)]. This rule has led to a number of difficulties over the years which are discussed below in relation to directors' current accounts and loan accounts.

Timing of receipt

[22.5] It should be noted that the tax treatment of a director's earnings, which used to differ significantly from the National Insurance contributions treatment of those same earnings, is now broadly aligned with the established NIC treatment, although minor differences remain. With effect from 6 April 1989, the basis of taxation of directors' general earnings was changed to that set out in the former *ICTA 1988, ss 202A, 202B* (created by *FA 1989, s 37*). Broadly, income from employment (ie excluding pensions and social security benefits) is now assessed for the tax year in which it is received, rather than for the tax year to which it relates. The change in the overall basis of assessment is also reflected in the introduction by *FA 1989, s 45* of a definition of the time when general earnings are treated as paid for the purposes of the PAYE collection system. [*ITEPA 2003, ss 15, 18*].

While *s 15* taxes income from an office or employment on the basis of its receipt, it relies on the definition in *s 18* of the time of receipt. This can be summarised in the case of directors as the earlier or earliest of the following times:

(a) when payment is made of or on account of the general earnings;
(b) when a person becomes entitled to payment of or on account of the general earnings;
(c) when sums on account of general earnings are credited to the director's current or loan account by the company;
(d) where the amount of the general earnings for a period is determined before the period ends, the time when the period ends; and/or
(e) where the amount of the general earnings for a period is not known until the amount is determined after the period has ended, the time when the amount is determined.

The PAYE rules introduced by *FA 1989, s 45* simply restate rules (a) and (b) above to 'the time when payment is actually made' and 'the time when a person becomes entitled to the payment' respectively, and broadly copy rules (c) to (e).

It will be noted that the effect of the above rules is to charge earnings to income tax when payment is made, whether already earned or on account of a sum which will be earnings in due course. This results in a situation broadly similar to that for National Insurance contribution purposes, which arises from the combination of the rule established in *Garforth v Newsmith Stainless Ltd* [1979] 2 AER 73 (see **15.5**) and *Social Security (Contributions) Regulations 2001, SI 2001/1004, Reg 22(2)* outlined above.

However, it should not be overlooked that rule (*d*) above is likely to be the rule which conflicts most readily with the National Insurance contribution law as follows.

Example

Gary Newsmith is a director of Lesstain Ltd. L has an accounting date of 5 July. G has no balance standing to his credit with L at 6 July 2016 and fees already voted and paid have exactly equalled his drawings up to that date. G has substantial earnings from other sources and takes only one payment annually from L in respect of his services. A meeting is held on 1 April 2017 at which G's fees for the year ending 5 July 2017 are determined at £50,000, but this amount is neither credited to his current account nor made available to him. Due to cash flow problems and the desire to tie G to the company, it is agreed that G will only become entitled to his emoluments on 4 October 2017.

G is taxable on these earnings in 2017–18, since that is the year in which the end of the accounting period falls, and L has to apply PAYE to the general earnings on 5 July 2017, despite the fact that G may not draw the general earnings before 4 October 2017. When that date arrives, L must deduct and account for National Insurance contributions via an FPS, since it is only then that the money is put unreservedly at G's disposal.

The above example is, of course, somewhat contrived and in reality there is likely to be little doubt about when PAYE and NICs are to be applied to a director's earnings and about the year into which earnings then fall. See earlier editions of this work for the contrast between the pre-6 April 1989 tax rules and the National Insurance rules.

If fees are voted to a director in advance, the fees will become earnings for contribution purposes on the date when he has an unreserved right to draw them.

Example

Dawn is a director of East Ltd. On 31 March 2016 E votes fees to D of £8,000 payable on the last Friday in each month for the next twelve months. D will have earnings for contribution purposes thus:

	£
29 April 2016	8,000
27 May 2016	8,000
24 June 2016	8,000
Etc	

Difficulties with National Insurance contribution liabilities arising from the operation of directors' current accounts were referred to above. For a full discussion of earlier DSS policies, please refer to past editions of this work.

The difficulty is caused by the fact that the typical close company director does not have a service contract and is remunerated in accordance with the Articles of Association. The standard 'Table A' articles under *Companies (Tables A to F) Regs 1985* (which still determine the position for the majority of directors currently) provide: '82 The directors shall be entitled to such remuneration as the company may by ordinary resolution determine and, unless the resolution provides otherwise, the remuneration shall be deemed to accrue from day to day.' This leads to a situation in many companies where the owner-directors simply take money as needed during the year, debiting the drawings to a drawings or current account and bringing that account back into credit by voting remuneration at the AGM, when the accounts for the year are approved. See also *Companies Act 2006, s 421*.

Clearly, a drawing by a director in *repayment of a loan* which he had earlier made to the company is *not* earnings since it is not a payment of earnings or a payment on account of a sum which would be earnings. Where a director's account goes into credit following the AGM, subsequent drawings against the *credit* balance are irrelevant for contribution purposes. However, if the account becomes overdrawn, or further overdrawn, as a result of the debiting of a particular transaction by the director, *Social Security (Contributions) Regulations 2001, SI 2001/1004, Reg 22(2)* becomes relevant.

Whether the director draws cash, equivalent to salary, or uses a company cheque to settle a personal bill, the company must consider whether the debiting of the transaction to the director's account constitutes a payment of earnings or deemed earnings. In other words, does the payment represent remuneration or profit derived from the employment, or an advance on such remuneration which would be treated as earnings by *Social Security (Contributions) Regulations 2001, SI 2001/1004, Reg 22(2)*?

Because *Social Security (Contributions) Regulations 2001, SI 2001/1004, Reg 22(2)* deems certain payments to be liable when they otherwise would not be so liable, care is needed to avoid double counting when fees are voted into such an account. Earnings are only liable once to Class 1 contributions, so any amounts charged under *Social Security (Contributions) Regulations 2001, SI 2001/1004, Reg 22(2)* must be excluded from earnings when fees are later voted into the account to clear or reduce the overdrawn balance. [*Social Security (Contributions) Regulations 2001, SI 2001/1004, Sch 3 Part X para* 2].

In the past, the then DSS misinterpreted the series of transactions which took place, insisting for a time that any payment of a director's personal bill was a payment of earnings, even if the bill was paid using money which already stood to the director's credit in a current account and which had already suffered a Class 1 liability at the time of credit to the account. The policy was revised in a 1994 supplement to the Manual for Employers on NIC for company directors, NI 35, and the new policy is set out in some detail in paras 30–31 of CA44 (2018).

The then DSS therefore accepted that, if a director's personal bill is paid by the company, liability will arise only if and to the extent that:

- the payment is treated by the company as remuneration and charged to the profit and loss account as such; or
- the payment is charged to the director's account with the company *and* the transaction makes the account overdrawn or further overdrawn *and* it is expected that the drawing is on account of an amount which will be voted into the account as earnings in due course.

Debiting amounts for cash drawings or personal bills to the account which leave it in credit will not constitute paying earnings. Similarly, debiting cash drawings or personal bills to the account which create or increase an overdrawn balance will not constitute earnings *provided* the overdrawing is not in anticipation of the future crediting of remuneration. If a director intends to clear the overdrawn balance by the introduction of cash from another source (eg dividends, matured life assurance policies, legacies, or other personal income), *Social Security (Contributions) Regulations 2001, SI 2001/1004, Reg 22(2)* is of no application and there can be no Class 1 liability. Remuneration taken in a form which does not constitute earnings for contribution purposes might also be used to clear the balance.

The DSS went further in the April 1995 edition of Leaflet CA 44 and HM Revenue and Customs has put its name to the same viewpoint in subsequent editions of CA 44. If a director draws money out of a current account making it overdrawn or further overdrawn and the director does not normally receive advance or anticipatory payments of remuneration, the amount overdrawn will not be regarded as earnings unless the company authorises payment of the amounts overdrawn. Authorisation may be in writing or by the other directors agreeing verbally that they know about the situation. According to the CA44 (2018), Para 31 guidance, Class 1 liability arises at the point where the amounts overdrawn are authorised.

This guidance is based correctly on the premise that, if a director takes money from the company, the payment to him cannot represent a payment of earnings if it is unauthorised. As was explained above, payment may take place only when an amount is placed unreservedly at the disposal of the director, so any unauthorised payment cannot constitute payment. An authorised drawing on account of future remuneration will be liable. However, the guidance is nevertheless flawed in that it ignores the requirements of *Social Security (Contributions) Regulations 2001, SI 2001/1004, Reg 22(2)* when dealing with an authorised payment. If an 'authorised' drawing is made in the knowledge that it will be debited to the director's account and the balance will be cleared in due course by something other than a vote of remuneration (eg dividends), *Social Security (Contributions) Regulations 2001, SI 2001/1004, Reg 22(2)* cannot apply to treat the payment as an advance of future earnings. There can accordingly be no Class 1 liability on the authorised drawing.

In typical situations, the position may be summarised by the following examples.

(a) *Account overdrawn, fees etc credited.* To the extent that the items creating the overdraft have already been treated as earnings for contribution purposes (see (c) and (d) below), the fees etc credited will not be earnings for contribution purposes, but any other part of the fees etc credited will be earnings. [*Social Security (Contributions) Regulations 2001, SI 2001/1004, Sch 3 Part X para 2*]. (CA44 (2018), Para 30).

> *Example*
>
> Sherlock is a director of Holmes Ltd. On 16 July 2016, his current account with H is overdrawn by £2,800 of which £2,000 has been treated as earnings for contribution purposes. On 20 July 2016 fees of £30,000 are voted to him and credited to the account. £28,000 of those fees are earnings for contribution purposes.

(b) *Account in credit, fees etc credited.* The whole of the fees credited will be earnings for contribution purposes. (CA 44, Para 30).

(c) *Account overdrawn, items debited.* All the items debited will be earnings for contribution purposes as long as the drawing is made in anticipation of an earnings payment (eg fees or bonuses). (CA 44, Para 31).

> *Example*
>
> Watson is a director of Elementary Ltd. On 21 June 2016, his current account with E is overdrawn by £5,000. On 25 June 2016, E pays W cash of £4,000. The £4,000 is debited to his account. The whole £4,000 is earnings for contribution purposes.

(d) *Account in credit, items debited.* To the extent that the total of the items debited do not exhaust the credit balance, they will *not* be earnings for contribution purposes, but to the extent that they throw the account out of credit and into overdraft they will be earnings as long as the drawing is made in anticipation of an earnings payment (eg fees or bonuses). (CA 44 (2016), Para 31).

> *Example*
>
> Moriarty is a director of Reichenbach Ltd. On 20 August 2016, his current account with R is in credit to the tune of £3,700. On 24 August 2016, R pays M cash of £5,000. The £5,000 is debited to his account. Only £1,300 is earnings for contribution purposes.

In (c) and (d) above, it is assumed that the director concerned was *authorised* to receive the amounts paid to him or *authorised* to have amounts paid to others on his behalf.

It must be stressed that the absence of, or lateness of, accounting entries relating to a director's current or drawings account will have no bearing on the date on which payments fall to be regarded as earnings. If a company pays cash to a director on 14 September 2016, that is the date on which (depending on the true state of the director's current account with the company on that date) earnings equal to the payment are paid to the director. Likewise, if fees are voted to the director unconditionally on 15 October 2016, that is the date on which (again subject to the true state of his current account up to that date) those fees are earnings paid to him.

For the treatment of fees paid to nominee directors see **29.68** EARNINGS FROM EMPLOYMENT: GENERAL.

It should be noted that, until 31 March 1989, where a disallowance of director's remuneration for corporation tax purposes was negotiated with the Inspector of Taxes and the amount disallowed was formally waived and refunded to the company by the director so as to obtain a reduction in what was then the Schedule E liability equivalent to the amount disallowed (see Inland Revenue Press Release 6 November 1967, later incorporated in Statement of Practice C4 Para 4), the DSS was not permitted to allow any similar reduction in Class 1 contribution liabilities. Thus, a director who, by reason of such a waiver, reduced his fees below the Upper Earnings Limit for a tax year would pay primary Class 1 contributions on some part, if not all, of the earnings which he had refunded to the company, and the company would suffer secondary Class 1 contributions on the whole of the amount refunded. (CA44 (2018), Para 30).

Although close company apportionment was abolished in 1989 and SP/C4 was withdrawn, it became clear from ICAEW Tax Faculty Technical Release Tax 11/93, para 38, that the practice outlined in SP/C4, para 4, was still being applied and that waivers were still used in exceptional circumstances, despite the fact that Class 1 liabilities have arisen. Such liabilities would be avoided only if it could successfully be argued that the fees waived had never been freely available to the director concerned but had been voted only on condition that the director would not be free to draw upon them until a deduction from profits for corporation tax purposes in respect of those fees had been agreed by HM Revenue and Customs (see **15.5** Class 1 Contributions).

Although what is now *SSCBA 1992, Sch 1 para 8(1)(h)* contains provision for refunds to be made of contributions paid by reference to earnings which have become repayable, the DSS made it known that it would use this power only in connection with repayments of contractual maternity pay (ie where an earner on maternity leave receives pay from her employer and, on deciding not to return to work, is obliged to refund the wages paid to her) and no further changes have been made to this provision since the 'transfer' of functions to the then Inland Revenue in April 1999. [*Refunds (Repayment of Contractual Maternity Pay) Regs 1990*]. In *Martin (Julian) v Revenue and Customs Comrs* [2014] UKUT 429 (TCC), [2015] STC 478, 164 NLJ 7627, a refunded bonus (triggered by his leaving a job before completing a minimum contractual period of service) was agreed to have reduced the taxpayer's earnings for income tax purposes. However, it is of no relevance to Class 1 liability, as the tax decision turned on *ITEPA 2003, s 11(2)*, which explicitly contemplates the possibility of earnings for the year being negative because of deductions from earnings.

However, that is not the only decision that highlights a difference between tax and NIC law. A close company (S) waived a loan to its controlling director (F). It was accepted that this gave rise to a charge to income tax under what is now *CTA 2010, s 455*, and that this took precedence over the employment income charge under *ITEPA 2003, s 188*. HMRC issued a ruling that the waiver of loan gave rise to a liability to Class 1 National Insurance contributions. S appealed. The First-Tier Tribunal dismissed the appeal. Judge Radford observed that 'the shareholders had not been consulted on the waiving of the loans', which had been approved by S's directors. Accordingly it appeared that the waiver was in respect of F's employment rather than in respect of his shareholding. Therefore it constituted remuneration which was subject to Class 1 contributions. *Stewart Fraser Ltd v HMRC* FTT [2011] UKFTT 46 (TC), TC00923. The decision does not mean that every loan waiver in favour of a shareholder-director will constitute a payment of earnings, although it seems that there will be such a presumption on the part of HMRC. If a loan to a participator is waived by a meeting of shareholders by way of a dividend, rather than by the board, HMRC's presumption ought to be rebuttable.

Calculation of contributions

[22.6] Calculation of primary and secondary Class 1 contribution liabilities in respect of the earnings of a company director proceeds largely in the same manner as does the calculation of contribution liabilities in respect of the earnings of any other employed earner. However, the following special rules apply:

(a) payments made to a company director may be regarded as earnings for contribution purposes before they would be so regarded in general law (see **22.4** above); *and*

(b) a company director's *earnings period* will be a *year* (or, if he is appointed a director during the course of a year, so much of the tax year as remains), whether or not he remains a director throughout the year or throughout so much of it as remains after his appointment (see **34.12** EARNINGS PERIODS); *and*

(c) where a company director has one or more other employed earner's employments the earnings of which fall to be aggregated with his earnings as a company director, special rules are to apply as to the length of the common earnings period (see **5.10** AGGREGATION OF EARNINGS);

(d) a company director's earnings period will be a *year* in respect of any earnings paid to him in any tax year *after he ceases to be a director* if those earnings relate to a period during which he was a director (see **34.12** EARNINGS PERIODS), and such earnings are under no circumstances to be aggregated with other earnings (see **5.8** AGGREGATION OF EARNINGS).

[*Social Security (Contributions) Regulations 2001, SI 2001/1004, Reg 8, Reg 22(2)*].

The combined effect of (a) and (b) above is to require Class 1 contributions in respect of each payment of earnings made to a company director during a tax year to be paid to HMRC within 14 days (17 days if payment is made electronically, whether compulsorily or voluntarily) of the end of the tax month (or, if quarterly payments are permitted, the quarter) in which each such payment of earnings is made, but to require the amount of contribution liability in respect of each such payment to be calculated by reference to the *annual* Upper and Lower Earnings Limits, and the primary and secondary Earnings Thresholds applicable for the tax year as a whole in which the payments fall (see **21.5** COLLECTION and EARNINGS LIMITS **28**). This being so, neither the normal exact percentage method nor the normal tables method of calculation may be used (see **15.9** CLASS 1 CONTRIBUTIONS: EMPLOYED EARNERS). Instead, a modified version of one or the other method must be applied.

The *modified exact percentage method* requires the carrying-out of the following procedure on each occasion of payment of earnings to a director during 2018–19.

(a) Add the amount of the payment of earnings in question to the total of all other payments of earnings to the director since 6 April 2018 or, if he was not appointed director until after 6 April 2018, since the date of his appointment.

(b) Compare the total arrived at in (a) with the annual (or, where the director was appointed after the start of the tax year, pro-rata annual) Lower and Upper Earnings Limits, and the primary and secondary Earnings Thresholds for the tax year in which the payment falls (see **33.4** EARNINGS LIMITS AND THRESHOLDS).

(c) If the total arrived at in (a):

(i) does not exceed the Lower Earnings Limit arrived at in (b), and the director has no other source of earned income, and there are no other employees for whom an FPS must be submitted, proceed no further for there is *no* liability on any of the payments to date in the tax year, including the payment in question, nor do any entries fall to be made on an FPS for RTI reporting purposes (but for pre-RTI years, no action beyond recording the payment on a P11 deductions working sheet was necessary);

(ii) does not exceed the Lower Earnings Limit arrived at in (b) but the director is liable to tax because he or she has a BR, D0 or D1 PAYE code, or because there are other employees for whom an FPS must be submitted, the earnings must be reported on an FPS on or before the date of payment (or, in qualifying micro-businesses, by the date of the last payment of earnings in the month), although contributions due will be shown as nil (for pre-RTI periods, see (i) above);

(iii) equals or exceeds the Lower Earnings Limit but does not exceed the Earnings Threshold, there is *no* liability on any of the payments to date in the tax year, including the payment in question, *but* entries will need to be reported on an FPS (pre-RTI they would have fallen to be recorded in columns 1a and 1b on the P11 deductions working sheet);

(iv) exceeds the Earnings Threshold but does not exceed the Upper Earnings Limit arrived at in (b), calculate contribution liabilities on the *total* arrived at in (a) and *deduct* therefrom the contribution liabilities already accounted for on *all* previous payments of earnings contained in the total. The remainders are the contribution liabilities on the payment in question due to be reported on an FPS (pre-RTI on a P11);

(v) exceeds the Upper Earnings Limit arrived at in (b), calculate the primary Class 1 contribution liability on an amount equal to the Upper Earnings Limit as arrived at in (iii) for the main rate (whether not contracted-out, contracted-out, married woman's reduced rate, etc), plus from 6 April 2003 the additional rate (currently 2%) on the excess and calculate the secondary Class 1 contribution liability on the total amount arrived at in (a), then *deduct* from the contribution liabilities so calculated the contribution liabilities already accounted for on *all* previous payments of earnings contained in the total. The remainders are the contribution liabilities on the payment in question to be reported on an FPS (pre-RTI recorded on a P11).

The *modified tables method* also requires step (a) above to be taken, but then, if the director concerned was a director at the beginning of the tax year, the total thus arrived at has to be *divided by 12*. If the director concerned was not appointed a director until after the start of the tax year, the total arrived at in (a) has to be divided by the number of remaining contribution weeks in the tax year including that in which his appointment took place. An average monthly (or, as the case may be, weekly) amount is thus obtained based on earnings to date. The monthly (or, as the case may be, weekly) contribution tables (and, if necessary, the contribution calculator located at the end of the contribution tables) is then used to ascertain the primary and secondary Class 1 contribution liabilities appropriate to such average earnings, *and those liabilities must then be multiplied by the divisor* which was used to obtain those average earnings. The total contribution liabilities already accounted for on the total earnings arrived at in (a) has then to be deducted from the total contribution liabilities thus calculated and the remainders are the contribution liabilities due on the payment of earnings in question. If the average earnings exceed the highest band figure in the contribution tables, the contribution calculator located at the end of the contribution tables has to be used to determine the extent of that secondary Class 1 liability. (CA44 (2018), Paras 38 to 44).

Example

Frederick is appointed a director of Great Ltd on 1 November 2018. There are 23 whole or part contribution weeks left in 2018–19, not counting for this purpose the one day which constitutes week 53 (Leaflet CA44 (2018), para 24). His earnings period as a director is therefore 23 weeks. As the weekly Earnings Thresholds and the Upper Earnings Limit for 2018–19 are £162.00 (employee), £162.00 (employer) and £892.00 respectively, F's Earnings Thresholds and Upper Earnings Limit are £3,726.00 (ie £162 × 23), £3,726 (ie £162 × 23) and £20,516.00 (ie £892.00 × 23). (The calculation of these limits and thresholds is necessary only if contributions in respect of earnings are to be calculated by use of the modified exact percentage method.) Not contracted-out earnings are paid to F as follows:

Date	*Payment*	*Cumulative*
	£	£
30 November	700	700
31 December	800	1,500
31 January	5,000	6,500
28 February	900	7,400
31 March	13,600	21,000

Contributions could be calculated by use of either the *modified exact percentage method* or the *modified tables method.*

The *modified exact percentage procedure* would operate thus:

Cum Pay			Cum Primary	*Primary payable*	Cum secondary	Secondary payable
£			£	£	£	£
700	Nil%	× £700	—	—	—	—
1,500	Nil%	× £1,500	—	—	—	—
6,500	Nil%	× £3,726	—	—		
	Nil%	× £3,726			—	—
	12%	× £6,500 – 3,726	332.88	332.88		
	13.8%	× £6,500 – 3,726			382.81	382.81
7,400	Nil%	× £3,726				
	Nil%	× £3,726				
	12%	× £7,400 – 3,726	440.88	108.00		
	13.8%	× £7,400 – 3,726			507.01	124.20
21,000	Nil%	× £3,726				
	Nil%	× £3,726				
	12%	× £20,516 – 3,726	2,014.80			
	2%	× £21,000 – 20,516	9.68			
			2,024.48	1,583.60		
	Nil%	× £3,726				
	13.8%	× £21,000 – 3,726			2,383.81	1,876.80
				£2,024.48		2,383.81

Alternatively, the *modified tables procedure* Table A (CA38) could have operated, thus:

Cum.Pay ÷ 23	Weekly table band	Primary per table × 23	Primary payable	Secondary per table × 23	Secondary payable
£	£	£	£	£	£
30.43	—	—	—	—	—
65.22	—	—	—	—	—
282.61	282.00	332.58	332.58	382.49	382.49
321.74	321.00	440.22	107.64	506.23	123.74
913.04	892 + 21	2,024.46	1,584.24	2,383.72	1,877.49
			£2,024.46		£2,383.72

The above procedures are set out in CA44 (2018), Paras 41 to 44 (and in earlier years in Employer's Help Book E13, pages 11 and 12). It will be noted that there are only minor discrepancies between the two results.

Payments on account and in advance

[22.7] Because it will very often be some time before a director's earnings in a tax year reach the Earnings Threshold for that year, the authorities have always been agreeable to amounts of contributions being paid on account during that period of nil liability. Furthermore, if the level of earnings which a director will attain by the end of the tax year can be estimated with some degree of certainty, the authorities are also agreeable to the primary and secondary Class 1 contribution rates appropriate to earnings at that anticipated level being applied throughout the year. The effect of both practices will be to spread contribution liabilities as evenly as possible over the period to the date on which the director's earnings reach the UEL for the director himself. (CA 44, Paras 45 to 48). If contribution-spreading of the type permitted is put into effect but, for some reason, the anticipated level of earnings is not attained, any overpayment of contributions which arises will be repayable. (CA 44, Para 61). In practice, this method is extremely cumbersome to operate in any event given the additional rate liability for the director on earnings above the Upper Earnings Limit, in addition to the zero rate to the Earnings Threshold and the positive main rate in between. The procedure introduced in 1999 described below will be preferred in most circumstances. Corrections submitted on an FPS or an EYU may also result in questions being asked by HMRC.

The former DSS did not consent to contribution liability being spread evenly over the whole earnings period if this would result in less contributions being accounted for month by month than were actually due. However, it has been permissible since 6 April 1999 to pay on account provided that there is a regular pattern of payments to the director, they exceed the relevant Lower Earnings Limit and the director agrees to this method being adopted (CA 44, Paras 6 to 9). Note that not all of these stated requirements seem to have the force of law. [*Social Security (Contributions) Regulations 2001, SI 2001/1004, Reg 8(6)*].

In neither of the above cases may the approach be simply adopted, however, without further attention at the end of the tax year. Either of these methods is only provisional and the annual (or pro-rata annual) earnings period is not displaced. Accordingly, it is necessary to carry out a check when making the final payment of earnings in the year applying the annual (or pro-rata annual) earnings period to the annual earnings as finally known, accounting for any variances in contributions which variations in the levels of pay, etc during the year have thrown up. The correct cumulative annual totals must be included in the final FPS for the year.

Non-executive and nominee directors

[22.8] Contribution liabilities in respect of earnings paid to a non-executive director are to be calculated and discharged in just the same way as they would be calculated and discharged in the case of any other director, except where:

- the director is a partner in a firm carrying on a profession, and
- being a director of a company is a normal incident of membership of that profession and of membership of the director's firm, and
- the director is required by the terms of his partnership to account to his firm for the payment, and
- the payment forms an insubstantial part of the gross returns of the firm.

In such circumstances, the payments made to the director are to be excluded from his earnings for contribution purposes. [*Social Security (Contributions) Regulations 2001, SI 2001/1004, Reg 27(1)(2)*]. (CA 44, Para 56). Instead, the payments will be included in the trading, etc profits subject to Class 4 liability as part of the profits of the partnership. *Social Security (Contributions) Regulations 2001, SI 2001/1004, Reg 27(1)(2)* gives legal force to an Extra-Statutory Concession (almost matching ESC A37, Para 1) which has been available since 6 April 1984. Further, from 6 April 1996, for the purpose of *Social Security (Contributions) Regulations 2001, SI 2001/1004, Reg 27(5)* only, 'company' has been defined so as to match the definition in *ITEPA 2003, Sch 1, Part 2*.

Since 6 April 1991, this rule has applied not only to company directors but also to building society directors.

It should be noted that neither the law nor the concession applies where a non-executive director, although holding his directorship as an incident of his profession, is a *sole practitioner*. In such a case, fees paid to him in his capacity as a non-executive director are liable to Class 1 contributions in the normal way. If such a practitioner chooses to include as a receipt of his practice fees which he has received in his capacity as a non-executive director, he will render those fees—which will already have suffered a primary Class 1 deduction—liable, as part of his profits or gains, to CLASS 4 CONTRIBUTIONS **20**. In such circumstances he may be excepted from part of his Class 4 liability and such exception may be more easily obtained from 6 April 2003 (see **20.6** CLASS 4 CONTRIBUTIONS).

(See CA Press Release 96/1, 15 March 1996.)

Nominee directors who do not benefit personally from the fees paid for their services are also covered by *Social Security (Contributions) Regulations 2001, SI 2001/1004, Reg 27(3)(4)*. The exclusion of their fees from earnings is discussed at **29.68** EARNINGS FROM EMPLOYMENT: GENERAL. See also CA 44, Para 56.

Multiple directorships

[22.9] Where a person is both a director and an employee of but a single company, his earnings in both capacities must be aggregated for contribution purposes (see AGGREGATION OF EARNINGS 5). (Leaflet CA 44, Para 50). If, however, his directorships (other than nominee directorships—see 29.65 EARNINGS FROM EMPLOYMENT: GENERAL) and/or employments extend to more than one company, contribution liabilities will arise in each company in respect of his earnings from that company without regard to his earnings from the other company or companies (see **15.2** CLASS **1** CONTRIBUTIONS) *unless* the circumstances are such that AGGREGATION OF EARNINGS **5** may, or must, take place. (Leaflet CA 44, Para 51).

Directors who are also self-employed

[22.10] A company director who is also a self-employed earner will generally be liable for Class 1, Class 2 and Class 4 contributions if, in the case of Class 1 and Class 4, his earnings reach a sufficiently high level for such liabilities to arise (see EARNINGS LIMITS AND THRESHOLDS **33**). He will not be so liable if he is not normally self-employed (see **14.18** CATEGORISATION) or has been *excepted* from, or has *deferred*, Class 2 (2014–15 and earlier years only) and/or Class 4 liabilities (see **18.4** CLASS **2** CONTRIBUTIONS; **20.5** CLASS **4** CONTRIBUTIONS; **27.8** DEFERMENT OF PAYMENT). If, however, the total contributions paid exceed his personalised ANNUAL MAXIMUM **7** he will be able to obtain repayment of the excess (see **55.8** REPAYMENT AND REALLOCATION).

Since 6 April 2000, the hiring of individuals through their own service companies to work in so-called 'disguised employment' has no longer benefitted from the fiscal advantages offered by a corporate structure. The use of such personal service companies had until then resulted in less tax and NICs being paid. It was intended that the changes would ensure that people working in 'disguised employment' will be paying the same tax and NICs as someone employed directly. However, it is not at all clear that HM Revenue and Customs has had the success in terms of extra income that it had expected from these provisions. Indeed, there was a subsequent proliferation of 'managed service companies' and 'composite companies', which the government legislated against in *Finance Act 2007* with effect from 6 April 2007. The same change for NIC and also the transfer of debt provisions came into effect in August 2007. See also **40** INTERMEDIARIES and CWG2, paras 122–123; Employer's Bulletin Issue 4, February 2000, page 11, **14.13 CATEGORISATION** and www.gov.uk/ir35-find-out-if-it-applies.

With the entry into force of the provisions of *NICA 2014, s 15* on 13 May 2014, those supplying their services as directors to client companies through the medium of a personal service company fell unequivocally within the IR35 regime, and the NIC legislation was updated in line with the tax legislation that had been changed from 6 April 2013 by *FA 2013, s 22*, following adverse press comment about certain high-profile public sector jobs being occupied by directors of personal service companies.

SSCBA 1992, s 4A imported the IR35 intermediaries regime into NIC law by creating, via the *Social Security Contributions (Intermediaries) Regulations 2000, SI 2000/727*, a deemed payment of Class 1 earnings on 5 April each year if the individual would have been regarded as 'employed in employed earner's employment by the client' if the corporate 'wrapper' was stripped away. The definition of 'employed earner' already included, before the 2014 change, only those working under a contract of service or in an office with 'general earnings', an income tax definition that had been inserted in an attempt at harmonisation of income tax and NICs law after *ITEPA 2003* was implemented. It was theoretically possible to work through a personal service company as a director of the client, charging a fee and drawing fees from the service company, without there being any 'general earnings'. HMRC already believed that personal service company owners working as directors of their client companies were within the IR35 rules for NIC before the tax rules were changed in 2013, so it seems the 2014 change to *SSCBA 1992* was intended to tidy up the legislation and close any possible loophole by reinstating the old National Insurance definition of 'employed earner'.

Changes during the earnings period

Attaining an age threshold

[22.11] Where, after 6 April 1983, a director attains pensionable age during the course of a tax year, his earnings period is, according to normal rules, the tax year during which the change occurs, but the only earnings to be taken into account for *primary* Class 1 contribution purposes are those both paid and due for payment before pensionable age is attained and those paid after pensionable age is attained but due for payment before that date (see **3.7** AGE EXCEPTION). (CA 44 (2015), Para 58.2).

Where, after 4 April 2005, a female director aged over 60 has a full gender recognition certificate issued so that thereafter he is then recognised as a man under state pension age, the earnings period rule is amended so that the otherwise annual (or pro-rata annual) earnings period will be split into two at the effective date. Employee contributions are then payable only in the second such earnings period in the year of change. [*Social Security (Contributions) Regulations 2001, SI 2001/1004, Reg 8(7)*, inserted by *Social Security (Contributions) (Amendment No 3) Regulations 2005, SI 2005/778*].

Where, during the course of a tax year, the *reduced liability election* of a director who is a married woman or widow ceases to be valid (see **54.8** REDUCED LIABILITY ELECTION), standard rate primary Class 1 contributions are payable on all earnings paid after the date on which the reduced rate certificate is cancelled. (CA44 (2018), Para 59).

Where a young director under the age of 21 reaches that age after 6 April 2015, when the 0% rate of secondary liability was introduced for under-21s, the company pays the normal rate of NICs on earnings paid or due to be paid from that birthday onwards. Reaching the age of 21 has no effect on primary liability. The category of contribution payable will change from Table M to Table A – not contracted-out, or from Table I to Table D – contracted-out. The exact percentage method must be used, but there is no apportionment of earnings between weeks worked under the age of 21 and weeks worked after that birthday; liability is determined by the payment date. (CA44 (2018), Para 58).

Similar principles apply where a director who is a qualifying apprentice reaches the age of 25 during the annual or pro rata earnings period: Table A replaces Table H and, for any earnings paid or due to be paid (ie, where unconditional entitlement arises) before the relevant birthday, the 0% secondary rate applies, but the standard rate applies from that birthday onwards. (CA44 (2018), Para 58.1).

Changes between COSR, COMP, etc employments

[22.12] Where, during the course of a tax year before 2016–17, when contracting out was still a feature of the NIC system, a director's employment changed from CONTRACTED-OUT EMPLOYMENT 23 to not contracted-out employment, or *vice versa* and total earnings reached or exceeded the annual (or pro-rata annual) Earnings Threshold but contracted-out earnings did not reach or exceed that amount, the primary Class 1 liability for the year was arrived at by applying the not contracted-out primary percentage to the chargeable earnings up to and including the annual (or pro-rata annual) Upper Earnings Limit (ie those exceeding the Primary Threshold) and charging the additional rate on the excess. The secondary liability was arrived at by applying the secondary not contracted-out percentage to the earnings which exceeded the Secondary Threshold.

If there was such a change but contracted-out earnings reached or exceeded the annual (or pro-rata annual) Earnings Threshold then the primary Class 1 liability for the year was arrived at by:

- treating the Earnings Threshold as comprising wholly contracted-out earnings,
- then applying the primary contracted-out percentage to the balance of contracted-out earnings up to and including the annual (or pro-rata annual) Upper Accrual Point,
- then, if the Upper Accrual Point had been exceeded, applying the primary not contracted-out percentage to any balance of not contracted-out earnings up to and including the annual (or pro-rata annual) Upper Earnings Limit, and
- then, if total earnings exceeded the Upper Earnings Limit, charging additional rate contributions on the excess.

The secondary liability was arrived at by applying the secondary contracted-out percentage to the contracted-out earnings which exceeded the Earnings Threshold but did not exceed the Upper Accrual Point and the secondary not contracted-out percentage to all the other earnings.

Up to the 2011–12 year if there was such a change where contracted-out earnings reached or exceeded the annual (or pro-rata annual) Earnings Threshold and the director had an appropriate personal pension, the primary Class 1 liability for the year will have been arrived at by:

- treating the Earnings Threshold as comprising wholly not contracted-out earnings,
- then applying the primary *not* contracted-out percentage to the balance of chargeable not contracted-out earnings up to and including the annual (or pro-rata annual) Upper Accrual Point (ie those exceeding the Earnings Threshold) together with (if the not contracted-out earnings alone do not reach the Upper Accrual Point) the primary contracted-out rate on any balance of earnings up to the Upper Accrual Point, and
- then, if the Upper Accrual Point has not already been exceeded, applying the primary not contracted-out percentage to any balance of contracted-out earnings up to and including the annual (or pro-rata annual) Upper Earnings Limit, and

- then, if total earnings exceed the Upper Earnings Limit, charging additional rate contributions on the excess.

The secondary liability will have been arrived at by applying the not contracted-out percentage to the not contracted-out earnings exceeding the Earnings Threshold, and the contracted-out percentage to the contracted-out earnings up to the Upper Accrual Point. Any balance of earnings above the Upper Accrual Point will have attracted the not contracted-out secondary rate.

It should be noted that, while contracting out via a money purchase arrangement was still possible, a director who chose to contract out with an appropriate personal pension continued to pay contributions at the not contracted-out rates (Table A). This would *not* therefore have been a 'change in employment status' for the purpose of the rules described above. Those rules would, however, have become relevant if the director had ceased to contribute to the personal pension and joined the company's contracted-out occupational scheme. With contracted out rebates for COMPS and APP arrangements having been abolished, from 6 April 2012 the above arrangements can no longer apply.

Example (1)

Greenfinch, a director of Starling Ltd, left S's occupational pension scheme on 16 April 2015. His earnings were £1,000 before the change and £13,000 after the change. As G's earnings from his contracted-out employment did not exceed the annual ET (£8,060), Class 1 liabilities arose as follows:

Primary:		
£8,060	× Nil% =	£0.00
£5,940	× 12% =	£712.80
£14,000		£712.80
Secondary:		
£8,112	× Nil% =	£0.00
£5,888	× 13.8% =	£812.54
£14,000		£812.54

Example (2)

Redwing was appointed a director of Starling Ltd on 7 May 2015 so his pro-rata limits were:

Lower Earnings Limit	£5,376 (ie £112 × 48)
Primary Threshold	£7,440 (ie £155 × 48)
Secondary Threshold	£7,488 (ie £156 × 48)
Upper Accrual Point	£36,960 (ie £770 × 48)
Upper Earnings Limit	£39,120 (ie £815 × 48)

He was not an employee of S at all prior to that date. He joined S's contracted-out salary-related (COSR) occupational pension scheme on 2 August 2015. His earnings were £11,550 before the change and £40,000 after the change. As R's earnings from his contracted-out employment exceeded the pro-rata Earnings Thresholds Class 1 liabilities arose as follows:

Primary:		
£2,064	× -1.4% =	(£28.90)
	(primary rebate from LEL to PT)	
£7,440	× Nil% =	£0.00
£29,520	× 10.6% =	£3,129.12
£2,160	× 12% =	£259.20
£12,430	× 2% =	£248.60
£51,550		£3,608.02
Secondary:		
£2,112	× -3.4% =	(£71.81)
	(secondary rebate from LEL to ST)	
£7,488	× Nil% =	£0.00
£29,472	× 10.4% =	£3,065.09
£14,590	× 13.8% =	£2,013.42
£51,550		£5,006.70

Example (3)

This example illustrates the position in 2011–12 for information. As is now the case with COSR employments, such calculations are no longer appropriate as contracting out by money purchase pension was abolished on 5 April 2012.

The basic facts are as in Example (2), using 48 weeks as the pro rata earnings period but 2011–12 weekly figures and rebate rates. However, Redwing had an APP before joining the occupational scheme. Class 1 liabilities arose as follows. The not contracted-out earnings took priority, so there was no rebate due on earnings between the LEL and the earnings threshold.

Primary:		
£6,672	× Nil% =	£0.00
£4,878	× 12% =	£585.36
£11,550		£585.36
£25,410	× 10.4% =	£2,642.64
£36,960		£3,228.00
£2,256	× 12% =	£270.72
£12,284	× 2% =	£245.68
£51,550		£3,744.40
Secondary:		
£6,528	× Nil% =	£0.00
£5,022	× 13.8% =	£693.04
£11,550		£693.04

£25,410	× 10.1% =	£2,566.41
£36,960		£3,259.45
£14,590	× 13.8% =	£2,013.42
£51,550		£5,272.87

Mitigation of Class 1 contribution liabilities

[22.13] Class 1 contribution liabilities in respect of earnings paid to company directors may be mitigated or avoided by various means. Payments may, for instance, be made in kind rather than in cash but that contribution-free method of paying remuneration is not confined to company directors. Most payments in kind are, in any event, subject to Class 1A contributions (see **16** CLASS 1A CONTRIBUTIONS: BENEFITS IN KIND). The one method which is generally confined to directors is the payment of remuneration by way of a dividend on shares, provided that the company's activities do not bring it within the scope of the intermediaries legislation or the managed service companies legislation (see **40** INTERMEDIARIES). A dividend, being derived from shares rather than from an employment, is not brought within the definition of earnings for Class 1 contribution purposes [*SSCBA 1992, s 3(1)*], subject to anti-avoidance provisions – see **31.6**). Nor is it liable to the extended Class 1A charge. Where a dividend is paid, therefore, it will generally attract no contribution liability. For a typical 'small' company (in corporation tax terms *CTA 2009, s 24*) the only taxes suffered will be the 20% corporation tax, plus the new dividend tax: if the shareholder is a basic rate taxpayer, any dividends over £5,000 per year are taxed at 7.5%; for higher rate taxpayers, the rate is 32.5%; and for additional rate taxpayers, it is 38.1%. Under the pre-2016–17 regime, a basic rate taxpayer suffered no income tax on dividends, and even where the shareholder was a higher rate taxpayer, with an effective income tax rate of 25% on the dividend received, the total tax cost of the shareholder's income will only have been 40%. For 2015–16, extracting a profit of £10,000 from a small company would typically have cost £4,000 if corporation tax was paid and the shareholder-director was a 40% taxpayer. To extract the £10,000 by way of bonus, there would have been an employer NI cost in the calculation.

From April 2015, there has been a single corporation tax rate for non-ring fence profits, initially set at 20%. At Summer Budget 2015, the Government announced legislation setting the rate at 19% for corporation tax years starting 1 April 2017, 1 April 2018 and 1 April 2019; and at 18% for the year starting 1 April 2020. [*Finance No 2 Act 2015, s 7*]. A further reduction to 17% for the year starting 1 April 2020 was announced at Budget 2016. [*Finance Act 2016, s 46*].

Caveat: Where a company is within the scope of the intermediaries or managed service companies rules (see **40** INTERMEDIARIES) any payment of dividend would be rendered ineffective for all practical purposes.

Example 1

Alan Bransdon-Smith and Geoff Legit are directors of Benevolent Ltd, a company not affected by the intermediaries, etc provisions, and each holds 500 £1 shares in that company. On 20 July 2015 it was clear that the corporation tax profits of Benevolent for the accounting period to 31 July 2015 would be approximately £100,000. Both had already been paid £60,000 each in salary, so had already used up their personal allowances and basic rate bands, but it was decided that the company could afford to pay out £10,000 immediately for each of them. This might be achieved by the payment of either bonuses or dividends.

If the company paid a bonus, it would be tax-deductible and subject to employer NICs, also tax-deductible. A dividend would attract no NICs charge but would have to be paid out of post-tax profits, so to determine the more tax-efficient payment method the comparison had to be made between £10,000 of cash to pay remuneration (including the employer NICs) and, allowing for a 20% corporation tax charge on profits, £8,000 of dividends.

An example comparison of the two routes for 2015–16 is as follows:

	Bonus route		*Dividend route*	
	£	£	£	£
Company position				
Pre-extraction profit		100,000		100,000
Bonus pool	20,000	(20,000)		
Class 1 secondary therein (13.8/113.8)	(2,425)			
Gross bonuses to directors	17,575			—
Taxable profit		80,000		100,000
Corporation tax @ 20%		(16,000)		(20,000)
Post-tax profit		64,000		80,000
Dividend		—		(20,000)
Retained Profit		£64,000		£60,000
Personal position				
Gross bonuses		17,575		—
Earnings above UEL already paid				
Primary NICs: 2% × £17,575		(352)		—
Post-NIC bonuses		17,223		—
Dividends		—		20,000
Income tax @ 40% / effective 25%		(7,030)		(5,000)
Post-tax and NI income		£10,193		£15,000

The bonus route cost the individuals in total £4,807, but saved the company only £4,000 because of the NIC costs. The dividend route was therefore more efficient.

The advantage for the dividend route applied, in principle, at all levels of income, but to varying degrees, as the very much simplified table below demonstrates. It follows the same process as above, assuming that the company was owner-managed so that all tax costs effectively fell on the owners; all income tax fell within the single tax band, there was no loss of personal allowance because taxable income did not fall between £100,000 and £121,200; the corporation tax fells into a single band, and leaving distributable profits in the company did not result in its falling into the quarterly instalment payment regime. It takes no account of the fact that PAYE would have been due within a few weeks of payment, whereas tax on the dividend would have been payable later under ITSA.

Dividend or bonus? Effective rates of tax for 2015–16

Income tax rate	**Total tax (IT + NIC) on bonuses**	**Total tax (IT + CT) on dividends**
	0% CT*	20% CT
20%**	40.25%	20.00%
40%	49.03%	40.00%
45%	53.43%	44.45%

* Where the company paid a bonus, it is assumed that it was fully deductible for corporation tax.

** The 10% dividend tax credit was assumed to frank the basic rate liability on the dividend.

The new dividend v bonus decision: 2016–17

The Government announced in the July 2015 Budget (but did not include in the July 2015 Finance Bill) a plan for April 2016 to remove the 10% dividend tax credit, and instead introduce a £5,000 dividend income exemption and, as already noted, an income tax rate on dividend income above the exemption of 7.5% for basic rate taxpayers, 32.5% for higher rate taxpayers and 38.1% for additional rate taxpayers. This is aimed at changing the economics of taking remuneration via dividends and stemming the tide of tax-motivated incorporation (referred to officially as 'TMI' in a 2015 consultation document, although the term seems to have disappeared in 2016 documents). The choices have become much more complex for those taxpayers over or nearing age 55 who can pay pension contributions for later extraction at a lower rate of tax.

The removal of the dividend tax credit and introduction of the £5,000 dividend income exemption was effected from 2016–17 [*Finance Act 2016, s 5*], and the dividend income exemption was then reduced to £2,000 from 2018–19. [*Finance (No 2) Act 2017, s 8*].

It was also announced that one-man companies would no longer be entitled to the employment allowance, ensuring that secondary NICs would be payable in future. The *Employment Allowance (Excluded Companies) Regulations 2016, SI 2016/344, Reg 2* inserted *NICA 2014, s 2(4A)* to specify that, with effect from 6 April 2016, a company cannot qualify for the employment allowance for a tax year if all the payments of earnings in relation to which the company is the secondary contributor in that year are paid to, or for the benefit of, the same employed earner, and when each of those payments is made, that earner is a director of the company.

HMRC takes the view that any second employee taken on by the company must trigger a NIC liability if the entitlement to the employment allowance is to be preserved, but this interpretation is plainly wrong. The new regulation merely requires that a payment of earnings be made to a second earner by the company as secondary contributor. A company that pays £1 of earnings is still a secondary contributor in relation to that payment, so a payment of £1 to a second earner is clearly sufficient to protect the entitlement. Many one-person companies will, however, not wish to enter into arguments with HMRC and will choose to protect the employment allowance to set against the secondary contribution liability in respect of the sole director's earnings by employing a casual worker who earns at least £162.08 in a week, generating 1p of secondary liability for the company in respect of that second earner.

The shareholder-director and his family may still benefit from taking cash out by way of a dividend, but the gap between the two routes has been narrowed by the imposition of the new dividend tax. At low levels of income such as those earned by self-employed workers with no particular skills and no great risks, who incorporate for tax reasons only (eg, using a personal service company at the behest of an agency), the gap will now often not be wide enough to cover the costs of running the company. Assuming income of £30,000, it seems likely that the benefit of taking dividends rather than remuneration might be only around £1,880, or £36 per week with which the worker would have to pay for the company administration.

Example

Gideon is the sole shareholder and director of Folders Ltd, with profits available for extraction after 6 April 2018 of £30,000. He works through an agency and has a (non-IR35) PSC in order to avoid the PAYE rules that apply to self-employed agency workers. Assuming a corporation tax rate of 19% he could declare a dividend of £24,300. Assuming he has no other income, he may pay tax as follows:

	£		Tax £	
Personal allowance	11,850		—	
Dividend nil rate band	2,000		—	
Basic rate band	10,450	7.5%	784	
	24,300		784	net = £23,516

Alternatively, he might pay remuneration to use up the whole sum, thereby paying no corporation tax, but suffering PAYE and NIC liabilities as follows:

	£		Tax/NIC £	
Personal allowance	11,850		—	
Employer NICs in £30,000 – £8,424	2,616			
Basic rate band	15,534	20%	3,107	
	30,000		3,107	
Primary threshold	8,424		—	
Employer NIC (as above)	2,616			
Main NIC rate	18,960	12%	2,275	
	30,000		2,275	net = £22,002

The advantage of £1,514 would have to cover company administration costs. Gideon might benefit by £784 by transferring half of the shares to his spouse, if she has a personal allowance and dividend nil rate band available, but even that advantage is comparatively small.

It should be noted that, where directors require income at regular intervals throughout the year, eg monthly, interim dividends may be paid at the required intervals. To avoid problems with HMRC arguing that such payments are earnings, it is important that the dividends are declared according to the requirements of the company's articles and company law, and that they are correctly documented.

Where it is undesirable that all shareholders should participate *pro rata* in any profits which are to be distributed, waivers (or part waivers) may be obtained from non- (or only part-) participating shareholders as necessary. For a waiver to be effective, however, it must be made and delivered to the company before the shareholder obtains the right to receive the dividend, which, in the case of an interim dividend, arises at the time of payment and, in the case of a final dividend, arises at the time the directors' recommendation is approved by the shareholders in general meeting. (*Lagunas Nitrate Co Ltd v Schroeder & Co and Schmidt* (1901) 85 LT 22, 17 TLR 625; *Re Severn and Wye and Severn Bridge Rail Co* (1896) 74 LTR 219). If a waiver is made voluntarily it must be made under seal.

See also HM Revenue and Customs Trusts, Settlements and Estates Manual TSEM4220 and TSEM4225, which explain that HMRC will invoke the settlements legislation where a waiver represents bounty in favour of a spouse or civil partner (see *ITTOIA 2005, s 624*) or minor child of the settlor (*ITTOIA 2005, s 629*). Where the waiver is made in order to benefit someone other than 'a spouse, civil partner or minor child, the settlements legislation will not apply unless there are arrangements under which the money will be paid to, or used to benefit, the settlor or spouse etc)'.

HMRC can be expected to examine critically any dividend waiver where the following factors are present, although this does not necessarily mean that any challenge to the waiver under the settlement rules would succeed and HMRC fails to explain the grounds for any such challenge.

- The level of retained profits, including the retained profits of subsidiary companies, is insufficient to allow the same rate of dividend to be paid on all issued share capital.
- Although there are sufficient retained profits to pay the same rate of dividend per share for the year in question, there has been a succession of waivers over several years where the total dividends payable in the absence of the waivers exceed accumulated realised profits.
- There is any other evidence, which suggests that the same rate would not have been paid on all the issued shares in the absence of the waiver.
- The non-waiving shareholders are persons whom the waiving shareholder can reasonably be regarded as wishing to benefit by the waiver.
- The non-waiving shareholder would pay less tax on the dividend than the waiving shareholder.

Possible drawbacks to arrangements of the kind described should not be overlooked. These include:

- the possibility that a dividend declared *before* the end of the accounting period to which it relates will (because the profits are not finally ascertained and not reasonably estimated at the time of payment) exceed the profits ultimately found to have been available for distribution and will thus be wholly or partly illegal. [*Companies Act 2006, ss 829, 830, 836*];
- the possibility that the value of any minority shareholdings will be enhanced if a high dividend record is established by the company;
- the fact that dividends are not earnings for pension purposes. This might be a major point for consideration in the case of any director who is approaching retirement age or a younger director who wishes to take maximum advantage of a good trading year to direct earnings into a tax-free savings scheme. However, shareholder-directors can, of course, have the company make employer contributions up to the available annual allowance(s) without needing earnings to qualify for tax relief on such payments (capping tax-relievable contributions at 100% of earnings only applies to employee pension contributions);
- the fact that entitlement to State benefits and statutory payments will be impaired unless remuneration by way of salary is maintained at a level equal to or above the Lower Earnings Limit (see **13.5** BENEFITS; **33.2** EARNINGS LIMITS AND THRESHOLDS);
- the risk that – especially where there is more than one class of share in issue – HM Revenue and Customs might invoke *ITEPA 2003, s 447(4)*. See **31.6** POST ACQUISITION BENEFITS;
- those with a repayable student loan will need to not overlook the fact that repayments will be due under the self-assessment system if unearned income is over £18,330 per annum (or £25,000 per annum for students whose courses started on or after 1 September 2012).

In February 1994, the Contributions Agency issued a note to the ICAEW and other professional bodies in which it admitted that, until August 1992, its view had been that *disproportionate* dividends were not genuine dividends but earnings. The note confirmed, however, that, from that date, its view was that a lawful dividend (ie one paid in accordance with the rights laid down in a company's Memorandum and Articles of Association and out of profits available for distribution) should not (even if disproportionate by reason of waivers) be regarded as earnings for contribution purposes. The note also went on to state that an unlawful dividend *would* be regarded as earnings, but there seems to be no justification for such a stance and this was superseded by HM Revenue and Customs National Insurance Manual NIM12012 (see below). A dividend, whether lawful or unlawful, is derived from shares, not from an employment, and is not therefore within the terms of *SSCBA 1992, s 3(1)*.

The National Insurance Manual states:

> 12012 Directors receive dividends as shareholders in the company and not in their capacity as Directors. Dividends are therefore not earnings for the purposes of National Insurance Contributions. If a company pays an unlawful dividend to its

Directors, or any other shareholder, the money is returnable to the company (Section 277 Companies Act 1985) and is not re-classified as earnings.

See also HM Revenue and Customs National Insurance Manual NIM02115. The manual (NIM12012) has not yet been revised to refer to *Companies Act 2006, s 847*.

Director's liability for company's contribution arrears

[22.14] Where a company is guilty of fraudulent evasion of its contribution liabilities and proceedings are taken against it under *SSAA 1992, s 114(1)* its guilt may extend to its directors if they have consented to or connived in commission of the offence, and they may be proceeded against for the same criminal offence (see **12.6** ARREARS OF CONTRIBUTIONS). [*SSAA 1992, s 115*]. The CA undertook its first criminal case against a director of a 'phoenix' company in 1995 for non-payment of NICs amounting to over £50,000. A fine and costs of £2,400 and £500 respectively were imposed on the director in this case. A 'phoenix' company is one which goes into liquidation only to set up again, very often with a similar name and close proximity to the original company, with the same assets transferred to it at an undervalue. See also Tolley's National Insurance Brief, September 1996 'Phoenix in the Frame'.

The pressure on 'phoenix directors' has been maintained subsequently and in this connection *Social Security Act 1998, s 64* from 6 April 1999 inserted *SSAA 1992, s 121C* (by virtue of *Social Security Act 1998 (Commencement No 4) Order 1999, Reg 2*). It established a new procedure and power for HMRC where a company's failure to pay contributions 'appears' to HM Revenue and Customs to be attributable to fraud or neglect on the part of one or more individuals who were officers of the body corporate, allowing culpable officers to be made personally liable for corporate NIC debts. As well as being liable for their proportion of debt based on their level of culpability, they are liable for accrued and future interest and penalties thereon. The previous sanctions had been limited to a fine of up to £1,000 and the deduction of the director's personal contributions from his NI account. Culpable officers who receive a personal liability notice under *s 121C* face the potential seizure of the culpable director's home and personal assets where relevant. See also DSS Press Release 98/020, 5 February 1998.

HMRC takes the view, seemingly correctly, that *s 121C* may be applied to a company secretary. However, if that is so it would appear not to extend to a corporate company secretary, *s 121C(1)(b)* referring as it does to 'individuals who . . . were officers' as opposed to the wider legal term 'persons'.

Directors, as well as others, might also fall foul of the new *s 121C* procedures where *any* person 'is knowingly concerned in the fraudulent evasion of any contributions which he or any other person is liable to pay'. [*SSAA 1992, s 114* as amended by *Social Security Act 1998, s 61,* effective from 6 April 1999; *Social Security Act 1998 (Commencement No 4) Order 1999, Reg 2*]. A person guilty of this offence is liable to imprisonment for a term not exceeding seven years, or a fine, or both.

Directors of managed service companies and MSC providers became potentially liable, by virtue of *ITEPA 2003, s 688A*, for any arrears of PAYE due from their companies or their client companies respectively, but this rule was not extended to NIC liabilities. *ITEPA 2003, s 688B*, introduced by *FA 2016, s 14(3)*, which also extended the *Income Tax (PAYE)* 2003 by adding *Regs 97ZG–97ZM*, created a new mechanism of personal liability notices that may be served on the directors or officers of a company that is an employment intermediary and that fails to deduct PAYE in respect of home-to-work travel expenses paid to the intermediary's workers. Again, this regime has not been extended to NICs. It is assumed that the threat of being made liable for the tax arrears alone will suffice as a deterrent to potential intermediary and MSCP directors.

Case law — 'phoenixism'

[22.15] In the case of *Inzani v Revenue and Customs Commissioners* [2006] STC SCD 279 Sp C 529 – the first appeal involving *s 121C* – I's appeal against the issue of a personal liability notice was dismissed. The company had never had a bank account and had only one customer. That customer paid net wages to the employees of I's 100%-owned company, but PAYE/NIC was not accounted for. The company was subsequently liquidated and the NIC due remained unpaid.

In *L Livingstone v HMRC* a Scottish company (M) failed to pay more than £60,000 in contributions for the two years ended 5 April 2007. It ceased trading in January 2007. HMRC issued a notice under *SSAA 1992, s 121C* that M's sole director (L), who was a chartered accountant, should be personally liable for the unpaid contributions. L appealed, contending that he had not been guilty of any 'fraud or neglect'. The First-Tier Tribunal reviewed the evidence in detail, rejected this contention and dismissed the appeal, holding on the evidence that M's failure to pay the contributions was attributable to L's neglect. Barton J observed that L 'was aware that these payments were not being made; and that the responsibility for making or withholding payments rested with him'. Furthermore, it was 'significant that when funds did become available from the sale of the business, he still made no payment to HMRC but intromitted with these funds in a manner which in part was beneficial to him personally'. L should have been aware that M was 'hopelessly insolvent', and the evidence indicated that he 'was negligent in the financial management of the Company and in particular in relation to the ongoing and increasing NIC liability'. [2010] UKFTT 56, TC00369. It should be noted that whilst the company had ceased to trade there was again – as in the case of *Inzani* Sp C 529 – no suggestion of 'phoenixism'.

In a case involving a company that went into liquidation in January 1997, one of its directors (Nash) had also been the controlling director of a second company until December 1996, when he resigned and was succeeded by his son. He was reappointed a director in July 1997 and remained a director until that company went into liquidation in December 1997. The former Inland Revenue took proceedings against Nash, contending that, by virtue of *Insolvency Act 1986, ss 216, 217*, he was liable for the tax debts of both companies. The Chancery Division granted judgment for the Inland Revenue, holding that the companies were associated within the meaning of *s 216*, and that N had been involved in the management of both companies at all material times. See *IRC v Nash* [2003] EWHC 686 (Ch), [2004] BCC 150, [2003] BPIR 1138. See also *HMRC v Holland & Holland (re Paycheck Services 3 Ltd and other companies)* Ch D [2008] All ER (D) 319.

More recently, in the case of *Mrs Christine Roberts* [2012] UKFTT 308, a director of a company that had paid no contributions to HMRC during its short trading life, despite paying wages and having funds to do so, was held personally liable for over £40,000 of arrears, one-third of the company's unpaid NIC liabilities. The director accepted that the Class 1 and Class 1A contributions, plus statutory interest, were unpaid, but denied personal culpability. The only area of dispute for the Tribunal to determine related to whether HMRC had proved on the balance of probabilities that the company's failure to pay contributions had been due to fraud or neglect on the part of one or more individuals. She claimed that all payment made by the company had in effect been dictated by the company's principal lender, which had exercised close control over the management of its debtor's funds, but she could produce no evidence to support that claim as all paperwork had been in the hands of administrators and had been lost. Actions had been based on advice from the company's advisers, a firm of corporate restructuring specialists. The tribunal found that she could not delegate her responsibilities as a statutory director to third party advisers and financiers, so held her liable.

Key Points regarding company directors and NICs

[22.16] Points to consider are as follows.

- Directors, whatever their actual payment interval, have an annual (or pro-rata annual) earnings period.
- Where the company pays the personal bills of a director then ordinarily this will constitute a payment of earnings subject to Class 1 NICs, unless the directors' account with the company is in credit.
- Where a married woman's reduced rate election ceases to be valid, or state pension age is reached, additional calculations will be required due to the incidence of the annual earnings period. Switches into and out of contracted-out pension schemes used to require the same type of extra calculation before contracting out was abolished with effect from 6 April 2016.
- In many cases it will be preferable to pay dividends in addition to only a small amount of salary, but all the drawbacks should be carefully considered first, and higher/additional rate taxpayers may find that the dividend tax reduces the advantage of dividends over bonuses quite significantly.
- Directors are not considered workers within the NMW rules unless the director has a contract of employment (written or oral, express or implied) with the employer.

- Directors may need to re-assess their plans in the light of changes made in April 2016 to the employment allowance and the new dividend tax rates.

23

Contracted-Out Employment

Cross-references. See **13.9** BENEFITS for additional pension component; CLASS **1** CONTRIBUTIONS **15**; **53.3** RATES AND LIMITS for contracted-out rates.

Other Sources. Former Leaflets CA 14, CA 14A, CA 15, CA 17, Tolley's Practical NIC Newsletter, May 2006, Tolley's Practical NIC Newsletter, December 2008.

Introduction to contracted-out employment

[23.1] When National Insurance contributions were first introduced as a state pension contribution, all contributions involved a flat-rate stamp on a card every week and, on retirement, a flat-rate pension. The design of the scheme being flawed from the outset, the scheme was always underfunded, as ministers chose not to charge the level of contributions needed to fund the desired benefits. There was never more than £500 million in the NI Fund between 1953 and 1973 (according to DHSS Social Security Statistics, 1974, Table 46), when pensioner numbers were never below 10 million, meaning there was just £50 or less per pensioner in the fund.

To raise money to bail out the NI Fund, which was in clear deficit, a system of 'graduated retirement benefits' was introduced in 1961, charging 4% of earnings between £9 and £18 per week, with the promise that graduated pensions would be paid at retirement (ie, lots of current income for the NI Fund, with most expenditure deferred into the long-term future). By 1975, the upper limit had risen to £62 per week, and the percentage had also crept upwards, but from the outset, employers who already offered a superannuation scheme were allowed not to pay the graduated contribution. In return for contracting to pay a higher flat-rate contribution (at least until 1966) and to forgo the extra benefits, employers paid no graduated contributions. This was known as 'contracting out'.

On 6 April 1978, the *Social Security Pensions Act 1975* came into force and brought into existence a new state earnings-related pension scheme (SERPS), introducing full earnings-related contributions and abolishing graduated contributions, but the contracting-out principle survived the changes.

Under SERPS, basic retirement pension, widow's pension, widowed parent's allowance and invalidity pension were each augmented by an *additional component*, the SERPS pension, which was earned by earnings-related contributions paid on such of a contributor's earnings as fell between the Lower and Upper Earnings Limits (see **33.2** EARNINGS LIMITS AND THRESHOLDS and **13.11** BENEFITS: CONTRIBUTION REQUIREMENTS). Invalidity pension was replaced by long-term incapacity benefit with no earnings related component and, from 27 October 2008, incapacity benefit was replaced by the employment and support allowance for new claimants.

The various widows' benefits were replaced by bereavement benefits in April 2001, available to both widows and widowers and, from 5 December 2005, a surviving civil partner whose partner died on or after that date.

SERPS became the State Second Pension (S2P) in 2002, providing a state earnings-related additional pension, payable to anyone who reached state pension age before 6 April 2016, when *Pensions Act 2014* introduced its replacement, the new single-tier state pension, which has no earnings-related component but may reflect partial SERPS/S2P entitlements earned before the change.

At 6 April 2016, with the abolition of SERPS/S2P (other than for existing pensioners at that date) and the introduction of the single-tier state pension (now known simply as the 'state pension' for new claimants), the system of contracting out came to an end. Every contributor now falls within the new state pension and pays the same standard rates of contribution.

Note that self-employed contributors were never asked to pay contributions at the same rate as employed earners, were never contributing towards a SERPS/S2P pension, and were unaffected by contracting out. It is no coincidence that Class 4 contributions have always been at a similar rate to contracted-out primary Class 1 contributions.

The state pension scheme

[23.2] The basic outline of the state pension scheme remained broadly the same from 1978 to 2016. The provisions of *SSPA 1975* (see **23.1**) entitled a worker who had earned at least at the LEL for enough years to a basic state pension, with, from 1978 to 2016, an extra earnings-related amount based on contributions paid or credited on earnings up to an upper limit.

In summary, earnings between the LEL and UEL (known as 'band earnings') were recorded each year, up to 5 April in the tax year before the individual's state pension age (or earlier death), and at that age were revalued for inflation in the period since they had been earned. The DSS / DWP then took 25% of that figure (later reduced to 20% to save the NI Fund some money), divided it by the number of years in the contributor's working life since 1978, and converted that into an annual addition to the basic pension: the SERPS pension, or additional component, paid in weekly instalments.

The 1975 scheme rules were later incorporated into the *Pension Schemes Act 1993*. Further changes effective from 6 April 2002 introduced a new 'State Second Pension' (S2P) to replace SERPS. From that date to 5 April 2009 earnings between the LEL and UEL attracted a three-tiered rate of pension accrual, biased towards lower earners to improve their retirement provision. Under SERPS, the earnings-related pension had been a flat 25% (later 20%) of all the band earnings. Under S2P, the band was sliced into three tiers. The accrual rate for the lower tier each year was set at 40%, the middle tier at 10%, and the top tier at 20%. At the top of the middle tier, the average rate of accrual was 20%, just as it had been under the later version of SERPS, so in effect those earners in the middle band were subsidising the S2P pensions of those in the lower tier, while those in the upper tier were neither better nor worse off than under SERPS.

From 6 April 2009 onwards an Upper Accrual Point (UAP) was introduced at a fixed permanent value of £770 per week (£40,040 per annum) so that employees in not contracted-out employment then (ie, up to 5 April 2016) only earned the S2P element of the state pension on earnings between the LEL and the UAP, and thereafter paid 12% on amounts above the UAP up to the UEL without earning any extra pension.

Employees who earned at least as much as the LEL, disabled people and certain carers will have been deemed to have earnings equal to the top of the bottom tier, the 'Low Earnings Threshold' (LET), set most recently at £15,300 for 2015–16. [*Social Security Pension (Low Earnings Threshold) Order 2015, SI 2015/186, Reg* 2.] The amount was uprated annually for inflation from its introduction in 2003. From 6 April 2010, S2P accrual was simplified to only two rates, namely from the LEL to the LET and from that point up to the UAP, with the low earnings band attracting a 40% accrual rate and the upper band a 10% rate [*Pensions Act 2007 (Supplementary Provisions) (No 2) Order 2009, SI 2009/3094*]. Because of the fixing of the UAP, each annual uprating of the LET improved the average rate of pension accrual of lower earners and reduced the average rate for higher earners.

Entitlements to SERPS/S2P earned up to 5 April 2016 are relevant to the 'foundation amount' of the new single-tier state pension for every contributor who reaches state pension age on or after 6 April 2016. The DWP will measure accrued state pension entitlements as at that date and, if the aggregate entitlement of the earner in respect of basic state pension, SERPS/S2P addition and pre-1975 graduated retirement benefits would at that point be better than the maximum flat-rate pension calculated under the new rules, the excess will form a protected addition to the new state pension. However, from the same date, it is impossible to accrue further SERPS or S2P additions, however much is paid in contributions.

Contracting-out

[23.3] As briefly mentioned above, S2P (and the former SERPS) was only one part of the UK's historical state pension regime. Not every employer wanted to pay into the SERPS scheme on its introduction in 1978, as many (mostly in the public sector) already had very adequate final salary pension schemes in place. Where an employer made independent arrangements for the provision of earnings-related pensions to its employees through a private occupational pension scheme, the employer was therefore allowed to elect to 'contract out' of the SERPS pension, replacing the additional component with an earnings-related pension from its own scheme. In exchange for removing the SERPS / S2P burden from the NI Fund, both employer and employee were entitled to pay a lower rate of contributions, known as a rebated rate or 'contracted-out' rate. The 'rebate' was reviewed by the Government Actuary every five years.

For salary-related schemes, the contracted-out rebate was always a flat rate for all employers and employees, and it simply reduced the contribution rates for both parties on 'band earnings' (ie, earnings in the band from LEL to UEL, or UAP from 2009). For money purchase schemes, from the point when they were introduced as a means of contracting out, the rebate was age-related, to ensure that contracting out remained attractive for those closer to state pension age. The minimum rebate (for 16-year-olds) was deducted from payroll contributions for everybody in an occupational money purchase scheme, and for older workers an extra age-related rebate was paid by the DSS or HMRC after the year-end.

A scheme was contracted-out of S2P *provided* the private scheme met certain stringent statutory requirements and there was an election by the employer for its occupational scheme(s) or the employee for his personal pension(s). [*PSA 1993, ss 40–49*.] The original arrangement in 1978, when contracting out was limited to final salary schemes (money purchase schemes were permitted but could not contract out), was that the private scheme then shouldered, in place of the state, the responsibility for providing a *guaranteed minimum pension* related to earnings, which was the replacement for the SERPS pension forgone. Schemes were designated 'contracted-out salary-related' or COSR, but because this open-ended responsibility deterred many small employers from making private arrangements for pensions, the reformed contracting out arrangements, from 6 April 1997, offered an employer, as an alternative commitment, responsibility for a *guaranteed minimum level of contributions* to a private occupational pension scheme. Such schemes were known as contracted-out money-purchase or COMP schemes. The guaranteed minimum contribution level was equivalent to the payroll element of the contracted-out rebate. (*Pensions Act 1993, ss 7, 8*.)

It also became possible for employees to choose personally to contract out, on a money-purchase basis only, by way of an appropriate personal pension (APP) policy. In such cases, the employer and employee paid the standard rate of NICs during the year and the DSS (later HMRC) paid the contracted-out rebate directly into the pension policy after the end of the year, once the year-end payroll tax returns had been processed and the level of NICs paid was known.

However, from April 2012 contracting out for money purchase schemes was abolished. The option to contract-out was then only available to those working for employers who offer benefits related to salary (COSR schemes), and that option was abolished on 5 April 2016.

In the past, in order to encourage the establishment of occupational pension schemes of either kind, the Secretary of State for Social Security (John Major MP at that time) had committed, where an occupational pension scheme had first become a contracted-out scheme on or after 1 January 1986 and before

6 April 1993, to making directly to the trustees of the scheme, for a limited period, an incentive payment equal to 2% of the upper band earnings of each employee within the scheme, or £1, whichever was the greater. The incentive was due for each tax week between 6 April 1988 and 5 April 1993 inclusive spent in such contracted-out employment [*SSA 1986, s 7*]. After 5 April 1993 the rate was 1% for a time and the incentive was limited to personal pension policyholders aged over thirty at the start of the tax year (*SSA 1986, s 3* as amended by *SSA 1993, s 1, PSA 1993, s 45* and *PSA 1995, s 138*).

From 6 April 2002, with the arrival of S2P and three tiers of pension accrual based on earnings levels, age-related rebates were banded by age *and* level of earnings, but only for money-purchase schemes (COMP and APP). Tables of such rebates for the years 2002–03 to 2006–07 were in TPN, June 2001, pages 47–48. Similar tables covering the years 2007–08 to 2011–12 were in TPN, May 2006, pages 39–40 having been set by *The Social Security (Reduced Rates of Class 1 Contributions, Rebates and Minimum Contributions) Order 2006, SI 2006/1009*. The rates for 2015–16, for COSR schemes only, were in *The Social Security (Reduced Rates of Class 1 Contributions, Rebates and Minimum Contributions) Order 2011, SI 2011/1036*. Contracting out by means of a money-purchase scheme was abolished from 6 April 2012, so money-purchase scheme rebates set in the 2011 regulations for periods after that date ceased to apply (since the abolition was planned before the 2011 regulations were made, it is open to question why they did not reflect the fact from their inception).

For 2015–16, for the last year of the S2P regime, the employment of an earner in employed earner's employment was *contracted-out employment* in relation to him during any period in which:

- he was under pensionable age; and
- his service was, for the time being, service which qualified him for a pension provided by an occupational pension scheme contracted out under *s 9(2)* (salary-related); and
- the scheme was a contracted-out scheme in relation to that employment; and
- a contracting-out certificate, issued by HM Revenue and Customs NIC&EO, was in force.

[*PSA 1993, s 7(1), s 8(1)*.]

Every employer was required to inform each of his employees, as part of the written particulars of his employment, whether or not his employment was a contracted-out employment. [*Employment Rights Act 1996, s 1(4)(d)*.] Employees who retrospectively became members of the employer's occupational scheme will, along with the employer, have been entitled to a refund of the difference between the not contracted-out contributions and the contracted-out contributions since the retrospective joining date. See CWG2 (2015) para 76.

Under COSR schemes, members were guaranteed a minimum pension, but this was not possible under COMP schemes. Before the abolition of contracting out by means of money purchase arrangements in April 2012, scheme members therefore had certain 'protected rights', which meant that their scheme had to pay a certain minimum level of pension (this restriction was lifted in 2012, well before the 2015 reforms to the rules for taking money flexibly out of private pension schemes). Protected rights could reduce their state pension. Where effect was given to protected rights NIC&EO needed, in certain circumstances, to establish the date this occurred. As a result of membership of a COMP scheme, the additional state pension entitlement of the member, or in the case of death, any widow(er) was reduced by an amount known as the contracted-out deduction (COD). In the case of a widow(er) the amount of COD was related to whether the member had died before state pension age (SPA). From 6 April 1996, in recognition of the fact that men and women could use their protected rights for pension/annuity purposes from age 60, the amount of the COD applied in the case of widows or widowers was related to whether or not effect had been given to the protected rights by the member before he or she died.

From 6 April 1998 until 5 April 2012, contracted-out money purchase schemes (COMPS) were allowed to open up a contracted-out salary related scheme (COSRS) part and operate as a contracted-out mixed benefit scheme (COMBS) either offering protected rights or salary-related benefits depending on which part of the COMBS an individual was in.

From April 2001, 'stakeholder pensions' were introduced (with no NIC impact and therefore no direct contracting out implications: they were just personal pensions and might be APPs if the employee chose to elect), and from April 2002 enhanced earnings-related state pension accrual for lower earners through the State Second Pension (S2P). In the report by the Government Actuary on 'Occupational and Personal Pension Schemes' (Cm 5076) the Secretary of State for Social Security stated:

> The reduced rates and rebates of National Insurance contributions set out in these reports will take effect from 6 April 2002. By then stakeholder pension schemes will have been in place for a year. I considered carefully whether it was appropriate to have different rebates for those contracted-out money purchase schemes or appropriate personal pensions that are set up as stakeholder schemes. I decided that, because the rebate represents the value of the State benefit forgone when someone contracts out of the State scheme, it should make no difference to the amount of the rebate whether the contracted-out scheme was set up as a stakeholder scheme or not. The Government Actuary has, therefore, reported on the same basis for all contracted-out money purchase schemes and for all appropriate personal pensions.

From 6 April 1997 onwards a new range of National Insurance contributions was introduced for members of contracted-out money purchase schemes. The new categories and the designation of the ready-reckoner tables were:

TYPE OF CONTRIBUTION	CATEGORY TABLE LETTER
COMPS CONTRACTED-OUT STANDARD RATE	F
COMPS CONTRACTED-OUT REDUCED RATE	G
COMPS CONTRACTED-OUT STANDARD RATE MARINER (Foreign Going)	H
COMPS CONTRACTED-OUT REDUCED RATE MARINER (Foreign Going)	K
COMPS CONTRACTED-OUT STANDARD RATE – FOR EMPLOYEES WITH DEFERMENT	S
COMPS CONTRACTED-OUT MARINER RATE – FOR EMPLOYEES WITH DEFERMENT	V

These reflected the minimum rebate that was granted via the payroll, with the age-related element being paid separately. Where the date of birth field on the P14 had been completed, a comparison was made with the date of birth held by NIC&EO which could result in enquiries being made to the individual or ultimately the scheme. Any age-related payment was, in these circumstances, suspended until NIC&EO enquiries were complete. Where the date of birth field on the P14 had not been completed, the date of birth held by NIC&EO was used to calculate any age-related rebate.

The date of birth used in the calculation was included in the payment details provided to the scheme.

Form P14 for years up to and including 2011–12 included a space for the Scheme Contracted-Out Number (SCON) to be entered against the relevant COMP earnings. [*Pensions Act 1995, s 137, s 138*].

Since S2P was abolished from 6 April 2016, with the introduction of the single-tier state pension by *Pensions Act 2014*, contracting out was also abolished at the same time. So that HMRC's records could enable the accurate identification of all members of COSR schemes in advance of the changeover, it was provided that all COSR members' payroll reports from 6 April 2014 to 5 April 2016 had to include both the Employer Contracting Out Number (ECON) and the SCON in every FPS for that employee if NICs were paid using tables D, E, L, N, O or W (see www.gov.uk/what-payroll-information-to-report-to-hmrc). Temporary SCONs, sometimes used by employers with old schemes with a long and complex history, were permitted for 2014–15 but were prohibited for 2015–16.

Case law

[23.4] An individual (W) had been in contracted-out employment from 1985 to 1991. He subsequently retired. In 2002, on reaching the age of 65, he began receiving a state retirement pension, the amount of which was reduced because he had been in contracted-out employment. He lodged an appeal to the Special Commissioners, contending that he should be treated as having paid the full rate of contributions. The Special Commissioners rejected this contention and dismissed his appeal, finding that he had paid contributions 'at the reduced rate applicable to contracted-out employment'. See *Wilkinson v HMRC* [2007] STC SCD 9 Sp C 567.

Contribution reduction – rebates

[23.5] Because an employed earner who was contracted-out of the State scheme would nevertheless receive the basic component of his pension from the State, and because that basic component was linked with contributions on earnings at the Lower Earnings Limit, the rate of contribution required on earnings up to that level was, until the introduction of the nil liability on that slice of earnings, the same as that required from an employed earner who was not contracted-out (see BENEFITS: CONTRIBUTION REQUIREMENTS **13**). With effect from 6 April 1999, however, that rate was nil. Prior to this the rate had been 2% on this slice of the earnings for a number of years.

Similarly, but because it is not linked with benefit entitlement at all, the rate of secondary Class 1 contribution required on earnings in excess of the Upper Earnings Limit was the normal rate of secondary Class 1 contribution, ie, the not contracted-out rate. [*PSA 1993, s 41(1)–(1E)*.] Because, however, contributions on earnings between the Lower Earnings Limit and Upper Accrual Point (between the LEL and UEL up to 5 April 2009) were linked with the additional component which a contracted-out earner forwent, those primary and secondary Class 1 contributions were reduced to a contracted-out rate by a 'rebate' (see **53.5** RATES AND LIMITS). [*PSA 1993, s 41(1)–(1E)*.]

Note that contracted-out rebates were given on earnings between the LEL and the UAP, not between the earnings threshold and the UEL, which is the basis of standard contributions liability. This means that earners whose earnings for a period exceeded the LEL but did not reach the ET should still have received a 'rebate', despite having paid no NICs for that period.

From 5 April 2002 until 5 April 2007, the percentages were 1.6% (employee) and 3.5% (employer) for contracted-out salary related schemes (COSRS) and the payrolled rebates were 1.6% and 1.0% respectively for contracted-out money purchase schemes (COMPS). COMPS members also received age-related rebates directly into their scheme from HMRC. [*Social Security (Reduced Rates of Class 1 Contributions, and Rebates) (Money Purchase Contracted-out Schemes) Order 1998, Reg 2(a)*].[*PSA 1993, s 41(1)* as amended by *Social Security (Reduced Rates of Class 1 Contributions) (Salary Related Contracted-out Schemes) Order 2001, Reg 2 and Social Security (Reduced Rates of Class 1 Contributions and Rebates) (Money Purchase Contracted-out Schemes) Order 2001, Reg 2(a)*]. See CWG2 (2012) page 32, para 68 onwards.

From 6 April 2007 to 5 April 2012 the employee and employer percentages were set at 1.6% and 3.7% respectively for contracted-out salary related schemes (COSRS) and the payrolled rebates were set at 1.6% and 1.4% respectively for contracted-out money purchase schemes (COMPS), again with age-related rebates for COMPS members paid after the year-end by HMRC. [*Social Security (Reduced Rates of Class 1 Contributions, Rebates and Minimum Contributions) Order 2006, SI 2006/1009*].

Note that money purchase schemes ceased to be contracted-out after April 2012, from which point members began to pay full standard rate NI contributions again.

In the case of APPs, employer and employee paid standard rate contributions through payroll and all rebates (basic and additional age-related rebates) were paid directly into the policy by HM Revenue and Customs on behalf of the Department for Work and Pensions. Rebates into APPs also ceased with effect from 5 April 2012. Before 6 April 2009, rebates applied between the LEL and UEL. From that date, though, there was introduced a new Upper Accrual Point (UAP), fixed indefinitely at £770 per week. [*National Insurance Contributions Act 2008, s 3*.] For not contracted-out contributors the practical effect of the UAP was simply that no additional S2P entitlement accrued beyond that level of earnings despite full rate contributions being due on the remaining earnings up to the increased Upper Earnings Limit for 2009–10 onwards, which was £815 per week in 2015–16, the last year of contracting out. For those in contracted-out employment, however, not contracted-out rates of contribution applied between the UAP and the Upper Earnings Limit. From 6 April 2012 there was no rebate for money purchase schemes, including APPs. For contracted-out salary related schemes the rebates were reduced to 1.4% for employees and 3.4% for employers until 5 April 2016.

Example 1

Aphid, Bollweevil, Chafer, Dungbeetle and Earwig were all employed in *contracted-out salary related scheme* employment with Flukeworm Ltd. During June 2015, their weekly earnings were £116, £142, £163, £810 and £860 respectively. Their contribution rates and those of F for 2015–16 were, therefore, determined as follows.

A £116 fell above the LEL (£112) but below the ST and PT (£156 and £155 for the employer and employee respectively), so no contributions were due.

However, the employer's contracted-out rebate was due on any earnings in the band from £112 to £116 ie £4 at 3.4% (14p), notwithstanding that there were no employer contributions due and there was an employee contracted-out rebate due of £4 × 1.4% (6p). As no employee contributions were due at this level of earnings, the employee rebate was given wholly to the employer, in addition to the employer's own rebate, so F deducted 20p from his liabilities in respect of other employees at the end of the month.

B £142 also fell below the ST and PT. Therefore, no contributions were due for the week.

However, the employer contracted-out rebate was due on the earnings from £112 to £142 ie £30 at 3.4% (£1.02), and there was an employee contracted-out rebate due of £30 × 1.4% (£0.42). As the employee's contribution was Nil the whole rebate (£1.44) went to the employer.

C £163 fell above both ST and PT. Therefore, contributions arose as follows:

on £112 (LEL)	Nil
on £43 (LEL to PT)	Nil
on £44 (LEL to ST)	Nil
on £8 (balance employee)	employee: (12 – 1.4)% = 10.6% × 8 = £0.85
on £7 (balance employer)	employer: (13.8 – 3.4)% = 10.4% × 7 = £0.73

However, the employer contracted-out rebate was due on the earnings from £112 to £156, ie £44 at 3.4% (£1.50) and there was an employee contracted-out rebate due on £43 at 1.4% (60p). As this was exceeded by the employee contributions due of £0.85, all of it could be used to reduce to £0.25 the deduction made from gross pay in respect of primary NIC. The employer benefitted only to the extent of the employer's own contracted-out rebate, reducing his liabilities in respect of other employees at the end of the month by £0.77.

D £810 fell above the UAP of £770 but below the UEL of £815, so the primary contracted-out rate was due up to the UAP, the primary not contracted-out rate of 12% was due on the balance, and secondary contributions were due on all earnings above the ST as follows.

on £112 (LEL)	Nil
on £43 (LEL to PT)	Nil
on £44 (LEL to ST)	Nil
on £615 (PT to UAP)	employee: (12 – 1.4)% = 10.6% × 615 = £65.19
on £614 (ST to UAP)	employer: (13.8 – 3.4)% = 10.4% × 614 = £63.86
on £40 (remainder)	employee: 12% = £4.80
	employer: 13.8% = £5.52
Rebate	(£0.60) (£1.50)
	£69.39 £67.88

The employer contracted-out rebate was due on the earnings from £112 to £156, ie, £44 at 3.4% (£1.50) and there was an employee contracted-out rebate due of £43 × 1.4% (60p). As this was exceeded by the employee contributions due, all of it benefitted the employee by reducing by 60p to £64.59 the contracted-out NIC deducted from gross pay (to which was added the £4.80 due on the excess over the UAP, giving a total deduction of £69.39). The employer benefitted only to the extent of the employer's own contracted-out rebate on this band of earnings (£1.50), paying a net £67.88 in total.

E £860 fell above the UEL of £815 so the primary contracted-out rate was due up to the UAP, the primary not contracted-out rate was 12% from UAP to UEL, additional rate primary contributions were due beyond the UEL, and secondary contributions were due on all earnings above the ST as follows

on £112 (LEL)	Nil
on £43 (LEL to PT)	Nil
on £44 (LEL to ST)	Nil
on £615 (PT to UAP)	employee: (12 – 1.4)% = 10.6% × 615 = £65.19
on £614 (ST to UAP)	employer: (13.8 – 3.4)% = 10.4% × 614 = £63.86
on £45 (UAP to UEL)	employee: 12% = £5.40
	employer: 13.8% = £6.21
on £45 (balance over UEL)	employee: 2% = £0.90 employer: 13.8% = £6.21
Rebate	(£0.60) (£1.50)
	£70.89 £74.78

In addition, the employer contracted-out rebate was due on the earnings from £112 to £156 ie £44 at 3.4% (£1.50) and there was an employee contracted-out rebate due of £43 × 1.4% (60p). As this was exceeded by the employee contributions due, all of it benefitted the employee by reducing by 60p to £64.59 the contracted-out NIC deducted from gross pay (to which was added the £6.30 due on earnings above the UAP, to give a total of £70.89 deductible). The employer benefitted only to the extent of the employer's own contracted-out rebate (£1.50), leaving a total liability of £74.78 net.

Termination of contracted-out employment

[23.6] Any payments of earnings (including statutory maternity pay, statutory paternity pay or statutory adoption pay) made to a former employee within the six weeks following the date of termination of his employment continued to attract contribution liabilities at the relevant contracted-out rates if his former employment was a contracted-out employment, except where payment was made after 5 April 2016. Any payment made thereafter, however, attracted contributions at the appropriate not contracted-out rates. [*PSA 1993, s 41(2)*.] It is worth emphasising that payments made after 5 April 2016 are not eligible for any contracting out rebate unless they represent entitlements that arose on before that date, and the payroll entries needed to be reported as 2015–16 transactions using an Earlier Year Update.

Reduced rate elections

[23.7] Married women and widows who had the right to pay contributions at a reduced rate (see REDUCED LIABILITY ELECTIONS **54**) might also have been in contracted-out employment. No further reduction of the reduced rate of primary contribution (5.85% in 2015–16) was available in respect of the contracted-out rebate, although the secondary contributor was entitled to the appropriate percentage reduction (ie 3.4% in 2015–16) in the secondary liability on those earnings falling between the LEL and the UAP (between the LEL and the UEL prior to 6 April 2009). [*PSA 1993, s 41(3)*.]

Effect on post-2016 state pensions

[23.8] When the Pensions Act 2014 scheme was being devised, it was recognised that those who had paid contracted-out contributions during their working life could not reasonably be paid the same single-tier state pension as those who had paid full standard rate. Their state pensions are reduced to recognise that their contracting out rebates will have been invested (assuming funded schemes were used) in order to replace the SERPS/S2P pension that they agreed to forgo when contracting out.

Those contributors who reached state pension age on or before 5 April 2016 will receive their state pension under the rules of the 1975 scheme and will be unaffected by Pensions Act 2014, unless they choose to make Class 3A contributions to enhance their 'old' entitlements.

Those who reach state pension age on or after 6 April 2016 will receive their state pension under the new regime. To recognise years of contribution under SERPS/S2P, two calculations are carried out by the DWP as at 6 April 2016, to compare how much pension would be payable under the old and new rules at that date. The higher amount is then the basis, or foundation amount, for future entitlements, and any excess over the new basis is a protected addition to the new-style pension.

This calculation involves making a deduction as at 6 April 2016 for past contracted-out years. The interaction of the new rules with past contracting out is explained in a DWP factsheet: www.gov.uk/government/uploads/system/uploads/attachment_data/file/210299/single-tier-valuation-contracting-out.pdf.

In summary, the calculation uses three different elements, to reflect the years where:

- A GMP was required (1978–79 to 1996–97): The calculation works out how much SERPS pension would have been payable based on the reported P14 earnings, and deducts the GMP due based on the rebates paid. The result is the contracted-out deduction (COD). Any net additional pension still due will be paid by the DWP at state pension age.
- 1997–98 to 2001–02: No additional pension was recorded so no offset is needed.
- 2002–03 to 2015–16: A modified form of the GMP calculation is used to take account of the S2P rules.

The 'foundation amount' is then arrived at as follows:

Basic state pension (old rules based on qualifying years)	A
Add: notional gross SERPS (1978–1997)	+ B
Deduct: contracted-out deduction (as explained above)	– C
Add: notional gross S2P (2002–2016)	+ D
Deduct: S2P contracted-out deduction (based on rebates to employer/scheme)	– E
Total 'old' scheme valuation at 6 April 2016	£ F

The single-tier valuation is then based on:

(Qualifying years ÷ 35) × current single-tier standard pension (£155.65 in 2016–17)	G
Deduct: rebate-derived amount re contracted-out years (ie, pension due from employer's scheme based on rebates paid to it)	– H
Total 'new' scheme valuation at 6 April 2016	£ I

The higher of £F or £I will become the foundation amount. The 'new' scheme pension will then be based on this amount (uprated annually) together with £4.45 (in 2016–17 money terms, uprated annually) per qualifying year between 6 April 2016 and the last 5 April before the contributor reaches state pension age.

It is clear that a career spent wholly in a contracted-out employment will lead to a state pension much lower than the headline £155.65 per week 'flat-rate' amount, and that everyone will have a personal 'flat rate'.

Key Points regarding contracted-out employment

[23.9] Points to consider are as follows.

- Reduced rates of NIC applied to both employer and employee where the employee was in a contracted-out private pension scheme. The rates were always different for salary-related schemes and money purchase schemes.
- The rebates applied from the LEL (even though no contributions were due until the PT/ST is reached) and the UAP (up to the UEL prior to 6 April 2009).
- Where earnings were low, some of the employee's rebate on earnings between the LEL and the PT might have been transferred for the benefit of the employer – there could not be a negative employee contribution.
- There were no contracted-out rebates in the case of COMP or APP schemes after 5 April 2012.
- The whole mechanism of contracting out became redundant, except for the purposes of calculating accrued state pension entitlements, from 6 April 2016 when the *Pensions Act 2014* changes came into force and introduced the new single-tier state pension, abolishing S2P and the earnings-related element of the state pension. All employers and employees now pay standard rate contributions (except, of course, for married women with reduced rate elections, employed deep sea mariners, and employers paying earnings to under-21s and apprentices under 25). This may mean that occupational pension schemes change their own pension contribution rates, as they will no longer have to accrue for the earnings-related element of the state pension that they are currently committed to paying when members reach state pension age. This is explicitly foreseen by the Pensions Act 2014 changes.
- The SERPS and S2P entitlements of not contracted-out contributors over many years will be protected if, at 6 April 2016, they would provide a better pension than the new single-tier pension, but those who have paid rebated contributions and been contracted-out for many years will receive less than the full standard single-tier pension to reflect the fact that they have paid less in contributions over the years.

24

Credits

Cross-references. See BENEFITS **13** for circumstances in which credits may be used to satisfy contribution conditions for benefit entitlement; EARNINGS FACTORS **28** for inclusion or otherwise of credited contributions.

Other Sources. Leaflet CF 411. HM Revenue and Customs National Insurance Manual NIM41000–41420. Tolleys Practical NIC, August 2007.

Introduction to credits

[24.1] National Insurance is a long-term matter, as contributors amass a contribution record towards their state pension over very many years. It is therefore relevant to be aware of how contributions may be credited to a contributor's record over his or her working life.

In relation to periods before 6 April 1987, a credit was a contribution which a person was entitled to have added to his contribution record without any payment being made, for the purpose of bringing his EARNINGS FACTORS **28** for any tax year to a figure which would enable him to satisfy contribution conditions of his own or some other person's entitlement to benefit. [Former *SSA 1975, s 13(4)*]. However, because of a change in the basis on which EARNINGS FACTORS **28** are calculated for 1987–88 and later years, that definition was, from 6 April 1987, extended to include an amount of notional earnings which a person is entitled to have added to his record of earnings for the purpose of increasing his earnings factors. [*SSCBA 1992, s 22(5)*].

The credit consists of an amount of earnings sufficient to raise the individual's earnings factor for the year in question to the annual Lower Earnings Limit. The earnings will be credited in multiples of the weekly Lower Earnings Limit (2018–19: £116). This condition remains tied to the Lower Earnings Limit, despite the fact that, from April 2000, employees have only paid contributions from a higher level of earnings, the Primary Threshold, which has been set at eg £162 for 2018–19. (See **15** CLASS **1** CONTRIBUTIONS).

Where two contribution conditions are specified in relation to a particular benefit, a credit may only be awarded for the purpose of enabling the *second* of those conditions to be satisfied (see **13.5** BENEFITS: CONTRIBUTION REQUIREMENTS). Where a person would be entitled to more credits than are required to bring his earnings factor to the required level, the award is to be limited to the minimum amount necessary for that purpose. [*Social Security (Credits) Regulations 1975, Reg 3(1)*, as amended by *Social Security (State Pension and National Insurance Credits) Regs 2009, SI 2009/2206, Reg 29*].

Credits of Class 3 count towards entitlement to all the basic contributory benefits as explained below. For S2P purposes, for periods before 6 April 2016 when the new state pension regime came into force, a person who earned at least at the LEL but below the Low Earnings Threshold ('LET' – see **13.12**) was given an earnings factor equal to the LET. 40% of the band of earnings between the LEL and the LET was then added to the contributor's notional S2P fund. This regime ceased to apply to contributions made from 6 April 2016 under the new single-tier state pension rules.

The rewriting of the state pension rules led to the extension of the credits regime by *State Pension (Amendment) (No 2) Regulations 2016, SI 2016/240*, so as to encompass the rights arising under both the old and new regimes. A new Part 8 was added to the *State Pension Regulations 2015, SI 2015/173* to create provisions relating to the eligibility for and crediting of contributions for the purposes of the new state pension. In practice, the principles of credits as outlined below remain unchanged, although a new type of credit was added in respect of spouses of armed forces personnel (see below). In summary, any credits of contributions or earnings under the provisions of the *1975 Regulations* are to be treated as credited for the purposes of the new state pension under *Pensions Act 2014*. [*State Pension Regulations 2015, Reg 29*].

The new regulations also ensure that any credits for periods before 6 April 2016 that would have counted towards any Category A retirement pension (ie, the basic state pension based on the contributor's own contributions) are taken into account in assessing the contributor's 'foundation amount', which may form the basis of a protected higher rate of new state pension for those who reach state pension age under the new rules having contributed for many years under the old SERPS/S2P rules. [*State Pension Regulations 2015, Reg 26*]. Since *Pensions Act 2014* abolished the Category A pension, special provisions were needed to ensure that the benefit of any earlier credits was not lost.

Types and rates of credit

[24.2] A credit may be of either a Class 3 contribution or (after 6 April 1987) earnings or (before 6 April 1987) a Class 1 contribution depending on the circumstances in which it falls to be awarded. The amount of the credit awarded is:

- in the case of a Class 3 contribution, the amount of a Class 3 contribution at the rate set for a Class 3 contribution in the year concerned; and
- in the case of a credit of earnings for a year, such amount as is needed to bring the person's earnings factor (see EARNINGS FACTORS **28**) to the level at which the second contribution condition for entitlement to benefit will be satisfied for that year (see **13.5** BENEFITS).

[*Credits Regs, Reg 3(2)*, as amended by *Credits Amendment Regs 1987, Reg 3(c)* for 1987–88 and subsequent years and *Reg 11* for 1986–87 and earlier years].

Where a person is entitled to a credit in respect of a week which is partly in one tax year and partly in another, he is entitled to be credited with earnings or a contribution for the tax year in which the week began and not for the tax year in which it ended. [*Credits Regs Reg 3(3)*, as amended by *Credits Amendment Regs 1987, Reg 3(d)*]. The same principle applies for the purposes of the new state pension. [*State Pension Regulations 2015, Reg 25*, as inserted by *State Pension (Amendment) (No 2) Regulations 2016*, with effect from 6 April 2016].

Age limitations

[24.3] A person cannot be brought within the contribution scheme until he attains the age of 16 and cannot continue in it after he has attained pensionable age, so credits will not be awarded to persons for any years before that in which the 16th birthday was reached or for any years in which state pension age was reached or subsequently (see AGE EXCEPTION **3**). Contributions before the date on which state pension age is reached and after the immediately preceding 5 April will not count towards the pension record. Before RTI was universal, the DWP could not know about such Class 1 contributions until after the end of the tax year, so it could not start to pay a state pension of the correct value from the 60th or 65th birthday if such contributions had to be taken into account. Even though RTI reports are now available, we now have Class 2 contributions due to be reported only by 31 January after the end of the tax year, under the *NICA 2015, Sch 1* reforms), so it is logical that there can be no credits for that same period.

Starting credits

[24.4] On the principle that a person who had entered the contribution scheme, but had not yet had the opportunity to do more than make minimal contributions, should not be penalised as regards his ability to benefit under the scheme, credits were, if necessary, awarded from 1975 onwards to all new scheme-entrants for both short- and long-term benefit purposes. From 2 October 1988 to 5 April 2010 starting credits were only awarded for long-term benefit purposes. No starting credits will be awarded for tax years from 6 April 2010 onwards or for earlier tax years where an application is made for a National Insurance number on or after 6 April 2010. [*Social Security (Credits) Regulations 1975, SI 1975/556, Reg 4* as amended by the *National Insurance Contributions Credits (Miscellaneous Amendments) Regulations 2011, SI 2011/709, Reg 2*].

Class 3 credits

[24.5] For the purpose of enabling a person to fulfil the second contribution condition (see 24.2 above) for entitlement to retirement pension, widowed parent's allowance (formerly widowed mother's allowance) or bereavement allowance (formerly widow's pension), that person is to be credited with sufficient Class 3 contributions to bring his earnings factor in respect of the tax year in which he attained the age of 16 and each of the two following tax years to the required level. [*Credits Regs 1975, Reg 4(1)*]. This type of credit was abolished from 6 April 2010 for the purposes of accruing entitlement to the basic state pension (but not for widow's and bereavement benefits), although past credits remain on the record. [*Credits Regs 1975, Reg 4(1A)*]. No such credits are given either in respect of tax years prior to 1975–76 unless the person was in Great Britain on 6 April 1975 and, though over the age of 16, was not then insured under the pre-1975 legislation. In such a case Class 3 credits for 1974–75 are to be awarded. [*Reg 4(2)*].

> *Example*
>
> At age 16, a contributor decided he wanted to be a PE teacher. Before he could go to university he had to stay on at school to study for 'A' levels.
>
> For the tax years containing the contributor's 16th, 17th and 18th birthdays, and provided these were in tax years 2009–10 or earlier, he had permanent Class 3 credits recorded on his NI account.

No starting credits will be awarded on their return to the UK to an employee of certain European Commission institutions who have opted to transfer their previous UK state pension rights to the Pension Scheme of the European Communities (PSEC). [*Transfer of State Pensions and Benefits Regs 2007, SI 2007/1398, Reg 8(4)*].

Education and training credits

[24.6] Credits are available both during, and at the end of, a period of training, and at the end of a period of full-time education or apprenticeship. Although they appear to belong together, approved training credits and termination credits are connected only superficially and must be considered in isolation from each other.

Approved training credits

[24.7] For the purpose of enabling the second contribution condition (see 24.2 above) for any benefit to be fulfilled, a person who has undergone a course of approved training was, until 3 September 1988, entitled to be credited with earnings equal to the Lower Earnings Limit then in force (see EARNINGS LIMITS AND THRESHOLDS 33 and 53.5 RATES AND LIMITS) in respect of each week of the course falling in 1987–88 or a later year and to a Class 1 credit in respect of each week of the course which fell in 1986–87 or an earlier year, provided that the following conditions were fulfilled.

- the course:
  - (i) was full-time; and
  - (ii) was not undertaken in pursuance of the employment of the person concerned as an employed earner; and
  - (iii) was approved by the Secretary of State for Social Security; and
  - (iv) was, when begun, not intended to last for more than twelve months or, in a case where the person concerned is a disabled person (within the meaning of *Disabled Persons (Employment) Act 1944*) who was undergoing training under *Employment and Training Act 1973* or *Enterprise and New Towns (Scotland) Act 1990* such longer period as was reasonable in the circumstances of the case; *and*
- the person concerned:
  - (a) had attained the age of 18 before the beginning of the tax year in which the week in question began; and
  - (b) had, for at least one of the last three tax years ending before the course began, derived from
    - (i) Class 2 contributions paid or credited; and either
    - (ii) Class 1 contributions paid or credited, if the year was 1986–87 or an earlier year; or
    - (iii) earnings upon which primary Class 1 contributions have been paid or treated as paid or from earnings credited, if the year is 1987–88 or a later year,

    an earnings factor amounting in the aggregate to at least 50 times the Lower Earnings Limit for that year, unless in the circumstances of his case there is reasonable ground for waiving this requirement; and
  - (c) was not a married woman with a reduced rate election in effect in any part of the week in question (see REDUCED LIABILITY ELECTIONS 54).

[*Credits Regs, Reg 7(1)–(3)*, as amended by *Credits Amendment Regs 1978, Reg 2(2); Credits Amendment Regs 1987, Reg 5* for 1987–88 and, until 3 September 1988, 1988–89 and *Reg 11* for 1986–87 and earlier years].

The term 'full-time' has been considered by the National Insurance Commissioners in the context of full-time education for child benefit purposes and held to carry its natural and ordinary meaning so that a course involving morning-only attendance was, though a full course, not a full-time course. (*R(F) 4/62*). If a course is to be approved by the Secretary of State, it must (in addition to being a full-time course) be 'vocational, technical or rehabilitative' (now obsolete DSS Leaflet NI 125). Approval was automatically granted to any such course run by the Training Commission (formerly the Manpower Services Commission), but, in other cases, a Certificate of Attendance at a Course of Training had to be sought by application on form CF 55C.

From 4 September 1988, the conditions under which approved training credits were awarded were changed and, in some respects, relaxed. From that date onwards it has been a requirement that the trainee had attained the age of 18 before the beginning of the tax year in which the relevant week of training began, was not a married woman with a valid reduced rate (see **54.2** REDUCED LIABILITY ELECTIONS) election, that the course, when it began, was not intended to continue for more than 12 months (or, in the case of a disabled person within the meaning of the *Disabled Persons (Employment) Act 1944* who was receiving the training under the *Employment and Training Act 1973* or, with effect from 1 April 1991, the *Enterprise and New Towns (Scotland) Act 1990*, such longer period as was reasonable in the circumstances) and that the course was either:

(a) a course of full-time training (20 hours or more per week); or
(b) if the trainee was a disabled person within the meaning of the *Disabled Persons (Employment) Act 1944*, a course of training which was attended for not less than 15 hours in the week in question; or
(c) a course of training introductory to either (a) or (b).

A disabled person is entitled to credits for a Government funded course which:

- lasts 15 hours a week or more; and
- lasts for longer than a year; or
- is a Guide-Dog for the Blind training course.

[*Credits Regs, Reg 7* as amended by *Credits Amendment (No 3) Regs 1988, SI 1988/1545, Reg 2, Reg 2* from 4 September 1988 and *Enterprise (Scotland) Consequential Amendments Order 1991, Art 3(a)*].

Some courses, particularly those arranged through the Department for Education and Employment, have a preliminary 12-week introductory course. Credits can be obtained for both the introductory course and the main course.

Courses sponsored by the Department for Education and Skills are acceptable for credits which will be awarded automatically or on application.

In respect of the years 1993–94 to 2007–08 some people were incorrectly awarded credits for approved training due to a mismatch between DWP general records and the NIRS2 computer. These were withdrawn and affected persons were invited to pay Class 3 contributions. However, the credits will be treated as having been correctly awarded for the purpose of certain retirement pension, incapacity benefit and contribution-based jobseeker's allowance entitlements already established. See Tolley's Practical NIC, August 2007. [*Credits Regs, Regs 8D, 8E, 8F*, inserted by *Social Security (National Insurance Credits) Amendment Regs 2007, SI 2007/2582*].

With effect from 29 April 2013, training credits will not be granted to a person in respect of any week in any part of which that person is entitled to universal credit. [*Credits Regs, Reg 7(4) as inserted by Universal Credit (Consequential, Supplementary, Incidental and Miscellaneous Provisions) Regulations 2013, SI 2013/630, Reg 70(3)*].

Termination credits

[24.8] The conditions under which, from 1 October 1989, termination credits of earnings equal to the Lower Earnings Limit will be awarded to a person for either of the last two years before the beginning of a relevant benefit year for the purpose of entitlement to contributions-based jobseeker's allowance (previously unemployment benefit) and short-term incapacity benefit (previously sickness benefit) are as follows:

- during at least part of the year concerned the person must have been either an apprentice or someone undergoing:
  (a) a course of full-time education (see above); or
  (b) a course of full-time training arranged under *Employment and Training Act 1973, s 2(1)* or, with effect from 1 April 1991, *Enterprise and New Towns (Scotland) Act 1990, s 2(3)*; or
  (c) any other full-time course the sole or main purpose of which was the acquisition of occupational or vocational skills; or
  (d) in the case of a disabled person within *Disabled Persons (Employment) Act 1944*, a part-time course attended for at least 15 hours a week which, if full-time, would fall within (b) or (c) above;
- the course or apprenticeship must have terminated;
- the year other than that for which credits are sought must be a year for which the EARNINGS FACTOR 28 is not less than 50 times that year's Lower Earnings Limit (see 33 EARNINGS LIMITS AND THRESHOLDS); and
- the year for which credits are sought must not be a year before the person attains the age of 18.

The credits are, however, conditional upon the course or the apprenticeship having commenced before the person attained the age of 21 and having terminated.

[*Credits Regs, Reg 8* as amended by *Credits Amendment Regs 1989, Reg 3, Enterprise (Scotland) Consequential Amendments Order 1991, Art 3(b), Incapacity Benefit Consequential Transitional Amendments and Savings Regs 1995, Reg 6* and *Social Security (Credits and Contributions) (Jobseeker's Allowance Consequential and Miscellaneous Amendments) Regulations 1996, SI 1996/2367, Reg 2(5)*].

Unemployment and incapacity credits

[24.9] For the purpose of enabling the second contribution condition for any benefit to be fulfilled (see **24.1** above), a person (provided not a married woman with a reduced rate election in force during any part of a week concerned—see REDUCED LIABILITY ELECTIONS **53**) is entitled to be credited with earnings equal to the Lower Earnings Limit then in force (see EARNINGS LIMITS AND THRESHOLDS **33** as well as **53.5** RATES AND LIMITS) in respect of each week of unemployment or incapacity falling in 1987–88 or a later tax year (see **24.15**, **24.16** below). This is subject to the proviso that, where the benefit concerned is *contributions-based jobseeker's allowance* or *contributions-based employment and support allowance (ESA(C))*, the person must, in respect of one of the last two complete tax years before the beginning of the benefit year in which the period of interruption of employment falls have:

- derived an EARNINGS FACTOR **28** of *not less than 25 times the weekly Lower Earnings Limit* for that year (26 times with effect from October 2010) (see EARNINGS LIMITS AND THRESHOLDS **33**). Where the benefit concerned is contributions-based jobseeker's allowance, the earnings factor must have been derived from earnings upon which Class 1 contributions have *actually been paid* or treated as paid. When the benefit concerned is sickness or short-term incapacity benefit or EAS(C), the earnings factor must have been derived from such earnings or from Class 2 contributions; or
- been entitled to (or, but for *Overlapping Benefits Regulations 1979*, would have been entitled to) either short-term incapacity benefit at the higher rate or long-term incapacity benefit (invalidity pension) (until 12 April 1995), carer's allowance (previously invalid care allowance), or unemployability supplement in respect of any day in, or any week falling in or partly in, that year; or
- claimed contributions-based jobseeker's allowance, sickness benefit or short-term incapacity benefit / EAS(C) or maternity allowance for some period of that year and has satisfied or may be treated as having satisfied the contribution conditions for such benefit; or
- been entitled to an approved training credit for any week in that year (see **24.8** above); or
- been entitled to a Class 1 credit or to be credited with earnings under these provisions for a week during that year and had exhausted his right to contributions-based jobseeker's allowance or unemployment benefit or sickness benefit or incapacity benefit for that week; or
- been entitled to be credited with earnings from a week which included a day which would have been a day of incapacity but for the fact that the person concerned was a local authority councillor and was, for the week in which the day fell, entitled to an attendance allowance payable under *Local Government Act 1972, s 173(1)* or *Local Government (Scotland) Act 1973, s 45(1)* which exceeded the permitted maximum amount of earnings under *Unemployment, etc Regs 1983, Reg 3(3)*.

[*Credits Regs 8A, 8B*, inserted by *Social Security (Credits and Contributions)(Jobseeker's Allowance Consequential and Miscellaneous Amendments) Regs 1996, SI 1996/2367, Reg 2* as amended by *Social Security*

(Credits) Amendment Regs 2003, SI 2003/521, Reg 2, The Social Security (Miscellaneous Amendments) (No 3) Regulations 2007, SI 2007/1749, Reg 8, Employment and Support Allowance (Consequential Provisions) (No 2) Regulations 2008, SI 2008/1554, Reg 48 and *Social Security (Credits) Amendment Regs 2010, SI 2010/385, Reg 2*.].

Credits under this regulation are awarded automatically for weeks of proven incapacity or unemployment between a claim for benefit and its determination even if the claim is disallowed for other reasons. If an appeal against disallowance of benefit is upheld, such credits are to be awarded for the period covered by the claim, if they have not already been awarded. (18 House of Commons Debates 6th Series Col 414, 24 February 1982).

In respect of the years 1993–94 to 2007–08 some people were incorrectly awarded credits for incapacity due to a mismatch between DWP general records and the NIRS2 computer. These were withdrawn and affected persons were invited to pay Class 3 contributions. However, the credits will be treated as correctly awarded for the purpose of certain retirement pension, incapacity benefit and contribution-based jobseeker's allowance entitlements already established. See Tolley's Practical NIC Newsletter, August 2007. [*Credits Regs, Regs 8D, 8E, 8F*, inserted by *Social Security (National Insurance Credits) Amendment Regs 2007, SI 2007/2582*].

With effect from 29 April 2013, unemployment credits rules were updated in consequence of the introduction of universal credit and the tightening of conditions for a claim for jobseeker's allowance.

Credits are now awarded for any week for the whole of which the person, in relation to old-style JSA (ie, under *s 1(2), Jobseekers Act 1995* before it was amended by the *Welfare Reform Act 2012*) satisfied, or was treated as having satisfied, the conditions for entitlement to JSA. It is also a condition that he must have notified the Secretary of State in writing, with suitable relevant evidence, of the grounds on which he claimed to be entitled to be credited with earnings on the first day of the period for which he claimed to be so entitled in which the week in question fell, or within such further time as might be reasonable in the circumstances of the case. [*Credits Regs, Reg 8A(2)(b), (3),(6)* as amended by *Universal Credit (Consequential, Supplementary, Incidental and Miscellaneous Provisions) Regulations 2013, SI 2013/630, Reg 70*].

For newer claims, which relate to new-style JSA (ie, under the *JSA 1995* as amended by *Welfare Reform Act (WRA 2012), Sch 14, Part 1*), fewer conditions of *JSA 1995, s 1(2)* apply but the applicant for credits must also have satisfied the work-related requirements as to work search and work availability under *JSA 1995, ss 6D and 6E*. The requirement to notify a claim on the first day of the period for which entitlement arises also applies. [*Credits Regs, Reg 8A(2)(ba), (3), (6)* as amended by *Universal Credit (Consequential, Supplementary, Incidental and Miscellaneous Provisions) Regulations 2013, SI 2013/630, Reg 70*].

Credits will be unavailable for any week in respect of which, in relation to the person concerned, an old-style JSA was reduced in accordance with *JSA 1995, ss 19, 19A or 19B* (eg, losing a job through misconduct or leaving a job voluntarily), or a new-style JSA was reduced in accordance with *JSA 1995, s 6J or 6K*, or where the person concerned was entitled to universal credit for any part of that week. [*Credits Regs, Reg 8A(5)* as amended by *Universal Credit (Consequential, Supplementary, Incidental and Miscellaneous Provisions) Regulations 2013, SI 2013/630, Reg 70*].

Week of unemployment

[24.10] A 'week of unemployment' under the pre-29 April 2013 version of the *Credits Regulations* was a week in which each of the days (excluding Sunday or some religiously acceptable alternative day) were *days of unemployment* for jobseeker's allowance purposes, or would have been such days had benefit been claimed within the prescribed time. In this latter event, a day would be a day of unemployment only if the person concerned attended a Jobcentre Plus office, etc and made a written declaration of unemployment and availability for employment on that day or provided alternative evidence of unemployment and availability for employment. Employment during a day would not preclude that day from being a day of unemployment provided that the person concerned was available on that day to be employed full-time in some employed earner's employment (including employment as a share fisherman—see SHARE FISHERMEN 56) *and* the employment in which he was engaged:

- did not engage him for a total of more than eight hours in the week; and
- was (if employed earner's employment) not his usual main occupation or was done for or organised through a charity etc.

Employment might also be disregarded if, even though failing to meet these conditions, the employment was engaged in on only one day of the week and the EARNINGS FROM EMPLOYMENT: GENERAL 29 in that day did not exceed the weekly Lower Earnings Limit then in force (see EARNINGS LIMITS AND THRESHOLDS 33) and he was engaged in no other employment in that week.

A day is not to be regarded as a day of unemployment (or availability for work) if the person concerned is a mariner subject to UK contributions who is on paid leave. A mariner or share fishermen (see SHARE FISHERMEN 56) employed as such on board any ship is treated as available for and actively seeking employment during any period when he is absent from the UK if he would be so available or actively seeking employment but for the fact that he is absent from the UK. In relation to new style JSA, he is also treated as complying with the work-related requirements in *JSA 1995, s 6(2)* during any period of absence from the UK if he would comply with those requirements but for that absence. [*Social Security (Mariners' Benefits Regulations 1975, SI 1975/529, Regs 2, 6* as amended by *Jobseeker's Allowance Regulations 1996, SI 1996/207, Reg 166*, and *Universal Credit (Consequential, Supplementary, Incidental and Miscellaneous Provisions) Regulations 2013, SI 2013/630, Reg 22*].

Week of incapacity

[24.11] A week of incapacity is a week in which each day (other than Sunday or some religiously acceptable alternative day):

- was a day of incapacity for work under *Social Security Contributions and Benefits Act 1992 (SSCBA 1992), s 30C* (incapacity benefit: days and periods of incapacity for work) (except where the person concerned was not entitled to incapacity benefit, severe disablement allowance or maternity allowance but was entitled to universal credit for any part of that week); or
- would have been such a day had the person concerned claimed short-term incapacity benefit or maternity allowance within the prescribed time (except where the person concerned was entitled to universal credit for any part of the week); or
- was a day of incapacity for work for Statutory Sick Pay purposes under *SSCBA 1992, s 151* and fell within a period of entitlement under *SSCBA 1992, s 153*; or
- was a day of limited capability for work for the purposes of *Part 1* of the *Welfare Reform Act 2007 (WRA 2007)* or would have been such a day had the person concerned been entitled to an employment and support allowance by virtue of *WRA 2007, s 1(2)(a)*; or
- would have been a day of limited capability for work for the purposes of *WRA 2007, Part 1* had that person claimed an employment and support allowance or maternity allowance within the prescribed time (except where the person concerned was entitled to universal credit for any part of the week); or
- would have been a day of limited capability for work for the purposes of *WRA 2007, Part 1* where the person concerned would have been entitled to an employment and support allowance but for the application of *WRA 2007, s 1A* (excessive claim duration) (except where the person concerned was entitled to universal credit for any part of the week); or
- fell in a week for any part of which an on employability supplement or allowance was payable by virtue of *SSCBA 1992, Sch 7*, or of *Naval, Military and Air Forces Etc (Disablement and Death) Service Pensions Order 2006, art 12*, or of *Personal Injuries (Civilians) Scheme 1983, art 18*.

A married woman with a reduced rate election in force may not receive a credit under this regulation.

Credits will only be awarded under these rules if the person has, before the end of the benefit year immediately following the year in which the day of incapacity fell, or within such further time as may be reasonable in the circumstances, notified the DWP in writing of the grounds on which the credit is claimed.

[*Credits Regs, Reg 8B*, as amended by *Employment and Support Allowance (Consequential Provisions) (No 2) Regulations 2008, SI 2008/1554, Reg 48(6)*, *Social Security (Credit) (Amendment) Regulations 2010, SI 2010/385, Reg 2; Employment and Support Allowance (Duration of Contributory Allowance) (Consequential Amendment) Regulations 2012, SI 2012/913, Reg 2*, and *Universal Credit (Consequential, Supplementary, Incidental and Miscellaneous Provisions) Regulations 2013, SI 2013/630, Reg 70*].

Over-60 credits

[24.12] Whilst this section refers to those aged over 60, in fact the credit is being slowly phased out over the period to 2018 in line with the rise in the female state pension age (see **3.9**). This was originally set up by limiting its application to men born before 6 October 1954. This meant that women would never be entitled to such credits. In addition, from the 2010 tax year men will only be entitled to receive the credits from the year in which they reach the State Pension Age of a woman with the same date of birth. A woman with a date of birth between 6 October and 5 November 1950 reached pension age on 6 May 2011. A man born in that period will now only be given the autocredits for the four tax years from 2011–12 to 2014–15. Under the *2016 Regulations* creating credits for the purposes of the new state pension, the phasing out process is reflected in the fact that the credits will now only be awarded to men born before 6 October 1953. [*State Pension Regulations 2015, Reg 32*, as inserted by *State Pension (Amendment) (No 2) Regulations 2016*, with effect from 6 April 2016].

For the purpose of enabling the second contribution condition for any benefit to be fulfilled (see **24.2** above), a person is (subject to the limitation described below) entitled, for 1987–88 and later years, to be credited with such earnings as are necessary to bring his EARNINGS FACTOR **28** to the required level in respect of the tax year in which he attained the age of 60 and each of the four succeeding years (but not any tax year in which he is absent from Great Britain for more than 182 days). [*Credits Regs, Reg 9A*, as amended by *Credits Amendment Regs 1987, Reg 9A*; *Credits Amendment Regs 1994, Reg 3* and *Social Security (State Pension and National Insurance Credits) Regs 2009, SI 2009/2206, Reg 30; State Pension Regulations 2015, Reg 32*].

Where, in any of the tax years concerned, a person is liable to pay a Class 2 contribution in respect of any week, he is to be credited with a Class 1 contribution or with earnings, as the case may be, only for weeks in respect of which no contribution of any class is payable and for which he is not entitled to a credit of any description under any other of the Credits Regulations. From 8 August 1994, a self-employed earner is eligible for such a credit of earnings equal to the Lower Earnings Limit only if he or she is liable to pay Class 2 contributions in respect of any week, or, is excepted from liability on the grounds that his or her earnings are expected to be less than the self-employed earners exception (SEE) limit set by *SSCBA 1992, s 11(4)* or, for years from 6 April 2015 onwards, the small profits threshold set by that subsection. [*Credits Regs, Reg 9A(3)*, as amended by *Supplementary Benefit etc Regs, Reg 2; Credits Amendment Regs 1987, Reg 9* for 1987–88 and later years and *Reg 11* for 1986–87 and earlier years; *Credits Amendment Regs 1994, Reg 3; Social Security (Credits and Contributions) (Jobseeker's Allowance Consequential and Miscellaneous Amendments) Regs 1996, SI 1996/2367, Reg 2; State Pension Regulations 2015, Reg 32(4)*].

Marriage termination credits

[24.13] For the purpose of enabling the second contribution condition for the then *unemployment benefit, sickness benefit and maternity allowance* to be fulfilled (see **24.2** above), a woman whose marriage had been terminated by the death of her husband or for any other reason was entitled, until 5 April 1987, to be credited with so many Class 1 contributions as were necessary to bring to the required level her EARNINGS FACTOR 28 for any tax year during the whole or part of which the marriage subsisted, provided that, during the tax year (if the marriage had by then taken place) before that in which the marriage ended, or during any subsequent tax year, she had derived an earnings factor of at least 25 times the weekly Lower Earnings Limit for the year in question from Class 1 or Class 2 contributions actually paid (see EARNINGS LIMITS AND THRESHOLDS 33). [*Married Women etc Regs, former Reg 2; Credits Regs, former Reg 10; Married Women and Widows Transitional Regs 1975, Reg 3; Credits Amendment Regs 1987, Reg 10*].

A marriage ended by divorce terminates on the date of the decree absolute. A voidable marriage which has been annulled is treated as if it was a valid marriage terminated by divorce at the date of the annulment. A woman who has obtained a decree absolute of presumption of death and dissolution of marriage is to be treated as a person whose marriage is terminated otherwise than on death, unless the date of her husband's death has been satisfactorily established. [former *Married Women etc Regs, former Reg 10*].

Widows/widowers

[24.14] Until 5 April 2017, where a person ceases to be entitled either to a bereavement (formerly widow's) allowance or to a widowed parent's (formerly widowed mother's) allowance (other than by reason of remarriage or cohabitation with a man as his wife), they are to be treated as having satisfied the first contribution condition for contributions-based jobseeker's allowance, incapacity benefit, contributory employment and support allowance or maternity allowance *and*, for the purpose of enabling the second contribution condition for any of those benefits to be fulfilled, they are to be credited with such Class 1 contributions as are necessary for every year up to and including that in which they ceased to be so entitled. The provisions were extended to former civil partners with effect from 5 December 2005. [*Married Women etc Regs, Reg 3(1)(a)(b)*, as amended by *Married Women and Widows Transitional Regs 1975, Reg 4 and Home Responsibilities Regs 1978, Reg 3(1); Credit Regs, Reg 8C inserted by Social Security (Benefits for Widows and Widowers) (Consequential Amendments) Regulations 2000, SI 2000/1483 and amended by Civil Partnership (Pensions, Social Security and Child Support) (Consequential, etc Provisions) Order 2005, SI 2005/2877* and *Employment and Support Allowance (Consequential Provisions) (No 2) Regulations 2008, SI 2008/1554, Reg 48(7)*].

A person will be *treated* as having ceased to be entitled to a bereavement allowance or widowed parent's allowance if, although they did not receive bereavement allowance or widowed parent's allowance, they would have been entitled to receive it but for their failure to claim, or delay in claiming, the benefit, or for their disqualification for receipt of the benefit for reasons other than cohabitation with a man as his wife, and the entitlement would have ceased. [*Married Women etc Regulations, Reg 3(7)*].

The bereavement benefits system is set to change from 6 April 2017, although the full detail is not yet known.

The current system involving bereavement payment, bereavement allowance and widowed parent's allowance is to be replaced with a new single bereavement support payment for new claims.

The aim is a simplified system concentrating support on the year immediately following the death. Widowed parent's allowance is currently paid until the youngest child leaves education, so this may be a significant change. It has been announced that national insurance contribution conditions are to be simplified, so it seems like that there will be an effect on how credits are awarded and converted into benefit entitlements.

A person who would currently otherwise be entitled to the credits referred to above but who is receiving a widow's industrial death benefit or a war or service widow's pension at a rate equal to or greater than the rate of contributions-based jobseeker's allowance, incapacity benefit or maternity allowance, will *not* be entitled to the credits for short-term benefit purposes until they have, in respect of any one year beginning after her husband's death, derived an earnings factor of at least 25 times that year's weekly Lower Earnings Limit from Class 1 or Class 2 contributions actually paid. [*Reg 3(5)(a)*].

Class 3 credits sufficient to enable certain widows and former widows (but not widowers) to fulfil the contribution conditions necessary for entitlement to long-term benefits were, as a transitional measure, granted for the tax years 1975–76 to 1977–78. [*Married Women etc Regs, Reg* 6, as amended by *Married Women and Widows Transitional Regs 1975, Reg 6(3)* and *Married Women and Widows Special Provisions Amendment Regs 1977, Reg 2*].

Credits for carer's allowance

[24.15] For the purpose of enabling the second contribution condition for entitlement to any benefit to be fulfilled, a person (other than a married woman with a reduced rate election in force for the week concerned—see REDUCED LIABILITY ELECTIONS **54**—or a person entitled to an unemployment or incapacity credit for that week—see **24.9** above) was, on or after 12 April 1976 but before 6 April 1987, entitled to a Class 1 credit in respect of each week for any part of which an invalid care allowance (now replaced by carer's allowance) was paid to him or, in the case of a widow, would have been so payable but for her receipt of other benefits. For qualifying weeks after 5 April 1987, the person is entitled to be credited with earnings equal to the Lower Earnings Limit then in force (see EARNINGS LIMITS AND THRESHOLDS **33** as well as **53.5** RATES AND LIMITS). Where carer's allowance (or previously invalid care allowance) is payable actual credits are available as stated but from 6 April 2002 to 5 April 2016, as earnings are deemed at the Lower Earnings Limit, S2P will have been enhanced too. If carer's allowance is not payable for the full tax year but caring has taken place for the whole of the year it will be possible to make a general claim for carer's credits (previously home responsibility protection) (see **24.23** below). The award of credits to recipients of carer's allowance should be automatic. [*Credits Regs, Reg 7A(1)(2)*, as inserted by *Invalid Care Allowance Regs 1976, Reg 19 and amended by Credits Amendment Regs 1978, Reg 2(2); Credits Amendment Regs 1987, Reg* 6 for 1987–88 and later years and *Reg 11* for 1986–87 and earlier years].

For the purposes of the new state pension, from 6 April 2016, new provisions were created to apply credits under the new regime. For these purposes, a person is to be credited with a Class 3 contribution in respect of any week in which the person, while, ordinarily resident in the UK and not legally detained is engaged in caring, which means caring for a person or persons in receipt of a relevant benefit, for a total of 20 or more hours in that week. The carer must make an application for such credits. Unlike under the previous regime, women who hold a reduced rate election may now qualify for credits under this regime and need not make specific application. [*State Pension Regulations 2015, Reg 37*, as inserted by *State Pension (Amendment) (No 2) Regulations 2016*, with effect from 6 April 2016].

Jury service credits

[24.16] For the purposes of enabling the contribution conditions for entitlement to any benefit to be fulfilled, a person (other than a married woman with a reduced rate election in force for the week concerned—see REDUCED LIABILITY ELECTIONS 54) is, from 6 April 1988, entitled to be credited with earnings equal to the Lower Earnings Limit then in force (see EARNINGS LIMITS AND THRESHOLDS 33 as well as 53.5 RATES AND LIMITS) in respect of each week for any part of which he attended at Court for jury service, provided that:

- their EARNINGS FROM EMPLOYMENT: GENERAL 29 as an employed earner for the week concerned are below the Lower Earnings Limit then in force, and
- they claim the credit in writing before the end of the benefit year which immediately follows the tax year in which the week falls or within such further time as may be reasonable in the circumstances of the case.

A person who in any part of the week is a self-employed earner is, from 8 August 1994, precluded from receiving jury service credits for that week.

Claims should be made to NIC&EO, Benton Park View, Newcastle upon Tyne NE98 1ZZ before the end of the calendar year following the tax year in which the jury service took place.

[*Credits Regs, Reg 9B*, as inserted by *Credits Amendment Regs 1988, Reg 2(3)* and amended by *Credits Amendment Regs 1994, Reg 4*].

In these circumstances the following letter is normally sent:

Letter to contributor who enquires about Jury Service credits

Dear [. . .]

Thank you for your enquiry about credits when you were on Jury Service.

I can confirm that someone who is called for Jury Service is entitled to a credit for each week they attend. Part of a week also counts. A married woman who has chosen to pay a reduced rate of contribution is not entitled to credits on the grounds of unemployment or Jury Service.

You only need credits to make up a deficiency in your contribution record for a particular year, so you may not need them. If you do, HM Revenue and Customs will notify you. You will also get a form on which you can claim the credits. When you return that form, we will ask you to provide a statement confirming the period you spent on Jury Service.

However, if you claim Employment and Support Allowance or Jobseekers Allowance before you claim the credits, tell your local Jobcentre Plus office about your Jury service. This will ensure that we take account of any credits due if they affect your benefit claim.

If you change your address, tell HMRC by calling 0300 200 3500.

Further information

Please get in touch with the person or manager of the section shown above if you:

- need further information
- are dissatisfied with the service you have received.

Yours sincerely,

Maternity, adoption, paternity and shared parental pay period credits

[24.17] For the purposes of enabling the contribution conditions for entitlement to any benefit to be fulfilled, a woman (other than a married woman with a reduced rate election in force for the week concerned—see REDUCED LIABILITY ELECTIONS 54) is, from 6 April 1987, entitled to be credited with earnings equal to the Lower Earnings Limit then in force (see EARNINGS LIMITS AND THRESHOLDS 33 as well as 53.5 RATES AND LIMITS) in respect of each week during a maternity pay period for which Statutory Maternity Pay was paid to her, provided that she claims the credit in writing before the end of the benefit year which immediately follows the tax year in which the week falls or within such further time as may be reasonable in the circumstances of her case.

From 6 April 2003 a credit is also awarded as above for any week where a person is in receipt of Statutory Adoption Pay, and from 6 April 2012 the entitlement was broadened to include any week where a person is in receipt of additional statutory paternity pay (ie, where the father has taken over the mother's right to statutory leave and pay).

From 31 December 2014, the provision was further extended to recipients of statutory shared parental pay, which is an alternative to SMP and SAP for babies due or adoptions finalised from 5 April 2015 onwards. Mother and father are now both entitled to claim a credit for the ShPP period within the time limit outlined.

[*Credits Regs, Reg 9C*, as amended by *Credits Amendment Regs 2003, Reg 2(3)* and *Social Security (Credits) (Amendment) Regulations 2012, SI 2012/766, Reg 2* and *Shared Parental Leave and Statutory Shared Parental Pay (Consequential Amendments to Subordinate Legislation) Order 2014, SI 2014/3255, Reg 2*.]

Stayed credits

[24.18] Where a person has been detained under a custodial sentence but:

- the sentence is quashed on appeal at the Court of Appeal, Crown Court or High Court, and
- they apply in writing to the NIC&EO Decision Making Team, and

- they do not continue to be detained under any other conviction,

then Class 1 credits may be awarded for the period of legal detention.

This provision is effective from 26 March 2001 but claims can be made for all earlier years. It only applies to those who have been wrongly convicted of a crime and so will not be of help to someone detained on remand.

[*Credits Regs, Reg 9D*, as inserted by *Social Security (Credits and Incapacity Benefit) Amendment Regs 2001, SI 2001/573, Reg 2*].

A married woman with a reduced rate election who has been wrongfully imprisoned for two years or more and lost her right to the election as a result can receive credits for the entire period of imprisonment (including the period that the election was still valid), though the election cannot be reinstated.

[*Credits Regs, Reg 9D(5)*, as inserted by *Social Security (Credits and Incapacity Benefit) Amendment Regs 2001, SI 2001/573, Reg 2*].

Credits for partners of members of HM Forces

[24.19] From 6 April 2010, Class 1 credits can be claimed by the spouses and civil partners accompanying members of HM Forces on assignment outside the UK. The partner does not have to be in the same country, eg the spouse could remain at a base in Germany while the Forces member is in Afghanistan. Claims must generally be made before the end of the tax year after the one in which the overseas assignment ended, though there is provision for early claims if needed to support a short-term benefit claim in the meantime. [*Credits Regs, Reg 9E*, as inserted by *Social Security (Credits) (Amendment) Regulations 2010, SI 2010/385*].

From 6 April 2016, a new Class 3 credit was introduced for people married to, or in a civil partnership with, a member of the UK Armed Forces who were accompanying them on a posting outside the UK. The new credit is available for tax years from 1975–76 onwards where there are gaps in their NI record. This change was made because of the new state pension rules which base entitlement to the state pension on a person's own national insurance record over many years, which could mean that those outside the UK serving the country lost out by being unable or ineligible to pay contributions.

The new type of Class 3 credit is available to a woman born on or after 6 April 1953 or a man born on or after 6 April 1951 who meets the marriage or civil partnership criteria (with a spouse or partner paying UK contributions) and has been on an accompanied assignment outside the UK at any time since 6 April 1975. An application must be made to HMRC. The new credit is available retrospectively, so widows and divorcees may apply in respect of any time in the past on an accompanied posting.

Class 1 credits are available at the same time and may be more beneficial than the new Class 3 credit, as they provide entitlement to a wider range of benefits. Any military spouse who has already applied for Class 1 credits need not apply for the Class 3 credit for the same posting. Note that the credits might not apply for a whole year: overseas postings rarely begin and end on 5 April, and the credits are awarded on a weekly basis, so contributors may need to consider paying voluntary contributions to make up a full qualifying year. [*State Pension Regulations 2015, Reg 33*, as inserted by *State Pension (Amendment) (No 2) Regs 2016*, with effect from 6 April 2016].

Miscellaneous credits

[24.20] Contribution schemes prior to the 1975 scheme provided for the awarding of credits and such credits are preserved for the purpose of satisfying the contribution conditions attaching to current benefits. [*Social Security (Consequential Provisions) Act 1975, s 2*].

Where for any year a contributor's earnings factor derived from Class 1, Class 2 or Class 3 contributions paid by, or credited to, him falls short of a figure which is 52 times that year's weekly Lower Earnings Limit for Class 1 contributions by an amount which is equal to, or less than, half that year's weekly Lower Earnings Limit (sometimes referred to as a 'near miss'), that contributor is to be credited with a Class 3 contribution for that year (see EARNINGS FACTORS 28). [*Social Security (Crediting and Treatment of Contributions*, and *National Insurance Numbers) Regulations 2001, SI 2001/769, Reg 3*].

Overseas employment credits

[24.21] Although not described as such within the legislation, a kind of credit will nonetheless be awarded to any person who:

- has been absent from Great Britain and, by virtue of *Social Security (Contributions) Regulations 2001, SI 2001/1004, Reg 146*, a reciprocal agreement or EC Reg 1408/71 or 883/2004 (see **51.9**, **51.23** and **51.38** OVERSEAS MATTERS) has paid Class 1 contributions at standard rate for the first 52 weeks of a continuing employment overseas or would have paid such contributions for the first 52 weeks of his employment overseas (or for such shorter period as his overseas employment continued) under *Social Security (Contributions) Regulations 2001, SI 2001/1004, Reg 146(2)(a)* but for the operation of a reciprocal agreement or *EC Regs*;
- has returned to Great Britain; and
- remained ordinarily resident in Great Britain throughout his absence (see **51.5** OVERSEAS MATTERS).

Any such person is to be treated as having paid Class 1 contributions on earnings at the Lower Earnings Limit for any tax week of absence for which Class 1 contributions have not in fact been paid if that tax week is relevant to a claim for contributions-based Jobseeker's Allowance or ESA(C) and the person concerned is not entitled to corresponding benefits under the social security scheme of the foreign country in which he was employed. Whether someone has remained ordinarily resident in Great Britain will be determined in the usual way. The guidance formerly on the HMRC website on this point has been removed.

Quite separately, there were special arrangements for people who worked or were detained without pay in Iraq during the 1990–1991 Gulf crisis. Those affected should have written to HM Revenue & Customs, NIC&EO, Benton Park View, Newcastle upon Tyne, NE98 1ZZ (www.gov.uk/national-insurance-credits#3).

NI credits for recipients of tax credits

[24.22] With effect from 6 April 1992 until October 1999, a person could be credited with earnings equal to the Lower Earnings Limit then in force in respect of each week for any part of which a disability working allowance (DWA) was paid to him. To qualify, the person in receipt of the DWA must either have been an employed earner or a self-employed earner who was excepted from Class 2 contributions on account of small earnings. No DWA credit could be awarded if the person was also entitled to an unemployment or incapacity credit, or was a married woman with a valid reduced rate election. [former *Credits Regs, Reg 7B*, as inserted by *Credits Amendments Regs 1991, SI 1991/2772, Reg 3*].

From October 1999 until April 2003, a person could be credited with earnings equal to the Lower Earnings Limit then in force in respect of each week for any part of which a disabled person's tax credit was paid to him. To qualify, the person in receipt of the tax credit must either have been an employed earner or a self-employed earner who was excepted from Class 2 contributions on account of small earnings, or had received a repayment of such contributions on the same grounds. No contributory benefits credit could be awarded if the person was also entitled to an unemployment or incapacity credit, or was a married woman with a valid reduced rate election — see REDUCED LIABILITY ELECTIONS 54. [former *Credits Regs, Reg 7B* as inserted by *Credits Amendments Regs 1991, Reg 3* and amended by *Social Security and Child Support (Tax Credits) Consequential Amendments Regs 1999, SI 1999/2566, Reg 2(1) and Sch 2 Part 1*]. Disabled Persons Tax Credits ceased from April 2003.

From April 2003, those receiving working tax credits and whose Class 1 earnings do not reach the Lower Earnings Limit or who are self-employed and have claimed small earnings exception can usually receive a contribution credit for retirement pension, widowed parent's allowance and widow(er)s pension purposes. This applies to any claimant other than a married woman with a valid reduced rate election—see REDUCED LIABILITY ELECTIONS 54, not just the disabled. However, in the case of those receiving a disability element of working tax credit (as specified in *Working Tax Credits (Entitlement and Maximum Rate) Regs 2002, Reg 20 (1)(b)(f)*) entitlement is to a credit for the purpose of all contributory (ie, including short-term) benefits. [*Credits Regs, Regs 7B, 7C* as amended by *Social Security (Working Tax Credit, Child Tax Credit) (Consequential Amendments) Regulations 2003, SI 2003/455, Sch 4, para 1* and *Civil Partnership (Pensions, Social Security and Child Support) (Consequential, etc Provisions) Order 2005, SI 2005/2877*].

From April 2016, a person is credited with earnings equal to the lower earnings limit for a week if for that week working tax credit is paid to a person who is an employed earner, a self-employed earner with small profits, or a self-employed earner excepted from paying Class 2 contributions under *Contributions Regulations 2001, Reg 43*. If both members of a couple have earnings and the working tax credit is paid in respect of the couple, the credit is awarded to the member of the couple to whom the working tax credit is paid. A woman with a reduced rate election is ineligible. [*State Pension Regulations 2015, Reg 30*, as inserted by *State Pension (Amendment) (No 2) Regulations 2016*, with effect from 6 April 2016].

Carers' credits

[24.23] A person who had to stay at home to look after a child or children or those caring for someone who had a long-term disability or illness and did not therefore undertake full time work was in many cases from 6 April 1978 to 5 April 2010 inclusive covered by home responsibilities protection (HRP) in relation to his or her pension rights.

HRP (see **24.24**) was replaced with effect from 6 April 2010 by new carers' credits. These are actual Class 3 credits and are governed by the *Social Security (Contributions Credits for Parents and Carers) Regulations 2010, SI 2010/19*. See also *SSCBA 1992, s 23A*.

Past years of HRP (to a maximum of 22 such years' entitlement) have been converted to carers' credits for those reaching state pension age after 5 April 2010.

New carers' credits will be awarded to those in receipt of child benefit for a child under the age of 12 or to their partner if the child benefit recipient herself already has a qualifying year by virtue of actual contributions paid.

Credits will also be awarded to foster parents and those caring for 20 or more hours per week and where the person cared for is in receipt of certain benefits (including Attendance Allowance or the highest rate of disablement pension). Gaps of up to 12 weeks in caring are permitted to allow for holidays, etc.

As with HRP, the new credit will be given automatically to those receiving child benefit in their own name. Partners and foster carers wishing to receive the credit must, in contrast, make a claim to HM Revenue and Customs. In the case of other carers a claim must be made to the Department for Work and Pensions. In either case the time limit is the end of the tax year following that in which the week or weeks subject to the claim fell. HMRC and DWP have the power to allow further time to claim if they consider it 'reasonable in the circumstances'.

Certain carers are excluded and these include those not ordinarily resident in the UK and those in prison or in legal custody.

A comment was made in the Budget speech on 22 April 2009 that grandparents of working age who stay at home to provide child-minding for their grandchildren will have their state pension position protected. The DWP undertook consultation on this and the extension to carers' credits became available from 6 April 2011, albeit limited to those who care for grandchildren aged 12 or younger for at least 20 hours a week. Only one of the grandparents is entitled to the award of the credits. [*Social Security (Credits) Regulations 1975, SI 1975/556, Reg 9F* as amended by the *National Insurance Contributions Credits (Miscellaneous Amendments) Regulations 2011, SI 2011/709*].

From April 2016, equivalent credits for the purposes of the new state pension are available for weeks where a specified person, ordinarily resident in the UK, provides care in respect of a child under the age of 12. Where a child is cared for by more than one person, only one may be credited with a Class 3 contribution for each relevant week. The list of eligible claimants is the same under the new rules. Equivalent credits have also been created for foster parents (or kinship carers in Scotland) who therefore may also claim a Class 3 contribution in respect of a week in which they are ordinarily resident in Great Britain and not in legal custody. [*State Pension Regulations 2015, Regs 35, 36*, as inserted by *State Pension (Amendment) (No 2) Regulations 2016*, with effect from 6 April 2016].

See also **19.1** VOLUNTARY CONTRIBUTIONS: CLASS 3 AND 3A.

Home Responsibility Protection credits

[24.24] Prior to 6 April 2010, HRP applied where the person who was being looked after received attendance allowance, constant attendance allowance or disability living allowance (middle and higher rates). The effect of this was that the years of home responsibility protection (HRP) were used to reduce the total number of years for which the contribution conditions for retirement pension had to be met (see **13.5** BENEFITS: CONTRIBUTION REQUIREMENTS). In addition, rules also provided for certain individuals with home responsibilities to be credited with contributions such as when receiving carer's allowance (previously invalid care allowance) in respect of severely disabled children. It also included the cases where Child Benefit was being received for a child under 16 years. In some circumstances for claims in respect of 2002–03 and subsequent years, an actual claim had to be made within three years of the end of the tax year in question. Each claim applied for the year in question and did not continue beyond that year and therefore a new claim had to be made each year. [*Home Responsibilities Regs, Reg 2*]. Enquiries in respect of home responsibility protection may be made to: HM Revenue and Customs, NIC&EO, DM Team, Room BP4302, Newcastle upon Tyne NE98 1ZZ. Tel 08459 158068.

The *Social Security Pensions (Home Responsibilities) (Amendment) Regulations 2005, SI 2005/48)* provided that where the recipient of child benefit was switched during the first three months of a tax year, it would be treated for the purpose of HRP as if made at the very start of that tax year. This change applied to switches made in 2004/05 onwards. The *Social Security Pensions (Home Responsibilities) Amendment Regulations 2008, SI 2008/498* went further and provided that HRP be given to a claimant where their partner was paid child benefit for a whole tax year and during that year they were residing together, sharing care for a child under 16 and where the child benefit claimant did not herself benefit from the HRP available due to having paid actual National Insurance contributions. The 2008 Regulations only applied where the claimant reached state pension age on or after 6 April 2008 (or in the case of bereavement benefit, the spouse's death is on or after 6 April 2008). Where a male partner had no NIC-able income and the female partner (who was the default claimant for child benefit) did, this was more flexible than the previous option to transfer which came into effect for 2004–05 onwards.

On 6 November 2003, the then Inland Revenue stated that it would be sending out deficiency notice letters to those it considered had not paid enough contributions or been credited with enough NICs to entitle them to a full pension. Where HRP for a particular year was in point that year will have been marked with a '*' to indicate that the credit was applicable. The Revenue also stressed that HRP years could reduce the number of qualifying years an individual needed to obtain a full pension by up to 50%. This did not apply where income support was being paid.

(See also CLASS 3 CONTRIBUTIONS: VOLUNTARY **19** and HM Revenue and Customs National Insurance Manual NIM41300–41415).

Universal credit

[24.25] With effect from 29 April 2013, if a person is entitled to universal credit under *WRA 2012, Part 1* for any part of a week, that person is entitled to be credited with a Class 3 contribution for the purposes of a category A or B retirement pension, widowed parent's allowance and bereavement allowance. [*Social Security (Credits) Regulations 1975, SI 1975/556, Reg 8G* as inserted by *Universal Credit (Consequential, Supplementary, Incidental and Miscellaneous Provisions) Regulations 2013, SI 2013/630, Reg 70*]. The entitlement was extended from 6 April 2016 for the purposes of the new state pension. [*State Pension Regulations 2015, Reg 31*, as inserted by *State Pension (Amendment) (No 2) Regulations 2016*, with effect from 6 April 2016].

Summary of how to obtain NI credits

[24.26] The following table summarises how to obtain NI credits.

Contributor's situation	Automatic award and type	Claim required and type
Claiming JSA and not in education or working 16 hours+ per week	Class 1	
Unemployed but not on JSA		Class 1 – apply to JCP
Claiming ESA or unemployability supplement or allowance	Class 1	
Eligible for ESA but not claiming		Class 1 – apply to JCP
On SMP, SAP, SPP, ShPP low earnings so that the year does not qualify		Class 1 – apply to NIC&EO
On maternity allowance	Class 1	

Contributor's situation	Automatic award and type	Claim required and type
Parent registered for child benefit for a child under 12	Class 3	
Parent who received child benefit for a child under 16 between 6 April 1978 and 5 April 2010 without HRP		Class 3
Wanting to transfer credits from a spouse/partner who received child benefit for a child under 12 between 6 April 2010 and the current year		Class 3 transfer
Wanting to transfer from a spouse/partner who received child benefit for a child under 16 before 6 April 2010		Class 3 transfer
Foster/kinship carer since 6 April 2010		Class 3
Foster/kinship carer between 6 April 2003 and 5 April 2010		Claim HRP for Class 3 credit
In receipt of carer's allowance	Class 1	
On income support and providing regular and substantial care	Class 3	
Caring for one or more sick or disabled persons for at least 20 hours a week		Class 3
Family member over 16 but under state pension age caring for a child under 12		Specified adult childcare Class 3 credits
On working tax credits with a disability premium (and small profits if self-employed)	Class 1	

Contributor's situation	Automatic award and type	Claim required and type
On working tax credits without a disability premium (and small profits if self-employed)	Class 3	
On universal credit	Class 3	
Men between the current women's state pension age and 65 ordinarily resident in the UK, not working, or not earning enough to make a qualifying year, or self-employed with small profits	Class 1	
Over 18 and on a government approved training course for up to a year mandated by Jobcentre Plus	Class 1	
As above but course not mandated by JCP		Class 1 – apply to NIC&EO
Employees who attend court on jury service		Class 1 – apply to NIC&EO
Spouse or civil partner of a member of the Armed Forces accompanying on an overseas posting after 6 April 2010 and returning to the UK		Class 1
As above but for overseas posting after 6 April 1975, reaching state pension age on or after 6 April 2016 and not in receipt of Class 1 credits		Class 3
Wrongly imprisoned with conviction quashed by Court of Appeal (Court of criminal appeal in Scotland)		Class 1 – apply to NIC&EO

Key Points regarding credits

[24.27] Points to consider are as follows.

- Credits are available for a wide range of circumstances that prevent work taking place (and thereby compulsory contributions being paid). These include sickness, unemployment, maternity, jury service, certain training, child-rearing and other caring duties.
- HRP was replaced by carers' credits from 6 April 2010. Previously, HRP merely reduced the number of qualifying years needed for full basic state pension entitlement.
- Past years of HRP have been converted to carers' credits for those reaching state pension age after 5 April 2010.
- Married women with reduced rate elections and the self-employed who are liable to Class 2 contributions are usually ineligible for credits (see exceptions above).

25

Crown Servants and Statutory Employees

Cross-references. See ARMED FORCES **11**; OVERSEAS MATTERS **51**; SUBPOSTMASTERS **57**.

Introduction to crown servants and statutory employees

[25.1] A significant percentage of the working population are employed in the public sector either as Crown servants or as employees of statutory corporations. A Crown servant is 'appointed to an office and is a public officer remunerated by moneys provided by Parliament so that his appointment depends not on a contract but on appointment by the Crown'. (*CIR v Hambrook* [1956] 2 QB 641). An employee of a statutory corporation will be a Crown servant if the Act creating the corporation expressly provides that the corporation is to act on behalf of the Crown, otherwise (even if the corporation is controlled by a government department) he will be an ordinary employee. (*Tamlin v Hannaford* [1950] 1 KB 18). Thus direct employees of the National Health Service are Crown servants, but employees of the British Broadcasting Corporation are ordinary employees. Employees of the old General Post Office were civil servants until 1969 when the Post Office became a statutory corporation rather than a department of state and the staff became ordinary employees (*Wood v United Leeds Hospitals* [1974] IRLR 204, 9 ITR 352, NIRC; *BBC v Johns (Inspector of Taxes)* [1965] Ch 32, [1964] 1 All ER 923, CA; *Malins v Post Office* [1975] ICR 60).

Employment protection legislation narrows the definition of Crown servants set out above so as to bring certain Crown servants and employees of Parliament within its ambit [*Employment Rights Act 1996, ss 191-195*] but such narrowing of definition is irrelevant in the context of contribution law.

Categorisation of crown servants and statutory employees

[25.2] Apart from members of the ARMED FORCES **11** who are Crown servants (see also *ERA 1996, s 192*) but are subject to special contribution provisions, a Crown servant is to be treated for contribution purposes as if he is a private person. [*SSCBA 1992, s 115(1)*]. This means that a liability for contributions on his earnings will arise only if he is an employed earner or self-employed earner according to the normal rules of CATEGORISATION **14**. A Crown servant cannot *per se* be in business on his own account and cannot, therefore, be a self-employed earner. The recent examples of those occupying the post of a Crown servant operating through their own service companies are outside the scope of this chapter. To be an employed earner, a Crown servant must, however, be gainfully employed in Great Britain under a contract of service or in an office with general earnings chargeable to income tax as employment income. [*SSCBA 1992, s 2(1)(a)*]. The traditional view has been that no contract of service can exist between the Crown and its servants (*Dunn v R* [1896] 1 QB 116) but a modern view is that it can. (*Kodeeswaran v A-G for Ceylon* [1970] AC 1111, [1970] 2 WLR 456, PC). Be that as it may, 'all servants . . . of the Crown hold office' (*Ridge v Baldwin* [1964] AC 40, [1963] 2 All ER 66, HL) and, assuming they are remunerated and that their earnings are chargeable to tax as employment income, that will be sufficient to bring them within the category of employed earner for contribution purposes. Prison governors, chaplains and medical officers also hold office under this legislation.

Police and prison officers

[25.3] A police officer is a ministerial officer exercising statutory rights independent of contract. (*A-G for New South Wales v Perpetual Trustee Co Ltd* [1955] AC 457). He falls in a class of his own being neither a Crown servant nor an ordinary employee. (*Ridge v Baldwin* [1964] AC 40, [1963] 2 All ER 66, HL). He does, however, hold an office with general earnings chargeable to income tax as employment income and is, therefore, an employed earner for contribution purposes.

On basic principles, police cadets are neither office holders nor persons under a contract of service, and cannot, therefore, be automatically categorised as employed earners or self-employed earners for contribution purposes. (*Wiltshire Police Authority v Wynn* [1981] ICR 649). (See APPRENTICES, TRAINEES AND STUDENTS **10**.) However, *Police Act 1996, s 28(3)* now deems the police authority that maintains a police force, for the purposes of any enactment relating to the functions of employers and of any rule of law with respect to the vicarious liability of employers, to be the employer of any police cadets undergoing training with the force.

A prison officer, while acting as such, has all the powers, authority, protection and privileges of a constable. [*Prison Act 1952, s 8*]. He, like a police officer, holds an office and is an employed earner for contribution purposes.

Crown servants etc employed overseas

[25.4] It will generally be the case that, if a Crown servant, an employee of a statutory corporation, or a person in the private service of such a person, is employed overseas but does not fall within the contribution exemption provisions of the *Diplomatic Privileges Act 1964* or the *Consular Relations Act 1968* (see **25.5** etc below), he will, if he is not permanently settled in the foreign state in which he is working and if there is a reciprocal agreement between the UK and that foreign state, or the foreign state is another EEA Member State, remain subject to the contribution legislation of Great Britain. [eg, *Social Security (Contributions) (Republic of Korea) Order 2000, SI 2000/1823, Art 7*, etc; *EC Reg 883/2004, Arts 11(3)(b), 13(4)*]. (See **51.22** and **51.23** OVERSEAS MATTERS.) Where a Crown Servant is posted to an overseas location within the EEA (see **51.2** OVERSEAS MATTERS) there is no requirement for certificates of coverage from the home state and no provision for such certificates in *EC Reg 883/2004*. Contributions are payable in the UK – the legislation says so. A certificate of coverage would only be relevant where the basic legislative requirement is not followed.

The payments made to persons in the service of the Commonwealth War Graves Commission or the British Council for the extra cost of living outside the UK are disregarded. [*Social Security (Contributions) Regulations 2001, SI 2001/1004, Sch 3 Part VIII para 13*]. The expenses of Westminster MPs, MSP, Welsh AMs and Northern Ireland MLAs incurred in European travelling on defined official business are tax-free under *ITEPA 2003, s 294* and, in consequence, are also excluded from earnings for NIC purposes. [*Social Security (Contributions) Regulations 2001, SI 2001/1004, Sch 3, Part VIII, para 16(d)*].

The former DSS had, historically, considered that certain allowances paid to Crown employees serving overseas were not subject to National Insurance contributions. However, it received legal advice suggesting that, on the basis of the legislation, contributions were in fact due from 6 April 1975. In response, the Government laid new regulations to put the previous, long-standing practice on a legislative footing from 6 April 1997 [*Social Security Amendment No 3 Regs 1997, Reg 2*]. The statutory exclusion from earnings depends upon tax exemption being granted by *ITEPA 2003, s 299* (formerly *ICTA 1988, s 319*) for Crown employees' foreign service allowances. The Contributions Agency decided not to pursue arrears of contributions from 6 April 1975 to 5 April 1997, '*since to do so would entail considerable administrative costs . . . and would not result in an overall increase in Government revenue*'. (National Insurance Fund Account 1996–97). [*Social Security (Contributions) Regulations 2001, SI 2001/1004, Sch 3 Part VIII para 12*]. In any case, much of the liability would have been time-barred for collection.

Contribution exemption

[25.5] The Vienna Convention on Diplomatic Relations (*Cmnd 1368*) and the Vienna Convention on Consular Relations (*Cmnd 2113*) have the force of law in the United Kingdom by virtue of the *Diplomatic Privileges Act 1964* and the *Consular Relations Act 1968*. Those conventions confer exemption from contribution liability on certain groups of persons employed in the state receiving a diplomatic mission or accepting the establishment of a consular post (see **25.6** to **25.9** below). Similar exemption is conferred on certain persons employed here by international organisations (see **25.10** below). Where the sending and receiving states are members of the EC, however, special rules apply (see **25.11** below).

Diplomatic agents etc

[25.6] A diplomatic agent is, as regards services rendered for the sending state but not as regards any other services, exempt from any social security provisions in force in the receiving state. [*Diplomatic Privileges Act 1964, Sch 1, Art 33(1)*].

Definitions

[25.7] A *diplomatic agent* is either the person charged by the sending state with the duty of acting as the head of a diplomatic mission or a member of the staff of such a mission having diplomatic rank (eg secretaries, counsellors and attachés). [*DPA 1964, Sch 1, Art 1*].

Similarly exempt from the social security provisions of the receiving state are:

- private servants who are in the sole employ of a diplomatic agent, provided they are neither nationals of nor permanently resident in the receiving state *and* they are covered by social security provisions in force in the sending state or some other state;
- the members of the family of a diplomatic agent forming part of his household, provided they are not nationals of the receiving state;
- any members of the administrative and technical staff of the mission, together with members of their families forming part of their respective households, provided they are neither nationals of nor permanently resident in the receiving state; and
- members of the service staff of the mission, provided they are neither nationals of nor permanently resident in the receiving state.

[*DPA 1964, Sch 1, Arts 33(2), 37*].

A *private servant* is a person who is in the domestic service of a member of the mission and who is not an employee of the sending state. *Members of the administrative and technical staff* are the members of the staff of a mission employed in the administrative and technical service of the mission (eg clerks, typists, archivists and radio and telephone operators). *Members of the service staff* are the members of the staff of a mission in the domestic service of the mission (eg butlers, cooks, maids and chauffeurs). [*DPA 1964, Sch 1, Art 1*].

Anyone who is not covered by these exemptions is subject to the social security provisions in force in the receiving state in the normal way, and any diplomatic agent employing such a person must observe the obligations which the social security provisions of the receiving state impose on employers. [*DPA 1964, Sch 1, Art 33(3)*].

Diplomatic list

[25.8] The head of a diplomatic mission will normally supply the Foreign and Commonwealth Office with a list of the staff of the mission etc and, once such persons have been accepted as *personae gratae*, exemption from liability will apply where appropriate. See The London Diplomatic List on www.gov.uk. Any question which arises as to whether a person is entitled to privilege or immunity is to be settled conclusively by a certificate issued by or under the authority of the Secretary of State (ie Foreign Secretary). See *Jimenez v CIR* [2004] STC SCD 371 Sp C 419. [*DPA 1964, s 4*].

All these provisions are subject to provisions to the contrary (if any) contained in bilateral or multilateral agreements affecting the sending and receiving states (see **51.20** OVERSEAS MATTERS). [*DPA 1964, Sch 1, Art 33(5)*]. In particular, they are subject to the EC regulations governing diplomatic staff described at **25.11** below.

Members of consular posts

[25.9] Identical provisions to those described at **25.7** above apply in the case of members of a consular post, members of their families forming part of their households, and members of the private staff who are in the sole employ of members of the consular post and are not nationals of or permanent residents of the receiving state. [*Consular Relations Act 1968, Sch 1, Art 48*].

A *member of a consular post* means a consular officer, a consular employee or a member of the service staff. A *consular officer* means the person charged with the duty of acting as head of a consular post and any other person entrusted with the exercise of consular functions. A *consular employee* means any person employed in the administrative or technical service of a consular post; and a *member of the service staff* means any person employed in the domestic service of the consular post. [*CRA 1968, Sch 1, Art 1*].

All those provisions are again subject to provisions to the contrary (if any) contained in bilateral or multilateral agreements affecting the sending and receiving states (see **51.20** OVERSEAS MATTERS). [*CRA 1968, s 1(7)*]. In particular, they are subject to the EC regulations governing consular staff described at **25.11** below.

International organisations

[25.10] Exemption as described at **25.6** to **25.9** above will, if conferred by Order in Council, be granted to senior officers and staff members of committees and missions of international organisations provided the persons concerned are neither nationals of nor permanently resident in the receiving state. [*International Organisations Act 1968, s 1, Sch 1 Part III*, as amended by *Diplomatic and other Privileges Act 1971* and *European Communities Act 1972, s 4(1), Sch 3 Part IV*]. Such organisations include the United Nations, the Commission of the European Communities, the Council of Europe, the International Labour Organisation, the World Health Organisation and the International Court of Justice. In reply to a question regarding whether the United Nations or its subsidiary organisations' employees in the United Kingdom are subject to employment law Baroness Amos stated:

> In general, United Kingdom employment law does not apply to employees of the United Nations or the specialised agencies of the United Nations; those bodies generally have internal regulations relating to employment contracts. The United Nations and specialised agencies have immunity from suit and legal process as set out in the International Organisations Act 1968 and legislation made thereunder.
> [Hansard Written Answers, 4 February 2003, Col 18].

Diplomatic and consular staff of EEA member states

[25.11] A person employed by a diplomatic mission or a consular post within the European Community or other European Economic Area Member State, or a member of the private domestic staff of an agent of such a mission or post, contrary to the rules described at 25.6 to 25.9 above, used to be subject to the social security legislation of the state in whose territory he was employed *unless*:

- he was a national of the EEA Member State which was the accrediting or sending state; and
- he opted to be subject to the social security legislation of that state.

[*EC Reg 1408/71, Art 16(1),(2)*].

However, these special rules were not reproduced when *EC Reg 883/2004* replaced *EC Reg 1408/71* in May 2010. All diplomats are treated as civil servants, now covered by the scheme for the Member State that they serve. [*EC Reg 883/2004, Art 11(3)(b)*]. Their private household staff are generally subject to the social security rules of the host state unless they are migrant workers and are able to request an A1 from their home state for the duration of their work in the host state.

Auxiliary staff of the European Communities may opt to be subject to the social security legislation of either:

- the Member State in whose territory they are employed; or
- the Member State to whose social security legislation they were last subject; or
- the Member State whose nationals they are.

In either case, the right of option may be exercised once only, at the time when the contract of employment is concluded, and takes effect from the date of entry into employment. [*EC Regs, 883/2004, Art 15* and *987/2009, Art 17*].

Non-exempt employees of exempt employer

[25.12] Where a non-exempt employed earner is employed by an exempt employer, the employer will not fall to be treated as a secondary contributor (see **14.32** CATEGORISATION). He will, therefore, have no liability to pay or account for primary or secondary Class 1 contributions payable on earnings paid to that non-exempt earner. In such cases, the exempt employer may voluntarily undertake a secondary contributor's responsibilities (see now withdrawn Leaflet CA 65, April 2003, pages 7–9) but, should he decline to do so, direct collection procedures (known as a DCNI scheme) will be imposed on the employed earner in relation to any liability for primary Class 1 contributions which arises (see now withdrawn Leaflet CA 65, April 2003, pages 9–11 and **21.30** COLLECTION).

This situation may arise where a UK national is employed overseas by an overseas government agency or body. Despite the fact that the individual is employed outside the UK, a diplomatic presence of some kind in the UK may be argued to create a UK place of business (see **51.8** OVERSEAS MATTERS) of that overseas government. An individual who is ordinarily resident in the UK and resident here immediately before the commencement of the employment with the overseas government may therefore be required to pay primary contributions for the first 52 weeks of absence from the UK under *Social Security (Contributions) Regulations 2001, SI 2001/1004, Reg 146*. The foreign government employer cannot be compelled to operate a payroll under the RTI rules.

German reciprocal agreement

[25.13] *Art 11(3)(b)* of *EC Reg 883/2004* making the employing state competent in the case of civil servants, does not apply where the surviving provisions of *Reciprocal Agreement (1961/1202) – Germany, Art 7(5),(6)* and *Reciprocal Agreement (1961/1513) – Germany, Art 5(5),(6)* are relevant as they take precedence by virtue of *Annex II* to *EC Reg 883/2004*. These provisions of the bilateral treaty deal, in effect, solely with the non-German civilian staff of British Forces Germany (although the whole agreement is still valid for Manxmen who go to work in Germany or Germans working in the Isle of Man, since these situations are not covered by the EC regulations).

It is provided that, if a person is employed in Germany by the British forces in a civilian capacity or by an organisation serving those forces and is not ordinarily resident in Germany, then the UK legislation applies to him as if he were employed in the UK. The 'competent authorities' (ie, DWP and its German counterparts) have agreed a list of the organisations to which the provisions apply (eg, the NAAFI).

Staff of the European School

[25.14] Staff members of the European School at Culham (ie headmaster, deputy heads, secondary school teachers, primary school teachers, kindergarten teachers and educational advisers) are excepted from any class of employment for social security contribution purposes provided that they are seconded to the School by an EEA Member State other than the UK and are subject to that state's social security legislation. [*EC (Privileges of the European School) Order 1990, Art 7(a)*].

Key Points regarding crown servants and statutory employees

[25.15] Points to consider are as follows.

- A Crown servant ordinarily is under a contract of service or holds an office and therefore cannot be classed as self-employed.
- Where Crown servants are sent to work abroad and are not within a diplomatic or consular status they are subject to the normal migrant worker rules.
- Allowances paid to certain Crown servants working abroad which are tax-free under ITEPA 2003, s 299, such as cost of living allowance (Commonwealth War Graves Commission), are free from NICs too.

26

Death of Contributor

Cross-references. See BENEFITS: CONTRIBUTION REQUIREMENTS 13; CLASS 3 CONTRIBUTIONS 19.

Other Sources. Simon's Taxes, Volume 2, para A8.269A; former Employer's Help Book E13 (2013), page 32; CWG2 (2018–19), para 1.15.

Introduction to death of contributor

[26.1] Liability for National Insurance contributions is *personal* to an earner and cannot, therefore, arise once an earner has died. [*SSCBA 1992, s 6(1), s 11(1)*]. However, contributions which have become due for payment before a person's death remain a debt due to HMRC by the estate of the deceased earner (in the case of Class 2 contributions) or by the secondary contributor concerned (in the case of Class 1 contributions).

Cessation of liability on death

[26.2] There is no liability for either primary or secondary Class 1 contributions in respect of payments of *inter vivos* earnings made to the earner's estate after his death. (Guidance CWG2 (2017), para 1.15). The employer should report the date of the employee's death as the date of leaving in the FPS reporting the final payment of earnings (there is no 'date of death' field in an RTI record). No other report to HMRC (eg, a P45) is now required from the employer.

Nor can there be a liability for a Class 2 contribution in respect of the week in which a self-employed earner dies, as liability for a Class 2 contribution does not arise until the last day of the contribution week. In contrast, any contributions that the individual was otherwise liable to pay may be paid notwithstanding the death of that person provided the amount is paid within the relevant time limits, see **26.4** below. [*Social Security (Contributions) Regulations 2001, SI 2001/1004, Reg 62*].

There are grounds for believing that it is NIC&EO policy to waive a claim for Class 2 contributions due from a deceased self-employed earner at the date of his death if, after distribution of the estate, the widow(er) is in financial difficulty, although the transfer of Class 2 collection into the self-assessment regime for 2015–16 onwards may mean that this policy is difficult to operate, given that the tax and NIC for the final accounting period will be assessed and collected together.

Class 4 contributions are payable in the same manner as income tax, and liability arises in accordance with self-assessments. [*SSCBA 1992, s 15(1)(2)(5)*]. Tax under *ITTOIA 2005, Part 2 Chapter 2* which would, but for a person's death, have been chargeable on him is, however, to be assessed and charged on his executors or administrators. It follows, therefore, that liability for Class 4 contributions on profits or gains to the date of death arises and also becomes a debt due from the estate of the deceased. It must be assumed that Class 2 will be similarly treated under the new regime from 2015–16.

Death of secondary contributor

[26.3] If a secondary contributor dies, anything which he would have been liable to do under the Contributions Regulations is to be done by his personal representatives or, if the secondary contributor was acting merely as an agent, by the person who succeeds him as agent or, if no one succeeds him, by the person on whose behalf he paid earnings. [*Social Security (Contributions) Regulations 2001, SI 2001/1004 Sch 4, para 27*].

Voluntary contributions

[26.4] If a person dies, any contributions which, immediately before his death he was entitled – but not liable – to pay, may be paid notwithstanding his death, subject to compliance with any time limits to which the deceased person would have been subject. [*Social Security (Contributions) Regulations 2001, SI 2001/1004, Reg 62*]. Thus, Class 2 contributions which the deceased was entitled but not liable to pay at the date of his death, and Class 3 contributions which he was entitled to pay, may be paid by *anyone* (not only his spouse but, for example, a former spouse) after his death. Such payments may be important, in relation to long-term benefits available to persons other than the contributor, on the contributor's record (eg retirement pension, widowed parent's allowance, and bereavement benefits). See **19.2** CLASS 3 CONTRIBUTIONS: VOLUNTARY. [*Social Security (Contributions) (Amendment No 6) Regs 2001, SI 2001/3728, Reg 2.*]

Note, however, that with the advent of the single-tier state pension under *Pensions Act 2014* from 6 April 2016, those reaching state pension age after that date are unable to create pension entitlements that may be inherited by a widow or widower, although those who reached that age before 6 April 2016 are potentially still able to enhance state pension entitlements by paying late contributions.

Class 3A contributions may be paid by those over state pension age to enhance their state pension under the rules of the 1975 state pension scheme – see **19.11** Class 3A.

Any extra pension so purchased may be inherited, in whole or in part, by the surviving spouse or civil partner. The amount due depends on age. See **19.16**.

However, in contrast to Class 3, it is not possible for the executors, administrators or surviving dependants to make Class 3A contributions on behalf of the deceased, but they are entitled to a refund of any such contributions paid by the deceased contributor within 90 days before death, net of any extra pension already received by the deceased since the date of payment. [*Social Security (Contributions) Regulations 2001, SI 2001/1004, Reg 56A.*]

Key Points regarding death of contributor

[26.5] Points to consider are as follows.

- No contributions are due on payments of earnings properly made after death – and in the case of employees, this also extends to the employer's liability.
- Where the deceased was an employer of 'earners' before his/her death then the personal representatives will stand in the shoes of the deceased employer and have to ensure that NICs are accounted for in relation to the 'earners'.
- For benefit purposes, consideration should be given to the payment of contributions which the personal representatives are eligible to make provided such contributions would enhance benefit entitlements for surviving dependants.
- The extra benefit purchased by a pensioner who pays a Class 3A contribution is treated like a SERPS pension, which means that 50% or more of it may be inherited. Class 3A contributions paid within the 90 days before the date of death will be refunded.

27

Deferment of Payment

Cross-references. See ANNUAL MAXIMUM 7; CLASS 1 CONTRIBUTIONS 15; CLASS 2 CONTRIBUTIONS 18; CLASS 4 CONTRIBUTIONS 20; COLLECTION 21; MULTIPLE EMPLOYMENTS 47; RATES AND LIMITS 53; REPAYMENT AND REALLOCATION 55.

Other Sources. Simon's Taxes Volume 2, Paras A8.268 and A8.307; Tolley's Practical NIC Newsletter, November 2002, page 87; CWG2 (2018 to 2019), para 3.5.2.

Introduction to deferment of payment

[27.1] Whenever a person who is employed in one employed earner's employment also becomes employed in one or more other such employments or is also self-employed, there arises the possibility that the total amount of contributions paid by him in the year will exceed his personalised ANNUAL MAXIMUM 7. Should this, in fact, occur, the excess amount of contributions paid is not lost and may be repaid, but it is obviously preferable that the payment of excess contributions is avoided wherever possible (see 55.8 REPAYMENT AND REALLOCATION).

To this end, HM Revenue and Customs will, on a contributor's application and if satisfied that the likelihood of over-payment is made out, arrange for deferment of the contributions which would otherwise be due in respect of one or more of the contributor's employments or self-employments. Whilst it may at first sound strange that deferment is still available from 6 April 2003, given the additional rate (currently 2%) above the upper limit for both Class 1 and Class 4 contributions, it will be appreciated that an individual is still liable to only one amount of contributions at the full rate (be it not contracted-out, contracted-out (before 6 April 2016), or reduced rate) no matter how many employments the individual may have and that the previous interaction with Class 4 contributions, where applicable, also continues. Consequently, deferment still exists to defer the difference between the main rate and the additional rate, ie currently 10% for Class 1 and 7% for Class 4 contributions.

As well as Class 1 deferment, NIC&EO in Newcastle grants about 60,000 Class 4 deferments each year and they handle about 13,000 Class 4 repayments after each year has closed.

Those applying for deferment (or their accountants on their behalf) needing to contact HM Revenue and Customs NIC&EO Deferment Group should do so initially on tel: 0300 056 0631.

It should be noted that deferment does not apply to Class 1 secondary (employer) contributions, which are due on all earnings above the secondary threshold in each employment. Employers' only involvement in deferment is in deducting a reduced amount from any employee for whom he holds a deferment certificate (see below).

Until 5 April 2015, it was possible to overpay Class 2 contributions when enough Class 1 contributions were being paid, so it was also possible to defer the Class 2 liability until the correct value was known. With the reform of Class 2 by *National Insurance Contributions Act 2015 (NICA 2015), Sch 1*, which moved collection into the ITSA system and deferred the date of collection until the ITSA filing deadline, deferment of Class 2 contributions is now no longer necessary, as the correct value should be known by the time the tax return is filed.

Class 1 deferment

[27.2] Where, in any tax year, an earner has earnings from two or more employed earner's employments, an arrangement may be authorised by HM Revenue and Customs under which the normal collection procedures are *not* to apply to earnings paid in respect of one or more of those employments but *are* to apply in respect of earnings paid in one or more of the others (see **21.2** to **21.19** COLLECTION). [*SSCBA 1992, s 19(1)(2); Social Security (Contributions) Regulations 2001, SI 2001/1004, Reg 68, Reg 84*]. Payment of contributions on the earnings to which the normal collection procedures are *not* to apply will then be deferred, save for the residual liability at the additional rate (currently 2% with effect from 6 April 2011) that applies to all earnings above the Earnings Threshold in the employments for which deferment is granted.

Such an arrangement will only be authorised where the earner has reason to believe that, during the year, he will pay contributions at the main rate in respect of earnings to which the normal collection procedures *are* to apply of a sum equal to at least 52 primary Class 1 contributions at the rate applicable to him on earnings at the weekly Upper Earnings Limit, or twelve such contributions at the monthly Upper Earnings Limit (see EARNINGS LIMITS AND THRESHOLDS **33** as well as **53.2–53.5** RATES AND LIMITS). [*Social Security (Contributions) Regulations 2001, SI 2001/1004, Reg 84.*] HMRC guidance (www.gov.uk/defer-national-insurance) puts the limits simply: deferment is available if the employee pays Class 1 contributions with more than one employer and earns £892 (the UEL for 2018–19) or more per week from one job or £1,054 (UEL + primary threshold for 2018–19) or more per week from two jobs over the tax year. The equivalent monthly figures for salaried employees are £3,863 and £4,565.

Application procedure

[27.3] Application for deferment is to be made by sending a completed form CA 72A, supported (if subsequently requested by HM Revenue and Customs) by payslips or other documentary evidence of earnings from each employment, to Deferment Services NIC&EO, HMRC, BX9 1BX (see 2.7 ADMINISTRATION). The application should reach Deferment Services as soon as possible *before 6 April* of the year for which deferment is sought in order that any arrangement made might be operative from the first pay day in the new tax year. Arrangements will not normally be made for a year if the deferment application has not been made on or before *14 February* in the year (ie before the end of PAYE week 45), or for a year in which the applicant will reach pensionable age (CA 72A guidance notes). In some circumstances, applications received after 14 February will be considered, but only with the agreement of the affected employers.

Form CA 72A and the guidance notes can be obtained from Deferment Services or downloaded from www.gov.uk.

From 6 April 2003 agent details were removed from forms CA 72A; individuals who wish their agent to act on their behalf should tick the relevant box on the CA 72A and attach form 64–8.

Contracted-out and not contracted-out employments

[27.4] An earner has no choice as to which of his employments are to be included in a deferment arrangement. That decision lies with Deferment Services. However, until 5 April 2016, when contracting out was abolished, there was a 'pecking order' of deferment where an earner was employed both in contracted-out employment and in not contracted-out employment. Deferment Services would always defer *not contracted-out contribution liability rather than contracted-out liability*, whenever this was possible. Before 6 April 2012, not contracted-out contributions would be deferred last if the earner had taken out an appropriate personal pension (because they generated a contracting out rebate after the year-end). In such a case, Deferment Services would try to defer the contracted-out liability. From 2012–13 any APP was ignored because no contracting-out rebate was then applicable to money purchase pension schemes.

Before April 2012, when contracting out through an occupational scheme could be by way of money purchase (COMP) schemes or salary-related (COSR) schemes, deferment was usually given in respect of COSR contracted-out employment, leaving payments in a COMP employment payable to the maximum extent that those earnings would allow.

Example

Afghan was employed by Beagle Ltd (contracted-out, salary £480 per week); Collie Ltd (contracted-out, salary £540 per week); and Doberman Ltd (not contracted-out, salary £450 per week). He sought Class 1 deferment for 2015–16. There were two possibilities: either liability on earnings from B might be deferred (leaving contributions payable on earnings from C and D which, together, would exceed the required amount for 2015–16 (ie weekly Upper Earnings Limit of £815 plus £155 per additional employment), or liability on earnings from D might be deferred (leaving contributions payable on earnings from B and C which, together, would also exceed the required amount). As A's employment with D was a not contracted-out employment, however, whereas his employment with B was not, deferment would be granted first in relation to A's employment with D.

Up to the 2011–12 year if the employment with B had been COSR, C had been COMP and A had had an APP in respect of earnings from D, then deferment would have been granted in respect of earnings from B leaving those from C and D to take priority. At the end of the tax year a balancing repayment would have been due which would have been made first out of the COMP earnings from C.

Contracting out was abolished with effect from 6 April 2016, so this element of the calculation has now ceased to be of relevance.

Notification and operating procedure

[27.5] An earner is notified of the NIC&EO Deferment Services decision on form CA 2717 and deferment certificates (CA 2700) are sent to the secondary contributors in the employments to which the deferment is to relate. (CWG2 (2017), para 3.5.2.) The certificate informs the secondary contributor of the period to which it relates and instructs the secondary contributor that, during that period, he is no longer to deduct the main primary Class 1 contributions from the earnings paid to the earner in question from the Earnings Threshold to the Upper Earnings Limit, but to deduct only the additional employee's rate (now 2%) on all earnings above the Earnings Threshold, unless he is given written notification that the arrangement has been cancelled (CA 2702), though it offers him no explanation as to why that should be so and gives him no indication that the earner has one or more other employments. [*Social Security (Contributions) Regulations 2001, SI 2001/1004, Reg 84*]. Nonetheless, although the Form CA2700 itself may remain silent on the matter, the astute employer who is conversant with the instructions in para 3.5.2 of CWG2 will be only too well aware that his employee has at least one other job.

The secondary contributor himself is unaffected by the arrangement and must continue to pay and account for *secondary* Class 1 contributions on the earner's earnings as normal, using Tables J (standard employees deferred), or Z (employees under 21 and apprentices under 25 deferred). The equivalent tables for foreign-going mariners are Q and P.

Tables L (COSR deferred) and K (under 21 COSR deferred) and the equivalents for foreign-going mariners (N and V) ceased to be relevant at 5 April 2016 (see **15.8** CLASS **1** CONTRIBUTIONS and CWG2 (2016), para 72).

Where an application is approved after *6 April*, one or more paydays may have passed before a deferment certificate can be sent to the secondary contributor (or contributors) concerned. In that event, the secondary contributor will be instructed to repay to the earner concerned all primary contributions above the additional rate thus far deducted from earnings paid to that earner since the previous 6 April. The secondary contributor will then be permitted to recoup from subsequent remittances to HMRC amounts already paid in respect of those refunded primary Class 1 contributions. Any unrecouped amount outstanding at the end of the tax year will be repaid by HMRC.

Post-deferment assessment

[27.6] If the earner's expectations are proved to have been correct after the tax year has ended, and it is found that maximum contributions have, in fact, been paid, exception from liability to pay contributions at the normal main rate in respect of the earnings on which contribution liability was deferred will be granted automatically. [*SSCBA 1992, s 19(3); Social Security (Contributions) Regulations 2001, SI 2001/1004, Reg 84*]. If, however, it is found that contributions actually paid have fallen short of the total contribution liability arising on all the earner's earnings (subject to the annual maximum), *direct collection* procedures (see **21.30** COLLECTION) will be instituted so as to recover the shortfall. [*Social Security (Contributions) Regulations 2001, SI 2001/1004, Reg 68*]. In making application for deferment, a contributor has to agree to pay any such shortfall within 28 days of demand (see form CA 72A and **27.11** below).

> *Example*
>
> Eel is employed by Flounder Ltd, Grunion Ltd and Hake Ltd. In March 2018, when his earnings from the three companies were £630, £300 and £490 per week respectively, he applied for Class 1 deferment for 2018–19. As his anticipated earnings from F and H together (£1,120) exceeded the required amount for 2018–19 (£892, plus £162 per additional employment) deferment was granted in respect of the primary Class 1 contribution liability which would otherwise have arisen on his earnings from G. If, when the year ends, it is found that earnings from F and H have, contrary to expectations, not together reached the Upper Earnings Limit throughout the year, HM Revenue and Customs will issue a demand for the balance of contributions due (relating those contributions to E's earnings from G but calculating the amount by reference to his actual total earnings in the year). If (as is more likely), however, the earnings from F and H have together exceeded the Upper Earnings Limit throughout the year, any excess contributions paid on those earnings will be refunded (see **55.8** REPAYMENT AND REALLOCATION) and the earnings from G will be automatically excepted from the liability at the main rate which, until its exception, had been merely deferred.

Change in circumstances

[27.7] Once a deferment arrangement has been brought into operation, there is an obligation on the earner to inform HM Revenue and Customs of the termination of any employment in which contributions should, as part of the arrangement, have continued to be payable.

Before 6 April 2016, it was also necessary to notify the change to contracted-out employment of any not contracted-out employment, but the abolition of contracting out from that date now renders this irrelevant.

Before 6 April 2012, the taking out of an appropriate personal pension was also notifiable, but this now has no relevance given the abolition of the NIC rebate.

Where a new employment is begun during a year for which deferment arrangements are already in effect, a further completed form CA 72A should be sent to Deferment Services in order that an additional deferment certificate may, if appropriate, be issued.

Class 2 and/or Class 4

[27.8] Where a person is both an employed earner and a self-employed earner during a tax year, HM Revenue and Customs may make special arrangements to avoid excess payments of contributions. For years up to 5 April 2015, they had first to be satisfied that the total amount of Class 1 contributions which was likely to be paid by or in respect of that person would exceed the Class 1 and Class 2 limiting amount for that year (see **7.4** ANNUAL MAXIMUM). HM Revenue and Customs could then make special arrangement with the person as to the manner and date for any (or any further) payment by him of Class 2 contributions in respect of that year (ie a 'deferment arrangement'). [*SSCBA 1992, s 19(1)(2); Social Security (Contributions) Regulations 2001, SI 2001/1004, Reg 90(3)(4).*] The specific legislation authorising alternative collection methods for Class 2 liabilities has not changed, but since the *NICA 2015* reform of Class 2, moving collection back to the ITSA deadline for the tax year, the need for deferment of Class 2 contributions has now disappeared.

Similarly, HM Revenue and Customs was permitted to issue a 'certificate of deferment' for any year of assessment if:

- there was doubt as to the extent, if any, of an earner's liability to pay Class 4 contributions at the main rate for that year; or
- it was not possible to determine whether or not the earner was, or would be, liable to pay Class 4 contributions at the main rate for that year.

That is now no longer possible (or indeed required). In years before 2015–16, the certificate of deferment would defer the earner's liability for Class 4 contributions at the main rate for such period as HM Revenue and Customs directed. However, contributions at the additional rate (currently 2%) were then due on all assessable profits above the lower annual limit. However, the reform of Class 2 from 6 April 2015 means that the correct Class 1, Class 2 and Class 4 liability should now almost always be known before the ITSA filing deadline of 31 January after the end of the tax year, so Class 4 deferment due to not knowing the total of Class 1 and Class 2 for the year is no longer necessary. The permission for HMRC to issue deferment certificates due to doubts about the liability is now restricted to tax years before 2015–16. [*SSCBA 1992, s 17 (2)(c); Social Security (Contributions) Regulations 2001, SI*

2001/1004, Reg 95 as amended by *Social Security (Contributions) (Amendment) Regulations 2003, SI 2003/193, Reg 12 and Social Security (Miscellaneous Amendments No 2) Regulations 2015, SI 2015/478, Reg 15*.]

Classes 1, 2 and 4 interaction

[27.9] There could have been doubt as to the extent of an earner's liability to pay Class 4 contributions whenever that earner had, in addition to earnings from self-employment, earnings from an employed earner's employment at or above the Earnings Threshold (see EARNINGS LIMITS AND THRESHOLDS 33). This is because, where the total of primary Class 1 and Class 2 contributions paid in a tax year fell short of that year's Class 4 personalised limiting amount any Class 4 liability was to be restricted to the amount of the shortfall, and if the combined Class 1 and Class 2 liabilities were *above* the Class 4 personalised limiting amount, any potential Class 4 liability at the main rate would have been extinguished entirely, leaving only the additional rate liability (currently 2%) still due (see 7.5 ANNUAL MAXIMUM).

Example

Inigo is a self-employed architect whose 2014–15 assessable Class 4 profits were £37,200. He was, however, also retained by Jones Ltd at an amount of £304 per week and expected the retainer to continue throughout 2014–15, but at an increased rate. His anticipated contribution liability for 2014–15 was, therefore:

	£
Class 1: £304: Nil% on £153 × 52 weeks	0.00
+ 12% on £151 (balance) × 52 weeks	942.24
Class 2: 52 × £2.75	143.00
	1,085.24
Class 4: £37,200 – £7,956 (lower limit) × 9%	2,631.96
	£3,717.20

As the estimated Class 1 and Class 2 total (£1,085.24) fell short of the 2014–15 Class 4 limiting amount (£3,200.31) (see 7.5 ANNUAL MAXIMUM), Class 4 contributions at the main rate will have been reduced from £2,631.96 to whatever the shortfall (estimated at £3,200.31 – £1,085.24 = £2,115.07) was ultimately found to be. Class 4 income so displaced (ie £2,631.96 – £2,115.07 = £516.89 × 100/9 = £5,743.22 will have then been liable at the additional rate (currently 2%) ie £114.86. However, because the amount might not have been determined with accuracy until 6 April 2015 or later, he could apply for deferment of Class 4 liability at the main rate and pay only the additional rate (currently 2%) in the meantime on all profits above the lower annual limit.

Had Inigo's anticipated earnings from his employed earner's employment been in excess of £805 per week, Class 2 liabilities could have been deferred also as, in that case, his Class 1 contributions alone would have approximated to his overall, personalised annual maximum.

Application procedure – Class 4

[27.10] If a person wished to defer his liability to pay Class 4 contributions for any tax year, he had to make formal application to HM Revenue and Customs in such manner as it approved. [*Social Security (Contributions) Regulations 2001, SI 2001/1004, Reg 97(1)*]. In practical terms, this meant that an applicant had to complete and send to HM Revenue and Customs NIC&EO Deferment Services, Benton Park View, Newcastle upon Tyne NE98 1ZZ (see 2.7 ADMINISTRATION) on form CA 72B (now withdrawn as it is no longer necessary). Where appropriate, this form (and renewal form RD 1301, issued automatically to previous year's successful applicants until the Class 2 reform in April 2015) served as an application for Class 2 deferment also.

The applicant had to be prepared to furnish HM Revenue and Customs with all such information and evidence as it required and inadequate or erroneous information could result in the revocation of any certificate of deferment which was issued. In such a case contribution liability would revive in respect of the whole year. These same rules will still apply to any retrospective applications for 2014–15. [*Social Security (Contributions) Regulations 2001, SI 2001/1004, Reg 97(4).*]

In practice, claims (except some renewal claims) were usually made well into the tax year to which the claim related as the application forms were not always physically available until sometime into the tax year. However, previously the legislation had required application to be made before the start of the tax year to which the claim related – a requirement often impossible to achieve.

Form CA 72B and the guidance notes were previously obtained from Deferment Services, but this information has now been archived (the form and notes are now available at www.gov.uk/government/publications/national-insurance-application-for-deferment-of-class-2-and-or-class-4-contributions-ca72b).

Since 6 April 2003 agent details have been absent from form CA 72B; individuals who wished their agent to act on their behalf had to use form 64–8.

The *Social Security (Contributions) (Amendment No 3) Regulations 2002, SI 2002/2366* ensured that the where there was a refund due of Class 4 contributions this could be made without restriction to the old six-year time limit (unless there was reasonable excuse for the lateness). Also, the five-years-and-ten-month time limit for reclaiming Class 4 where contributions were paid above the 'limiting amount' was removed.

Notification and procedure

[27.11] Notification of a Class 4 deferment decision was made to an applicant on form CA 2703. Where the decision was favourable, a certificate of deferment was issued to the contributor and a note to that effect was also sent to the relevant HM Revenue and Customs income tax office. Responsibility for the calculation and collection of any Class 4 contributions ultimately payable over and above the additional rate (currently 2%) then became the responsibility of NIC&EO (see **21.52** COLLECTION) even if the certificate was revoked. [*Social Security (Contributions) Regulations 2001, SI 2001/1004, Reg 98(a), Reg 99(1)(b)*]. The office handling the contributor's self-assessment tax matters continued to note the self-assessed profits or gains for Class 4 purposes, however, and certified these to NIC&EO for each deferment year. [*Social Security (Contributions) Regulations 2001, SI 2001/1004, Reg 99(3)*].

Any deferred contributions which were ultimately found to be due were payable within 28 days of demand. [*Social Security (Contributions) Regulations 2001, SI 2001/1004, Reg 99(6)*].

Key Points regarding deferment of payment

[27.12] Points to consider are as follows.

- Deferment applies only to the individual's personal contributions and does not affect employer liabilities.
- It is in the multi-employment contributor's own interests to apply for deferment as soon as possible, as deduction of 10% of the 12% primary contributions can be avoided, which is preferable to having to wait for a refund after the end of the tax year.
- Where deferment is granted, there remains liability at the additional rate (currently 2%) on all earnings above the Primary Threshold (Class 1) until the end of year assessment performed by NIC&EO.
- If maximum Class 1 contributions (53 weeks of primary contributions on earnings at the UEL) are paid, no Class 2 contributions should be due and Class 4 should be payable only at the 2% additional rate.
- In cases of multiple employments, where possible, not contracted-out jobs used to be granted deferment leaving contracted-out jobs taking the priority that was required.
- Class 4 deferment may still be available for 2014–15, but has been abolished for later years.

28

Earnings Factors

Cross-references. See BENEFITS **13**; CLASS 3 CONTRIBUTIONS **19**; CREDITS **24**; LATE-PAID CONTRIBUTIONS **42**.

Introduction to earnings factors

[28.1] An earnings factor is the criterion for judging a person's:

- satisfaction of contribution conditions for benefit entitlement (see **13.5** BENEFITS);
- eligibility for credits (see **24.1** CREDITS);
- need to pay Class 3 contributions (see **19.2** CLASS 3 CONTRIBUTIONS); and
- for those reaching state pension age before 6 April 2016, level of entitlement to the additional State pension (see **13.11** BENEFITS).

The need for such a common unit of contribution measurement arises out of the fact that certain contributions are earnings-related (with contribution rates depending on the level of earnings) whereas others are not. Additionally, within certain classes of contribution, rates differ according to the status of the contributor without his entitlement to benefit being necessarily thereby reduced. The rules changed in April 2016 with the advent of the single-tier state pension under *Pensions Act 2014*, from which point no further accrual of additional state pension has been possible.

Relevant contributions and earnings

[28.2] Relevant contributions and earnings for the purposes of accruing benefit entitlement are as follows:

- for 2016–17 onwards, earnings up to the primary threshold upon which primary Class 1 contributions are payable or treated as paid (including the amount of earnings up to that threshold on which nothing is paid, provided that the Lower Earnings Limit is equalled or exceeded) at a rate other than the reduced rate (see REDUCED LIABILITY ELECTION 54); and

- so far as 2009–10 to 2015–16 are concerned, earnings insofar as they did not exceed the Upper Accrual Point upon which primary Class 1 contributions were payable or treated as paid, (including the amount of earnings up to the employee's earnings threshold on which nothing was paid, provided that the Lower Earnings Limit was equalled or exceeded) at a rate other than the reduced rate (see REDUCED LIABILITY ELECTION 54); and
- so far as 1987–88 and tax years up to and including 2008–09 were concerned, earnings insofar as they did not exceed the UEL upon which primary Class 1 contributions were payable or treated as paid, (including, from 6 April 1999, the amount of earnings up to the Lower Earnings Limit on which nothing was paid, and from 6 April 2000 the amount of earnings up to the employee's earnings threshold on which nothing was paid, provided in either case that the Lower Earnings Limit was equalled or exceeded) at a rate other than the reduced rate (see REDUCED LIABILITY ELECTION 54); and
- so far as 1986–87 and earlier tax years were concerned, primary Class 1 contributions paid at a rate other than the reduced rate (see REDUCED LIABILITY ELECTION 54).

[*SSCBA 1992, s 22(1)(2)(4)* and *s 6A*, inserted by *Welfare Reform and Pensions Act 1999, Sch 9, para 3* as amended by *National Insurance Contributions Act 2002, Sch 1 para 7(2), National Insurance Contributions Act 2008, s 3*, and *Pensions Act 2014, s 2(4)(5)*.]

Secondary Class 1 contributions, Class 1A contributions, Class 1B and Class 4 contributions are ignored. The Secretary of State for Work and Pensions has authority to make regulations providing for reduced rate primary Class 1 contributions to yield an earnings factor but this has never yet been exercised. This power remains with the Secretary of State notwithstanding the transfer of various powers and functions to HM Revenue and Customs and the Treasury under *SSC(TF)A 1999*. [*SSCBA 1992, s 19(6)*.] Note that, under the April 2016 state pension changes, a woman with a reduced rate election may nevertheless be treated as if she had an earnings factor for the purposes of establishing state pension entitlement, despite the fact that all previous legislation precluded such treatment. Under the single-tier state pension rules, women may not rely on their husband's contribution record, which might have meant that women with a reduced rate election had no entitlement whatsoever to a state pension if they reached state pension age on or after 6 April 2016. *Pensions Act 2014, ss 11–12, Schs 6–7* provide transitional protection for such women.

Prior to 6 April 1987, what was counted was the notional amount of a person's earnings for a tax year calculated by reference to contributions paid and credited and thereafter it is calculated by reference to earnings payable or treated as paid. [*SSCBA 1992, s 22(1)(2)*.]

Computational procedure 2016–17 onwards

[28.3] The computation of an earnings factor must proceed in a prescribed manner. [*SSCBA 1992, ss 22(3); Earnings Factor Regulations, Reg* 2.] For 2016–17 onwards, it is necessary to assess the earnings factors for earlier years using the rules set out at [28.4] below and, for 2016–17 and later years:

(a) calculate the earnings factor derived from earnings up to the UEL on which primary Class 1 contributions have been paid (ie, at the main rate) or treated as paid (ie, at the nil effective rate applicable between the LEL and the primary threshold) and from earnings credited – although any real or deemed earnings in excess of the LEL are in fact now irrelevant for the purpose of calculating state pension entitlement (see **28.5** below); and
(b) calculate separately the earnings factor derived from Class 2 and Class 3 contributions paid and from Class 3 contributions credited (see **28.6** below); and
(c) under so-called 'near miss' provisions, if there were earnings on which primary Class 1 contributions were paid or treated as paid, subject the aggregate earnings factor arrived at under (a) to various tests and increase that earnings factor as appropriate (see **28.7** below); and
(d) round down each separate number and combine earnings factors arrived at under (a)–(c) above.

[*SSCBA 1992, s 22; Earnings Factor Regulations, Reg* 2 as amended by *Social Security Contributions Act 2002, Sch 1, paras 8, 9*.]

Computational procedure 1987–88 to 2015–16

[28.4] The calculation of an earnings factor must proceed in a prescribed manner. [*SSCBA 1992, ss 22(3); Earnings Factor Regs, Reg* 2]. For 1987–88 to 2015–16 it is necessary to:

(a) calculate the earnings factor derived from earnings up to the UEL on which primary Class 1 contributions have been paid (ie, at the main rate) or treated as paid (ie, between the LEL and primary threshold) and from earnings credited – but earnings in excess of the UAP (UEL in the case of 2008–09 and earlier years) are to be ignored when calculating any additional S2P pension for those who reached state pension age before 6 April 2016 (see **28.5** below); and
(b) calculate separately the earnings factor derived from Class 2 and Class 3 contributions paid and from Class 3 contributions credited (see **28.6** below); and
(c) if there were earnings on which primary Class 1 contributions were paid or treated as paid, subject the aggregate earnings factor arrived at under (a) to various tests and increase that earnings factor as appropriate (see **28.7** below); and
(d) combine earnings factors arrived at under (a) to (c) above.

[*SSCBA 1992, s 22(3); Earnings Factor Regs, Reg 2* as amended by *Social Security Contributions Act 2002, Sch 1 paras 7, 8*].

Class 1 contributions

[28.5] The earnings factor derived from:

- earnings on which a person has paid, or is treated as having paid Class 1 contributions (see **15.11** CLASS 1 CONTRIBUTIONS; **21.5** COLLECTION and **42.4** and **42.5** LATE-PAID CONTRIBUTIONS), and
- earnings with which he has been credited (see **24.7**, **24.9** and **24.12–24.15** CREDITS)

is an amount equal to the amount of those actual and credited earnings rounded down to the nearest whole pound. [*Earnings Factor Regs, Reg 2, Sch 1 para 2* as substituted by *Earnings Factor Amendment Regs 1991, Reg 3*].

Where a person's earnings upon which Class 1 contributions have been paid or treated as paid fall to be recorded as separate sums (by reason, for example, of the person having two or more separate employments during the year), the earnings factor derived from those earnings is to be equal to the aggregate of the amounts arrived at by rounding down each sum separately to the nearest whole pound. [*Earnings Factor Regs, Reg 2, Sch 1 para 3* as substituted by *Earnings Factor Amendment Regs 1991, Reg 3*].

Example

For the first four weeks of 2014–15, Amos was employed by Baruch and had earnings of £202.23, £30.31, £201.76 and £780.24. He was then made redundant and was unemployed for twelve weeks after which he was self-employed for 28 weeks before obtaining part-time employment with Caleb for the remaining nine weeks at a weekly wage of £105.60. He reached state pension age in 2015–16. His earnings factor in respect of earnings credited and earnings on which Class 1 contributions were paid is calculated as follows.

Earnings from B on which Class 1 contributions actually paid or treated as paid because the Lower Earnings Limit was equalled or exceeded:	
£202 + £201 + £770 (NB £30.31 ignored as below LEL and £10.24 of £780.24 ignored for S2P purposes as above UAP) =	1,173.00
Earnings credited during unemployment assuming that a successful claim to Jobseeker's Allowance was made:	
12 × £111.00 (LEL)	1,332.00
Earnings from C on which Class 1 contributions paid:	
None (£105.60 was below LEL)	—
	£2,505.00

The Class 1-derived earnings factor used to be used for two purposes, but with the abolition of S2P at 6 April 2016 and the introduction of the new single-tier state pension, it has only one surviving use.

It is still compared with the qualifying earnings factor or standard level (see below) to test for entitlement to the old 'basic' state pension and the new 'single-tier' state pension, and short-term contributory benefits such as JSA.

However, for those who reached state pension age before 6 April 2016, any surplus of the earnings factor above the qualifying earnings factor arising from not-contracted-out contributions also then earned the contributor entitlement to an additional pension component, originally known as SERPS and later known as S2P, the state second pension that was directly related to the level of not-contracted-out earnings since 1978. This second element of the earnings factor calculation became irrelevant from 6 April 2016 when the state pension moved to the single-tier basis.

Class 2 and Class 3 contributions

[28.6] The earnings factor derived from Class 2 or Class 3 contributions paid or credited in respect of a year is the weekly Lower Earnings Limit for the year for Class 1 purposes (see EARNINGS LIMITS AND THRESHOLDS **33**) multiplied by the number of Class 2 or Class 3 contributions paid or credited for the year (see **24.5** and **24.16** CREDITS) and rounded to the nearest whole pound. [*Earnings Factor (Amendment) Regs 1991, Reg 2, Sch 1 paras 8, 9*]. Since the DSS decided that in future the LEL would be a whole pound figure, the provision for rounding to the nearest whole pound has been of no practical effect since 1985–86.

Example

Amos (see example at **28.5** above) paid Class 2 contribution of £2.75 for each of his 28 weeks of self-employment. His earnings factor derived from these contributions was 28 × £111 = £3,108. His aggregate earnings factor for the year then became, therefore, £3,108 + £2,505 = £5,613.

Following the transition from the 1978 pension regime (ie, basic plus SERPS/S2P) to the 2016 regime (ie, single-tier), the earnings factor calculation is much simpler.

Example

For the first four weeks of 2016–17, Amos' younger brother, Daniel was employed by Enoch and had earnings of £202.23, £30.31, £201.76 and £780.24. He was then made redundant and was unemployed for 12 weeks after which he was self-employed for 28 weeks before obtaining part-time employment with Florian for the remaining nine weeks at a weekly wage of £105.60. He will not reach state pension age in 2016–17. His earnings factor in respect of earnings credited and earnings on which Class 1 contributions were paid is calculated as follows.

Earnings from B on which Class 1 contributions actually paid or treated as paid because the Lower Earnings Limit was equalled or exceeded:	
£202 + £201 + £780 (NB £30.31 ignored as below LEL and £780.24 need not be ignored for S2P purposes as there is no longer a UAP) =	1,183.00
Earnings credited during unemployment assuming that a successful claim to Jobseeker's Allowance was made:	
12 × £112.00 (LEL)	1,344.00
Earnings from C on which Class 1 contributions paid:	

None (£105.60 was below LEL)	—
Earnings factor derived from Class 2 contributions: 28 × £112	3,136.00
	£5,663.00

Since this does not reach the qualifying earnings factor (QEF) for the state pension (52 × £112 = £5,824), Daniel will need to pay a Class 3 voluntary contribution of £14.10 for one week to increase his earnings factor by £112, up to £5,775, which is only £49 below the QEF, which will be credited under the 'near miss' rules – see [28.7] below.

Earnings factor shortfalls

[28.7] Where a person has actual earnings upon which Class 1 contributions have been paid or treated as paid (as opposed to earnings merely credited) and:

- his earnings factor derived from those earnings (see **28.5** above), or
- the aggregate of his earnings factors derived from those earnings and from any earnings credited and from Class 2 or Class 3 contributions paid or credited (see **28.5** and **28.6** above),

falls short of:

- the qualifying earnings factor (see below) by an amount not exceeding £50, or
- the standard level (see below) by an amount not exceeding £50, or
- one-half of the standard level by an amount not exceeding £25,

the aggregate earnings factor is, *for the purpose of satisfying the contribution conditions of benefit entitlement only* (see **28.1** above), to be increased by the amount of the shortfall and rounded up to the next whole pound. [*Earnings Factor Regs, Reg 2, Sch 1 para 4* as amended by *Earnings Factor Amendment Regs 1991, Reg 3*].

The 'qualifying earnings factor' is an earnings factor equal to the weekly Lower Earnings Limit for the year in question multiplied by 52 (see EARNINGS LIMITS AND THRESHOLDS 33). [*SSCBA 1992, s 122(1)*].

The 'standard level' is a level equal to the weekly Lower Earnings Limit for the year (not the Earnings Threshold) multiplied by 50 (see EARNINGS LIMITS AND THRESHOLDS 33). [*Earnings Factor Regs 1979, Sch 1 para 1(1)*].

For 2010–11 to 2017–18 the shortfall criteria are:

	2010–11	2011–12	2012–13	2013–14	2014–15	2015–16, 2016–17	2017–18	2018–19
	£	£	£	£	£	£	£	£
Qualifying earnings factor (52 × £LEL)	5,044	5,304	5,564	5,668	5,772	5,824	5,876	6,032
Standard level (50 × £LEL)	4,850	5,100	5,350	5,450	5,550	5,600	5,650	5,800
½ standard level	2,425	2,550	2,675	2,725	2,775	2,800	2,825	2,900

Example – pre-6 April 2016

Amos (see previous example) had an earnings factor derived from actual earnings in respect of which Class 1 contributions have been paid of £1,173 and an aggregate earnings factor derived from such earnings and from credited earnings and from Class 2 contributions paid of £5,613. The aggregate earnings factor fell short of the qualifying earnings factor for 2014–15 by £159 and, since this is greater than £50, his aggregate earnings factor is (for benefit purposes only) unable to be increased to £5,772. If Amos were to pay a single Class 3 contribution of £14.10 this would increase the aggregate earnings factor to £5,724 since it is equivalent to earnings of £111 for that year on which Class 1 contributions were paid (see 28.5 above). This revised earnings factor for Amos is now within £50 (£5,772 – £5,724 = £48) of the qualifying earnings factor and will therefore automatically be raised to that level enabling a successful claim as regards certain benefits.

Notification of deficient earnings factor

[28.8] It is NIC&EO practice to identify, through a scan of the computer record about 18 months after the end of the tax year, those contributors who have not paid or been credited with enough contributions or earnings to make the year count towards the basic state pension. It will notify an employed earner (but not a solely self-employed contributor) of a deficient earnings factor for a year by means of a letter showing the gap that needs to be made up to make the year qualify. (The letter is a CA 8334, previously RD 170, of which there are two versions, for UK and non-resident contributors). The contributor is also sent instructions on how to pay, a leaflet CA 93, and a reply form CA 93A.

If the earnings factor stated in CA 8334 falls short of the qualifying earnings factor, the NIC&EO will inform him of the number of Class 3 contributions he will need to pay to rectify matters. Such a statement may be requested if, as may happen, one is not automatically received. The CA 8334 is produced automatically by the computer in the next-but-one tax year to the one in which the deficiency arose, but *only if* at least one contribution was paid or credited for that year (the system assumes that the contributor was not working or was employed abroad outside the UK NIC scheme if nothing is paid). The notice specifies the contributions paid as an employed person, the number of Class 2 and Class 3 contributions and the number of credited contributions on the contribution record for the year. If the record is deficient (ie the year will not count for pension purposes), the notice invites payment of Class 3 contributions of a specified amount and recommends payment by the following 5 April, warning that the contributions may still be paid after that date but may be at a higher rate. In the case of Amos (see **28.5** above) he should ordinarily receive his CA 8334 sometime from September 2016 to early 2017.

There were difficulties with the deficiency notices issued in autumn 2006 in respect of 2004–05. Many such notices were issued to people who in fact had significant earnings liable to Class 1. This was as a result of the still unprocessed P35s and P14s following the employer e-filing debacle for those 2004–05 forms submitted by employers. Where this was the case it was inevitably the situation that the entire workforce was questioning employers, as if the whole PAYE scheme remained unprocessed by HMRC, then consequently every employee would have received a deficiency notice. It is believed that around 700,000 rogue deficiency notices were issued at that time, though HMRC denied the accuracy of that figure, without offering one that it did consider to be accurate. When the returns were subsequently processed, affected individuals were sent 'correction letters'. These contained no apology nor explanation but merely stated:

> Your National Insurance Account
>
> We wrote to you previously to tell you that it appeared that you hadn't paid or been credited with enough National Insurance contributions for the tax year 04/05 to count towards your state pension.
>
> I am pleased to tell you that your record has been updated and now shows that there is no shortfall for the year 04/05. This means that you have enough contributions for that year to count towards your basic State Pension.
>
> If you'd like to talk to someone about this, please call 08459 155996.

Similar issues arose in respect of the 2005–06 and 2006–07 deficiency notices issued from autumn 2007 and autumn 2008 respectively.

Another issue that affected the 2004–05 deficiency notices was that inadequate commentary was provided to recipients about the change to the number of qualifying years for those retiring on or after 6 April 2010 (see **13.5**). In January 2007, the Paymaster General announced that refunds 'might' be made to those who had paid National Insurance contributions voluntarily after 25 May 2006 – the date of issue of the White Paper revealing this change. Refunds would be made to those who applied and meet the following conditions:

- they reached state pension age on or after 6 April 2010;
- paid contributions voluntarily on or after 25 May 2006 and before the Pensions Bill received Royal Assent (this was 26 July 2007); and
- they had not been aware of the changes when the contributions were paid. HMRC said that this meant that at the time of payment they had not received information from HMRC about the changes.

Three special forms were available for this purpose and could be downloaded from www.hmrc.gov.uk.

Following a mismatch between NIRS2 and the DWP computer, acknowledged in 2007, some contributors had or will have had credits previously awarded for incapacity and training removed from their records. HMRC advised affected persons through a special deficiency notice and gave them the opportunity to make up any shortfall by way of Class 3 or (if applicable) Class 2 contributions. The *Social Security (Contributions) (Amendment No 8) Regulations 2007, SI 2007/2520* enabled people affected by the removal of these credits to pay Class 3 contributions (or Class 2 if self-employed at the relevant time) in respect of the years 1993–94 to 2007–08 inclusive on or before 5 April 2014 (but not before 1 October 2007). The penalty rates (see

42.8 LATE-PAID CONTRIBUTIONS) were also disapplied.

Key Points regarding earnings factors

[28.9] Points to consider are as follows.

- Contributions made at the married woman's reduced rate have no earnings factor attached to the payments, although there is transitional protection for some of the women affected under the state pension reform introduced by *Pensions Act 2014* in April 2016.
- A week's Class 2 or Class 3 contribution and most credits are equivalent to having earnings as an employee at exactly £116 in the week for the 2018–19 tax year.
- Deficiency notices alert contributors to shortfalls and are generally issued 18–21 months after the end of the tax year to which they relate.
- Given that each year some 1.5 million items of contributions or credits cannot be matched with a contributor (although the RTI system has helped reduce this number) it should be confirmed that all contributions paid or credited in a tax year are included on a shortfall notice before any consideration is given to paying voluntary contributions. The new personal tax account should facilitate this.
- Any surplus in the earnings factor from not-contracted-out contributions earned entitlement to an S2P addition to the basic state pension in respect of years before 6 April 2016.

29

Earnings from Employment: General

Cross-references. See CLASS 1 CONTRIBUTIONS 15; CLASS 1A CONTRIBUTIONS 16 for treatment of cars and fuel supplied by an employer to an employee; EARNINGS FROM EMPLOYMENT: EXPENSES 30 and EARNINGS FROM EMPLOYMENT: READILY CONVERTIBLE ASSETS, ETC 31.

Other Sources. Tolley's Tax Planning 2016–17; Tolley's Income Tax 2016–17; Tolley's National Insurance Brief, February 1997; Leaflet CWG2 (2018 to 2019), CWG5 (2018). See also Leaflets 480 (2018) and 490 (2018); HM Revenue and Customs National Insurance Manual NIM02000, Company Taxation Manual CTM60060. Note that from 2017, leaflets CWG2 and CWG5 are available only in electronic format at www.gov.uk/government/collections/payroll-publications-for-employers.

Introduction to earnings from employment: general

[29.1] The term 'earnings', when used in the context of social security legislation, includes any remuneration or profit derived from any employment, trade, business, profession, office or vocation. It applies equally, therefore, to the income of an employed earner and that of a self-employed earner, though the amount of a person's earnings for any period, or the amount of his earnings to be treated as comprised in any payment made to him or for his benefit, are to be calculated or estimated in the manner and on the basis prescribed in the legislation and such prescriptions do, in fact, differ in the case of employed earners and self-employed earners. [*SSCBA 1992, ss 3(1)(2), 122(1); Social Security (Contributions) Regulations 2001, SI 2001/1004, Reg 25*]. See HM Revenue and Customs National Insurance Manual NIM02000.

The term 'remuneration' is not defined in social security legislation. When liability to pay contractual remuneration was limited by law in 1975 in an attempt to counter inflation, 'remuneration' was statutorily defined as including, in relation to any person, 'any benefit, facility or advantage, whether in money or otherwise, provided by the employer or by some other person under arrangements with the employer, whether for the first-mentioned person or otherwise, by reason of the fact that the employer employs him'. [*Remuneration, Charges and Grants Act 1975, s 7*].

It seems, however, that, in common law, remuneration is not so wide a concept as that. In *S & U Stores Ltd v Lee* [1969] 2 All ER 417, [1969] 1 WLR 626, DC it was said that the term 'remuneration' carries a narrower meaning than what was at that time 'emoluments' (the corresponding term to 'earnings' at that time in use for tax purposes) but is 'not mere payment for work done, but is what the doer expects to get as the result of the work he does, insofar as what he expects to get is quantified in terms of money'. This definition was clarified in *S & U Stores Ltd v Wilkes* [1974] 3 All ER 401, [1974] ICR 645, NIRC where it was held that in order to ascertain a person's remuneration in the context of employment protection law, one must:

(a) include any sum which is paid as a wage or salary without qualification;
(b) disregard the value of any benefit in kind (eg free accommodation) and any sum paid in cash by someone other than the employer (eg the Easter offering received by a minister of religion);
(c) examine any sum which is agreed to be paid by way of reimbursement or on account of expenditure incurred by the employee and see whether *in broad terms* the whole or any part of it represents a profit or surplus in the hands of the employee, and, to the extent that it does represent such a profit or surplus, include that sum.

It was stressed that (c) calls not for an involved accountancy exercise but for a broad common sense view of the realities of the situation.

S & U Stores v Wilkes was not a National Insurance case but was concerned with redundancy pay. Its authority is, therefore, at best persuasive in the present context. Furthermore, the addition of the word 'profit' to the definition of earnings for contribution purposes will, it seems, catch the items which are to be disregarded under (b) above, but *not* anything disregarded under (c) as being a legitimate reimbursement of expenses. The view that the word 'profit' brings payments in kind within the meaning of the word 'earnings' in *SSCBA 1992, s 3(1)* is rejected by at least two leading Counsel but the former DSS clearly believed that it does as *Social Security (Contributions) Regulations 2001, SI 2001/1004, Reg 25, Sch 3 Part II para 1* was specifically introduced to *remove* such payments from the amount of earnings on which Class 1 contributions are exigible. See HM Revenue and Customs National Insurance Manual NIM02015. (See **29.28** below).

The calculation or estimation of earnings is not merely a matter of deciding what should be *included* but of deciding also what should be *excluded*. The various regulations concerned govern both aspects of the computation and provide for certain receipts to be disregarded entirely and for certain items of expenditure to be deducted from receipts. [*SSCBA 1992, s 3(3); Social Security*

(Contributions) Regulations 2001, SI 2001/1004, Sch 3]. Regulations may also provide that where a payment or benefit is provided to two or more earners proportions shall be attributed to each earner [*SSCBA 1992, s 3(2A)*, inserted by *SSA 1998, s 48*].

Earnings paid in a foreign currency are to be converted to their sterling equivalent at the exchange rate current at the date of payment.

It should be noted, in the context of employees, that where an item is *not* earnings for Class 1 purposes it may well, from 6 April 2000, fall within the extended charge to Class 1A National Insurance contributions. See CLASS 1A CONTRIBUTIONS: BENEFITS IN KIND **16**.

Earnings for Class 1 purposes

[29.2] For the purpose of Class 1 contributions the amount of a person's earnings is, subject to the exclusion of various types of payment (see **29.7** to **29.68** below), to be calculated on the basis of that person's gross earnings (see **29.51** below) from the employment or employments concerned. [*Social Security (Contributions) Regulations 2001, SI 2001/1004, Reg 24, Sch 2*].

The fact that, in this Chapter, various types of payment will be stated or argued to be outside the scope of Class 1 contributions will not, of itself, prevent a Class 1A charge arising in respect of the provision of benefits in kind (only cars and fuel were relevant for Class 1A purposes before 6 April 2000). Where a Class 1A charge arises on the provision of a benefit in kind there will often be no difference in the National Insurance cost to the employer since the main Class 1 (employer) and Class 1A (employer-only) rates are identical. In limited circumstances before 6 April 2016, it could actually have been more if the Class 1 NIC was at the contracted out rate. That is because Class 1A will always be at the standard rate. However, no Class 1A contribution is payable by employees. See Table in CLASS 1A CONTRIBUTIONS: BENEFITS IN KIND **16**. Even where an employer opts to payroll all eligible benefits in kind, with the result that no P11D is submitted for the employee concerned, there will be a Class 1A rather than a Class 1 liability: the payrolling process only deals with the tax liability, and Class 1A liability will arise on the value of the payrolled benefits (see **16.2** above).

In the absence of any directions to the contrary, payments received by an employed earner will fall to be attributed or not attributed to his employments on the same causative principle as was enunciated in the leading tax case of *Hochstrasser (Inspector of Taxes) v Mayes* [1960] AC 376, [1959] 3 All ER 817, HL. In that case it was stated that not every payment made to an employed earner by his employer is necessarily derived from his employment but that, for a payment to be so derived, the payment must be made 'in return for acting as or being an employee' and for no other reason. It is not sufficient to render a payment assessable that an employee would not have received it unless he had been an employee.

Despite the words of Lord Radcliffe in the *Hochstrasser* case quoted above, there has always been a tendency, when considering whether or not an item constitutes earnings, to seek only a link to services rendered or to be rendered (ie to see whether the item in question has been received in return for *acting* as an employee) and to disregard the alternative causative link of status (ie to see whether the item has been received in return for *being* an employee). The case of *Hamblett v Godfrey* [1987] STC 60 serves as a strong reminder that that alternative causative link cannot be ignored. June Hamblett, a civil servant employed by GCHQ at Cheltenham by the Crown, had her right to belong to a trade union and certain other employment protection rights withdrawn, and in recognition of her loss of those previously-enjoyed rights she was paid £1,000. The court found that the £1,000 was not received by her in return for *acting* as an employee but that, as all the rights in question were directly connected with her employment, it *was* received by her in return for *being* an employee and was, therefore, an emolument (as the term then was) for tax purposes. The former DSS is understood to have found this judgment of particular interest and, in the light of the court's decision, reconsidered its views on what should not be included in earnings for contribution purposes.

The more recent case of *Wilcock v Eve* [1995] STC 18 concerned whether an ex gratia payment to a former employee could be charged to tax as income from employment. The judgment contains a useful review of the case law in this area, although part of the then Inland Revenue's case turned on the benefits in kind legislation in what is now *Income Tax (Earnings and Pensions) Act 2003* (*ITEPA 2003*), which is irrelevant to Class 1 contributions, as the test for P11D purposes merely requires a benefit to be provided 'by reason of' employment, which is much wider than 'from' the employment.

Mr Eve was employed by a company which was sold out of a group to its management. Had he remained an employee of a group company for five months longer, he would have been entitled to exercise share options under an approved SAYE share option scheme and would have made a tax-free gain of around £10,000, depending on the share price on the actual day of exercise. The vendor company decided, a year after the notional exercise date, to pay him £10,000 as compensation for the loss of his rights under the SAYE scheme, which had been caused by its decision to sell the subsidiary. It was under no contractual obligation to do so, nor had any promise been made to the taxpayer: indeed, Mr Eve knew nothing of the payment until it was received. The company's reason for making the payment was given as a wish to maintain its reputation of dealing fairly with its employees and ex-employees.

The then Inland Revenue claimed that the payment was either an emolument (as it was called then) from the employment, taxable under what became *ICTA 1988, s 19* (repealed by *ITEPA 2003, ss 722, 724, Sch 6 paras 1, 6, Sch 8; ITEPA 2003, Part 2 Chapter 2*) or, alternatively, a benefit by reason of employment, taxable under what became *ICTA 1988, s 154* (repealed by *ITEPA 2003, ss 722, 722, Sch 6 paras 1, 24, Sch 7; ITEPA 2003, ss 201–215*). Only the former argument would be relevant to Class 1 liability. In support of the *s 19* argument, the then Inland Revenue relied on the decisions in *Laidler v Perry* [1966] AC 16; *Brumby v Milner* [1976] 1 WLR 1096 and *Hamblett v Godfrey*. The first concerned £10 vouchers habitually given to employees at Christmas, held to be taxable emoluments. The second concerned a company merger which led to a payment being made to employees following the winding up of a profit-sharing trust, again held to be taxable emoluments.

Carnwath J felt able to distinguish Mr Eve's case from the three main authorities cited by the Inland Revenue. While accepting that an emolument 'from' employment is not necessarily confined to something in the nature of a reward for continuing employment (following *Hamblett*), he noted a distinction between rights intimately linked with the employment (eg trade union rights) and rights enjoyed in some other capacity (eg as a house-owner required to move). In his view, the share option scheme rights would have fallen on the borderline, were it not for the decision in *Abbott v Philbin HL* 1960, 39 TC 82. There it had been held that the *grant* of an option might be a taxable emolument, but the value realised on *exercise* was not — only the introduction of what became *ICTA 1988, s 135* (repealed by *ITEPA 2003, ss 722, 725, Sch 6 paras 1, 15, Sch 7; ITEPA 2003, ss 471–487*) deemed a share option gain to be taxable under the former Schedule E, and then not by deeming it to be an emolument from the employment, but by simply including it within the former Schedule E charge. In the absence of *s 135*, the exercise of Mr Eve's option after five years would not have constituted a taxable emolument on basic principles. Carnwath, J held that the payment made by the vendor to compensate him for the loss of the right to exercise the option should have the same character, ie it was not 'from the employment' but from his rights as the owner of an option.

Where payments of expenses and benefits are subject to Class 1 NICs but not to PAYE, they are to be reported under the Real Time Information requirements the next time the regular payroll is run or 14 days after the end of the tax month in which the payment in question is made, whichever is the earlier.

Tax legislation, practice and extra-statutory concessions

[29.3] Although the underlying principle is the same whether the nature of a payment is being determined for contribution purposes, tax purposes, Statutory Sick Pay purposes, Statutory Maternity Pay purposes, Statutory Paternity Pay purposes, Statutory Adoption Pay purposes or State benefit purposes (see 29.2 above), the Secretary of State for Social Security was *not bound* by decisions in other areas. Indeed, the legislation in each area has its own incompatible rules of inclusion and exclusion. Earnings for the purposes of deciding the availability of benefits are governed by separate regulations for each type of benefit, and earnings for the purposes of deciding the earnings level in connection with Statutory Sick Pay, Statutory Maternity Pay, Statutory Paternity Pay and Statutory Adoption Pay are governed by *Statutory Sick Pay General Regs 1982 Statutory Maternity Pay (General) Regulations 1986* and *Statutory Paternity and Statutory Adoption Pay (General) Regulations 2002* respectively, which, despite their obvious similarities, are confined in their application to the area of law to which they belong.

Where the nature of a payment falls to be determined solely on general principles, however, a person may be *estopped* from arguing that a payment which he has conceded to be earnings for one purpose is not earnings for another. 'Blowing hot and cold in this way is something which the law does not tolerate'. (*R(P) 4/67*. See also *R(P) 1/69*).

In order to facilitate the working of the tax system and to avoid undue harshness in the application of certain provisions of tax law, HM Revenue and Customs has published a large number of extra-statutory concessions and statements of practice, both now available only at www.gov.uk/government/publications/extra-statutory-concessions-ex-inland-revenue. It must not be assumed, however, that, where there is an area of common concern to both tax and National Insurance contributions, such concession will apply to contribution matters (either before or after the transfer the transfer of NIC responsibility to the Inland Revenue on 1 April 1999). (See, for example, **22.4** COMPANY DIRECTORS.) HM Revenue and Customs' authority for making concessions for tax is weak (as well illustrated in the *Wilkinson* case [2007] STC SCD 9 Sp C 567), but the authority in social security law is non-existent. Concessions made up to now have, therefore, tended to be given statutory force by secondary legislation. The insertion of what is now *Social Security (Contributions) Regulations 2001, SI 2001/1004, Reg 40* ensured that general earnings not charged to income tax by reason of ESCs:

- A2 (luncheon vouchers) (now enacted for tax purposes in *ITEPA 2003, s 89*),
- A6 (miners' coal) (now enacted for tax purposes in *ITEPA 2003, s 306*),
- A11 (residence in the UK),
- A22 (long service awards) (now enacted for tax purposes in *ITEPA 2003, s 323*),
- A37 (director's fees received by partnerships and other companies),
- A56 (employee accommodation in Scotland),
- A57 (staff suggestion schemes) (now enacted for tax purposes in *ITEPA 2003, ss 321, 322*),
- A58 (travelling and subsistence allowance when public transport disrupted) (now enacted for tax purposes in *ITEPA 2003, s 265*),
- A59 (disabled persons' home to work travel) (now enacted for tax purposes in *ITEPA 2003, ss 246, 247*),
- A65 (workers on offshore oil and gas rigs or platforms; free transfer to and from mainland) (now enacted for tax purposes in *ITEPA 2003, s 305*),
- A66 (employees' journeys home – night travel and breakdown in car sharing arrangements) (now enacted for tax purposes in *ITEPA 2003, s 248*),
- A70 (small gifts to employees by third parties and Christmas parties) (now enacted for tax purposes in *ITEPA 2003, ss 264, 279, 324*),
- A72 (pension schemes, etc) (now enacted for tax purposes in *ITEPA 2003, s 307*),
- A74 (meals provided for employees) (now enacted for tax purposes in *ITEPA 2003, ss 266, 367*),
- A85 (transfers of assets) (now enacted for tax purposes in *ITEPA 2003, s 326*),
- A91 (living accommodation provided by reason of employment), and
- A97 (Jobmatch programme),

were all excluded from the extended Class 1A contributions charge introduced with effect from 6 April 2000. Some are now no longer referred to in National Insurance legislation as *ITEPA 2003* has given legal force (as indicated above) to a number of situations which, prior to 6 April 2003, were covered by mere concessions. In addition, certain exceptions from earnings for Class 1 purposes are regularly added to the *Social Security (Contributions) Regulations 2001, SI*

2001/1004, Sch 3, such as van fuel at **30.14**, HM Forces' Operational Allowance, Council Tax Relief, Continuity of Education Allowance and payments under the Armed Forces Early Departure Scheme at **11.4** ARMED FORCES and payments to lone parents from the In-Work Emergency Discretion Fund (IWEDF) in the first few months of starting work after a period of unemployment and New Deal participation at **10.4** APPRENTICES, TRAINEES AND STUDENTS (although it is wholly unclear why a social security benefit might be classed as earnings at all). [*Social Security (Contributions) (Amendment No 8) Regs 2000, SI 2000/2207, Reg 4; Social Security (Contributions) (Amendment No 3) Regs 2001, SI 2001/596, Reg 7 and Social Security (Contributions) Regulations 2001, SI 2001/1004, Sch 3 Part X para 8; Social Security (Contributions) (Amendment No 2) Regs 2008, SI 2008/607, Reg 4; FA 2008, ss 46, 48 and 51*]. See also **16.1** CLASS 1A CONTRIBUTIONS: BENEFITS IN KIND.

Gross earnings

[29.4] The definition of 'earnings' discussed at **29.1** above means that all wages, salaries, commissions and overtime payments fall to be included. See HM Revenue and Customs National Insurance Manual NIM02030, NIM02075, NIM02150 and NIM02265.

There are many other kinds of payment which are made to employees and which, in certain circumstances, will fall, or not fall, to be included in earnings. These are discussed below in the order set out at the beginning of this Chapter.

It should be noted that, where an item falls to be included in earnings, the requirement that Class 1 contribution liability is to be assessed on the basis of *gross* earnings precludes all deductions. [*Social Security (Contributions) Regulations 2001, SI 2001/1004, Reg 24, Sch 2*]. That preclusion extends to deductions permitted for tax purposes such as relief for:

- superannuation and personal pension contributions [*FA 2004, Sch 36*];
- expenses of the employment [*ITEPA 2003, ss 327–352*] but see **29.70**;
- foreign earnings [*ITEPA 2003, s 353*];
- personal allowances [*Income Tax Act 2007, ss 35–55*];
- interest on qualifying loans [*Income Tax Act 2007, ss 383–412; ITTOIA 2005, s 52*]; and
- charitable donations under the payroll giving scheme [*ITEPA 2003, ss 713–715*]. See also HM Revenue and Customs National Insurance Manual NIM02175.

It should also be noted, in the context of employees, where an item is *not* earnings for Class 1 purposes it may, from 6 April 2000, nonetheless fall within the extended charge to Class 1A National Insurance contributions.

Timing problems

[29.5] The timing of a payment will often create confusion as to whether or not the payment forms part of earnings for contribution purposes.

The mere fact that a payment of an amount which is clearly earnings is made *in advance* of the period to which it relates does not prevent that amount being earnings at the date of payment if such payments are regularly made in advance. The question is one of unconditional entitlement. If, for example, an employee's contract provides that he is to receive a salary monthly in advance, his unconditional entitlement to the salary arises at its due date each month irrespective of the fact that he has yet to perform a month's work in connection with the payment. If, on the other hand, an employee who is not entitled to be paid until the end of the month requests and obtains a 'sub' or advance payment in the second week of the month, the amount paid to him is not earnings until the due date arrives. (HM Revenue and Customs National Insurance Manual NIM02055). In that case, the 'sub' or advance is, in reality, a loan, see **29.49** below.

The basic principle applies equally to a payment made before the commencement of the employment, provided that the payment is sufficiently referable to that employment. See *Shilton v Wilmshurst* [1991] 1 AC 684 HL. See **29.7** below.

These principles apply equally to advance payments (if any) made to agricultural workers engaged on six-monthly or yearly hirings. Unless advance payments are made at regular intervals, they are to be treated as loans, not earnings, and the whole amount payable for the hiring will be earnings at (and not until) the end of the hiring period.

All payments made to COMPANY DIRECTORS **22** in advance or on account of fees yet to be voted are earnings at the point of payment (see **22.4** COMPANY DIRECTORS). (CWG2 (2017), para 5.1).

Where pay is held back from an employee or set aside until some later date or event (eg Christmas or the annual holiday), the question whether the reserved amount is earnings or not again depends on whether or not the employee is unconditionally entitled to it at the date of reservation. If he is, the amount is earnings at that point; if he is not, the amount does not become earnings until entitlement does arise or payment is actually made (whichever is the earlier). For holiday pay, see **29.25** below.

Care must be taken in the kind of situation described above to ensure that amounts of pay are not treated as earnings *twice* for contribution purposes. Any payment made to an employee which would otherwise be earnings for contribution purposes is to be *excluded* from the computation of his earnings if, and to the extent that, it represents sums which have previously been included in earnings for Class 1 contribution purposes. [*Social Security (Contributions) Regulations 2001, SI 2001/1004, Reg 25, Sch 3 Part X para 2*].

Arrears of pay (eg from a backdated pay award) become earnings only when entitlement to them arises—normally on the date of payment. See HM Revenue and Customs National Insurance Manual NIM02065.

Where a payment of earnings was made either before an employment begins or after an employment has ended, it might at first seem that no Class 1 liabilities can arise as regards that payment—despite the fact that *Social Security (Contributions) Regulations 2001, SI 2001/1004, Reg 3(5)* is framed on a contrary assumption. Under the primary legislation, the Class 1 charge is confined to situations where, in any tax week, earnings are paid to or for the benefit of an earner in respect of any one employment of his which *is* employed earner's employment. [*SSCBA 1992, s 6(1)*]. It is not plainly extended to a payment of earnings in respect of an employment which *was* or which *will be* employed earner's employment. The term 'which is' in the present principal *Act* replaced the more ambiguous term 'being' in the former principal *Act* with effect from 1 July 1992 and thus arguably narrowed the range of interpretation which the charging section is able to sustain. [*SSA 1975, s 4(2)*]. See **29.7** and **29.8** below.

But the matter was put beyond doubt in *RCI Europe v Woods (Inspector of Taxes)* [2003] EWHC 3129 (Ch), [2004] STC 315, 76 TC 390. This was a Special Commissioner's case regarding NIC liability on restrictive covenants. In respect of the change in wording from 'being' to 'is' the Commissioner stated 'It is not likely that by changing the wording from 'being' to 'which is' and leaving the regulations to continue that [sic] a consolidation Act changed its meaning in such a significant way as to exclude liability for contributions on payments in respect of a former employment.' On another point the Commissioner quoted from Lord Lowry in *Hanlon v Law Society* [1981] AC 124 at paragraph 193:

> 'Subordinate legislation may be used in order to construe the parent Act, but only where the power is given to amend the Act by regulations or where the meaning of the Act is ambiguous.'

Further, the Commissioner stated that; 'as *Bray v Best* [1989] STC 159, [1989] 1 WLR 167 was reversed at about the same time as s 4(4) of the 1992 Act [*ICTA 1988*] was originally enacted I do not find this point helpful in deciding whether s 4(4) applies.' The Commissioner concluded in summing up that 'The draftsman of s 4(4) of the 1992 Act had to incorporate payments taxed under s 313 of the 1988 Act into the contributions legislation. He deliberately excluded payments in kind in s 313(4) because they were not at the time liable to contributions. He did not make any other changes to a section that applied in terms to a person who holds, has held, or is about to hold an office or employment. If an employed earner were restricted to someone currently employed he would surely have made a further modification to restrict the application of the section rather than merely applying contributions to "any sum paid to or for the benefit of an employed earner which is chargeable to tax by virtue of section 313". Accordingly I consider that contributions are payable on the payments in question.' On appeal to the Chancery Division the company again failed in its aim; normal expectations would lead to the conclusion that contributions were to be paid on all earnings whether paid before the employment commenced, during it, or after it had ended. The legislation had, the court stated, not intended to make liability depend on the happenstance of when (in this case) the restrictive covenants were entered into or whether earnings were actually paid whilst the employment continued in force. If so the date of any agreement or payment would be open to engineering or manipulation so as to make liability for making those contributions in effect voluntary. When the case reached the High Court, Lightman J had no doubt that 'is' referred to the nature of the employment in question and not to its subsistence at the time of payment.

The general matter of timing is also of importance where an HM Revenue and Customs compliance officer carrying out National Minimum Wage functions on behalf of the Department for Business, Energy and Industrial Strategy requires an employer to pay arrears of pay because the minimum wage had not been paid. NIC will arise at the time of payment of the arrears but PAYE is due for the periods in which the pay accrued (ICAEW Tax Faculty TAXGUIDE 7/00).

Assignment, waiver or sacrifice of entitlement to pay

[29.6] Once an unconditional entitlement to remuneration arises from an employed earner's employment, the amount of the entitlement is earnings for contribution purposes irrespective of the use to which it is put. Thus, for example, a member of a religious order may covenant to his or her order the whole of the remuneration to which he or she is entitled under, say, a contract to teach in a local school, but the remuneration remains nonetheless earnings for contribution purposes.

Likewise, charitable gifts under the Payroll Giving scheme deducted from pay for tax purposes remain part of earnings for contribution purposes. (CWG2 (2018 to 2019), para 2.5).

If, however, an employed earner waives his entitlement to remuneration *before* that entitlement arises, that remuneration will not be earnings for contribution purposes since the employee thereby disclaims his right to the remuneration. If, however, the employee directs the remuneration to be paid elsewhere, he has effectively assumed control over that remuneration, which is accordingly treated as his earnings.

Waivers and repayment of remuneration already paid must (with the exception of contractual maternity pay — see 29.23 below), therefore, be disregarded for contribution purposes, even if they are recognised for tax purposes. (See 22.4 COMPANY DIRECTORS).

Similarly, either individually or under a larger scheme initiated by the employer, an employee may 'sacrifice' part of his salary, ie the cash salary is reduced and replaced by non-taxable benefits in kind—typically childcare vouchers, one mobile phone for personal use, etc. The rationale for such arrangements does not stem from tax and NIC legislation but from contract and employment law and therefore HM Revenue and Customs will not comment on such arrangements before they come into being. However, once such an arrangement is in actual operation, HM Revenue and Customs will look closely at the terms to ensure that the sacrifice is real and cannot readily be reversed and the full cash salary paid. See HM Revenue and Customs National Insurance Manual NIM02330.

Starting payments

[29.7] The former DSS asserted and HM Revenue and Customs continues to assert that all 'golden hellos' and 'golden handcuffs' are earnings for contribution purposes. (CWG2 (2017), para 5.1 and see HMRC National Insurance

Manual NIM02185). This is quite simply wrong. Certainly, if the payment is made as a reward for services to be rendered to the payer in the future, it will be earnings. (*Hochstrasser (Inspector of Taxes) v Mayes* [1960] AC 376, [1959] 3 All ER 817, HL; *Riley (Inspector of Taxes) v Coglan* [1968] 1 All ER 314, [1967] 1 WLR 1300).

This will be so even if the payment is made by a party who has no direct or indirect interest in the performance of the contract of service which the recipient is being induced to enter and takes the form of a 'golden goodbye' from his former employer. (*Shilton v Wilmshurst* [1991] STC 88).

But, if the 'golden hello' is an inducement for a person to surrender a personal advantage and a compensation for the loss caused to him by such surrender (other than the loss of earnings in his previous employment!), the amount should, on the grounds that it is not derived from the *employment*, not be regarded as earnings for contribution purposes. (*Jarrold (Inspector of Taxes) v Boustead* [1964] 3 All ER 76, [1964] 1 WLR 1357; *Pritchard (Inspector of Taxes) v Arundale* [1972] Ch 229, [1971] 3 All ER 1011; *Glantre Engineering Ltd v Goodhand* [1983] STC 1; *Vaughan-Neil v IRC* [1979] STC 644).

In accordance with this principle (and despite the statements originally in CWG2 (2000), page 76), the former DSS is understood to have agreed that (in line with Inland Revenue treatment from 6 April 1987) a sum of up to £6,000 paid unconditionally by a Rugby League Football club to an individual as part of a signing-on fee and representing compensation for the individual player's loss of amateur status was not earnings for contribution purposes. (Taxation, 19 July 1990, page 448). The inclusion in the original DSS leaflet CA 28, page 76, Item 25, of a sentence advising employers to contact their local Social Security office in cases of doubt, suggests that discretion may have been exercised. It was reported in *Taxation* (26 January 1995, page 383) that the agreement between the Rugby Football League and the Inland Revenue had been updated, increasing the allowable tax-free payment to £8,500 with effect from 1 December 1993. The introduction of professional players into rugby union has now rendered this type of payment obsolete in the context of this particular sport, but the principle holds good.

Many top professional clubs now make payments for the use of a player's image as well as for his or her playing services. Famous managers can also have image rights. HMRC is automatically suspicious of, and automatically reviews in detail, any such image rights payments, but it is indisputable that a payment made genuinely for the right to exploit the image of any person, be that a sportsman or any other type of celebrity, will not represent a payment for acting as or being an employee. The rights are divorced from the employment and can be assigned to another party without any adjustment to the employment contract. HMRC's real challenge is usually to prove that the licence fee paid for the use of the image is wholly unrealistic, and not commensurate with the value received by the payer, such that some or all of the payment is in reality remuneration in disguise.

HMRC has tenaciously clung to the position that there is no such thing as an image right in UK law, as there is no legal process that protects the intellectual property rights that identify an image or personality, but it is often indisputable that a famous sportsperson has an image the use of which can be licensed in exchange for a royalty. It is also indisputable that image rights can be protected by the UK courts, albeit under a different label: see *Fenty v Arcadia Group Brands* [2015] EWCA Civ 3, [2015] 1 WLR 3291, [2015] IP & T 223, in which the pop star Rihanna and her 'corporate licensing vehicles' successfully sued Topshop under a passing off action for using her image on garments without permission.

HMRC has to accept that image rights are a valid legal concept in certain foreign jurisdictions, but it usually treats them as equivalent to personal goodwill under UK agreements. Since there is frequently an assignment of rights when players move from club to club, HMRC's views are summarised principally in its CGT Manual at CG68405–68440. However, it reportedly struck a deal with the Premier League in 2000 after Dennis Bergkamp and David Platt succeeded against the Inland Revenue's challenge to their image rights arrangements in *Sports Club plc v Inspector of Taxes* [2000] STC (SCD) 443. Under that deal, footballers can now designate a maximum of 20% of payments from the club employing them as image rights, provided the payments are made to a UK-registered company. (See *The Independent*, 6 April 2016, 'Panama Papers: Image rights prove football is the Panama of all Panamas'.)

Leaving payments

Generally

[29.8] Given the comments at **29.5** and **29.7** above (and in the absence of any new challenge to the decision in *RCI Europe v Woods (Inspector of Taxes)* [2003] EWHC 3129 (Ch), [2004] STC 315, 76 TC 390, any regular payments of earnings made to an employed earner after he has left his employment will fall to be included in earnings for contribution purposes, whether, at the time of payment, he has commenced employment with a different employer or not. (CWG2 (2018 to 2019), para 1.14.)

Also to be included in earnings is any additional payment made to the employed earner such as a deferred bonus, pay arrears from a back-dated pay award or (provided it does not represent amounts which have already been included in earnings—see **29.5** above) and accrued holiday pay entitlement (but see **29.9** below for an alternative view).

Other payments made on or after the termination of an employment may, or may not, be earnings for contribution purposes, depending on the circumstances. The same general principle enunciated earlier holds good. If the payment is made to the employed earner in return for his acting as or being an employee, it will be earnings; if it is made for some other reason or on other grounds, it will not. For this reason, it will be very difficult to argue that any payment made to an employed earner on or after termination in satisfaction of an entitlement arising under the earner's contract of service is not earnings; and the same problem will arise wherever it can be shown that there was a firm expectation and understanding that the payment would be made, for then there may be an *implied* term in the contract or service that such a payment will be made.

See HM Revenue and Customs National Insurance Manual NIM02500.

Compensation for loss of office

[29.9] In accordance with the general principle laid down at **29.8** above, any payment which is made voluntarily by an employer to compensate an employed earner for the loss of his office or employment (rather than as a disguised additional reward for past services—see *Bray (Inspector of Taxes) v Best* [1989] 1 All ER 969, [1989] 1 WLR 167, HL) will *not* be earnings for contribution purposes. (*Henley v Murray (Inspector of Taxes)* [1950] 1 All ER 908, 31 TC 351, CA; *Clayton v Lavender* (1965) 42 TC 607). But an involuntary payment, ie one made under the express or implied terms of the employed earner's contract of service (see **29.8** above), will be caught. (*Henry (Inspector of Taxes) v Foster* (1932) 16 TC 605; *Dale (Inspector of Taxes) v de Soissons* [1950] 2 All ER 460, 32 TC 118, CA; *Williams v Simmonds* [1981] STC 715). A negotiated sum arising out of an agreement with an employer constituted a payment derived from employment and therefore taxable under the former Schedule E Case I. (*Richardson v Delaney Ch D* [2001] STC 1328). See also Leaflet CWG2 (2016), p 94.

It is arguable that even accrued holiday pay included in a termination payment may, in appropriate circumstances, be treated as a compensation payment. If the contract of employment is silent on the treatment of accrued holiday entitlement at the time of termination, it is possible that any payment in respect of holiday entitlement accrued but not taken could quite correctly be characterised as compensation rather than earnings. However, in many businesses, it is the invariable practice to pay accrued holiday pay on termination and it may therefore have become an implied contractual term for all the employees concerned. In such circumstances, the payment is very likely to be earnings. The introduction of a right to paid holiday under the *Working Time Regulations 1998, SI 1998/1833* should mean that the minimum statutory payment for untaken holiday at termination is automatically regarded as a reward for having worked during the holiday year up to the date of termination, rather than compensation for the loss of holiday entitlement.

If the circumstances under which termination has taken place are such that the employed earner has a claim against the employer for breach of contract, ie wrongful dismissal, or for discrimination on prohibited grounds, but the employed earner agrees (preferably *following* termination) to accept a compensation payment in satisfaction of his claim for damages, the payment by the employer will hardly be voluntary but it will nonetheless *not* be regarded as earnings for contribution purposes. It will, in fact, be treated as damages (see 29.10 below). (CWG2 (2016), page 78.) If a settlement of compensation is negotiated *before* the contract has been terminated, care must be taken to ensure that the negotiations do not merely result in a variation of the contract so as to provide for an agreed sum on termination; for such a sum will constitute earnings for contribution purposes.

The former DSS sought to recover contributions in respect of employers' payments intended as compensation for breach of contract. The Department argued that they were in fact restrictive covenant payments, liable by virtue of

SSCBA 1992, s 4(4). Whilst that section would at first sight appear to be inapplicable because such payments are made to compensate the former employee for his loss of rights and not in return for any restriction on his future actions, the section uses the very wide definition of 'restrictive covenant' contained in what is now *ITEPA 2003, s 225*. That refers to where an individual gives a restrictive undertaking in connection with the individual's current, future or past employment (whether or not the undertaking is legally enforceable or is qualified) and means an undertaking which restricts the individual's conduct or activities. This definition, the then DSS maintained, included situations where the individual agreed not to pursue his legal remedy for breach of contract in consideration of his former employer's paying him a certain sum, which was often quantified, under normal breach-of-contract principles, by reference to the salary that he had lost.

This interpretation was at odds with the former DSS's own original guidance in the 1995 leaflet CA 28, page 90, item 95, namely, 'If an employee seeks redress through the courts and payment is made to prevent, or as a result of, legal action, no NICs are due.' This view has now been accepted: see CWG2 (2018 to 2019), para 5.11.2, Item 7 which states 'the termination was a breach of contract. For example . . . you agree, or the Courts or an Employment Tribunal rule, that the employee was unfairly or wrongly dismissed' and at Item 8 'Payments for the employee giving a restrictive covenant' are NICable. However, that guidance also states in Item 7 that if the payment of compensation on termination of employment is contractual or contains a contractual element, the contractual element should be included in gross pay. As contributions can only be levied in respect of earnings (see **29.1** above), the contract referred to in the guidance must therefore be the contract of employment and not the agreement that the employee reaches with his employer. This is borne out by the example given of a contractual element, namely arrears of pay.

This point has been confirmed in a legal case where the taxpayer entered into a written agreement with the employer agreeing to withdraw an appeal to the employment tribunal and accept voluntary redundancy. In addition, the taxpayer agreed to abide by a confidentiality agreement as well as not issuing any further employment tribunal proceedings. The employer therefore paid a lump sum as well as the normal lump sum benefits available under its retirement benefit scheme. The Special Commissioners determined that it was necessary to construe the agreement and other evidence so as to determine the substance and the reality of what the payment was made for. The preamble to the agreement stated that it related to the taxpayer's severance from the employer on grounds of voluntary redundancy *and* withdrawal of the appeal to the tribunal. £20,000 was assigned to the withdrawal of the appeal and £180,000 was assigned by the Special Commissioners to the voluntary termination. This latter part (of which £95,075 was not in respect of allowable pension contributions) was therefore paid in consideration or in consequence of or in connection with the termination of the employment and was accordingly taxable under the former *ICTA 1988, s 148*. IR Statement of Practice 3/96, which ensured that no charge to tax arose under *ITEPA 2003, s 225* (formerly *ICTA 1988, s 313*) where there was no agreement to discontinue legal proceedings or not to commence legal proceedings, was only to apply if the settlement did not provide for a value to be attached to an undertaking to discontinue legal proceedings. It is interesting to note that the Commissioner took the view that chargeable values were attributed by the parties to such agreements so that it prevented IR Statement of Practice 3/96 applying with the result that the amount was chargeable under *s 313*. Clearly therefore the contractual agreement between the two parties ensured that tax and NICs were correctly exigible from the £95,075 notwithstanding the exemption provided under *ICTA 1988, s 188*. The importance of the wording of the Statement of Practice is clear *viz*: 'But this does not affect the application of [*s 313*] to sums that are attributable to other restrictive undertakings which individuals give in relation to an employment, whether these are contained in a job termination settlement or otherwise.' *Appellant v Inspector of Taxes* [2001] STC SCD 21 Sp C 268. [*ITEPA 2003, ss 401–416*].

In Revenue Interpretation, 17 October 2003, the then Inland Revenue stated in regard to compromise agreements:

> Normally, a compromise agreement made at termination deals with genuine claims and the settlement sum is paid in consideration for settling those claims. Where that is the case, the settlement sum is exhausted by reference to those claims and no sum remains to be attributable to the undertaking not to litigate. That remains the case whether or not the repayment clause exists.
>
> Consequently, enquiries will not normally be raised on this point alone. The Revenue will raise the question only if the claim appears to be spurious, for example the amounts are clearly in excess of a reasonable sum for settlements of the claims.

Damages

[29.10] Damages are not earnings for contribution purposes, and that extends to payments made to compromise an action for damages. (*Du Cros v Ryall* (1935) 19 TC 444). Thus, the former DSS regarded as damages which are not earnings for contribution purposes any payment made by an employer to his former employee in connection with a breach of contract if:

- court proceedings have started, or
- there is a threat of court proceedings, or
- the payment is made to prevent legal action being taken.

This continues to be the view of HM Revenue and Customs. See HM Revenue and Customs National Insurance Manual NIM02110. In the Employment Appeals Tribunal (EAT) case of *Orthet Ltd v Vince-Cain* [2004] IRLR 857, involving damages for injured feelings in a sex discrimination case, issues were raised regarding the grossing up of awards which exceed the £30,000 tax exemption limit. Courts and tribunals should take into account the potential loss of damages because of the tax deduction by HM Revenue and Customs where the amount exceeds £30,000. In view of this the award may have to be grossed up when calculating the damages. The precedent for this is *Shove v Downs Surgical plc* [1984] IRLR 17 EAT where it was considered that damages should be grossed up so that claimants receive the amount after deductions such as tax and NICs. [*ITEPA 2003, s 401*]. It is, however, important to note that not every employment tribunal award need be grossed up: where an award is made to a 'worker' (for national minimum wage, working time or auto-enrolment purposes) who falls into that category by reason of being a self-employed person who has committed to provide personal service, rather than because there is a contract of employment (see, eg, *Employment Rights Act 1996, s 230(3)*), the payment will not fall to be taxed under *ITEPA 2003* or included in Class 1 earnings for NICs purposes – the worker is still self-employed for these purposes.

Following the initiative of the Office of Tax Simplification, HMRC and HM Treasury published a consultation document on 24 July 2015 in which the idea of aligning the NIC rules with the tax rules was advanced, albeit with reformed tax rules that would reduce the £30,000 exemption. The proposals were not well received, and were withdrawn pending the issue of a further consultation document on revised proposals, which appeared in August 2016. In summary, from April 2018, the government proposes now to maintain the exemption for income tax of the first £30,000 of a damages payment and the exemption for employee NICs for the whole of any such payment. There will be a new secondary Class 1 liability (without primary) on any excess of a damages payment over £30,000. HMRC have since indicated that the 'secondary' charge will be a Class 1A liability. Further, it is anticipated that payment of the Class 1A charge will be in 'real time' as opposed to after the end of the tax year as is the normal situation with Class 1A payments (see www.gov.uk/government/publications/income-tax-and-national-insurance-contributions-treatment-of-termination-payments/income-tax-and-national-insurance-contributions-treatment-of-termination-payments). Any payment that the employee would have received if he had worked his notice period, even if the notice period is dispensed with and the payment in lieu of notice is a damages payment, will be subject to PAYE and Class 1 NICs. [*Social Security (Contributions) (Amendment No 2) Regulations 2018, SI 2018/257, Reg 2(2)(b)*].

The application of the Class 1A NICs charge has since been deferred until April 2019. At the time of writing, the publication of the National Insurance Bill is still awaited.

Termination payments

[29.11] Since NICs are chargeable only in respect of payments of earnings (ie remuneration or profit derived from employment), compensation payments in respect of the termination of employment are usually excluded from liability (since they represent payments for no longer working). Certain damages payments for personal injury are also excluded from tax liability, but if they are paid in direct connection with the termination, they cease to be tax-exempt while maintaining their NIC-free nature.

In the case of *Moorthy v Revenue & Customs* [2010] UKUT 13 (TCC), M was a director of a company who was made redundant in 2009–10. He received a statutory redundancy payment of £10,000, tax-free, but he claimed against the company for unfair dismissal and age discrimination.

After negotiations, he entered into a compromise agreement (which would now be a settlement agreement) under the rules in Employment Rights Act 1996 and accepted an 'ex-gratia' lump sum of £200,000 in 2010–11. The company treated the first £30,000 as tax-free and deducted PAYE, but not

NICs, from the balance. When M submitted his self-assessment tax return, he reclaimed the tax on the basis that the £200,000 had been personal damages in respect of the discrimination he had suffered and the injury to his feelings.

In negotiations between M and HMRC, HMRC had offered to accept £30,000 as a tax-free payment for injury to feelings, along the lines of the *Vento v Chief Constable of West Yorkshire Police* [2002] EWCA Civ 1871, [2003] IRLR 102, [2003] ICR 318), in addition to the £30,000 exemption under ITEPA 2003, s 401, but M rejected the offer and took the case for a full refund to tribunal.

The tribunal ruled that the whole of the £200,000, plus the statutory redundancy payment, should be deemed to be earnings for PAYE purposes, because they constituted payments in connection with the termination of the employment and were therefore within the scope of s 401. Only one £30,000 exemption was available, and HMRC had had no right to offer to accept by concession an extra £30,000 in respect of injury to feelings.

Personal damages for injury to feelings are normally wholly tax-free, but if they are directly connected with the termination of an employment, a tax charge arises under s 401. See also *Walker v Adams* (2003) SpC 269 (a religious discrimination case) and *Oti- Obihara v Revenue & Customs* [2010] UKFTT 568 (TC) (a racial discrimination case).

A consultation document was issued during the summer of 2016 following an announcement in Budget 2016 (see www.gov.uk/government/consultations/simplification-of-the-tax-and-national-insurance-treatment-of-termination-payments) and the final decision was confirmed in outline in the Autumn Statement 2016, at para 4.10. The consultation also proposed removing the foreign service exemption as a simplification and tax-raising measure, but this was not mentioned in the Autumn Statement. It must be presumed that the normal separate, tax and NIC rules on cross-border workers will continue to apply in determining whether either or both levies must be paid.

Finance Act 2018 removed the foreign-service exemption from termination payments where the payment is made on or after 6 April 2018 and the employee is UK tax resident in the year in which the termination award is made. The Statutory Residency Test is to be used to determine UK tax residency. The exemption is retained for seafarers. [*Finance Act 2018, s 10*].

Dividends

[29.12] Although it would appear that the principal causative factor in receiving the payment of a dividend is the ownership of the necessary shares, and not any employment of the employee, the DSS and HMRC have in the past asserted that Class 1 contributions were potentially due.

HMRC now states plainly that dividends are not earnings: see CWG2 (2018 to 2019), para 5.1 and the NI Manual, para NIM02115. The decision in *Revenue and Customs Comrs v PA Holdings Ltd* [2011] All ER (D) 237 (Nov), [2011] EWCA Civ 1414, in which the Court of Appeal unanimously decided that the dividends paid in the circumstances of the case were indeed earnings, may encourage them to revisit their earlier view. However, the case had unusual facts: the pool for the payment of bonuses had been paid to an offshore trust and routed to the employees through special purposes companies set up by the trustees, the shares in which had been transferred to the employees with no tax liability because of an exemption in the employment-related securities rules. When these companies declared 'dividends', it was open to the court to consider the reality of the situation and re-characterise the payments as earnings. The PA Holdings Ltd scheme had involved a tax-deductible payment by the employer to the trustees, which is as expected for bonus payments but not for dividends. Furthermore, the company's employees were generally already shareholders in the company, so the routing of the bonus pool via specially created shareholdings was unnecessary if it simply wanted to pay a dividend. The contrived nature of the scheme allowed it to be defeated.

HMRC subsequently confirmed to the ICAEW that its view of normal dividends paid by private companies to their shareholders had not changed and was unlikely to change. They are not earnings, nor are they tax-deductible for the employing company, and the shareholder-director is at liberty to choose whether to take money out of the company by way of earnings or a distribution of taxed profits. The imposition of a new dividend tax from 6 April 2016 is intended in part to reduce the advantage of dividends over remuneration in owner-managed businesses.

Employment protection payments

[29.13] Certain payments made under the *Employment Rights Act 1996* and the *Trade Union and Labour Relations (Consolidation) Act 1992* to an employed earner are earnings on basic principles or are to be treated as earnings for contribution purposes. See HM Revenue and Customs Manuals NIM02130. These are:

(a) guarantee payments (NIM07006);
(b) medical suspension payments (NIM07011);
(c) maternity suspension payments (NIM07016);
(d) arrears of pay under an order for reinstatement (NIM07021);
(e) arrears of pay under an order for re-engagement (NIM07031);
(f) pay due as a result of an order for the continuation of a contract of employment (NIM07041);
(g) pay due as a result of a protective award (NIM07052).

[*SSCBA 1992, s 112; Social Security (Contributions) (Employment Protection) Regulations 1977, SI 1977/622, Reg 2(a)(b); Employment Rights Act 1996, s 240, Sch 1 para 51(1)(4)*].

An award by an employment tribunal of compensation for unfair dismissal is *not* regarded as earnings for contribution purposes.

The amount to be *included* in earnings is, in a case falling within:

- (a) or (b), the amount actually paid;
- (c), the amount actually paid or, if normal wages are paid, the gross wage net of any maternity pay handed over to the employer;

- (d) or (e), the gross amount of the award including wages in lieu of notice, *ex gratia* payments and other benefits;
- (f), the gross amount of the award including payments under the contract of employment, damages for breach of the contract in respect of any part of the pay period covered by the order and any lump sum payment in lieu of notice;
- (g), the gross amount of the award including payments under the contract of employment and damages for breach of the contract in respect of a period falling within the protected period.

(See CWG2 (2018 to 2019), para 5.1.)

The above rules are to apply even if the actual amount payable to the earner is, after PAYE and National Insurance deductions and deductions made by the awarding tribunal, very small or non-existent (CWG2 (2018 to 2019), para 5.12).

If an award includes an element which would normally have been excluded from earnings for contribution purposes (eg loss of tips direct from customers), that element of the award should be excluded for contribution purposes.

Where there is difficulty in ascertaining the gross amount which is to be included in earnings for contribution purposes, the clerk to the awarding tribunal may be consulted.

It should be noted in connection with the above that a British expatriate employee of a British employer can bring a claim for unfair dismissal if he or she is posted abroad to work for a business conducted in Britain or if posted to a political or social British enclave abroad, such as a military base. Indeed, an employee can bring a claim in the employment tribunal for unfair dismissal by a foreign company if the employment is based in Britain. [*Employment Rights Act 1996, s 94(1)*]. See *Lawson v Serco Ltd; Botham v Ministry of Defence; Crofts v Veta Ltd* [2006] TLR 27.

See also HM Revenue and Customs National Insurance Manual NIM02198, NIM02313, NIM02314 and NIM07000.

Ex gratia payments

[29.14] An *ex gratia* payment is simply a payment not compelled by any legal right. (See *Edwards v Skyways Ltd* [1964] 1 WLR 349). It thus strictly covers voluntary compensation for loss of office (see **29.9** above). The term is more commonly confined, however, to payments which an employer makes to an employed earner following termination of the earner's contract of service but which he has no obligation to make and which are not primarily compensatory in nature. It is axiomatic that a contract of service cannot provide for an *ex gratia* payment on termination. Such payments are not earnings for contribution purposes provided they are made in recognition of loyalty, length of service etc rather than to the past services provided. See HM Revenue and Customs National Insurance Manual NIM02140.

HM Revenue and Customs advises that, if it is an employer's normal practice to make '*ex gratia*' payments when employees leave, such payments constitute earnings for contribution purposes. (CWG2 (2016), page 94, Item 1). This is correct only if the employer's past practice has given rise to an implied term in the contract of service of the person to whom the *ex gratia* payment is now being made; and for that to be so the practice must have been well known to the employees. A past practice, however consistent, will not bring an *ex gratia* payment into earnings for contribution purposes if the practice has been kept confidential or is explicitly non-contractual. See *Quinn v Calder Industrial Materials Ltd* [1996] IRLR 126 in which former employees claimed that the employer was in breach of contract in failing to pay enhanced redundancy compensation that had been paid to former colleagues in previous redundancy projects. The company had issued a policy document some years earlier containing guidelines on such additional redundancy payments. The terms of the policy had not been communicated to the employees or their trade unions, but they became generally known. On the four occasions between 1987 and 1994 when the need for redundancies had arisen, enhanced payments had been made. However, such payment was not made automatically but required a decision from higher management on each occasion.

The industrial tribunal concluded that the employees in this case had failed to establish either that the policy had been drawn to their attention by the management, or that it had been followed without exception for a substantial period. Accordingly, although the employees had expected to receive the enhanced payments, they were not contractually entitled to them.

See also **29.2** above for details of *Wilcock v Eve* concerning an *ex gratia* payment to a former employee.

In the case of *McBride v Blackburn* [2003] STC SCD 139 Sp C 356 a Lloyd's Name and a member of two groups of syndicates acted as an officer of an association formed to conduct litigation against Lloyd's. He received no remuneration as such but on the successful prosecution of the litigation he received payments in recognition of his services. Were the receipts from an office or employment within former *ICTA 1988, s 19* or were they *ex-gratia* gifts of an exceptional nature paid to him personally and not for his work or services? The weight of the evidence pointed towards each of the payments being what was then 'emoluments' because, although *ex-gratia*, they were paid by the members of each association following the passing of resolutions at the respective general meetings for or in respect of the services which had been rendered rather than as gifts. The payments were referred to as rewards that had been earned as, in part, recognition of the extra work that had been undertaken to save the association incurring secretarial costs which might have proved irrecoverable and as, in part, compensation for having worked for no salary and the possibility of *ex-gratia* payment as an inducement to ensure continuity of personnel. The Special Commissioners found that the payments were 'not gifts in recognition of services or "peculiarly due" to personal qualities, nor were they gifts to mark participation in an exceptional event. The payments were made by "the employer" namely the associations, and were decided upon before the offices were at an end. We accept that other remuneration was not paid; that there was no element of recurrence; and that the recipients were not entitled to the payments at the commencement of their offices, but those factors are not conclusive.' [*ICTA 1988, s 19* repealed by *ITEPA 2003, ss 722, 724, Sch 6 paras 1, 6, Sch 8; ITEPA 2003, Part 2 Chapter 2*].

Golden handshakes

[29.15] 'Golden handshake' is not a term of precise meaning and is generally used to cover the whole of any lump sum which an employee receives on leaving his employment, however that lump sum is constituted. In order to determine the contribution consequences of making the payment, therefore, each of its separate elements will need to be identified and examined in the light of **29.8** to **29.14** above and **29.16** to **29.19** below. The former DSS was quite wrong in the past in stating that all golden handshakes should be treated as earnings.

See HM Revenue and Customs National Insurance Manual NIM02620.

Payments in lieu of notice

[29.16] The legal principles underlying the guidance are these. The phrase 'payment in lieu of notice' ('PILON') may be used both where (a) a contract of service ends on an agreed date with an agreed payment, and (b) where the contract is terminated immediately with the employee having the right to damages for breach of contract or compensation for unfair dismissal. In the former case, the employee surrenders no rights. He merely receives what he is entitled to receive by virtue of his contract of service. (*Dale (Inspector of Taxes) v de Soissons* [1950] 2 All ER 460, 32 TC 118, CA). In the latter case, the employer might decide to make a payment to meet any anticipated claim for damages which the employee might have in respect of the failure to work out his notice and to earn his wages. The true nature of the latter payment is to meet any anticipated claim for loss by the employee; it is not referable to the provision of services and it should thus be regarded as damages (see **29.10** above). (*Dixon v Stenor Ltd* [1973] ICR 157; *Gothard v Mirror Group Newspapers Ltd* [1988] ICR 729; *Delaney v Staples* [1990] ICR 364; *Foster Wheeler (London) Ltd v Jackson*, [1990] ICR 757, [1990] IRLR 412, EAT).

The former DSS confirmed its position to be as follows:

> Legal advice available to the Department confirms that any payments made under the provisions of a contract of service will, unless excluded by regulations, attract NIC liability. Payments in lieu of notice are made because the provisions of a contract cannot be fulfilled. As such they are regarded as damages for breach of contract and not earnings. Clearly a payment which is provided for in a contract cannot represent damages for breach of contract.
>
> (Letter to editor, 4 April 1990).

There has, in the past, been some difficulty over a typical clause in a service contract reserving a right to the employer to make a payment in lieu of notice. Generally, this clause, which may also provide for liquidated damages, is intended to protect the employer after termination. If the employer is in fundamental breach of the contract, the former employee may be able to refuse to abide by restrictive covenants in the contract, citing the employer's breach as a defence if enforcement of those covenants is sought. Reservation of the right to pay damages under the contract allows the employer to avoid such actions by the ex-employee because early termination will not involve a fundamental breach of the contract, which could otherwise result in the termination of the covenants.

The view was supposedly clarified by the former Contributions Agency when they stated:

> Because a PILON is a payment to compensate an employee's legal claim for damages for loss due to a breach of contract and to forestall a legal action for such breach its compensatory character prevents it being regarded as earnings. It does not, therefore, attract liability for NICs.
>
> In addition to specifying the period of notice, a contract of employment may provide *expressly* for a sum to be paid *instead* of that notice. In other words, the contract provides that in the event of the employment being terminated prematurely, a payment in lieu of notice *will* be made.
>
> This payment too is intended to replace the employee's entitlement to damages in the event of notice *not* being given. It too has the character of a payment made to forestall a legal action, and to compensate for a breach of contract.
>
> But, the payment *is* earnings for NIC purposes. This is because it is something to which the employee becomes entitled as part of the terms on which they agreed to provide their services. It is therefore treated as, and constitutes part of, the employee's rewards for their labour.
>
> (CA Specialist Conference written responses, 20 February 1996.)

If payment is made, it is often difficult to determine whether the payment is contractual 'earnings' (and therefore subject to Class 1 liability) or non-contractual compensation (and therefore not earnings). In *Dale v de Soissons*, the contract of employment provided for a payment of £10,000 as 'compensation for loss of office' if termination occurred after twelve months of a contract which purported to be for three years. The court held that, in fact, termination after twelve months did not constitute a breach, as specific provision had been made for just such an eventuality. A breach would only have occurred if the £10,000 had not been paid on termination after one year. The £10,000 paid was therefore held to be an emolument from the employment rather than compensation derived from the termination. The Contributions Agency subsequently used this line of argument to charge Class 1 contributions on payments in lieu.

This matter was further addressed by the CA as follows:

> If the contract provides that in the event of the fixed term being curtailed in any way the employer will make a payment in lieu of remuneration for the remaining period, then the right to that payment arises from the terms of the contract. The employer and employee have agreed that as part of the terms on which the employee will provide his services, that the employee shall in certain circumstances be entitled to certain payments. The right to the payment specified in the contract forms part of the rewards for the employee's services. It is earnings, and attracts liability for NICs.
>
> If the contract does not provide for the making of a payment in lieu of remuneration in the event of the employer terminating the contract before the expiry date, then

> any payment on account of lost remuneration is compensatory only. It is not earnings, and therefore there is no liability for NICs.
>
> If an employee has contracted to work for a fixed term and the employer has contracted to provide work for that period, any termination by the employer in advance of the expiry date constitutes a breach of contract by them, and entitles the employee to claim damages. The employer's payment is compensation for a legal claim to damages, and is made to forestall such a claim. For the reasons given in paragraph 7 it does not constitute earnings and does not attract liability for NICs.
>
> (CA Specialist Conference written responses, 20 February 1996.)

However, in the subsequent case in the Court of Appeal of *EMI Group Electronics Ltd v Coldicott* [1999] STC 803 the question of whether pay in lieu of notice at the option of the employer is taxable as emoluments or compensation has fallen on the side of the authorities. In this case the former Inland Revenue had asserted that termination payments made to two senior executives in lieu of their notice, written into their contracts, were assessable to PAYE (and NICs). The specific part of the termination provisions was as follows:

> NOTICE OF TERMINATION
>
> The senior manager is required to give the Company three months' notice in writing of the intention to terminate employment. The Company will give its senior managers six months' notice in writing of its intention to terminate employment, except during the first six months' of service, when this will be reduced to three months' notice.
>
> The Company reserves the right to make payment of the equivalent of salary in lieu of notice and to terminate employment without notice or payment in lieu for gross misconduct.

In the Court of Appeal, Chadwick LJ supported the decisions reached by the Commissioners and the High Court and came to the conclusion that ' . . . there is nothing in the authorities which requires this court to reach the conclusion that a payment in lieu of notice, made in pursuance of a contractual provision, agreed at the outset of the employment, which enables the taxpayer company to terminate the employment on making that payment, is not properly to be regarded as an emolument *from* that employment. In my view, for the reasons which I have set out, such a payment is an emolument from the employment.' Leave to appeal to the House of Lords was refused. Now that the matter has been resolved it might be in the interests of employers to review the discretionary pay in lieu contracts and in the above circumstances deduct PAYE and NICs (where relevant).

See also Tolley's Practical NIC, June 1999, page 41.

Delaney v Staples, although a *Wages Act* case, is illuminating. Lord Browne-Wilkinson, LJ stated there that 'a payment in lieu is not a payment of wages in the ordinary sense since it is not a payment for work to be done under the contract of employment.' Something that is not wages for work done or a reward for services cannot be remuneration or profit derived from the employment on the principles outlined above in relation to *Hochstrasser v Mayes*.

Furthermore, the principles applied in *Hamblett v Godfrey* need not present a difficulty. Following Carnwath, J's reasoning in *Wilcock v Eve* (see **27.2** above), Miss Hamblett was taxed on the £1,000 compensation she received not simply because she was an employee under a contract of service but because the payment was derived from a right intimately linked with that employment. It is submitted that, where payment in lieu is *permitted, but not required*, by the contract of employment, but only at the discretion of the employer, no contractual *right* to the payment exists and any payment made cannot be earnings. Thus, no contribution liability can arise in this circumstance and this was confirmed, for the first time, in CWG2 (1998), page 81 (although the then Inland Revenue still asserted that such payments are both taxable and subject to PAYE). The CA view was in line with what was expressed in its Specialist Conference written responses, 20 February 1996. Before its demise, the Contributions Agency, however, rebutted that advice (CA National Insurance News No 12, Winter 1998/99) and the 1999 and subsequent editions of CWG2 again revert to the statement that such payments *are* liable to contributions. This is supported by the outcome of the *EMI* case referred to above. See CWG2 (2017), para 5.11.2, Item 1 and HM Revenue and Customs National Insurance Manual NIM02570.

Termination without notice need not always involve invoking a PILON clause in the employment contract. In January 2001 the employment law case *Rowley v Cerberus Software Ltd* [2001] EWCA Civ 78, [2001] ICR 376, [2001] IRLR 160 considered a contractual clause providing that the employer 'may' make a PILON. The Court of Appeal held that the word 'may' meant that the employer was free to give neither notice nor a PILON but instead to breach the contract and pay damages for that breach. That conclusion clearly applies wherever the contractual clause is not prescriptive in requiring a payment where notice is not given. Such action was financially beneficial to the employer in *Cerberus* because the sum payable as compensation for breach of contract, initially calculated by reference to lost remuneration in the notice period, could be reduced or 'mitigated' to take account of the fact that the ex-employee had found alternative employment during what would have been the notice period. This reduced the loss caused by the employer's action and so lessened the sum due as damages. By contrast, if the employer had exercised the right to pay a PILON instead of giving notice (and so terminated the contract lawfully), the payment would need to have been equal to the gross salary that would have been payable during the notice period.

Some commentators have argued that the *Cerberus* decision means that the *EMI* case has effectively been overruled. The basis of this view is that *Cerberus* means that an employee has no right to sue for a payment and so it cannot be general earnings from employment. HM Revenue and Customs does not accept this analysis and holds the view that former *ICTA 1988, s 131*, which defined an emolument for the purpose of former *ICTA 1988, s 19*, was not expressed in contractual terms. [Now *ITEPA 2003, s 62*]. It thinks that there are many taxable payments that are not dependent on any contractual obligation. In the *EMI* case, it states, the employee equally had no right to sue for the PILON, but it was nevertheless held to be taxable as an emolument from employment because the employer had exercised its discretion and so ensured that the source of the payment was the employer-employee relationship, as evidenced in that case by the contractual terms.

In the August 1996 Tax Bulletin article, it was stated that '. . . even where there is no such contractual arrangement, an employer may regularly make a PILON instead of giving whatever notice is due. It is then possible that an implied contractual term of service may come into being, and where it does the payment is also properly regarded as made under contractual arrangements. All the facts of an individual case, including the employee's knowledge of an established practice, would need to be considered in deciding whether this was so.' HM Revenue and Customs now accepts that it is unlikely that an implied contractual term in relation to PILONs can exist. Contract law suggests that if something conflicts with an express or written contractual term, then it cannot be implied. Since contracts generally include a right to receive notice of termination of employment (whether directly or through the *Employment Rights Act 1996*) then an implied right to receive a PILON would appear to conflict with the express term that the employee is entitled to receive notice of termination.

Despite that, however, HM Revenue and Customs maintains that a non-contractual PILON may in some circumstances fall within what was *ICTA 1988, s 19* and so then also, in practice, be liable for NICs. This view affects those cases where, as a response to the *EMI* decision, PILON clauses were deleted from contractual arrangements as well as other cases where no contractual provision for PILON exists. In such cases it is commonly asserted that any PILON made is in breach of contract and so liable to tax only under what was *ICTA 1988, s 148* and not liable to NICs. Where a PILON is paid as an automatic response to a termination, it may – says HM Revenue and Customs – be within the scope of what was *ICTA 1988, s 19* and similarly liable for NICs, for example, if every time there is a redundancy, all employees receive a payment in lieu of any period of unworked notice. [*ITEPA 2003, Part 2 Chapter 2; ITEPA 2003, ss 401–416*]. In such circumstances the payment is an integral part of the employer-employee relationship for the workplace, albeit non-contractual, and has its source in that relationship and nowhere else. See Tax Bulletin, Issue 63, February 2003.

SCA Packaging Ltd made more than 100 employees redundant, and made payments in lieu of notice. It did not deduct tax from the payments. HMRC issued determinations under the *Income Tax (Employments) Regulations 1993, SI 1993/744, Reg 49*, in respect of all the relevant employees, without consideration of the three different contractual arrangements in use. The employees had a written contract that included only a notice period, but the trade unions had negotiated a series of memoranda with the company to regulate how redundancies would be handled. The key clause in the relevant memorandum stated that payment in lieu would be made on termination, and the court held that this memorandum had been incorporated into the contracts of employment. The Chancery Division dismissed the company's appeal against all of the determinations for two of the three classes of employee.

Interestingly, however, the Special Commissioner had held that, for the one member of the office staff whose contract had not been extended by the redundancy memorandum, HMRC could not simply imply a contractual right to a PILON on the basis that everyone else had received one. It was not permissible to imply a term into a contract where it was not necessary to make sense of the contract: in the particular worker's contract, there were termination provisions, but they did not include a PILON clause.

It is worthy of note that HMRC did not appeal against the Special Commissioner's decision to uphold the company's appeal in the case of the claimed implied PILON clause.

In the High Court, Lightman J observed that the bulk of the employees were entitled under their contracts 'to specified payments in lieu of notice . . . There was no variation or discharge of their contracts of employment. The payments were payments made under and pursuant to the provisions in their contracts of employment . . . in circumstances which their contracts expressly contemplated, namely payment in lieu of notice. An event contemplated and provided for in their contracts occurred triggering the clause in their contracts entitling them to payment and the payment must constitute emoluments from the employees' employment.' However, because there was no appeal to the High Court, he was not asked to opine on the one case where HMRC had tried to imply a PILON clause and failed before the Special Commissioner. It must be surmised that HMRC was anxious to avoid a decision in the High Court that would be a precedent in other cases where it was similarly arguing that employees could have implied PILONs because it had happened before or happened with others in the organisation. An adverse finding at that level would have meant HMRC having to drop its argument for a liability on so called 'auto-PILONs'. *SCA Packaging Ltd v Revenue and Customs Comrs* [2006] STC (SCD) 426 ; *SCA Packaging Limited v Customs and Excise Commissioners* [2007] EWHC 270(Ch).

In a more recent case in the same subject area, a woman (C) began employment with a company in 1996. In 2003 her responsibilities were changed. She took the view that this amounted to 'constructive dismissal'. Her employers took the view that the circumstances did not amount to 'constructive dismissal', and that she had resigned. However, following negotiations, she was paid a lump sum representing three months' salary as a 'goodwill gesture'. HMRC issued an amendment to her self-assessment, charging tax on the basis that the payment was a taxable emolument because a right to be paid in lieu could be inferred from custom and practice. She appealed, contending that it was a compensation payment within *ITEPA 2003, s 401*, and qualified for the £30,000 exemption under *ITEPA 2003, s 403*. The First-Tier Tribunal accepted this contention and allowed her appeal, applying the principles laid down in *EMI Group Electronics Ltd v Coldicott*, above, and accepting C's contention that the circumstances amounted to 'constructive dismissal'. The Tribunal found that 'the threshold for custom and practice to have the effect of implying terms into employment agreements is high' and that there was no evidence before it of any implied right to a PILON. HMRC again declined to appeal to the Upper Tribunal and risk creating an unwelcome precedent. *Clinton v Revenue and Customs Comrs* [2009] UKFTT 337 (TC), [2010] SWTI 487. It should be noted that the £30,000 exemption does not apply for National Insurance purposes.

An individual (G) began working for a company in 2002. In August 2004 he was made redundant, and was paid £76,872 in lieu of notice. In his tax return, he claimed a repayment on the basis that the first £30,000 of this was exempt from tax. HMRC issued an amendment charging tax on the basis that the payment had been made in accordance with G's contract of employment, and was therefore a taxable emolument which did not qualify for exemption. G appealed. The First-Tier Tribunal dismissed his appeal, applying the principles laid down in *EMI Group Electronics Ltd v Coldicott* (see above). *Goldberg v HMRC* [2010] UKFTT 346, TC00628.

In the common case where an employee is told that he or she is being made redundant and must take 'garden leave' the question arises whether the payment is part of the redundancy or a PILON. In *Redundant Employee v McNally (Inspector of Taxes)* [2005] STC (SCD) 143 an employee being made redundant was contractually entitled to three months' notice. She was paid her salary for these three months, but was not required to attend her employer's office. HM Revenue and Customs issued an amendment to her self-assessment charging tax on the salary which she received. She appealed, contending that the payments qualified for the £30,000 exemption under *ITEPA 2003, s 403(1)*. The Special Commissioner rejected this contention and dismissed her appeal, finding that she had effectively been required to take 'garden leave' for three months and holding that her salary remained taxable. In an appeal to the Chancery Division the Judge, Park J, stated:

> I accept, as did Dr Avery Jones, that the last sentence of paragraph 3 of the letter (which refers to 'your pay in lieu of notice') would be more consistent with Miss Ibe not having been given notice but instead having been dismissed summarily. However, as Lord Browne-Wilkinson said in *Delaney v Staples*, the expression "Payment in lieu of notice" is also used in garden leave cases. The feature of paragraph 3 of the letter whereby the pay to Miss Ibe was to be made through the payroll in the normal manner on the 25th of each month is more indicative of the employment continuing for three months. If an employment is terminated without notice but the employer is willing to pay an amount equal to three months' salary in lieu of notice, one would certainly expect that amount to be paid in one lump sum and to be paid at an early date.

The appeal was dismissed. See *Ibe v McNally* Ch D [2005] STC 1426.

If it can be demonstrated that the payment is derived directly from the termination rather than from the services (ie it would not have been made if the employment had not been terminated and no right to receive it was written into the contract), it should not represent earnings. Even if the payment might have been made in another form in due course, it is likely that it would still not be liable. In *Henley v Murray*, a director with a fixed term contract was asked by the board to resign early. He was paid on termination the amount he would have received if the appointment had continued to the contractual termination date. The sum was held by the Court of Appeal not to be assessable. The payment was clearly *related to and based on* the contract, but was derived from its termination, not from its being carried out. Also, if the employer and the employee both agree that the employment should terminate forthwith on payment of *a sum in lieu of notice* this subsequent agreement between the parties does not constitute a term on which the employee agreed to provide their labour. It is in fact the price the employer is prepared to pay the employee to forego notice to which they would otherwise be entitled and no NICs would be due in respect of it, but for the outcome of the *EMI* case referred to above. For a review of the tax position see IR Tax Bulletin, August 1996, pages 325–327 and IR Tax Bulletin 63, February 2003.

In *Mimtec Ltd v CIR* [2001] STC SCD 101 under an agreement reached with the trade union, employees to be made redundant would each be entitled to receive a specified payment 'in recognition of any entitlements under the consultation process including pay in lieu of notice, etc.' Payments were made and the first dismissal was made prior to the 90-day consultation period, there was a failure to comply, resulting in a 'protective' award. See *Trade Union and Labour Relations (Consolidation) Act 1992, ss 188, 189 and 190*. The Inland Revenue took the view that these payments were emoluments but the court determined:

> In contrast to the statutory rights to join unions etc, which are conferred on persons who are employed, the right to a protective award under the 1992 Act is given because the person in question, e.g. the taxpayer company's employee, has been deprived of his employment by redundancy without proper consultation. The right to the award arises because the employer and employee relationship has been terminated. The 1992 Act is the source of the protective awards, not the employer and employee relationship. Thus, had they been made, they would not have ranked as emoluments within s 19 of the 1988 Act.

It should be noted, though, that such payments are always deemed to be earnings for NIC purposes – see **29.13** above.

The HMRC and HM Treasury consultation document of 24 July 2015 on reforming the tax and NIC rules relating to termination payments suggested that all PILONs will in future be treated in the same way (ie, taxable and NICable, subject to an exemption lower than the current £30,000), in order to simplify decision-making for employers and HMRC (it will also raise more revenue for the Exchequer, since employer NICs will apply to termination payments, but this point was not a feature of the consultation).

Subsequently, all PILONs whether or not contractual, are now treated as earnings from employment and are subject to PAYE tax and Class 1 NICs from 6 April 2018. The legislation provides a formula to calculate how much of a termination award is to be treated as a PILON, referred to as 'Post-Employment Notice Pay' (PENP). The formula is:

$$\left(\frac{BP \times D}{P}\right) - T$$

Where:

BP is the employee's basic pay from the employment in respect of the last pay period of the employee to end before the trigger date, but excluding overtime, bonus, commission, gratuity and allowances. Also excluded are the value of benefits in kind and income related to securities and securities options, and amounts received in connection with the termination of the employment. Importantly, any amounts that the employee has given up, eg salary sacrifice arrangements, must be added back.

D is the number of days in the PENP.

P is the number of days in the last pay period to end before the trigger date.

T is the total of the amounts of any payment or benefit received in connection with the termination which:

(a) would fall within section 401(1)(a) but for section 401(3) of ITEPA 2003;
(b) is taxable as earnings under Chapter 1 of Part 3 of ITEPA 2003;
(c) is not pay in respect of holiday entitlement for a period before the employment ends; and
(d) is not a bonus payable for termination of the employment.

The 'trigger date' is:

(a) if the termination is not a notice case, the last day of the employment, and
(b) if the termination is a notice case, the day the notice is given.

The 'post-employment notice period' is the period:

(a) beginning at the end of the last day of the employment; and
(b) ending with the earliest lawful termination date.

Example

Finn is given notice by Dorsal Ltd owing to redundancy on 15 June; the contract specifies two months' notice on either side with no PILON clause. Finn's annual salary is £40,000, of which 10% (£4,000) is sacrificed in return for employer pension contributions. In the pay period before the trigger date (15 June), his May salary comprised of £3,000 basic pay and a £500 bonus. The PENP ends on 15 August.

The basic pay to be used in the PENP calculation is £3,333, ie basic pay £3,000 plus the salary sacrifice £333. The bonus is ignored and the PENP calculation is thus:

$$\left(\frac{3,333 \times 61}{31}\right) - 0 = £6,558.48$$

The legislation provides that where the last pay period is a whole month, and the notice period is also in whole months, then 'D' and 'P' can be expressed in months (P will then be '1'). Using the details above, this gives a PENP value as follows:

$$\left(\frac{3,333 \times 2}{1}\right) - 0 = £6,666$$

Using months, where possible, may be more preferable since it removes the vagaries that arise owing to the differences in the number of days in a month. In the above example, if the last pay period had been February (in a non-leap year) the PENP would have been £7,261.18 because the denominator would be 28.

[*Finance (No. 2) Act 2017, s 5; Social Security (Contributions) (Amendment No 2) Regulations 2018, SI 2018/257, Reg 2*].

Redundancy pay

[29.17] Any payment by way of redundancy pay, whether provided for within the terms of a contract or not, is to be excluded from earnings. [*Social Security (Contributions) Regulations 2001, SI 2001/1004, Reg 24, Sch 3 Part X para 6*]. (CWG2 (2018 to 2019), paras 5.1, 5.11.1 and 5.11.2, Item 7). The exclusion stated applies to all redundancy payments, not merely to statutory redundancy payments. A redundancy payment is merely compensation for the loss of the accrued right in a person's job (*Lloyd v Brassey* [1969] 2 QB 98, [1969] 1 All ER 382, CA) which, were it not excluded from earnings for contribution purposes by regulation, would fall to be excluded or included by reference to the principles set out at **29.9** above. A redundancy payment is made in return for an employee ceasing to be an employee rather than for acting as or being one. (See *Mairs v Haughey* [1992] STC 495, and **29.2** above). See HM Revenue and Customs National Insurance Manual NIM02580.

In practice, for these purposes, the definition of 'redundancy' is drawn from *Employment Rights Act 1996, Part XI* and *s 199(2)* or *s 209*. Redundancy, for employment protection purposes, is defined as dismissal wholly or mainly due to the fact that the employer has ceased, or intends to cease, to carry on the business for the purposes of which the employee was employed or has ceased or intends to cease to carry on that business in the place where the employee was employed. Alternatively, redundancy can occur where the requirements of that business for employees to carry out work of a particular kind, or for employees to carry out work of a particular kind in the place where they were so employed, have ceased or diminished or are expected to cease or diminish.

The CA added further clarification:

> 'A company may embark on a series of comprehensive redundancies where payments in lieu of notice are common, and become an expectation by those who are affected. However, it is unlikely to be the intention of any employer that whatever may be offered by way of a payment in lieu of notice as part of a redundancy package shall become incorporated into an employee's existing terms of and conditions of service, and, as a consequence, form part of the rewards that employee receives in exchange for providing services. The usual intention is that the payment should be received as compensation for losing the right to provide services. The payment therefore remains one to compensate the employee for the breach of contract in giving no notice or less than the requisite amount of notice, and does not attract liability for NICs.'
>
> (CA Specialist Conference written responses, 20 February 1996.)

Redundancy may be indirect, eg an employee may leave as a result of a reduced need for employees elsewhere in the business (CWG2 (2018 to 2019), para 5.11.2, Item 6).

> ***Example***
>
> The direct sales department of Benevolent Ltd is made redundant in September 2016. It is decided that they should leave the company immediately rather than serve their full three months' notice and they will receive a Payment In Lieu of Notice (PILON) as well as their month's salary and a redundancy payment of one month's pay for each year served with the company as follows:

	PILON	Redundancy	Total
Mark	£4,500	£15,000	£19,500
Luke	3,700	11,250	14,950
John	5,400	27,000	32,400

Their staff handbook states that '*You will be expected to work your full period of notice before leaving the company. The company reserves the right to make payment of the equivalent salary in lieu of notice and to terminate employment without notice or payment in lieu for gross misconduct*'. It should also perhaps be made clear that PILONs are subject to PAYE and NICs as straightforward earnings, whereas statutory redundancy payments are not taxable as general earnings, but instead are subject to tax over the £30,000 limit because they are within *ITEPA 2003, s 401* and classed as 'specific employment income' by *ITEPA 2003, s 7(4)(6)*.

As far as Benevolent Ltd's obligations regarding unfair dismissal are concerned the maximum basic award for unfair dismissal from an Employment Tribunal from 6 April 2018 is £508 per week and the maximum compensatory award is £83,682. See also *Keeley v Fosroc International Ltd* [2006] EWCA Civ 1277, [2006] IRLR 961, [2006] 40 LS Gaz R 33 for the importance of stating contractual and non-contractual terms in company literature. In addition, if Benevolent Ltd refused to reinstate an employee following a tribunal decision that was not in their favour the company might have to pay an additional award. Statutory redundancy pay is calculated on length of service up to a maximum of 30 weeks (based on a maximum of 20 years' service after age 41) multiplied by the person's weekly pay up to a maximum of £508 per week. The maximum amount of statutory redundancy pay is therefore £15,240 from 6 April 2018. However, it should be borne in mind that no financial limit exists in respect of findings of discrimination on the grounds of race, sex, disability, religious beliefs or sexual orientation.

The redundancy letter sent by Benevolent Ltd to the employees is along the following lines:

Dear Mark/Luke/John

I refer to my letter of [. . . . .] and our meeting today.

I confirm that the position remains as set out in my letter. The company, with regret, does not see any practical alternative to the reorganisation and thus the reduction in staff which, unfortunately, means that your employment will end because of redundancy.

While careful thought has been given to the points raised by you, these do not change our view that your redundancy is unavoidable in the circumstances.

Since there is currently no work for you to perform and there is no likelihood of the overall situation changing, the company will not ask you to work your notice but will pay you in lieu of it. Your employment will therefore end today.

You will receive the following payments:

£[. . . . .] week's pay in lieu of notice

£[. . . . .] redundancy payment based on [. . . . .] years' service, your age and a weekly wage of £[. . . . .].

Letter continues

In *Porter v Revenue and Customs Comrs* [2005] STC (SCD) 803 an individual (P) had been employed for many years by a group of companies which operated an employee incentive scheme known as a 'stock bonus plan'. In late 1998 he was made redundant. In February 2001 he received a disbursement of £64,726 under the 'stock bonus plan'. The Inland Revenue issued a ruling that this was a taxable emolument. P appealed, contending that it should be treated as a termination payment under what is now *ITEPA 2003, s 403*. The Special Commissioner accepted this contention and allowed the appeal, holding on the evidence that the payment had been made in settlement of claims that P could have 'made in an action for breach of employment rights'. It was not simply 'satisfaction of an existing entitlement to remuneration earned during the period of employment'. Accordingly, it was not an emolument from P's employment, but fell within *ITEPA 2003, s 403*.

Restrictive covenant payments

[29.18] Guidance on this topic is that payments made by an employer to an employed earner in consideration of the earner agreeing not to compete against the employer are earnings for contribution purposes. (CWG2 (2017), para 11.5.2, Item 8). That has been correct advice since 21 July 1989 for, since that date, any sum paid to or for the benefit of an employed earner which is chargeable to tax by virtue of what is now *ITEPA 2003, ss 225, 226* (other than by *s 226* — until 10 July 1997), ie a cash payment made to an employee in return for some undertaking, such as an undertaking not to compete, is to be treated as earnings for contribution purposes. [*SSCBA 1992, s 4(4)(a)*]. See HM Revenue and Customs National Insurance Manual NIM02320.

In the case of *ITEPA 2003, ss 225, 226* it is important that no payment is classed as a 'reward' for the employee's taking part in an agreement not to issue any further employment tribunal proceedings, see above and *Appellant v Inspector of Taxes* [2001] STC SCD 21 Sp C 268. It is worth observing that *ITEPA 2003, s 226* relates to circumstances where valuable consideration other than money is given. As *SSCBA 1992, s 4(4)* was not originally to apply in such a case, it had previously been possible for an employer to transfer, say, gilts to a former employee in consideration for a restrictive covenant without the gilts being earnings for contribution purposes. However, this 'loophole' was blocked, with effect from 10 July 1997. [*Social Security Act 1998, s 50 (1)(3)*].

It is worth emphasising that payments in respect of restrictive covenants are, in principle, capital: the employee sells his right to do certain things after termination of the employment (see *Beak v Robson* [1943] 1 All ER 46). They are accordingly *not* earnings within *SSCBA 1992, s 3(1)(a)* unless *Sec 4(4)(a)* puts them there; and a careful reading of *Sec 4(4)* will show that it cannot put them there unless, *at the point of payment*, the person to whom or for whose benefit they are paid is not just an 'earner' but an '*employed earner*', ie someone 'gainfully employed in Great Britain either under a contract of service, or in an office (including an elective office) with general earnings chargeable to income tax as employment income'. [*Sec 2(1)(a)*]. It can therefore be argued that if, at the time of payment of a restrictive covenant payment, the person concerned is *not* such an 'employed earner' (because, for example, he is between jobs), *Sec 4(4)(a)* does not appear at first sight to apply to him and the payment cannot, therefore, ever reach *Sec 6(1)*, the Class 1 charging section. However, despite this, the decision in *RCI (Europe) Ltd v Woods* was to the opposite effect (see below and **29.7**).

In 1994 a company (R) terminated the employment of one of its directors (H), under an agreement whereby H agreed to a 'restrictive undertaking' not to compete with the company, in return for R making five payments to him, totalling £2,200,000. Some of the payments were made after termination of the employment. The Inland Revenue (having subsumed the Contributions Agency in 1999) issued a determination that R was liable to account for National Insurance contributions on the payments, by virtue of *SSCBA 1992, s 4(4)(a)*. The Special Commissioner dismissed R's appeal, holding that all five payments were within what is now *ITEPA 2003, ss 225, 226*. Accordingly, the effect of *SSCBA 1992, s 4(4)(a)* was that R was required to account for NICs on the payments. *RCI (Europe) Ltd v Woods* [2003] STC SCD 128 Sp C 355; [2003] STC 315. This decision was confirmed on appeal to the Chancery Division of the High Court. See **29.5** above. In a similar case *Kent Foods Ltd v HMRC* [2008] STC SCD 307 Sp C 643 a company (E) acquired the shares of another company (K) from its controlling director (D) and his wife. D remained a director of K after the change of ownership. E and D entered into a 'non-compete agreement' under which E paid £250,000 to D in 2000–01 and a further £250,000 in 2001–02, in return for D agreeing not to enter into competition with E for a three-year period. HMRC issued a determination that National Insurance contributions were chargeable on the payments under *SSCBA 1992, s 4(4)*, and that K was liable to account for those contributions under *SSCBA 1992, s 6(4)*. K appealed. The Special Commissioner dismissed the appeal, holding that the payments were within *ICTA 1988, s 313* (see now *ITEPA 2003, s 225*). Accordingly, the effect of *SSCBA 1992, ss 4(4), 6(4)* was that K was required to account for National Insurance contributions on the payments.

See also **29.9** above for commentary on the policy of applying *s 4(4)* to termination payments.

Pensions

[29.19] The legislation in respect of pensions changed from 6 April 2006 following the introduction of a new tax regime for pensions. Until that time, any payment by way of a pension was to be excluded from earnings for contribution purposes. [former *Social Security (Contributions) Regulations 2001, SI 2001/1004, Reg 25, Sch 3 Part VI para 1* as amended by *Social Security (Contributions) (Amendment No 2) Regs 2006, SI 2006/576, Reg 8(2)*].

From 6 April 2006 this previously very wide exception has been (save for the items in the later list in this section) restricted to contributions to and benefits from pension schemes registered under *ITEPA 2003, s 308*. [*Social Security (Contributions) Regulations 2001, SI 2001/1004, Reg 25, Sch 3 Part VI paras 2, 3* as inserted by *Social Security (Contributions) (Amendment No 2) Regs 2006, SI 2006/576, Reg 8(2)*]. See HM Revenue and Customs National

Insurance Manual NIM02700 and CWG2 (2009), page 81 (but CWG2 (2015), page 64 directed any employer to 'Ask [HMRC] for details' where payments are made from an EFRBS because of the complexity of the disguised remuneration rules – this was removed from the 2016 edition, which included several pages of guidance on disguised remuneration but did not mention EFRBS in that context. However, it has now been reinstated in CWG2 (2018 to 2019), para 5.11.2, Item 13 and 5.11.3). The exemption for payments out of registered pension schemes now extends to any payment under the flexi-access rules introduced by *Taxation of Pensions Act 2014*, such as Uncrystallised Funds Pension Lump Sums (CWG2 (2016), page 95, Item 12). The CWG2 guidance on flexi-access pensions was expanded in the 2nd edition for 2016–17, issued in August 2016, by the addition of paras 24a and 24b to explain the complex PAYE and RTI processes that the introduction of flexibility has created. These paras are now CWG2 (2018 to 2019) para 2.2.6 and para 5.11.2, Item 13. Paragraph 5.11.2, Item 12 states that the items should not be included in gross pay for NICs purposes, since there is no liability.

The following exceptions apply both before (from 6 April 1999) and after the 6 April 2006 changes.

- No NICs are to arise on certain benefits from a FURBS which are attributable to payments made to schemes prior to 6 April 1998. Broadly, benefits which would be 'relevant benefits' under the now repealed *ICTA 1988, s 612* were the fund 'approved', will escape NIC liability. [*Social Security (Contributions) Regulations 2001, SI 2001/1004, Reg 25, Sch 3 Part VI para 4; ITEPA 2003, ss 586–588*]. Whilst this exception was not in practice needed before 6 April 2006 due to the very wide general exception already mentioned, it is the only one now statutorily available for FURBS where contributions were made before 1998.
- No NICs are to arise on benefits from a FURBS which are attributable to payments made to schemes on or after 6 April 1998 but before 6 April 2006 and which have themselves been subjected to National Insurance contributions (but see further below). [*Social Security (Contributions) Regulations 2001, SI 2001/1004, Reg 25, Sch 3 Part VI para 5* as amended by *Social Security (Contributions) (Amendment No 2) Regs 2006, SI 2006/576, Reg 8(4)*].
- No NICs are to arise on payments into certain French, Irish, Canadian, South African, Chilean and Danish schemes. [*Social Security (Contributions) Regulations 2001, SI 2001/1004, Reg 25, Sch 3 Part VI para 7* as amended by *Social Security (Contributions) (Amendment No 2) Regs 2006, SI 2006/576, Reg 8(6)*].
- No NICs are to arise on payments into or benefits arising from employer financed retirement benefit schemes (EFRBS), employer financed pension-only schemes (EFPOS) or payments from EFRBS and EFPOS where the benefits are of a kind which would have been permitted had the scheme been a registered pension scheme. Also, this extends to any payments by way of an employer's contribution into a superannuation fund to which *ICTA 1988, s 615(3)* applies and any resulting annuity paid from such fund which does not have income tax

deducted therefrom. [*Social Security (Contributions) Regulations 2001, SI 2001/1004, Reg 25, Sch 3 Part VI paras 8, 9, 10, 11* inserted by *Social Security (Contributions) (Amendment No 2) Regs 2006, SI 2006/576, Reg 8(7)* and para 11 as amended by *Social Security (Contributions) (Amendment No 5) Regs 2006, SI 2006/2829, Reg 4* with effect from 16 November 2006].

- Refunds of NICs may be obtained in respect of payments to a scheme before application was made for HM Revenue and Customs approval or, notwithstanding the exception mentioned above, if contributions were nonetheless paid, and the scheme was subsequently granted approval. [*Social Security (Contributions) Regulations 2001, SI 2001/1004, Reg 53*, omitted with effect from 6 April 2006 by virtue of *Social Security (Contributions) (Amendment No 2) Regs 2006, SI 2006/576, Reg 5*].

The effectiveness of the first above-listed exemption is questioned in 'Yet another stealth tax?' (Tolley's Practical Tax, 4 August 2006). *Social Security (Contributions) (Amendment No 2) Regulations 2006, SI 2006/576, Reg 8* effectively withdrew the exemption for benefits paid on and after 6 April 2006 by an unregistered scheme which are referable to contributions made to the scheme before 6 April 1998. This happened because the exemption as it is now written in *Sch 3, Part VI, para 4* is given by reference to 'relevant benefits' as defined in *ICTA 1970, s 612*. However, that provision was itself withdrawn as a result of the changed tax regime. HM Revenue and Customs confirmed to the Tax Faculty of the ICAEW early in 2007 that it was not the intention to withdraw that exemption and that they would continue to apply it as if *s 612* was still a current tax provision. They did not though have any plans to formally amend the NIC legislation.

The following exceptions applied only from 6 April 1999 up to and including 5 April 2006.

- No NICs were to arise on an employer's contributions to an HM Revenue and Customs approved scheme, including funds under what was *ICTA 1988, s 607* and *ITEPA 2003, ss 590, 591*, nor (for the avoidance of doubt) on benefits deriving from such schemes. [*Social Security (Contributions) Regulations 2001, SI 2001/1004, Reg 25, Sch 3 Part VI para 3*, as amended by *Social Security (Contributions) (Amendment No 2) Regs 2006, SI 2006/576, Reg 8(2)* and amended by *Social Security (Contributions) (Amendment No 5) Regs 2006, SI 2006/2829, Reg 3* with effect from 16 November 2006].
- No NICs were to arise on payments into a new scheme for which HM Revenue and Customs approval under *ICTA 1988, s 604* had been made (subject to various conditions and, also, certain small self-administered schemes are excluded). [*Social Security (Contributions) Regulations 2001, SI 2001/1004, Reg 25, Sch 3 Part VI para 6* as amended by *Social Security (Contributions) (Amendment No 2) Regs 2006, SI 2006/576, Reg 8(5)*; *ICTA 1988, s 604* repealed from 6 April 2006; *FA 2004, Sch 36*].

- Provision was made for the apportionment of payments into a FURBS which related to two or more earners [*SSCBA 1992, s 3(2A); Social Security (Contributions) Regulations 2001, SI 2001/1004, Reg 24, Sch 2 para 13*, as amended by *Social Security (Contributions) (Amendment No 2) Regs 2006, SI 2006/576, Reg 7*].

Although no longer necessary, the term 'pension' was not defined in the pre-2006 legislation and there is no judicial definition of the term. It has been held, however, that, for payments to be pension payments:

(a) the employment in respect of which the payments are made must have ceased;
(b) the employment need not have ceased because of retirement but may have ceased through, for example, incapacity;
(c) the payments need not be for past services in the sense of being deferred pay but may be on account of, for example, disability; and
(d) the payments need not continue for life but may end, for example, on the ceasing of disability.

(*Johnson v Holleran* [1989] STC 1).

This accords with the usual meaning of the term 'pension' which is a periodic allowance made to a person who has retired or become disabled or permanently incapacitated, reached old age, or become widowed or orphaned.

Until 5 April 1993, DSS Leaflet NI 269 stated that 'for a payment to be regarded as a pension the employment must have ceased,' but this was subsequently deleted.

As regards (c) above, it is important to note that, though a payment need not relate to *past* services in order to be a pension, if it relates to *present or future* services it will *not* be a pension in accordance with any accepted understanding of the term.

Former DSS guidance was that neither periodic payments by way of pension for long service, retirement, ill health or widowhood nor lump sum commutation payments in respect of such pensions are earnings for contribution purposes. The DSS appeared to draw no distinction between pensions under schemes approved under *ICTA 1988, s 590* and unapproved pension schemes such as are referred to in what was *ICTA 1988, s 595* (now *ITEPA 2003, s 386*). It did, however, stress that if payments are made under a trust arrangement during the course of employment, such payments will constitute earnings for contribution purposes (1995 DSS Leaflet CA28, page 83, item 72). This comment presumably related to attempted contributions avoidance by means of payments through funded unapproved retirement benefits schemes or 'FURBS' trusts where money was paid out of the trust before retirement – see **29.20** below. Payments from pension trust funds after the employment has ended are arguably, however, to be excluded from earnings. [*ICTA 1988, ss 590–594 repealed from 6 April 2006; FA 2004, Sch 36*].

Funded Unapproved Retirement Benefit Schemes (FURBS)

[29.20] FURBS were heavily marketed in the 1990s as a supposed NIC avoidance scheme and the rules were sometimes written in such a way that a relatively young person could take a supposed pension but then commute that payment into a lump sum. This way FURBS had been used regularly as a conversion medium for annual bonuses which were then in turn converted into cash in the hands of that employee with no Class 1 NICs liability. It was announced on 22 July 1997 that clauses would be included in the Social Security Bill to bring FURBS contributions into charge to NICs from 6 April 1999. However, the CA then declared:

> 'Having examined the issue, we consider that we may have been somewhat cautious in our view of the current legislation in relation to FURBS. We also know that there has been comment regarding the guidance we have issued. We have never issued specific guidance on FURBS. However we are aware that there is a need to provide clear guidance on the issue of FURBS.'
>
> CA Specialist Conference, 29 October 1997.

Subsequently, the Agency confirmed in a Press Release on 17 November 1997 that in their view FURBS contributions had always, technically, been liable to contributions and that they expected employers to comply by 6 April 1998. They also stated that they might look again at earlier alleged FURBS transactions where payments had been made out of the FURBS very quickly. This view by the Agency and reiterated in Tax Bulletin, June 2003, p1037, as it applied to a genuine FURBS, had been widely thought to be incorrect but was never challenged until *Telent plc* in 2007 – see below; DSS Press Release 97/127, 22 July 1997; CA 47/97, 17 November 1997; CA National Insurance News extracts, Summer 1997 and CA National Insurance News extracts, Spring 1998). See HM Revenue and Customs National Insurance Manual NIM02155.

Further provision was made by *The Social Security (Contributions and Credits) (Miscellaneous Amendments) Regulations 1999, SI 1999/568* (since consolidated) which applied until the 6 April 2006 change to the tax regime. Those regulations made various provisions from 6 April 1999 up to and including 5 April 2006 with regard to FURBS and other pension schemes. These were all arguably superfluous, since any payment 'by way of a pension' was at that time to be excluded from earnings and a pension contribution — whilst it was clearly a payment to or for the *benefit* of the earner — was arguably excluded by former *Social Security (Contributions) Regulations 2001, SI 2001/1004, Reg 25, Sch 3 Part II para 1*, but these regulations stem from the authorities' highly questionable belief that payments by employers to pension schemes are, nonetheless, earnings.

In *Telent plc v Revenue and Customs Commissioners* [2008] STC SCD 202 Sp C 632, the company (T) made payments to a funded unapproved retirement benefit scheme and into an unapproved life assurance scheme for the benefit of a specific senior employee (B). HMRC issued a determination that these payments were 'earnings' of B. The company appealed, contending that the effect of the QB decision in *Tullett & Tokyo Forex International Ltd v Secretary of State for Social Security*, see above, was that Class 1 NICs were not due because the FURBS contributions had merely bought a future right to a pension, a right that should have been treated as a payment in kind. The Special Commissioner reviewed the evidence in detail, rejected this contention and dismissed the appeal. The Commissioner distinguished *Tullett & Tokyo Forex International Ltd* on the grounds that that case referred to a 'payment in kind', whereas the payments made by T were not within the definition of 'payments in kind'. The Commissioner also observed that for a charge to arise under *SSCBA 1992, s 6(1)*, 'earnings must be "paid to or for the benefit of" the employed earner.

It was clear to many observers that the principle of the case had been wrongly decided, because there was no immediate benefit to anyone. The employee could not access the money while it was held by the trustees, so the rule in *Garforth v Newsmith Stainless Ltd* was disregarded in ruling that the FURBS contribution was a payment of earnings. However, the decision was not finally shown to have been incorrect until the Supreme Court decision in *Forde & McHugh Ltd v Revenue and Customs Commissioners* [2014] UKSC 14.

There, in what was acknowledged to be a 'lead' or test case, it was argued successfully by the taxpayer that the payment of earnings was contingent, and until that contingency was met, there was no 'payment'.

The Court of Appeal had decided that the 'employee received a present right to future benefit' and would receive the benefit at some time in the future, yet nevertheless decided that there had been a payment of earnings equal to the money and securities put into the fund. But the implication of HMRC's successful argument before that court was that a payment into a FURBS was a payment of earnings and the payment of that same money out of the FURBS was also a payment of earnings.

Lord Hodge in the Supreme Court described this proposition as 'remarkable' (para 15). Mr McHugh, said HMRC, 'was immediately better off because he had the hope of receiving the trust fund in the future, and his family would benefit if he did not survive until his retirement age.' The lower courts had looked solely at what the employer paid, but the Supreme Court held that the word 'earnings' itself connotes receipt of something by a worker in exchange for his work, so if Mr McHugh had received nothing but a promise of future benefit, common sense dictated that the point of receipt by the worker should be the point when earnings were paid to him or for his immediate benefit, not when paid to the FURBS trustees who held a fund to which he had no immediate right of access.

HMRC had also failed to address the question of valuation: Mr McHugh had not received the cash and gilts paid by the employer to the FURBS trustees, but a right to money at some indeterminate future point, the value of which was not the value of the cash and gilts in the fund at the outset.

The case was not solely about FURBS: the courts were in agreement that 'earnings' for NIC purposes means something different than 'emoluments' for income tax purposes. So while income tax law treats cash or money's worth as emoluments, but then has to deem a payment of emoluments for certain benefits in kind that cannot be turned into cash by surrender or sale, NI law encompasses everything given by employer to employee as a reward for his service but then excludes payments in kind, pensions and certain other items to arrive at the basis of the Class 1 charge.

It remains to be seen how long it will take HMRC to redraft *Schedule 3* to the *Social Security (Contributions) Regulations 2001, SI 2001/1004* to reflect the analysis of the Supreme Court in *Forde & McHugh Ltd*, as it currently purports to exclude from earnings contributions to registered pension schemes and certain foreign equivalents, and payments to Employer-Financed Retirement Benefits Schemes (EFRBS). Since they are not earnings in the first place, as we now know for certain, the regulations are otiose and misconceived. The treatment of money in an EFRBS is now dealt with under the disguised remuneration regime in *ITEPA 2003, Part 7A*, with consequences for NICs by virtue of *Reg 22B*, but paying money into the EFRBS initially is now known not to constitute a payment of earnings.

The Press Release accompanying the 1999 Regulations again stated that where payments have been made to a discretionary FURBS before 6 April 1999 the Contributions Agency would 'closely scrutinise such arrangements and [would] seek National Insurance if it [could] establish a payment of earnings to or for the benefit of an employee'. However, the 2006 changes and the *Forde & McHugh* decision have neutered any outstanding cases of dispute regarding contributions made into a FURBS from 1998. Indeed, HMRC owes money to a number of employers who were persuaded by flawed arguments to pay NICs and interest to settle disputes over contributions to FURBS after the change in policy noted above.

Pension scheme inducements

[29.21] No National Insurance contributions are to arise on payments as inducements or incentive payments to members of defined benefit occupational pension schemes when those members agree to a reduction in their benefits or to a transfer out of a defined pension scheme into a defined contribution scheme provided these payments enhance the transfer value of the pension fund that is being transferred between the schemes. Inducements paid in cash, etc to pension scheme members themselves that encourage such members to give up future pension rights or move their rights from one pension to another are, according to the HMRC view announced on 24 January 2007, earnings within *SSCBA 1992, ss 3(1)(a), 6(1)*. Where inducement payments had already been paid before 24 January 2007 and no National Insurance accounted for or where HMRC had confirmed that inducement payments were not liable or an employer made an offer to a member before 24 January 2007 based on HMRC's previous understanding of the law such payments will also not have been subjected to tax and NICs. See HMRC's Press Release statement dated 24 January 2007. The HM Revenue and Customs advice is perhaps overly restrictive. It appears to base its related tax view on *ITEPA 2003, s 394* which is within *Part 5* of *ITEPA 2003*. *Part 5* is headed 'Income which is not earnings' which suggests quite clearly that such income is not considered to be within 'general earnings' on general tax principles. Similarly, it will almost certainly also not be 'earnings' on general principles for NIC, yet there is nothing in *SSCBA 1992* and the associated regulations to deem such amounts to be earnings for NIC purposes. It is doubtful whether any such payment to a member (ie, other than an enhancement of benefits) is, on basic principles, a reward for acting as or being an employee. It is derived from scheme membership and scheme transfer, and it is not sufficient for HMRC to argue that the payment would not have been made if the individual had not been an employee. However, the motivation for the payment will be the deciding factor, as illustrated by the test case of *Kuehne + Nagel Drinks Logistics Ltd and others v Revenue and Customs Commissioners*.

Following a company reconstruction, workers at KNDL under a new employer found that they would no longer be members of a defined benefit (ie salary related) pension scheme. There ensued the threat of strikes and concern about the future attitude of workers and whether they would work willingly and satisfactorily. To head off the strike threat, compensation payments were made for the loss of pension rights and the payers and some employees contended that these were neither taxable nor liable to NICs. The First-tier Tribunal [2009] UKFTT 379, TC00314 held that the payments were taxable. They stemmed from two sources – the pure compensatory factor and the clearly employment-related issue that they were made to prevent the strikes and promote future harmony. Just because there was a non-employment reason for the payment did not prevent the other reason being the means by which HMRC could attach tax liability. The judge said that if the payment had been a sum simply and solely to recognise the removal of a voluntary pension or the removal of an expectation of a pension then it would not have been treated as from employment. (This may provoke other future cases involving the reduction of pension benefits). Further, the judge also considered that the test to be applied for NIC purposes was identical to that in the case of the employment income tax charge. The employer and employee appeals were accordingly dismissed. The FTT decision was supported by the Upper Tribunal in [2010] UKUT 457(TCC) and the Court of Appeal [2012] EWCA Civ 34, [2012] STC 840.

Pay during absence

General

[29.22] An employed earner may be absent from his employment for a variety of reasons: sickness, maternity/paternity, holiday, jury service, trades union activities, etc but may still receive payments from his employer or from third parties during such absences. The question whether or not such payments are earnings for contributions purposes is to be answered by looking at the contract of service (written or oral, express or implied) and seeing whether the payments arise under or from the contract or not. If they do, they are earnings.

It is sometimes the case that an employer who pays his employee during the employee's absence because of sickness or maternity will require the employee to pass to him any social security benefits received. In those circumstances, only the payments by the employer *net* of the benefits handed over are earnings for contribution purposes because that is all that the employer is actually paying to the employee. (See 29.23; HM Revenue and Customs National Insurance Manual NIM02250).

Maternity pay, SMP, SPP, SAP and ShPP

[29.23] Any sum paid to or for the benefit of an employed earner in whole or part satisfaction of any entitlement of that person to Statutory Maternity Pay, Statutory Paternity Pay, Statutory Adoption Pay or Statutory Shared Parental

Pay is to be treated as earnings for contribution purposes. [*SSCBA 1992, s 4(1)*, as amended by *Employment Act 2002, s 53, Sch 7 paras 2, 3* and *Children and Families Act 2014, s 126, Sch 7 paras 6, 8*]. However, maternity allowance (as contrasted with SMP or SAP), claimed by the self-employed and women who do not qualify for SMP but have the relevant contribution record (and whose employer has issued an SMP1 refusal), is paid by the DWP, not the employer, and is not classed as earnings for tax or NIC purposes (see EIM76361).

The ECJ decision in *Gillespie and others v Northern Ireland Health and Social Services Board and others* C-342/93, [1996] All ER (EC) 284 ensures that retrospective pay rises must also apply to those on maternity leave. Also see *Alabaster (1) Woolwich Plc (2) v Secretary of State for Social Security* C-147/02, [2004] All ER (D) 558 (Mar) in March 2004, where, if a pay rise is awarded that would affect a woman on maternity leave, or who is about to start maternity leave, her SMP must be increased by the employer to take into account the rise in pay even where that is effective during or after the SMP payment period. From 6 April 2005, SMP rules adhere to this ECJ case decision so as to require the employer to re-calculate the average weekly earnings depending on where the effective date of the pay rise falls. From 1 April 2007, statutory maternity leave is for 52 weeks and can be taken in full no matter how long the employee has been with the employer and this applies to agency workers too. Also from the same date the 26-week SMP payment period was increased to 39 weeks. [*Statutory Maternity Pay (General) (Amendment) Regs 2005, SI 2005/729; Work and Families Act 2006 (Commencement No 1) Order 2006, SI 2006/1682; Work and Families Act 2006 (Commencement No 2) Order 2006, SI 2006/2232; Statutory Maternity Pay, Social Security (Maternity Allowance) and Social Security (Overlapping Benefits) (Amendment) Regulations 2006, SI 2006/2379*]. See Employers Bulletin Issue 19, February 2005 and former Employers Helpbook E15 (2013) and Tolley's Practical NIC Newsletter, June 2005.

Women eligible for SMP for a maternity pay period which starts on or after 1 April 2018 will receive:

- the higher rate of 90% of their average earnings for the first six weeks; and
- up to 33 weeks at £145.18 or 90% of average weekly earnings, whichever is less.

If an employer chooses to pay an employed earner the whole or part of her normal pay during a period of maternity leave in consideration for her promise to return to work at the end of her leave, that pay, too, is, on general principles, earnings for contribution purposes. Contractual maternity pay refunded by an employee who fails to return to her employment after her maternity leave ends can be excluded retrospectively from earnings and a refund claimed. [*Refunds (Repayment of Contractual Maternity Pay) Regs 1990, Reg 2*].

Example

The wages department of Maternity Pay Ltd is told by one of its long-standing workers, Barbara Bump, that she is pregnant and is expecting to give birth on 7 November 2018. After checking her medical evidence (MATB1) and reviewing the action required on form SMP3, the wages department checks to see what the entitlements are using the 'Maternity and paternity calculator for employers' tool on the www.gov.uk website. The qualifying week is calculated by the tool and it commenced on 22 July 2018. Barbara has been continuously employed since before 3 February 2018 (ie more than 26 weeks up to and including the fifteenth week before the baby is due) so she will meet the condition of continuous employment. Barbara's average earnings for the eight weeks ending on the last pay-day on or before the Saturday of the qualifying week must be looked at and this figure is £196.18 which is more than the Lower Earnings Limit for NICs (2018–19, £116). A bonus payment for exceeding her sales quota is paid on 15 August amounting to £750.

Barbara wants to start her maternity absence on 9 October 2018 (ie within 11 weeks from the due date) so the start of the Maternity Pay Period is that date. The higher rate of SMP is payable for the first six weeks:

Average earnings £196.18 × $^{9}/_{10}$ = £176.57 per week.

Maternity Pay Ltd must continue to pay SMP at the lower rate of £145.18 for the subsequent 33 weeks. Note that because the bonus payment was made after the qualifying week this amount would not fall to be included in the calculation of average weekly earnings, as such. However, any subsequent pay rises (and this may include some bonuses too) from the start of the set period (2 June 2018 in this case) to the end of the leave must be included in a reworking of the average earnings figure and arrears of SMP paid as necessary.

From 6 April 2003 onwards new rules were introduced that offer pay and leave for fathers who help the mother care for a child in the first few weeks following a child's birth. This is termed as statutory paternity leave with up to two weeks' worth of Statutory Paternity Pay (SPP). SPP and paternity leave may be due to someone who is a biological father, a partner/husband who is not the biological father or a female partner in a same sex couple. In order to calculate the SPP that is due, the date the baby is due and the date the baby is born are important in the calculation. The father can choose to take one week's or two consecutive weeks' leave within 56 days of the date of birth. 'Fathers' (as defined above) eligible for SPP are, for payments in pay periods beginning on or after 1 April 2018 (but note that this is fixed by reference to the closest Sunday to 6 April rather than always being the same date) and provided that average weekly earnings in the set period equal or exceed the Lower Earnings Limit, receive:

- 90% of their average earnings; or
- £145.18, whichever is less.

The 'father' is given form SC3 which tells him that his entitlement to SPP depends on how long he has been employed by the employer and his average earnings. Both these conditions of payment are based at the time 15 weeks before the week the baby is due. The length of time the father has worked for the employer to receive SPP and paternity leave is split into two as follows:

- By calculating when the child is due by reference to the latest start date for employment by reference to the online tool at www.gov.uk/maternity-paternity-calculator which will confirm whether or not SPP is due to be paid.

- If the date at the point above confirms SPP and leave are due then the employee must continue to be employed until the child is born in order to receive entitlement.

The parent is required to advise the employer at least 15 weeks before the birth date of both the expected birth date and the time when he or she expects to be absent from work (in the above example, the father would have to notify the employer before 22 July 2018).

[*Statutory Paternity Pay and Statutory Adoption Pay (General) Regulations 2002, SI 2002/2822*; *Welfare Benefits Up-rating Order 2014, SI 2014/147*].

From 6 April 2003 onwards new rules were introduced that offer pay and leave for employees (male or female) that help them when adopting a child who is placed with them. This is termed 'adoption leave' with Statutory Adoption Pay (SAP) being available. SAP and adoption leave may be due to someone who is adopting on his or her own or with his or her partner. If the employee is adopting with his or her partner the couple must choose who gets the SAP and the adoption leave and who gets the SPP and paternity leave (see above – the 'paternity' leave and pay can be taken by the mother in an adoption case). Until 5 April 2004, only married couples could adopt together. The employee must give evidence of 'matching' for SAP and adoption leave, or the declaration of family commitment for SPP and paternity leave. Entitlements are summarised online at www.gov.uk/employers-adoption-pay-leave. It is a legal entitlement to a certain amount of pay (see below) and to take time off work at or around the time the child is placed with the adopter. The period of claim for adoption pay lasts 39 weeks (26 weeks before 1 April 2007) and the adopter employee who is eligible for SAP will, for payments in pay periods beginning before 5 April 2015 and provided that average weekly earnings in the set period equal or exceed the Lower Earnings Limit, received:

- 90% of his or her average earnings, or
- from April 2015, £139.58, whichever is less.

From 5 April 2015 SAP was brought into line with SMP so that provided average weekly earnings in the set period equal or exceed the Lower Earnings Level receive:

- the higher rate of 90% of their average earnings for the first six weeks; and
- up to 33 weeks at the SAP lower rate or 90% of average weekly earnings, whichever is less.

The lower rate from 1 April 2018 is £145.18.

The adopter employee may claim adoption leave which is available for 52 weeks in all but only the first 39 weeks will be covered by SAP. SAP depends on how long the employee has been employed, and his or her average earnings. The date the adoption agency tells the employee that he or she has been 'matched' with a child is the crucial date for these purposes.

[*Statutory Paternity Pay and Statutory Adoption Pay (General) Regulations 2002, SI 2002/2822*; *Welfare Benefits Up-rating Order 2014, SI 2014/147*].

With effect from April 2011 until 5 April 2015, fathers who had earned at least at the LEL for the relevant eight weeks of the qualifying period were entitled to take over part of a mothers' entitlement to maternity or adoption leave and pay so that the mother could return to work early. Such 'additional paternity leave' could be from two to twenty-six weeks and the father received 'additional SPP' at the same level as his entitlement to ordinary SPP, ie, in 2014–15, £138.18 per week or 90% of his average weekly earnings in the reference period if less. The mother had to take off at least two weeks after the birth. The ASPP was treated as earnings in the same way as SMP, SAP and SPP.

For births due, or adoptions certified, on or after 5 April 2015, entitlement to share leave became governed by the *Shared Parental Leave Regulations 2014, SI 2014/3050*, and the entitlement to statutory shared parental pay by the *Statutory Shared Parental Pay (General) Regulations 2014, SI 2014/3051*. Note that the new rules were legislated in December 2014 so that they could apply to the parents of babies due on or after 5 April 2015 but born prematurely. Those families with babies due or adoption certificates issued before the change could take leave and receive SMP/SAP/SPP under the existing rules, so SMP, SAP and SPP would have been payable in the first part of 2015–16 under those rules. The new rules applied only if the expected date of childbirth or matching for adoption occurred on or after 5 April 2015, so two sets of rules ran in parallel for part of 2015–16.

Under the ShPP rules, parents can now choose how to share the full period of maternity leave and pay, potentially taking three blocks of leave each, consecutively or concurrently, and the rate of ShPP payable is set at the same level as the SMP/SAP lower rate, ie, £145.18 per week or 90% of average earnings in the qualifying period if lower. The RTI records include fields for recording and reporting the relevant partner's details so that HMRC can match up related entitlements and ensure that overpayments (or, more to the point, over-recoveries out of remittances of PAYE and NICs) do not occur.

Another statutory payment, Statutory Parental Bereavement Pay, is expected to be introduced from 2020. The *Parental Bereavement (Pay and Leave) Bill*, a private member's bill but with widespread cross-party support, is currently wending its way through Parliament. This proposes to give employed parents who lose a child under the age of 18 a 'day-one' right to take two weeks leave. Entitlement to pay (Statutory Parental Bereavement Pay (SPBP)) will be dependent on the parent having a minimum of 26 weeks continuous service and having average weekly earnings equal to the NIC lower earnings limit.

SPBP will be payable at the lesser of the statutory flat rate (£145.18 in 2018–19) and 90% of average weekly earnings. As with the other statutory payments, excluding SSP, employers will be able to recover a percentage of the SPBP. Recovery will be effected by employers reducing their NICs payments to HMRC.

Sick pay and SSP

[29.24] Any sum paid to or for the benefit of an employed earner in whole or part satisfaction of any entitlement of that person to Statutory Sick Pay (SSP) is to be treated as earnings for contribution purposes. [*SSCBA 1992, s 4(1)*].

(See www.gov.uk/employers-sick-pay.) The weekly rate of Statutory Sick Pay from 6 April 2018 is £92.05 per week and is payable for days of incapacity for work for employees with average weekly earnings of £116 or more. It should be noted that where an employee has been in receipt of the Employment and Support Allowance (ESA) and is sick within 12 weeks the ESA may be claimed, instead of SSP from his/her employer. Further, in certain circumstances an employee who is sick again within 104 weeks of being entitled to ESA will also be able to claim ESA, instead of SSP from the employer. Jobcentre Plus will supply an ESA220 letter to the employee to give to the employer.

Following the abolition from 6 April 1991 of the employer's right to recover 80% of SSP paid, SSP ceased to be a State benefit and became 'pay'.

The right of recovery was restricted to small employers by the introduction of a 'percentage threshold scheme' in April 1995, but even that right of recovery was abolished from 6 April 2014 (see **15.12**).

At one time, women over state pension age but below 65 were entitled to SSP. For such women, although SSP constituted earnings, no primary contributions were due because they were over State pension age. However, all age restrictions were removed from SSP with effect from 1 October 2006 as a result of an EU directive on age discrimination. SSP may therefore be payable to under-16s and those of any gender over state pension age, but in both cases no NICs liability will arise for the individual. Employer liability still technically arises in respect of SSP paid to employees over state pension age, although the rate of SSP is so low that it will always fall under the LEL.

See also **29.23** regarding average weekly earnings, which applies also to Statutory Sick Pay. The employee must have been paid earnings at least equal, on average, to the Lower Earnings Limit for an eight-week period before the period of incapacity for work.

As regards agency workers and short-term contract workers, there are no special restrictions.

Any occupational sickness payment is to be treated as remuneration derived from an employed earner's employment if such a payment is made to or for the benefit of an employed earner in accordance with arrangements (eg with trustees or with an insurance company) under which the secondary contributor in relation to the employment concerned has made, or remains liable to make, payments towards the provision of that sickness payment. [*SSCBA 1992, s 4(1)*].

Where, however, the funds for making such a sickness payment are in part attributable to contributions made by the employed earner himself, the part of any sickness payment so attributable is to be disregarded. [*SSCBA 1992, s 4(2); Social Security (Contributions) Regulations 2001, SI 2001/1004, Sch 3 Part X para 7*]. See also HM Revenue and Customs National Insurance Manual NIM02345.

A 'sickness payment' is any payment made in respect of absence from work due to incapacity for work by reason of some specific disease or bodily or mental disablement. [*SSCBA 1992, s 4(3)*]. There are specific provisions to preclude the claiming of SSP where a pregnant woman is absent in 'the disqualifying period'. Where a sickness payment falls to be treated as earnings under these provisions, it is to be made through the person who is the secondary contributor in relation to the employment concerned unless it is payable by some other person who has agreed to make the payment and has arranged to provide the secondary contributor with all the information he needs in order to be able to pay and account for any Class 1 contribution liability arising. [*SSCBA 1992, Sch 1 para 11; Social Security (Contributions) Regulations 2001, SI 2001/1004, Reg 23*]. Authorisation may be needed for such an alternative arrangement. Occupational sick pay paid for a period after an earner's contract of service has ended, for example, as an ill-health pension, is not to be so regarded, even if it would otherwise fall to be regarded as earnings under the above provisions.

It is often the case where, for example, an employee is covered by permanent health insurance that the insurer's liability, when a claim is made in respect of a long-term absence from work through incapacity, specifically includes both the wages and the employer's Class 1 contribution liability on the 'earnings' paid to the invalid employee. Contributions are paid until State pension age and a full contribution record is thereby maintained.

Holiday pay

[29.25] Holiday pay (whether or not a holiday is actually taken) is earnings for contribution purposes and falls to be included in gross pay when paid *unless* it represents sums to which the earner concerned had an earlier unconditional right but which, with his consent, were set aside (eg under a holiday credits scheme operated by the secondary contributor concerned) until such time as a holiday was taken (CWG2 (2018 to 2019), para 2.7.3). The pay set aside is treated as earnings when it is set aside, rather than when it is withdrawn from the fund.

Until 30 October 2007, there was an exclusion from earnings for payments via holiday funds, but it was abolished because of perceived abuse by employers in industries where holiday funds were not traditionally in use. It remained available to construction industry employers, who had been traditional users of holiday stamp schemes, until 30 October 2012, but was then abolished completely. [*Social Security (Contributions) Regulations 2001, SI 2001/1004, Reg 25, Sch 3 Part X para 12*, as revoked by *Social Security (Contributions) (Amendment No 9) Regulations 2007, SI 2007/2905*.]

See **34.9** EARNINGS PERIODS for special rules concerning the assessment of contribution liability on holiday pay. See also HM Revenue and Customs National Insurance Manual NIM02200.

Payments made under schemes falling within the pre-2012 rules for holiday funds outlined above (which are widespread in the building and civil engineering, electrical contracting and heating, ventilating and domestic engineering industries) were entirely excluded from gross earnings. The amounts expended by the secondary contributor in the purchase of the special stamps which are used to build up entitlement under such schemes were also excluded. (CWG2 (2012), page 23, Item 39). Holiday payments under such schemes have, from 1 January 1982, been subject to a basic rate tax deduction [*The Income Tax (Pay As You Earn) Regulations 2003, SI 2003/2682, Regs 134–140*].

Payments made under the kind of arrangement described above should have been excluded from gross earnings only if the set-aside sums which they represented had (as they should have) been included in gross earnings at the time the earner acquired his unconditional right to them (see **15.4** CLASS 1 CONTRIBUTIONS). In cases where the earner's right to a set-aside amount was restricted to such time as he took his holiday, the amount should have been excluded from gross earnings until the restriction was removed.

See **29.8** for the treatment of holiday pay paid after the earner concerned has left his employment.

Note that holiday pay due to 'workers' (under the *Working Time Regulations 1998, SI 1988/1833*) who are not employees but self-employed workers committed to offering personal service is not classed as earnings for Class 1 purposes. It forms part of the profits of the worker taxed under *ITTOIA 2005*.

Lost-time payments

[29.26] Payments made to an employed earner to compensate him for the loss of earnings he has sustained in undertaking jury service or engaging in trade union activities etc is *not* earnings for contribution purposes *providing* the payment is made by someone other than the employer or, if made by the employer, is made on behalf of some other person or organisation. See also HM Revenue and Customs National Insurance Manual NIM02220.

Damages advances

[29.27] It is sometimes the case that, if an employed earner has an accident at work, his employer will, instead of paying him sick pay, make a loan to him pending settlement of his claim for damages. Once the claim is settled and the amount of damages (if any) is ascertained, the whole or part of the loan becomes repayable. If, at that point, the employed earner is released from the obligation to repay any part of the loan which does not represent damages, that part becomes earnings for contribution purposes (see **29.48** below).

HM Revenue and Customs guidance here is that the loans should be included in gross pay unless the employee is obliged to make repayment whether or not his damages claim is successful. See also HM Revenue and Customs National Insurance Manual NIM02110.

Payments in kind

General

[29.28] It should be noted that most payments in kind that are not subject to Class 1 contributions because they are not 'earnings' will, from 6 April 2000, attract a Class 1A liability.

Any payment in kind or by way of the provision of board or lodging or of services or other facilities is (with some specific exceptions — see **31** EARNINGS FROM EMPLOYMENT: READILY CONVERTIBLE ASSETS, ETC) to be excluded from earnings for Class 1 contribution purposes. [*Social Security (Contributions) Regulations 2001, SI 2001/1004, Reg 25, Sch 3 Part II para 1*].

The terms of that regulation clearly presuppose that payments in kind *are* earnings and that, but for the excluding effect of the regulation's terms, would remain so. That presupposition has been increasingly brought into question outside the former DSS and HM Revenue and Customs. In particular, it has been said that the terms 'remuneration' and 'profit' which are used by *SSCBA 1992* to define earnings are (unlike 'emoluments' in the former *ICTA 1988, s 131(1)* which were defined so as to include 'perquisites') not sufficiently wide to bring benefits in kind within their ambit. The point becomes of increasing importance as the scope of *Social Security (Contributions) Regulations 2001, SI 2001/1004, Reg 25, Sch 3 Part II para 1* is restricted further (see **31** EARNINGS FROM EMPLOYMENT: READILY CONVERTIBLE ASSETS, ETC). [*ITEPA 2003, s 62*]. However, the analysis of the Court of Appeal and later the Supreme Court in *Forde & McHugh Ltd v Revenue and Customs Comrs* [2014] UKSC 14 appears to have laid any doubt to rest. Lord Hodge took the view that 'earnings' in the broadest sense of the word has included benefits in kind since the *National Insurance Act 1946* was introduced, because specific provision was made, and has been made ever since, in secondary legislation to exclude typical payments in kind from earnings. Parliament clearly had in mind that benefits in kind were, in principle, included if it legislated from the start of the new NI regime in 1948 explicitly to exclude them.

The former DSS view was that if a payment in kind is to be brought within the excluding provisions of *Social Security (Contributions) Regulations 2001, SI 2001/1004, Reg 25, Sch 3 Part II para 1* it must be 'payment by a means which cannot be directly negotiated for a known cash value' and must, therefore, be something which cannot 'be exchanged for cash by surrender' but which 'can only be turned into cash if a willing purchaser can be found' ('Review of DSS/Inland Revenue Definitions of Gross Earnings: Consultation Paper', July 1991). For items which fail this test see **29.29** below.

A further condition which, though axiomatic, is often overlooked is that the goods or services concerned must belong to the employer before they can constitute a payment in kind to the employee. If, for example, an employee contracts for a package holiday abroad and his employer pays the bill, the employer has not made a payment in kind (ie a holiday package) to the employee: he has paid off the employee's debt for a package holiday which has 'belonged' to or been the liability of the employee from the outset (see **29.51** below). In the case of a holiday, even if the contract is properly made with the employer rather than the employee, tickets will be passed to the employee. From 6 April 1999, this latter act will have attracted a contributions liability, since the tickets are likely to constitute a non-cash voucher which has been provided to the employee. And even if no such voucher is involved, there will instead, albeit only from 6 April 2000, be a Class 1A liability.

Even if a particular item can withstand both the tests described, it may still be taken out of the excluding provisions of *Social Security (Contributions) Regulations 2001, SI 2001/1004, Reg 25, Sch 3 Part II para 1* by operation of *Social Security (Contributions) Regulations 2001, SI 2001/1004, Reg 25, Sch 3 Part II para 2* but if it is not, then the item may very well, from 6 April 2000, attract a Class 1A charge.

As the wording of *Social Security (Contributions) Regulations 2001, SI 2001/1004, Sch 3 Part II para 1* makes plain, free board and lodging provided for an employed earner is not earnings for contribution purposes; but the expression 'or other facilities' is somewhat vague. The word 'facilities' has three common meanings: the means of rendering something readily possible; things specially arranged or constructed to provide recreation; and moneys available for use or borrowing. But the former DSS had expressed no view on which of those meanings it considered the word to carry. Some have sought to argue that the term is wide enough to cover not only the provision to an employee of a company credit card but even any personal expenditure for which the card is used (see **29.56** below). That argument was rejected, however, in *R v Department of Social Security, ex p Overdrive Credit Card Ltd* [1991] 1 WLR 635, [1991] STC 129, DC.

Premium bonds etc

[29.29] A payment to an employed earner in the form of National Savings and Investments premium bonds or national savings certificates cannot be regarded as a payment in kind within *SI 2001/1004, Sch 3 Part II para 1* as the nature of such bonds and certificates is such that they are capable of encashment by mere surrender and thus fail one of the fundamental tests which the then DSS believed that the law imposes (see **29.28** above). They are, therefore, earnings for Class 1 purposes. (See CWG2 (2015), page 64).

Commodities

[29.30] See **31.6** and **31.18** EARNINGS FROM EMPLOYMENT: READILY CONVERTIBLE ASSETS, ETC.

Retail vouchers and warrants

[29.31] Since 1 December 1993, vouchers which can be exchanged for any commodity traded on an investment exchange recognised under the *Financial Services Act 1986* or on the London Bullion Market or for shares, unit trusts, loan stock, gilts, debentures and other securities, have constituted earnings. [*Social Security (Contributions) Regulations 2001, SI 2001/1004, Sch 3 Part IV para 12*]. From 24 August 1994 vouchers exchangeable for alcoholic liquor or gemstones were added to this list, while vouchers exchangeable for tradeable assets were added on 6 April 1995 and vouchers exchangeable for readily convertible assets on 1 October 1998. [*Contributions Amendment No 3 Regs 1994; Contributions Amendment No 4 Regs 1995 Sch 1B para 3* as inserted by *Social Security (Contributions) Amendment (No 3) Regs 1998, Reg 10*]. (CWG2 (2013), page 78 – later editions do not associate vouchers and readily convertible assets, although the rules have not changed). See also HM Revenue and Customs National Insurance Manual NIM02410 and **31** EARNINGS FROM EMPLOYMENT: READILY CONVERTIBLE ASSETS, ETC.

Since 6 April 1999 Class 1 NICs have also been due on the provision of all other non-cash vouchers. Whilst cash vouchers were already chargeable to NICs, retail vouchers became liable for NICs in the same way as cash earnings. [*Social Security (Contributions) Regulations 2001, SI 2001/1004, Sch 3 Part II para 2(1)(b)*].

The 1999 legislation adopted the very wide definition in what is now *ITEPA 2003*, ie it does not include a cash voucher but, subject to that, means any voucher, stamp or similar document or token capable of being exchanged (whether singly or together with other such vouchers, stamps, documents or tokens and whether immediately or only after a time) for money, goods or services (or for any combination of two or more of those things) and includes a transport voucher and a cheque voucher. [*ITEPA 2003, s 84(1)(2)*]. The separate rules for vouchers for readily convertible assets are retained. [*Social Security (Contributions) Regulations 2001, SI 2001/1004, Sch 3 Part IV para 12*].

The amount on which NICs are to be calculated is the expense incurred in, or in connection with, the provision of vouchers. The figure may be reduced by any amount made good by the employee or, in the case of vouchers exchangeable only for meals, any excess of cost over the face value of the vouchers. In the case of childcare vouchers (see **29.32**) the face value can be increased by the supplier's administration charges. [*Social Security (Contributions) Regulations 2001, SI 2001/1004, Sch 2 para 14; Social Security (Contributions) Regulations 2001, SI 2001/1004, Sch 3 Part V para 7(3)* as amended by *Social Security (Contributions) (Amendment No 3) Regulations 2005, SI 2005/778, Reg 9(2)*].

Where either a non-cash or a cash voucher is provided to or for the benefit of more than one earner and the respective proportions are known at the time of 'payment', then those proportions are applied to the expense incurred as identified in the manner mentioned above. Otherwise, the expense is simply to be divided equally among the recipients. [*SSCBA 1992, s 3(2A); Social Security (Contributions) Regulations 2001, SI 2001/1004, Sch 2 para 15(1)(2)*].

For 2003–04 onwards where an employer subsidises a public bus service that entitles employees to transport by way of a non-cash voucher within *ITEPA 2003, s 243* the tax and NICs treatment is now aligned. [*Social Security (Contributions) Regulations 2001, SI 2001/1004, Sch 3 Part V para 5A(b)* inserted by *Social Security (Contributions) (Amendment No 7) Regulations 2003, SI 2003/2958, Reg 5*].

The following non-cash vouchers remain (or remained until the dates shown below) NIC-free, in line with income tax reliefs:

- Transport vouchers supplied to employees in the industry under arrangements in force on 25 March 1982. [*Social Security (Contributions) Regulations 2001, SI 2001/1004, Sch 3 Part V para 2*].
- Certain voucher use where the £5 per night (£10 if abroad) personal incidental overnight expenses (formerly personal incidental expenses, or 'PIEs') limit applies [*Social Security (Contributions) Regulations 2001, SI 2001/1004, Sch 3 Part V para 1(2)(b)*].
- Sporting and recreational facilities for employees. In addition, from 2005–06 onwards, where an employer provides free or subsidised sporting and recreational facilities that are exempt for that employer's staff then no benefit arises in respect of other employees of other employers who work on the same site and use the same facilities (*ITEPA 2003, ss 261–263*). [*Social Security (Contributions) Regula-*

tions 2001, SI 2001/1004, Sch 3 Part V para 5B(b), as amended by *Social Security (Contributions) (Amendment No 7) Regs 2003; Income Tax (Exemption of Minor Benefits) (Amendment) Regs 2004, SI 2004/3087, Reg 2*].

- A non-cash voucher up to £150 in respect of one or more annual staff functions within the tax limits (*ITEPA 2003, s 264* as amended by *Income Tax (Exemption of Minor Benefits) (Increase in Sums of Money) Order 2003, SI 2003/1361, Reg 2*). [*Social Security (Contributions) Regulations 2001, SI 2001/1004, Sch 3 Part V para 5B(c)*, as amended by *Social Security (Contributions) (Amendment No 7) Regs 2003*].
- Leave travel facilities for the armed forces (in line with *ITEPA 2003, ss 228, 266, 296*). [*Social Security (Contributions) Regulations 2001, SI 2001/1004, Sch 3 Part V para 5B(d)*, as amended by *Social Security (Contributions) (Amendment No 7) Regs 2003, SI 2003/2958*].
- A non-cash voucher to mark service of twenty years or more where the cost does not exceed £50 per year of service and no similar award has been made in the previous ten years. (*ITEPA 2003, s 323* as amended by *Income Tax (Exemption of Minor Benefits) (Increase in Sums of Money) Order 2003, SI 2003/1361, Reg 3*) [*Social Security (Contributions) Regulations 2001, SI 2001/1004, Sch 3 Part V para 6(d)*, as amended by *Social Security (Contributions) (Amendment No 7) Regs 2003*].
- A non-cash voucher providing home to work travel for disabled persons unable to use public transport [*Social Security (Contributions) Regulations 2001, SI 2001/1004, Sch 3 Part V para 5(a)*, as amended by *Social Security (Contributions) (Amendment No 7) Regs 2003*].
- A non-cash voucher in connection with the provision of cars for disabled employees. [*Social Security (Contributions) Regulations 2001, SI 2001/1004, Sch 3 Part V para 5(b)*, as amended by *Social Security (Contributions) (Amendment No 7) Regs 2003*].
- A non-cash voucher provided in connection with transport home after either late night working or following the breakdown of car-sharing arrangements. The exemption only applies if the late night working is on an irregular basis and in the case of taxi hire public transport has ceased to be available. See also **30.14** EARNINGS FROM EMPLOYMENT: EXPENSES. [*Social Security (Contributions) Regulations 2001, SI 2001/1004, Sch 3 Part V para 5(c)*, as amended by *Social Security (Contributions) (Amendment No 7) Regs 2003*].
- A non-cash voucher where that voucher evidences entitlement to use works transport services (within *ITEPA 2003, s 242*), support for public bus services (within *ITEPA 2003, s 243*) or the provision of cycles or cyclist's safety equipment (within *ITEPA 2003, s 244* as amended by *FA 2005, s 16(3)*). [*Social Security (Contributions) Regulations 2001, SI 2001/1004, Sch 3 Part V para 5A(a)(b)(c)*, as amended by *Social Security (Contributions) (Amendment No 7) Regs 2003*].

- A non-cash voucher which can be used only to obtain travelling and subsistence facilities during a public transport strike. [*Social Security (Contributions) Regulations 2001, SI 2001/1004, Sch 3 Part V para 5B(a)*, as amended by *Social Security (Contributions) (Amendment No 7) Regs 2003*].
- Subject to various conditions, childcare vouchers within *ITEPA 2003, s 270A* – see **29.32** below. [*Social Security (Contributions) Regulations 2001, SI 2001/1004, Sch 3 Part V para 7*; *Social Security (Contributions) (Amendment No 3) Regs 2006, SI 2006/883*].
- Non-cash vouchers exchangeable for meals on the employer's premises or in a canteen where meals are provided to staff generally, if on a reasonable scale. Where an employer provides free or subsidised meals that are exempt for that employer's staff then no benefit arises in respect of other employees of other employers who work on the same site and use the same facilities. As a direct result of a change made to *ITEPA 2003, s 317* by *FA 2010, s 60*, vouchers were excluded from this exemption from 6 April 2011 if awarded under salary sacrifice arrangements. [*Social Security (Contributions) Regulations 2001, SI 2001/1004, Sch 3 Part V para 5B(e)*, as amended by *Social Security (Contributions) (Amendment No 7) Regs 2003; Income Tax (Exemption of Minor Benefits) (Amendment) Regs 2004, SI 2004/3087 Reg 2*].
- The first 15 pence per working day in respect of vouchers exchangeable only for meals (ie "Luncheon Vouchers") was excluded from 26 July 2001 to 5 April 2013. [*Social Security (Contributions) Regulations 2001, SI 2001/1004, Sch 3 Part V para 6A*, revoked by *The Social Security (Contributions) (Amendment and Application of Schedule 38 to the Finance Act 2012) Regulations 2013, SI 2013/622*].
- Non-cash vouchers provided by third parties not exceeding £250 per annum per employee, where the provision is made other than in recognition of the performance of particular services, either past or anticipated (*ITEPA 2003, ss 270, 324* as amended by *Income Tax (Exemption of Minor Benefits) (Increase in Sums of Money) Order 2003, SI 2003/1361, Reg 4*). [*Social Security (Contributions) Regulations 2001, SI 2001/1004, Sch 3 Part V paras 6(a), 6(e)* as amended by *Social Security (Contributions) (Amendment No 7) Regs 2003*].
- A non-cash voucher in connection with transport by way of mainland transfers of offshore oil and gas workers (within *ITEPA 2003, s 305*). [*Social Security (Contributions) Regulations 2001, SI 2001/1004, Sch 3 Part V para 6(b)*, as amended by *Social Security (Contributions) (Amendment No 7) Regs 2003*].
- A non-cash voucher provided under a staff suggestion scheme (within *ITEPA 2003, s 321*). [*Social Security (Contributions) Regulations 2001, SI 2001/1004, Sch 3 Part V para 6(c)*, as amended by *Social Security (Contributions) (Amendment No 7) Regs 2003*].
- Provision of pensions information and advice that is available to all employees and is not general financial or tax advice up to £150 in total in any year of assessment. [*ITEPA 2003, ss 201–215; Income Tax (Exemption of Minor Benefits) (Amendment) Regs 2004, SI 2004/3087, Reg 2*].

- Provision of vouchers for the cost of eye care tests and/or corrective glasses for VDU use regarding the employment. [*Social Security (Contributions) Regulations 2001, SI 2001/1004, Sch 3 Part V para 5BA(d)*, inserted by *Social Security (Contributions) (Amendment No 4) Regs 2006, SI 2006/2003, Reg 2*; *ITEPA 2003, s 320A*; *FA 2006, s 62*].
- Provision of vouchers for only *one* mobile phone where the voucher is used as a means of making the phone available to the employee. [*Social Security (Contributions) Regulations 2001, SI 2001/1004, Sch 3 Part V para 5B(f)*, inserted by *Social Security (Contributions) (Amendment No 4) Regs 2006, SI 2006/2003, Reg 2*; *ITEPA 2003, s 319*; *FA 2006, s 62*].
- From 14 August 2007, provision of vouchers for health screening or a medical check-up in certain circumstances. This change was intended to be in accordance with HM Revenue and Customs' longstanding practice that where an employer provides employees with such facilities they should not be treated as taxable and follows the legal status of the practice having been called into question. It is anticipated that HMRC will not seek arrears of any technical liability that may have arisen previously. [*Social Security (Contributions) (Amendment No 6) Regulations 2007, SI 2007/2091*]. However, the legislation (and the associated tax legislation) has had the effect of tightening up the previous practice. The matter was under review and HMRC has said that it will not seek to collect tax/NIC on these items for 2006–07, 2007–08 and 2008–09 where they would not have been payable on the basis of the previous non-statutory treatment. The matter is legislated for generally in the *Finance Act 2009* but new legislation putting the previous non-statutory treatment on a proper footing from 6 April 2009 was necessary in respect of such provision by way of non-cash vouchers. [*Social Security (Contributions) Regulations 2001, SI 2001/1004, Sch 3 Part V para 9*, inserted by *Social Security (Contributions) (Amendment No 6) Regulations 2007, SI 2007/2091* and amended by *Social Security (Contributions) (Amendment No 3) Regulations 2009, SI 2009/600, Reg 7*; *The Employer-Financed Retirement Benefits (Excluded Benefits for Tax Purposes) (Amendment) Regulations 2009*; *ITEPA 2003, s 320B* as inserted by *FA 2009, s 55*].

[*Social Security (Contributions) Regulations 2001, SI 2001/1004, Sch 3 Part V paras 2–8* and *The Income Tax (Exemption of Minor Benefits) (Increase in Sums of Money) Order 2003, SI 2003/1361; Income Tax (Exemption of Minor Benefits) (Amendment) Regs 2004, SI 2004/3087*].

The CA originally envisaged that that there would be no exceptions to this rule even to the extent that no *de minimis* limit for seasonal rewards/gifts will be allowed. However, in regulations that came into force on 6 April 2000 the following categories of non-cash voucher became disregarded for NICs:

- vouchers provided to, or for the benefit of, an employee by a person who is not the secondary contributor who provides that voucher [*Social Security (Contributions) Regulations 2001, SI 2001/1004, Sch 3 Part V para 8*] instead the third party – not the employer – has the Class 1A liability on the provision; and

- vouchers to obtain goods and services in connection with a company car which are exempt for tax reasons. [*ITEPA 2003, ss 239, 269*]. [*Social Security (Contributions) Regulations 2001, SI 2001/1004, Sch 3 Part V para 1(2)(a)*].

See HM Revenue and Customs National Insurance Manual NIM02416–02451.

Child care vouchers

[29.32] Qualifying childcare provision was made tax-free by *ICTA 1988, s 155A* in April 1990, and the provision of on-site nursery facilities by the employer is still classed as wholly tax-free. Vouchers were classed as taxable income but were NIC-free, because giving out vouchers was classed as payment in kind until 6 April 1999. When the government then brought non-cash vouchers generally into earnings for NIC purposes, it introduced an unlimited NIC exemption for qualifying childcare vouchers provided by an employer in order to entice employers to make a contribution towards childcare costs (although it did not give any tax relief). This led to complaints about lack of harmonisation, so the law was eventually changed from 6 April 2005.

The employer could then provide such vouchers tax- and NIC-free, but only up to a specified limit of £50 per week plus administration charges in 2005–06. This was increased to £55 per week (or £243 per month) plus administration charges from 6 April 2006. Large numbers of employers took up the idea, implementing salary sacrifice schemes to convert taxable pay into tax-free childcare payments, and saving much more in tax and NICs than the government had ever intended. [*Social Security (Contributions) Regulations 2001, SI 2001/1004, Sch 3 Part V para* 7 as amended by *Social Security (Contributions) (Amendment No 3) Regulations 2005, SI 2005/778, Reg 9*; *ITEPA 2003, s 270A* as amended by *FA 2005, s 15*; *Social Security (Contributions) (Amendment No 3) Regs 2006, SI 2006/883*; *FA 2006, s 63*.]

From 6 April 2011, the scope of the exclusion was limited for new joiners to employer-supported childcare schemes in an attempt to limit the cost of the tax and NIC relief. Since that date, employers have been obliged to assess each (post-2011) scheme member's basic earnings and decide whether they would be basic, higher or additional rate taxpayers for the coming year, or for the remainder of the year of joining. Basic rate taxpayers may still be given tax- and NIC-free vouchers worth £55 per week, but higher rate taxpayers were limited to £28 per week and additional rate taxpayers to £22 per week, which was adjusted to £25 per week when the additional rate was reduced to 45% on 6 April 2013. [*Social Security (Contributions) Regulations 2001, SI 2001/1004, Sch 3 Part V para 7A* inserted by *Social Security (Contributions) (Amendment No 4) Regulations 2011, SI 2011/1000, Regs 2, 5* and *SI 2013/622, Reg 40(a)(ii)*.]

The limit applies to each employee (not each child) and must be used for registered childcare or approved home-childcare. In order to qualify, the benefit must be available to all employees and the childcare must be registered or approved. Unlike other non-cash vouchers, where the amount of earnings is the cost to the employer (which will sometimes be less than the face value), the childcare vouchers limit is based on the face value plus any administration charges. Only the excess over the allowable face value (and no element of associated administrative charges) is liable to Class 1, although in practice few employers hand out more than the tax-free limit. As some employees do not use childcare all year round, some may want to take more than the weekly limit of vouchers at some times of the year and none at others. *Sch 3, Part V, para 7* allows past unused relief to be used in a later earnings period in the same tax year. The relief for childcare vouchers is not due however if 'other childcare' is also provided by the employer – see **16.9**. [*Social Security (Contributions) (Amendment No 3) Regulations 2005, SI 2005/778, Reg 10*].

See IR Press Release IR 99/03, 11 December 2003. [*Social Security (Contributions) Regulations 2001, SI 2001/1004, Sch 3 Part V para 7*].

Under the provisions of the *Childcare Payments Act 2014*, a new Tax-Free Childcare Scheme (TFCS) has been introduced from 21 April 2017. The introduction was originally planned for October 2015, but a coalition of childcare voucher providers whose businesses were likely to be ruined by the replacement of tax- and NIC- free vouchers by the TFCS instituted a judicial review, ultimately unsuccessful, that delayed implementation. Taxpayers (including the self-employed) will be able to pay up to £8,000 per year per child into a voucher fund and have it topped up to £10,000 by a tax credit. Tax credit and universal credit recipients, and any family where at least one parent is an additional rate taxpayer, will generally be excluded. The TFCS was fully rolled-out on 14 February 2018, and following earlier Government announcements, it was expected that no further members will be permitted to join the old-style Employer-Supported Childcare voucher schemes from 6 April 2018. Employees will have the right to switch from the ESC to the TFCS, which most will do because the benefit is worth more than under the ESC. Since parents will be paying for the childcare themselves, with help from the tax credit, the vouchers will not constitute payments of earnings for NIC purposes and there will be no scope for salary sacrifice arrangements. This was a large factor in the underlying rationale for the change, and the problem for the current ESC voucher providers, whose role as a middle-man in the childcare voucher market will disappear, because the TFCS will simply see money paid into an account with National Savings and Investments and paid from there to registered childcare providers (or HMRC, in the case of employer NICs on nannies' wages).

However, on 13 March 2018 the Secretary of State for Education announced in Parliament that employer supported childcare schemes (mainly childcare voucher schemes) would remain open for a further six months to new entrants. Childcare voucher schemes will now be closed to new entrants on 4 October 2018. [*Income Tax (Limited Exemptions for Qualifying Childcare Vouchers and other Childcare) (Relevant Day) Regulations 2018, SI 2018/462, Reg 2*].

Gifts and awards

[29.33] According to the former DSS, any payment made to an employed earner, however described, will be earnings for contribution purposes if it is made under contract or in accordance with a scheme or an established practice or in fulfilment of a firm expectation that it would be made. The first three conditions are clearly correct because, in any of those circumstances, the payment will be one of the rewards in return for which the employed earner is, in fact, providing his service (see **29.2** above). But the last condition is questionable *if the payment is purely personal* (see **29.34** below). See also HM Revenue and Customs National Insurance Manual NIM02165. See also *McBride v Blackburn* [2003] STC SCD 139 Sp C 356.

Birthday presents etc

[29.34] In accordance with the principle described at **29.33** above, guidance is that gifts from an employer to an employed earner are earnings for Class 1 purposes if they are paid under the employee's contract of service or the employee could expect such a payment because, for example, it is an acknowledged practice within the company to make such payments. Only personal and totally unexpected gifts may be excluded. But that cannot be right. A birthday gift made each year to an employee because of a close *personal* relationship between the employer and the employee will not be earnings for contribution purposes whether it is expected or not. See also **29.46** below. It will not be made to the person 'in return for acting as or being an employee' (*Hochstrasser v Mayes* [1960] AC 376, [1959] 3 All ER 817, HL). The kind of gifts most likely to pass this test are birthday, anniversary and wedding presents; though the former DSS recognised that a gift in recognition of long service or the passing of an examination (see **29.36** below) may also qualify. See also HM Revenue and Customs National Insurance Manual NIM02165. See also *Bridges v Bearsley* [1957] 2 All ER 281 which involved acts of bounty towards two directors of a company by the heirs to a deceased chairman's estate that owned the company.

Bonus payments

[29.35] Bonus payments made in the normal course of an employment, eg for productivity, performance, job completion, Christmas, will always be earnings for contribution purposes in accordance with the principle described at **29.1** and **29.2** above. See also HM Revenue and Customs National Insurance Manual NIM02070.

There appear to be only two circumstances in which that may not be so. The first is where the bonus is paid by some unconnected third party who bears the ultimate cost. The former DSS was, for example, understood not to regard as earnings a bonus paid by a car manufacturer to a car salesman working for one of the manufacturer's distributors in recognition of his performance. But it may well be regarded as a gratuity or offering falling within the special rules described at **29.37** below. Certainly, there would seem to be no other justification for the practice as such a bonus is quite clearly 'derived from' the salesman's employment. The case of *Booth v Mirror Group Newspapers plc* [1992] STC 615, [1992] BTC 455 should have caused the then DSS to review its policy but there was never any evidence of such a review. Although the case concerned the deductibility of PAYE from payments to a non-employee, the PAYE provision on which the case turned is imported into contributions law as what is now *Social Security (Contributions) Regulations 2001, SI 2001/1004, Sch 4 para 1(2)*. This defines 'employer' and 'employee' respectively as 'the secondary contributor' and 'any person in receipt of earnings'. *Social Security (Contributions) Regulations 2001, SI 2001/1004, Sch 4 para 1* provides that 'every employer, on making . . . payment of earnings in respect of which earnings-related contributions are payable . . . may deduct earnings-related contributions in accordance with this Schedule'. Official thinking now is, however, that cash amounts paid by third parties are liable to Class 1, which is due from the employer. But the employer may very well not know that a payment has been made, or if so its quantum. There is no provision for third parties to be required to give such information in these circumstances so it is difficult to see how employers can comply with this supposed view of the law. *Sch 4 para 6* implies that the employer pays Class 1 on payments that the *employer* makes to the employee (and not on such payments made by others).

The second circumstance is where the bonus is paid to an employee of a UK company by a non-group overseas company with which the UK company does *not* carry on business in association (see **5.4** AGGREGATION OF EARNINGS) and the overseas company bears the full cost. In such circumstances, the amount may not be regarded as earnings for contribution purposes, even if the payment is made via the UK company. But, again, the only justification for such treatment would seem to be the special rules on tips and gratuities described at **29.37** below.

Examination awards and scholarships

[29.36] Former DSS guidance was originally that examination awards were earnings for contribution purposes if paid by an employer who had an organised scheme for making such awards or if the employed earner could have expected to receive such an award on passing an examination. Although this accords with the general principle laid down at **29.2** above, the guidance was wrong as examination awards are not normally made for 'acting as or being an employee' (*Ball v Johnson* (1971) 47 TC 155). In the case on which the guidance was based, Midland Bank Ltd required certain of its employees to sit for (though not necessarily to pass) the Institute of Bankers examinations and, though it did not consider itself bound to do so, Midland Bank made awards to employees who succeeded in passing the examinations. The then DSS subsequently corrected its guidance and said that examination awards are earnings only if the employee's contract of service or terms of employment require the examinations to be passed for the employment to continue. HMRC continues to follow the same approach and also points out that an examination prize could, in some circumstances, be made as a personal gift (**29.33**). See HM Revenue and Customs National Insurance Manual NIM02105.

Scholarships funded by employers and awarded on a discretionary basis to employees' children are not earnings of the employee because they are paid neither 'to' nor 'for the benefit of' the employee as would be required by *SSCBA 1992, s 6(1)* if a Class 1 liability were to arise. Save for Class 1A contributions, where various tax definitions form the basis of the charge, there are no 'connected person' rules in contribution law that enable the benefit received by another family member to be imputed in such circumstances to the earner.

Gratuities, tips and service charges

[29.37] A payment made to an employed earner in respect of gratuities or offerings is to be entirely excluded from earnings for contribution purposes provided that the payment is neither directly nor indirectly:

- made by the secondary contributor (ie the employer) and does not comprise or represent sums previously paid to the secondary contributor; or
- allocated by the secondary contributor to the earner.

[*Social Security (Contributions) Regulations 2001, SI 2001/1004, Sch 3 Part X para 5*]. See also HM Revenue and Customs National Insurance Manual NIM02390.

From 23 February 2004, the above exception does not apply in the case of most payments made by persons who are connected with the secondary contributor nor made by a trustee. 'Trustee' does not include a tronc-master.

[*Social Security (Contributions) Regulations 2001, SI 2001/1004, Sch 3 Part X para 5(4)–(6)*, inserted by *Social Security (Contributions) (Amendment) Regs 2004*].

Tips have been held not to be earnings within the meaning of *Employment Protection (Consolidation) Act 1978, s 8*. Before 1 October 2009, they were not counted as wages for national minimum wage purposes if they were not paid through the payroll, but since that date tips are never wages for those purposes. [*National Minimum Wage Act 1998*; *National Minimum Wage Regulations 1999, SI 1999/584, Reg 31(1)(e)*.] They have always been held to be remuneration chargeable to income tax as earnings (see, eg, *Confone v Spaghetti House* [1980] ICR 155; *Calvert (Inspector of Taxes) v Wainwright* [1947] KB 526, [1947] 1 All ER 282; *Figael Ltd v Fox* [1990] STC 583). In all likelihood, therefore, tips and gratuities would, but for *Social Security (Contributions) Regulations 2001, SI 2001/1004, Sch 3 Part X para 5*, be earnings for contribution purposes. The effect of *Social Security (Contributions) Regulations 2001, SI 2001/1004, Sch 3 Part X para 5* is, however, to exclude from an employed earner's earnings any tip or gratuity paid to him directly by a consumer or paid into a staff box or to someone acting independently of his employer, eg a troncmaster or tronc committee, *unless*:

- the employer decides how the amount of tips collected in that way are to be divided among the employees; *and*
- the employer or a connected person is involved in the payment process.

It should be noted that both conditions have to be satisfied before a contribution liability arises. It should also be noted that this treatment differs from the tax treatment. Payments made through a tronc are subject to PAYE deductions at the hand of a troncmaster even if free from contribution liability.

A gratuity or tip is essentially a *voluntary* payment which the payer is under no obligation to make. Accordingly, any amount which a customer is required by the management of an hotel, restaurant, etc to pay for services is *not* a tip, gratuity or offering but a *service charge* and, as such, if distributed to employees, is part of their earnings for contribution purposes. (CWG2 (2017), para 2.8.) See also HM Revenue and Customs National Insurance Manual NIM02390.

In the National Minimum Wage case *Nerva v United Kingdom* (Application 42295/98) (2002) 36 EHRR 31, [2002] IRLR 815, ECtHR, the European Court of Human Rights ruled that tips paid by cheque or credit card were the property of the employer and could be used to pay the basic staff wage. Some commentators and HM Revenue and Customs compliance officers had suggested that there could therefore be a Class 1 liability on such tips paid by a 'troncmaster' where none had existed previously. See also Tolley's Practical NIC Newsletter, March 2003 page 17; Tolley's Practical NIC Newsletter, February 2004 page 12; Tolley's Practical NIC Newsletter, March 2004 page 19; Tolley's Practical NIC Newsletter, March 2005 page 17.

Early in 2004 HM Revenue and Customs attempted to clarify matters by issuing booklet E24 'Tips, Gratuities, Service Charges and Troncs' which covered income tax, NIC, VAT and National Minimum Wage. 'Issued' in this case meant that it was only available on HM Revenue and Customs' website and the Employer's CD-Rom. The booklet contained more detail than any editions of CWG2 and was helpful in confirming that where tips are added by a customer to a cheque or credit card or debit card payment and the amount is passed on in full to a troncmaster, the mere initial receipt by the employer will not automatically give rise to a Class 1 NIC liability when the tips are shared out by a tronc to the employees. More controversially, the first edition of the booklet suggested that NIC liability would arise in various circumstances which the law would not seem to support. It stated, for example, that if the troncmaster is appointed by the employer rather than a committee of employees then the employer has 'interfered' with the allocation of the tips. First, it is doubtful whether the word 'interfere' can be properly used in this way. More importantly, the relevant part of the legislation would require the employer to 'allocate' the distribution and 'allocate' is not the same as 'distributing' or 'interfering'. However, a revised booklet E24 in 2005 clarified the word 'allocated' as meaning directly or indirectly by the employer and the word 'interference'. Subsequently, the issue of Tax Bulletin 77 in June 2005 made further clarification by stating:

> 'If the employer determines both these matters [which employees receive payment and how much each receives] directly, or indirectly through another person, he will be allocating the payments and the second condition cannot be satisfied. If someone else, such as a troncmaster, genuinely determines these matters the second condition can be satisfied.'

The first edition of E24 also asserted that where the employer withheld an amount representing credit card commission and similar charges before handing such amounts over to the troncmaster for distribution, this also amounted to the employer influencing the share of tips received by any employee such that there would then be a Class 1 liability on the share-out. Again this was always highly questionable, and this was also specifically reversed in the 2005 edition of E24. See Tolley's Practical NIC Newsletter, March 2004 page 19 and Taxation magazine, 8 April 2004, p 27; Tolley's Practical NIC Newsletter, March 2005 page 17.

A further announcement was made in February 2006, that mere entitlement to participate in a tronc expressed in a contract of employment is not of itself enough to attract a Class 1 liability. This was reiterated in a Tax Bulletin article in April 2006 which went further:

> If tips paid by customers are paid to employees through an independently-run tronc, they are not liable for Class 1 NICs even where they go to meet a
>
> - contractual obligation, or
> - legal requirement such as the National Minimum Wage (NMW).
>
> Customers are obliged to pay compulsory service charges so if such payments are the source of payments made to employees, they are not tips or in respect of tips. Such payments are earnings and liable for Class 1 NICs.
>
> Amounts paid by a customer as service charges, tips, gratuities and cover charges count towards NMW pay if they are paid by the employer to the employee via the employer's payroll and the amounts are shown on the pay slips issued by the employer. Tips and gratuities given directly to the worker by a customer do not count towards NMW pay. Tronc money paid directly from the tronc to an employee does not count towards NMW pay. However, if the tronc money is passed to the employer, and is both paid to the employee via the employer's payroll and reflected on payslips issued by the employer, then it will count towards NMW pay. It will also count towards NMW pay where the troncmaster operates PAYE on tronc distributions and uses the employer to pass the net payments to each employee, provided the amounts are paid to the employee via the employer's payroll and are reflected on their payslips.
>
> In the event that an employer pays amounts to a tronc which exceed the total value of the tips paid by customers, the excess is not a payment of or in respect of a tip, so Class 1 NICs are due on the excess.
>
> HMRC consider that where the employer promises or guarantees a certain amount from the tronc, that may indicate that the employer has sufficient de facto control over the operation of the tronc to constitute an indirect allocation by the employer. Further investigation may be required to establish the true nature of the arrangements.

See Tax Bulletin 82.

This was followed in early autumn 2006 by a further revised version of the E24 tips booklet – which at last appeared to be correct and in accordance with the law. The current edition is E24 (2015). See also Tolley's Practical NIC Newsletter, November 2006 page 83.

Where, due to HM Revenue and Customs' previous insistence of liability, amounts had been overpaid on the basis of the incorrect interpretation of the law, employers were entitled to the appropriate refund which would, where appropriate, have included a refund of interest and penalties paid. This was so whether the payment was through a contract settlement or otherwise. Where some or all of the overpayment was through a contract settlement HM Revenue and Customs should have written to the employer by 31 May 2006 to make arrangements for the appropriate refund. See Tax Bulletin 82.

On 13 June 2008, HM Revenue and Customs was successful in its appeal concerning the National Minimum Wage at the High Court (*Revenue and Customs Comrs v Annabels (Berkeley Square) Ltd* [2008] ICR 1076, [2008] All ER (D) 170 (Jun), EAT). The Employment Tribunal had heard that sums held by a troncmaster belonged to the employees. But the High Court decision was that such sums when distributed cannot form part of an employer's National Minimum Wage obligation. In the Court of Appeal in May 2009 Annabel's appeal against the decision in the lower court was rejected and leave to appeal further was refused. However, as many affected businesses now handle tips rather differently the success on the part of HM Revenue and Customs may be of limited value in its application to other cases. Perhaps for this reason, the Government subsequently announced in July 2008 that the National Minimum Wage legislation would be changed (which happened from 1 October 2009, as already noted) so that tips can no longer be counted in any circumstances as part of an employee's NMW entitlement. No changes were made to the NIC legislation as none were needed.

See **5.12** AGGREGATION OF EARNINGS for the treatment of gratuities, tips, etc which, though earnings for contribution purposes in accordance with the rules described above, are paid separately from other earnings.

It must be noted that the gratuities and offerings to which *Social Security (Contributions) Regulations 2001, SI 2001/1004, Sch 3 Part X para 5* relates are not subject to any limitation either as to amount or to the type of business or circumstances in which they are received. Thus, until the 23 February 2004 change noted above and amended early in 2005, the provisions might have applied to any voluntary third party payment to an employed earner (see **29.35** above)—even, perhaps, from trustees (see below).

The unusual case of *Channel 5 TV Group Ltd v Morehead* [2003] STC SCD 327 Sp C 369 concerned gratuities paid in February 2000 by a non-resident investor in Channel 5 to a number of Channel 5 employees following the sale of its 18% interest. The payments were not contractual, entirely gratuitous and were not received under any expectation that payment would be made. Although the then Inland Revenue had claimed that National Insurance was due on the payments, Channel 5 claimed that the exemption under what was then *Reg 19(1)(c)* of the *1979 Regs* applied, but the Inland Revenue claimed that this was inapplicable as, in their view, the payments had been made or allocated by the appellant, the appellant's directors having supplied the non-resident investor with details of the employees necessary to enable the payments to be made.

The Special Commissioners found that whilst one meaning of 'gratuity' was 'tip' that was not its only meaning and the *Regulations* gave no indication of any restriction on the meaning of 'gratuity'. They stated various authorities for this view:

- *Smith v Incorporated Council of Law Reporting for England and Wales* [1914] 6 TC 477.
- *Holloway v Poplar Corporation* [1904] 1 KB 173.
- *McGarry v R* [1954] IR 64.

- *McGrath v Secretary of State for Northern Ireland* [1994] National Insurance 98.
- *Henley v Murray* [1950] 31 TC 351.

The Commissioners found that the payments were gifts given by the investor and that there was no obligation to make the gifts. Thus the payments were gratuities within the terms of former *Reg 19(1)(c)*. However, at least one of two conditions needs to be met before the exemption applies. The first is that the payment is not made by the employer and the second is that it is not allocated by the employer. The Commissioners had little trouble in finding that these are alternative conditions, not cumulative, but observed that the 2001 consolidation of the Contribution Regulations makes this even clearer. The Commissioners also found that the employer – Channel 5 – had not allocated the payments. It had, however, indirectly assisted with the process by supplying names of recipients, the net amount to be paid to each and the details necessary to deal with tax payments to the then Inland Revenue. The Commissioners held that this did not constitute either 'making' or 'allocating' the payments.

As the decision was that the payments did not attract an NIC liability, the question of whose liability it was did not arise. Nonetheless, it was observed in passing that had that been the case it would have been Channel 5. *1979 Regs, Sch 1, para 3A* applied so that the third party was liable to pay as agent for the secondary contributor. If the third party did not pay because, for example, it was outside the jurisdiction as in this case then the liability remained with the employer (*SSCBA 1992, s 6(3)*). The changes made with effect from 23 February 2004 and amended in early 2005 – see above, are undoubtedly a direct response to the decision in this case.

In *Knowledgepoint 360 Group Ltd v Revenue and Customs Comrs* [2011] UKFTT 438, payments made to employees in respect of shares and share options in an employee benefit trust which was wound up following the sale of the company which created the trust were held not to be gratuities.

Honoraria

[29.38] An honorarium is usually taken to mean a voluntary fee paid for services; and the former DSS followed this in referring to payments made for services which are not within an employee's contract of service or terms of employment and giving as an example voluntary payments made to an employee who serves in an unpaid capacity as the secretary of the firm's sports club. Guidance was once that such payments were not earnings for contribution purposes, but this guidance changed in the 2003 edition of CWG2. (See now CWG2 (2017), para 5.1.) The rationale for the previous treatment is that if a person's working arrangement in any particular capacity is such that he has no *entitlement* to reward, the arrangement cannot constitute a contract of service or an office with general earnings and the person cannot, therefore, be an employed earner within the terms of *SSCBA 1992, s 2* (see **14.4** CATEGORISATION). And were that so, there is no employment from which he can derive remuneration or profit and it follows, therefore, that anything he does derive from his activity cannot be earnings within *SSCBA 1992, s 3*.

Nonetheless, the position was reversed from 2003 – see HM Revenue and Customs National Insurance Manual NIM02205 (which for a considerable time at first was not updated in line with CWG2). The Manual makes clear that arrears arising prior to the change of view in 2003 should not be collected. See also *McBride v Blackburn* [2003] STC SCD 139 Sp C 356.

Incentive payments

[29.39] In certain circumstances, an employer may make payments to an employee which are best described as 'sweeteners'. They do not relate to the service rendered by the employee but are intended to make changes in the terms and conditions of the employment more acceptable to the employee, eg a change from weekly to monthly pay, a change from cash payments to bank credits, a change in working hours or work times or even an inducement to the employee to accept lower pay. All such payments are earnings for Class 1 purposes because they are payments made to the person 'for . . . being an employee' (see **29.1** above). See HM Revenue and Customs National Insurance Manual NIM02275, NIM02280.

However, see **29.19** in the case of incentives to give up ongoing membership of defined benefit pension arrangements, etc.

Offerings etc to clergy

[29.40] Offerings, fees, etc made to, and received directly by, a MINISTER OF RELIGION 45 (eg Easter, Christmas offerings, baptism, marriage, funeral fees), are to be excluded from his earnings for Class 1 purposes, provided they do not form part of his stipend or salary. The logic is that parishioners make personal gifts as tokens of esteem, not payments of earnings. See also HM Revenue and Customs National Insurance Manual NIM02260. [*Social Security (Contributions) Regulations 2001, SI 2001/1004, Sch 3 Part X para 13*]. However, for tax purposes, Easter offerings, customarily paid to the incumbent, were held to be taxable as part of the income from his employment in *Blakiston v Cooper* 5 TC 247, HL.

Prizes and incentives

[29.41] A cash prize awarded to an employee as a result of a competition which his employer runs in connection with his business (but which, presumably, is open only to employees) is earnings for Class 1 purposes on general principles (see **29.1** above). (CWG2 (2017), para 5.1.)

Likewise, any percentage of prize money which is paid to an employee of a horse racing stable is earnings for contribution purposes. In such cases, the trainer will be the secondary contributor as regards the share of prize money whether he is the actual employer or not. In contrast, a September 1992 decision made by the Secretary of State confirmed that prize money from the Jockey Club was paid on a voluntary basis and so not liable by virtue of *Social Security (Contributions) Regulations 2001, SI 2001/1004, Sch 3 Part X para 5*. HM Revenue and Customs stresses that this is only appropriate where the payment is not:

- made directly or indirectly by the secondary contributor and the sum does not comprise or represent sums previously paid to the secondary contributor; or
- directly or indirectly allocated by the secondary contributor to the earner.

More recently, however, the Jockey Club has returned to its original role as a members club. The distribution of prize money to stables is now the responsibility of the British Horseracing Authority (BHA), the rules of which are quite specific on the distribution of such moneys and follow exactly the previous Jockey Club procedures. The stable employees decide the distribution criteria under BHA rule 119 and in line with 'tronc' arrangements, income tax but not NIC is accounted for by the trainer on such distributions.

See HM Revenue and Customs National Insurance Manual NIM02300 and the Bloodstock Taxation Guide issued by the British Horseracing Board.

In other exceptional circumstances, some similar cases might now be caught by the changes made from 23 February 2004 – see **29.37** above.

Where an employer operates an incentive scheme for employees or third parties which does not provide cash rewards, the incentive or award is not earnings for Class 1 contribution purposes because of the general payment in kind rules, see **29.28**; there may, however, be a Class 1A liability. If the employer meets all or part of his employee's tax liability in respect of the award, this forms part of earnings for contribution purposes, whether or not the award was provided by the employer or by a third party. If, however, it is a third party, with whom the employee has no contract of employment, who meets the tax liability, that tax arguably does not constitute earnings for Class 1 contributions purposes. From 6 April 2000, Class 1A is due on the tax paid by the third party (if any). If the award itself is in cash, normal earnings rules apply so that if the award is from a third party the tax ought not to constitute earnings for contributions purposes. [*SSCBA 1992, s 6(1)*]. However, the authorities assert that the employer should account for Class 1 contributions on cash paid to his employees by a third party, even though he may well not have all the required information to do this (see also **29.35** above).

Where an issuer of charge cards, cheque guarantee cards, credit cards or debit cards makes a reward payment in cash to another person's employee (typically staff in retail stores) who has assisted in identifying lost or stolen cards in the course of his or her employment, no Class 1 liability is to arise (CWG2 (2017), para 5.1). This provision took effect from 26 July 2001 but the authorities have never pursued contributions on such items previously and have said that they will continue this practice prior to the formal legislation having come into effect. See HM Revenue and Customs National Insurance Manual NIM02108. Where a retailer pays its own till staff an incentive for spotting a lost or stolen card, any such payment will be classed as earnings.

[*SI 2001/1004, Sch 3, Part X, para 15*, inserted by *Social Security (Contributions) (Amendment No 5) Regulations 2001, Reg 5*].

Staff suggestion scheme payments

[29.42] Awards made under a staff suggestion scheme are not regarded as forming part of earnings for contribution purposes provided they meet the criteria set out in *ITEPA 2003, s 321* (formerly Extra-Statutory Concession A57):

- the making of suggestions is outside the scope of the employee's normal duties;
- there is no contractual entitlement to the awards;
- there is no expectation that an award will be made in any particular case; and
- awards are conditional upon discretion as to
  - (a) the eligibility of the suggestion;
  - (b) the acceptance/rejection of the suggestion; and
  - (c) the award made.

[*Social Security (Contributions) Regulations 2001, SI 2001/1004, Sch 3 Part X para 8(f)*, as amended by *Social Security (Contributions, Categorisation of Earners and Intermediaries) (Amendment) Regulations 2004, SI 2004/770, Reg 28* and *Social Security (Contributions) (Amendment No 2) Regs 2010, SI 2010/188*]. See also HM Revenue and Customs National Insurance Manual NIM02350. (CWG2 (2017), paras 2.6.6, 5.1, in which the employer is invited to ask HMRC about the details of such a scheme.)

Profit-related pay

[29.43] Despite the fact that part of an employee's pay may be linked to, and vary with, the profits of his employer's business, the whole of that pay is earnings for contribution purposes on general principles (see **29.1** above).

See also HM Revenue and Customs National Insurance Manual NIM02305.

Profit-sharing scheme payments

[29.44] See 31.26 EARNINGS FROM EMPLOYMENT: READILY CONVERTIBLE ASSETS, ETC.

Surrender of share option payments

[29.45] See 31.27 in earlier versions of this work for details.

Trivial benefits

[29.46] Prior to April 2016, the value of a trivial benefit that could be excluded from tax and NICs liability was something of a hit and miss affair owing to what was accepted as trivial by HMRC. The OTS interim report 'review of employee benefits and expenses' (August 2013) found trivial amounts for 'non-work' flowers ranged from £0–£50 (see footnote 6, page 67 of the OTS interim report).

From 28 November 2016 for NICs purposes (but 6 April 2016 for PAYE purposes), a trivial benefit not exceeding £50 in value will not attract Class 1 or Class 1A NICs liability. There are a number of conditions, all of which must be met, to qualify for the exemption. These are that:

- the cost of providing the benefit does not exceed £50 (or the average cost per employee if a benefit is provided to a group of employees and it is impracticable to work out the exact cost per person);
- the benefit is not cash or a cash voucher;
- the employee is not entitled to the benefit as part of any contractual obligation (including under salary sacrifice arrangements); and
- the benefit is not provided in recognition of particular services performed by the employee as part of their employment duties (or in anticipation of such services).

The birthday gift referred to in **29.34** above will be covered by this exemption, assuming it's not a close company.

Additional conditions are imposed in respect of closed companies for the exemption to be met, namely:

- where the trivial benefit is provided to directors and other office holders of close companies will be subject to an annual cap of £300;
- where the director's or other office holder's family or household member is also an employee of the company, they will be subject to a £300 cap in their own right; and
- although subject to an annual cap, each trivial benefit (if more than one) cannot exceed £50.

[*Social Security (Contributions) Regulations 2001, SI 2001/1004, Sch 3 Part V para 6(da)* as inserted by *Social Security (Contributions) (Amendment No 4) Regulations 2016, SI 2016/1067, Reg 5*.] See also HM Revenue and Customs Company Taxation Manual CTM60060.

Trust fund payments

[29.47] Until 6 October 1987, payments *to* trustees (other than payments in connection with an occupational sick pay scheme—see **29.24** above) were to be excluded from earnings for contribution purposes, provided any share of the payments which an earner was entitled to have paid to him was, or may have been, dependent not on the secondary contributor concerned but on the exercise by the trustees of a discretion or the performance by them of a duty arising under the trust; and payments *by* trustees were, in those circumstances, also to be excluded from earnings. [*Reg 19(1)(e)* as amended by *Contributions Amendment No 4 Regs 1983, Reg 3(a) and revoked by Contributions Amendment No 3 Regs 1987, Reg* 2].

Between 6 October 1987 and 6 April 1990, such payments by trustees were, in certain circumstances, to continue to be excluded from earnings if the establishment of the trust (or a predecessor trust) pre-dated 6 April 1985. [*Social Security (Contributions) Regulations 2001, SI 2001/1004, Reg 26*].

The exclusion from earnings of payments to and by trustees was withdrawn by legislation because it had become a popular means of contribution avoidance for an employer to settle on trust for his employees amounts which the trustees would then distribute to the employees as beneficiaries. But it must be questioned whether that avoidance route had at that time, in fact, been closed and whether, in the case of purely *discretionary* employee trusts, the former *Reg 19(1)(e)* was ever needed to open it! If the trustees of a trust at that time made gratuitous, discretionary payments to the employees of the settlor, free from any interference by the settlor as to how much each or any employee should receive, were not the payments gratuities which fell squarely within the excluding provisions of *SI 2001/1004, Sch 3 Part X para 5* (see **29.37** above)? If that is correct, DSS guidance to the effect that, from 6 April 1990, payments from all trust funds would be earnings subject to Class 1 was incorrect. (See 1995 leaflet CA 28, page 83, Item 72). These comments are not applicable following the 23 February 2004 change – see **29.37** above. See also HM Revenue and Customs National Insurance Manual NIM02404.

Further, employer's tax relief for contributions made to trusts on and after 27 November 2002 is deferred until the employee receives a payment that is liable to tax and NICs. These provisions do not adversely affect companies contributing to such trusts that qualify for relief under the pre-existing statutory corporation tax deduction for employee share schemes. In addition, the nine-month leeway that applies for accruals of general remuneration is also retained. In line with this tax change, the *Social Security (Contributions) (Amendment No 5) Regulations* (*SI 2002/2929*) – effective from 28 November 2002 – regulated who pays the NIC, ie the employer (or former employer) and not the trustees. The regulations were unhelpful in introducing a different concept of 'intermediary' to that applicable in the case of IR35 legislation (see 40 INTERMEDIARIES). They also did not provide an obligation for the trustees to notify details to the person liable to pay NIC in order that the latter was thereby enabled to discharge his own legal obligations. The whole position has, of course, been changed by the introduction of *ITEPA 2003, Part 7A* from April 2011, which imposes a tax charge and, through *Reg 22B* (inserted by *SI 2011/2700, Regs 2,3* from 6 December 2011), a Class 1 charge on the same amount of deemed earnings where a third party such as an employee trust takes a 'relevant step'.

Damages payments

[29.48] Where an employer makes payments to recompense an employee for injuries sustained in the course of his employment, the payments do not constitute earnings for contribution purposes unless the employer has a contractual liability to make such payments. (CWG2 (2017), para 5.1.) The measures were widened by HM Revenue and Customs to cover situations in which a third party may discharge the damages which would fall outside the scope of the current tax exemption. (See Inland Revenue Press Release 29 February 1996). See also HM Revenue and Customs National Insurance Manual NIM02110. The same principle applies here as with termination payments that constitute compensation rather than a payment for carrying out the duties or simply being an employee.

Loans and debt payments

[29.49] The official guidance is that a loan made by an employer to an employee is not earnings unless and until it is written off, in whole or in part, at which point the amount which is written off becomes earnings. (CWG2 (2018 to 2019), para 5.1.) This applies not only to loans which the employer funds himself but also to loans funded by a third party in accordance with arrangements made by an employer.

This guidance may be of questionable validity, however. The mere making of a book entry pursuant to a decision by an employer not to seek repayment of a loan is not sufficient to extinguish the loan in law. The debt can be abandoned by the employer only by a release under seal or in return for some consideration by the employee—and whether the current services of the employee are sufficient consideration for that purpose without any agreement being made to that effect is open to question.

The former DSS was silent as to the position where a loan by an employer to an employee becomes statute-barred under the *Limitation Act 1980* by a lapse of six years. Such debts are not extinguished, they merely become unenforceable, so, arguably, they can never give rise to earnings. However, see the comments of the former Chief Executive of the DSS, Mrs Faith Boardman, in Payroll Manager's Review, April 1996 on this point and **14.25** CATEGORISATION.

A problem which guidance has never addressed is that of joint liability. An employee may enter into a contract as an agent for his employer as an undisclosed principal and thereupon the employer becomes primarily liable to discharge the debt that is created. If, however, the employer will not or cannot pay, the employee himself is liable—though with a right of indemnity against the employer. If, in such circumstances, the employer *does* pay, can it be said that he has discharged the employee's debt and thus made a payment of earnings? Surely not, for the employee's debt was only contingent and was in any case balanced by the right of indemnity and *both* are extinguished when the employer pays. The employee gains no money's worth. The former DSS did *implicitly* take a contrary view, however, as evidenced by its view on petrol purchases in earlier years (see **30.21**).

See **29.58** for details of the relief for payments in respect of employee liabilities and indemnity insurance.

See HM Revenue and Customs National Insurance Manual NIM02270. In the light of anti-avoidance legislation introduced in 2011 and relating to 'disguised remuneration' for tax purposes, HMRC's attitude to the National Insurance treatment of loans to employees has hardened, both before and after the incorporation of the disguised remuneration rules into NIC law by *Reg 22B* deeming the taxable value of a relevant step to be earnings for Class 1 purposes with effect from 6 December 2011.

Where an employer who has himself made a loan to an employee assigns to a bank, building society etc the *chose in action* (ie the right to interest and repayment of principal) created by the loan and, in consequence, pays interest additional to the interest payable by the employee, that additional interest is *not* earnings of the employee for contribution purposes. See also HM Revenue and Customs National Insurance Manual NIM02210.

In law, student loans repaid by the employer in the case of certain teachers would generally be treated as a payment and would be earnings for contribution purposes as they constitute a discharge by the employer of the employee's personal debt, as a specific exception applies only to repayments made by the former student. [*Social Security (Contributions) (Amendment No 4) Regulations 2002, SI 2002/2924, Reg 4* inserting new *Social Security Contributions Regulations 2001, SI 2001/1004, Sch 3 Part X para 16*]. However, agreement has been reached between the Department for Education and Skills and HM Revenue and Customs that both the tax and the National Insurance liability is met centrally by DfES so that the qualifying teachers receive the full face value of the loan write-off and do not themselves have to pay tax or National Insurance on those amounts.

HMRC has argued for many years that loans, made by the trustees of employee benefit trusts to the directors and senior employees of the employers who settled those trusts, should be treated as earnings, on the basis that there is little likelihood that the loans will ever be repaid and that they are therefore tantamount to free cash in the hands of the employees. The principal challenge was made in litigation against trust and loan schemes operated by Glasgow Rangers FC and its holding company, Murray Group Holdings Ltd, but HMRC lost the argument before both the First-tier and the Upper Tribunal (see *Revenue and Customs Comrs v Murray Group Holdings Ltd and others* [2014] UKUT 0292). The tribunals found for the employer, principally because there is detailed legislation to deal with beneficial loans made to employees and there was nothing in the documentation or the behaviour of the employer or employees to cause them to fall outside that legislative framework. It was not open to HMRC to re-characterise the payments made to the employees as anything other than what they were in law. It did not help HMRC's case that it had, in *MacDonald v Dextra Accessories Ltd* [2005] UKHL 47, persuaded the House of Lords that similar payments to that employer's EBT, which had also made large beneficial loans to directors, did not constitute earnings at that point but were simply 'potential emoluments'. HMRC's aim in *Dextra* had been to deny the company a corporation tax deduction because the cash in the trust had not been paid out to employees as remuneration within nine months of its year-end, but that argument was irrelevant to the position of the football club, which had large accumulated tax losses. A claim for PAYE and NICs on the trust payments in *Murray* seemed to some like opportunism rather than the application of the plain terms of the law.

HMRC v Murray Group Holdings

[29.50] The seemingly never ending case of Advocate General for *Scotland v Murray Group Holdings Ltd* [2015] CSIH 77, [2016] STC 468; affd sub nom *RFC 2012 Plc (in liquidation) (formerly Rangers Football Club Plc) v Advocate General for Scotland* [2017] UKSC 45, [2017] 4 All ER 654, [2017] STC 1556, was finally brought to an end when the Supreme Court found in favour of HMRC.

In brief, Rangers Football Club (RFC) paid earnings into a trust instead of directly to the footballer concerned. The footballer could then obtain a loan from the trust which would be greater than if the earnings had been subject to PAYE and NICs through the payroll. The Supreme Court found that:

- the sums paid into the trust constituted earnings of the footballer(s) and therefore should have been subject to PAYE and NICs;
- it is not necessary that a payment is made for the purposes of PAYE only if the money is paid to or at least placed unreservedly at the disposal of the employee;
- discretionary bonuses made available to RFC's employees through the same trust mechanisms also fell within the tax charge as these were given in respect of the employee's work.

It seems that HMRC was perhaps adopting a 'belt and braces' approach in case the judgment went against it, in introducing the various disguised remuneration measures concerning the provision of loans provided through third parties. The legislation, rather controversially, is retrospective; applying to loans provided on or after 6 April 1999 where there is an amount of the loan outstanding immediately before the end of 5 April 2019. See **29.69** below.

[*Finance (No.2) Act 2018, s 34 and Sch 11; Social Security (Contributions) (Amendment No 2) Regulations 2018, SI 2018/257, Reg 2*]

Discharge of personal debts

[29.51] Where an employer discharges a debt which his employee owes to a third party, the amount paid by the employer is money's worth in the hands of the employee and is, accordingly, earnings for contribution purposes. (See *Hartland v Diggines* (1926) 10 TC 247; *Nicoll v Austin* (1935) 19 TC 531). But, as previous DSS guidance has rightly emphasised, it is important in this context to determine whether a debt being discharged by the employer *is* the employee's debt or is the *employer's* debt. (CWG2 (2017), para 5.2.6.) The question to be asked is: Who has made the contract? The same problem arises with credit cards (see **29.56** below). If the employer makes the contract and discharges the liability which arises under it, then, to any extent to which the employee enjoys or consumes or utilises the services or goods contracted for, the employee receives a payment in kind (see **29.28** above) and there is likely to be a Class 1A NIC liability. If, however, the employee makes the contract and the employer discharges it, the employee receives earnings liable to Class 1 NIC (but see **22.4** COMPANY DIRECTORS).

Repayments of capital and/or interest made by an employer in respect of a loan obtained by an employee from a third party, eg a bank, building society or other financial institution, are earnings for contribution purposes as they constitute a discharge by the employer of the employee's personal debt.

Examples of other payments which are commonly made by an employer but which, because they discharge an employee's debts, are earnings of the employee, are the payment of home telephone bills (see **30.12**), private credit card accounts, home electricity bills, premiums on retirement annuity contracts entered into by the employee, employee's premiums under personal pension policies, premiums on private medical cover arranged by the employee (see HM Revenue and Customs National Insurance Manual NIM02230), club membership fees, school fees for the employee's children. In some instances – typically, for example, home telephone and school fees, it may be possible for the original contract for the supply of services to be made with the employer, or for the original contract with the employee to be replaced by one with the employer. Great care is required to ensure that what is intended in this regard is, as a matter of contract law, actually achieved.

School fees

[29.52] The fact that great care is required to ensure that intentions are, as a matter of contract law, actually achieved is no better demonstrated than in the instance of school fees. At one time the former CA asserted that the *Education Acts* do not permit parents to delegate responsibilities regarding education to others so that an employer's contract with a private school is impossible. This view is incorrect. The *Education Act 1996, s 7*, merely imposed a duty on parents 'to cause' their children to receive education. Education other than by attendance at school is expressly permitted and the *Act* appears to be silent as to the manner in which education at school is obtained, other than by providing that 'pupils are to be educated in accordance with the wishes of their parents'. [*EA 1996, s 9*.]

The Secretary of State for Social Security accepted in a determination pre-1 April 1999 that the *Education Act* could not be interpreted in the way claimed by the CA. The case of *Ableway Ltd v CIR* [2002] STC SCD 1 Sp C 294 illustrates that in practice there are many difficulties to overcome in establishing a valid employer's contract. In this case, the original deposit was paid by the parent – not the employer. In addition, the parent signed the application forms, and at the hearing the school bursar gave evidence that in the event of non-payment the school would sue the parent for non-payment as that is the person with whom it thought it had its contract.

In a further similar case *Frost Skip Hire (Newcastle) v Wood* [2004] STC SCD 387 Sp C 420 payment of school fees by a limited company owned and run by the husband and wife directors was found to be chargeable to Class 1 NICs. In this particular case the Commissioner accepted the then Inland Revenue's submission that the application form and prospectus signed by the director parents of the child showed that a contractual relationship existed between the parents and the school. This was notwithstanding that subsequently the school, acting on the wife's request, altered the name and address to which the school fees invoice would be sent to that of the company. Once the child was offered a place and the parents had accepted the place for their child at the school, at that moment the parents acquired a legal right to have their child educated at the school and the school became legally entitled to receive the fees. The fact that the billing changed was for the convenience of the parents and did not alter the underlying contractual obligation to pay the fees. The disputed Class 1 NICs were therefore due on the amount of the school fees paid by the company.

See also *Glynn v IRC* [1990] STC 227.

From 6 April 2000, such items paid under an employer's contract have attracted a Class 1A charge.

Subscriptions

[29.53] From 6 April 2000, the payment of an employee's professional subscription by the employer (or re-imbursement) was not liable to any NIC (*SI 2001/1004, Sch 3 Part X para 11*) if the body to which it was paid appeared in the HM Revenue and Customs list approved for the purpose of *ITEPA 2003, ss 343–344*. Prior to April 2000, whilst many thought that it should have been possible to achieve the same result under the general specific and distinct business expenses rule, in practice the DSS and later HMRC asserted that Class 1 liability existed unless membership of the body was a contractual or professional requirement. See also HM Revenue and Customs National Insurance Manual NIM05695.

From 6 April 2016, following a concerted attempt to restrict the use of salary sacrifice arrangements, it was explicitly provided that the *para 11* exclusion should be subject to *Sch 3, Part 8, para 1A*, which prohibits a disregard in the calculation of earnings for any amount paid or reimbursed pursuant to relevant salary sacrifice arrangements as provided for in *ITEPA 2003, s 289A*, any round sum allowance deemed to be earnings by *Contributions Regulations 2001, Reg 22(13)* and any amount paid to an employed earner in respect of anticipated expenses that have yet to be incurred (whether or not such expenses are actually incurred after the payment is made). [*SI 2001/1004, Sch 3, Part X, para 11* as amended by *Social Security (Contributions) (Amendment) (No 2) Regulations 2016, SI 2016/352, Reg 6(3)*].

Security licences and DBS (CRB) checks

[29.54] Fees payable by a person employed or to be employed at an airport in the UK for a criminal record check are also added to the list of allowable items in *ITEPA 2003, s 343* and thus there is no Class 1 liability either. [*Social Security (Contributions) Regulations 2001, SI 2001/1004, Sch 3, Part X para 11; Income Tax (Professional Fees) Order 2003, SI 2003/1652, Reg 1*]. See also HM Revenue and Customs National Insurance Manual NIM05659.

Fees payable by persons working in the private security industry that have to be licensed under *Private Security Industry Act 2001*, such as nightclub door staff, security guards, wheel clampers, private investigators, security consultants and keyholders are also added to the list of allowable items in *ITEPA 2003, s 343* and thus there is no Class 1 liability either. [*Social Security (Contributions) Regulations 2001, SI 2001/1004, Sch 3, Part X para 11*]. See also NIM06175.

Fees paid under various provisions of the *Police Act 1997* relating to updating criminal record checks for the Disclosure and Barring Service (which replaced the Criminal Records Bureau and Independent Safeguarding Authority from 1 December 2012), when paid by employers on behalf of employees, are now also excluded from earnings. [*Social Security (Contributions) Regulations 2001, SI 2001/1004, Sch 3, Part X, para 23* with effect from 10 June 2013 by virtue of *The Social Security (Contributions) (Amendment No 2) Regulations 2013, SI 2013/1142*]. See also NIM05681.

Discharge of tax

[29.55] Discharge of an employee's tax liabilities by an employer constitutes a payment of earnings in accordance with the principle described at **29.51** above (see *Hartland v Diggines* (1926) 10 TC 247). (CWG2 (2018 to 2019), para 5.1.) See also HM Revenue and Customs National Insurance Manual NIM02370.

Under the stated rule, contribution liability will also arise on the tax which providers of awards under a *taxed award scheme* pay on behalf of their own employees. However, where a payment of tax is made under a *taxed award scheme* in respect of awards made to employees of other businesses, the third party pays Class 1A National Insurance on the income tax borne. See CWG5 (2018), para 42.

More problematical is the position where an employer makes a settlement with HM Revenue and Customs which is based on estimated, undeclared and unpaid liabilities of employees and which has the effect of extinguishing such liabilities. This is often still occasionally referred to as a Class 6 settlement. Does such a settlement by the employer constitute a payment of earnings equal to the tax element of the settlement? The former DSS believed that it does; but it is arguable that that is not so. The matter is left beyond doubt where payment is made in an organised way eg through a PAYE Settlement Agreement (see **17** CLASS **1**B CONTRIBUTIONS: PAYE SETTLEMENT AGREEMENTS), but there may still be grounds for the non-liability view to be taken in some other circumstances eg where a settlement is made following a PAYE/NIC audit.

Credit card transactions

[29.56] If an employer discharges the balance on an employee's personal credit card, that is clearly a payment of earnings on the general principle described at **29.51** above. Where, however, the employer has supplied his employee with a company credit card and the employer discharges the balance on that card, the situation is more complex.

The official guidance is that, where a company credit card is used to pay for actual business expenses, payment to the card company by the employer in respect of that part of the balance on the card will not constitute earnings. (CWG2 (2018 to 2019), para 5.1.) So far as the payment of *non*-business expenses by company credit card is concerned, however, the position is more complex.

Until 6 April 1994, the then DSS view, as set out in a letter dated 8 August 1989, was that an employee could never be acting as agent for his employer as either a disclosed or undisclosed principal when he purchased goods or services which were wholly or partly for private or personal use—even if his employer had authorised him to do so. Accordingly, an employee who used a company card to obtain private goods or services was, until 6 April 1994, regarded by the then DSS as incurring a personal debt to the supplier which was then discharged by the card company. (See *Re Charge Card Services Ltd* [1989] Ch 497, [1988] 3 All ER 702, CA). When the employer then reimbursed the card company he thus (in the DSS's view) became a creditor of the employee under the employee's agreement (express or implied) to reimburse the employer for any private purchases made on the card unless the employer waived that obligation.

The then DSS changed its mind and subsequently considered that if an employee is given prior authority to make a non-business purchase and if the employee reaches agreement with the supplier in advance of the contract being made that the purchase is to be made on behalf of the employer, the value of the goods or services so purchased does not form part of earnings for NI purposes (See 1995 leaflet CA 28, page 74, Item 14 and CA National Insurance News, Issue 3, p 4). The current position remains, therefore, that if the contract for the supply of goods or services is clearly between the employer and the supplier, with the employee acting as agent for his employer, then the goods or services become the property of the employer from the outset and, if the employee is allowed to retain them without being called upon by his employer to pay for them, they become a payment in kind (see **29.28** above and CWG2 (2018 to 2019), para 5.1).

Unfortunately, the revised guidance does not include any indication of when the contract is regarded as being entered into. This will depend on the nature and circumstances of the transaction. In the case of the purchase of car fuel, the contract is entered at the point of fill-up on the station forecourt (*Richardson v Worrall* [1985] STC 693; *R v DSS ex p Overdrive Credit Card Ltd* [1991] STC 129). The procedure described in the previous paragraph is referred to as 'the litany' and is derived from the *Overdrive* case (see **30.20**). However, some petrol station forecourts have the option to pay at the kiosk or swipe the credit card at the pump—this results in the purchase becoming the property of the employee in both cases unless 'the employee explained in advance of the contract being made *and* the supplier accepted that the purchase was made on your [the employer's] behalf.' (CWG2 (2018 to 2019), para 5.1.) Likewise, it seems that a contract for a meal in a restaurant will be entered at the point at which an order for food, wine, etc is given. But in a self-service store (just as in any other kind of shop) the contract is entered at the till, ie when (and only when) the customer offers to buy the goods in question, the offer is accepted and consideration is exchanged (*Pharmaceutical Society of Great Britain v Boots Cash Chemists (Southern) Ltd* [1952] 2 QB 795, [1952] 2 All ER 456,CA). See also HM Revenue and Customs National Insurance Manual NIM02090; NIM02191.

The first edition of CWG5 advised that from a date shortly after enactment of the *Child Support, Pensions and Social Security Act 2000*, which was 28 July 2000, new Regulations would be introduced to provide specifically that a Class 1 liability will arise in respect of the use of an employer's credit card, etc in order to obtain personal goods and services (CWG5, obsolete January 2000 edition, page 8). However, the same comment was removed from Issue 2 in November 2000 and the regulations referred to have not, to date, actually been introduced, although in theory the disguised remuneration provisions (in conjunction with *Reg 22B*) might achieve this aim if the credit card provider is regarded as a third party making a loan to an employee under arrangements with the employer.

Insurance premiums

[29.57] The general rule concerning the discharge by an employer of an employee's debts applies in most instances where an employer pays the premiums under an insurance contract entered into by the employee including insured sick pay schemes (see **29.58** below). (CWG2 (2018 to 2019), para 5.1.) However, see **30.27** for the exclusion of NICs liability of insurance for medical costs/expenses for a period when an employee carries out duties abroad.

One exception to that rule arises where contributions are paid by an employer under approved personal pension arrangements made by his employee. Under *ITEPA 2003, s 308(1)*, such contributions are not to be regarded as general earnings of the employment chargeable to tax and, where that is the case, the payment is to be excluded from earnings for contribution purposes also. *[Social Security (Contributions) Regulations 2001, SI 2001/1004, Sch 3 Part VI para 2; Social Security (Contributions) (Amendment No 2) Regulations 2006, SI 2006/576, Reg 8]*. The fact that, under a personal pension contract, contributions can be made by either the employee or the employer or both of them often causes confusion. It is essential for both income tax and NIC purposes that where the employer wishes to pay a premium that the insurance company's application form is correctly completed showing the relevant amount as an *employer's* contribution. Although the number of personal pension contracts where the employer makes a contribution is thought to be in the minority, where that is so it is often found, on an employer compliance visit, that the contributions have been stated on the application form to be *employee's* contributions and treated as such by the insurance company. Where that is so the employer is meeting the personal obligation of the employee and Class 1 contributions are due. The matter can easily be rectified for the future by varying the employee's contribution downwards with the employer then contracting to make an *employer's* contribution. Where the employer merely bears the cost of an employee's contribution then, as well as attracting an unnecessary Class 1 charge, there could be other tax difficulties. An employee's contribution is made net of basic rate tax (ie, out of net pay), which the pension fund reclaims from HMRC, whereas an employer makes payments gross (ie, without deducting any tax), meaning that the pension fund should not reclaim any tax from HMRC.

Where an employer pays contributions to an approved occupational pension scheme, which may include provision for death-in-service benefit of up to four times salary to be paid to the deceased employee's dependants, no indebtedness of the employee is being discharged, nor is the employee acquiring anything other than a future entitlement to pension. Such contributions are not treated as payments of earnings, especially in light of the *Forde & McHugh* decision (see **29.28** above). Contributions to approved schemes were, from 6 April 1999, specifically excluded from earnings as were such contributions to registered pension schemes under the new April 2006 tax regime for pensions, although as noted above, the *Forde & McHugh* decision by the Supreme Court means that these exclusions by regulation were unnecessary because the DSS and Inland Revenue analysis was flawed. [*Social Security (Contributions) Regulations 2001, SI 2001/1004, Reg 25, Sch 3 Part VI paras 2, 3*, as amended by *Social Security (Contributions) (Amendment No 2) Regulations 2006, SI 2006/576, Reg 8*].

Note that there is no cap on the earnings disregard for contributions purposes equivalent to the annual allowance that applies for income tax purposes. This means that, even if the employer makes a contribution that exceeds the employee's cumulative annual allowance, triggering a tax charge that will be accounted for through the employee's self-assessment return, or by the trustees if the employee elects for the 'scheme pays' option, the payment still does not constitute a payment of earnings for NIC purposes.

Where an employer pays a premium on a life policy and then assigns the policy to an employee, a payment of earnings now takes place (see **31.2** EARNINGS: READILY CONVERTIBLE ASSETS, ETC).

See **29.58** below for details of the relief given in respect of employee liabilities and indemnity insurance.

Employee liabilities and indemnity insurance

[29.58] Directors and officers of companies may incur a liability to a third party in carrying out their official duties. Costs and losses may be incurred by them in a personal capacity, eg where the third party brings an action for actual or alleged breach of trust, breach of duty, neglect, error, misstatement, misleading statement or omission. Further liabilities may arise from fraud, dishonesty or malicious conduct, although these are actions of a different kind. Since the introduction of new provisions in *Companies Act 1989*, it has been possible for an employer to insure against a liability to indemnify directors or officers for losses or costs resulting from their actions as such, although agreements to indemnify against certain liabilities may be void under *Companies Act 2006, s 232*.

Since 6 April 1995 for income tax and 18 July 1995 for NIC there is relief for such payments, whether made by employer or employee, where they relate to a 'qualifying liability' or a claim that the officer is subject to such a liability. A 'qualifying liability' in relation to an office or employment is a liability to someone other than the employer, imposed either (a) in respect of acts or omissions of a person in his capacity as an office-holder or in any other capacity in which he acts in the performance of the duties of that employment or office; or (b) in connection with any proceedings relating to or arising out of a claim that a person is subject to a liability imposed in respect of any such acts or omissions. Relief is denied where it would be illegal for the employer to insure against a liability to indemnify the employee. For both tax and NIC purposes, the exclusion for indemnities provided for ex-employees may only cover the last six years before the payment, so if a former employee is the subject of a claim over six years after leaving, any payment by the former employer will constitute earnings for NIC purposes, whether or not the act giving rise to the indemnity was lawful.

From 6 April 2016, following a concerted attempt to restrict the use of salary sacrifice arrangements, it was explicitly provided that the *para 10* exclusion should be subject to *Sch 3, Part 8, para 1A*, which prohibits a disregard in the calculation of earnings for any amount paid or reimbursed pursuant to relevant salary sacrifice arrangements as provided for in *ITEPA 2003, s 289A*, any round sum allowance deemed to be earnings by *Contributions Regulations*

2001, Reg 22(13) and any amount paid to an employed earner in respect of anticipated expenses that have yet to be incurred (whether or not such expenses are actually incurred after the payment is made).

[*Social Security (Contributions) Regulations 2001, SI 2001/1004, Sch 3 Part X para 10* as amended by *Social Security (Contributions) (Amendment) (No 2) Regulations 2016, SI 2016/352, Reg 6(2); ITEPA 2003, s 346*]. (See also CA National Insurance News, Issue 4, page 10 and Booklet 480 (2016) paras 7.9–7.11).

Premiums for employee cover

[29.59] Where employers insure against their liability to indemnify a director or officer, the proceeds of a claim paid to the employee's creditor would, assuming *Social Security (Contributions) Regulations 2001, SI 2001/1004, Sch 3 Part VIII para 9* could not apply, represent Class 1 earnings were it not for this relief. The premium paid by the employer would be to cover its own liabilities and would be of no relevance to the employee's income tax or Class 1 contributions position. However, some policies cover not only the employer for liabilities to indemnify employees, but also the employees directly for costs the employer may not legally reimburse. Before the specific tax relief was introduced, the payment of a premium by the employer for such cover represented a taxable benefit to the employee, as it was not necessary for such insurance to be carried. In practice, the total premium was often apportioned for tax purposes on a negotiated basis between company cover (no benefit) and officer cover (to be reported on P11D). As the premium was a payment in kind, no Class 1 liability arose in respect of it in those days. If a claim was made by the employee under the 'employee cover' part of the policy, the proceeds were non-taxable, as he was the insured person and the premiums had been taxed at the inception of the policy. Again, no Class 1 liability would arise as no 'earnings' were paid. Under s *346*, even the premiums for employee cover, to the extent that they relate to qualifying liabilities, are now exempt from income tax. In addition, liability insurance reimbursed by the employer from 18 July 1995 is not liable for NICs. Also, the CA did not seek NICs for payments made in the period 6 April 1995 to 17 July 1995 (CA 28 Supplement April 1996). [*Social Security (Contributions) Regulations 2001, SI 2001/1004, Sch 3 Part X para 10; ITEPA 2003, s 346*].

See also HM Revenue and Customs National Insurance Manual NIM05660.

Allowances and bounties

[29.60] If an employer requires an employee to work away from his main place of work or to work from home, the employer will usually make payments to cover accommodation, meals and incidental expenses. To the extent that such payments are specific and distinct payments of, or contributions towards, expenses actually incurred by the employee in carrying out his employment or travelling to and staying at a temporary workplace they will not be earnings for contribution purposes. [*Social Security (Contributions) Regulations 2001, SI 2001/1004, Reg 25, Sch 3 Part VIII para 9*].

Bounties etc to serving members of HM Forces

[29.61] Certain allowances, bounties and gratuities paid to serving members of HM Forces are to be *excluded* from earnings for contribution purposes, as were early departure scheme payments made from 6 April 2005 to 5 April 2013, although this last exclusion was not legislated until *NICA 2014, s 16* did so retrospectively in March 2014. Lump sums under the Scheme were once more, from 1 April 2015, exempted from tax and NICs by *FA 2015, s 15* and *Social Security (Miscellaneous Amendments No 2) Regulations 2015, SI 2015/478, Reg 21(2)* (see **11.4** ARMED FORCES).

Concessionary fuel for miners

[29.62] Under *ITEPA 2003, s 306* (formerly Inland Revenue Extra-Statutory Concession A6) free coal supplied to miners or cash allowances in lieu of such free coal are exempt from income tax. Free coal is excluded from earnings for contribution purposes also as a payment in kind (see **29.28** above) but, strictly, a cash allowance in lieu was not until 6 April 1996 when a batch of income tax ESCs were legislated for NIC. [*Social Security (Contributions) Regulations 2001, SI 2001/1004, Reg 25, Sch 3 Part X para 14*, as substituted by *SI 2004/770, Reg 28*]. See also HM Revenue and Customs National Insurance Manual NIM02095.

Councillor's attendance allowance

[29.63] Attendance allowances paid to local councillors are earnings. This was determined in an unemployment benefit case (*R(U) 2/94*) and confirmed similar earlier decisions based on different legislation. In a supplementary decision there was held to be a rebuttable presumption that expenses incurred by a councillor relate to attendance at council meetings and therefore deductible from attendance allowance. However, basic and special responsibilities allowances are not earnings [*Social Security (Computation of Earnings) Regulations 1978*] but include a substantial element of reimbursed expenses and need, therefore, to be taken into account before an expenses deduction is allocated against the payment of attendance allowance. In many cases, of course, such payments will fall below the Lower Earnings Limit and/or Earnings Threshold in any event, or the councillor will have other employment and contributions otherwise payable on his allowances as such will be deferred (see **27** DEFERMENT OF PAYMENT). See also HM Revenue and Customs National Insurance Manual NIM05640 and *The Income Tax (Pay As You Earn) Regulations 2003, SI 2003/2682, Regs 118–121*.

Travel expenses paid to members of local authorities for attending meetings technically cover the costs of travelling to a permanent workplace where meetings are always held in the same council premises. To prevent tax and NIC charges arising on the payment of such expenses in future, *F(No 2)A 2015, s 29* inserted a new *ITEPA 2003, s 295A* exempting such expenses from income tax. From 6 April 2016, the payments are also excluded from earnings for NIC purposes. [*Contributions Regulations 2001, Sch 3, Part 8, para 17*, inserted by *Social Security (Contributions) (Amendment) (No 2) Regulations 2016, SI 2016/352, Reg 5(8)*].

Police rent allowances

[29.64] A police rent allowance is earnings for contribution purposes as is any grant paid to cover income tax on the allowance or on the value of the accommodation as a benefit in kind. (See HM Revenue and Customs National Insurance Manual NIM06100).

Overseas earnings

[29.65] If an employee is, or is treated as being, an employed earner for contribution purposes, the fact that he receives payments from an overseas source does not prevent those payments being earnings for contribution purposes if they would otherwise be earnings in accordance with the rules described in this chapter. (See also Tax Bulletin 81 and OVERSEAS MATTERS 51).

If the earnings are paid in a foreign currency the amount of the earnings is to be determined by converting them into their sterling equivalent using the exchange rate current at the time of payment. (See now-withdrawn leaflet NI 132, April 2002, page 6).

According to NI 269 in April 1993, where an employee in the UK received a payment from an overseas company the former DSS did not expect contributions to be accounted for by a UK employer if the overseas company was not trading in association with the UK company or its parent company when the overseas company actually made the payment to the employee or via the UK company *and* incurred the full cost of the payment. (The question of who bore the cost was not mentioned in CA 28, April 1995.) The rationale of this view is discussed at 29.35 above. Payments from overseas *must*, however, be included in gross pay if the UK employer carries on business in association with the overseas company and the overseas employer has a place of business in the UK, in which case aggregation of earnings (5.5) is required. See also the AGENCY WORKERS 4 rules in respect of payments from intermediaries or foreign employers supplying workers into the UK through a UK intermediary.

Special payments to mariners

[29.66] Certain special payments made to mariners while incapacitated overseas are *excluded* from earnings for contribution purposes (see 45.8 MARINERS).

VAT

[29.67] Where goods or services on which VAT is chargeable are supplied by an employed earner in the course of his employment and earnings paid to him in respect of that employment include the remuneration for the supply of those goods or services, an amount equal to the VAT so chargeable is to be excluded from his earnings for contribution purposes. Any VAT which forms part of a payment of earnings, for example, VAT on an employee's telephone bill which has been paid by the employer, forms part of earnings for contribution purposes. See HM Revenue and Customs National Insurance Manual NIM02405. [*Social Security (Contributions) Regulations 2001, SI 2001/1004, Reg 25, Sch 3 Part X para 9*].

Nominee directors' fees

[29.68] A payment by a company to or for the benefit of one of its directors, in respect of any employed earner's employment of the director with the company, is to be excluded from the computation of the director's earnings for contribution purposes provided that:

- the director was appointed to his office either:
  - (a) by a company which had the right to make the appointment by virtue of its shareholding in, or agreement with, the company making the payment, or
  - (b) by a company which is not the company making the payment and which is not controlled by the director and/or any person connected with him, and
- the director, by virtue of an agreement with the company which appointed him, is required to account for the payment to that company, and
- the payment forms part of the profits brought into charge for corporation tax or income tax of the company that appointed him.

[*Social Security (Contributions) Regulations 2001, SI 2001/1004, Reg 27*].

For these purposes, 'control' has the meaning attached to it in *Income Tax Act 2007, s 995*, and 'any person connected with the director' means the spouse, civil partner, parent, child, son-in-law or daughter-in-law of the director. [*Social Security (Contributions) Regulations 2001, SI 2001/1004, Reg 27(4)(d); Social Security (Contributions) (Amendment No 6) Regulations 2005, SI 2005/3130, Reg 4*].

'Family' means spouse, civil partner, parent, child, son-in-law or daughter-in-law.

This regulation, which was originally made on 6 January 1988, corresponds almost exactly to Inland Revenue ESC A37 Paras 2 and 3 and gives the force of law to the former DSS concession which was available before that date. From 6 April 1996 contribution law and the ESCs were brought fully into line by adopting for the purpose of *Reg 27* the definition of 'company' that is contained in *Income Tax Act 2007, s 992 (2)(3)*.

Following consultation, ESC A37 has now been placed on a statutory footing and incorporated into *ITEPA 2003*, *ITTOIA 2005* and *CTA 2009*.

[*Enactment of Extra-Statutory Concessions Order 2018, SI 2018/282, Arts 4, 5 and 6*].

The position is summarised in Leaflet CA44 (2018), para 56 and explained in a flowchart.

The rules can give rise to difficulty where the company which makes the appointment has no UK presence whatsoever, since the fees for which the director must account to that company may be included in profits which are subject to neither corporation tax nor income tax.

Employment income provided through third parties

[29.69] In addition to all of the above, specific anti-avoidance legislation may deem additional amounts to be earnings for the purpose of Class 1 NIC.

Following a long history of HMRC action to challenge remuneration structures using employee benefit trusts or other vehicles to defer, reduce or avoid income tax liabilities, *Finance Act 2011, Sch 2* introduced a new *Part 7A* into the *Income Tax (Earnings and Pensions) Act 2003*. The legislation is commonly known as 'the disguised remuneration provisions' following on from the language used in HMRC consultations leading up to its introduction. The scope of the legislation is very wide. It applies where:

- there is an arrangement which relates to an existing, former or prospective employee or a 'relevant person' linked to the employee. 'Arrangement' for these purposes includes an agreement, scheme, settlement, transaction, trust or understanding, and 'employee' for these purposes includes non-executive directors and office holders;
- the arrangement is, 'in essence', wholly or partly a means of providing rewards, recognition or loans in connection with employment;
- a 'relevant third party' operating the arrangement takes a 'relevant step' (see below); and
- it is reasonable to suppose that, in essence, the step is taken pursuant to the arrangement or there is some other connection (direct or indirect) between the relevant step and the arrangement.

The trigger point for the legislation is when the third party takes a 'relevant step' in relation to the employee or a person linked with the employee. A 'relevant step' can be any of the following:

- a payment of money (including the making of a loan);
- the transfer of an asset;
- earmarking money or assets for an employee (however informally) with a view to making a later relevant step;
- a step that enables the person to acquire shares, interests in shares or share options;
- making an asset available as if the asset has been transferred outright;
- making an asset available as security; and
- granting a lease of premises for a period or more than 21 years.

As the legislation is of such potentially wide application, in the period between publication of the legislation in draft and its final form, a large number of exclusions were drafted – now contained in *Income Tax (Earnings and Pensions) Act 2003, ss 554E-554X*.

Where this legislation applies to produce a charge to income tax, and if the relevant step is taken on or after 6 December 2011, the value of the relevant step counts as employment income for tax purposes. That amount is also treated as 'earnings' for the purposes of Class 1 NIC (regardless of whether it is a payment in cash or a benefit in kind).

New guidance was added to the CWG2 in 2012 as para 167 (now para 5.15.8 in CWG2 (2018 to 2019)).

[*Social Security (Contributions) Regulations 2001, SI 2001/1004, Reg 22B*, as inserted by *Social Security (Contributions)(Amendment No 5) Regulations 2011, SI 2011/2700, Reg 3*.]

Key Points regarding earnings from employment: general

[29.70] Points to consider are as follows.

- There is currently no £30,000 exemption in respect of termination payments as there is for income tax. Such a payment is either NIC-free or liable in full, but the law is set to change in April 2019 so that there will be an employer-only Class 1A contribution on compensation in excess of £30,000.
- Genuine *ex-gratia* payments, where there is no expectation of receipt and no element reward for past, present or future services are likely to be NIC-free.
- There is no NIC liability on redundancy pay either up to or beyond the statutory redundancy payment limit – provided the redundancy is genuine and other payments are not masked within the overall payment.
- Statutory Payments constitute NIC-able earnings.
- Child care vouchers are NIC-free and tax-free up to the value of £55 per week for those employees who joined employer-supported childcare schemes before 6 April 2011. A lower value may apply to later joiners. Only the excess over this amount attracts liability.
- Many other non-cash vouchers, and all retail vouchers, attract liability in full.
- Payment of bills for non-business expenses that the employee has personally contracted for attracts a Class 1 NIC liability.
- Reimbursed expenses are not earnings for National Insurance purposes if the payments to the employee are 'specific and distinct' payments of, or contributions towards, expenses 'actually incurred' by the employee in carrying out his employment. [*Social Security (Contributions) Regulations 2001, SI 2001/1004, Sch 3, Pt VIII, para 9*]. There is no requirement for the original expenses to have been incurred 'wholly, exclusively and necessarily' in the performance of the duties of the employment, such as there is for tax purposes. However, expenses paid under salary sacrifice arrangements, or as round sum allowances that are not approved by HMRC, or in respect of anticipated expenses that have yet to be incurred can, from 6 April 2016, not be excluded from earnings under the normal rule for travel expenses and will generally give rise to a Class 1 liability for both employer and employee when paid. Note that travel and subsistence expenses paid to workers employed through intermediaries are subject to different rules, and home-to-work travel expenses can no longer

be paid NIC-free (see INTERMEDIARIES 40 and LABOUR ONLY CONTRACTORS 41).

30

Earnings from Employment: Expenses

Cross-references. See CLASS 1 CONTRIBUTIONS 15; CLASS 1A CONTRIBUTIONS 16 for treatment of cars and fuel supplied by an employer to an employee.

Other Sources. Tolley's Tax Planning 2016–17; Tolley's Income Tax 2016–17; Booklet CWG2 (2018 to 2019). See also Booklets 480 (2018) and 490; HM Revenue and Customs National Insurance Manual NIM05000.

Introduction to earnings from employment: expenses

[30.1] The term 'earnings', when used in the context of social security legislation, includes any remuneration or profit derived from any trade, business, profession, office or vocation. It applies equally, therefore, to the income of an employed earner and that of a self-employed earner, though the amount of a person's earnings for any period, or the amount of his earnings to be treated as comprised in any payment made to him or for his benefit, are to be calculated or estimated in the manner and on the basis prescribed in the legislation and such prescriptions do, in fact, differ in the case of employed earners and self-employed earners. [*SSCBA 1992, s 3(1)(2); Social Security (Contributions) Regulations 2001, SI 2001/1004, Reg 25*]. See HM Revenue and Customs National Insurance Manual NIM02000. See also **29.1**.

The calculation or estimation of earnings is not merely a matter of deciding what should be *included* but of deciding also what should be *excluded*. The various regulations concerned govern both aspects of the computation and provide for certain receipts to be disregarded entirely and for certain items of expenditure to be deducted from receipts. [*SSCBA 1992, s 3(3); Social Security (Contributions) Regulations 2001, SI 2001/1004, Sch 3*].

In *S and U Stores Ltd v Wilkes* [1974] 3 All ER 401, [1974] ICR 645, NIRC it was held that in order to ascertain a person's remuneration in the context of employment protection law, one must:

(a) include any sum which is paid as a wage or salary without qualification;
(b) disregard the value of any benefit in kind (eg free accommodation) and any sum paid in cash by someone other than the employer (eg the Easter offering received by a minister of religion);
(c) examine any sum which is agreed to be paid by way of reimbursement or on account of expenditure incurred by the employee and see whether *in broad terms* the whole or any part of it represents a profit or surplus in the hands of the employee, and, to the extent that it does represent such a profit or surplus, include that sum.

It was stressed that (c) calls not for an involved accountancy exercise but for a broad common sense view of the realities of the situation.

S & U Stores v Wilkes was not a National Insurance case but was concerned with redundancy pay. Its authority is at best persuasive in the present context. Furthermore, the addition of the word 'profit' to the definition of earnings for contribution purposes will, it seems, catch the items which are to be disregarded under (b) above, but *not* anything disregarded under (c) as being a legitimate reimbursement of expenses. The view that the word 'profit' brings payments in kind within the meaning of the word 'earnings' in *SSCBA 1992, s 3(1)* is rejected by at least two leading Counsel but the former DSS clearly believed that it does as *Social Security (Contributions) Regulations 2001, SI 2001/1004, Reg 25, Sch 3 Part II para 1* was specifically introduced to *remove* such payments from the amount of earnings on which Class 1 contributions are exigible. See HM Revenue and Customs National Insurance Manual NIM02015. (See **29.28**).

Tax legislation, practice and extra-statutory concessions

[30.2] In order to facilitate the working of the tax system and to avoid undue harshness in the application of certain provisions of tax law, HM Revenue and Customs has published a large number of extra-statutory concessions and statements of practice now available only at www.gov.uk/government/publications/extra-statutory-concessions-ex-inland-revenue, although many of them have now been incorporated into the legislation because of doubts about HMRC's legal capacity to make concessions. National Insurance law also follows a number of past extra statutory concessions for tax purposes which are now enshrined within *Income Tax (Earnings and Pensions) Act 2003 (ITEPA 2003)* and remaining ESCs which are replicated in National Insurance law, albeit not in income tax law.

It is also important to note, at the outset, that tax law and NIC law have classically dealt with expenses in a fundamentally different way. The basic principle is that an individual is taxed and subject to Class 1 contributions on 'earnings', which it might be assumed must, by definition, be something that makes him better off as a result of carrying out his duties. Where genuine expenses are met by an employer, there is at common law (and therefore for both tax and NIC purposes, absent deeming rules) no payment of earnings because all the employer has done by reimbursing expenses is to fill a hole in the employee's pocket caused by his spending money on the employer's behalf.

For example, if an employee is asked by his employer to deliver a parcel to a customer by taking a taxi across town, and the taxi fare is reimbursed out of the petty cash tin, the employee is no better off by reason of that reimbursement. The employer owes him the money as soon as he incurs the expense on the employer's behalf, and the employer settles the debt when he presents the proof of expenditure. The payment of the taxi fare is not a payment of earnings on common law principles.

In this simple scenario, that is the end of the story as far as NICs are concerned. Tax law, however, takes a different approach, albeit an approach that changed from 6 April 2016 as a result of *FA 2015* simplification measures.

Under the pre-2016 rules, the P9D employee remained untaxed on the same grounds that continue to apply to NIC liability. However, once an employee had emoluments or earnings at a rate of at least £8,500 pa, any payment of expenses was deemed to be earnings (reportable on a P11D unless covered by a dispensation) and taxable, so the employee wishing not to be taxed had then to show that the expense was deductible as having been wholly, exclusively and necessarily incurred in carrying out the duties, or was for necessary travel. In other words, while the NIC rules simply disregarded anything that did not enrich the employee (there was no need for an exclusion, as expense reimbursements do not enrich the recipients who have spent the money in the first place), the tax rules treated everything as taxable, even in the absence of any enrichment, and required employees to claim and justify a deduction, or required their employers to agree a dispensation for expenses that would have been deductible on the making of a claim. The only exception was statutorily authorised mileage allowance payments for employees using their own cars, which were exempt.

Under the April 2016 rules, introduced by *FA 2015, s 11*, the tax rules were modified, but not so as to bring them into line with the NIC rules. Instead, any payment by the employer is still, in principle, deemed to be earnings, but any expense payment that would be deductible is, instead, exempted from tax, provided it is not paid under a salary sacrifice arrangement. Dispensations have been abolished as they are no longer needed if employees no longer need to claim a deduction. The P9D rules have been codified and limited, applying in specific terms to ministers of religion and certain live-in carers. *ITEPA 2003, ss 289A–289E* set out the rules for the exemption of both deductible expenses and certain round-sum allowances, either at a standard statutory rate or at a bespoke rate agreed by the employer with HMRC.

None of this should in principle have been relevant to Class 1 NICs, under which genuine expenses were simply not earnings. But life is never quite that simple: simplification means yet more legislation, bringing NIC rules into line with the new tax rules. Instead of keeping the longstanding simple approach of accepting that reimbursed expenses were not earnings, *Social Security (Contributions) (Amendment) (No 2) Regulations 2016, SI 2016/352, Reg 4* amended the *Contributions Regulations 2001* by inserting a new *Reg 22(12)* to deem a number of items to be earnings that would not be earnings on common law principles:

- amounts paid or reimbursed to an employed earner in respect of expenses;
- amounts provided pursuant to relevant salary sacrifice arrangements within the meaning of *ITEPA 2003, s 289A(5)*; and
- amounts that are not payment or reimbursements of relevant motoring expenditure within the meaning of *Reg 22A(3)*.

A new *Reg 22(13)* also deems round-sum allowances to be earnings, ie, any amount paid or reimbursed to an employed earner in respect of expenses which is calculated according to a set rate rather than by reference to the actual amount incurred where such a rate is not a statutory rate set by HMRC regulations or approved by HMRC after negotiation with the employer.

Having added new rules to create earnings where none existed before, the same set of regulations goes on to take back out the same items as the tax legislation exempts, and prevent an exclusion from earnings of:

- any amount paid or reimbursed pursuant to relevant salary sacrifice arrangements as provided for in *ITEPA 2003, s 289A(5)*;
- any amount paid or reimbursed to an employed earner which falls within new *Reg 22(13)* (ie, a round sum allowance at other than the statutory rate that has not been agreed with HMRC); and
- any amount paid to an employed earner in respect of anticipated expenses that have yet to be incurred (whether or not such expenses are actually incurred after the payment is made).

[*Contributions Regulations 2001, Sch 3, Part VIII, para 1A*, inserted by *Social Security (Contributions) (Amendment) (No 2) Regulations 2016, SI 2016/352, Reg 5(2)*].

In order to fully align the tax exemptions and NIC exclusions for expenses, *Contributions Regulations 2001, Sch 3, Part VIII, para 3* was also amended by *Reg 5(3)* of the same amending regulations so that the definition of 'travel expenses' now means amounts necessarily expended on travelling in the performance of the duties of the office or employment, or other expenses of travelling which are attributable to the necessary attendance at any place of the holder of the office or employment in the performance of the duties of the office or employment and are not expenses of:

- ordinary commuting;
- travel between any two places that is for practical purposes substantially ordinary commuting;
- travel between any two places that is for practical purposes substantially private travel; or
- private travel.

Regulation 5(4) inserted a new *Contributions Regulations 2001, Sch 3, Part VIII, para 3ZA*, providing definitions of 'workplace' and 'permanent workplace' that match the equivalent tax rules in *ITEPA 2003, s 339*.

It is perhaps worth noting that the tax and NIC rules are not completely aligned, in that a taxpayer who incurs expenses in excess of the amounts reimbursed by the employer may make a claim for a further deduction, by means of submitting a P87 claim form, a letter or a self-assessment return. No such relief is available in respect of Class 1 NICs: relief only applies in respect of amounts paid by the employer to the employee.

See also **29.2**.

Gross earnings

[30.3] The definition of earnings discussed at **30.1** and **30.2** means that all wages, salaries, commissions and overtime payments fall to be included. See HM Revenue and Customs National Insurance Manual NIM02030, NIM02075, NIM02150 and NIM02265.

In addition, there are many kinds of expense payment which are made to employees and which, in certain circumstances, will fall, or not fall, to be included in earnings for contribution purposes and these are detailed in the subsequent paragraphs.

Relocation payments

[30.4] If an employer requires an employee to move house for the purposes of his employment, the employer will normally make various payments in connection with the move. To the extent that such payments are specific and distinct payments of, or contributions towards, expenses actually incurred by the employee in carrying out his employment they will not be earnings for Class 1 contribution purposes. From 6 April 2016, however, they will not be NIC-free if they fall within the salary sacrifice, round-sum allowance and anticipatory payments categories introduced into the deeming provisions of *Reg 22*. [*Social Security (Contributions) Regulations 2001, SI 2001/1004, Reg*

25, Sch 3, Part VIII, para 9, as amended by *Social Security (Contributions) (Amendment) (No 2) Regulations 2016, SI 2016/352, Reg 5(7)*]. See also HM Revenue and Customs National Insurance Manual NIM02104, NIM06110.

In order to align NICs more closely with the tax rules on removal expenses, Class 1 National Insurance contributions are collected only on those removal allowances that are not within one of the *eligible* categories for tax relief. Expenses that can never fall within the exemption, such as the employer paying children's school fees for a period, will fall within Class 1 when the employer meets the employee's personal liability. Allowances such as legal and estate agent's fees, stamp duty land tax and removal expenses, etc exceeding £8,000 for each move under *ITEPA 2003, s 271* will not incur a Class 1 NICs charge even though a tax liability exists, but a Class 1A charge is due. CWG2 (2017), para 58. [*Social Security (Contributions) Regulations 2001, SI 2001/1004, Sch 3, Part VIII, para 2*].

Since 6 April 2000, the excess over £8,000 has not been liable to Class 1, but it is liable to Class 1A — whether such expenditure constitutes benefits or reimbursed expenses. This comes about because the exclusion in *SI 2001/1004, Sch 3, Pt VIII, para 2* specifically excludes the application of *ITEPA 2003, s 287*, the £8,000 limit, for NIC purposes. This treatment applies only to items which would have been eligible for tax relief but for the limit of £8,000 being exceeded. Expenses which are not qualifying expenses under the tax legislation will follow the usual rules, ie Class 1 liability if the employee incurs the expense and the employer reimburses it, Class 1A if a benefit is provided or an expense incurred under an employer's contract. A typical instance where Class 1 liability arises on relocation is where a Post Office redirection of mail is obtained and paid for by the employer.

Care must be taken when relocating an employee overseas, as the employee may cease to be taxable in the UK immediately upon departure if the split-year residence rule applies. Even if the posted worker remains covered by the UK NIC scheme, the removal expense relating as it does to overseas work in a non-resident period should not be taxable. It should therefore not attract a Class 1A charge, which is dependent on an earner being 'chargeable to income tax under *ITEPA 2003* on an amount of general earnings'. If no amount is chargeable under *ITEPA 2003* because of non-residence, *SSCBA 1992, s 10* cannot levy a Class 1A charge.

(CWG2 (2018 to 2019), para 5.9; CWG5 (2018), para 32; HM Revenue and Customs National Insurance Manual NIM06110.)

Subsistence and other allowances

[30.5] If an employer requires an employee to work away from his main place of work or to work from home, the employer will usually make payments to cover accommodation, meals and incidental expenses. To the extent that such payments are specific and distinct payments of, or contributions towards, expenses actually incurred by the employee in carrying out his employment they will not be earnings for contribution purposes. The NICs treatment has effectively been aligned with the tax treatment since 6 April 1998, albeit in an indirect manner and under legislation that did not entirely match up. This has been remedied, as already outlined above, by importing from 6 April 2016 the revised tax deeming provisions and reliefs inserted into *ITEPA 2003 by FA 2015*. [*Social Security (Contributions) Regulations 2001, SI 2001/1004, Reg 25, Sch 3, Part VIII, para 9*, as amended by *Social Security (Contributions) (Amendment) (No 2) Regulations 2016, SI 2016/352*]. See also HM Revenue and Customs National Insurance Manual NIM06180.

The official guidance is that reimbursement of the actual amount spent will fall within the terms of that excluding regulation, as will any part of a round-sum allowance which corresponds to an actual, identifiable business expense.

From 6 April 2016, it must fall within the scope of *ITEPA 2003, s 289A or s 289B* without falling within *Reg 22(12) or 22(13)* as explained above. From 6 April 2009 until 5 April 2016, HMRC-specified round sums (so-called 'benchmark scale rates') could be applied in certain circumstances if the employer preferred to use a fixed rate rather than actual expenditure (see EIM05231). Provision was made in *ITEPA 2003, s 289B* (inserted by *FA 2015, s 11*) for flat rate expense reimbursement rates to be approved by HMRC for exemption of such expenses from income tax from 6 April 2016, and, as already noted, the NIC regulations were amended so as to adopt the same rules from the same date. (CWG2 (2018 to 2019), paras 5.3 and 5.6.)

Under the non-statutory HMRC benchmark rules:

- A rate of up to £5.00 could be paid for breakfast cost where a worker has left home earlier than usual and before 06:00, and has incurred an expense in buying breakfast away from home after the qualifying journey has started.
- A rate of up to £5.00 may be paid where the worker has been away from his home/normal place of work for a period of at least five hours and has incurred the cost of a meal.
- Where the worker has been away from his home/normal place of work for a period of at least ten hours and has incurred the cost of a meal or meals a rate of £10 will be allowed.
- However, a further rate of up to £15.00 may be paid where the employee has to work later than usual, finishes work after 20:00 having worked his normal day and has to buy a meal which he would usually have at home.

The new statutory meal allowance rates from 6 April 2016 followed the same pattern, albeit with slightly different wording and with extra obligations for the employer, such as having a checking regime in place to ensure that the allowances claimed were in respect of qualifying travel and were actually being spent as intended, and not knowing or suspecting that the conditions would not have been met. [*ITEPA 2003, s 289A(2)–(4)*]. Anything exempted from income tax by s 289A is also excluded from earnings for NIC purposes. [*Social Security (Contributions) Regulations 2001, SI 2001/1004, Sch 3, Part VIII, para 8A*, inserted by *Social Security (Contributions) (Amendment) (No 2) Regulations 2016, SI 2016/352, Reg 5(6)*].

The rates were set by the *Income Tax (Approved Expenses) Regulations 2015, SI 2015/1948* as early as 21 December 2015 so as to give HMRC the power to agree bespoke rates in advance of implementation on 6 April 2016. The standard rates are now expressed, for both income tax and NIC purposes, as an amount that does not exceed:

- £5 where the duration of the qualifying travel in the day is five hours or more;
- £10 where the duration of the qualifying travel in that day is 10 hours or more; or
- £25 where the duration of the qualifying travel in the day is 15 hours or more and is ongoing at 8 pm.

A supplementary allowance not exceeding £10 per day may be added to either of the first two allowances where the allowance is paid for a period that is ongoing at 8 pm.

[*Income Tax (Approved Expenses) Regulations 2015, SI 2015/1948, Reg 2(2)*].

Employers wishing to use the benchmark scale rates for subsistence payments originally simply needed to notify HMRC of their intention by ticking the appropriate statement/box on form P11DX before starting to use the system. If employers wished to pay higher sums free of tax and NIC, they needed receipts, etc as evidence, or (until 6 April 2016) a dispensation. See Revenue and Customs Brief 24/09.

In line with the changes to the legislation affecting the tax position on travel and subsistence in 1998 the then DSS decided to mirror the tax position for NICs. In view of this the DSS reviewed the subsistence payments made to employees who were unexpectedly recalled to work. This applied to employees who work in the construction and computer industries amongst others and such payments were regarded as earnings for NICs purposes. For employers who did not wish to adopt the benchmark rates in the years before they became statutory, reasonable reimbursed subsistence allowances, evidenced by receipts, were not liable to NICs. It was not clear what constituted 'reasonable' in this instance but the CA stated that 'reasonable' in connection with mileage rates meant at that time the FPCS rates. HMRC Booklet 480 (2017), Appendix 8 states that it includes alcoholic refreshments as well as non-alcoholic. This would indicate that using a standard agreed model is sufficient and therefore the use of the dispensation (eg Form P11DX) will have facilitated this by enabling rates paid for food, accommodation, etc to be agreed in advance as being 'reasonable'. (See CA Specialist Conference notes, 29 October 1997; CA National Insurance News, Winter 1997–98 and Booklet 490 'Employee Travel—A Tax and NICs Guide for Employers'.) The statutory rates are now automatically exempt unless paid under a salary sacrifice arrangement.

The main expenses HMRC cover by a P11DX dispensation were:

- travel, including subsistence costs associated with business travel;
- fuel for company cars;
- hire car costs;
- telephones;

- business entertainment expenses;
- credit cards used for business; and
- fees and subscriptions.

See Form P11DX at www.gov.uk/government/publications/paye-expenses-and-benefits-dispensation-p11dx. The form became redundant with the abolition of dispensations from 6 April 2016.

All of these expenses are now automatically exempt from tax and excluded from earnings for NIC if the criteria outlined above are met.

Lorry drivers

[30.6] Where lorry drivers use a sleeper cab in preference to alternative accommodation they usually still receive a general overnight subsistence payment. This payment is intended to cover an evening meal and breakfast, washing facilities, upkeep of any bedding in the cab and secure parking facilities. In these circumstances, HM Revenue and Customs has for many years accepted that for both tax and NIC purposes 75% of the Road Haulage Association's nationally agreed overnight subsistence payment can be disregarded. It was, of course, open to employers to disregard a greater amount for NIC purposes where there was evidence of actual expenditure available, which showed that this was appropriate (HM Revenue and Customs National Insurance Manual NIM05684 and EIM66110-66130). Under the 2016 rules, employers can agree a bespoke rate with HMRC under *ITEPA 2003, s 289B*, on the same basis as before but with appropriate sample checking to ensure that expenses at least equal to the reimbursed level are being incurred, which will then be exempt from income tax and excluded from NICable earnings.

Incidental overnight expenses

[30.7] Regulations were introduced to reflect the *Finance Act 1995, s 93* provision of relief for employees who incur incidental expenses when they are away from home up to a maximum of £5 per night in the UK and £10 per night outside the UK. (Booklet 480 (2017), Appendix 8 and Booklet 490, para 8.4.) The relief for incidental overnight expenses (formerly called personal incidental expenses – PIEs) was introduced into *ITEPA 2003, s 240* because items such as newspapers and telephone calls home, when paid for by an employer (whether by non-cash voucher, credit tokens, cash payments, etc), would not qualify for relief under s 336 as the expenses were not *necessarily* incurred in the performance of the duties. Although this tax relief is now paralleled in contributions regulations, it is questionable whether the change was necessary before 6 April 2016, when expense reimbursements were deemed for the first time to be NICable earnings, as the test in *Sch 3, Part VIII, para 9* was less strict than the income tax equivalent in *s 336* and would arguably have allowed the exclusion from earnings of costs incurred because the employee was carrying out the employment away from home. The statutory NIC exemption is now found in *Social Security (Contributions) Regulations 2001, SI 2001/1004, Sch 3, Part X, para 4*. See HM Revenue and Customs National Insurance Manual NIM06015.

Board and lodging

[30.8] Where an employer provides free board and lodging for an employee, the board and lodging are to be excluded from earnings for contribution purposes. [*Social Security (Contributions) Regulations 2001, SI 2001/1004, Reg 25, Sch 3, Part II, para 1*]. Note that any reimbursement of board and lodging costs, as opposed to direct provision under a contract made by the employer, will only have been excluded from earnings before 6 April 2016 if it was a specific and distinct payment of, or contribution towards, expenses actually incurred by an employed earner in carrying out his employment. Under the 2016 rules, it should be tax-exempt and excluded from NICable earnings if the conditions outlined above are met. [*Social Security (Contributions) Regulations 2001, SI 2001/1004, Reg 25, Sch 3, Part VIII, para 9*]. (See **41.12** LABOUR-ONLY CONTRACTORS in respect of agricultural workers).

It should be appreciated that where there is an employer's contract there may be a taxable benefit in kind and an associated Class 1A charge, subject to reliefs in respect of job-related accommodation.

A payment of, or contribution towards, expenses incurred by an employee in staying in board and lodging near his place of work does not form part of earnings for contribution purposes if those expenses were incurred as the result of a disruption to public transport caused by a strike or other form of industrial action. [*Social Security (Contributions) Regulations 2001, SI 2001/1004, Sch 3, Part X para 8(a)* as amended by *Social Security (Contributions) (Amendment No 2) Regs 2010, SI 2010/188; ITEPA 2003, s 245*].

Club membership fees

[30.9] HMRC considers that the joining of a club or society by an employee, even if the membership has a business motivation, always confers some personal benefit on the member. Accordingly, guidance is that, unless the employer contracts for the membership of his employee, any subscription paid by the employer will be earnings for contribution purposes in accordance with the principle described at **29.51**. (HM Revenue and Customs National Insurance Manual NIM05690). Even if the employer makes the contract there will be a Class 1A liability instead, according to HMRC. (HM Revenue and Customs National Insurance Manual NIM05690.) This is a blanket statement of, at best, dubious validity, since certain club memberships serve purely business purposes and qualify for income tax relief under the notoriously more difficult 'wholly, exclusively and necessarily' test. While many club memberships may be intended to initiate or foster business relationships, employer payments will often be taxable because the employee can do the job without joining the club (see, eg, *Brown v Bullock* (1961) 40 TC 1 in which the fees failed the 'necessarily' test for tax purposes) but in other cases there will be a valid business reason that is acceptable for tax and, it must be assumed, NIC purposes (see, eg, *Elwood v Utitz* (1965) 42 TC 482 in which an employee based in Northern Ireland joined two London clubs in order to obtain discounted facilities and accommodation when he had to visit London on business, with any personal benefit to him being held merely incidental).

Meal allowances

[30.10] Meal allowances which are paid in connection with an employee's employment away from his main place of work are subsistence allowances (see **30.5** above) and their treatment has already been explained.

See HM Revenue and Customs National Insurance Manual NIM05685.

Other meal allowances are earnings for contribution purposes if the payment is made in cash or by a voucher which can be redeemed for cash or for cash or food. The first 15p per day of a voucher exchangeable only for food and drink, and not for cash, was, however, kept free of NIC under a 'Luncheon Voucher' exemption from 26 July 2001 (introduced after lobbying following the inclusion of non-cash vouchers within Class 1 for the first time) until it was revoked with effect from 6 April 2013 as a simplification measure. [*Social Security (Contributions) Regulations 2001, SI 2001/1004, Reg 25, Sch 3 Part V para 6A* as amended by *Social Security (Contributions) (Amendment No 5) Regulations 2001, SI 2001/2412, Reg 5* and *SI 2013/622, Reg 40(a)(i)*.] (See **29.31**.)

Mortgage payments

[30.11] A mortgage provided by an employer for his employee is a loan and its treatment for contribution purposes is as described at **29.49**. (CWG2 (2018 to 2019), para 5.1.)

Repayments by an employer of the interest on, or the principal of, a mortgage loan obtained by his employee other than from the employer are earnings of the employee for contribution purposes as they are a discharge or partial discharge by the employer of the employee's personal debt (see **29.51** and CWG2 (2018 to 2019), para 5.1). See also HM Revenue and Customs National Insurance Manual NIM02240.

Telephone charges

[30.12] Guidance on payments made in connection with an employee's home telephone has been as follows.

If the employer is the subscriber, ie, the contract is between the employer and the telephone company, payments by the employer are not earnings for contribution purposes. (CWG2 (2018 to 2019), paras 5.1 and 5.2.6.) That is because such payments, to the extent that they benefit the employee, are payments in kind (see **29.28** and **29.51**). Provision in this manner will almost certainly attract a Class 1A charge – see **16.38**.

If, as is more usual, the employee is the subscriber, ie, the contract is between the employee and the telephone company, the whole of any payments by the employer in respect of the *rental* element of telephone bills will be earnings for contribution purposes, whether a record of private and business calls is maintained or not, *unless* a record is kept which shows that the telephone is used *exclusively* for business calls. Where payments are made by the employer in respect of *calls and other charges*, those payments, too, will be earnings for contribution purposes *unless and only to the extent that* they relate to business calls. See HM Revenue and Customs National Insurance Manual NIM06190.

The basis of this guidance was, first, the general principle that, where an employer discharges an employee's personal debts, he is placing money's worth in the hands of the employee (see **29.51**) and, secondly, that a payment in connection with a business expense may be excluded from earnings only if it is a specific and distinct payment of or contribution towards an expense actually incurred in carrying out the employment. [*Social Security (Contributions) Regulations 2001, SI 2001/1004, Reg 25, Sch 3 Part VIII para 9*]. The HMRC view is that, whereas a business call made on a private telephone is an identifiable expense actually incurred in carrying out the employment, the expense of renting a telephone which is used in part for private purposes is incurred in the course of domestic living and not in carrying out the employment. Accordingly, in HMRC's view, no apportionment is possible. This view has not changed under the 2016 expenses rules.

The Contributions Agency accepted that if the employer had a dispensation from the Inland Revenue allowing all or part of reimbursed telephone bills to be disregarded for income tax purposes, then that agreement could be used for contributions purposes as well (see HM Revenue and Customs National Insurance Manual NIM05500). The same principle continued to apply as it also did to expenses other than telephone costs where a dispensation was in operation. Again, the 2016 changes made by FA 2015 and the associated regulations outlined above have not affected this basic position.

Motor and travelling

[30.13] Many changes have taken place in the field of motor and travelling expenses and their NIC treatment over the years. The following paragraphs summarise the current position.

Home to work travel expenses

[30.14] It is well established in income tax law that the costs incurred by an employee in travelling from his home to his normal place of work are expenses incurred in placing himself in a position to carry out his employment, not in carrying out the employment itself. Accordingly, any payment by an employer of, or as a contribution towards, any such expenses *incurred by the employee* is earnings for contribution purposes. In the case of *Warner v Prior* [2003] STC SCD 109 Sp C 353 a supply teacher worked from home and travelled to different schools in the area and claimed the cost of travelling as an expense. It was held that the expense of travel to and from home to the schools was not allowable as 'her secondary place of work at home was dictated by where she lives and not by the requirements of the job itself.' Also in *HP Lewis v HMRC* [2008] Sp C 690 a Revenue officer (L) had worked for many years at HMRC offices within daily commuting distance of her home in Warwickshire. In 2000 she successfully applied for a post in London. She was allowed to work at the London office for two or three days each week, and from her home for two or three days each week. She claimed a deduction for the costs of travelling from Warwickshire to London. HMRC rejected the claim on the basis that this expenditure was 'ordinary commuting', which was not deductible by virtue of *ITEPA 2003, s 338*. The Special Commissioner upheld HMRC's ruling and dismissed L's appeal. See HMRC Booklets 480 (2017), Chapter 4 and 490, Chapter 3. There are now six exceptions to the rule stated above.

The first arises where the employee is a *disabled person* for whom training or employment facilities (ie sheltered workshops) are being provided under the *Disabled Persons (Employment) Act 1944, s 15*. If an employer defrays or contributes towards the expenses which such an employee incurs in travelling from his home to his main place of work, the employer's payments are to be excluded from earnings for contribution purposes. [*Social Security (Contributions) Regulations 2001, SI 2001/1004, Sch 3, Part V, para 5(a) and Part X, para 8(b)* as amended by *Social Security (Contributions) (Amendment No 2) Regs 2010, SI 2010/188; ITEPA 2003, s 246*]. See HMRC Booklet 480 (2017), paras 5.22, 11.17, 13.5 and 490, para 8.22. This exception was introduced to bring disabled people in sheltered workshops into line with disabled people in open employment for whom State-provided help with travelling expenses does not count as earnings for contribution purposes. (DSS Press Release, 8 December 1987). Payments made by the former Department of Employment or by an employer to assist with a disabled person's travel expenses were similarly excluded. See HM Revenue and Customs National Insurance Manual NIM06390.

The second exception arises where the employee is temporarily working at some place of work other than his usual place of work, eg at the premises of one of his employer's clients or on detached duty at some branch of the business other than the branch at which he normally works. If the employer pays or contributes towards the expenses which such an employee incurs in travelling from his home to his temporary place of work and, at the outset, the temporary placement is not expected to last for more than 24 months, the employer's payments are to be excluded from earnings for contribution purposes. Before 6 April 2016, there appeared to be some basis in law for a rule that had regard to a temporary workplace. It would have appeared to lie in *Smith v Stages* [1989] AC 928, [1989] 1 All ER 833, HL (a vicarious liability case) where it was held that an employee who, for a short time has to work for his employer at a different place of work some distance away from his usual place of work will be acting in the course of his employment when travelling from and returning to his ordinary residence if he travels in his employer's time.

From 6 April 2016, the NIC position was moved onto a statutory footing that matches the income tax position, as explained at **30.2** above.

Where any period of work at a temporary workplace is not expected to exceed 24 months, tax or NICs are not required to be deducted from the payments. However, if the period at the temporary workplace is expected from the outset to exceed 24 months then the favourable treatment will not apply. The employee need not return to the original permanent workplace. The recurrence of temporary employment in manipulation of the 24-month period will not be allowed but travel between employments or offices in the same group of companies will be allowed (see Extra-Statutory Concession A4, CA National Insurance News, Winter 1997–98, page 10 and HMRC Booklet 490, Chapter 3). [*ITEPA 2003, ss 338, 339; Social Security (Contributions) Regulations 2001, SI 2001/1004, Sch 3, Part VIII, para 3*].

Example (1)

Q works for 007 Support Ltd and normally works at and lives near the company's London site. He is asked to go to the Hereford site for a period of seventeen months from 3 August 2015. He commutes on a weekly basis and 007 Support Ltd reimburses his travel costs. The Hereford site counts as a temporary workplace and neither tax nor Class 1 NIC liabilities will therefore arise in relation to the reimbursed costs.

Example (2)

Ms M who is Q's assistant normally works at the London site but is required to travel to the Hereford site for one day, 18 May 2015. She normally travels into London using her season ticket. She drives directly to Hereford from her flat in Ashford which is a round trip of 436 miles. 007 Support Ltd reimburses the full costs of her day's journey to Hereford. The theoretical round trip from the London office to Hereford is 296 miles, which is significantly less than the actual costs incurred travelling from home. If the employer had only reimbursed her for the 296 miles being the theoretical round trip from her normal office location to Hereford (because she would have had to incur the cost of travelling between Ashford and London anyway), Ms M would have been able to claim a tax deduction via a P87 or her self-assessment return for the additional cost of the journey not originally allowed, ie 140 miles. There would however only be Class 1 NIC relief on the amount actually reimbursed by the employer, and no retrospective NIC relief for the cost she had incurred in excess of the reimbursement.

Example (3)

S is a salesman for the southern part of England for 007 Support Ltd and will be working in the Hereford area for a week as back-up to Q. He is due to call on at least twenty companies including the one where Q will be working. S has what is known as a 'travelling appointment' and therefore the reimbursement of the costs of travelling have not been taxed (relief being due under *ITEPA 2003, s 337*) and will continue to remain non-taxable under the new rules. No NICs are due in these circumstances.

Example (4)

X who has been on leave at his home in Canterbury is suddenly called in to test a new flak jacket at the London office's testing ground. This recall to the office is unexpected due to the fact that he was covered for the week he was on leave. However, the person who was covering his leave period has been taken ill and hence X is recalled to the office. The cost of his travel from Canterbury to

London is paid by the company but is taxable and NICable in full as it falls within the definition of 'ordinary commuting'.

Note that this second exception does not apply, with effect from 6 April 2016, to workers supplied via an intermediary (ie an umbrella company or a personal service company). The detail of this exception, which makes reimbursed travel costs between home and a deemed permanent workplace, taxable and NICable, is explained at **40.9** INTERMEDIARIES.

The third exception relates to costs incurred on fuel, repairs etc for use in a car made available to the employee in connection with his employment. [*Social Security (Contributions) Regulations 2001, SI 2001/1004, Sch 3, Part VIII, para 7*.] This exception was extended to company-owned vans with effect from 21 July 2008. [*ITEPA 2003, s 239*, as amended by *Finance Act 2008, s 48(1)*].

The fourth exception applies when there is a disruption to public transport caused by a strike or some other form of industrial action, or when an employee has worked to 9 pm or later at the request of his employer and this has not happened more than 60 times already in that year so that it does not then form part of the normal pattern of the employment. [*Social Security (Contributions) Regulations 2001, SI 2001/1004, Sch 3, Part X, para 8(a)(c)* as amended by *Social Security (Contributions) (Amendment No 2) Regs 2010, SI 2010/188*.] See also Booklet 490 and HM Revenue and Customs National Insurance Manual NIM06370. This corresponds to the income tax exception set out in *ITEPA 2003, ss 245, 248* (formerly ESC A58 and A66). (See HMRC Booklet 480 (2017), Chapter 5). The exception also applies when travel (including foreign travel) expenses are paid under ITEPA 2003, ss 341, 342, 369–371, 376. There was a revision in early 2008 of HMRC guidance on this subject which confirmed that, in practice, it was often very difficult to fall within the stipulated parameters. See also Booklet 490, HM Revenue and Customs National Insurance Manual NIM06370 and HMRC Employment Income Manual EIM21831. See example at **17.5** CLASS 1B CONTRIBUTIONS: PAYE SETTLEMENT AGREEMENTS.

Where the employer (rather than the employee) incurs the expense of the employee's home to work travel—by, for example, arranging a taxi on the company account—the benefit enjoyed by the employee is a payment in kind (see **29.28**) and is *not* earnings for Class 1 purposes although a Class 1A charge arises. Before 6 April 2016, when the distinction between P9D and P11D employees was abolished, the Class 1A charge would have arisen only in respect of P11D employees, but now all employees fall within the benefits code and potentially attract a Class 1A NIC liability. The same comment was applicable to the purchase of, for example, a rail season ticket until 6 April 1999, but that is no longer so because non-cash vouchers were then brought into Class 1 liability.

The fifth exception relates to the travel expenses of unpaid directors of not-for-profit companies, following the introduction of a statutory exemption for expenses previously disregarded under ESC A4. *ITEPA 2003, ss 241A, 241B* and *340A* were inserted by the *Enactment of Extra-Statutory Concessions Order 2014, SI 2014/211*. Where the director is obliged to incur expenses as the holder of the unpaid employment and they are attributable to the director's necessary attendance 'at any place' in the performance of the duties of the employment, they are excluded from earnings by *SI 2001/1004, Sch 3, Pt VIII, para 3A* with effect from 6 April 2014 by virtue of *SI 2014/608, Reg 4*.

The sixth exception, from 6 April 2016, relates to the travel expenses of local authority members attending official council meetings that became statutorily tax-free by virtue of *ITEPA 2003, s 295A* (inserted by *F(No 2)A 2015, s 29*). These also became NIC-free under *Contributions Regulations 2001, Sch 3, Part VIII, para 17*, inserted by *Social Security (Contributions) (Amendment) (No 2) Regulations 2016, SI 2016/352, Reg 5(8)*.

Site-based employees

[30.15] 'Site based' employees such as those in the construction industry or computer support industries often have no normal place of work. They work at various sites consecutively spending weeks or months at each site. The expense of travel in getting from home to site is not incurred in the performance of the duties. These expenses were therefore included in gross pay for NICs until 6 April 1998. The employee was deemed to be travelling *to* the job as opposed to the travelling appointment situation, mentioned below, where he is travelling *on* the job. If the employee then has to travel between sites it will be treated as travel between two (or more) places of work and is therefore in the course of employment. 'Reasonable' reimbursed travelling expenses between sites will not be liable for NICs. See Inland Revenue Tax Bulletin, issue 33, page 477 *et seq*; CA Press Release 10/98; CA National Insurance News, issue 9, page 10.

In a travelling appointment, the employee has to travel as part of his duties. He is travelling *on* the job rather than *to* the job, as in the case of a person with a normal place of employment. In such a case, the employment generally commences when the employee leaves home and therefore his travelling expenses are incurred in the performance of the duties of that employment. In these cases, expenses paid should not be included in gross pay for NICs. The expenses of travelling to the boundary of the area of the area of responsibility are liable to tax and NICs if the employee lives outside the area within which he is required to travel as part of his job (see Booklet 490).

When the tax and NIC treatment of travel expenses for intermediary workers was reformed with effect from 6 April 2016, nothing changed the treatment of site-based workers supplied by intermediaries. While *FA 2016, s 14* inserted *ITEPA 2003, s 339A* to deny tax relief to certain intermediary workers for the costs of travelling between home and work, the relief affected was only that previously available for travel to a temporary workplace under ss 338–339. The tax relief for the travel costs of site-based workers (eg, district nurses, meter readers, in-home carers, etc) is given by s 337, which was unaffected. The same applies for the changes in *Social Security (Contributions) (Amendment) (No 2) Regulations 2016, SI 2016/352* that introduced the statutory relief from NIC liability.

In the case of offshore oil and gas rig workers, the reimbursement of expenses incurred by those workers in the course of transferring to or from the mainland is disregarded for NIC purposes. This also includes the provision of overnight accommodation in the vicinity of the mainland departure point. See Booklet 480 (2017), para 5.22. [*Social Security (Contributions) Regulations 2001, SI 2001/1004, Reg 25, Sch 3, Part VIII, para 6; ITEPA 2003, s 305 and former ESC A59*].

Recall expenses

[30.16] In the past if an employee was recalled from his home to work by his employer, his travelling expenses, if reimbursed by his employer, were not earnings for contribution purposes. (CWG2 (1997), page 83, Item 147). The basis for this rule lay in *Blee v LNER* [1938] AC 126 where it was held that a man who is called out at night to deal with an emergency may be acting in the course of his employment when travelling from his home to his place of work to deal with the emergency. The exclusion did not apply where the employee was required by the terms of his contract of service to be on call. (CWG2 (1997), page 84, Flowchart). See also **16.9** CLASS **1**A CONTRIBUTIONS: BENEFITS IN KIND.

This changed when the CA's National Insurance News, Winter 1997–98, page 10 stated that the new rules regarding employee's travel and subsistence payments in *Finance Act 1997* were to be mirrored by the then DSS:

> However, the Department of Social Security has now concluded that all such payments should be subject to National Insurance contributions. This aligns the National Insurance contributions position with that for tax. The Contributions Agency will not be seeking any arrears from the employer who has relied on published past guidance and not paid National Insurance contributions on these payments, but new employer guidance from April 1998 will confirm National Insurance contributions are due in these circumstances.

See HM Revenue and Customs National Insurance Manual NIM05610.

There is an exception to this where the employee has to perform duties at home and while travelling to an emergency at a permanent workplace. In these circumstances the cost of the travel may be excluded.

See HM Revenue and Customs National Insurance Manual NIM06350.

Season travel tickets

[30.17] In accordance with the principles described at **29.51** a reimbursement by an employer in respect of a season travel ticket purchased by an employee will be earnings for contribution purposes. Where, however, the employer himself purchases the ticket either by buying it from the supplier directly or by giving the employee a cheque made payable to the supplier and appointing the employee its agent, the payment is a payment in kind (see **29.28**) and, until 6 April 1999, attracted no NIC liability. However, even though the employer may arrange for an employer's contract, the handing over of the season ticket constitutes, from 6 April 1999, the provision of a 'voucher, token, stamp or similar document exchangeable for goods or services' and Class 1 liability will arise. Similar remarks also now apply to the provision of holidays, etc under an employer's contract. (CWG2 (2018 to 2019), paras 2.6.2–2.6.6, 5.1 and 5.2.6.)

Likewise, any voucher or warrant which is redeemable only for travel and not for cash is a payment in kind but attracts Class 1 NICs as a transport voucher.

See HM Revenue and Customs National Insurance Manual NIM02335.

Use of company car

[30.18] Where an employer provides an employee with a car for his use, the benefit enjoyed by the employee is a payment in kind (see **29.28**). (CWG2 (2018 to 2019), para 5.1.) The employer of the person to whom the car is made available may be liable to pay CLASS 1A CONTRIBUTIONS **16** in respect of the car benefit and, if applicable, fuel benefit, although having the benefit of free fuel for private use in a company car will usually cost an employee more in tax alone than he or she would pay to buy all fuel for private motoring. See also *Vasili v Christensen* [2003] STC SCD 428 Sp C 377 and other cases cited at **16.19**.

See **16.12** CLASS 1A CONTRIBUTIONS: BENEFITS IN KIND.

Use-of-own-car allowances

[30.19] Where an employee uses his own car for the purposes of his employment he may be recompensed in various ways and this may give rise to difficulties from a contribution point of view.

From 6 April 2002, only the statutory mileage rate (AMAP — see **30.22**) can escape Class 1 liability, even where there are full records and it can clearly be demonstrated that the actual costs incurred were higher.

If an employer discharges specific debts which the employee incurs in connection with a car which he owns personally but uses for the purposes of his employment, eg road fund licence, insurance, servicing, AA/RAC membership, DSS guidance was that the whole of each payment was earnings for contribution purposes. The basis for that guidance was, first, the general principle that, where an employer discharges an employee's personal debts, he is placing money's worth in the hands of the employee (see **29.51**) and, second, that a payment in connection with a business expense may be excluded from earnings only if it is a specific and distinct payment of or contribution towards an expense actually incurred in carrying out the employment. [*Social Security (Contributions) Regulations 2001, SI 2001/1004, Reg 25, Sch 3 Part VIII para 9*]. The former DSS was of the view that a person's expenses incurred in running a car for private purposes were incurred in the course of domestic living and not in carrying out the employment so that, even though the car might be put to some business use, what is now *Social Security (Contributions) Regulations 2001, SI 2001/1004, Reg 25, Sch 3 Part VIII para 9* was of no relevance.

It is no longer possible for tax relief to be claimed on borrowings used to fund the purchase of a private car or van that is also driven for business purposes. In addition, capital allowances for the cost of a car or van that is used for business purposes are denied. All costs are deemed to be covered by the approved mileage allowance payment (AMAP) that an employer may pay tax- and NIC-free under *ITEPA 2003, Part 4, Chapter 2* and *Social Security (Contributions) Regulations 2001, SI 2001/1004, Sch 3, Part VIII, paras 7A–7C*. Therefore when considering changing a company car lease scheme (and free petrol) to privately owned vehicles, these two points should be borne in mind.

The AMAP for tax purposes is currently 45ppm for the first 10,000 business miles, but it is then reduced to 25ppm for further mileage in the year. For NIC purposes, it is a uniform 45ppm whatever the business mileage in the year. The employer need not track mileage so as to ensure that a split rate is applied in the earnings period when mileage passes 10,000 for the year (although it will probably be doing so anyway for tax purposes). Each separate (unrelated) employment attracts its own separate 10,000 miles limit on the higher rate for tax purposes.

The increase in scale charges caused by regular lowering of the starting point of the CO_2 scale for company cars, combined with the AMAP rate, may make it worthwhile for employees to own cars personally rather than have company cars, depending on the exact circumstances.

Example

If Benevolent Ltd was to pay amounts in excess of the statutory AMAP figures then the excess would be subject to tax and NICs. As stated above the company might be better off to 'buy out' the car fuel benefit of those employees who are intending to switch to their new cars. This can be seen from this example using 2018–19 figures of the new company car costing £20,000 with carbon dioxide (CO_2) emissions of 180 grams per kilometre. If an employee of Benevolent Ltd is a higher rate taxpayer travelling 10,000 private miles and 10,000 business miles per year, petrol prices are £5.00 per gallon and fuel consumption averages out at 30 miles per gallon what will be the effect of a 'buy out' of free fuel and the withdrawal of the company car scheme?

2018–19			*Employee*	*Employer*
			£	£
Fuel scale charge	£23,400 × 37% = £8,658 × 40%	=	3,463	
Private mileage costs	10,000 × £5.50 ÷ 30mpg *(for simplicity, VAT is disregarded)*	=		1,833
Car scale benefit	£20,000 × 37% = £7,400 × 40%	=	2,960	
Class 1A charge	(£7,400 + £8,658) × 13.8%	=		2,216
			6,423	4,049

From the above calculations it can be seen that the employee will have a car benefit and free fuel benefit cost of £6,423 for the year and the cost to the employer (even excluding leasing costs of £199 per month) is £4,049 per annum.

Giving up the benefit of free fuel would save the employee £3,463 in tax, leaving him with £1,630 extra cash after buying his own fuel for private motoring (£1,833), and the employer would save £1,195 (£8,658 × 13.8%) in Class 1A NICs.

In this particular case the employee might be better advised to forgo not only the free fuel but also the new company car, purchasing or leasing his own with a 'buy out' scheme from the company. He would immediately save £4,590 (£6,423 – £1,833). The company could also pay him £4,500 (10,000 × 45p) tax- and NIC-free to cover the costs of business mileage. With fuel costing 18.3p per mile, he would have an additional £2,670 towards the cost of providing and running his own car, to add to the £4,590 saving. This makes a total 'buy out' savings fund of about £7,260 out of which he would pay for buying or leasing, maintaining and insuring his own car.

However, the matter may not be so clear cut for the *employee* where the mileage is very high eg 30,000 miles per annum with high private mileage (eg, long-distance commuting every day). Here the savings in fuel to the employee paid for by the company will be higher and it might not be worth giving up the fuel benefit (or indeed the company car, since high mileage normally equates to high maintenance and faster depreciation costs).

Lump sum mileage allowance payments are liable to NICs and local government (and some other) employers pay such amounts to 'essential car users'. In these circumstances the AMAP rate may be deducted from the essential car user allowance when computing the Class 1 liability each month. The CA stated at their Specialist Conference on 29 October 1997:

> If FPCS [the forerunner of AMAP] rates were used we would be quite happy. If people were using higher rates than FPCS then we would establish whether or not there was a profit to the individual and we would charge NICs, if there was. If there wasn't then we'd accept it.

However, from 6 April 2002, it has no longer been possible to claim relief in excess of the statutory mileage rate, even when evidence shows that actual expenditure exceeds this amount (see above).

It is crucial to note that, while an employee may claim a retrospective income tax deduction for mileage based on the AMAP rate, there is no equivalent for the purposes of NIC. The employer may exclude from earnings in each earnings period the cost of business mileage at the AMAP rate, but the balance of any round sum allowance for motoring paid in that period must be subjected to Class 1 liability. Total People Ltd managed to persuade the Court of Appeal that it should be entitled to a NIC refund based on total business mileage for the year (see *Cheshire Employer & Skills Development Limited (formerly Total People Limited) v Revenue and Customs Comrs* [2012] EWCA Civ 1429) but HMRC persists in denying refunds to other employers with similar essential user schemes in defiance of the court's ruling, claiming that its facts were unique. See further **30.22** below.

Petrol

[30.20] The table below summarises the NIC position for both employer-supplied cars and employee-supplied cars where the employer provides or pays for fuel.

It should be noted that, where appropriate, the rules about what constitutes acceptable evidence of a business expense may need to be borne in mind.

Method of fuel supply	Employer supplied cars	Employee supplied cars or vehicles on which Class 1A NICs are not payable
Employer's credit card/agency card/petrol vouchers/employer's garage account.	Class 1A NICs on scale charge.	No Class 1 NIC liability if it was explained in advance that fuel was being bought on behalf of the employer. P11D report and Class 1A on cost to employer.
Supply from company fuel pump.	Class 1A NICs on scale charge.	No Class 1 NIC liability, fuel is benefit in kind subject to Class 1A NICs on cost to employer.
Reimbursement of fuel bills paid by employee, including use of employee credit cards.	Class 1A NICs on scale charge.	There is no Class 1 NIC liability if only business mileage is involved and the rate does not exceed the AMAP rate. If both business and private mileage are involved, Class 1 NICs are due on the full amount paid less.
Round sum allowance.	A Class 1 NIC liability on whole amount, unless clearly related to fuel purchase, in which case Class 1A NICs on scale charge instead.	Class 1 NIC liability on whole amount. If any business miles can be identified, employer may exclude (business miles × AMAP rate) in the earnings period.
Mileage allowance—business mileage only.	A Class 1 NIC liability may arise on the excess if the employer pays more than the HMRC advisory mileage rate for the engine size and fuel type but it is paid only for genuine business travel.	A Class 1 NIC liability may arise on the excess if the employer pays more than the AMAP rate but it is paid only for genuine business travel.
Mileage allowance—business and private mileage included.	Class 1A NICs on scale charge.	Class 1 NICs are due on the amount paid if both business *and* private mileage are involved. *But*, if the *actual* business mileage can be identified, the amount on which NICs is due can be reduced by the business element (business miles × AMAP rate).

See earlier editions of this work as regards the position prior to 2000, pre-Class 1A, and the consequences of the case *R v DSS, ex p Overdrive Credit Card Ltd* [1991] STC 129.

Mileage allowances for business travel – company cars

[30.21] HM Revenue and Customs first published in guidelines 'advisory rates' of fuel-only mileage allowances for petrol and diesel company cars in February 2002, and those for LPG followed in May 2002. No income tax or NICs will arise on payments at rates up to those stated below for business mileage. However, if payments above these figures can be substantiated for business mileage (eg, where a sales representative regularly tows a display trailer behind a car with a large engine) then HM Revenue and Customs will accept them.

These rates may also be used in making calculations where employees are required to reimburse the cost of private fuel paid for by the employer. Even in circumstances where the cost of fuel to be reimbursed by the employee should arguably be higher, HM Revenue and Customs will not so argue for cars of 3000cc or less. This gives some certainty to employers who keep to the guidelines in that they can now expect that their agreed reimbursements from the employee will not be overturned.

HM Revenue and Customs guideline rates for NICs in pence per mile

	Petrol			**Diesel**			**LPG**		
From	*Up to 1400cc*	*1401 to 2000cc*	*Over 2000cc*	*Up to 1600cc*	*1601 to 2000cc*	*Over 2000cc*	*Up to 1400cc*	*1401 to 2000cc*	*Over 2000cc*
1.3.18	11p	14p	22p	9p	11p	13p	7p	8p	13p
1.12.17	11p	14p	21p	9p	11p	13p	7p	9p	14p
1.9.17	11p	13p	21p	9p	11p	12p	7p	8p	13p
1.6.17	11p	14p	21p	9p	11p	13p	7p	9p	14p
1.3.17	11p	14p	22p	9p	11p	13p	7p	9p	14p
1.12.16	11p	14p	21p	9p	11p	13p	7p	9p	13p
1.9.16	11p	13p	20p	9p	11p	13p	7p	9p	13p
1.6.16	10p	13p	20p	9p	10p	12p	7p	9p	13p
1.3.16	10p	12p	19p	8p	10p	11p	7p	8p	13p
1.12.15	11p	13p	20p	9p	11p	13p	7p	9p	13p
1.9.15	11p	14p	21p	9p	11p	13p	7p	9p	14p
1.6.15	12p	14p	21p	10p	12p	14p	8p	9p	14p
1.3.15	11p	13p	20p	9p	11p	14p	8p	10p	14p
1.12.14	13p	16p	23p	11p	13p	16p	9p	11p	16p
1.9.14	14p	16p	24p	11p	13p	17p	9p	11p	16p
1.6.14	14p	16p	24p	12p	14p	17p	9p	11p	16p
1.3.14	14p	16p	24p	12p	14p	17p	9p	11p	17p
1.12.13	14p	16p	24p	12p	14p	17p	9p	11p	16p
1.9.13	15p	18p	26p	12p	15p	18p	10p	11p	16p
1.6.13	15p	17p	25p	12p	14p	18p	10p	12p	18p
1.9.12	15p	18p	26p	12p	15p	18p	10p	12p	17p
1.6.12	15p	18p	26p	12p	15p	18p	11p	13p	19p
1.3.12	15p	18p	26p	13p	15p	19p	13p	12p	18p
1.9.11	15p	18p	26p	12p	15p	18p	11p	12p	18p
1.6.11	15p	18p	26p	12p	15p	18p	11p	13p	18p
1.3.11	14p	16p	23p		13p	16p	10p	12p	17p
1.12.10	13p	15p	21p		12p	15p	9p	10p	15p
1.6.10	12p	15p	21p		11p	16p	8p	10p	14p
1.12.09	11p	14p	20p		11p	14p	7p	8p	12p

Mileage allowances which are not related to actual business mileage are merely round sum allowances (see **30.23** above).

Mileage allowances for business travel – cars provided by employees

[30.22] From 6 April 2002, a statutory mileage allowance for cars and vans owned personally was introduced for income tax purposes, known as the Approved Mileage Allowance Payment (AMAP) rate. It was initially set at 40p per mile for the first 10,000 business miles per annum and 25p thereafter for tax purposes. It was then applied with adaptation for NIC purposes. [*ITEPA 2003, ss 229–236*]. The standard 40ppm rate was stated to apply to *all* business miles for NIC purposes. On 6 April 2011 the rate increased to 45ppm for all purposes. The lower 25p rate for income tax purposes was left unchanged. The rates for motorcycles and cycles are respectively 24 pence and 20 pence per mile and these have been unchanged since their introduction. See CWG2 (2018 to 2019), para 5.4.2 and IR Press Release, 7 August 2001, Tolley's Practical NIC Newsletter, January 2005 and *SI 2002/307* inserting *SI 2001/1004, Reg 22A*. See HM Revenue and Customs National Insurance Manual NIM05700.

Where lump sum allowances are paid to a car-user see **30.25**.

> *Example*
>
> Frank works at different sites and has no permanent workplace. He travels in his own 1600cc car to and from the sites where he is working. Over the whole of the tax year he travels 18,000 miles on business to and from the different sites. He is entitled to tax relief for the cost of his travel.
>
> Frank's employer pays him 50 pence a mile for his business travel. This is more than the HM Revenue and Customs AMAP rate. For the particular tax year the authorised rates are 45 pence for each of the first 10,000 business miles and, for income tax only, 25 pence for each mile over 10,000. Frank gets a tax return. As Frank's employer pays more than the AMAP, the excess over the AMAP (Booklet 480 (2018), para 16.7) needs to be returned on the P11D. So his P11D shows the excess mileage allowances of £2,500 (£9,000 – (£4,500 + £2,000)) he has been paid for the tax year.
>
> Frank cannot choose to calculate the tax relief for his business travel by using his actual motoring costs incurred.
>
> The deemed cost of 18,000 business miles using AMAP rates is £6,500 (the first 10,000 miles at 45 pence = £4,500, plus the next 8,000 miles at 25 pence = £2,000). This applies for tax purposes.
>
> For Class 1 NICs purposes Frank's employer will have to include in earnings £900 in total (ie, 18,000 miles at (50p – 45p) 5ppm), but the calculation ought to be carried out in each earnings period based on the business mileage in that period.

As already mentioned above, Total People Ltd paid allowances to its employees and challenged HMRC's interpretation of the NIC rules. The company provided the services of apprentices and trainees to employers, and supervised their training. It employed about 160 training advisers, who had to visit the trainees at their places of work. It paid these advisers a mileage allowance, plus an annual payment which was described as a 'lump sum' but was actually paid in 12 monthly instalments. The lump sum was based on the estimated actual running costs of a typical car used by the employee group in question. Initially the company accounted for National Insurance contributions on these payments. Subsequently it submitted a repayment claim on the basis that the effect of *Social Security (Contributions) Regulations 2001, SI 2001/1004, reg 22A* was that it had not been required to pay NIC on these payments. HMRC rejected the claim on the basis that the payments were 'earnings' on which contributions were payable. The First-Tier Tribunal allowed the company's appeal, holding on the evidence that the payments 'were paid as motoring expenditure'; they were not 'additions to salary' and 'were not paid as earnings'. *Total People Ltd v HMRC* [2010] UKFTT 379 (TC). HMRC appealed and the decision was reversed: [2011] UKUT 329 (TCC). The company's appeal was allowed by the Court of Appeal: [2012] EWCA Civ 1429. See an article by John Messore and Peter Moroz in *TAXline*, December 2012.

Volunteer drivers will not pay National Insurance on any mileage allowances above the AMAP rates as volunteer driving is not gainful employment for National Insurance purposes. Nor is there a liability for Class 2 or Class 4 National Insurance on any profits made from volunteer driving (HM Revenue & Customs leaflet IR 122, now withdrawn, and webarchive.nationalarchives.gov.uk/20140109143644/http://www.hmrc.gov.uk/mileage/volunteer-drivers.htm now in the National Archives).

Mileage allowances for business travel – car passenger payments

[30.23] A statutory rate of 5p per mile can be paid to the car driver where a colleague is carried as a passenger on a business journey. No separate claim by the driver for income tax relief can be made if the employer does not make such a payment, nor is there relief if the payment is made to the passenger rather than the driver, or if the passenger is self-employed. The passenger payment can, however, be made whether the car is privately owned or a company car (in the latter instance the passenger payment will therefore be the only payment made to the employee unless fuel is not provided and the advisory rate per mile is also paid for that). See IR Press Release, 7 August 2001 and CWG2 (2018 to 2019), para 5.4.2. [*Social Security (Contributions) Regulations 2001, SI 2001/1004, Reg 25, Sch 3, Part VIII, para 7C*].

Previously, the former DSS did not regard payments made to employees to cover the additional expense of carrying passengers and/or equipment specifically relating to the employment in the employee's car as part of earnings for contribution purposes. (See 1995 leaflet CA 28, page 88, Item 87).

Mileage allowances for business travel – bicycles and motorbikes

[30.24] A rate was first published in 1999 in respect of pedal cycles being 12p per business mile from 6 April 1999, raised to 20p per mile from 6 April 2002, and for motorcycles it has been 24p per mile since 6 April 2000.

NICs do not arise if employees are paid at or below these rates for business use of their pedal cycles or motorcycles. [*Social Security (Contributions) Regulations 2001, SI 2001/1004, Reg 25, Sch 3, Part VIII, para 7B*].

Essential car user allowances

[30.25] Some employers (typically, until recently, local authorities) make two forms of payment to employees who use their own cars for the purposes of their employment. The first is a periodic round sum allowance representing a proportion of the vehicle standing charges (often known as an essential car user allowance) and the second is a (usually low) mileage allowance. If (as will normally be the case) the mileage rate used is less than the relevant AMAP rate, the excess of the AMAP rate over the rate used may be applied to the relevant business mileage and the resulting amount may be deducted from the round-sum allowance for the earnings period.

Originally, by concession before April 2002, only the reduced round sum allowance was then regarded as earnings. Special notes were available from the DSS to assist local authorities etc in making the necessary calculations. The NJC 'Purple Book' rates of allowance were *not* accepted by the DSS as an alternative to FPCS rates.

However, at the CA Specialist Conference in Newcastle on 27 October 1997 this point was addressed with the following reply:

> We would look at what was paid and was it reasonable in the circumstances. If FPCS rates were used we would be quite happy. If people [Local Government] were using higher rates than FPCS then we would establish whether or not there was a profit to the individual and we would charge NICs if there was. If there wasn't then we'd accept it.

In the HM Revenue and Customs National Insurance Manual NIM05745 (now withdrawn) this was confirmed: 'Some HAs [Health Authorities] have in the past argued that their CWC or HMDS rates do accurately reflect the employee's actual business costs and that no NICs are payable. This is not a view held by HMRC.'

The AMAP scheme from 6 April 2002 formalised the impact on essential car user allowances. Broadly, if business mileage is skewed into later parts of the year and/or the essential user allowance is paid in advance or infrequently, then unnecessary Class 1 NIC costs are likely to arise, due to the normal application of the earnings period rules. Whilst HM Revenue and Customs' attention has been drawn to this inequity, no positive guidance has yet been forthcoming. See Tolley's Practical NIC Newsletter, January 2005 page 3. Class 1 NIC costs will be minimised if lump sums are paid in arrears and/or at fairly regular intervals (eg monthly or quarterly). The *Total People Ltd* decision mentioned above must be borne in mind in this context.

It is interesting to note that in a written answer to the House of Lords concerning mileage allowances paid to members of the House of Commons and Lords (and other Civil Service Departments) on 7 February 2002 the Lord Privy Seal stated that even then 53.7p per mile was paid on mileage up to 20,000 per annum. See Hansard 7 February 2002, Cols WA 105 and 106. The mileage allowances paid to members of local authorities that became statutorily exempt from 6 April 2016 are based on the AMAP rates.

Parking fees and fines, etc

[30.26] An employer's reimbursement of parking fees incurred by an employee in connection with business-related journeys does not form part of earnings for contribution purposes because they are expenses actually incurred by the employee in carrying out his employment. [*Social Security (Contributions) Regulations 2001, SI 2001/1004, Reg 25, Sch 3, Part VIII, para 9*]. (CWG2 (2018 to 2019), para 5.1.) Evidence is required of the parking fees incurred, however, and, in the absence of such evidence, the reimbursements must be included in gross pay. See HM Revenue and Customs National Insurance Manual NIM05615. There is no explanation of how an employee is supposed to evidence parking meter payments where the meter dispenses no receipt, or where payments are made by mobile telephone, as is now common, but amounts involved are probably insignificant.

An employer's reimbursement or payment of parking fees incurred by an employee at his normal place of work constituted earnings for contribution purposes on general principles until 6 April 2001. This was so despite statutory exemption for PAYE income tax purposes. However, from 6 April 2001 the position was harmonised (see CWG2 (2018 to 2019), para 5.1). [*Social Security (Contributions) Regulations 2001, SI 2001/1004, Sch 3, Part VIII, para 8; ITEPA 2003, s 237* as amended by *FA 2005, s 16(2)*]. See HM Revenue and Customs National Insurance Manual NIM05625.

Where an employer contracts with a car park or uses his own land to provide car parking facilities for his employees, no Class 1 liability arose even before 6 April 2001 as the facility was a payment in kind. A contract made by the employer could nonetheless attract Class 1 contributions from 6 April 1999 if a ticket (ie a non-cash voucher) was provided or, if not, a Class 1A charge from 6 April 2000 until the 6 April 2001 exemption was introduced.

Fines incurred for illegal parking are not generally regarded as expenses incurred in carrying out an employment and any payment or reimbursement by an employer in that regard will normally constitute earnings for contribution purposes if the employee is liable to pay the fine. If, instead, a 'notice to owner' is issued by virtue of which the employer becomes liable to pay the fine no liability to Class 1 contributions arises. See HM Revenue and Customs National Insurance Manual NIM05630.

If an employer pays a parking fine in respect of a car which he provides for his employee he is meeting his own personal liability as keeper of the car and not a liability of the employee. Consequently, there is no benefit to the employee and no NIC liability will arise. See *Tolley's Practical NIC September 1993*, pp 68-69 and *R v Parking Adjudicator, ex p Wandsworth London Borough Council* [1998] RTR 51 CA.

Exceptionally, in a Secretary of State for Social Security determination under the pre-1 April 1999 procedures (see **9** APPEALS AND REVIEWS), parking fines were held not to be earnings where the employee's duties were to empty gaming machines, etc at customers' premises in central London and his written contract of employment specifically required that the vehicle be parked as near the customer's entrance as physically possible, regardless of any parking restrictions, for security reasons. It seems odd that a contract requiring unlawful actions was held to be valid, as it would normally be void.

The London congestion-charging scheme came into effect on 17 February 2003. HM Revenue and Customs has confirmed that all normal rules relating to employees' expenses, benefits and travel as well as self-employed deductions apply. The employees' use of their own vehicles incurring a congestion charge will only be tax and NICs exempt where the journey is in connection with business. Where the company car is used and the benefit charge includes expenditure on items such as insurance, road tax and the congestion charge then no additional benefit arises for tax and NICs. Alternatively, it was until April 2016 far simpler for the congestion charge to be included in a dispensation so that they could be paid free of tax and NICs in respect of business journeys but this will have involved the employer in additional administration in the short term. The costs are now exempt for business journeys as they would be deductible. See *Simon's Tax Intelligence*, 6 March 2003 page 292. See HM Revenue and Customs National Insurance Manual NIM05635. Similar rules apply to congestion charges imposed by other towns and cities.

Overseas expenses and allowances

[30.27] An employer's specific and distinct payment of or contribution towards expenses which an employee actually incurs in carrying out his employment while overseas is excluded from earnings for contribution purposes in accordance with the normal rule. [*Social Security (Contributions) Regulations 2001, SI 2001/1004, Reg 25, Sch 3, Part VIII, para 9*].

Due to the difficulty in obtaining receipts, etc HM Revenue and Customs announced on 5 March 2008 tables of benchmark rates, details of which are to be found at www.hmrc.gov.uk/manuals/eimanual/EIM05250.htm onwards. The tables themselves are based on information provided by the Foreign and Commonwealth Office. HM Revenue and Customs reviews rates from time to time. The current rates are to be found at: www.gov.uk/government/publications/scale-rate-expenses-payments-employee-travelling-outside-the-uk. The rates are not statutory and therefore do not fall under *ITEPA 2003, s 289A* from 6 April 2016, but HMRC will agree to their use under the alternative provisions of *s 289B*, with the result that they will also be free of NIC liability.

Accommodation and subsistence payments at or below the published rates will not be liable for income tax or National Insurance contributions for employees who travel abroad, and employers need not include them on forms P11D. However, if an employer decides to pay less than the published rates its employees are not automatically entitled to tax relief for the shortfall. They can only obtain relief under the employee travel rules. The tax/NIC free amounts are in addition to any incidental overnight expenses (PIEs) that employers may also reimburse tax/NIC free.

Of course, employers do not have to use the published rates – they are entirely optional. It is always open to an employer to reimburse his employees' actual, vouched expenses, or to negotiate a scale rate amount which he believes more accurately reflects his employees' spending patterns.

Round sum allowances paid by an employer to an employee who is or has been working overseas do not fall within the excluding provisions of *Social Security (Contributions) Regulations 2001, SI 2001/1004, Reg 25, Sch 3, Part VIII, para 9* (except to the extent that actual expenses covered by the allowance are identified or they are subject to a bespoke rate agreement with HMRC from 6 April 2016) and they are, therefore, earnings for Class 1 contribution purposes. The former DSS gave as examples of such round sum allowances payments to compensate for the higher cost of living abroad; payments as an inducement to persuade the employee to work abroad; and bonuses for working abroad.

The CA stated that 'Cost of living allowances (COLAs) . . . are generally based on a shopping basket of goods and services more highly priced in the country where the employee is working and compared with the UK equivalent. They are not therefore incurred as an expense . . . ' and therefore must be taken into account for NIC purposes on earnings. (See CA National Insurance News, Issue 4, page 9 and CA Specialist Conference written responses, 20 February 1996 and this was reaffirmed by the CA Specialist Conference written responses, 4 February 1997.) See also CWG2 (2018 to 2019), para 5.10 and HM Revenue and Customs National Insurance Manual NIM06000.

A tax equalisation payment to an employee by his employer will normally cover an actual liability incurred but is not regarded as an expense incurred by the employee in carrying out his employment. Accordingly, it cannot be excluded from earnings by virtue of *Social Security (Contributions) Regulations 2001, SI 2001/1004, Reg 25, Sch 3, Part VIII, para 9*. (See HM Revenue and Customs National Insurance Manual NIM02380).

CWG2 (1997) referred employers to their local Contributions Agency Office for advice on paying travel expenses for employees and/or their families returning to the UK on home leave. The advice for 1998 and subsequent years is contained in booklet 490 'Employee Travel – A Tax and NICs Guide for Employers'. Any payment of, or contribution towards, expenses which, under *ITEPA 2003, ss 341, 342, 370, 371, 373, 374, 376* (travel expenses and foreign travel expenses where the duties of an office or employment are performed wholly or partly outside the UK) are deductible from the general earnings of the employment chargeable to tax is excluded from earnings for Class 1 purposes. [*Social Security (Contributions) Regulations 2001, SI 2001/1004, Sch 3, Part VIII, paras 4, 4A, 4B, 4C, 4D and 5, introduced by Contributions Amendment No 4 Regs 1993 with effect from 6 April 1993* and amended by *Social Security (Contributions, Categorisation of Earners and Intermediaries) (Amendment) Regulations 2004, SI 2004/770, Reg 28; Social Security (Contributions) (Amendment No 6) Regulations 2005, SI 2005/3130, Reg 5*].

Note also that where an employee or director, although fit enough to carry out duties at his normal place of work in the UK, because of his poor state of health cannot undertake travel abroad on business without being accompanied by a spouse, then the cost of the spouse's travel will not be charged to NICs. The former CA took the view that legislation to mirror ESC A4(d) (under which the income tax exemption arose) was not required because the CA was advised that the terms of what is now *Social Security (Contributions) Regulations 2001, SI 2001/1004, Reg 25, Sch 3, Part VIII, para 9* are wide enough to cover this matter. (CA Specialist Conference, 20 February 1996 and see also HMRC Booklet 480 (2018), paras 10.1–10.6). It is assumed that similar treatment will be accorded to the travelling expenses of an accompanying civil partner.

From 6 April 1998 onwards the payment of medical expenses by an employer to an employee in respect of expenses the employee incurs when carrying out his duties abroad was removed from NICs liability. This applies to actual medical costs and expenses or insurance against such costs. CA Press Release CA10/98, 16 March 1998 and *Social Security (Contributions) Regulations 2001, SI 2001/1004, Reg 25, Sch 3, Part VIII, para 14*. The former Contributions Agency did not publish any guidance on this issue before 6 April 1998. Instructions are that where a case comes to light involving arrears for periods prior to this date, payment of 'arrears should not be requested unless it is clear that the employer ignored specific advice that a liability existed' (HM Revenue and Customs National Insurance Manual NIM05688). Such arrears would now be time-barred for collection so the matter is academic.

Training expenses

[30.28] Payments made by an employer to an employee to reimburse him for fees, books, travel, etc in connection with courses which are work-related or are required or encouraged by the employer (eg first aid courses) are not earnings for contribution purposes. (IR Tax Bulletin, April 2003 page 1022, CWG2 (2018 to 2019), para 5.1 and see also HMRC Booklet 480 (2018), Chapter 5 and Appendix 9). [*Social Security (Contributions) Regulations 2001, SI 2001/1004, Reg 25, Sch 3, Part VII, para 2; Income Tax (Earnings and Pensions) Act 2003, ss 250–254*]. See also HM Revenue and Customs National Insurance Manual NIM02395.

Payments to participants in Employment Retention and Advancement Schemes (arranged under *Employment and Training Act 1972, s 2(1)*) and payments to participants in a Return to Work Credit Scheme were excepted from liability with effect from 1 October 2003 [*SI 2001/1004 Regs, Sch 3 Part VII paras 8, 9* as inserted by *Social Security (Contributions) (Amendment No 6) Regulations 2003*, and further amended from 10 December 2003 by *Social Security (Contributions) (Amendment No 7) Regulations 2003, SI 2003/2958, Reg 5*]. See HM Revenue and Customs National Insurance Manual NIM02398.

From 6 April 2004, payments to participants in either Working Neighbourhoods Pilots or In-Work Credit schemes (under *Employment and Training Act 1973 s 2(1)*) were not subject to NIC [*Social Security (Contributions) Regulations 2001, SI 2001/1004, Sch 3 Part VII paras 10, 11* inserted by *Social Security (Contributions, Categorisation of Earners and Intermediaries) (Amendment) Regulations 2004, SI 2004/770, Reg 28*]. See HM Revenue and Customs National Insurance Manual NIM02400.

From 6 April 2005, part-time employees who are provided with outplacement counselling services and/or a retraining course have benefitted from the same income tax exemption that full-time employees can receive. The outplacement courses may last for up to two years. No NICs are payable, either Class 1 or Class 1A. [*ITEPA 2003, ss 310, 311* as amended by *FA 2005, s 18*].

Not every training expense is excluded from earnings. Two airline pilots whose contracts provided that, if they left their employment within three years, they would have to reimburse part of the cost of their training, both resigned their employment within the three-year period and subsequently made reimbursement payments as required by their contracts. They claimed that these should be allowed as deductions. HMRC rejected the claims and the Special Commissioner dismissed the pilots' appeals, observing that the payment was required 'because of the termination of the contract', rather than in the performance of the employees' duties. See *Hinsley v HMRC; Milsom v HMRC* [2007] STC SCD 63 Sp C 569.

From the academic year starting 1 September 2007 and later years, payments of up to £15,480 per annum to an employee for periods of attendance on full-time educational courses at a recognised educational establishment will not attract a Class 1 NICs charge nor will there be a Class 1A liability. This amount was initially £15,000 per annum from 1 September 2005 (when this relief was introduced) to 31 August 2007. The amount relates to earnings payable to the earner in respect of attendance at the educational establishment eg lodging, travel subsistence but excludes tuition fees. This aligns the NICs position with the previous tax treatment of payments in the Statement of Practice 4/86 (SP 4/86) which was revised on 16 March 2005 and again on 15 August 2007. Previously the payments would have been chargeable to Class 1 NICs where the payments were made under an employment contract, although such payments made under a training contract were not chargeable. [*Social Security (Contributions) Regulations 2001, SI 2001/1004, Reg 40, Sch 3 Part VII para 12; Social Security (Contributions) (Amendment No 2) Regulations 2005, SI 2005/728, Regs 3, 4; Social Security (Contributions) (Amendment No 7) Regulations 2007, SI 2007/2401, Regs 1, 2*]. See HM Revenue and Customs National Insurance Manual NIM02402.

Eye tests, etc

[30.29] Following the introduction of the *Health and Safety (Display Screen Equipment) Regs 1992*, the former Contributions Agency stated that it would not regard as 'earnings' the reimbursement by an employer of an employee's expenditure on an eyesight test when the employee is required to use a VDU (ie, visual display unit or computer monitor) in the course of his employment. Nor will Class 1 contributions be sought in respect of the provision or reimbursement of the cost of spectacles needed solely for use with a VDU in the course of the duties of an employment. Where a general need for spectacles is identified and, in addition to the special prescription for VDU use, the employer discharges the whole of the employee's liability for the spectacles acquired, the cost in excess of the VDU-only prescription will be regarded as earnings. If, however, the spectacles are purchased under a contract between the employer and the optician, the provision of the spectacles to the employee will be a payment in kind which will attract a Class 1A charge for years prior to 6 April 2006. See HM Revenue and Customs National Insurance Manual NIM02145. From 6 April 2006, no tax or NICs is charged to an employee if the employer makes the payment for eye care tests and/or corrective glasses for VDU use whether this is by direct payment to the provider or reimbursement to the employee or by providing a voucher in whole or in part payment to secure the test or corrective glasses. This change in legislation applied from 6 April 2006 [*FA 2006, s 62*] for income tax purposes and from 14 August 2006 in respect of NICs. [*Social Security (Contributions) (Amendment No 4) Regulations 2006, SI 2006/2003*].

Tool allowances

[30.30] Where an employee is given an allowance to purchase tools and those tools are available to the employee for private use, the allowance will be earnings and cannot be excluded as a business expense. Where, however, the tools are not available to the employee for private use, then the allowance will be excluded from the calculation of earnings as a business expense. [*Social Security (Contributions) Regulations 2001, SI 2001/1004, Sch 3, Part VIII, para 9*].

Working rule agreements

[30.31] Working Rule agreements are drawn up by representatives of employers and trade unions to govern national rates of pay and conditions of work of manual workers in the construction industry and allied trades. Since 6 April 1993 the treatment of expenses for Class 1 NICs purposes has been in alignment with the tax treatment of expenses covered by a Working Rule agreement accepted as meeting the requirements for the special taxation procedures. It also follows that where travel and subsistence expenses are paid under a Working Rule agreement and are accepted as tax free then they will be excluded also from liability for Class 1 contributions, being accepted as business expenses. From 6 April 2016, when the new rules on bespoke expenses allowances were introduced as *ITEPA 2003, s 289B*, matched by the NIC rules as described above, employers were required to agree explicitly with HMRC in advance of the tax year that WRA rates could be used, and to renew that agreement at least every five years. [*Social Security (Contributions) Regulations 2001, SI 2001/1004, Sch 3, Part VIII, para 9*]. See HM Revenue and Customs National Insurance Manual NIM06420.

Key Points regarding earnings from employment: expenses

[30.32] Points to consider are as follows.

- Relocation expenses over £8,000 will, if they are tax-allowable apart from exceeding the limit, be liable to Class 1A, not Class 1, even where the item is a reimbursed expense rather than an employer-contracted benefit in kind.
- Even if the employer makes all the contractual arrangements, the provision of a season ticket is liable to Class 1 contributions as the ticket constitutes a non-cash voucher/transport voucher.
- AMAPs are statutory rates of reimbursement for the business use of an employee's own vehicle. Even where actual expenditure for the business mileage undertaken can be proven to exceed the statutory rate, no additional relief is available.
- However, for NICs the standard rate can (but need not be) used for all business miles including those over 10,000 per annum. Any excess over the AMAP rate paid by the employer, or any allowance paid for private mileage, constitutes earnings for NIC purposes.
- Advisory fuel rates issued by HMRC for reimbursement of company car business mileage are normally issued quarterly. Employers may apply the new rates from those dates or, if preferred, within the following month.
- Advisory fuel rates can be paid free of tax and NICs to company car drivers where no fuel is provided and business mileage is undertaken or, can be used, where fuel *is* provided, to compute (in all but very rare cases) the amount of private fuel reimbursement to avoid a fuel benefit scale charge.

31

Earnings from Employment: Employment-Related Securities, Readily Convertible Assets, etc

Cross-references. See CLASS 1 CONTRIBUTIONS 15; EARNINGS FROM EMPLOYMENT: GENERAL 29; NATIONAL INSURANCE NEWS.

Other Sources. Tolley's Tax Planning 2016–17; Tolley's Income Tax 2016–17; Tolley's National Insurance Brief, February 1997; Leaflet CWG2 (2018–19); Leaflet CWG5 (2018). See also Leaflet 480 (2018); HM Revenue and Customs National Insurance Manual NIM06800–06915. HM Revenue and Customs Employment Related Securities Manual; Tax Bulletin Special Edition 7, December 2003, Tax Bulletin Special Edition, April 2005.

Introduction to earnings from employment: employment-related securities, readily convertible assets, etc

[31.1] The term 'earnings', when used in the context of social security legislation, includes any remuneration or profit derived from any trade, business, profession, office or vocation. The amount of a person's earnings for any period, or the amount of his earnings to be treated as comprised in any payment made to him or for his benefit, is to be calculated or estimated in the manner and on the basis prescribed in the legislation and such prescriptions do, in fact, differ in the case of employed earners and self-employed earners. [*SSCBA 1992, s 3(1)(2), s 122(1)*]. See HM Revenue and Customs National Insurance Manual NIM02010.

Earnings which are 'payments in kind' are not susceptible to deduction of contributions at source and were in consequence not generally liable to Class 1 until the introduction of the anti-avoidance provisions referred to later in this chapter, but in any event most items not attracting a Class 1 charge, attract instead – but only from 6 April 2000 – a Class 1A (employer-only) charge – see CLASS **1**A CONTRIBUTIONS: BENEFITS IN KIND **16**.

Financial instruments

[31.2] In contrast to, for example, premium bonds etc (see **29.29** EARNINGS FROM EMPLOYMENT: GENERAL), most financial instruments are incapable of encashment by mere surrender and require a willing buyer and a mutually agreed price before they may be converted into cash by sale, unless they are held to redemption. On basic principles, therefore, such instruments would *prima facie* appear to offer themselves as potential vehicles for the payment of remuneration in kind, ie in a form which does not attract Class 1 liabilities.

Gilt-edged securities are the prime example of such financial instruments: they are readily available, readily valued (with only a small bid-offer spread), easily transferred and readily sold for cash settlement. However, in the face of widespread contribution avoidance using gilts, the Government acted through an amendment to the *Contribution Regulations 1979* to render their use ineffective with effect from 12 May 1988. Employers' attention then switched to other financial instruments, such as equities, units in unit trusts and life assurance policies. This perceived abuse of the payment in kind rule was blocked with effect from midnight on 6 November 1991 by *Contributions Amendment No 6 Regs 1991*. For detailed descriptions of the use of gilts, units etc in this way reference should be made to earlier editions of this work.

The 1991 regulations amended the *Contributions Regs 1979, Reg 18, Reg 19 as substituted by Social Security (Contributions) Regulations 2001, SI 2001/1004, Sch* 2, *Sch* 3 in order to bring a wide range of financial instruments, including certain life assurance policies, into charge for Class 1 purposes when used to remunerate employees or directors. Technically, the old *Regulation 19(5)* prevented the 'conferment of any beneficial interest in' the specified assets being treated as a payment in kind under what is now *Social*

Security (Contributions) Regulations 2001, SI 2001/1004, Sch 3 Part II para 2. A list of financial instruments, based on (but with much wider scope than) the list of 'investments' in what was then *Financial Services Act 1986, Sch 1 Part I* (now *Financial Services and Markets Act 2000, Sch 1 Part I*), was added as *Contribution Regs 1979, Sch 1A*, which became *Social Security (Contributions) Regulations 2001, SI 2001/1004, Sch 3 Part IV*, headed 'Payments by way of specific assets not disregarded as payments in kind'. As the assets in question are not cash, valuation provisions were added by what is now *Social Security (Contributions) Regulations 2001, SI 2001/1004, Sch 2*.

The original list was further extended with effect from 1 December 1993 by *Contributions Amendment No 7 Regs 1993* which added two further items to the original *Schedule 1A*. The amendment was intended to block the use of gold bullion, but it is of much wider application. When employers' attention switched to assets outside that wider application, eg diamonds and fine wines, the list was extended yet again with effect from 23 August 1994 to include gemstones and alcoholic liquors (see **31.17** and **31.18**) and, with effect from 6 April 1995 to include any 'readily convertible' assets for which 'trading arrangements' existed (see **31.22**). On 5 December 1996 an exemption in respect of shares in the employing company was removed. Then due to perceived defects in the 'trading arrangements' definition, this was further extended to include, for PAYE purposes from 6 April 1998, 'readily convertible assets' (see **31.21**). This definition also extended to National Insurance contributions with effect from 1 October 1998 by the amendment of the then *Reg 18* and the inclusion of the former *Sch 1B*. The legislation was overhauled substantially in 2003 but whilst the tax changes took effect on 16 April 2003, the equivalent NIC changes took effect only from 1 September 2003. [*Social Security (Contributions) (Amendment No 3) Regs 1998*]. (Now in CWG2 (2018–19), paras 5.1, 5.13, 5.14, and 5.15.1–5.15.6.)

As a result of the various changes outlined above, any payment in kind will now only be free of Class 1 liability if it satisfies the two tests already outlined (ie whatever is given or provided must be non-encashabale and must be supplied by the employer to the employee) *and* falls outside the groups of assets specified by *Social Security (Contributions) Regulations 2001, SI 2001/1004, Sch 3 Parts III, IV*. (If it does fall outside those provisions, a Class 1A charge is nonetheless likely to arise.)

The investments which may not now be treated under *Social Security (Contributions) Regulations 2001, SI 2001/1004, Sch 3 Parts II, III and IV* as payments in kind when given by employer to employee are considered further below and each attracts a Class 1 National Insurance liability except where stated. As regards shares, other securities and options where the legislation follows very closely the income tax provisions, we do not attempt to replicate all the detailed nuances of the tax rules. For this, reference should be made to Tolley's Income Tax 2016–17 or to more specialised works on shares and securities. However, there are a number of instances – particularly in respect of unexercised options granted some time ago – where the national insurance treatment differs from the tax treatment and/or different choices are available to the employer providing the options.

All the anti-avoidance rules against schemes exploiting the payment in kind rule have been aimed at cash conversion schemes, where assets can be easily traded for a fairly certain value. Where employers choose to give employees, eg, works of art or expensive cars without making arrangements for their resale, *Social Security (Contributions) Regulations 2001, SI 2001/1004, Sch 3 Part IV* does not apply. However, without such trading arrangements, most employees will presumably be reluctant to accept such assets by way of remuneration, particularly when 40% or 45% of the cost to the employer must be paid in income tax in due course. It therefore seems unlikely that *Social Security (Contributions) Regulations 2001, SI 2001/1004, Sch 3 Part IV* will be further extended to such items, especially since such transactions now attract a Class 1A charge and most recipients of such assets are likely to have earnings subject to Class 1 already in excess of the Upper Earnings Limit. In some circumstances, HM Revenue and Customs may nonetheless contend that the asset in question is the subject of 'trading arrangements'. With the advent of the 'readily convertible asset' rules, the attention of those looking to reduce their NIC liabilities switched to other areas of the legislation.

However, further evidence of the government's desire to clamp down on 'avoidance' can be found in the *Finance Act 2004*, which introduced a requirement to notify avoidance schemes to the authorities. Whilst those provisions at first dealt only with various taxes (including income tax) and not National Insurance (presumably because it was thought that any scheme that purports to avoid Class 1 National Insurance will also avoid PAYE – even if not an ultimate income tax liability – and so would fall to be notified for those non-NIC reasons), provision was made for similar requirements in respect of National Insurance-only avoidance schemes with effect from 1 May 2007 – see **8.5, 31.3**. Advisors and employers notified 23 NIC avoidance schemes in the first year, but the application of the DOTAS regime and various decisions by the tribunals and courts against past NIC avoidance schemes have led the number of NIC schemes to dwindle to nil. The September 2014 DOTAS statistics from HMRC (see www.gov.uk/government/statistics/tax-avoidance-and-disclosure-statistics) noted that no new NIC avoidance schemes had been notified to HMRC's Counter Avoidance Directorate in the previous year. An update was due by 1 May 2015, but nothing more recent has been published.

Securities (including shares)

[31.3] Securities given to employees are now not automatically regarded as a payment in kind; thus a Class 1 NIC liability can exist unless the transfer falls under a tax-advantaged share scheme (until April 2014, referred to as an HMRC-approved share scheme). [*Social Security (Contributions) Regulations 2001, SI 2001/1004, Reg 22(5)–(10)*; *Social Security (Contributions) Regulations 2001, SI 2001/1004, Sch 3 Part IV para 1*, both as amended by *Social Security (Contributions) (Amendment No 5) Regs 2003, SI 2003/2085, Reg 11*.]

Whilst there is an exception in *Social Security (Contributions) Regulations 2001, SI 2001/1004, Sch 3, Part IX, para 7A* only where there is an acquisition of securities, securities options or interests in securities within *ITEPA 2003, s 471(5)* and the security acquired is not a readily convertible asset, occasions outside approved share schemes where the securities are not actually or deemed to be readily convertible assets will be few and far between. [*Social Security (Contributions) (Amendment No 5) Regulations 2003, SI 2003/2085, Reg 12.*]

It should be noted that from 1 September 2003 a security which is not a readily convertible asset, but in respect of which a corporation tax deduction is not available, is nonetheless to be treated as a readily convertible asset. This matches the PAYE rule. [*Social Security (Contributions) Regulations 2001, SI 2001/1004, Sch 3 Part III para 1*, applying *ITEPA 2003, s 702*; *ITEPA 2003, s 702(5A)*, inserted by *Finance Act 2003, s 140, Sch 22.*]

'*Securities*' is a term that does not merely take its common sense meaning. For NIC purposes, it means, per *Social Security (Contributions) Regulations 2001, SI 2001/1004, Reg 1(2)*, the same as in *ITEPA 2003, s 420* which is as follows:

- shares in a body corporate (wherever incorporated) or in any unincorporated body constituted outside the UK;
- rights under contracts of insurance other than excluded contracts of insurance. [*ITEPA 2003, s 420(1)(aa)*; *Finance Act 2005, s 20*];
- debentures, debenture stock, loan stock, bonds and certificates of deposit;
- warrants and other instruments that entitle their holders to subscribe for securities;
- certificates and other instruments conferring rights in respect of securities held by persons other than the persons on whom the rights are conferred and the transfer of which may be effected without the consent of those persons;
- units in a collective investment scheme;
- futures; and
- rights under contracts for differences or contracts similar to contracts for differences.

[*Social Security (Contributions) Regulations 2001, SI 2001/1004, Reg 1(2)*, as inserted by *Social Security (Contributions) (Amendment No 5) Regs 2003, SI 2003/2085, Reg 4*].

Given the direct link with *ITEPA 2003, s 420* 'securities' includes, with effect from 14 August 2007, alternative finance investment bonds (ie, those falling within *Finance Act 2005, s 48A*). [*Employment Income (Meaning of Securities) Order 2007, SI 2007/2130.*]

Thus from 1 September 2003, a Class 1 National Insurance liability will generally arise whenever there is a 'chargeable event' for income tax purposes under *ITEPA 2003, s 427*. This applies not just to shares and share options, but all securities and also options over such securities (see **31.8**).

Under general UK law a limited liability partnership (LLP) is regarded as a 'body corporate' but HM Revenue and Customs will not normally regard any UK partnership, limited partnership or LLP as a 'body corporate'. Under the 'salaried member' regime for LLPs created by *Finance Act 2014, s 74, Sch 17*, imported into NIC as *SSCBA 1992, s 4A* and the *Social Security (Limited*

Liability Partnership) Regs 2014, regulations made thereunder, while perceived avoidance is tackled by deeming profit shares to be employment income, no steps were taken to treat membership interests as securities or readily convertible assets.

Because the definition in *ITEPA 2003, s 420* is so wide, some of the former heads set out below on which a Class 1 National Insurance charge arose under the specific provisions mentioned ceased to have effect from 1 September 2003, as they now fall within the general charge instead, so separate provision is no longer required.

'*Company*' was defined under the NIC legislation but is not mentioned in terms in *ITEPA 2003, s 420*, which takes the approach of defining the scope of the word 'securities'. The word includes shares or stock in any body corporate constituted under the law of any country or territory and any unincorporated body constituted under the law of a country or territory outside the UK. This does not encompass UK LLPs which do not issue shares or stock to members, although a membership interest in a property investment LLP might conceivably fall within another part of the definition, namely as a unit in a collective investment scheme. Unlike the original *FSA 1986* definition, the NIC definition of 'company' also explicitly included bodies incorporated under the law of any part of the UK relating to building societies within the meaning of *Building Societies Act 1986, s 119(1)*, and industrial and provident societies registered or deemed to be registered under the *Industrial and Provident Societies Act 1965* or the *Industrial and Provident Societies Act (Northern Ireland) 1969*. The *Income Tax (Earnings and Pensions) Act 2003 (ITEPA 2003)* definition of 'securities' sweeps up all these bodies automatically. [*ITEPA 2003, s 420*, and previously *Social Security (Contributions) Regulations 2001, SI 2001/1004, Sch 3 Part IV para 1*.]

It should be noted that, while there was a general trend after 1987 to reward employees in quoted securities, which are usually readily saleable, this category covers both listed and unlisted shares and, from 1 September 2003, securities generally.

Retrospective anti-avoidance legislation was put in place with effect from 2 December 2004. *ITEPA 2003, s 420(8)* was amended to include the proviso that a right or opportunity to acquire securities or an interest in securities will not be treated as a securities option where the main purpose (or one of the main purposes) of the employer in making it available was to avoid tax or NICs. This creates a tax and NIC charge where otherwise none might apply. While an option over readily convertible assets is not taxable or NICable at the point of grant, an option granted as part of a tax avoidance scheme will be treated as a security rather than as an option. These anti-avoidance provisions apply notwithstanding the 2 December 2004 date where something is done on or after that date as part of the arrangements made before that time under which it was made available.

The *National Insurance Contributions Act 2006* provided the power to introduce regulations that would have backdated effect to that date, such regulations being in line with action taken in a Finance Bill [*NICA 2006, ss 1-4*]. The first such regulations were the *Social Security (Contributions)*

(Amendment No 2) Regs 2007, SI 2007/1057 applying Class 1 liability (with effect from 2 December 2004) to amounts chargeable by virtue of *F(No 2)A 2005, s 20, Sch 2* and *FA 2006, s 92*. See **21.3**.

Under *ITEPA 2003, s 428(9)* the taxable amount on a chargeable event is reduced on a pro-rated basis if the consideration for the disposal is less than the actual market value. From 2 December 2004 such a chargeable event that affects such securities and is part of a scheme or arrangement to avoid tax and NICs will not benefit from such pro-rating. [*ITEPA 2003, s 428(10)*; *Finance Act 2005, s 20*].

Previously, regulations excluded from earnings payment by way of shares or stock (including a payment by way of or derived from shares appropriated under what was then an *ICTA 1988, s 186* profit sharing scheme) where such shares or stock formed part of the 'ordinary share capital' of the secondary contributor, a 'company' which has 'control' of that secondary contributor, or a 'company' which either is or has 'control' of a 'body corporate' which is a member of a consortium owning either that secondary contributor or a body corporate having control of that secondary contributor. From 5 December 1996, that exclusion from earnings did not apply if the shares were outside an approved scheme and the shares were tradeable assets. From 1 October 1998 the exclusion did not apply if the shares were readily convertible assets. See HM Revenue and Customs National Insurance Manual NIM06904–06908. [Former *Social Security (Contributions) Regulations 2001, SI 2001/1004, Sch 3 Part IX paras 2 and 8*.]

Further guidelines regarding securities and securities options were set out by the then Inland Revenue in Tax Bulletin Special Edition 7, December 2003 and, as regards workers from or going abroad, in Tax Bulletin Special Edition, April 2005, although some of the policy statements in the latter are of questionable validity, and some have by now been superseded by changes in the legislation.

There can be difficulties where options are granted or shares are awarded outright to employees of a UK subsidiary with a foreign parent (typically but not necessarily in the US). The foreign parent will often overlook supplying details of share/share option events to the UK subsidiary (and in some cases may resent having to do so) and it is the case that in circumstances such as these there are often instances of failure to deal with NIC and PAYE correctly. This can be costly.

National Insurance contributions rules are driven by treaty and wider social policy considerations which do not impinge on income tax. Therefore, the 2008 rules affecting residence for tax purposes and the remittance basis which provide for the apportionment of specific employment income under *ITEPA 2003, Part 7* for income tax and PAYE purposes do not generally apply for the purposes of National Insurance contributions (except for employment-related securities income from 6 April 2015 – see below). Rather, the National Insurance contributions rules are subject to their own provisions relating to internationally mobile employees within the UK legislation and/or international social security agreements.

HM Revenue and Customs used to contend that, in the context of the EC Regulations, securities income could be time-apportioned, though it is questionable whether this was correct. With a view to finally putting some of the questionable policies in TBSE 2005 on a sound footing, HMRC introduced from 6 April 2015 statutory time-apportionment of gains for 'internationally mobile employees' (ie, where employees work in more than one state during the currency of an option or share scheme). See **51.64** regarding expatriates and employment-related securities for a full explanation of how the new rules have been framed.

[*Social Security (Contributions) Regulations 2001, SI 2001/1004, Sch 3, Part 9, para 18, inserted by Social Security (Miscellaneous Amendments No 2) Regulations 2015, SI 2015/478, Reg 21*].

In *McLoughlin v Revenue & Customs Commissioners* [2006] STC SCD 467 Sp C 542 the provision of shares to an employee some years after he had been promised a share of the proceeds upon the incorporation of the partnership employing him was held by the Commissioners to be employment income at the time the shares were provided. McLoughlin contended unsuccessfully that the offer and not the employment was the source of the shares.

Founder shares

[31.4] All shares and other securities acquired in connection with employment fall within the employment-related securities regime – this includes the acquisition of securities even if not received under any formal scheme or plan, and also includes the acquisition of shares on the formation of a company (sometimes called 'founder's shares') by persons who go on to become employees and/or directors. Further, since the legislation also applies to office holders, a charge could potentially arise in respect of a company secretary despite his not also being either a director or employee.

In the case of a founder's share, if the founder pays full unrestricted market value at acquisition (which will typically be the case where a new company is created with £2 of share capital) then there will be no charge as the quantum of the 'benefit' obtained is zero. However, if any value is subsequently passed to the founder otherwise than through natural commercial growth or dividends out of commercial profits then both PAYE and Class 1 NIC are likely to arise under the employment-related securities rules.

Corporate restructures

[31.5] The introduction by *Finance Act 2003, Sch 22* of the (then) new employment-related securities regime created some new uncertainties. *ITEPA 2003, s 421B(3)* provides that where a right or opportunity to acquire securities or an interest in securities is made available by a person's employer (or a person connected with the employer) that right is to be treated as made available by reason of the employment unless the right or opportunity is made available by an individual and it is made available in the course of the domestic, family or personal relationships of that person. This may clearly cause concern in relation to – inter alia – the treatment of earn-outs in a company sale where these are satisfied by loan notes in the acquirer, shares in the acquirer, or a mixture. A right of this kind could fall within the definition of a securities option (*ITEPA 2003, s 420(8)*). Thus in the appropriate circumstances a Class 1 National Insurance charge would arise. However, the former Inland Revenue confirmed that where an earn-out fully represents the consideration for the sale of the (target) company's shares (as will usually be the case), the potential National Insurance charges will not be applied. Conversely, where all or part of an earn-out relates to value provided to an employee as a reward for services over a performance period, the remuneration element will constitute taxable earnings under the *ITEPA 2003* regime, with potential Class 1 liability accordingly. (Memorandum of Understanding (MoU) between the then Inland Revenue and British Venture Capital Association, 25 July 2003).

Subsequently, in August 2006, HM Revenue and Customs announced that where shares are acquired under a ratchet but in accordance with arrangements consistent with those set out in sections 1 to 5 of the MoU no *ITEPA 2003, Chapter 4* benefit charge will arise on either the disposal of shares or earlier operation of the ratchet. Where the ratchet meets the conditions in section 6(2)(a)(b) of the MoU the gains realised on exit will be subject to capital gains tax only.

In other circumstances charges may be possible under *Chapters 3B*, *3C* and *4* and *s 62* (general earnings).

Key indicators that HM Revenue and Customs will take account of in determining whether an earn-out is further sale consideration rather than remuneration are whether:

- the sale agreement demonstrates that the earn-out is part of the valuable consideration given for the securities in the old company;
- the value received from the earn-out reflects the value of the securities given up;
- where the vendor continues to be employed in the business, the earn-out is not compensation for the vendor not being fully remunerated for continuing employment with the company;
- where the vendor continues to be employed, the earn-out is not conditional on future employment, beyond a reasonable requirement to stay to protect the value of the business being sold;
- where the vendor continues to be employed, there are no personal performance targets incorporated in the earn-out; and
- non-employees or former employees receive the earn-out on the same terms as employees remaining.

The following factors may also be relevant:

- negotiations between the seller and buyer as to the level of the earn-out in relation to the value of the consideration given for securities in the old company;

- any clearance that might have been obtained under *TCGA 1992, s 138* and *TA 1988, s 707* (now the *Income Tax Act 2007, ss 701, 702* and the *Corporation Tax Act 2010, ss 748, 749*) demonstrating the bona fide nature of the transactions, and the level of the earn-out linked to profitability or other key performance indicators of the business; and
- evidence that future bonuses were reclassified or commuted into purchase consideration would indicate that the earn-out was, at least partly, remuneration rather than consideration for the disposal of securities.

[Employment Related Securities Manual ERSM110940]

See also Employment Related Securities Manual ERSM30520, ERSM30530 and ERSM90500.

Post-acquisition benefits

[31.6] *ITEPA 2003, s 447* (in *Chapter 4*) imposes a tax charge on what are termed 'post-acquisition benefits' derived from employment-related securities. It applies to UK resident employees, and to cross-border employees in a split year for the part of the year in which they are resident in the UK. It is a mopping up provision which taxes any benefits which have not been caught elsewhere in *ITEPA 2003, Chapters 2-3D*, or otherwise taxed as employment income for the employee or another associated person.

Where a tax charge arises under this provision there will also be a Class 1 National Insurance liability if what is received is cash or a readily convertible asset (see **31.21**). The charge may apply to any benefit received after 16 April 2003, regardless of when the securities were received, but only applies to those that are employment-related. This means that securities that can be shown to have been acquired through a personal relationship, such as gifts from friends and family, are unaffected. The most common benefits that HMRC have in mind here are dividends, if paid as employment reward or if the anti-avoidance clause is breached, but benefits can equally include things such as free ferry journeys, vouchers and bonus shares.

Non-employee investors should, of course, not be affected. A benefit may only come into charge in this way if it is not taxed elsewhere or where something has been done which affects the employment-related securities as part of a scheme or arrangement, the main purpose (or one of the main purposes) of which is the avoidance of tax or National Insurance contributions. [*ITEPA 2003, s 447(4)*]. Whilst dividends will be otherwise charged to tax already, it is the second leg just mentioned that may impose extra charges on dividends in certain circumstances. HM Revenue and Customs says that this does not mean that it will challenge all small companies who choose to pay dividends as their chosen method of profit extraction (HM Revenue and Customs Employment Related Securities Manual ERSM90060). Further, if either the IR35 rules or the managed service company rules (see **40 INTERMEDIARIES**) apply to the company, *s 447* will not apply, as those deemed income rules will have taxed the income already. There are also possible exceptions where the company is employee-controlled or the majority of the company's shares of the class in question are not employment-related securities. [*ITEPA 2003, s 449*].

The Paymaster General at the time (Dawn Primarolo MP) made the following statement in the Standing Committee on Finance (No 3) Bill 2005 on 21 June 2005 to clarify the scope of an amendment in this connection:

> 'These arrangements are devised to deal with the minority of cases where there are complex, contrived arrangements to avoid paying Income Tax and National Insurance on employment rewards. The Government have made clear their intention to close that activity down permanently.
>
> There has been some debate about whether small businesses are caught by the provisions, so I am grateful to have the opportunity to offer small businesses some reassurance.
>
> A change being made to *Chapter 4* of the *Income Tax (Earnings and Pensions) Act 2003* will remove, where avoidance is involved, the provision that automatically exempts benefits received in connection with securities from a full Income Tax and National Insurance charge, if Income Tax has been paid elsewhere. I am aware, from representations made directly to me and my department, that professionals have expressed concern about the possible scope of the change. I want to make it clear that this change does not bring all benefits derived from securities into a tax and National Insurance charge. A reference to benefits in the context of the schedule means the employment reward—the passing of value to an employee in return for the employee's labour. Where investors are carrying out their normal investment transaction, this charge will not affect them.
>
> The purpose test introduced in *section 447* of the 2003 Act has been carefully designed to target complex, contrived avoidance arrangements that are used mainly to disguise cash bonuses. If taxpayers use contrived arrangements to get round anti-avoidance legislation—to avoid paying the proper amount of tax and National Insurance—they cannot expect to be excluded from the charge. However, it will be absolutely clear from what I say about the purpose test that this measure will not affect the taxation of those small businesses that do not use contrived schemes to disguise remuneration to avoid tax and National Insurance.'

Where dividends from special purpose vehicle companies (eg, set up to pay bonuses), or dividends from special shares in an employing company, are used for avoidance (being disguised cash bonuses or additional remuneration) HM Revenue and Customs considers that *ITEPA 2003, Chapter 4* applies and the dividends are liable to full income tax and Class 1 NIC. See ERSM90210.

Restricted securities

[31.7] Shares (and other securities) are treated from 16 April 2003 as 'restricted securities' if they are subject to forfeiture or have other restrictions which result in the securities having a lower market value than would otherwise be the case.

Where the securities are readily convertible assets (see **31.21**) and are subject to forfeiture in less than five years or there are other restrictions, Class 1 NIC will be due, not when the securities are acquired, but when the restrictions are lifted or the risk of forfeiture expires. The amount so liable will be the amount by which the market value has increased as a result of the change. However, it is possible to enter into an election under *ITEPA 2003, s 431* (on acquisition), *s 430* (post acquisition chargeable event) or *s 425* (shares subject to forfeiture) to pay Class 1 NIC (and PAYE) on the unrestricted market value (less any price paid or value given) at the time of the award or other chargeable event. Any future growth in value then falls outside the employment related securities regime, outside the scope of NIC liability and will be subject only to capital gains tax unless HMRC levies a charge under *Chapters 3–4A* of *Part 7* of *ITEPA 2003* (convertible securities, manipulation of market value, acquisition at under-value, or post-acquisition benefit). There is no refund of tax or NIC if the subsequent market value is lower.

Such an election must be jointly made by both the employee and employer, in a form approved by HM Revenue and Customs and must be made within 14 days after acquisition of the securities in question. The election is irrevocable. Once signed, the original or a copy of the election must be retained by the parties to it. Neither need be submitted to HM Revenue and Customs. They may, however, be requested for inspection as part of an employer compliance review or similar enquiry. Specimen forms of election can be found at the links shown in the Employment Related Securities Manual ERSM30370 (forfeiture) and Employment Related Securities Manual ERSM30450 (restricted securities).

In the case of shares acquired under tax-advantaged (formerly known as 'approved') schemes (see **31.12**) but which nonetheless carry one or more restrictions there is a deemed election under *ITEPA 2003, s 431A* so that the tax-advantaged position is obtained on the full unrestricted market value of the shares.

As regards restricted securities, HMRC Shares & Assets Valuation is reported as accepting that shares in companies which impose identical restrictions on all their shares through the Articles of Association (and on which no additional restrictions have been imposed) are not restricted securities (Taxation, 2 December 2004, page 240).

For some years, there has been uncertainty about the correct treatment of so-called 'restricted stock units' or RSUs, which are arrangements used to incentivise employees over a longer period by linking their reward to shares and other securities without actually transferring to them any of those shares or securities. Typically, bonuses or the ability to claim a bonus would be linked to the performance of the employer's share price, and rights might be forfeited in certain circumstances. It has not been clear whether the charge to tax on any rewards so received should be under the part of the legislation that deals with income tax on earnings or the specific rules that deal with securities options (see below). Since the NIC treatment follows the tax treatment in most employment-related securities situations, the correct choice can have a significant effect on NIC liabilities.

Finance Act 2016, s 17 made changes to *ITEPA 2003, s 418* with effect from 6 April 2016 to ensure that acquisition of RSUs or events such as exercise are clearly to be charged to tax under the rules that deal with securities options, rather than those that deal with earnings. *ITEPA 2003, s 227* was amended to ensure that any transaction falling within the new *s 418(1A)* would be excluded from earnings for tax purposes, which automatically has the same effect for NIC purposes. Liabilities arising under the securities options rules are particularly relevant to internationally mobile employees (IMEs), and the changes lead to gains on RSUs that give rise to a NIC liability (ie, as if an option has been exercised) now being time-apportioned as described at **51.64** below.

Securities options

[31.8] A Class 1 NIC liability will generally arise where securities (which are or are deemed to be readily convertible assets – see **31.21**) are acquired by an employee (or an associated person) as a result of:

- the exercise of an employment-related securities option;
- where such an option is assigned or released for cash or for a readily convertible asset; or
- the employee (or a person associated with the employee receives a benefit in cash or money's worth (eg, compensation for loss of the option where there is a company takeover, etc).

'Phantom options' are not options for this purpose and the cash received is subject to NIC and tax in the same way as any other bonus.

Where an employer reserves a right to pay cash at the time of exercise of an option, then as there is no absolute right to receive securities, again the cash or securities are subject to NIC and tax as for any other cash payment. The position is different where it is the employee who has the right to have the exercise value paid in cash – here any cash received is subject to NIC and tax as such, but any securities received are liable as an option exercise.

There can be difficulties where options are granted or shares are awarded outright to employees of a UK subsidiary with a foreign parent (typically but not necessarily in the US). The foreign parent will often overlook supplying details of share/share option events to the UK subsidiary (and in some cases may resent having to do so) and it is the case that in circumstances such as these there are often instances of failure to deal with NIC and PAYE correctly. This can be costly, especially when an employee fails to make good the PAYE due on an acquisition of employment-related securities within the 90 days allowed, which can trigger a benefit in kind charge under *ITEPA 2003, s 222*.

A rights issue in respect of employment-related securities is an employment-related securities option chargeable under *ITEPA 2003, Chapter 5*. In practice because the issue reduces the value of shares already held, the chargeable amount will, except in very unusual circumstances, be zero.

As noted at **31.7** above, the securities options rules clearly apply to restricted stock units with effect from 6 April 2016 (and arguably applied in any case before that date).

Transfer of secondary liability to employee

[31.9] Concern was expressed, particularly on behalf of e-commerce and high-tech companies, at the charging of the employer's National Insurance contribution at the then 12.2% rate on wholly unpredictable gains arising on the exercise of unapproved options. Following the 2000 Budget, the Government legislated to allow all or part of the employer's NIC liability to be met by the employee by mutual agreement. Alternatively, liability may be formally transferred to the employee. [*SSCBA 1992, Sch 1, paras 3A, 3B*, as amended by *National Insurance Contributions and Statutory Payments Act 2004, ss 3, 4*; *SI 2001/1004, Reg 69*.] Model agreements can be found in HM Revenue and Customs' ERSM170750. HM Revenue and Customs has also made available two new approved forms of joint election under *ITEPA 2003, s 431* for use with EMI options accessible through its website. See also IR Press Releases, 5 and 10 September 2003; CWG2 (2018–19), para 5.15.1; Society of Share Scheme Practitioners November 1996; Budget Press Release and IR Press Release 189/00.

Legislation was introduced into the *National Insurance Contributions Act 2006* to ensure that elections only provide that the facility for employers to pass on the secondary NICs liability to employees is limited to the original intended purpose which was to deal with future unpredictable secondary employers' liabilities. The additional amendment ensures that an employee and employer entering into an election to transfer secondary NICs cannot transfer any retrospective liability. See **21.3**. [*Social Security Contributions (Share Options) Act 2001, s 1(6)*; *Social Security (Contributions) Regulations 2001, SI 2001/1004, Sch 5 para 1*; *Social Security (Contributions) (Amendment No 3) Regulations 2007, SI 2007/1175, Reg 2*].

No relief against the National Insurance liability is given for any employer's National Insurance that is in fact met by the employee. [*Social Security (Contributions) Regulations 2001, SI 2001/1004, Sch 2 para 7(2)*.] However, the employer liability borne by the employee is deducted in computing the latter's income tax liability.

'Dot-com' freezing election

[31.10] Where options were granted on or after 6 April 1999 but before 19 May 2000, the legislative change in **31.9** was of no help. A further measure contained in the *Social Security Contributions (Share Options) Act 2001* enabled companies to elect to 'freeze' the Class 1 liability to the 7 November 2000 value of the shares if an election was made, and payment also made, within 92 days of the Act receiving Royal Assent. This 92 day period expired on 10 August 2001. [*Social Security Contributions (Share Options) Act 2001* and *Social Security (Contributions) Regulations 2001, SI 2001/1004, Sch 4 para 23, Sch 5 paras 1–3*]. If however, there would have been no liability as at 7 November 2000 either because the shares and options were not 'readily convertible assets' or because the market value was at that time less than the exercise price then no formal election was required, as the Act provided that, in these circumstances, an election was deemed to have been made.

Once either an actual or deemed election existed, then there was no NIC liability on any uplift in value after 7 November 2000. The number of options granted in the relevant period is now likely to be minimal, but care must be taken with any such surviving old options exercised now so as to avoid paying NICs again because the freezing rule is overlooked.

Example

Alex joined Benevolent Ltd on 1 May 2000 and on that day he received share options in an unapproved scheme over 50,000 ordinary 25 pence shares at an exercise price of £2.78 per share, the market value at that date. These shares were valued at £1.50 per share on 7 November 2000. Benevolent's shares are readily convertible assets (RCAs). The options were exercised on 17 May 2007 when the market value of the shares was £5 each.

Value on exercise	50,000 × £5 =	£250,000
Exercise price	50,000 × £2.78 =	£139,000
Realised gain		£111,000

However, as the options were 'underwater' on 7 November 2000 the deemed election under *SSSOA 2001* produced a nil liability rather than a liability on the 'gain' of £111,000. In the event of an employer compliance visit, it might well have been that the officer was unaware of this provision and might simply have assessed 'arrears' of NIC due. Benevolent will have needed to assert its legislative authority for the nil liability that the law required.

University 'spin-outs'

[31.11] *ITEPA 2003, Part 7, Chapter 4A* covers shares and securities issued or put under option by university 'spin-out' companies. Some discussions took place between the former Inland Revenue and the University Companies Association (UNICO), as result of which the latter issued a Memorandum of Understanding on 14 April 2004. See ERSM100340. However, on the day of the Pre-Budget Report 2004, it was announced that reliefs were to be introduced for these companies. *Finance Act 2005, ss 20, 21* duly introduced *Chapter 4A.*

The legislation prevents both income tax and National Insurance charges arising on researchers in respect of an increase in the value of shares in the spin-out company due to the transfer of intellectual property covered by the research institution's intellectual property-sharing policy. The relief only applies at the time of transfer of the intellectual property, or at the time the researcher acquires his shares, provided the latter is not more than 90 days after the former. Where the spin-out company issues restricted shares, a charge would normally apply when the restriction is lifted, subject to the right of the employer and employee to elect that the effect of any restrictions should be disregarded such that tax and National Insurance is charged on the unrestricted value at acquisition. The legislation enabled an election to be made no later than 15 October 2005 for income tax and NICs to be deferred unless or until the company was successful. Further, some relief also applies to spin-out companies set up before 2 December 2004, but again only if an election was made by 15 October 2005. See Taxation 19 May 2005, page 185.

See ERSM100000.

Tax-advantaged schemes

[31.12] Excluded from earnings are certain payments by way of an option or share award granted under what was, until 6 April 2014, usually known as a 'Revenue-approved share scheme'.

Most gains and payments under these schemes (other than cash for surrendering rights) are excluded from NIC liability, even if they involve transactions in readily-convertible assets, provided there is no income tax charge. Under the simplification agenda promoted by the Office of Tax Simplification, *FA 2014, Sch 8* introduced new nomenclature. In particular, all the tax-advantaged schemes are now registered and self-certified by the employer rather than being 'approved' by HMRC. As a result, reference to them is now made according to the location of the main rules in *ITEPA 2003* as follows:

- a share incentive plan is now a 'Schedule 2 SIP';
- a savings-related SAYE scheme is now a 'Schedule 3 SAYE option scheme'; and
- a company share option plan is now a 'Schedule 4 CSOP'.

Enterprise Management Incentive (EMI) option schemes (for which the legislation is found in *Schedule 5*) were already self-certified and have not been re-named.

Also excluded from earnings for NIC purposes are 'unapproved' options (ie, those outside the above framework) where neither the option nor the underlying securities (either at grant or exercise) are readily convertible assets. [*Social Security (Contributions) Regulations 2001, SI 2001/1004, Sch 3 Part IX*.]

In the case of the EMI there is an individual limit of £250,000 (£120,000 before 16 June 2012) which is the maximum unrestricted value of shares that an employee may have under option at the time of grant. [*ITEPA 2003, Sch 5, para 6*.] At the same time, the company must have less than 250 (full-time equivalent) employees (*para 12A*) and no more than £30 million gross assets (*para 12*). See www.gov.uk/hmrc-internal-manuals/employee-tax-advantaged-share-scheme-user-manual/etassum50000. There is no lower limit on the exercise period, which can therefore be very short, but if the option is not exercised within ten years of grant its tax advantages are lost.

One non-tax advantage of EMI over unapproved options is that HM Revenue and Customs will agree market values in advance of the grant of the options. Provided the exercise price is no lower than market value there will not generally be a charge to income tax or Class 1 National Insurance on the exercise. If the exercise price is below market value, then income tax will be payable on exercise and if the shares are actually or deemed by *ITEPA 2003 s 702(5A)* to be readily convertible assets, the tax will be due in the form of PAYE and there will be Class 1 National Insurance contributions liability.

No charges arise on grant, whether the price is full market value or at a discount. Where EMI options are granted at a discount, an income tax charge and almost certainly a Class 1 National Insurance charge will arise, when the options are exercised, on the discount at grant that was built in to the options from the outset.

Where an option falls out of the EMI regime because of a 'disqualifying event' (eg, the employee ceases to be eligible, or the company is taken over and comes under the control of another company), the employee is allowed 90 days (40 days before 17 July 2013) to exercise with the full EMI tax advantages, but thereafter the option becomes unapproved. The result is that any built-in discount at grant and any post-event gain are treated as earnings for both tax and NIC purposes.

EMI is attractive to companies as they can obtain corporation tax relief on the value of shares at exercise less the exercise price paid, and for the option holder in a typical case there will be neither income tax nor National Insurance charges on exercise on the gain over the market value at grant (or exercise price if higher). Any such gain on exercise falls only within the capital gains tax regime.

There will always be a charge to Class 1 NIC if an approved option is assigned or released either for cash or for a readily convertible asset (see **31.21**).

Similarly there will be Class 1 NIC (and PAYE) liability where a CSOP option over a readily convertible asset is exercised on or after 9 April 2004 in circumstances that do not attract tax relief (eg, less than three years after the last exercise, or after grant, unless exercised as a 'good leaver' within six months of leaving, ie, due to injury, disability, redundancy, retirement within the scheme rules, or on a TUPE transfer, or on the employing company leaving the group operating the scheme, or more than ten years after grant). Scheme rules must now permit the personal representatives to exercise within 12 months of the employee's death, which should be without a NIC charge in any event because the relevant contributor is deceased. [*Sch 4, para 25* as amended by *FA 2014, Sch 8, para 175*.]

Tax charges may arise under a SIP in accordance with *ITEPA 2003, ss 500-508*. The rules apply to those who at the time of award are UK resident earners or those with UK duties taxable under *Part 2, Chapters 4* or *5*.

If the participant enjoys a capital receipt from free, matching or partnership shares within five years of the award, or dividend shares within three years of their acquisition, any value received is treated as employment income. No charge arises if the recipient is deceased. [*ITEPA 2003, s 501*.]

Any amounts of partnership share money returned to the participant will equally be treated as employment income. [*ITEPA 2003, s 503*.]

If anyone pays the employee in respect of the cancellation of a partnership share agreement, the payment will also be treated as employment income. [*ITEPA 2003, s 504*.]

If free, matching or partnership shares are withdrawn from the plan (but not forfeited) within three years of the award or acquisition, the market value at the exit date is treated as employment income. [*ITEPA 2003, ss 505(2), 506(2)*.] If the period between grant and withdrawal of free or matching is between three and five years, the lesser of the market value at the award date and the market value at the exit date is treated as employment income, after deduction of any amount already taxed under *s 501*. [*ITEPA 2003, s 505(3)*.]

In the case of partnership shares withdrawn in the same timescale, the deemed employment income is the lesser of the partnership share money used to buy the shares and the market value at the exit date. [*ITEPA 2003, s 506(3)*.]

If the holder of shares in a SIP assigns, charges or otherwise disposes of a beneficial interest in them, the market value at the point of disposal is treated as employment income. [*ITEPA 2003, s 507*.]

Social Security (Contributions) Regulations 2001, SI 2001/1004, Reg 22(8) deems to be earnings for NIC purposes any of the amounts subject to PAYE by virtue of *ITEPA 2003, ss 500-508* above.

Employee priority share allocations

[31.13] Any payment by way of any benefit which is free of income tax liability by virtue of *FA 1988, s 68(1)* or, from 1 September 2003, *ITEPA 2003, s 542* is excluded from earnings. [*Social Security (Contributions) Regulations 2001, SI 2001/1004, Sch 3 Part IX para 5* as amended by (*Social Security (Contributions) (Amendment No 5) Regulations 2003, SI 2003/2085, Reg 12(7)*)].

Securities pre-1 September 2003

[31.14] The history of NIC being applied to share awards and share options is long and convoluted. For information about the position before the *ITEPA 2003* rules were applied, ie, 1 September 2003, readers should refer to earlier editions of this work.

Other exclusions

[31.15] As well as the previously mentioned exclusions for shares and options which are not readily convertible assets and the grant of share options which are not exercisable more than ten years after grant, there are also the following exceptions:

- certain conditional shares where there exists no charge under *ITEPA 2003, s 425* (other than by virtue of *s 425(2)*) and that interest is treated as earnings. See HM Revenue and Customs Manuals NIM06911. The exception does not, however, apply where an election has been made under *ITEPA 2003, s 425(3)*. [*Social Security (Contributions) Regulations 2001, SI 2001/1004, Sch 3 Part IX para 9*, as amended with effect from 1 September 2003 by *Social Security (Contributions) (Amendment No 5) Regulations 2003, SI 2003/2085, Reg 12(11)*];
- anti-avoidance legislation was brought in from 2 December 2004 to ensure that employment-related securities that are, or are an interest in, redeemable securities will now come within *Chapter 2* of *ITEPA 2003, Part 7* to ensure that if additional value is transferred to an employee at a later date when the restriction is lifted then this will be chargeable to tax and NICs. Where securities are within *Chapter 2*, the requirement that those securities were restricted securities or a restricted interest in

securities at acquisition is removed from 2 December 2004, even where the securities were acquired before that date. However, where certain partly-paid shares or securities that have restrictions on sale where employment ceases through, for example, misconduct, do not come within *Chapter 2* unless one of the main reasons was the avoidance of tax and NICs, in which case the securities would be included. [*ITEPA 2003, ss 424, 428*; *Finance Act 2005, s 20*.] See also below for the restriction in pro-rating under *ITEPA 2003, s 428(10)*;

Options to acquire certain assets

[31.16] Options to acquire or dispose of the following may not be treated as a payment in kind when the beneficial ownership of the option is transferred to an employee or director.

(a) Currency of the UK or of any other country or territory.

(b) Gold, silver, palladium or platinum.

(c) Any asset within any other paragraph of *Social Security (Contributions) Regulations 2001, SI 2001/1004, Sch 3 Part IV*.

(d) Options to acquire or dispose of any of the options listed in (a) to (c) above.

This paragraph covers only options over the commodities in question, not the underlying assets themselves. From 1 December 1993, those are however included in *Sch 3 Part III* (see **31.21** and **31.22**). Until that date, commodities within (c) might have been used in appropriate circumstances to pay remuneration free of Class 1 liability.

[*Social Security (Contributions) Regulations 2001, SI 2001/1004, Sch 3 Part IV para 6*.]

Alcoholic liquor

[31.17] With the inclusion of gold bullion in what is now *Social Security (Contributions) Regulations 2001, SI 2001/1004, Sch 3 Part III*, some employers began to pay bonuses in the form of cases of fine wines stored in bond (ie where no VAT or duty had been paid or was payable on a transfer). From 24 August 1994, the exclusions also embraced any alcoholic liquor within the meaning of *Alcoholic Liquor Duties Act 1979, s 1* in respect of which no duty has been paid under that Act. *ALDA 1979, s 1* does not cover angostura bitters or methylated spirits. Because of *Social Security (Contributions) Regulations 2001, SI 2001/1004, Sch 3 Part IV para 12* (below), payments of bonuses in the form of vouchers exchangeable for alcoholic liquor ceased at the same time to be effective in avoiding Class 1 liability.

[*Social Security (Contributions) Regulations 2001, SI 2001/1004, Sch 3 Part IV para 9*.]

Gemstones

[31.18] From 24 August 1994, *Sch 3 Part IV* was also extended to include any gemstone, defined as including stones such as diamond, emerald, ruby, sapphire, amethyst, jade, opal or topaz and organic gemstones such as amber or pearl, whether cut or uncut and whether or not having an industrial use. Because of *Social Security (Contributions) Regulations 2001, SI 2001/1004, Sch 3 Part IV para 12* (below), payments of bonuses in the form of vouchers exchangeable for diamonds, etc ceased at the same time to be effective in avoiding Class 1 liability.

[*Social Security (Contributions) Regulations 2001, SI 2001/1004, Sch 3 Part IV para 10.*]

Certificates conferring rights in respect of assets

[31.19] Also excluded from relief under *Social Security (Contributions) Regulations 2001, SI 2001/1004, Sch 3 Part II para 1* are certificates or other instruments which confer:

- property rights in respect of (a) any securities (see **31.2** above), (b) certain debentures and other securities for loans, (c) loan stocks and public and local authorities, (d) alcoholic liquor (see **31.17** above) or (e) gemstones (see **31.18** above); any asset falling within (a), (d) or (e) only from 1 September 2003);
- any right to acquire, dispose of, underwrite or convert an asset, being a right to which the holder would be entitled if he held any such asset to which the certificate or instrument relates; or
- a contractual right (other than an option) to acquire any such asset otherwise than by subscription.

[*Social Security (Contributions) Regulations 2001, SI 2001/1004, Sch 3 Part IV para 11.*]

Insurance contracts

[31.20] Before 6 November 1991, some employers were remunerating their employees by taking out investment-type life assurance policies and assigning the benefit to those employees, then paying money or transferring a holding of gilts to the insurer to increase the value of the policy.

Accordingly another category of asset within the scope of the anti-avoidance regulations is any contract, the effecting and carrying out of which constitutes long-term business falling within Class I (life and annuity business), Class III (linked long-term business) or Class VI (capital redemption business) specified in *Financial Services and Markets Act 2000 (Regulated Activities) Order 2001, SI 2001/544, Sch 1, Part II*. The other classes of business in *FSMA 2000, Sch 1* are birth and marriage contracts, permanent health contracts and tontines, none of which would be of importance in the context of employee remuneration.

Where the provisions of a contract of insurance are such that the effecting and carrying out of the contract constitutes both long-term business and general business (within the meaning of *FSMA 2000*) or long-term business despite the inclusion of subsidiary general business provisions, the contract is deemed to be long term business for the purposes of *Social Security (Contributions) Regulations 2001, SI 2001/1004, Sch 3 Part II para 2(1)(a)(ii)*. [*Social Security (Contributions) Regulations 2001, SI 2001/1004, Sch 3 Part II para 2(3)*.]

As *Social Security (Contributions) Regulations 2001, SI 2001/1004, Sch 3 Part II para 2* is confined to circumstances in which a beneficial interest is conferred, some employers tried to circumvent the regulations by making payments into single premium life policies already owned by their employees, arguing that this merely inflated the value of the policy but did not represent the conferment of a beneficial interest. Alternatively, the employer made the single premium life contract himself with a nominal premium, assigned the benefit of the almost worthless policy to the employee and followed this with a large payment into the policy. While the initial transfer conferred a beneficial interest, the value of the earnings was minimal, and the second premium did not confer an interest in the policy. It is doubtful whether this route successfully avoided Class 1 liability but it was in any event stopped from 2 December 2004 by anti-avoidance legislation (see below). The second premium was in cash, not kind, it clearly represented remuneration or profit derived from the employment, and was made for the benefit of the earner. It was therefore arguably chargeable to Class 1 contributions under *SSCBA 1992, s 6(1)*. The counter-argument was that the payment must also have been received in kind, as 'earnings' are defined in *SSCBA 1992, s 3(1)(a)* as remuneration or profit derived from an employment, ie by reference to their receipt rather than their payment. The Contributions Agency challenged a number of such schemes and the initial absence of further anti-avoidance legislation suggested that the DSS lawyers may have felt that none was needed to defeat the schemes at that time. *Finance Act 1998, s 66* inserting what is now *ITEPA 2003, s 697* as amended by *Income Tax (Employments) (Notional Payments) (Amendment) Regs 1998, SI 1998/189*, sought to make the authorities' intentions clear as regarded the operation of PAYE from 6 April 1998 (enhancement expenditure on existing assets). The same change took place for NIC purposes with effect from 1 October 1998.

Nonetheless three unreported cases were won in the High Court by the employers in 2000, under the pre-1999 Secretary of State Questions 'appeal' procedure. [*Tullett and Tokyo Forex International Ltd and others v Secretary of State for Social Security* QB [2000] EWHC Admin 350; 25 May 2000 CO/2038/1999]. The then Inland Revenue decided to apply the decision in other life policy cases. The *Telent* appeal, discussed at **29.20**, is relevant here. Telent contended that the effect of the QB decision in *Tullett & Tokyo Forex International Ltd v Secretary of State for Social Security* was that Class 1 NICs were not due on contributions it had made to a FURBS. The Special Commissioner reviewed the evidence in detail, rejected this contention and dismissed the appeal. The Commissioner distinguished *Tullett & Tokyo Forex International Ltd* on the grounds that that case referred to a 'payment in kind' – gilts were transferred to the life office – whereas the payments made by Telent were not within the definition of 'payments in kind'. The Commissioner also observed that for a charge to arise under *SSCBA 1992, s 6(1)*, 'earnings must be "paid to or for the benefit of" the employed earner. The effect of any disregard (under *Social Security Regulations 2001, Sch 3 Part II para 1*) is that the relevant element of the individual's earnings is to be excluded from the calculation of his or her total earnings for NIC purposes; the element in question remains "earnings" as defined, but is not chargeable.' See *Telent plc v HMRC* [2008] STC SCD 202 Sp C 632. The more recent Supreme Court decision in *Forde & McHugh Ltd v Revenue and Customs Comrs* [2014] UKSC 14 suggests that *Telent* was wrongly decided, although for a different reason that has no bearing on the payment in kind issue. It might, however, have been useful in supporting the decision in *Tullett & Tokyo*.

Anti-avoidance legislation was brought in from 2 December 2004 to ensure that contracts of insurance, other than excluded contracts, come within the definition of securities (and are thus liable to Class 1 National Insurance). These contracts other than excluded contracts will also not be regarded as instruments creating or acknowledging indebtedness or where there are rights under insurance contracts. Rights under such contracts will not be regarded as rights under contracts for differences or contracts similar to contracts for differences within point 8 above. [*ITEPA 2003, s 420(1)(aa)(b) and (g)*.]

Certain insurance contracts having the same meaning as contracts within *Financial Services and Markets Act 2000 (Regulated Activities) Order 2001, SI 2001/544, Sch 1, Part II* continue to be excluded contracts within the new anti-avoidance provisions as follows:

- contracts for an annuity that is or will become pension income;
- contracts of long-term insurance, other than an annuity contract, which are not capable of acquiring a surrender value on conversion or in any other circumstances;
- contracts of general insurance provided that the contract would not be accounted for as a financial asset or liability in accordance with generally accepted accounting practice within *ITEPA 2003, s 420(1A)(c)*; *FA 2004, s 50*.

[*Social Security (Contributions) Regulations 2001, SI 2001/1004, Sch 3 Part II para 2(1)(a)(ii)*].

Readily convertible assets

[31.21] Following the introduction of the previous *Sch 1A para 9C* (now *Sch 3 Part III*) a number of companies and their advisers continued to advocate the use of the items referred to below and similar items in order to avoid the incidence of NIC. The authorities said that they did not accept the 'narrow interpretation' of this law but to prevent further doubt a new term 'readily convertible asset' was introduced for PAYE purposes from 6 April 1998 (*FA 1998, s 65*, amending what is now *ITEPA 2003, ss 696, 702*) and also applies for NIC purposes from 1 October 1998. [*Social Security (Contributions) Regulations 2001, SI 2001/1004, Sch 3 Part III paras 1*, 2, as amended by *Social Security (Contributions) (Amendment No 5) Regulations 2003, SI 2003/2085, Reg 10(2)*.]

See HM Revenue and Customs National Insurance Manual NIM06909 and SE11803.

Social Security (Contributions) Regulations 2001, SI 2001/1004, Sch 3 Part III para 1 imposes a liability in respect of a readily convertible asset which *ITEPA 2003, s 702(1)* defines as:

- an asset capable of being sold or otherwise realised on a recognised investment exchange (within the meaning of the *FSMA 2000, s 285 (1)(a)*) or on the London Bullion Market (see below) eg stocks, shares and other financial instruments, gold bullion and other precious metals, etc;
- an asset capable of being sold on the New York Stock Exchange;
- an asset capable of being sold or otherwise realised on a market for the time being specified in PAYE regulations;
- an asset consisting in the rights of an assignee, or any other rights, in respect of a money debt that is or may become due to the employer or any other person;
- any property that is subject to a fiscal warehousing regime eg oriental or Persian carpets stored in 'bond';
- anything that is likely (without anything being done by the employee) to give rise to, or to become, a right enabling a person to obtain an amount or total amount of money which is likely to be similar to the expense incurred in the provision of the asset eg an interest in a trust which comes to an end shortly after being assigned to an employee;
- an asset for which trading arrangements (see **31.22**) are in existence;
- an asset for which trading arrangements (see **31.22**) are likely to come into existence in accordance with any arrangements of another description existing when the asset is provided or with any understanding existing at that time eg jewellery which can be sold under an existing arrangement or under a future arrangement where steps have been taken already to ensure a sale at the time of provision of the items;
- an asset which is already owned by the employee and the value of which is enhanced by the employer eg an additional life assurance premium paid into an employee's policy considerably increasing the value of the policy.

[*Social Security (Contributions) Regulations 2001, SI 2001/1004, Reg 1(2), ITEPA 2003, ss 697, 700(1)–(3)*.]

Social Security (Contributions) Regulations 2001, SI 2001/1004, Sch 3 Part III para 2 also extends the provisions to any other readily convertible asset treated by *ITEPA 2003, s 697* as falling within these provisions (ie expenditure to enhance an existing readily convertible asset).

From 1 December 1993, commodities or any others assets capable of being sold on an investment exchange which has been recognised under *Financial Services and Markets Act 2000, s 285(1)(a)* are excluded from *Social Security (Contributions) Regulations 2001, SI 2001/1004, Sch 3 Part II para 1*. The regulation therefore plugs the gap that payments in gold bullion and other traded commodities used to exploit.

The UK investment exchanges recognised under the *Financial Services and Markets Act 2000, s 287* as at 1 July 2017 are:

- ICE Futures Europe

- BATS Trading Limited
- CME Europe Limited
- Euronext UK Markets Limited
- ICAP Securities & Derivatives Exchange Limited
- London Stock Exchange plc
- The London Metal Exchange Ltd

The overseas investment exchanges recognised under the *Financial Services and Markets Act 2000, s 287* by the Treasury as at 4 November 2014 are:

- Australian Securities Exchange Limited
- Chicago Board of Trade (CBOT)
- EUREX (Zurich)
- National Association of Securities Dealers Automated Quotations (NASDAQ)
- New York Mercantile Exchange (NYMEX Inc)
- SIX Swiss Exchange AG
- The Chicago Mercantile Exchange (CME)

The definition of 'readily convertible assets' changed further with the enactment of the *Finance Act 2003*. Securities which are not eligible for the new statutory corporation tax deduction are now deemed to be 'readily convertible assets' whether or not, in fact, they are such assets (*Social Security (Contributions) Regulations 2001, SI 2001/1004, Sch 3 Part III para 1*, applying *ITEPA 2003, s 702*; *ITEPA 2003, s 702(5A)*, inserted by *Finance Act 2003, s 140, Sch 22*).

Assets which are not 'readily convertible assets' are not liable to either Class 1 or Class 1A contributions.

The definition of 'readily convertible assets' can cause difficulty in groups.

Example

Sapphire is a private company that runs a football club. It is owned by Keith who holds the shares through his corporate vehicle. Sapphire is in fact under the control of a company that is not listed. This means that S's shares are not corporation tax deductible and are therefore treated as readily convertible assets even though there is no market in them. If Keith sells any Sapphire shares at less than full value to any of the club's employees, there will be a PAYE and Class 1 NIC liability.

Where the application of *ITEPA 2003*, s 698 means that a PAYE charge arises on a notional payment and the employee does not make good the PAYE within 90 days of the end of the tax year (90 days from the date of the transaction before 6 April 2014 – the time limit was extended by *FA 2014, s 19* for payments of income treated as made after that date), then a benefit in kind may be deemed to arise under *s 222* if the conditions are met. However, the reimbursement time limit does not extend to Class 1 National Insurance, so late reimbursement of NICs does not crystallise a further charge as long as it is eventually made good. The time limit on the statutory right for the employer to recover the primary NICs is the end of the tax year following the year in which the transaction occurs. Although the National Insurance liability is clearly to Class 1 contributions, it is often assumed – incorrectly – to be Class 1A. Note that the *s 222* benefit in kind will, unless the employee is outside UK NIC (or outside the *ITEPA 2003* charge due to non-residence), attract a Class 1A liability as deemed non-cash earnings. [*Social Security (Contributions) Regulations 2001, SI 2001/1004, Reg 22(4)-(10)*.]

Where under the company articles of association or under a shareholders' agreement there is a requirement to sell the shares at 'fair value', this can mean pro-rated value with no minority discount. Any excess over statutory market value will be taxable under *Chapter 3D, s 446X*. *Section 698* requires that the shares be treated as readily convertible assets, so PAYE and Class 1 contribution liability will exist.

Similar considerations may apply where something other than fair value is specified. In *Gray's Timber Products Ltd v HMRC (aka Company A v HMRC)* CS [2009] CSIH 11 a company's managing director (G) had been allotted a 6.63% shareholding in its holding company (B) under an agreement whereby, if B were sold to a third party, G would be entitled to one-third of any increase in B's value between the date of his share purchase and the date of disposal. In 2003 all the shares in B were purchased by an unconnected company (J) for £5,903,219. The effect of the earlier agreement was that £1,451,172 of this was allocated to G for his shares (so that he received substantially more per share than the other shareholders). HMRC issued a determination that G's shares had been sold for more than their market value, giving rise to a charge to income tax under *ITEPA 2003, ss 446X-446Z*, on which the company was required to account for PAYE (because the company shares were being sold, they were automatically readily convertible assets at that point). The Special Commissioner upheld the determination and dismissed the company's appeal, holding that 'to calculate the market value of each and every £1 ordinary share in (B), ie including (G's) shares . . . one simply takes the total paid by (J) for (B), namely £5,903,219, and divides that figure by the number of ordinary shares issued, 222,037. That results in a market value of £26.59 per share'. The Court of Session upheld this decision (by a 2-1 majority, Lord Osborne dissenting). Lord Mackay of Drumadoon held that, on the evidence, G had disposed of his shares for a consideration which exceeded their market value. The sum which J paid to G was not the market value of his shares. It was clear that G 'received a disproportionately greater amount for his shares in the equity share capital of the company than its other shareholders did'. Had the original allotment of shares been of a different class, with different capital rights, the outcome could have been different.

For an indication of the official views on readily convertible assets see Tax Bulletin, Issue 36, August 1998 and HM Revenue and Customs National Insurance Manual NIM06909. [*Social Security (Contributions) Regulations 2001, SI 2001/1004, Sch 2 para 5*.] The following are extracts from the 'Open Letter' referred to in the Tax Bulletin article. The letter stresses that the questions relate only to PAYE and not NIC but are a useful indicator, nevertheless:

> **'Q4. How can employers know whether trading arrangements are likely to come into existence in accordance with any arrangements or an understanding that was in place when the asset was provided?**

The new provisions do not bring within PAYE every circumstance in which shares are awarded and trading arrangements arise at a later date. PAYE must be operated only where trading arrangements derive from arrangements or an understanding that was in place when the shares were awarded. This is a broadly based provision and such arrangements or understandings may exist in a variety of circumstances. Employers will generally know, or will be able to find out, whether such arrangements or understandings exist and whether they are likely to give rise to trading arrangements.

Q5. Can trading arrangements exist where the employer incurred no cost in issuing shares awarded to employees?

Yes. Where shares are newly issued the cost to the employer of awarding them to employees may be minimal. If arrangements are in place which enable an employee to obtain an amount greater than this minimal figure those arrangements will be trading arrangements.

Q6. The new rules require employers to operate PAYE on the 'best estimate that can reasonably be made' of the amount chargeable to tax under Schedule E. How can employers calculate this figure?

The new measure recognises that valuing shares and options within an income tax month can sometimes cause difficulty. It allows employers who operate PAYE on a best reasonable estimate of the amount chargeable to tax under Schedule E. This can be arrived at by reference to any amounts obtained or capable of being obtained by the employee for the asset and any contributions made by the employee to the cost of the share and/or share option.

Where an employee is awarded or otherwise acquires unquoted or restricted shares the employer may need to estimate the value of the shares in order to work out the figure on which to operate PAYE. Employers can check whether the Inland Revenue thinks that their valuation is reasonable by writing to:

Shares Valuation Division (PAYE valuations), Fitzroy House, Castle Meadow Road, Nottingham NG2 1BD.

Employers should provide full details of the transactions and make it clear that they want their valuation checked for the purpose of operating PAYE. It is important to be aware that these checks are informal 'health checks' for PAYE purposes only. It will not normally be possible or necessary to provide a formal valuation in the time scale within which employers must operate PAYE.

Q7. What happens if there is a difference between the 'best estimate that can be reasonably be made' at the time the employer has to operate PAYE and the amount which is finally chargeable to tax under Schedule E on the employee?

Where PAYE is operated on the basis of an estimated figure neither the Inland Revenue nor the employee is obliged to accept that valuation when working out the final amount chargeable to tax under Schedule E. That is because the 'best estimate that can reasonably be made' rule enables employers to identify within the Income Tax month the amount on which they must operate PAYE whereas the amount to be included in the employee's Self Assessment must be a precise measure of the amount chargeable to tax under Schedule E. The employer's obligation is to operate PAYE at the right time on an amount which is the best estimate that can reasonably be made, at that time, of the amount chargeable to tax under Schedule E. Where the employer has done this any discrepancy between the amount on which PAYE is operated and the final amount chargeable to tax under Schedule E will be dealt with after the end of the year through the employee's Self Assessment. In the Self Assessment the employee must return the correct amount on which Schedule E is chargeable and the amount of PAYE tax deducted and accounted for.

Where the employer has operated PAYE on a figure which is less than the best estimate that can reasonably be made of the amount chargeable to tax under Schedule E he will have failed to operate PAYE correctly and action under Regulation 49 will be considered.

Q18. Is there a formal clearance procedure for establishing whether PAYE should be operated on awards of shares?

No. Employers will need to form a judgement as to whether they have to operate PAYE on awards of shares just as they do for other payments or awards made to employees. Local Tax Offices will deal with enquiries on this subject in the same way as they respond to requests for assistance. However, there is no formal clearance procedure and Tax Offices will normally be only able to reply to enquiries in general terms. Where an employer is concerned about the value of shares awarded to an employee the Shares Valuation Division of the Capital Taxes Office may be contacted in writing for a 'health check' on the employer's proposed valuation.

These notes are for guidance only and reflect the tax position at the time of writing. Please bear in mind that they are not binding in law and in a particular case there may be special circumstances which will need to be taken into account. They do not affect your right of appeal about your own tax.

Inland Revenue, May 1998

In the case of calculating the 'best estimate', an employer will need to consider a combination of a number of factors including; the cost of the asset to the employer, the market value of the asset when it was awarded, where the asset was sold and the amount the employer received for it and any contribution to the cost of the asset by the employee.

Trading arrangements

[31.22] With effect from 6 April 1995, *Contributions (Amendment) (No 4) Regs 1995* added to the former *Sch 1A*, payment in the form of 'any other asset, including any voucher, for which trading arrangements exist and any voucher capable of being exchanged for such an asset.' For this purpose the previous meaning of 'trading arrangements' was as given in the former *ICTA 1988, s 203K(2)(a)* (*Reg 1(2)* as amended by *Contributions Amendment (No 6) Regs 1996, SI 1996/3031, Reg 2*). [*Social Security (Contributions) Regulations 2001, SI 2001/1004, Sch 3 Part III*, as amended by *Social Security (Contributions) (Amendment No 5) Regulations 2003, SI 2003/2085, Reg 10(2)*].

The definition in *s 203K* was introduced by *FA 1994, s 131* with effect from 3 May 1994 as part of the then Inland Revenue's revision of the PAYE rules to ensure that payment in kind for contributions avoidance purposes did not automatically entail a deferral of the tax liability on the same transactions. From that date, payment in the form of tradeable assets became subject to PAYE (see (now) *ITEPA 2003, ss 696, 701*).

References to enabling a person to obtain an amount include both a reference to enabling a class or description of persons which includes that person to obtain the amount and a reference to enabling an amount to be obtained by any means, including in particular by using an asset or goods as security for a loan or an advance. [*ITEPA 2003, s 702(2)*.]

An amount is 'similar to' an expense incurred if it is greater than, equal to or not substantially less than that expense. [*ITEPA 2003, s 702(5)*.]

This amendment to *Social Security (Contributions) Regulations 2001, SI 2001/1004, Sch 3 Part III* effectively ended the use of a number of further avoidance schemes where dealers were prepared to make arrangements, formal or informal, for assets to be sold to employers and bought back from employees at a price close to the original selling price. Bonuses paid in the form of platinum sponge (ie industrial powder rather than the metal ingots traded on the London Metal Exchange), demonetised gold coins (not being bullion deals which are regulated by the London Bullion Market Association) (see **31.3**), long-case clocks and rare metals (eg lithium, rhodium, cobalt, antimony, molybdenum etc), which had received some press attention, seem to have been the target of the amendment. See *NMB Holdings Ltd v Secretary of State for Social Security* [2000] TLR 10; C0/357/2000 October 2000 and HM Revenue and Customs National Insurance Manual NIM02394. See also **8.5**.

Vouchers and non-cash vouchers

[31.23] Any voucher, stamp or similar document that can be exchanged for a readily convertible asset (see **31.21**) (previously various of the assets in the previous sections) is, from 1 December 1993, also excluded from Sch 3 Part II para 1 and thus there is Class 1 NIC liability. Until 6 April 1999, non-encashable vouchers for use in High Street stores remained outside the scope of earnings provided that, as will usually be the case, they could not be exchanged for items described in *Social Security (Contributions) Regulations 2001, SI 2001/1004, Sch 3 Part IV*. However, all non-cash vouchers are liable to Class 1 NICs from 6 April 1999 with the exception of childcare vouchers within the rules described at **29.32**. Certain other vouchers are excepted – see **29.31**. Where a third party provides workers with awards in non-cash vouchers as part of an incentive scheme that third party must pay the Class 1A liability that arises. (CWG5 (2018), paras 36 to 42.)

[*Social Security (Contributions) Regulations 2001, SI 2001/1004, Sch 3 Part IV para 12*.]

Timing and valuation

[31.24] No specific timing provisions were added to the regulations bringing notional payments (transfers of assets within what are now *Social Security (Contributions) Regulations 2001, SI 2001/1004, Sch 3 Parts II, III and IV*) into earnings for Class 1 purposes. Because of this, the transfer to the employee must be treated as if it were a cash payment of earnings when it is made. No separate year-end reporting procedures were introduced, as none were required. However, if the transfer is to be treated as a cash payment, the employer must know the value to be included in gross pay for Class 1 purposes. No valuation provisions were included in the revised regulations in respect of life policies assigned by way of remuneration, but from 2 December 2004 these follow the general rules for securities. However, detailed provisions have always existed to deal with the other categories set out above. These are as follows.

(a) *The basic rule*

The amount of earnings chargeable to National Insurance contributions is to be the best estimate that can reasonably be made of the amount of income likely to be chargeable to tax in respect of, as the case may be, the provision or enhancement of the asset (ie, from 1 September 2003, 'general earnings'). In the case of a voucher exchangeable for such assets, similar rules apply. [*Social Security (Contributions) Regulations 2001, SI 2001/1004, Sch 2 para 5*, as amended by *Social Security (Contributions) (Amendment No 5) Regulations 2003, SI 2003/2085*.]

Any difference between the employer's 'best estimate' and the finally agreed value for tax purposes will be dealt with through the employee's self-assessment. The National Insurance position should remain undisturbed, unless the estimate used was manifestly ascertained without proper care. Similarly, provided a reasonable value is used on any HM Revenue and Customs return forms, such as Form 42 or Form 35, such returns will not be considered to be incorrect where subsequently a different value is agreed.

For most assets the value which therefore has to be ascertained is 'money's worth' having regard to:

- the cost of the asset to the employer;
- the value of the asset when it was awarded;
- if the employee has already sold the asset, the amount received for it (if known);
- and any contribution towards the cost of the asset made by the employee may be deducted.

However, if the asset is charged to income tax under the securities legislation then the market value must be obtained by reference to *TCGA 1992, ss 272–273*. This general rule is as follows:

- 'Market value' in relation to any assets means the price which those assets might reasonably be expected to fetch on a sale in the open market.
- In estimating the market value of any assets no reduction may be made in the estimate on account of the estimate being made on the assumption that the whole of the assets is to be placed on the market at one and the same time.

Subject to *subsection (4)* below, the market value of shares or securities in The Stock Exchange Official Daily List shall, except where in consequence of special circumstances prices quoted in that List are by themselves not a proper measure of market value, be as follows:

(A) the lower of the two prices shown in the quotations for the shares or securities in the Stock Exchange Daily Official List on the relevant date plus one-quarter of the difference between those two figures, or

(B) halfway between the highest and lowest prices at which bargains, other than bargains done at special prices, were recorded in the shares or securities for the relevant date,

choosing the amount under paragraph (A) if no bargains were recorded for the relevant date, or otherwise choosing the lower between (A) and (B).

Subsection (4) says that subsection (3) does not apply to shares or securities for which The Stock Exchange provides a more active market elsewhere than on the London trading floor; and, if the London trading floor is closed on the relevant date, the market value shall be ascertained by reference to the latest previous date or earliest subsequent date on which it is open, whichever affords the lower market value.

In July 2014, the Government announced a consultation on changing the 'quarter-up' rule, a change that did not subsequently appear in any of the Finance Acts in 2015 or 2016.

TCGA 92 s 273 provides the modifications for unquoted securities as follows:

(1) The provisions of subsection (3) below shall have effect in any case where, in relation to an asset to which this section applies, there falls to be determined by virtue of *section 272(1)* the price which the asset might reasonably be expected to fetch on a sale in the open market.

(2) The assets to which this section applies are shares and securities which are not quoted on a recognised stock exchange at the time as at which their market value for the purposes of tax on chargeable gains falls to be determined.

(3) For the purposes of a determination falling within subsection (1) above, it shall be assumed that, in the open market which is postulated for the purposes of that determination, there is available to any prospective purchaser of the asset in question all the information which a prudent prospective purchaser of the asset might reasonably require if he were proposing to purchase it from a willing vendor by private treaty and at arm's length.

If the asset comprises unquoted or restricted shares employers may if they wish check whether the amount on which they propose to operate PAYE and Class 1 NIC is officially considered to be reasonable. Where this facility is required the employer should provide full details of the transaction(s) to Shares and Assets Valuation (PAYE Valuation), Fitz Roy House, Castle Meadow Road, Nottingham NG2 1BD.

As to recognised stock exchanges see HMRC Capital Gains Tax Manual para 50250.

(b) *Unit trusts*

Units in a unit trust (as defined in Financial Services and Markets Act 2000, s 237) must be valued when an employer confers a beneficial interest in them on an employee. Where the items have a published selling price, the earnings are to be calculated or estimated by reference to the lowest selling price on the date of payment. If no selling price was published on the date of payment, the price applies which was the lowest published on the last previous date before the date of payment. [*Social Security (Contributions) Regulations 2001, SI 2001/1004, Sch 2 para 3*].

(c) *Options (within Sch 3, Part IV)*
An option is valued by reference to the value of the underlying asset on the day on which the beneficial option is conferred, less the amount (or least amount, if it is variable) of the consideration to be given in order to acquire the asset under the option. [*Social Security (Contributions) Regulations 2001, SI 2001/1004, Sch 2 para 4*.]

(d) *Alcoholic liquor, gemstones and vouchers*
The amount of earnings comprised in a payment in the form of assets within *Social Security (Contributions) Regulations 2001, SI 2001/1004, Sch 3 Part IV paras 9, 10, 12* is to be calculated or estimated on the basis of the cost of the asset in question. [*Social Security (Contributions) Regulations 2001, SI 2001/1004, Sch 2 para 6*]. In the case of alcoholic liquor or gemstones this only applies after 1 September 2003 if the asset is not in any event a 'readily convertible asset' – but where it is not this will differ from the valuation for PAYE purposes under *ITEPA 2003, ss 696, 702*, which refers to the 'amount which, on the basis of the best estimate that can reasonably be made, is the income likely to PAYE income in respect of the provision of the asset' under the trading arrangements. [*ITEPA 2003, s 696(2)*]. See also (a) above.

(e) *Other items within Sch 3, Part IV*
Where (a), (b), (c) or (d) above do not apply then where a payment of earnings comprises the conferment of a beneficial interest in any asset specified in *Social Security (Contributions) Regulations 2001, SI 2001/1004, Sch 3 Part IV*, the amount of those earnings for Class 1 purposes is to be calculated or estimated at a price which that beneficial interest might reasonably be expected to fetch if sold in the open market on the day on which it is conferred. [*Social Security (Contributions) Regulations 2001, SI 2001/1004, Sch 2 para 2(1)*.]
Where any such asset is not quoted on a recognised stock exchange (as defined by *ICTA 1988, s 841* now *ITA 2007, ss 1005, 1010*) (see www.gov.uk/recognised-stock-exchanges), it is to be assumed that there is available to any prospective purchaser of the beneficial interest all the information which a prudent prospective purchaser might reasonably require before buying by private treaty at arm's length. [*Social Security (Contributions) Regulations 2001, SI 2001/1004, Sch 2 para 2(2)*].

Commodities

[31.25] As mentioned in **31.15** above in relation to *Social Security (Contributions) Regulations 2001, SI 2001/1004, Sch 3 Part IV para 6* above, until 1 December 1993 transfers of commodities to employees were not within the scope of the revised regulations and so any commodity for which there was a ready market could potentially be used to pay remuneration. The most popular seemed to be gold bullion. For a discussion of remuneration planning using gold bullion, readers should consult earlier (2002–03) editions of this work. HM Revenue and Customs National Insurance Manual NIM02180 and NIM02394, now withdrawn, used to give guidance on this topic. NIM4007 used to give guidance on readily convertible assets generally, but has for some time appeared as 'Withdrawn and currently being redrafted'. See 8.5 anti-avoidance in respect of litigation regarding the 'gold coins' bonus scheme.

Profit-sharing scheme payments

[31.26] Any payment by way of, or derived from, shares appropriated under a profit-sharing scheme to which former *ICTA 1988, s 186* applied was to be excluded from earnings for Class 1 purposes. [Former *Social Security (Contributions) Regulations 2001, SI 2001/1004, Sch 3 Part IX para 8*.] This provision ceased to apply from 1 September 2003, with the introduction of charges covered by *ITEPA 2003, Part 7* (*Social Security (Contributions) (Amendment No 5) Regulations 2003, SI 2003/2085, Reg 12(10)*).

Key Points regarding earnings from employment: employment-related securities, readily convertible assets, etc

[31.27] Points to consider are as follows.

- The exercise of any 'unapproved' options over securities or the award of any securities themselves where the securities are readily convertible assets will attract Class 1 National Insurance liability.
- Some assets which are not readily convertible assets can be deemed by *ITEPA 2003, s 702(5A)* to be readily convertible assets.
- In the case of unapproved securities options it is possible at the time of grant to transfer the liability that will arise on exercise to the employee. This protects the employer from an unquantifiable future liability. The employee will obtain tax relief on the employer National Insurance that is borne.
- There are a number of exceptions to liability to give transitional relief where the rules changed in the past or in the case of a 7 November 2000 election (or deemed election). Employers need to take care not to accede to claims for National Insurance arrears where such reliefs apply.
- Where an amount received by an employee in respect of unapproved or approved / registered shares or options is treated as taxable employment income, the amount will generally be deemed to be earnings for contributions purposes.
- The NIC liability in respect of gains on employment-related securities realised by internationally mobile employees (IMEs) was put onto a logical statutory footing from 6 April 2015 (see

51.64).

32

Earnings from Self-employment

Cross-references. See CLASS 2 CONTRIBUTIONS 18 for small income exception; CLASS 4 CONTRIBUTIONS 20.

Other Sources. Simon's Taxes, Volume 2, paras A8.302 and 316; Tolley's Tax Planning 2016–17; Tolley's Income Tax 2016–17; Tolley's National Insurance Brief, February 1997. See also Leaflet 480 (2018); HM Revenue and Customs National Insurance Manual NIM21000-22003 and 24000-24715.

Introduction to earnings from self-employment

[32.1] The term 'earnings', when used in the context of social security legislation, includes any remuneration or profit derived from an 'employment', defined by *Social Security Contributions and Benefits Act 1992 (SSCBA 1992)*, s 122 as any trade, business, profession, office or vocation. It applies equally, therefore, to the income of an employed earner and that of a self-employed earner, though the amount of a person's earnings for any period, or the amount of his earnings to be treated as comprised in any payment made to him or for his benefit, are to be calculated or estimated in the manner and on the basis prescribed in the legislation and such prescriptions do, in fact, differ in the case of employed earners and self-employed earners. [*SSCBA 1992, s 3(1)(2); Social Security (Contributions) Regulations 2001, SI 2001/1004, Reg 25*].

From 6 April 2015

[32.2] As outlined below, the rules for Class 2 and Class 4 measurement of earnings used to be different. However, Class 2 was reformed by *National Insurance Contributions Act 2015 (NICA 2015), Sch 1* with effect from 6 April 2015. As well as moving the collection of Class 2 into the income tax self-assessment regime, the changes also included a redefinition of 'relevant profits' for Class 2 purposes.

Earnings for Class 2 purposes are now defined in *SSCBA 1992, s 11(3)* (as substituted by *NICA 2015, Sch 1, para 3*) as 'profits, from the [self-] employment, in respect of which Class 4 contributions are payable under section 15 for the relevant tax year (or would be payable if the amount of the profits were to exceed the amount specified in subsection (3)(a) of that section in excess of which the main Class 4 percentage is payable) [ie, the lower annual limit]'.

The small profits threshold for Class 2 and the lower annual limit for Class 4 have been set at different levels (£6,205 and £8,424 respectively for 2018–19), so liability for Class 2 can exist without liability for Class 4, but the underlying measure of earnings is now the same. As noted at 32.4 below, Class 4 liability arises in respect of earnings that are profits or gains chargeable to income tax under *Income Tax (Trading and Other Income) Act 2005 (ITTOIA 2005), Part 2*, Chapter 2, ie, profits of a trade, profession or vocation. [*SSCBA 1992, s 15(1)*].

Where a self-employed earner incurs a trading loss, the 'profits' will now fall below the Class 2 small profits threshold, making the payment of Class 2 contributions for the year optional. There are no provisions importing the Class 4 loss relief rules for Class 2 purposes, so it is possible that a trader will have no Class 4 liability due to losses brought forward, but nevertheless still have the Class 2 liability because profits for the year in question exceed the small profits threshold.

Where a person is in employment as a self-employed earner in the UK but begins to carry on the business wholly elsewhere in the EEA such that there are no UK profits taxable under *ITTOIA 2005*, the term 'relevant profits' is extended to encompass non-UK profits. It then means profits from the self-employment in respect of which Class 4 contributions *would be payable if* the earner was resident in the UK in that year, the business was carried on by the earner in the UK, the amount of the profits was to exceed the Class 4 lower annual limit (NB: not the Class 2 small profits threshold), and any double tax relief under *Taxation (International and Other Provisions) Act 2010, s 2* was to be disregarded. [*Social Security (Contributions) Regulations 2001, SI 2001/1004, Reg 148B* as inserted by *NICA 2015, Sch 1, para 17*].

None of the other measures outlined below (eg, income from carrying on a property letting business that does not amount to a trade) are now of any relevance, other than to enable contributors to make voluntary Class 2 contributions under *SSCBA 1992, s 11(6)* (as amended) if they are classed as self-employed earners without income from a trade or profession.

Any possible distinction between earnings for Class 2 and Class 4 seems likely to become a thing of the past if the government's plans, announced in the Budgets of March and July 2015 and again in March 2016, to abolish Class 2 and reform Class 4 to introduce a new contributory benefit test in April 2019 come to pass. The detail of this reform is yet to be worked out and will be subject to consultation.

Before 6 April 2015

[32.3] Although CLASS 2 CONTRIBUTIONS **18** are not earnings-related, before the *NICA 2015* changes from 6 April 2015, it used to become necessary to ascertain earnings for Class 2 purposes where exception from liability was sought on the grounds that those earnings were less than a specified amount, or where it was sought to demonstrate by reference to earnings that the earner was not ordinarily self-employed at all (see **14.18** CATEGORISATION and **18.4** CLASS 2 CONTRIBUTIONS).

The earnings to be compared with the limit set for a tax year were the earnings *in respect of* that year. [*Social Security (Contributions) Regulations 2001, SI 2001/1004, Reg 45(1), revoked by Social Security (Miscellaneous Amendments No 2) Regulations 2015, SI 2015/478, Reg 24*]. In this connection, earnings meant the applicant's *net earnings* from employment as a self-employed earner. [*Social Security (Contributions) Regulations 2001, SI 2001/1004, Reg 45(2)(a), revoked as above*] and, in calculating those earnings, where the contributor also had earnings from employed earner's employment in the same year which were shown in the accounts of his business, those earnings were disregarded. [*Social Security (Contributions) Regulations 2001, SI 2001/1004, Reg 45(2)(b), revoked as above*]. Employment credits and training grants received under the 'New Deal 50 plus' scheme and payments under schemes based on *Welfare Reform and Pensions Act 1999, s 60(1)* were excluded. [*Social Security (Contributions) Regulations 2001, SI 2001/1004, Reg 45(2)(b), revoked as above*].

The term 'net earnings' was interpreted as meaning the figure which would appear in a profit and loss account prepared in accordance with normal accounting principles. Accordingly, deductions might be made from gross earnings for expenses incurred in running the business and an allowance might be made for depreciation. No deduction might, however, be made for income tax payments or for Class 2 or Class 4 contributions payable; a Business Start-Up Allowance (formerly Enterprise Allowance) paid under *Employment and Training Act 1973, s 2(2)(d)* and income from any source other than self-employment had to be disregarded; and adjustments had to be made for drawings from the business (including any 'salary' drawn by the earner) and the value of any withdrawals from stock for the person's own use. (Leaflet CA 02, now withdrawn). The application for exception was to be accompanied by an estimate of gross earnings and expenses prepared in this way and until 27 May 1996 it was also necessary to enclose, with the application for exception, evidence of earnings eg the last accounts or tax papers — these did not latterly need to be supplied unless requested subsequently by HM Revenue and Customs (see form CF 10).

Where a figure of net earnings from self-employment has been required in connection with the application of the 'earnings rule' for benefit claim purposes, which has not been changed by the Class 2 reforms, the National Insurance Commissioners have accepted that accounts which have clearly been drawn-up by someone versed in commercial accountancy are sufficient evidence that the net earnings are as shown by the net profit in those accounts (see reported decision *R(P) 1/76* in the pension series). They have also accepted, however, that where the accounts include income from capital assets (such as rents), the net profit should be reduced by such income (see reported decision *R(U) 3/77* in the unemployment benefit series). These decisions, though useful indicators of probable DSS thinking, were not binding on the Department in the contribution field (see **29.3**).

The National Insurance Commissioners accepted that, in connection with the application of the 'earnings rule', the net earnings relevant to a particular tax year were the 'actual net earnings for that year', even though those earnings might be taxed in a later tax year (see reported decision *R(P) 1/73* in the pension series). This is clearly the force of the phrase 'in respect of' in *Social Security (Contributions) Regulations 2001, SI 2001/1004, former Reg 45(1), now revoked as above.*

It was therefore necessary, if a person's accounting period overlapped 5 April, to time-apportion the profits shown by his accounts in order to arrive at an earnings amount appropriate to a Class 2 exception application.

Example

Jerry was an unsuccessful builder. His accounting year ended on 30 June and his accounts for the last two years before April 2015 showed results as follows

Year to		£
30.6.2013	Profit	18,000
30.6.2014	Loss	(1,500)

For the purpose of an application for Class 2 exception in 2014–15, his profits for 2013–14 were

	£
$^3/_{12}$ × £18,000	4,500
$^9/_{12}$ × £(1,500)	(1,125)
	£3,375

Where a person had more than one self-employment, the net earnings from each had to be arrived at as illustrated, then aggregated (see **5.16** AGGREGATION OF EARNINGS). (Leaflet CA 02, now withdrawn). Whilst it is clear from the above example that exemption from Class 2 would have been straightforward some thought ought to have been given as to whether that was the best course of action – Class 2 contributions were relatively inexpensive and they do provide significant benefit entitlements.

HMRC announced at the beginning of April 2013 that sleeping and other inactive limited partners who took no active part in the running of the business were no longer outside the scope of Class 2 and Class 4 NIC. In consequence there was allegedly a liability to pay Class 2 and Class 4 NIC but because of the previously incorrect advice no action would be taken to collect any contributions for years before the 2013–14 tax year, although individuals would be given the opportunity to pay arrears of Class 2 if it would enhance their benefit entitlements.

HMRC are now of the view that sleeping or inactive partners are gainfully employed and so fall within *SSCBA 1992, s 2(1)(b)*. They consider that 'employment' as defined in *SSCBA 1992*, s 122 includes 'business', and the *Partnership Act 1890, s 1(1)* supports this view in that 'Partnership is the relation which subsists between persons carrying on a business in common with a view of profit'.

Whether such a view can be sustained must be questionable given the number of Tribunal decisions where individuals have been denied the right to pay Class 2 contributions and their benefit rights adversely affected where it was ruled they had insufficient activity to be said to be a self-employed earner.

Individuals who fell within this ruling and were not below age 16 or over state pension age should have considered whether they were entitled to an exception from liability on the grounds of small earnings.

As noted above, *NICA 2015* changed the basis described above with effect from 6 April 2015, although the principles underlying liability for sleeping and inactive partners have not really changed: if their income is taxable under *ITTOIA 2005*, Part 2, Chapter 2 so that it falls within the definition of earnings for Class 4 purposes, it seems clear that such partners should be classed as self-employed earners for Class 2 purposes. See also 14.19, 20.2, 20.4 and 58.3 in respect of whether profits allocated to a sleeping partner should not be treated as 'immediately derived' from carrying on a trade and therefore subject to neither Class 2 nor Class 4 liability.

Subpostmasters

[32.4] It is important to note that although, as indicated above, one of the instructions to a person with earnings from self-employment was: 'Do not count as earnings any income . . . from sources other than self-employment', that instruction related only to the way in which an account of earnings should have been drawn-up. If a self-employed earner (or his accountants) ignored that advice and included on revenue account receipts from a source other than self-employment, it was maintained that those moneys thereby became a receipt of the trade and thus part of the earner's income from self-employment. Treasury Counsel advised the former DSS with particular reference to SUBPPOSTMASTERS (57.6) that where a subpostmaster included his PO remuneration (Class 1 earnings) in the accounts relating to his ancillary business,

> The payments he puts into his business are plainly receipts of the business. Indeed, the accounts show how the gross salary appears in the accounts as an undifferentiated receipt on revenue account. There would be no other way of dealing with them in accordance with proper commercial accounting practice. It would be different if the payments were appropriated to capital expenditure or by way of a loan (other than a short-term loan analogous to an overdraft) (see eg *Ryan v Crabtree Denims* [1987] STC 402).

The case referred to by Treasury Counsel concerned the correct treatment for tax purposes of an interest relief grant made to a company in difficulties by the Dept of Trade for the purpose of keeping the business alive. Hoffman J held that, because the grant was not specifically earmarked for either a revenue or a capital purpose (ie it was an undifferentiated receipt) and because there was nothing in the circumstances of the case to suggest that it was for a capital purpose, the grant fell to be treated as a revenue receipt.

The application of the principle in *Ryan* to the situation of subpostmasters etc is surely open to challenge but a challenge now seems unnecessary following the amendment to the definition outlined above. See CA National Insurance News, Issue 2, page 6 concerning the entitlement to relief for the small earnings exception by reference only to the actual earnings from the business itself and not to the total receipts of the business which would have included those other earnings. The change to *Reg 45(2)* noted above and detailed in SUBPOSTMASTERS (see **57.6**) affected subpostmasters and groups of mainly professional people such as accountants and doctors. The problem of whether exception should have been granted in the past may never now be settled. To avoid problems, a self-employed earner should, perhaps, have ensured that any of his earnings which were not from self-employment were paid into some bank account other than that used for the main business, and should then have made a capital introduction to the main business, taking care that the amount introduced did not appear in his trading and profit and loss account but in his capital account on the balance sheet as an introduction of capital. It is suggested that, in contradiction of Counsel's advice, this was an 'other way of dealing with' non-trading income 'in accordance with proper commercial accounting practice'. Where earnings of the kind in question had previously been included in the profits and, by concession, charged to tax under what was Schedule D, the tax computation would, of course, have needed to include an addition of those earnings to the profit shown by the accounts. It is assumed that, provided such an addition had been made in the computation, HM Revenue and Customs would have continued to permit the income concerned to be assessed under former Schedule D, but, if that was not so, it should be noted that the increased tax liability would have generally outweighed the Class 2 savings and would have made the treatment suggested inappropriate. From 1995, however, Leaflet CA 02 (now withdrawn) advised 'Where you also have earnings from employed earner's employment in the same year and those earnings are shown in the accounts of the business, as a business receipt, those earnings can be disregarded when calculating the profits from your self-employed business.'

Earnings for Class 4 purposes

[32.5] A self-employed earner's earnings for Class 4 purposes are all annual profits immediately derived from the carrying on or exercise of one or more trades, professions or vocations, being profits or gains *chargeable to income tax* under *ITTOIA 2005, Part 2 Chapter 2*. [*SSCBA 1992, s 15(1)*]. They are subject to various deductions, additions and reliefs as prescribed in *Sch 2 para 2, para 3* and described at **32.7** to **32.13** below.

The effect of this provision is to exchange the actual basis on which earnings are otherwise assessed throughout the contribution scheme for whichever basis is adopted for income tax purposes. The current year basis (including the opening rules) under 'self-assessment' has been applicable since 1997–98. [*ITTOIA 2005, ss 7(2), 198(1)(2), 200(3), 201(1)*].

The reference in *SSCBA 1992, s 15(1)* to profits or gains chargeable to income tax under what was Case I or II of Schedule D was to be taken as including a reference to profits consisting of a payment of Business Start-Up Allowance (formerly Enterprise Allowance) made:

- on or after 18 March 1986, or
- before 18 March 1986 as part of a distinct series of payments of which one or more is made on or after that date

under *Employment and Training Act 1973, s 2(2)(d)* or *Enterprise and New Towns (Scotland) Act 1990, s 2(4)(c)* and chargeable to tax under what was Case VI of Schedule D by virtue of *ICTA 1988, s 127*. [*ITTOIA 2005, s 207(1)(3)*].

New Deal and Flexible New Deal payments, paid before September 2011 under the same acts, were also classed as income for tax and Class 4 purposes (although they were not classed as earnings for Class 2 purposes because they were considered an 'unemployability supplement' for the purposes of *Reg 44* of the *Social Security (Contributions) Regulations 2001, SI 2001/1004 (revoked from 6 April 2015 by SI 2015/478, Reg 24)*. However, New Deal 50-Plus payments were exempt from income tax and both classes of contribution (excluded by *Reg 45(2)(b)(ii), also now revoked*).

More recent allowances to encourage self-employed enterprise, such as the New Enterprise Allowance, have in contrast been exempted from income tax and are disregarded for Class 4 purposes (and, consequently, for Class 2 purposes from 6 April 2015 onwards). [BIM40401].

As described at **32.2** above HMRC have ruled that sleeping and other inactive partners are liable to Class 4 NIC from 6 April 2013 onwards, although this contradicts the decision of the National Insurance Commissioners described at 14.19 which determined that a sleeping partner could not be an earner if he did nothing to earn the money other than make an investment in the partnership. Membership of a limited liability partnership (LLP) is slightly different in nature, but it is not clear that members should be treated any differently than sleeping partners in general partnerships. An individual LLP member may receive a profit share, and if he or she is not deemed to be a salaried member and thereby fall within Class 1 (see 18.11 and 20.2), he or she is, from 6 April 2015, deemed to be self-employed because 'employment' is now deemed to include membership of an LLP which carries on a trade, profession or business with a view to profit. [*Social Security (Limited Liability Partnership) Regulations 2014, Reg 2A* as inserted by *Social Security (Limited Liability Partnership) (Amendment) Regulations 2015, Reg 4*]. It is therefore clear that any profit share from a trade or profession will potentially be earnings for Class 4 purposes, but the same question must still arise over whether an inactive member can be an 'earner' in view of the National Insurance Commissioners' decision.

Capital allowances

[32.6] Former provisions ceased to be of practical application under 'self-assessment' from 1997 and relief is now obtained for capital allowances as if the amount computed were a deductible trading expense in arriving at profits/losses.

Loss relief

[32.7] Loss relief available for tax purposes under *Income Tax Act 2007 (ITA 2007)*, s 83 by carry-forward against subsequent profits is available for Class 4 purposes also, as is carry-back of terminal loss relief under *ITA 2007, s 89*. [*SSCBA 1992, Sch 2 para 3(1)(c)(d)*]. The fact that a loss might have originated before the introduction of Class 4 contributions (6 April 1975) did not affect its availability for use for Class 4 purposes under *Sch 2 para 3(1)(c)*.

Loss relief available for tax purposes under *ITA 2007, ss 64, 72* by set-off against general income is available for Class 4 purposes also, provided the loss arises from activities of which any profits would have been earnings for Class 4 purposes. [*SSCBA 1992, Sch 2 para 3(1)(a)*]. Loss relief under *ITA 2007, s 64* is not available for losses of 2013–14 and subsequent years calculated using the cash basis, which may only be relieved against later profits of the same trade or by way of terminal loss relief (see BIM70000 onwards), and the Class 4 position follows the tax position.

Because capital allowances are treated as if they were a trading expense, loss relief is therefore also available for capital allowances.

In most instances where such relief is available, however, it will be claimed for tax purposes against income which is not profits or gains for Class 4 purposes. Accordingly, where, in any tax year beginning on or after 6 April 1975, a deduction in respect of a loss falls to be made in computing a person's total income (or, for 1989–90 or earlier years, that of his spouse) for tax purposes and all or part of the loss falls to be deducted from income other than his trading profit or gains, the loss is, to that extent, to be carried forward for Class 4 purposes and set off against the first available trading profit or gains for subsequent years. [*SSCBA 1992, Sch 2 para 3(3)(4)*].

Example

Kit has a sportswear business. His trading results (adjusted for tax purposes) are

Year to		£
5 July 2013	Profit	12,000
5 July 2014	Loss	(17,200)
5 July 2015	Profit	4,000
5 July 2016	Profit	19,400

K is single and his assessable amounts of profit and other income are

	Tax and Class 4	*Investment Income*
	£	£
2013–14	12,000	1,500
2014–15	NIL	1,700
2015–16	4,000	1,800
2016–17	19,400	2,200

If K claims relief for his 2014–15 loss of £17,200 under *ITA 2007, s 64*, it will be set against 2014–15 investment income, ie £1,700 profits, then against 2013–14 earned income ie £12,000 profits and then against 2013–14 investment income ie £1,500. The balance of the loss (£2,000) is then carried forward against profits of the same trade only. This will result in revised assessable amounts of profit and income, thus

	Tax and Class 4	*Investment Income*
	£	£
2013–14	NIL	NIL
2014–15	NIL	NIL
2015–16	2,000	1,800
2016–17	19,400	2,200

For Class 4 purposes, however, only £14,000 of the loss has been relieved (£12,000 in 2013–14 and £2,000 in 2015–16) and the remaining £3,200 must, therefore, also be carried forward to 2016–17 (and subsequent years, if necessary, as in the example), giving revised Class 4 profits as follows

	Class 4
	£
2013–14	NIL
2014–15	NIL
2015–16	NIL
2016–17	18,200

The *Finance Act 2009* extension of loss relief carry back built temporarily on the existing trade loss relief against general income in *ITA 2007, s 64*. It will have applied where a claim had been made under *s 64* to set a trade loss for 2008–09 against general income of 2008–09, the previous year (2007–08), or both, and relief for the loss could not be fully given under the claim. Where a *s 64* claim had been made for set-off of a trade loss for 2008–09 against general income in that way, a claim could also have been made to carry back unrelieved losses against profits from the same trade for 2007–08, 2006–07 and 2005–06. Loss relief available for tax purposes under *Finance Act 2009* was available for Class 4 purposes also, provided the loss arises from activities of which any profits would have been earnings for Class 4 purposes. [*SSCBA 1992, Sch 2 para 3(1)(a)*.] The loss relief arising in 2008–09 could have been carried back under *FA 2009, Sch 6 paras 1, 2* to set against trading profits of 2006–07 and 2005–06 but was subject to a £50,000 cap.

In the Budget on 22 April 2009, it was announced that this extended relief would also be available in respect of a further year's losses, viz those of the basis period for 2009–10, as well as those of the basis period for 2008–09. [*FA 2009, Sch 6 paras 1, 2*.] See the example below.

Example

Anna Bolik had a gym business. Her trading results (adjusted for tax purposes) were

Year to		£
31 March 2008	Profit	65,000
31 March 2009	Profit	60,000
31 March 2010	Profit	30,000
31 March 2011	Loss	(100,000)

Anna was single and her assessable amounts of profit and other income were

	Taxable Profit	*Investment Income*
	£	£
2007–08	65,000	5,000*
2008–09	60,000	5,000*
2009–10	30,000	5,000*
2010–11	Nil	5,000*

* Gilt edged security paid gross.

If Anna had claimed relief for her 2010–11 loss of £100,000 under *ITA 2007, s 64*, it would have been set against 2010–11 investment income ie £5,000, then against 2009–10 investment income ie £5,000 and then against 2009–10 trading income ie £30,000. The balance of the loss (£60,000) would then have been carried back under *FA 2009* against trading profits of 2008–09 and then 2007–08 up to a limit of £50,000 with any remaining balance carried forward to 2011–12. As Anna's loss to carry back beyond 2009–10 exceeded £50,000 that was the maximum amount that could be relieved across the two years collectively, relief being given in the later year first. This will have resulted in revised assessable amounts of profit and income, thus

	Profit after loss	*Investment Income*
	£	£
2007–08	65,000	5,000
2008–09	10,000	5,000
2009–10	Nil	Nil
2010–11	Nil	Nil

Whilst for tax purposes £10,000 of losses were to be carried forward, for Class 4 purposes, however, only £80,000 of the loss had been relieved (£30,000 in 2009–10 under *ITA 2007, s 64* and £50,000 in 2008–09 under *FA 2009, Sch 6 para 1*) and the remaining £20,000 had, therefore, also to be carried forward to 2011–12 (and subsequent years, if necessary, as in the example), giving revised Class 4 profits as follows

	Class 4
	£
2007–08	65,000
2008–09	10,000
2009–10	Nil
2010–11	Nil

There is a view that the words 'of any relevant trade, profession or vocation' mean that a loss incurred in a trade, etc and carried forward for Class 4 purposes (whether or not *any* part has already been set against income not liable to Class 4) in *SSCBA 1992, Sch 2 para 3(4)(a)* may be deducted from profits in any other trade, etc being carried on in future years. These days this might typically occur where a self-employed person invests in a film partnership as a trading venture which, because of capital allowances and initial investment costs, incurs trading losses in its early years. The matter is not free from doubt however as *SSCBA 1992, Sch 2 para 3(1)* says that relief 'shall be available under, *and in the manner provided by . . . Income Tax Act 2007*'. Para 6053 of the Inspector's Manual (removed however in May 2004) did state that losses carried forward remained with the trade that generated those losses.

No relief is available for Class 4 purposes for constructive losses available for tax purposes in respect of annual payments carried forward under former *ICTA 1988, s 387* (as amended by *ITTOIA 2005, Sch 1 para 163*) or interest carried forward or backward under *ITA 2007, ss 88, 94*. [*SSCBA 1992, Sch 2 para 3(2)(c)(d)*]. In the HM Revenue and Customs Inspector's Manual it used to state that any loss which was allowed for income tax purposes against non-NIC income, eg PAYE income, would remain unrelieved for NIC purposes and would be carried forward to use against the first available subsequent year and so on until it was fully allowed. As a result trading tax losses carried forward may be different from NIC losses carried forward and NIC losses should be separately recorded. Also relief for an employment income loss may occasionally be given for income tax in an assessment on trading profits: it is not to be allowed for NIC. This guidance is now found at NIM24610.

HMRC's Business Income Manual now states that 'set off of losses for the purposes of Class 4 NIC is covered in the National Insurance manual' (BIM85010), while NIM24610 simply states that a trading loss is to be relieved for NIC purposes in the same manner as for income tax under *ITA 2007, ss 64, 72, 83, 89* and *93*, and then refers readers back to a list of pages in the Business Income Manual.

Loss relief restrictions

[32.8] HMRC Brief (Brief 18/07) issued on 2 March 2007 described a new anti-avoidance measure whereby loss relief under *ICTA 1988, 380, 381* and *FA 1991, s 72* termed as 'sideways loss relief' was restricted from that date for 'non-active' or limited partners who carried on a trade at any time during the tax year and who did not devote a significant amount of time (ie less than 10 hours a week) to the business. Broadly the restrictions imposed a purpose test and an annual limit of relief of £25,000. The purpose test applied to the capital contribution made by the partner to the partnership so that restrictions applied in respect of contributed capital where one of the main purposes was to obtain a reduction in tax liability by means of sideways loss relief. It is important to appreciate that whilst this measure was aimed at film partnerships it will apply to every partnership. Once the restricted relief is computed for tax purposes, that amount will then attract Class 4 relief in the various ways described above. Further similar anti-avoidance measures were introduced that apply to *individuals* with effect from 12 March 2008 to restrict the amount of 'sideways loss relief' that broadly followed the existing rules. [*ITA 2007, ss 64,*

70, 72, 74, 103C; FA 2007, s 26, Sch 4 para 1; FA 2008, Sch 21]. It should also be noted that, where film partnerships have been held to be non-trading businesses (eg, *Eclipse Film Partners No 35 LLP v Revenue and Customs Comrs* [2014] EWCA Civ 184, 164 NLJ 7597, [2014] SWTI 742 – leave to appeal to the Supreme Court was refused), the denial of sideways loss relief for income tax purposes will be equally valid for Class 4 purposes, and should the films produced by the partnerships result in a profit in due course, there should be no Class 4 liability on the investment return. See also **52.1** PARTNERS.

Personal reliefs

[32.9] No allowance for personal reliefs under *ITA 2007, ss 35–55* may be made for Class 4 purposes. [*SSCBA 1992, Sch 2 para 3(2)(a)*].

Retirement annuities and personal pension premiums

[32.10] No relief for premiums or other consideration under annuity contracts and trust schemes under *ITEPA 2003, ss 605–608* may be given for Class 4 purposes [*SSCBA 1992, Sch 2 para 3(2)(f)*] nor for personal pension contributions under *ITEPA 2003, s 639*. [*SSCBA 1992, Sch 2 para 3(2)(g)*]. (*Maher v CIR* [1997] STC SSCD 103).

Interest and other annual payments

[32.11] Relief for payment of interest under *ITA 2007, s 383* is not to be given *per se* for Class 4 purposes, but *is* to be given to the extent to which it falls within the relieving provision next described. [*SSCBA 1992, Sch 2 para 3(2)(b)*].

Relief was allowed in respect of annuities and other annual payments under former *ICTA 1988, ss 348, 349(1)* up to and including 5 April 2007. [former *SSCBA 1992, Sch 2 para 3(5)(a)*]. Whilst the legislation suggested for a time that equivalent relief was no longer available under *ITA 2007* (which was a mere consolidation), the omission was an oversight and relief was restored, with backdated effect to 6 April 2007 by *Income Tax Act 2007 (Amendment) Order 2010, SI 2010/588*, and extended to:

- commercial payments made by individuals (*ITA 2007, s 900(2)*);
- patent royalties (*ITA 2007, s 903(5)*);
- certain royalties where the owner's abode is abroad (*ITA 2007, s 906(5)*); and
- payments required to be made under deduction of income tax and made as a result of a direction under *ITA 2007, s 944(2)* – tax avoidance involving non-UK residents.

[*SSCBA 1992, Sch 2 para 3(5)(c)(d)(e)*, inserted by *Income Tax Act 2007 (Amendment) Order 2010, SI 2010/588, Reg 2*].

Relief is to be allowed in respect of payments of *interest* for which relief from income tax is or can be given under *ITA 2007, s 383*, but only so far as incurred wholly or exclusively for the purpose of any relevant trade, profession or vocation. [*SSCBA 1992, Sch 2 para 3(5)(b)*].

There can be little doubt that the 'or' separating 'wholly' and 'exclusively' is a drafting error and that the intention was to reproduce the highly restrictive phrase of *ITTOIA 2005, s 34(1)(a)*. In the event, the intention failed and a much wider test of allowability lies in its place. 'Wholly' relates to the amount of the expenditure; 'exclusively' relates to the motive behind the expenditure. The 'and' of *ITTOIA 2005, s 34(1)(a)* ensures that both criteria must be met for tax allowability while the 'or' of *SSCBA 1992, Sch 2 para 3(5)* clearly bears the meaning that satisfaction of either criterion will suffice.

Relief for payments which satisfy the prescribed conditions is to be given by deducting from profits the gross amount of the payments made in the tax year concerned, and any such amounts which, because of an insufficiency of profits, cannot be relieved in the year of payment are to be carried forward and relieved as soon as possible. [*SSCBA 1992, Sch 2 para 3(5)(b)*]. The amount carried forward does not reduce profits in the following year for the purposes of the post-2015 Class 2 small profits threshold, which relies on there being profits in respect of which Class 4 contributions would be payable if they reached the Class 4 lower annual limit.

Professions: 'catching-up' charge under Finance Act 1998

[32.12] The 'catching-up' charge required as a result of the change requiring non-corporate business accounts to be prepared on the basis that they show a true and fair view with effect from the period of account beginning after 6 April 1999 was taxable as miscellaneous income under *ITTOIA 2005, Part 2, Chapter 17* (ie, akin to the former Schedule D, Case VI charge) and therefore not subject to Class 4 contributions. A negative adjustment was allowable as a deduction in computing profits and so will have been deducted also in computing the amount on which Class 4 contributions were to be charged. [*ITTOIA 2005, ss 228, 229*].

Although the charge will not have attracted a Class 4 liability, it will nonetheless have counted as 'relevant earnings' for pension contribution purposes before A-Day. [*ITTOIA 2005, s 232(4)*].

Professions and others: UITF40 adjustment

[32.13] The prior year adjustment that arose where there was change in accounting approach in the first year that ended on or after 22 June 2005 and the profits thereafter were calculated in accordance with Application Note G as interpreted by UITF40, could be taxed over a period of three to six years. [*FA 2006, s 102, Sch 15*]. The taxpayer could nonetheless elect that the charges were accelerated. In any case, these amounts were taxable as miscellaneous income under *ITTOIA 2005, Part 2, Chapter 17* (ie, akin to the former Schedule D, Case VI charge) and therefore not subject to Class 4 contributions.

Although the charge will not have attracted a Class 4 liability, it will nonetheless have counted as 'relevant earnings' for pension contribution purposes. [*ITTOIA 2005, s 232(4)*].

Key Points regarding earnings from self-employment

[32.14] Points to consider are as follows.

- Earnings for Class 2 purposes before 6 April 2015 were specifically defined and had to be measured on a strict 6 April to 5 April basis by time-apportioning, where necessary, the profits shown by the accounts.
- Earnings for Class 2 purposes are, from 6 April 2015, calculated on the same basis as for Class 4 following changes in *NICA 2015*.
- Class 4 profits are as measured for tax purposes with all deductions replicated, including loss reliefs.
- Rather oddly, 'catch-up' charges for certain professions are not subject to Class 4.
- HMRC announced that from 6 April 2013 sleeping partners are subject to Class 2 and 4 NIC, although the change in interpretation is not without its challengers (see PARTNERS 52). Sleeping partners in investment partnership and investment LLPs will be entitled to pay Class 2 contributions voluntarily but should have no Class 4 earnings.

33

Earnings Limits and Thresholds

Cross-references. See **5.3** AGGREGATION OF EARNINGS for anti-avoidance rule relating to Lower Earnings Limit in multiple employments; **13.5** BENEFITS: CONTRIBUTION REQUIREMENTS for use of Lower Earnings Limit in setting contribution conditions; CLASS **1** CONTRIBUTIONS **15**; CLASS **4** CONTRIBUTIONS **20**; **23.5** CONTRACTED-OUT EMPLOYMENT for significance of Lower Earnings Limit in relation to basic component of State pensions; **24.2** CREDITS for use of Lower Earnings Limit in setting value of Class 1 credits; **28.7** EARNINGS FACTORS for use of Lower Earnings Limit in setting qualifying earnings factor and standard level of contribution; EARNINGS PERIODS **34** for relation of earnings limits and thresholds to earnings periods; **53.2** and **53.8** RATES AND LIMITS.

Other Sources. Simon's Taxes, Volume 2, para A8.259.

Introduction to earnings limits and thresholds

[33.1] The earnings limits and thresholds are generally changed annually and set by Statutory Instrument. Even where no changes take place (as for 2010–11, save for the Lower Earnings Limit) a review is nonetheless undertaken.

Class 1 limits and thresholds

[33.2] For every tax year there is set both a Lower Earnings Limit ('LEL') and an Upper Earnings Limit ('UEL') for Class 1 contributions purposes. From 6 April 2015, there is also an 'upper secondary threshold' ('UST') applicable to employer liability at the 'age-related secondary percentage' (initially 0%) in respect of the earnings of employed earners under the age of 21 on the date of payment. From 6 April 2016, a similar 'apprentice upper secondary threshold' (AUST) was created with the introduction of the 0% age-related secondary percentage for employers of apprentices under the age of 25.

The LEL is the level of weekly EARNINGS FROM EMPLOYMENT: GENERAL **29** at which entitlement to a record for state benefit purposes begins to arise, and it was until April 2012 linked to the level of the single person's state pension. Before

6 April 2000, a liability for primary Class 1 contributions arose once earnings from employed earner's employment reached the LEL. A new, higher, earnings threshold (the 'Primary Threshold') was then introduced, harmonising the starting point for Class 1 with the single personal allowance, and the LEL became a trigger for benefit purposes only (including entitlement to Statutory Sick Pay and Statutory Maternity Pay).

Until 5 April 1999, the LEL was also the starting point for secondary Class 1 contributions, but a 'secondary threshold' was then introduced, also equal to the single personal allowance. Secondary contributions have no impact on benefit entitlements, and the PAYE-NIC harmonisation measure was no more than an attempt at simplification.

The Upper Earnings Limit ('UEL') is the maximum amount of weekly earnings in respect of which *primary* Class 1 contributions at the main rate are payable. Until 6 October 1985, the UEL capped secondary Class 1 contribution liabilities also, but that cap was then removed. Until 6 April 2003, the UEL also served as the point at which primary (employees) liability was capped – but since that date there has been an additional rate (originally 1%, now 2%) of primary contribution payable on earnings above the UEL. And until 6 April 2009, the UEL was also the level of earnings up to which earnings-related state pension would be earned, but thereafter, until 6 April 2016, such entitlement only accrued up to the Upper Accrual Point (see below). The UAP became irrelevant for benefit purposes on 6 April 2016 when the single-tier state pension was introduced and the State Second Pension (S2P) was abolished. [*Social Security (Contributions) Regulations 2001, SI 2001/1004, Regs 10, 11* as amended by *Social Security (Contributions) (Amendment) Regulations 2005, SI 2005/166, Regs 3, 4* and *Social Security (Contributions) (Amendment) Regulations 2009, SI 2009/111, Reg 3; Pensions Act 2014, Sch 13*.]

The LEL and *not* the Earnings Threshold (see below) continues to mark the level of weekly earnings at which entitlement to basic contributory benefits is secured (see **13.5** BENEFITS: CONTRIBUTION REQUIREMENTS and EARNINGS FACTORS **28**).

From 6 April 1999, there has been a Secondary (ie, employer's) earnings Threshold (ST). It was set at the same level as the Primary earnings Threshold (PT) from 6 April 2000 until 6 April 2011, when the two diverged, but they were brought back into alignment from 6 April 2014. For 2014–15 it was set at £153 per week / £7,956 per annum for both. For 2015–16, the employer and employee thresholds diverged once more. The ST was set at £156 per week/£8,112 per annum and it remained at that level for 2016–17.

From 6 April 2017, following the recommendation from the OTS ('The closer alignment of income tax and national insurance', OTS, 7 March 2016) and announced at 2016 Autumn Statement, the employer and employee thresholds were aligned again. The two thresholds have been set at £162 per week/£8,424 per annum for 2018–19. [*Social Security (Contributions) Regulations 2001, SI 2001/1004, Regs 10, 11* as amended by *Social Security (Contributions) (Rates, Limits and Thresholds Amendments and National Insurance Funds Payments) Regulations 2018, SI 2018/337, Regs 7 and 8*.]

From 6 April 2000, the Primary (ie employee's) earnings Threshold (PT) has represented the point at which employees' liability begins. For 2018–19, it has been set at £162 per week/£8,424 per annum. [*Social Security (Contributions) Regulations 2001, SI 2001/1004, Regs 10, 11* as amended by *Social Security (Contributions) (Limits and Thresholds) (Amendment) Regulations 2018, SI 2018/377, Regs 7 and 8*.]

The LEL is retained due to the government policy of protecting the contributory benefit entitlement of those earning from the LEL up to the PT, even though no contributions are payable by the employee in such circumstances.

As noted above, from 6 April 2009 to 5 April 2016, entitlement to added S2P pension ceased to accrue once earnings reached the Upper Accrual Point (UAP) of £770 per week (a permanently fixed cash amount), though main rate primary contributions continued to attract liability up to the UEL. [*National Insurance Contributions Act 2008, s 3*.] The UAP became irrelevant other than for historical purposes once the new single-tier state pension was introduced on 6 April 2016, as there is no earnings-related element to a state pension entitlement that first arises after that date.

The UST is fixed under *Social Security Contributions and Benefits Act 1992 (SSCBA 1992), s 9A* (introduced by *National Insurance Contributions Act 2014, s 9*). It was set at introduction on 6 April 2015 at the same level as the UEL [*Social Security (Contributions) Regulations 2001, SI 2001/1004, Reg 10 as inserted by Social Security (Contributions) (Limits and Thresholds) (Amendment) Regulations 2015, SI 2015/577, Reg 3(h)*].

The AUST from 6 April 2016 was similarly fixed under *SSCBA 1992, s 9B* (introduced by *NICA 2015*, s 1) at the same level as the UEL. Both the UST and the AUST have been legislated in such a way that they may be amended independently, of each other and of the UEL, in future, as may the 0% rates that apply to under-21s and under-25 apprentices.

The *National Insurance Contributions (Rate Ceilings) Act 2015, s 3* provides that the UEL specified in regulations for any tax year commencing after the passage of the Act during the current Parliament (ie, 2016–17 to 2019–20) shall not exceed the weekly equivalent of the proposed income tax higher rate threshold for that tax year. The aggregate value of the single personal allowance and the basic rate band proposed in the annual Autumn Statement or Pre-Budget Report will become the UEL for the tax year commencing on the following 6 April 2016. [*NICRCA 2015, s 3(3)*.] The rate ceiling has now been rendered obsolete with the June 2017 general election and the subsequent commencement of a new Parliament.

The weekly amount is to be arrived at by dividing the annual value by 52 and rounding up or down to the nearest pound. [*NICRCA 2015, 3(4)*.]

Prescribed amounts

[33.3] The limits and thresholds are set annually by regulations. The LEL was, until 2012, linked to the (rounded down) amount of the basic category A retirement pension at the start of the tax year for which the earnings limits are being set (or the immediately following 6 May if an increase in the basic component is to take effect by then). The UEL was, until 6 April 2000, statutorily linked to the basic pension and LEL, but it became linked to the Primary (ie employee's) Threshold. [*SSCBA 1992, s 5(1)(2)(3)*.] That link was broken from 6 April 2009, so that the UEL each year may simply be set by regulations. Since the category A retirement pension is payable only to existing pensioners from the start of the new single-tier state pension in April 2016, the former link is no longer relevant and it remains to be seen how the LEL, UEL, UST and AUST are set in future.

In the case of the LEL, the weekly amount prescribed had, before 6 April 2011, to be an amount equal to or not more than 99p less than the basic pension. [*SSCBA 1992, s 5(2)*, now repealed).] However, the old statutory practice was then abandoned so that the LEL was not automatically linked to the basic pension, although the divergence was still small. As the pre-2016 scheme basic pension payable from the week commencing 6 April 2016 was set at £119.30, the Lower Earnings Limit would have been set at £119 per week from 6 April 2016 if the old rules had been used, but it was in fact set at £112. [*Social Security (Contributions) Regulations 2001, SI 2001/1004, Reg 10* as amended by *Social Security (Contributions) (Limits and Thresholds) (Amendment) Regulations 2015, SI 2015/577, Reg 3*.] The link with the basic category A retirement pension was broken by *Pensions Act 2007, ss 7, 8*, commenced by *SI 2010/2650*.

For the Upper Earnings Limit, the weekly amount prescribed used to be equal to seven times the Primary Threshold or had to exceed or fall short of that sum by not more than half of that amount. [*SSCBA 1992, s 5(3)*, as amended by *Welfare Reform and Pensions Act 1999, s 73*.] However, from 6 April 2009, these restrictions on what the amount at which the UEL might be set were removed. [*National Insurance Contributions Act 2008, ss 1, 2*.] The UEL for 2017–18 was set at £866 per week or £45,000 per year, and was increased for 2018–19 to £892 per week or £46,350 per year. [*Social Security (Contributions) Regulations 2001, SI 2001/1004, Reg 11* as amended by *Social Security (Contributions) (Limits and Thresholds Amendments and National Insurance Funds Payments) Regulations 2018, SI 2018/377, Regs 7 and 8*.]

For the UST, *Social Security (Contributions) Regulations 2001, SI 2001/1004, Reg 11(3B)* was inserted by *Social Security (Contributions) (Limits and Thresholds) (Amendment) Regulations 2015, SI 2015/577, Reg 4* so as to provide that the equivalent monthly and annual values of the UST follow the same formula as the UEL. A similar result was achieved for the AUST by *Social Security (Contributions) (Limits and Thresholds Amendments and National Insurance Funds Payments) Regulations 2016, SI 2016/343, Reg 5*.

As noted above, under *NICRCA 2015, s 3*, the weekly amount of the UEL in future is to be arrived at by dividing the annual value (ie, the single personal allowance plus the basic rate band proposed in the Budget Statement) by 52 and rounding up or down to the nearest pound. [*NICRCA 2015, 3(4)*.] It must be assumed that the UST and AUST will follow suit, until there is a policy change.

The Earnings Thresholds are specified quite separately and were once intended to match the weekly equivalent of the personal tax allowance. See **33.2**. [*Social Security (Contributions) Regulations 2001, SI 2001/1004, Reg 10*; *Social Security (Contributions) (Limits and Thresholds) (Amendment) Regulations 2012, SI 2012/804, Reg 4*.]

The UAP was fixed permanently for 2011–12 onwards at the same weekly and other amounts as represented the UEL for 2008–09, but it ceased to be relevant on 6 April 2016 when S2P was abolished.

For other prescribed amounts for 2017–18 and earlier years see **53.2 RATES AND LIMITS**.

Pro-rata earnings limits and thresholds

[33.4] Where an employed earner's earnings period is other than a week, the weekly LEL (relevant to benefits), UEL (relevant to state pension entitlement up to 5 April 2009 and the boundary between main and additional rate primary contributions) and UAP (relevant to contracted-out primary contributions and state pension entitlement from 6 April 2009 to 5 April 2016) are replaced by a prescribed equivalent. [*SSCBA 1992, s 5(4)*.] As noted above, the rules for the UST and AUST follow those for the UEL. The equivalent limits are as follows.

(a) Where the earnings period is a multiple of a week, the weekly limits multiplied by that multiple.
(b) Where the earnings period is a month, the weekly limits multiplied by 4 $^1/_3$.
(c) Where the earnings period is a multiple of a month, the monthly limits (before rounding, see below) multiplied by that multiple.
(d) In any other case, one-seventh of the weekly limits multiplied by the number of days in the earnings period concerned.

[*Social Security (Contributions) Regulations 2001, SI 2001/1004, Reg 11(2)* as amended by *Social Security (Contributions) (Amendment) Regulations 2009, SI 2009/111, Reg 3(4)*.]

The amounts determined under (b) and (c) above are, if not whole pounds, to be rounded up to the next whole pound, whereas the calculation under (d) is to be made to the nearest penny and any amount of one-half penny or less is to be disregarded. [*Social Security (Contributions) Regulations 2001, SI 2001/1004, Reg 11(4)(5)* as amended by *Social Security (Contributions) (Amendment) Regulations 2009, SI 2009/111, Reg 3(7)*.] Thus, for 2018–19 the monthly and yearly LEL is:

	LEL
Monthly:	
£113 × 4 $^1/_3$ =	£503
Yearly:	
£113 × 52 =	£6,032.00

The UAP equivalents from 2009 to 2016 were arrived at on the same basis:

Monthly: £770 × 4 1/3 = £3,366.66 = £3,337

Yearly: £770 × 52 = £40,040

The Earnings Thresholds, from 6 April 1999, are not, however, computed for longer earnings periods in the same way — nor is the UEL with effect from 6 April 2009.

The equivalent Earnings Thresholds are specified in regulations. Those for 2018–19 are contained in *Social Security (Contributions) (Rates, Limits and Thresholds Amendments and National Insurance Fund Payments) Regulations 2018, SI 2018/377, Regs 7 and 8 and Social Security (Contributions) Regulations 2001, SI 2001/1004, Regs 10, 11* as follows:

The employee's (primary) threshold was set at:

- £162 per week, where the earnings period is a week;
- £702 per month, where the earnings period is a month; and
- £8,424 per year, where the earnings period is a year.

The employer's (secondary) threshold was set at:

- £162 per week, where the earnings period is a week;
- £702 per month, where the earnings period is a month; and
- £8,424 per year, where the earnings period is a year.

The rules for setting the non-weekly limits are:

- where the earnings period is a whole number of weeks, divide the annual limit by 52, multiply by the number of weeks contained in the earnings period and round up to the next whole pound;
- where the earnings period is a whole number of months, divide the annual limit by 12, multiply by the number of months contained in the earning period and round up to the next whole pound;
- in any other case, divide the annual limit by 365, multiply by the number of days in the earnings period and round to the nearest penny (½p being rounded down).

For the monthly and yearly thresholds for 2016–17 and earlier years see **53.3** RATES AND LIMITS.

[*Social Security (Contributions) Regulations 2001, SI 2001/1004, Reg 11(3)(4)(5)*, as amended by *Social Security (Contributions) (Amendment) Regulations 2009, SI 2009/111, Reg 3(7)(8)*].

The equivalent amounts for the UEL, UST and AUST have, to date, been specified in regulations. Those for 2018–19 are contained in *Social Security (Contributions) Regulations 2001, SI 2001/1004, Reg 2A*, as amended by *Social Security (Contributions) (Rates, Limits and Thresholds Amendments and National Insurance Funds Payments) Regulations 2018, SI 2018/377, Regs 7 and 8* as follows:

- £892 per week, where the earnings period is a week;
- £3,863 per month, where the earnings period is a month; and
- £46,350 per year, where the earnings period is a year;

and

- where the earnings period is a whole number of weeks, divide the annual limit by 52, multiply by the number of weeks contained in the earnings period and round up to the next whole pound;
- where the earnings period is a whole number of months, divide the annual limit by 12, multiply by the number of months contained in the earning period and round up to the next whole pound; and
- in any other case, divide the annual limit by 365, multiply by the number of days in the earnings period and round to the nearest penny (½p being rounded down).

This rule was extended to the UST by *SSCBA 1992, s 9A(8)*, so the UEL equivalents apply equally to the UST.

As noted above, the UST has been legislated separately from the UEL so that the UST may deviate from the UEL in future (as indeed may the age-related secondary rate).

National Insurance Contributions Act 2015, s 1 created in *SSCBA 1992, s 9B* an 'apprentice UST' or 'AUST' (and apprentice age-related secondary rate of 0%) applicable from 6 April 2016. These have also been created as separate provisions so that the UEL, UST and AUST may be set at different levels in future, although they are all initially set at the same value.

[*Social Security (Contributions) Regulations 2001, SI 2001/1004, Reg 11(2A)(4)(5)*, as amended by *Social Security (Contributions) (Amendment) Regulations 2009, SI 2009/111, Reg 3 (5)(7)(8)*.]

As noted above, the weekly equivalent of the annual UEL is in future to be set by reference to the income tax higher rate threshold. [*NICRCA 2015, s 3*.]

The significance of the earnings limits and thresholds

[33.5] It may be possible in a small number of cases to employ several people each earning less than the earnings thresholds so that neither employees' nor employers' contributions arise but basic benefit entitlement is nonetheless thereby earned. See Tolley's National Insurance Brief, April 1998 and *Social Security Act 1998, s 51*.

Class 4 limits

[33.6] Class 4 contributions are calculated at a main percentage rate on so much of the adjusted profits as falls between a *lower annual limit* and an *upper annual limit* and, from 6 April 2003, the additional Class 4 percentage (originally 1% and currently 2%) on so much of those profits or gains as exceeds the upper profits limit. (See **32.2** to **32.11** EARNINGS FROM SELF-EMPLOYMENT). [*SSCBA 1992, s 15(3)(3ZA)* as amended by *National Insurance Contributions Act 2002, s 3(1)*.] These limits may be altered by order of the Treasury as a result of the review of contributions and general level of earnings which, in the absence of statutory direction to the contrary, must be carried out annually. [*SSAA 1992, s 141(3)(4)(d)* as amended by *National Insurance Contributions Act 2002, Sch 1 para 16*.] For 2018–19 the lower limit was set at £8,424 and the upper annual limit was set at £46,350. [*Social Security (Contributions) (Rates, Limits and Thresholds Amendments and National Insurance Funds Payments) Regulations 2017, SI 2017/415, Reg 5.*]

It has become the convention that the Class 4 lower and upper annual limits are set at the same level as the Class 1 LEL and UEL. The Queen's Speech after the 2015 general election committed the government to continuing to follow this practice, although the point was not included in the NIC (Rate Ceilings) Act 2015, which tied the Class 1 UEL to the proposed income tax higher rate threshold for each tax year for the duration of the current Parliament (ie, until 2018). The government has instead proposed consultation on a reform involving the merger of Class 2 into Class 4, with a redefinition of the link to benefits, although it seems unlikely at this stage that the new Class 4 upper annual limit will deviate dramatically, if at all, from the Class 1 UEL.

For limits for 2016–17 and earlier years see **53.15** RATES AND LIMITS.

34

Earnings Periods

Cross-references. See **5.10** AGGREGATION OF EARNINGS for establishment of common earnings period; CLASS 1 CONTRIBUTIONS **15**; COMPANY DIRECTORS **22**; EARNINGS FROM EMPLOYMENT: GENERAL **29**; EARNINGS LIMITS AND THRESHOLDS **33**.

Other Sources. Simon's Taxes, Volume 2, para A8.248; Tolley's National Insurance Brief, March 1997, pages 17–19; Leaflets CWG2 (2018 to 2019), CA39, CA43, CA44, Employer's Help Book E12 (2013); HM Revenue and Customs National Insurance Manual NIM08000.

Introduction to earnings periods

[34.1] An earnings period is a period to which earnings paid to or for the benefit of an employed earner are deemed to relate, irrespective of the period over which those earnings are earned, and by reference to which assessment of contribution liability takes place. Where earnings are paid at *regular intervals*, the earnings period is determined by the periodicity of such payments but, where payment is *irregular*, the earnings period is determined by the application of certain rules provided by regulations made under *SSCBA 1992, Sch 1 para 2*. Special rules apply to company directors whether their earnings are paid at regular intervals or not (see **34.12** below) and to mariners who are paid in respect of voyage periods (see **34.13** below).

An earnings period cannot normally be *less than seven days* in length and the first earnings period in any tax year is deemed to begin on the first day of that tax year. [*Social Security (Contributions) Regulations 2001, SI 2001/1004, Reg 3(1)*]. See HM Revenue and Customs Manual NIM08020. Where an earnings period is either a week or a month or a multiple of a week or a month, its end will, therefore, always correspond with the end of either a tax week or a tax month in the PAYE calendar. See *The Income Tax (Pay As You Earn) Regulations 2003, SI 2003/2682, Reg 2*. HM Revenue and Customs National Insurance Manual NIM08002 was for a time incorrect in suggesting the contrary. Any period between the end of the last earnings period of normal length and the beginning of the next tax year is itself to be treated as an earnings period of normal length however short it might actually be. [*Social Security (Contributions) Regulations 2001, SI 2001/1004, Reg 3(2)*]. Where the normal earnings period is a week, the final earnings period of a week in a tax year will always contain either one or two days, but no more (known as 'week 53' in payroll operation).

In accordance with the rule stated in the foregoing paragraph, the earnings period of an employed earner who is paid at intervals of less than a week is a week and it will, therefore, be necessary to aggregate all payments made to him during each contribution week (ie, by the same employer – separate employments have separate and independent earnings periods) in order to calculate any Class 1 contribution liabilities on his earnings. (CWG2 (2018 to 2019), para 1.7.) Arguably this is wrong where an individual is hired to work on, say, only Monday and there is no expectation of any further work but is hired again on Friday. Each payment should attract its own earnings period of seven days. It is not clear how HMRC's RTI system would react to two FPSs for the same week if they applied separate weekly earnings periods. It would appear that HMRC have circumvented this potential problem as para 1.7 goes on to state that 'all the payments made in an *Income Tax week*' [emphasis added] should be added together to determine whether NICs are due.

Regulations ensure that under normal circumstances (but for exceptions see **34.8**, **34.9** and **34.12** below) an earner can, at any one time, have but one earnings period per employment and that he is never outside an earnings period.

Pay patterns

Single regular pay pattern

[34.2] 'Regular intervals' are intervals of substantially equal length at which, in accordance with an express or implied arrangement between an employed earner and a secondary contributor, payments of earnings normally fall to be made. A 'regular pay pattern' is established where there is a succession of such intervals, each of which begins immediately after the end of the interval which precedes it. Where only one such pattern exists in relation to a particular earner, that earner's earnings period is identical to his normal pay interval. [*Social Security (Contributions) Regulations 2001, SI 2001/1004, Reg 1(2), Reg 3(1)*]. See Leaflet CWG2 (2018 to 2019), para 3.1.1.

Example

Aubrey and Beardsley both work in an art studio. A is paid £200 per week and B is paid £870 per month; therefore A's earnings period is one week and B's earnings period is one month. A's first earnings period in the tax year will begin on 6 April and end on 12 April (see **34.1** above). His second will start on 13 April and end on 19 April. B's first earnings period will begin on 6 April and end on 5 May. His second will start on 6 May and end on 5 June. If A's weekly wage of £200 is paid to him on 13 April it will, therefore, fall in and be related to his second earnings period for the tax year, ie PAYE week 2 ended 19 April. If B's monthly salary of £870 is paid to him on 8 May it will fall in and be related to his second earnings period for the tax year also, ie PAYE month 2 ended 5 June.

Not all employees are paid either weekly or monthly. An employee may, for example, be paid every ten days, and, in that event, he will have 37 earnings periods in the year: 36 of ten days each and the thirty-seventh of five or six days. Class 1 primary contribution liabilities on earnings paid in each of those 37 such earnings periods will be ascertained in 2018–19 by reference to the Upper Earnings Limit of £46,350 ÷ 365 × 10 = £1,269.86, and an Earnings Threshold of £8,424 ÷ 365 × 10 = £230.79 (see **33.4** EARNINGS LIMITS AND THRESHOLDS). Class 1 secondary contributions would be calculated on the same basis when the primary and secondary thresholds are the same. In these circumstances, employers may only use the exact percentage method of calculation. The numbers are calculated exactly, then rounded to the nearest penny, with any amount of exactly 0.5p rounded down. (CWG2 (2018 to 2019), para 1.7.)

Some employees may work and be paid only every other week or every other fortnight during the year. In such cases, the employee should be treated as having a two- or four-weekly earnings period and his earnings should be divided by two (if he works every other week) or four (if he works every other fortnight) and Class 1 contribution liabilities should be calculated by looking up the weekly figure in the tables and then multiplying the answer by 2 or 4 as appropriate. (CWG2 2018 to 2019, para 1.7).

Multiple regular pay pattern

[34.3] Because an earner (other than an ex-company director—see **34.12** below) may not at one and the same time have two or more earnings periods as regards a single employment (see **34.1** above), difficulties arise where *two or more regular pay patterns run concurrently*. The difficulties are resolved, except where a direction is issued, by equating the earnings period with the length of the *shorter or shortest* interval at which any part of earnings is paid or treated as paid—except in certain circumstances where earnings fall to be aggregated (see **5.10** AGGREGATION OF EARNINGS). [*Social Security (Contributions) Regulations 2001, SI 2001/1004, Reg 6(3)*].

Example (1)

Clive is a salesman for Dubbleglays Ltd. He is paid a monthly salary, a quarterly commission and an annual bonus and has, therefore, three regular pay intervals: a month, a quarter and a year. As the shortest of these is a month, C's earnings period is a month and all the earnings paid to him in a year will be related to one or other of the twelve such periods it contains. If, therefore, he is paid £830 commission on 8 May for the quarter ended 31 March, £600 salary on 15 May for the month of May and £2,500 bonus on 29 May for the year ended 31 December of the preceding year, his earnings for the earnings period from 6 May to 5 June (PAYE month 2) will be £3,930, irrespective of the fact that only £600 of the total is earned within the month and the remainder relates to previous tax years and was earned over a period of between three and twelve months.

It will be observed that, because an earnings period of one month attracts an Upper Earnings Limit appropriate to only one month (2018–19, £3,863, see **33.4** EARNINGS LIMITS AND THRESHOLDS), £67 of the earnings in PAYE month 2 in the above example escapes Class 1 *primary* contribution liability at the main rate, attracting instead a liability at only 2% (and also *not* escaping Class 1 *secondary* liability), and that, as a matter of general principle, the greater the amount of earnings paid at the longer pay intervals of a multiple regular pay interval earnings arrangement, the greater the Class 1 primary contribution avoidance which may be achieved. In order that such avoidance activity may be countered, however, HM Revenue and Customs are empowered, where satisfied that the greater part of earnings is normally paid at intervals of greater length than the shorter or shortest, to reverse the rule by merely notifying the earner and the secondary contributor that they are doing so. Thereafter (but not retrospectively), the length of the *longer or longest* interval will be the length of the earnings period. [*Social Security (Contributions) Regulations 2001, SI 2001/1004, Reg 3(2B)*, as amended by *Social Security (Contributions) (Amendment No 3) Regulations 2002, SI 2002/2366, Reg 4*]. Where that longer or longest interval is a year, the first earnings period following a *Reg 3(2B)* direction is to consist of the number of weeks remaining in the tax year, commencing with the week in which the direction takes effect. [*Social Security (Contributions) Regulations 2001, SI 2001/1004, Reg 3(3)*].

Example (2)

For the tax year, Everard (one of Clive's colleagues—see above example) had total earnings of £15,200 comprising

	£	*Pay interval*
Salary	7,200	month
Commission	14,000	quarter
Bonus	4,000	year

if a similar pattern had also subsisted at least during the preceding tax year or two HM Revenue and Customs will, because the greater part of earnings were paid at quarterly and annual intervals, be able to direct that, from the date of the direction onwards, and for all future years, E is to have an annual earnings period. If such a direction were to be made on, say, 5 June, E's earnings periods for the tax year would be

month to	5 May
1 month to	5 June
44-week period to	5 April

(Ignore part weeks covering 5 April or 4 and 5 April in a leap year when calculating a pro rata earnings period – leaflet CA44 (2018), para 24.)

His earnings period for the next and all future tax years would be the tax year concerned.

The use of the phrase 'practice' in the wording of *Social Security (Contributions) Regulations 2001, SI 2001/1004, Reg 3(2)* would suggest that HM Revenue and Customs will be unable to use its powers under that regulation until an arrangement to which the regulation would otherwise apply has been repeated sufficiently to establish it as the rule rather than the exception, and this is confirmed in HM Revenue and Customs National Insurance Manual NIM09512.

Where HM Revenue and Customs is unable to issue a *Reg 3(2B)* direction (eg because less than half the earnings are paid at the longer interval), it may instead issue a similar direction under *Social Security (Contributions) Regulations 2001, SI 2001/1004, Reg 31* which applies where HM Revenue and Customs is satisfied as to the existence of a practice in respect of the payment of earnings whereby the incidence of Class 1 contributions is avoided or reduced by means of irregular or unequal payments (see **8.21** ANTI-AVOIDANCE). Such directions are usually only issued where the loss to the NI Fund is at least £250 in a year for a single employee. See HM Revenue and Customs National Insurance Manual NIM09650.

Irregular payments treated as paid at regular intervals

[34.4] Where a payment of earnings which would normally fall to be made at a regular interval is made at some other interval it is to be treated as made on the date on which it would normally fall to be made. [*Social Security (Contributions) Regulations 2001, SI 2001/1004, Reg 7(1)(a), Reg 7(2)(a)*]. (CWG2 (2016), para 60 and chart on pages 10–11).

Example (1)

Fred works for Gimlet, a self-employed joiner, and is paid £280 per week. G falls ill and for three weeks F is unpaid despite working normally. In the fourth week G is again able to attend to his business and F is paid £1,120. For Class 1 purposes, however, F is to be treated as receiving £280 on each normal payday and his earnings period remains a week.

Note that the deeming is for the purposes of assessing NICs, ie, the calculation and the earnings period rule. The actual payment would be reported on an FPS on or before the date of payment.

In the First-tier Tribunal case of *Mehta* [2015] UKFTT 0396, a question arose at the time of the contributor's retirement about the correct earnings period for his time as a new starter who missed the payroll closing date in February 1995, the month of joining, but was paid an advance in that month (outside payroll), then the correct total pay to date, including the advance recovered, in March 1995, his second month of employment. The employer had treated the advance as an on-account amount and shown just one month's earnings at the UEL on Mr Mehta's P60 for the year (ie, everything had been treated as March earnings). For that year, his total NICable earnings on HMRC's records were therefore shown as slightly below the level needed to make the year qualify for state pension purposes. If the employer had correctly processed his February salary in February, or as a separate month's earnings in March, he would have paid more contributions and his relevant earnings for the year would have exceeded the qualifying earnings factor, and most importantly an extra year would have been credited to his state pension record. The FTT found in his favour: the employer had disregarded the correct procedure in not using an earnings period of two months for the first payment, which was what it represented, and HMRC had incorrectly rejected his claim to have the liability recalculated. He was therefore to be treated as having paid the correct amount and having a qualifying contribution record for the year in dispute, which increased his state pension.

The rule does not only apply to a regular payment that is mistimed. In the same way, earnings paid at irregular intervals are to be treated as paid at regular intervals if the pay arrangement in force ensures that *one and only one* payment is made in each of a succession of periods consisting of the same number of days, weeks or calendar months. The deemed date of payment in such a case will be the last day of the deemed regular interval. [*Social Security (Contributions) Regulations 2001, SI 2001/1004, Reg 7(1)(b), 7(2)(b)*]. (Leaflet CWG2 (2018 to 2019), para 3.1.2 and examples in para 1.7.) The DSS (now DWP) said that payments are made at regular intervals if, for example, payments are normally made at 17-day intervals but some of the payments are made at 16-day or 18-day intervals.

Example (2)

Henry is paid on the last Thursday of each calendar month. He is, therefore, to be treated as paid at regular monthly intervals corresponding with PAYE months and the deemed payday will be the last day of each such month.

Where earnings are paid *in respect of regular intervals* but at *irregular intervals*, each payment is to be treated as made on the last day of the regular interval in respect of which it is due. See HM Revenue and Customs Manual NIM08050. [*Social Security (Contributions) Regulations 2001, SI 2001/1004, Reg 7(1)(c), Reg 7(2)(b)*].

Where earnings are paid irregularly, eg at intervals of 4–4–5 weeks, perhaps because of the need for quarterly accounting, the earnings periods will be 4–4–5 weeks. Where, however, employees are paid monthly but the calculation differs because sometimes they are paid for four weeks and sometimes five, the earnings period is a month.

The only circumstance in which these rules are *not* to apply is where, in consequence of treating an irregular payment of earnings as paid at a regular interval, a payment of earnings made in one tax year would be treated as made in another. See CWG2 (2018 to 2019), para 3.1.5. [*Social Security (Contributions) Regulations 2001, SI 2001/1004, Reg 7(3)*].

Example (3)

Ingrid starts work on 3 March 2016 but the payment of £1,000 due to be made to her on 28 March 2016 is made to her with her April salary of £1,000 on 25 April 2016. Under the rule stated earlier, £1,000 of this would have been treated as paid on 28 March 2016 but as it was actually paid in a different tax year this is not possible. Although the payments are kept separate for NIC purposes the rates and limits to be used are those in force at the time of payment and the £2,000 is treated as having been paid in the later tax year. Ingrid is in not contracted-out employment and not eligible to pay the reduced rate. The total contributions due are, from CA38 (2018), page 25 using the figure of £999, £77.14. Each payment of £1,000 attracts such liability.

In such a case, however, the earnings have to be shown separately so that an earner may, if he wishes, apply for the contributions paid in the year to which the earnings do not truly belong to be allocated to the other year for benefit entitlement purposes. [*Social Security (Contributions) Regulations 2001, SI 2001/1004, Reg 58*]. See HM Revenue and Customs National Insurance Manual NIM08312. See also CA National Insurance News, Issue 8, summer 1997, pages 8 and 9.

Despite these rules, and without the legislation having been changed, HM Revenue and Customs instructed employers not to apply *Reg 7(3)* where they were due to pay wages on 6 April 2007 (Good Friday, a non-banking day) and therefore made the payment early. Such payments were to be treated as paid on the due day 6 April. Similar arrangements would apply if the payments were due on Easter Monday and brought forward to Maundy Thursday. This was the first time since the introduction of earnings related contributions (and also the first time since the PAYE system was introduced in the 1940s) that Good Friday had fallen on the first day of the tax year. The same instructions applied again for 2012. (CWG2 (2011), page 12 and CWG2 (2012), page 9). These instructions will not apply in the above case of Ingrid as the payment was merely late for the employer's convenience and not in any way related to non-banking days. HMRC appeared to be disregarding the law at the turn of a tax year if a payment was due on a non-banking day, eg Sunday 6 April 2014, and was made on Friday 4 April. HMRC subsequently revised its guidance: such a payment is to be treated as being made on 6 April as appropriate, but reported on an FPS when paid, albeit with the regular payday shown as the payment date (CWG2 (2018 to 2019), para 1.8).

Other irregular payments

[34.5] A special rule applies where earnings are paid at irregular intervals but earnings neither follow nor can be treated as following a regular pay pattern. In such cases, the earnings period is to be the length of that part of the employment for which the earnings are paid or a week, whichever is the longer. See HM Revenue and Customs National Insurance Manual NIM08100. [*Social Security (Contributions) Regs 2001, SI 2001/1004, Reg 4(a)*]. (Leaflet CWG2 (2018 to 2019), para 3.1.3.)

Example (1)

On 15 July, Jack is employed by Kwest Films Ltd as a researcher but, because of his age, he is not entitled to the adult minimum wage. He is to be paid £10 per hour to work in his own time and at his own convenience. He has, however, to meet the following deadlines

'Health Service' material	31 August
'Aids' material	28 October
'Disarmament' material	31 October

J works 106 hours on the first project, 151 hours on the second and 12 hours on the third. Earnings periods and earnings will be as follows

	£
48 days from 15 July to 31 August	1,060
58 days from 1 September to 28 October	1,510
Week ended 1 November (though only a four-day fixed period)	120

Example (2)

Logan is employed by Mulch Ltd as a gardener. He is paid on an irregular basis for occasional attendance at various locations at such times and for such periods as he considers necessary. His rate of pay is £8 per hour. Part of his work record is

23 October to 5 November	80 hours
18 November	6 hours
30 November to 10 December	63 hours

L's earnings periods and earnings are as follows

	£
14 days to 5 November	640
Week ended 22 November	48
11 days to 10 December	504

Where it is not reasonably practicable to determine the period of that part of the employment for which earnings are paid, the earnings period is to be the period from the date of the last preceding payment of earnings in respect of the employment to the date of payment. Where there has been no previous payment, the period is to be measured from the date the employment began. In any event, the minimum length of the earnings period must be one week. [*Social Security (Contributions) Regulations 2001, SI 2001/1004, Reg 4(b)(i)*]. Where such a payment is made before the related employment begins or after it ends, the earnings period is to be a week. [*Social Security (Contributions) Regulations 2001, SI 2001/1004, Reg 4(b)(ii)*].

Each session of a person in a sessional fee-paid office is to be treated as a separate employment and, accordingly, under *Social Security (Contributions) Regulations 2001, SI 2001/1004, Reg 3(1)* a weekly earnings period is to apply unless, exceptionally, a session lasts for longer than a week. In that event, the earnings period is, instead, to be the length of the session.

In practice, persons paid per session are normally paid on a regular basis. For example, a teacher at an evening class may work on Tuesday, Thursday and Friday evenings but payment is made on a weekly or, more often, a monthly basis. The payments in such cases are aggregated and the earnings period will be a week or a month.

Each payment per session may sometimes have a separate earnings period of a week, for example, in the case of a relief barmaid who fills in at short notice for someone who has failed to turn up. At the end of the session she may receive £30 and at that time it is not known if she will work again. If she does in fact work again that day or week the payments are not aggregated. This may prove a challenge for some RTI software. Although the employer should be able to set the 'irregular employment' indicator in software, HMRC's RTI instructions used to be as follows:

> 'You must follow the same payroll procedures for temporary or casual employees as you do for your permanent employees. The length of their employment with you or the amount they are paid doesn't make any difference to your payroll responsibilities.
>
> If you employ people on a temporary or casual basis and your business pays them, you must:
>
> - calculate, record and deduct PAYE tax and National Insurance contributions (NICs) in the same way as any other employee
> - include the employee's details on your FPS when you pay them.'
>
> (www.hmrc.gov.uk/payerti/employee-starting/special-situations/temps.htm#1)

Guidance on temporary and casual hires is now restricted to harvest workers and beaters (www.gov.uk/paying-harvest-casuals-and-casual-beaters). This may stem from the fact that the former guidance did not accord with NIC regulations on earnings periods, as each payment to the barmaid should be treated separately, not in the same way as multiple payments to a permanent employee in a single earnings period.

Payments under Employment Rights legislation

[34.6] Special earnings period rules are to be applied to payments made under employment rights legislation (see **29.13** EARNINGS FROM EMPLOYMENT: GENERAL), except in the case of company directors where the annual earnings period (or pro-rata earnings period in the year of appointment) will apply. See HM Revenue and Customs National Insurance Manual NIM09000-09030. Except in the case of directors the position is as follows.

In the case of *awards under orders for reinstatement or re-engagement or for the continuation of a contract of employment*, the earnings period is to be the period to which the award relates or a week, whichever is the longer. [*Social*

Security (Contributions) Regulations 2001, SI 2001/1004, Reg 5(a)]. If certain amounts due under the order are payable by instalments those instalments are to be aggregated and the rule is to be applied as stated. Where the award is paid with the first regular payment of earnings following reinstatement or re-engagement, the award must be assessed separately according to the stated rule. (CWG2 (2018 to 2019), paras 5.12, 5.12.1, 5.12.2.)

In the case of a *protective award*, the earnings period is to be the protected period or that part of it for which the sum is paid or a week, whichever is the longer. [*Social Security (Contributions) Regulations 2001, SI 2001/1004, Reg 5(a)*]. Where, therefore, earnings have been paid to an earner for part of the protected period, the earnings period to be applied in relation to wages paid for the remaining part of the protected period is to be that remaining part of the protected period. Any earnings paid during the period covered by the award (eg overtime arrears) must be dealt with separately for contribution purposes. (CWG2 (2018 to 2019), para 5.12.3.)

Where, in consequence of these rules, an earnings period falls wholly or partly in a tax year or years other than that in which relevant contributions are paid, contributions may, on request and in order to protect the earner's contribution record for the purposes of benefit entitlement, be treated as paid proportionately in respect of the year or years in which the earnings period falls. [*Social Security (Contributions) Regulations 2001, SI 2001/1004, Reg 5(b)*].

SSP, SMP, SPP, SAP and ShPP payments

[34.7] Where a payment of Statutory Sick Pay, Statutory Maternity Pay, Statutory Paternity Pay, Statutory Adoption Pay or Statutory Shared Parental Pay is made by HM Revenue and Customs on behalf of the Secretary of State for Work and Pensions rather than by an employer (eg where the employer has become insolvent and a period of entitlement or a maternity pay period has not expired), the earnings period is, in the case of such a payment of SSP, a week or the period for which the payment is made, whichever is the longer, and, in the case of such other payments for any week, the earnings period is a week. [*Social Security (Contributions) Regulations 2001, SI 2001/1004, Reg 9; Social Security (Contributions) (Amendment) Regulations 2003, SI 2003/193, Reg 4; Social Security and Tax Credits (Miscellaneous Amendments) Regulations 2015, SI 2015/175, Regs 2, 3.*]

Change of regular pay interval

[34.8] Where, because of a change in the regular interval at which any part of an employed earner's earnings is paid or treated as paid, an earner's earnings period is changed and the new earnings period is longer than the old, a payment of earnings at the old interval may fall within the first new earnings period. In that event, contributions on all payments made during the new earnings period are not to exceed the contribution which would have been payable had all those payments been made at the new interval. [*Social Security (Contributions) Regulations 2001, SI 2001/1004, Reg 18(3)*]. Accordingly, employers are instructed to calculate the Class 1 contribution liabilities on the total of all payments of earnings made in the new earnings period and then to deduct from those amounts the contribution liabilities already calculated on payments of earnings made at the old interval within the new earnings period. See HM Revenue and Customs Manual NIM08500 and 08510. (CWG2 (2018 to 2019), paras 1.9, 1.10.)

Example (1)

Nuthatch and Osprey are both employed by Partridge Ltd. N is paid £400 per week and O is paid £250 per week. In June 2016, they become salaried employees and begin to be paid monthly at £1,800 and £1,050 per month, respectively. The last weekly wage is paid to each of them on 7 June and their first monthly salaries are paid on 28 June. The first new earnings period is the month from 6 June to 5 July and their last payments of weekly wage fall within this period. Contributions have already been calculated on that wage as follows.

		*Primary**		*Secondary**	
		%	£	%	£
N	£400	Nil/12	28.56	Nil/13.8	32.84
O	£250	Nil/12	10.56	Nil/13.8	12.14

If contributions on the payment of salary on 5 July are calculated without regard to that wage payment, those contributions will be

		*Primary**		*Secondary**	
		%	£	%	£
N	£1,800	Nil/12	131.76	Nil/13.8	151.52
O	£1,050	Nil/12	41.76	Nil/13.8	48.02

If, however, contributions are calculated on the total payments in the earnings period, contributions will be

		*Primary**		*Secondary**	
		%	£	%	£
N	£2,200	Nil/12	179.76	Nil/13.8	206.72
O	£1,300	Nil/12	71.76	Nil/13.8	82.52

*First £702 (monthly) or £162 (weekly) at Nil%.

Under *Social Security (Contributions) Regulations 2001, SI 2001/1004, Reg 18(3)*, the contributions due on the two separate parts of earnings are not to exceed the contributions due on the total and they do not. However, the CWG2 guidance requires the recalculation to be performed regardless of any comparison and thus, N's separate contributions (primary, £28.56 + £131.76 = £160.32 and secondary, £32.84 + £151.52 = £184.36) become primary, £179.76 and secondary £206.72, and O's separate contributions (primary £10.56 + £41.76 = £52.32 and secondary, £12.14 + £48.02 = £60.16) are to be uplifted to £71.76 primary and £82.52 secondary. Thus, primary contributions of £151.20 (£179.76 – £28.56) and secondary contributions of £173.88 (£206.72 – £32.84) are to be paid on the first payment of monthly salary to N, while primary contributions of £61.20 (£71.76 – £10.56) and secondary contributions of £70.38 (£82.52 – £12.14) are to be paid on the first monthly payment of salary to O on 28 June. The legal validity of this instruction in CWG2 in these circumstances is highly questionable, but the outcome is sensible.

If, in the circumstances described above, the date of the change to a longer pay interval before 6 April 2016 was also the date of a change from not contracted-out employment to CONTRACTED-OUT EMPLOYMENT 23, the Class 1 liabilities on the total payments in the new earnings period would have been calculated at the appropriate contracted-out rates. (CWG2 (2015), page 10.)

It should be noted that, provided the regular interval in respect of which earnings are paid remains unchanged, a mere change of pay day or a change in 'week in hand' or 'lying-time' arrangements does *not* bring the *Social Security (Contributions) Regulations 2001, SI 2001/1004, Reg 18* rule into operation. This is because the earnings period (which is determined by the regular pay interval) also remains unchanged. Instructions are, therefore, that, where in consequence of such a change, two regular payments fall within the same earnings period, contribution liabilities are to be calculated on each payment separately (CWG2 (2018 to 2019), para 1.11).

Example (2)

Quail is employed by Roadrunner Ltd and is paid, on a Friday, a weekly wage of £180 for the previous week. In the earnings period ended 20 July 2016, the arrangement is changed and, having received £180 on 20 July (in respect of the working week ended 12 July), Q also receives a further £180 on 20 July (in respect of the working week ended 19 July) in accordance with the new arrangement. It follows, therefore, that Q has received two payments in his one-week earnings period ended 20 July. Were these payments to be aggregated, Class 1 liabilities would be

Primary	£360 @ Nil%/12%	=	£23.76
Secondary	£320 @ Nil%/13.8%	=	£27.32

Instead, however, liabilities are to be

Primary	2 × (£180 @ Nil%/12%)	=	2 × £2.16	=	£4.32
Secondary	2 × (£180 @ Nil%/13.8%)	=	2 × £2.48	=	£4.96

This same principle of separate assessment is applicable where an employed earner's regular pay interval is changed so that the new interval is shorter than the old interval and, in consequence, the first of the new earnings periods is contained within the last of the old earnings periods. (CWG2 (2018 to 2019), para 1.9.)

Example (3)

Snipe is employed by Teal Ltd at a salary of £800 per month. He receives £800 on 6 August 2018 but then, from 1 September 2018, his pay arrangement is changed to one under which he receives a weekly wage of £200. His first weekly wage under the new arrangement is paid on 2 September 2018. It follows that, in the contribution month ended 5 September, S has received two payments of earnings. Were these payments to be aggregated and treated as relating to the monthly earnings period ended 5 September 2016, Class 1 liabilities would be

Primary	£1,000 @ Nil%/12%	=	£35.76
Secondary	£1,000 @ Nil%/13.8%	=	£41.12

Instead, however, liabilities are to be

			£
Primary	(on a monthly earnings period basis)	£800 @ Nil%/12% =	£11.76
	(on a weekly earnings period basis)	£200 @ Nil%/12% =	£4.56
			£16.32
			£
Secondary	(on a monthly earnings period basis)	£800 @ Nil%/13.8% =	£13.52
	(on a weekly earnings period basis)	£200 @ Nil%/13.8% =	£5.24
			£18.76

Holiday pay

[34.9] Where a payment of earnings (other than a payment on termination of the employment) includes a payment in respect of one or more week's holiday (see 29.25 EARNINGS FROM EMPLOYMENT: GENERAL), the earnings period may be the length of the interval in respect of which the payment is made. Alternatively, the holiday pay may simply be treated for contribution purposes as pay in the weeks in which earnings would normally have been paid. See HM Revenue and Customs Manual NIM09100–NIM09170. [*Social Security (Contributions) Regulations 2001, SI 2001/1004, Reg 19*].

Note that holiday pay payments to 'workers' under the *Working Time Regulations 1998, SI 1998/1833* who are not employees under a contract of service, but are entitled workers by virtue of being self-employed but contracted to provide services personally, are not subject to PAYE or Class 1 liability and are simply included in the workers' accounting profits.

The first method is referred to as 'method B' and the second as 'method A'. (See CWG2 (2018 to 2019), para 2.7.5.) Where method B is adopted and the length of the interval in respect of which the payment is made includes a fraction of a week, that fraction is to be treated as a whole week. [*Social Security (Contributions) Regulations 2001, SI 2001/1004, Reg 19(a)*].

Where, having received holiday pay on which contributions have been calculated, an employed earner decides not to take his holiday but to work instead, the additional contribution liability on earnings for the holiday weeks is to be calculated as follows.

If method A was used, the earnings for each week are to be aggregated with the holiday pay apportioned to each week and contribution liabilities are to be calculated on the weekly aggregate amounts. The contribution liability for each week as already calculated on the holiday pay is then to be deducted from the contribution liability on the aggregated amount, and the result will be the contributions due on the earnings for the week. (See CWG2 (2018 to 2019), para 2.7.5.)

If method B was used, the contributions are to be calculated in the normal manner using the National Insurance Tables on the earnings for each week of holiday without taking any account of contributions paid on the holiday pay already paid for the holiday period. (See CWG2 (2018 to 2019), para 2.7.5.)

Where, although an employed earner takes the holiday for which he has been paid, payments fall due to him during his holiday period (eg overtime payable one week after the week in which it was earned), liability for contributions on those payments is to be calculated as follows.

If method A was used, the payment falling due for each week is to be aggregated with the holiday pay apportioned to each week and contribution liabilities are to be calculated on the weekly aggregated amounts. The contribution liability for each week as already calculated on the holiday pay is then to be deducted from the contribution liability on the aggregated amount, and the result will be the contributions due on the payment falling due in the week. (See CWG2 (2018 to 2019), para 2.7.6.) When the payment which fell due during the holiday period is actually paid, it must, of course, be excluded from earnings for contribution purposes.

If method B was used, payments falling due during the holiday period are not to be taken into account as earnings for contribution purposes until they are actually paid, whereupon they are to be aggregated with any other earnings paid in the same earnings period. (See CWG2 (2018 to 2019), para 2.7.6.)

Example

Utrillo and Vermeer are both employed by Whistler Ltd. Each is paid a wage of £260 and holiday pay (for the following two weeks) of £250 each per week on 28 June 2018. U works during his holiday period and earns £180 paid to him on 5 July and £220 paid to him on 12 July. His wage on 19 July is £260. V takes his holiday but £40 in overtime pay becomes due for payment to him on 5 July. This is paid (along with a wage of £250) on 19 July after his return to work.

If W adopts *method A*, final calculations will be as follows.

U	£	*Primary*	£	*Secondary*	£
28 June 2018	260	Nil%/12%	11.76	Nil%/13.8%	13.52
5 July 2018	430	Nil%/12%	32.16	Nil%/13.8%	36.98
12 July 2018	470	Nil%/12%	36.96	Nil%/13.8%	42.50
19 July 2018	260	Nil%/12%	11.76	Nil%/13.8%	13.52
	£1,420		£92.64		£106.52

V	£	*Primary*	£	*Secondary*	£
28 June 2018	260	Nil%/12%	11.76	Nil%/13.8%	13.52
5 July 2018	290	Nil%/12%	15.36	Nil%/13.8%	17.66
12 July 2018	250	Nil%/12%	10.56	Nil%/13.8%	12.14
19 July 2018	250	Nil%/12%	10.56	Nil%/13.8%	12.14
	£1,050		£48.12		£55.46

If W adopts *method B*, final calculations will be as follows.

U	£	*Primary*	£	*Secondary*	£
28 June 2018	760	Nil%/12%	10.92	Nil%/13.8%	12.56
	÷ 3 = 253		× 3 = 32.76		× 3 = 37.68
5 July 2018	180	Nil%/12%	2.16	Nil%/13.8%	2.48
12 July 2018	220	Nil%/12%	6.96	Nil%/13.8%	8.00
19 July 2018	260	Nil%/12%	11.76	Nil%/13.8%	13.52
	£1,420		£53.64		£61.68
V	£	*Primary*	£	*Secondary*	£
28 June 2018	760	Nil%/12%	10.92	Nil%/13.8%	12.56
	÷ 3 = 253		× 3 = 32.76		× 3 = 37.68
5 July 2018	—	—	—	—	—
12 July 2018	—	—	—	—	—
19 July 2018	290	Nil%/12%	15.36	Nil%/13.8%	17.66
	£1,050		£48.12		£55.34

Aggregable earnings

[34.10] Where earnings paid in respect of two or more employed earner's employments fall to be aggregated, special rules apply for the purpose of establishing a common earnings period (see **5.10** AGGREGATION OF EARNINGS).

Earnings paid on or after cessation of employment

[34.11] The rules which follow are in accordance with *Social Security (Contributions) Regulations 2001, SI 2001/1004* and guidance. Note that, as explained at **29.5** EARNINGS FROM EMPLOYMENT: GENERAL, there has in the past been an argument that payments made after an employment has ended were no longer within the ambit of the Class 1 contribution charge. See *RCI Europe v Woods (Inspector of Taxes)* [2003] EWHC 3129 (Ch), [2004] STC 315, 76 TC 390.

Where an employment in respect of which earnings have been paid or treated as paid according to a regular pay pattern comes to an end and, at the end of the employment, two or more payments of earnings are made in respect of regular pay intervals, the payments should *not* be aggregated and treated as falling into a single earnings period but each payment should be regarded as falling into a separate earnings period (determined according to general rules) and contributions should be calculated accordingly. (See CWG2 (2018 to 2019), para 1.14.) If the employee was in contracted-out employment and left before 6 April 2016 (eg Table D in CA39 would have applied) and the payment was made more than six weeks after leaving then the NICs should have been worked out using the equivalent not contracted-out rate (ie Table A in CA38) (see CWG2 (2015), page 12).

Example

Xerxes was employed by Yesteryear Ltd on a weekly wage of £300 payable each Friday in respect of the working week ended on the previous Friday. He left the employment on 10 May 2015, which fell within the earnings period Friday 10 May to Thursday 16 May (see 34.2 above). On the day he left, 10 May, he was paid his wage for the working week ended 3 May 2015 and also for the working week ended 10 May 2015. His earnings for the earnings period ended 17 May 2015 were £300, *not* £600, and his earnings for the earnings period ended 24 May 2015 were (although by then he had left his employment) £300 also.

If, in addition to regular earnings, holiday pay is paid to an employed earner when he leaves his employment, the way in which it should be treated for contribution purposes will depend on whether the employed earner's contract of service terminates on the date he leaves or only after a period of holiday following his last day of work. In the latter event, contribution liability on the holiday pay may be calculated using either of the normal methods (see **34.9** above). In the former event, however, it should be aggregated with regular earnings paid at the date of leaving.

Where an employment in respect of which earnings have been paid or treated as paid according to a regular pay pattern comes to an end and, after the end of the employment, a payment of earnings which is not in respect of a regular interval is made by way of an addition to a payment of earnings made before the employment ended (see **29.22** EARNINGS FROM EMPLOYMENT: GENERAL), the earnings period in respect of those additional earnings is to be the week in which the payment is made regardless of what the length of the regular pay interval has been. [*Social Security (Contributions) Regulations 2001, SI 2001/1004, Reg 3(5)*]. Examples of such payments are arrears of pay from a back-dated pay increase, holiday pay in respect of a holiday which an employee has not taken by the time he leaves his employment, and a one-off payment such as an unexpected bonus. In leaver cases before 6 April 2016, if the employee was in contracted-out employment (eg Table D in CA39) and the payment was made more than six weeks after leaving then the NICs should have been worked out using the equivalent not contracted-out rate (eg Table A in CA38) (see CWG2 (2015), page 12). The same principle still applies where Statutory Maternity Pay, Statutory Paternity Pay, Statutory Adoption Pay or Statutory Shared Parental Pay is paid after a contract of service has ended and it is paid at a different interval from that at which regular earnings were paid or is paid in a lump sum. (See CWG2 (2018 to 2019), para 2.3.2.)

Where a payment made to an employed earner after he has left his employment *is* in respect of a regular pay interval, the earnings period into which the payment falls is an earnings period determined according to the general rules. If, for example, a monthly-paid employed earner leaves his employment part way through a month and his final monthly salary payment is made at the end of that month, his earnings period as regards that payment is the month in which he leaves, just as it would be had he continued in the employment. (See CWG2 (2018 to 2019), para 1.14.) Likewise, the earnings period into which there falls a payment of Statutory Maternity Pay, etc paid after a contract of service has ended is to be of the same length as the earnings period in use before the employee left if the Statutory Maternity Pay, etc is paid at the same interval as that at which regular earnings were paid. (See CWG2 (2018 to 2019), para 2.3.2). Any payment of SMP, SPP, SAP or ShPP made when a contract of service ends is, if paid with the last regular payment of earnings, to be aggregated with that last regular payment of earnings.

Where the earner who has left is under the age of 21 or an apprentice under the age of 25 at the time of leaving, but has reached the relevant birthday before receiving the post-termination payment, the employer works out the NIC liabilities using the usual earnings period, the contributions rates and limits current at the time of payment, and the correct NI category letter for an employee over the age of 21 or 25 as appropriate.

Tables H, M, and Z apply according to the age and status of the earner at the date of payment. However, note that Table H cannot apply to a post-termination payment to an earner who is at that time no longer an apprentice, so unless the earner is under 21, Table A will apply.

Payments to company directors and ex-company directors

[34.12] Until 6 April 1983, COMPANY DIRECTORS **22** were subject to the same earnings periods rules as all other employed earners. Now, however, when a person is, or is appointed, or ceases to be, a director of a company, the amount (if any) of Class 1 contributions payable in respect of earnings paid to or for his benefit in respect of any employed earner's employment with *that* company (whether the employment is as a director or not) are to be assessed on the amount of all such earnings paid (whether at regular intervals or not) in the earnings period specified under the following special rules. [*Social Security (Contributions) Regulations 2001, SI 2001/1004, Reg 8(1)*].

Where a person is a company director at the beginning of a tax year, the earnings period in respect of his earnings is to be *that tax year*, whether or not he remains a director throughout the year (see **22.6** COMPANY DIRECTORS). [*Social Security (Contributions) Regulations 2001, SI 2001/1004, Reg 8(3)*].

Example (1)

Anchovy is a director of Barracuda Ltd. His drawings (treated as earnings) are £3,600 per month. On 30 June 2018, he resigns his office and begins to work as an ordinary employee of Carp Ltd (a completely unconnected company) who pay him a weekly wage. An earnings period of one year is to apply to his earnings for the months April, May and June 2018 of £10,800 from B. A weekly earnings period will then apply in respect of his earnings from C.

Social Security (Contributions) Regulations 2001, SI 2001/1004, Reg 8(3) is designed to ensure that any payments made to an ex-director in the year in which his directorship ceases will not escape the April 1983 rules (eg a bonus paid by B to A in August 2018, in the example above).

Any payments to an ex-director in any year *after* that in which his directorship ceased are, if they are in respect of any period during which he was a company director, also caught by the rules in that the earnings period in respect of those earnings is to be the *tax year* in which they are paid. [*Social Security (Contributions) Regulations 2001, SI 2001/1004, Reg 8(5)*].

Example (2)

Anchovy (see previous example) continues to work for C in the next tax year but in May of that year is paid a bonus of £10,000 by B in respect of the year ended 31 March. The bonus will attract an annual earnings period and, as the annual Upper Earnings Limit for the later year will inevitably be in excess of £10,000, will be subject to contribution liability at the main rate, on the excess over the Earnings Threshold for 2019–20, irrespective of the level of earnings received from C during that year. Only if the total contributions paid for 2019–20 exceed his annual maximum for that year will a repayment of excess primary contributions be due.

Where (on one or more than one occasion) a person is appointed a company director during the course of a tax year, the earnings period in respect of such earnings as are paid in so much of the year as remains in the period commencing with the week in which he is appointed (or, as the case may be, first appointed) is to be the number of weeks in that period. [*Social Security (Contributions) Regulations 2001, SI 2001/1004, Reg 8(2)*]. 'Week' means tax week. [*Social Security (Contributions) Regulations 2001, SI 2001/1004, Reg 1(2)*].

Example (3)

Dace is appointed a director of Eel Ltd on 3 June. He resigns on 1 September and becomes a salaried employee of E. He is re-appointed a director on 1 December of that same year. 3 June lies in the tax week commencing 1 June (Tax week 9) and the number of tax weeks to 5 April is, therefore, 44. (NB: There are 53 tax weeks in *every* tax year although the last 'week' will consist of only one or two days but the odd day or two days can, generally, be ignored (CA44, para 24)). Despite his resignation and subsequent re-appointment, D will have a 44-week earnings period by reference to which all his earnings from E (whether in respect of his directorships or not) will be assessed.

It should be noted that it is the date of *appointment* that is relevant, not the date on which a company *begins to trade* or (following a period of suspension) recommences trading nor the date on which salary first starts to accrue.

Example (4)

Moby Ltd was formed on 22 April 2018 and Dick was appointed a director on that date. The company begins to trade on 1 March 2019 and on 31 March 2019, Dick is paid £20,000. Dick's earnings period is 50 weeks (UEL: 50 × £892 = £44,600), not five weeks (UEL: 5 × £892 = £4,460), and thus the whole of the £20,000 falls below the UEL and suffers Class 1 contributions at the main rate on the excess above the Earnings Threshold.

It should be noted that in practice employers are instructed to assume a basis of a 52-week year in carrying out the pro-rata calculation. However, if the director is appointed in week 53, the pro-rata period is one week. (Leaflet CA 44, para 24).

Special earnings periods rules apply where earnings of a company director fall to be aggregated, and aggregation is actually prohibited in certain circumstances where a person has been, but is no longer, a company director (see **5.8**, **5.10** AGGREGATION OF EARNINGS).

Payments to mariners

[34.13] Where employed MARINERS **45** are paid at regular intervals (eg a week or a month), the length of the earnings period by reference to which contributions are to be calculated will be ascertained in the normal way (see 34.2 etc above). Where, however, a mariner receives a general settlement of his earnings at the end of a voyage, his earnings period is to be determined by reference to the voyage period and special rules have applied from 6 April 1982. [*Social Security (Contributions) Regulations 2001, SI 2001/1004, Reg 120(1)*].

A 'voyage period' is a pay period comprising an entire voyage or series of voyages and it includes any period of paid leave which immediately follows the day on which the termination of the voyage or series of voyages occurs. It is measured in weeks which are periods of seven consecutive days. [*Social Security (Contributions) Regulations 2001, SI 2001/1004, Reg 115*].

The length of a 'voyage-paid' mariner's earnings period will depend on whether the voyage period falls wholly in one tax year or partly in one and partly in one or more other tax years and whether or not, during the voyage period, one or more than one *relevant change* occurs. A 'relevant change' is a change (other than a change in the amount of the mariner's earnings or in contribution rates or earnings limits) affecting the calculation of Class 1 contributions, eg the mariner attaining pensionable age. [*Social Security (Contributions) Regulations 2001, SI 2001/1004, Reg 120(2)*].

Where a voyage period falls wholly in one year but, during the voyage period, one or more than one relevant change occurs, earnings periods are to be:

- the period beginning with the day on which the voyage began and ending with the day immediately before the first change occurs;
- each period beginning with the day on which the immediately preceding change occurs and ending on the day immediately before the next succeeding change occurs; and
- so much of the voyage period as remains.

[*Social Security (Contributions) Regulations 2001, SI 2001/1004, Reg 120(3)(b)*].

Where a voyage period falls partly in one and partly in one or more other tax years but, during the voyage period, no relevant change occurs, the earnings periods are to correspond with the parts of the voyage period falling in each tax year. [*Social Security (Contributions) Regulations 2001, SI 2001/1004, Reg 120(4)*].

Where a voyage period falls partly in one and partly in one or more other tax years but, during the voyage period, one or more than one relevant change occurs, the earnings periods are to be periods corresponding to the parts of the voyage period between its beginning and end arrived at by allowing each relevant change and each tax year-end to act as a division point. [*Social Security (Contributions) Regulations 2001, SI 2001/1004, Reg 120(5)*].

Where a voyage period does not comprise an exact number of weeks, any remaining period of three days or less are ignored. Any remaining period four, five or six days is treated as a further whole week. [*Social Security (Contributions) Regulations 2001, SI 2001/1004, Reg 120(6)*].

When the termination of an entire voyage or series of voyages is immediately followed by a period of leave on pay, the earnings for the period of leave are treated as if earned during that period and are to be excluded from the earnings of any other earnings period. Where relevant (ie, the period of leave spans two tax years) the leave pay is deemed to accrue evenly over the entire leave pay period. [*Social Security (Contributions) Regulations 2001, SI 2001/1004, Reg 120(7)*].

Example

Flounder was engaged by Gudgeon Ltd to serve on a voyage which began on 13 December 2017. The voyage ends on 14 April 2018 and F is then paid £3,500 which includes leave pay to 16 June 2018. F attained the age of 65 on 14 March 2018. His earnings are attributable to periods of work and leave as follows.

	£
13 December 2017 to 13 March 2018	1,800
14 March 2018 to 5 April 2018	400
6 April 2018 to 14 April 2018	200
15 April 2018 to 16 June 2018	1,100

In accordance with the rules described above, F's earnings periods and the bases of contribution calculation are as follows.

Earnings period 1.	13 December 2017 to 13 March 2018 (13 weeks): primary and secondary Class 1 contributions due at 2017–18 rates on £1,800.
Earnings period 2.	14 March 2018 to 5 April 2018 (3 weeks): secondary Class 1 contributions due at 2017–18 rates on £400.
Earnings period 3.	6 April 2018 to 16 June 2018 (10 weeks): secondary Class 1 contributions due at 2018–19 rates on £1,300.

Key Points regarding earnings periods

[34.14] Points to consider are as follows.

- Most employees will, in practice, have an earnings period of a week or a calendar month, although some employers operate a 'lunar' payroll where all employees are paid every four weeks, with an equivalent earnings period.
- The minimum possible earnings period is a week.
- Directors have an annual earnings period with special rules for the year of appointment, the year of resignation and, to prevent the rules being circumvented, payments made in tax years following resignation.
- There are different rules for mariners who are not paid on a regular basis.

35

Enforcement

Cross-references. See ADMINISTRATION 2; AGENCY WORKERS 4; APPEALS AND REVIEWS 9; ARREARS OF CONTRIBUTIONS 12; COLLECTION 21.

Other Sources. HMRC Debt Management and Banking Manual.

Introduction to enforcement and NICs

[35.1] HM Revenue and Customs may authorise any of its officers to exercise powers to monitor and enforce compliance with contribution law. [*SSAA 1992, s 110ZA*, as amended from 6 April 2005 by *National Insurance Contributions and Statutory Payments Act 2004, ss 7, 8*, applying the provisions of *TMA 1970, ss 20, 20B, 20BB*]. Additionally, the Secretary of State for Work and Pensions may make arrangements with HM Revenue and Customs or some other department for any of the powers or duties of his inspectors to be carried out by an inspector or officer employed by HM Revenue and Customs or that other department. [*SSAA 1992, s 110(5)* as amended by *Social Security Contributions (Transfer of Functions, etc.) Act 1999, Sch 5 para 2, para 3*].

Officers of HM Revenue and Customs

[35.2] When HMRC compliance officers carry out an inspection of an employer's records, National Insurance liability can only be assessed according to social security, and not tax, legislation. Neither the merger in April 1999 with the Contributions Agency nor that in 2005 with HM Customs & Excise changed this fundamental fact, although there have since then been several changes to HMRC powers that, in effect, import tax law into NIC law (see 35.6 below).

In *Pawlowski v Dunnington* [1999] STC 550 the taxpayer waited until the Collector of Taxes (now known as Debt Management and Banking or DMB) was seeking payment through the County Court before arguing that the Collector had not put forward any evidence to support the determinations that had been issued. The Collector's claim was dismissed and it was held that the taxpayer was able to put forward a public law defence.

In addition, *Child Support, Pensions and Social Security Act 2000, s 67* introduced new social security investigation powers via *Schedule 6* of that *Act*. This section was brought into force with effect from 2 April 2001 by the *Child Support, Pensions and Social Security Act (Commencement No 8) Order 2001, SI 2001/1252*. Although these provisions are stated to be required to investigate fraudulent benefit claims — a laudable aim — the provisions are very widely drawn and, in particular, they permit the Secretary of State for Work and Pensions to authorise *any* official of *any* Government department to carry out such investigation work on behalf of the DWP, for example, an employer compliance officer. Provision is made to enable enquiries to be made by fax or e-mail as well as by correspondence or in person. Enquiries may be made of, amongst others, employers, employees, the self-employed, agencies, and trustees or managers of pension schemes. Where appropriate, there is the power to require not only the production of records but to insist upon their creation where they do not already exist. There is a power of entry, but not with force, and a power to interview anyone found on the premises (as defined) but not, apparently, the power to interview persons alone. In practice, where DWP staff (eg, when dealing with a claim for universal credit) need to check what an employer has done or what its records show, it requests HMRC to carry out the check on its behalf.

It has been said that these provisions will typically be used to 'ask' (sic) an employer for details of employees in order to obtain information about people who may be committing benefit fraud by working whilst claiming benefit, or to obtain information from a self-employed person who may be working whilst claiming benefit. Where an employer has a history of colluding with staff in order that they can commit benefit fraud, the employer may be asked for a list of all employees which would then be cross-referenced against benefit records.

Right of entry

[35.3] An HM Revenue and Customs officer has the right of entry at all reasonable times to any premises (except a private dwelling-house not used for the purposes of trade or business) where he has reasonable grounds for supposing that persons are employed or that an employment agency or similar business is being carried on. A private dwelling-house is not within the exception unless it is in use as such at the time and it is for the person challenging an inspector's right of entry to prove that is so. (*Stott v Hefferon* [1974] 3 All ER 673, [1974] 1 WLR 1270, DC).

Where an inspector or officer of, or under the control of, some other Government department has a similar right of entry to any premises HM Revenue and Customs may make arrangements with that department (eg DWP) for such a person to have the powers and carry out the duties of HM Revenue and Customs officer. This right of entry is wide ranging and can extend to farmhouses, private property, nursing homes, lodging houses, etc.

Every officer is furnished with a certificate of his appointment and must, on applying for admission to premises, produce it if asked to do so. The fact that there might be no one on the premises to whom the certificate can be produced does not, however, negate right of entry to those premises. (*Grove v Eastern Gas Board* [1952] 1 KB 77, [1951] 2 All ER 1051, CA).

Obstruction of an officer properly seeking entry is an offence and carries a penalty (see **35.8** below), but entry cannot be forced if refused and social security legislation makes no provision for obtaining of search warrants. [*Sec 111(1)(a)* as amended by *SSC(TF)A 1999, Sch 5 para 4(2)(3)*].

However, where documents are promised but the information is not forthcoming HM Revenue and Customs can apply for 'a notice to produce documents'.

Tax and NICs powers alignment

[35.4] From 6 April 2005 the effect of *National Insurance Contributions and Statutory Payments Act 2004, ss 7, 8*, applying the provisions of *TMA 1970, ss 20, 20B, 20BB* was that the tax and the National Insurance powers of HM Revenue and Customs officers to inspect records and obtain information relating to Class 1, Class 1A, Class 1B and Class 2 contributions were aligned. *Taxes Management Act 1970 (TMA 1970), ss 20, 20B* and *20BB* applied to National Insurance contributions – with appropriate modifications – as a replacement for the previous version of *Social Security Contributions and Benefits Act 1992 (SSCBA 1992), s 110ZA*. With regard to the 2005 change, no provision was required for Class 3 contributions as they are entirely voluntary, and Class 4 contributions were already within that regime. See **35.14** below. [*National Insurance Contributions and Statutory Payments Act 2004 (Commencement) Order 2004, SI 2004/1943* and *Social Security (Contributions) (Amendment No 4) Regulations 2004, SI 2004/2096*].

From 1 December 2007, *TMA 1970, ss 20, 20B* and *20BB* were superseded since HM Revenue and Customs can now apply for search warrants under *Police and Criminal Evidence Act 1984*. [*Police and Criminal Evidence Act 1984 (Application and Customs) Order 2007, SI 2007/3175; Civil Evidence Act 1995; Finance Act 2008 (FA 2008), s 118, Sch 36 paras 65, 69*]. Previous HMRC powers to investigate cases of tax evasion were substantially increased by the *Serious Crime Act 2007*. *Chapter 3* extended certain investigatory powers of officers of Her Majesty's Revenue and Customs to former Inland

Revenue matters (which powers were previously limited to former Customs matters). This legislation amended the *Regulation of Investigatory Powers Act 2000* to include 'HM Revenue and Customs'. In particular *s 32* covering 'Authorisation of Intrusive Surveillance' now allows HMRC to sanction through senior authorising officers the carrying out of intrusive surveillance. The list of senior authorising officers now includes 'any HM Revenue and Customs officer designated for the purposes of this paragraph by the Commissioners for HM Revenue and Customs.' *The Wireless Telegraphy Act 1949* (misleading messages and interception and disclosure of wireless telegraphy messages) was changed so that for the purpose of assessing or collecting any tax, duty, levy or other imposition, contribution or charge payable to a government department a designated person must obtain an authority to use any wireless telegraphy apparatus with intent to obtain information as to the contents, sender or addressee of any message (whether sent by means of wireless telegraphy or not) and shall not be guilty of an offence under the Act in so doing. A designated person includes HMRC. HMRC therefore now has substantially more powers to look into peoples' personal affairs to obtain information that HMRC believe will support their suspicions that tax, National Insurance or another duty is being evaded. This now encompasses the interception of e-mails, tapping telephone lines, planting bugging devices and use of other intelligence services to secure a conviction.

Right of examination and inquiry

[35.5] An officer has the right of examination and inquiry to whatever extent is necessary for the purpose of ascertaining whether or not the requirements of social security legislation have been, or are being, complied with.

Until 6 April 2005, this right extended to the examination (alone, if the inspector thought fit) of anyone whom he found on premises he had entered *or* anyone whom he had reason to believe was, or had been, liable to pay contributions. Thus, a person who, being found in premises which an officer had entered, admitted to being an employee committed an offence if he refused to disclose the identity of his employer. (*Smith v Hawkins* [1972] 1 All ER 910, [1972] 1 WLR 141).

Previously, the former Inland Revenue had indicated following the merger in 1999 that the power, whilst it existed, to require a person to be interviewed alone would be exercised exceedingly sparingly.

Right to require information and documents

[35.6] From 1 April 2009 the provisions of *FA 2008, Schedule 36* apply to National Insurance contributions as they do to tax. [*Social Security Contributions and Benefits Act 1992, s 110ZA*, as substituted by *FA 2008, Sch 36, para 84*.]

As regards employers, the records inspected under the *FA 2008, Sch 36* regime will be those required to be maintained under *Social Security (Contributions) Regulations 2001, SI 2001/1004, Sch 4 para 26(1)*, as amended by *Social Security (Contributions) (Amendment No 3) Regulations 2009, SI 2009/600, Reg 8(4)*.

An employer must keep, in addition to those documents required to be submitted to HM Revenue and Customs, all Class 1 contribution records for not less than three years after the end of the tax year to which they relate and, in the case of Class 1A and Class 1B, documents or records relating to the amount payable for a like period.

'Contribution records' means wages sheets, deductions working sheets (ie forms P11, RT11 for post-RTI paper filers, and the electronic records that are now required for RTI), and other documents or records relating to the calculation of payment of earnings and the amount of contributions payable on those earnings as well as documents, records and 'any information' about the amounts of Class 1A and/or Class 1B payable by the employer. [*Social Security (Contributions) Regulations 2001, SI 2001/1004, Sch 4 para 26(4)*, as amended by *Social Security (Contributions) (Amendment No 3) Regulations 2009, SI 2009/600, Reg 8(4)*].

The contribution records or other documents and records may be kept in any format. [*Social Security (Contributions) Regulations 2001, SI 2001/1004, Sch 4 para 26(2)* as amended by *Social Security (Contributions) (Amendment No 3) Regulations 2009, SI 2009/600, Reg 8(4)*.]

Where agency employers are required to maintain 'non-PAYE records' (ie, records not required to be sent to HMRC under any other provision of the PAYE regulations) in support of the quarterly returns they make under *Reg 84F, PAYE Regulations 2003*, containing details of payments made to agency workers without deduction of PAYE or NICs, *Regulation 84H* requires that the records be kept for not less than three years after the end of the tax year to which they relate, also in any form or by any means. The reporting requirements, introduced by the *Income Tax (Pay As You Earn) (Amendment No 2) Regulations 2015, SI 2015/171, Reg 2* with effect from 6 April 2015 are part of a drive to combat NIC avoidance, but there is no reason to replicate the reporting requirements in NI legislation as no contributions need to be paid or reported. HMRC's power in *FA 2008, Sch 36, para 1* to require a person to provide information, or produce a document, automatically covers these new returns where HMRC can show that the information or document is reasonably required by an officer for the purpose of checking the taxpayer's tax position.

Pre-April 2009 obligations

[35.7] Prior to April 2009, the obligations imposed on employers and other contributors in relation to NICs were contained wholly within the social security legislation. There was a duty to give an officer information when he reasonably required it. Anyone:

(a) who was the occupier of premises liable to inspection (see **35.3** above);
(b) who was, or had been, employing another;
(c) who was carrying on an employment agency or similar business;
(d) who was a servant or agent of any person falling within (a) to (c) above;
(e) who was, or had been, liable to pay contributions; or
(f) who was, or had been, a trustee or manager of a personal or occupational pension scheme,

had to furnish an officer with all such information, and produce for his inspection all such documents, as he might reasonably require for the purpose of ascertaining whether any contributions due were payable, had been payable, or had been duly paid, by, or in respect of, any person. This included all wages sheets, deduction working sheets and other documents and records relating to the calculation of earnings, earnings-related contributions and Class 1A contributions. An officer could decide that he/she needed to check information about working practices of the company to see if it had reached the correct view on the application of the IR35 legislation when the form P35 was filed. This could prove difficult as evidenced in *Tilbury Consulting Ltd v Gittins* [2004] STC SCD 1 Sp C379. [*Social Security (Contributions) Regulations 2001, SI 2001/1004, Sch 4 para 26(1); The Income Tax (Pay As You Earn) Regulations 2003, SI 2003/2682, Reg 97(1)(2)*].

Any documents reasonably required were to be produced at the prescribed place. [*Social Security (Contributions) Regulations 2001, SI 2001/1004, Sch 4 para 26(1)*]. This meant such place in Great Britain as the employer and the officer might agree upon. If no agreement was reached, they had to be produced at the place in Great Britain at which they were normally kept or, if there was no such place, at the employer's principal place of business in Great Britain. [Former *Social Security (Contributions) Regulations 2001, SI 2001/1004, Sch 4 para 26(2)*]. The officer was empowered to take copies of, or make extracts from, any documents produced to him and, if it appeared to him to be necessary, at a reasonable time and for a reasonable period, to take away any such document, providing a receipt to the employer. If any of the documents removed was reasonably required for the conduct of the business, the officer had to provide a copy, free of charge, within seven days of its being taken away. [Former *Social Security (Contributions) Regulations 2001, SI 2001/1004, Sch 4 para 26(3); The Income Tax (Pay As You Earn) Regulations 2003, SI 2003/2682, Reg 97(3)(4)(5)*].

A reduction in powers to call for documents by virtue of *National Insurance Contributions and Statutory Payments Act 2004, ss 7, 8* with effect from 6 April 2005 was referred to in the NICSP Bill debates as follows by the then Paymaster General, Dawn Primarolo:

> The clause removes some powers currently available to the Inland Revenue. It takes the existing Inland Revenue powers to obtain information in tax investigation cases and applies them to certain classes of National Insurance contributions. [Classes 1, 1A, 1B or Class 2]. The clause has been widely welcomed and is a reduction in powers for the Inland Revenue. It was thought that, on transfer, the Contributions Agency had considerable wider-ranging powers than the Revenue, with regard to power of entry, power of examination and the power to compel the production of information documents. Some concern about that was raised at the time. The clause removes those substantial powers and introduces the well-known, and trusted powers that the Inland Revenue now uses, with all the safeguards provided by the Taxes Acts.
>
> Standing Committee D debates, 13 January 2004, Col 28.

Offences and penalties

[35.8] From 6 April 2009 a revised penalty regime was introduced, which survived until 5 April 2015. See **21.31** as regards Class 1 contributions.

In respect of the commencement of liability to pay – or cease to pay – Class 2 contributions, the rules changed with the reform of Class 2 by *National Insurance Contributions Act 2015* with effect from 6 April 2015. Under the 2009 regime, the penalty for failure to notify HMRC was as follows, based on the lost contributions, the reason for the failure, the way the failure was disclosed or came to light, and how the matter was dealt with by the contributor and his agent:

Behaviour	*Maximum penalty*	*Maximum mitigation after*
Deliberate and concealed	100%	Unprompted disclosure 70% (penalty 30% minimum); Prompted disclosure 50% (penalty 50% minimum)
Deliberate but not concealed	70%	Unprompted disclosure 50% (penalty 20% minimum); Prompted disclosure 35% (penalty 35% minimum)
Other cases	30%	Unprompted disclosure – minimum penalty between 0%* and 10%

* In case of an unprompted disclosure notified less than 12 months after 31 January following the end of the year in which the person became liable to pay Class 2.

[35.9] The 2009 rules may still be applied for some time to pre-2015 failures to notify. In the Table above 'unprompted disclosure' means that the person has no reason to believe that HMRC has discovered or is about to discover the failure to pay the required contributions. Prompted disclosure is likely to apply otherwise. Where the person has made a prompted disclosure in 'Other cases' above, which attracts a 30% penalty, this may be reduced to as low as 10% where HMRC becomes aware of the failure to notify less than 12 months after 31 January following the end of the year in which the person became liable to pay Class 2 contributions. In all other circumstances the 30% penalty will not be reduced below 20%. 'Other cases' would encompass circumstances where the person liable to pay Class 2 makes an unprompted disclosure by notifying HMRC and then assisting in determining the quantity of unpaid contributions and allowing HMRC access to records to check the amount unpaid contributions quantified. [*Social Security (Contributions) Regulations 2001, SI 2001/1004, Regs 87B, 87C, 87D* as inserted by *Social Security (Contributions) (Amendment No 3) Regulations 2009, SI 2009/600, Regs 5*]. See also the archived material at webarchive.nationalarchives.gov.uk/20140109143644/http://www.hmrc.gov.uk/about/new-penalties/index.htm.

Regulations 87B–87G dealing with the 2009 regime penalties for failure to notify and related provisions were revoked by *Social Security (Miscellaneous Amendments No 2) Regulations 2015, SI 2015/478, Reg 24* with effect from 6 April 2015. This is a natural consequence of the reform of Class 2 by *NICA 2015, Sch 1*, which introduced a new *SSCBA 1992, s 11A*, to apply to liability for payment of compulsory Class 2 contributions in respect of businesses carried on in the UK under the revised *SSCBA 1992, s 11(2)* the provisions of:

- *Taxes Management Act 1970* (Part 2 (returns), Part 4 (assessment and claims), Part 5 (appeals), Part 5A (payment of tax), Part 6 (collection and recovery) and Part 10 (penalties));
- *Finance Act 2007, Sch 24* (penalties for errors, incorporating very similar disclosure discounts to those described above);
- *Finance Act 2009, ss 101–102* (interest);
- *Finance Act 2009, Schs 55 and 56* (penalties for failure to make returns etc or for failure to make payments on time);
- *Finance Act 2014, Pt 4* (follower notices and accelerated payments) and *Part 5* (promoters of tax avoidance schemes); and

any other provisions of the Income Tax Acts as to assessment, collection, repayment or recovery. A provision that remains in force but will soon lose any significance due to the ubiquity of RTI filing was one that for now still applies to a specified employer who was required to file PAYE records electronically. The rule applies in respect of 2004–05 onwards (ie by 19 May 2005 *et seq*) for large employers and in respect of 2005–06 onwards (ie by 19 May 2006 *et seq*) for medium-sized employers, and for most other employers in respect of 2009–10 onwards (ie by 19 May 2010 *et seq*). A penalty for non-compliance was applied where there was no reasonable excuse. The penalty depended on the number of employees for whom particulars had to be included with the specified information and could vary from £600 to £3,000 for 1,000 or more employees. [*Reg 90P*, inserted by *Social Security (Contributions, Categorisation of Earners and Intermediaries) (Amendment) Regulations 2004, SI 2004/770, Reg 23* and amended by *Social Security (Contributions) (Amendment No 4) Regs 2010, SI 2010/721, Reg 9; Income Tax (Employments) (Amendment) Regulations 2003, SI 2003/2494, Reg 7; The Income Tax (Pay As You Earn) Regulations 2003, SI 2003/2682, Reg 210*].

SSA 1998, s 61 introduced, by way of new *SSAA 1992, s 114A* and with prospective effect from 6 April 1999, a new criminal offence of fraudulent evasion of NICs. Although aimed at large scale and repeated evasion and the non-compliance of directors of 'phoenix' companies, the provision was far wider, covering far more circumstances than merely that situation. In addition, it was to extend to 'any person' involved with fraudulent evasion, which could have included professional advisers, on the one hand, or junior payroll clerks, on the other. In the event, the Contributions Agency takeover by the Inland Revenue on 1 April 1999 led to the repeal of *s 114A* before it ever came into force. There are other methods which provide, in certain circumstances, for contribution and associated penalty and interest debts to be transferred to directors personally (see **12.1** and **12.6** ARREARS OF CONTRIBUTIONS and **22.14** COMPANY DIRECTORS). In practice, these provisions are rarely used.

False statements or documents

[35.10] A person commits an offence if, for any purpose connected with contribution law, he:

- knowingly makes any false statement or false representation; or

- produces or furnishes, or causes or knowingly allows to be produced or furnished, any document or information which he knows to be false in a material particular. (*Barrass v Reeve* [1980] 3 All ER 705, [1981] 1 WLR 408).

A statement or representation will be false if, even though no specific part of it is untrue, the statement or representation, looked at as a whole, intentionally gives a false impression. (*Aaron's Reefs v Twiss* [1896] AC 273). It follows that an omission from an otherwise true statement or representation will, if that omission creates, clearly and intentionally, an impression and belief which is wrong, render the statement or representation false. (*R v Bishirgian* [1936] 1 All ER 586, 25 Cr App Rep 176, CCA). It will be false 'not because of what it states, but because of what it does not state, because of what it implies'. (*R v Kylsant* [1932] 1 KB 442).

A corporate body, even though itself is incapable of having a wrongful intent, will be guilty of making false statements or representations if it makes such statements or representations through its human agents. (*DPP v Kent and Sussex Contractors Ltd* [1944] KB 146, [1944] 1 All ER 119, DC).

In the context of the 2014 reform of the agency rules in *Income Tax (Earnings and Pensions) Act 2003 (ITEPA 2003), ss 44–47* and the *Social Security (Categorisation of Earners) Regulations 1978*, the production of a fraudulent document purporting to evidence the fact that an agency worker is not subject to a right of supervision, direction or control can also have the consequence that the person producing the fraudulent document is deemed to be the employer, and thereby becomes responsible for all PAYE and NIC liabilities in respect of the workers concerned. [*Income Tax (Earnings and Pensions) Act 2003, s 44(4)(5) and Social Security (Categorisation of Earners) Regulations 1978, SI 1978/1689, Sch 3, para 2(c)*.]

The reform of travel and subsistence rules in *Finance Act 2016* by the insertion of *ITEPA 2003, s 339A* with backdated effect from 6 April 2016 included further provisions on fraudulent documents. The aim of the changes was to block any tax deduction for the costs of home-work travel by workers supplied by an intermediary (ie, umbrella company or personal services company) who are subject to a right of supervision, direction or control by any person as to the manner of carrying out the work, and so are, in effect, just like any ordinary employee of the client organisation who cannot claim the costs of ordinary commuting tax-free.

Under *s 339A(7)(8)*, if the client or a 'relevant person' (ie, someone other than the client, the worker or a person connected with the intermediary who has a UK presence and is a party – or is connected to a party – to a contract with the intermediary related to the provision of the worker's services) provides the intermediary at any time with a fraudulent document intended to constitute evidence of an absence of supervision, direction and control with the result that PAYE is not deducted or accounted for, the worker is to be treated as employed by the provider of the fraudulent document in respect of the services. The provider is therefore liable for any under-deducted PAYE in respect of the deemed employment, and any interest and penalties that follow.

Furthermore, *ITEPA 2003, s 688B*, inserted at the same time *as s 339A*, empowers the making of PAYE regulations such that the liability for any arrears that arise in the absence of fraudulent documents may be transferred to the directors or officers of the intermediary company or LLP. The provisions on 'relevant PAYE debts' are set out in new *Regs 97ZG–97ZM* of the *Income Tax (PAYE) Regulations 2003*.

Contravention of regulations

[35.11] If a person contravened or failed to comply with any requirement of contribution regulations and no *special* penalty was provided, he was liable, from 20 April 1999 to 5 April 2009, to a penalty of £100 and such penalty was recoverable as if it had been contributions payable to HM Revenue & Customs. [*1979 Regs, Reg 132* as amended by *Social Security (Contributions) Amendment (No 3) Regs 1999, Reg 3*].

Non-payment of contributions

[35.12] For the offence of failure to pay a contribution which is due see **12.6** ARREARS OF CONTRIBUTIONS.

Prosecution

[35.13] HM Revenue and Customs some years ago revised its policy regarding criminal prosecution for offences relating to various areas of business and this also applied to cases relating to NICs. The ambit of the prosecution policy extended to:

- deliberate concealment or deception;
- false or forged documents, certificates, statements or claims, prepared with the intention to deceive;
- conspiracy or corruption;
- money laundering offences;
- the 'informal' economy;
- a second or subsequent serious offence against HM Revenue and Customs;
- additional books or records for accounting, tax, NICs or tax credit claims;
- organised or systematic fraud in respect of tax, NICs, stamp duty, or tax credit claims;
- unusual frauds of novelty or ingenuity; and
- 'phoenixism'. See **22.14**.

The potential for prosecution in respect of the above applied equally to the persons involved in the administration of taxation and those in the field of law and government, as well as to the general public.

Proceedings for an offence under contribution law at one time could be conducted before a magistrates' court by anyone authorised for that purpose by HM Revenue and Customs, or before the county courts even if the person authorised was not a barrister or solicitor. [*SSC(TF)A 1999, s 4, Sch 4*.] These provisions are still in place to enable the recovery through the courts of contributions where income tax recovery provisions are not applicable, although they are not used for criminal offences.

HMRC will ask the magistrates to order the debtor to pay the debt in full by a fixed date together with the costs of the case. If payment is not then made, bailiffs may be used to take goods for sale, or HMRC may make an individual bankrupt or wind up a company.

A Revenue and Customs Prosecutions Office was set up as a non-departmental public body, independent of HMRC, in April 2005 under *Commissioners for Revenue & Customs Act 2005* to take over responsibility for HMRC prosecutions of criminal offences in England, Wales and Northern Ireland (in Scotland it was merely a Specialist Reporting Agency supporting the Procurator Fiscal). The RCPO was merged into the Crown Prosecution Service on 1 January 2010. Following this reorganisation of both policy and personnel, HMRC no longer has responsibility for criminal prosecutions. The decision whether to bring a criminal prosecution is made by an independent prosecuting authority which, in England and Wales, is the Crown Prosecution Service. In Scotland it is the Crown Office and Procurator Fiscal Service, and in Northern Ireland it is the Public Prosecution Service for Northern Ireland.

HMRC does however retain responsibility for investigating crime involving NICs. The staff authorised to use criminal investigation powers are in the Criminal Investigation Directorate, which is responsible for all criminal investigations undertaken by HMRC where criminal investigation has been determined to be the appropriate response to tax fraud. There is a complete separation of civil and criminal investigations, and no one in HMRC dealing with civil enquiries such as those made into PAYE and NIC returns can use any criminal powers to further their enquiries.

The circumstances in which HMRC will now generally consider starting a criminal rather than a civil investigation are:

- operations of organised criminal gangs or systematic frauds where losses represent a serious threat to the tax base;
- where an individual holds a position of trust and responsibility;
- where materially false statements are made or materially false documents are provided in the course of a civil investigation;
- where, pursuing an avoidance scheme, reliance is placed on a false or altered document or such reliance or material facts are misrepresented to enhance the credibility of a scheme;
- where deliberate concealment, deception, conspiracy or corruption is suspected;
- cases involving the use of false or forged documents;
- where the perpetrator has committed previous offences or there is a repeated course of unlawful conduct or previous civil action;
- cases involving theft, or the misuse or unlawful destruction of HMRC documents;
- where there is evidence of assault on, threats to, or the impersonation of HMRC officials; and

- where there is a link to suspected wider criminality, whether domestic or international, involving offences not under the administration of HMRC (including money laundering).

Although HMRC committed to ministers to increase the number of prosecutions each year to at least 1,000, it will normally investigate using the civil fraud investigation procedures under Code of Practice 9.

On 17 December 2015, the National Audit Office reported on HMRC's efforts at tackling tax fraud (Report HC 610, Session 2015–16), that HMRC had focused on less complex cases to meet its target of increasing prosecutions by 1,000 per year, with a quarter of all prosecutions involving less than £10,000 of taxes. The National Audit Office pointed out that HMRC had initially estimated that there would be £295m of yield from the deterrent effect of an additional 1,000 prosecutions, but that HMRC had admitted that this was unverifiable and that its own research could find no evidence that the extra prosecutions led to changes in behaviour or increases in tax revenues. In the Budget in July 2015, the government announced that HMRC would receive additional funding for criminal investigations into serious and complex tax crime, particularly focusing on wealthy individuals and corporates, with the aim of increasing prosecutions in this area to 100 per year by 2020. The NAO also found that the prosecutions undertaken had focused on income tax, VAT and tobacco duty, with no mention of National Insurance Contributions.

Where HMRC succeeded in providing enough evidence for a prosecution to be initiated, about one-third of cases resulted in a custodial sentence, 16% a suspended sentence, 41% a non-custodial sentence and 9% an acquittal.

Distraint of goods and chattels

[35.14] Where a person is served with a certificate under *SSAA 1992, s 118* as to underpaid contributions issued by an authorised officer and he neglects or refuses to pay the contributions, interest or penalties within seven days, an authorised officer may distrain upon that person's goods or chattels. [*SSAA 1992, s 121A*].

The period was originally 30 days but reduced to seven days by *NICSPA 2004, s 5(1)* with effect from 1 September 2004.

Where Scottish law was in point, and contributions, interest or penalties remained unpaid after 14 days from the issue of a certificate, an authorised officer could, until 23 November 2009, issue to the sheriff for the grant a summary warrant authorising recovery of the unpaid amount by way of an attachment, an earnings arrestment or an arrestment and action of furthcoming or sale. The provision was repealed by *FA 2008, s 129, Sch 43, para 14*, but see below. [*SSAA 1992, s 121B(1)*].

Alternatively, the Commissioners may use the *Tribunals, Courts and Enforcement Act 2007, Sch 12* procedure to recover any sum payable. This procedure applied only to England and Wales until 23 November 2009, when a similar procedure was extended to Scotland [*FA 2008, ss 127–129* and *FA 2008 (Section 8 and Part 2 of Schedule 43 (Appointed Day, Transitional Provisions and Savings) Order 2009 (SI 2009/3024)*.]

HM Revenue and Customs will use distraint as its first choice where recovery of contributions is required, before resorting to court action – either the magistrates or the county court.

Laying an information

[35.15] A duly authorised officer will commence proceedings for debt recovery by attending the Office of the Clerk to the Justices and laying an information (ie, an official complaint or charge) under *Magistrates' Courts Act 1980* alleging the offence of failure to pay. It is the duty of the Clerk to ensure that authorisation is produced but, if it is not and if no objection is raised before HMRC's case is closed, the summons must be considered good. (*Price v Humphries* [1958] 2 QB 353, [1958] 2 All ER 725, DC).

Time limits

[35.16] Proceedings must be brought before a magistrates' court not later than the first anniversary of the day on which the contribution become due (ie, the offence of non-payment is committed) or, if later, within three months of the date on which evidence justifying a prosecution comes to the attention of the Secretary of State, except in the case of Class 2 contributions (or interest or penalties in respect of Class 2 contributions) when the time limit is the end of the year following the tax year in which the contributions fell due. [*SSAA 1992, s 116*.]

Provided an information is received at the Office of the Clerk to the Justices for the relevant area within the time limit allowed, it is 'laid' within the time, even though it may not be personally considered by a magistrate or the Clerk to the Justices until after the time limit has expired. (*R v Dartford Justices, ex p Dhesi*, [1982] 3 WLR 331).

The certificate of an authorised officer as to unpaid contributions, interest or penalties is sufficient evidence of the outstanding amount in any proceedings before any court, until the contrary is proved. [*SSAA 1992, s 118* as amended by *Social Security Act 1998, s 62*].

In the debates on the National Insurance Contributions and Statutory Payments Bill, Clause 5 the then Paymaster General, Dawn Primarolo stated with regard to Class 2:

> Clause 5, and Clause 6 for Northern Ireland, deal with a minority (3 per cent) of NICs that are not collected with tax. They are mainly the flat rate Class 2 contributions that are paid by the self-employed. The purpose of this clause is to align the Inland Revenue's procedures for recovering that type of NIC debt with those for recovering tax debts. Tax legislation and procedures have applied to debt recovery contributions collected with tax since the mid 1970s.' and
>
> 'The period of notice for distraint action in England and Wales is changed from 30 days to seven, in line with the procedures for recovering tax debt and accepted good practice. The period of notice for a summary warrant in Scotland is changed from 30 days to 14, in line with the tax legislation and procedures under the Debt Arrangement and Attachment (Scotland) Act 2002.

Standing Committee D, 13 January 2004, Col 23.

In the county court the time limits under *Limitation Act 1980* (see **12.11**) apply.

Where court action is taken by HM Revenue and Customs this will normally follow warnings that such action would ensue. When formal court papers are received it is essential to act upon them quickly – whether or not an appeal has been made against Notices of Decision. Under the Civil Procedures Rules, rule 12, the defendant must file an acknowledgement within 14 days of the date of service of the particulars. In the absence of this the claimant (HM Revenue and Customs) is entitled to obtain a default judgment and a court order to make the debt enforceable. It may be possible to apply to have such a judgment set aside but this is time consuming and not without costs. Assuming that any Notices of Decision are already the subject of an appeal the response would therefore typically be to file an application for an indefinite stay of the proceedings pending full determination of the appeal before the tribunal and/or higher courts, citing *SSAA 1992, s 117A(5)* as statutory authority.

HMRC rarely uses these powers except when a dispute has dragged on for several years and there is a danger that any liabilities would become unenforceable because of the six-year rule in the *Limitation Act 1980*. It has instead followed exclusively civil recovery procedures and, from 6 April 2014, is able to collect arrears of Class 2 contributions by adjusting PAYE codes.

The summons

[35.17] Following an information being laid, a summons will, without delay prejudicial to the defendant and within a reasonable time before the hearing, be issued and served on the person cited in the information. It will state the general matter of the information and the place and time the defendant is to appear. The summons must be issued by the justices before whom the information was laid. (*R v Fairford Justices, ex p Brewster* [1975] 2 AER 757; *R v Jenkins* (1862) 26 JP 775; *Dixon v Wells* (1890) 54 JP 725).

If the alleged offender is a limited company, the company itself must be summoned, and where, instead, a director or the company secretary is summoned the case must be dismissed. (*City of Oxford Tramway Co v Sankey* (1890) 54 JP 564). A summons will be properly served on a company only if it is left at, or posted to, its registered office. In the case of a company registered in Scotland carrying on business in England and Wales, a summons may be served at its principal place of business in England and Wales if process is served through an English or Welsh court, but the person issuing the summons must send a copy of it by post to the company's registered office. [*Companies Act 1985, s 725; Companies Act 2006, s 1258*].

An error in the defendant's name as it appears in the summons will not invalidate the proceedings provided that the identity of the defendant is clear or the defendant appears to the summons.

Where a summons is defective because of a clerical error (eg the statement therein of the wrong section number of the relevant enactment under which the offence is alleged to have taken place) but the person summoned has not been misled by the error and pleads guilty when the charge is put to him without reference to either the section of the enactment or the enactment itself, the justices are entitled to amend the summons before the final disposal of the case. (*R v Eastbourne Justices, ex p Kisten*, The Times, 22 December 1984.)

Representation

[35.18] The committal hearing takes place in open court. [*Magistrates' Courts Act 1980, s 4(2)*]. An HM Revenue and Customs officer, although not a barrister or a solicitor, may conduct the proceedings for the offence before the magistrates or county court. [SSAA 1992, s 116(1) as amended by *SSC(TF)A 1999, Sch 1 para 21 and Sch 4 para 3(2)*]. This will normally be a debt manager from HMRC's Debt Management and Banking team. The proceedings will not be invalidated if they are conducted by a different officer to the one who laid the information which gave rise to the summons. (*R v Northumberland Justices, ex p Thompson* (1923) 87 JP 95). Either party may be represented by a barrister or a solicitor and an absent party so represented is deemed to be present. The court may, however, proceed in the absence of the defendant even where he is unrepresented provided it is proved to the satisfaction of the court that the summons was served on the accused within a reasonable time before the trial. [*MCA 1980, s 11*].

Witnesses

[35.19] Either party may call witnesses and is able to seek a witness summons if a required witness is unwilling to attend voluntarily. Such a summons may require the production of documents, etc.

The argument that there is a commercial risk in the issue of a witness summons was not upheld on the basis that the interests of justice are served best by issuing the witness summons. See *Tilbury Consulting Ltd v Gittins* [2004] STC SCD 1 Sp C 379.

36

Entertainers

Cross-references. See CATEGORISATION **14**; **20.6** CLASS **4** CONTRIBUTIONS for relief for Class 1 contributions paid by a self-employed earner; INTERMEDIARIES **40**; LABOUR-ONLY CONTRACTORS **41**.

Other Sources. Simon's Taxes, Volume 2, Para A8.219A; Tolley's Tax Planning 2015–16, Tolley's National Insurance Brief, August 1996, specialist sector; Tolley's Practical NIC, July 2003, November 2004 and February 2006; Note: CWG2 (2014), page 5 was out of date from 6 April 2014 in respect of entertainers, but CWG2 (2016) is correct where it makes reference to them.

Introduction to entertainers and NICs

[36.1] The categorisation of entertainers (which term includes actors, singers, musicians, or anyone 'in any similar performing capacity') for contribution purposes has been a continual source of difficulty and a number of cases have come before the Secretary of State for Social Security and the courts over the years.

Many entertainers are in business on their own account and are treated as self-employed on basic principles. They become employees if they take on an employment contract with a business, which may be their own personal service company or may be an entertainment business acting like any other employer. Many self-employed entertainers find work through an agency, and most workers who are supplied by an agency to provide personal service to an end client who supervises their work are deemed by the *Social Security (Categorisation of Earners) Regulations 1978* to be employees of the agency. However, actors, singers, musicians and other entertainers in any similar performing capacity have been specifically excluded from the agency deeming rules for many years. Instead, specific deeming rules for entertainers who met certain criteria applied from 1998 to 2014, treating them as employees of the producer of the entertainment in question.

[*Categorisation Regs, Reg 2, Sch 1 Part I paras 2(b), 5A* as amended by *Social Security (Categorisation of Earners) Amendment Regulations 1998, SI 1998/1728, Reg 3*; *Social Security (Categorisation of Earners) Amendment Regulations 2003, SI 2003/736, Reg 3*; and *Social Security (Categorisation of Earners) Amendment Regulations 2014, SI 2014/635, Regs 2, 4*; see also *ITEPA 2003, s 352(4)*].

Whilst the 1998 more general change to the Categorisation Regulations (see **36.4**) classified most artistes as employees in any event, those provisions did not come into play if the individual was already an employee in any case by application of common law.

Exactly what was meant by 'any similar performing capacity' was not without doubt and arguably did not include performers such as comedians, dancers, jugglers and so on. It is understood a test case was being prepared to challenge the matter, but this now seems unlikely to proceed in light of the abolition of the NIC deeming rule in 2014.

Actors and stage and screen performers

[36.2] The position concerning stage performers has been one of great difficulty over recent decades. Publicity during the early part of 1990 highlighted a hardening of the then Inland Revenue's attitude towards theatrical performers, in that any performer working under the standard Equity contract was argued automatically to be an employee (ie, within the former Schedule E) for income tax purposes but was allowed, by virtue of *ITEPA 2003, ss 328, 329, 352* (originally *ICTA 1988, s 201A* introduced by *FA 1990, s 77* and amended by *FA 1991, s 69* replaced by *ITEPA 2003, ss 722, 723, Sch 6 paras 1, 28(c), Sch 7*), a deduction for certain agents' fees. Attempts during Finance Bill debates to grant automatic or voluntary Schedule D status to actors came to nothing. On a purely concessionary basis, however, the then Inland Revenue agreed that any such performer who could prove that he or she had been dealt with before 6 April 1987 under Schedule D could continue on that basis indefinitely (known as 'reserved Schedule D status'), but any new entrant to the profession after that date would automatically have their receipts dealt with for tax purposes as employment income. The change of policy by the Inland Revenue did not go unchallenged, and the position has changed several times over the last 25 years.

Case law

[36.3] The then Inland Revenue based its Schedule E argument on the *Fall v Hitchen* case (see below) which established that the Esher Standard Contract for Ballet (a standard Equity contract) was a contract of service rather than a contract for services. In the past, it was furthermore argued that any contract which extended over three months or more (whether or not an Equity contract and whatever the true nature of the Equity contract might be) could not be regarded as merely one of a series of successive contracts which were entered into in the course of exercising a profession such as that which was found to be exercised in the *Davies v Braithwaite* case (see below).

The DSS view continued to be that the Equity contract was clearly a contract of service, however long the engagement, principally because it gave a very detailed degree of control over the performer and it required personal service to be provided. The then Inland Revenue's past treatment of performers and the then-current treatment by HM Revenue and Customs of those with reserved Schedule D status were seen as purely concessionary, aimed at simplifying the collection of tax and no more. The DSS expected the producer in each case to deduct and account for Class 1 contributions, irrespective of the income tax treatment unless it was a clear cut case of Schedule D status. Despite the Inland Revenue's views, in September 1993 the Special Commissioners ruled that live theatre work by actors Sam West and Alec McCowen should be taxed under Schedule D and not Schedule E. The Inland Revenue stated that it would not appeal against the Commissioners' decision. The basis of the decision was understood to be that a series of roles played amounted to incidents in a professional self-employed career, which enabled the Special Commissioners to distinguish the case from *Fall v Hitchen*. This accorded with the decision in *Hall v Lorimer* later in the same year (see **41.15** LABOUR-ONLY CONTRACTORS).

Until the *McCowen* and *West* decisions (see **41.15** LABOUR-ONLY CONTRACTORS), neither the DSS nor the then Inland Revenue gave due weight to the *Davies v Braithwaite* decision and any performer who wished to retain self-employed status entered into only renewable short-term contracts and considered not using the Equity standard contract but rather a contract drawn up with different terms and conditions which supported any claim to self-employed status.

Categorisation

[36.4] The DSS eventually admitted in Press Release 98/202 (15 July 1998) that its view that actors and musicians were always employees could not, in fact, be sustained. However, many such persons were, under new regulations with effect from 17 July 1998, to be categorised specifically as if they were employees for NICs purposes. This would not affect the income tax position where status would continue to be determined according to basic case law principles. These regulations were to cease to have effect on 1 February 1999 but that cessation date was subsequently removed by further regulations. [*Categorisation Regs, Sch 1, para 5A*, as inserted by *Categorisation Amendment Regs 1999*].

In the summer of 2003 the Inland Revenue issued notes on the application of the special NIC rules to entertainers (including workers in the film and television industries). These notes stressed that in many cases the special categorisation rules would apply to treat individuals engaged as if they were employees and so bring them within the scope of Class 1 contributions. Such contributions were payable by 'entertainers' except those whose remuneration '[did] not consist wholly or mainly of salary'. Whilst 'entertainer' was defined in the legislation 'salary' was not, until 6 April 2003 (see below).

Case law suggested to the Inland Revenue that a sum would be salary if it was paid in respect of services rendered or to be rendered, and was payable under the terms of a contract, and was computed by reference to time and payable at a fixed time, and was in respect of services which had an element of continuity or recurrence. See *Re Shine, ex parte Shine* [1892] 1 QB 522 and *Greater London Council v Minister of Social Security* [1971] 2 All ER 285. They said that specific advice should be sought from them in all cases of dispute or difficulty but that, as a general rule of thumb, sums payable under most contracts which imported Equity conditions in relation to hours of work, etc were likely to be regarded as salary. Because of the need for an element of recurrence 'it seemed unlikely that remuneration for a one-off engagement for one day or less could reasonably be described as 'salary'. The Inland Revenue stressed that the special categorisation rules applied if the entertainer was remunerated 'wholly or mainly' by salary. The *ITV Services* decision (see below) then cast serious doubt on that view. Where that was the case, though, all payments from the engagement were liable to National Insurance contributions, and not just the salary element.

Until November 2006 ITV treated several actors as employed earners and accounted for Class 1 contributions on the amounts it paid them. From December 2006 it ceased to account for Class 1 NICs, treating the actors as self-employed. HMRC issued determinations charging NICs on the payments, and the company appealed. The First-Tier Tribunal reviewed the evidence in detail and allowed the appeal in part, issuing a decision in principle that the company was required to account for NICs in respect of most of the types of contracts, but not where the actors were 'engaged to perform a specific role in a specific programme, engaged for a specific period of engagement, and received a single total inclusive fee'. *ITV Services Ltd v HMRC* FTT [2010] UKFTT 586 (TC), TC00836. The original decision was upheld by the Upper Tribunal (FTC/12/2011; [2012] UKUT 47 (TCC)) and it was also ruled that payments under All Rights Contracts and certain Bespoke Agreements were salary and Class 1 NIC was due. A further appeal by ITV to the Court of Appeal was also unsuccessful ([2013] EWCA Civ 867).

Revenue & Customs Brief 29/13 issued on 2 October 2013, set out the HMRC view on how matters should be addressed both going forward and for past years. HMRC was of the view that although the contracts reviewed by the Court of Appeal were specific to actors engaged by ITV, the comments made and the principles established were clear enough to apply to all entertainers. They therefore expected all engagers of entertainers to comply with the legislation as determined by the Court of Appeal decision.

For past years HMRC expected compliance with the Court of Appeal decision, as it was in accord with their interpretation of the legislation. Where, however, HMRC had given a written opinion that contributions were not payable because the payments made were not by way of salary, no action would be taken to recover any Class 1 contributions for periods before 6 April 2011. Where such an opinion had been given on a specific contract and the engager had used that opinion for other entertainers in identical circumstances again no action would be taken to recover contributions before 6 April 2011.

Definition—'salary'

[36.5] As stated above, the term 'salary' in the context of entertainers was specifically defined from 6 April 2003 to 5 April 2014 (when the special entertainer status rules were abolished) as follows:

- payments made for services rendered;
- paid under a contract for services;
- where there was more than one payment, payable at a specific period or interval; and
- computed by reference to the amount of time for which work had been performed.

[*Categorisation Regs, Sch 1, para 5A* inserted by *Social Security (Categorisation of Earners) Amendment Regs 2003, SI 2003/736*, revoked by *Social Security (Categorisation of Earners) (Amendment) Regulations 2014, SI 2014/635*.]

In addition, the person specified as the secondary contributor was, from 6 April 2003 to 5 April 2014, the producer of the entertainment in question (previously the person who engaged the entertainer).

[*Categorisation Regs, Sch 3, para 10*, inserted by *Social Security (Categorisation of Earners) Amendment Regs 2003, SI 2003/736*, revoked by *Social Security (Categorisation of Earners) (Amendment) Regulations 2014, SI 2014/635*.]

In the *ITV Services* case, the Court of Appeal reviewed at some length what was meant by the final condition outlined above. They concluded that in many cases a lump sum payment made for an engagement during which an entertainer might be on call would not satisfy this condition. That, however, was of little help because usually included within such a lump sum were daily payments agreed under a PACT or Equity arrangement and such payments were sufficient to make the lump sum 'salary' as defined in the *Categorisation Regs*.

Many producers were attempting to avoid Class 1 NIC liabilities by insisting on entering into contracts with an entertainer's service company. That placed any contribution liability on the service company and in an attempt to minimise contribution liabilities much of the remuneration was taken in the form of dividends. HMRC has been seeking to challenge this via the intermediaries (ie, IR35) provisions. See **40 INTERMEDIARIES**. A challenge was put to HMRC that there was a mismatch between the intermediaries provisions and the *Categorisation Regulations 1978*, as entertainers are not employees in all cases but are simply treated as such for NIC purposes. HMRC rejected this argument and a case was planned for the First-Tier Tribunal which was supposed to be heard sometime in 2013, but that date slipped. HMRC initially agreed to stop pursuing their challenge whilst considering the technical argument but it lifted its moratorium. It did, however, agree to take no enforcement action or make formal decisions for any entertainer who stated in writing he wished to follow the argument put forward in the test case. HMRC encouraged those who took advantage of this offer to make a payment on account. HMRC was in discussion with a number of producers regarding the treatment of those entertainers at the top of their profession who are collectively known as 'key talent' and also on how 'residual' payments (in effect, payments for further use of the production, such as repeat fees for satellite channels) should be treated for NIC assessment purposes. This was not a formal consultation and the discussions were shrouded in secrecy.

These discussions resulted in HMRC issuing on 15 May 2013 a consultative document entitled 'National Insurance and Self-employed entertainers'. HMRC had recognised that the legislation did not fit neatly with the way many entertainers were being remunerated, and specifically so where that remuneration included royalties or additional use payments. The consultative document provided four potential solutions:

(1) provide for separate secondary contributors for NIC due on initial performance payments and additional use payments;
(2) provide that initial performance payments be subject to Class 1 NIC but additional use payments be subject to Class 4 liabilities;
(3) repeal the existing legislation and introduce a higher rate special Class 2 contribution for entertainers to be paid in addition to Class 4 NICs; and
(4) repeal the existing legislation and have entertainers pay Class 2 and 4 NIC in the same way as any other self-employed individual.

The fourth option was the one preferred by HMRC, as it would appear to have been the easiest to introduce, as the 1993 deeming rules were repealed from 6 April 2014. The downside of the change is that entertainers will no longer be able to claim Jobseekers' Allowance when they are not working unless they work through a service company and pay themselves a salary at or above the LEL for at least two tax years.

HMRC issued a summary of responses to the consultation on 23 October 2013. Some 11,800 responses were received with 11,700 supporting the self-employed proposal set out at option (4) above. The large response was primarily because of some 7,600 replies from members of the Musicians Union who used standard wording prepared by the union.

HMRC considered various comments on how benefit entitlement would be affected and, in particular, rights to Universal Credit (which do not depend on having paid NICs) but concluded that the way forward was to regard entertainers as self-employed for NIC purposes. That was achieved by amending the *Social Security (Categorisation of Earners) Regulations 1978, SI 1978/1689* from 6 April 2014 to remove the recategorisation of entertainers (see *Social Security (Categorisation of Earners) (Amendment) Regulations 2014, SI 2014/635*). One point to keep in mind is that, despite the legislative change, entertainers engaged via a contract of service will still be within Class 1 NIC. Whether the contractual arrangements in such circumstances need to be revised to ensure Class 2 liability applies instead is for individual consideration. HMRC confirmed the relevance of the contractual position in Revenue & Customs Brief 35/13, which also explained the contribution treatment for periods before 6 April 2014.

Pre-purchase payments, royalties, etc

[36.6] The change in April 2003 was made because, since the 1998 Regulations, it had become commonplace for film actors and, to a lesser extent, TV actors to receive pre-purchase payments in lieu of future rights and royalties/repeat fees as part of their remuneration package. Such payments invariably outweighed the other sums due under the contract and so the requirement to be caught for Class 1 NIC ('wholly or mainly salary') was not met. Thus the 2003 change merely required the inclusion of 'any' salary in the package to trigger categorisation as an employed earner. Subsequent rights payments were subject to Class 1 NICs even if the contract period had ended and the repeat programme was not broadcast by the original production company. In the case of the BBC, their BBC/PACT agreement (January 2004), which enabled them to take out a licence to use the original programme and pay the original production company for its showing, resulted in the original production company continuing to be treated as the secondary contributor with regard to the deduction of NICs from rights payments.

With the repeal of the entertainers' rules in the *Categorisation Regs 1978* from 6 April 2014, any royalties, repeat fees, etc paid after that date will be treated as self-employed income unless the entertainer was working under a contract of service for the original production.

Actors resting

[36.7] The advantage of Class 1 liability to performers is, of course, that when they are 'resting' they may qualify for contributions-based Jobseeker's Allowance ('JSA(C)'), which is not means-tested. JSA(C) would not be available to Class 2 contributors. It is possible that this may be the underlying reason for any enthusiasm shown by actors' representatives for treatment as employees. Equity, for example, were particularly keen for the employee status to continue for the bulk of their members. For this reason, individuals entitled to make the reclaim of contributions announced in summer 2003 may have chosen to forgo that refund to maintain greater benefit entitlement. This did not, however, prevent their engagers reclaiming the secondary contributions that were paid.

There was a disadvantage while the deeming rule was still in force in that each engagement was treated as a separate employment for Class 1 purposes with the result that contributions in excess of the individual's personalised ANNUAL MAXIMUM (see 7.4) might have been paid. In certain circumstances, of course, Class 1 DEFERMENT OF PAYMENT (see 27.2) might have been available or repayments obtained (see REPAYMENT AND REALLOCATION 55).

Pre-1998 case law now relevant

[36.8] Prior to the 1998 announcement, case law was pertinent to ascertaining the status of actors and entertainers, and many cases had been decided over the years. Following the repeal of the special categorisation rules for entertainers, the basic principles elucidated in these old cases have become important once more. Almost all the published decisions in this area were arrived at by application of the control test (see **14.11** CATEGORISATION). As the degree of control exerted over an entertainer tends to be much greater in the case of extended or resident (rather than short or single) engagements, the duration of the contract is of great significance. Entertainers who appear regularly in a radio or TV series may have a contract of service and therefore be treated as employed earners on basic principles. This applies even though they may do other work which is classed as that of a self-employed earner.

A number of decisions had been made by the courts before 1998 concerning the employment status of actors and performers and these are now potentially once more of application to cases where employed earner status is determinable by application of basic case law.

In *Gould v Minister of National Insurance* [1951] 1 KB 731, [1951] 1 All ER 368, the engagement of Gould and his partner was for one week and the only control of any significance was a reserved right on the part of the theatre management to prohibit the whole or part of Gould's act. The performing of the act itself was, however, quite outside the management's control and rested solely on Gould's skill, personality and artistry. Gould was, accordingly, held to be a *self-employed* earner.

In *Stagecraft Ltd v Minister of National Insurance* 1952 SC 288, 1952 SLT 309, Ct of Sess, however, the engagement was for almost six months and the two comedians involved were under the direction of a producer and were obliged to collaborate with other artists involved in the performances produced. The two comedians were, accordingly, held to be *employed* earners.

Similarly, in *Campbell v Minister of National Insurance* (1952) (unreported except as part of the Minister of State's formal decision *M28 (1952)* against which the case was brought on appeal), a film actress was held to be an *employed* earner as her contract with the film company by which she was engaged extended over two years during which time the company had complete control over her. The fact that the actress had to bring her personal talents to her performance was held to have no bearing on the situation.

Similarly, in *Fall v Hitchen* [1973] STC 66 (a tax case), a professional ballet dancer was held to be an *employed* earner because the company by which he was engaged had secured his virtually exclusive services for a minimum period of rehearsals plus 22 weeks during which the dancer was to work specified hours for a regular salary. Here the judge said 'the expression "contract of service" appears to be coterminous with the expression "employment"'. See HM Revenue and Customs Employment Status Manual ESM7055.

In *Davies (Inspector of Taxes) v Braithwaite* [1931] 2 KB 628, 18 TC 19 (also a tax case), the important point was made that if a person finds a method of earning a livelihood which does not involve acquiring a post and continuing to occupy it, but which involves rather 'a series of engagements' and moving from one to the other, each of those engagements cannot be considered an employment but is a mere *engagement in the course of exercising a profession* (per Rowlatt J at p 203). See HM Revenue and Customs Employment Status Manual ESM7020. This principle is embodied in the economic reality test (see **14.14** CATEGORISATION) and also accords with the decision in *Hall v Lorimer* [1994] STC 23 (see **41.15** LABOUR-ONLY CONTRACTORS). See HM Revenue and Customs Employment Status Manual ESM7160. Although that test was applied only in the *Fall* case of those referred to above, it would, it is suggested, have produced results consistent with the decisions reached.

Musicians

[36.9] From July 1998 the position was as set out in **36.2** above.

With the exception of those musicians who are with the major London orchestras, other musicians and singers who are permanent members of major orchestras and choruses are generally liable for tax and NICs as employees. Session musicians and their deputies (who are generally engaged through Musicians Union approved contractors) are outside the scope of both old and new versions of the *Categorisation Regulations*. In the House of Lords in reply to a question regarding the involvement of the Musicians Union in the discussions leading to the original 1998 changes, Lord McKenzie of Luton stated that the Musicians Union made written representations and had meetings with Ministers and officials in the former Department of Social Security. The Union was a major supporter of the move to repeal the deeming rule for entertainers that happened in 2014.

London orchestras

[36.10] From autumn 2005 there was much press coverage about London orchestras having a liability under the entertainers' categorisation rules – arrears reputedly amounting to £33 million.

In the face of all the publicity HM Revenue and Customs stated on 8 November 2005:

> H M Revenue and Customs (HMRC) has learned that a number of orchestras have not operated Class 1 National Insurance on certain categories of musicians since 1998. HMRC is currently discussing with the Arts Council, the Association of British Orchestras, Opera and Theatre Music Forum, National Musicians Union and the Department for Culture, Media and Sport the implications of the orchestras' failure to deduct Class 1 National Insurance. The Association of British Orchestras and Opera and Theatre Music Forum will be writing to their members to explain the current position of the discussions and the action needed by orchestras.

This was followed by a flurry of written questions in the Commons. The then Paymaster General, Dawn Primarolo, said that the widespread failure of orchestras to deduct Class 1 National Insurance contributions did not become evident (following the 1998 change) to the then Inland Revenue until 2004. The Revenue then 'undertook customer support activity' in the orchestra sector. She also stated that the Department for Culture, Media and Sport was involved in the discussions leading up to the changes of summer 1998 affecting entertainers.

The Arts Council issued a press release during summer 2006 confirming that in conjunction with other bodies such as the Association of British Orchestras and the Musicians' Union, it arranged for collective legal representation and technical assistance for a group of 33 leading performing arts organisations and entered into discussions with HMRC which took place over nine months. HMRC concluded a detailed review of both contracts and 'employment' practices and was able to confirm that where payments to musicians under those contracts did not constitute a 'salary', there was no Class 1 National Insurance liability.

Arguably, that statement did no more than state what was in the amended Regulations, and the true reason for the agreement of no liability may never become clear. The 2014 repeal of the deeming rule should have negated any of the earlier problems for the future.

Club musicians

[36.11] The status of individual club musicians is more problematic because 'the forms of engagement of musicians working in clubs vary and the employment status of any individual musician will depend on the particular facts'. (Hansard 5 December 1983 Vol 150 Col 26). Where, however, the facts reveal (as they often will) that the engagement is an ongoing one and that the musician is closely controlled by the management of the club in which he performs and that such control extends beyond the mere dictation of the dates, times and duration of his appearances, to the dictation of the very content and style of his performances (see **14.11** CATEGORISATION), it will be difficult to resist the contention that the musician is an employed earner under a (possibly unwritten) contract of service to the club. Where such musicians had a regular performing slot and were paid by time, they could have fallen under the deeming rules as employed earners before 6 April 2014.

Disc jockeys

[36.12] Disc jockeys will usually be treated as self-employed even though they are often engaged under Equity contracts because they are (arguably) not included in the definition of 'entertainer'. In a case where the disc jockey provided additional services which came within the definition of 'entertainer' then he may have been treated as an employee and subject to Class 1 NICs along with the 'employer' under the pre-6 April 2014 rules. An exception to this would have been where a disc jockey came from another EEA state or a country with which the UK had a reciprocal agreement, in which case the presentation of an E101 or similar document ensured that the 2003 Regulations could not apply in that particular individual's case. See **51.9** OVERSEAS MATTERS.

Other musicians

[36.13] A number of decisions were made by the courts concerning the employment status of musicians who play in bands and orchestras that ceased to be relevant between the July 1998 announcement by the DSS and the repeal of the deeming rule in April 2014, but they may now be of possible application again.

In the early case of *Performing Right Society Ltd v Mitchell & Booker (Palais de Danse) Ltd* [1924] 1 KB 762 it was held that the members of a dance band were *employed earners* because the band was subject to 'continuous dominant and detailed control on every point, including the nature of the music to be played'.

In the Minister of State's decision *M14 (1950)*, it was held that the leader of a dance band engaged by an hotel was a *self-employed* earner but that the members of his band were *employed earners* by reason of the fact that, while the leader was not himself subject to detailed control, he exercised detailed control over the members, handled the hotel's complaints concerning the band, and paid them wages from the weekly engagement fee which he received from the hotel.

That decision contrasts with that of the Employment Appeal Tribunal in *Winfield v London Philharmonic Orchestra Ltd* [1979] ICR 726 (an employment law case) where it was held that the members of the orchestra were *self-employed earners*. That conclusion followed from the finding that the relationship between the company and the individual players was not that of 'a boss and his musician employees' but that an orchestra was 'a co-operative of distinguished musicians running themselves with self and mutual discipline'.

In *Addison v London Philharmonic Orchestra Ltd* [1981] ICR 261 (an employment law case), it was held that an associate player and three additional players of the London Philharmonic Orchestra were *self-employed* earners. This was because, when playing with the orchestra, each remained essentially a freelance musician and pursued his or her own profession as an instrumentalist. Their skills and interpretative powers were contributed by them to the orchestra as independent contractors.

Similarly, in *Midland Sinfonia Concert Society Ltd v Secretary of State for Social Services* [1981] ICR 454, it was held that musicians engaged to perform in an orchestra in individual concerts and rehearsals by separate invitation and remunerated solely in respect of each engagement are *self-employed* earners. That decision reversed the determination by the Secretary of State on 21 July 1978 that the individuals concerned were employed earners.

The most modern 'musician' case concerning status was *Jowitt v London Symphony Orchestra Ltd*, 5 November 1990, EAT 301/90. Mr Jowitt was co-principal clarinettist with the London Symphony Orchestra. Although he was being treated as self-employed for tax and National Insurance purposes and was registered for VAT, upon having his appointment terminated by the LSO because of a disagreement, he complained to an industrial tribunal that, as an *employee* of the orchestra, he had been unfairly dismissed within the terms of the *Employment Protection (Consolidation) Act 1978*.

The question of Mr Jowitt's true status fell to be determined by the Employment Appeals Tribunal and, on the basis of the facts, the EAT decided that Mr Jowitt was indeed *self-employed*.

In *Warner Holidays Ltd v Secretary of State for Social Services* [1983] ICR 440, two musicians (and a comedian) were held to be *employed earners*. The case was distinguished from the various 'orchestra' cases referred to above in that it did not concern concert or session musicians but musicians who were holiday camp entertainers. Warners had full and exclusive control over them and paid them fixed salaries. The economic reality test was applied and it was found that none of the persons were performing their services as persons in business on their own account.

Circus performers

[36.14] From July 1998 to April 2014, the position was as set out in **36.2** above.

Before 1998, various cases covering the employment status of circus performers had been heard and may now be of possible application again because employed earner status is now determinable by the application of basic case law without the need to have regard to the *Categorisation Regulations*.

One such case was *Whittaker v Minister of Pensions and National Insurance* [1967] 1 QB 156, [1966] 3 All ER 631, in which it was held that a trapeze artist engaged by Bertram Mills Circus and paid by the performance was an *employed* earner. Although on the basis of the *Gould* case (see **36.8** above) it had been decided by the Minister of State that Miss Whittaker was self-employed, there were additional factors which made that decision incorrect. Miss Whittaker had a dual role with the circus, being under contract to act as an usherette when not performing and to assist in moving the circus when it transferred to a new location. These factors clearly pointed to control by the company in a sufficient degree to make the contract one of service.

In the Minister of State's decision *M66 (1958)*, it was similarly held that a circus clown engaged not only to clown but also to drive one of the circus vehicles and to assist in erecting and dismantling tents was an *employed* earner.

Perhaps significantly, the entertainers in the *Warner* case (see **36.12** above) had also accepted a dual role: each had general duties in addition to his obligations as a performer.

Voiceovers

[36.15] The status of individuals engaged in voiceovers has been unclear and conflicting advice was given by the DSS and HMRC, but in a letter dated 24 July 2012, Specialist Employer Compliance stated in connection specifically with the entertainers' rule in the *Categorisation Regs*:

> Anyone providing a voiceover to a recorded documentary or presentation where they are using their own normal voice does not fall within the Special NIC Rules for Entertainers. This is because the work being done is not considered to be 'performing in a similar capacity to an actor'.
>
> Anyone providing a voiceover which is performed in character for the purpose of dramatised material or who speaks in a dialect which is not their normal speaking voice would fall within the Special NIC Rules for Entertainers because it is considered that they are 'performing in a similar capacity to an actor'.

A Narrator or a Continuity Announcer, who provides the links between programmes, would not be classed as an entertainer for Class 1 NIC purposes.

Reporters and newsreaders

[36.16] HM Revenue and Customs accepted that TV presenters and news reporters were not 'entertainers' for the purpose of the *Categorisation Regs*. There was therefore a number of actors, and their engagers, to whom HM Revenue and Customs had insisted that Class 1 NIC applied in the past but the legislation did not – until the change on 6 April 2003 – sustain this view. Affected persons could apply for refunds in respect of the period from 17 July 1998 to 5 April 2003 inclusive, provided the claim was made by 5 April 2005. At first, there was no time limit to repayment claims, but the Inland Revenue subsequently announced that these had to be made by 5 April 2005. See Inland Revenue Guidance Notes, October 2004.

Radio industry

[36.17] In 2008, HMRC agreed a set of status guidelines for the radio industry which are similar to those that are used in the TV industry. The guidelines are not incorporated into HMRC's Employment Status Manual, but are available at www.radiocentre.org/files/hmrc_radio_industry_guidelines_2008-0.pdf.

The guidelines, highlighted by an article in *Taxation*, Issue 4513 in 2015, proceed on the basis that any presenter or DJ on the 'staff payroll' is likely to be engaged under a contract of service, and other types of contract are likely to be contracts for services if all or most of the following points apply:

- the contract is for a specific programme at a specific interval for a fixed term (eg, where a presenter presents a programme once a week on a fixed-term contract);
- the method of remuneration is by way of a fee per programme. In this situation there is more risk of not being paid compared to an employee who is paid a regular wage or salary;
- there is no roll-over situation (eg the engager gives no guarantee to negotiate the next contract);
- the radio presenter/DJ is free to pursue other engagements that do not conflict with the radio presentation (ie the contract is non-exclusive);
- there is no requirement to provide cover for staff shortages. This would suggest that the right of control by the engager over the radio presenter/DJ is low;
- there is no right on the part of the radio station to move the radio presenter/DJ from task to task (eg presenting to scripting, editing, producing, voicing etc) without the agreement of the radio presenter/DJ;
- the presenter has creative input into the programme;
- the engager does not have the right to control the manner in which the radio presenter/DJ carries out the work outside of observing the regulatory requirements of the industry (ie Ofcom Code, BBC Trust etc).

These points are intended to enable engagers to recognise self-employment features of a contract with a presenter. However, they are told to keep in mind that it is also important that:

- the contract accurately reflects the true terms and conditions and is not simply a case of wording the contract to reflect a contract for services;
- in practice, the actual services required of the presenter do not extend over and beyond what they are contractually required to do.

The guidelines also mention other personnel in the industry, stating that all except a defined list must be subject to PAYE and Class I NIC deductions. The grades where self-employment is accepted are summarised as follows:

- *Engaged on a freelance basis for a specific subject*:
  - story editor;
  - writer (excluding reporter);
  - sound recordist/mixer (where the contract requires substantial provision of equipment).
- *Engaged on a freelance basis for a period of less than nine months*:
  - producer;
  - co-producer;
  - executive producer;
  - associate producer (except where engaged primarily for general research);
  - director;
  - art director;
  - casting director;
  - musical director;
  - musical associate;
  - editor;
  - composer.
- *Translators*: The work must be performed other than on premises provided by the engager.
- *Language assessors*: Where used on an occasional basis to check style and delivery of foreign language broadcasts.
- *Cricket scorers*: Providers of occasional information, eg tip offs, racing tips, news and sport engaged for a period of less than nine months.
- *Freelance news and sports reporters and commentators*: This category is not intended to cover reporters and commentators who present their finished work on the air as they are covered above as radio presenters. This category is intended to cover reporters (often with a full-time job with a newspaper), who are paid on a per-contribution basis for the supply of news and sporting information and stories, who are commissioned as and when news and sports stories arise.
- *Score readers*: This heading covers both musical scores and sporting scores.
- *Auditioners*: Where they are engaged for a period of less than nine months. This category covers somebody who does not normally work within the radio industry and is engaged when there is a lot of

auditioning to be done, eg for a talent show. Often an established entertainer in their own right. Normal auditioning would be done by a producer or director and is not covered by this category.

- *Contributors to concerts publicity and prospectus*: Non-staff contributors where payment is made on a per-contribution basis. An example would be a person of renown in the musical world who contributed a piece on Beethoven for a concert prospectus.
- *Specialist researchers*: Where the worker has either an existing profession outside TV/radio (eg academic, legal adviser, doctor etc) or specialist knowledge of the programme content to be researched and the worker is engaged for a specific project and is not a regular contributor. Excluded are those people used by the radio industry to carry out research over a wide variety of fields, eg, in news and current affairs, investigative journalism.
- *Special effects man*: Where the contract requires provision of necessary equipment by the worker.

IR35 and entertainers

[36.18] HMRC believes that, to avoid PAYE and Class 1 NICs, many TV and radio workers in 'employed' grades have set up limited companies where they are the majority shareholder and a director. In HMRC's words, 'It is usually *alleged* [emphasis added] that the service company supplies the services of the individual to the television or radio company' (ESM4113). Whether this kind of undisguised prejudice should appear in HMRC's official guidance is a moot point, but it is at least clear how HMRC views the use of service companies by those who would ordinarily be treated as employees of the producer organisation.

HMRC believes that such arrangements 'often fail' and the worker remains an employee of the broadcaster. Compliance staff are also instructed to consider whether the IR35 legislation applies to any such service company, but this could only be relevant if the arrangements have not in fact failed and the worker is not an employee of the production company.

Before the repeal in 2014 of the special categorisation rule for entertainers, HMRC often argued that the mere fact that an artiste was deemed to be an employee of the producer by those regulations was enough to invoke the IR35 rules in respect of the artiste's service company. With the repeal, the argument is no longer relevant and it is unclear whether any of the old disputes will ever reach a tribunal.

However, the introduction of the 'off-payroll working in the public sector' rules from 6 April 2017 may possibly have an effect on those working for the BBC – see INTERMEDIARIES 40 and LABOUR-ONLY CONTRACTORS 41.

Status queries

[36.19] Queries about status could in the past be directed to local HM Revenue and Customs offices in the first instance, except that those in the TV industry were advised to telephone the TV and Broadcasting Unit at Trinity

Bridge House in Salford, which has now moved to Floor 2, Weardale House, Washington, NE37 1LW on 0191 419 8800. The unit deals with BBC TV and radio, and all the independent TV broadcasting, satellite, cable and radio companies. Queries about workers engaged by foreign broadcasting companies are dealt with by Specialist Employer Compliance at Grayfield House in Edinburgh (tel: 0131 453 8780). These offices still remain relevant and will support any Local Compliance officers with status enquiries in connection with entertainers.

Key Points regarding entertainers and NICs

[36.20] Points to consider are as follows.

- Many entertainers such as actors who have been treated as employed earners for NIC since 1998 while still paying tax on a self-employed basis may now once more be self-employed for both purposes.
- Under the pre-6 April 2014 rules, Class 1 NICs were applicable in respect of residual payments and royalties where some salary (as defined) had been received as part of the overall remuneration package. Any payment of fees, residuals or royalties after that date should be subject to Class 2 and Class 4 liability rather than Class 1, even if the original performance was subject to Class 1, if the entertainer was not under a contract of service for the performance.
- The use of service companies by entertainers and the subsequent payment in the form of dividends is being strongly challenged by HMRC. An agreed test case was being prepared for the First-Tier Tribunal, but no recent developments have been made public.
- From 6 April 2014 entertainers not engaged under a contract of service are treated as self-employed for NIC purposes.

37
Examiners

Cross-reference. See CATEGORISATION **14**.

Other Sources. Tolley's National Insurance Brief, June 1995. HM Revenue and Customs Employment Status Manual ESM4150.

Introduction to examiners and NICs

[37.1] Anyone who is gainfully employed as an examiner (other than through an agency – see **4.5** AGENCY WORKERS) will, irrespective of whether or not his employment is under a contract of service or in an office with general earnings chargeable to tax as employment income, be treated as falling into the category of *self-employed earner* provided:

(a) the person employing him is responsible for the conduct or administration of an examination leading to a certificate, diploma, degree or professional qualification;
(b) his duties are to examine, moderate, invigilate or act in a similar capacity, or to set questions or tests for examinations of the kind referred in (a); and
(c) his contract is one under which the whole of the work to be performed is to be performed in less than 12 months.

[*Social Security Contributions and Benefits Act 1992 (SSCBA 1992), s 2(2)(b), Categorisation Regs, Reg 2(3); Sch 1 Part II para 6.*]

The restriction in (c) above is often circumvented by the simple practice of providing a series of consecutive contracts none of which is for a period of 12 months or more.

Dual status

[37.2] This regulation is of particular application to those persons who are given short-term (even if renewable) contracts relating to particular examinations, eg GCSE and college and university examinations. Its effect is to give most examiners dual status: employed earner status for tax purposes and self-employed earner status for National Insurance purposes. In the years leading up to 1984, many examiners were treated as self-employed for tax purposes also but, over those years, more than 100,000 were re-categorised as employed by the former Inland Revenue. (Hansard 16 January 1984 Vol 52 Col 14.) Examiners are generally treated as employees for PAYE purposes because they are integral to the process of examining students and are closely controlled in their work (ESM 4152). Special PAYE arrangements generally applied until 5 April 2014, but standard RTI arrangements now apply, for tax purposes only (PAYE 70245).

Examiners to whom this chapter applies are, if their earnings are sufficiently high, liable for special Class 4 contributions (see **20.8** CLASS 4 CONTRIBUTIONS) based on those earnings.

38

Homeworkers and Outworkers

Cross-reference. See CATEGORISATION **14**.
Other Sources. Leaflet CWG2 (2016); Leaflet 480 (2016), para 5.16; Tolley's Practical NIC Newsletter, September 2003, page 68.

Introduction to homeworkers and outworkers and NICs

[38.1] A person who performs services in his own home or on other premises not under the control or management of the person for whom he performs them may be either an employed earner or a self-employed earner depending on the nature of the relationship between the parties and whether that relationship indicates the presence of a contract of service or of a contract for services. (See also AGENCY WORKERS **4** and CATEGORISATION **14**.)

Specific activities

[38.2] The Secretary of State for Social Security formally decided that a person making rugs in her own home for a company engaging disabled persons was not under a contract of service and was, therefore, a *self-employed earner*. (*M17 (1951)*). He also decided that a person making up coats for a tailor, unsupervised, in his own home was *self-employed*, (*M25 (1952)*), and that an outworker engaged in scissor grinding and finishing who employed his own assistants, supplied his own tools, equipment and materials, was free to process goods for whom he wished, chose his own production methods, was paid by the piece processed, and was unsupervised, was a *self-employed earner*, despite the fact that he rented and occupied premises in the factory of his main customer and undertook the whole of that customer's grinding and finishing work. (*M35 (1953)*).

In *Westall Richardson Ltd v Roulson* [1954] 2 All ER 448, [1954] 1 WLR 905, the court held that another outworker in the Sheffield cutlery trade—a mirror finisher of cutlery whose working arrangements were virtually identical with those described in *M35* above—was also a *self-employed earner* for, although there was 'some element of service or servitude in his position' there was 'a far greater element of independence and freedom'.

Conversely, an industrial tribunal found in *D'Ambrogio v Hyman Jacobs* [1978] IRLR 236 that a machinist working at home and using equipment and materials supplied to her by the person for whom she worked was an *employed earner* because the person for whom she worked called at her home daily and exercised a high degree of control over her—something the Secretary of State for Social Security had found lacking in the two cases referred to earlier.

Although control is of great importance, however, lack of it will not be decisive. In *Airfix Footwear Ltd v Cope* [1978] ICR 1210, the Employment Appeal Tribunal upheld a finding that a person who assembled shoe parts in her own home was an *employed earner* and in *Nethermere (St Neots) Ltd v Gardiner and Taverna* [1984] ICR 612 the Court of Appeal upheld an Employment Appeal Tribunal decision that a person who made up boys' trousers in her own home was an *employed earner*. In both these cases, the courts emphasised the failure of the economic reality test of self-employment (see **14.14** CATEGORISATION) and stressed the ongoing and dependent nature of the working relationship between the persons concerned and the persons for whom they worked. It will be noted that, had the economic reality test been applied in *Westall Richardson Ltd v Roulson* (see above), it would have fully supported the outcome.

Agency and intermediary workers

[38.3] The only circumstance in which the categorisation of a homeworker or outworker is in no doubt is where the person falls within the AGENCY WORKERS **4** (see **4.5**) category and is, by *reason of the nature of the services he renders*, required to render that service in his own home or on other premises not under the control or management of the person to whom he is supplied. Such a person is to be categorised as an *employed earner*. [*SSCBA 1992, s 2(2)(b); Categorisation Regs, Reg 2(2), Sch 1 Part I para 2(2)(a)*].

One example of such a situation will arise where an audit clerk supplied by an agency to an accountant is, according to normal practice, sent to work on an audit at the premises of one of the accountant's clients. (Earlier editions of now withdrawn leaflet CA 25).

Anyone who, though an agency worker and though working at home or on other premises not under the control or management of the person to whom he is supplied, does not do so by reason of the nature of the services is, however, to be categorised according to whether he is under a contract of service or not, and *not* under the special rules relating to AGENCY WORKERS **4** (see **4.15**), under which he will be an excluded worker. [*Categorisation Regs, Reg 2(2), Sch 1 Part I para 2(2)(a)*.] CWG2 (2016), page 74.

Employees working at home

[38.4] There is another form of 'homeworker' in the modern era being employees with a separate place of work who choose, or who are required, to carry out part of their duties at home.

In the 2003 Budget, the Chancellor announced a minor tax relief for modern-day homeworkers amounting to £2 per week where the employer reimbursed additional expenditure incurred. This was increased to £3 per week with effect from 6 April 2008 and to £4 per week (£18 per month) from 6 April 2012 (CWG2 para 143). The relief is given for 'reasonable additional household expenses', and the weekly limit is the guideline amount of reimbursement that HMRC will accept without requiring evidence of the extra costs incurred.

The associated 2003 Budget press release referred to the fact such reimbursement was already not liable to Class 1 contributions. At first reading, this was surprising but it must be appreciated that the statement referred only to reimbursement by the employer and also only to 'additional' expenditure (which may be difficult to measure in any event, eg extra electricity, water, insurance etc). Reimbursements of expenses incurred in carrying out the employment will not ordinarily constitute NIC able earnings as they do not represent remuneration or profit to the employee. The DSS and later Inland Revenue policy was always to accept that, for NIC purposes, any business expenditure that could be evidenced satisfactorily was disregarded in the calculation of earnings, and that basic principle has not changed. The NIC rules, unlike the *Income Tax (Earnings and Pensions) Act 2003 (ITEPA 2003)* benefits code rules (until the new exemption provisions applied from 6 April 2016), do not sweep up every payment of expenses and then allow a deduction only for expenses incurred wholly, exclusively and necessarily in the performance of the duties.

The Chancellor's proposal was enacted in the *Finance Act 2003*, when *s 137* inserted *ITEPA 2003, s 316A*. This ensures that where an employer makes a payment to an employee in respect of reasonable additional household expenses which the employee incurs in carrying out duties of the employment at home under homeworking arrangements then no liability to tax arises in respect of that payment. 'Homeworking arrangements' means arrangements between the employee and employer under which the employee regularly performs some or all of the duties at home. The amount of the relief being restricted to £4 per week as being 'reasonable' is somewhat small in comparison to the expenses incurred by homeworkers and it is questionable that the Class 1 primary and secondary savings in NICs and tax on £216 per annum is worth the cost of substantially altering the employees' contracts and monitoring the payments. This may, however, be a beneficial side effect where a company is keen to relocate workers to a home environment to free up office space for other commercial considerations.

NICs relief is also given for equipment or services (including broadband internet access necessitated by the employment) provided at the employee's home by the employer for homeworking including furniture and normal office supplies. See Leaflet 480 (2016), para 5.17 and CLASS 1A CONTRIBUTIONS: BENEFITS IN KIND 16.

Home to work travel

[38.5] The tax case *Kirkwood (Inspector of Taxes) v Evans* EWHC 30 (Ch), [2002] 1 WLR 1794, [2002] STC 231 concerned 'working from home' contracts. The taxpayer lived in King's Lynn but worked on detached duty in Southampton. During this period the work he was engaged on was moved to the Leeds office and the taxpayer moved with the work but kept his home in King's Lynn. He travelled to Leeds on a weekly basis, staying in Leeds two or three nights of the week. For the first five years he received an allowance towards his travelling and subsistence costs and then took advantage of a home-working scheme. He then travelled to Leeds once a week to deliver and collect work and was provided with the necessary equipment eg a computer to do his job from home. He claimed relief in respect of the trips to and from Leeds and for the use of part of his home as an office. The High Court decided that the expenses claimed by the taxpayer were not deductible: even though his usual place of work was in King's Lynn, and he travelled to and from another place of work each Friday, the main place of work was nevertheless his home, and at the time home-to-work travel was not deductible. Even under the current rules, he would not have been travelling from home to a temporary workplace, as Leeds was a permanent workplace every Friday, so even now no deduction would be available. Whilst this was a case involving *ICTA 1988, s 198* (now *ITEPA 2003, ss 336-338)* it does have implications from the NICs point of view in that expenses paid to individuals such as the taxpayer in this case will attract tax and NICs. This creates a heavy burden on the taxpayer. Patten J stated in his judgment:

> Firstly . . . the home-working scheme was optional. Mr Evans was permitted to work from home but he was not required to do so. He took up the option because for perfectly understandable reasons it was more convenient for him to remain at home for most of the week rather than to travel to Leeds. Working at home was not therefore a necessary incident of his employment. Secondly, however, even if one ignores the optional nature of the scheme it is not a requirement of the home working agreement that the taxpayer should maintain a separate room to work in. In these circumstances the costs of heating and lighting the workspace in his home were not wholly, exclusively and necessarily incurred in the performance of his duties. They were expenses which seem to me to be equally attributable to the maintenance of his home as such.

See also *Refson v HMRC* Ch D [2009] STC 64 which confirms HMRC's treatment of home to office travel expenses even where there is the suggestion of legitimate expectation regarding the non-taxability of those expenses.

It appears therefore that where such schemes are optional, the first point, they are likely to fail. The fact that a room is not exclusively set aside for the work may, irrespective of the first point, preclude an allowance for the proportionate utility expenses, although it would seem entirely reasonable for the worker to argue that he incurred extra utility costs when he was at home working, compared to when he was in his employer's office working, and reimbursement should therefore not constitute earnings for NIC purposes to the extent that the reimbursement merely covered those extra costs. As has been mentioned above in relation to earlier cases (38.2) the control over Mr Evans was such that he was considered an employee even though working from home but had the contract of service been such that it was a condition of his work to be located at King's Lynn and have an exclusively office-orientated workplace there then the matter might have been viewed differently.

[38.6] *ITEPA 2003, s 339A*, introduced with effect from 6 April 2016, deems each engagement for an 'intermediary' worker (ie, in broad terms, agency, umbrella and PSC employees) to constitute a separate employment. The effect is to deny an income tax exemption for reimbursed home-to-work travel ('travel for necessary attendance' within *ss 338–339*) for intermediary workers travelling to and from what would ordinarily be classed as a temporary workplace. Although the new rules are translated into the *Contributions Regulations 2001*, they explicitly do not affect intermediary workers who provide their services wholly in the client's home, since these are 'excluded services'. [*ITEPA 2003, s 339A(1)(a), (11); Contributions Regulations 2001, Sch 3 Pt 8 paras 3ZB(1)(a), (8)*, as introduced by *Social Security (Contributions) (Amendment) (No 2) Regulations 2016, SI 2016/352, Reg 5*.] This exclusion benefits, eg, district nurses, domestic cleaners, meter readers, etc, supplied through an agency.

Workers in the home of others

[38.7] Home care workers provided with board and lodging by the client family ('live-in carers') might have been adversely affected by the *Finance Act 2015 (FA 2015)* abolition from 6 April 2016 of the £8,500 limit for charging taxable benefits based on cost to the employer. While their actual accommodation would ordinarily have been excluded from earnings as it is job-related, the associated benefits (eg, food, heating, etc that were not chargeable on P9D employees) might have fallen into charge for the first time. *FA 2015, s 14* therefore introduced a specific exemption from the residual liability to charge on taxable benefits as *ITEPA 2003, s 306A*. This automatically excluded the potentially chargeable benefits from the scope of Class 1A NICs, which hang on the peg of taxable benefits.

Key Points regarding homeworkers and outworkers and NICs

[38.8] Points to consider are as follows.

- Traditional homeworkers – making or packing goods, for example – and having no separate place of employment may be self-employed depending on the nature of the work and degree of control.
- Those who have an office but who choose or are required to work from home some of the time will have difficulty obtaining relief for what remains essentially 'home to work' travel.
- HMRC will not normally question the payment by the employer of up to £4 per week towards additional household costs incurred where an employee regularly works at home under agreed flexible working arrangements.
- Employers may pay more than £4 per week tax- and NIC-free if supporting evidence is retained to show that the expenses are wholly additional to those normally incurred by the employee by living in the house. A dispensation may no longer be granted by HMRC for higher amounts to be paid without supporting

evidence, since the dispensation regime was abolished on 5 April 2016, but additional costs that can be proven may be exempted instead.

39
Husband and Wife, and Civil Partners

Cross-references. See CATEGORISATION 14; CLASS 1 CONTRIBUTIONS 15; CLASS 2 CONTRIBUTIONS 18; CLASS 4 CONTRIBUTIONS 20; PARTNERS 52.

Other Sources. Tolley's Income Tax 2016–17; Tolley's Tax Planning 2016–17; CWG2 (2018 to 2019); CA44 (2018).

Introduction to husband and wife, and civil partners and NICs

[39.1] A person who is employed by his or her spouse or civil partner for the purpose of the spouse's or civil partner's employment (which in this context means either employment under a contract of service or self-employment – see further below) is to be treated as falling within the category of employed earner despite the probable absence of a contract of service. [*SSCBA 1992, s 2(2)(a)(b); Categorisation Regs, Reg 2(2), Sch 1 Part I para 3; Social Security (Categorisation of Earners)(Amendment) Regulations 2005, SI 2005/3133, Reg 3(2)*].

Employment of a person by his or her spouse or civil partner otherwise than for the purpose of the spouse's or civil partner's employment is to be entirely disregarded whether under a contract of service or not. [*SSCBA 1992, s 2(2)(a); Categorisation Regs, Reg 2(4), Sch 1 Part III para 8; Social Security (Categorisation of Earners)(Amendment) Regulations 2005, SI 2005/3133, Reg 3(3)*].

Where a person is to be treated as an employed earner under these regulations, that person's spouse or civil partner will fall to be treated as the *secondary contributor*. [*SSCBA 1992, s 7(2); Categorisation Regs, Reg 5(1), Sch 3 para 3; Social Security (Categorisation of Earners)(Amendment) Regulations 2005, SI 2005/3133, Reg 4*]. He will be responsible for paying and accounting for contributions in the normal way (see CLASS 1 CONTRIBUTIONS 15, COLLECTION 21).

While social security legislation dealing with certain means-tested benefits explicitly treats couples living together as man and wife, the contributions legislation uses the term 'spouse' in the ordinary legal sense, which excludes the concept of common law spouse.

Employed by spouse or civil partner

[39.2] The expression 'employment of the spouse or civil partner' in the *Categorisation Regs* is not confined to spouse's or civil partner's self-employment (though that is the usual case where this regulation applies) but extends to spouse's or civil partner's employed earner's employment also.

Example

On 22 October 2018, Alf, a sales representative, is disqualified from driving and, in order not to lose his job, employs Bet, his wife, as his chauffeuse. He pays B £180 a week. B will suffer a primary Class 1 contribution of £2.16 (ie £162 @ Nil% + £18 @ 12%) and A will have to pay a secondary Class 1 contribution of £2.48 (ie £157 @ Nil% + £18 @ 13.8%).

NB. It *may* be that both A and B will escape contribution liability entirely if B is unremunerated and A's employer, discovering that B is acting as his unpaid chauffeuse, pays B, on his own volition and merely in token recognition of the help she is giving A, £180 a week. A wife who helped her public school housemaster husband in his work was sent monthly cheques by the school bursar in monetary recognition of her contribution to the school and the Secretary of State for Social Security formally decided that she was neither gainfully employed by her husband nor under a contract of service with the school nor ordinarily self-employed for the purposes of gain (*M47 (1956)*). The income tax position would, of course, be based on tax legislation and the conclusion would probably be different.

It has been generally accepted by both HM Revenue and Customs and, in the past, the then DSS (now DWP) that a self-employed earner's spouse has an almost inevitable involvement in the business (eg telephone answering, book-keeping, making appointments). This being so, remuneration at a modest level will usually be justifiable provided it is physically paid. (*Copeman v William Flood & Sons Ltd* (1940) 24 TC 53; *Abbot v IRC* (1996) STC SCD 41 Sp C 58). It will avoid complications with tax and National Insurance if such remuneration is below the level at which either would be levied. For 2018–19, this is the amount of the Earnings Threshold ie £162 per week for both employee and for employer, although FPS returns will still be required if earnings are £116 per week or more so that contributions can be credited. It should not be overlooked that payment below the LEL ie £116 for 2018–19, which also does not attract a contribution liability, does prevent the accumulation of a contribution record which in turn affects future benefit entitlement of the spouse (see EARNINGS FACTORS 28).

In contrast, where a husband and wife in fact run a business jointly (eg a public house), it may be that the wife is in partnership with her husband (rather than being employed by him) and is entitled to a half share in the profits whether she has ever claimed a share or not. (*Nixon v Nixon* [1969] 1 WLR 1676, *Re*

Cummins [1972] Ch 62, R(P)1/76). In that event both the husband and the wife should be self-employed earners and a Class 2 and Class 4 liability may accordingly arise for each of them unless NIC&EO argues that one spouse spends so little time working in the business (eg less than an hour or two per week) that he or she is to be treated as being other than ordinarily self-employed and accordingly has no Class 2 liability, however much is received as a share of the profits. It should be noted that such a decision would apparently contradict the advice given previously to Adjudication Officers, which was that 'the owner of a business, representing . . . that the profits from the business are income, should be regarded as gainfully employed continuously in the business *even if taking little or no direct part in the running of it*.' (Author's italics). HMRC issued a press release at the end of March 2013 indicating that sleeping partners and other inactive partners are engaged in employment and should be subject to Class 2 and 4 NIC liabilities. Such liabilities will not be enforced for periods before the 2014–15 tax year and seem unlikely to be due at all in the case of sleeping partners in limited partnerships and LLPs that are demonstrably no more than investment vehicles rather than 'businesses'. From 6 April 2015, following the *National Insurance Contributions Act 2015* reform of Class 2, such partners are classed as self-employed earners and therefore eligible to pay Class 2 contributions, but only have a liability to pay if their earnings are classed as income from a trade or profession that is taxable under *Income Tax (Trading and Other Income) Act 2005 (ITTOIA 2005), Pt 2, Ch 2*. See CLASS 2 CONTRIBUTIONS: SELF-EMPLOYED EARNERS 18 for more detail.

Since a 'common law spouse' is not a spouse in contribution law, the employment of such a person as a housekeeper by the other partner in the relationship would not be disregarded under *Categorisation Regulations, Reg 5(1), Sch 3, para 3*. A wage of at least £116 per week therefore creates a contribution record on which claims to benefit may be based. Creating such an employment relationship brings with it, of course, numerous other complications in tax and employment law terms, and is not an arrangement to be adopted lightly.

National Minimum Wage implications

[39.3] With the introduction of the National Minimum Wage (NMW), now set at £7.38 per hour from 1 April 2018 for adults aged 21 to 24, and the National Living Wage (NLW) set at £7.83 per hour from 1 April 2018 for adults aged 25 and over, as per www.gov.uk/national-minimum-wage-rates, the employer spouse or civil partner should ensure that not only does the calculation come below the Earnings Threshold but also it should not come below the NMW/NLW for the hours actually worked, although this will not necessarily be the case where husband and wife or civil partner are director/company secretary of a small company and are paid a wage below the NMW without an employment contract. This is because there are certain exclusions from the *National Minimum Wage Act 1998* but detailed consideration of the NMW provisions is outside the scope of this work. See www.gov.uk/national-minimum-wage/who-gets-the-minimum-wage, Inland Revenue Employer's Bulletin Issue 9, September/October 2001 and Inland Revenue Tax Bulletin Issue 50, December 2000.

Arctic Systems case

[39.4] In the Inland Revenue Tax Bulletin, February 2004 comment was made in respect of the employment of spouses in the business in connection with the settlement anti-avoidance provisions of *ICTA 1988, Part XV* (now replaced by *ITTOIA 2005*) as follows:

> There has been some misunderstanding about how the legislation applies where spouses are involved. We have not suggested that a "non-fee-earning" spouse makes no contribution to a business. The question, in the context of the settlements legislation, is "What contribution does the spouse make and how commercial is the reward for it?" The settlements legislation applies not only where there is a benefit to the settlor's spouse but also where the settlor retains an interest in the settlement *whoever the beneficiary may be.* In a service company it is usually the person with the specialist knowledge who retains the interest because s/he controls the source of income . . .
>
> . . . if one spouse undertakes an average of eight hours secretarial work a week for a company, and the going rate for a secretary in that area is £6 per hour (£2,496 per year), then we would consider it uncommercial if the spouse was in fact receiving £5,000 a year from the company.
>
> Deciding what is and what is not a commercial salary is not an exact science. It is impossible to give definitive guidance as each case depends on the facts. When in doubt it is useful to consider whether an individual employed at arm's length would have accepted the same salary if their friend/relative was not also benefiting from the arrangement.

It is clear therefore that HM Revenue and Customs will look closely at salary payments made to spouses with regard to the settlements legislation and indeed it did so in the *Arctic Systems* case, more correctly known as *Jones v Garnett (Inspector of Taxes)* [2007] UKHL 35, [2007] 4 All ER 857, [2007] 1 WLR 2030.

However, the hypothecation of one spouse's income to the other under the settlements legislation in *ITTOIA 2005* is of no relevance to National Insurance contributions.

Even if HM Revenue and Customs determined on the facts of a case that there has been a bounteous settlement on a spouse, the effect of such a decision would, if the recipient spouse did no work, create additional income tax. However, the NIC position should not be affected as the tax charge under what is now *ITTOIA 2005, ss 622, 624, 625, 626, 627, Sch 2 para 132(1)(3)* is outside of *ITTOIA 2005, Part 2, Chapter 2*, which is the basis of any Class 4 NIC liability. Given the House of Lords judgment in *Jones v Garnett* there is unlikely to be any HM Revenue and Customs challenge at present, though the prospect of so-called 'income shifting' legislation at some future unspecified time might change the position, both generally and possibly in introducing a Class 4 charge on 'shifted' partnership income.

Joint employment

[39.5] Where spouses and civil partners are jointly employed in employed earner's employment (eg as wardens of a hostel or managers of a hotel) and earnings in respect of that employment are paid to them jointly, the amount of the earnings of each is, for Class 1 contribution purposes, to be calculated on the same basis as that on which it is calculated for tax purposes. (See CWG2 (2018 to 2019), para 1.16; CA44 (2018), para 67.) In the absence of such a calculation, it will be calculated upon such basis as HM Revenue and Customs may approve. [*Social Security (Contributions) Regulations 2001, SI 2001/1004, Reg 20; Social Security (Contributions) (Amendment No 6) Regulations 2005, SI 2005/3130, Reg 3*]. In ascertaining the amount of earnings for benefit claim purposes, the Social Security Commissioners divided such sums according to the proportion of the work performed by each spouse.

A wife who worked with her husband (and children) as a cherry picker on a farm was held to be an employed earner in joint employment with her husband, even though the husband alone was paid for their combined pickings. (*M8 (1950)*).

Both spouses will be treated as gainfully employed where they are appointed jointly to an employment or, where only one has been appointed, there is an express or implied term of the contract of service that the other should assist in the duties. In the absence of any such term, the spouse's services are deemed voluntary and gratuitous. He or she is then deemed not to be gainfully employed.

The *Civil Partnership Act 2004* came into effect on 5 December 2005. Extension of the above provisions of the *Categorisation Regs* to registered same-sex civil partners was included in *Social Security (Categorisation of Earners) (Amendment) Regulations 2005, SI 2005/3133*. The position has not been affected by the *Marriage (Same Sex Couples) Act 2013*, since the only changes needed to place married same-sex couples on an equal footing with civil partners were minor changes of wording (see the *Marriage (Same Sex Couples) Act 2013 (Consequential and Contrary Provisions and Scotland) Order 2014, SI 2014/560*). The social security rules apply after 13 March 2014 to same-sex married couples as they do to civil partners.

Self-employed wife

[39.6] For Class 4 contribution purposes, a wife is to be regarded as a *femme sole* for the purpose of *calculating* her Class 4 contribution liability and so, for example, any losses which her husband has incurred in self-employment cannot be set off against her profits. Once calculation of the Class 4 liability has taken place, that liability is also, under the independent taxation rules, to be *assessed on and recovered from* her.

Partnership

[39.7] The principles stated above apply equally where a husband and wife carry on business together in partnership. Each is liable (if the share of trading profits exceed the small profits threshold) to pay Class 2 contributions unless specifically excepted from such liability (see CLASS 2 CONTRIBUTIONS 18) or unless, in the case of the wife, a reduced rate election is in force (see REDUCED LIABILITY ELECTIONS 54). One matter to remember in spouse partnerships is that it must be a genuine partnership with each spouse's share of profit/losses being appropriate to his or her contribution to the business. If it was not found to be genuine then the partnership arrangement might be treated as a settlement by one spouse on the other, and the profits involved would be treated as belonging to the 'settlor' spouse – see **39.4** above. (Also see INTERMEDIARIES **40**). [*ITTOIA 2005, ss 622, 624, 625, 626, 627, Sch 2 para 132(1)(3*]. See Tax Bulletin Issue 64, April 2003, p1011. The settlement anti-avoidance provisions for income tax are, from 5 December 2005, also extended to same-sex couples registered under the *Civil Partnership Act 2004*.

In the former Inland Revenue's Tax Bulletin, February 2004 comment was made in respect of partnerships between husband and wife in connection with the settlement anti-avoidance provisions of *ICTA 1988, Part XV* (now replaced by *ITTOIA 2005*) as follows:

> We have also had feedback on application of the legislation to partnerships where some argue that the unlimited liability of the partners means that the settlement legislation cannot apply. We do not accept that. It is important, in relation to partnerships, to look at the whole arrangement to see whether someone is getting a disproportionate return on their contribution because they are related to, or friends with, the settlor. If they are then the legislation applies even if a partnership is being used.

HM Revenue and Customs does, however, state that where the partnership involves some risk or an outright gift by or to the other partner then it is unlikely that the settlement legislation will apply. However, contrast this with the example below:

Example

An Accountant A commences an accountancy business as a sole trader. The business is successful and a few years later, when profits are £80,000 per annum, he introduces his wife Mrs A as a partner and a deed is created sharing profits equally. Mrs A contributes no capital and does not carry out any work in the partnership but receives £40,000 as her share of the profits.

In this case HM Revenue and Customs might seek to apply the settlements legislation and assess the £40,000 on the husband A. The lack of any gift of assets/capital by Mr A to Mrs A means that the exclusion in *ITTOIA 2005, s 626(1)–(4)* cannot apply and the settlement provision does apply for tax purposes. However, as the tax liability falls outside *Chapter* 2 of *Part* 2 of *ITTOIA 2005* the Class 4 liability of either spouse cannot be affected in any event. [*SSCBA 1992, s 15(1)(b)*].

Key Points regarding husband and wife, and civil partners and NICs

[39.8] Points to consider are as follows.

- Spouses and civil partners engaged by their spouse or civil partner for the purposes of their business or employment will always be categorised as employed earners, but it is not possible to manufacture a liability to Class 1 or an entitlement to deemed contributions by employing a legally married spouse or civil partner for purely domestic purposes.

- An outright gift from one spouse or civil partner to the other of ordinary shares with standard rights as to income, capital and ownership benefits should escape the income tax settlement provisions, unless new legislation is brought into effect, and should have no effect on the National Insurance position.
- The income tax settlement rules are not replicated in National Insurance law.

40

Intermediaries

Cross-references. See AGENCY WORKERS **4**; AIRMEN **6**; APPEALS AND REVIEWS **9** for means of contesting categorisation decisions; COMPANY DIRECTORS **22**; ENTERTAINERS **36**; EXAMINERS **37**; HOMEWORKERS AND OUTWORKERS **38**; HUSBAND AND WIFE, AND CIVIL PARTNERS **39**; LABOUR-ONLY CONTRACTORS **41**; PARTNERS **52**.

Other Sources. Tolley's National Insurance Contributions Brief, July 1996, pages 53–55 and August 1996, pages 57–60; Tolley's Practical NIC Newsletter, November 2004 page 83, January 2005 page 6, March 2007 page 17, May 2007 page 33, March 2008, April 2008; HM Revenue and Customs leaflets CWG2 (2018–19); CA44 (2018); 480 (2018) and 490.

Introduction to intermediaries

[40.1] It is a basic principle of NICs that liability arises only in relation to earnings, ie, remuneration or profit derived from working. Dividends are investment income, not earnings, even in companies owned by a sole-shareholder director: see **29.12**.

As businesses in the 1990s reacted to increasing employment protection obligations and costs by using more subcontractors, whose contracts could be terminated easily, the DSS and the Inland Revenue began to challenge the status of such workers, believing them to be *de facto* employees rather than self-employed subcontractors. As more and more businesses were challenged over their subcontractors' status, contractors began insisting that their subcontractors worked through limited companies in order to protect the contractors from potential PAYE and Class 1 NIC liabilities. The trend was accelerated when the Chancellor of the Exchequer, Gordon Brown, in 1999 both abolished ACT and introduced a 10% corporation tax rate for profits up to £10,000, and basic rate taxpayers receiving dividends from such small companies had no further tax to pay. The subcontractors themselves were therefore actively encouraged by the government to incorporate their one-man businesses into 'personal service companies' (PSCs) and pay themselves principally in dividends. The logical consequence of large numbers of traders incorporating their businesses to avoid PAYE and NIC was a large fall in receipts by the Exchequer. The law of unintended consequences meant that another change was required.

Under proposals first announced by the Chancellor in the March 1999 Budget, contained in a Press Release numbered 'IR35', enacted as *Finance Act 2000 (FA 2000), Sch 12* and *Social Security Contributions (Intermediaries) Regulations 2000 (SI 2000/727)* and still in force, people who would otherwise be employees or office holders of their clients are no longer able to avoid paying Class 1 National Insurance contributions by working through personal service companies and other intermediaries and paying themselves by way of dividend instead of earnings. These rules have applied since 6 April 2000. See also *Social Security Contributions and Benefits Act 1992 (SSCBA 1992), s 4A* and Tax Bulletin, Issue 51, February 2001, page 819.

Almost parallel provisions were introduced for income tax and NIC, with one major difference. The provisions of *Income Tax (Earnings and Pensions) Act 2003 (ITEPA 2003), Part 2, Chapter 8* (the consolidation of *FA 2000, Sch 12*) looked for so called 'disguised employment' but did not affect the 'disguised' holding of an office such as a directorship. In other words, the worker was brought within the IR35 rules if, with the corporate (or partnership) wrapper stripped away, he would be an employee working under a contract of employment. The deeming provision for tax purposes was not extended to the holding of a disguised office until 6 April 2013, following pressure in the media over a number of high profile public sector executives working through PSCs. In contrast, for NIC purposes, disguised office holders were in the same boat as disguised employees from the inception of the regime: the *Social Security Contributions (Intermediaries) Regulations 2000, Reg 6* merely looked for arrangements involving an intermediary for an individual worker to personally perform services in circumstances where, had the arrangements taken the form of the contract between the worker and the client, the worker would have been regarded under NIC law as an employed earner, a term which includes holding an office with earnings.

After the introduction of the IR35 rules described above a number of 'providers' marketed outsourced administration via managed service and 'composite' companies enabling a wide variety of workers to operate through the medium of a limited company where they would not ordinarily have done so. A managed service company (MSC) would typically be a one-man company for which a provider undertook all the administration (statutory filings, payroll, tax returns, billing, cash handling) in exchange for a weekly or monthly fee, while the 'one-man' simply found and delivered the work. A composite company would be broadly similar in concept but would typically involve a provider selling an 'alphabet share' (A share, B share, C share, etc) in a service company that had a number of shareholders, each holding a different class of share so that differential dividends might be paid to reflect their individual billings. It was important to ensure that the composite company profits did not exceed £300,000 pa so that corporation tax was payable only at the small companies rate, so as to maximise the profits available for distribution.

Whilst a few of these workers might arguably have been self-employed but for the existence of the corporate structure, the overwhelming majority would have been employees or treated as employees under the agency worker rules. The marketed schemes seemed to rely for their effect on HMRC's lack of available resources to police 'IR35', coupled with the ability to wind up companies leaving unpaid tax/NIC debts under the IR35 rules, and then to form a completely different entity to carry on the same activities. The Government, having lost patience, announced in the December 2006 Pre-Budget Report that such companies would be brought into a new MSC scheme, similar to IR35 – yet with subtle differences – from 6 April 2007 for PAYE and 6 August 2007 for National Insurance. In addition, provisions were introduced to enable debts unpaid by the 'scheme provider' to be transferred and then enforced against the directors, scheme provider and a wide range of third parties.

As IR35 and the MSC regime failed to close down all the intermediary employers who were regarded by HMRC as exploiting the tax and NIC rules, and some continued to operate in ways that reduced liabilities, the Government announced in the Autumn Statement 2013 that it would be taking action from 6 April 2014 against certain onshore and offshore intermediaries. The new rules were introduced by *FA 2014* and the *Social Security (Categorisation of Earners) (Amendment) Regulations 2014, SI 2014/635*. The onshore intermediaries targeted were those supplying self-employed contractors outside the scope of the agency rules described more fully in AGENCY WORKERS 4, who had succeeded in staying outside the scope of Class 1 by removing any obligation on the worker to provide personal service. The offshore intermediaries targeted were of two basic kinds. The first was the offshore umbrella employer supplying staff to onshore businesses where no-one was operating the long-standing host employer rules that should have meant that the onshore end-user was obliged to account for PAYE and NICs if the actual employer did not do so. The second was in the oil and gas sector, where most businesses working on the UK Continental Shelf were using workers engaged by non-UK employers that were, quite legitimately, outside the scope of secondary Class 1 liability. The changes were put out to consultation after the Autumn Statement and were finalised in the *Finance Act 2014* and *Social Security (Contributions) (Amendment No 2) Regulations 2014, SI 2014/572*.

See AGENCY WORKERS **4** and OIL-RIG WORKERS **50** for a full exposition of the 2014 rule changes for these types of intermediary arrangement. The remainder of this chapter focuses on the IR35 and MSC rules as laid down by *ITEPA 2003, ss 48–61J* and the parallel *Social Security (Contributions) (Intermediaries) Regulations 2000, SI 2000/727.*

Intermediaries and IR35

[40.2] The 'IR35' procedure ultimately enacted after consultation on the March 1999 announcement was a revised approach which responded to concerns expressed during consultation that the rules as at first announced were too wide in scope, and that they would make it impossible for people to work through intermediaries even if they were prepared to accept full liability to tax and NICs.

In a highly unusual (on its facts) employment tribunal case that proceeded to the Court of Appeal, it was held that in appropriate circumstances there may be an implied contract of employment between an agency worker and the client/end-user – even if the contract with the agency states that the worker is employed or engaged by the agency (*Cable & Wireless plc v Muscat* [2006] EWCA Civ 220, [2006] ICR 975, [2006] IRLB 14). This would render the IR35 legislation redundant in most cases, but HMRC does not accept that that is the effect of the legal decision. See Taxation 26 May 2005 and 18 May 2006. The taxpayer was not a typical IR35 worker: he had been an employee of the company and had been compulsorily transferred into a structured intermediary arrangement with a view to avoiding PAYE, NIC and other employer obligations. The court found that he had, in fact, never ceased to be an employee of the Cable & Wireless company in question, but the facts were so specific to the case that it is dangerous to generalise from the decision.

The main points of the rules as finally introduced, are:

- The rules rely on the *long-standing* tests (see **14.9–14.15** CATEGORISATION) which have always been used to determine the boundary between employment and self-employment for tax and National Insurance contributions purposes. Using these familiar tests will help understanding of the rules and ensure they are targeted on the right people. Unfortunately, in *F S Consulting v McCaul* [2002] STC SCD 138 Sp C 305 it was stated by the Special Commissioner that the *Social Security (Categorisation of Earners) Regulations 1978* and the *Social Security Contributions (Intermediaries) Regulations 2000* were not mutually exclusive and either could be applicable, or in fact both. [*Categorisation Regs 1978, SI 1978/1689 Reg 2(4), Sch 1 Part III para 9*].
- The responsibility for ensuring that the new rules are followed is that of the *intermediaries* themselves, not the clients. As a result of this approach, there is no need for a certification scheme to allow clients to identify intermediaries who could continue to receive gross payments. Note that the 2014 oil and gas worker changes, in contrast, did introduce a certification scheme to give clients some comfort that they

would not be liable for unpaid contributions in respect of workers supplied through an intermediary. HMRC seems to have a learned a lesson from the abject failure of IR35 to raise significant amounts of money.

- The *intermediaries* are responsible for applying PAYE and National Insurance contributions to all earnings from relevant engagements, after a limited allowance for expenses and pension contributions. See Example in **40.15**. Only where the intermediaries are offshore should the liability arise on a UK agency in the supply chain or the end user.

An intermediary may be a company or a partnership.

The yield (tax and NICs combined) from, and number of, IR35 investigations (now known as compliance interventions) was disclosed in February 2015 in response to a Freedom of Information Act request by Pamela Nash MP as follows:

Tax Year	No of IR35 enquiries	*Yield*
2000–2001	16	nil
2001–2002	261	nil
2002–2003	1,016	£946,275
2003–2004	1,166	£1.9m
2004–2005	771	£1.4m
2005–2006	656	£2.3m
2006–2007	158	£1.9m
2007–2008	104	£1.7m
2008–2009	25	£1.4m
2009–2010	12	£155,502
2010–2011	23	£220,000
2011–2012	59	£1.2m
2012–2013	256	£1.1m
2013–2014	192	£430,000

When providing this information (Hansard Written Question 220788, 2 February 2015), David Gauke MP (then Financial Secretary to HM Treasury) stated as a fact that the cost to the Exchequer of not having IR35 in place 'would be around £520m a year', although the methodology behind this number was not disclosed and must be questionable in view of past ministerial replies.

Kitty Ussher MP in 2009 refused to disclose the numbers of investigations or the increase in yield from them (Hansard 15 June 2009, Column 53W–54W) on the grounds that: 'Disclosure of HM Revenue and Customs' compliance data relating to the legislation would result in a risk of non-compliance with the legislation.'

'IT Now', the monthly journal of the British Computer Society, reported in July 2009 Government yield of £9.2m under the IR35 legislation from April 2002 to March 2008, compared to the £220m initially expected.

John Healey MP, one of Mr Gauke's predecessors in the Treasury role, stated to the House of Commons (HC Deb, 21 June 2005, Column 937W) that 'It is . . . not possible to isolate the increase in yield to the Exchequer arising from this legislation alone.' In 2004, Dawn Primarolo, then Paymaster General with responsibility for the Inland Revenue, was asked in Parliament by Mark Prisk MP how many investigations under the IR35 regulations had been started, resulted in additional yield and been concluded with no investigation yield. In a written answer (Hansard, 6 January 2004, Column 224W) she replied that IR35 challenges were part of the overall Employer Compliance effort of the Inland Revenue and it was not possible with any accuracy to isolate data relating solely to this legislation.

The original estimates of the yield from the introduction of the personal service company legislation were in Chapter A of the Budget 2000 Red Book, which has been removed from the internet archive.

In July 2015, HMRC launched its next 'Intermediaries Legislation (IR35)' discussion document on potential changes to the IR35 regime that would, it claimed, make the system more effective and easier to police, as well as 'levelling the playing field between direct employees and those who work in a similar manner to direct employees but through their own limited companies'.

In short, HMRC proposed to transfer the obligation to assess whether a PSC worker was in disguised employment to the engager, on the basis that the engager would have direct knowledge of how the worker was acting and whether he or she might legitimately be treated as self-employed in the absence of the PSC. The plan had so many obvious flaws and would have imposed so many unreasonable burdens on business that its scope was reduced in the next iteration of the consultation so as to encompass only contracts between PSCs and 'public sector' bodies (as defined in the *Freedom of Information Act 2000*) and to take account of the existence of thousands of employment agencies involved in the arrangements between those parties.

The revised outline plan was set out in a consultation document entitled 'Off-payroll working in the public sector: reform of the intermediaries legislation' that was issued on 26 May 2016. From April 2017, where workers are engaged through their own limited company (PSC), responsibility to apply the intermediaries rules will fall to the public sector body, agency or other third party paying the worker's company. That organisation will be liable to pay any associated income tax and NICs. Whoever pays the PSC will be required to operate PAYE and NIC deductions based on 95% of the amount paid. The base figure is to exclude materials costs, but it seems unlikely that an IR35 contractor would be providing materials.

The document clearly represented an incomplete understanding of how PSCs work and presented a number of unworkable proposals, all without detail. It remains to be seen when that detail might be worked out, and how, if at all, public sector bodies and the agencies supplying them might design, test and implement systems changes by April 2017 to meet the proposed requirements.

Software houses in particular are unlikely to be able to write the required systems changes in time since, at the time of writing, it is already too late and no detailed specification of the requirements is available. It is also open to question whether HMRC's systems will be able to cope with the fact that each PSC worker will have to have a payroll record under the employer reference for his or her own PSC in the RTI system, while the same worker will be required to have a payroll record in respect of the same work under the employer reference for the public sector body or the agency supplying the worker to that body. The consultation document assumes (arguably, somewhat naively) that the PAYE and NIC deducted by the public sector body or the agency supplying the worker, based on 95% of the amount paid, will be matched against any income drawn by the worker from the PSC, which might be a completely different sum, in a different tax year or accounting period.

The proposal for a start date of April 2017 follows several other recent faux pas by HMRC where policy implementation has taken no account of the practicalities. For example, when the new agency rules were introduced in April 2014, the intended imposition of extra reporting requirements had to be deferred until April 2015 because neither HMRC nor external systems could be readied for April 2014. Similarly, the introduction of a statutory option to payroll benefits in kind from 6 April 2016, on the basis of regulations not finally laid before Parliament until 23 November 2015, resulted in elections into the new regime by only about one-third of those employers already payrolling benefits under an informal agreement with HMRC. April 2018 seems like a more realistic commencement date for the IR35 changes outlined in the latest version of the consultation document, as it will allow more time for the problems to be identified and for the policy and all of the relevant systems to be changed to cope.

Intermediaries and the public sector

[40.3] Nevertheless, HMRC pressed ahead and the new 'Workers' services provided to public sector [sic] through intermediaries' legislation (often referred to as 'off-payroll working in the public sector') has been enacted from 6 April 2017 via *Finance Act 2016, s 6, Sch 1*. The equivalent amendments to Social Security legislation were made by *Social Security (Miscellaneous Amendments No 2) Regulations 2017, SI 2017/373, Reg 2(13)* inserting *Part 2, Regs 13–23 into Social Security Contributions (Intermediaries) Regulations 2000, SI 2000/727*.

Public sector bodies are those listed in the Freedom of Information Act 2000 and the Freedom of Information (Scotland) Act 2002. But in an example of the law of unintended consequences, last minute amendments had to be made to FA 2016 and the Social Security legislation to exclude some private sector retail businesses including high street pharmacies and opticians, which were incorrectly brought into scope because they provide services on behalf of the National Health Service (NHS). [*The Social Security (Miscellaneous Amendments No 3) Regulations 2017, SI 2017/613.*]

In outline, the public sector end-user is seen as the only person or entity that is able to determine whether the contract falls within IR35, because it knows whether the work is subject to close supervision, direction and control in the same way as for an employee. If the end-user contracts directly with a PSC, and it determines that the contract is a IR35 contract, it will be obliged to operate

PAYE and NIC on 100% of the invoice value excluding materials. It was originally proposed that the PAYE charge should be based on just 95%, to match the 5% expense allowance in the IR35 rules, but this was changed as a response to feedback during the consultation, allegedly to recognise that workers will no longer have to bear the administrative burden of deciding whether the IR35 rules apply. Given that HMRC has previously claimed that there is 90% non-compliance with the IR35 rules, the expected yield from this change that is listed in Table 2.1 of the Statement, at just £115 million over five years, seems somewhat low.

If the PSC supplies its worker through an agency, the agency that pays the PSC will have the obligation to account for the PAYE and NIC if the public sector client informs it that the contract is within IR35.

Whether it is the client or the agency that is liable to account for deductions, it must do so under RTI. Provisions have been made to prevent double taxation (what is now *ITEPA 2003, Part 2, Ch 10, s 61W*), and a similar prevention of a double National Insurance liability arising has been included in the equivalent Social Security regulations. [*Social Security Contributions (Intermediaries) Regulations 2000, SI 2000/727, Part 2, Reg 23* inserted by *Social Security (Miscellaneous Amendments No 2) Regulations 2017, SI 2017/373, Reg 2(13)*.] The RTI system seems unlikely to be able to cope with the same income being paid out twice on separate employer references. To avoid the double taxation and NICs liabilities, the payment by the PSC of the net 'deemed direct earnings' will need to be included in the PSC's FPS as a payment not subject to tax and NI. Whether the increase in such payments will raise questions within HMRC remains to be seen. Given that this will require changes in HMRC systems, the new rules taking effect in April 2017 may have to be introduced with very light touch regulatory action. HMRC has not yet explained how double taxation will be avoided and it seems little thought may have been given to this beyond the need to make some provision along these lines. If the client or agency deducts PAYE and accounts for it under RTI, it will pay employer National Insurance contributions, and when the PSC itself pays out the net money as wages, it will also be liable to account for PAYE and NIC, unless provision is made for the income to be streamed and excluded from liability under both regimes. The RTI system seems unlikely to be able to cope with the same income being paid out twice on separate employer references.

No equivalent action is proposed, yet, for private sector contracts. Given the new danger for public sector bodies that they may be held liable for any missed deductions if their assessment of the contracts is incorrect, it may be presumed that most will take a safety first approach to the new regime and require most contractors to go onto their, or their agents', payroll unless they can credibly certify that their business and the contract in question are outside IR35. A consultation, expected to take place in 2018, on extending the off-payroll working in the public sector rules to the private sector was announced at Autumn Budget 2017.

The worker is treated as having earnings from employment if one of the following conditions is met [*Social Security Contributions (Intermediaries) Regulations 2000, SI 2000/727, Part 2, Reg 14(9)–(11)* inserted by *Social Security (Miscellaneous Amendments No 2) Regulations 2017, SI 2017/373, Reg 2(13)*].

Condition A (Reg 14(9)):

(a) the intermediary is a company; and
(b) the conditions in regulation 15 are met in relation to the intermediary

Condition B (Reg 14(10)):

(a) the intermediary is a partnership;
(b) the worker is a member of the partnership;
(c) the provision of the services is by the worker as a member of the partnership; and
(d) the condition in regulation 16 is met in relation to the intermediary.

Condition C (Reg 14(11)):

(a) the intermediary is an individual.

The further conditions in Regulation 15 in respect of Condition A are as follows:

'(1) The conditions mentioned in regulation 14(9)(b) are that—
 (a) the intermediary is not an associated company of the client that falls within subparagraph (2), and
 (b) the worker has a material interest in the intermediary.
(2) An associated company of the client falls within this paragraph if it is such a company by reason of the intermediary and the client being under the control—
 (a) of the worker, or
 (b) of the worker and other persons.
(3) The worker is treated as having a material interest in the intermediary if—
 (a) the worker, alone or with one or more associates of the worker, or
 (b) an associate of the worker, with or without other associates of the worker, has a material interest in the intermediary.
(4) For this purpose "material interest" has the meaning given by section 51(4) and (5) of ITEPA 2003.
(5) In this regulation "associated company" has the meaning given by section 449 of CTA 2010.'

The condition in Regulation 16 in respect of Condition B is:

'(1) The condition mentioned in regulation 14(10)(d) is—
 (a) that the worker, alone or with one or more relatives, is entitled to 60 per cent or more of the profits of the partnership, or
 (b) that most of the profits of the partnership derive from the provision of services under engagements to which one or other of this Part and Part 1 applies—
  (i) to a single client, or
  (ii) to a single client together with associates of that client, or
 (c) that under the profit sharing arrangements the income of any of the partners is based on the amount of income generated by that partner by the provision of services under engagements to which one or other of this Part and Part 1 applies.
(2) In sub-paragraph (1)(a) "relative" means spouse or civil partner, parent or child or remoter relation in the direct line, or brother or sister.
(3) For the purposes of this regulation section 61(4) and (5) of ITEPA 2003 apply as they apply for the purposes of Chapter 8 of that Act.'

The earnings from the employment, the 'deemed direct earnings' from which the income tax and NICs should be deducted, are calculated in four steps as follows.

Step 1: identify the amount or value of the chain payment made by the person who is treated as making the deemed direct earnings, and deduct from that amount so much of it (if any) as is in respect of value added tax.

Step 2: deduct, from the amount resulting from Step 1, so much of that amount as represents the direct cost to the intermediary of materials used, or to be used, in the performance of the services

Step 3: deduct, at the option of the person treated as making the deemed direct earnings, from the amount resulting from Step 2, so much of that amount as represents expenses met by the intermediary that under ITEPA 2003 would have been deductible from the taxable earnings of the employment under ITEPA 2003, s 10, in accordance with ITEPA 2003, s 327(3)–(5), if:

(a) the worker had been employed by the client; and
(b) the expenses had been met by the worker out of those earnings.

Step 4: if the amount resulting from the preceding Steps is nil or negative, there are no deemed direct earnings. Otherwise, that amount is the amount of the deemed direct earnings.

Note that there is no 5% reduction as there is under 'normal' IR35 rules.

[*Social Security Contributions (Intermediaries) Regulations 2000, SI 2000/727, Part 2, Reg 17(1)* inserted by *Social Security (Miscellaneous Amendments No 2) Regulations 2017, SI 2017/373, Reg 2(13)*].

The liability to deduct income tax and NICs from the deemed direct earnings applies to payments made on or after 6 April 2017, even though the services may have been rendered, or the contract entered into, before that date.

HMRC has provided a new interactive online tool (Employment Status Service (ESS)) to give a real-time and definitive HMRC view on whether or not the rules apply to a particular engagement. The service is available at www.tax.service.gov.uk/check-employment-status-for-tax/setup. The service is anonymous and doesn't store any information entered or the result given. The results can be printed, and it is recommended that they are printed, as a record of the status returned from the inputs made.

HMRC has stated that it will 'stand by the result given unless a compliance check finds the information provided isn't accurate'. However, results achieved through contrived arrangements designed to get a particular outcome from the service will be treated as evidence of deliberate non-compliance with its associated higher penalties.

No equivalent action is proposed, yet, for private sector contracts. Given the new danger for public sector bodies that they may be held liable for any missed deductions if their assessment of the contracts is incorrect, it may be presumed that most will take a safety first approach to the new regime and require most contractors to go onto the public sector body's, or the contractor's agent's, payroll unless they can credibly certify that their business and the contract in question are outside IR35.

[*Social Security Contributions (Intermediaries) Regulations 2000, SI 2000/727, Part 2* inserted by *Social Security (Miscellaneous Amendments No 2) Regulations 2017, SI 2017/373, Reg 2(13)*].

The legislation appears to create a different sort of employee (a second class employee?). The contractor is an employee in all but name, yet seems not to be entitled to the statutory payments and other rights accruing to employees. HMRC's technical note (www.gov.uk/government/publications/off-payroll-working-in-the-public-sector-reform-of-the-intermediaries-legislation-technical-note/off-payroll-working-in-the-public-sector-reform-of-the-intermediaries-legislation-technical-note) states that 'statutory payments and other employment rights are unaffected by the new legislation', ie these rights are available through the PSC rather than the public sector body. This includes not having to apply the employer duties in respect of workers under the pension auto-enrolment regulations. However, while this may be the intention, there does not appear to be anything in the legislation that specifically precludes the worker from claiming these statutory rights from the public sector body.

Definitions

[40.4] *Any* intermediary is potentially affected by the IR35 rules, and *will* be affected if:

- a worker is supplied by an intermediary to a customer (end-user),
- that worker* controls* the intermediary, and
- had the contract been between the worker and the customer direct, the relationship would have been such that the worker would be regarded for the purposes of *SSCBA 1992* as employed in employed earner's employment rather than self-employment.

  The exact scope of this rule has changed several times since 2000, not necessarily intentionally, and has not always had the same scope for NIC and income tax purposes.

  On 6 April 2000, when the IR35 rules were introduced, an 'employed earner' for NIC purposes was a person gainfully employed in the UK, either under a contract of service *or in an office with 'emoluments chargeable to income tax under Schedule E'*. [*SSCBA 1992, s 2(1)(a)*]. The IR35 definition therefore encompassed both employees and office holders, but only for NIC purposes. The *FA 2000, Sch 12* rules for income tax extended only to workers who would have been 'an employee' ie, under a contract of service. It did not extend to those earners in an office with Schedule E emoluments but with no contract of employment.

  On 6 April 2003, for income tax purposes, *Income Tax (Earnings and Pensions) Act 2003 (ITEPA 2003)* substituted the concept of 'general earnings' for 'Schedule E emoluments', which did not affect the tax aspects of IR35, but in a misguided attempt to harmonise income tax and NIC rules, *ITEPA 2003, Sch 6, para 171* inserted 'general earnings' into *SSCBA 1992, s 2(1)(a)*, replacing the reference to emoluments quoted above. The definition of 'general earnings' for NIC purposes, inserted into *SSCBA 1992, s 122*, was derived directly from *ITEPA 2003, s 7*, which was not congruent with the concept of earnings for

NIC purposes, since it excluded, eg, anything classed as 'specific employment income', such as share awards and option gains taxable under *ITEPA 2003, Part 7*, and pre-2006 FURBS, UURBS and post-2006 EFRBS contributions and termination payments taxable under *Part 6*. For practical purposes, only a highly unusual office holder, remunerated solely by means of shares and options, is likely to have been affected by this change.

From 6 April 2013, office holders supplying their services through a PSC became subject to the IR35 provisions for income tax when *FA 2013, s 22* added office holders to employees in *ITEPA 2003, s 49(1)(c)*, bringing the tax rules almost into line with the NIC rules.

From 14 May 2014, *NICA 2014, s 15(1)* deleted 'general' from 'general earnings' in *SSCBA 1992, s 2(1)(a)*, bringing the two sets of IR35 rules almost completely into line, as the NIC definition of earnings that was then applied does not exclude share awards and option gains.

* Subject to provisions affecting certain associated companies (as defined by *CTA 2010, ss 449-451, 1069(3)* and *ITA 2007, s 995*), the IR35 rules apply to income generated by workers who have a material interest in a company. A material interest is where the worker or an associate, either alone or with (other) associates or family members has beneficial ownership, or the ability to control – directly or indirectly – more than 5% of the ordinary share capital of the company, or possession of or entitlement to acquire rights entitling the holder to receive more than 5% of any company distributions or, if a close company, entitlement to receive more than 5% of the assets in a winding up. [*Social Security Contributions (Intermediaries) Regs 2000, Reg 5(1)–(4)*].

Engagements which fall into the above categories are termed 'relevant engagements' and all earnings from them fall within the 'IR35' scheme. Note that some intermediaries will have both 'relevant engagements' and other engagements. The latter are not affected by the IR35 intermediaries legislation (although the agency reporting provisions may apply if the PSC director finds work through third parties such as employment agencies). Similarly, the engagements of some employees of a company or a partner in a partnership will be 'relevant engagements' and those of others may not. For those very few intermediaries who cannot work outside the scope of IR35, this can cause accounting and tax complexity. The position may also be complicated by a change in the way of working or the terms of engagement, because the changes may take a relevant engagement out of the ambit of IR35, or vice versa (eg, because the engagement has clearly become permanent: see *JLJ Services Ltd v Revenue and Customs Comrs* [2011] UKFTT 766 (TC).

'Associate' in relation to an individual is as defined by *ICTA 1988, s 417 (3)* and *(4) (now Income Tax Act 2007, s 253(1)(2))* and in relation to a company is as defined by *ICTA 1988 s 839* (*now Income Tax Act 2007, ss 993, 994*). In relation to a partnership it means any associate of a member of the partnership. [*Social Security Contributions (Intermediaries) Regs 2000, Reg 3*].

For all purposes of these Social Security Regulations (and the associated tax provisions) persons living together as husband and wife or as civil partners are treated as if they were married to each other or had entered into a civil partnership, as the case may be. This extension of the definition to include civil partners and same sex couples living together took effect from 5 December 2005 on the coming into effect of the *Civil Partnership Act 2004*. Where appropriate, a calculation of deemed earnings for 2005–06 was required for the period from only 5 December 2005 to 5 April 2006. [*Social Security Contributions (Intermediaries) Regs 2000, Regs 2(5), 6; Social Security Contributions (Intermediaries)(Amendment) Regs 2005, SI 2005/3131, Reg 4(3)*].

Note that the holding of a directorship with a corporate intermediary is irrelevant – it is purely 'control', as tightly defined above, that is the relevant factor. The holding of a directorship in the end-client organisation while being supplied by an intermediary was a cause of several disputes, particularly in the public sector, in 2012 and 2013. It was argued, with justification, that where a worker was supplied by an intermediary to hold an office, without carrying out the duties of an employment as if employed under a contract of service, the IR35 provisions could not bite on the personal service company. As outlined above, HMRC conceded defeat in the argument, as *NICA 2014, s 15* and *Sch 2* amended *SSCBA 1992, s 2(1)(a)* and *s 7* with effect from 14 May 2014 so as to ensure that any relevant NICable earnings of office holders are now also caught.

Anything done by or to an associate of an intermediary is treated as if done by or to the intermediary itself. [*Social Security Contributions (Intermediaries) Regs 2000, Reg 2(3)(a)*].

A payment or other benefit provided to a member of an individual's family or household is treated as provided to the individual and this reference to an individual's family or household is construed as in *ITEPA 2003, s 721(4)(5)*. [*Social Security Contributions (Intermediaries) Regs 2000, Reg 2(3)(b), (4)*].

Engagements where services are provided in domestic circumstances, eg a nanny, chauffeur, butler, etc, were excluded for NICs until 1 September 2003. The equivalent income tax change was in respect of services performed after 9 April 2003. [Former *Social Security Contributions (Intermediaries) Regs 2000, SI 2000/727, Reg 6(1)(a)*].

[*Social Security Contributions (Intermediaries) Regulations 2000, SI 2000/727, Reg 2(5), Reg 6(1)(a); Social Security Contributions and Benefits Act 1992 (Modification of Section 4A) Order, SI 2003/1874; Social Security Contributions (Intermediaries) (Amendment) Regulations 2003, SI 2003/2079, Reg 5; Social Security Contributions (Intermediaries)(Amendment) Regulations 2005, SI 2005/3131, Reg 4(3)*; see also *FA 2003, s 136*].

Identifying engagements where the rules will apply

[40.5] The intermediaries rules apply for NIC purposes (the different tax position is outlined above) to engagements ('relevant engagements') on or after 6 April 2000 where:

- a worker provides services under a contract between a client and an intermediary; and

- but for the presence of the intermediary, the income arising would have been treated as coming from an office or employment held by the worker under the existing rules used to determine the boundary between employment and self-employment income for tax/NICs purposes, if the individual had contracted directly with the client.

[*Social Security Contributions (Intermediaries) Regs 2000, SI 2000/727, Reg* 6].

Guidance on the existing rules was included in the now obsolete HM Revenue and Customs leaflets IR175 and IR2003 which have now been replaced with 'online information' at www.gov.uk/guidance/ir35-find-out-if-it-applies.

The rules are to be applied in respect of each engagement, in the same way as they apply to individuals who operate without intermediaries. See **40.12** Contracts below.

The rules do not apply to such engagements where:

- prior to 2003 (see **40.1** above), the client was an individual and not in business (so services for a householder were not affected); or
- the worker only receives income from the intermediary in a form which falls within PAYE/Class 1 (eg straightforward employees of consultancy firms) and has no other rights to income or capital from the intermediary. Exceptions have been made for income from certain investments (eg holdings of small numbers of shares in the employing company). Similar rules exempt some partners in larger partnerships.

Tax and NICs treatment where the rules apply

[40.6] Under the modified approach ultimately enacted, personal service companies (or partnerships), and not the clients, are responsible for operating the legislation. It is not (yet) necessary for the clients to check whether the legislation applies when they enter into a contract with such an intermediary. There is no certification scheme (as had originally been planned) other than, since 6 April 2014, for oil and gas workers on the UK continental shelf.

The intention is that all the money received by the intermediary in respect of a relevant engagement, minus certain specified deductions listed in **40.9** below, should be treated as paid to the worker in a form subject to PAYE and Class 1 NICs.

The fact that the onus is placed on the company or partnership supplying the workers' services to operate 'IR35' means that there is now even greater pressure applied by end-users to ensure that their suppliers of labour are intermediaries rather than individuals.

As outlined above, HMRC intends to introduce new legislation from April 2017 (but realistically it may only be feasible by April 2018) to make public sector engagers responsible for checking the IR35 status of PSC workers they engage and deducting PAYE and NICs. If the PSC worker is supplied through an agency, the agency (or the body that actually pays the PSC's invoice, if different) will be responsible, and will need basic standing payroll data from the worker for that purpose.

The intermediary

Where the intermediary is a company

[40.7] Where a company intermediary receives income in respect of a relevant engagement, then:

- the intermediary will operate PAYE and pay NICs on any payments of salary to the worker during the year, in the normal way, including making a claim for employment allowance against the secondary contributions due in respect of actual payments of earnings during the year (if there is more than a sole director on payroll, for 2016–17 onwards).
- if, at the end of the tax year, the total of the worker's employment income from the intermediary, including benefits in kind, amounts to less than the intermediary's income from all that worker's relevant engagements, then the difference (net of allowable expenses described below) will be deemed to have been paid to the worker as salary on 5 April, and PAYE/NICs will be due, but no employment allowance may be claimed against the secondary contributions due in respect of the notional payment (and the July 2015 Budget speech announced that one-man companies would be disqualified from claiming the allowance in any event from 6 April 2016, the details later being set out in *Employment Allowance (Excluded Companies) Regulations 2016, SI 2016/344*).
- Where salary is deemed to arise in this way:
  - (a) equivalent deductions will be allowed in arriving at corporation tax profits; and
  - (b) no further tax/NICs will be due if the worker subsequently withdraws the money from the company as a dividend.

The deemed payment will be aggregated with other payments already made in the tax year concerned and the total amount will be charged as if the recipient was a director (ie annual or pro-rata annual earnings period will apply) whether or not the person is in fact a director. [*Social Security Contributions (Intermediaries) Regulations 2000, SI 2000/727, Reg 8(2)*].

Where the intermediary is a partnership

[40.8] Where a partnership receives gross payment under a relevant contract:

- Income of the partnership from all relevant engagements in the year (net of allowable expenses described in **40.9** below) will be deemed to have been paid to the worker on 5 April as salary from a deemed employment held by the worker, and PAYE/NICs will be due accordingly, albeit with no claim for employment allowance.
- Any amount deemed to be income within PAYE/Class 1 under the previous point will not be included when computing the worker's share of taxable partnership profits.

However, HM Revenue and Customs' current practice of including small amounts of employment income in the calculation of taxable profits for the self-employed, including partners, will apply also in these cases.

The deemed payment will be aggregated with any other payments already made in the tax year concerned and the total amount will be charged as if the recipient were a director (ie annual or pro rata annual earnings period will apply). [*Social Security Contributions (Intermediaries) Regulations 2000, SI 2000/727, Reg 8(2)*].

In addition, the provisions only apply to partnerships where:

- an individual, either alone or with one or more relatives*, is entitled to 60% or more of the profits, or
- all or most of the partnership's income in the relevant tax year is derived from the provision of services, in a form which would fall within the definition of relevant engagements, to a single client or associate(s) of that client, or
- the profit sharing arrangements in the partnership provide for the income of any of the partners to be based on the amount of income generated by those partners through relevant engagements, eg through a 'first drawing', etc.

If none of the above tests applies to a partnership, the IR35 rules do not affect it.

* Relative means spouse or civil partner, parent or remoter forebear, child or remoter issue, or brother or sister. [*Social Security Contributions (Intermediaries) Regulations 2000, SI 2000/727, Reg 5(6); Social Security Contributions (Intermediaries) (Amendment) Regulations 2005, SI 2005/3131, Regs 4(3), 5*].

If the rules do apply then, since there is no employment of a partner by his partnership, there will be no deduction in the calculation of the deemed payment for salary already paid and Class 1 thereon, nor for benefits in kind and Class 1A contributions thereon, nor for employer pension contributions. The IR35 rules were not changed to recognise the PAYE and Class 1 NIC charge levied in respect of 'salaried members' of LLPs, but Step 6 of the calculation of the worker's attributable earnings in *Social Security Contributions (Intermediaries) Regulations 2000, SI 2000/727, Reg 7* plainly allows the deduction of any secondary Class 1 contributions and Class 1A contributions paid by the intermediary for the year in respect of earnings of the worker.

Expenses

[40.9] An intermediary is allowed to deduct only the following expenses from payments in respect of a relevant engagement in calculating whether any 'deemed payment' is required:

- all expenses otherwise eligible for deduction under the normal tax rules for employees (*ITEPA 2003, s 336*): ie qualifying travelling expenses including AMAP scheme payments and those expended wholly and exclusively and necessarily in the performance of the duties of the employment, including professional subscriptions and professional indemnity insurance (guidance on the expenses rules is included in HM Revenue and Customs booklets 480 and 490); plus

- any employer pension contributions made to a registered pension scheme (an approved scheme prior to 6 April 2006) which are allowable under normal rules together with any of the Pensions Act levies; plus
- a further flat rate 5% allowance of the gross payment for the relevant contract to cover other miscellaneous expenses, such as running costs of the intermediary; plus
- the amount of the employer's NICs payable for the year, plus any due on the deemed payment, and including any Class 1A.

[*Social Security Contributions (Intermediaries) Regs 2000, SI 2000/727, Reg 7(1)*, as amended by *Social Security Contributions (Intermediaries) (Amendment) Regulations 2002, SI 2002/703, Regs 4, 5* and *Social Security Contributions (Intermediaries) (Amendment) Regulations 2005, SI 2005/3131, Regs 6, 7; Pensions Act 2004, ss 117, 174, 175*].

From 6 April 2016, *Finance Act 2016, s 14* inserted *ITEPA 2003, s 339A* to remove tax relief in respect of travel expenses between home and work (ie, under *ss 338–339*) for supervised or directed workers supplied by intermediaries, which includes all PSCs that are not managed service companies within *ITEPA 2003, Part 2, Ch 9* (albeit with a slightly extended definition – see below). The equivalent changes were introduced into contributions legislation by *Social Security (Contributions) (Amendment) (No 2) Regulations 2016, SI 2016/352, Reg 5*, which inserted a new *para 3ZB* into *Contributions Regulations 2001, Sch 3, Part 8*.

Paragraph 3ZB provides that, where a worker personally provides services other than in the client's home and those services are provided via an employment intermediary, each engagement is now to be regarded as a separate employment, mirroring the new income tax rules. This severely limits the scope to claim a deduction for home-to-work travel expenses, although expense deductions will still be available where the duties involve travelling to other temporary workplaces during the course of an engagement (ie, in the same way as relief would apply to a permanent employee of the client).

For most intermediary workers, this rule does not apply if it is shown that the manner in which the worker provides the services is not subject to (or to the right of) supervision, direction or control by any person, but where the engagement falls within the IR35 rules in *ITEPA 2003, Part 2, Ch 8* and the PSC is not a managed service company, this exclusion does not apply.

Where a PSC is not within *Chapter 8* of *Part 2* 'merely because the circumstances in *s 49(1)(c)* . . . are not met' (ie, there is no disguised employment, such as where a genuinely self-employed contractor has decided to operate through a limited company) and the company is not a managed service company, *para 3ZB* does not apply, so home-to-work travel payments should still be tax- and NIC-free

For the purpose of both of these tests, the definition of 'managed service company' is extended beyond the meaning given by *ITEPA 2003, s 61B* to include those PSCs that would be managed service companies if all of the income was not paid out as employment income and therefore disregarded under *s 61B(1)(c)*. The MSC is excluded in both situations because the rules in *Chapter 9* of *Part 2* already tax any NIC payments that reimburse the costs of travel between home and work.

As with all new legislation, a targeted anti-avoidance rule was included. In determining whether the block on relief for home-to-work travel expenses should apply, no regard is to be had to any arrangements the main purpose, or one of the main purposes, of which is to secure that this rule does not to any extent apply.

In practical terms, the new rules mean that a PSC worker whose engagement falls within IR35 will no longer be able to extract money from his or her company as tax- and NIC-free travel expenses and thereby sidestep the IR35 rules that require PAYE and NIC deductions.

Early cessations, etc

[40.10] Calculation and payment is required before the end of the tax year if:

- The worker ceases to be a member of a corporate intermediary;
- The worker ceases to hold office with a corporate intermediary (eg resigns as a director but everything else remains the same);
- The worker ceases to be employed by a corporate intermediary;
- A partnership intermediary is dissolved, ceases to trade or a partner resigns/retires;
- The worker is an employee of a partnership and that employment ceases.

[*Social Security Contributions (Intermediaries) Regs 2000, Reg 8(4)–(6)*].

Failure cases

[40.11] A common mistake is to assume that, once the self-assessment enquiry windows have closed for the individual and company tax returns, that is the end of the matter. This is not so. Whilst non-compliance may well be picked up from this source, the matter is ultimately one of PAYE/NIC compliance with the usual four- and six-year time limits. Where necessary, HM Revenue and Customs will apply its normal approach in the case of PAYE/NIC failure as set out in factsheets CC/FS1–19. Penalties will be applied in the case of careless or deliberate conduct (factsheet CC/FS7). The former EC Employer Compliance series of factsheets has been replaced by Compliance Operational Guidance – see www.gov.uk/hmrc-internal-manuals/compliance-operational-guidance/cog903620.

Where an intermediary fails to deduct and account for PAYE/NICs on payments to the worker under the new rules, the normal penalty provisions for employer failures will apply. If the intermediary does not meet its obligations to account for PAYE/NICs then the amount may be collected from the worker — as happens in certain circumstances under general PAYE and NIC legislation.

Contracts

[40.12] As mentioned above the terms of contracts used by service company workers are all-important. These contracts often require the worker to perform his/her duties at the client's premises, using the client's equipment, work standard hours and be paid at an hourly rate, etc but will, where there is no overriding reason such as security clearance for it to be otherwise, explicitly permit the sending of a substitute. The existence of a substitution right, provided it is real rather than bogus, is without further complication sufficient to ensure that the IR35 notional contract cannot be a contract of service, since personal service is a fundamental component of any employment contract. The right to send a substitute is fundamentally incompatible with a contract of service and will exclude the application of IR35. This is now not always so, following the 2014 change to the 'false self-employment' rules for onshore employment intermediaries – see AGENCY WORKERS 4 – if the work is routed through an agency, but those new rules should not apply if the worker is already employed by his own company such that any remuneration paid by the intermediary is already classed as employment income. However, despite this, according to *Income Tax (Pay As You Earn) Regulations 2003, SI 2003/2682, Regs 84E–84G*, as inserted by *Income Tax (Pay As You Earn) (Amendment No 2) Regulations 2015, SI 2015/171, Reg 2(3)*, from 6 April 2015 any agency supplying workers employed by another company (including an 'IR35' company) and paying such an intermediary gross is required to report online the gross payments every quarter and, in the case of companies, include the company registration number.

Where the period of the contract is less than a month the position will be considered on a case by case basis.

It will always be important to consider both contracts: the contract between the PSC and the end client, and the contract between the worker and his PSC. A further contract may be relevant to the context of the review if an agency is involved.

HM Revenue and Customs 'Clearance Service' for existing contracts

[40.13] People working through intermediaries can seek from HM Revenue and Customs an opinion on the notional employment status under a contract. Requests can be made by post or fax, to IR35 Customer Service Unit, HM Revenue and Customs, Ground Floor North, Princess House, Cliftonville Road, Northampton NN1 5AE. Phone: 0300 123 2326; Fax: 03000 533 404. An email address is also provided on the HMRC website: www.gov.uk/government/organisations/hm-revenue-customs/contact/ir35-enquiries: ir35@hmrc.gov.uk.

A copy of the contract should be sent together with all relevant information, including details of any recent history of work engagements which have the characteristics of self-employment. The worker's National Insurance number, the company's HM Revenue and Customs reference number and the company's postcode should also be provided. Unless HM Revenue and Customs has already seen the contract it will not give an opinion over the telephone. Contracts sent by e-mail should have all material converted to Rich Text Format (RTF) with any logos removed. The 'subject' line of the message should contain the tax reference number for the personal service company followed by the postcode.

Opinions will only be given by HM Revenue and Customs on signed contracts, not on drafts.

HM Revenue and Customs used to aim to reply to any requests for advice within 28 days of receiving all the details, but it now states that 'HMRC gives contract review requests priority and aims to deal with them as quickly as possible. If you don't or can't provide all the information, it may not be possible for HMRC to form an opinion.'

Because many service company workers in the IT industry are, HM Revenue and Customs believes, engaged through agencies on standard contract terms, it has given specific guidance on these standard contracts. These contracts, say HM Revenue and Customs, require the worker to work where the client requests, for an agreed number of hours per week, at an agreed rate of pay, keep a time sheet checked by the client, be subject to the direction of the client and not sub-contract their work to anyone else. Where these contract terms apply, and the engagement is for a month or more, HM Revenue and Customs' publicly stated view is that the intermediaries legislation *does* apply, unless the worker can demonstrate a recent history of work including engagements which have the characteristics of self-employment. Where the contract is for less than a month then, although the engagement may still have been one of disguised employment, the status position will be considered on a case by case basis.

Case law

[40.14] In *Lime It v Justin* [2003] STC SCD 15 Sp C 342 a company (L) was incorporated in April 2000 to provide information technology services. Shortly after its incorporation, it entered into a contract with a company providing 'executive recruitment services', under which it provided the services of its controlling director (F) to another company (M) in relation to specific projects, including organising and managing a computer support function, introducing a new email system, organising remote access, and changing to 'Windows 2000'. The contract lasted for almost one year. The former Inland Revenue issued a ruling that the arrangements were within the *Social Security Contributions (Intermediaries) Regulations 2000, SI 2000/727*, and that L was liable to pay Class 1 National Insurance Contributions in respect of F's income under the contract. L appealed. The Special Commissioner reviewed the evidence in detail and allowed the appeal, observing that M contracted for particular projects, and that F 'did not work a regular pattern of hours; the hours were dictated by the requirements of the work'. L had 'suffered delays in being paid in the way that businesses do'. F 'did not work alongside any other employees (of M) as part and parcel of the (M) organisation', and L 'operated as a normal small business with its own office working for four other clients'. Accordingly, if F had contracted directly with M, 'she would not have been employed under a contract of service; she would have been in business on her own account'.

Since *Lime It v Justin* [2003] STC SCD 15 Sp C 342 there have been a number of IR35 cases with just under half won by the taxpayers and just over half by what is now HM Revenue and Customs. But in addition, many cases taken on by the Professional Contractors Group (see **40.1** above) have been conceded by the authorities prior to reaching the Commissioners and these have been the majority of cases where the personal service contracts have been properly drafted and implemented ensuring that there is no IR35 case to answer. See *Battersby v Campbell* [2001] STC SCD 189 Sp C 287; *F S Consulting v McCaul* [2002] STC SCD 138; *Synaptek Ltd v Young (Inspector of Taxes)* [2003] EWHC 645 (Ch), [2003] STC 543, 75 TC 51 where the *F S Consulting* case was distinguished and this was followed by *Future Online Ltd v Faulds* [2004] STC SCD 237 Sp C 406; ChD [2005] STC 198 which had some similarities to the *Synaptek* case. See also *Tilbury Consulting Ltd v Gittins* [2004] STC SCD 1 Sp C 379 and 390 with regard to appeal procedure regarding witness summons in IR35 cases and *Ansell Computer Services Ltd v Richardson* [2004] STC SCD 472 Sp C 425 regarding 'mutual obligation'. See Tolley's Practical NIC Newsletter, November 2004 pages 83–85.

In *Usetech Limited v Young* [2004] STC SCD 213 Sp C 404, a case which was lost by the taxpayer company in the High Court, Park J held that the Commissioner had been entitled to find that, if there had been a contract between the software designer and the company for whom the services were provided, it would have been a contract of employment, rather than a contract for freelance services.

In *Carter Lauren Construction Ltd v Revenue and Customs Comrs (also known as Island Consultants Ltd v Revenue and Customs Comrs)* [2007] STC (SCD) 482, [2007] SWTI 1329 a company (C) provided the services of its controlling director (H) to a water company (S), through an employment agency, on a series of three-month contracts for a five-year computer project. HMRC issued a ruling that C was liable to pay Class 1 NICs in respect of H's income under the contract. The Special Commissioner upheld HMRC's ruling, holding that under the 'hypothetical contract' required by the regulations, 'the factors predominantly point towards employment'. See also *MKM Computing Ltd v HMRC* [2008] STC SCD 403 Sp C 653; *Dragonfly Consulting Ltd v HMRC* [2008] STC SCD 430 Sp C 655; Ch D [2008] STC 3030; *First Word Software Ltd v HMRC* [2008] STC SCD 389 Sp C 652; *Datagate Services Ltd v HMRC* [2008] STC SCD 453 Sp C 656; and *Alternative Book Company Ltd v HMRC* [2008] STC SCD 830 Sp C 685.

In 1998 *MKM Computing Ltd* agreed to provide the services of E (a controlling director) to a company (P) which supplied contract workers. P agreed to provide E's services to another company (L). The Special Commissioner upheld HMRC's ruling and dismissed MKM's appeal, finding that the controlling director, E, was 'part and parcel of (L's) organisation' and holding that under the hypothetical contract required by the regulations, he would have been an employee. In *Dragonfly Consulting Ltd* Ch D [2008] STC 3030; EWHC 2113 (Ch) a company (D) was incorporated to provide the services of its controlling director (B), who was a computer software engineer. In 2000, D agreed to provide B's services to an agency (P) which in turn agreed to provide B's services to the Automobile Association. The Special Commissioner reviewed the evidence in detail, rejected the contention that B was self-employed and dismissed the appeal. The Commissioner observed that B 'worked fairly regular hours during each engagement, . . . worked on parts of a project which were allocated to him as part of the AA's teams, . . . was integrated into the AA's business, . . . and had a role similar to that of a professional employee'. The Chancery Division upheld the decision on appeal. Henderson J observed that there were 'slight, but potentially significant differences' between the wording of the statutory test laid down for NIC purposes and that laid down for income tax purposes. He observed that 'the NIC test requires the arrangements themselves to be embodied in a notional contract, and then asks whether the circumstances (undefined) are such that the worker would be regarded as employed; whereas the income tax test directs attention in the first instance to the services provided by the worker for the client, and then asks whether the circumstances . . . are such that, if the services were provided under a contract directly between the client and the worker, the worker would be regarded as an employee of the client'. However, these differences did not affect the result in this case. On the evidence, the Commissioner was entitled to conclude that 'the nature and degree of the control by the AA under the hypothetical contract' pointed towards employment.

First Word Software Ltd (F) was incorporated to provide the services of its controlling director (N), who was a computer consultant. In 2000, F agreed to provide N's services to a company (P) which provided software services to another company (R). HMRC issued a ruling that the arrangements were within the *Social Security Contributions (Intermediaries) Regulations 2000, SI 2000 No 727*, and that F was liable to pay Class 1 NICs in respect of the payments which it made to N. F appealed, contending that if the services had been performed under a contract between N and R, N would not be regarded as an employee of R. The Special Commissioner reviewed the evidence in detail, accepted this contention and allowed F's appeal, finding that the relevant contract contained a right of substitution and 'the intention of the parties was that (N) was not obliged to perform the services personally'. On the evidence, N 'acted as a subcontractor, with responsibility for part only of a larger project, and not as an employee'.

In *Datagate Services Ltd* [2008] STC SCD 453 Sp C 656, a company (D) was incorporated to provide the services of its controlling director (B), who was a computer software consultant. In 2000, D agreed to provide B's services to a company (T) which provided software services to another company (M). HMRC took the view that the arrangements were within *SI 2000 No 727*, and that D was liable to pay Class 1 NICs on the basis that the payments it received under the contract were employment earnings which it paid to B. D appealed, contending that if the services had been performed under a contract between B and M, B would not be regarded as an employee of M. The Special Commissioner accepted this contention and allowed the appeal, finding that there was no 'ultimate right of control on the part of (M)' and that B was 'in business on his own account and was not a person working as an employee in someone else's business on the hypotheses that the legislation requires'.

A company (N) was incorporated to provide the services of its controlling director (B), who was an IT analyst. In 1998, N agreed to provide B's services to another company (L) which carried on an agency business, providing IT contractors to companies engaged in IT projects. L arranged for B to work for a third company (Z). HMRC issued a ruling that the arrangements were within *SI 2000 No 727*, and that N was liable to pay Class 1 NICs on the basis that the payments it received under the contract were employment earnings which it paid to B. N appealed, contending that if the services had been performed under a contract between B and Z, B would not be regarded as an employee of Z. The First-Tier Tribunal reviewed the evidence in detail, accepted this contention, and allowed the appeal. Judge Kempster concluded that 'the overall picture painted is one of a contract for self-employment'. *Novasoft Ltd v HMRC* [2010] UKFTT 150, TC000456.

A company (M) was incorporated to provide the services of its controlling director (F), who was a design engineer. In 2003 M entered into a contract with another company (G), under which F's services would be provided to a large manufacturing company (AS). On the following day G entered into a contract with a fourth company (H), regulating the terms under which F was to work for AS. HMRC took the view that the arrangements were within the *Social Security Contributions (Intermediaries) Regulations 2000, SI 2000/727*, and that M was liable to pay Class 1 National Insurance contributions on the basis that the payments it received under the contract were employment earnings which it paid to F. M appealed, contending that if the services had been performed under a contract between F and AS, F would not be regarded as an employee of AS. The First-Tier Tribunal accepted this contention and allowed the appeal, holding that the arrangements appeared to be typical of a contract for services, rather than a contract of service. Judge Cornwell-Kelly observed that the terms of the relevant contract gave AS the right to cancel it without giving notice. He held that this condition was 'characteristic of a contract for services but quite foreign to the world of employment'. *MBF Design Services Ltd v HMRC* FTT [2011] UKFTT 35 (TC), TC00912.

Under the new off-payroll working in the public sector rules a TV presenter (A) provided her services to the BBC via her PSC (CAM Ltd). Despite having taken professional advice in relation to the contractual arrangements and with the encouragement of the BBC, the First-tier Tribunal found that A was within the off-payroll working in the public sector (IR35) rules. *Christa Ackroyd Media Ltd v HMRC* FTT [2018] UKFTT (TC), TC0069.

It is clear from the above cases that, depending on the facts, the tribunals review the evidence presented to them carefully and can come to differing conclusions, but these are invariably based on the evidence provided. Further useful comment on some of these cases can be obtained from Tolley's Practical NIC Newsletter of March 2008 and April 2008.

In *Netherlane Ltd v York* [2005] STC SCD 305 SpC 457 procedural matters were addressed in connection with regard to preparing evidence in an IR35 case. See APPEALS AND REVIEWS 9. See Tax Bulletin, February 2001 Appendix 1.

Calculating the IR35 deemed payment — example

[40.15] The following example illustrates calculation of the deemed payment.

Example

Graham, an IT consultant working through his own service company, has secured a job with Benevolent Ltd through an agency to work on the computerised accounts system for seven months from October 2015 to April 2016 inclusive. In accounts, a team leader (another IT contractor) tells Graham what work he is to carry out but he is left to his own experience to determine 'how' the work is carried out. Graham is expected to be in attendance at Benevolent Ltd a regular 40 hours per week. Graham's company is paid an hourly rate for his services at 1.5 times the normal hourly rate. Billed monthly, Benevolent Ltd pays the agency who in turn are invoiced by Graham's company. The total invoices for the seven months amounted to £35,000 (excluding VAT). Graham draws a salary of £10,234 from his company over the period. Allowable expenses up to 5 April 2016 amount to £750 and there are pension contributions of £2,000. The main indications in favour of self-employment are the ability to work for others and the existence of Graham's company. In contrast, the engagement is relatively long and he must carry out the services personally. Also Benevolent Ltd provides the equipment and working accommodation and he works the usual working hours of the client. There is also minimal financial risk to Graham and his company. The engagement with Benevolent Ltd seemingly would have been an employment had it been between Graham and the client direct rather than through the service company. The IR35 rules therefore apply as follows:

Relevant income received (October, November, December, January, February; March not paid as at 5 April 2016; April 2016 not yet invoiced)		£25,000
Deduct		
Pension contributions paid	£2,000	
Expenses paid (allowable)	£750	
Flat rate allowance (5% of £25,000)	£1,250	
Salary paid in year to 5 April 2016	£10,234	
Class 1 secondary NICs on salary paid in year (on £10,234 – £8,112) @ 13.8%	£293	
Employment allowance	(£293)	(£14,234)
Net deemed payments before NICs		£10,766
Employer's NICs (£10,766 × 13.8/113.8)		(£1,306)
Deemed payment		£9,460

NOTES: i) Employer's NIC on £9,460 @ 13.8% = £1,306; ii) Employment allowance of up to £2,000 is available against *actual* salary (but not the notional payment) for 2015–16 (but will not be available for 2016–17 as Graham is the sole employee).

The post-expense figure before NICs (ie £10,766) is multiplied by 100/113.8 to reach the deemed payment figure since the employer's Earnings Threshold has already been taken into account on the £10,234 salary. Clearly, an adjustment will be necessary if none or only part of the Earnings Threshold has not been set against salary payments already made in the tax year in question. In any year, other fractions will be applicable if the married woman's reduced rate applies. For years before April 2016, the contracted-out rate might have been relevant, although it is unlikely that a PSC will have had a contracted-out salary-related scheme in place. It is also unlikely that any earner under 21 will operate through an IR35 PSC, but if that happens in 2015–16 or later years, the secondary NIC rate would be 0% on earnings up to the upper secondary threshold. The apprentice rate for under-25s will also not apply from April 2016, as the apprentice is certain not to be employed by his or her own PSC. If any of the travel expenses relate to home-to-work travel, they will no longer be excluded from income in 2016–17 or later years where the engagement falls within IR35.

The PAYE and NICs on the first deemed payment under the IR35 legislation were payable on or before 19 April 2001 and that in the above example were due and payable on 19 April 2016 (22 April if paid electronically). Late payment will incur an interest charge and possible penalty and therefore an accurately-estimated amount of PAYE/NICs should have been paid.

Under RTI, the deemed payment must be reported on a FPS by the April due dates (ie, 5th April for the FPS, 19th/22nd April for the payment). The final return of the year should be flagged as such, but it is unlikely that the value of the deemed payment will be known by 5 April, so HMRC instructs PSCs to report the best estimate by 5 April (by simply adding the value to any other wages on the FPS).

Corrections that will usually be necessary once the correct deemed payment calculation has been finalised will be reported on an EYU before 31 January following the end of the tax year, with any extra tax due also being paid by that date. Interest will be due, but no penalty will apply. (See www.gov.uk/ir35-what-to-do-if-it-applies#report-payments.)

The service company (ie Graham's own company) is responsible for the compliance aspect of PAYE/NICs under the intermediaries rules, although this duty may transfer to the client or the agency from April 2017 if current HMRC plans come to fruition. Further details regarding computation can be found at www.gov.uk/ir35-what-to-do-if-it-applies#calculate-the-deemed-employment-payment.

Extra-Statutory Concession C32 was announced on 4 April 2001 permitting intermediaries in the construction industry to take account of the CIS deductions when paying tax and NICs on the deemed payment. See IR Press Release 64/2001, 4 April 2001. [*Social Security Contributions (Intermediaries) Regs 2000, SI 2000/727, Reg 7*]. This concession is now obsolete. It should be noted that, in accordance with the wording of the legislation, the NICs to be deducted are those paid or payable *for* the year in question, not those actually paid *in* the year.

See Tax Bulletin, February 2001.

Provisional payments, deferred penalties and P35 completion

[40.16] Except where *Social Security Contributions (Intermediaries) Regs 2000, SI 2000/727, Reg 8(4)–(6)* is in point (see **40.10**), the deemed payment arises on 5 April and therefore falls to be included on the FPS for that period. In the past, it would have been shown on forms P14 and P35 of the same tax year. Whilst HM Revenue and Customs accepts that this does not leave some affected businesses a great deal of time to make the necessary calculations, it still requires payment on 19 April (22 April if paid electronically) after the end of the relevant year and interest will be charged on normal terms.

However, it is accepted that final figures may not be available, in which case a provisional payment should be made – with a further payment (or claim for repayment) later. In years before 2014–15, if the 19/22 April payment was provisional, HMRC should have spotted this by virtue of the two service company questions having been answered correctly on the P35 (reduced to one question on the final FPS or EPS – field 117 in the submission for 2013–14) for the year. Debt Management staff should take no interest if the deemed payments included in the final FPS and the EYU are paid by the due dates.

The old form P35 had be submitted by 19 May, but under RTI the FPS is supposed to be filed on or before the date of the deemed payment, which is likely to be impossible for most IR35 intermediaries, so HMRC instructs relevant intermediaries to include a provisional calculation of the deemed payment on an FPS on or before 5 April. By 19 May, the previous provisional figures might have been finalised, but under RTI this is much less likely. If the old P35 numbers were not final, Debt Management had to be informed that the return, as well as the previous payment, was provisional. A provisional return had to be finalised as soon as possible thereafter by means of an amended P35, with the outstanding payment or request for the appropriate repayment. In any event, finalised P35 details had to be submitted no later than 31 January following the end of the tax year otherwise penalties would be imposed at that point. This relaxation was originally made for 2000–01 returns only, but was then extended indefinitely. Under RTI, as noted, any amendment to the reported figure (after 19 May) is included in an EYU (Earlier Year Update).

The two service company questions first appeared when form P35 was amended from 2006–07. Firstly, did the intermediaries legislation apply to the employer? Secondly, was the return final? With the introduction of MSCs from 2007–08 (see **40.18**) the questions were replaced for the 2007–08 P35 and for subsequent years with different questions, the first of which merely asked 'Are you a service company?' in general terms without tying the meaning of the question to the IR35 and MSC legislation (see **40.18**). The second asked whether the IR35 rules had been operated. It was widely thought that this was a 'fishing expedition' whereby HM Revenue and Customs would collect details of all companies providing services – whether either set of legislation was in point or not. In the circumstances, HM Revenue and Customs said that it would not act on any answers to these questions for the 2007–08 returns.

For the 2014 year-end, under RTI, the two questions were combined into a single question with HMRC guidance indicating what was intended by the question: 'Service company - answer: "Yes" if you are a service company - "service company" includes a limited company, a limited liability partnership (but not a sole trader) - AND have operated the Intermediaries legislation. Otherwise indicate "No".'

Some software providers did not pick up on this change and continued to ask simply whether the employer was a service company, which looks equivalent to the old first question, so many of their employer clients will have incorrectly ticked 'yes', not realising that they were thereby signalling that they had operated the IR35 rules.

HM Revenue and Customs stated that no penalties would be charged under *TMA 1970, s 98A* if the above procedures were complied with and the provisional calculations were done in good faith. In particular, penalties would not be sought for late filing if the P35 was received by 19 May, showing remuneration paid during the year, plus an amount on account of the deemed payment, with tax and NIC correctly calculated on the aggregate figure, Debt Management was informed that – respectively – the 19/22 April payment and the subsequent P35 were provisional, and a supplementary return including the correct final figure for the deemed payment was then sent in to HM Revenue and Customs by 31 January following the end of the tax year. This position remains essentially unchanged in the new, post-RTI guidance.

Concerns were expressed to the former Inland Revenue that accountants with many intermediary clients would not be able to do the necessary calculations for all affected clients in the short time from 6 April to 19 April each year, even in those years when Easter did not fall within that period. They stated that since only a provisional payment and, if necessary, provisional return were required 'the worker need not necessarily consult his accountant before making the payment on 19 April'. This would seem to suggest that the required level of accuracy in fixing a provisional payment did not need – perhaps – to be too high. Nonetheless, in practice, astute clients were likely to require this service on a speedy basis in order to mitigate interest charges at punitive rates. The introduction of RTI has meant that the timescale has shifted, with many more provisional numbers submitted, but HMRC has had to accept this as a natural consequence of the shortening of the reporting timetable under RTI.

A statement dated 7 January 2004 from the former Inland Revenue advised:

> As part of an employer compliance review an officer may decide that he/she needs to check information about working practices with the client to see if the service company had reached a correct view on the application of the IR35 legislation when the P35 was filed. To facilitate an approach to the client the officer will ask for the worker's permission.

Caveats

[40.17] HM Revenue and Customs is adamant that the new rules cannot be overcome by use of an offshore company, with the rules applying wherever the intermediary is incorporated or resident. This appears to be correct since, under the normal rules relating to Class 1 contributions, it is the place where the work is performed which determines liability. In any event, the policy position of the Government and HM Revenue and Customs should be borne in mind. It should therefore be assumed that any assertions of non-liability before 6 April 2014, when the rules changed, due to the intermediary being offshore would only be upheld through recourse to the appeals system, with all the attendant risk and cost that that would entail. See Tax Bulletin April 2003, pp 1016-1020.

HM Revenue and Customs has also stated that it has powers to obtain details of payments made to offshore companies from the records of UK-based clients and agencies, although the new provisions on offshore intermediaries from

April 2014 suggest that these claimed powers do not work: if an offshore intermediary refuses to disclose actual wage payments to the UK end-user and refuses to pay the employer NICs, there is in practice little that HMRC can do to calculate liabilities and enforce collection. It remains to be seen how the 2014 changes work in practice and whether onshore intermediaries or liable end clients can indeed obtain the information they need in order to comply.

Where an intermediary does not have a place of business in the UK at which to serve legal process for amounts due, HM Revenue and Customs states that it will use powers that it has to transfer unpaid PAYE/NIC debts to the worker(s) in question, although again it first has to know how much has been paid to the worker(s), which is sometimes impossible under current information powers. This aspect was not addressed by the 2014 changes imposing the liability on an onshore party to the arrangements, so it remains to be seen how compliant the intermediary population will be.

Another area that HM Revenue and Customs is looking at and which may affect some companies only partly caught by the intermediaries legislation is applying the settlement provisions under *ITTOIA 2005, ss 622, 624, 625, 626, 627, Sch 2 para 132(1)(3)*. This would be where a company is set up and the spouse receives dividends from company profits, thereby avoiding PAYE and NICs on a portion of the company profits which would have incurred tax and NICs if paid as salary.

HM Revenue and Customs took the stance that if one of the principal fee earners was avoiding tax at the higher rate and NICs by ensuring that dividends were paid to the spouse then there should have been an apportionment of some or the whole of the dividend back to the principal. This would apply in cases where the wife, say, who has a small administrative role in the company has been allotted shares which attract the requisite dividend payment. See *Jones v Garnett (Arctic Systems Ltd)* Ch D [2005] All ER (D) 396; STC 1667 Sp C 432; HL [2007] All ER 857, which although concerning shares/dividend payments and not NICs, does indicate the stronger line that HM Revenue and Customs are taking in this area.

This case, known as the *Arctic Systems* case, involved a challenge to a structure created with the intention that it should be a means of providing regular bounty in the future, that amounted to an 'arrangement' within *ICTA 1988, s 660G* (now *ITTOIA 2005, ss 620(1)–(3), 648(1)–(5)*). Accordingly, the effect of what is now *ITTOIA 2005, ss 622, 624, 625, 626, 627, Sch 2 para 132(1)(3)* was that the wife's income was chargeable on the husband. Furthermore, there had not been an 'outright gift', so that *s 626* did not apply.

The taxpayers' appeals were ultimately successful in the House of Lords. One other aspect of this situation, the purported saving of National Insurance on dividend income, might also arguably be caught by *F(No 2)A 2005, Sch 2* insofar as 'something has been done which affects employment-related securities as part of a scheme or arrangement for the main purpose (or one of the main purposes) of which is the avoidance of tax or national insurance contributions' [*ITEPA 2003, s 447(4)*]. See also *HMRC v PA Holdings Ltd* [2011] EWCA Civ 1414, decided by the Court of Appeal on 30 November 2011. It should, however, be noted that any re-allocation of income from one spouse to the other under the settlement rules in *ITTOIA 2005* will not be taxable under *ITEPA 2003*, but under *ITTOIA 2005*, and the settlement rules are of no relevance to the Class 1 NIC liability of any party.

See also 39.2 HUSBAND AND WIFE, AND CIVIL PARTNER.

Managed service companies and composite companies

[40.18] *Finance Act 2007* inserted a new *Chapter 9* into *ITEPA 2003* which defines a 'managed service company' (MSC) (as an additional enforcement measure against what were effectively bulk IR35 schemes) and subjects payments received by persons relating to services provided through such companies ie bodies corporate or partnerships, as employment income. Note that this applies even if the worker would, but for the corporate structure, be self-employed – such a person will need to operate through his own company doing as much management as possible himself in order to fall within the 2000 'IR35' rules to the exclusion of the 2007 MSCs rules. [*FA 2007, s 25, Sch 3*]. In addition, there are provisions to enable debts unpaid by the 'scheme provider' to be transferred and then enforced against the directors, scheme provider and a wide range of third parties. See also CWG2 (2017), para 4.7.2 and CA44 (2017), para 69.

Definition—Managed service companies

[40.19] A 'managed service company' will meet four requirements:

(i) the business of the company consists wholly or mainly of providing, directly or indirectly, the services of an individual or individuals to other persons;

(ii) payments, directly or indirectly, to the individuals providing their services or those of their associates, are made which equate to the majority (or all) of the consideration that the company is paid for the provision of those services;

(iii) the way in which the individual is, or his associates are, paid results in their receiving more money than they would have received, after PAYE and NICs have been deducted, if all the payments had been employment income; and

(iv) a person, termed an 'MSC provider' (MSCP), whose business is that of promoting and facilitating the use of companies to provide the service of individuals, is 'involved' with the company.

In the case of (iv) above there are three points:

- the MSC's business is that of promotion and facilitation of companies;
- the business is not simply that of promoting or facilitating companies, but specifically promoting or facilitating companies to provide the services of individuals; and
- the MSCP is 'involved with' the company.

For these purposes *involved with* is defined within *ITEPA 2003, s 61B(2)* as being where any associate or associate of the MSCP benefits financially, influences or controls those services or payments, influences or controls the company's finances or any activities, and, gives or promotes an undertaking to make good any tax loss.

The *Social Security Contributions (Managed Service Companies) Regulations 2007, SI 2007/2070* apply with effect from 6 August 2007 the rules in *ITEPA 2003, Chapter 9* described above. Because the start date for National Insurance contributions was not until 6 August 2007, two separate types of calculation applied for 2007–08 – one dealing only with PAYE from 6 April 2007 to 5 August 2007 and the other covering both National Insurance contributions and PAYE after 5 August 2007. It should also be noted that the standard earnings periods rules apply – this contrasts with the 'IR35' rules where an annual earnings period applies automatically. The power to make these regulations is in the *Social Security Contributions and Benefits Act 1992 (Modification of Section 4A) Order 2007, SI 2007/2071*. The fact that a mere Statutory Instrument provides the power to make other Regulations is due to the powers in *SSCBA 1992, s 4A(9)* inserted by *Welfare Reform and Pensions Act 1999* upon the introduction of 'IR35'.

As regards directors or office holders of MSCs and MSCPs (and associates of those persons), the debt transfer provisions also did not take effect until 6 August 2007 and did not take effect for NIC purposes until 6 January 2008 in the case of other persons (such as agencies). Where a transferred debt is duly paid, that sum is not an allowable deduction in the payer's computation of taxable profits. [*Social Security (Contributions) (Amendment No 5) Regulations 2007, SI 2007/2068*, inserting new Regs 29A to 29L into the *Social Security Contributions Regs 2001*] See also *Income Tax (Pay As You Earn) (Amendment No 2) Regulations 2007, SI 2007/2069*. Security may be required for the payment of Class 1 contributions.

Assurances—Managed service companies

[40.20] The position of a genuinely self-employed person who operates through a service company remains unclear as regards the involvement of one or more MSC providers. In the debate stages of the Finance Bill on 30 April 2007, John Healey MP (the then Financial Secretary to the Treasury) said:

> If someone is genuinely operating on their own account and essentially running their own affairs and engaging their labour through a managed service company, they clearly will not be caught by the provisions before us.

On 15 May 2007 Healey stated:

> Freelancers or agency workers who are in some way in business on their own account and run their own affairs, either through a personal service company or some sort of umbrella company, are simply not affected by the legislation.

It would appear from these comments that even where a MSC provider is 'involved' with a service company it may still be possible to avoid the MSC rules if it can be demonstrated that the worker is clearly in business on his own account.

A major difference between the MSC rules and the IR35 legislation until 6 April 2016 was that those who fell within IR35 could claim travel and subsistence costs and a flat-rate general expenses deduction of 5%. The IR35 worker has one employer, the PSC, and until 6 April 2016 had the potential for claiming for the cost of travel between home and work if he had a series of temporary workplaces. This was not the case under the MSC rules because the worker may only claim business travel expenses in the same way as a permanent employee of the end client. The MSC rules removed the tax/NICs advantage in respect of home-to-work travel altogether, which is why the provisions in *Contributions Regulations 2001, Sch 3, Part 8, para 3ZB*, introduced on 6 April 2016 for intermediary workers, exclude MSCs from their scope – the block on relieving such expenses already existed, created when the MSC rules were introduced. [*ITEPA 2003 s 61G(3)*].

> Employees are able to claim travel and subsistence costs for home-to-work travel free of tax and NICs when they are at temporary workplaces. MSC schemes make use of these rules on the basis that each of the worker's assignments represents a temporary workplace since the worker is treated as having one overarching employment with the MSC.
>
> [Regulatory Impact Assessment, paragraph D8]

MSCs—Example

[40.21] *ITEPA 2003, s 61D(2)* sets out when a worker is treated as receiving earnings from employment in relation to the MSC which are then subject to PAYE and NICs payable on a monthly basis. If such a worker receives a payment or benefit, directly or indirectly eg through a spouse, then that worker is deemed to have received an equivalent 'deemed employment payment' which is subject to PAYE and NICs as employment income. The date on which the worker receives the deemed employment payment is the date the MSC must deduct and account for PAYE and NICs.

HMRC published guidance in July 2007 which helps interpret difficult parts of the legislation. The guidance is however poorly presented in parts and littered with hyperlinks to the HM Revenue and Customs intranet and thus not directly of use to public readers. It is however available at www.gov.uk/hmrc-internal-manuals/employment-status-manual/esm3500.

Example

Maxwell is an IT consultant working through an employment agency Intermedia which facilitates his services to Benevolent Ltd through a MSC (of which he is the sole shareholder and director) within *ITEPA 2003, s 61B(1)*. The employment agency pays Maxwell's managed service company, and his wife is provided with a car by Intermedia as Maxwell does not drive and she undertakes the driving for him to and from Benevolent Ltd's office. The employment agency service company secured the job with Benevolent Ltd for seven months from October 2016 to April 2017 inclusive. Benevolent Ltd pays the employment agency Intermedia who in turn are invoiced by the MSC which then naturally receives gross payment. The total invoices for the seven months amount to £35,000. Maxwell draws a salary of £10,000 from his company over the period. The car provided directly to Maxwell's wife to get him to and from work is a Chrysler Cruiser and that benefit and the free fuel provided for the car are valued using the CO2 scale at £3,300 after taking into account the non-availability portion. Benevolent Ltd would appear not reasonably to have known that they were dealing with a MSC that is a provider of Maxwell's services but Intermedia, who set up the contract and service agreement, would be within *ITEPA 2003, s 61B(1)*. Benevolent Ltd is excluded under *ITEPA 2003, s 61B(3)(4)*. Allowable expenses (ie, excluding home-to-work travel costs) up to 5 April 2017 amount to £750 and there are pension contributions of £2,000. The MSC rules therefore apply as follows:

Employment payment or benefit (October, November, December 2015, January, February; March not paid as at 5 April 2017 and April 2017 not yet invoiced): *ITEPA 2003, s 61D(1)(b)*		£25,000
Add		
Car benefit through associate (ie wife): *ITEPA 2003, s 61D(1)(b)*		£3,300
Deduct		
Pension contributions paid	£2,000	
Expenses paid (allowable): *ITEPA 2003, s 61B(2)*	£750	(£2,750)
		£25,550*
* Employer's NICs calculated on the above inclusive amount and then deducted to calculate employee's PAYE and NICs £25,550 – £8,112 × 13.8/113.8		(£2,115)
Deemed employment payment subject to PAYE, employee's and employer's Class 1 NICs: *ITEPA 2003, s 61E(1)*		£23,435

NOTE: For ease of presentation this example is shown with annual figures, but in practice calculations will be required on the occasion of each separate payment to the worker, ie generally weekly or monthly. Unlike the IR35 calculation, the MSC calculation takes no account of actual salary payments. Home-to-work travel costs reimbursed by the MSC have been taxable and NICable since the MSC provisions were introduced in 2007 and were unaffected by the changes to the IR35 expenses rules on 6 April 2016.

Key Points regarding intermediaries

[40.22] Points to consider are as follows.

- Only very limited deductions are allowable in the IR35 deemed payment calculation, and home-to-work travel costs became an additional exclusion at 6 April 2016.
- The deductions in the case of an MSC are even more tightly restricted.
- Calculations are done on a cash basis for both receipts and payments, not on an accruals basis.
- An IR35 deemed payment can be paid out subsequently as a dividend (but not salary) and the double tax on the dividend (at rates above the basic rate deemed covered) eliminated.
- Where there is an unpaid liability by a MSC then recovery may be sought from:
  (a) a director, office holder or associate of the MSC provider;

(b) a MSC provider;
(c) the person who has been closely involved in the provision of the worker's services by the MSC such as an agency; and
(d) any other person who has encouraged or been actively involved in the provision of the worker's services. [*ITEPA 2003, s 688A*].

- The provisions for PSCs and MSCs changed in April 2017 insofar as the company provides the personal services of its shareholder-director to a public sector body, when that body, or the agency arranging the contract, is likely to become responsible for identifying whether IR35 applies and, if it does, operating PAYE and NICs deductions on the payment, excluding VAT and materials, made to the PSC or MSC and reporting the figures as earnings of the shareholder-director concerned.

41

Labour-only Contractors

Cross-references. See AGENCY WORKERS **4**; CATEGORISATION **14**; **20.6** CLASS 1 CONTRIBUTIONS for relief for Class 1 contributions paid by a self-employed earner; COLLECTION **21** for treatment of deductions made by contractors from amounts paid to subcontractors in the construction industry; ENTERTAINERS **36**; EXAMINERS **37**; HOMEWORKERS AND OUTWORKERS **38**; INTERMEDIARIES **40**; LECTURERS, TEACHERS AND INSTRUCTORS **44**.

Other Sources. IR Tax Bulletin, April 1997, pages 405–413; Tolley's Practical NIC Newsletter, November 2004; Leaflets CIS 340, CIS 359 and fact sheets CIS 341–349 and ES/FS1, ES/FS2. HMRC Employment Status Manual; Taxation, 1 March 2018, page 8; Taxation, 29 March 2018, page 8.

Introduction to labour-only contractors

[41.1] The term 'labour-only contractor' means anyone who supplies, or purports to supply, services consisting entirely of his own labour to another, not as an employee but as an independent contractor. It does, therefore, include persons working in the building and construction industry, but is by no means confined to such persons. Where the worker finds work and is paid via an agency, see also **4** AGENCY WORKERS (for rules that are likely to deem him to be an employee of the agency, whether or not he is genuinely self-employed) and where the worker trades through a personal service company see also **40** INTERMEDIARIES. Those labour-only workers who are employed by an 'umbrella' company have a contract of employment and are employees, even if the clients for whom they work see them as contractors, albeit supplied via an intermediary.

HMRC attitude

[41.2] Labour-only contractors tend to be viewed with some suspicion by HM Revenue and Customs since the contracts or agreements on which their status rests may be found to be matters of mere form disguising their true status as employed earners and devised with the objective of reducing contribution liability (see **8.1** ANTI-AVOIDANCE). This suspicion on the part of HM Revenue and Customs was further underlined by the Budget Day Press Release on 9 March 1999; the now notorious 'IR35' regarding the restriction placed on personal service companies from 6 April 2000 and followed up by consultation document *Tackling Managed Service Companies* issued on 6 December 2006 and *Finance Act 2007, Sch 3*. See **40** INTERMEDIARIES. The tax legislation and final NIC regulations mean that those undertaking such services will have additional or, in some cases, new PAYE and NICs deductions to account for. The legislation is not targeted at any particular occupation or business sector but 'IR35' has predominantly involved the information technology sector.

Employment Status Indicator tool

[41.3] HM Revenue and Customs has set up a web tool which aims to advise the employment status of individuals by calculating the situation from information supplied. See www.gov.uk/employment-status-indicator. The Employment Status Indicator is not the final determinant of status and should not be relied upon as anything other than a guide (or 'indicator' as the name suggests), though HMRC stated in late 2007 that it will be bound (provided the answers given to the ESI questions accurately reflect the terms and conditions under which the services are provided at the relevant time of the contract) by the ESI outcome where the engager or its authorised representative provides copies of the printer-friendly version of the ESI Result screen, bearing the 14 digit ESI reference number, and the Enquiry Details screen. The user should also retain a copy of the written contract (if available) in relation to the engagement to which the print-out refers along with any other documentation relied upon when completing the ESI. A CIS helpline has also been set up for status advice on 0300 200 3210. See also Tolley's Practical Tax, 17 February 2006, page 29 and www.gov.uk/topic/business-tax/construction-industry-scheme.

Case law

[41.4] Of particular importance in the wider group of labour-only contractors are casual workers. The case of *O'Kelly v Trusthouse Forte plc* [1984] QB 90, [1983] 3 All ER 456, CA (discussed at **41.12** below) underlined the fact that the employment status of a casual worker who works regularly for one employer will depend on whether or not there exists an ongoing obligation on the part of the person who employs him to supply him with work and an ongoing obligation on the part of the worker to take work which is offered (see **14.9** CATEGORISATION). In the absence of such mutual obligations there can be no 'umbrella' contract of service and each engagement (however regular) will generally constitute a contract for services rather than a contract of service. In those circumstances, the casual worker will (unless he obtains his engagements through an agency under the conditions described at **4.5** AGENCY WORKERS) fall to be categorised as a *self-employed earner*. Many cases coming before the Courts more recently have been concerned with 'IR35' and have analysed contracts in great detail. However, occasionally a case comes to court which is not of the IR35 variety. One such case was *Demibourne Ltd v HMRC* [2005] STC SCD 667 Sp C 486 where a company operated a hotel. It had employed a maintenance worker (B), who retired at the age of 65. Following his retirement, B continued to do regular maintenance work at the hotel, but the company treated him as self-employed. HMRC issued a ruling that he was an 'employed earner', within the charge to PAYE and Class 1 NICs. The Special Commissioner upheld HMRC's ruling and dismissed the company's appeal, holding that the changes which took place when B reached the age of 65 were not 'sufficient to replace the relationship of employer and employee with one between client and independent contractor'. The conclusion of the court was that:

> Whatever the parties may have believed that they were doing in arriving at the agreement concerning Mr Bone's engagement, the overall effect of the contractual terms, taken together with the course of conduct as between the parties, was to continue a relationship as master and servant.

In the context of the case, only employer NIC (and PAYE) liability was at stake, since the worker was over state pension age throughout the period in dispute, but the principles of status determination for labour-only workers were well illustrated by the decision.

Class 2 and 4 paid in error following recategorisation

[41.5] As a result of the *Demibourne* case referred to in **41.4** the accounting and tax professional bodies sought agreement with HMRC concerning the formalisation of the long standing arrangement of offsetting tax paid by an individual whilst they are self-employed against the PAYE settlement liability. HMRC has determined that where Class 4 contributions have been paid in error then in accordance with *Social Security (Contributions) Regulations 2001, SI 2001/1004, Reg 101* those payments can be treated as made on account of other contributions properly payable by the same person. Where Class 4 contributions were paid in error by an individual re-categorised as an employee, they may be set against any primary Class 1 contributions payable by a secondary contributor for that employee. The payment of Class 4 contributions does not impact on the state benefit entitlements of the individual.

Where Class 2 contributions are paid which are of the wrong class, or at the wrong rate, or of the wrong amount, HMRC may also treat them as paid on account of contributions properly payable. Where Class 2 contributions were paid in error by an individual re-categorised as an employee they may be set against any primary class 1 NICs payable by a secondary contributor for that employee. See **14.25** CATEGORISATION.

Categories of labour-only contractors

Sales representatives

[41.6] Commercial agents who are remunerated on a commission-only basis are a source of categorisation difficulty in that the written terms under which they perform their services are seldom conclusive evidence of employment or self-employment.

In *Egginton v Reader* [1936] 1 All ER 7, 80 Sol Jo 168 it was held that a sales representative who was remunerated by commission only, sought sales where he thought fit, was free to act as a representative of other companies, and was not subject to any orders or directions from the company which he represented, was a *self-employed earner*. A sales representative operating on similar terms was also held to be a *self-employed earner* in *Chadwick v Pioneer Private Telephone Co Ltd* [1941] 1 All ER 522.

In *Willy Scheidegger Swiss Typewriting School (London) Ltd v Minister of Social Security* (1968) 5 KIR 65 it was decided, following *Rolls Razor Ltd v Cox* [1967] 1 QB 552, [1967] 1 All ER 397, CA, that sales representatives who were paid only by results, were liable to dismissal if sales targets were not reached, worked to no fixed hours or days, had to meet their own expenses, and were at liberty to undertake non-competitive work, were, despite an obligation to pursue the sales policies of the company and to obey all its lawful orders, *self-employed* earners.

In the formal determination against which the *Scheidegger* case was an appeal, the Minister had, on those facts, decided that the sales representatives were employed earners, emphasising the control implicit in the terms relating to the carrying out of sales policies and obedience to lawful orders.

Control (or lack of it) was the deciding factor in two earlier determinations by the Secretary of State for Social Security relating to the status of sales representatives. In *M9 (1950)* a commercial agent who was remunerated on a commission-only basis, visited only such persons and firms as he thought fit, and held another non-competing agency, was held to be a *self-employed* earner. In *M22 (1952)*, however, a commercial agent who, though remunerated on a commission-only basis, was bound by contract to serve the company faithfully and at all times to obey instructions, was held to be an *employed* earner.

Those decisions were reinforced by the Employment Appeal Tribunal decision in *Tyne & Clyde Warehouses Ltd v Hamerton* [1978] ICR 661. There it was held that a sales representative who, each week, was instructed when and where to work and was required to follow detailed selling techniques laid down for him in a staff manual, was held to be subject to a sufficient degree of control for him to be regarded as an *employed earner*, despite the fact that he was remunerated solely by commission.

Drivers and driving instructors

[41.7] In *Ready Mixed Concrete (South East) Ltd v Minister of Pensions and National Insurance* [1968] 2 QB 497, [1968] 1 All ER 433, CA, a person contracted to carry concrete in a vehicle provided by himself for the purpose was held to be *self-employed*, even though he was obliged to wear the uniform and colours of the concrete manufacturer and work to his orders. The contract was held to be inconsistent with a contract of service (and to be, in fact, a contract of carriage) in that control did not extend far enough for the person to cease to be an independent contractor.

In contrast, in *Global Plant Ltd v Secretary of State for Health and Social Security* [1972] 1 QB 139, [1971] 3 All ER 385, a driver of a hired-out industrial plant vehicle, who regarded himself as a self-employed earner and purported to be engaged on a contract which gave him freedom to work when he chose and to send a suitably qualified substitute to work in his stead, was held to be an *employed earner* since, in practice, he worked the normal hours of a full-time employee, attended sites as directed by the company, submitted to the instructions of site foremen, was remunerated on an hourly basis and generally behaved in all respects as would an employee.

Many heavy goods vehicle drivers, having entered into arrangements for the lease of the vehicles they operate from the haulage firm for which they principally work, have operated as self-employed earners, but the status of such drivers was once the subject of a concerted attack by the former DSS with the result that many such drivers were recategorised as *employed earners*. However, it is interesting to note in the IR Tax Bulletin, Issue 8 the Inland Revenue acknowledged the existence of 'long distance self-employed lorry drivers'.

HM Revenue and Customs is clear in its Employment Status Manual where it says: 'Drivers who only provide their labour, driving vehicles owned, maintained and insured by contractors, are likely to be employees. Drivers who also provide the means of transport, that is the vehicle, are likely to be self-employed even if they work mainly for one principal. The vehicle may be one which they own or lease' (HM Revenue and Customs Employment Status Manual ESM4210). Until 5 April 2014, drivers who found their work and were paid through agencies were able to stay outside Class 1 and PAYE liability if they worked under contracts that gave them to the right to send a substitute driver, as the agency rules in the *Categorisation Regs 1978* did not deem such situations to be employment. *Finance Act 2014* and the *Social Security (Categorisation of Earners) (Amendment) Regulations 2014, SI 2014/635* reformed the law in this area in a campaign against perceived (by HMRC) 'false self-employment', so that such drivers will now only be accepted as self-employed if they are not subject to a right of supervision, direction or control as to the manner of performance of the work. See 4 AGENCY WORKERS for full details.

The employment status of a taxicab driver will depend on the arrangements under which he works. At one extreme there are drivers who merely operate cabs owned by some other person in accordance with contracts of service under which they receive a wage; such drivers are *employed earners*. At the other extreme, there are owner-drivers who are independent of any other person; such drivers are *self-employed earners*. Between these two extremes, however, there are two other kinds of taxicab drivers—'settle' or 'on-the-flat' drivers and 'on-the-clock' drivers—the status of whom is problematical. Under a settle agreement a driver pays for his own fuel and hires his cab from the owner for a fixed weekly amount which entitles him to its use for twelve hours of every day in the week and to all his takings. Under the less common on-the-clock agreement, the owner of the cab pays for all fuel and at the end of each week receives from the driver a percentage of the fares registered on the clock. The driver is left with the remainder of the registered fares and any tips he has received. The consensus of judicial thought seems to be that in neither case will the driver be the employee of the cab owner since neither type of contract is a contract of service. The relationship in both cases is probably that of bailor and bailee (*Smith v General Motor Cab Co Ltd* [1911] AC 188; *London General Cab Co v IRC* [1950] 2 All ER 566, 29 TC 407; *Challinor v Taylor* [1972] ICR 129), so that, in the absence of a categorisation regulation which imposes employed earner status (such as that, long since repealed, which existed under *National Insurance (Classification) Regulations 1948*), drivers under either type of agreement will now, under normal circumstances, be regarded as *self-employed earners* for contribution purposes.

In *BSM (1257) Ltd v Secretary of State for Social Services* [1978] ICR 894 it was held that a written contract between a driving instructor and a car-owning operating company expressly intended to establish the instructor as a self-employed earner succeeded in doing so, since the terms of the contract itself were consistent with the relationship of engager and independent contractor and the relationship was in fact as stated by the contract, ie the company took bookings and payment, and the instructor would be available at stated times but could notify the office that he would not be available and could send a substitute if necessary; payment would be by the lesson and the operating company would make no provision for sickness, holidays or pension.

Motorcycle despatch riders

[41.8] The employment status of motorcycle despatch riders will also depend on the arrangements under which they operate. Where (as is usually the case) the rider owns his own motorcycle, provides his own protective clothing, personally bears the costs of road tax, insurance, fuel, repairs etc, and is remunerated only by reference to actual mileage and/or the contract price, it is arguable on the basis of the economic reality test (see **14.14** CATEGORISATION) that he is truly in business on his own account and is a self-employed earner fulfilling contracts for carriage. Against this, however, must be set the fact that the rider will generally obtain work only from a single firm which will, itself, obtain the contracts for the delivery of mail or goods which the rider will then execute. Furthermore, the rider's radio will usually be hired to him by the firm for which he works, and the firm will usually insure itself in respect of general liability for the goods etc carried.

Construction workers

[41.9] Although the construction industry tax deduction scheme, first introduced in 1975, is of no direct application for contribution purposes, the then DHSS had, historically, stated that it would normally accept a certificate issued under the scheme as evidence of self-employment unless investigation revealed that a contract of service was in existence. (Hansard 13 November 1981 Vol 12 No 8 Pt II Col 188). Whether a contract of service does exist or not will be determined by application of the usual tests (see **14.9** to **14.13** CATEGORISATION).

Thus, in *Ferguson v John Dawson & Partners (Contractors) Ltd* [1976] 3 All ER 817, [1976] 1 WLR 1213, CA, a 'lump labourer' who regarded himself as a self-employed earner was held to be under a contract of service (and, accordingly, an *employed earner*) as his employers controlled not only the work he did but also the method and manner in which he did it, even supplying him with the necessary tools.

DSS practice then moved towards disregarding a 714 certificate issued by the former Inland Revenue. It was presumed that the then Inland Revenue had not made detailed enquiries into a subcontractor's employment status before issuing a 714 certificate (replaced until 6 April 2007 by CIS5, CIS5 (Partner) or CIS6), unless there was evidence to the contrary. With the 1999 merger, self-employed status is questioned simultaneously for both tax and National Insurance purposes.

Example

Subbies Ltd has taken on John, Paul, George and Jimbo to service a new contract to build a motel on the outskirts of Guildford. Following an earlier employer compliance visit the current work force are being treated as employees and Class 1 contributions are being deducted. However, the new workers all declare that they are subcontractors within the CIS. Subbies Ltd needs to verify this by calling HMRC's CIS Helpline on Tel 0300 200 3210 (or +44 161 930 8706) as it is not clear from the booklet CIS340 what their status is and HMRC advises using the Employment Status Indicator Tool at www.gov.uk/employment-status-indicator.

John runs his own small construction business and will be providing the subcontract work in building the slipway off the dual carriageway leading to the motel. Paul is to provide electrical and plumbing expertise for the duration of the contract and is expected to be on site for three months. George is a self-employed site supervisor and estimator who provides his services on an irregular basis for Subbies Ltd from his office at home and has previously had an Employment Tribunal decision declare him to be self-employed (but see below). Jimbo is a qualified carpet fitter and will lay all the carpets in the motel. Subbies Ltd should be aware that carpet fitting does not come within the CIS and the only question that arises is therefore whether Jimbo is employed by Subbies Ltd or is self-employed.

Clearly a lot more information is required from Subbies Ltd on the terms of the engagements but initially the likely view by reference to CIS349 'Are your workers employed or self-employed? – advice for contractors' might be that John could be self-employed; if the circumstances indicate that he provides his own heavy equipment and workforce to do the slip road this would be a decisive factor and, if there was a penalty clause for delays in the completion of the road which might delay the building of the motel, this would further reinforce a determination of self-employment.

Paul's situation seems to indicate that he will supply his own small tools with no financial risk amongst other things. He will probably be an employee for the duration of the contract even though it is relatively short.

George is providing hard hat and white collar services and is already classed as self-employed. However, these facts do not mean that Subbies Ltd should automatically treat him as self-employed even though he may provide white collar services from his home base. Also, the Employment Tribunal determination has no binding force on the decision in these particular circumstances.

Jimbo is a self-employed carpet and lino fitter who supplies his own tools for each job he undertakes.

Subbies Ltd should have starter declarations (formerly forms P46) completed by Paul and George and deduct tax and Class 1 NICs from the first and subsequent payments. Subbies Ltd files online using the HMRC's CIS Online service. Subbies Ltd will also have to submit monthly returns of payments made to subcontractors as well as nil returns where relevant, and this will only cease when trading has ceased. Any monthly return, even if it is a nil return, will attract a penalty if it is late. John's situation should be reviewed with the IR status officer with the full facts and supporting documents as quickly as possible. See IR Tax Bulletin, April 1997, page 413. See HMRC guidance note issued in connection with monthly returns issued on 24 May 2006. Jimbo is most probably self-employed and this would be supported by comments by the General Commissioner in *Castle Construction (Chesterfield) Ltd v Revenue and Customs Comrs* [2009] STC (SCD) 97 (see below) regarding categories of workers on a construction project.

In connection with the above example reference might be made to *Lewis (t/a MAL Scaffolding) & Others v HMRC* [2006] STC SCD 253 Sp C 527 where HMRC issued rulings that a number of construction industry workers, who worked for the proprietor of a scaffolding business, were 'employed earners' and liable to Class 1 NICs. HMRC also issued determinations under *Income Tax (PAYE) Regulations 2003, SI 2003/2682, Reg 80* to the proprietor. The proprietor and the workers appealed, contending that they were independent subcontractors. The Special Commissioner reviewed the evidence in detail, accepted this contention, and allowed all the appeals.

The Commissioner specifically declined to follow an earlier decision of the Employment Tribunal, which had held that two of the workers were employees and entitled to payments in lieu of holiday at the termination of their contracts. The Commissioner observed that 'the relevant regulation has its own, extended, definition of employee for the purposes of the benefits claimed by the claimants. They could be self-employed and also entitled to holiday pay.' On the evidence, the relationship between the proprietor and the workers was 'an informal and undocumented verbal contract for services and not any form of contract of service'.

In *Castle Construction (Chesterfield) Ltd v HMRC* [2009] STC 97 Sp C 723, HMRC issued rulings that 321 construction industry workers, who worked for a building company, were 'employed earners' and liable to Class 1 National Insurance contributions. It also issued determinations under *Income Tax (PAYE) Regulations 2003, SI 2003/2682, Reg 80*. The company appealed, contending that the workers were self-employed subcontractors. The Special Commissioner reviewed the evidence in detail and held that 314 of the workers (including all the bricklayers and scaffolders) were self-employed, but that the seven truck or lorry drivers were employees. The Commissioner observed that, in 2000, following a previous enquiry, HMRC had accepted that the bricklayers working for the company were self-employed subcontractors. They worked under terms that were 'reasonably common and traditional in the building industry'. The truck and lorry drivers were in a different position, since they were 'subject to more potential control'. An interesting point to note in the decision is that the judge criticised mildly the HMRC compliance officer concerned for issuing a blanket 'employee' opinion covering the bricklayers before she had interviewed any of them.

In *Wright v Revenue and Customs Comrs* [2009] UKFTT 53 (TC), [2009] SFTD 84 a case of sub-contracted 'employed earners' was remitted to the First-tier Tax Tribunal and W's appeal was dismissed but the Tribunal judge went on to consider the degree of control in such matters.

In *Littlewood (t/a Window and Door Services) v Revenue and Customs Comrs* [2009] STC (SCD) 243, a partnership carried on a business of installing windows, doors and curtain walling in commercial buildings. It treated its workers as self-employed subcontractors, and operated the Construction Industry Scheme. HMRC issued determinations under *Income Tax (PAYE) Regulations 2003, SI 2003/2682, Reg 80* on the basis that the partnership should have treated the workers as employees. The partnership appealed. The Special Commissioner allowed the appeal, applying the principles laid down in *Ready Mixed Concrete (South East) Ltd v Minister of Pensions and National Insurance* [1968] 2 QB 497, [1968] 1 All ER 433, CA, holding that the partnership 'did not exercise control over the workers', so that the contracts were contracts for services rather than contracts of service.

All the changes over the years affecting the construction industry and its workers may well have been a result of a Privy Council case concerning a construction worker: *Lee Ting Sang v Chung Chi-Keung* [1990] ICR 409. Mr Lee was a mason who was injured while working for Mr Chung, a subcontractor, on a construction site in Hong Kong. His application for compensation under the Hong Kong Employees' Compensation Ordinance had been refused on the grounds that he was a self-employed worker, not an employee. On appeal from the judgment of the Court of Appeal of Hong Kong, the Privy Council held that Mr Lee was, in fact, an *employed earner*. Referring with approval to the tests laid down by Cooke J in *Market Investigations Ltd v Minister of Social Security* (see **14.14** CATEGORISATION), Lord Griffiths said:

> The applicant did not provide his own equipment, the equipment was provided by his employer. He did not hire his own helpers; this emerged with clarity in his evidence when he explained that he gave priority to [Chung Chi-Keung's] work and if asked by [Chung Chi-Keung] to do an urgent job he would tell those he was

> working for that they would have to employ someone else: if he was an independent contractor in business on his own account, one would expect that he would attempt to keep both contracts by hiring others to fill the contract he had to leave. He had no responsibility for investment in, or management of, the work on the construction site, he simply turned up for work and chipped off concrete to the required depth upon the beams indicated to him on a plan by [Chung Chi-Keung]. There is no suggestion in the evidence that he priced the job which is normally a feature of the business approach of a subcontractor; he was paid either a piecework rate or a daily rate according to the nature of the work he was doing. It is true that he was not supervised in his work, but this is not surprising, he was a skilled man and he had been told the beams upon which he was to work and the depth to which they were to be cut and his work was measured to see that he had achieved that result. There was no question of his being called upon to exercise any skill or judgment as to which beams required chipping or as to the depths that they were to be cut. He was simply told what to do and left to get on with it . . . Taking all the foregoing considerations into account the picture emerges of a skilled artisan earning his living by working for more than one employer as an employee and not as a small businessman venturing into business on his own account as an independent contractor with all its attendant risks. The applicant ran no risk whatsoever save that of being unable to find employment . . .

Lord Griffiths specifically advised that the application of the 'integration' test (see **14.13** CATEGORISATION) (which had been relied on in the Hong Kong courts) is likely to be misleading in the context of the employment status of construction workers.

Leaflet CIS349 reiterated the standard tests of control (see **14.11** CATEGORISATION), mutual obligations (see **14.4** CATEGORISATION) and integration (see **14.13** CATEGORISATION) it does go into the practicalities of the industry in determining whether someone is an employee or self-employed. In this connection, the leaflet summarises the common industry indicators as follows:

Employment

- The contractor has the right to control what the worker has to do – where, when and how it is done – even if the contractor rarely uses that control;
- The worker supplies only his or her own small tools;
- The worker does not risk his or her own money and there is no possibility that he or she will suffer a financial loss;
- The worker has no business organisation, for example, a yard, stock, materials, or workers. (These examples are not exhaustive);
- The worker is paid by the hour, day, week or month.

Self-employment

- Within an overall deadline, the worker has the right to decide how and when the work will be done;
- The worker supplies the materials, plant or heavy equipment needed for the job;
- The worker bids for a job and will bear the additional cost if the job ends up costing more than the worker's original estimate;
- The worker has a right to hire other people who answer to him or her and are paid by him or her to do the job;

- The worker is paid an agreed amount for the job regardless of how long it takes.

Needless to say the above lists are not conclusive; the determining factor will be the actual terms and conditions that apply to that particular job. The transition from apprenticeship to normal working will not normally result in the individual being self-employed unless there is a material change in the terms and conditions applying.

The obvious criteria that employers might be advised to concentrate on are:

- hourly/daily paid subcontractors;
- continuous employment periods eg exceeding two years;
- transport provided to and from home;
- holiday and sick pay provided.

Any other relevant matters should also be taken into account.

One of the main reasons for the April 2014 change in the *Categorisation Regs 1978* to counter so-called 'false self-employment' was a growth in recent years of contracting in the construction industry via so-called 'payroll companies'. When the change was announced, the impact assessment noted that some 200,000 labour-only construction workers were working in this way, relying on the agency worker rules and a right of substitution to escape from PAYE and Class 1 NIC liability. See **4** AGENCY WORKERS for the full rationale and details of the changes.

Market researchers

[41.10] The Secretary of State for Social Security formerly determined that a woman conducting surveys on the listening and viewing habits of the public was not an employed earner because she was given only general guidance in her duties and was not subject to detailed control. (*M48 (1956)*). However, it was held in *Market Investigations Ltd v Minister of Social Security* [1969] 2 QB 173, [1968] 3 All ER 732 that, because of the degree of control exercised by Market Investigations Ltd over their interviewers and because, approaching matters from a different angle, the interviewers could not truly be said to be performing their services as persons in business on their own account, the interviewers were *employed earners* (see **14.2** CATEGORISATION). At page 737 of the *Market Investigations Ltd* case, Cooke, J describes the 'economic reality test'.

> 'The fundamental test to be applied is this: "Is the person who has engaged himself to perform these services performing them as a person in business on his own account?" If the answer to that question is "yes", then the contract is a contract for services. If the answer is "no", then the contract is a contract of service. No exhaustive list has been compiled and perhaps no exhaustive list can be compiled of considerations which are relevant in determining that question, nor can strict rules be laid down as to the relative weight which the various considerations should carry in particular cases. The most that can be said is that control will no doubt always have to be considered, although it can no longer be regarded as the sole determining factor; and that factors, which may be of importance, are such matters as whether the man performing the services provides his own equipment, whether he

> hires his own helpers, what degree of financial risk he takes, what degree of responsibility for investment and management he has, and whether and how far he has an opportunity of profiting from sound management in the performance of his task.'

It is clear from the decision in *Hall v Lorimer* (see **41.15** below) that Cooke, J's list is *not* a checklist but merely an indication of the factors to be weighed in any case and this is clear from the wording of HMRC literature which uses words such as 'probably', 'usually' and 'guidelines'.

Armed with the decision in *Market Investigations* HM Revenue and Customs is in no doubt that all market researchers are employed persons and any allegation of self-employment is to be referred to the local Status Inspector (HM Revenue and Customs Employment Status Manual ESM4220). Further, the modified PAYE arrangements in respect of payments to market research interviewers, which applied to members of the British Market Research Association and the Market Research Society, ceased from 6 April 2007. Market researchers will also often be sourced via an agency and, given that their working methods are strictly set out in their instructions, are likely to be deemed employees under the AGENCY WORKERS 4 rules.

Office workers

[41.11] In *Rennison & Son v Minister of Social Security* (1970) 10 KIR 65, 114 Sol Jo 952 it was held that employees of a firm of solicitors remained *employed earners* despite their entering into a contract with the firm which stipulated that they were to be treated as self-employed earners in partnership with each other. The arrangement involved the weekly payment of a lump sum to the cashier (who was one of the parties to the arrangement) and his division of it between himself and the others on the basis of hours worked at an hourly rate. The arrangement would now be caught by the rules relating to AGENCY WORKERS 4 but the case is of importance in showing that arrangements which are clearly artificial and which do not change the reality of a relationship will almost always be overturned by the court. Office 'temps' working through agencies could, until 6 April 2014, escape deemed employee status by ensuring that they had a right of substitution, but that route has now been closed. See AGENCY WORKERS 4 for the full rationale and details of the changes.

Catering staff

[41.12] In *O'Kelly v Trusthouse Forte plc* [1984] QB 90, [1983] 3 All ER 456, CA the Court of Appeal restored the decision of an industrial tribunal that so-called 'regular casuals' (ie casual staff engaged on a regular basis to such an extent that some of their number had no other work) who formed the main part of the banqueting staff of the banqueting business carried on by Trusthouse Forte at the Grosvenor House Hotel were in business on their own account as independent contractors supplying services to the company. Although the regular casuals were remunerated for work actually performed; performed their work under the direction and control of Trusthouse Forte; were (when they attended functions) part of Trusthouse Forte's organisation and were represented in the staff consultation process; wore clothing and used equipment provided by Trusthouse Forte; were paid weekly in arrears under deduction of income tax and National Insurance contributions; were organised on the basis of a weekly rota and required permission to take time off from rostered duties; were subject to a disciplinary and grievance procedure and received holiday pay or an incentive bonus calculated by reference to past service, *there was no obligation on Trusthouse Forte to offer them work and there was no obligation on them to take the work offered.* In the absence of such mutual obligations, there could be no 'umbrella' contract of service and each engagement constituted a separate contract for services.

In such circumstances, no liability for Class 1 contributions can arise unless the persons concerned are categorised as employed earners by regulation (see **14.29** CATEGORISATION).

It should be noted, however, that mutual obligations may arise out of custom and almost certainly will so arise where a worker is offered and accepts work on a day-in, day-out basis over a significant period of time. (*Airfix Footwear Ltd v Cope* [1978] ICR 1210; *St Neots Nethermere Ltd v Gardiner* [1984] ICR 612). Even work offered and accepted on a week-in, week-out basis where the number of days varies will, in some instances, suffice. In *Four Seasons (Inn on the Park) Ltd v Hamarat 17.4.85 EAT 369/84*, for example, mutual obligations were held to have come into existence between a wine waiter and a hotel for which, since 1976, he had worked exclusively for between one or two and six days a week. The industrial tribunal (distinguishing the case from the *O'Kelly* case) found that 'if the applicant had not undertaken work offered to him by the respondent, further work would have been withheld. Equally, if the respondent had not offered further work to the applicant, he would have removed his services to some other form of employment'. The tribunal's decision that Mr Hamarat was, therefore, an employed earner was upheld by the Employment Appeal Tribunal.

Even where mutual obligations are found to be absent in situations where there is a regular succession of short-term contracts, each contract may (exceptionally) be found to be a contract of service rather than a contract for services. Thus, in *Letheby and Christopher Ltd v Bangurah* 19 May 1987 EAT 639/86, a Mrs Bangurah who worked on a regular but casual basis as a waitress and barmaid for a race-course catering company was found to have worked under a series of individual contracts which the EAT, though not having to decide the point, seems to have regarded as contracts of employment.

The catering industry became the subject of the then Inland Revenue's investigations from the latter part of 2002, which involved matters such as the payment of cash amounts by suppliers to chefs in return for their recommendation and use of the suppliers goods and services. Clearly these payments arose out of the chefs' employment position and therefore was part of their tax and NICable remuneration. See statement by the then Inland Revenue Chairman Nicholas Montagu to CIOT 9 January 2003. See Simon's Tax Intelligence, 16 January 2003.

Agricultural workers

[41.13] The employment status of most agricultural workers is determinable, without difficulty, by application of the normal tests (see CATEGORISATION **14**). Regular full-time farm workers will be under contracts of service and will be *employed earners*, while contractors such as threshers, ploughmen and hauliers who supply their own equipment and perform their tasks unsupervised and in their own way will generally be *self-employed earners*. (HM Revenue and Customs Employment Status Manual ESM4001). Former Inland Revenue Leaflet, P5, Para 15, (now withdrawn) advised that gangmasters who supply and pay squads for potato, onion and beet-lifting, pea, fruit and hop-picking, etc were to be regarded as *self-employed earners* provided they were not in the regular employment of the grower to whom they supplied the services in question, as were milkers who contracted to milk cows at a price per gallon or per cow and rat catchers, rabbit catchers, thatchers etc who went from farm to farm performing their services. A statement involving 16 questions slanted towards employment status was obtained in some cases by the former CA from the farmer as to the working arrangements of the farm worker and it is often this statement that forms the basis of contentious issues.

Although most of that advice is probably still sound, the question of the status of a gangmaster must now always be considered in the light of *Andrews v King* [1991] STC 481. There it was held that Mr Andrews, a master of a potato picking and/or grading gang was *not* a self-employed earner. For a period of just over two years, Mr Andrews was engaged on various days by J W Stanberry Ltd, potato merchants, in connection with potato picking and/or grading. He would telephone the company on an evening and if he found there was work available for the following day, he would contact the men necessary, supply transport and arrange for them and himself to be on site the next morning. Payment was made to Mr Andrews who, after deducting petrol contributions, divided the pay between himself and the gang members. Referring with approval to the tests laid down by Cooke J in *Market Investigations Ltd v Minister of Social Security* (see **14.14** CATEGORISATION), Sir Nicolas Browne-Wilkinson V-C said:

> Beyond the selection of the members of the gang the taxpayer had no rights of control. Where and when the work was to be done were matters for Stanberrys. The work of the whole gang including the taxpayer was supervised by Stanberrys. There is no indication that [Mr Andrews] had any powers of control over the members of the gang. The evidence was that he was subject to the control of Stanberrys. Turning to the question whether the taxpayer provided equipment for carrying out the work, it is clear that he did not. The only equipment he provided was a van which was not used to do the work but to get to the place of work. Even in relation to the van, the direct cost of getting there in the form of petrol was not paid by him alone but was shared by the other members of the gang. As to the question whether or not he hired his own helpers, he certainly selected them but he did not himself pay them any wages. He did not engage men, pay them and then provide a gang en bloc to Stanberrys in return for a fixed charge. Having selected his gang, they all went together to the place of work selected by Stanberrys and the total sum paid for the work by Stanberrys was a sum which all the members of the gang had agreed, not [Mr Andrews] by himself. The net proceeds, after deduction of petrol money, were divided equally between them. In my judgment it is impossible to call that 'hiring helpers'. As to the question whether or not [Mr Andrews] was running any financial

> risk, I can see none beyond the risk run by many casual labourers in agriculture that if there is no work because of weather conditions there is no payment. There was no question of investment or management so far as [Mr Andrews] was concerned. There was no question of his profiting from sound management since he took the same reward as all other members of the gang. He had no extra remuneration reflecting in any way the quality of his management in the selection and production of the gang at the workplace. Looking at those elements and standing back and considering the case as a whole, one asks the basic question: Was [Mr Andrews] in business on his own account? I cannot see that he was carrying on any business . . .

Where a gangmaster *is* self-employed, he has a responsibility to deduct and account for PAYE and Class 1 National Insurance contributions on the amounts he pays to the individual squad members. (See CWG2 (2018 to 2019), para 4.4.2). Because many gangmasters fail to discharge that responsibility, HM Revenue and Customs established an Agricultural Compliance Unit which is charged with the task of enforcing compliance. HM Revenue and Customs says:

> Agricultural gangmasters are middle men who supply casual labour for farmers, canning factories and other agricultural concerns at peak times. Gangmasters should normally operate PAYE and account for National Insurance contributions on the wages they pay to work forces they supply. They should also account for tax on their own business profits. There is fierce competition for work among gangmasters. Many gangmasters do fulfil all their tax obligations, but others do not. They may also disregard social security, employment, and health and safety laws. Their overheads are thus substantially lower than the 'legitimate' gangmasters, who may find their prices are undercut, and their businesses threatened.
>
> (IR Press Release, 2 September 1988).

The Gangmaster (Licensing) Act 2004, s 7 has required gangmasters to obtain a licence since 1 October 2006 and they must be entered on a public register. It is a criminal offence for a gangmaster in many trades to operate without a licence (*section 12(4)*). Specifically excluded are (*inter alia*) the short term loan of workers between farms, the supply of individual specialist farm workers and the supply of labour to process non-farm products which include an agricultural component (such as cosmetics). Under the *Act* a gangmaster is required to co-operate with the licensing authority to provide identity to their workers and/or agents, not to withhold personal documents from workers, to produce for inspection by the principal their licences/identification and to keep licences for a period of five years starting with the date on which the licensable conduct was performed. See also DEFRA Committee Report 'Gangmasters: Government Reply to the Committee's Report', 17 December 2003, HC 122. [*Agricultural Wages Act 1948, s 17; Employment Agencies Act 1973, s 13(3); Working Time Regulations 1998; The Gangmaster (Licensing) Act 2004; Gangmasters Licensing (Exclusions) Regs 2006; Gangmasters Appeals Regs 2006; DEFRA Press Release 107/06, 13 March 2006; Gangmasters (Licensing Conditions)(No 2) Amendment Rules 2008, SI 2008/638*]. See also www.gov.uk/gangmasters-licensing-authority.

The forms of engagement of dairy herdsmen vary in practice and the employment status of any individual herdsman will depend on the particular facts. (Hansard 5 December 1983 Vol 50 Col 26). (HM Revenue and Customs Employment Status Manual ESM4002).

In the case of contract milkers a specific contract (Agreement LL 12) has typically been entered into if they were to be self-employed and this was the result of discussions between the former CA, National Farmer's Union and Milk Marketing Board (at the time). The CA contended that the self-employed milker must adhere strictly to the contract and if they do not they become relief milkers and are treated as employees. Where the milker takes full responsibility for the care, breeding and milking of the herd and engages and meets the expense of other workers to help with the fulfilment of his or her obligations, the milker is likely to be self-employed. The National Farmers Union provides advice to contract milkers on the implications of their prospective terms and conditions. (HM Revenue and Customs Employment Status Manual ESM4002). The two large agencies supplying contract milkers do so on a self-employed contract basis.

Workers engaged for a fixed sum payable at the end of a six-month or annual 'hiring', eg at Whitsun or Martinmas, are *employed earners*.

Where a farmer provides his workers with free board and lodging, this is a benefit in kind and is generally disregarded for Class 1 contribution purposes (see **29.60** EARNINGS FROM EMPLOYMENT: GENERAL). However, where a board and lodging allowance is paid, whether to the employee or, after deduction from wages, to the accommodation provider, contributions may be due on the gross wage.

Particular difficulties arise in relation to *irregular casual workers* engaged for no fixed period in the field or orchard in work such as fruit picking and remunerated on a piece-work basis. In such circumstances, the grower generally has no way of identifying individual workers, controlling their hours of work or recording their earnings, and, accordingly, in 1975, the National Farmers' Union negotiated a working arrangement with the then DHSS under which the DHSS agreed not to seek contributions in respect of such workers. In 1978, further discussions between the NFU and the DSS resulted in a DSS agreement not to disturb the earlier working arrangement. (NFU Cyclo 918/74/78 Econ Y57 of 17 May 1978). This position was confirmed in Parliament in 1983. (Hansard 28 July 1983 Col 591). In 1984, the issue was again reviewed by the NFU and the DSS with the result that, so far as the irregular casual category of workers was concerned:

> The previously agreed arrangements for National Insurance contributions, as set out in the May 1978 statement, remain unchanged except that since the original agreement was reached the DSS have made clear that the simple notation of names and addresses will not necessarily make irregular casuals ineligible for this category.
>
> (NFU Cyclo 456/29/84 Econ O29 of 29 February 1984).

The DSS was at pains to point out, however, that

> it is not a case of irregular casuals having no liability for NICs. Rather, the department has taken a realistic approach to the particular characteristics and difficulties of this industry, and has decided not to attempt to enforce liability.
>
> (Letter from DSS, 5 June 1987).

In other words, the forms of engagement of most casual crop pickers are such that they will generally be *employed earners*. (Hansard 5 December 1983 Vol 50 Col 26). They are merely treated as non-employed as a matter of convenience. The position is confirmed as follows, if the employee is engaged on an irregular basis:

- to work outdoors harvesting perishable crops;
- is paid off at the end of each engagement, eg at the end of the day; or
- has no contract for further employment,

For many years, NICs were not collected where it was impossible for the employer to identify individuals and records their earnings.

If the identity details were known, NICs were due when the earnings for each engagement exceeded the ET:

- the NICs due were worked out at the time the earnings were paid; and
- form P11 etc was completed as detailed in the former Employer Helpbook E13.

(Current information: CWG2 (2018 to 2019), para 4.4.1.)

The arrival of RTI created problems for many farmers using harvest casuals. The guidance on liability now states:

- 'if earnings do not exceed the Primary Threshold (PT) or Secondary Threshold (ST) no NICs are payable;
- if earnings reach or exceed the Lower Earnings Limit (LEL) but do not exceed the PT the employee is treated as having paid NICs when claiming benefit;
- if earnings exceed the PT, Class 1 NICs are payable by the employee;
- if earnings exceed the ST, Class 1 NICs are payable by the employer.'

(CWG2 (2018 to 2019), para 4.4.1.)

The RTI-specific guidance states ' . . . employers of harvest casuals who pay someone on more than one occasion should note that they can report payments to a particular employee on a weekly basis provided that:

- each individual payment is below the Lower Earning Limit (LEL) of [£116]. Employers should report any payments above the LEL separately;
- the weekly Full Payment Submission (FPS) report is made within the seven-day period allowed for the earliest payment (the seven-day period begins on the day after the day on which the earliest payment is made).

For reporting purposes, the harvest casual is treated as starting on the date of the first payment and treated as leaving on the date of the last payment covered by the FPS.'

Regular casual workers also are regarded as *employed earners* but in their case no concessionary treatment is available. A regular casual is regarded as a person who is known to the grower, is usually paid weekly and will normally move from one casual job to another as the season proceeds. Class 1 contribution liabilities are to be accounted for in the normal way as regards earnings paid to such persons (Hansard 28 July 1983 Col 591). See Leaflet CWG2 (2018 to 2019), para 4.4.1.

The Agricultural Compliance Unit, it is understood, took an interest in large fruit farms with large numbers of casual pickers. Where, for example, foreign students are recruited overseas by an agency offering work for a particular season, the ACU argues that they are not casual harvest employees and that full PAYE and NIC procedures should be operated. This position has been bolstered by the 6 April 2014 changes to the *Categorisation Regs 1978* to create a liability for offshore employment intermediary, their UK agents or UK end clients. Where students work continuously then tax and NICs will be in point and a starter declaration will need to be completed.

The true status of both regular and irregular casuals is, in any event, questionable following the decision in *O'Kelly v Trusthouse Forte plc*. (See **41.12** above).

In Minister of State's decision *M34 (1953)* it was decided that a father and son who cleared areas of standing timber as dictated by the forest manager were *self-employed earners* since they determined their own methods of performance of their task and supplied most of their own equipment. By contrast, it was held in *M40 (1953)* that two timber fellers who were more closely controlled, in that the company foreman would dictate the trees to be felled and the method of felling, were *employed earners*.

Journalists

[41.14] In *Beloff v Pressdram Ltd* [1973] 1 All ER 241, [1973] FSR 33, it was held that a political and lobby correspondent of the Observer newspaper was an *employed earner* even though the Observer exercised little control over her work and even though she engaged in other forms of journalism and authorship while working for the Observer newspaper. The court applied both the 'integration test' (see **14.13** categorisation) and the 'economic reality test' (see **14.14** categorisation) and found that the woman in question was 'an integral part of the business' carried on by the Observer and was not in business on her own account.

Earlier, the Secretary of State for Social Security had determined that a newspaper correspondent who worked in Great Britain for an Italian newspaper was an *employed earner*. (*M33 (1953)*). Although he worked here without supervision, his activities were subjected to a high degree of control in that he was required not only to devote substantially the whole of his time to the regular transmission of news but was required also to submit one or two special articles each month and to write articles on given subjects when instructed to do so.

Although a number of journalists enjoyed self-employed status previously, Inland Revenue activity in the years leading up to 1984 resulted in more than 700 being re-categorised as employed earners. (Hansard 16 January 1984 Vol 52 Col 14).

Film and TV industry workers

[41.15] On 30 March 1983, the then Inland Revenue announced that, having carried out a review of the employment status of workers engaged on 'freelance' terms within the film and allied industries and having had an extensive series of discussions with representative bodies within the industry, it had come to the conclusion that 'a number of workers engaged on "freelance" terms within the industry are engaged as employees under contracts of service, either written or oral' and that, where those workers had been treated as self-employed, re-categorisation would take place from 6 April 1983. (Press Release). By the end of 1983, over 7,000 such workers had been re-categorised as employed earners. (Hansard 16 January 1984 Vol 52 Col 14).

The then Inland Revenue identified in Summer 2003 the following casual and freelance staff in the film, television and production industry as genuinely *self-employed*. HMRC reissued the guidance in April 2011 but there is no change to the original rulings.

ADVANCE RIGGER	Where the contract requires substantial provision of equipment. (*See Note 5)*
*ANIMAL HANDLER	
*ANIMATION DIRECTOR	
*ANIMATION PRODUCTION CO-ORDINATOR	
ANIMATOR	Where the work is performed other than on premises provided by the engager and the contract requires substantial provision of equipment. (*See Note 5*)
*ANIMATRONIC MODEL DESIGNER	
*ART DIRECTOR	
ASSISTANT ART DIRECTOR	Where the work is performed other than on premises provided by the engager. (*See Note 5*)
ASSISTANT COSTUME DESIGNER	Where the work is performed other than on premises provided by the engager or the contract requires substantial provision of materials. (*See Note 5*)
*ASSOCIATE PRODUCER	Except where engaged primarily for general research
*AUDITIONER	
BACKGROUND ARTIST	Where the work is performed other than on premises provided by the engager. (*See Note 5*)
CAMERA OPERATOR	Where the contract requires substantial provision of equipment. (*See Note 5*)
CAMERAPERSON	Where the contract requires substantial provision of equipment. (*See Note 5*)
*CASTING DIRECTOR	

*CHAPERONE/TUTOR	
*CHOREOGRAPHER	
*COMPOSER	
CONSTRUCTION MANAGER	Where the contract requires substantial provision of equipment. (*See Note 5*)
CONTINUITY	Where script breakdown is an integral part of the contract.
CONTRIBUTOR	Where the payment is made on a per contribution basis.
*CO-PRODUCER	
COSTUME DESIGNER	Where the work is performed other than premises provided by the engager or the contract requires substantial provision of materials. (*See Note 5*)
*CRICKET SCORER	
*DIRECTOR	
*DIRECTOR OF PHOTOGRAPHY	
DRESSMAKER	Where the work is performed other than on the premises provided by the engager. (*See Note 5*)
DRIVER	Where contract requires the driver to provide his own vehicle.
*EDITOR	
*EXECUTIVE PRODUCER	
*FIGHT ARRANGER	
*FILM STYLIST	
*FIRST ASSISTANT DIRECTOR	
GAFFER	Where the contract requires substantial provision of equipment. (*See Note 5*)
GRAPHIC ARTIST	Where the work is performed other than on premises provided by the engager. (*See Note 5*)
GRAPHIC DESIGNER	Where the work is performed other than on the premises provided by the engager. (*See Note 5*)
GRIP	Where contract requires substantial provision of equipment. (*See Note 5*)
HAIRDRESSER	Where the contract requires substantial provision of equipment (including wigs), or 50% or more of the work is performed other than on premises provided by the engager. (*See Note 5*)

*HEAD OF ART DEPARTMENT	
HEAD OF DEPARTMENT RIGGER	Where the contract requires substantial provision of equipment. (*See Note 5*)
LANGUAGE ASSESSOR	Where used on an occasional basis to check style and delivery of foreign language broadcasts.
LETTERING ARTIST	Where the work is performed other than on premises provided by the engager. (*See Note 5*)
LETTERING DESIGNER	Where the work is performed other than on premises provided by the engager. (*See Note 5*)
LIGHTING CAMERAPERSON	Where responsible for designing lighting or photography.
LIGHTING DIRECTOR	Where responsible for designing lighting or photography.
*LINE PRODUCER	
LOCATION MANAGER	Where the contract requires provision of facilities by the worker.
MAKE-UP ARTIST	Where the contract requires provision of a standard make-up kit by the worker, or 50% or more [of the work] is performed other than on premises provided by the engager. (*See Note 5*)
*MATRON	
MODEL CAMERA	Where the contract requires substantial provision of equipment. (*See Note 5*)
MODEL DESIGNER	Where the engagement requires the provision of facilities and equipment/materials by the individual. (*See Note 5*)
MODEL MAKER	Where the engagement requires the provision of facilities and equipment/materials by the individual. (*See Note 5*)
*MODELLER	
MUSICAL ARRANGER	Where the work is performed other than on premises provided by the engager. (*See Note 5*)
*MUSICAL ASSOCIATE	
MUSICAL COPYCAT	Where the work is performed other than on premises provided by the engager. (*See Note 5*)
*MUSICAL DIRECTOR	
*MUSICAL SCORE READER	

*NURSE	
*PHOTOGRAPHIC STYLIST	
*POST PRODUCTION SUPERVISOR	
PRINTER	Where the work is performed other than on premises provided by the engager. (*See Note 5*)
*PRODUCER	
PRODUCTION ACCOUNTANT	Where the contract requires provision of relevant facilities by the worker.
PRODUCTION ASSISTANT	Where script breakdown is an integral part of the contract.
*PRODUCTION BUYER	
*PRODUCTION DESIGNER	
*PRODUCTION MANAGER	
*PRODUCTION SUPERVISOR	
PROPERTY MASTER	Where the contract requires substantial provision of equipment (including props). (*See Note 5*)
PROPERTY HAND	Where the contract requires substantial provision of equipment (including props). (*See Note 5*)
PROVIDER OF OCCASIONAL INFORMATION	Embraces tip-offs, racing tips, news, sports news and similar information.
*PUBLICIST	
SCENIC ARTIST	Where 50% or more of the work is performed other than on premises provided by the engager. (*See Note 5*)
SCENIC DESIGNER	Where 50% or more of the work is performed other than on premises provided by the engager.
SCRIPT READER	Where the work is performed other than on the premises provided by the engager. (*See Note 5*)
SCRIPT SUPERVISOR	Where script breakdown is an integral part of the contract.
*SCRIPTWRITER	Excluding reporting scripts.
*SCULPTOR	
*SENIOR FLOOR MANAGER	
*SENIOR SPECIAL EFFECTS TECHNICIAN	
SET DECORATOR	Where the contract requires set design performed other than on premises provided by the engager.

SET DRESSER	Where the contract requires set design performed other than on premises provided by the engager.
SOUND MAINTENANCE ENGINEER	Where the contract requires substantial provision of equipment. (*See Note 5*)
SOUND MIXER	Where the contract requires substantial provision of equipment. (*See Note 5*)
SOUND RECORDIST	Where the contract requires substantial provision of equipment. (*See Note 5*)
SPECIAL EFFECTS SUPERVISOR	Where the contract requires provision of necessary equipment by the worker.
SPECIAL EFFECTS WIREPERSON	Where the contract requires provision of necessary equipment by the worker.
SPECIALIST RESEARCHER	Where the worker has either an existing profession outside the Film Industry (Academic, Legal Adviser, Doctor, etc) or specialist knowledge of the programme content to be researched and the worker is engaged for a specific project and the worker is not a regular contributor.
*SPORT STATISTICIAN	
STAGE MANAGER	Where the contract requires provision of equipment (including props). (*See Note 5*)
STILLS PHOTOGRAPHER	Where the contract requires provision of all cameras by the worker.
*STORY-WRITER	Excluding news reporting.
STORYBOARD ARTIST	Where the work is performed other than on the premises provided by the engager. (*See Note 5*)
*STYLISTS	Film or photographic styling.
TRACER	Where the work is performed other than on the premises provided by the engager. (*See Note 5*)
TRANSCRIPT TYPIST	Where the work is performed other than on the premises provided by the engager. (*See Note 5*)
TRANSLATOR	Where the work is performed other than on the premises provided by the engager. (*See Note 5*)
TRANSPORT MANAGER	Where the worker provides vehicles.
*TUTOR	

VIDEO TECHNICIAN	Where the contract requires substantial provision of equipment. (*See Note 5*)
WARDROBE	Where the work is performed other than on premises provided by the engager or the contract requires substantial provision of materials. (*See Note 5*)
*WARM-UP	
WIGMAKER	Where the work is performed other than on the premises provided by the engager. (*See Note 5*)
WIREPERSON	Where the contract requires provision of necessary equipment by the worker.
WRITER	Excluding reporter.

Note 5

5. DEFINITIONS

Premises provided by the engager

These embrace studios, locations or other facilities provided by or at the direct expense of the engager, whether or not the engager is occupier of those premises.

Substantial provision of materials/equipment

This means that the provision of major items which play an important and fundamental role in the work of the grade in question and which are of significant value, such provision being an integral requirement of the contract of engagement. It does **not** include tools of the trade (see below). The significance of the provision of equipment in determining tax status is the financial risk which such provision entails. It follows that in general equipment must be owned by, or at the permanent disposal of the worker. Provision of hired equipment, whether or not hired in the worker's name, is relevant only if obtained entirely independently of the engager. Such provision should be disregarded if the financial risk is effectively underwritten by the engager. If a worker is treated as self-employed by virtue of the substantial provision of equipment, the engager must retain full details of the equipment provided for production to this office on request.

Tools of the trade

It is customary for most craftsmen to provide their own tools, whether engaged as employees or as self-employed contractors. Such tools should be disregarded in considering the value of equipment provided, even though the contents of a joiner's or electrician's toolbox may have substantial intrinsic value.

Workers in the film industry who do not fall within any of the categories listed are regarded by HM Revenue and Customs as employees, and the former Inland Revenue's view was also adopted by the then HM Customs and Excise for VAT purposes with effect from April 1988.

A similar list exists for the radio industry.

It should also be noted that HM Revenue and Customs has instructed film companies to continue to treat as employees individuals who fall outside the categories listed above and operate through a partnership or a limited company. Such persons may also, from 6 April 2000, be affected by the 'intermediaries' provisions or from 6 April/6 August 2007 by the MSC provisions, see **40** INTERMEDIARIES. At the time of writing, HMRC had instigated enquiries into a significant number of entertainers using dividends from service companies as a means to minimise NIC liabilities. A test case in respect of an Equity member was expected to be heard by the FTT in 2013, but in the event no case was listed and the matter is still in dispute with a number of actors.

The DSS attitude to voice-over artists was that they were employed earners because of the right of close supervision and control over method and manner of performance which is available to producers. No account was taken of the brevity of any particular voice-over contract, since each engagement is regarded in itself as an employed earner's employment, although this policy is inconsistent with the decisions in *Hall v Lorimer* (see below) and the Special Commissioners' hearing on the status of actors Alec McCowen and Sam West (see **36.2** ENTERTAINERS). This view appears to have softened in that HMRC have said the special NIC rules for entertainers do not apply to voiceovers unless the presentation is in character and that the normal status tests should be applied. This would appear to be correct as the individual performing the voiceover would not fall within the definition of entertainer.

In November 1993, the Court of Appeal confirmed the 1992 High Court decision that, on the particular facts of the case, a freelance vision mixer was self-employed (*Hall v Lorimer* [1993] BTC 473). He worked over a four-year period on 580 separate engagements for a maximum number at any one time of 22 clients. He was free to accept or reject offers of work and when engagements clashed he sometimes provided a substitute with the consent of the TV company. The former Inland Revenue at one time believed the decision of the single Special Commissioner who had heard the case had been incorrect in law. Lorimer did not provide any equipment and, except for a few occasions, he provided no staff. He worked where and when he was required and was subject to the control of the programme's director. There was allegedly no economic risk other than that of having no work and he could not profit from sound management of his business. It was contended that these facts clearly showed him to have undertaken a series of contracts of employment. Mummery J accepted that the then Inland Revenue's argument that Lorimer was not a small businessman was formidable and that the distinction between employment and self-employment was very fine, especially where only personal services were provided, but the Special Commissioner had applied the correct tests to the established facts and had been entitled to reach the conclusion that Lorimer was self-employed.

There were a number of factors weighing against self-employed status:

- the production company controlled the time, place and duration of the work;
- Lorimer provided no equipment and only rarely provided staff;
- he ran no financial risk, other than the possibility of an occasional bad debt and of not being able to find work; and

- he had no part in the investment and management of the production and no opportunity for profit.

Importantly, the judgment acknowledged these alleged weaknesses but pointed out that these things were the production company's business but *not part of Lorimer's business*. His business was different:

- he had his own office;
- he exploited his abilities in the market place;
- he bore his own financial risk, which was higher than that of an employee;
- his opportunity to profit from being a good vision mixer was through using his skill and efficiency to increase demand for his services; and
- he incurred substantial costs which an employee would not incur: bad debts, car running costs, office costs, all different in nature and scale from those likely to be incurred by an employee.

The then Inland Revenue asserted that the case did not change the law, but many commentators disagreed. The Inland Revenue issued a note on 17 August 1994 on the application of the case to the film and TV industry, implicitly trying to restrict the scope of the decision, but it is arguably of application wherever labour-only subcontractors work, as the Inland Revenue subsequently acknowledged in its own guidance on IR35/intermediaries.

TV presenters

[41.16] Many TV presenters provide their services through their own personal service company (PSC) (see INTERMEDIARIES 40). Often, this is at the behest of the TV company itself.

The introduction of the off-payroll working in the public sector rules in 2017 [*Social Security (Miscellaneous Amendments No 2) Regulations 2017, SI 2017/373*] has raised questions over these arrangements where the presenters are working for the BBC – the BBC being one of the public authorities listed in *Schedule 1* to the *Freedom of Information Act 2000*.

The 'leading' case currently is *Christa Ackroyd Media Ltd* (TC 6334). Ms Ackroyd supplied her services to the BBC through her PSC, Christa Ackroyd Media Ltd. Despite having taken professional advice with regards to the contractual arrangements, and having been encouraged to contract through a PSC by the BBC, the First-tier Tax Tribunal determined that Ms Ackroyd would have been an employee if she had been engaged directly by the BBC. This is the first time in several years that HMRC have won an IR35 case at the First-tier Tax Tribunal and the outcome has given rise to a number of contrasting views by experienced commentators in this area, one view being that the reasoning behind the decision is thought to be 'seriously flawed' (see Taxation Magazine, 1 March 2018, page 8; Taxation Magazine 29, March 2018, page 8).

Although not setting a precedent, its impact may be felt in any subsequent cases involving TV presenters working for the BBC through PSCs, as it may well also do for other broadcasting organisations if and when the off-payroll working in the public sector rules are extended to the private sector. Each future case will turn on its own particular circumstances, such that another First-tier Tax Tribunal may come to a different decision.

Domestic workers

[41.17] A domestic worker, or a cleaner who is employed in a private household or elsewhere, will generally be categorised as an *employed earner* simply by reason of the contract of service which will normally exist between that person and the person for whom he works (see CATEGORISATION **14**). Thus, a handyman working seven hours a week has been held by the Secretary of State for Social Security to be an *employed earner*, as has a jobbing gardener working two days a week and as has a resident housekeeper. (*M21 (1952)*, *M64 (1958)* and *M58 (1958)*). Where, however, circumstances are such that a contract of service does not exist or its existence is difficult to establish, categorisation rules operate to resolve the categorisation questions which arise.

Engagements where services are provided in domestic circumstances, eg a nanny, chauffeur, butler, etc, were excluded from the intermediaries legislation for NICs until 1 September 2003. After 31 August 2003 domestic workers operating through intermediaries within the scope of IR35 fall into line with *FA 2003, s 136* so that their engagement is within 'IR35'. The equivalent income tax change took effect in respect of services performed after 9 April 2003. [*SSCBA 1992, s 4A* as amended by *Social Security Contributions and Benefits Act 1992 (Modification of Section 4A) Order 2003, SI 2003/1874*].

Note that the employer of a person for domestic duties in his or her own home (ie, in connection with the employer's personal, family or household affairs) was originally not eligible for the Employment Allowance in respect of that worker, even if the worker also worked part of the time in the employer's trading business. [*NICA 2014, s 2(3)*.] This was relaxed from 6 April 2015 by *Employment Allowance (Care and Support Workers) Regulations 2015, SI 2015/578* which inserted a new *s 2(3A)* to protect from the *s 2(3)* exclusion any employee whose duties relate wholly to the employer's personal, family or household affairs and are performed for an individual who needs care on the grounds of old age, disability, substance dependency, illness or mental disorder.

A business employing domestic staff and selling their services to its customers will, of course, still qualify for the allowance, except in relation to any staff working in the proprietor's own home. A company employee working as domestic staff in a director's home will not disqualify the company from claiming the allowance, but the director will be liable to tax in respect of the benefit in kind and the company to Class 1A NICs based on the same value.

Agencies supplying 'umbrella' employees to clients in their own homes are classed as providing 'excluded services' for the purposes of the April 2016 rules in *Income Tax (Earnings and Pensions) Act 2003, s 339A* denying relief for the costs of home-to-work travel to most intermediary workers. Any such expenses can therefore still be paid tax- and NIC-free.

Employment by a close relative

[41.18] Where a person is employed in a private dwelling-house in which both he and his employer reside and the employer is the person's parent, step-parent, grandparent, child, step-child, grandchild, brother, sister, half-brother or half-sister, the employment is to be entirely *disregarded* for contribution purposes, provided it is not employment for the purposes of any trade or business carried on in the house by the employer. [*SSCBA 1992, s 2(2)(a); Categorisation Regs, Reg 2(4), Sch 1 Part III para 7*].

The kind of employments to which this regulation may relate include employment outdoors as a gardener, chauffeur or handyman or employment indoors as a cook, cleaner, secretary, housekeeper or companion. (DSS Leaflet NI 11, now withdrawn).

Employment by one's spouse or civil partner (NB: only legally married couples are in scope – 'common law' spouses are not) is also to be disregarded in similar domestic circumstances (but see **39.2** HUSBAND AND WIFE, AND CIVIL PARTNERS). [*SSCBA 1992, s 2(2)(a); Categorisation Regs, Sch 1 Part III para 8*].

Employment of a spouse or civil partner for the purposes of the employing spouse's business or employment will not be disregarded, and the contract will be regarded as a contract of employment. [*Categorisation Regs 1978, Reg 2(2), Sch 1 Part I para 3*.]

In the former Inland Revenue's Tax Bulletin, February 2004 clarification was also given in respect of the employment of spouses in a business in connection with the settlement anti-avoidance provisions *ss 660A–G* of *ICTA 1988, Part XV* (now *ITTOIA 2005, ss 622, 624, 625, 626, 627, Sch 2 para 132(1)(3)*) as follows:

> Deciding what is and what is not a commercial salary is not an exact science. It is impossible to give definitive guidance as each case depends on the facts. When in doubt it is useful to consider whether an individual employed at arm's length would have accepted the same salary if their friend/relative was not also benefiting from the arrangement.

It is clear therefore that HM Revenue and Customs will look closely at salary payments made to spouses – and perhaps other relatives – on the strength of the settlements legislation. In the House of Lords case, *Jones v Garnett* [2005] All ER (D) 396; [2006] CA STC 283 Sp C 432; [2007] HL STC 1536, HMRC was ultimately unsuccessful in arguing that dividends paid on shares were taxable on the donor and not his wife, to whom he had given the shares. Whilst no NICs are payable on dividends, the case does clearly emphasise the interest HM Revenue and Customs are showing in this area. Perhaps not surprisingly, only one day after the House of Lords verdict the government announced new legislation to deal with the "loophole" supposedly created — however, this was deferred indefinitely by the November 2008 Pre-Budget Report and has not reappeared. The legislation relating to NICs does not have an equivalent to *ITTOIA 2005, ss 622, 624, 625, 626, 627, Sch 2 para 132(1)(3)* for the time being, but it is important that when employing spouses remuneration paid should be commensurate with their duties. [*ITTOIA 2005, ss 620(1)–(3), 622, 624, 625, 626, 627, 648(1)–(5), Sch 2 para 132(1)(3)*].

The *Categorisation Regulations 1978* make no reference to the employment of a person by a *close relative of his or her spouse or civil partner* and, in such circumstances, the question as to whether or not the person is an employed earner will have to be determined by reference to the legal relationship, if any, which has been created between the parties. If the relationship is, and was intended to be, merely domestic with no intent to create legal relations (see *Simpkins v Pays* [1955] 3 All ER 10, [1955] 1 WLR 975), no contract of service will exist and the person will not be an employed earner.

Cleaners of commercial or industrial premises

[41.19] Employment as an office cleaner or in any similar capacity in any premises other than those used as a private dwelling-house is an employment in respect of which a person is to be treated as an *employed earner* irrespective of whether or not a contract of service exists between the person employed and the person for whom the services are performed. [*SSCBA 1992, s 2(2)(b); Categorisation Regs, Reg 2(2), Sch 1 Part I para 1*]. See HM Revenue and Customs Employment Status Manual ESM4018.

This special categorisation rule does not apply to proprietors of office cleaning businesses even if they perform some cleaning activities themselves. Nor does it apply to window cleaners. (See **41.20** below). The rule *does* apply to telephone kiosk cleaners, however. (See **41.21** below). See HM Revenue and Customs Employment Status Manual ESM4018.

Where the person engaged is supplied by, or through, an agency and is remunerated from or through the agency, there can be no contract of employment (see **4** AGENCY WORKERS), but the agency is to be treated as the secondary contributor (see **14.32** CATEGORISATION). In any other case, the person with whom the person employed contracted to do the work is to be treated as the secondary contributor, unless that person is a company in voluntary liquidation, when the liquidator will be the secondary contributor. [*Categorisation Regs, Sch 3 para 1, para 4*].

Window cleaners

[41.20] The DSS did not regard the special categorisation rule described at **41.19** above as applying to window cleaners. Accordingly, their employment status falls to be determined by application of the normal CATEGORISATION **14** rules.

Kiosk cleaners

[41.21] Following an inquiry held in London on 31 January 1989, the Secretary of State for Social Security decided that British Telecom telephone kiosk cleaners subcontracted to do their work by a contract cleaning firm *do* fall within the special categorisation rule described at **41.19** above. The Secretary of State conceded that, but for the special rule, such cleaners would have been self-employed earners as they used their own materials and invoiced the principal contractor for the work done on a monthly basis; but he held that the special rule applied because telephone kiosks—even the open hood-covered types—are 'premises' within the meaning of *Categorisation Regs, Sch 1 Part I para 1* and because—even though the kiosk cleaners did more than merely clean the kiosks—they were employed 'in a similar capacity' to office cleaners, again within the meaning of that paragraph. Despite that decision, however, the *Categorisation Regs* were amended with effect from 16 October 1990 to ensure the employed earner status of anyone employed as 'a cleaner of any telephone apparatus and associated fixtures' other than of apparatus or fixtures in a private house. [*Categorisation Regs, Sch 1 Part I para 1(b)* as amended by *Categorisation Amendment Regs 1990, Reg 2*]. The secondary contributor is identified under the rules described at **41.19** above. See HM Revenue and Customs Employment Status Manual ESM4018.

Au pairs

[41.22] If the arrangement under which an 'au pair' works in a private household is one which satisfies the conditions of stay laid down by the Home Office s/he is likely to be regarded as not being gainfully employed and thus no contribution liabilities will arise even if they are paid 'pocket money' of about £70–£85 per week.

The relevant guidance states that this rule applies to au pairs if:

- they are a foreign national living with a family in the UK;
- they are an EU citizen or have entered the UK on a Youth Mobility Visa or student visa;
- they are here on a cultural exchange programme;
- they have got a signed letter of invitation from the host family that includes details of their stay, eg accommodation, living conditions, approximate working hours, free time, pocket money;
- they learn about British culture from the host family and share their own culture with them;
- they have their own private room in the house, provided free of charge;
- they eat their main meals with the host family, free of charge;
- they help with light housework and childcare for around 30 hours a week, including a couple of evenings babysitting;
- they get reasonable pocket money;
- they can attend English language classes at a local college in their spare time;
- they are allowed time to study and can practise their English with the host family;
- they sometimes go on holiday with the host family and help look after the children; and
- they can travel home to see their family during the year.

An au pair will usually be aged 17 or more but not older than 27 and have no dependents.

If these conditions are *not* met, the normal CATEGORISATION **14** rules will apply. (See *M67(1958)*).

Until 3 July 1993 the Immigration Rules excluded male 'au pairs'. Despite the relaxation of the rules, it is understood that the DSS did not alter its departmental practice to reflect this, although this arguably contravenes

European Community law on equal treatment, at least for EEA nationals. Note that visa requirements apply to au pairs from non-EEA states and, for a transitional period, for au pairs from Croatia, which joined the EU on 1 July 2013, Tier 5 visas are available under the Youth Mobility Scheme (see www.gov.uk/government/organisations/uk-visas-and-immigration).

Locum doctors, dentists, opticians etc

[41.23] The DSS did not generally regard a locum as being an employed earner unless he or she entered a contract of service with the person for whom he or she was 'standing in'. Although it might be expected that attacks by the then Inland Revenue on locum opticians might have changed DSS attitudes, this did not appear to be the case.

In April 1989, charges for sight-tests were introduced and test fees began to be paid by Specialeyes (Optical Services) Ltd (a major high-street chain of dispensing opticians) to the opticians who it engaged to carry out sight-testing on a self-employed basis at its various branches. In a case taken before the Special Commissioners the then Inland Revenue contended that the 'self-employed' opticians were, in fact, employees of Specialeyes Ltd.

On the basis of the following facts, the Special Commissioners decided that the locum opticians were *self-employed*:

- The opticians negotiated a fixed fee for each test performed and were paid on the basis of a monthly claim supported by their own invoices.
- Specialeyes provided all major items of non-portable equipment but the opticians provided their own retinoscopes and ophthalmoscopes.
- The opticians attended the branches to perform sight tests only and (unlike employee opticians at some of the branches) undertook no other duties.
- Specialeyes was not obliged to offer any of the opticians work and the opticians were free to refuse engagements offered without penalty and to stipulate their own hours of availability; though, in practice, many worked up to six days a week.
- The locum opticians received none of the benefits enjoyed by employee opticians: fixed salary, sick pay, holiday pay, medical insurance, company car.
- The opticians insured themselves against malpractice claims.
- Some of the opticians had their own practices elsewhere.

The Special Commissioners accepted Specialeyes' contention that there was no global contract between it and any particular optician but that there was rather a series of individual contracts each of which covered but a single engagement; and they further agreed with Specialeyes that each such individual contract was a contract for services rather than a contract of service—mainly on the grounds that Specialeyes had very little control over the activities of the opticians.

The Special Commissioners were dismissive of the suggestion that, as the opticians were clearly part of Specialeyes' 'team', the application of the 'integration test' (see **14.13** CATEGORISATION) showed that the opticians were employees of Specialeyes. The Commissioners held that the fact that the company could not function without the opticians did *not* mean that the opticians were 'part and parcel' of Specialeyes' organisation.

From 1 August 2005, the NHS no longer pays locum opticians direct for NHS work, payment instead being made to the organisation using the locum's services. This may prompt enquiry from HM Revenue and Customs as to the employment status in respect of the payments then made by the organisation to the locum out of the NHS funds received. (See also **40.3** INTERMEDIARIES AND THE PUBLIC SECTOR.)

It was, for a time, policy to categorise locum pharmacists according to the status of the pharmacists they replaced, so that the local chemist shop might treat a locum as self-employed when he or she replaced the self-employed proprietor, while the pharmacy chains would be expected to treat the locums as casual employees. This policy, while a convenient rule of thumb, had no basis in law. The status of the locum should depend solely on the tests discussed above and on the terms of the contract under which the work is carried out. Accordingly HM Revenue and Customs now says that where the locum is engaged on a sessional or daily basis, performs only the statutory requirements of a pharmacist's job, which is essentially dispensing and supervision of the sale of 'pharmacy only' medicines and advising on medicines for the treatment of common ailments then the engagement is likely to amount to self-employment. However, if the locum takes over the full range of duties of the employed pharmacist (which may include supervision of staff more generally, cashing-up, re-ordering non-pharmacy stock such as perfumes, sunglasses, toothpaste and so on) then the pharmacist is more likely to be an employee. There is a standard form of agreement devised by the National Pharmaceutical Association (NPA) which is commonly utilised for the engagement of locum pharmacists. Whilst a written document by itself cannot determine status staff are instructed that where they are satisfied that the NPA agreement is followed it is likely that the locum will be self-employed.

See HM Revenue and Customs Employment Status Manual ESM4270.

Some locum dentists and doctors find work through agencies, so the rules applicable to AGENCY WORKERS **4** may be relevant. Since qualified professionals are unlikely to be subject to supervision, direction or control, it is likely that no PAYE or Class 1 liabilities will arise, but there may be a reporting obligation for the business that finds them work.

School inspectors

[41.24] The Office for Standards in Education (OFSTED) – or the Office of Her Majesty's Chief Inspector (Wales) in Wales – invites tenders for the work involved in the inspection of schools and similar establishments (including city technology colleges, city colleges for technology of the arts and maintained nursery schools). The tendering bodies may be sole traders, partnerships, companies, local authorities, syndicates or other similar organisations. The person in charge of the inspection work will always be a 'Registered Inspector', ie a person registered under the *School Inspections Act 1996*. However, the work involves a team of other Inspectors including a 'Lay

Inspector'. A Lay Inspector is a person without personal experience in the management of any school or the provision of education in any school (otherwise than as a Governor or in any voluntary capacity). Sometimes a Registered Inspector or team member is engaged for a specific inspection by the tendering body, and there is no ongoing financial or contractual arrangement between the tendering body and the Inspector. On other occasions the engagement of a team member is on a similar basis, but the engagement is direct with the Registered Inspector. HM Revenue and Customs accepts that where a number or all of the following factors are present, the Inspector may well be a self-employed earner.

- Payment is computed on the basis of a fixed sum for completion of the Inspector's work, rather than payment computed by reference to an hourly rate for the hours actually worked.
- No additional expenses are paid eg travelling, accommodation or subsistence.
- No major facilities are provided by the engager to the Inspector, for example an office at the engager's premises, word processing equipment, or secretarial assistance for pre-inspection preparation and post-inspection reporting.
- Payment is only made to the Inspector on receipt of an invoice.
- VAT is charged and paid where appropriate.
- There is a common intention to create self-employment.

See also HM Revenue and Customs Employment Status Manual ESM4300-4301.

Key Points regarding labour-only contractors

[41.25] Points to consider are as follows.

- The Employment Status Indicator Tool is very useful but will not give a clear decision in all instances.
- Where re-categorisation takes place the Class 2 and Class 4 contributions should normally be set off against the Class 1 contributions due.
- Self-employed workers in the construction industry are particularly likely to have their given status challenged by HMRC.
- HMRC has listed a wide range of trades in the film, radio and TV industries where it will accept, subject to conditions in some cases, that the worker is self-employed.
- Many formerly self-employed labour-only contractors working through 'payroll companies' will have become deemed employees with effect from 6 April 2014 as a result of changes to the categorisation rules aimed at curbing 'false self-employment', and those paid gross because they are outside the scope of PAYE and NICs may find that their earnings are reported to HMRC quarterly by the agency from July 2015.

- Similarly with those self-employed labour-only contractors providing services to the public sector, who may find themselves caught by the 'off-payroll working in the public sector' rules applicable from 6 April 2017.

42

Late-paid Contributions

Cross-references. See ARREARS OF CONTRIBUTIONS **12**; BENEFITS **13**; COLLECTION **21**; **26.4** DEATH OF CONTRIBUTOR; ENFORCEMENT **35**; RATES AND LIMITS **53**.

Other Sources. HM Revenue and Customs National Insurance Manual NIM23005 and NIM23002.

Introduction to late-paid contributions

[42.1] There is a 'due date' of payment for every Class 1, Class 1A, Class 1B, Class 2 or Class 4 contribution for which liability arises (see **21.5**, **21.42**, **21.45**, **21.46** and **21.48** COLLECTION). If payment is not made on or before that date, collection may be enforced and the person from whom the payment is due may (subject to *Limitation Act 1980, s 9(1)* — see **12.10**) be proceeded against for recovery of the ARREARS OF CONTRIBUTIONS **12**. There is also a 'required date' by which Class 3 contributions are to be made by anyone entitled to pay them (see **42.2** LATE-PAID CONTRIBUTIONS).

Where the due or required date for payment has passed, however, a contribution then paid may nevertheless, in certain circumstances, be admitted for the purpose of satisfying the contribution conditions for benefit entitlement. In effect, the provisions relating to such late-paid contributions impose a secondary 'due date'.

Rules where good reasons for delay

Delay due to ignorance or error

[42.2] Where a person who is entitled to pay a Class 3 contribution or is entitled, but not liable, to pay a Class 2 contribution, fails to pay that contribution by its due or required date and HM Revenue and Customs is satisfied that the failure is attributable to *ignorance or error* and not to failure to exercise due care and diligence, the contribution may be paid within such further period as HM Revenue and Customs may allow. [*Social Security (Contributions) Regulations 2001, SI 2001/1004, Reg 50, Reg 61*]. From 8 October 2002, *Social Security (Contributions) (Amendment No 3) Regulations 2002, SI 2002/2366, Regs 7, 18* ensure that such decisions are made by officers of the Board of HM Revenue and Customs and can also therefore be the subject of an appeal to the tax tribunal. In assessing whether a contributor had failed to exercise due care and diligence, HM Revenue and Customs might be expected to take into account the person's circumstances. For example, youth and inexperience or age and infirmity may explain why a person failed to pay a contribution on time. Similarly, the contributor's level of intelligence and standard of education might be taken into account. See HM Revenue and Customs National Insurance Manual NIM23005.

Furthermore, where the time has passed within which a late-paid contribution is, for benefit entitlement purposes, to be recognised as paid (see **42.6** to **42.7** below), HM Revenue and Customs may, if similarly satisfied, direct that the late-paid contribution is to be treated as paid on such earlier day as is considered appropriate. [*Social Security (Crediting and Treatment of Contributions, and National Insurance Numbers) Regulations 2001, SI 2001/769, Reg 6*]. From 8 October 2002, *Social Security (Contributions) (Amendment No 3) Regulations 2002, SI 2002/2366, Regs 18 and 19* ensure that such decisions are to made by officers of the Board of HM Revenue and Customs and can also therefore be the subject of an appeal to the tax tribunal.

1996–97 to 2001–02 Class 3 extension

[42.3] On 7 April 2003, HM Revenue and Customs announced that the time limit for payment of Class 3 contributions would be extended to 5 April 2008 in respect of the years 1996–97 to 2001–02 inclusive, and that the 'penalty rate' (see **42.8**) would not be applied. This, it seems, applied whether payment of Class 3 contributions for those years arose through the issue of a deficiency notice or otherwise. However, there was then a further extension to 5 April 2009, where a deficiency notice relating to these years was not received until after 1 November 2003 so as not to further disadvantage those whose notice was issued later rather than sooner. The time limit was further extended to 5 April 2010 in the case of individuals who reached State retirement age before 24 October 2004. [*Social Security (Crediting and Treatment of Contributions, and National Insurance Numbers) Regulations 2004, SI 2004/1361; Social Security (Contributions) Regulations 2001, SI 2001/1004, Regs 50A, 65A* inserted by *Social Security (Contributions) (Amendment No 3) Regulations 2004, SI 2004/1362*].

After the 2004 regulations above were made, the former Inland Revenue advised the Institute of Chartered Accountants in England and Wales that the 5 April 2008 time limit was extended to 5 April 2009 in all cases, notwithstanding that few recipients would have been aware of this extra year due to their accompanying literature referring to the 2008 time limit. Whilst neither the then Inland Revenue nor HM Revenue and Customs publicised this fact, reassurance that it was so was in HM Revenue and Customs National Insurance Manual NIM25043 which initially made no reference to a time limit of 5 April 2008 in any circumstance. It now makes clear that the time limit for those who had reached state pension age by 23 October 2004 was 5 April 2010, while for those with a later state pension age it was indeed 5 April 2009.

See **42.8** for subsequent relaxations in certain circumstances.

Delay or failure attributable to secondary contributor

[42.4] Where a primary Class 1 contribution which is payable on a contributor's behalf by a secondary contributor (see **21.5** COLLECTION), either under the normal collection rules or, since 6 April 2007, under the anti-avoidance rules for retrospective charging of contributions, is paid after the due date or is not paid and HM Revenue and Customs is satisfied that the failure or delay was neither consented to, nor connived at by, nor attributable to any negligence on the part of, the primary contributor then the primary contribution is to be treated as paid on the due date. [*Social Security Contributions and Benefits Act 1992 (SSCBA 1992), Sch 1 para 8(1)(c); Social Security (Contributions) Regulations 2001, SI 2001/1004, Reg 60.*] To connive at something is to 'wink at' it or to take no exception to it. It has been described as intentional concurrence. (*Godfrey v Godfrey* [1965] AC 444, [1964] 3 All ER 154, HL).

Where, in these circumstances, payment is not made relative to, and before a day in respect of which, contributions based jobseeker's allowance (JSA(C)) or contributions-based employment and support allowance (ESA(C)) is claimed, the primary contribution is, for the purpose of the first contribution condition of entitlement (see **13.5** BENEFITS), to be treated as paid on the date on which the earnings to which it relates are paid and for any other contribution condition treated as paid on the due date. [*Social Security (Contributions) Regulations 2001, SI 2001/1004, Reg 60*]. From 8 October 2002, *Social Security (Contributions) (Amendment No 3) Regulations 2002, SI 2002/2366, Regs 11, 18* ensure that such decisions are made by officers of the Board of HM Revenue and Customs and can also therefore be the subject of an appeal to the tax commissioners.

Because of the nature of a *director's* responsibilities in relation to the business of his company, however, Class 1 contributions unpaid by a company will generally *not* be treated as having been paid so far as the company's directors are concerned. (Hansard 12 April 1984 Vol 58 No 141 Cols 376–377).

The *Finance Act 2007* introduced a new framework of penalty impositions relating to PAYE matters which included NICs liabilities with specific regard to 'careless', 'deliberate' and 'concealed' actions which result in loss of tax and NICs. This new framework of penalties is detailed in **21.31 COLLECTION.** [*Finance Act 2007 (FA 2007), s 97, Sch 24 paras 3, 5(3).*]

Example

Benevolent Ltd has 500 employees who are all provided with late night taxis each year prior to Christmas when a large, regular and anticipated time-sensitive order is placed by an overseas customer. The taxi fares amount to an average of £50 per employee during the year ended 5 April 2018. Of the employees affected, 400 are basic rate taxpayers and the other 100 pay tax at the 40% rate. Also, 100 employees receive expenses amounting to £2,000 in total relating to home to work travel (all higher rate taxpayers). Benevolent Ltd has agreed a PSA with HMRC and owes £14,727 by 19 October 2018 (22 October if paid electronically). See **17.5** for detailed calculations.

Benevolent Ltd's wages clerk is taken seriously ill at the time the payment is due to be made and an agency bookkeeper is brought in to cover. The RTI PAYE returns are attended to but unfortunately the PSA calculations and payment due at the latest by 22 October 2018 are overlooked. An application is made by the company to avoid the penalty by reason of 'reasonable excuse' due to the bookkeeper's serious illness at the time of the due payment date. However, although serious illness can constitute a reasonable excuse for HMRC, it is unlikely to apply in this case because it applies in a case of 'the person who would have made the payment'. In this case it is likely to be a director who actually signs off such a large payment. If the relevant director had been taken seriously ill at the time the payment was due and no other person was able to sign-off the payment, HMRC might be more likely to accept it as a 'reasonable excuse'.

As the payment is not paid until after the due date, a 5% penalty is due ie £14,727 × 5% = £736.35. If the amount is not paid within five months of the 'penalty' date of 21 November (ie 30 days from the due date), then a further 5% penalty will be payable. If the amount has not been paid within 11 months of the 'penalty' date a further 5% is payable.

Delay by reason of a deferral arrangement

[42.5] Class 1 or Class 2 contributions which, under an approved deferral or other arrangement, are paid after the date on which they would otherwise have fallen due for payment are, for the purpose of the contribution conditions for entitlement to benefits, to be treated as paid on that due date. [*SSCBA 1992, Sch 1 para 8(1)(d); Social Security (Crediting and Treatment of Contributions, and National Insurance Numbers) Regulations 2001, SI 2001/769, Reg 8*].

Other rules

General rule in other circumstances

[42.6] Subject to the provisions described in **42.1** to **42.5** above, any Class 2 or Class 3 contribution which is paid before the end of the sixth tax year following the tax year in which its due or required date lies is, for the purpose of satisfying contribution conditions for entitlement to benefit in respect of periods after payment of the contribution, to be treated as paid on the date on which it is *actually* paid. If it is paid after the end of that sixth year, it is (subject to an extension) to be treated for benefit purposes as *not* paid. Before the mid-1980s the time limit was only two years. [*SSCBA 1992, Sch 1* *para 8(1)(d); Social Security (Contributions) Regulations 2001, SI 2001/1004, Reg 48(3)(b)(i)* and by *Social Security (Crediting and Treatment of Contributions, and National Insurance Numbers) Regulations 2001, SI 2001/769, Reg 4, Reg 5*].

Where the normal six-year time limit is extended for the reasons set out in **42.3** (1996–97 to 2001–02 inclusive) and **42.8** (1993–94 to 2007–08 inclusive), the payment is also treated as made in time for benefit entitlement purposes.

See Tolley's National Insurance Contributions 1995–96, pages 358–9 for relaxations as to the required timing of payments of Class 3 for 1981–82 and earlier years.

Special rules relating to short-term benefits

[42.7] A late-paid Class 1 or Class 2 contribution may count towards satisfaction of the *second* contribution condition for the purpose of entitlement to:

- contributions-based jobseeker's allowance or contributions-based employment and support allowance only if it is paid:
  - (a) *before* the start of the relevant benefit year, or
  - (b) if it is paid *after* the start of the relevant benefit year, only after 42 days have elapsed. In practice, this means that benefit could be disallowed for up to six weeks;

  and
- maternity allowance only if it is paid *before* the beginning of the period for which maternity allowance is payable.

After 6 April 2014, where a Class 2 contribution is paid under *Reg 63A* by an adjustment to the earner's PAYE code, it is treated as paid on 5 April of the tax year *in* which (not *for* which) it is paid. Where this happens it is treated for the purpose of entitlement in respect of any period before that 5 April date as not having been paid, which may disqualify the earner from certain benefits.

[*Social Security (Crediting and Treatment of Contributions, and National Insurance Numbers) Regulations 2001, SI 2001/769, Reg 4(1B), (7), (7A), (8)* as amended by *Employment and Support Allowance (Consequential Provisions) (No 2) Regulations 2008, SI 2008/1554, Reg 49(3) and Social Security (Crediting and Treatment of Contributions, and National Insurance Numbers) (Amendment) Regulations 2013, SI 2013/3165, Regs 1, 2.*].

Rate at which late Class 2 and Class 3 contributions payable

[42.8] As there are no provisions to the contrary, late-paid *Class 1* contributions will be payable at the rate current at the time when their payment was due (although late payment penalties may be charged and interest will be charged automatically for any late remittance from 19 April 2014 onwards).

Social Security Contributions and Benefits Act 1992, s 12 and a number of regulations have made specific provision for many years for late-paid Class 2 contributions (including a contribution at other than the standard rate paid by share fishermen and volunteer development workers). Until the 6 April 2015 reform of Class 2 by *National Insurance Contributions Act 2015 (NICA 2015), Sch 1*, the rules applied equally to compulsory and voluntary Class 2 contributions, but the long-standing provisions now only apply to contributions made under *SSCBA 1992, s 11(6)*, which applies only to voluntary contributions, which may be the traditional type of voluntary contribution, or the new type that may be paid by earners whose profits do not reach the small profits threshold, or by women who wish to protect their entitlement to maternity allowance.

Late-paid compulsory Class 2 contributions under *SSCBA 1992, s 11(2)* are now subject to the same rules as Class 4, ie, the provisions of *Taxes Management Act 1970 (TMA 1970)*, and *Finance Act 2009 (FA 2009)* with none of the escalation of rates described below. The following comments are directed at contributions paid late in respect of years before 6 April 2015 and, where stated, voluntary contributions under *s 11(6)* for later years.

If such a contribution is paid within the tax year in which the contribution week to which it relates falls, the rate at which the contribution is payable is (there being no statutory provision to the contrary) the rate at which the contribution would have been payable had it been paid on its due date. See HM Revenue and Customs National Insurance Manual NIM23002 (NB: yet to be updated for the *NICA 2015* changes.)

The rate at which late-paid *Class 2* contributions (only s 11(6) voluntary contributions for periods after 6 April 2015) are payable is determined according to the following rules:

(a) The normal late payment rule is that where HM Revenue and Customs has agreed to accept payment of arrears by instalments in accordance with an undertaking made by the contributor, the rate at which a Class 2 contribution payable in accordance with that undertaking is to be paid in respect of any particular contribution week is
   (i) if the undertaking was entered into in the tax year in which the contribution week fell or in the immediately following tax year, the rate at which it would have been payable had it been paid on its due date; and
   (ii) if the undertaking was entered into in any other tax year, the highest rate in the period from the due date to the date of the undertaking.

   It seems highly unlikely that voluntary contributions will now be subject to any kind of payment undertaking, which implies some kind of compulsion to pay. The relevant regulation presumably remains in force solely to cover pre-April 2015 undertakings.
   [*Social Security (Contributions) Regulations 2001, SI 2001/1004, Reg 63*].

(b) Where HM Revenue and Customs has agreed to accept payment of arrears by instalments in accordance with an undertaking made by the contributor, the rate at which a Class 2 contribution payable *otherwise than* in accordance with that undertaking is to be paid in respect of any particular contribution week is

(i) if the contribution is paid in accordance with a further undertaking entered into in a later year, the highest rate in the period from the due date to the date of the further undertaking; or

(ii) if there has been a further undertaking but the contribution is paid *otherwise than* in accordance with that further undertaking, the highest rate in the period from the due date to the date of payment.

Again, this clearly relates solely to compulsory contributions under the pre-April 2015 rules.

[*Social Security (Contributions) Regulations 2001, SI 2001/1004, Reg 63(2)(c)*].

(c) Where, following notification by HM Revenue and Customs in the last month of a tax year of the amount, a Class 2 contribution is paid within one calendar month from the date of notification but in the tax year immediately following notification, the rate at which that contribution is payable is the rate at which it would have been payable had it been paid on the last day of the tax year of notification. It seems this will also affect only compulsory contributions under the pre-April 2015 rules.

[*Social Security (Contributions) Regulations 2001, SI 2001/1004, Reg 64*].

(d) Where a Class 2 contribution is paid late but it is shown to the satisfaction of HM Revenue and Customs that the late payment was attributable to ignorance or error on the part of the contributor (other than ignorance or error due to his failure to exercise due care and diligence), the rate at which that contribution is payable is the rate at which it would have been payable had it been paid on the date on which the period to which it relates commenced. From 8 October 2002, *Social Security (Contributions) (Amendment No 3) Regulations 2002, SI 2002/2366, Regs 3, 13* ensure that such decisions are made by officers of the Board of HM Revenue and Customs and can also therefore be the subject of an appeal to the Tax Tribunal. See *Revenue and Customs Comrs v Thompson* [2005] EWHC 3388 (Ch), [2007] STC 240, [2005] SWTI 1812 where it was determined in respect of 'ignorance or error' that a taxpayer had to prove total ignorance of National Insurance regulations and statutory obligations to make payments, or point to circumstances existing at the time which robbed him of all knowledge and understandings that payments were due at the relevant time. Disruption following marriage break-up leading to failures to pay Class 2 contributions was not a demonstration of failure due to ignorance or error, where Class 2 contributions had been paid previously and change of address was not notified to the authorities.

[*Social Security (Contributions) Regulations 2001, SI 2001/1004, Reg 65*].

(e) Where a Class 2 contribution was paid late by a person who was entitled but not liable to pay, was in respect of the year 2005–06 and that person would reach pensionable age on or after 6 April 2010, then the rate at which that contribution was payable was the weekly rate (ie £2.10) which would have been payable had it been paid during the year 2005–06 provided payment was made before 6 April 2012.

[*Social Security (Contributions) Regulations 2001, SI 2001/1004, Reg 65C* inserted by *Social Security (Contributions) (Amendment No 2) Regulations 2008, SI 2008/607, Reg 3*; revoked (as spent) by *Social Security (Miscellaneous Amendments No 2) Regulations 2015, SI 2015/478, Reg 24*.]

(f) Where a Class 2 contribution was paid late by a person who was entitled but not liable to pay, was in respect of any of the years 1993–94 to 2007–08 inclusive and that person had been notified of the removal of approved training and/or incapacity credits for those years due to the correction after 1 July 2007 of official computer error, the rate at which that contribution was payable was by reference to the weekly rate which would have been payable had it been paid during the year in question provided the contribution was paid before 6 April 2014.
[*Social Security (Contributions) Regulations 2001, SI 2001/1004, Reg 61A, Reg 65ZA* inserted respectively by *Social Security (Contributions) (Amendment No 8) Regulations 2007, SI 2007/2520, Reg 7, Reg 8*; revoked (as spent) by *Social Security (Miscellaneous Amendments No 2) Regulations 2015, SI 2015/478, Reg 24*.]

(g) Where a Class 2 contribution was paid late by a person who was entitled but not liable to pay, was in respect of the year 2006–07 and the contributor would have reached pensionable age on or after 6 April 2010 and he or she was precluded from regular employment by responsibilities at home in any year and received HRP, the rate payable was that payable for the year in question, provided payment was made before 6 April 2013.
[*Social Security (Contributions) Regulations 2001, SI 2001/1004, Reg 65D* inserted by *Social Security (Contributions) (Amendment No 6) Regulations 2008, SI 2008/3099, Reg 2*; revoked (as spent) by *Social Security (Miscellaneous Amendments No 2) Regulations 2015, SI 2015/478, Reg 24*.]

(h) Where a Class 2 contribution (only *s 11(6)* voluntary contributions from 6 April 2015) is paid late but (a) to (g) do not apply, the rate at which that contribution is payable is
   (i) if it is paid in the tax year in which it is due or in the immediately following tax year, the rate at which it would have been payable had it been paid on its due date; or
   (ii) if it is paid at a date later than that stated in (i), the highest rate in the period from the due date to the date of payment. This is not necessarily the same as the rate in force on the date of payment.

[*SSCBA 1992, s 12(3)*].

Example

Alec became self-employed on 6 April 1999 and, knowing he was liable to pay Class 2 contributions, failed to do so. On 29 June 2013, HM Revenue and Customs discovered the failure and required Alec to pay the arrears. The Class 2 weekly rate was £6.55 from 6 April 1999 to 5 April 2000, £2.00 from 6 April 2000 to 5 April 2004, £2.05 from 6 April 2004 to 5 April 2005, £2.10 from 6 April 2005 to 5 April 2007, £2.20 from 6 April 2007 to 5 April 2008, £2.30

from 6 April 2008 to 5 April 2009, £2.40 from 6 April 2009 to 5 April 2011, £2.50 from 6 April 2011 to 5 April 2012, £2.65 from 6 April 2012 to 5 April 2013 and £2.70 from 6 April 2013 to the date of payment. The payment of the contributions for the contribution year 1999–2000 took place after the end of the tax year following the contribution year and the rate at which those contributions had to be paid was, therefore, the highest (as in *(b)*(ii) above) of all the rates stated, ie £6.55 for each of the 52 weeks. The payment of the contributions for the contribution years 2000–01, 2001–02, 2002–03, 2003–04, 2004–05, 2005–06, 2006–07, 2007–08, 2008–09 and 2010–11 also took place after the end of the tax year following the contribution year and the rate at which those contributions must be paid is, therefore, the highest of the eight rates, £2.00, £2.05, £2.10, £2.20, £2.30, £2.40, £2.50 and £2.65, ie £2.65. The payment of the contributions for the contribution year 2012–13 and for the period from 6 April 2013 to 30 June 2014, however, took place before the end of the tax year following the contribution year and the rates at which those contributions had to be paid were, therefore, the rates at which they would have been paid had they been paid on their due dates, ie £2.70 or £2.75 per week. By reason of special rule *(a)* above, this position would have remained unchanged even if Alec had entered into an arrangement with HM Revenue and Customs and, under that arrangement, had paid some or all of the arrears in an even later tax year when contribution rates might have increased once again, unless he failed to honour the undertaking. In view of the provisions of the *Limitation Act 1980*, it is questionable whether Alec should have acceded to the request for payment for periods prior to June 2006.

The single-tier pension arrangements from 6 April 2016 require 35 years of contributions to have been paid or credited before a full single-tier pension is payable. In order to ensure that contributors who reach state pension age on or after 6 April 2016 are not disadvantaged by the fact that the DWP's systems could not produce pension forecasts before all returns for 2015–16 had been processed, the time limits for paying voluntary Class 2 NIC for the tax years from 2006–07 to 2015–16 were extended to 5 April 2023. In addition, the higher rate provisions have been suspended so that for the tax years 2006–07 to 2010–11 the amount payable is the rate for 2012–13 (£2.65) and for the years 2011–12 to 2015–16 the rate payable for that particular year. [*Regulation 61B of the Social Security (Contributions) Regulations 2001, SI 2001/1004* as inserted by Reg 37 of the *Social Security (Contributions) (Amendment and Application of Schedule 38 to the Finance Act 2012) Regulations 2013, SI 2013/622* and amended by *Social Security (Miscellaneous Amendments No 2) Regulations 2015, SI 2015/478, Reg 5*.]

Where a Class 3 contribution is paid late but is paid within the two tax years immediately following that to which it relates, the rate at which the contribution is payable is the rate at which the contribution would have been payable had it been paid in the tax year to which it relates. [*SSCBA 1992, s 13(4)(6)*]. Where, however, a Class 3 contribution is paid late and the payment is made after the end of the second tax year after that to which it relates, the rate at which the contribution is payable is, unless the contribution is of a kind referred to in the special rules set out below, the highest of the Class 3 contribution rate which would have applied had the contribution been paid in the tax year to which it relates, the Class 3 contribution rate applying at the date of payment or any other Class 3 contribution rate applying in the intervening period. [*SSCBA 1992, s 13(6)*]. See HM Revenue and Customs National Insurance Manual NIM25028. See, however, **28.8** and **42.3** in relation to an easing of the rules that followed where the Class 3 contributions were for any of the years 1996–97 to 2001–02 inclusive.

The special rules referred to above are as follows:

- Where, following notification by HM Revenue and Customs in the last month of a tax year of the amount, a Class 3 contribution is paid within one calendar month from the date of notification but in the tax year immediately following notification, the rate at which that contribution is payable is the rate at which it would have been payable had it been paid on the last day of the tax year of notification.
[*Social Security (Contributions) Regulations 2001, SI 2001/1004, Reg 64*].
- Where a Class 3 contribution is paid late and it is shown to the satisfaction of HM Revenue and Customs that there was a period commencing at some date prior to the end of the second tax year after the tax year within which the contribution was due, where the contribution was not paid during those two subsequent tax years because of ignorance or error on the part of the contributor (other than ignorance or error due to his failure to exercise due care and diligence), the rate at which that contribution is payable is the rate at which it would have been payable had it been paid on the date at which the period of non-payment through ignorance or error began.
[*Social Security (Contributions) Regulations 2001, SI 2001/1004, Reg 65(4)(5)*].
- Where a Class 3 contribution was paid late, was in respect of the year 2005–06 and the contributor would have reached pensionable age on or after 6 April 2010, then the rate at which that contribution was payable was the weekly rate (ie £7.35) which would have been payable had it been paid during the year 2005–06 provided payment was made before 6 April 2012.
[*Social Security (Contributions) Regulations 2001, SI 2001/1004, Reg 65C* inserted by *Social Security (Contributions) (Amendment No 2) Regulations 2008, SI 2008/607, Reg 3*, and revoked (as spent) by *Social Security (Miscellaneous Amendments No 2) Regulations 2015, Reg 24*.]
- Where a Class 3 contribution was paid late, was in respect of the year 2006–07 and the contributor would have reached pensionable age on or after 6 April 2010 and he or she had received any Home Responsibilities Protection (HRP), the rate payable was that appropriate to 2006–07 provided payment was made before 6 April 2013.
[*Social Security (Contributions) Regulations 2001, SI 2001/1004, Reg 65D* inserted by *Social Security (Contributions) (Amendment No 6) Regulations 2008, SI 2008/3099, Reg 2*, and revoked (as spent) *by Social Security (Miscellaneous Amendments No 2) Regulations 2015, Reg 24*.]
- Where a Class 3 contribution was paid late, was in respect of any of the years 1993–94 to 2007-08 inclusive and the contributor had been notified of the removal of approved training and/or incapacity credits

for those years due to the correction after 1 July 2007 of an official computer error, the rate at which that contribution was payable was by reference to the weekly rate which would have been payable had it been paid during the year in question provided the contribution was paid before 6 April 2014.

[*Social Security (Contributions) Regulations 2001, SI 2001/1004, Reg 65ZA* inserted by *Social Security (Contributions) (Amendment No 8) Regulations 2007, SI 2007/2520, Reg 8*, and revoked (as spent) by *Social Security (Miscellaneous Amendments No 2) Regulations 2015, Reg 24*.]

- Where a retrospective Class 3 contribution is paid following the issue of a full gender recognition certificate to a person whose acquired gender is male (which extends the state pension age and period of eligibility to make further qualifying contributions) and that contribution is paid in the year of issue of the certificate or the following tax year, the rate of contribution is that applicable for the year to which the contribution relates.

  [*Social Security (Contributions) Regulations 2001, SI 2001/1004, Reg 65B* inserted by *Social Security (Contributions) (Amendment No 3) Regulations 2005, SI 2005/778, Regs 2, 7*.]

In *HMRC v Kearney*, a British citizen (K) had worked in Kenya from 1948 to 1971 and whilst he was in Kenya, he did not pay any national insurance contributions until 1971, when he was permitted to pay backdated contributions for the previous six years. He subsequently applied to pay backdated Class 3 contributions to cover the period from 1948 to 1965, in order to qualify for a full pension. HMRC rejected the claim on the basis that his failure to pay these contributions was attributable to his 'failure to exercise due care and diligence', within *Social Security (Contributions) Regulations 2001, SI 2001/1004, Reg 50*. The General Commissioners decided he could pay arrears of contributions. The Chancery Division upheld HMRC's decision. Lewison J held that the National Insurance authorities were not required to chase up a former contributor who had failed to pay where that contributor was not obliged to pay National Insurance, but merely entitled to do so. On the evidence, it appeared that K had failed to make any enquiries, either of the National Insurance authorities or his employer, as to the consequences of his working outside the UK. The Court of Appeal upheld the original Commissioners' decision and Arden LJ observed that 'the facts of this case are unusual', since K had left the UK at the age of 19, and that 'in 1948 the NIC scheme was a novel and unfamiliar concept'. See *Kearney v HMRC* CA [2010] EWCA Civ 288.

A similar decision was reached by the First Tier Tribunal in the case of *John Redman Goldsack* (TC784) who had also been in East Africa. This contrasts with the decision in the case of *Anthony Marshall* (TC849) where he was found not to have exercised due care and diligence.

Contribution arrears: recovered through court on conviction

[42.9] Where a contributor has been convicted of an offence of failing to pay under *SSAA 1992, s 114(1)* or penalised as a result under *s 119(1)*, unpaid contributions are recoverable through the court as a penalty (see **12.14** ARREARS OF CONTRIBUTIONS), the amount recovered is to be treated as being the contributions which it represents. [*SSAA 1992, s 121(4)(5)*]. Insofar as the amount represents primary Class 1 or Class 2 contributions, it is to be treated as contributions paid in respect of the persons with regard to whom they were originally payable. [*Sec 121(6)*]. Accordingly, the provisions described in this chapter will apply to such recoveries in the same way and to the same extent as they apply to other late-paid contributions.

Class 2 contribution arrears recovered through PAYE

[42.10] *Regulation 14A* of the *Income Tax (Pay As You Earn) Regulations 2003, SI 2003/2682* was inserted with effect from 6 April 2012 to allow HMRC to collect 'relevant debts' owed to it (defined by *ITEPA 2003, s 684(7AA)*) through a taxpayer's PAYE code. From 6 April 2013, Class 2 arrears may be collected by this method from a contributor who is in employed earner's employment. If any Class 2 liability falls to be computed under the late payment rules in *SSCBA 1992, s 12(3)*, *Reg 63A* of the *Social Security (Contributions) Regulations 2001, SI 2001/1004* provides that the amount collected is the highest weekly rate of a Class 2 contribution in the period beginning with the week to which the relevant debt relates and ending with the date of issue of the PAYE code that is intended to recover the debt.

The first such codes were issued for use in 2014–15, but only after HMRC had requested direct payment of the Class 2 arrears.

Such Class 2 contributions are treated for the purposes of benefit entitlement as if they are paid on the last day of the tax year in which they are paid, so the contributor who fails to pay and forces HMRC to use the PAYE system to collect the arrears may, in consequence, lose entitlement to benefits. [*Social Security (Crediting and Treatment of Contributions, and NI Numbers) Regulations 2001, SI 2001/769, Regs 4(1B), 7, 7A* as inserted by *Social Security (Crediting etc) (Amendment) Regulations 2013, SI 2013/3165, Reg 2*.]

Interest on overdue Class 1 contributions

[42.11] A person who fails to pay contributions by their due date may be proceeded against summarily (see ARREARS OF CONTRIBUTIONS **12**). He could also, from 19 April 1993, be liable for interest on overdue amounts of Class 1, Class 1A and Class 1B contributions and on Class 4 contributions which attract an interest charge under *TMA 1970, s 86* (see Inspector's Manual, para 6035, issue 12/97 and Enforcement Manual, para 2514, issue 10/97). [*SSCBA 1992, Sch 1 para 6(2); The Income Tax (Pay As You Earn) Regulations 2003, SI 2003/2682, Regs 82, 83*]. Interest is charged on late-paid primary and secondary Class 1 contributions in respect of 1992–93 and subsequent years, and on Class 1A contributions for 1991–92 and subsequent years from the reckonable date until payment. It is also charged on late payments of Class 1B contributions for 1999–2000 onwards. [*Social Security (Contributions) Regulations 2001, SI 2001/1004, Reg 76, Sch 4 para 17, para 18*].

In the case of Class 1 primary or secondary contributions, as with PAYE, the reckonable date before 2014–15 was the fourteenth day after the end of the year in respect of which the contributions were due (the seventeenth if payment for 2004–05 onwards was made electronically – whether compulsorily or otherwise), and in the case of a Class 1A contribution it was and still is the day after it was due to be paid. See **53.16** RATES AND LIMITS. [*SSCBA 1992, Sch 1 para 6(3)* which refers to *FA 1989, s 178* as amended by the *Taxes (Interest Rate) (Amendment No 4) Regs 1996, SI 1996/3187*].

Following the end of the first year of mandatory RTI reporting, the interest rules for Class 1 and PAYE were changed. Unusually, the NIC change was made by tax legislation. *Finance Act 2009, s 101* had already set out new rules for late payment interest that were to apply across the tax system to 'any amount that is payable by a person to HMRC under or by virtue of any enactment', but only once a commencement order was passed. *FA 2009, s 102* dealt with repayment interest on the same basis. The new basis commenced for PAYE and NIC purposes on 6 May 2014 so as to cover the 2014–15 Month 1 deductions due to be paid to HMRC by 19 May 2014.

Finance Act 2009, Sections 101 and 102 (Interest on Late Payments and Repayments), Appointed Days and Consequential Provisions Order 2014, SI 2014/992 provides that, from 6 May 2014, any amount payable by an employer to HMRC for Class 1 NICs (or PAYE or CIS deductions) falls under the new interest rules in *FA 2009, ss 101-102. The Social Security (Contributions) (Amendment No 3) Regulations 2014, SI 2014/1016* corrected an omission from *Schedule 4* to the *Social Security (Contributions) Regulations 2001, SI 2001/1004* to deal with retrospective reports of adjustments for over-declared contributions and consequent repayment interest calculations, also from 6 May 2014.

From that date, the late payment interest rule for Class 1 in *Social Security (Contributions) Regulations 2001, SI 2001/1004, Sch 4 para 17* was replaced by the rules in *FA 2009, s 101(3)(4)*: interest runs from the date that payment is due until the date of payment. Interest will also now be charged automatically on underpayments that arise because of retrospective adjustments reported on FPS (for earlier pay periods) or EYU (for earlier tax years) under RTI, but only for 2014–15 onwards.

Interest is charged at the same rate as for late-paid income tax (set at 3% since 29 September 2009).

Overpayments also attract repayment interest, again at the same rate as refunded PAYE (0.5% since the same date).

With RTI came the monthly updating of employer accounts, which the employer can track through the liabilities and payments viewer (LPV) or 'Business Tax Dashboard'. The way interest is calculated, whether charged or refunded, will depend on the timing of payments and adjustments, which will be reflected in the employer's tax account.

Payments reported on a FPS and deductions on an EPS will be recognised as on time if they are reported and paid over before the 19th of the following tax month.

If a correction is made on a subsequent FPS, it will affect the numbers for the tax month to which it relates only if submitted by the 19th of the tax month following the month of payment (ie, an error spotted and rectified quickly, shortly after the submission of the original FPS).

If submitted in a later period, it will count for that later period, and the amount reported via the original FPS and EPS will be treated as due for the original period, so any under-payment will generate an automatic interest charge.

Where a FPS adjusts the amount of Class 1 contributions due for an earlier period in the same tax year because of an error of over-declaration and an over-payment, the amount is treated as having been overpaid to HMRC 14 days after the end of the tax month (or quarter, for small employers who pay quarterly) in which the correction is made. [*Schedule 4, Paras 10(4), 11(3B)*].

Where an EYU adjusts the amount of Class 1 contributions due for an earlier tax year because of an error of *over*-declaration and an *over*-payment, the amount is treated as having been overpaid to HMRC 14 days after the end of the final tax period in the tax year covered by the return. [*Schedule 4, Paras 11ZA(3A).*]

In both cases, the 14-day period is extended to 17 days where electronic payment is made.

Note that the EPS did not originally include a field to indicate the tax month to which it refers, although this was eventually introduced in October 2014 to improve HMRC's allocation of deductions.

Interest on other overdue contributions

[42.12] *Regulations 76-79* of the *Social Security (Contributions) Regulations 2001, SI 2001/1004* deal with the payment of interest on Class 1A contributions. On under-payments, interest runs from the reckonable date until the date of payment. The reckonable date for normal purposes is 19 July, but this is extended to 22 July for electronic payers. Repayment interest on over-payments normally runs from the date of payment to the date of repayment, but if the contributions were paid early (eg, because the business ceased in a year) the earliest start date for the repayment interest calculation is 14 days after the end of the tax year in respect of which the contribution was paid.

The provisions of *Schedule 4, Reg 17* as they were before the RTI changes continue to apply to Class 1B contributions, for which interest starts to run at the normal payment date (ie, 19 October after the end of the relevant tax year, or 22 October for electronic payers).

There are no late payment interest provisions for Class 3 contributions, which are voluntary.

From 6 April 2009 until 5 April 2015 there was a penalty in respect of Class 2 contributions where the self-employed person or his agent failed to notify HM Revenue and Customs of commencement. See **18.1**. The penalty, which could be up to 100% of the lost contributions, could be imposed where there had been a failure to notify the commencement of the self-employment by 31 January following the end of the tax year in which the liability first arose. This replaced the £100 fine which applied in earlier years. [*Social Security (Contributions) Regulations 2001, SI 2001/1004, Regs 87A-87G* as amended by the *Social Security (Contributions) (Amendment No 3) Regulations 2009, SI 2009/600.*]

From 6 April 2015, the collection of Class 2 contributions was reformed so that the contributions are now collected through the self-assessment system alongside Class 4 contributions, under changes made by *National Insurance Contributions Act 2015, Schedule 1*, which inserted a new *s 11A* into *SSCBA 1992*. From 2015–16, the provisions of *FA 2009, ss 101–102* apply interest charges and repayment interest to Class 2 liabilities as if they were income tax or Class 4 liabilities. The provisions of *FA 2009, Schs 55–56* now also apply to impose penalties for failure to make returns and failure to pay, and the *FA 2007, Sch 24* penalties for inaccuracies have also been extended to Class 2. [*Social Security Contributions and Benefits Act 1992, s 11A*, inserted by *NICA 2015, Sch 1, para 3.*] The provisions of *Social Security (Contributions) Regulations 2001, SI 2001/1004, Regs 87(3)–(8), and 87B–87G* were revoked from 6 April 2015 by *Social Security (Miscellaneous Amendments No 2) Regulations 2015, SI 2015/478, Reg 24.*

Regulation 87A survived to preserve the status quo ante for the notification or commencement or cessation of payment of Class 2 or Class 3 from 6 April 2009 to 5 April 2015, and a new *Regulation 87AA* created a reformed notification obligation, from 6 April 2015, for a person who commences or ceases to be a self-employed earner, or is entitled to pay a Class 3 contribution and either wishes to do so or cease doing so. Such a person is now required to 'immediately notify' to HMRC, in writing or by an approved method of electronic communications, the date on which the self-employment commenced or ceased or the date on which payment of Class 3 contributions is to commence or cease. The term 'immediately' is not defined, but the contributor is to be treated as having immediately notified HMRC in accordance with the new rule if he has notified HMRC within such further time, if any, as HMRC may allow. [*Social Security (Contributions) Regulations 2001, SI 2001/1004, Reg 87AA, as inserted by Social Security (Miscellaneous Amendments No 2) Regulations 2015, SI 2015/478, Reg 11.*]

Where an assessment had been made for the purpose of making good to the Crown a loss of tax wholly or partly attributable to a failure or an error on the part of the taxpayer, and a related Class 4 assessment was made also, the contributions charged by the Class 4 assessment already carried interest, just as the tax carried interest. (See also HMRC Press Release 27/05 on 6 September 2005 and NIM24705). [*SSCBA 1992, Sch 2 para 6* as amended by *SS(CP)A 1992, Sch 4 para 8*]. The interest charges provided by *FA 2009, s 101* for income tax were applied to Class 4 from 31 October 2011 by *FA 2009 Sections 101 to 103 (Income Tax Self-Assessment) (Appointed Day and Transitional and Consequential Provisions) Order 2011, SI 2011/701.*

It should be noted that there was at one time a separate penalty under *TMA 1970, s 7* (failure to notify liability) in relation to Class 4 contributions. It was known for the former Inland Revenue, on occasions, to attempt to impose a double penalty (eg, before 6 April 1988), £100 in respect of failure to notify a liability to tax, and an additional £100 in respect of failure to notify a liability to Class 4 contributions. It was questionable whether the imposition of the latter penalty was valid, but the penalty provisions of *TMA 1970, Part X* were specifically stated to apply to Class 4 contributions '*as if those contributions were*' income tax chargeable under *Chapter 2 of Part 2 of IT(TOI)A 2005*. [*SSCBA 1992, s 16(1)*]. This was interpreted by some HMRC Officers as meaning that they were added to the income tax liability and by others as meaning that the liability was separate and distinct and, therefore, open to additional penalties. The position after 6 April 1988 was that the maximum penalty for failure to notify was the tax liability in respect of income from each undeclared source for a year under assessments made more than twelve months after the end of the year. The penalty in respect of Class 4 liability assessed in this way may therefore have equalled the contributions due in respect of the undeclared income.

However, the penalty for failure to notify was reformed by *FA 2008, Sch 41* with effect from April 2010, so Class 4 failures from 2009–10 are covered by the new rules. Instead of the flat-rate penalty of the old regime, the level of the penalty will now depend on the potential lost revenue (PLR) and the type of failure, so the penalty will be linked to a PLR figure that includes both income tax and Class 4 contributions in the case of a new sole trader or partnership. The *NICA 2015* change outlined above has extended this approach to Class 2 liabilities.

HMRC's Compliance Handbook refers to failure to notify liability to income tax, capital gains tax and Class 4 NICs (see CH71300) and cross-refers to its Enquiry Manual, EM4550, but the latter makes no reference whatsoever to National Insurance liabilities, despite the merger of the Contributions Agency and its enforcement activities into the Inland Revenue as long ago as 1999.

Floods, foot and mouth disease deferment

[42.13] Following the first outbreak of foot and mouth disease during 2001, any businesses (not just farming businesses) that were affected did not have to pay interest on tax or NICs deferred as a result of the serious financial difficulties encountered. The initial period of deferral for those farming businesses affected was three months but this could have been extended by agreement if necessary. In March 2002 the deferral of tax and NICs was extended for businesses that could demonstrate that they were still adversely affected by the foot and mouth disease. A similar approach applied in respect of the 2007 outbreaks. IR Press Releases 18/2001, 28 March 2001, 19 March 2002 and 55/2007, 8 August 2007 [*Finance Act 2001, replaced by Finance Act 2008, s 135(2)(13) and Social Security Contributions (Deferred Payments and Interest) Regulations, SI 2001/1818; Finance Act 2008, s 135*].

Following the summer 2007 floods in certain parts of the UK, any businesses that were affected did not have to pay interest on tax or NICs deferred as a result of any serious financial difficulties encountered. [*Finance Act 2008, s 135*].

Further, any businesses that were affected by the Autumn 2009 floods in certain parts of the UK could agree a revised payment schedule for tax or NICs as a result of any serious financial difficulties encountered because of the floods.

For details of repayment supplement payable where refunds of contributions are received late, see **55.3** and **55.12** REPAYMENT AND REALLOCATION. See also **53.16** RATES AND LIMITS.

Key Points regarding late-paid contributions

[42.14] Points to consider are as follows.

- The basic time limit for payment of Class 2 and Class 3 contributions used to be six years after the end of the tax year to which they relate, but Class 2 became like Class 4 from 6 April 2015 and liabilities may be subject to a four-year limit (see *TMA 1970, s 34*) in the absence of careless or deliberate understatement. However, increased rates will be due if voluntary Class 2 contributions are paid more than one year after the end of the tax year to which they relate – two years in the case of Class 3.
- There are various extensions to the basic rule caused by problems with the implementation of the NIRS 2 computer – lack of deficiency notices in the second part of the 1990s, credits incorrectly awarded and later removed – and later problems with the NPS system, such as the implementation of the April 2010 and April 2016 state pension changes, particularly the late notification to older working women of the effects the latter would have on their state pension.
- Where a business or an individual contributor suffers disruption as a result of flood or foot and mouth disease, payments may be deferred by agreement and time limits extended.

43

Leaflets and Forms

Introduction to HMRC leaflets and forms

[43.1] Tax and NICs are complex, but the taxpayers and contributors are obliged to comply nonetheless. HMRC (and its predecessors) has for many years published numerous guidance booklets, leaflets and factsheets to assist taxpayers and contributors and their agents in interpreting the legislation and complying with it. Over the last few years, much of the guidance has been migrated to the online channel and paper guidance has been largely discontinued, particularly the guidance provided to employers and unusual contributors (eg, mariners). Many forms are now online 'i-forms' that can be completed on screen and either filed electronically or printed and mailed.

Each leaflet and the online guidance carries the warning that it gives general guidance only and should not be treated as a complete and authoritative statement of the law (unlike certain VAT notices, PAYE and NIC guidance does not carry any authority). There is no estoppel (ie a conclusive admission which cannot be denied by the party it concerns) against the Crown. HM Revenue and Customs and the Department for Work and Pensions cannot, therefore, be prevented from denying statements contained in their leaflets. No legal reliance may therefore be placed in their contents. (*Southend-on-Sea Corporation v Hodgson (Wickford) Ltd* [1962] 1 QB 416, [1961] 2 All ER 46). If, however, HM Revenue and Customs and the Department for Work and Pensions were to ignore considerations which, according to one of its leaflets, were relevant and were to reach a decision based on other considerations, it would have misdirected itself according to its own criteria and its decision could be quashed on judicial review by an order of *certiorari*. (*R v Secretary of State for the Home Department ex p Khan* [1985] 1 All ER 40, [1984] 1 WLR 1337, CA.) Note that there is a strict 90-day time limit on making an application for judicial review of an administrative decision.

Leaflets

[43.2] HM Revenue and Customs, together with the Department for Work and Pensions and its agencies, used to produce various leaflets, many of which were specifically aimed at employers (ie manuals, tables and fact cards), and these are listed below. Many employer booklets and forms were printed for the last time for 2013–14 and are now available solely online. RTI guidance and forms for those who cannot use computers are still available on paper, but only in response to a specific request to the HMRC Orderline.

Leaflets regarding National Insurance Contributions are issued by HM Revenue and Customs (except for SA series leaflets, which are issued by the Department for Work and Pensions). HM Revenue and Customs first withdrew a significant number of NIC leaflets during 2005 and 2006 and the remaining few are primarily only available online. DWP leaflets have now generally also been withdrawn and replaced by online guidance via www.go v.uk. See **43.3** for application forms formerly contained in now withdrawn leaflets.

The list below therefore names the various leaflets that should still enable readers to find the relevant information via a search of the HMRC website or, with more likelihood of success, via a search engine, the website of another relevant department or agency. Where a document no longer appears on the HMRC website, those carrying out a web search will often be taken to the re-written web guidance, which is not in leaflet form and is rarely as comprehensive as the previous printed guidance. They may also find their search re-directed to the National Archives copy of previously available material. A search for the leaflet or booklet number on www.gov.uk (including the department name as well as the booklet reference) will often be productive, although often not as productive as reading the originals. Some of the most important guidance booklets for employers are made available in PDF format, either from the HMRC website (flagged as 'H' below) or the www.gov.uk website (flagged as 'G' below). The content of others is now carried, in much shortened form, as web pages (flagged as 'W' below). In some cases, links to booklets flagged as 'PDF' files now take the reader to web pages rather than a PDF version of a booklet, as the maintenance of the HMRC web information is under-resourced. The guidance on contracted-out employment became obsolete at 5 April 2016 as far as contributions are concerned, but the old information may be relevant for several years as outstanding queries about records are resolved.

National Insurance Leaflets (mainly discontinued, but possibly still available by web search engine)

	Number	**Date of last pub**	**Name**
W	AO 1		The Adjudicator's Office for complaints about HM Revenue and Customs and the Valuation Office Agency
	C/FS	Sep 11	Complaints and putting things right
G	CA 14	Jun 02	Termination of Contracted-out Employment Manual for Salary Related Pension Schemes and Salary Related Parts of Mixed Benefits Schemes
	CA 14A	Apr 02	Termination of Contracted-out Employment Manual for Money Purchase Pension Schemes and Money Purchase Parts of Mixed Benefits Schemes
	CA 14C	May 10	Contracted-out Guidance for Salary Related Pension Schemes and Salary Related Overseas Schemes
	CA 14D	May 10	Contracted-out Guidance for Money Purchase Pension Schemes and Money Purchase Overseas Schemes

National Insurance Leaflets (mainly discontinued, but possibly still available by web search engine)

Number		Date of last pub	Name
	CA 14E	May 10	Contracted-out Guidance for Mixed Benefit Pension Schemes and Mixed Benefit Overseas Schemes
G	CA 14F	Apr 03	Technical Guidance on Contracted-Out Decision Making and Appeals
G	CA 15	Feb 05	Cessation of Contracted-out Pension Schemes Manual
	CA 16	Nov 08	Appropriate Personal Pension Scheme Manual – Procedural Guidance
	CA 16A	May 10	Appropriate Personal Pension Scheme Manual – Guidance for Scheme Managers
	CA 17	Nov 08	Employee's guide to minimum contributions
	CA 19	Apr 03	Using the Accrued GMP Liability Service
	CA 20	Mar 03	Using the Contracted-out Contributions/ Earnings Information Service
	CA 21	Jul 04	Using the National Insurance Number/Date of Birth Checking Service
	CA 22	Oct 02	Contracted-out Data Transactions using Magnetic Media
G	CA 33	Apr 16	Class 1A National Insurance contributions on Car and Fuel Benefits – A guide for employers. For use from 6 April 2016
	CA 37	Apr 13	Simplified Deductions Scheme for employers. Obsolete April 2013
G	CA 38	Mar 16	Standard rate NI Tables (Tables A, H, J, M, Z). For use from 6 April 2016
G	CA 39	Mar 15	Contracted-out contributions for employers with Contracted-out Salary Related Schemes (Tables D, E, L, I, K). For use from 6 April 2015. Obsolete 5 April 2016
G	CA 40	Feb 16	Employee only contributions tables for employers or employees authorised to pay their own contributions (Tables A, B, H, M). For use from 6 April 2016
G	CA 41	Feb 16	Not contracted-out Tables (Tables B and C). For use from 6 April 2016
G	CA 42	Apr 16	Foreign-Going Mariner's and Deep Sea Fisherman's contributions for employers (Tables R, T, Q, W, G, Y, P). For use from 6 April 2016
G	CA 44	Feb 16	National Insurance for Company Directors. For use from 6 April 2016
	CA 84	Oct 02	Stakeholder Pension Scheme Manual – Procedural Guidance (obsolete)
	CA 85	May 03	Contracted-out Stakeholder Pension Scheme Manual (obsolete)
	CA 89	Aug 11	Payroll Cleanse (service withdrawn with RTI introduction)
	CC/FS1a	Oct 15	General information about compliance checks
	CC/FS1b	Dec 15	General information about checks by compliance centres
	CC/FS1c	Nov 15	Compliance checks: large and complex businesses
	CC/FS2	Apr 09	Compliance checks: checking a customer's tax position
	CC/FS3	Oct 15	Compliance checks: visits by agreement or advance notice
	CC/FS4	Apr 09	Compliance checks: unannounced visits for inspections
	CC/FS5	Apr 09	Compliance checks: unannounced visits for inspections approved by the tribunal
	CC/FS7a	Nov 15	Compliance checks: penalties for inaccuracies in returns or documents
	CC/FS7b	Nov 15	Compliance checks: penalties for not telling HMRC about an under-assessment
	CC/FS9	Nov 15	Compliance checks: The Human Rights Act and penalties

National Insurance Leaflets (mainly discontinued, but possibly still available by web search engine)

Number		**Date of last pub**	**Name**
	CC/FS10	Nov 15	Compliance checks: suspending penalties for careless inaccuracies in returns or documents
	CC/FS11	Nov 15	Compliance checks: penalties for failure to notify
	CC/FS13	Nov 15	Compliance checks: publishing details of deliberate defaulters
	CC/FS14	Oct 15	Compliance checks: managing serious defaulters
	CC/FS19	Oct 14	Compliance checks: employer and contractor returns and old penalty rules
	CC/FS21	Oct 15	Compliance checks: alternative dispute resolution
	CC/FS22	Oct 15	Compliance checks: sending HMRC electronic records
	CC/FS23	May 15	Compliance checks factsheets: third party information notices
	CC/FS24	Aug 15	Compliance checks: tax avoidance schemes – accelerated payments
	CF 411	Jun 16	Home Responsibilities Protection (HRP replaced by carer's credits April 2010)
G	CWG 2	Dec 15	Employer Further Guide to PAYE and NICs for use from 6 April 2016
G	CWG 5	Dec 15	Class 1A National Insurance contributions on benefits in kind: A guide for employers for use from 6 April 2016
	E 10	Dec 12	Employer Help Book. Finishing the tax year up to 5 April 2013 (paper only)
W	E 11		Employer Web Page. Starting the tax year from 6 April 2014
	E 12	Apr 13	Employer Help Book. PAYE and NICs rates and limits for 2013–14
W	E 13		Employer Web Page. Day-to-day payroll (now for non-RTI filers)
G	E 14		Employer Web Page for Statutory Sick Pay
G	E 15		Employer Help Book for Statutory Maternity Pay
G	E 16		Employer Help Book for Statutory Adoption Pay
G	E 18	Oct 12	How you can help your employees with childcare
G	E 19		Employer Help Book for Ordinary and Additional Statutory Paternity Pay
G	E 24	Mar 14	Tips, Gratuities, Service Charges and troncs. A guide to Income Tax, National Insurance contributions, National Minimum Wage issues, and VAT
	EC/FS1	May 11	Employers and contractors – reviewing your records (obsolete)
	EC/FS2	Aug 10	Large employers and contractors – reviewing your records (obsolete)
	EC/FS3	Mar 11	Compliance checks – what happens during and at the end of a check (obsolete)
	EC/FS4	Aug 10	Compliance checks – types of penalty (obsolete)
	EC/FS5	Aug 10	Employers and contractors compliance checks – your obligations (obsolete)
H	ES/FS1	Jun 08	Employed or self-employed for tax and National Insurance contributions (obsolete)
H	ES/FS2	Oct 08	Are your workers employed or self-employed for tax and National Insurance contributions (obsolete)
H	HMRC 1	Feb 16	HM Revenue & Customs decisions – what to do if you disagree
H	IR 115	Apr 13	Paying for Childcare – getting help from your employer
	IR 121	Jul 12	Approaching retirement A guide to tax and National Insurance contributions

National Insurance Leaflets (mainly discontinued, but possibly still available by web search engine)

Number	Date of last pub	Name
H NI 38	Apr 15	Social Security abroad
DWP SA 4		Social security agreement between the United Kingdom and Jersey and Guernsey
DWP SA 8		Social security agreement between the United Kingdom and New Zealand
DWP SA 14		Social security agreement between United Kingdom and Israel
DWP SA 17		Social security agreement between United Kingdom and the Republics of the former Yugoslavia
DWP SA 20		Social security agreement between the United Kingdom and Canada
DWP SA 22		Social security agreement between the United Kingdom and Turkey
DWP SA 23		Social security agreement between United Kingdom and Bermuda
DWP SA 27		Social security agreement between United Kingdom and Jamaica
DWP SA 29		Your social security insurance, benefits and healthcare rights in the European Community
DWP SA 33		Social security agreement between the United Kingdom and United States of America
DWP SA 38		Social security agreement between United Kingdom and Mauritius
DWP SA 42		Social security agreement between the United Kingdom and Philippines
DWP SA 43		Social security agreement between the United Kingdom and Barbados
H SE 1	May 13	Thinking of working for yourself?
W SS/FS1	Jul 14	Securities in respect of PAYE and NIC

Number	Date	Name
G DWP11	Apr 16	Benefit and pension rates
G NP45		Bereavement Benefits – technical guidance (pre-2016 scheme)
G DWP032	Nov 14	Our service standards
DWP042	Apr 16	Your State Pension statement explained
NP 46	Aug 08	A guide to State Pensions (pre-2016 scheme, obsolescent)

Application forms

[43.3] A number of leaflets that HM Revenue and Customs completely withdrew in 2005 and 2006 (ie it is not simply the case that they are only available on the internet) contained important application/claim forms. These can now be downloaded from www.gov.uk and are as follows:

Former leaflet	Form	Form title
CA 02	CF 10	Application for small earnings exception for Class 2 (obsolete for 2015–16 and later years)
CA 08	CA 5603	To pay voluntary Class 3 National Insurance contributions
CA 09	CF 9A	NI contributions for widows – application for updated reduced rate certificate or for cancellation of election

Former leaflet	Form	Form title
CA 13	CF 9	Married woman application for a certificate of election or to change to full liability

The CA72 leaflet was withdrawn and no longer appears anywhere. The application forms, however, are still needed and may be downloaded from www.gov.uk:

CA 72	CA 72A	Application for deferment of payment of Class 1 contributions
CA 72	CA 72B	Application for deferment of payment of Class 2 and/or Class 4 contributions (obsolete for 2015–16 onwards)

Other forms (though some are duplicated from the above list) can be downloaded from http://webarchive.nationalarchives.gov.uk/20140109143644/http://www.hmrc.gov.uk/nic/forms.htm (now a National Archives page) as follows

Form	Form title
CA 1586	National Insurance Services to Pension Industry Forms – list and order form
CA 5601	Application to pay Class 2 National Insurance contributions by Direct Debit (voluntary contributions only from April 2015)
CA 5403	Get your NI number in writing (for individuals)
CA 5603	To pay voluntary National Insurance contributions
CA 6855	Employer's application for National Insurance Number Trace (superseded by NVR NINO verification request under RTI)
CA 72A	Application for deferment of payment of Class 1 contributions
CA 72B	Application for deferment of payment of Class 2 and/or Class 4 contributions (obsolete for 2015–16 onwards)
CA 82	Notice of appeal against a decision made by HM Revenue and Customs
CF 9	Married woman application for a certificate of election or to change to full liability
CF 9A	National Insurance contributions for widows

Forms in connection with international matters are as follows

Form	Form title
CA 3821	National Insurance Contributions – For employers whose employees are going to work in a European Economic Area (EEA) member state
CA 3822	National Insurance Contributions – Application for a certificate of continuing UK liability, including form A1 or E101 – when employees are going to work abroad
CA 3837	National Insurance Contributions – Application for form A1 or E101 when a self-employed person goes to work in the European Economic Area (EEA)
CA 8421i	Application for form A1 or E101 when an employee is employed in two or more countries of the EU
CA 8454	Application for certificate S1 or other portable health form
CA 9107	National Insurance Contributions – For employers whose employees are going to work in a Reciprocal Agreement country
CF83	Application to pay National Insurance contributions abroad (available at www.gov.uk/government/uploads/system/uploads/attachment_data/file/414910/NI38_CF83.pdf).

HM Revenue and Customs publications

[43.4] The HMRC Tax Bulletin was published every other month until December 2006. From April 1999 it contained relevant National Insurance material. This was in place of the CA 'National Insurance News', the final issue of which was No 12, Winter 1998–99. All Tax Bulletins can be viewed on the HMRC website at webarchive.nationalarchives.gov.uk/20110620155444/hmrc.gov.uk/bulletins/index.htm and relevant extracts from both CA National Insurance News and Tax Bulletins can be found in the 2008–09 and previous editions of this work. Much of the HM Revenue and Customs practice set out in the Bulletins is now contained in the appropriate Manual. Information on PAYE and NICs is now provided to employers by HMRC's Employer Bulletin, a bi-monthly web publication.

Contributors' Charter

[43.5] The former HMRC Code of Practice 1 – leaflet COP 1 was replaced in May 2007 by the new fact sheet C/FS Complaints and putting things right (though its stated issue date is April 2007). The latest version was issued in February 2015.

A new HM Revenue and Customs Customer Charter came into effect on 11 November 2009 and has legal recognition, although it is widely felt to have little value even after its recent review. [*Finance Act 2009, s 91.*]

44

Lecturers, Teachers and Instructors

Cross-references. See ANNUAL MAXIMUM **7**; CATEGORISATION **14**; CLASS **1** CONTRIBUTIONS **15**; CLASS **2** CONTRIBUTIONS **18**; DEFERMENT OF PAYMENT **27**; **41.3** LABOUR-ONLY CONTRACTORS for the position of driving instructors.

Other Sources. Leaflet CWG2 (2017). ESM4500. See Tolley's Practical NIC, January 2004.

Introduction to lecturers, teachers and instructors and NICs

[44.1] Most lecturers, teachers and instructors will indisputably fall to be categorised as employed earners by reason of their being employed under contracts of service or holding offices with general earnings chargeable to income tax (see **14.2** to **14.17** CATEGORISATION). The main exceptions will be teachers in private schools which are being run by those teachers in partnership, and head teachers who are the proprietors of the private schools in which they teach. Such teachers will fall to be categorised as self-employed earners.

Student teachers will, if they are gainfully employed in Great Britain, generally be categorised as employed earners on normal principles (see **44.5** below). So, too, will most part-time teachers because of the degree of control to which they will be subject. Even if a particular part-time teacher would fall to be categorised as self-employed on general principles, however, he or she may until 5 April 2012 have fallen to be *treated* as an employed earner by virtue of regulations (see **44.2** below). Despite the fact that some student teachers receive a 'signing-on' ex gratia payment when they become teachers, the tax and NICs treatment will be no different to any other employed earner. One area, however, where such newly appointed teachers differ from other students taking up full-time employment is the matter of student loans repayable through the payroll. Student teachers benefit from reductions in student loans outstanding on their becoming newly qualified teachers, and payments made to them under powers granted by *Education Act 2002, s 186* are excluded from earnings. [*Social Security (Contributions) Regulations 2001, SI 2001/1004, Sch 3 Part X, para 16; Education (Teacher Student Loans) (Repayment etc) Regulations 2002, SI 2002/2086, Reg 11*.] See also **29.49**.

In a number of cases between 2003 and 2011, qualified teachers returning to the teaching profession after leaving received payments within the Employment Retention and Advancement Scheme. Those payments were not taken into account for tax purposes or Class 1 NICs liability. [*Social Security (Contributions) Regulations 2001, SI 2001/1004, Sch 3 Part VII, para 8; Social Security (Contributions) (Amendment No 6) Regulations 2003, SI 2003/2340, Reg 3; Taxation of Benefits under Government Pilot Schemes (Return to Work Credit and Employment Retention and Advancement Schemes) Order 2003, SI 2003/2339*].

The fact that a member of a religious order who is employed as a teacher may arrange for the whole of his or her remuneration to be paid to the order will not prevent that person falling to be categorised as an employed earner if he or she has a contractual entitlement to the remuneration in question.

Categorisation

Employed earners by regulation

[44.2] Anyone who, between 6 April 1978 and 5 April 2012, was engaged as a lecturer, teacher, instructor or in any similar capacity in an educational establishment (see below for definition) by any person providing education was treated as falling within the category of employed earner *provided*:

- he was not an agency worker (see AGENCY WORKERS 4); and
- the instruction was not given as public lectures; and
- the number of days on which the instruction was given had not been limited, by prior agreement, to three days or less in three consecutive months; and
- he gave the instruction in the presence of the person to whom the instruction was given, except where the employment was in the Open University; and
- his earnings were paid by, or on behalf of, the person providing the education.

[*SSCBA 1992, s 2(2)(b); Categorisation Regs, Reg 2(2), 1 Sch Part I para 4* as amended by *Categorisation Amendment Regs 1984, Reg 2*]. See CWG2(2011), page 6.

Where the person *was* an agency worker (see AGENCY WORKERS 4) he still fell to be categorised as an employed earner but under those special categorisation rules and not under these rules. The current version of the agency provisions for income tax (*Income Tax (Earnings and Pensions) Act 2003, s 44*) and NICs (*Categorisation Regulations, Reg 2(2), 1 Sch Part I para 2*) continue to apply to self-employed teachers working through an agency in educational establishments. Those teachers employed by their own personal service company or an umbrella company are, of course, already employed under a contract of employment, so no deeming rules are required to bring them within the scope of PAYE and Class 1 NICs. Even so, they may find themselves caught by the 'workers' services provided to public sector via intermediaries' legislation, effective from 6 April 2017 (*FA 2017, s 6, Sch 1*). See **40.3** INTERMEDIARIES AND THE PUBLIC SECTOR.

The special recategorisation of teachers, lecturers and instructors was abolished in April 2012 after a government consultation that established that the rules had not been achieving their aim of providing extra social security protection to the target group and had merely been causing unnecessary administrative problems.

Definitions pre-2012

[44.3] A lecture was regarded as 'public' if members of the public could attend, whether they did or not and whether or not they were charged for admission. A lecture that was part of a course or that was only open to a particular group of persons or to the members of a particular society was not regarded as 'public'.

The phrase 'in three consecutive months' in the third bullet point above was presumably intended to mean in an overall period of three months but could also have been interpreted as meaning in each of three consecutive months. The then DSS rejected this latter interpretation.

The clause 'in the presence of the persons to whom instruction is given' precluded instruction by correspondence and videotape (except where the educational establishment was the Open University); and the qualification concerning pay precluded the payment of fees directly to the instructor by individual students. (Leaflet CA 26, now withdrawn.)

An 'educational establishment' included any place where instruction was provided in any course or part of a course designed to lead to a certificate, diploma, degree or professional qualification, or any like place where courses were substantially similar but did not lead to a certificate, etc. [*Categorisation Regs, Reg 1(2)*]. The term accordingly covered universities, colleges and schools of all kinds including schools of arts and crafts and languages. (Leaflet CA 26, now withdrawn). The former DSS did not regard a teacher's own home as an educational establishment. The issue of what constituted an 'educational establishment' was one of the matters considered in the unreported case *St John's College School, Cambridge v Secretary of State for Social Security* [2001] ELR 103 (HM Revenue and Customs Employment Status Manual ESM7230). HM Revenue and Customs' commentary on the case stated that an 'educational establishment' did not necessarily have to be a building. For instance, if instruction was provided in the open air as part of a course designed to lead to a certificate, diploma, degree or professional qualification, then that place (ie the open air) would be an 'educational establishment'. Further, the course provided did not have to be part of the 'educational establishment's' own curriculum; *Reg 1(2)* required simply that the 'educational establishment' was a 'place' where such instruction was given. In practice, HMRC's view was that courses at any place where the instruction was provided fell within the Regulations where the completion of the course represented a substantive achievement. HMRC's view of what represented a 'substantive achievement' was the attainment of a recognised qualification, licence or skill which provided access to a particular job or the authority to conduct a particular activity in the workplace. In the First Aid training sector, the requirement that a course represent a substantive achievement caused difficulty because of the diverse nature of courses provided by the sector (different courses being delivered by the same trainer in the same week), the nature of the courses, the circumstances under which they were provided, to whom they were provided and where they were provided. HM Revenue and Customs noted that it was clear that there were wide-ranging and firmly held views in the sector on the application of the regulations and it reviewed the regulations to see whether they should be amended in view of the nature of training delivery. See Revenue & Customs Brief 25/09 'The First Aid Training Sector' and HM Revenue and Customs Employment Status Manual ESM4503. Further consultation seeking comment was issued on 7 October 2011 with a closing date of 6 January 2012. The guidance at ESM 4503 was withdrawn pending further consideration. Traditional education establishments such as schools, colleges and universities were advised to consider the regulations as they stood but with immediate effect vocational training providers were instructed not to consider or apply the regulations.

HMRC considered the responses to the original consultation document and reconsidered available documentation relating to the original Regulations. Having concluded that the Regulations applied more widely than was originally intended, HMRC considered the impact on both those in the traditional academic education sector and those in the vocational training sector. Specifically, HMRC considered the policy objective of protecting benefit entitlements and whether the Regulations were capable of wider practical application. They took into account such factors as changes in the delivery of academic education since the 1970s, the blurring of the boundary between academic and vocational tuition and the increase in vocational and recreational training. After taking these factors into account HMRC concluded that the Regulations no longer achieved their original policy intention. HMRC concluded that the Regulations were originally introduced in 1978 to apply only in what could be termed traditional education but were extended following the decision in the *St John's College* case. Given that there appeared not to be contributory benefit implications coupled with Government initiatives promoting simplification, the conclusion reached was that the Regulations relating to lecturers, teachers, instructors or those in a similar capacity were no longer necessary and they were, accordingly, repealed from 6 April 2012. [*The Social Security (Categorisation of Earners) (Amendment) Regulations 2012, SI 2012/816*].

HMRC consulted with all interested parties regarding the consequences of repealing the provisions and particularly whether there were any potential negative consequences for individuals and they issued a Tax Information and Impact Note showing that the effects would be minimal.

It is possible that, before the repeal, because of earlier published HMRC guidance or because of HMRC instructions to secondary contributors, some training providers, particularly in the vocational or recreational sector, incorrectly applied the regulations to payments made to trainers engaged under self-employed contracts. If the regulations were incorrectly applied Class 1 NIC may have been paid in error and HMRC will now consider claims for the refund of any incorrectly paid contributions. Refunds are restricted to the last two tax years up to the repeal.

Refunds may be due to trainers or instructors or those who engaged them where NICs were paid in error on the basis of the HMRC guidance. Refunds will not be due where educational training providers applied the regulations and the HMRC guidance. This is because prior to 6 April 2012 there was no dispute or doubt that the regulations applied to such training. Educational training meant that provided at a school, college, university or similar educational establishment. Refunds are also not appropriate where the instructor was engaged under a contract of employment and Class 1 NIC correctly paid.

HMRC believe there are three categories of training providers who may be eligible to apply for refunds. They are:

- first aid training providers who were advised specifically by HMRC that Class 1 NIC was due. HMRC are writing direct to such entities;
- other vocational and recreational training providers who were specifically advised by HMRC that Class 1 NIC was due; and
- any other training provider who followed the guidance which had been given to other entities but without HMRC having been directly involved.

Where a Class 1 NIC has been incorrectly paid it is open to trainers not to seek a refund and to allow the contributions to count towards their entitlement to contributory benefits. This does not prevent the engager seeking a refund of its share of the contribution. Where trainers elect to have a refund of Class 1 NIC the amount due to be refunded will be reduced by the amount of any Class 2 and 4 NIC due or for any other amount due to HMRC. This will include previous NIC, income tax and VAT. The normal time limit of six years under *Limitation Act 1980* applies to refund claims.

Any engager or trainer seeking a refund should write to:

The Employment Status Team
HMRC
PT (Product & Process)
Area 1E 09
100 Parliament Street
London SW1A 2HQ

The letter should include sufficient information for HMRC to identify the engager, the precise nature of the business, the years for which a refund is being claimed, the amount being reclaimed, the names and NI numbers of the trainers and evidence of why Class 1 NIC was paid. (See Revenue & Customs Brief 28/12 issued 17 October 2012.)

Peripatetic teachers

[44.4] The former Contributions Agency used the regulations in relation to self-employed peripatetic music teachers giving instruction in non-local authority schools. If the teacher was paid by or on behalf of the school, Class 1 contributions were due from both the individual and the school. However, if the teacher contracted directly with the parents of the children in question and received payment directly from the parents, the arrangement was outside the scope of the regulations.

The position was similar in relation to university lecturers, etc whose employers were also the subject of special interest by the former Contributions Agency.

The person falling to be treated as the secondary contributor in a case falling within these provisions was the person providing the education. [*Categorisation Regs, Reg 5, Sch 3 para 6* as amended by *Categorisation Amendment Regs 1984, Reg 4*]. From 6 April 2012, whether such peripatetic teachers are employed or self-employed is determined by applying the normal status tests.

Other lecturers, teachers and instructors

[44.5] Where a person did not fall to be categorised as an employed earner under the regulation described at **44.2** above and was not in an office with income chargeable to income tax as employment income, the normal tests had to be applied to determine whether he was, in fact, under a contract of service (see **14.5** to **14.7** CATEGORISATION). See also HM Revenue and Customs Employment Status Manual ESM4500.

Under *Education and Inspections Act 2006* every maintained primary, secondary and special school was, between September 2005 and April 2008, to be allocated a School Improvement Partner (SIP) by the local authority. The SIP was required to produce a report for the local authority based on his or her review of the performance of each school and each head teacher. The SIP worked under contract to the local authority which had the responsibility for setting the SIPs' remuneration and reviewing their overall performance management. Given the skills required, many SIPs will also have been employed full-time in other schools (eg, as a head teacher). It seems likely that the duties as a SIP fell within the category of an employed earner – especially as each SIP would appear to have been an 'office holder'. HMRC could be expected to strongly resist any attempts to treat such persons as self-employed in relation to their SIP activities.

Sports professionals

[44.6] In 1954, the Minister of Pensions and National Insurance determined that a golf professional who was paid a weekly salary by a golf club and provided with a shop and workshop rent-free, with free heating and lighting, was a *self-employed earner* since the club exercised no control over the way in which he performed his duties, imposed no fixed hours of attendance, imposed no constraints on his outside activities, and left it to him to agree tuition times and fees with club members. (*M44 (1954)*).

Similarly, in 1955, the Minister of Pensions and National Insurance determined that a professional lawn tennis coach appointed by the Lawn Tennis Association to give instruction to school-teachers and youth leaders on the teaching of lawn tennis was a *self-employed earner* since the coach was not controlled in his methods of teaching, was not obliged to accept engagements for any particular course, and was remunerated by a fee for each tuition session. (*M51 (1956)*).

Case law

[44.7] The leading case concerning the employment status of part-time lecturers etc is *Argent v Minister of Social Security* [1968] 3 All ER 208. Argent gave acting instruction at the Guildhall School of Music and Drama and was remunerated at an hourly rate. He was free to undertake other engagements, was given no guidance as to his teaching methods and had no administrative duties. On the facts it was held that, applying all three tests described at **14.5** to **14.17** CATEGORISATION, Argent was a *self-employed earner*.

The *Argent* case contrasts with an earlier case in which the Minister of Pensions and National Insurance held that a self-employed architect and surveyor who was also a part-time lecturer in the Department of Building in a College of Technology was an *employed earner* as regards his lecturing post by reason of the degree of control which the college exercised over him. Unlike Argent, he was obliged to carry out various specific administrative duties, to adhere to the syllabus laid down in the college prospectus, and to be subject to the head of the department in which he taught (*M20 (1952)*).

In *Davis v New England College of Arundel* [1977] ICR 6 it was found that Davis, who had previously been a freelance self-employed lecturer, had, upon his engagement by the college, come under its control, been integrated into its organisation and become an *employed earner*, despite the fact that, at his own request, he had been treated as self-employed by the college.

In *Narich Pty Ltd v Comr of Pay-roll Tax* [1984] ICR 286, the Judicial Committee of the Privy Council held that lecturers ('leaders') who conducted Weight Watchers classes in New South Wales, pursuant to contracts with a company which was the franchisee throughout Australia of Weight Watchers International Inc, were employees of that company despite a clause in their contracts that they were independent contractors and not employees. The lecturer was 'tied hand and foot' by the contract with regard to the manner of performing the work under it and in those circumstances the only possible conclusion was that the lecturer was an employee. This Privy Council decision was followed more recently in the similar case of *Weight Watchers (UK) Ltd v Revenue and Customs Comrs* [2011] UKUT 433 (TCC), [2011] SWTI 3270, [2011] All ER (D) 229 (Nov), where the same principles were discussed and followed. Permission to appeal on one point on continuous mutuality of obligation was granted to the company ([2012] EWCA Civ 1155) but the matter was not pursued.

In *Sidey v Phillips* [1987] STC 87, it was held that a barrister who lectured part-time for both Thames Polytechnic and the Inner London Education Authority was an *employed earner* in relation to both engagements. The contracts which regulated the relationship between Mr Sidey and those who paid him, though not closely adhered to, pointed 'inescapably to the establishment of master and servant relationships'. There was lawful authority to command so far as there was scope for it. All of the above were cases decided on basic principles rather than on the special categorisation rules for teachers.

Disclosure arrangements

[44.8] A disclosure opportunity, the 'Tax Catch Up Plan for tutors and coaches', announced by HMRC in 2011 was aimed at those who provided private tuition, instruction and coaching, either as a main or secondary income, which had not been returned to HMRC. Where such individuals had undisclosed income they needed to make contact with HMRC by 6 January 2012 and make full disclosure and payment by 31 March 2012. It is likely that the bulk of such coaching and training will have fallen outside the scope of the *Social Security (Categorisation of Earners) Regulations 1978, SI 1978/1689* but there could well have been some income which was treated as being derived from employed earner's employment and Class 1 NIC will have been due. It was expected that HMRC would make follow up enquiries with secondary contributors as appropriate.

Key Points regarding lecturers, teachers and instructors and NICs

[44.9] Points to consider are as follows.

- Teachers taking extra classes (eg music, sports) after school for which the parents were billed by the school on behalf of the teacher will generally have been treated as employed earners by the *Categorisation Regulations*, but only before 5 April 2012.
- The definition of 'educational establishment' was extremely wide and, according to HM Revenue and Customs, included customers' premises visited by first aid trainers.
- Since 6 April 2012 and the abolition of the special provisions in the *Social Security (Categorisation of Earners) Regulations 1978, SI 1978/1689*, the employment status of teachers and lecturers has been determined using the normal tests, including the agency rules for those working through intermediaries.

45

Mariners

Cross-references. See CLASS 1 CONTRIBUTIONS **15**; COLLECTION **21**; EARNINGS FROM EMPLOYMENT: GENERAL **29**; EARNINGS PERIODS **34**; OVERSEAS MATTERS **51**; **53.3** RATES AND LIMITS; SHARE FISHERMEN **56**.

Other Sources. Simon's Taxes, Volume 2, para A8.291; Leaflet CA42 (2018–19); Taxation magazine, 29 March 2001; Tolley's Practical NIC Newsletter October 2003, October 2004, January 2007 and June 2007; HMRC National Insurance Manual NIM29002–NIM29034.

Introduction to mariners and NICs

[45.1] The social security system is, like the tax system, subject to territorial limitations (see **51.3** OVERSEAS MATTERS). Where an insured person works outside the UK (ie, outside the 12-mile limit), he ceases to be 'gainfully employed in Great Britain', with the result that he can be neither an 'employed earner' nor a 'self-employed earner' for contributions purposes (see **14.2** and **14.18** CATEGORISATION). This implies that there is no liability to pay Class 1, Class 2 or Class 4 contributions.

In the absence of special rules to change the position, UK residents employed in the shipping and fishing industries would often cease to be compulsorily insured when they left UK territorial waters and might have to rely on voluntary contributions under Class 2 or Class 3 to maintain their entitlement to the basic State pension (and, under Class 2, contributory employment and support allowance and maternity allowance).

The system generally copes with many temporary overseas absences for those normally within Class 1 liability by either ignoring short absences altogether or deeming the individuals concerned to continue to be 'employed earners' for 52 weeks after departure from the UK. There is a corresponding 52-week period of non-liability for those sent to work only temporarily in the UK by non-UK employers (see 51.9 OVERSEAS MATTERS). [*Social Security (Contributions) Regulations 2001, SI 2001/1004, Reg 145, Reg 146*]. This, however, is not appropriate for mariners who spend long periods at sea but nevertheless have a permanent connection to the UK and should be covered by the country's social security system.

Worker coverage

[45.2] Because of the brevity of the stays of workers in the shipping and fishing industries in many different jurisdictions and the length of time they spend outside national jurisdictions, they may not qualify for the protection of any state's social security system. To provide such protection for essentially UK-based workers in fishing and international sea transport, the *Social Security (Contributions) Regulations 2001, SI 2001/1004, Regs 115–119* include provisions governing the UK NIC liabilities of 'mariners', broadly limiting liability to those domiciled in the UK or resident in the UK, subject to the provisions of reciprocal agreements and EC regulations as they apply to nationals of EEA member states and certain dependents.

HMRC has centralised all NIC work for affected persons at Marine NICs, HMRC, 15th Floor, East Wing, Ty Glas Road, Llanishen, Cardiff, CF14 5FP. HMRC Centre 1, Edinburgh, deals with people in the oil and gas industry who work on vessels on the UK Continental Shelf.

Definitions related to mariners

[45.3] Subject from 6 April 2014 to an exception for certain UK Continental Shelf workers (see further below), a mariner is a person who is or has been in employment under a contract of service:

- as a master or member of the crew of any ship or vessel (See HMRC Manual NIM29008); or
- on board any ship or vessel in some other capacity (ie as a supernumerary, eg a cattleman, shop assistant, hairdresser—see Leaflet CA 23, now withdrawn) for the purposes of the ship, vessel, her crew or any passengers, cargo or mails she carries, provided the contract was entered into in the UK with a view to its whole or part performance while the ship or vessel is on her voyage. (See HMRC Manual NIM29008).

  Crew members will include deck and engine room hands, navigating and engineering officers, cooks and stewards.

[*Social Security (Contributions) Regulations 2001, SI 2001/1004, Reg 115*].

The term technically includes a radio officer, but not any member of the ARMED FORCES 11. A 'radio officer' used to be a mariner employed in connection with the radio apparatus of any ship or vessel and holding a certificate of competence in radio telephony granted by the Secretary of State, or by an authority empowered in that behalf by the legislature in some part of the Commonwealth or Ireland and recognised by the Secretary of State as equivalent to a certificate granted by it. The legislation has failed to keep pace with the real world in this area, as the old system (dating from the early Marconi days) of having a radio operator on board who was employed by the company that supplied leased radio equipment to shipping lines is now history. Modern ships have complied since 1 February 1999 with Global Maritime Distress and Safety System (GMDSS) communication standards, which no longer require a radio officer aboard all ships when they sail. Most ocean-going ships are now in constant satellite-based electronic communication with the company offices and the specialist radio officer no longer exists, having been replaced by IT professionals employed by the shipping line.

[*Social Security (Contributions) Regulations 2001, SI 2001/1004, Reg 115*].

The terms 'ship' and 'vessel' are not further defined for National Insurance purposes, except to include hovercraft for the purposes of certain of the mariners' rules. [*Social Security (Contributions) Regulations 2001, SI 2001/1004, Reg 115*]. However, in merchant shipping law, a 'vessel' is any ship, boat or other vessel used in navigation, and a 'ship' is any vessel used in navigation not propelled by oars. [*Merchant Shipping Act 1995, s 313*].

In a Special Commissioners case it was determined that an oil drilling rig which was being towed by two tugs to its drilling site could be classed as a 'ship' for the purposes of *ITEPA 2003, ss 40, 385*. The fact that the drilling unit 'did not appear at first glance to be what the layman would describe as a ship' and it had no rudder was irrelevant: the oil rig 'was operating as a ship' and its 'movements were under the control of a master mariner' on the bridge of the unit — it was therefore, for these purposes, a ship and its crew were within the definition of 'seafarer' for income tax purposes. (See *Lavery v MacLeod* [2000] STC SCD 118 Sp C 230).

In a further three cases, the same decision was reached by the Special Commissioners, but the Chancery Division decided on appeal that a 'jack-up' drilling rig with floating hull and retractable legs was not a ship. It is thought it could not be realistically said that the function of the rig was navigation. (*Clark v Perks*; *MacLeod v Perks*; *Guild v Newrick and Granger ChD* [2000] STC 1080; [2000] STC 428; [2001] STC 1254). However, the Court of Appeal ([2001] EWCA 1228) overturned this and held that a 'jack-up' rig should indeed be treated as a ship for the purposes of the seafarer's earnings deduction and that this definition would have the necessary tax implications. The Inland Revenue subsequently accepted that the decision on what constituted a 'ship' or 'vessel' would also apply to National Insurance contributions. By the time of the final decisions, the tax definition had been changed by *Finance Act 1998* and was further amended by *Finance Act 2004* for tax purposes, but the NIC legislation remained unaffected until 6 April 2014 (see further below).

A semi-submersible vessel, carrying out exploration for mineral resources, was excluded from the definition of a 'ship' for the purposes of seafarer's earnings deduction (SED) by *ITEPA 2003, s 385*, introduced by *FA 2004, s 143*, since it was an 'offshore installation' within the meaning of the *Mineral Workings (Offshore Installations) Act 1971*. In a tax case the General Commissioners dismissed an appeal and the Court of Session (Inner House) upheld their decision as one of fact. Lord Penrose observed that 'it is undoubtedly the case that different regulations classify structures in different ways according to their purpose, and on occasion depending on the department of government sponsoring their promulgation. But the regulatory point of reference in this case is clear and specific and nothing can turn on the possible application of provisions that have not been incorporated for tax purposes'. *Palmer v HMRC* CS [2006] CSIH 8. See also *Langley v Revenue and Customs Comrs* [2008] STC (SCD) 298 and *Torr & Others v HMRC* [2008] STC SCD 772 Sp C 679 at OIL-RIG WORKERS, DIVERS, ETC 50.

Since 6 April 2007, *ITA 2007, s 1001* has provided a freestanding definition of 'offshore installation' for the purposes of the Taxes Acts, including the seafarer's earnings deduction rules, but there is no connection with the National Insurance rules, so the ruling in *Perks* (above) remains of general relevance, even after the changes made from 6 April 2014.

From about November 2011 HMRC began advising shipping industry employers that, where a mariner was on a vessel operating on the UK Continental Shelf and engaged in duties defined in the Petroleum Act 1998, s 11(2), the provisions in *Social Security (Contributions) Regulations 2001, SI 2001/1004, reg 114* (which deems oil and gas workers in the UK sector of the continental shelf to be working in the UK) took priority and so a Class 1 primary NIC liability would always arise. Whether a secondary liability arose would depend on whether the employer had a place of business in Great Britain or whether the host employer rules applied. It is extremely doubtful that such a policy could have been correct and it would appear to have had no basis in law, and particularly so where the vessel was flying an EU flag – the social security rules for persons normally employed at sea clearly take priority.

Partly to remove the doubts about the validity of this policy, partly to increase the yield from secondary contributions from employers in the North Sea, and partly to combat perceived avoidance and unfairness, the social security regulations governing mariners working on ships or vessels in the oil and gas industry were changed from 6 April 2014. The change, made by the *Social Security (Contributions) (Amendment No 2) Regulations 2014, SI 2014/572*, affects the employers of certain mariners working on ships in the UK Continental Shelf area (UKCS) of the North Sea who are performing certain work in connection with offshore installations.

Employment of any kind in connection with UKCS operations has been treated for many years as being carried out inside the 12-mile limit even if the worker is a greater distance offshore and therefore not present 'in the UK'. [*SSCBA 1992, s 120*; *Social Security (Contributions) Regulations 2001, SI 2001/1004, Reg 114*.] This ensures that UK-based workers on oil and gas rigs do not slip out of social security coverage, although the deeming rule has never applied to their employers, who frequently have no UK presence and are therefore outside the secondary contribution net.

However, there have also been the parallel rules described in this chapter applying solely to mariners employed as such on ships, wherever those ships operate, to achieve the same aim. It has always been a moot point whether mariners working on ships within the geographical limits of the UKCS were covered by the UKCS rules or the mariners' rules, but until 6 April 2014 mariners were treated as such and dealt with under *Regs 115–125* rather than *Reg 114*.

As part of a package of measures combating evasion and perceived avoidance through the use of non-UK employment companies to supply workers into the UK without a secondary NIC liability, and especially to work on the UKCS, the UKCS rules were amended from 6 April 2014 so that they take precedence over the mariners' rules for work in some cases. If a mariner classed as a 'continental shelf worker' (a term that is not specifically defined but with an almost unmistakable meaning in the context of *section 120* and *Reg 114*) is employed, whether under a contract of service or not, in any 'designated area' (ie, the UKCS), in connection with an offshore installation in the oil and gas industry, *Reg 114* now defines who the secondary contributor is to be.

However, the new rule does not apply to all mariners: the regulations exclude from their scope a 'continental shelf worker' on a ship who works in a specified capacity and whose presence on board is required in order to meet the requirement of *Regulation 5(1)(c)* of the *Merchant Shipping (Safe Manning, Hours of Work and Watchkeeping) Regulations 1997, SI 1997/1320*. The table of roles and certifications is now set out in Table 1 to *Reg 114* and encompasses various grades of skilled mariners: a master or chief mate on a ship of any size, various grades of engineers, and ratings who hold certificates under *Regs 7* and *8* of the *Merchant Shipping (Training and Certification) Regulations 1997, SI 1997/348*. The aim of the regulations is to treat the employers of workers on vessels that are also offshore installations as falling under the UKCS workers' rules rather than the mariners' rules, except where the mariners are present on offshore installations because of the requirements of the safe manning legislation.

It should be noted that the 2014 changes apply only to oil and gas workers on the UKCS. Those mariners working on vessels supporting the offshore wind industry, which are sometimes very similar to the vessels supporting oil and gas exploration and exploitation, are not affected by the UKCS rules: their position is governed by *Regs 115–124*, 'Case C'.

Categorisation

[45.4] Not all members of the crew of a ship etc are under contracts of service and, if they are not, they are neither employed earners nor mariners within the terms of *Social Security (Contributions) Regulations 2001, SI 2001/1004, Reg 115* and the rules described in this chapter do not apply to them. It was held, for instance, in *McLeod v Hellyer Brothers Ltd* [1987] IRLR 232 that trawlermen who worked under crew agreements regulated by the *Merchant Shipping Act 1970* were *self-employed* earners if their agreements terminated at the end of each voyage and thereupon the shipping company had no obligation to offer further work and the trawlermen had no obligation to take any further work which was offered. This is because the agreements which trawlermen signed on engagement aboard a fishing vessel were contracts for services. Where, however, a series of such agreements is entered into between the same parties and covers a substantial period of time *and* the minimum of mutual obligations necessary to support a contract of service exist during the interval between the individual crew agreements, it is open to a court to infer the existence of an overriding arrangement which governs the whole relationship and which constitutes a global or umbrella contract of service. (*Boyd Line Ltd v Pitts* [1986] ICR 244).

Although, by definition (see **45.3** above), a mariner is a person under a contract of service, that alone is not sufficient to result in his categorisation as an employed earner: it is also necessary that he be gainfully employed *in Great Britain* (see **45.1** above). [*SSCBA 1992, s 2(1)(a)*]. Because any mariner (other than one employed exclusively in British territorial waters) would necessarily fail to comply with this requirement, however, regulations have been made under *SSCBA 1992, s 117* which provide that a mariner is to be *treated as* an employed earner (although not necessarily liable to Class 1 contributions – see **45.5** below for exception) if he is employed as a mariner on board either:

- a British ship; or
- a non-British ship where:
  - (a) the employment on board is under a contract entered into in the UK with a view to its whole or part performance while the ship is on her voyage; *and*
  - (b) the person paying his earnings (or, if the mariner is the ship's master or a crew member (but not a supernumerary), the ship's 'owner' or managing 'owner') has a place of business in Great Britain. (See NIM29011).

[*Social Security (Contributions) Regulations 2001, SI 2001/1004, Reg 118(a)(i)–(iii)*.]

A contract is treated as entered into in the UK when the offer of work is accepted there. If a UK mariner signs a contract in the UK and posts it back to an overseas employer, acceptance is regarded as complete as soon as the document is put in the post box. (See NIM29013).

A mariner who does not fall to be treated as an employed earner under these provisions is nonetheless to be so treated if he is employed on any ship etc as either:

- a radio officer and:
  - (a) his contract is entered into in the UK; and
  - (b) his employer or the person paying his earnings has a place of business in Great Britain;

  or
- a master, crew member or radio officer (but not as a supernumerary) and:
  - (a) his contract is not entered into in the UK; but
  - (b) the person paying his earnings has his principal place of business in Great Britain.

[*Social Security (Contributions) Regulations 2001, SI 2001/1004, Reg 118(a)(i)–(iii)*]

A 'British ship' is any ship or vessel in the service of the Crown, any ship or vessel registered at a port in Great Britain, or any hovercraft registered in Great Britain. [*Social Security (Contributions) Regulations 2001, SI 2001/1004, Reg 115*]. Accordingly, ships of the Royal Navy, cable ships, weather ships and Customs launches are all included, as are ships held by Her Majesty by Demise Charter or requisition.

For the meaning of 'place of business' see **51.8** OVERSEAS MATTERS.

The term 'owner' has an extended meaning for the purposes of the mariners' rules. In relation to a ship or vessel it means both:

- the person to whom the ship belongs and who, subject to the right of control of the captain or master of the ship, is entitled to full control of that ship; and
- where the ship has been demised, the person who for the time being is entitled as charterer to possession and, subject to the right of control of the captain or master, to control of the ship by virtue of the demise or any sub-demise.

The 'managing owner' is the owner of the ship who, where there is more than one owner, is responsible for its control and management.

[*Social Security (Contributions) Regulations 2001, SI 2001/1004, Reg 115*].

Exception from liability under British scheme

[45.5] The conditions of residence or presence in Great Britain which must normally be fulfilled for contribution liabilities to arise, set by *Social Security (Contributions) Regulations 2001, SI 2001/1004, Reg 145–148* do not apply in the case of mariners. [*SSCBA 1992, s 117; Social Security (Contributions) Regulations 2001, SI 2001/1004, Reg 117(1)(a)*]. Subject to EC regulations and reciprocal agreements providing to the contrary, a mariner's liability is to be conditional on him being domiciled or resident in Great Britain. (See HMRC National Insurance Manual NIM29009).

[*Social Security (Contributions) Regulations 2001, SI 2001/1004, Reg 117(1)(b)*].

A mariner who does not live in Great Britain but stays in the country between voyages is not treated for social security purposes as UK-resident, even if paid while ashore, provided that he works for a shipping company as a mariner and does not take up work ashore. (Earlier editions of now withdrawn leaflet CA 23). The statutory residence test that applies for income tax purposes is of no relevance to this NIC rule, although the statutory residence test may be relevant for income tax purposes and any claim for seafarer's earnings deduction.

In addition, by virtue of the joint arrangements made for the purpose of co-ordinating the social security schemes of Great Britain and Northern Ireland and the agreement between Great Britain and the Isle of Man, a mariner employed on a Northern Irish ship is treated as working on a British ship and *vice versa* and a similar arrangement operates with Isle of Man ships. (Leaflet CA23, page 14 and CA 24, pages 8 and 9 – both now withdrawn).

[*SSAA 1992, ss 177–179; Reciprocal Agreements—Isle of Man, Art 2*].

Because the normal rules on residence and presence in *Social Security (Contributions) Regulations 2001, SI 2001/1004, Reg 145* are disapplied for mariners and their employers, the 'host employer' rule in *Categorisation Regs 1978, Sch 3, para 9* (see **51.15** OVERSEAS MATTERS) cannot apply to deem the UK user of the personal services of a mariner employed by a non-UK employer to be the secondary contributor in relation to the mariner's earnings. This led to the employment of some shipboard workers in the UK by entities set up outside the UK so as to avoid secondary liability. Dawn Primarolo MP, then Paymaster General, announced on 23 April 2003 that the Government would act to prevent avoidance of employer's National Insurance contributions by shipping companies operating in UK territorial waters and the change duly took effect from 13 October 2003. The change did not affect those mariners employed wholly or mainly outside territorial waters (or their employers).

The Inland Revenue reviewed the previous legislation and believed that arrangements of the type mentioned above always fell within it so that secondary contributions were in fact due. However, it did not seek payment of contributions on earnings paid in such circumstances before 13 October 2003 and, from that time, clarified the existing exemption in *Social Security (Categorisation of Earners) Regulations 1978, Sch 3, para 9* for foreign employers of 'mariners'. The fact that the *Categorisation Regs* apparently needed to be specifically amended would seem to suggest that the then Inland Revenue was perhaps in reality less certain of its view of the previous law than the Paymaster General's statement would at first suggest. The reference in the former Inland Revenue's Press Release to not seeking payment of contributions on earnings paid prior to 6 October 2003 (later changed to 13 October) appears to have related to employers' contributions only, as it seems that steps were taken to recover arrears of primary contributions (together with interest) direct from affected employees where these had not previously been paid directly by them.

Since this change, primary and secondary Class 1 contributions have now been payable where a mariner is engaged in duties wholly or mainly in UK waters classified as A, B, C or D under the *Merchant Shipping (Categorisation of Waters) Regs 1992* and included in the Merchant Shipping Notice 1776(M). Category A and B waters are inland rivers and canals, while Category C and D waters are tidal rivers and estuaries, docks, ports and harbours, and some defined areas of the sea in inshore waters. The 2014 changes described above are the first to tackle the avoidance of secondary liability for mariners at sea. [*Social Security (Categorisation of Earners) Regulations 1978, SI 1978/1689, Sch 3 para 9*, as amended by *Social Security (Categorisation of Earners) (Amendment No 2) Regulations 2003, SI 2003/2420, Reg 5*].

HMRC believe that the mariner provisions contained in *Regulations 115* et seq do not apply to mariners on vessels on the UKCS where the vessel is engaged in activities defined in *s 11(2)* of the *Petroleum Act 1998*. Such a view has been hotly contested and to clarify matters, whilst at the same time ensuring payment of secondary NIC, the amended legislation already mentioned was introduced from 6 April 2014.

EC Social Security Regulations

[45.6] In practice, the identity of the insuring state in relation to most mariners will be determined under the reciprocal agreements between the UK and foreign states (for which see **45.7**) or under the provisions of the EC social security regulations. Only where such regulations or agreements are of no application will the rules stated at **45.5** above apply. See NIM29004–NIM29007.

The current EC Social Security Regulations (which came into effect on 1 May 2010) direct that a mariner normally employed on board a vessel flying the flag of the EC/EEA Member States is to be subject to the contribution legislation of that state because the activity is deemed to be activity carried out in that state [*EC Reg 883/2004, Art 11(4)*] *unless* he is remunerated by an undertaking or person whose registered office or place of business is in another Member State and the mariner is resident in that Member State, in which case liability arises in the latter state. Further, the undertaking or person paying the remuneration is considered to be the employer. This makes clear that this provision applies when someone other than the employer remunerates the mariner.

EC Member States may, by mutual agreement, provide for exception to these provisions in the interests of certain mariners or groups of mariners, but, to date, no states have made any such provision. [*EC Reg 883/2004, Art 16(1)*]. Such agreements are usually considered by the Member States concerned on a case-by-case basis and both Member States must agree to any arrangement proposed. However, a point worthy of note in such special agreement cases is that HMRC will not normally accept an *Article 16* application to stay within the home system in respect of mariners who, whilst correctly paying employee NIC, are employed by offshore companies who are not required to pay employer NIC. The HMRC view is that full NIC (ie, employee and employer) must normally be payable before entering into such special agreements. This policy may change in view of the April 2014 changes to counter avoidance in relation to secondary contributions, although they cover only mariners working in the UKCS.

Since 1 June 2002, EC Social Security Regulations have applied to workers entering and leaving Switzerland because that country entered into a special agreement with the EC. It covers only EC and Swiss nationals, ie, it does not apply to those EEA countries that are not EC members. Switzerland and the EFTA Member States (Norway, Iceland and Liechtenstein) have now adopted *EC Reg 883/2004* from 1 April and 1 June 2012 respectively.

In the case of *Kik v Staatssecretaris van Financien (Case C-266/13)* the European Court considered the social security position under the EC Regulations of a Dutch mariner, resident in the Netherlands, who was employed by a Swiss company to work on a Panamanian-flagged pipe-laying vessel, partly in the North Sea and partly in international waters further afield (see **51.37** INTERNATIONAL TRANSPORT WORKERS). The Panamanian registration meant that none of the normal provisions relating to European mariners would apply. Mr Kik carried out none of his duties in the Netherlands or in Dutch territorial waters, so his principal link to European social security was his employer in

Switzerland. He was held to be subject to Swiss social security legislation. Only if Swiss legislation was limited to voluntary cover would he be covered by the social security law of the Member State in which he was habitually resident.

Where mariners wish to remain insured in their home scheme despite the normal EEA rules, applications for form A1 should be made to HMRC NIC&EO International Caseworker on application forms CA3821 and CA3822. Such certificates are not normally needed by mariners because contribution liabilities will generally arise in the Member State where the vessel is registered. An A1 is only required where there is an exception to this rule.

Until 1 April 2012 for Switzerland and 1 June 2012 for Iceland, Norway and Liechtenstein the 'old' EC Social Security Regulations (*EC Reg 1408/71*) continued to apply (see **51.22** and **51.23**). The 'old' rules will also still apply in the UK in the case of third country (ie, non-EEA and non-Swiss) nationals (see **51.22** and **51.23**) and where applicable are slightly different to the current rules set out in *EC Regulation 883/04*. They direct that a mariner employed on board a vessel flying the flag of the EC/EEA Member States is to be subject to the contribution legislation of that state (*EC Reg 1408/71, Art 13(2)(c)*) *unless*:

- he has been posted on board that vessel by his employer to perform work there for his employer but is normally employed in another state or on board a vessel flying another state's flag, in which case he is to remain subject to the contribution legislation of that other state (see NIM29004) (*EC Reg 1408/71, Art 14b(1)*);
- that vessel is in a port of, or within the territorial waters of, another Member State and the mariner concerned is not normally employed at sea, in which case he is to be subject to the contribution legislation of that other state (*EC Reg 1408/71, Art 14b(3)*); or
- he is resident in another Member State and paid by an employer or other person whose registered office or place of business is also in that other Member State, in which case he is to be subject to the contribution legislation of that other State (*EC Reg 1408/71, Art 14b(4)*).

Applications for form E101 are, as with the A1 under the new regulations, sent to HMRC NIC&EO International Caseworker on forms CA3821 and CA3822.

The reciprocal agreements and double contribution conventions

[45.7] The reciprocal agreements and double contribution conventions currently in force between the United Kingdom and Barbados, Bermuda, Chile, Israel, Japan, Jamaica, Jersey and Guernsey, Korea, Mauritius, Turkey, the USA, and the successor states of the former Yugoslavia (excluding Slovenia and Croatia, which are now EU members) all make special provisions concerning mariners. (See NIM29006). Reciprocal agreements with all of the 'old' EEA Member States except Greece make such special provision also, but those agreements were in many cases superseded by the EC regulations referred to above in the case of EEA nationals up to and including 31 May 2003. Thereafter, there is no nationality restriction to the application of *EC Regs 1408/71* (see **51.20** OVERSEAS MATTERS) and so the old reciprocal agreements with EC/EEA members are no longer of any practical application at all. It should be noted that the UK has 'opted-out' of equivalent provisions in the current EC Regulations and so *EC Reg 1408/71* continues to apply to third country nationals.

Certificate of mariner's non-liability

[45.8] A mariner who, after application of all these rules, found himself not liable to pay contributions under the British scheme could at one time (if he was to be employed on a British ship etc) apply for confirmation of his position from the DSS and, later, HMRC. The procedure whereby certificates of non-liability were issued no longer applies, on the basis that the legislation confirms there is no liability, but anyone in doubt may call HMRC's Marine NICs helpline for assistance (03000 582419 or +44 3000 582419 from overseas). Enquirers may be asked to complete a standard mariner's questionnaire (www.gov.uk/government/uploads/system/uploads/attachment_data/file/423012/marinerquestionnaire.pdf) to provide HMRC with all the information relevant to answering any questions about liability.

Earnings

[45.9] A mariner's earnings are to be calculated according to the normal rules (see EARNINGS FROM EMPLOYMENT: GENERAL **29**) and, until 5 April 2012, there were certain disregards and any interim payment by way of an advance or any payment of part of his earnings to some other person at his behest, were disregarded until the earnings they represented actually fell due. [Former *Social Security (Contributions) Regulations 2001, SI 2001/1004, Reg 123*].

A special payment (as defined by the National Maritime Board) made to a mariner who had to be left abroad because of sickness or the risk of infection was excluded from earnings entirely. [Former *Social Security (Contributions) Regulations 2001, SI 2001/1004, Reg 123(1)(c)*].

These disregards were removed from 6 April 2012 on the repeal of *Reg 123*. [*Social Security (Contributions) (Amendment No 2) Regulations 2012, SI 2012/817*].

Calculation and collection of contributions

[45.10] Calculation of primary and secondary Class 1 contribution liabilities in respect of the earnings of a mariner proceeds largely in the same manner as does the calculation of the contribution liabilities in respect of the earnings of any other employed earner *except that*:

(a) where a mariner is paid his earnings in the form of a general settlement at the end of a voyage or series of voyages, special rules are to be applied for the ascertainment of his earnings periods and the apportionment of earnings to those periods (see **34.13** EARNINGS PERIODS); and
(b) where the mariner is the master or crew member of a 'foreign-going' ship, secondary Class 1 contribution liability will arise at reduced rates (see **45.12** and **45.13** below).

Collection procedures (see COLLECTION **21**) are modified only insofar as the employer is required to submit a special post-voyage period return to HMRC within 14 days of the end of a voyage or series of voyages. The ready reckoner tables CA42 Foreign-Going Mariner's and Deep Sea Fisherman's contributions for employers make it clear that mariners generally fall under the RTI system for reporting and collection, but that there may be some employers who can still use paper returns (eg, the RT11 deductions working sheet, which replaced the P11).

[*Social Security (Contributions) Regulations 2001, SI 2001/1004, Sch 4 para 24*].

The prescribed secondary contributor

[45.11] In relation to mariners who are not within the 2014 regulations that changed the rules for continental shelf workers, the shipowner will, as a mariner's employer, usually fall to be treated as the secondary contributor in relation to earnings paid to a mariner, but only if he is resident or has a place of business (see **51.5** and **51.14** OVERSEAS MATTERS) in Great Britain. From 1 May 2010 EU legislation extends this to an employer or payer of wages in any EEA country as long as the employment is on a UK-flagged vessel.

[*Social Security (Contributions) Regulations 2001, SI 2001/1004, Reg 117(1)(c)*].

A radio officer was usually employed by a marine radio company rather than by a shipowner. Where that was the case, the marine radio company fell to be treated as the secondary contributor (Leaflet CA 24, page 13 – now withdrawn).

If the employer of a mariner does not satisfy either of these conditions but the person who actually pays the mariner does, that person (even if he is acting merely as agent for the employer) is to be treated as the secondary contributor in the employer's stead.

[*Social Security (Contributions) Regulations 2001, SI 2001/1004, Reg 122*].

The *Oleochem* case is a demonstration of why the rules for continental shelf workers were changed from April 2014 (see above).

A Scottish company (S) had a wholly-owned Jersey subsidiary (J), which employed 42 process chemists, who worked in the oil industry on various 'floating production storage & offload facilities' (FPSOs) in the North Sea. J paid PAYE and primary Class 1 National Insurance contributions in respect of these chemists, but did not pay secondary contributions. HMRC were not satisfied that all the 42 chemists worked exclusively on FPSOs, and issued rulings that S was required to pay secondary Class 1 contributions in respect of the chemists' earnings. S appealed. The Special Commissioner reviewed the evidence and issued a determination that the chemists who worked on FPSOs during the relevant period were 'mariners' within *Social Security (Contributions) Regulations 2001, SI 2001/1004, Reg 115*. They were employed by a company which did not have a place of business in Great Britain, so that the condition of liability laid down by *SI 2001/1004, Reg 117(c)* was not satisfied. Furthermore, there was no other statutory enactment by virtue of which S could be treated as a secondary contributor in respect of the chemists' earnings. The Commissioner formally directed HMRC 'to inform the appellants which of the 42 chemists they dispute were deployed on FPSOs'. *Oleochem (Scotland) Ltd v HMRC* [2009] STC SCD 205 Sp C 731.

After the changes brought about by the *Social Security (Contributions) (Amendment No 2) Regulations 2014, SI 2014/572*, where a mariner works on a ship or vessel that works in the UKCS and that is not used wholly or mainly for the transport of supplies, as a safety or standby vessel, or for the laying of cables, there is a risk that the offshore employer of such a worker will trigger the application of a secondary liability for a business in the UK that is deemed to be the secondary contributor. If the ship or vessel qualifies as an 'offshore installation' (see NIM33860 and *Social Security (Contributions) Regulations 2001, SI 2001/1004, Reg 114D*) and the mariner is not within the grades specified in the table in *Reg 114* the secondary liability will fall on:

- the employer, if it has a presence in the UK;
- an associated company in the UK if the employer has no such presence; or
- the oil field licensee if the employer has no such presence and no UK associated company.

If there is more than one UK associated company of the employer, the liability falls on the associated company that has the greatest taxable total profit (within the meaning of *CTA 2010, s 4*) for the accounting period preceding the tax year in which the contributions are due.

[*Social Security (Contributions) Regulations 2001, SI 2001/1004, Reg 114(4).*]

Because some businesses in the UKCS use workers supplied by third parties, many of which have no UK presence, new *Regs 114A–D* also provide rules from 6 April 2014 for a system of certification of relevant employers by HMRC as being compliant, so that their clients can be certain that no liability will attach to them under the rules just described. See OIL RIG WORKERS 50.

Mariners on vessels that are 'structures . . . put to a relevant use while in water' could find that they are oil rig workers rather than mariners for NIC purposes.

A 'relevant use' is a use for the purposes of exploiting mineral resources, exploration with a view to such exploitation, for the storage of gas in or under the shore or the bed of any waters, for the recovery of gas so stored, for the conveyance of things by means of a pipe, or a use mainly for the provision of accommodation for individuals who work on or from structure which is, is to be, or has been put to any of the above uses while in the water, or for the purposes of decommissioning any structure which has been used for or in connection with any of the relevant uses above [*Reg 114D(c)*]. It will generally be clear whether the structure is being put to a relevant use.

However, the phrase 'put to use while in water' means put to use while standing in any waters, stationed (by whatever means) in any waters, or standing on the foreshore or other land intermittently covered with water [*Reg 114D(d)*]. This may present a difficulty of interpretation because certain ships and vessels operate in connection with oil and gas extraction while stationary without being anchored (eg because the water is too deep) or moored to a structure that stands on the seabed. HMRC has confirmed that the phrase 'stationed (by whatever means)' will not encompass, for example, a dive support vessel that remains stationary using dynamic positioning, provided that it changes its position. HMRC will use the guidance issued for the purposes of the seafarer's earnings deduction at EIM33018-33109 as the basis of determining whether a vessel is stationary: as a rule of thumb, and with no force of law, HMRC will accept that a vessel that spends five or fewer days at one location (whether anchored, moored, or kept in place by dynamic positioning) should not be regarded as performing its duties while standing stationed, so it will not be an offshore installation and those on board should be accepted as mariners.

Contribution rates

[45.12] Primary and secondary Class 1 contributions in respect of a mariner's earnings are normally payable at the same rates as would be applicable were the mariner an ordinary employed earner, including the nil secondary rate for the earnings of under-21s and apprentices under 25 (see 53.3 RATES AND LIMITS). Where, however, a mariner is a master or crew member on a '*foreign-going*' ship (see 45.13 below), secondary Class 1 contributions other than at the nil rate (at either contracted-out or, before 6 April 2016, not contracted-out rate) are reduced and for these purposes see the special mariners' contribution tables CA 42 *Foreign-Going Mariner's and Deep Sea Fisherman's contributions for employers*. See 45.13 below.

Foreign-going rebated contributions

[45.13] Where a mariner is a master or crew member of a 'foreign-going ship', the appropriate percentage rate of the secondary Class 1 contributions payable in respect of his earnings is reduced by 0.5%. The reduction originally reflected the reduced likelihood of a worker who spent most of the year away at sea claiming short-term social security benefits, such as sickness benefit (later short-term incapacity benefit, now ESA), maternity benefit (now SMP/SAP/SPP/ShPP) and unemployment benefit (now JSA), although that logic has been eroded with changes to statutory payments and JSA entitlements and liabilities, so it is arguably now an anachronism.

Foreign-going mariner rates were reflected in tables R, T, W, N and O, from 6 April 1984 onwards, and also in tables H, K and V from 6 April 1997 onwards, and table Q from 6 April 2003 onwards. Tables W, H and K ceased to be applicable after 6 April 2012 when the contracted-out money purchase rebates were abolished. New tables P, V and Y were introduced from 6 April 2015 for foreign-going mariners under the age of 21 whose earnings attract a nil rate of secondary contribution up to the upper secondary threshold (initially the same as the UEL). New table G was introduced from 6 April 2016 to cover the nil secondary rate applicable to qualifying apprentice mariners under the age of 25 on foreign-going ships. Tables N, O and W were withdrawn at the same time, reflecting the abolition of contracting out by *Pensions Act 2014, s 24* and *Pt 2* of *SI 2016/352*.

[*Social Security (Contributions) Regulations 2001, SI 2001/1004, Reg 119.*]

A 'foreign-going ship' is (in contradistinction to a home-trade ship) a ship or vessel which is employed in trading or going beyond the UK (including, for this purpose, Ireland), the Channel Islands, the Isle of Man and the continent of Europe between the river Elbe and Brest inclusive; and any fishing vessel proceeding beyond the limits of:

- on the south, latitude 48°30' N (ie, approximately the latitude of Brest in Brittany);
- on the west, longitude 12°W (about 60 nautical miles west of Valentia, Western Ireland);
- on the north, latitude 61°N (ie, the latitude of the Southern Faroe Islands, about 40 nautical miles north of Shetland).

[*Social Security (Contributions) Regulations 2001, SI 2001/1004, Reg 119(2)*].

'Employment' in this context includes any period of leave, other than study leave, accruing from the employment.

[*Social Security (Contributions) Regulations 2001, SI 2001/1004, Reg 119(3)*]. Where home-trade agreements are opened between successive foreign-going voyages, rebated secondary contributions may be made in respect of all the earnings arising provided the home-trade agreements are merely incidental to the distribution and collection of foreign cargo at ports within the home-trade limits and the ship is not actually engaged in trade between those ports. (Leaflet CA 24, page 12 – now withdrawn).

HMRC mariners' tables

[45.14] Special tables (see **15.8** CLASS **1** CONTRIBUTIONS) are prepared by HMRC to facilitate the complex calculations to which (a) and (b) in **45.10** may, on occasions give rise, though contributions may be calculated using the exact percentage method if this is preferred (see **15.8** CLASS **1** CONTRIBUTIONS). With the advent of mandatory RTI reporting, few employers may be expected to use the paper tables.

[*Social Security (Contributions) Regulations 2001, SI 2001/1004, Reg 121(2)*].

The Tables associated with foreign-going mariners are as follows:

Table R	Mariner
Table T	Mariner – married woman's reduced rate
Table W	Mariner, over State pension age – Non-pensioned, and COSR cases up to 5 April 2016 (and not contracted-out deferred contributions up to 5 April 2003 and COMPS to 5 April 2012)
Table Q	Mariner – not contracted-out deferred contributions (from 6 April 2003)
Table N	Mariner – Contracted-out salary related (COSR) up to 5 April 2016
Table H	Mariner – Contracted-out money purchase (COMPS) – only appropriate before 6 April 2012

Table O	Mariner COSR – married woman's reduced rate up to 5 April 2016
Table K	Mariner COMPS – married woman's reduced rate – only appropriate before 6 April 2012
Table V	Mariner COMPS – deferred contributions only appropriate before 6 April 2012
Table P	Mariner – not contracted out, deferred, under 21 (from 6 April 2015)
Table V	Mariner – Contracted-out salary related (COSR), under 21 from 6 April 2015 to 5 April 2016 only
Table Y	Mariner – not contracted out, under 21 (from 6 April 2015)
Table G	Mariner – not contracted-out, under 25 qualifying apprentice (from 6 April 2016)

Note: Tables were never produced for COSR mariners with deferment certificates, and none were produced at 6 April 2015 for mariners under the age of 21. The COMP tables became redundant on 6 April 2012, and the COSR tables followed on 6 April 2016, when contracting out was abolished.

Modification of compliance rules

[45.15] Where a mariner is unable, because of his absence from Great Britain by reason of his employment as a mariner, to comply with any time limits on acts which he is liable to perform under contribution law, he is to be treated as complying if he performs the acts as soon as is reasonably practicable. [*Social Security (Contributions) Regulations 2001, SI 2001/1004, Reg 124(2)*].

46

Ministers of Religion

Cross-reference. See CATEGORISATION **14**.

Other Sources. Simon's Taxes, Volume 2, para A8.219; Tolley's National Insurance Brief, December 1995, page 89; Taxation, 15 March 2007, page 296; CWG2 (2017), para 1.1. HM Revenue and Customs National Insurance Manual NIM02260 and NIM02315.

Introduction to ministers of religion and NICs

[46.1] As a matter of general law, Church of England clergy and stipendiary readers in the Church of England and Church of Scotland are office holders rather than employees. Their functions have traditionally been regarded as vocational and spiritual in nature and therefore incompatible with the existence of a contract, which must in law involve an intention to create legal relations. In addition, certain clergymen will hold other offices, eg every prison is statutorily required to appoint an Anglican chaplain (see further below). Ministers of the Methodist Church, ministers of the Congregational Church, ministers of the Presbyterian Church, officers of the Salvation Army, Sikh *granthis* or priests and Islamic *khateebs* have been held to be neither office holders nor employees under contracts of service, although it is nevertheless not unknown for HMRC to argue that certain ministers are office holders. (*Re Employment of Church of England Curates* [1912] 2 Ch 563; *Barthorpe v Exeter Diocesan Board of Finance* [1979] ICR 900; *Re Employment of Methodist Ministers* (1912) 107 LTR 143; *Methodist Conference (President) v Parfitt* [1984] QB 368, [1983] 3 All ER 747, CA; *Parker v Orr* (1966) 1 ITR 488; *Lewis v Scunthorpe Congregational Church* (1978) unreported; *Davies v Presbyterian Church of Wales* [1986] 1 All ER 705, [1986] 1 WLR 323, CA; *Rogers v Booth* [1937] 2 AER 751; *Santokh Singh v Guru Nanak Gurdwara* [1990] ICR 309; *Birmingham Mosque Trust Ltd v Alavi* [1992] ICR 435). For tax purposes, a Roman Catholic priest may pay income tax through a church payroll where the church income is his main source, or otherwise under a PAYE Direct Payment arrangement (see PAYE70230). For contribution purposes these ministers of the non-established churches, including the Roman Catholic church, would ordinarily be classed as self-employed. However, *any* 'minister of religion' is to be treated as falling within the category of employed earners unless his remuneration in respect of his employment (disregarding any payment in kind) does not consist wholly or mainly of stipend or salary. [*Categorisation Regs, Sch 1 Part I para 5*].

Definitions

[46.2] The term 'minister of religion' is defined neither in *SSCBA 1992* nor in the *Categorisation Regs* but it has been held by the courts that to be a minister of religion a person must be 'set apart in sacred matters as superior to the rest of the religious community, the laity'. It must be 'for them and them alone to perform the important sacred rites . . . to preach and interpret the gospel and the doctrines of the church with authority'. The 'dominant feature' must be 'the differentiation between clergy on the one hand and laity on the other'. (*Walsh v Lord Advocate* [1956] 3 All ER 129, [1956] 1 WLR 1002, HL, *per Lord Patrick and Lord Mackintosh*), a point accepted more recently in *Methodist Conference (President) v Parfitt* [1984] QB 368, [1983] 3 All ER 747, [1984] 2 WLR 84, when a Methodist minister claimed unfair dismissal and the Court of Appeal found that the doctrinal standards of the church did not provide for a contractual relationship between the church and the individual minister. It follows from this that remunerated 'apostles', 'elders' and the like in the unstructured, charismatic, non-denominational churches ('New Churches') are not 'ministers of religion' since a feature of such churches is the absence of a distinction between clergy and laity: any member may teach, preach and administer the sacraments. Similarly, a member of the Jehovah's Witnesses — though termed 'a minister of God' — is not a 'minister of religion' since *all* members are termed 'ministers of God'. Likewise, a Sikh priest (ie a *granthi*) should probably not (contrary to practice) be regarded as a 'minister of religion' in this context because there is no system of ordination or formal training for the priesthood in the Sikh religion. The employment status of all such persons falls, therefore, to be decided according to normal criteria. Persons who will be regarded as ministers of religion by application of the stated test are ordained ministers and deaconesses of any denomination, trained deaconesses of the Methodist Church and the Baptist Church, evangelists under the Home Missions Committee of the Methodist Church, commissioned officers of the Salvation Army, Jewish ministers and rabbis and Muslim imams.

In *R(P)7/54* (a reported decision of the National Insurance Commissioner in the retirement pension series) it was accepted that members of an enclosed devotional order are engaged neither under contracts of service nor under contracts for services. The latter view of the then DSS was, however, that such persons were employed earners and that Class 1 contribution liabilities arose on the whole of their earnings even if those earnings were covenanted in whole or in part to the order. (Letter from DSS 5 June 1987 and the 1996 edition of (now obsolete) DSS Leaflet CA 28, page 79, Item 53.)

A stipend or salary or any regular payment of a similar kind, however described, must be payable *as of right* for it to be recognised as such for the purpose of the categorisation rule and must form the *major* part (ie over half) of the minister's remuneration. In deciding whether or not the stipend or salary represents over half of a minister's total remuneration, such benefits as free housing, the provision of a motor vehicle etc are to be disregarded. [*Social Security (Contributions) Regulations 2001, SI 2001/1004, Sch 3 Part X para 13*]. (See also HM Revenue and Customs National Insurance Manual NIM02260 and NIM02315). This rule should not be disturbed by the *Finance Act 2015 (FA 2015), s 13* reform abolishing the P9D and creating special exemptions for ministers of religion (see *Income Tax (Earnings and Pensions) Act 2003 (ITEPA 2003), ss 290C–290G*) with effect from 6 April 2016. It should be noted that those rules also do not attempt to define the term 'minister of religion', so the case law mentioned here should apply.

Because the remuneration payable to ministers of the Elim Pentecostal Church is, under the constitution of that church, the last call on church funds and is not payable if no funds remain after all other expenses have been met, that remuneration does not constitute 'stipend or salary' for the purposes of the regulations. Accordingly, an Elim Pentecostal minister — though a 'minister of religion' — is excluded from the categorisation rules and is, according to normal criteria, regarded as a self-employed earner.

A Roman Catholic priest has likewise for many years been regarded as self-employed because of the absence of a right to remuneration, although some small stipends may be payable and the matter is known to have been under review.

HMRC accepts that if a minister receives offerings, gifts or fees direct, which are not part of their stipend or salary, then the payments do not constitute earnings and no NICs are due on them (NIM02260).

Case law

[46.3] Recent case law, including a case decided by the House of Lords, have added to the confusion about which ministers are to be treated as employees. In *Percy v Board of National Mission of the Church of Scotland* [2005] UKHL 73, [2006] 2 AC 28, [2006] 4 All ER 1354, Ms Percy, who was ordained as a minister within the Church of Scotland, claimed sexual discrimination. The employment tribunal, employment appeals tribunal and the Court of Session had held her not to be an employee within the meaning of the *Sex Discrimination Act 1975*. In an appeal to the House of Lords she submitted that she was engaged 'under a contract to personally execute any work or labour'. The House of Lords upheld her appeal and pertinently stated that the fact that someone is an office holder does not mean that he or she cannot be working under a contract. This case was then followed by the employment appeal tribunal *New Testament Church of God v Stewart* [2007] IRLR 178 where there was no written contract between Rev Stewart and the Church but he was paid through the payroll and was a member of the pension fund. Rev Stewart was dismissed by the Church and the tribunal held that there was a legal relationship between him and the Church sufficient to create a contract of service and his unfair dismissal was confirmed. This case was subsequently heard in the Court of Appeal where the judges agreed unanimously with the employment tribunal's findings but did state that their decision 'does not involve a general finding that ministers of religion are employees.' These cases, particularly the *Percy* case, may now call into question the previously held view that such Ministers of Religion are neither office holders nor employees under contracts of service. See Taxation Magazine 15 March 2007, page 296. In particular, in *Preston v President of the Methodist Church* [2011] EWCA Civ 1581, [2012] QB 735, [2012] 2 All ER 934, the decision in *Parfitt* was regarded by the EAT and the Court of Appeal as having been superseded by the decision in *Percy*. The concept of a rebuttable presumption that there was no intention to create legal relations of an employer-employee nature between a church and its clergy had by then been abandoned. In effect, the primarily spiritual role of a minister could not by itself justify denying the existence of contractual relations. However, the Supreme Court (*President of the Methodist Conference v Preston* [2013] UKSC 29, [2013] 2 AC 163, [2013] 4 All ER 477) disagreed, restoring the status quo ante, holding that (absent any special arrangements) the appointment of a Methodist minister was made solely under the church's constitution rather than under a contract.

The most recent case of note involving Church of England clergy is *Sharpe v Bishop of Worcester (in his corporate capacity)* [2015] EWCA Civ 399, [2015] IRLR 663, in which a rector claimed to have been unfairly dismissed and to have suffered a detriment as a result of having been a 'whistleblower'. To win the former point, he had to show that he was an employee under a contract of service, while the latter depended on his falling into the scope of the term 'worker'. The Court of Appeal decided that there was 'no contract, let alone one of employment' (Davis LJ at 132). Doubts were also expressed about whether employment tribunals and lay courts had the right to interfere with matters of ecclesiastical law (Lewison LJ at 184), although this is arguably of relevance solely to the Church of England, whose authority is recognised in English law.

Several employment tribunals have ruled that a church organist is an employee of the Church of England and will have full employment rights. See, eg, *Sholl v PCC of St Michael & All Angels w St James, Croydon & Ors* [2011] ET 2330072/2010. In contrast to the question of the status of ministers, the consideration of vocation and spiritual issues is unlikely to be relevant to lay people in the church, so normal principles of categorisation will normally apply, albeit occasionally complicated by matters of canon law, which affects certain matters such as the appointment of a church organist.

Employment in other capacities

[46.4] A minister of religion may, of course, also be employed in some other capacity and may thus be an employed earner on general principles. Thus, the Secretary of State for Social Security has formally determined that a member of the Church of England clergy appointed director of education for a diocese of the Church of England is engaged under a contract of service and is an *employed earner*. (*M60 (1958)*). Similarly, it has been held that an ordained priest appointed Church of England chaplain at a general hospital by a Hospital Management Committee is engaged under a contract of service and is an *employed earner*. (*M61 (1958)*).

The Churches' Legislation Advisory Service (see www.churcheslegislation.org.uk) notes in its guidance note on 'Case law on church employment' that, in the Church of England, certain non-parochial clergy fulfilling specific functions for specific periods (such as clergy employed directly by the Archbishops' Council), although few in number, are undoubtedly employed under contract.

For the purposes of EC social security legislation, a missionary priest who was supported by contributions from his parishioners was regarded as *self-employed*. (*Van Roosmalen v Bestuur van de Bedrijfsvereniging voor de Gezondheid, Geestelijke en Maatschappelijke Belangen, Case 300/84, 29 October 1986, The Times*).

Secondary contributors

[46.5] In the case of employment as a minister of the Church of England, the *Church Commissioners* for England fall to be treated as the secondary contributor. [*Categorisation Regs, Sch 3 para 7*].

The secondary contributor in relation to any other employment as a minister of religion is, however, to be identified by examining the source of his remuneration. In this connection, 'remuneration' includes any payment in respect of stipend or salary which would be earnings for contribution purposes under the normal rules *excluding* any specific or distinct payment made towards the maintenance or education of a dependant of the person receiving the payment (see EARNINGS FROM EMPLOYMENT: GENERAL 29). [*Categorisation Regs, Reg 1(2)*].

Where the whole of such remuneration is paid from one fund, the person responsible for the administration of that fund is to be treated as the secondary contributor. [*Categorisation Regs Sch 3 para 8(a)*]. This will be so even if the fund is assisted by another fund in order to be enabled to make the payment.

Where, however, a minister is remunerated directly from one fund but receives *regular additional payments* from one or more other funds, the person responsible for the administration of the fund out of which such payments are made to the greatest number of ministers is to be treated as the secondary contributor. [*Categorisation Regs, Sch 3 para 8(b)(i)(ii)*]. This generally means, in practice, that where some payments are made from a local fund and others from a central fund, the person responsible for administering the central fund falls to be treated as the secondary contributor, irrespective of the comparative values of the local and central payments.

Where a minister is remunerated from more than one fund but each fund makes payments to an equal number of ministers, the person responsible for administering the fund from which a minister first receives a payment of remuneration in the tax year is to be treated as the secondary contributor. [*Categorisation Regs, Sch 3 para 8(b)(iii)*].

There will be a secondary contributor as regards each separate employment in which a minister of religion is engaged and for which he is separately remunerated (eg the Church Commissioners with regard to stipend and a local authority with regard to teaching work undertaken). Where, however, a minister has but one employment there will be but one secondary contributor, identified according to the rules stated and that secondary contributor will be responsible for paying and accounting for *all* contributions due in respect of payments made to the minister, however many funds are involved.

Earnings

[46.6] Stipends and salaries are earnings. However, fees for conducting weddings, funerals, etc can be legally assigned by deed to a Diocesan Board of Finance and in such cases the fees are not treated as earnings. It is also not unknown for retired ministers, already in receipt of a church pension, to conduct weddings and funerals and receive fees for doing so. HMRC regards this as neither employment nor the carrying on of a trade or profession on a commercial basis, so such income is taxed as miscellaneous income under *ITTOIA 2005* and is not earnings for NIC purposes.

HM Revenue and Customs regards reimbursements to ministers of religion for household expenses (eg heating and lighting, cleaning) as payments towards expenses actually incurred in the employment (*ITEPA 2003 ss 290A, 290B, 351*). Such expenses are explicitly excluded from income tax liability by *ITEPA 2003, s 290C(2)(a)* with effect from 6 April 2016 as a result of *FA 2015, s 13(2)*. In so doing it is recognised that ministers of religion pursue a pastoral vocation which encompasses their whole way of life and of which their families form an integral part and also that they may be required to live in and maintain ecclesiastical property to discharge their vocation. From 6 April 2010 by law and previously by practice there is therefore excluded from earnings for Class 1 purposes any reimbursements for heating and lighting, and cleaning. In fact, NIM05698 states succinctly:

> It would be very difficult, if not impossible, to establish exactly how the reimbursement of expenses is divided between the business and private use of the accommodation. We therefore exclude from Class 1 NICs any reimbursement of expenses in respect of heating, lighting and cleaning.

[*Social Security (Contributions) (Amendment No 2) Regs 2010, SI 2010/188, Reg 2* and *Enactment of Extra-statutory Concessions Order 2010, SI 2010/157*; *Social Security (Contributions) Regulations 2001, SI 2001/1004, Sch 3, part 10, para 8*, as amended.]

However, prior to 6 April 2010, this principle did not extend to Class 1A contributions, which will have been in point where – as might often be the case – the employer had entered into the contracts for these services.

Normal rules apply to most other expenses, including telephone and motor expenses. If a minister of religion is living in a property owned by their Church and that Church is responsible for the council tax, water or sewerage charges, NICs are not due on the payment (see HM Revenue and Customs National Insurance Manual NIM 02103).

Particular issues may arise in respect of travel expenses, where no special rules apply: a mileage allowance up to 45ppm may be paid free of NICs in respect of business mileage, but it is important to recognise whether a particular journey is travel in the performance of duties, or for necessary attendance at any place in the performance of duties, or substantially ordinary commuting. A minister travelling around his parish to visit his parishioners, the school, the hospital, etc as part of his duties will usually be travelling to a temporary workplace. However, where a minister is appointed to a living without having to move to the vicarage or rectory in the parish, such that he or she commutes from outside the area to carry out his duties, it may be that the mileage between home and the church or parish office constitutes ordinary commuting and as such any mileage allowance must be treated as earnings for NIC purposes, as none of the exclusions in *Part VIII* of *Sch 3* to the *Contributions Regs 2001* may apply.

Compensatory payments

[46.7] In order to clarify the NIC treatment of compensatory payments made to individuals who resigned from the Church of England and gave up their living over the ordination of women priests, the Contributions Agency Technical Services issued a circular in November 1995 setting out the position:

> The Church of England's decision to allow the ordination of women priests has meant that a number of the clergy consider that they have no option but to resign on the grounds that their conscience does not allow their continuance in the Church. The scheme to draw up a system of benefits to compensate those that felt they had to resign was introduced in early 1994 under the Ordination of Women (Financial Provisions) Measure but it only covers the Church of England. To benefit from the measure introduced, those clergy resigning as a matter of conscience must do so between 25 August 1993 and 24 February 2004. On resignation the individual must have been in paid ecclesiastical service of not less than five years within the Province of Canterbury or the Province of York. (This covers the whole of England, Europe, the Channel Islands and the Isle of Man but nowhere else within Great Britain and Northern Ireland). The individual resigning must
>
> - cease to hold employment or ecclesiastical office, and
> - cease to receive remuneration in the form of stipend or salary.
>
> Three categories of payment arise from the Measure and these are periodical payments, resettlement grants and discretionary retraining grants. The payments made under the provision of the Measure are compensatory payments, not rewards for past services or inducements to continue to perform services, and therefore are not earnings. As a result there is no NIC liability on these payments.

These details (together with further information about the payments that were made to such individuals) are now to be found at HM Revenue and Customs National Insurance Manual NIM02630.

Key Points regarding ministers of religion and NICs

[46.8] Points to consider are as follows.

- Accommodation outgoings reimbursed to Ministers of Religion are not taxable or subject to Class 1 NICs and this includes heating/lighting, gardening in qualifying premises and cleaning of qualifying premises.

- Where a minister provides teaching duties at say an independent school's chapel, college or university religious instruction see LECTURERS, TEACHERS AND INSTRUCTORS 44 for the position prior to 6 April 2012.
- HM Revenue and Customs is currently contending that many leaders in the 'New Churches' have become office holders and thus liable to Class 1 contributions. There is, however, no current guidance in HMRC's NI Manual or Employment Status Manual, which suggests that HMRC does not feel it is on solid ground.

47

Multiple Employments

Cross-references. See AGGREGATION OF EARNINGS 5; ANNUAL MAXIMUM 7; CLASS 1 CONTRIBUTIONS 15; CLASS 2 CONTRIBUTIONS 18; DEFERMENT OF PAYMENT 27; REPAYMENT AND REALLOCATION 55.

Other Sources. HM Revenue and Customs National Insurance Manual NIM10010 with embedded NIM Appendix 3 questionnaire and NIM12023.

Introduction to multiple employments

[47.1] It is a general principle of contribution law that a separate potential liability is to arise in respect of each employed earner's employment in which a person is engaged and in respect of any self-employment. [*SSCBA 1992, s 2(5), s 6(4)*]. In contrast all self-employments in which a person may engage are treated as one since a person has only one 'self' by whom he may be employed.

In some circumstances, earnings from one or more of a person's employed earner's employments may, or must, be *aggregated* (see AGGREGATION OF EARNINGS 5) in which case those multiple employments become effectively a single employment.

In other circumstances, where it is clear that contributions paid in one or more employed earner's employments will comfortably exceed the annual maximum contribution liability of the contributor concerned, liability on earnings from any remaining employments and self-employments may be deferred and those earnings ultimately excepted from liability at the main rate. Since 6 April 2003, all earnings in excess of the Earnings Threshold in deferred employments have attracted the additional rate (currently 2%) – whether not contracted-out, contracted-out or married woman's reduced rate (see ANNUAL MAXIMUM 7 and DEFERMENT OF PAYMENT 27).

Where there are employments with earnings which may neither be aggregated with other earnings nor temporarily disregarded under a liability-deferment arrangement, however, contributions in excess of the annual maximum standard contribution liability may well be paid and, in that event, a repayment of contributions will need to be obtained (see 55.8 REPAYMENT AND REALLOCATION).

Avoidance of excessive secondary contributions

[47.2] Although the effect of the various provisions referred to at **47.1** above is to limit an earner's combined primary standard Class 1 contribution liabilities to an annual maximum – adjusted and personalised since 6 April 2003 in respect of the additional rate of 1% or 2% – secondary Class 1 contribution liabilities arising on the earner's earnings remain completely unaffected.

Given the absence of any Upper Earnings Limit for secondary contributions from 6 October 1985, consolidating payments due under separate jobs into one contract will increase secondary (and primary) contribution liabilities by allowing only one slice of earnings up to the Earnings Thresholds to be charged at 0%.

Example

Angelica is a director of Basil Ltd, Camomile Ltd and Dill Ltd. For the year 2018–19, director's fees on which Class 1 liability arises are £5,000 from B, £9,000 from C, and £10,000 from D. Class 1 contribution liabilities are as follows.

			Primary		*Secondary*	
	£		%	£	%	£
B	5,000	(below ET)	—	—	—	—
C	9,000		Nil/12	69.12	Nil/13.8	79.49
D	10,000		Nil/12	189.12	Nil/13.8	217.49
	24,000			258.24		296.98

If, however, B, C and D had made an arrangement whereby all A's fees were paid through, say, B (with B making service charges to C and D to recover their share of such fees), Class 1 contribution liabilities would have been

B	24,000	Nil/12	1,869.12	Nil/13.8	2,149.49

As such an arrangement produces liabilities over seven times the primary and secondary Class 1 liability, it should, of course, be avoided. If it *is* avoided, however, HM Revenue and Customs may attempt to enforce the higher liability by contending that B, C and D are carrying on business in association and by insisting that, in those circumstances, AGGREGATION OF EARNINGS 5 must take place. In that event, the impracticability exemption should be pleaded if it is appropriate in the circumstances of the case (see **5.7** AGGREGATION OF EARNINGS).

Companies economically unassociated

[47.3] It follows that, where companies are economically unassociated (ie are *not* carrying on business in association for contribution purposes) but are constitutionally associated to a sufficient degree to permit the making of advantageous arrangements between themselves, the fragmentation of a single employment into multiple employments may prove extremely beneficial, subject to convincing HMRC that any recharges do not mean that the companies are sharing personnel and therefore 'carrying on business in association'. If, for instance, using the facts in the example in **47.2**, A was a director only of B with director's fees of £24,000, the contribution bill could have been substantially reduced by reducing her fees from B to £7,000 pa and appointing her a director of C and D with fees of £8,000 pa and £9,000 pa respectively. (See HM Revenue and Customs National Insurance Manual NIM10010 and Appendix 3 – NB, the latter is not included in the manual's index but is accessible from the given page.) Given that both employee and employer thresholds are just over £8,400 per annum it would be possible to remove all liabilities if the fees were spread evenly over all the directorships. Such steps, however, may encourage HMRC to have a closer look at matters.

At the CA Specialist Conference in Newcastle on 29 October 1997 it was stated:

> There are many aspects that we would need to look at to arrive at a decision on trading in association, such as: whether or not they are sharing resources; whether or not they are sharing staff; if they are involved in contracts where they would both share — it is not enough to merely identify premises and directors.

It is perhaps worth noting that the rules on connected employers for employment allowance purposes, introduced in April 2014, take a much more detailed, prescriptive, formulaic approach, based broadly on the rules in the tax legislation for close company connections, when determining whether an employer is excluded from claiming the allowance because of economic interdependence between related businesses.

Apportionment of secondary contributions

[47.4] Where a *single payment* of earnings is made in respect of two or more employed earners' employments under different secondary contributors, and those secondary contributors are *not* carrying on business in association with each other, the payment of earnings is to be *apportioned* to the secondary contributors in proportion to the earnings due from each and contribution liability is to be calculated accordingly. [*SSCBA 1992, Sch 1 para 1(7); Social Security (Contributions) Regulations 2001, SI 2001/1004, Reg 17(b)*].

Where the secondary contributors *are* carrying on business in association *as regards the two or more employments in question*, contribution liability may be determined by treating the entire payment as due from the secondary contributor by whom it is made. [*Social Security (Contributions) Regulations 2001, SI 2001/1004, Reg 17(a)*]. As has been noted, the NIC&EO applies an economic, not a constitutional test, in determining whether or not businesses are being carried on in association (see **5.4** AGGREGATION OF EARNINGS).

Key Points regarding multiple employments

[47.5] Points to consider are as follows:

- The £8,424 (for employee and employer) NIC thresholds provide the opportunity to spread more fees over different directorships where the businesses are not trading in association.
- The splitting of remuneration among loosely-connected businesses is likely to lead to closer official scrutiny of the associations between the businesses.

48

National Insurance Fund

Cross-references. See ADMINISTRATION 2; **13.1** BENEFITS for description of benefits payable out of the National Insurance Fund.

Other Sources. Simon's NIC, Part I, Section 1, Section 2, Chapter 8.1.

Introduction to the national insurance fund

[48.1] On 1 April 1975, the National Insurance (Reserve) Fund (established under *National Insurance Act 1946* on 5 July 1948) and the Industrial Injuries Fund (established under *National Insurance (Industrial Injuries) Act 1946*) were wound up and their assets and liabilities were transferred to the National Insurance Fund. This fund was originally under the control and management of the Ministry of Pensions and National Insurance, then the Secretary of State for Health and Social Security, and then the Department of Social Security, but following the transfer of the former Contributions Agency to the then Inland Revenue on 1 April 1999, the National Insurance Fund now comes under the control and management of HM Revenue and Customs. Periodically, accounts of the fund are prepared at Treasury direction and, after being examined, certified and reported on by the Comptroller and Auditor-General, are laid before Parliament. [*SSAA 1992, s 161* as amended by *SSC(TF)A, Sch 3 para 5* and *Commissioners for Revenue and Customs Act 2005, Sch 4 para 47*]. The most recent report covers the 2016–17 tax year, published on 17 October 2017. The most significant points in the report were that income to the GB

Fund (ie, excluding the Northern Ireland fund) was £98.29 billion and payments out were £99.54 billion. This left a balance in the Fund at 31 March 2017 of £21.9 billion compared with £23.7 billion at 31 March 2016.

Quinquennial review

[48.2] Every five years the Fund and the social security scheme in general are to be subjected to a review by the Government Actuary who, having regard to current contribution rates, expected future contribution yields and other relevant factors, is to determine the extent to which the fund may be expected to bear a proper relationship to the demands made upon it in respect of benefits, and is to report to the Treasury who then lays the report before Parliament. [*SSAA 1992, s 166* as amended by *SSC(TF)A 1999, Sch 3 para 55*].

Quinquennial reviews covered the periods from 1975 to 1980, 1980 to 1985, 1985 to 1990, 1990 to 1995, 1995 to 2000 and 2000 to 2005. That for the five years to 5 April 2005 was not published until March 2010 (just ahead of the expiry of the subsequent five-year period), while the report for that period was itself not published until 17 July 2014. One of the major items settled by the quinquennial review was once the appropriate level of the contracting-out rebate for the next five years. The five-yearly pattern of review of the contracting-out rebate was broken, however, with a reform to this rebate from 6 April 1997 on the introduction of contracting out via money purchase schemes. Changes thereafter followed on the subsequent five-yearly anniversaries, ie 6 April 2002, 6 April 2007 and 6 April 2012 (see **23** CONTRACTED-OUT EMPLOYMENT). Following the abolition of contracting out on 5 April 2016, this element of the quinquennial reporting process is no longer necessary.

The 2010 report projected the future of the NI Fund to 2075 and factored in, albeit without great detail, the effects of the *Pensions Act 2014*, which was then set to introduce the single-tier state pension from April 2016, abolish S2P and contracting out from the same date, and programme rises in the state pension age. One of the findings of the 2010 review was that, without the *Pensions Act 2014* changes, the NI Fund would reach a nil balance by 2027 and would need to be supported by significant transfers from tax revenues each year thereafter. Without the reforms, the combined Class 1 contribution rate (employer + employee) would have had to rise to around 35% by 2075 to cope with paying pensions to an ever large proportion of pensioners in the population.

The 2015 report projected the future of the NI Fund to 2080–81 and is slightly more positive in that the projected deficit and subsequent increase in contribution rates were less than projected in the 2010 report. The NI Fund is expected to be exhausted by around 2032–33; combined Class 1 contribution rates in 2070–71 would have to rise to around 26% (previously 35%) and to around 27% by 2080–81.

Annual review

[48.3] In practice, the National Insurance Fund is reported upon each year (though less fully than under the quinquennial review), because a report by the Government Actuary is required whenever a draft order for changes in contribution rates etc is to be made by the Treasury.

In each tax year there is required to be carried out a review of the general level of earnings, taking into account changes in that level which have taken place since the last review, with a view to determining whether an order should be made varying for the ensuing tax year the weekly rate of Class 2 contributions (see **18.6** CLASS **2** CONTRIBUTIONS), the Class 2 exception or small profits level (see **18.4** CLASS **2** CONTRIBUTIONS), the rate of Class 3 contributions (see **19.8** CLASS **3** CONTRIBUTIONS), and/or the annual lower and upper profits limits for Class 4 contribution purposes (see **20.9** CLASS **4** CONTRIBUTIONS). [*SSAA 1992, s 141*].

Following such a review, there may be made, if it is thought expedient to do so, an order changing (within defined limits) the various rates and levels mentioned and also the maximum percentage rates for primary and secondary Class 1 contributions (see **15.5** CLASS **1** CONTRIBUTIONS) and the percentage rate for Class 4 contributions (see **20.9** CLASS **4** CONTRIBUTIONS). [*SSAA 1992, s 143*]. Whenever there is laid a draft of any such order before Parliament, there must, however, be laid with it a copy of a report by the Government Actuary on the likely effects of the order on the National Insurance Fund. The order is usually laid with the Government Actuary's report in January each year. [*SSAA 1992, s 142(1), s 144(1)* as amended by *SSC(TF)A 1999, Sch 3 para 45, Sch 3 para 48* respectively].

The 2018–19 estimates

[48.4] On the basis of figures set out in the Government Actuary's report of January 2018 on the draft *Social Security Benefits Up-rating Order 2018*; the draft *Social Security (Contributions) (Rates, Limits and Thresholds Amendments and National Insurance Fund Payments) Regulations 2018*; the income and outgoings of the National Insurance Fund for 2018–19 are likely to be as set out below.

	£ million	*£ million*	*£ million*		*£ million*
Contributions (see 48.6)				Retirement pensions	96,083
Class 1 primary	51,463			Widows' bereavement benefit	491
		51,463		Incapacity benefit	0
				Employment and support allowance	4,608
Class 1 secondary	74,403			Maternity allowance	454
		74,403		Contribution based JSA	301
				Guardian's allowance	2
SMP, SAP, SSP refunds		(2,653)		Pensioner's Christmas Bonus	124
Class 1A and 1B		1,534		Total contributory benefits	102,061

Class 2	508		Other payments	0
Class 3	16		Summary total benefit payments	102,061
Class 3A	No longer payable			
Class 4	2,935			
		128,206		
			Personal pension and stakeholder pension rebates and incentives (see 48.15)	–
Treasury grant (see 48.7)		NIL	Redundancy payments (see 48.13)	295
Consolidated fund (see 48.7 and 48.11)		2,645	NHS allocation (see 48.12)	24,937
State scheme premiums (see 48.8)		43	Northern Ireland transfers (see 48.14)	612
Investment income		174	Administration (see 48.15)	726
Other receipts		0	Other net payments	206
Excess of receipts over payments		(2,229)	Roundings	2
		128,839		128,839

Balance in hand

[48.5] The National Insurance Fund is not a true fund in that it has no significant balance available for investment. The anticipated balance in hand of £26.18 billion at the end of 2018–19 should be sufficient to support around 13 weeks of benefit expenditure and the remainder of fund expenditure must be met from current contributions and other fund income (such as a grant from the Exchequer). For this reason the scheme is described as a 'pay-as-you-go' scheme.

Before 2010–11 the balance in the Fund had tended to grow. Even with the recession reducing expected contribution receipts and increasing benefit expenditure the balance was not too significantly impaired. 15–20 years ago, the balance was often only sufficient to cover six to eight weeks' benefit expenditure, a level which it has now exceeded. On the basis of the central assumptions adopted by the Government Actuary in his January 2018 report, the balance in the National Insurance Fund is projected to rise to around £40.5 billion by 5 April 2023, representing some 35% of benefit expenditure. This differs very significantly from the small balance of £4.8 billion (4.5% of benefit expenditure) forecast for April 2020 in the Government Actuary's Report in January 2015 (NB: the comparative fund balances shown in the January 2016 report as having been forecast in the 2015 report were incorrect, as the 2016 figures shown excluded the adjusted Class 1 estimates actually used in the 2015 forecasts – 2016 showed the figures for 2015 before that adjustment). This significant drop in the projected balance in 2015's report was due to a combination of the higher NIC thresholds, the lowering of the UEL and the increased pensions expenditure caused by 'triple lock' uprating by 2.5% while earnings inflation, which determines how quickly contributions income grows, was much lower. The projection went very close to a position where a Treasury Grant would be needed, and the report suggested that the NI Fund would need to be topped up from general tax revenues by some £6.6 billion in 2015–16 if it was to maintain a level of two months' benefit entitlements. The major change in the fund's fortunes in the 2016 projections arises from the abolition of contracting-out rebates, which increases fund income by some £6 billion per year without a corresponding immediate increase in state pension expenditure.

Contributions

[48.6] It will be noted that, together, the main primary, additional primary and secondary Class 1 contributions account for around 97% of total contributions. It is not surprising, therefore, that because the fund's largest outlay relates to retirement benefits, the contribution scheme is sometimes described as an unfunded pension scheme supported by a payroll tax. Contributions in respect of employees in contracted-out salary-related occupational pension schemes were received up to April 2016 net of the contracted-out rebate. Since late 2012, the only rebates paid to money purchase schemes (occupational and personal) have been in respect of late claims for periods before 6 April 2012, when contracting out on a money purchase basis was abolished.

Consolidated Fund and Treasury Grant

[48.7] Until 6 April 1989, the National Insurance Fund was subsidised from general taxation by means of a Treasury supplement. That supplement was abolished by *SSA 1989, s 3* but, to compensate for the resulting loss of fund income, industrial injuries benefits, Statutory Sick Pay and Statutory Maternity Pay became payable out of general taxation rather than (as formerly) the National Insurance Fund. This change came into force with effect from 1 April 1990. [*SSCBA 1992, s 1(5); SSAA 1992, s 165(1)(b)*]. Recovery of SSP was abolished for most employers from 6 April 1994 and for the remainder from 6 April 2014 (see **48.11** below) but the relief given by the Percentage Threshold Scheme for 1995–96 and subsequent years up to its abolition was funded from taxation, although employers would initially recover it through their contributions remittances. The *Social Security Act 1993, s 2*, reintroduced the Treasury grant for 1993–94 onwards. However, while no Treasury Grant was required in the years 1998–99 to 2013–14 inclusive, the *Rerating Order* for 2014–15 set the Treasury Grant at a maximum of 5% of benefit expenditure, and this maximum was increased to 10% for 2015–16 (*Social Security (Contributions) (Re-rating and National Insurance Funds Payments) Order 2015, SI 2015/588, Reg 4*). No Treasury supplement or grant is expected to be needed for 2016–17 or the next five years.

State scheme premiums

[48.8] State scheme premiums are compensation payments which an employer must make to the State if, having taken responsibility for an employee's pension through a contracted-out pension scheme (see CONTRACTED-OUT

EMPLOYMENT 23), he subsequently transfers the responsibility for that employee's pension back to the State and the employee requalifies for S2P additions for the year or years in question. These rules are almost redundant from 6 April 2016 since contracting out was then abolished, although leavers in 2016–17 might still be eligible for refunds of contracted-out pension contributions made to employer COSR schemes in 2015–16, so the fund still included an estimate in 2016–17 for such premium payments and also in 2018–19.

Investment income

[48.9] At Treasury direction, monies in the National Insurance Fund may, from time to time, be paid over to the National Debt Commissioners for investment. [*SSAA 1992, s 165(3)*]. Because there is never a significant amount of fund income available for investment, however, the income generated by investment never represents more than 3% of total fund income (see 48.5 above) and, due to the current low rates of return available and low balance in the Fund, is only 0.03% for 2017–18.

Benefits

[48.10] Not all State benefits are paid from the National Insurance Fund. In particular, the non-contributory benefits listed at **13.1** BENEFITS are not so paid nor is the winter fuel allowance. See also 48.7 above as regards industrial injuries benefits.

Statutory sick pay, statutory maternity pay, statutory paternity pay, statutory adoption pay and statutory shared parental pay

[48.11] Under *SSCBA 1992, Part XI*, an employee's entitlement to sickness benefit (now employment and support allowance (ESA(C))) was removed but a corresponding responsibility was imposed on his employer to pay him Statutory Sick Pay (SSP) during that period at specified levels if he qualified. The SSP scheme continues in force.

From 1985 to 1991, the employer paying SSP was entitled to recover 100% of any SSP paid out, plus an amount of compensation for the employer NICs suffered on paying out what was, after all, a state benefit (the compensation rate in 1990–91 was 7%).

From 6 April 1991 to 5 April 1994, the employer's recovery was limited to 80% of the SSP so paid, with no compensation added, but recovery was then abolished, except for qualifying 'small' employers who had retained in April 1991 the right to recover 100% of their SSP payments for employees absent for at least six weeks. This small employer relief (SER) remained available until 5 April 1995, when SER was replaced by a new 'Percentage Threshold Scheme' (PTS). From 6 April 1995 to 5 April 2014, any employer qualifying under the PTS (payroll size was unimportant, but in practice only small employers could qualify) were entitled to recover some of the SSP paid to employees: if their SSP liability in any month exceeded 13% of their gross NIC liability, they could reclaim the excess. A reduction in the rate of Class 1 secondary contributions from 10.4% to 10.2% from 6 April 1994 was billed as compensating larger employers for the additional payroll cost arising from the abolition of the 80% recovery. Its abolition in 2014 was purportedly to fund a new 'Health & Work Service', to provide occupational health advice by way of a telephone helpline to SMEs, starting in late 2015.

In cases where it applied, the PTS recovery was effected by the employer deducting an equivalent amount from Class 1 contributions due to be remitted to HMRC. Thus, in PTS cases the NI Fund actually received an amount of secondary Class 1 contributions net of SSP.

The SER principle (but with 92% recovery from 4 September 1994 for all except eligible small employers, who continued to receive varying amounts of compensation – see **15.11**) operated in relation to Statutory Maternity Pay (SMP) which, from 6 April 1987, replaced maternity allowance for employed women, except for those women who did not qualify for SMP. SMP has, since inception, also been payable by the employer, now for up to 39 weeks of maternity absence (it was 18 weeks initially, then 26 weeks from April 2003 until April 2007), to any female employee who is expecting or bears a child. SMP first came into force for employees expecting a child on or after 21 June 1987. See **15.11** **CLASS 1 CONTRIBUTIONS**.

From 6 April 2003 the procedures for reimbursing employers in respect of the payment of Statutory Paternity Pay (SPP) and Statutory Adoption Pay (SAP) followed those described above for SMP, with the same 92% recovery rate and the same SER rules, currently allowing 103% recovery (reduced from 104.5% on 6 April 2011).

For women expecting a baby due to be born on or after 5 April 2015 (ie, the start of the first benefit week of 2015–16, rather than the start of the tax year), or adopting a child from the same date, the SMP and SPP rules were overtaken by new rules on statutory shared parental pay (SShPP) and leave. In summary, the mother's maternity leave and SMP/SAP may now, subject to conditions, be shared with the child's father/adoptive father, although the rate of payment and the level of reimbursement out of the NI Fund remain unchanged. A woman may opt to claim SMP, but can choose SShPP instead if she returns to work earlier.

The fund estimates at **48.4** above show the gross contributions as expenditure while the payments of SSP, SMP, SPP, SAP and ShPP are shown as income from the Consolidated Fund, as they are now made from general taxation as explained at 48.7 above.

National Health Service allocation

[48.12] A part of contributions received by the National Insurance Fund has always (since 1948) been allocated as a contribution to health service funds, although the NHS is principally funded from general taxes.

In the case of primary (main rate) and secondary Class 1 contributions, the part so allocated is a specified percentage applied to an amount of *earnings*; in the case of Class 1A and Class 1B contributions it is a specified percentage of the amount in charge to those classes of contributions; in the case of Class 2 and Class 3 contributions, a specified percentage of the *total contributions* of those classes; in the case of Class 4 contributions, a specified percentage applied to the amount of earnings in respect of which the contributions at the main rate have been paid; and in the case of Class 3A contributions, introduced by *Pensions Act 2014, Sch 15*, 15.5% of the amount estimated to be the total of those contributions [*SSAA 1992, s 162(5)(6), as amended by PA 2015, Sch 15, para 13*]. The Class 3A provision is unusual, in that this class of contribution is payable only by those already over state pension age, who are normally not required to make any contribution to NHS costs.

In the case of Class 1 contributions, until 5 April 2000, the percentages applied to the amount of earnings above the LEL on which contributions had been paid. From 6 April 2000, when the LEL ceased to be the starting point for liability, the allocation in respect of secondary contributions is the specified percentage applied to all earnings above the Secondary Threshold. In respect of primary contributions at the main rate the allocation is based on earnings between the Primary Threshold and the Upper Earnings Limit.

The relevant percentages may be varied by order of the Treasury, provided the increase or decrease is, in the case of primary or secondary Class 1 contributions and Class 4 contributions, not more than 0.1% and 0.2% respectively of the relevant earnings; in the case of Class 1A and Class 1B contributions, not more than 0.1% of the amount estimated to be the aggregate of the cash equivalents of the benefits used in calculating those contributions; and, in the case of Classes 2, 3 and now 3A, not more than 4% of the relevant contributions. [*SSAA 1992, s 162(7)(8) as amended by Pensions Act 2014, Sch 15, para 13.*] Variations which go beyond these limits require full legislation.

When the Chancellor imposed a 1%-point increase in Class 1 and Class 4 rates (with a new 'additional rate' on earnings or profits above the UEL / UAL) in April 2003, the whole of that £8bn increase was hypothecated to the NHS. When the additional rate became 2% in April 2011, the extra NI Fund income was not directed to the NHS but to increasing pensions at a rate above inflation.

Where secondary Class 1 contributions are reduced in the case of foreign-going mariners 45, the health service allocation was reduced to 1.6% from April 2003 (previously 0.6%). [*SSAA 1992, s 162(12); Contributions (Re-rating) Order 1989, Art 6*].

The NHS allocation out of secondary contributions in respect of under-21s and apprentices under 25 is somewhat anomalous, in that the legislation directs HMRC to pay an NHS allocation of 1.9% of all earnings between the secondary threshold and the UEL. Younger employees are not separately mentioned, so the 1.9% figure is due under the general rule because they have NICable earnings, even though there are in fact no secondary contributions collected on earnings in that band from such young earners.

The various percentage rates are set out below.

	Class 1 rate %								*Class 4 rate %*	
	Primary (main)	*Primary (additional)*	*Secondary*	*Class 1A %*	*Class 1B %*	*Class 2 %*	*Class 3 %*	*Class 3A %*	*Class 4 (main)*	*Class 4 (additional)*
2015–16 to 2018–19	2.05	1.00	1.90	1.90	1.90	15.50	15.50	15.50	2.15	1.00
2003–04 to 2014–15	2.05	1.00	1.90	1.90	1.90	15.50	15.50	n/a	2.15	1.00
1998–99 to 2002–03	1.05	—	0.90	0.90	0.90	15.50	15.50		1.15	—
1992–93 to 1997–98	1.05	—	0.90	0.90	—	15.50	15.50		1.15	—

[*SSAA 1992, s 162(1)(5), as amended by PA 2015, Sch 15, para 13.*]

Redundancy Fund

[48.13] On 31 January 1991 the Redundancy Fund was merged with the National Insurance Fund. Redundancy payments made by the State from that date now form part of benefit expenditure as shown, although their administration was until the July 2016 Whitehall reorganisation the responsibility of the Department for Business, Innovation & Skills rather than the DWP. It is likely in future to be the responsibility of the new Department for Business, Energy and Industrial Strategy ('BEIS').

Northern Ireland transfers

[48.14] The Joint Authority which co-ordinates the operation of social security in Great Britain and Northern Ireland is empowered to make financial adjustments between the National Insurance Fund and the Northern Ireland National Insurance Fund. [*SSAA 1992, s 177(3)*]. See **51.49** OVERSEAS MATTERS.

Pension scheme rebates and incentives

[48.15] Contributions in respect of employees who contracted out of S2P by means of an appropriate personal pension or an appropriate stakeholder personal pension were paid at the not contracted-out rate. HMRC NIC&EO (Pension Scheme Services, formerly known as 'NISPI' and, in the more distant past, Contracted-Out Employments Group or 'COEG') was then responsible for paying all the contracted-out rebate and (where relevant) age-related rebates (see **23.3** CONTRACTED-OUT EMPLOYMENT) to the personal pension provider. Similar arrangements also applied in the case of contracted-out money purchase arrangements. All these arrangements ceased with effect from 6 April 2012, although late claims for rebates were still shown in the Government Actuary's report in January 2014.

49

National Insurance Number

Cross-reference. See ADMINISTRATION 2.

Other Sources. Simon's Taxes Volume 2 Para A8.808–812; Leaflet CWG2 (2017), Employer's Help Book E13 (2013), pages 6, 7, HM Revenue and Customs National Insurance Manual NIM39000–39760 and Home Office Leaflet 'Prevention of illegal working—guidance for employers'; Tolley's Practical NIC Newsletter, July 1999, Tolley's Practical NIC Newsletter, November 2005; Message Implementation Guidelines for PAYE Full Payment Submission (2017/18).

Introduction to the National Insurance Number

[49.1] Under arrangements authorised by the Secretary of State for Work and Pensions, a National Insurance number (often referred to by HMRC as a 'NINO') is generally notified to a person born in the UK within the year preceding his sixteenth birthday under the so called 'Juvenile Registration Process'. [*Crediting and Treatment of Contributions, and National Insurance Numbers) Regulations 2001, SI 2001/769, Reg 9(3)*]. It is notified to him on a NINO notification letter which is given to him shortly before his statutory school-leaving date is reached. Up to November 2011 the number would have been notified via the issue of a NI Number card. Number cards have been replaced by a letter as part of a cost saving exercise. Cards issued after January 1984 up to October 2011 were plastic and resembled a credit card. The notification of a National Insurance number marks a person's registration with the state social security scheme. Employees who have never been given an NI number can apply to their nearest 'hub' (see **49.3**). Foreigners who come to the UK to work for a UK employer must apply for a NINO, but those who remain employed by a foreign employer and insured under the scheme in their state of origin, under EEA rules or a bilateral social security convention, are not entitled or required to apply and do not need a NINO.

National Insurance number format

[49.2] A National Insurance number consists of two prefix letters (see later), six figures and a suffix letter (eg AB 12 34 56 C) and it is by this number as it appears on returns, claims, elections and contribution collection documentation that a person's contribution record (against which claims to benefit are checked by the DWP) is maintained and updated in the NPS computer by HMRC (see 2.7 ADMINISTRATION and HM Revenue and Customs National Insurance Manual NIM39105, NIM39110). The letters D, F, I, Q, U and V are not used as either the first or second letter and O will never be used as the second letter. The prefix 'MA' is a Manx NI number, which cannot yet be processed by the RTI system but should not result in error messages (the Manx NI scheme is broadly similar to the UK scheme and records are administered by HMRC on behalf of the Manx Treasury). Prefixes 'BG', 'GB', 'KN', 'NK', 'NT', 'TN' and 'ZZ' are not to be used.

The suffix letter A, B, C or D is a legacy of the days when NI stamps were stuck on cards and returned to the Ministry of Pensions & NI (the predecessor of the DHSS and DSS) annually: cards with an 'A' suffix were sent back to Longbenton in March each year, 'B' cards were returned in June, 'C' in September and 'D' in December.

National Insurance numbers are, furthermore, used as reference numbers in the separate computerised PAYE system, and HM Revenue and Customs had transferred names, addresses, dates of birth and titles of contributors from the DSS's predecessor computer to the NIRS 2 system before NI and PAYE records were merged in the NPS. Contrary to popular belief, the numbers issued do not represent a code that reflects the holder's age, employer, address, etc.

Where HMRC issues forms showing NI numbers, in some cases the NI number shown differs from that already in use by an employer. In this situation, the NI number issued by HMRC should be used. Should the employee dispute that this is the correct NI number then he will need to contact HMRC. (See CWG2 (2017), para 1.2.2.)

Where the DWP cannot issue an NI number, but a PAYE record is required (eg for a young child in receipt of a dependant's pension from an occupational pension scheme), the former Inland Revenue would issue and use a temporary number until such time as the DWP was able to issue a true NI number. The temporary number was made up of the letters TN (ie temporary number) followed by the person's date of birth (expressed as six digits: DD-MM-YY) and a suffix of M (male) or F (female). However, such temporary numbers are now not acceptable and instead the date of birth and gender fields on the Full Payment Submission (FPS) when the employee is paid should be completed and the NINO box left blank. References beginning with 00 are issued temporarily to tax credit claimants who do not have a NINO but should not be entered on payroll records, as they will be rejected when filed. Other administrative prefixes include CR, FY, MW, NC, PP and PZ (eg, for expatriates who have a PAYE liability but no NIC liability).

Because HMRC's system used to reject submissions with no NINO, some employer legacy systems still insist on the entry of a validly-formatted NINO before they will submit payroll data. It is understood that some thousands of employees' returns are therefore still submitted showing AA 11 11 11 A or AB 12 34 56 C, although this is no longer necessary for HMRC's system.

Example

Kite Design Systems Ltd has a computerised payroll system and two new joiners in July 2016 who have no NI numbers. Jane is a university graduate born on 27 September 1987 and Bill is a previously long-term expatriate now seconded to the UK office. Bill will not disclose his date of birth to the employer. If the contributors do not know their NI numbers, they can ask HMRC for written confirmation of it by completing form CA5403, but this takes time and they are likely to reach their first payday before that confirmation is received.

If Jane and/or Bill do not produce an NI number shortly after starting work for the completion of the starter declaration, the payroll manager can ask the NIC&EO to find the number by submitting a National Insurance Number Verification Request (an 'NVR') through the payroll software (or HMRC's Basic PAYE Tools online) before paying them.

Alternatively, the first FPS should show a blank NI number field, but include full name, date of birth and gender fields, and HMRC's RTI system will try to match the employee's details to a record and issue an electronic notification. If there is a match, the employer will receive an online secure message advising the correct NI number for future use, and the employee will receive a form P217 in the post confirming the NI number.

Supplies of the old CA6855 form can no longer be obtained from HMRC as the 'NINO tracing service' has been closed down after the introduction of the NVR system. If Jane and Bill have claimed Social Security benefits since leaving school, they should already know their NI numbers.

Rules relating to NI numbers

Application for NI number

[49.3] Anyone who is resident or present in Great Britain (see **51.4** and **51.5** OVERSEAS MATTERS) and over the age of 16 and not exempt from UK National Insurance coverage by virtue of EC regulations or a treaty must, if he has not received notification as described at **49.1** above and is an employed earner or a self-employed earner or wishes to pay a Class 3 contribution, apply to the Secretary of State for a number. [*Social Security (Crediting and Treatment of Contributions, and National Insurance Numbers) Regulations 2001, SI 2001/769, Reg 9(1)(1A)(2)*, as amended by *Social Security (National Insurance Numbers) Amendment Regulations 2006, SI 2006/2897, Reg 2*; *Social Security (National Insurance Numbers) Amendment Regulations 2008, SI 2008/223, Reg 2*]. In practical terms, such an application will be made initially by telephone to the National Insurance Registrations helpline (0300 200 3502 or 0345 600 0643) at Jobcentre Plus (JCP). Most applicants will be invited to an appointment at a JCP office so that their identity may be verified before the issue of a NINO. Where a person is neither an employed earner nor a self-employed earner, there is no obligation to apply for an NI number unless and until that person wishes to pay a Class 3 contribution or claim a benefit.

With effect from 11 December 2006, any person applying for a NINO for work purposes must produce evidence of the right to work in the UK of the kinds set out in the *Immigration (Restrictions on Employment) Order 2007, SI 2007/3290* as amended by the *Immigration (Restrictions on Employment) (Codes of Practice and Amendment) Order 2014, SI 2014/1183)*.

With effect from 1 March 2007 anyone applying for a student loan who does not have a NINO (typically foreign-born students) will be required to apply for one, but the process will be initiated by the Student Loans Company, who will establish the student's right to reside in the UK before referring the applicant to the JCP.

From 1 April 2006 Jobcentre Plus created about 15 large scale interview locations ('hubs') with about 30 satellite offices dedicated to NINO work. Appointments for application interviews should be booked by initially contacting the helpline above. Employers bringing more than one employee in from overseas can book up to nine appointments via the helpline. Employers of staff coming from the EU or who hold UK work permits can use a fast-path application system which entitles them to complete a NINO application form CA5400 so that the employee does not need to visit a hub or satellite location to register. The employer, however, has to be on the DWP approved list. From around April 2012 agents acting on behalf of employers have been unable to request CA5400 forms. Guidance formerly in HM Revenue and Customs National Insurance Manual NIM39720 has now been hidden from the public, presumably because of concerns about fraud that relies on false NINOs. Numbers requested by post are usually issued within ten days of the completed form being received. The number is entered on a DWP letter and sent to the applicant. As already mentioned letters are now issued instead of number cards in all instances from November 2011 onwards. At the National Insurance number application appointment the individual will have to produce documentary evidence of identity, eg:

- current valid passport;
- a current immigration status document issued by the Home Office;
- EL3;
- an identity card issued by an EU/EEA Member State;
- a biometric immigration document; or
- various other official documents evidencing the holder's right to stay and work in the UK.

[*Immigration (Restrictions on Employment) Order 2007, SI 2007/3290*, Lists A and B, paras 1–6, as amended.]

The above documents are listed in detail in *Schedule 1* of *Social Security (Crediting and Treatment of Contributions, and National Insurance Numbers) Regulations 2001, SI 2001/769, Reg 9(1A)*, as amended by *Social Security (National Insurance Numbers) Amendment Regulations 2008, SI 2008/223, Reg 2 and Social Security (Miscellaneous Amendments) Regulations 2015, SI 2015/67*, as well as Appendix A of the Home Office's leaflet 'Prevention of illegal working—guidance for employers'.

If the person is unable to provide these documents an interview will normally take place and the individual will be asked to provide as much documentary evidence as possible including birth certificate, marriage certificate (if applicable), full driving licence (if applicable) and paid fuel/telephone bills in the person's name.

After establishing their identity and completing application form CA5400 the forms are sent to NIC&EO National Insurance Registration Section after the NINO details have been registered on the NIRS 2. Once the application has been made, the employee will be sent form CA5404, which can be shown to the employer as verification that the employee has applied for a number. It should be noted that under the *Asylum and Immigration Act 1996, s 8* such forms would not be sufficient as specified documents and thereby fail as a defence to a charge of employing an illegal worker. (See also Leaflet CWG2 (2017), para 1.2.3 and HM Revenue and Customs National Insurance Manual NIM39325.)

Employees on oil and gas platforms on the UK Continental Shelf are treated as working in the UK even if they are physically outside the 12-mile limit. Unless they are covered by a certificate from an overseas social security regime (eg, Norway, USA), they need a NINO. Those who commute to the rig from elsewhere in Europe and never set foot in the UK are able to apply for a NINO via the DWP's oil and gas team in Glasgow rather than having to come to the UK for an appointment with DWP.

Disclosure

[49.4] Anyone who has a National Insurance number must supply it to anyone who is liable to pay earnings-related contributions in relation to his earnings. [*Social Security (Contributions) Regulations 2001, SI 2001/1004, Reg 66, Reg 104(1)*].

An employee who cannot produce his National Insurance number should complete form CA5403 and send it to Newcastle. It is also possible to call on 0300 200 3502. The number will not be confirmed over the telephone, due to security concerns, but HMRC will write with the details.

Where an employee has lost the plastic number card, it is no longer possible to obtain a replacement, and confirmation will be by letter. A secondary contributor who is unable to obtain a National Insurance number from an employee of his should, if the number cannot be obtained by the employee from the contact centre, follow the RTI procedure outlined above and, having established the right of the employee to work legally in the UK, file the first FPS with a blank NI number field.

Immigration, Asylum and Nationality Act 2006

[49.5] The *Immigration, Asylum and Nationality Act 2006, ss 15–25* replaced from 29 February 2008 the *Asylum and Immigration Act 1996, s 8*, which created a criminal offence for an employer, who may be prosecuted for employing someone without the necessary immigration entitlement to work in the UK. This impacts on the employer who may be committing an offence unwittingly, but those employers who have made the NI number checks (and the document checks and, in certain cases, online checks required by UK Visas & Immigration) may not be liable to prosecution and a possible maximum fine of £20,000 per illegal employee if, despite having taken those steps, it turns out that they were employing an illegal worker. Enquiries regarding a person's right to work in the UK should be directed to the Home Office UK Visas & Immigration 'Sponsorship, Employer & Education' helpline on 0300 123 4699 and an i-form at www.immigrationstatuscheck.service.gov.uk/employers.

Whilst the employer is making checks on a potential new employee the checks must be consistent with the *Equality Act 2010*, covering such matters as race, sex and age discrimination laws. There is guidance issued by the Home Office on the *Immigration, Asylum and Nationality Act 2006* (see above) and this guidance includes advice on how to ensure that checks are not carried out by employers in a discriminatory way by employers.

Example

Death's Door Ltd has decided to take on extra staff as from 17 September 2016 and has interviewed a number of candidates. Having decided to make two of the applicants an offer of employment, the *Immigration, Asylum & Nationality Act 2006* obligations apply and are dealt with by Death's Door Ltd's personnel department by an insertion in the letter of offer as follows:

Dear . . . .

Following your interview with . . . . I am pleased to offer you the position of . . . . in the . . . . with this Company commencing on Monday, 17 September 2016. The salary offered for the position is £ . . . . per annum.

Under the *Immigration, Asylum & Nationality Act 2006*, we require evidence that you are permitted to work in the United Kingdom. A documented National Insurance number (shown on eg, a form P45, P60 or payslip, or tax assessment), together with a British or EEA or Swiss Passport or British birth certificate would fulfil this requirement. A copy of the original form will be made for our records or alternatively the form may be retained by us if you do not need it. If you do not have any of the above documents please contact the Human Resources Department as there are other documents which will also suffice for this purpose. The document should be sent with your other acceptance documents or brought with you on your date of start.

Please confirm your acceptance by signing and returning to me the attached copy of this letter and the Schedule of Principal Terms, together with other starter forms enclosed.

Etc.

Departmental records

[49.6] HMRC's records of NICs, currently on the NPS system, are crucial to contributors' benefit claims and remain so until they reach state pension age or die (and even thereafter because they might entitle a dependant to a benefit). It is therefore extremely important that they are correct and complete, throughout a working life that might span fifty years (or longer once state pension age rises above age 66).

HM Revenue and Customs (NIC) offices are all eventually to have direct access to contribution records at Longbenton.

Any UK resident individual or his personal advisers may now obtain details of his contribution record only through an online request to NIC&EO in Newcastle (see www.gov.uk/check-national-insurance-record). If the purpose of the request is to check how many qualifying years are on record for state pension purposes, the alternative i-form at www.gov.uk/check-state-pension will, for those with a NINO and a British passport, who can pass an instant online security check, provide an immediate list of all years of the working life, showing whether each is a full or partial year, taking into account earnings and credits.

The CA Specialist Conference in Newcastle on 29 October 1997 stated:

> We try and identify discrepancies and look into any differences, in terms of the National Insurance number we check – does it relate to that person? Is it correct? We want to make sure the names fully match those recorded against the National Insurance number. We check the address and also run against other Departmental records, for example Jobseeker's Allowance, Income Support records, to see if there is any overlap, such as someone working and claiming benefit. This is part of the Department's anti-fraud efforts.

Inaccuracies may sometimes occur in NIC&EO records, though such inaccuracies are, in many cases, attributable to errors or omissions in the returns made by employers (see **21.20** COLLECTION). At the 1996 Contributions Agency Specialist Conference, for instance, it was mentioned that about ten million of the returns received each year were *partially deficient* so that contributions could not immediately be credited to any particular contributor. Of these, about one million were such that it was necessary to contact the employer to resolve matters. Many of those one million had the employee's National Insurance number missing and this was the only defect. It was the case, from 6 April 1981, that the DSS did not try to trace the identity of individual contributors where computer techniques alone had failed and the contributions in question did not exceed the contributions which would be payable on earnings up to twice the Lower Earnings Limit. (Hansard 6th Series Vol 1 Col 123).

The compulsion on most employers' PAYE schemes to file electronically reduced very significantly the number of NINO and contributions errors as more problem P14s were picked up at the time of filing and rejected instantaneously for the employer to 'correct', and the introduction of RTI filing has led to further improvements in data cleansing.

It had been thought that the use of duplicate NINOs for various reasons including fraud was rife. However, in a reply to a written question in the House of Commons in 2004, the suggestion was that the problem seems to have been exaggerated, as the figures supplied stated that in the year 2003 the numbers of individuals using more than one NINO amounted to 303 and the extent of NINOs being used by more than one person in 2006 was 1,984. More recently, experience suggests that the most likely problem with records is the creation by HMRC's RTI system of duplicate records, where the system has treated a changed parameter in an FPS as an indication that a new employment has been created.

In all there are around 82 million National Insurance numbers held on the DWP Customer Information System (House of Commons Answer February 2011). The number is this large due to records of some 19,500,000 deceased persons not being removed as their contributions history may affect future benefit entitlements of their spouse or civil partner.

The computer record may be difficult to challenge and any such challenge will constitute an application for a decision of an officer of the Board of HM Revenue and Customs and be subject to possible appeal (see APPEALS AND REVIEWS 9).

Direct independent access to the records is, however, available to the Parliamentary Commissioner for Administration (the Ombudsman) and, on one occasion, certain errors and omissions were found. (House of Commons Paper 395, Session 1980–81, p 55, Case C 135/80). The Parliamentary Commissioner may only investigate a matter when a complaint made to a member of the House of Commons by a member of the public who claims to have sustained injustice in consequence of maladministration is referred to him. [*Parliamentary Commissioner Act 1967, s 5(1), s 8*].

In the effort to trace individuals' National Insurance records, for many years before the introduction of RTI filing, the form P46, signed by new employees who did not have a form P45, was sent by the HM Revenue and Customs tax office on to NIC&EO for their attention. This was expected to assist in the tracing and anti-fraud measures which are carried out (Inland Revenue Press Release, 9 October 1996). If the National Insurance number stated on the form was incorrect, or where no number was stated, the employer was informed, within seven to ten days, of the correct number. If the form disclosed no NINO, the local office advised the employer of the correct number. If the number was incorrect a notice giving the correct number was sent by NIC&EO to the employer (on form P46-5T) and to the employee (on form P217). If the employer applied to NIC&EO for notification of the number on form CA6855, it was advised either on that form or on CA6856. As outlined above, the procedure is now online under the RTI system, which incorporates into its specification the use of a NVR (NINO verification request) by employers who wish to check an employee's NI number before using it in a FPS. If the employer's payroll software does not offer the NVR facility, HMRC's Basic PAYE Tools may be used by any employer, irrespective of the number of employees on its payroll.

As part of the political debate before the EU referendum in June 2016, John Redwood MP asked the Home Secretary to make a statement on the number of NINOs issued to EU migrants (Hansard, 12 May 2016, c 717). The aim appeared to be to highlight the level of immigration from the EU following the issue of a paper by the Office for National Statistics on the same day. While the ONS provisionally estimated that annualised long-term international migration to the UK had reached 265,000 in the year to 30 June 2015, 697,000 NINOs had been issued to EU citizens in the same period. Over the previous five years, 2.2 million NINOs had been issued to adult overseas nationals, but only 1 million new immigrants had appeared in the statistics. This discrepancy was explained by the minister as being due to the fact that EU citizens often come to the UK to work for only short periods, for which they need a NINO, but they do not stay for long enough to be classed as immigrants. The estimates of immigrant numbers were based on the ONS's International Passenger Survey, which it regarded as a much more robust method of estimating migrant numbers than the issue of NINOs.

The numbers of new NINOs issued to EU nationals between March 2003 and March 2015 may be summarised as follows. The table was broken down by the ONS into three types of EU worker: those from the 'old' Europe, before expansion into Eastern Europe ('EU15'), those from the new accession states excluding Romania and Bulgaria ('EU8') and those from Romania and Bulgaria who were subject to work restrictions for seven years ('EU2').

Overview of NINO Registrations data for EU citizens (source: ONS, 12 May 2016)

Year ended 31 March	*EU15*	*EU8*	*EU2*
2004	85,548	19,842	8,361
2005	80,735	107,746	7,799
2006	97,832	269,279	5,706
2007	102,735	308,902	6,840
2008	107,465	293,865	36,923
2009	120,125	215,070	39,965
2010	91,335	151,320	30,201
2011	134,943	186,853	35,924
2012	143,855	168,941	35,571
2013	176,055	178,819	28,218
2014	190,398	181,804	64,920
2015	237,915	194,682	192,938

Valid National Insurance Number prefixes

[49.7] Where an employee provides a National Insurance number the employer may wish to check the number against the valid NI number prefixes (payroll software will often check the validity of the two-letter prefix, although the rest of the number and the suffix cannot be validated). These prefixes are shown in the Table below:

Valid National Insurance Number Prefixes
AA AB AE AH AK AL AM AP AR AS AT AW AX AY AZ
BA BB BE BH BK BL BM BT
CA CB CE CH CK CL
EA EB EE EH EK EL EM EP ER ES ET EW EX EY EZ
GY
HA HB HE HH HK HL HM HP HR HS HT HW HX HY HZ
JA JB JC JE JG JH JJ JK JL JM JN JP JR JS JT JW JX JY JZ
KA KB KE KH KK KL KM KP KR KS KT KW KX KY KZ
LA LB LE LH LK LL LM LP LR LS LT LW LX LY LZ
MA MX

NA NB NE NH NL NM NP NR NS NW NX NY NZ
OA OB OE OH OK OL OM OP OR OS OX
PA PB PC PE PG PH PJ PK PL PM PN PR PS PT PW PX
RA RB RE RH RK RM RP RR RS RT RW RX RY RZ
SA SB SC SE SG SH SJ SK SL SM SN SP SR SS ST SW SX SY SZ
TA TB TE TH TK TL TM TP TR TS TT TW TX TY TZ
WA WB WE WK WL WM WP
YA YB YE YH YK YL YM YP YR YS YT YW YX YY YZ
ZA ZB ZE ZH ZK ZL ZM ZP ZR ZS ZT ZW ZX ZY
The characters D, F, I, Q, U and V are not used as the first or second letter in a prefix. Character O is not used as the second letter.
Various of the newer prefixes in the 'P' and 'S' ranges listed above are still being introduced currently.

(Quality Standard Validation Specification from April 2011).

Note to above Table: GY and JY prefixes are issued by the Guernsey and Jersey authorities and up to April 1975 the Channel Islands NINO was used on the mainland if an individual came to work here. The GY or JY NINO of a worker coming to the mainland for the first time after April 1975 is, however, not valid and such workers need to apply for a UK NINO just like any other worker arriving from abroad. Payroll software does, of course, need to be capable of accepting GY and JY NINOs until all affected workers (ie pre-1975) have passed state retirement age.

Rather perversely, whilst the above valid NINO prefixes are freely made available to employers as indicated, the equivalent paragraph in HM Revenue and Customs National Insurance Manual (NIM39115) states 'This text has been withheld because of exemptions in the Freedom of Information Act 2000'!

The following prefixes have been used internally by HMRC for a variety of reasons but are not accepted as valid NI numbers for the purposes of collecting or recording contributions:

- OO – tax credit cases where no NINO held;
- CR – Account Investigations use only;
- FY – old Attendance Allowance cases;
- MW – migrant workers before 1987 only;
- NC – personal and stakeholder pension payees with no NINO;
- PP – pensions scheme members only;
- PY & PZ – tax only cases (typically inbound expatriate workers) before 2002; and
- TN – temporary number formerly used by employers for P14 filing, now prohibited.

Any employee providing an NI number with any of these prefixes should be advised to contact HMRC so the correct number can be traced.

Prefix KC has recently begun to be issued to new registrants who have recently arrived in the UK to work. It was not initially added to the specification, so some payroll software rejects it. In such cases, employers are advised to leave the NINO field in the payroll record blank until the software has been updated to include the new KC number format.

As a consequence of the rejection of the KC prefix, HMRC has moved away from the above table of valid prefixes and has advised payroll software developers to validate NINOs as follows:

> 'National Insurance Number Prefix Validation Rules
>
> 1. The characters D, F, I, Q, U and V are not used as either the first or second letter of a NINO prefix.
> 2. The letter O is not used as the second letter of a NINO prefix.
> 3. Prefixes BG, GB, KN, NK, NT, TN and ZZ are not to be used.'

See Message Implementation Guidelines for PAYE Full Payment Submission (2017/18), Appendix B.

50

Oil-rig Workers, Divers, etc

Cross-references. See MARINERS **45**; OVERSEAS MATTERS **51**; SHARE FISHERMEN **56**.

Other Sources. Taxation magazine, 29 March 2001, page 636; Tolley's Practical NIC, January 2009, page 1.

Introduction to oil-rig workers, divers, etc and NICs

[50.1] As most of the UK continental shelf (UKCS) is outside the territorial waters of the UK, employment there is not employment in Great Britain and would, therefore, apart from regulations made under *SSCBA 1992, s 120*, be beyond the scope of contribution legislation, since anyone working outside the UK falls outside the definition of 'employed earner' unless he is deemed by regulation to be present in the UK (see **14.4** CATEGORISATION and **51.3** OVERSEAS MATTERS). Anyone who is employed (whether under a contract of service or not) in connection with the exploitation of resources or the exploration of the sea bed and subsoil in any area designated under *Continental Shelf Act 1964, s 1(7)* (ie by *Continental Shelf (Designation of Areas) Orders*) is, however, to be treated for contribution purposes as if those areas *are* in Great Britain, where the employment is in connection with any activity mentioned in *Petroleum Act 1998, s 11(2)*. Compliance with the general requirements of residence or presence is to be judged accordingly (see **51.4** and **51.5** OVERSEAS MATTERS). [*Social Security (Contributions) Regulations 2001, SI 2001/1004, Reg 114*]. Thus, anyone who would be an employed earner/self-employed earner were he engaged in relevant activities in Great Britain will be an employed earner/self-employed earner for contribution purposes if he is engaged in those activities in a designated area of the continental shelf (referred to below for brevity as the UKCS).

Oil-rig workers, divers and diving supervisors will be the main types of worker to whom these provisions apply. It should be noted that the deeming regulation applies only to persons in 'prescribed employment'. A person's own liability is to be determined as if the UKCS were in Great Britain, but this is not extended to his employer, who may operate in the North Sea without having a place of business in the UK or European Economic Area for NIC purposes (although the company is likely to have a deemed branch for corporation tax purposes). This usually meant, until 6 April 2014, that an employer had no secondary Class 1 liability even if the company was employing workers on the UKCS, provided it was not UK- or EEA-resident and had no presence onshore or within the 12-mile limit that amounted to a UK or EEA place of business.

This changed from 6 April 2014 as a result of *NICA 2014* and an amendment to the *Social Security (Contributions) Regulations 2001, SI 2001/1004* that was introduced to ensure that non-UK employers of UKCS workers paid employer NICs in the UK, and to stop avoidance achieved in the past by routing UKCS employments deliberately via an offshore intermediary.

NICA 2014, s 12 amended *SSCBA 1992, s 120* to insert with effect from 6 April 2014 a new definition of 'continental shelf worker' (CSW): a person in any prescribed employment (whether employed or self-employed) in connection with continental shelf operations. A new sub-section *(4)* was also inserted to allow for the deeming of secondary contributors and the creation of a new certification process to protect businesses using CSWs from unexpected liabilities when the CSWs are employed by another entity. New provisions inserted as *Social Security (Contributions) Regulations 2001, SI 2001/1004, Reg 114(4)(5)* identify the relevant secondary contributor and new *Regs 114A–114D* create the framework for certification. See further below.

Since November 2011 HMRC has been advising employers that mariners on vessels operating on the UKCS engaged in the relevant activities fall within the old CSW provisions rather than the specific mariner provisions. It is doubtful whether such advice was ever correct without the necessary legislative change, and that change has now been made. That was particularly so where the vessel was operating under an EEA flag and HMRC had agreed that the EU social security provisions took priority over UK domestic law. There is now a list of mariners' grades that will always be dealt with under the mariner rules in priority to the UKCS rules even if the work is carried out within the UKCS area.

HMRC contact centre

[50.2] For workers such as divers and those on oil rigs, etc specialist HMRC staff, based in Edinburgh, are available to give advice. Divers and diving contractors are normally dealt with by HMRC in Aberdeen. The postal address for enquiries is HM Revenue and Customs – Local Compliance, Marine Group S0970, Newcastle Upon Tyne NE98 1ZZ.

Continental Shelf Act 1964

[50.3] Orders made under the *Continental Shelf Act 1964* over many years were consolidated by the *Continental Shelf (Designation of Areas) Order 2013, SI 2013/3162* with effect from 31 March 2014, but they continue to have effect in respect of early orders made before the coming in to force of the *Territorial Sea Act 1987, s 2(4)*. The UKCS is now delineated by reference to a schedule of World Geodetic System coordinates specifying the boundaries of what is now, subject to a few exceptions, the UK's 'exclusive economic zone', which is the area up to 200 miles from coastal baselines agreed in treaties with all countries bounding the UK zone.

Definitions—'ship' and 'vessel'

[50.4] The terms 'ship' and 'vessel' are not further defined for National Insurance purposes, except to include hovercraft for the purposes of certain of the mariners' rules. [*Social Security (Contributions) Regulations 2001, SI 2001/1004, Reg 115*]. However, in merchant shipping law, a 'vessel' is any ship, boat or other vessel used in navigation, and a 'ship' is any vessel used in navigation not propelled by oars. [*Merchant Shipping Act 1995, s 313*]. In a Special Commissioners case it was determined that an oil drilling rig which was being towed by two tugs to its drilling site could be classed as a 'ship' for the purposes of *ITEPA 2003, ss 40, 385*. The fact that the drilling unit did 'not appear at first glance to be what the layman would describe as a ship' and it had no rudder, the oil rig 'was operating as a ship' and its 'movements were under the control of a master mariner' on the bridge of the unit—it was therefore, for these purposes, a ship. (See *Lavery v MacLeod* [2000] STC SCD 118 Sp C 230). In a further three cases in the Court of Appeal a 'jack-up' drilling rig with a floating hull and retractable legs was a ship—it is now accepted that 'rigs' can indeed be ships and this applies for the purposes of *s 115(1)* in the application of NIC earnings rules. (*Perks v Clark (HMIT); Perks v MacLeod (HMIT); Newrick and Granger v Guild (HMIT), CA* [2000] STC 1080).

Offshore drilling activities involve one of a number of vessels:

- drilling ships which comprise a drilling rig mounted amidships which may be a converted tanker or a custom built ship;
- semi-submersible rigs which float but have submerged thrusters which position it as well as being anchored to the sea bed;
- jack-up rigs which are towed from location to location and can be carried or towed for long distances.

In addition, a number of other vessels are used, such as floating production, storage and offloading (FPSO) vessels, floating storage units (FSUs) and floating accommodation ships ('flotels'). Seismographic survey ships and dive support vessels will generally not be classed as 'offshore installations' for the purposes of NICs or seafarer's earnings deduction unless they are stationed (whether moored to a rig, at anchor or using dynamic positioning) for more than five days in one location. See EIM33108–9.

Case law—'offshore installation'

[50.5] The Inland Revenue had accepted as 'ships' the first two types of drilling vessels noted above but not the last, although following the decision in the Court of Appeal in the above case this did change. See Taxation 29 March

2001, page 636 and Tax Bulletin 57, February 2002, page 915. However, the position was reversed for income tax purposes by *Finance Act 2004*. It took until 6 April 2014 for the National Insurance legislation to be changed along the same lines. See also EIM33101, *Torr and Others v Commissioners for Revenue and Customs* SpC 679 and *Spowage and Others v HMRC* [2009] UKFTT 142 (TC 110) for a discussion of how the actual use of a vessel rather than its description will determine whether it is, at a particular time, a ship or an offshore installation.

In a case relating to 1998–99, an individual (P) was employed on an offshore semi-submersible vessel, carrying out exploration for mineral resources. He claimed foreign earnings deduction under the income tax legislation then in force (see now *ITEPA 2003, s 379*). HMRC rejected his claim on the basis that the vessel was excluded from the definition of a 'ship' by *ITEPA 2003, s 385*, since it was an 'offshore installation' within the meaning of the *Mineral Workings (Offshore Installations) Act 1971*. [*ITA 2007, s 1001*.] The General Commissioners dismissed P's appeal and the Court of Session in Scotland upheld their decision as one of fact. Lord Penrose observed that 'it is undoubtedly the case that different regulations classify structures in different ways according to their purpose, and on occasion depending on the department of government sponsoring their promulgation. But the regulatory point of reference in this case is clear and specific and nothing can turn on the possible application of provisions that have not been incorporated for tax purposes.' *Palmer v HMRC* CS [2006] CSIH 8. In a more recent case an individual (L) was employed from 1999 to 2004 on a self-propelled oil drilling rig. He claimed foreign earnings deduction under income tax legislation then in force (see now *ITEPA 2003, s 379*). HMRC rejected his claim for the period during which the rig was in use, and the period before the rig was brought into use, on the basis that it was an 'offshore installation' within the meaning of the *Mineral Workings (Offshore Installations) Act 1971*, and was therefore excluded from the definition of a 'ship' by *ITEPA 2003, s 385*. However HMRC did accept that the rig was not an 'offshore installation' after it had been taken out of use, and therefore qualified as a ship for part of 2002/03. The Special Commissioner dismissed L's appeal, applying the Court of Session decision in *Palmer v HMRC* CS [2006] CSIH 8. *Langley v Revenue and Customs Comrs* [2008] STC (SCD) 298. In *Torr & Others v HMRC* [2008] STC SCD 772 Sp C 679 the decision resulted in HMRC reclassifying many oil industry vessels as outside the definition of a 'ship' for income tax purposes. Now EIM33103 states:

> The effect of this provision is that a structure that satisfies the definition of offshore installation will remain within the definition unless it has **permanently ceased** to be used as an offshore installation with no prospect of resuming such use **and** it has been put to an entirely new use.

This results in a further re-designation by HMRC of what is a 'ship' when considering oil industry vessels. See HMRC example below and HMRC Notice 16 December 2008.

Example

On 6 April 2007, a mobile drilling rig in port in Rotterdam obtained a contract for work in the Dutch sector of the North Sea from 1 May. It left Rotterdam on 30 April and carried out exploration drilling for gas until 31 July. On completion of its contract, it returned to Rotterdam and remained idle until 31 December. On 1 January 2008, it obtained a new drilling contract in the Gulf of Mexico and left Rotterdam on 1 February arriving in Mexican waters on 28 February where it drilled for oil between 1 March and 5 April.

The rig was an offshore installation throughout 2007–08. At any one time, it was either in use, to be used or it had been used for "exploration with a view to exploiting mineral resources by means of a well". This includes all periods in transit between locations and the periods when the rig was not used. Therefore, earnings attributable to any duties performed on the rig in 2007–08 are not eligible for SED.

Imposing secondary contributions

[50.6] As noted above, employers in the oil and gas industry have typically not been liable to pay secondary Class 1 NICs because they usually have no UK presence to which such a liability could attach. This was not always a matter of deliberate avoidance, but a feature of how the industry works. When drilling companies first moved into the North Sea, they were typically ultimately US-owned or US-controlled businesses, and their non-US workforce outside the US was employed by subsidiaries in various countries. Rigs might be owned by Swiss companies and operated by Panamanian or BVI-registered companies, which employed all the permanent workforce and hired in contractors for specialist roles. Provided they did not open an office in the UK, their presence on the UKCS was not sufficient to bring them within the scope of UK NICs, although they would have a deemed branch for corporation tax purposes. Typically, they would need a UK subsidiary to manage their logistical needs onshore and the operation of payroll would be subcontracted to such an associate, but accounting only for PAYE and primary NICs.

The lack of an employer liability came to be seen as unfair, and DSS and HMRC tried several times to seek liabilities based on inappropriate parts of the NIC legislation (eg, under the agency rules in the *Categorisation Regs 1978*). The liability has now been imposed, as noted above, by deeming one of a number of entities within UK jurisdiction to be the secondary contributor in relation to the earnings of continental shelf workers from 6 April 2014.

As already mentioned, the definition of offshore installation for tax purposes used to be irrelevant for NICs purposes. *Social Security (Contributions) Regulations 2001, SI 2001/1004, Reg 114* now uses it as peg on which to hang a secondary liability. Where a CSW is employed on or in connection with an offshore installation, the secondary contributor will now be:

- where the employer is present in the UK, the employer;
- where the employer has no such presence but has an associated company present in the UK, that associated company (and if there is more than one, the liability falls on the one with the greatest taxable total profit, in terms of *CTA 2010, s 4*, in the accounting period preceding the tax year in which the contributions are due); and

- where the employer has no presence and no UK associates, the oilfield licensee.

[*Social Security (Contributions) Regulations 2001, SI 2001/1004, Reg 114(4)* as inserted by *Social Security (Contributions) (Amendment No 2) Regulations 2014, SI 2014/572, Reg 2*.]

These rules override the mariner rules in *Social Security (Contributions) Regulations 2001, SI 2001/1004, Regs 115-125* to the extent that there is any conflict. [*Social Security (Contributions) Regulations 2001, SI 2001/1004, Reg 114(7)*.] HMRC stated in the explanatory memorandum to *SI 2014/572* that the original policy intention was that those on oil and gas industry vessels should not be treated as mariners and that the change merely restores that original intention. It seems more likely that the rewriting of the policy intention was caused by schemes hoping to take advantage of a statutory disregard in *Para 9* to *Schedule 3* to the *Social Security (Categorisation of Earners) Regulations 1978, SI 1978/1689* for employers of mariners by claiming all oil and gas workers on ships and vessels are mariners.

Those regarded by HMRC as 'genuine' mariners, however, working on ships in the UKCS and listed in Table 1 in *Reg 114(5)* (described in the explanatory memorandum as 'traditional marine crew occupations'), are excluded from the new rules about continental shelf workers on offshore installations where they are in roles that are required in order to meet the stipulations in the *Merchant Shipping (Safe Manning, Hours of Work and Watchkeeping) Regulations 1997, SI 1997/1320, Reg 5(1)(c)*. This exception will ensure that certain marine crewmen on the various floating vessels used in the offshore oil and gas industry will still be treated as mariners rather than CSWs. The definition of 'offshore installation' set out in *Reg 114D* also ensures that the crew on safety and standby vessels, re-supply vessels and cable-laying vessels will not be moved from the mariners' rules to the UKCS rules, even if the ships stay on station close to a rig for so long that they might sometimes be temporarily classed as an offshore installation.

The new rules have left a number of questions unanswered.

The definition of 'offshore installation' in *Reg 114D* looks for a 'structure which is, is to be, or has been, put to a relevant use while in water'.

'Relevant use' is defined by reference to what might be expected: the exploitation of mineral resources, exploration for that purpose, storage and recovery of gas under the shore or the bed of any waters, the conveyance of things by means of a pipe, use mainly for the provision of accommodation for individuals who work on or from the structure for the aforementioned uses while in water or the decommissioning of any such structures.

However, a structure will not be an offshore installation if it has permanently ceased to be put to a relevant use, it is not and is not to be put to any other relevant use, and since permanently ceasing to be put to a relevant use, it has been put to use which is not a relevant use. It is unclear how decommissioning any structure might be a relevant use if the structure is excluded from being an offshore installation once it has permanently ceased production and has been moved on to other tasks.

Certain businesses servicing the oil and gas sector are also uncertain about the status of their workers because 'put to use while in water' is defined as standing in any waters, stationed (by whatever means) in any waters, or standing on the foreshore or other land intermittently covered with water. Dive support vessels, for example, tend to be stationary for a few days at a time while diving takes place, but they will rarely be anchored because the water is too deep, so they use dynamic positioning thrusters to maintain their location. In the past, HMRC has taken five days as a rule of thumb minimum for measuring whether a vessel is stationary (eg, moored to a stationary rig), but the new regulations include no statutory *de minimis* provisions. The crew of a dive support vessel will include mariners in the excluded grades but will also include dive masters, ROV pilots and hydrographic surveyors. If the vessel is classed as stationary it could be an offshore installation, with resulting secondary liabilities for the employer(s) of these non-mariner crewmembers, while the crew of a standby vessel, required to remain on station in a field for safety reasons would attract no such liabilities. HMRC indicated to the ICAEW in early 2015 that the definition of 'stationed' will be interpreted in accordance with the long-standing practice in connection with the seafarer's earnings deduction set at out at EIM33108–9.

Certification

[50.7] Oilfield licensees tend not to operate the exploration and production facilities themselves but to subcontract the work to specialists. A rig might be taken on a bareboat charter and operated by an unconnected company, which might provide the offshore installation manager and general crew but might hire in teams of workers from other unconnected companies to cover particular aspects of the operation, such as mud technology, seismology, well stimulation, health and safety, catering, etc. They in turn might hire in their own sub-contractors. It is therefore difficult for a licensee to know for certain whether a particular worker might be employed by a non-UK employer who has not paid the secondary contributions due and whether, therefore, there is a potential liability about to fall on the licensee under the new rule in *Social Security (Contributions) Regulations 2001, SI 2001/1004, Reg 114(4)(c)*.

To reduce uncertainty for oilfield licensees in their choice of offshore contractors, and indeed employers and intermediaries in the chain of suppliers of staff to UKCS businesses, *Social Security (Contributions) Regulations 2001, SI 2001/1004, Regs 114A–114D* introduced a process of certification of labour suppliers. An employer who meets conditions set out in *Reg 114A*, which includes giving a confirmation that the employer understands and intends to discharge the obligations set out in the NIC regulations, may (but need not) apply in writing to HMRC for a UKCS continental shelf workers certificate (and a parallel PAYE certificate). HMRC will issue the combined certificate to a compliant business.

Offshore employers can apply to HMRC for a certificate by writing to:

Oil and Gas Certificates Unit
Grayfield House
Bankhead Avenue
Edinburgh EH11 4UY

The certificate holder commits to operating PAYE and NIC deductions and fulfilling all the associated obligations of a normal employer and certain additional duties imposed in respect of offshore contracts, so that HMRC is informed in advance of the full details of the oilfield licensee to which continental shelf workers are to be supplied. [*Social Security (Contributions) Regulations 2001, SI 2001/1004, Reg 114B*.]

After that information has been supplied, HMRC will issue a UKCS oilfield licensee certificate to the relevant licensee, containing specified details about the parties and the contract. Holding the certificate exempts the licensee from any liability for contributions in respect of any continental shelf worker that it covers. [*Social Security (Contributions) Regulations 2001, SI 2001/1004, Reg 114C*.]

For HMRC guidance in this area, see NIM33760–NIM33870.

Divers and diving supervisors

[50.8] For 1978–79 and subsequent years, a diver or diving supervisor working as an employee in the designated areas referred to at **50.1** above, whose work involves diving operations concerned with the exploration or exploitation of the seabed, its subsoil and their natural resources is to be treated as carrying on a trade for tax purposes. [*ICTA 1988, s 314; ITTOIA 2005, s 15*]. Note that the definition is unlikely to extend to diving work in connection with, eg, salvage of sunken vessels or the installation or maintenance of offshore wind farms, which do not involve exploitation of the seabed or subsoil and their natural resources. Diving work on dock installations and ship repairs is also outside the scope of the deeming rules (but may well fall within the Construction Industry Scheme for self-employed divers). Although, in consequence of the deeming, earnings from seabed diving are asscssed under *ITTOIA 2005, Part 2 Chapter 2* and should, therefore, attract a Class 4 contribution liability, the diver is, if he is under a contract of service, to retain his status as an employed earner for contribution purposes and is to be excepted from such contributions on so much of his profits as are derived from that employment and his earnings will attract a Class 1 contribution liability under the normal rules (see CLASS 4 CONTRIBUTIONS 20). [*Social Security (Contributions) Regulations 2001, SI 2001/1004, Reg 92*]. In practice, oil and gas industry contractors or the diving employers usually payroll all earnings but use an NT code for PAYE. Divers and diving supervisors submit their accounts to Scotland North Area, Aberdeen, which issues guidance notes on their tax treatment – see HM Revenue and Customs National Insurance Manual NIM24630. The current notes state that the rules do not extend to 'diving superintendents', although that term is not further defined by HMRC, who rely on industry terminology, and some confusion may arise where an employer uses the term to describe a 'diving supervisor' (also not defined by HMRC but by the industry), who may also act as a 'diving supervisor' at the same time if in charge of the gas panel and communications panel.

Rig-workers

[50.9] It is generally the case that rig-workers spend a number of weeks on a rig followed by a short period of leave and then repeat the cycle. Payment is made for hours worked and includes an element of leave pay. For the NIC treatment of reimbursed expenses of cost of travel and subsistence see 30.4 EARNINGS FROM EMPLOYMENT: EXPENSES and 50.14.

Because of this work-pattern, primary Class 1 contribution liabilities may be minimised in some cases if a *weekly* pay interval is established wherever possible (see below). This may be achieved, however, only by actually *paying* earnings at weekly intervals (ie, by transfer of pay to the credit of a rig-worker's bank account with a parallel full payment submission): mere weekly *calculation* followed by, say, a monthly payment is not sufficient. A weekly pay interval will establish an EARNINGS PERIOD 34 of a week and, as a rig-worker will frequently earn an amount in excess of the weekly Upper Earnings Limit (see EARNINGS LIMITS AND THRESHOLDS 33) in the weeks he is actually working, this will result in more earnings escaping a primary contribution liability at the main rate which (because of the period of leave a monthly or longer earnings period would include) they would otherwise wholly or partly attract.

Case law—'retainer' payments

[50.10] In *Mason v Revenue and Customs Comrs* [2008] STC (SCD) 1231, from 1983 to 1998 an electrician (M) had been employed on drilling rigs in the North Sea. His employers reduced his monthly salary by withholding a small 'retainer', which they then paid two weeks later. For NIC purposes, his employers treated him as having two-weekly pay periods rather than four-weekly pay periods. The consequences were that the employers avoided paying NIC on the 'retainer' payments, on the basis that these payments fell below the lower limit for NICs for the fortnightly earnings period, and that they paid less NIC than they would otherwise have done in respect of the balancing payments, on the basis that much of the payment exceeded the UEL for NICs for the fortnightly earnings period (ie, until the cap was removed from employer contributions). The effect of the way in which his employers had paid him was that he received a lower state pension than he would have done if his employers had paid him monthly. The First-Tier Tribunal reviewed the evidence in detail and dismissed the appeal, observing that it was a common pattern of work 'to be offshore for a two-week period, and then to have a two-week period back in Aberdeen or elsewhere on the mainland, effectively as a rest period'. In such cases, 'the workers were paid when they worked and basically not paid when they had their "weeks off"'. The Upper Tribunal upheld this decision, and held that 'it would be inappropriate to speculate, without evidence, as to the reasons or reasons why the Secretary of State did not at any stage exercise his discretion to review and reform the practice in question'. *JAL Mason v HMRC (No 2)* [2010] UT unreported 16 July 2010 ([2008] Sp C 712).

It is understood that HMRC have considered whether this deliberate splitting of earnings would constitute an abnormal pay practice but concluded that it would not because this method of payment was relatively common in the oil and gas industry, where staff typically work a regular 'rotation'.

Example

Angus works as a mud technician on a rig in Morecambe Bay. His earnings in the four weeks to 22 November 2018 are as follows:

	£
5 November 2018	1,650
12 November 2018	1,665
19 November 2018	1,685
26 November 2018	Nil
	£5,000

If A is paid weekly, Class 1 liabilities will arise as follows:

W/ended	*Earnings*	*Main Primary (ET to UEL) 12% £892–£162*	*Additional Primary above UEL 2% Above £892*	*Secondary (above ET) 13.8% Above £162*
	£	£	£	£
05.11.18	1,650	On £730 =87.60	On £758 = 15.16	On £1,488 =205.34
12.11.18	1,665	On £730 =87.60	On £763 = 15.26	On £1,503 =207.41
19.11.18	1,685	On £730 =87.60	On £793 = 15.86	On £1,523 =197.99
29.11.18	Nil			
	£5,000	£262.80	£46.28	£610.74

If A is paid monthly, however, the contribution liabilities would become:

Month ended	*Earnings*	*Main Primary ET to UEL 12%*	*Additional Primary Above UEL2%*	*Secondary Above ET 13.8%*
		£3,863–£702	Above £3,863	Above £702
29.11.18	£5,000	On £3,161 = £379.32	On £1,137 = £22.74	On £4,298 = £593.12

By being paid weekly, A would gain £92.98 (£402.06 – £309.08), although his employer would lose £17.62 (£610.74 – £593.12). The saving to A is because greater amounts overall fall above the UEL and so only attract liability at the 2% rate instead of the main primary rate of 12%, offset by the loss of a week's Earnings Threshold. The cost to the employer is the loss of a further Earnings Threshold in the weekly payment model because of the week in which no payment is made. The monthly thresholds, of course, are not a simple multiple of the weekly figures, except where the employer operates a lunar payroll schedule (ie, payment every four weeks).

Modification of compliance rules

[50.11] Where a person in prescribed employment on the continental shelf is, because of his employment in that capacity and by reason of his being outside Great Britain (see 51.3 OVERSEAS MATTERS), unable to comply with any time limit imposed on acts which, under contribution law, he is required to perform, he is to be deemed to have complied if he performs the acts as soon as is reasonably practicable. [*Social Security (Contributions) Regulations 2001, SI 2001/1004, Reg 114(3)*].

Norwegian continental shelf

[50.12] Until 31 December 1993, the contribution liability of individuals sent to work in Norway (onshore or within the 12-mile limit) who were previously insured in either the UK or Norway was governed by the reciprocal agreement on social security with Norway. Under that agreement it is a basic rule that a worker is insured where he is 'gainfully occupied', in an employed or self-employed capacity. If a self-employed person works in both the UK and Norway, his liability falls to be determined under the legislation of the state where he is ordinarily resident. [*Social Security (Norway) Order 1991, Art 5*].

Where any person insured in the UK or Norway and employed by an employer with a place of business in either state was, before 1 January 1994, sent by his employer to work in the other state (ie onshore or within the 12-mile limit) for a period not expected to last for more than three years, home state liability continued for the period of the detached duty. No host state liability arose. It was a condition that the home state employer had to continue to pay the worker and that application for a certificate of continuing liability was requested from the home authorities within four months and was presented to the host state authorities within two months of its issue. In practice, the treaty time limits are closely monitored by the Norwegian authorities.

These rules continue to apply to workers who are sent temporarily to the Norwegian sector outside the 12-mile limit. The same time limit for application applies, but workers ordinarily resident in the UK in employment offshore on the Norwegian Continental Shelf whose employers have a UK place of business benefit from the above rule without the three-year time limit on the duration of the certificate of coverage. [*Article 6.*] Note the restriction to employers within the jurisdiction of the contracting parties: employers with no UK or Norwegian presence will be denied the benefit of the treaty where possible. Similar provisions applied to Norwegian residents working in the British sector outside the 12-mile limit for an employer with a Norwegian place of business. [*Art 6(5)*]. Self-employed persons ordinarily resident in the UK could continue to pay UK contributions without time limit when going to work in the Norwegian offshore sector, before 1 January 1994, despite not fulfilling the necessary conditions of residence or presence in the UK. [*Art 6(6)*].

Since the ratification of the treaty establishing the European Economic Area on 1 January 1994, the EC regulations have governed the contribution liabilities of cross-border workers, insofar as nationals of EEA member countries working onshore or inside the Norwegian 12-mile limit are concerned. Transitional provisions ensured that workers already working within Norway on 1 January 1994 would not be subject to the EC regulations until the expiry of the existing three-year period within their home scheme. [*Art 2A*].

The EC social security regulations are more restrictive than the reciprocal agreement between the UK and Norway in that the latter provides for automatic cover by the 'home' scheme for three years, whereas the old EC regulations only provided for a period of twelve months with a possible twelve-month extension, and this could generally be extended to five years in total. [*EC Reg 1408/71, Art 14(1)(a)(b), Art 17*]. *EC Reg 883/04, Article 12* only provides for a maximum cover of 24 months. However, *EC Reg 883/04, Art 16* permits this period to be extended by agreement between the appropriate national authorities and this can generally be for up to five years. For mariners see *EC Reg 883/04, Art 11(4)* – general rules. It should be noted that, unlike the old EC social security rules, the post-2010 EC rules do not provide separate rules for the 'posting' of mariners who are now covered under *EC Reg 883/04, Article 12*. It should be noted that *EC Reg 883/04* was only adopted by Norway on 1 June 2012. Before that date *EC Reg 1408/71* applied but the rules were broadly similar.

The British and Norwegian social security authorities have agreed that the designated areas of the continental shelf outside the 12-mile limit will *not* be classed as within the EEA (ie Svalbard, Jan Mayen). Offshore workers in international waters are therefore still subject to the provisions of the UK–Norway reciprocal agreement. [NIM28004.]

If the UK leaves the EEA, as seems likely, the reciprocal agreement should automatically cover all oil and gas workers moving between the UK and Norway, and indeed onshore workers generally, although it seems likely that there will be some transitional arrangements for workers holding form A1 under the EEA rules.

The UK, Netherlands and Denmark

[50.13] Neither the UK nor the Netherlands regards its respective sectors in the designated areas as part of the EC/EEA. *EC Reg 883/04*, therefore, does not in principle apply to offshore staff working on the UK and Dutch sectors. The European Commission, however, urged the Dutch Government to adapt its national laws for people working on the Dutch continental shelf. On 5 March 2010 it was announced that the Dutch Minister of Social Affairs proposed a change in legislation (the '*Wet NCP*' = Act on Social Security Dutch Continental Shelf) which would result in all employees working on the Dutch continental shelf being covered by all Dutch social insurance schemes (at the time they were only covered for sickness and disability) in the same way as if working onshore. The law was adopted by the Dutch Parliament and applied from 1 January 2013. The same rule was extended to non-resident self-employed persons from 1 January 2013. It is now theoretically possible, therefore, for EEA nationals working temporarily in the Dutch sector to apply for an A1 under *EC Reg 883/04* to remain insured in their normal home state.

Denmark has, however, for a number of years agreed to regard its sector as covered by the EC regulations. The UK has no plans to include the UKCS as part of its territorial definition for EU social security purposes but now accepts that transfers to and from the Danish or Dutch sectors may be covered by an A1 on the basis that the treatment is reciprocated by the Danish and Dutch authorities.

Despite the manual having been updated for the 2014 changes to the rules for offshore intermediaries, NIM28003 still states simply that the EEA rules do not apply to the UKCS, while NIM28004 then directly contradicts this by noting that 'The EC regulations override the 1991 Norwegian reciprocal agreement but, except for Denmark, do not apply to the Continental Shelf'. The guidance appears to have been written by different HMRC staff at different times. It will have to be rewritten if the UK-Denmark and UK-Netherlands reciprocal agreements are revived as a result of the UK's leaving the EU.

Expenses related to oil-rig workers, divers, etc

[50.14] The former Inland Revenue concession ESC A65 was given the force of law for contribution purposes with effect from 6 April 1996. Where the employee incurs expenses of travel from the mainland to offshore oil and gas rigs or platforms (or vice versa) or in respect of reasonable overnight accommodation in the vicinity of the mainland departure point and the employer reimburses such expenses no contribution liability is to arise (see Leaflet 480 (2016), para 5.22. [*ITEPA 2003, s 305*]. Clearly, if the employer contracted for the provision of these items they would be payments in kind (see **29.28** EARNINGS FROM EMPLOYMENT: GENERAL and Booklet 490 (2015), Chapter 8.25 and 8.26).

[*Social Security (Contributions) Regulations 2001, SI 2001/1004, Sch 3 Part XIII para 6*].

51

Overseas Matters

Cross-references. See AIRMEN 6; ARMED FORCES 11; CROWN SERVANTS AND STATUTORY EMPLOYEES 25; LEAFLETS 43; MARINERS 45; OIL-RIG WORKERS, DIVERS, ETC 50; SHARE FISHERMEN 56.

Other Sources. Simon's Taxes, Volume 2, para A8.7; Tolley's Tax Planning 2016–17; Tolley's National Insurance Brief, January 1996; Tolley's Practical NIC Newsletter, January and February 2002, May 2004, October 2004; former Leaflets NI 38, SA 29; HM Revenue and Customs National Insurance Manual NIM33000–NIM33870.

Introduction to overseas matters relating to NICs

[51.1] Whenever an individual or his employer has any overseas involvement the National Insurance contribution position can become very complicated, and the complications are different from those encountered under the tax rules.

It is worth noting that the cross-border rules highlight why social security rules are not primarily about taxing people but about providing them with social protection in the welfare state: unlike in the UK and the US, in many other developed countries the social security system is designed as the main provider of adequate retirement pensions and healthcare. It is important to recognise that the UK is unusual among developed nations in using the social security system to provide only a subsistence-level state pension, and providing healthcare based on residence rather than contributions. The UK's immigration health surcharge ('IHS' – see www.gov.uk/healthcare-immigration-application) for incoming expatriates who hold a visa is a fairly recent innovation.

When a 'migrant worker' (a term which covers investment bankers as well as seasonal fruit pickers) comes to the UK on assignment, it often matters materially to his or her benefit entitlements where contributions fall due, and those contributions may be as much about building up a solid pension entitlement (and maintaining sickness and unemployment insurance) as paying a levy of some kind to a national taxing authority. NHS treatment may be covered by EU regulations on social security coordination, a bilateral reciprocal health agreement or the IHS. An EU national visiting with a European Health Insurance Card is treated under the EC social security regulations in the same way as a UK citizen, but the Department of Health bills the visitor's home authority. For the rest of the world, NHS services are covered, even if private medical insurance is held, by payment of the IHS, which is generally £200 per person per year of the visa (eg, a US expatriate seconded to the UK on a five-year visa with spouse and child would pay an IHS of £3,000, although those on student visas pay less). Visitors coming to the UK for less than six months do not pay the IHS: instead, they pay for treatment when it is provided. In the UK, the IHS regime is outside the social security regime.

Responsibility for regulating the social security 'overseas connection' in relation to contribution liabilities lies largely with HM Revenue and Customs, National Insurance Contributions & Employer Office, International Caseworker section (which signs international certificates), Centre for Non-Residents (Newcastle) at Benton Park View, Newcastle upon Tyne, NE98

1ZZ. The International Caseworker section has around 200 staff, dealing solely with the National Insurance contributions of individuals who are abroad temporarily or permanently, and requests from overseas authorities for agreements in respect of their insured workers temporarily in the UK. It does not deal with the issuing of NI numbers to newly-arrived foreign employees: that is a matter solely for the DWP's Jobcentre Plus team. The Department of Health, through the NHS Business Services Authority, is responsible for the coordination of reciprocal health cover.

Whatever the circumstances surrounding the individual's crossing of international borders, three basic social security principles must be understood. See 51.2 below.

Basic principles regarding overseas matters and NICs

[51.2] *First*, as far as the UK social security regulations are concerned (see 51.3 below for the territorial boundaries of the United Kingdom) the world can for the moment (and as far as contributions records history is concerned, for the foreseeable future) be divided into three distinct groups insofar as international social security applies:

- The EC Social Security Regulations – apply to the Member States of the European Economic Area (EEA), comprising from 1 July 2013 the 28 Member States of the European Union together with Iceland, Norway and Liechtenstein (see NIM33008). The EC Regulations also apply to Switzerland (by virtue of the EU/Switzerland Agreement, see **51.20**);
- Reciprocal Agreement countries ('RA' – non-EEA countries) – apply to those countries with which the UK has a bilateral or multi-lateral social security agreement, as listed at **51.52** below (see NIM330124), and;
- Rest of the World ('ROW' – non EEA/Agreement countries) – where British contribution legislation may continue to apply to a worker from the UK or begin to apply to a foreign worker arriving in the UK (see below and NIM33014).

Although the term 'European Union' is now widely used, the 'union' is based on the European Communities and has no direct legal effect on social security matters. *Art G(1)* of the Maastricht Treaty provided that the term 'European Community' would replace 'European Economic Community' in the Treaty of Rome under which the original EEC was established. All directives and regulations affecting social security in the EU are made by the Council of the European Communities. For this reason, references below are to the 'EC' rather than the 'EU'.

The purpose of the EC regulations and the reciprocal agreements is to co-ordinate the provision of social security cover for migrant workers, so that people are clear about which state is responsible for providing their benefits (long-term such as pensions, and short-term such as unemployment and sickness cover) and collecting contributions, and that only one Member State at any particular point in time is 'competent' or responsible for both aspects.

The Treaty of Rome enshrined four 'fundamental freedoms' intended to foster the creation of a common market. *Article 48* provided for one of those, the freedom of movement for workers within the Community and the abolition of any discrimination based on nationality between workers of the Member States as regards employment, remuneration and other conditions of work and employment. The aim of the EC social security regulations is to remove a barrier to that free movement by providing for non-discrimination, protecting benefit entitlements and preventing dual contribution liability (see *Terhoeve v Inspecteur van de Belastingdienst Particulieren/Ondernemingen Buitenland, ECJ C-18/95*). The second relevant treaty freedom, freedom of establishment, extended the same principles to self-employed workers, who were brought within the scope of the EC regulations on social security for migrant workers in the early 1970s. These all apply to the UK at least until the UK formally ceases to be a member of the EU.

Secondly, the EC regulations and reciprocal agreements use certain terms repeatedly and it is important that their meaning is understood, especially when they do not mean the same in the context of the EC regulations as they might in ordinary English day-to-day or legal usage. The terms 'presence' (see **51.4** below), 'residence and ordinary residence' (see **51.5** below) and 'domicile' (see **51.6** below) are all vital to the understanding of how domestic legislation and the overseas agreements will affect a particular individual. Note that the Finance Act 2013 statutory residence test does not apply for National Insurance purposes, so the term 'ordinary residence', while abolished for tax purposes, continues to have relevance. For the employer (the secondary contributor—see **51.14** below) the key phrases are 'place of business' and 'registered office' (see **51.8** below).

Finally, subject to certain conditions, an individual who moves abroad may sometimes, even if not liable to contribute to the UK National Insurance scheme, continue to do so on a *voluntary* basis and thus maintain his entitlement to some UK State benefits, eg the basic retirement pension. Such voluntary contributions will usually be either of Class 2 or Class 3 and are discussed at **51.16** and **51.17** below. UK state pensioners resident overseas may also, until 5 April 2017, pay the new Class 3A contribution to enhance their entitlement to the UK state pension, albeit subject to the restriction that, if they live in a non-EEA and non-RA state, the additional pension that they 'buy' will not be uprated each year for inflation.

Territorial connecting factors

[51.3] *Security Contributions and Benefits Act 1992 (SSCBA 1992), SSAA 1992* and *SS(CP)A 1992* relate to England, Wales and Scotland and, for a small number of provisions, to Northern Ireland (see **51.49** below). [*SSAA 1992, s 192; SSCBA 1992, s 177.*] England, Wales and Scotland are described collectively as Great Britain. [*Royal and Parliamentary Titles Act 1927.*] The United Kingdom consists of Great Britain and Northern Ireland. [*Interpretation Act 1978, Sch 1.*] Although certain taxation powers have been devolved to the Holyrood parliament, there is no effect yet (and none is planned) on NIC legislation and contribution liability, although some responsibility for non-contributory benefits has been devolved. [*Scotland Act 2016, Pts* 2 and 3.]

Northern Ireland has its own social security system (see **51.49** below). The regulations dealing with the international aspects of social security contain mixed references to Great Britain and the UK and, because of joint arrangements between the Secretary of State for Work and Pensions and the Northern Ireland Office, the two terms are effectively interchangeable in nearly all cases.

References in the legislation to Great Britain are to be treated as including a reference to the territorial waters of the United Kingdom adjacent to Great Britain (ie, inside the 12-mile limit – see below). [*SSCBA 1992, s 172(a)*]. References to the United Kingdom include a reference to the territorial waters of the United Kingdom. [*SSCBA 1992, s 172(b)*].

The Scilly Isles, Orkney, Shetland and the Western Isles are all part of Great Britain and the UK but the Isle of Man and the Channel Islands are not (see **51.50** and **51.51** below). Special social security provision is made for the non-UK islands in various bi-lateral and multi-lateral treaties.

The territorial waters of the United Kingdom include inland waters, the area of sea which lies upon the landward side of the low water line along the coast, and any part of the open sea which lies within twelve nautical miles on the seaward side of the low water line. [*Territorial Waters Order in Council 1964, Arts 2–5; Territorial Sea Act 1987, s 1*]. Note that the twelve nautical mile territorial limit (just over 14 land miles) does not equate with the Continental Shelf which has implications for oil-rig workers working on the Norwegian Continental Shelf and their employers. See **50.12** OIL-RIG WORKERS, DIVERS, ETC.

Whether or not a person is prima facie subject to British contribution legislation is to depend on whether or not he is present, resident or ordinarily resident in Great Britain. [*SSCBA 1992, s 1(6)*]. In the case of an airman or mariner it may also depend on whether or not he is domiciled in England and Wales, or Scotland or Northern Ireland (see **6.3** AIRMEN and **45.5** MARINERS). In the case of employers, a key term is 'place of business'.

Presence

[51.4] Whether or not an individual is present in Great Britain at any particular time is a matter of *fact*. (*Colt Industries Inc v Sarlie* [1966] 1 All ER 673, [1966] 1 WLR 440). Presence on a British ship on the high seas or in the territorial waters of a foreign state or presence in a British embassy overseas is, therefore, not presence in Great Britain. (National Insurance Commissioners' decisions *R(S) 23/52, R(U) 18/60* and R(I) 44/61; *Haughton v Olau Lines (UK) Ltd*, [1986] 2 All ER 47, [1986] 1 WLR 504). For EC purposes an activity on board a vessel flying the flag of a Member State is deemed to be an activity pursued in that Member State. [*EC Social Security Regulations 883/2004, Art 11.4*]. As there are no express provisions to the contrary, however, a company registered in England and Wales or Scotland will be present in Great Britain even if all its business activities take place overseas. [*Companies Act 2006, ss 1046, 1158*]. It is arguable, however, that a registration with no activity does not create a place of business.

In determining whether or not a non-resident and non-ordinarily resident director of a British company is present here for *contribution* purposes, HM Revenue and Customs has regard to contribution law, not tax law, and considers where the director lives and/or works, and the number, length and purpose of his visits in the particular tax year concerned. If the director lives and/or works in one or more EEA Member States (see **51.20** to **51.41** below), including the UK, the provisions of the appropriate regulations govern the contribution liability of both director and company.

The position of a director from a state other than an EEA state is, however, governed by an extra-statutory practice. If a director who usually lives overseas (ie is neither resident nor ordinarily resident in the UK) visits merely to attend board meetings and his visits are only fleeting visits (extending over no more than two nights each) which number ten or fewer in the tax year, the visits will be ignored and the director will be regarded as not being present here. HMRC has confirmed that a two-night rule applies despite its guidance referring in places to two days. Alternatively, if there is only one board meeting in a tax year and that visit does not last more than two weeks, the visit will also be ignored. However, if neither condition is met, the director will be regarded as present here and contribution liabilities on fees etc paid to him in the tax year will ensue. (Leaflet CA 44, para 66).

Three points of interest are worthy of note. First, the wording of the guidance appears to preclude from the concessionary treatment a non-resident director who visits for only one board meeting of between three and fourteen days' duration where the company in fact holds more than one board meeting in a tax year. This would seem a strange result, since the concession is aimed at allowing temporary presence to be ignored. HMRC states that any activity outside the terms of the concession means NICs are due and also that it has no intention of varying this position. Secondly, the policy is stated in CA 44 to be that it (at present) 'will not seek payment of Class 1 NICs' (CA 44, para 66), highlighting the concessionary nature of the policy. Thirdly, Leaflet CA 44 makes a distinction between those directors ordinarily resident in an EEA Member State and those ordinarily resident elsewhere; the EC Regulations on Social Security are looked at by HMRC prior to the test at paragraph 66 of leaflet CA 44. At one time this easement did not apply in the case of a state with which the UK has a reciprocal agreement on social security and it seems odd that it does, given that one of the purposes of an agreement is to ensure that contributions are payable somewhere so that social security benefit coverage is maintained (see **51.48–51.56** below).

Residence and ordinary residence

[51.5] The statutory residence test (SRT) introduced by *Finance Act 2013, Sch 45* relates solely to tax and is of no relevance to social security. For that reason, everything that follow relates solely to NIC law unless explicit reference to the 2013 tax rules is made.

Neither residence nor ordinary residence is defined in the social security legislation and the terms must, therefore, carry their ordinary meanings. As the ordinary meaning of these terms has been much debated in the context of earlier income tax law, however, and as regard may be had to relevant decisions on the ordinary meaning of words in one statute when considering the meaning of those words in another statute, it is suggested that the long-accepted meanings of the terms for tax purposes before the SRT's introduction must carry great weight in the present context. (*Goodman v J Eban Ltd* [1954] 1 AER 763). It is worth observing, however, that a person could under the pre-2013 rules be found to be not ordinarily resident for contribution purposes when he was ordinarily resident for tax purposes. (*R(P) 1/78*). This position did not change simply by virtue of the transfer of the former Contributions Agency on 1 April 1999 to the then Inland Revenue and leaflet HMRC6 re-iterated the point at page 70 of the October 2011 edition. See also *Revenue and Customs Comrs v Grace* [2009] EWCA Civ 1082, [2009] STC 2707, [2009] SWTI 2834.

Residence is something more than mere presence (see **51.4** above). However, there cannot be residence without there being physical presence at some time during the period of residence. (*Lloyd v Sulley* (1884) 2 TC 37; *Reed v Clark* [1985] STC 323). If a person maintains a fixed place of abode in Great Britain, he will be resident for any tax year in which he makes any visit, however brief, and non-ownership of the property will not prevent this being so, though the maintenance of a fixed place of abode is by no means an essential of residence. (*Cooper v Cadwalader* (1904) 5 TC 101; *Lowenstein v De Salis (Inspector of Taxes)* (1926) 10 TC 424, 161 LT Jo 235; *Lysaght v CIR* (1928) 13 TC 511). A person's intentions and wishes have no bearing on whether he is resident or not, for residence is a matter of *degree* and *fact*. Family ties, though on their own not conclusive, may indicate where a person is resident, though a person may be resident in more than one place at one time. (*Inchiquin (Lord) v CIR* (1948) 31 TC 125; *Turnbull v Foster* (1904) 6 TC 206).

In *Levene v CIR* (1928) 13 TC 486 it was stated that 'to dwell permanently or for a considerable time; to have one's settled or usual abode; to live in or at a particular place' is an accurate meaning of the word 'reside'.

Days of arrival and departure are days of residence for contribution purposes. (*R(S)1/66*). Note also that in the important (pre-SRT) income tax case on residence of *Gaines-Cooper v HMRC* [2011] UKSC 47 the appellant in applying the wording in the then current IR20 (later replaced by HMRC6) chose to ignore days of arrival and departure in calculating total days spent in the UK. The Special Commissioners stated 'However, in this appeal we must apply the law rather than the provisions of IR20' and added back the days of arrival and departure. Clearly therefore the HMRC6 leaflet may be used as guidance but any reliance on its contents may be misplaced. Whilst the case does not have a direct impact on NICs it is a good indicator of the problems that individuals face if they are claiming non-residence and non-domicile status. The Supreme Court did not disagree with the Special Commissioners.

As with the SRT, the change to the tax definition of residence from 6 April 1993 made by *FA 1993, s 208* (ie regarding the existence of 'available accommodation') was of no direct application in considering residence for contribution purposes, nor were the tax changes made with effect from 6 April 2008. A temporary edition of leaflet IR20 was made available in May 2008 (dated April 2008) which also confirmed (para **11.3**) that the changed tax rules were of no application to NIC.

Ordinary residence is something other than mere residence and, indeed, it is clear from *Social Security (Contributions) Regulations 2001, SI 2001/1004, Reg 145(1)(a)* (where ordinary residence is prescribed as an alternative condition to residence for contribution liability to arise) that a person may be ordinarily resident in Great Britain when he is neither resident nor present here.

The consensus of judicial thought is that 'ordinary' contrasts with casual or occasional or extraordinary and that 'ordinarily resident' refers to 'a man's abode in a particular place or country which he has adopted voluntarily and for settled purposes as part of the regular order of his life for the time being, whether of short or long duration'. (*Shah v Barnet London BC* [1983] 1 AER 226, *per Lord Scarman* at p 235). It follows that a person may be outside Great Britain for extensive periods of time and yet still be ordinarily resident here.

The DSS (now DWP) generally used to regard a person as continuing to be ordinarily resident in Great Britain where he was absent for up to five years, provided the intention to return was not abandoned. If the intention to return was abandoned during the five years, ordinary residence ceased. (*R(G)1/54*). Where the absence extended, or was likely to extend, beyond five years, however, the DSS considered each case individually taking into account the intended length of absence, whether a home or accommodation was being maintained in Great Britain and whether personal effects and furniture were being stored or disposed of. This guidance was formerly given in DSS Leaflet NI 38, but later editions of the leaflet (now published by HMRC) make no reference to a period of five years since that old rule is no longer used by HM Revenue and Customs.

The ordinary residence indicators at pages 6 and 7 of the 2015 edition of Leaflet NI 38 give the type of factors which are used currently to decide on ordinary residence. Legal advice was received by the former CA to the effect that the five-year rule could no longer be sustained. Ordinary residence is a matter of fact, and each case must be decided on its own merits. The CA transfer to what is now HM Revenue and Customs may yet mean that the question of ordinary residence will be re-visited in due course (because of the different rules which applied between the former CA and what is now HM Revenue and Customs) but this has not happened yet (see HMRC6, page 73). See *Gaines-Cooper v HMRC* [2007] STC SCD 23 Sp C 568; Ch D [2008] STC 1665 above regarding ordinary residence for income tax purposes.

Note that the term 'residence' in the context of the EC Regulations is specifically defined as 'habitual residence', which is more akin to the British concept of ordinary residence, contrasted in EC Regulation terms with the more short-term 'stay', which covers a short-term visit or secondment – see 51.36 below.

Domicile

[51.6] Unlike presence, residence and ordinary residence, domicile is a matter of law not of fact (ie, law as applied to the facts). Furthermore, it is a matter of general personal law and neither tax law nor social security law. Fundamentally, it is used as the determinant of the system of personal law to which a person should be subject wherever he might be (eg, for the purposes of inheritance of property under a will). Beyond tax law, it is used in the common law jurisdictions of the UK, the Commonwealth and the USA. To these nations, with a number of diverse legal systems within their jurisdictions, domicile is the determinant of the relevant personal law.

A person is domiciled in the country in which he is considered, under English law, to have his *permanent home*. Every person has a domicile but no person may have more than one. (*IRC v Bullock* [1976] 3 AER 353). At birth each person acquires a *domicile of origin* which, regardless of the country of birth, is that of the father if the father is alive and married to the mother at the time of birth, or that of the mother if the father is dead, the parents are divorced, or the child is illegitimate. (*Forbes v Forbes* (1854) Kay 341; *Udny v Udny* (1869) LR 1 Sc & Div 441).

After birth, a child's domicile normally follows that of the person on whom he is legally dependent. (*D'Etchegoyen v D'Etchegoyen* (1888) 13 PD 132). Where, however, his father and mother are alive but living apart, his domicile is that of his mother if he has his home with her and has no home with his father. [*Domicile and Matrimonial Proceedings Act 1973, s 4*].

Once a child attains the age of 16 or marries under that age (ie under foreign law), he may set aside his domicile of origin (or dependency if different to his domicile of origin) by acquiring a *domicile of choice*, but only by positive, unambiguous action and intent. [*DMPA 1973, s 3(1)*]. However, if that domicile of choice is then abandoned in *actuality*, whether by intent or not, the domicile of origin and not the domicile of dependency, if different, will revive. (*Udny v Udny* (1869) LR 1 Sc & Div 441).

In an income tax case, the issue of domicile of choice has been explored. *Civil Engineer v CIR* [2002] STC SCD 72 concerned an individual who left Hong Kong, his domicile of choice, without the intention of returning. This was held to revive his domicile of origin in the UK.

Until 31 December 1973, a woman automatically acquired the domicile of her husband on marriage but, from 1 January 1974, the domicile of a married woman is to be ascertained by reference to the same factors as in the case of any other individual capable of having an independent domicile, except that a woman already married at that date will retain her husband's domicile until it is changed by acquisition or revival of another domicile. [*DMPA 1973, s 1, s 17(5)*]. In practice, of course, a husband and wife will frequently be domiciled in the same country, but this is not always the case. A widow who was married before 31 December 1973 retains her domicile of dependency until she acquires a domicile of choice: *Re Wallach Weinschenk v Treasury Solicitor* [1950] 1 All ER 199).

FA 1996, s 200(2) introduced, for certain inheritance tax purposes, a relief whereby a person living overseas and registering to vote in the UK would not have that factor taken into account. Since, however, domicile is a matter of general law (see above), this inheritance tax change would seem to have no bearing on contribution matters whatsoever and the domicile concept for all purposes other than inheritance tax, including contributions purposes, will continue to follow general law principles.

In the past the UK Government has, on a number of occasions, sought to review the domicile concept, eg the 1987 Law Commission Report, 1988 Consultation Paper and numerous earlier Commissions and Committees set up to look at the subject. In the Budget of 2003 the Chancellor of the Exchequer stated that a White Paper would be issued for discussion. This occurred but the paper made no proposals and initial representations from some areas of industry and commerce stated their disquiet at the idea of taxing certain capital and income where residence in the UK has exceeded a certain period. The alternative tax changes eventually implemented for non-domiciled taxpayers by *Finance Act 2008*, while changing the tax rules for non-domiciled individuals, skirted round the fundamental concept of domicile itself and it is therefore thought that there will now be no change to the domicile concept for some time to come. Political debate before the 2015 general election highlighted the fact that the 'non-domiciled' tax status has been a feature of the system since the early days of income tax, as it was felt that British plantation owners settled in the Caribbean should not be taxed on their worldwide income to pay for the European (Napoleonic) war effort. It remains to be seen whether this debate will lead to reform, and whether any such reform will affect the social security system; domicile is generally relevant only to **AIRMEN 6** and **MARINERS 45** for social security purposes.

All efforts to date to change the significance of domicile for tax purposes have been limited to just that: they do not extend to NIC provisions, other than where there is an automatic knock-on effect, such as where profits from a trade are taxable in the UK under *Income Tax (Trading and Other Income) Act 2005, Pt 2, Ch 2 (ITTOIA 2005)*, which leads to a Class 4 liability. A consultation document including a draft Finance Bill clause, issued in February 2016, proposed to change the taxation of non-domiciled persons by extending the IHT deemed domicile rule to income and capital gains taxes for anyone who had been UK resident for 15 of the last 20 years, or who had been born in the UK but later acquired a different domicile, by adding a new *s 835BA* to *Income Tax Act 2007*. The clause did not appear in the subsequent Finance Bill.

Nationality

[51.7] Nationality is not prescribed as a connecting factor under the British contribution scheme but may be such a factor under certain of the EC regulations and under reciprocal agreement rules. For the purposes of the EC regulations, each Member State defines the scope of its own nationality laws and, in the case of the UK, the definition includes:

- British citizens;
- persons who are British subjects by virtue of *British Nationality Act 1981, Part IV* and who have the right of abode in the UK and are therefore exempt from UK immigration control;
- British Dependent Territories citizens who acquire their citizenship from a connection with Gibraltar.

Other British Subjects and British Dependent Territories citizens are excluded, as are Commonwealth Citizens who do not fall within the headings above and British Overseas Citizens and British protected persons. However, from 2002 some British Overseas Territories Citizens (the new name for British Dependent Territories Citizens) may also be British citizens (*British Overseas Territories Act 2002*).

Channel Islanders and Manxmen are generally excluded under the above rules but an exception is made in the case of any Channel Islander or Manxman who is classed as 'patrial', ie, if:

- he, a parent or grandparent was born, adopted, naturalised or registered in the UK, or
- he has at any time been ordinarily resident in the UK for five years.

[*Act of Accession, Protocol No 3, Art 2*].

Under the provisions of *BNA 1981*, those persons who, immediately before the commencement of the *Act*, were Citizens of the UK and Colonies *and* had the right of abode in the UK under the provisions of *Immigration Act 1971*, were reclassified as 'British citizens'. See also now the *Nationality, Immigration and Asylum Act 2002*.

Children born in the UK on or after 1 January 1983 are 'British citizens' if one or both parents is a British citizen or settled in the UK at the time of the birth. A child born in the UK may be registered as a British citizen before he or she reaches the age of eighteen if either parent becomes a British citizen or becomes settled, or if the child has spent the first ten years of his or her life in the UK, with no more than 90 days' absence in any one year.

A child born outside the UK on or after 1 January 1983 is a British citizen if, at the time of the birth, one parent is a British citizen otherwise than by descent (ie birth, adoption, registration or naturalisation). The child will also be a British citizen if, at the time of the birth, one parent was a British citizen in Crown Service under the UK Government or in service designated as closely associated with HM Government's activities outside the UK, provided the parent was recruited for that service in the UK. A similar rule applies where, at the time of birth, one parent was a British citizen serving outside the UK under a European Community institution, provided the parent was recruited in a EC Member State.

A person holding British citizenship continues to hold that status without time limit unless it is formally renounced or, in exceptional circumstances, the Home Secretary exercises a discretionary power to deprive that person of British citizenship (eg in cases of treason) or some other act 'seriously prejudicial to the vital interests of the UK or a British overseas territory'. [*NIAA 2002, s 4*.] A person who becomes British by naturalisation or registration may also have that status removed by the Home Secretary if the status has been obtained by means of fraud, false representation or concealment. [*NIAA 2002, s 5*.]

Under reciprocal agreements between the UK and other states, a definition of British nationality may apply which differs from that in the context of EC regulations. All of the bilateral agreements with EC states, for example, define a 'UK national' as 'a citizen of the United Kingdom and Colonies'. This category of nationality was abolished by *British Nationality Act 1981* with effect from 1 January 1983 and was replaced by three categories: 'British Citizen', 'British Dependent Territories Citizen' and 'British Overseas Citizen'. Under *BNA 1981, s 51(2)*, however, the term 'citizen of the United Kingdom and Colonies' is, in any enactment passed before 1983, to be deemed to include the three new categories. This means, therefore, that each agreement covers not only the typical UK-resident British citizen but also includes, eg approximately 1,300,000 Malaysians who are also British Overseas citizens, together with citizens of numerous island relics of Britain's imperial past. A British Overseas Citizen will typically have a British passport but have no right to live and work in the UK. Until sovereignty over Hong Kong returned to China on 30 June 1997, citizens of Hong Kong would also have qualified, but almost all of them lost their right to British Overseas Citizen status at that date. Robin Cook MP, the then Foreign Secretary, stated on 16 March 1999 'I can announce today that we will be offering British citizenship to all those residents of Overseas Territories who wish to take it up'.

Other reciprocal agreements refer to 'British subjects' and 'British protected persons', which brings what are now Commonwealth citizens within the scope of their provisions.

The UK is also a signatory to the two 'European Interim Agreements on Social Security Schemes' brought into force for UK purposes in 1959. The agreements were drawn up under the auspices of the Council of Europe to cover, in one case, old age, invalidity and survivors' benefits and, in the other, short-term benefits for sickness, maternity, employment injury, unemployment and family allowances. Their effect is limited to persons not already covered by the EC regulations or a reciprocal agreement. Nationals of the participating states are granted favoured status, so that they are not to be prejudiced by reason of nationality and they are to receive the benefits of agreements entered into by other participating states. In effect, until the advent of the European Economic Area this meant that Norwegians, Swedes and Icelanders were allowed to benefit from the provisions of the UK's reciprocal agreements, where they were not otherwise covered by a treaty of their own, by means of granting them deemed UK nationality. The agreements imposed an ordinary residence qualification, however, so they were intended to apply in practice only to those who had moved on a permanent basis between states. This position seems likely to be restored automatically post-Brexit.

Place of business

[51.8] A 'place of business' is regarded for contributions purposes as being any premises which the employer occupies and of which, or part of which, the employer is the lawful tenant or occupier, and where the employee(s) or agent(s) carries out activity in the UK which furthers the employer's business. (Previously, this was stated more briefly as any place from which a person can, as of right, conduct his business, or from which his agent has power to conduct business on his behalf.) A business incorporated in under the *Companies Acts* is normally regarded as having a place of business in Great Britain. (Leaflet NI 132, April 2002, Page 3, now withdrawn). Under the *Companies Act 2006*, *s 1046*, any overseas company which establishes a place of business within Great Britain must, within one month of so doing, deliver to the registrar of companies a list of the names and addresses of some one or more persons resident in Great Britain authorised to accept service of process on behalf of the company. The then DSS confirmed (see below) that the delivery to the registrar of such a list will be 'a strong indication' though 'not in itself conclusive proof' of the existence of a place of business in Great Britain, but failure to deliver such a list will not be evidence that a place of business does not exist.

The premises occupied by a UK subsidiary of an overseas parent company or by the UK parent company of an overseas subsidiary are *not* regarded (see below) as constituting a place of business of the overseas company unless there is tangible evidence that the overseas company has the legal right to occupy part of the UK company's premises for business purposes. This view has been upheld in Canadian law. (*Imperial Oil v Oil Workers International Union* 69 WWR 702).

The courts have held that, in deciding whether a company has established a place of business in Great Britain for the purposes of the Companies Acts, one must see whether the company has here 'a local habitation of its own'. (*Lord Advocate v Huron and Erie Loan and Savings Co* 1911 SC 612). The concept is of 'some more or less permanent location, not necessarily owned or even leased by the company, but at least associated with the company and from which habitually and with some degree of regularity business is conducted'. Thus, the meeting of clients or potential customers in an hotel room may constitute the carrying on of business but the company will not have, in the hotel room, a place of business. (*Norris, Re, ex p Reynolds* (1888) 5 Morr 111, 4 TLR 452, CA; *Re Oriel Ltd* [1985] 3 AER 216, *per Oliver LJ*). This accords with the judgment in *South India Shipping Corporation Ltd v Export-Import Bank of Korea* [1985] 2 AER 219 that a place of business is some specific location readily identifiable with the company by members of the public from which it can be deduced that some substantial business activity is being carried on. In line with these later definitions, a fixed address from which activity such as the sending out of advertisements or the soliciting of finance is conducted has been held to be a place of business, while mere ownership of property in Great Britain or the retention of books and records here has been held not to be evidence of the establishment of a place of business here. (*A/S Dampskib 'Hercules' v Grand Trunk Pacific Railway Co* [1912] 1 KB 222; *Badcock v Cumberland Gap Park Co* [1893] 1 Ch 362).

A 'visible sign or physical indication' that the company has a connection with particular premises will be indicative of the establishment of a place of business, but the absence of such signs or indications will not be conclusive evidence that a place of business has not been established. (*Deverall v Grant Advertising Inc* [1954] 3 AER 389).

The then DSS had in the past asserted that the use of a desk and chair may result in that furniture constituting a place of business, but from 6 April 1995 it said that whether an employer has a place of business is a question of fact and may depend on how the business operates: 'Generally an employer can be said to have a place of business in the UK if the employer has a fixed address or occupies premises where he is present with the consent of, the lawful owner or tenant, *and* an activity takes place which need not necessarily be remunerative in itself, but is in furtherance of the purposes of the business. The business does not need to be of a trading or commercial nature.' (Leaflet CWG2 (2016), page 68). Some of the pointers that will be looked for in deciding whether there is a fixed address of the kind described are a name plate on the door or premises; headed letter paper; an entry in the telephone directory; a lease or rent agreement or some sort of financial transaction for the use of the premises; a registered office; registration as a company incorporated outside the UK, but with a place of business in the UK for the purposes of the *Companies Act 2006*; and the existence of any other premises in Great Britain. In a note supplied to the ICAEW by the then DSS, the DSS said that so far as the 'carrying out of a business activity' is concerned 'it is not necessary for the staff in this country to be carrying out the main activity of the company, eg a foreign bank may have a branch in this country which is not actually banking; a foreign building firm may have an office here which is not actually building etc [but] as long as the office in Great Britain is carrying out some sort of activity for the company, eg collecting orders and posting them on to the foreign company, this is sufficient for it to be said that the company is carrying out its business here.' The DSS note stressed that an overseas organisation may have a place of business in Great Britain even if it has no employees under contract of service here, eg where partners or office-holding directors of the overseas entity work from a UK base. [ICAEW Faculty of Taxation Technical Release Tax 21/92, Annex F, December 1992]. For EC social security purposes, since 1 May 2010, a place of business in one EU country has been deemed to be a place of business in all the others. [Article 5, EC Regulation 883/2004.]

It is maintained that an embassy in Great Britain is a place of business of the relevant overseas government and this is probably correct (although the embassy will undoubtedly possess crown immunity and therefore not be liable for any secondary NICs in respect of its staff's UK wages). See **25.6** CROWN SERVANTS AND STATUTORY EMPLOYEES.

The former Inland Revenue changed for tax purposes the terminology used for UK branches or agencies of foreign entities to 'permanent establishments' and 'representative offices', which is based on the standard wording used in the OECD model Tax Convention. At present this has no impact on NIC legislation and procedures.

It had long been accepted by DSS that an individual who works from home would not create a place of business for the overseas employer unless there were obvious signs of the employer being present there. That view seems to be changing with HMRC asking specific questions about whether the employee receives any payment for the use of the premises, which would indicate that the employer does indeed occupy the premises by right.

Employed earners

[51.9] Unless the EC regulations are, or a reciprocal agreement is, of application and provide or provides to the contrary, anyone who falls to be categorised as an employed earner by reason of being gainfully employed in

Great Britain (see **14.4** CATEGORISATION) is, subject to the exceptions stated below, to be liable for primary Class 1 contributions in respect of the earnings from his employment if, at the time of his employment, he is:

(a) resident in Great Britain (see **51.5** above); or
(b) present or but for any temporary absence would be present in Great Britain (see **51.4** above); or
(c) ordinarily resident in Great Britain (see **51.5** above).

[*Social Security (Contributions) Regulations 2001, SI 2001/1004, Reg 145(1)(a)*].

These rules apply to all workers moving to and from 'Rest of the World' (ROW) territories (ie, non-EEA states or social security treaty partner states).

It should be noted that the fact that a person's contract of employment may be made under foreign law or that his employer may be based overseas is irrelevant. It is the place in which a person works that determines where he is gainfully employed. In *Crofts and Others v Cathay Pacific Airways Ltd and Others* CA [2005] TLR 31, an employment tribunals case, five pilots were employed by Veta Ltd, a subsidiary of Cathay Pacific Airways, who had appealed against an employment tribunals decision on breach of contract and unfair dismissal claims. The employment tribunal had found that the pilots were employed in Great Britain within *Employment Rights Act 1996, s 94(1)* notwithstanding that *section 196(2)* (repealed by *Employment Relations Act 1999, s 32(3)*) of the same act excluded international pilots who necessarily spent most of their working hours outside Great Britain. However, the Court of Appeal in a majority decision held that findings of the tribunal led to the conclusion that the Veta pilots were employed in Great Britain because the contract required them to live and work in the way it did ie flying in and out of Heathrow with Great Britain as a base rather than Hong Kong. Therefore they were employed in Great Britain for the purposes of *Employment Rights Act 1996, s 94(1)* and unfair dismissal claims were within the tribunal's jurisdiction.

52 week NIC exemption – ordinarily resident outside Great Britain

[51.10] Where an employed earner coming from a ROW jurisdiction would be liable to pay contributions under the above rule by reason of falling within (a) or (b) in **51.9** above, but does not fall within (c), no main primary, additional primary, secondary Class 1 or Class 1A liability is to arise in respect of earnings from the employment until a continuous period of 52 weeks of residence has elapsed beginning with the contribution week following the date of his last entry into Great Britain provided the employee is:

- not ordinarily resident in Great Britain;
- not ordinarily employed in Great Britain;
- in the UK in pursuance of an employment that is mainly outside the UK;
- employed by an employer with a place of business outside the UK (see **51.8** above); and
- employed for a time in GB as an employed earner.

[*Social Security (Contributions) Regulations 2001, SI 2001/1004, Reg 145(2)*].

In the case of Class 1A liability where *Reg 145* is in point, an apportionment of benefits will need to be adjusted on Form P11D(b) if necessary. Once liability for Class 1 ceases, any benefits in kind provided thereafter should be outside the scope of Class 1A. In addition, if the employee becomes non-resident upon leaving to take up full-time work abroad, there should be no benefits that remain taxable in the UK, which should preclude a Class 1A liability.

In the context of employment law, it has been said that in deciding where a person ordinarily works one should look at the terms of his contract, express or implied, in order to ascertain where, looking at the whole period contemplated by the contract, his *base* is to be; and that, where the contract is of no assistance the matter should be resolved by looking at the conduct of the parties and the way they have operated the contract. (*Maulik v Air India* [1974] ICR 528; *Wilson v Maynard Shipbuilding Consultants AB* [1978] ICR 376; *Todd v British Midland Airways Ltd* [1978] ICR 959; *Janata Bank v Ahmed* [1981] ICR 791, [1981] IRLR 457, CA; *Sonali Bank v Rahman* [1989] ICR 314). It is suggested that this approach is equally valid in deciding whether or not a person is ordinarily employed in Great Britain.

The meaning of 'place of business' is discussed at **51.8** above, but the phrasing of *Social Security (Contributions) Regulations 2001, SI 2001/1004, Reg 145(2)* suggests that the expression, where first used, denotes the *principal* place of business, ie the *siège sociale* or central seat of government and control of a corporation. That being the case it is irrelevant that the employer may also have a place of business in Great Britain.

A 'contribution week' is a period of seven days beginning with midnight between Saturday and Sunday. [*Social Security (Contributions) Regulations 2001, SI 2001/1004, Reg 1(2)*.] Applying this rule, the first week of a contribution year may start on any day from 6 to 12 April inclusive. Note that this is not the same as the tax week for PAYE purposes, which always starts on 6 April each year and every seven days thereafter, with the last day (or two in a leap year) of the year counting as week 53.

The DSS (now DWP) considered that the reference in the Regulation to 'the date of the earner's last entry' should not be looked at in isolation—but should be considered in the context of the Regulation as a whole. The 'continuous period of 52 weeks' is, in the DSS' view, a test of continuous residence and not a test of continuous presence in the UK. The test of 52 weeks continuous residence has been applied to seconded workers from abroad since 1948 when the National Insurance scheme began, and the policy intention has not changed since then. Once the worker has been resident in the UK for a continuous period of 52 weeks after having been sent here 'for a time', Class 1 NICs become due. The date of the worker's last entry in the UK for this purpose will be the date of the worker's last entry in order to take up the employment 'for a time'. (Letter from the Contributions Agency, 11 February 1994). Accordingly, the DSS rejected any suggestion that a short period of absence from the territory of Great Britain in, say, the fifty-first week of residence will trigger off a fresh 52-week period of non-liability when the employee returns to GB. It is understood that this view was supported in an unreported determination of a question by the Secretary of State for Social

Security in 1994 on the contribution liabilities of a Japanese employer with a number of Japanese employees in the UK for varying periods (not that there is now a reciprocal agreement or social security treaty between the UK and Japan – see below). The essence of the decision was that the words 'last entry' should be taken to mean 'last entry at or before the commencement of such employment', ie *first* entry to take up the employment in the UK. (See Tolley's National Insurance Brief, Vol 4, No 1, pages 1–3). However, the matter is far from resolved, as the determination by the Secretary of State for Social Security is open to challenge in a new case through the courts as being unreasonable. It may be argued that 'last' cannot possibly have meant 'first' and that the plain English of the regulation should only take a different meaning if the result of the natural meaning of the words is absurd. Since the 2000 agreement between the UK and Japan on social security Japanese workers detached to the UK for more than *five* years at the outset will be subject to UK social security legislation as though they were ordinarily resident in the UK. See **51.52** below.

With effect from 3 April 2006 the Home Office announced that work permit holders must complete at least five years of continuous 'work permit employment' to be eligible for indefinite leave to remain in Great Britain ie permanent residence. This change also affected other business- and employment-related immigration such as the Highly Skilled Migrant Programme (HSMP), Innovators, UK Ancestry Applicants and Investors. These categories were for an initial period of *up to* two years followed by an extension of up to a further three years. It follows, therefore, that the same facts should be applied for income tax, work permit and NIC issues.

See **10.14** APPRENTICES, TRAINEES AND STUDENTS for a similar 52-week exception in the case of certain students and apprentices not ordinarily resident in Great Britain. It should be noted, however, that this particular 52-week exemption was withdrawn from 6 April 2012, although the normal rule for employed apprentices and students will apply.

Example

Pak-lok, a Malay engineer who is ordinarily employed in Kuala Lumpur for a Malay company, is sent to Birmingham for a nine-month period of service with an associated British company. His sister accompanies him and finds employment in a restaurant.

P's sister is 'present' during the nine months and falls to be categorised as an employed earner by reason of her contract of service with the proprietor of the restaurant for whom she works. Her earnings will, therefore, attract primary and secondary Class 1 contribution liabilities from the outset. P's earnings will, however, attract no contribution liabilities under the British contribution scheme for, although he, like his sister, is 'present' and falls to be categorised as an employed earner during the period of presence, he is neither 'ordinarily resident' in Great Britain, nor 'ordinarily employed' in Great Britain, nor employed in Great Britain for a *continuous* period of 52 or more weeks, *and* his employment is 'mainly outside the UK' by an employer whose place of business is outside the UK. While his earnings will attract tax in respect of his UK duties (and the UK host company will probably operate a payroll to account for that tax), there should be no liability to Class 1 NICs on his salary or Class 1A NICs in respect of his benefits in kind.

Employment outside UK

[51.11] Where a person is gainfully employed outside Great Britain in a ROW jurisdiction in an employment which, were it in Great Britain, would be an employed earner's employment, that employment is to be treated as an employed earner's employment and primary, additional primary and secondary Class 1 liabilities are to arise in respect of the person's earnings for the employment, with Class 1A liability for the employer only if:

- the employer has a place of business in Great Britain (see **51.8** above);
- the earner is ordinarily resident in Great Britain (see **51.5** above); and
- immediately before the commencement of the employment the earner was resident in Great Britain (see **51.5** above). For HMRC's view on the definition of *immediately* see HMRC Press Release on 25 November 2009.

Example

Massey is made redundant by Ferguson Ltd in the UK, and decides to seek work overseas. She takes up a two-year contract as an employee of Deer Pty in South Africa, which has no UK presence. Her weekly earnings for Class 1 contribution purposes are £841.67 in £sterling terms. However, there is no Class 1 liability, because the first of the three conditions for such liability is not met. While Massey remains ordinarily resident, having gone abroad for only two years, and she was resident immediately before taking up the South African contract, she is working for a wholly non-UK employer, so she cannot be classed as an employed earner. If the period in South Africa leaves her with a gap in her contribution records, she needs to consider paying voluntary contributions under Class 2 (see **51.12** below).

If the three conditions are met, liability will continue, however, only during the period of 52 contribution weeks from the beginning of the contribution week in which the overseas employment commenced. [*Social Security (Contributions) Regulations 2001, SI 2001/1004, Reg 146(1)(2)*.]

In the case of Class 1A liability where *Reg 146* is in point, an apportionment of benefits will need to be adjusted on Form P11D(b) if necessary, as only in respect of benefits provided before the expiry of the 52 weeks will Class 1A liability arise, and then only if the benefit in question is taxable in the UK such that it is reportable on a P11D. In the example of *Massey* above, there can also be no Class 1A liability because she is not an employed earner in relation to the new employment.

52 weeks of continuing NIC liability

[51.12] The 52 weeks of continuing NIC liability are, according to HMRC to include weeks of sickness or leave or temporary duty for which the employee is remunerated. This is surely correct and this was reasserted by Tax Bulletin, Issue 79 where it stated:

This means that an employee who has employment based in the UK who goes abroad for a time on a short business trip or holiday abroad, and who departs from or returns to the UK, can continue to be within the UK scheme.

The DSS previously asserted that weeks of *unpaid* leave in GB were not to be included—an assertion which seemed wrong in law. However, the August 1995 and subsequent editions of Leaflet NI 132, the last edition before its withdrawal being dated April 2002, agreed that the 52-week period of liability is *not* extended if periods of unpaid leave fall within it (page 8). Again, the DSS formerly asserted that where an employee was to return abroad after a remunerated period of sickness or leave in GB and the 52 weeks of continuing liability came to an end before or during that leave, etc. Class 1 liability would be treated as arising again after the leave, etc had lasted for 26 weeks and that a further 52-week period of liability would begin—even if no actual duties had been performed in GB. Again, there appeared to be no grounds in law for imposing such liabilities since paid leave in the UK does not bring the employment outside the UK to an end. Leaflet NI 132 (August 1995 editions onwards, now withdrawn) was not therefore subsequently so presumptive and seemed to suggest that a fresh period of 52 week liability will only arise when:

- a quite separate and distinct secondment abroad takes place, or
- the return to the UK is other than on temporary duty, incidental to the overseas employment (eg a briefing or further training), or
- the return to the UK is other than on temporary duty, *not* incidental to the overseas employment but the stay in the UK is for six weeks or more.

The period of six weeks mentioned above does not have the force of law but it was admitted in the leaflet to be a concession to ease administration.

The earnings upon which Class 1 liabilities continue to arise for 52 weeks are the gross earnings from the employment concerned (converted into their sterling equivalent, if necessary, at the rate of exchange applicable at the date of payment) irrespective of where, or by whom, those earnings are paid.

Example

Mary, who is employed by Quite Ltd in the UK, is seconded to Contrary, Quite's Taiwan subsidiary, for eighteen months. She is paid £800 a month by Quite and 2,000 NT$ by Contrary. On the date of her first payment by Quite and Contrary, the exchange rate is 48 NT$ to £1. Her earnings for Class 1 contribution purposes are £841.67. The actual exchange rate needs to be similarly dealt with on each occasion of future payments where Class 1 liability exists. There is no such liability, however, in respect of payments made *after* the first 52 weeks have elapsed.

The question whether (and which) overseas allowances form part of earnings for contribution purposes is discussed at **51.57** below.

It is important to note that 'employer' in the context of *Social Security (Contributions) Regulations 2001, SI 2001/1004, Reg 146(1)(2)* means the employer to whom the earner is under a contract of service while overseas. (DSS Leaflet CF(N) 1030, Para 1 (now withdrawn)). Accordingly, whenever an employee is seconded overseas to work for an associated or subsidiary company, it will be important to decide whether or not the employee remains under contract to the UK company or whether that contract has been replaced by a contract with the overseas company. There is no concept of 'economic employer' such as that adopted for the purposes of income tax and the dependent personal services or employment income article of double tax treaties.

If the employee is given a new contract with the overseas company, and if the overseas company has no place of business in Great Britain (see **51.8** above), Class 1 liability will *not* continue after the date on which the contract with the UK company was terminated. In cases where the position is in doubt, HM Revenue and Customs will look at the precise terms of employment overseas and consider whether the employer/employee relationship implicit in a contract of service still exists between the original employer and employee or whether in fact that relationship now exists between the employee and the associate or subsidiary company overseas. In coming to a decision, HM Revenue and Customs will ask four principal questions.

(a) Which company has the right to dictate what work the employee will perform during his time overseas and the manner in which he will perform it?
(b) Which company has the right to suspend or dismiss the employee?
(c) Is the UK company able to recall the employee at any time?
(d) By which company are the employee's earnings funded?

The DSS (now DWP) acknowledged that an employee's continued membership of a UK company's pension scheme while he is overseas is a factor in deciding with which company his contract lies, but said that 'it should not be taken as decisive'. (DSS Leaflet CF(N) 1030, now withdrawn, Para 3). It is possible that the overseas entity is a participating employer in the UK pension arrangements.

Where an employee sent overseas by a UK employer changes jobs with the same employer, the 52-week period of continuing liability is brought to an end, because condition (c) above is not met in relation to the new job.

Example

Ralph, who works for Albert Ltd in London, is posted to become general manager of the personnel office of Albert's Sydney office. Liability to Class 1 contributions should continue for the first 52 weeks, but Ralph is moved after six months onto a dam-building project in Malaysia. Class 1 liability ceases at this point, even though Ralph is still employed by Albert. Had, however, it been agreed before leaving Great Britain that Ralph would move to Malaysia after six months, Class 1 NIC would continue for the first 52 weeks.

In instances where there is a fresh employment with an overseas employer, anomalous results can arise from the breadth of the 'place of business' definition in **51.8**. Employees and overseas employers may be unaware of the existence of a deemed place of business in Great Britain so that direct collection of primary and secondary Class 1 contributions is due, but overlooked.

Example

Bill is unable to find work in the UK but goes to Saudi Arabia and is immediately taken on by X Ltd, who recruit him locally, on a three-year contract. Unbeknown to Bill, X Ltd has a place of business in Manchester because it rents an office there at Y Ltd and, when Bill applies to pay voluntary Class 2 contributions, this fact is picked up by HM Revenue and Customs. Accordingly, because all the conditions for 52 weeks of the UK Class 1 liability as laid down in *Social Security (Contributions) Regulations 2001, SI 2001/1004, Reg 146(1)* are met, HM Revenue and Customs approaches the UK place of business of X Ltd at Y Ltd (who has never heard of Bill) and asks for Class 1 contributions in respect of Bill's earnings from X Ltd.

Whilst collection of both primary and secondary contributions can be enforced against the entity having a UK place of business, the diplomatic immunity enjoyed by embassy officials prevents this being effective where an embassy is a UK place of business. In such a case, collection of secondary contributions cannot be enforced against the employee, and whilst he is outside the UK, it is not possible to enforce collection of his primary contributions, either. Collection can, however, be enforced when he is within the UK, eg upon his return at the end of the contract. [*Social Security (Contributions) Regulations 2001, SI 2001/1004, Sch 4, Reg 30*]. It should be possible to avoid the unexpected liabilities described in these paragraphs if condition (c) above is not met. This can be achieved by a period of time elapsing between the employee ceasing to be resident in the UK and the employment overseas commencing. As mentioned above, EC regulations and reciprocal agreements may override the ROW provisions of *Social Security (Contributions) Regulations 2001, SI 2001/1004, Reg 146*. For example, where entertainers came from an EEA Member State or where there was a reciprocal agreement in operation with the UK and the 'entertainer' supplied an A1 or E101 or their equivalent, then the 2003 changes to the Categorisation Regulations that affected entertainers until 5 April 2014 did not apply and, notwithstanding that the individual was in receipt of a 'salary' (as defined in the 2003 Regulations), Class 1 NICs will not have been applicable. See also **36** ENTERTAINERS.

Working overseas and voluntary NICs

[51.13] Where a person takes up overseas employed earner's employment with an employer who has no place of business in the UK, neither the employee nor the employer is liable to contribute to the UK National Insurance scheme in respect of that employment. This means that, on his return to the UK, the employee may not (depending on the length of time spent overseas) be eligible for short-term social security benefits (eg contributions based jobseeker's allowance, contributory employment and support allowance) and his State pension entitlement may also be prejudiced by the lack of a contribution record. The long-term benefit position may be safeguarded by the payment of Class 3 voluntary contributions (see **51.17** below). The individual's entitlement to short-term incapacity benefit, maternity allowance and widow's payment may be protected, subject to certain requirements as to past residence or past payment of contributions, by the payment of voluntary *Class* 2 contributions in respect of each year relevant to benefit entitlement for which his or her contribution record or EARNINGS FACTOR **28** is deficient. [*Social Security (Contributions) Regulations 2001, SI 2001/1004, Reg 147*]. Such contributions must normally be paid within six years of the end of the fiscal year for which they are paid. [*Social Security (Contributions) Regulations 2001, SI 2001/1004, Reg 148*]. In practice, contributions should be paid promptly as late payment may result in otherwise valid claims to short-term benefit becoming inadmissible.

Example

George and Mildred have both worked in the UK for many years. George obtains a new job in Saudi Arabia where he is recruited locally for three years. He leaves his old job, as does Mildred, and they both move to accommodation in Saudi Arabia for the three years. Mildred does not obtain any employment during the three years, but pays Class 3 (voluntary) contributions (see **51.17** below) to protect her benefit entitlement. This only covers basic retirement pension, however. George's income from employment is not subject to UK Class 1 contributions but he is entitled to pay Class 3 contributions. Because he is working, however, he is also entitled to pay Class 2 contributions instead. He pays Class 2 contributions as they are cheaper than Class 3 and provide greater benefit coverage. Two months before the end of George's contract, both he and his wife fall seriously ill and George is unable to complete his contract. After a further month George and Mildred return to the UK ie one month early. Whilst ill in Saudi Arabia, neither George nor Mildred can receive UK employment and support allowance as it is a benefit requirement that they are present in the UK. On return George can claim contributory benefits immediately, but Mildred cannot as she did not pay, nor was she entitled to pay, contributions which give rise to eligibility for contributory employment and support allowance. Had the three-year job been in Germany rather than Saudi Arabia, George could have claimed benefit for the whole of the first two months as under EC law, presence in another EEA Member State is treated as presence in the UK as necessary.

Class 2 contributions used to cost only 10 pence per week more than Class 3 contributions until 6 April 2000 and are considerably cheaper thereafter, so they should be considered for the last three complete tax years ended before the start of the calendar year of return to the UK, upon which the conditions for short-term benefit entitlement are based (see **13.5** BENEFITS).

However, where a person continues to pay UK contributions under the 52-week rule described above, the entitlement to contributions-based jobseeker's allowance and contributory employment and support allowance is already protected, subject to certain conditions, by virtue of *Social Security (Unemployment, Sickness and Invalidity Benefit) Regulations 1983, Reg 20*.

Where an employee works overseas for several years, it is likely that a gap will be created in his or her contribution record. However, in the year of departure (or, if the 52-week rule applies, the following year), it is possible that enough Class 1 contributions will be paid from 6 April to the point of departure (or cessation of liability after 52 weeks, as the case may be) to make the year a qualifying year for all basic benefit purposes (although S2P/SERPS entitlements might have been reduced in years up to 5 April 2016), since the year qualifies if Class 1 contributions are paid or deemed paid on earnings equal to the annual LEL for the year. Similarly, in the year of return, unless the return to UK employment is shortly before 5 April, it is possible that enough Class 1 contributions will be paid in that year to make the year a qualifying one. From 2016–17 onwards, earnings need only reach the LEL. For earlier years from 2009 to 2016, an employee paid £770 per week or more (or monthly or other equivalent) needed to be paid such an amount for only eight weeks (8 × £770 = £6,160) since he would then have paid contributions on the LEL for the equivalent of a whole year (2015–16: 52 × £112 = £5,824). In either case, if the year does not qualify, NIC&EO may issue a deficiency letter to the contributor after the end of the year inviting payment of voluntary contributions. Such a notice will not be issued automatically for any of the years where *no* contributions are paid.

Example

Lionel is seconded to his firm's South African subsidiary company for four years from 12 July 2012. His wife Jean gives up her current employment and finds new employment in South Africa beginning on 1 September 2012. Lionel's income is subject to primary and secondary contributions for the first fifty-two weeks only. When he returns to the UK on 12 July 2016 he is immediately covered for short-term benefits so he does not need to pay Class 2 (or Class 3) contributions whilst abroad. As regards State pension entitlement, his earnings at the start of 2012–13 are likely to be sufficient for that year to become a 'qualifying year'. A similar position applies at the end of 2016–17. Lionel needs to consider payment of Class 2 or Class 3 contributions for 2013–14, 2014–15 and 2015–16 to enhance basic State pension and bereavement benefit entitlement.

On becoming employed in September 2012, Jean is entitled to pay Class 2 contributions and does so throughout the remainder of their time in South Africa. Jean expects to have a baby in August 2016. She cannot make a valid claim for Maternity Allowance whilst in South Africa as she has to be present in the UK, so she defers her claim until arrival back in the UK. Had Lionel's secondment been to Luxembourg and Jean had worked there and paid Luxembourg social security contributions, she could have claimed UK Maternity Allowance from eleven weeks before the birth, as presence in, and payment of contributions to, a fellow EEA Member State satisfies, under EC law, the conditions as to presence for UK benefit entitlement. Had Jean paid only Class 3 contributions while in either South Africa or Luxembourg no Maternity Allowance would be due as Class 3 buys only entitlement to State pension and bereavement benefits.

Following a dispute ever since the introduction in April 2000 of the £2 per week Class 2 rate (now £2.80 per week), the then Centre for Non-Residents (Newcastle) finally accepted in late 2002 that workers sent to work abroad in ROW countries (ie, other than EC/EEA countries or those with whom there is a reciprocal arrangement) who cease to have Class 1 liability abroad after 52 weeks can pay Class 2 contributions instead of Class 3. Regardless of the extra benefit coverage, this is beneficial from April 2000 due to the reduction in the rate of Class 2 at that time. In view of the fact that NICO's advice was initially to the contrary, affected individuals could have applied to have the Class 3 contributions already paid converted to Class 2, and the balance refunded. Such claims are now time-barred under the general six-year rule.

Secondary contributors

[51.14] A person who would be the secondary contributor in respect of earnings paid to an employed earner (taking no account of questions of residence and presence) *is* to be the secondary contributor and is to be liable to pay secondary Class 1 contributions and collect primary Class 1 contributions in the normal way *if*, at the time the contributions become due, he is either resident (see **51.5** above), or present (see **51.4** above), or has a place of business (see **51.8** above), in Great Britain. [*Social Security (Contributions) Regulations 2001, SI 2001/1004, Reg 145(1)(b)*]. (See CLASS **1** CONTRIBUTIONS **15** as well as **21.5** COLLECTION).

Article 5 of *EC Regulation 883/2004*, combined with *Article 21* of *EC Regulation 987/2009*, introduces an equality of treatment provision and an explicit rule requiring an employer present or resident in one Member State to have the same obligations and duties of an employer in another Member State, including paying any employer contributions due, either directly or through the employee.

Where a liability for *primary* Class 1 contributions arises but not (by virtue of *Reg 145(1)(b)*) a liability for secondary Class 1 contributions, the person who would otherwise have been liable for secondary contributions may pay them *voluntarily* if he wishes to do so and will then also collect the primary contributions due. [*Social Security (Contributions) Regulations 2001, SI 2001/1004, Reg 145(1)(b)*]. If he declines to do so, however, direct collection from the earner of the primary Class 1 contributions will be arranged (see **21.30** COLLECTION).

'Host Employer' rules

[51.15] New rules applied from 6 April 1994 under which a UK employer may be treated as the secondary contributor in relation to workers seconded to him by a foreign employer who has no place of business in the UK. See **4.13** AGENCY WORKERS for a DSS note concerning the position prior to the introduction of this legislation. The rules provided that, where a person was employed by a foreign employer and, in pursuance of that employment, his personal service was first made available to a host employer on or after 6 April 1994 and was rendered for the purposes of the host employer's business, the host employer to whom the personal service was made available was treated as the secondary Class 1 contributor. [*Categorisation Regulations, Sch 3 para 9* as inserted by *Categorisation Amendment Regulations 1994, Reg 4*]. For this purpose, a 'foreign employer' was a person who did not fulfil the conditions as to residence or presence in Great Britain described earlier and who, if he had fulfilled those conditions, would have been the secondary contributor in relation to any payment of earnings to or for the benefit of the person employed; and a 'host employer' was a person who had a place of business in Great Britain. [*Categorisation Regulations, Reg 1(2)* as amended by *Categorisation Amendment Regulations 1994, Reg* 2]. HMRC has subsequently admitted that this legislation was not as robust as it had originally believed. Employers were able to circumvent the provisions by having provided to them some form of composite service rather than personal service. HMRC has attempted to rectify matters by changes to the provisions from 6 April 2014 so as to catch so-called 'offshore employment intermediaries' and attach the secondary liability to an entity with a UK presence.

Paragraph 9 was rewritten from 6 April 2014 so as to encompass six different set of circumstances and identify for each the host employer responsible for accounting for NICs:

(1) Where a foreign employer provides an employee to work directly and personally for a host employer, or be personally involved in the provision of services to the host employer, the host employer will be the secondary contributor.
(2) Where a worker is supplied by a foreign agency to a UK end client, the end client is the host employer and secondary contributor.
(3) Where a foreign employer supplies a worker to work for a UK end client under a contract between that end client and a UK agency, the UK agency that has the contractual relationship with the end client is the host employer and secondary contributor.
(4) Where a foreign agency supplies a worker to a UK end client under a contract between that end client and a UK agency, the same result applies as in 3. Above.
(5) Where a UK employer supplies a worker to a business outside the UK under a contract between that foreign person and a UK agency, and the worker is 'eligible' to pay UK contributions in relation to that employment, the UK employer or UK agency that has the contractual relationship with the foreign business is the secondary contributor.
(6) Where a foreign employer supplies a worker to a business outside the UK under a contract between that foreign person and a UK agency, and the worker is 'eligible' to pay contributions in the UK in relation to that employment, the UK agency that has the contractual relationship with the foreign business using the worker's services is the secondary contributor.

In situations 3 and 4, the production of fraudulent documents by an end client to a UK agency, or by any other person resident in the UK with a contractual relationship with the UK agency, purporting to show that the worker was not subject to a right of supervision, direction or control as to the manner of performing the work will render the end client or that other person liable to be treated as the employer and secondary contributor.

The above host employer rules only apply to mariners if they work on vessels deployed wholly or mainly in category A, B, C or D waters, ie, canals, rivers and estuaries.

It is not immediately clear why situations 5 and 6 refer to a worker being 'eligible' to pay UK contributions, since eligibility is a matter for voluntary contributors rather than compulsory contributors. As may be seen at **[18.10]** and **[19.2]**, many contributors are eligible to pay contributions of Class 2 or 3 while overseas, but the UK agency involved in supplying the worker is unlikely to have the personal information necessary to determine whether the worker is 'eligible' to pay such contributions, especially where the worker is already on the payroll of another company, be that onshore or offshore. It would seem logical that HMRC expects the UK agency, if deemed to be the employer, to apply the 52-week rule as if it was sending its own employees overseas on assignment, but that is not how the legislation has been framed, and no guidance has been issued as to the intended meaning.

See AGENCY WORKERS **4** and OIL RIG WORKERS, DIVERS, ETC **50** for further details.

It should be noted that the pre-2014 'host employer' rules were of no application where the seconded worker was already working for the UK employer on 6 April 1994 and that, even where they were of application by reason of a seconded worker beginning to work for a UK employer on or after that date, no primary or secondary Class 1 liability will generally have been imposed on the host employer until 52 weeks of the secondment had elapsed. (See *Social Security (Contributions) Regulations 2001, SI 2001/1004, Reg 145(2)* as described at **51.14** above).

However, it should not be overlooked that the old rules did not, and the new rules do not, only apply to seconded workers. Employees hired locally in the UK on or after 6 April 1994 by a 'foreign employer' for work in the UK with a UK 'host employer' will have an immediate primary Class 1 liability. As the 'host' is deemed to be the secondary contributor in relation to the earnings paid, there will also be an immediate secondary liability, and the 2014 changes should ensure that a UK entity, be that an employer or a UK agency, is held liable provided the worker would have attracted a Class 1 liability if supplied by a UK agency to a UK business.

In certain cases where an employee is not ordinarily resident in the UK but has been assigned to the UK from a ROW country and has worked for the foreign employer in the UK, then returned to work for the ROW employer, but has his salary paid for both the UK and foreign duties, HMRC says that a NIC refund may be available based on an apportionment of the respective UK and non-UK duties. See Tax Bulletin, Issue 79. The reasoning adopted by HMRC is questionable but, nonetheless, providing travel documents and business diaries can sustain a claim to apportionment, repayment in respect of NIC paid for the relevant non-UK duties will be allowed. Claims to repayment and a calculation reflecting the apportionment should be sent with a copy of the appropriate final FPS together with a statement on the following lines:

From Benevolent Ltd

NIC&EO
Refunds Multi Erroneous
Room BP1001
Benton Park View
Longbenton
Newcastle Upon Tyne NE98 1ZZ

Dear Sir,

I refer to the employees listed on the attached Appendix. I can confirm that work undertaken outside the UK by the individuals, during the relevant period, was by reason of their continuing employment with their offshore employer (where different offshore employers are involved these have been notified accordingly). I can confirm that the total earnings relating to the overseas workday element of the continuing overseas employment were:

- paid and effectively borne by the overseas employer,
- not paid by any UK employer or by any UK resident person,

and that no costs relating to the overseas workday element of the continuing overseas employment have been or will be borne or incurred, directly or indirectly, by any person who is resident in the UK.

Appendix

Name & NI number	Pay Period (from payroll record)	NICs paid Employee	NICs paid Employer	Earnings on which NICs paid in pay period	Overseas days in pay period
Total days in pay period	Revised earning in pay period	Revised Employee NIC	Revised Employer NIC	Employee NIC Refund	Employer Refund

HM Revenue & Customs confirmed that where an employee was resident but not ordinarily resident in the UK and had earnings from employment inside and outside the UK, the practice set out in tax Statement of Practice 1/09 (formerly SP 5/84) could usually be applied to the Class 1A liability. An apportionment was required under the SP between income chargeable under *ITEPA 2003, ss 25, 26*. That chargeable under *s 26* then required further apportionment to reflect the extent of UK remitted earnings (although how the employer was supposed to know about these sums, which are not necessarily processed through PAYE, was never explained). It also confirmed that where, under a double taxation agreement, there was a taxable benefit in the UK but relief was claimed as a credit against the benefits, the Class 1A liability was not extinguished. [Tax Bulletin 79.] This view may require revision in the light of *Willett Ltd v HMRC* (2012) TC02301 (see **16.3**). However, it should probably be unaffected by the rewriting of the *s 26* rules in 2013 when the three-year rule for ordinary residence was codified in *s 26A* to recognise the introduction of the statutory residence test and the abolition for tax purposes of ordinary residence.

Self-employed earners

[51.16] Unless the EC regulations are, or a reciprocal agreement is, of application and provides to the contrary, anyone who falls to be categorised as a self-employed earner by reason of being gainfully self-employed in Great Britain (see **14.18** CATEGORISATION) (albeit limited from 6 April 2015 to those with Class 4 income from a trade or profession) is liable to pay a Class 2 contribution for a contribution week if:

- he is ordinarily resident in Great Britain (see **51.5** above); or
- he has been resident in Great Britain (see **51.5** above) for at least 26 of the 52 immediately preceding contribution weeks.

He is, however, *entitled* to pay such a contribution for any contribution week in which he is merely present in Great Britain (see **51.4** above). [*Social Security (Contributions) Regulations 2001, SI 2001/1004, Reg 145(1)(d)*].

> *Example*
> Miguel arrived in Great Britain from Belize on 27 August 2015. He took a short lease on some premises in Leeds (intending to return to Belize in a year or two) and started a hairdressing business. As he is not 'ordinarily resident' in Great Britain, the first week for which he will be *liable* to pay a Class 2 contribution is that ended 6 March 2015, for not until then will he have been 'resident' for 26 of the immediately preceding 52 weeks (bearing in mind that a contribution week starts on a Sunday). He is, however, *entitled* to pay Class 2 contributions, if he so wishes, from the date he begins to trade. [*Social Security (Contributions) Regulations 2001, SI 2001/1004, Reg 145(1)(c).*]

Note that, before 6 April 2015, Class 2 liability would have arisen for anyone in self-employment, which encompassed earning income from a trade, profession, vocation, office or 'business', in accordance with the definition of 'employment' in *SSCBA 1992, s 122*. With the reform of Class 2 by *National Insurance Contributions Act 2015, s 2 (NICA 2015)*, compulsory liability now arises under *SSCBA 1992, s 11(2)* only for those self-employed people with income from a trade or profession that is taxed under *ITTOIA 2005, Pt 2, Ch 2*, but the Class 2 residence and presence conditions outlined above have not been changed.

Before *NICA 2015* reformed the basis of Class 2, payment of contributions by direct debit or billing by NIC&EO would ordinarily continue irrespective of where the earner was working and living. However, where a UK self-employed earner works for an extended period in the EEA or Switzerland and remains insured in the UK under *EC Regulation 1408/71* or *EC Regulation 883/2004*, it is possible that there will now be no relevant profits taxable under *ITTOIA 2005* in the UK, which would mean that there could be no Class 2 liability under the 6 April 2015 rules. *Regulation 148B* was therefore inserted into the *Contributions Regulations 2001* to redefine 'relevant profits' in such circumstances to mean profits that would have been subject to Class 4 if the earner had been resident and working in the UK in the year, disregarding the lower annual profit limit and any double tax relief granted under arrangements made under *Taxation (International and Other Provisions) Act 2010, s 2*.

This type of absence abroad could mean that the earner is no longer required to file an income tax self-assessment for a particular tax year, which means that, while there may still be a UK liability, the normal post-2015 Class 2 collection process will not work. This is recognised by new *Reg 148C* with effect from 6 April 2015, which disapplies the normal collection requirements (via the ITSA return and process) set by *SSCBA 1992, s 11(5)*, creating instead an obligation to pay the Class 2 liability for any relevant weeks by 31 January after the end of the tax year (ie, the normal self-assessment deadline). The earner is also obliged to make 'a return in such form as may be approved by HMRC'. That form or process involves telling HMRC of the situation (via +44 191 203 7010 from outside the UK) so that HMRC can issue a bill for the year. The bill should ordinarily be issued in October, with payment of any compulsory contributions due by 31 January, as for self-assessment taxpayers.

No time limit is specified for contributions paid voluntarily, so the normal six-year limit (or the extended limits introduced because of the change in the state pension system) should apply.

Records of how the relevant profits (which are outside UK tax liability and therefore outside normal UK jurisdiction) have been calculated must be retained for six years from the 31 January filing deadline.

[*Social Security (Contributions) Regulations 2001, SI 2001/1004, Reg 148C.*]

Example

Michael owns and runs an antiques business in the UK and sees an opportunity to make money from an upsurge in interest in 19th century Austrian art, so he relocates to Vienna for two years. He applies for and is granted an A1 certificate so that he remains insured under UK social security legislation while he is pursuing his business in Austria and is not subject to Austrian social security costs (which would amount to over 25% of his profits up to an upper earnings limit of around €68,000).

Since he becomes non-resident in UK terms, his profits from the Viennese venture are taxable only in Austria and he has no trading profits in the UK. However, he remains liable to pay compulsory UK contributions because his Austrian profits are deemed to be 'relevant' for Class 2 purposes. [*Social Security (Contributions) Regulations 2001, SI 2001/1004, Reg 148B.*] In addition to dealing with the Austrian tax authorities, he will be required to make a return of, and pay, his Class 2 contributions to HMRC in the UK, and to keep records for a further six years to support his calculation of profits. [*Regulations 148C.*]

A person who is self-employed outside Great Britain with no continuing liability under EC or treaty rules is also entitled to pay Class 2 contributions (but only to the extent to which he would be entitled to make such contributions were he present in Great Britain) if *immediately* before he last left Great Britain he was ordinarily an employed earner or a self-employed earner *and*:

(a) he has been resident in Great Britain (see **51.5** above) for a continuous period of three or more years at some time prior to the period for which the Class 2 contributions are to be paid; *or*

(b) he has in each of any three earlier tax years paid:

    (i) contributions of any Class from which an earnings factor of at least 52 times the then-current Lower Earnings Limit for Class 1 purposes has been derived (see EARNINGS FACTORS **28**); or

    (ii) where one or more of those years falls before 6 April 1975, an average of 52 contributions of any class under the former principal *Act*.

[*Social Security (Contributions) Regulations 2001, SI 2001/1004, Reg 147(1)(a)(2)(3)*].

Following legal advice HMRC has advised that its interpretation of 'immediately' was too narrow. It had been HMRC practice to look at the position in the week before leaving the UK. The legal advice was that it should consider an individual's employment arrangements over a longer period. The same legal advice confirmed that the requirement to have been employed for a minimum of three years before being able to pay voluntary contributions was also wrong and a much shorter period could well be appropriate.

Example

Gavin came to the UK to study and obtained his doctorate in mining engineering from Leeds University. He took up a lecturing post at the university for three academic terms and then moved to Australia to work for one of the mining giants. He satisfied the three-year residence test and was ordinarily employed in the UK, albeit for only nine months. He had been employed for as long as he could have been in the UK so Gavin could pay voluntary Class 2 contributions.

Example

Jennie obtained her degree at St Andrew's University. She intended looking for a teaching post but in the end she settled for a number of temporary jobs for around 18 months. She then took three months off before going to Russia where she taught English for four years. She was ordinarily an employed earner in Great Britain so she could pay voluntary Class 2 contributions even though she was not employed in the months immediately before leaving Great Britain.

Time spent in another EEA country and/or Turkey may help to meet condition (a) above.

This entitlement is subject to the contributions being paid within the time limits relating to Class 3 contributions set down at **42.6** LATE-PAID CONTRIBUTIONS. [*Social Security (Contributions) Regulations 2001, SI 2001/1004, Reg 48(3)(b)(i), 148(a)*].

Whether it makes sense for either Gavin or Jennie to pay voluntary contributions will depend on their long-term plans and where they intend to live once they reach UK state pension age. Only if they live in the UK, the EEA or a treaty country will their state pension be uprated each year by inflation. If they retire permanently to a ROW country, the UK state pension should still be payable (as the rules currently stand), but it will be frozen at the level at which it is first paid.

Class 3 contributors

[51.17] Unless the EC regulations or a reciprocal agreement is of application and provides to the contrary, anyone who wishes to pay Class 3 contributions may, subject to normal constraints, do so if he is resident in Great Britain during that year for which they are to be paid (see **19.2** CLASS 3 CONTRIBUTIONS). [*Social Security (Contributions) Regulations 2001, SI 2001/1004, Reg 145(1)(e)*].

Where a person is gainfully employed in an employed earner's employment *outside the United Kingdom* which is to be treated as an employed earner's employment attracting Class 1 contribution liabilities for the first 52 weeks (see **51.9** above), that person is entitled to pay Class 3 contributions for any tax year during the whole or part of which the overseas employment subsists, provided he would be entitled to make such contributions were he present in Great Britain and Northern Ireland (as the case may be). [*Social Security (Contributions) Regulations 2001, SI 2001/1004, Reg 146(2)(b), Reg 148(b)*].

The payment of Class 3 contributions provides cover for UK basic pension rights and bereavement benefit rights. Class 3 NICs can be paid by direct debit, annual remittance or by an agent in the UK (see below) acting on behalf of the contributor. In addition, the voluntary contributions may be paid from abroad by direct debit from a UK bank account or cheque (sterling or foreign currency), banker's draft or BACS to HM Revenue and Customs, NIC&EO, Room BP1301, Longbenton, Newcastle upon Tyne NE98 1ZZ. Annually HMRC NIC&EO will advise the individual of the increase in Class 2 or 3 contributions by letter. See www.gov.uk/national-insurance-if-you-go-abroad.

An employer may agree to act as the employee's agent for the payment of Class 2 or 3 contributions and arrangements may be made for payment to be made annually to HM Revenue and Customs NIC&EO International Caseworker in Newcastle. (Leaflet NI 38.)

Apart from the entitlement described, any person who fulfils the past-contribution or past-residence conditions under which a self-employed earner outside Great Britain and Northern Ireland may voluntarily pay Class 2 contributions (see **51.14** above) may pay Class 3 contributions, provided he would be entitled to make such contributions were he present in Great Britain and Northern Ireland. [*Social Security (Contributions) Regulations 2001, SI 2001/1004, Reg 147(1)(b)(2)(3), Reg 148(b)*].

From 1 May 2010 voluntary contributions cannot be paid to a scheme in an EU member state unless the contributor has already been a compulsory member of that country's scheme [*EC Regulation 883/2004, Art 14.3*].

These entitlements are subject to the contributions being paid within the time limits set down at **42.6** LATE-PAID CONTRIBUTIONS. [*Social Security (Contributions) Regulations 2001, SI 2001/1004, Reg 48(3)(b)(i), Reg 148(a)*].

Officials and servants of Community institutions and other such workers may transfer their national pension rights to the Community pension scheme (PSEC). In such a case the individual may not pay Class 3 contributions for the period to which the transfer relates. [*Social Security (Contributions) Regulations 2001, SI 2001/1004, Regs 146, 148, 148A* as amended and inserted by *Social Security (Contributions)(Amendment No 4) Regulations 2007, SI 2007/1838*]. Where rights have been so transferred, no starting credits will be awarded on their return to the UK [*Transfer of State Pensions and Benefits Regulations 2007, SI 2007/1398, Reg 8(4)*].

Class 3A contributors

[51.18] There are no residences, ordinary residence, domicile or nationality restrictions on paying Class 3A contributions. The eligibility criteria inserted into *SSCBA 1992, s 14A* are very straightforward: a person is eligible to pay a Class 3A contribution if the person was, by 5 April 2016, already entitled to a Category A, Category B or Category D retirement pension or graduated retirement benefit, or had deferred entitlement to Category A or Category B retirement pension or graduated retirement benefit. [*Section 14A(2), inserted by Pensions Act 2014, s 25* and *Sch 15, para 3*.]

In summary, this means any person in receipt of a UK state old-age pension. Category A is the pension earned with the contributor's own contributions, Category B is the spouse's pension payable by reason of the other spouse's contributions, and Category D is the over-80 addition, while graduated retirement benefit is payable to those who paid graduated contributions at any time between 1961 and 1975.

Entitlement to pension would have been earned by paying UK contributions. Workers of any nationality could have worked and been paid in the UK, and are entitled to their state pension as a result. The state pension top-up for which Class 3A contributions are paid is simply an addition to that pension, treated as if it were a SERPS pension. This means that it is payable anywhere in the world, although annual uprating will only apply to pensioners who live in an EEA or treaty state.

Class 4 contributors

[51.19] Any earner who, for tax purposes (ie, using the SRT), is not resident in the UK in a year of assessment is to be excepted from liability for Class 4 contributions. [*Social Security (Contributions) Regulations 2001, SI 2001/1004, Reg 91(b)*]. See also Class 4 NIC under EC/RA rules and **51.33** below.

EC Social Security Regulations

[51.20] For social security purposes (but not necessarily for other purposes) the European Community presently consists of:

- Austria (from 1 January 1995);
- Belgium;
- Bulgaria (from 1 January 2007);
- Croatia (from 1 July 2013);
- Cyprus (from 1 May 2004);
- Czech Republic (from 1 May 2004);
- Denmark (excluding the Faroe Islands and including Greenland from 1.4.73 to 31.1.85 but not thereafter);
- Estonia (from 1 May 2004);
- Finland (from 1 January 1995);
- France (including Corsica, Guadeloupe, Martinique, Réunion, French Guiana and Saint-Pierre et Miquelon, but excluding Monaco);
- Germany (consisting of, until 3.10.90, the Federal Republic, ie West Germany and West Berlin but, thereafter, both the former Federal Republic and the former German Democratic Republic);
- Greece (including Crete and the Greek Islands);
- Hungary (from 1 May 2004);
- Ireland;
- Italy (including Sicily, Sardinia, Trieste and Elba, but excluding Vatican City and San Marino);
- Latvia (from 1 May 2004);
- Lithuania (from 1 May 2004);

- Luxembourg;
- Malta (from 1 May 2004);
- the Netherlands (excluding the former Netherlands Antilles, although this may change after the planned review of the 2010 dissolution of the island group: Bonaire, Sint Eustatius and Saba, which are currently 'special municipalities' of the Netherlands and are classed as 'overseas countries and territories' in EU terms – entitled to help from the European Development Fund but not EU members – may become EU territory);
- Poland (from 1 May 2004);
- Portugal (including Madeira and the Azores);
- Romania (from 1 January 2007);
- Slovakia (from 1 May 2004);
- Slovenia (from 1 May 2004);
- Spain (including the Balearic Islands of Majorca, Minorca, Ibiza and Formentera, the Canary Islands and the Spanish enclaves of Ceuta and Melilla in North Africa);
- Sweden (from 1 January 1995); and
- (only for the next few years perhaps) the United Kingdom of Great Britain and Northern Ireland (including Gibraltar for social security purposes but excluding the Isle of Man and the Channel Islands). (See HM Revenue and Customs National Insurance Manual NIM33003.)

A European Economic Area Agreement was reached in Oporto on 2 May 1992 among the seven EFTA states (Austria, Finland, Iceland, Liechtenstein, Norway, Sweden and Switzerland) which was intended to promote co-operation between the EC and EFTA, including in the field of social security co-ordination, with effect from 1 January 1993. However, following a referendum in December 1992, Switzerland failed to ratify the agreement and implementation by the remaining participants was therefore delayed until 1 January 1994. Liechtenstein ratified the agreement but, because its economy was so closely bound up with the Swiss economy, could not participate initially but eventually became an EEA member on 1 May 1995.

From 1 January 1994, the EC social security regulations *1408/71* and *574/72* (see below) applied to the other five EFTA states as if they were EC members. Austria, Finland and Sweden became full members of the EU on 1 January 1995, leaving only Norway, Iceland and Liechtenstein as EFTA members covered by the EC regulations under the EEA Agreement.

From 1 June 2002 the EC Social Security Regulations have applied to workers entering and leaving Switzerland because the country entered into a special agreement with the EC. It covered only Swiss and EC nationals. It did not apply to those EEA countries that are not EC members (ie, Iceland, Liechtenstein and Norway) nor to the most recent entrants to the EC, viz Bulgaria and Romania. The three EFTA countries have separate agreements with Switzerland. The agreement was renewed after a referendum in Switzerland in 2009, so Switzerland is now effectively treated as an EU state for the purposes of social security and the freedom of movement of workers, although a referendum in 2014 obliged the Swiss federal government to introduce quotas on migrant workers, a move that is incompatible with its agreement with the EU and which has been met with a refusal to negotiate from Brussels.

Bulgaria and Romania joined the European Union on 1 January 2007 but could not benefit from the EU-Switzerland agreement until 1 June 2009 at the earliest, and the Swiss have the option to exclude their citizens from free movement until 2019. Croatia joined on 1 July 2013, but was not permitted to benefit from the EU-Swiss agreement until 2016 or 2017, with a quota system initially. FYR Macedonia and the other countries which made up the former Yugoslavia, as well as Albania (an official candidate for membership only since 27 July 2014 and Turkey, wish to join in the future, and all but Bosnia and Herzegovina and Kosovo have formally applied. Switzerland made a formal application to join in May 1992, but the Swiss public voted to cancel the application a few months later, and instead the arrangements outlined above were negotiated some years later.

All articles of EC Treaties and Regulations which are of relevance to British contribution law take direct effect in Great Britain under *European Communities Act 1972, s 2* and decisions of the Court of Justice of the European Union in Luxembourg on contribution matters also take direct effect here under *ECA 1972, s 3*.

The principal regulations currently are *EC Regulation 883/2004* and *EC Regulation 1408/71* (dealing with the application of social security schemes of Member States to employed persons and their families moving within the Community) together with *EC Regulation 987/09 and EC Regulation 574/72* (fixing the procedure for implementing *EC Regulations 883/2004* and *EC Regulation 1408/71* respectively). *EC Regulation 1408/71* was amended, *inter alia*, by *EC Regulation 1390/81* (extending *EC Regulation 1408/71* to self-employed persons), *EC Regulation 3795/81* (extending the implementing regulation), *EC Regulation 2332/89* (extending *EC Regulation 1408/71* in respect of minimum periods of insurance) and *EC Regulation 2195/91*. All these regulations were made under *EC Treaty 1957, Art 51*, which has now been superseded by the *Treaty on the Functioning of the European Union (TFEU), Art 48*).

The new EC Regulations 883/2004 and 987/09 entered into force on 1 May 2010.

The regulations prevail over inconsistent internal law of a Member State and over prior bilateral and multilateral agreements unless these are expressly excepted. It should be noted that until 1 June 2003 EC Regulations only applied to EC nationals or stateless persons and refugees residing within the Community, whereas the coverage of other reciprocal agreements depended (as it still does) on their specific terms.

From 1 June 2003 and prior to 1 May 2010, the previous EC nationality, etc restriction was lifted except in the case of Denmark, Switzerland, Iceland, Liechtenstein and Norway (*Council Regulations 859/2003*). From the latter date, the UK refused to accept that anyone but EC nationals might be covered by the new *Reg 883/2004*, so they remain covered by *Reg 1408/71* (in other words, for example, an Australian working in London and sent on assignment to Berlin would be covered by the pre-2010 rules).

A list of all bilateral agreements between the UK and other states is given at **51.52** below and those relating to EC Member States are **in bold**. Apart from the agreements with the Federal Republic of Germany (in which case certain articles have been retained in accordance with *EC Regulation 1408/71 Annex III, Point A, para 19*, as renumbered by *Council Reg 629/2006*) and *Annex II* of *EC Regulation 883/2004 none* of the agreements has been excepted for UK purposes and *all* are superseded by EC regulations. However, given the extension of the application of the EC Regulations to non-EC nationals, etc from 1 June 2003 the previous reciprocal agreements (other than that with Germany in some instances) are now effectively redundant as far as the mainland is concerned, though some will continue to have relevance for movements involving workers from the Channel Islands and/or Isle of Man in some circumstances. Indeed, the new agreement with the Netherlands that took effect on 1 June 2007, unlike the old agreement, covers 'persons' and is not restricted to nationals of the UK and the Netherlands. The new agreement also covers the Channel Islands and this will be of particular importance to those workers moving between the Channel Islands and the Netherlands in the horticultural trades.

New EC Regulations (EC Regulations 883/2004 and 987/2009) from 1 May 2010

[51.21] The following is a list of key changes.

- Short-term assignments: an employee assigned from one Member State to another for a period of up to two years (previously up to one year) will remain insured in their home country unless the assignee is sent to replace another posted worker.
- Multi-state workers: previously, a person working partly in the country in which he was habitually resident paid contributions in that country. Under the new rules such an individual will still pay in the country of habitual residence provided there is regular activity in that country and the employer is in that country. Where the employer is in another EC country, the individual has to 'pursue a substantial part of his activity' (at least 25% of work time and/or remuneration) in the home country for this to apply. These rules have been significantly revised from 28 June 2012. See below.
- Long term assignments: despite the new rules, HM Revenue and Customs has confirmed that it will continue to issue certificates for up to five years where it is in the individual's best interests to do so.
- Previously, in certain circumstances, individuals employed in one Member State and self-employed in another would pay contributions in both Member States. Under the new rules they will only pay where they are employed.
- Authorities in different Member States will help each other collect unpaid contributions from employers who do not have a presence in the State where the contributions are payable.
- From 1 May 2010 where an employee is paying UK NIC, employer's NIC will also be payable even if the employer has no place of business in the UK provided the employer has a place of business or other presence in a Member State.
- The new rules for the self-employed are broadly the same as those for employees.

- Transport workers: there are no longer special rules for international transport workers such as aircrew or lorry or coach drivers who normally work in two or more Member States. These groups will be subject to the same rules as other people. The legislation was amended for aircrew from 28 June 2012 so that contributions will be payable in the Member State where the employee has his designated home base.
- Mariners – the rules have been simplified; the general 'flag rule' continues whereby a mariner is subject to the social security legislation of the Member State of the flag the ship is flying; the exception rules continue to apply where the mariner is paid by an employer in a different Member State and where the mariner resides.

Exceptions are as follows.

- For Third Country Nationals (ie Rest of the World), HMRC has advised that the UK will continue to use the old rules in *EC Regulations 1408/71 and 574/72*. The Danish social security authorities have also taken this stance. Since 1 January 2011, *EC Regulation 1231/2010* has formally extended modernised coordination to nationals of non-EU countries legally resident in the EU and in a cross-border situation. Their family members and survivors are also covered if they are in the EU. It does not apply to Denmark or the United Kingdom.
- Employees who already had an E101 certificate on 1 May 2010 can continue to use this until it expires. However, all other rules contained in the new legislation took immediate effect from 1 May 2010 ie an EU but non-UK employer with no place of business in the UK was required to assume all the NIC responsibilities of a UK company, that is:
  (a) register with HMRC as a payer of National Insurance Contributions (NIC);
  (b) pay over secondary (employers') and primary (employees') NIC; and
  (c) operate employer-delivered benefits such as Statutory Sick Pay, Statutory Maternity Pay and Statutory Paternity Pay.
- The EEA countries (Iceland, Liechtenstein and Norway) did not agree to adopt the new rules from 1 May 2010 but did so from 1 June 2012. The old rules (in *EC Regulations 1408/71 and 574/72*) applied in the interim period.
- Switzerland did not immediately adopt the new rules but did so from 1 April 2012. The old rules (in *EC Regulations 1408/71 and 574/72*) applied in the interim period.

Applications for A1/E101 forms.

- The E101 certificate was replaced by a new form (officially a 'portable document') A1 where the new Regulations are of application (ie in the case of Iceland, Liechtenstein, Norway and Switzerland, and third-country nationals, E101s were still used).
- From 1 May 2010 all applications other than those for third-country nationals are considered first under the new provisions.
- Employees with E101s issued under the old rules which were valid beyond 1 May 2010 could opt for the new rules to apply to them if they wished.

- Multi-state worker applications will have to be made to the authorities in the state where the individual is habitually resident irrespective of whether that is where contributions are expected to be payable.

Healthcare.

- European Health Insurance Cards (EHICs) will continue to be the appropriate healthcare insurance document for assignments up to 24 months.
- E106 forms and E109 forms have been replaced by form (portable document) S1. As before, this will be the appropriate healthcare insurance form for longer term assignments of more than 24 months. It will also be used where a person's family lives in a different Member State to the Member State where the employee pays contributions.

Both old and new regulations distinguish between employed persons and self-employed persons and provide specifically that all persons who are employed earners or self-employed earners within the meaning of the legislation of Great Britain are to be regarded as employed persons and self-employed persons respectively under EC regulations. [*EC Regulation 883/2004, Art 1(a) & (b) and EC Regulation 1408/71, Annex I, Point L*]. Accordingly, the European Court will not interfere with the determination of status (pre-April 1999) or an appeal under the procedures effective from 1 April 1999 (see APPEALS AND REVIEWS 9). This can occasionally lead to conflicts of laws, where for example one state treats a company director as an employee while another, where the director also works, applies self-employed status. In such cases, the basic principles of the treaty freedoms will point towards the correct outcomes.

The fundamental principle underlying the regulations is that a person should at no time be subject to the contribution legislation of more than one Member State. *EC Regulation 1408/71, Art 14f* (civil servants) *or Art 14c(b)* used to allow dual competence in certain very limited circumstances. *EC Regulation 883/2004* does not contemplate any dual social security contribution liability. [*EC Regulation 1408/71, Art 13(1)*]. (*Nonnenmacher v Bestuur der Sociale Verzekeringsbank Case 92/63* [1964] ECR 281). A migrant worker should normally be subject to the contribution law of the state in whose territory he is employed or self-employed even though he may reside in another state or even though (if he is an employed person) the registered office or place of business of his employer may be situated in another state. [*Art 13(2)*]. In *Bestuur der Sociale Verzekeringsbank v van der Vecht Case 19/67* [1967] ECR 345 the court held that this principle must be upheld even where a worker who is employed in the territory of a Member State, other than that in which he resides, and in which his employer's undertaking is situated, travels at his employer's cost between his place of residence and his place of work.

In accordance with this principle, the state in which a person resides could not enforce payment of contributions on earnings on which the earner has already paid contributions in the state of his employment (being another state) prior to the coming into force of *EC Regulation 1408/71*. (*Perenboom v Inspecteur der Directe Belastingen, Nijmegen Case 102/76* [1977] ECR 815).

In a case that was put to the then Contributions Agency (CA) International Services with regard to the UK insurability of a group of workers in the UK who were all at the time employed by a company operating from the Netherlands: the question arose as to the treatment for NIC purposes of the workers from the Netherlands. The CA replied that workers coming to the UK from other EEA countries, such as the Netherlands, were liable to pay UK Class 1 contributions from the outset under *EC Regulation 1408/71, Art 13(2)(a)* provided they were EEA nationals unless, of course, they were able to produce an E101 certificate. The EEA workers were not exempt from their first 52 weeks contribution liability under the terms of *Social Security (Contributions) Regulations 2001, SI 2001/1004, Reg 145(2)* due to the application of *Art 13(2)(a)* mentioned above. The EC Regulations take precedence over domestic legislation and aim to protect the Social Security position of those workers covered. However, given the extension of the application of the EC Regulations from 1 June 2003, the previous reciprocal agreements (other than that with Germany in some limited instances) are now effectively redundant as far as the mainland is concerned, though some will continue to have relevance for movements involving workers from the Channel Islands and/or Isle of Man in some circumstances.

It should be noted that the EC regulations on social security for migrant workers do not cover all aspects of the social security systems of Member States: social assistance programmes (in effect, means-tested benefits, such as universal credit and housing benefit in the UK) are not coordinated and there is no automatic entitlement to such benefits for new arrivals from another EEA Member State. The benefit case CIS/2680/2004 (12-8-2004) highlights the distinction. The claimant was refused income support by virtue of having failed the habitual residence test under the UK state benefits code. The claimant was born in Somalia, lived in Holland in 1997 but then moved to the UK in August 2003, fleeing domestic violence. It was held that the claimant was outside the scope of *EC Regulation 1408/71* as she had never worked in the EU/EEA, and therefore was not an employed or self-employed person as required by *Art 2(1)*. Although she had been covered by the Dutch social assistance system as regards child benefit and insurance for pension on residence grounds (ie, rather than being required to pay contributions – as in the UK) this did not make her a worker as required by *Art 2(1)*.

Throughout the EC, liability as a secondary contributor in respect of earnings paid to an employed person *follows* the primary liability of *the earner*, and is now unaffected by the fact that the secondary contributor may reside in a state other than that under the contribution law of which the earner's liabilities arise. It was held under the 1971 regulations that a French football club engaging German musicians not subject to French contribution law was under no liability to pay contributions to the Caisse under French contribution law in respect of earnings paid to the musicians, but was liable to pay contributions under the legislation to which the musicians were subject. (*Caisse Primaire d'Assurance Maladie, Sélestat v Association du Foot-ball Club D'Andlau Case 8/75* [1975] ECR 739). This last element of the decision was, however, odd, because the German musicians were evidently insured in Germany as self-employed persons, so no employer contributions would have been due.

Clearly, this cross-border liability raises enforcement problems which *EC Regulation 1408/71, Art 92* partially resolved by providing for the collection and enforcement of contribution payments due to one Member State in the territory of any other Member State under inter-state agreements scheduled in *EC Regulation 574/72, Annex 5*. No such agreements were made with the UK.

However, *EC Regulation 883/2004, Art 84* and *EC Regulation 987/09, Art 21* (see above) added some bite to the 'toothless' *Art 92* of *EC Regulation 1408/71*. As previously mentioned, from 1 May 2010 where an employer has its place of business in another Member State, there is now – even where there is no place of business in the UK – a corresponding employer NIC liability in respect of those employees paying NIC.

The general principle (enunciated earlier in this section) that the contribution legislation to which a person is to be subject is to be identified by the location of his employment, is modified in relation to certain types of earner by *EC Regulation 1408/71* and *EC Regulation 883/2004* as explained in ensuing sections.

Posted workers – EC Regulation 883/2004

[51.22] Where an earner who is employed in the territory of one Member State by an undertaking to which he is normally attached is sent by his employer to work in another Member State, he is to remain subject to the contribution laws of the first state provided that:

(a) the period of employment in the second state is not expected to last for a period in excess of twenty-four months; and
(b) he is not being sent to replace another person whose period of employment in the second state is at an end.

[*EC Regulation 883/2004, Art 12(1)*].

HMRC has confirmed that the person being replaced must also be a posted worker before the exclusion can apply. This was being disputed by some social security authorities but the position has been made clear and *Art 12* amended by virtue of *Art 1(5)* of *EC Regulation 465/2012*.

See also below regarding EC Administrative Decision 181, replaced by Decision A2, which extends *Art 12* to ensure that there must be a continuing direct relationship between the worker and employer. This requires that a person who is being sent abroad must already be in employment in the home country with the employer and must not now be *replacing* another person as in (b) above. A minimum period of one month of employment in the sending country will generally be required before the employee can be accepted as a posted worker.

An employed earner's continuing liability to pay contributions under the contribution legislation of the Member State in which he was employed before being posted to another Member State is certified by the first Member State on a form A1. UK employers must apply to HM Revenue and Customs NIC & EO International Caseworker for A1 certificates, using CA3821 and CA3822 which can be downloaded from the gov.uk website (see **43.3** LEAFLETS AND FORMS). When an employer applies for forms A1 for the first time, International

Caseworker will examine the case and the details shown on CA3821 to confirm whether or not the employer meets the criteria set out in Decision A2. The former Contributions Agency (CA) gave the example (CA Specialist conference, 4 February 1997) that where a workforce was substantially in another country and all that constituted the UK employer was, say, a typist and fax machine, no E101s (as they were then) would be issued. This still applies; the UK employer must undertake 'substantial activities' in the UK before A1s can be issued by HMRC in respect of outbound workers. This is a measure intended to prevent companies being set up as employment agencies in the UK, which has a comparatively low NIC rate, solely to avoid subjecting workers and their employers to high rates of social security contribution elsewhere (eg, France, Italy, Belgium, Sweden).

It is a popular misconception that the certificate A1 is issued *only* in temporary secondment situations. This is not so. The document certifies continuing Social Security coverage in the 'home' state and is of equal application where work is carried out in more than one EU state (see **51.27** below). Well over 50,000 A1s/E101s are issued each year.

E101s already in existence when the new general regulations, mentioned above under *EC Regulations 883/2004*, came into force are likely to continue to their expiry.

As previously stated, the main changes from 1 May 2010 are:

- home coverage for postings is now automatic for postings of up to two years;
- Form A1 replaced form E101;
- Form E102 is no longer necessary within the EU except for third country nationals;
- an employee recruited with a view to being posted must, before the start of the employment, have been immediately subject to the legislation of the Member State. '*Immediately*' means that the employee must have been subject to the sending country's legislation for at least one month prior to the posting;
- EC institutions can, in exceptional circumstances, give some leeway to the one month rule; and
- AC Decision No 181 (see **51.24**) has been replaced by Decision No A2.

Cases not covered by *EC Regulation 883/2004* (eg Third Country Nationals) will continue be determined under *EC Regulation 1408/71* – see below.

'Posted' workers – EC Regulation 1408/71

[51.23] Where the new Regulations do not apply (eg, to third country nationals), the previous Regulations will be applied and the old 12 months rule will therefore apply. The same application forms will be used as mentioned above and the old style E101 will be issued.

In the event of the period of employment unexpectedly exceeding twelve months, the contribution laws of the first state may continue to apply for a further period of up to twelve months provided a request that that might be so is made to the appropriate authority in the state of employment before the first period of twelve months has elapsed and provided that the authority consents to the extension, certified on form E102. Consent cannot, however, be given for an extension in excess of twelve months unless the two states have entered into a special agreement permitting longer extensions and have notified the Commission of the Communities of that agreement. [*Arts 14(1)(b), 17*]. The application should be submitted to the country in which the employee is working and that country's version of the E102 should be used. Such applications should now only apply to third country nationals leaving the UK.

Exceptions to the general posting rule

[51.24] Extensions under *Art 17* prior to 1 May 2010 were available in appropriate circumstances wherever an EEA national moved within the EEA. On 12 December 1984, the Administrative Commission on Social Security for Migrant Workers issued a formal 'Recommendation' to all Member States that they should 'conclude . . . agreements pursuant to Article 17 . . . applicable to employed persons who, by virtue of their special knowledge and skills or because of special objectives set by the undertaking . . . with which they are employed are posted abroad to a Member State other than the one in which they are normally employed . . . for a period exceeding 12 months. These agreements should lay down that these employed persons remain subject to the legislation of the sending state for the full duration of their assignment provided that the workers concerned agree to this condition'. [*ACR 16*].

HM Revenue and Customs NIC&EO International Caseworker followed the recommendation in granting E101 coverage for up to five years where it was satisfied that the various conditions laid down in *ACR 16* were met. This did, however, also require the consent of the authorities in the other state concerned. In the case of some states, considerable delays could occur. It is understood that, in exceptional circumstances, an even longer extension might be granted.

A specific application setting out the circumstances will need to be made to the social security authority in the home country. HMRC NIC&EO will usually support such an application where:

(a) the employee has special skills or knowledge in the job in question; or
(b) the employer has specific objectives in the other country for which the employee's services are required; or
(c) it will be in the employee's own best interests to remain in the home country scheme.

In the case of (a) it will be necessary to show that the knowledge or skills are not available on the local labour market in the other EC/EEA member state and that the job cannot be done without such knowledge or skills. In the case of (b) it is necessary to show that the employee is familiar with the employer's specific objectives in the other EC/EEA member state.

The full text of ACR 16 was as follows:

> 'RECOMMENDATION No 16 of 12 December 1984 concerning the conclusion of agreements pursuant to Article 17 of Council Regulation (EEC) No 1408/71(85/C 273/03)

THE ADMINISTRATIVE COMMISSION OF THE EUROPEAN COMMUNITIES ON SOCIAL SECURITY FOR MIGRANT WORKERS, Having regard to the opinion of the Advisory Committee on Social Security for Migrant Workers, adopted at its 15th meeting on 11 April 1984, Whereas Article 17 of Regulation (EEC) No 1408/71 lays down that two or more Member States, the competent authorities of those States or the bodies designated by those authorities may, by common agreement, provide for exceptions to the provisions of the aforementioned Regulation concerning the determination of the legislation applicable in the interests of certain categories of employed or self-employed persons, or of certain such persons; Whereas certain employed persons, by virtue of their special knowledge and skills or because of specific objectives set by the undertaking or organization with which they are employed, are posted abroad to the territory of a Member State other than the one in which they are normally employed in the interests of, in the name of, or on behalf of that undertaking or organization for a period of more than 12 months; Whereas it is recommended that in the interests of these employed persons, they should be allowed to choose between being subject to the legislation of the Member State of employment or remaining subject to the legislation of the Member State where they are normally employed for the duration of the posting abroad, RECOMMENDS to the competent authorities of the Member States that they conclude, or have concluded by the bodies designated by these competent authorities, agreements pursuant to Article 17 of Regulation (EEC) No 1408/71 applicable to employed persons who, by virtue of their special knowledge and skills or because of specific objectives set by the undertaking or organization with which they are employed are posted abroad to a Member State other than the one in which they are normally employed in the interests of, in the name of, or on behalf of that undertaking or organization for a period exceeding 12 months. These agreements should lay down that these employed persons remain subject to the legislation of the sending State for the full duration of their assignment provided that the workers concerned agree to this condition. J. DOWNEY Chairman of the Administrative Commission.'

From 1 May 2010, *Art 16* of the new EC Regulations, broadly speaking, provides much the same provisions as its predecessor in *EC Regulation 1408/71, Art 17*. In other words, it is possible, in certain cases, to extend the posting period for up to a maximum of five years, provided it can be demonstrated to the EC institutions in both the sending and receiving Member States that there are good reasons for doing so and that both EC institutions agree.

ACR 16 (ie, Administrative Commission Recommendation 16, rather than *Art 16* of the Regulation) has, however been withdrawn following the introduction of *EC Regulations 883/2004* and *987/09* from 1 May 2010. Nonetheless, it is understood from HMRC that when considering an *Art 16* application, they will continue to apply the normal criteria they have developed over a number of years and they do not expect the operation of the *Art 16* rules to be significantly different from the *Art 17* rules. In practice, and despite the HMRC statement mentioned above, it is understood that HMRC rejected some applications, especially under heads (a) and (b) above or where the time to be spent abroad was to be longer than that for which the employee had previously paid UK contributions. There is no justification or legal backing for this and such decisions should be challenged.

In the European Court case (*C-202/97*) of *Fitzwilliam Executive Search Ltd (t/a Fitzwilliam Technical Services) v Bestuur van het Landelijk Instituut Sociale Verzekeringen* [2000] All ER (EC) 144 an Irish company's workers in the Netherlands who were in possession of E101s issued by the Irish state were also subjected to the Netherlands' system and the company was required by the Netherlands authorities to pay the employer's contributions. The Advocate General in the case stated:

> In my view, the host state may not impose its own social security system unless and until the E101 certificate issued by the other state has been withdrawn by the issuing authority. The fact that the certificate is based on a standard form drawn up by the Administrative Commission whose decisions cannot bind national authorities is irrelevant since it is the completion of that form by the competent institution which constitutes the certificate and the certificate draws its authority from art 11 of Regulation 574/72 (compare, however, the reasoning of the court in *Knoch's* case (paras 50–54)).

This opinion was supported by the ECJ. It is clear therefore that one state may not usurp a competent institution of a Member State. A Member State to which workers are posted must take account of the fact that those workers are already subject to the social security legislation of the state in which the undertaking employing them is established. See also *Knoch v Bundesanstalt fur Arbeit C-102/91* [1992] ECR I-4341. Despite the clear guidance from the ECJ (now CJEU), problems persist with certain Member States: on 26 March 2015, the European Commission referred Belgium to the court for refusing to recognise mobile workers' A1 'portable documents' certifying that they pay social security in another Member State. Belgian law, in clear breach of treaty obligations and disregarding consistent jurisprudence, enables local enforcement authorities to decide unilaterally not to recognise certificates from other Member States without first requesting verification of validity from the issuing states. The Commission had already sent a 'reasoned opinion' to the Belgian authorities in September 2014 warning that the domestic rules were illegal and that action would be taken through the CJEU if the law and practices were not changed.

An earner is employed in the territory of one Member State if the relationship between him and the person paying him is that of employer and employee and the employment commenced in that state. It is irrelevant that the employee may have been engaged for the sole purpose of working in the second state (*Bestuur der Sociale Verzekeringsbank v Van der Vecht Case 19/67* [1967] ECR 345) and that the employer may have had an existing commitment to supply labour in that second state. (*Manpower v Caisse Primaire d'Assurance Maladie, Strasbourg Case 35/70* [1970] ECR 1251). It is sufficient that a direct relationship continues to exist between the employer and the employee. (Administrative Commission Decision 128 OJ 1986 C 141, but see below as this decision was superseded and refined successively by AC Admin Decisions 162 and 181).

In accordance with *Art 14(1)* and *Art 14b (1)* of *Reg 1408/71* and the judgments of the European Court cited above, therefore, the former NICO International Services took the view that

> consideration can only be given to the provision of a form E101 (by this Department) where either,

(a) a person has been sent to another EEA country in continuation of his United Kingdom employment, ie has been sent abroad by the employer he normally works for in the United Kingdom, *or*

(b) a person has been recruited in the United Kingdom with a view to immediate employment elsewhere within the EEA by a United Kingdom employer who normally carries out activities in this country comparable to those upon which the person sent abroad is to be employed and there is a direct relationship between the United Kingdom employer and the person concerned during his employment in the other EEA country. If the services of the person are hired to an undertaking in another EEA country and that undertaking makes the person's services available to another undertaking, then the direct relationship will be deemed to have broken and United Kingdom social security legislation will not be applicable.

These quotations (and the reference to EEA should also include Switzerland) are taken from the standard response to a request for the issue of a form E101 in circumstances where the direct relationship between employer and employee appears to International Caseworker to have been broken. This view reflects the contents of Decision 181 (and its predecessors) referred to above. They are of particular relevance to the not-infrequently encountered arrangement under which the services of a UK worker are made available, on a labour-only subcontract basis, to an EEA undertaking through an EEA intermediary, but where the whole arrangement is channelled, for tax purposes, through a 'one-man' company formed in the UK to 'employ' and 'post overseas' the individual concerned. From 6 April 2000, such arrangements might also have been inhibited by the intermediaries legislation or, from 6 April 2007, the managed service companies legislation — see 40 INTERMEDIARIES. The offshore intermediaries changes to the Categorisation Regulations 1978 in April 2014 could also be relevant.

Following EC Administrative Decision 181 (dated December 2001, effective from 1 January 2002), updating Decision 162 (dated 31 May 1996) for workers posted to other EEA countries/Switzerland the competent State (ie the State where contributions are paid) can exercise more control over those companies and employment agencies employing people for immediate posting abroad. This applies in particular, but not exclusively, to employment agencies which must usually carry out similar work in the UK to that undertaken abroad and seeks to prevent 'fly by night' agencies being set up with no presence in the UK. Companies must undertake *substantial* business in the UK. This seeks to prevent the situation where a foreign employer sets up business in the UK and recruits workers for immediate posting abroad. In this case the employer would otherwise get form E101 from HMRC but then the employer returns abroad having paid no NICs. EC Administrative Decision 181 further tightened the rules under which E101s (both for employees and the self-employed) were issued and helped to prevent fraud. This decision arose out of the *Fitzwilliam* (see above) and *Banks* (see below) cases where the Netherlands and Belgium, respectively, sought unsuccessfully to ignore the E101 requirements.

Where an employment situation meets the criteria of International Caseworker set out above, a form E101 or A1 will be issued provided the employer of the employed earner concerned supplies International Caseworker with the full details of the posting.

EC Decision A2 of 12 June 2009 replaced AC Decision No 181 with effect from 1 May 2010. The principles in EC Decision No A2 are broadly the same as its predecessor AC Decision No 181. It should be noted that as a result of the *Banks* case below, a provision was included in AC Decision No 181 which allowed a retrospective application of form E101. Although there is not a similar provision in AC Decision No 2 to allow a retrospective application for form A1 (the new E101), HMRC has confirmed that retrospective applications will still be allowed.

Applications forms CA3821 and CA3822 must be completed by employers, or their agents, as appropriate.

Healthcare

[51.25] In addition to the form A1 (form E101 prior to 1 May 2010 for individuals covered by *EC Regulation 1408/71*) confirming continuing liability to contributions under the British scheme, NICO International Services formerly issued a certificate E111 or E128 confirming entitlement to full healthcare cover for the worker and any accompanying family. However, this ceased from 19 August 2004. For a time there were transitional arrangements, but since 1 January 2006 the only permissible replacement has been the European Health Insurance Card, which covers both work and leisure travel in the EEA and Switzerland. Application forms for this are online (www.gov.uk/european-health-insurance-card#before-you-start) or by post, with a telephone helpline (0300 330 1350 or 0191 218 1999). The healthcare is provided at the cost of the issuing country: visitors are treated locally where they need the care, as if they were insured there, but the bill is sent to the EHIC-issuing country. For example, someone who is going to France will only be covered for 70% of the cost, whereas in Germany the individual will receive free medical and dental treatment, subject to a €10 prescription charge, just like the local population. For further information see www.nhs.uk/nhsengland/Healthcareabroad/pages/Healthcareabroad.aspx. The healthcare provider in question bills the usual fund, which recharges the costs to the UK Department of Health if the traveller is insured in the UK.

Under current rules, an EHIC is the appropriate healthcare insurance document for assignments up to 24 months under *Art 12* and for all assignments in multi-state cases under *Art 13*. Form S1 is the appropriate healthcare insurance form for Article 16 cases in longer term assignments of more than 24 months and for where a person's family lives in a different Member State to the Member State where the employee pays contributions.

Self-employed workers going overseas

[51.26] A person who, though normally *self-employed* in one Member State, performs work in another Member State for a period expected not to exceed twenty-four months is to remain subject to the contribution law of the state in which he is normally self-employed. See *Banks and Others v Théâtre Royal de la Monnaie C-178/97* [2000] TLR 5. The application form for an A1/E101 for a self-employed person is CA3837 (see **43.3** LEAFLETS AND FORMS). Before 1 May 2010 or for Third Country Nationals in any event, if owing to unforeseeable circumstances, the duration of the work to be done extended beyond the duration originally anticipated, continuing liability could be extended for a further period of not more than twelve months, provided a request for the extension was made to the appropriate authority before the end of the initial twelve-month period. [*Article 14a(1).*] *EC Reg 883/2004, Art 16* can now extend the period for as long as the home and host authorities will accept.

EC Regulation 883/2004, Art 12.2 refers to the self-employed person as a person 'who normally pursues an activity as a 'self-employed person' in another Member State. *EC Regulation 987/2009, Art 14.3* defines a person who 'normally pursues an activity as a self-employed person' as a person who:

- habitually carries out substantial activities in his home country;
- has pursued his activity for some time;
- pursues a similar activity in the other Member State; and
- continues to maintain a business structure in his home country which would enable continuity of their self-employed activity on return.

Put simply, *Art 12.2* applies to a self-employed person who, whilst normally self-employed in his home country, takes up his self-employed activity on a temporary basis in another Member State with the intention of resuming that activity on his return.

It should be noted that the self-employed person who pursues a 'similar activity' refers to the type of self-employed activity rather than the self-employment itself. For example, this condition would probably be satisfied in the case of a person who is a self-employed plumber in the UK and takes up work as a self-employed heating engineer in Ireland or Poland.

Also of note is the time limit envisaged by the phrase 'must have already pursued his activity for some time' in *EC Regulation 987/2009*, Under AC Decision A2 this is defined as a two-month period, although a shorter period can be considered depending on the circumstances.

Generally speaking, Class 4 contributions will not be payable by individuals from abroad who have an A1/E101 form from an EC authority (or a certificate of continuing liability from a Reciprocal Agreement country) whether that individual is UK tax resident or not. Similarly, those individuals assigned to work abroad who have form A1, E101 or a certificate of continuing liability for a Reciprocal Agreement country, will not be liable for Class 4 contributions for any complete tax year they are not tax resident in the UK.

HMRC confirmed that the above rules do not apply to split year payments (originally under ESC A11 for tax purposes, now in statute after the introduction of the statutory residence test in 2013), on the ground that there is no NIC equivalent to the ESC A11 (and nothing has changed after 2013). HMRC says that UK NIC legislation requires the payment of Class 4 NIC on profits over the tax year and there are no plans at the moment to align the Class 4 NIC rules with the tax rules on split years.

Multi-state employments

Employed persons

[51.27] Since the aim of the EC regulations on social security for migrant workers is to resolve any conflict of laws and reduce or eliminate barriers to free movement created by national social security rules, there are provisions that go beyond temporary postings to encompass those who regularly work in two or more Member States. In the old regulations, there were even specific rules for 'frontier workers', but from 1 May 2010 there were major changes to the rules for multi-state workers that attempted to simplify the situation. *EC Regulation 883/2004, Art 13.1* applies.

The multi-state worker rules apply to individuals who normally work in two or more Member States and includes individuals who are international transport workers who may be aircrew or lorry drivers previously covered under *EC Regulation 1408/71, Art 14.2(a)*. Similar rules apply to the self-employed; see *Art 13.2*.

Under *EC Regulation 1408/71, Art 14.2(b)* once an individual partly performed an activity in the Member State of residence that individual would normally be subject to the legislation of that Member State. In the UK, these rules still apply to non-EEA nationals who work in the UK and elsewhere in the EU. Under the new rules from 2010 for EEA nationals, where the employer is not in the State of residence the individual must 'pursue a substantial part of his activity' (at least 25% of work and/remuneration) in the home country for this to apply. This is a significant difference between both sets of Regulations. Where the employee and employer are in the same State the 25% rule does not apply but the activity in the home State needs to be regular. Whilst we have yet to see guidance on this, it is unlikely that a day a month will be sufficient.

The rules for workers employed concurrently in more than one Member State are now found in *EC Reg 883/2004, Art 13.1 (as amended by EC Reg 465/2012)*.

Most such workers will be covered by a simple rule: if they pursue a substantial (25%) part of their activities in the state in which they are habitually resident, that will be the competent state, responsible for their contributions and benefits.

The position becomes more complex where workers do not pursue a substantial part of their activity in the Member State of residence. The identification of the competent state then depends on the location and the number of employers:

- If there is a single employer, the competent state is the Member State in which that employer has its registered office or place of business.
- If there are two or more employers which both have their registered office or place of business in a single Member State that will be the competent state.
- If there are two employers based in different Member States, but one of those states is where the worker is habitually resident, the other state will be competent.

- If there are two or more employers in different Member States, neither or none of which is the state of the worker's habitual residence, the state of habitual residence will be competent.

From 1 May 2010 until 28 June 2012, the rule was much more simply presented. A worker was subject to the legislation of the Member State of habitual residence if he pursued a substantial part of his activity in that Member State, or if he was employed by various undertakings or various employers whose registered office or place of business was in different Member States. If he did not pursue a substantial part of his activities in the Member State of habitual residence, the competent state was the state in which the registered office or place of business of the employer was situated. It will be seen that the current rule (introduced by *EC Reg 465/2012*) is more nuanced than the original version. Anyone who would have been subject to a change of competent state as a result of the 2012 regulations should have remained subject to the legislation of the original Member State for a transitional period lasting for as long as the relevant situation remained unchanged and, in any case, for no longer than ten years from the change in the regulations. Such a person could, however, request that the new rules apply instead. [*EC Reg 883/2004, Art 87a, inserted by EC Reg 465/2012, Art 1.11*.]

Normally pursues an activity

[51.28] Until 28 June 2012, the phrase 'normally pursues an activity as an employed person in two or more Member States' referred to a person who:

- while maintaining an activity in one Member State, simultaneously exercised a separate activity in one or more other Member States, irrespective of the duration or nature of the separate activity; or
- continuously pursued alternating activities, in two or more Member States, irrespective of the frequency or regularity of the alternation.

[*EC Regulation 987/2009, Art 14.5*].

From 28 June 2012, *Art 14.5* has been slightly amended and now refers to a person who:

- simultaneously, or in alternation, for the same undertaking or employer or for various undertakings or employers, exercises one or more separate activities in two or more Member States.

[*EC Regulation 465/2012, Art 12.2(a)*].

Substantial activity

[51.29] For the purposes of determining *substantial activity* of an employed person, account must be taken of the working time and/or remuneration. If in the context of undertaking an overall assessment it emerges that less than 25% of the person's working time and/or less than 25% of the person's remuneration is earned in a Member State, this is an indicator that the activity in that Member State is not substantial. HMRC says that when looking at this it may not only look to past periods, but to future periods too, to take account of changing circumstances (see also *Art 14.10*). For example, for long distance lorry drivers, time spent loading/driving in Member States will be factored into the equation when calculating 'substantial activity'.

HMRC also says that although it is obligatory to take account of working time and/or remuneration, this list is not exhaustive and other criteria may be taken into account (although at the time of writing it is not clear what those 'other criteria' are).

[*EC Regulation 987/2009, Art 14.8*].

Note: also see Transitional Provisions – *EC Regulation 883/2004, Art 87.8.*

Person employed by various employers in different Member States

[51.30] The legislation of the Member State of residence applies to a person employed by various employers whose registered offices are in different Member States. 'Registered office or place of business' is defined as where the essential decisions of the undertaking are adopted and where the functions of its central administration are carried out.

[*EC Regulation 987/2009, Art 14.5a* as inserted by *EC Regulation 465/2012* from 28 June 2012].

Person does not have a substantial activity in the Member State of residence

[51.31] If the person does not perform a substantial activity in the Member State of residence, the legislation of the Member State in which the registered office or place of business employing him is situated applies.This is significantly different from the position before 1 May 2010, when *any* work in the state of residence would make the state of residence competent.

Revised rules from 28 June 2012

The way the legislation was worded for individuals working in more than one country made it relatively easy in many circumstances to create contribution liabilities in a country where the costs were low. In an attempt to block some of the less acceptable practices, the rules described above apply from 28 June 2012, with the transitional provisions mentioned.

Flight crew

There were special provisions for flight crew and others engaged in international transport within *EC Regulation 1408/71* but the revised rules from 1 May 2010 did not include such separate provisions. The position of flight crew fell to be determined in the same way as for any other individual employed in more than one Member State. This caused significant problems and in an attempt to clarify matters the contribution liabilities are now to arise in the country where the member of the flight crew has his or her home base.

[*EC Regulation 883/2004, Art 11.5* as inserted by *EC Regulation 465/2012*].

'Home base' for this purpose is defined in *Annex iii* to *EC Regulation 3922/91* and this concept should be familiar to those entities operating airlines. In the preamble to *EC Regulation 465/2012* it is stated, '. . . the applicable legislation for flight crew and cabin crew members should remain stable and the home base principle should not result in frequent changes of applicable legislation due to the industry's work patterns or seasonal demands'.

There is no additional comment on how the contribution liabilities should be determined in such cases but it would appear *Art 16* should apply with the relevant competent authorities agreeing the position.

> *Example*
>
> Robert is employed by a UK-based airline from 3 July 2012 on a permanent contract. He lives near Gatwick Airport and his regular pattern of work is that, on Sunday evening, he flies as a passenger to Barcelona and for the next six days he flies in and out of Barcelona Airport on a mixture of domestic and EU flights. He then flies back to Gatwick as a passenger. His home base is Barcelona so contributions are payable in Spain. It falls to the UK employer to make arrangements to pay over what is due in Spain.

> *Example*
>
> Jim is a UK resident pilot employed by a French airline which has a base at Heathrow from which he flies regularly. As Jim only spends around 15% of his working time in the UK, he was paying French social security contributions from May 2010. Jim's home base is Heathrow and under the revised legislation from 28 June 2012 he could opt to pay contributions in the UK from that date. The French employer would then have needed to make arrangements to pay over UK NIC.

> *Example*
>
> Bjorn is employed by Europe Wide Travel, which operates out of a number of different places in the EU. He is an experienced pilot and is used by his employer to cover holidays and other absences. He works from a number of different 'home' bases in a year. The home base rule cannot apply in Bjorn's case and it will be up to the competent authorities in the different countries in which he works to agree where contributions are payable. The likely result is that he will pay in the country where he is habitually resident.

Employer is based outside the EC

[51.32] If a person is employed in two or more Member States by an employer established outside the territory of the EC and if that person resides in a Member State without performing a substantial activity there, he is subject to the legislation of his Member State of residence.

[*EC Regulation 987/2009, Art 14.11*].

> *Example*
>
> Mark resides in the UK where he is employed in Manchester as a representative for an Australian pharmaceutical company. He works at the Manchester office for four days each week and each Friday he works at the company's branch office in Amsterdam. Mark lives in the UK and has substantial work there. He is subject to UK NIC.

Example

As above but Mark is now an employee of the Dutch parent company. he works in Manchester one day a week and travels all over the EU the rest of the time. As he does not have at least 25% of his activity in the UK he pays contributions (and accrues benefit entitlements) where the employer has its registered office, ie the Netherlands.

Example

Jenni lives in France. She is a financial consultant who works for an employer based in Spain and another employer based in Portugal. As Jenni has more than one employer in different EU Member States she pays contributions where she is resident. She lives in France and so she is subject to French social security legislation.

Example

Kevin is an HGV driver who lives in Ireland. He is employed by a company whose registered office is in the UK. Kevin's job is to transport goods throughout most EC countries. As he does not pursue any of his activity in Ireland where he is resident, he is subject to the legislation of the UK.

Example

John lives in the UK. He is employed by a company based in the US. John works for X Bank in the Netherlands and in Denmark. As he does not have an employer in the EC, he is subject to the social security legislation where he is resident. That is the UK so he pays NIC.

Applications for form A1 or E101 where the UK is the competent state are made to HM Revenue and Customs NIC&EO International Caseworker by the worker him/herself [*EC Reg 987/2009, Art 16.1*] on form CA8421 on paper or online – see **43.3**. It would be difficult to require an application from the employer: which employer would be responsible?

Where the certificate is granted, the worker is treated for the purposes of the relevant legislation as though he was pursuing all his activities as an employed (or self-employed) person and receiving all his income in the Member State concerned. [*EC Reg 883/2004, Art 13.5*.]

The provisions of *EC Regulation 1408/71, Art 14.2(b)* still apply to eg Third Country Nationals, as follows.

A person who normally pursues his employment in the territory of two or more EEA countries is to be subject to the contribution law of the state in which he resides if:

- he partly pursues his employment there; or
- he is attached to several businesses or employers and those businesses or employers have their registered offices or places of business in a number of Member States.

[*EC Regulation 1408/71, Art 14(2)(b)(i)*].

In any other case, he is to be subject to the contribution law of the state in which his employer has his place of business or its registered office. [*Art 14(2)(b)(ii)*]. For the meaning of 'place of business' see **51.8** above.

Contributions are also due as if the individual undertook all activities in the competent State. [*EC Regulation 1408/71, Art 14d*].

The former *Article 14(2)* was held to apply in the case of a person who was employed in several Member States by *different* employers. It thus covers a German national resident in Germany and employed in Germany by a German company but also employed in France by a French company. (*Bentzinger v Steinbruchs Berufsgenossenschaft Case 73/72* [1973] ECR 283).

The amount of work carried out in the state of residence was irrelevant under the pre-2010 rules (and as they now apply to third-country nationals).

Example

Gerald has his home in Manchester but has for many years worked as a sales representative in France for Rheinwein GmbH, a German wine producer which has its registered office in Mainz and a branch in Manchester. In accordance with the requirements of the *Companies Act 2006*, Rheinwein had, upon setting up the Manchester branch, filed with the Registrar of Companies the name and address of a British resident whom it authorised to accept service of process on its behalf. On 1 July 2009, Gerald's territory had been extended to cover Belgium and, on 1 August 2010, it was again extended; this time to cover Great Britain.

Until 30 June 2009, Gerald's earnings would have been subject to French contribution law under *EC Regulation 1408/71, Art 13(2)(a)*. From 1 July 2009, however, they will have been subject to German contribution law under *EC Regulation 1408/71, Art 14(2)(b)(ii)*, and, from 1 August 2010 and assuming that the duties carried out in the UK are 'substantial' (ie, at least 25% of his work), they became subject to British contribution law under *EC Regulation 883/2004, Art 13*. From 1 August 2010, Rheinwein was the secondary contributor under the British scheme in accordance with both *Social Security (Contributions) Regulations 2001, SI 2001/1004, Reg 145(1)(b)* and the general EEA principle that liability as a secondary contributor follows the primary liability of the earner. Collection of contributions will, if necessary, be enforced against Rheinwein through the person authorised to accept service of process for its Manchester branch.

Self-employed multi-state workers

[51.33] A person who normally pursues an activity as a self-employed person in two or more Member States is subject to:

- the legislation of the Member State of residence if he pursues a substantial part of his activity in that Member State; or
- the legislation of the Member State in which his centre of interest of is situated, if he does not reside in one of the Member States in which he pursues a substantial part of his activity.

The key features of *Art 13.2* are:

- normally pursues an activity as a self-employed person;
- substantial activity; and
- centre of interest.

Normally pursues an activity as a self-employed person in two or more Member States

[51.34] A person who normally pursues an activity as a self-employed person in two or more Member States is someone who simultaneously or alternately pursues one or more separate self-employed activities, irrespective of the nature of those activities.

[*EC Regulation 987/2009, Art 14.6*].

Substantial activity as a self-employed person

[51.35] This means that a quantitatively substantial part of all activities of the self-employed person is pursued in a Member State. Account must be taken of:

- the turnover;
- the working time;
- the amount of services rendered; and/or
- the income.

[*EC Regulation 987/2009, Art 14.8*].

HMRC says that if, when carrying out an overall assessment, less than 25% of the criteria mentioned above is in the UK this is a general indication that the self-employed person does not undertake substantial activities in the UK. However, HMRC also says that it can consider 'other factors' depending on the facts of the case. At the time of writing it is not clear what those 'other factors' comprise.

Centre of interest

[51.36] 'Centre of interests' is to be determined under the following criteria:

- all the aspects of the person's occupational activities, in particular the locality in which the fixed and permanent premises are situated;
- the habitual nature or the duration of the activities pursued;
- the number of services rendered; and
- the intention of the person concerned as revealed by all the circumstances.

[*EC Regulation 883/2004, Art 13.2(b) and EC reg 987/09, Art 14.9*].

HMRC says that when deciding the centre of interest, it is not only the current position that must be considered, but also the expected position in the following twelve months.

Example

Dorothy is a self-employed IT consultant who lives in the south of France. She works partly in other Member States and partly in the UK but not in France. There are no permanent or fixed premises in any of the Member States where

Dorothy works. Dorothy works mostly in London and that is where most of her income comes from. Her intention is to build up the business in London and she is negotiating the purchase of permanent business premises there. Accordingly, Dorothy is subject to UK legislation as:

- she does not reside in any of the Member States where she works; and
- as evidenced by her intention to purchase business premises in London, the UK is the centre of her business activities.

The meaning of 'resides' has been considered by the European Court of Justice. According to *EC Regulation 883/2004, Art 1(j)* 'residence means habitual residence' and, in the light of that definition, the European Court held in *Anciens Etablissements D'Angenieux fils ainé v Willy Hakenberg* 13/73 [1973] ECR 935, ECJ, that Hakenberg, a French national who worked in Germany as a business representative for several French undertakings, was 'resident' (within the terms of the European social security coordination regulations) in France despite the fact that for nine months of each year he lived in a caravan in Germany. The court decided that the state in which a person must be held to reside is the state with which the person has the strongest personal connections. Such connections need not be numerous but must have a degree of permanency greater than any connections with other states. The question to be asked is with which country is the person most closely and permanently connected? Where are his roots? The length of stay in a particular state is not the only factor to be considered. Other considerations of fact which establish a recognisable connection between the person himself and a territory must also be taken into account. Thus, in *di Paolo v Office National de l'Emploi Case 76/76* [1977] ECR 315, it was held that the state in which a worker resides is the state in which, although occupied in another state, he continues *habitually* to reside *and where the habitual centre of his interests is also situated.* In *Rigsadvokaten v Ryborg* C-297/89 [1991] ECR I-1943, [1993] 1 CMLR 218, ECJ, it was held that the fact that a person spent nights and weekends for more than a year with a girlfriend in one state while maintaining accommodation and working in another state was not, in itself, sufficient reason to conclude that the person had moved the permanent centre of his interests to the first-mentioned state. In a judgment in February 1999 the Court of Justice held that British law could not prevent a British national, who had spent a considerable time working abroad, from claiming Income Support immediately upon return to Great Britain with the intention of residing here for the foreseeable future. *Article 10a* prevented the operation of the restriction in income support law as regards persons from abroad since its operation would discriminate against those that exercised their right to freedom of movement. (*Swaddling v Adjudication Officer* C-90/97 [1999] ECR I-1075, [1999] All ER (EC) 217, ECJ).

The former Contributions Agency historically took such habitual residence as being broadly equivalent to the concept of 'ordinary residence' in English law (see **51.5** above) but it must be questioned whether it was correct to do so. For example, a German national will, it seems, be regarded by International Caseworker as ordinarily resident in the UK if he is employed here for substantial tours of duty over three or four years, yet he may well not be 'habitually resident' here in the sense in which the European Court construes those words. If Germany remains the permanent centre of his interests and the place to which he returns when the demands of his work permit it, he is habitually resident in Germany, and, that being so, he will, if he has employment in Germany as well as in the UK, be subject to German contribution legislation only, not UK contribution legislation. See CA Specialist Conference reply 8, 4 February 1997 concerning the continued non-alignment of the two terms 'ordinarily resident' and 'habitually resident'.

In 1985, the National Insurance Commissioners held (in a benefit case) that the view of the then Inland Revenue on ordinary residence for tax purposes 'has no relevance whatsoever to the determination of habitual residence' (*R(U)7/85*) and, in another case, they gave detailed consideration to, and then applied, the judgment, in the *di Paolo case* referred to above. (*R(U)7/85*.)

In the House of Lord's decision of *Nessa v Chief Adjudication Officer HL*, [1999] TLR 27 October 1999 (another benefit case) it was held that it was not sufficient merely to arrive with the intention of settling in the UK to achieve 'habitual residence'. Habitual residence in the context of social security legislation has to be construed as a matter of ordinary language so that the claimant had to take up residence and live in the UK for a period which showed that the residence was in fact 'habitual'. Voluntariness of presence and an intention to reside do not immediately and alone establish habitual residence.

International transport workers

[51.37] The provisions of *EC Regulation 1408/71*, *Art 14(2)(b)* were not to apply to anyone who was employed in two or more EEA Member States as a member of the travelling personnel of an undertaking engaged in the international transport of passengers or goods by road, rail, inland waterway or air the registered office or place of business of which was in one of those Member States. Such a person was to be subject to the contribution legislation of *that Member State*, (ie the Member State in which the undertaking had its registered office or place of business) unless:

- the undertaking had a branch or permanent representation in a state other than that in which it had its registered office or place of business and the employee was employed by that branch or permanent representation, in which case the employee was to be subject to the law of that state; or
- the employee was employed principally in the Member State in which he resided, in which case he was to be subject to the law of that state, whether or not the employer had a branch or permanent representation in that state.

[*Art 14(2)(a)*].

As previously stated, *Art 14.2(a)* no longer applies to most migrant workers, having been superseded by *EC Regulation 883/2004* from 1 May 2010 (see **51.21**). All multi-state workers are covered by the same rules except flight crew from 28 June 2012 (see **51.30** above). However, *EC Regulation 1408/71* continues to apply to Third Country Nationals, for example.

See also the meaning of 'substantial' in relation to *Art 13* – Multi-State employments: air crew and long distance lorry drivers (see **51.27**).

The position of mariners or seafarers, who regularly leave EEA sovereign territory, can be complex. *EC Reg 883/2004, Art 11.4* makes them subject in principle to the legislation of the Member State whose flag is flown by the vessel on which they are working, unless they are remunerated for that work by an undertaking whose registered office or place of business is in another Member State and that is the state in which they live. In such cases, the legislation of the state of residence will apply.

Their position becomes more complex when they become employed on a vessel flagged in a non-EEA state but are employed by a company in an EEA state or Switzerland. In the case of *Kik* (Case C-266/13), the contributor was a Dutch national, resident in the Netherlands, working on board a Panamanian-flagged vessel. At first, he was employed by a Dutch company and insured under Dutch social security legislation. However his employment was transferred to a Swiss company and he argued that, under Dutch domestic legislation, his social security cover ceased. The pipe-laying vessel on which he worked was positioned, at various times, above the continental shelf adjacent to the UK or the Netherlands and in international waters, so the Dutch authorities claimed that he should have been insured under their scheme. On appeal, the CJEU held that the relevant EC coordination regulations (in this case, *EC Reg 1408/71*) extended to workers such as Mr Kik, who was a national of a Member State in which he resided and in which his income was subject to tax, and was employed, on a vessel flying the flag of a non-Member State, successively by employers in different Member States. He was not working in the Netherlands, so his only employment link to the EEA was his Swiss employer. Switzerland was therefore the competent state. The court pointed out that the only exception to this would have been if Switzerland made his social security coverage voluntary or did not ensure him at all, in which case he would be subject to the legislation of his Member State of residence.

Simultaneously employed/self-employed

EC Regulation 1408/71

[51.38] A person who is simultaneously employed in one Member State and self-employed in another is generally subject to the legislation of the state in which he is in paid employment and this has been so for many years under both the old and new regulations. [*EC Regulations 1408/71, Art 14c; 883/2004, Art 13.3*].

A dual contribution liability could arise in certain cases set out in *Annex VII* to *EC Regulation 1408/71*. This rule used to have a somewhat unexpected consequence due to the differing treatment of company directors in some EEA states. Foreign states do not necessarily treat company directors as employees in the same way as the UK.

In German law, for example, a company director who is also a shareholder in the company may be treated as self-employed, and in Belgium a company director will usually be treated as self-employed. If the German or Belgian company had a UK subsidiary of which he was a paid director, *Art 14c* made the director liable only to UK contribution law, despite the fact that he habitually resided in Germany or Belgium, but International Caseworker would consider an application under *Art 17* of *Reg 1408/71* to retain him under German or Belgian social security legislation. However, any such application would need to be agreed by both home and host authorities, and it is unlikely that the Belgian authorities would have agreed to forgo contributions on the Belgian self-employed earnings of a director of the Belgian company who was also a paid director of a UK company. The Annex VII provisions permitted liability to arise in the UK on the UK earnings and in Belgium on the Belgian earnings. The only escape from Belgian liability would have been under the rules for multi-state self-employment (ie, if the director was also self-employed in some capacity in the UK at the same time), which would have made the state of habitual residence competent for all EU social security purposes.

From 1 May 2010 under *EC Regulation 883/2004* mentioned above in **51.21**, there are no provisions for such dual social security liability. However, it will still be possible, if highly unusual, to have the dual liability arrangements that currently are allowed as set out in *Annex VII* to *EC Regulation 1408/71* in the case of third-country nationals.

Similarly, under *EC Reg 1408/71*, an individual who was normally self-employed in two or more Member States was subject to the contribution law of the state in which he (habitually) resided if he pursued any part of his activity there. Otherwise, he was to be subject to the contribution law of the state in which he pursued his main activity. [*EC Regulation 1408/71, Art 14a(2).*] The exception was that if, in its application, this rule would prevent the person joining a pension scheme, even on a voluntary basis, he could choose to be subject to the contribution law of the other state or, if there were two or more other states, the law of whichever state those states themselves decided upon. [*EC Regulation 1408/71, Art 14a(4).*] In deciding where a self-employed earner pursued his main activity, account was taken, first and foremost, of the locality in which the fixed and permanent premises from which the person pursued his activities was situated. If this approach was inconclusive, however, account was then taken of criteria such as the usual nature or duration of the activities pursued the number of services rendered, and the income arising from those activities. [*EC Regulation 574/1972, Art 12a(5)(d).*] Under the new *EC Reg 883/2004, Art 13.2*, the rule is similar but much simplified: if the self-employed person pursues a substantial part (meaning at least 25%) of his activities in his state of habitual residence, that state is competent to collect contributions and provide benefits. If he resides elsewhere, the competent state is where the centre of interest of his activities is to be found.

Where there is employment and / or self-employment in more than one Member State, application must be made to International Caseworker for certificate A1 or E101, using form CA8421 (see **43.3** LEAFLETS AND FORMS).

Company directors who are regarded as self-employed in other Member States

[51.39] As noted above, in Belgium, company directors are regarded as self-employed. In the UK, company directors are regarded as employed persons. Under the previous *EC Regulation 1408/71*, a person who was a director in both the UK and Belgium (ie, of separate companies) would be liable for two separate social security contributions as Belgium had an exception in *Annex VII* to *EC Regulation 1408/71*, which meant that Belgian social security liability applied even where there was a liability for UK NIC. Under *EC Regulation 883/2004*, such a person is insured in one Member State only – the country of employment (*Art 13.3*) which would be the UK in this case. In the case of a Belgian national who is a board director in Belgium and a board director in the UK, then, this begs the question as to whether, under *EC Regulation 987/09, Art 21* there would be a liability for UK secondary NIC even where the Belgian entity has no place of business in the UK. HMRC opinion is that there *is* such a liability. However, on the authority of *Banks* (see **51.26**) – where liability is determined on the person's status in their home country (ie self-employed in this case) – one may also come to the conclusion that *Art 13.3* does not apply; rather, the person is regarded as self-employed in both countries.

[*EC Regulation 987/2009, Art 21*].

The employment status of company directors in the Netherlands was, under *EC Regulation 1408/71*, deemed to be as employed persons (a person who undertook a self-employed activity in the Netherlands on behalf of a limited company in which he had a 'significant interest' within the meaning of Netherlands legislation was deemed to be an employed person). See *EC Regulation 1408/71, Annex VI, J, Netherlands, Point 7*.

There is no equivalent provision in *EC Regulation 883/2004*. Following a policy review, the Netherlands authorities have decided that the insurability position of directors will follow the rules of the employee insurance schemes under their new rules instead of the National Insurance schemes as applicable under their old rules.

Therefore, a company director in the Netherlands will not be regarded as an employed person – and therefore will be regarded as a self-employed person – where, for instance he has at least 50% of the voting rights; the company directors and their close relatives own at least 2/3rds of all shares; and they cannot be fired against their own will. Any director of a limited company who does not satisfy these criteria will be regarded as an employee.

Some directors will, therefore, be regarded as self-employed and others will not.

It remains to be seen whether a company director in the Netherlands (or Germany) who also has a directorship in Germany (or the Netherlands), will come under *Art 13.3*.

Frontier employments

[51.40] Until 1 May 2010, a person employed in an undertaking which straddled a frontier common to two Member States was subject to the contribution law of the state in which the employer had its registered office or place of business or, if the person was self-employed, the state in which he himself had his place of business. [*EC Regulation 1408/71, Art 14(3), Art 14a(3)*].

There are no special provisions contained in *EC Regulation 883/2004*; any such individual will be covered by the normal insurability rules.

Transitional provisions

[51.41] *EC Regulation 883/2004, Art 87.8* says that if, as a result of *EC Regulation 883/2004*, a person is subject to the legislation of a Member State other than that determined in accordance with *Title II* of *Regulation (EEC) No 1408/71*, that 'old' legislation continues to apply while the relevant situation remains unchanged but in any case for no longer than ten years from the date of application of the new Regulation unless the person concerned requests that he be subject to the legislation applicable under *EC Regulation 883/2004*.

By and large, the transitional provisions mean that if, at 1 May 2010, an individual was insured under the former *EC Regulation 1408/71* and if as a result of *EC Regulation 883/2004* his insurability changed, the individual continues to be covered under *EC Regulation 1408/71* unless:

- he requests that his case be dealt with under *EC Regulation 883/2004*; or
- his situation changes.

An E101 form or an E102 form issued prior to 1 May 2010 will continue to be valid until:

- the individual's situation changes; or
- his circumstances change, whichever is the earlier.

Article 87.8 will have particular relevance to those individuals covered under the multi-state rules who, provided their situation remains the same, will continue to be covered under the rules determined by *EC Regulation 1408/71, Arts 14.2(a)* and *14.2(b)*.

A relevant change (ie in the individual's situation) includes:

- taking up a new (additional) activity;
- the cessation of an activity;
- the end of the work contract;
- substantial change of working time;
- change in status of the worker or self-employed person;
- change of employer (but not a transfer of business according to Council Directive 2001/23);
- interruption of the posting for more than two months;
- change in the country in which the work is performed, except temporary changes which do not lead to a change of the work contract;

- change in the country where the employer's business is situated; or
- a significant change in the percentage of duties performed in the Member State of residence such that it would produce a change under rules in *EC Regulation 1408/1971*.

HMRC points out that this list is not exhaustive.

EC Regulation 987/2009 – new features when implementing EC Regulation 883/2004

Article 6 – Provisional application of legislation

[51.42] Unless provided for in the Implementing Regulation, where there is a difference of opinion between the institutions of two or more Member States concerning the determination of applicable legislation, the person concerned must be made provisionally subject to the legislation of one of those Member States in the following order of priority:

- the legislation of the Member State where the person actually pursues employment or self-employment if the employment or self-employment is pursued in only one Member State;
- the legislation of the Member State of residence where the person concerned performs part of his activity there;
- the legislation of the Member State which originally received the request where the person pursues an activity or activities in two or more Member States.

In the unlikely event that an agreement cannot be reached between the Member States concerned, the matter may be escalated to the Administrative Commission. This should not be any earlier than one month after the date on which the difference arose. The Administrative Commission's aim would be to resolve the matter within six months.

Where it is concluded that the provisional decision means that the person is not subject to the legislation of the Member State of that provisional decision, then the legislation of the competent Member State should apply retrospectively from the date when the provisional decision was made.

If any contributions were incorrectly paid to the Member State which gave the provisional decision, that Member State must reconcile the financial situation of the person concerned.

Article 19 – Provision of information to persons concerned and employers

[51.43] The competent institution of the Member State whose legislation is applicable (for the UK this is HMRC, acting by International Caseworker) must inform the person concerned and, where appropriate his employer(s) of the obligations required under that legislation. That institution must also provide the necessary assistance to complete any formalities required under its legislation.

At the request of the person concerned or of his employer, the competent institution of the Member State whose legislation is applicable must provide 'an attestation' (form A1) confirming the period for which that legislation is applicable.

Article 20 – Co-operation between institutions

[51.44] Institutions must communicate with each other, in respect of a person or persons to whom their legislation is applicable, all of the necessary information required to establish the date on which that legislation becomes applicable and the contributions due in respect of that person or persons and his or their employer(s).

The competent institution of the Member State whose legislation becomes applicable to a person must make the information available to the authority of the Member State to whose legislation the person was last subject, showing the date on which that legislation takes effect.

Article 21 – Obligations of the employer

[51.45] *Article 21* of the new EC Implementing *Regulation, 987/2009* – which supersedes the somewhat 'toothless' *Art 92* in *EC Regulation 1408/71* – says that an employer whose registered office or place of business is outside the Member State whose legislation is applicable must fulfil all the obligations as laid down by that legislation ie the obligation to pay contributions as specified by that legislation, as if the registered office or place of business was situated in that Member State.

An employer and employee may agree for the employee to fulfil the employer's obligations in a Member State if the employer does not have a place of business in that Member State. The employer must notify the Member State concerned of the arrangement.

This is a major change and in simple terms provides for payment of secondary (employer) NIC where such would not otherwise be payable under the terms of *EC Regulation 1408/71*. For example, if an employee is resident in and working in the UK for an employer situated in another Member State who does not have a place of business in the UK, then there will be a secondary NIC liability on the part of the foreign employer.

Where a migrant worker is subject to one of the multi-state rules, all his earnings are deemed to accrue and all his activities to take place in the competent state. [*EC Reg 883/2004, Art 13.5*.]

Electronic data (EESSI)

[51.46] The European Commission intended with the reform of the regulations in May 2010 that institutions should eventually communicate electronically via an Electronic Exchange of Social Security Information (EESSI), a common IT platform across all competent institutions. It is estimated that there are some 800 million intra-community messages each year passing between some 15,000 institutions. These will include forms A1 and E101 and associated correspondence, but the system covers all cross-border social security coordination, so the volume of correspondence on benefits matters will be much greater than that on contributions certificates.

Member States were originally supposed to adopt EESSI by the end of 2012, but this was postponed to 31 December 2018 (according to an official timeline issued in mid-2015), because the European Commission was still working on the specification for the Europe-wide network in late 2013, and the whole project was relaunched in 2014, with the first 'pilot builds' of national access gateways only some time in 2015. HMRC has yet to give an indication of the date from which they will be ready to use EESSI, but it seems likely the UK's full participation in the project will depend among other things on the UK government's electronic ID assurance programme being in place first. The European Commission issued only in March 2016 an invitation for proposals (CEF-TC-2016-1) for a system that 'will facilitate the connection of national systems, for which Member States are responsible, to the central EESSI electronic communication (Core) platform to ensure interoperability and communication as well as the business implementation of the EESSI project'. The proposal opportunity closed on 19 May 2016, but the Commission stated in accompanying documents that it still intended to make available, as planned, an 'Integration Ready Release version of EESSI' which would allow Member States to start integration activities as of 1 January 2017.

Decision E4 (2014/C 152/04) of the Administrative Commission for the Co-ordination of Social Security Systems in March 2014 formally postponed the date by which Member States should implement EESSI until two years after the central EESSI system has been 'developed, tested and delivered into production, ready for Member States to start the integration to the central system'. As noted above, the latest revised implementation date for EESSI was shown as 31 December 2018 (ie, two years from the scheduled release), in the 'EESSI Read' newsletter, Issue 2, in June 2015. Although this newsletter was supposedly quarterly, it has not been followed by any further public newsletters, and all Commission documents about the delayed system appear to be available only to insiders.

In view of the UK's referendum result, it seems likely that the UK's participation in the EESSI project will be put on hold, although it may yet be needed in the framework of any future social security cooperation agreement between the UK and the remaining EU.

Structured electronic documents (SEDs)

[51.47] 'E' forms, theoretically, ceased to exist from 1 May 2010. Some of the 'E' forms previously issued by HMRC to individuals have been replaced by a series of so-called 'portable documents'. For example, form E101 has been replaced by form A1 (also known as an 'attestation'); forms E106 and E109 have been replaced by form S1; and form E301 (NIC record for Unemployment Benefit claims in another Member State) has been replaced by form U1. There is no portable document to replace the previous forms E104 and E205 (NIC records for Sickness/Maternity and Pension claims), which means that HMRC will need to revert to a previous practice of providing statements of insurance, probably in a standard format.

Information HMRC previously provided to other EU institutions on forms E104, E205 and E301 are replaced by a series of Structured Electronic Documents (SEDs).

SEDs will initially be used in paper format, and then via EESSI once the system comes on-line. Some SEDs have been available from 1 May 2010; others became available later. Some 300 SEDs have been approved for electronic exchange of information via email.

HMRC has now started to collect all applications for contributions-related certificates by means of so-called 'i-forms' (eg, the *CA3821i* via gov.uk), online questionnaires that will ask all the necessary questions and collect the necessary facts, in digital format from the outset. Holding the incoming data digitally from the start should have eased the transition to the EESSI system once it had been finalised, but it also facilitates HMRC's digital agenda in helping to reduce clerical work at Longbenton.

Bilateral agreements

[51.48] Agreements providing for reciprocity in matters of social security between the UK and other nations are from time to time entered into by the Crown and given effect to by Order in Council under *SSAA 1992, s 179*. All such agreements entered into with other EEA Member States have been largely superseded by the EC regulations (but only in respect of EEA nationals until 1 June 2003). In *R(U)7/85* and *R(U)4/86*, the National Insurance Commissioners held that bilateral agreements were irrelevant where the states concerned were EC Member States, although a small number of provisions of the UK-Germany bilateral agreement survive in respect of Rhine Army civilian staff. There is nothing to prevent agreements with such states being made in the future, however, and, provided they are based on the principles and in the spirit of the EC regulations and are notified to the President of the EC Council, they will be of full effect.

The amended European Economic Area treaty between the EC and European Free Trade Association Member States, excluding Switzerland, was ratified with effect from 1 January 1994. From that date the relevant reciprocal agreements ceased to apply to persons to whom the EC regulations on social security are applicable.

Because Switzerland did not ratify the treaty establishing the EEA, *SI 1969 No 384* remained in force for a time, but this changed in 2002 and it is now relevant only to Manxmen and Channel Islanders, who are within the scope of the UK-Swiss reciprocal agreement – see **51.20** and **51.54**.

It should be noted that the reciprocal agreements may be of wider application than the EC rules, and if there is no conflict with the EC rules the reciprocal agreement will still apply. An instance of this is in the case of the reciprocal agreement with Norway, where the provisions covering Continental Shelf workers are applied by Norway because the coverage conditions under the Agreement are better than under the EC Social Security Regulations, and the EC only extends as far as the 12-mile limit rather than covering the whole continental shelf, so extra provisions are needed for migrant rig workers.

Similarly, the reciprocal agreements will continue to apply to EEA (but non-EC) nationals whose detached duty overseas had already begun on 1 January 1994, and will continue as long as necessary to give effect to existing treaty commitments (see HM Revenue and Customs National Insurance Manual NIM33014).

A description of the usual form of a reciprocal agreement and the topics normally covered is given at **51.52** below together with a list of the current agreements.

The bilateral Social Security Agreement (Reciprocal Agreement) with the Netherlands has been revised to cover non-EC/EEA nationals, particularly Channel Islanders, and came into effect on 1 June 2007. Similarly, the agreement with Ireland was also updated with effect from 1 October 2007, and a new double contributions convention (DCC) between the UK and Chile entered into force on 1 June 2015.

Generally speaking, Class 4 contributions will not be payable by individuals from abroad who have a certificate of continuing liability from a reciprocal agreement/DCC country – whether that individual is UK tax resident or not (see also **51.27**).

Northern Ireland

[51.49] Although technically quite separate from the British contribution scheme, the Northern Ireland scheme is virtually identical to it and currently operates under *Social Security Contributions and Benefits (Northern Ireland) Act 1992* and its accompanying regulations. Rates of contributions are maintained at the same level as the British rates.

There is no reciprocal agreement between Great Britain and Northern Ireland but reciprocity and co-ordination of the two schemes is secured by joint arrangements made by the Secretary of State for Work and Pensions with the Northern Ireland Department, the object of which is to ensure that the legislation provides a single system of social security for the UK. Such joint arrangements are given effect by a Joint Authority consisting of the Secretary of State and the Head of the Northern Ireland Department. [*SSAA 1992, s 177*.] The arrangements were amended slightly as at 6 April 2016 to reflect the introduction in Great Britain of the new single-tier state pension, but there was no effect on contribution liabilities. Similarly, the NI scheme in Northern Ireland, as part of the UK, is automatically covered by the range of reciprocal agreements discussed here. Those that include coordination and totalisation of state pension entitlements are also affected by the introduction of the new state pension by *Pensions Act 2014*, so the Department for Social Development has been a party to various amendments to those agreements (see, eg, *Social Security (Reciprocal Agreement) (Isle of Man) Order 2016, SI 2016/157*).

Isle of Man

[51.50] As in the case of Northern Ireland, the Isle of Man has a contribution scheme separate from but very similar to that of Great Britain. UK social security legislation is generally adopted by an Order of Tynwald, although earnings thresholds and rates have diverged over the years, and the Manx system has neither Class 1A nor Class 1B. The link is not, however, as strong as that binding Great Britain and Northern Ireland but consisted until 6 April 2016 of an agreement made in July 1948 (extending the new UK NI regime to the island, with certain modifications) and subsequently merely of an Exchange of Letters which have been introduced into the British scheme by *Social Security (Isle of Man) Orders 1977 and 1989* and by *Social Security (Isle of Man) No 2 Order 1989* and under which rights acquired in one country are to be fully honoured in the other territory on a reciprocal basis.

The Agreement is not like the UK's traditional Agreements with other countries. In simple terms it:

- treats an individual or his employer as resident in either territory;
- broadly speaking, it provides for the two NI schemes to operate as one;
- provides for the transfer of NI contributions (NICs) and NICs records from one jurisdiction to the other; and
- it treats anything done on the mainland as done in the Isle of Man and vice versa, so that employers in the Isle of Man set up for UK workers are liable as UK employers.

The UK 1948 order was revoked on 6 April 2016 to be replaced by a new agreement which achieves broadly the same ends but encompasses both the old *SSCBA 1992* and the new *Pensions Act 2014* arrangements for the state pension. [*Social Security (Reciprocal Agreement) (Isle of Man) Order 2016, SI 2016/157*.]

Channel Islands

[51.51] Two separate and dissimilar social security schemes subsist in the Channel Islands: that of Jersey and that applying to the Bailiwick of Guernsey which comprises Guernsey, Alderney, Herm, Brecqou, Jethou and Lithou (which is currently not inhabited, except for tourists visiting its nature reserve). Reciprocity with the British scheme is effected by *Social Security (Jersey and Guernsey) Order 1994, SI 1994/2802*, amended from 6 April 2016 by *Social Security (Reciprocal Agreements) Order 2016, SI 2016/158* to reflect the 2016 changes to the UK state pension from that date by adding references to the state pension payable under *Pensions Act 2014*. It should be noted that the tripartite reciprocal agreement on social security between the UK, Jersey and Guernsey is expressed to extend only to Jersey and 'the Islands of Guernsey, Alderney, Herm and Jethou', so Sark and Brecqhou are not included.

Having noted that the two jurisdictions have their own social security regimes and that they are signatories to a tripartite agreement with the UK, it must also be mentioned that Channel Islanders will often qualify to be within the scope of the UK's bilateral or reciprocal social security agreements with other states (but not the EU regulations) because the geographical definition of the 'UK' in those agreements sometimes includes either or both Channel Islands, as well as the Isle of Man. This allows residents of Jersey, for example, to work temporarily in the Netherlands, under the terms of the UK-Netherlands agreement, without necessarily becoming immediately subject to the Dutch social security regime. The new 2015 agreement with Chile simply treats the three territories as if they were part of the UK.

Reciprocal Agreements and Double Contribution Conventions

[51.52] Agreements currently exist between the United Kingdom and the countries in the table below. Those with EU or EEA Member States are in **bold**. They are mainly superseded for the moment by the EC regulations, except for Manxmen and, in some cases, as noted above, Channel Islanders moving to and from the UK. Pension benefits for those with a contribution history spanning periods when the reciprocal agreement applied and when the EU regulations applied will take into account both sets of rules.

The territorial extension of the agreement to the Bailiwick of Guernsey, Jersey or the Isle of Man is indicated by G, J or M. Certain treaties also include a right for temporary visitors from one of the other contracting parties to qualify for immediately necessary medical treatment, which is consistent with the regime in many countries of treating the health service as part of the social security system. These agreement are indicated below with a '†' symbol.

The treaties that deal with contributions all include provisions governing the position of temporary migrant workers, keeping them within their 'home' social security regime for various periods when they remain in employment with their 'home' employer. In some cases, those periods may be extended when an assignment takes longer than expected. The length of the initial secondment period and the possible extension period are indicated in the table. Treaties marked # are double contributions conventions (DCC), with no provision for coordination of social security benefits.

State	Notes	Posting period(s)	Main implementing regulations
Austria	G J M †	2 years	*SI 1981 No 605* *SI 1987 No 1830* *SI 1992 No 3209*
Barbados	G J M †	3 years	*SI 1992 No 812* *SI 2005 No 2765*
Belgium	–	1 year	*SI 1951 No 1801* *SI 1958 No 771*
Bermuda	G J M †	1 year	*SI 1969 No 1686*
Bosnia-Herzegovina	M	1 year + 1 year	*SI 1958 No 1263*
Canada#	M	5 years	*SI 1995 No 2699* *SI 1998 No 263*
Chile#	G J M	5 years	*SI 2015 No 828*
Croatia	M	1 year + 1 year	*SI 1958 No 1263*
Denmark	M	1 year	*SI 1960 No 211*
Finland	M	4 years	*SI 1984 No 125* *SI 1992 No 3210*
France	M	6 months	*SI 1951 No 972* *SI 1958 No 597*
Germany	M	1 year	*SI 1961 No 1202*

State	Notes	Posting period(s)	Main implementing regulations
			SI 1961 No 1513
Gibraltar	–	EEA rules	*SI 1974 No 555*
Guernsey	J M	3 years	*SI 1994 No 2802*
Iceland (*now EEA*)	J M	1 year	*SI 1985 No 1202*
			SI 1992 No 3211
Ireland (formerly Irish Rep)	M	1 year	*SI 2007 No 2122*
Israel	M	2 years + 3 years	*SI 1957 No 1879*
			SI 1984 No 354
Italy	M	6 months	*SI 1953 No 884*
Jamaica	G J M	3 years	*SI 1997 No 871*
Japan#	G J M	5 years	*SI 2000 No 3063*
Jersey	G M	3 years	*SI 1994 No 2802*
Kosovo	M	1 year + 1 year	*SI 1958 No 1263*
Luxembourg	M	6 months	*SI 1955 No 420*
Macedonia (former Yugoslavia)	M	1 year + 1 year	*SI 1958 No 1263*
Malta	G M	3 years	*SI 1996 No 1927*
Mauritius	M	2 years	*SI 1981 No 1542*
Montenegro	M	1 year + 1 year	*SI 1958 No 1263*
Netherlands	G J M	3 years	*SI 2007 No 631*
New Zealand (benefits-only treaty)	M	n/a	*SI 1964 No 495*
			SI 1983 No 1894
Norway (onshore now EEA)	J M †	3 years onshore	*SI 1991 No 767*
		No limit offshore	*SI 1992 No 3212*
Philippines	M	3 years	*SI 1989 No 2002*
Portugal	G J M	1 year	*SI 1979 No 921*
			SI 1987 No 1831
Republic of Cyprus	G J M	3 years	*SI 1983 No 1698*
			SI 1994 No 1646
Republic of Korea#	G J M	5 years	*SI 2000 No 1823*

State	Notes	Posting period(s)	Main implementing regulations
Serbia	M	1 year + 1 year	*SI 1958 No 1263*
Slovenia	M	1 year + 1 year	*SI 1958 No 1263*
Spain	G J M	1 year	*SI 1975 No 415* *SI 1976 No 1916*
Sweden	G J M	1 year	*SI 1988 No 590* *SI 1992 No 3213*
Switzerland (EC rules apply from 1 June 2002 except to G J M)	G J M	2 years	*SI 1969 No 384*
Turkey	M	negotiable	*SI 1961 No 584*
United States of America	G J M	5 years	*SI 1984 No 1817* *SI 1997 No 1778*

A number of these agreements have been amended by *SI 1976 No 225; SI 1979 No 290; SI 1982 No 1528; SI 1988 No 591; SI 1995 No 767* and/or *SI 1996 No 1928; SI 2001 No 407*; and/or *SI 2005 No 2765*. The last-named came into force from 5 December 2005 and made modifications to existing agreements to ensure that references to 'civil partners' are included and 'husband' and 'wife' are altered to 'spouse', which also dealt in advance with the UK's introduction in 2014 of same-sex marriage. Those listed above **in bold** involve EC or EEA Member States and have been superseded for most purposes by the *EC Regulations*. EEA states with which the UK had no pre-existing reciprocal agreement on social security at the date of accession (eg, Greece, Liechtenstein) are not listed. The UK state pension reform from 6 April 2016, when the single-tier state pension was introduced by *Pensions Act 2014* for those newly reaching state pension age, was reflected in those agreements involving pensions coordination by *Social Security (Reciprocal Agreements) Order 2016, SI 2016/158* deeming for domestic law purposes appropriate references to the new pension to be included.

The states that were formerly part of Yugoslavia all continued to operate and benefit from the UK-Yugoslavia reciprocal agreement when that country broke up. Slovenia was the first ex-Yugoslav state to join the EU, and Croatia followed in 2013, which left only Manxmen covered by the agreement as far as those two states were concerned. When Montenegro voted to leave its union with Serbia, it also adopted the former agreement, and the UK continues to deal with Kosovo under that same agreement after its secession from Serbia.

From 1 June 2002 the EC Social Security Regulations have applied to workers entering and leaving Switzerland. This is because Switzerland entered into a special agreement with the EC which was renewed in 2009. It covers only Swiss and EC nationals. It does not apply to those EEA countries that are not EC members (ie, Iceland, Liechtenstein and Norway) nor to Bulgaria and Romania before 2009 or Croatia before 2013. The three EFTA countries have separate agreements with Switzerland, so the EC rules do not apply, for example, to a British worker moving from Switzerland to, eg, Norway. Channel Islanders and Manx contributors who move between Switzerland and their home island should be covered by the UK-Swiss reciprocal agreement, whereas if they move between a job on the UK mainland and a job in Switzerland they will be a third-country nationals under the EEA rules.

Revisions are expected in due course to the existing agreement with Turkey. Turkey has had an 'association agreement' with the EU since 1963 under which equality of treatment is guaranteed and which allows for certain social security benefits rights, such as the aggregation of intra-EU periods of insurance (but not aggregation with Turkish periods) and the export of state pension rights (eg, when a Turkish 'Gastarbeiter' retires from a job in Germany and returns to Turkey), but there is no coordination of contribution liabilities. An example of the issues covered by the agreement may be seen in *Sürül v Bundesanstalt für Arbeit* [Case C-262/96].

The UK relies on its bilateral treaty with Turkey to deal with the liabilities of migrant workers. Turkey is a signatory to the European Convention on Social Security (CETS no 078), created in Paris in December 1972 under the auspices of the Council of Europe, which is unrelated to the EU. The UK is a CoE member but not a signatory to this convention. Twelve current EU members and Moldova are parties to the convention, which allows a 12-month period of continuing home insurance for posted workers along the same lines as *EC Reg 1408/71*. The UK-Turkey bilateral treaty permits all temporary postings to be subject to continuing home insurance, although 'temporary' is not defined. Turkish domestic legislation since 21 August 2013 has allowed posted workers who can evidence continuing insurance in their home state to stay outside Turkish liability indefinitely, so it would seem that 'temporary' means simply 'not permanent'. If, before the UK leaves the EU, Turkey's membership application is accepted by the EU following the cooperation shown during the Syrian refugee crisis, the provisions of EC Regulation 883/2004 will replace those of the bilateral agreement for UK citizens (although totally free movement seems likely to be restricted for a transitional period).

Australia was originally a party to a benefits-only reciprocal agreement with the UK (see *SI 1958/422* and *SI 1992/1312*) but withdrew from the arrangements from 1 March 2001 because the UK refused to apply annual uprating of the UK state pension payable under the treaty to former UK contributors who retired to Australia, leaving Australia to pay its means-tested pension to top up those pensions. The agreement was therefore revoked by *SI 2000/3255*, except insofar as existing benefit entitlements already claimed or in payment under the agreement as at 28 February 2001 were protected.

Not every EU state had a social security agreement with the UK before its accession to the EU. Greece's first relationship with the UK social security came through that accession. The UK had reciprocal health agreements with old Soviet Bloc countries such as Hungary, Czechoslovakia, etc, but no reciprocal agreements on contributions and cash benefits.

In the IR Press Release 66/01 of 30 March 2001 the purpose of a DCC is stated to be:

> . . . promote the free movement of labour and assist in maintaining the UK's position as an attractive inward investment location. Among other things, DCCs provide that, where a worker is sent on detachment from one country to the other, he and his employer are liable to contribute only to the "home" country's scheme – and they thus eliminate the liability to contribute simultaneously to the social security schemes of both countries.

A reciprocal agreement or DCC begins by defining its territorial scope, the persons to whom it relates (eg nationals, or in some cases residents, of the contracting states or 'insured persons') and the branches of social security law involved. It then sets out the rules for determining under which state's contribution law a person connected with both states is to fall. The principle usually (but not invariably) adopted is that:

- an employed person who is employed in the territory of one party is to be subject to the legislation of that party even if he is *resident* (see **51.21–51.23** above) in the territory of the other party or even if the person or undertaking by which he is employed has its principal place of business or is resident in the territory of the other party; and
- a self-employed person who follows his occupation in the territory of one party is to be subject to the legislation of that party even if he resides in the territory of the other party.

These general rules are then followed by various derogations from them dealing with:

- temporary postings from the territory of one party to the other (the provisions usually being similar to those described at **51.22** above);
- workers in international transport (the provisions usually being similar to those described at **51.38** above);
- mariners (**45.6**);
- CROWN SERVANTS AND STATUTORY EMPLOYEES **25**;
- armed forces (**11.3**).

The remainder of the agreement then deals with entitlement to benefits.

> *Example*
>
> Alex, Bill and Sandy are employed by Shipfitters Ltd who provide internal servicing for maritime vessels. A large contract is undertaken by their representative office at Silver Sands, Barbados. The three are required to work in Barbados on the contract for eight months and then return to the UK. As the three workers are not going to be working in Barbados for more than three years they will continue to be within the UK contributions scheme. Shipfitters Ltd must apply to HMRC on form CA9107 for certificates of continuing UK NIC liability. HMRC's International Caseworker team normally issues two certificates in respect of each employee. The employer keeps one copy and the other copy is held by the employee in case it is required by the office in Barbados or the social security authorities there. UK contributions liability continues. During the first three months Bill is injured and Sandy is released from his contract. Under the Barbados/UK reciprocal agreement, both have paid sufficient contributions into the UK scheme but Sandy cannot claim jobseeker's allowance whilst remaining in

Barbados as the agreement does not provide for this particular benefit. Bill is entitled to be paid Statutory Sick Pay by Shipfitters Ltd even though he is in Barbados (as Class 1 contributions will have been paid in the relevant eight-week period) and if for some reason he did not meet the qualifying conditions for SSP, he would instead be entitled to claim employment and support allowance whilst in Barbados on the strength of his previous contributions history. The agreement also provides for the payment of state pensions in either territory. See SA 27, *The Social Security (Barbados) Order 1992, SI 1992/812, Arts 7, 13.*

Full reciprocal agreements generally provide for 'totalisation' of benefit entitlements. This involves taking into account insurance periods completed under both parties' legislation in computing entitlements. In the context of long-term benefits, this generally has the effect that a worker will receive a partial retirement pension from both states, provided he has a record of contributing in both. The UK from April 2016 will require at least ten years contributions before a contributor may claim any state pension. This rule also applied before April 2010. If a migrant worker from a treaty state has contributed for only seven years before reaching the UK state pension age in 2017, instead of having no UK entitlement, he will be able to use his foreign insurance periods in the treaty state to pass the ten-year test and be eligible for payment of 7/35ths of a UK state pension.

In the EU context, insurance records in all Member States will be recognised collectively in the calculation, but the process for bilateral treaty states is different: each is normally dealt with in isolation. This can give rise to lower entitlements. To recognise the unfairness for British-based contributors who have spent time working in one or more of Australia, Canada and New Zealand as well as in one or more EEA states over the course of their working lives, the UK modified its approach to the totalisation calculations with effect from 1 April 2015 when the *Social Security (Application of Reciprocal Agreements with Australia, Canada and New Zealand) (EEA States and Switzerland) Regulations 2015, SI 2015/349* came into force.

Where a person is an EEA or Swiss national, habitually resident in the EEA or Switzerland, and can demonstrate 'a genuine and sufficient link to the UK social security system' (undefined in the regulations), and there is a benefit claim involving some element of *EC Regulation 1408/71* or *883/2004*, each of the three treaties is modified so that insurance periods or residence anywhere in the EEA or Switzerland are treated as UK insurance periods. The effect is to treat the affected contributors as if they had paid NICs in the UK during the periods in which they were resident in Australia, Canada or New Zealand.

Brexit

[51.53] No EEC or EU state has ever left the organisation before, although Greenland voted to leave the EEC while remaining an autonomous part of Denmark, as indicated above. It is therefore impossible to know what the future holds for migrant workers once the UK is no longer a Member State. The details are yet to be discussed.

Where an old reciprocal agreement is still in force, principally for the benefit currently of Manx and Channel Island migrants, it could be expected to encompass UK mainland workers automatically after the EC Regulations cease to apply to the UK. None of the reciprocal social security agreements assume or provide for free movement of workers: they simply coordinate contribution obligations and, where they extend to benefits, identify which state is responsible.

Where the agreements apply only to British citizens, the position of non-British migrant workers could prove problematic and it will have to be settled as part of the Brexit negotiations.

It may be assumed that entitlements already accrued will be protected, if the negotiations are conducted in good faith for the benefit of all concerned, but totalisation may become more complex unless the replacement treaty between the UK and the other EEA states provides for totalisation of contribution records across all Member States as if they were a single entity.

Until Brexit happens, pension entitlements for EU migrant workers are comparatively straightforward: each state recognises contribution histories in other states, and a person who pays social security contributions for ten years in each of, for example, Germany, Italy, France and the UK should qualify, in broad terms, for a quarter of the social security pension in each of those states, based on the contributions paid while liable under each state's regime. If workers have to rely on bilateral agreements instead, the entitlements will be worked out separately between each pair of states according to the provisions of the relevant bilateral agreement.

The *Gottardo* case (C-55/00) may provide a pointer towards possible future complications, although Mrs Gottardo was only able to claim protection from discrimination because she was an EC national, and it is far from certain how UK citizens might be regarded as ex-EU citizens post-Brexit.

She was born Italian but married a French national and herself became a French national on marriage. She had started her career in Italy, then moved to Switzerland, and in later life had worked in France and retired there. Switzerland at the time was not party to any EEC agreement and did not have a bilateral social security agreement with France, although it did have an agreement with Italy.

She was entitled to partial pensions from both France and Switzerland because her contribution records there were adequate on a standalone basis. She claimed a partial pension from the Italian National Social Security Institute (the INPS) on the basis of her record in all three states because she did not have enough qualifying years in Italy on a standalone basis.

The Italy-Switzerland (I-CH) agreement provided for cross-border totalisation of pension records if it was necessary to enable the retiring contributor to reach the minimum contribution level to qualify for even a partial pension. However, because the Swiss and Italian periods in aggregate were insufficient even for that, Mrs Gottardo claimed to take her French contributions into account as well.

The I-CH agreement provided for third-country contributions to be added to the total *if* both states had a bilateral agreement with that third state, but because there was no such agreement between Switzerland and France, and

Mrs Gottardo was a French national and therefore not entitled to benefit from the I-CH agreement, the INPS refused to recognise the Swiss years. She therefore did not have enough notional years on her record to qualify for the partial Italian pension claimed. She claimed that her rights as an EC migrant worker were thereby infringed, and the European Court of Justice agreed. The INPS was not entitled to discriminate against her, because she had exercised her rights of free movement as an EC citizen, and she was entitled to rely on the I-CH agreement and claim her partial Italian pension.

Given the number of EU migrant workers who have passed through the UK in the last 43 years, and the number still living here now, the post-Brexit employment of the DWP team in Longbenton that deals with migrant worker entitlements seems assured for many years to come.

The UK/USA reciprocal agreement

[51.54] On 13 February 1984, agreement was reached between the UK government and the government of the United States of America as to reciprocity between the two nations in matters of social security. The agreement, for the most part, took effect on 1 January 1985. A number of amendments to the agreement were announced from 1 September 1997 onwards. As far as contribution matters are concerned, the agreement prevents dual liability by continuing the individual's social security coverage under the system of the country to whose economy the individual has the more direct connection, thus exempting the individual from coverage in the other country. For example, *Art 4(2)* says:

> Where a person who is covered under the laws of coverage of one Party and is normally employed by an employer in the territory of that Party is sent by that employer to work in the territory of the other Party, the person shall be subject only to the laws on coverage of the former Party . . . provided that the period of work . . . is not expected to exceed 5 years . . . .

The UK authorities interpret the above to mean that the employer has to be in the UK but the employee(s) to whom *Art 4(2)* is to apply can already be abroad on another assignment (CA Specialist Conference, 20 February 1996). This is now the standard approach to the issue of certificates of coverage, and is recognised explicitly in the wording of some agreements (eg, the 2015 treaty with Chile).

The US social security system is mainly founded on the Federal Insurance Contributions Act (usually referred to as FICA), which charges two contributions: a capped element for Old Age, Survivors and Disability Insurance (OASDI) and an uncapped amount for Medicare, together known as FICA tax. There are separate contributions for unemployment insurance under the Federal Unemployment Tax Act (FUTA). Self-employed workers pay both the employer and employee portions of FICA tax.

The US authority's interpretation is that six months' FICA contributions are usually required before they will consider that the provisions cover the employee. Also, in the above quotation from *Art 4(2)* the insertion of the word *normally* from 1 September 1997 is a shift of emphasis so that the UK employer may no longer take on an employee and send him/her straight to the US and expect the provisions of the agreement to apply. There will be at least a few months, rather than weeks, of employment required by the UK employer before the employee is sent to the US. Ideally, six months is considered a starting point although the then DSS International Services confirmed that there is no actual period and each case will be looked at on its own merits.

Where an employee has two contracts, one with a UK company for work in the UK and the other with a US affiliate for work in the US, the UK earnings will generally be subject to UK NIC while the US earnings will be insurable in the USA under FICA. There is considered to be no dual contribution liability under such circumstances and the treaty accordingly provides no relief. This is a consequence of the specific wording of a number of modern agreements, including that with the US.

The provisions described do not apply to MARINERS **45** or AIRMEN **6** (see HM Revenue and Customs National Insurance Manual NIM29000 and 27000). [*Art 4(2)*]. Such persons are, if they would otherwise be subject to the contribution law of both parties, to be subject only to the contribution law of the party in whose territory they ordinarily reside (see **51.5** above). [*Art 4(5)*].

A person who is *self-employed* and would otherwise be subject to the contribution law of both parties to the agreement is subject to the contribution law of the party in whose territory he ordinarily resides.

This above amendment to the old *Art 4(3)* means that dual coverage is now also eliminated for individuals who work in third countries and who would be otherwise be covered under both the UK and US schemes. The change does not affect those US individuals coming to the UK who will continue to pay their contributions in the US. [*Art 4(3)*]. See also Tolley's Practical NIC, Vol 6, No 9. The criterion of ordinary residence is similarly to be applied where a person who, in relation to a single activity, is regarded as self-employed under the contribution law of one of the parties and regarded as employed under the contribution law of the other party. [*Art 4(4)*].

A person who ordinarily resides in the UK and who is neither employed nor self-employed is subject only to UK law but since no insurable earnings exist, this provision is only relevant to the coordination of benefit entitlements. [*Art 4(6)*].

If none of these provisions applies, a person employed within the territory of one of the parties is, as regards that employment, subject to the laws of only that party, and, if that means he is subject only to UK law, he is treated as ordinarily resident in the UK for the purpose of UK contribution law (see **51.5** above). [*Art 4(1)*].

Government employees of one party to the agreement are, if they are employed in the territory of the other party and do not fall within the special rules relating to CROWN SERVANTS AND STATUTORY EMPLOYEES **25**, to be subject only to the contribution law of the first party (see HM Revenue and Customs National Insurance Manual NIM33018 – now only available via the National Archives website). [*Art 5(1)(2)*].

Where, because of the provisions described above, the contribution laws of one of the parties to the agreement are applicable, the appropriate agency of that party, eg HM Revenue and Customs is, upon the request of an employer, employee or self-employed person, to issue a certificate stating that to be the case. That certificate must then be accepted by the other party as proof of exemption from its contribution law of the person concerned. [*Sch 2, Art 3(1)(2)*].

Multilateral agreements

[51.55] Apart from the EC Treaty itself, the most important multilateral treaties affecting contribution law are the EC 'Co-operation Agreements' and 'Association Agreements' entered into between the EC and Switzerland, Algeria, Morocco, Tunisia, (the Maghreb states) and the 'Euro-Med Association Agreements' (EMAA) with various other states bordering the Mediterranean. A multilateral agreement with the Maghreb states was entered into in the 1970s but has now been superseded by newer agreements with individual states under the EMAA project. That with Switzerland came into effect on 1 June 2002 and was renewed in 2009. When the remaining treaties are fully implemented, the EC regulations on contribution law will extend to the other states mentioned also, although limited to recognition of insurance periods and the right to export pension entitlements, not to the certification of migrant workers to remain insured in their home state. There are also similar agreements in the cases of Former Yugoslav Republic of Macedonia and Israel and there are proposals for further developments in association agreements with Turkey, Albania, Montenegro and San Marino.

Since the principal reason for social security reciprocity is to coordinate benefit entitlements across borders, it might be expected that the UK would have provisions in UK law to coordinate entitlements accruing under the various treaties and the EU regulations (now encompassing Switzerland), but until 1 April 2015 that was not the case. The EU rules operate across the EU, but not in conjunction with the UK's other treaty obligations, so while pension entitlements between the UK and the USA might be calculated on the basis of the number of years spent contributing in each of the two countries, the calculation would not take into account any periods contributing in an EU member state. A separate calculation might take place between the UK and a relevant EU state, and between that same state and the USA, but there would not be one, all-encompassing totalisation of entitlements. Even after 1 April 2015, the UK's provisions are not very generous.

By virtue of *SI 2015/349*, as noted above, the UK will now recognise residence and contributions in Australia, New Zealand and Canada for a person who has had a social security presence in those countries, is an EEA national (including a British citizen), habitually resident in an EEA state or Switzerland, who can demonstrate a genuine and sufficient link to the UK social security system and who has exercised the right to work cross-border and thereby brought the EEA migrant worker rules into play.

In effect, for the purposes of determining entitlement to a UK state retirement pension, periods of residence in the three Commonwealth countries will be treated as if they had been periods of contribution under the UK NI scheme.

In accordance with *Article 21* of the *Treaty on the Functioning of the European Union* (which empowers the Council to make social security regulations to foster the free movement of workers), the 2015 regulation ensures that residence anywhere in the EEA or Switzerland is treated as UK residence for EEA or Swiss nationals who are migrant workers with a link to the UK.

Measuring earnings for expatriates

[51.56] It is frequently the case that where a UK company posts one of its employees overseas, liability for contributions on that employee's earnings is to continue by reason of the rules laid down in *Social Security (Contributions) Regulations 2001, SI 2001/1004, Reg 146(1)(2)*, *EC Regulation 883/2004, Art 12*, or in the reciprocal agreement (if any) between the UK and the country to which the employee is posted. Until 6 October 1985, this presented an employer with few difficulties as the secondary Class 1 contribution liability was limited to contributions on earnings at the Upper Earnings Limit, however great the employee's earnings might be. Following the removal of the Upper Earnings Limit for secondary Class 1 contribution purposes on 6 October 1985, however, the position changed completely. Expatriate remuneration arrangements are usually such as to compensate the employee for cost of living, accommodation, child education, and taxation increases, and such compensation will usually result in the employee's gross pay entitlement being significantly larger than that of his UK counterpart.

Example

Henry worked for International Widgets Ltd at a salary of £64,000 pa On 6 April 2014 he was posted to America for a period of four years. International Widgets agreed with Henry that, to maintain his earnings level at the equivalent of £64,000, he should, while working in America, be paid £99,000. International Widgets' increased contribution costs are £4,830, being 13.8% × (£99,000 – £64,000). Henry himself also has an unlimited liability to primary contributions, although that on earnings above the UEL is only at 2%.

Faced with increases of this order, UK companies operating on an international level may wish to consider breaking the direct relationship between themselves and the employees whom they wish to post overseas, and to arrange for such employees to terminate their employment and to enter employment overseas with, for example, an expatriate employment bureau or an overseas associated or subsidiary company which has no place of business in Great Britain (see **51.8** above). In the above example if the UK company paid £64,000 and the balance was paid from the US company the balance may not be liable to PAYE depending on the exact circumstances and the employee's residence status (see *Bootle v Bye (Inspector of Taxes)* [1996] STC (SCD) 58), although US tax liability is likely to arise in any event.

If the direct relationship is not broken, then the UK employer will no doubt wish to exclude as much of the increased cost from earnings for NIC purposes as possible. Overseas payments and allowances may, however, be excluded from earnings only if they are specific and distinct payments of or contributions towards such items as hotel accommodation, meals, clothing or if they are payments made in accordance with a scheme that complies with the requirements laid down in connection with a subsistence allowance scheme. NICs should be charged on payments described as compensation for working abroad (ie not business expenses), inducements, or bonuses for working abroad as well as COLAs (see **29.65** EARNINGS FROM EMPLOYMENT: GENERAL and DSS 1996 Leaflet CA 28, April 1995, page 91, Items 100 and 101, CA 28 Supplement (1996) April 1996, page 8). See also CA Specialist Conference, written response 24, 4 February 1997. Where the employee is provided with benefits in kind rather than cash, Class 1A NIC will be avoided as long as the benefit is not taxable in the UK.

The practice followed by some companies of calculating contribution liabilities only on the notional UK equivalent of earnings paid to an employee who has been posted overseas is incorrect and has no foundation in law or HM Revenue and Customs practice. The authorities are aware of the practice of accounting for contributions on such 'phantom salaries' and assess arrears due in appropriate cases.

Payroll matters

[51.57] Paying expatriate employees, inbound or outbound, can be fraught with difficulty. Information flows can be slow, currency conversions need to be factored in, pay may be delivered in more than one jurisdiction, the value of gross-ups and expenses might not be ascertainable until the year has ended, double taxation relief is hard to estimate, etc. This has always made payroll compliance more complex than it would be for a purely UK-oriented payroll.

No UK contributions due

[51.58] The position is easy where the inbound expatriate has a certificate of coverage or A1/E101: the NI fields are simply left blank. There is no need to report 'Table X' contributions. The same applies to those who are exempt for the first 52 weeks of UK presence.

Where non-resident directors are taxable on fees paid for their UK duties but excluded from UK NICs by concession (see NIM12031), no NI data should be shown on the FPS.

Special schemes

[51.59] Where life is more complex, employers may apply to HMRC to operate a 'Modified NICs' procedure if they second employees overseas with NIC liabilities but no PAYE due, or have employees in the UK who are non-resident and not liable for UK tax and receive part of their earnings abroad. The Modified NICs arrangement allows the employer to account for contributions through payroll on a best estimate basis throughout the year and submit a NIC Settlement Return (NSR, a paper-only return at the moment) by 31 March after the end of the tax year.

For inbound employees who are subject to an 'EP Appendix 6' agreement (modified PAYE in tax equalisation cases) and have a UK host employer liable to account for the contributions due on earnings that are at least equal to the

UEL, the employer can enter into an 'EP Appendix 7A' agreement, set out at PAYE82003 (NB: these are now in the PAYE Manual rather than the Employment Procedures Manual, despite the persistence of the 'EP' names). Only one FPS will be required each month irrespective of how many separate payments are made.

There is then an obligation to submit an FPS each month (or quarter, if there are five or fewer employees involved) on an estimated basis and to undertake a review between December and 5 April, correcting the cumulative values on the next FPS. Any underpayment does not attract late payment penalties or late payment interest if the agreement is operated correctly. There are also extensions and special arrangements for Class 1A contributions on benefits in kind. A final NSR and correcting payment with an EYU complete the year's compliance.

Even where no EP Appendix 6 agreement is in place, HMRC will allow the employer to file a best estimate FPS for the month and correct it in the following month (eg, because of exchange rate fluctuations changing the taxable amount paid from overseas).

For outbound employees, the equivalent application is set out at PAYE82004, known as an 'EP Appendix 7B' agreement. This covers workers who are liable to UK NICs while away without remaining taxable in the UK.

FPS filing deadlines

[51.60] From the introduction of RTI, it has often been the case that employers cannot file a correct FPS in respect of an expatriate's earnings on or before the date of payment of those earnings. HMRC expects that the late reporting of expatriate and employment-related securities income would normally take place no later than the next regular monthly payroll date, and that the relevant payment would normally be made to HMRC within the normal PAYE deadlines for that month. This relaxation will not apply in the case of those paid solely by the UK employer (www.gov.uk/paying-employees-working-abroad).

From April 2014, the FPS was modified to include a late reporting reason, and the first is 'A. Notional payment: Payment to Expat by third party or overseas employer'. 'G' is also likely to be relevant: 'Reasonable excuse'.

One of the accepted exceptions from the 'on or before' rule for filing payroll information by FPS is where earnings and notional payments are delivered by overseas employers and third parties to employees for duties performed on assignment in the UK or overseas. If the UK employer is operating 'reasonable and currently accepted payroll/administrative practices' and it isn't possible to operate PAYE and / or calculate NICs to be deducted by the PAYE deadline, HMRC 'will apply a common sense approach in-year where employers in these situations have a reasonable excuse for not reporting the information by the end of the pay period or the 19th of the following month'. (See www.gov.uk/running-payroll/fps-after-payday.)

Expat NINOs

[51.61] One regular problem with inbound expatriates is the lack of a NINO. The NINO is now not a mandatory field for RTI purposes. Many inbound expatriates will not be eligible to apply for a NINO if they have a certificate of coverage and are not subject to UK social security law, but those given a UK contract may need one. If they apply via Jobcentre Plus, it will typically take many weeks before the number is issued, and one or more paydays may pass in the meantime. The employer is simply required to ensure that the remaining employee standing data is correct, and is requested (but not required) to record the employee's passport number in the FPS as a unique identifier. Once the DWP issues the new arrival with a NINO, the RTI system should notify the employer who has submitted an FPS for the employee with a blank NINO field.

Foreign employers – EEA

[51.62] Where a foreign employer is liable for UK contributions as a result of *Article 21, EC Reg 987/2009*, even if it has no UK presence for PAYE it must arrange for RTI returns to be made and secondary contributions to be paid, possibly by a host employer or the employee.

Direct collection NI schemes

[51.63] Sometimes employees employed by a non-UK company have no UK employer, so they pay their tax through self-assessment and operate a DCNI scheme. From 6 April 2014, they are required to operate RTI. See HMRC PAYE Manual PAYE20090.

Expatriates and employment-related securities

[51.64] The OTS recommended in January 2013, in a report on unapproved employee share schemes, that the taxation of shares and share options awarded to 'internationally mobile employees' (IMEs) be changed. The tax rules were changed by *FA 2014, s 52* and *Sch 9*, but since the NIC charge arises under different legislation, and there are additional complications arising from the European regulations on migrant workers, the government launched a further consultation in July 2014.

The proposal was to change UK law so that gains from employment-related securities (referred to oddly in the consultation as 'earnings-related securities') would be apportioned according to the economic activity in each relevant country, which follows the OECD model for direct taxes. This would result in the amount subject to NICs being aligned more closely with the amount liable to income tax, albeit with differences caused by the effect of differing international obligations (ie, tax treaties do not work like the EU social security coordination regulations).

From 6 April 2015, under the *FA 2014, Sch 9* rules, ERS deemed income for IMEs is apportioned for income tax purposes on a time basis over a 'relevant period' determined under the new *Income Tax (Earnings and Pensions) Act 2003 (ITEPA 2003), s 41G*.

New Chapter 5B (*ss 41F–41L*) replaced *Ch 5A* of *Pt 2* of *ITEPA 2003*, which had its origins in the *Finance Act 2008* changes to the rules for non-domiciled employees. No longer will ERS gains be taxed according to where the employee was resident at the date of award of shares or options.

The new regime essentially, for both income tax and NIC purposes, deems any gain on ERS to accrue evenly over the workdays in the relevant period and then treats those gains in exactly the same way as cash earnings. This gives different results for tax and NIC.

The 'relevant period' for share options will, in UK law, be measured from the date of grant to the date of vesting, although the US measures it from grant to exercise, a point which is recognised in the UK-US double tax treaty in relation to share option gains.

The relevant period for share awards will be from award to lifting of restrictions.

If the worker fulfils any of the 'international mobility conditions' in *s 41F(2)* (eligibility for the remittance basis, a non-resident, or in a split year) during any part of the relevant period, the deemed 'securities income' (SI) for the relevant period is then allocated between UK and foreign source, and split into:

- taxable specific income (TSI) – UK tax as it arises,
- chargeable foreign securities income (CFSI) – taxed on a remittance basis if that is appropriate, or
- unchargeable foreign securities income (UFSI) – not taxable in the UK as employment income.

The NIC rules were similarly reformed from 6 April 2015 by the insertion of a new *para 18* into *Contributions Regulations 2001, Sch 3, Pt 9 by Social Security (Miscellaneous Amendments No 2) Regulations 2015 (SI 2015/478, para 21(3))*. However, the concepts of TSI, CFSI, and UFSI are unknown in NIC law, so the approach is necessarily different.

The NIC legislation now proceeds on the basis that any taxable gain on employment-related securities is deemed by *SSCBA 1992, s 4(4)(a)* or *Contributions Regulations 2001, Reg 22* to be earnings for NIC purposes. The new *para 18* then excludes from earnings so much of any such earnings as would meet the conditions set out in the paragraph, which identify earnings paid during a period when the earner is not subject to UK liability because of *Reg 145*, the EC regulations or a reciprocal agreement. Earnings for this purpose are to be measured by treating amounts which count as employment income under *Ch 2* to *5 of Pt 7* of *ITEPA 2003* as having been paid in equal instalments on each day of the relevant period (as determined in accordance with *s 41G*, outlined above). In effect, the gain on the employment-related securities is time apportioned between periods spent working abroad and periods spent working in the UK.

The 2015 provisions are an attempt to deal with the problem that an employee to whom an amount of income is attributed because of time spent working in the UK may often not be subject to UK NICs, and equally might be subject to UK NICs on all his employment income while being taxable in the UK on only that element relating to UK working time.

They avoid potential overcharging of contributions, by excluding UK liability in respect of days when the IME is probably subject to foreign social security rules. They have simplified the regime by ensuring that ERS deemed income attributable to days when the individual was not in the UK NIC system will be disregarded and not subjected to a UK NIC liability. Where an expatriate goes on assignment to a 'rest of the world' country (ie, non-EEA and non-reciprocal agreement) and remains subject to UK liability for the first 52 weeks, with the gain vesting after the 52-week period has expired, any part of the gain time-apportioned to that 52-week period will be subject to UK NICs.

In effect, the law will disregard any gain that is attributable to a period when international social security rules mean that a foreign country, rather than the UK, is the competent state in social security terms. For each day between the date of grant and the date of vesting, the IME will be subject to the legislation of one country. If that country is the UK, the ERS deemed earnings attributable to that day will be subject to UK NICs. Otherwise they will not.

At first blush, the new rules seem logical and sensible, and are very well explained in new guidance added to the Employment-Related Securities Manual (see ERSM 162,000 onwards). The equivalent guidance for NIC is to be found at NIM06870 onwards. However, it is questionable whether the rules are totally effective.

Take, for example, the worked example of 'Edith' at ERSM162845, which appears under the heading of 'International from 6 April 2015: PAYE and NICs – from 6 April 2015' but omits to explain the NIC position:

> 'Edith is a Hong Kong citizen who has been assigned to the UK for 2 years from 1 May 2013 and is awarded an option over shares in her UK-employer company on 1 June 2014, in year 2 of her stay in the UK. Edith leaves the UK and returns to Hong Kong on 30 April 2015, where she continues to work for the same group. Her option vests on 30 November 2015 but she does not exercise it until 30 May 2016. For 2016/17 Edith is not UK resident and remains back home in Hong Kong. She claims the remittance basis in 2013/14, 2014/15 and the UK part of 2015/16.'

The guidance explains how much of the £10,000 again she makes in May 2016 is treated as taxable specific income, chargeable foreign securities income, and unchargeable foreign securities income, but does not mention the NIC position. Applying the *Para 18* provisions, she has a relevant period from 1 June 2014 to 30 November 2015, and in that period she works in the UK from 1 June 2014 to 30 April 2015. From 1 May 2015 she clearly falls outside UK NIC liability by virtue of Regulation 145: she is no longer an employed earner after leaving the UK to resume her ordinary residence in Hong Kong. It is therefore straightforward to calculate how much of the gain should be disregarded as a proportion of the total gain in the relevant period.

However, it should not be overlooked that the gain in fact arises only in May 2016, when she is clearly outside UK liability completely. Class 1 liability arises under *SSCBA 1992, s 6* 'where in any tax week earnings are paid to or for the benefit of an earner . . . in respect of any one employment of his which is employed earner's employment'. While HMRC might argue that the gain does arise in respect of an employment which used to be employed earner's employment, it has yet to explain how Edith, who is not an employed earner at the time of payment, can be liable in that tax week. Neither has it explained how the exercise of a share option constitutes a payment of any kind: *SSCBA 1992, s 4(4)(a)* merely deems the game to be earnings and is not deemed payment to take place. As the decision in *Abbott v Philbin (Inspector of Taxes)* [1959] 2 All ER 270, [1959] 1 WLR 667 shows, while the grant of an option constitutes an occasion of payment, the exercise of that option does not. It is very arguable that *Para 18* excludes from earnings an amount that is possibly deemed to be earnings but is not in fact chargeable at all. The contrast between the PAYE and NIC rules is remarkable: PAYE is charged on employment-related securities principally under *ITEPA 2003, s 698*, which provides explicitly that the PAYE rules in *ss 684–691* and *s 696* have effect as if the employee were provided with PAYE income on the relevant date. In other words, the deemed to gain is chargeable because there is a deemed payment. No equivalent exists in the NIC legislation.

Key Points regarding overseas matters and NICs

[51.65] Points to consider are as follows.

- NIC treatment differs markedly from that for income tax.
- The NIC treatment will depend on which of three categories the other country(ies) involved fall into – those to which the EC Regulations apply, reciprocal agreement/DCC countries and those other countries (ROW) not falling into the former categories.
- Compared with income tax, there are very few countries with which the UK has a reciprocal social security agreement, and most such agreements are equally or more concerned with coordinating benefit entitlements.
- The EC rules changed from 1 May 2010 but Switzerland only adopted these updated rules on 1 April 2012 and Norway, Iceland and Liechtenstein on 1 June 2012.
- Within the EC, form A1 has replaced the E101, except for non-EEA nationals, and is available for postings of up to 24 months.
- Under the 2010 EC rules a UK company may have to pay foreign contributions in some cases and some employers based abroad will need to set up a UK PAYE/NIC scheme for NIC purposes.
- Special rules apply to the contribution position of aircrew and mariners.
- The rules relating to where contribution liabilities arise for multi-state workers changed significantly from 29 June 2012.
- Transitional rules may allow the 2010 and 2012 changes to be ignored for up to ten years.
- The introduction of RTI has meant that 100% compliance in respect of expatriate employees has become impossible. HMRC has undertaken to apply common sense to any employer failings where there is a reasonable excuse for late filing or late payment.

- The social security implications of the UK leaving the EU in the next few years are wholly unclear. The coordination rules of the EC regulations will not wholly cease to be relevant, as historical entitlements based on intra-EEA rules are likely to be protected, but it would seem most pragmatic for all parties to the exit treaty to agree to continue to operate the established rules as between the UK and all the other Member States without the associated freedom of movement entitlements. The number of cases within the scope of the treaty will clearly diminish if the UK restricts the flow of migrants, but it will by no means cease, so new rules will be absolutely necessary if there is to be any semblance of business as usual. It remains to be seen whether entrenched political positions in Brussels and London will allow for such pragmatism to prevail. At the time of publication, it is too early to make any predictions.

52
Partners

Cross-references. See CATEGORISATION **14**; COLLECTION **21**; EARNINGS FROM EMPLOYMENT: GENERAL **29**; HUSBAND AND WIFE, AND CIVIL PARTNERS **39**.

Other Sources. Simon's Taxes, Volume 2, para A8.223; Tolley's Practical NIC, Vol 3 No 8, page 61.

Introduction to partners and NICs

[52.1] Partnership is the relationship which subsists between persons carrying on a business in common with a view of profit. [*Partnership Act 1890, s 1*]. It is a question of *fact* whether a particular person is truly a party to such a relationship or is merely a senior employee who is being held out as a partner (see 52.5 below). The usual tests must, therefore, be applied in order to establish the truth of the relationship (see **14.9** to **14.14** CATEGORISATION). The absence of a formal partnership agreement under *Partnership Act 1890* is not definitive of the existence or non-existence of a partnership. See *Burrell (t/a The Firm) v Customs and Excise Comrs* [1997] STC 1413.

The partnership 'relationship'

[52.2] If the truth of the relationship is that the person *is* a partner but that he merely invests capital in the firm and takes no part in its management, he is neither an employed earner nor a self-employed earner for contribution purposes since he is not *gainfully employed* either under a contract of service or otherwise. [*SSCBA 1992, s 2(1)*]. This was established by the National Insurance Commissioners many years ago (*R(S)10/79, CP 5/75*) on the basis that, while the sleeping partner may have a motive of gain, there is no employment of any kind, so he cannot be 'employed'.

After that decision was promulgated, this applied to limited partners (unless there was some actual involvement in the running of the business) and to sleeping partners. This view was shared by HMRC, the Contributions Agency and the DSS for many years, but on 5 June 2013 HMRC issued a press release saying that sleeping partners and other inactive limited partners (NB, not LLP members) were and always had been liable to pay Class 2 NIC as a self-employed earner and Class 4 on their taxable profits.

HMRC now considers these partners to be gainfully employed as self-employed earners because 'employment' as defined in *Social Security Contributions and Benefits Act 1992 (SSCBA 1992), s 122* includes 'business' which falls squarely within the definition already given from the *Partnership Act 1890, s 1(1)* and *SSCBA 1992, s 2(1)(b)* imposes no requirement for the partner to be active. Since the law upon which the National Insurance Commissioners opined has not changed since, it is not clear why HMRC's opinion changed or indeed whether the revised view is valid.

In a similar vein HMRC said Class 4 NICs were due because, for there to be a partnership, the persons making up the partnership must be carrying on a business in common with a view of profit and *SSCBA 1992, s 15* imposes no requirement for the partners to be active. HMRC is clearly wrong where the partnership is not trading but investing, since Class 4 applies only to the profits of a trade or profession taxable under *ITTOIA 2005, Part 2, Chapter 2*.

This revised view will almost certainly be rejected as a blanket opinion should HMRC ever decide to impose its new policy. Because of the allegedly incorrect view previously promulgated by HMRC no action will be taken to collect arrears for earlier years (ie, before 2013–14) but Class 2 contributors can pay these contributions if they would enhance benefit rights. HMRC was to issue further guidance on how this could be done in due course, but the view was challenged and was reviewed in a consultation on 'Simplifying the National Insurance Processes for the Self-Employed', a document first issued in July 2013, which resulted in the reform of Class 2 from 6 April 2015 by *National Insurance Contributions Act 2015 (NICA 2015), Sch 2*.

The analysis in the June 2013 note was questionable.

On basic principles, it cannot always be assumed that a partnership is a business that falls within *s 1(1)* of the *Partnership Act 1890*, although there is arguably a presumption to that effect. Property investors who jointly acquire buildings as an investment might not be carrying on a business in partnership even if they consider themselves partners. In the case of *Rashid v Garcia* [2003] STC (SCD) 36 a contributor who owned and let four properties, some residential and some commercial, as his only source of income, was held not to have been carrying on a business and was therefore unable to pay Class 2 contributions (which he wanted to do so as to qualify for incapacity benefit). Had he held the properties through a company, there would probably have been less doubt about the status of the venture, but the Special Commissioner held that Mr Rashid was not carrying on a business in the context of the NIC legislation. He said (at 40):

> The context here is that 'business' is included along with trade, profession, office or vocation in the definition of employment, implying activity in contrast to mere investment . . . Whether property rental is a business in any particular case is a matter of degree. . . . Standing back and looking at all the evidence although I think that the case is near the borderline in the end I am not satisfied that there is

> sufficient activity for it to constitute a business. In my view, it is an investment which by its nature requires some activity to maintain it, rather than a business.

It has always been the case that NICs apply to earned income – contributors must have 'earnings' (remuneration or profit derived from an employment) before they have a liability – so it is very doubtful that any investment income was ever intended by Parliament to be subject to a contribution liability (or in consequence generate a contributory state benefit entitlement).

Sleeping and limited partners are generally investors, and will always be so in typical investment limited partnerships, although it would be hard to argue that investors in film and IP partnerships, who generally claim loss reliefs from trading in the initial stages, are not in business. The Class 2 position before the reform at 6 April 2015 will depend on the facts. The Class 4 position will also depend on whether, and when (eg, where the profits are deferred by members of an AIFM firm by an election under *ITTOIA 2005, s 863H*), the income generated falls to be taxed under *ITTOIA 2005, Part 2, Chapter 2* as profits of a trade or profession (see **20** CLASS 4 CONTRIBUTIONS).

The *NICA 2015* reform of Class 2 means that from 6 April 2015 a partner *in a business* without profits that are taxable under *Income Tax (Trading and Other Income) Act 2005 (ITTOIA 2005), Part 2, Chapter 2* (ie, Class 4 profits) will be classed as a self-employed earner and will be eligible, but not required, to pay Class 2 contributions. [*SSCBA 1992, s 11(6)*]. A partner in a venture which is not a business (and therefore by definition is not trading) will not be classed as a self-employed earner and will therefore be liable to neither Class 2 nor Class 4 contributions.

Another aspect to consider with regard to partnerships is the potential effect of the IR35 position. See **40** INTERMEDIARIES and Tax Bulletin, February 2001.

If the truth of the relationship between the individual and the organisation is that a contract of service exists (whether disguised by a partnership deed or not) the person will be an employed earner liable to pay primary Class 1 contributions on the earnings paid to him (whether described as profits or not). In that event, the true partners will be liable as secondary contributors in respect of his employment (see **14.32** CATEGORISATION and **52.6** below) (see also 'Profit sharing arrangements with employees' Tolley's Practical NIC, Vol 3, No 8, p 61).

If the truth of the relationship is that the person is a partner in the business in the full sense of the word, he will be a self-employed earner liable to pay Class 2 contributions unless his share of the actual trading profits is (before 6 April 2015) below the small earnings exception limit or (from 6 April 2015) below the small profits threshold (see **18.4** CLASS 2 CONTRIBUTIONS). He will also be liable for Class 4 contributions on his share of profits or gains chargeable to income tax under *ITTOIA 2005, Part 2 Chapter 2* (see CLASS 4 CONTRIBUTIONS **20** as well as **52.7** below).

A partnership may in fact exist where it was not intended. In the VAT case of *Tracey Jane Sumner (trading as Extravaganza Hair Workshop)* (Case 17784) two hair stylists arranged to work at the same premises although their intention was that they would not form a partnership. Expenses were shared but net income was apportioned and both parties submitted sole trader accounts with different year ends. However, even after reference to the *Partnership Act 1890* and *Sixth Directive of the European Community, Art 4*, the tribunal determined that there was in existence a partnership despite the intention by the traders for there not to be one.

The *Finance Act 2014* changed the tax treatment of salaried members of LLPs (see below), but not salaried partners in general partnerships.

Settlement provisions

[52.3] One matter to remember in partnerships between spouses (and those of civil partners from December 2005 onwards – see **39** HUSBAND AND WIFE, AND CIVIL PARTNERS) is that it must be a genuine partnership with one spouse or civil partner's share of profit/losses being appropriate to his or her contribution to the business. If it was not found to be genuine then the partnership arrangement might be treated for income tax purposes as a settlement by the one party on the other party and the monies involved would be treated as the settlor's for tax purposes. This would therefore lead to additional tax at their marginal rate. [*ITTOIA 2005, ss 622, 624, 625, 626, 627, Sch 2 para 132(1)(3)*]. However, as the settlements charge is under what was Schedule D, Case VI, rather than under *ITTOIA 2005, Part 2, Chapter 2*, there cannot be any additional Class 4 liability. [*SSCBA 1992, s 15 (1)(b)*]. In the Inland Revenue Tax Bulletin, Issue 69, February 2004 (Example 21) clarification was given in respect of a partnership between spouses in the business in connection with the settlement anti-avoidance provisions of *ITTOIA 2005*) particularly with regard to the former *s 660A* notwithstanding a genuine partnership deed being in place:

> *Example*
>
> Mr Y, an architect, commences business as a sole trader. The business is successful and a few years later annual profits are in the region of £80,000. The business has significant capital and there are no employees. The business is transferred to a new partnership of Mr and Mrs Y. A deed is created under which profits are to be shared equally. Mrs Y subscribes no new capital and carries out no work whatsoever for the partnership. Profits for the year are £80,000 and £40,000 belong to Mrs Y. This is arguably a bounteous arrangement transferring income from one spouse to another. The settlements legislation is likely to apply and Mrs Y's share of profits will probably continue to be assessed on Mr Y.

Clearly in the case of the settlement provisions regarding the partnership division of profits, this example suggests a bounteous arrangement in which Mr Y should include Mrs Y's partnership income of £40,000 in his self-assessment tax return and make a note in the 'Additional information' section of the return. In this case HM Revenue and Customs would seek to apply the settlements legislation and assess the £40,000 on the husband, Mr Y. However, as stated above, the Class 4 liability will be unaffected.

The former Inland Revenue introduced further legislation that limits or precludes partnership loss relief by set off against other income and gains under *ITTOIA 2005, ss 303–305, 878(5)*. This legislation applies to accounting periods ending on or after 10 February 2004 where a partner in a partnership does not spend a significant amount of time (ie ten hours a week) in running or operating the trade. Broadly the restrictions impose a purpose test and an annual limit of relief of £25,000. Further similar anti-avoidance measures were introduced that apply to individuals with effect from 12 March 2008 to restrict the amount of 'sideways loss relief' that broadly followed the existing rules. See 32.7.

Limited liability partnerships

[52.4] Members of limited liability partnerships have generally been accepted as subject to NIC (and tax) as if they were partners in a conventional partnership, but legislation was introduced to ensure that partnerships under the *Limited Liability Partnerships Act 2000 (LLPA 2000)* engaged in certain property and other investment activities did not obtain this treatment. See Tax Bulletin, Issue 50, December 2000. [*SSCBA 1992, s 15(3A)*].

It is debatable whether all LLP members should have been treated as self-employed earners before 6 April 2015, when *Social Security Contributions Limited Liability Partnership) (Amendment) Regulations 2015, SI 2015/607, reg 4* deemed them to be so.

Limited Liability Partnerships Act 2000, s 4(4) provided that a member should not be regarded for any purpose as employed by the LLP unless, if he and the other members were partners in a partnership, he would be regarded for that purpose as employed by the partnership. The National Insurance Commissioners determined many years ago that sleeping and inactive partners taking no part in running the business of the general or limited partnership were not to fall within the category of self-employed earner because they were not, in fact, 'employed' doing anything (see *R(S)10/79, CP 5/75*). See 18.11 for a full description of the issue. This affects only Class 2, though: the share of trading profit of an LLP member has been subject to Class 4 liability since the start of LLPs in the UK. *SSCBA 1992, s 15(3A)* was introduced with the rest of the LLP legislation on 6 April 2001 by *LLPA 2000, s 13* and commenced by *SI 2000/3316*. It simply provided that, if there was an income tax charge on a member in respect of a profit from the carrying on of a trade or profession by the LLP, Class 4 contributions were payable if they would have been payable had the trade or profession been carried on in partnership by the members. The Class 4 charge did not rely on the member being classed as self-employed under the NIC legislation, which is perhaps counter-intuitive.

Restrictions were imposed via *s 13* of the *National Insurance Contributions Act 2014*. This disapplied *s 4(4)* of the *Limited Liabilities Partnerships Act 2000* for the purposes of *SSCBA 1992* with effect from 6 April 2014 by creating a new category of 'salaried member'. The aim was to prevent avoidance of secondary Class 1 liability that was being achieved by deliberately turning many employees into salaried 'partners' in a LLP, albeit without their having many of the usual attributes of partners. The measure also attempted to raise significant contribution yield by forcing professional practices to account for Class 1 contributions in respect of their salaried and fixed share members.

A member of a LLP who meets three conditions will now be treated as a salaried member and fall within the category of employed earner for both PAYE and NIC purposes (PAYE and Class 1 primary contributions will be due from the member and he or she will be entitled to SSP, SMP, etc). The LLP (ie, those members seen as genuinely sharing the profits) will be liable as the secondary contributor and will be able to claim a tax deduction for the salaries, benefits in kind and Class 1 and Class 1A NIC liabilities. As a deemed employed earner, the salaried member cannot be liable to pay Class 4 contributions on his profit share.

Another device used to reduce tax and NIC liabilities was the introduction into the LLP of a corporate member to which a profit share was allocated. Typically, this would be owned and controlled by one or more of the human members, who would then extract the profit by way of dividend, thereby marginally reducing the income tax liability and avoiding altogether the NIC liability on the diverted profits. There were also opportunities to allocate excess losses to partners who were individuals while excess profits were allocated to corporate members, often taxed only at 20%.

The legislation was changed as follows.

The status of 'salaried member' was created by *Finance Act 2014, Sch 17* inserting new provisions as *ITTOIA 2005, ss 863A to 863G*, while the perceived exploitation of partnerships with mixed membership was addressed by the insertion of *ITTOIA 2005, ss 850C–850E, ITA 2007, ss 116A, 127C* and *CTA 2009, s 1264A*. These were imported into the NIC regime by *NICA 2014, ss 13–14*.

NICA 2014, s 14 provided, by inserting new *SSCBA 1992, s 4AA*, for the Treasury to use regulations to override any rule in the *LLPA 2000* treating any member as self-employed (see *SSCBA 1992, s 4AA(6)*) and to deem the LLP to be the secondary contributor in relation to the earnings of a member deemed to be an employee. The regulations may also prescribe how earnings in respect of the deemed employee's deemed employment with the LLP are to be determined and when they are paid.

NICA 2014, s 13 amended *SSCBA 1992* by inserting a new *s 18A* to permit the Treasury to make regulations to modify the way in which the liability to Class 4 contributions of a partner in a firm is determined, or otherwise modify the law relating to Class 4 contributions when a provision of the Income Tax Acts is passed that relates to partners in firms.

Under the *Social Security Contributions (Limited Liability Partnership) Regulations 2014, SI 2014/3159*, a member will, for 2014–15 and later years, be a 'salaried member' if he, either directly or through an intermediary, meets the three *ITTOIA* 2005 conditions:

(1) It is reasonable to expect that at least 80% of the total amount payable by the LLP for the member's services will be fixed or, if variable, variable without reference to, or in practice unaffected by, the overall profits or losses of the LLP (ie, the member is seen to be entitled to disguised salary).
(2) The member has no significant influence over the affairs of the LLP.

(3) The member's capital contribution to the LLP is less than 25% of the disguised salary likely to be paid by the LLP in the relevant tax year.

Where a member does not meet one or two of the conditions (eg, his capital contribution to the LLP exceeds 25% of his likely 'salary'), he remains a self-employed earner and is subject to Classes 2 and 4 rather than Class 1. Where all three conditions are met but his circumstances change and he ceases to meet one of the conditions (eg, by increasing his capital contribution), his position may be reassessed and he will fall outside the deeming provisions and will once more become subject to Class 2 and 4 instead of Class 1. [*ITTOIA 2005, s 863B(1)(b)*].

The regulations apply where a person is treated by *ITTOIA 2005, s 863A* as being employed by an LLP under a contract of service (including where that is the case by virtue of *ITTOIA 2005, s 863G*, the anti-avoidance rule aimed principally at the diversion of profit shares to corporate members from which the individual benefits), and the 'deemed tax employment' would be employment in the UK.

For NIC purposes, the person, known as the 'salaried member', is treated as employed in employed earner's employment by the LLP. The 'salaried member' does not become an employee or gain any employment protection rights – the measure was simply aimed at raising PAYE and Class 1 NICs. Any amount treated by *ITTOIA 2005, s 863A* or *s 863G(4)* as employment income from the deemed tax employment, except for benefits in kind that would be taxed under the benefits code of *ITEPA 2003*, is treated as Class 1 earnings paid to or for the benefit of the salaried member. The secondary contributor in relation to such earnings is the LLP. Where the anti-avoidance rules are invoked in a case where the profit share attributable to the individual is diverted to a corporate member of the LLP, and the employment income is deemed to arise by *ITTOIA 2005, s 863G(4)*, the earnings are treated as paid by the LLP to the salaried member when they arise to the corporate member. [*SI 2014/3159, reg 3(1),(2)*].

The salaried member is entitled to statutory payments (SSP, SMP, SAP, SPP) from the LLP by virtue of the deemed employee status. [*SI 2014/3159, reg 3(4)*].

In order to deal with the possibility of double contribution liability where an interposed corporate member provides salary or a benefit in kind to the individual who is deemed to be an employee of the LLP, the regulations inserted a new *Social Security (Contributions) Regulations 2001, SI 2001/1004, reg 40A* and *Sch 3, Part 10, para 25*. These ensure that, where Class 1 or Class 1A contributions are payable under the LLP deeming rules, any subsequent payment of earnings or provision of a benefit to the salaried member by an employer that relates to the original payment from the LLP to the corporate member is not subject to further Class 1 or Class 1A contributions. [*SI 2014/3159, reg 5*].

Forestalling avoidance by the use of corporate LLP members might also have a knock-on effect on the anti-avoidance provisions of the intermediaries rules (IR35) where the LLP supplies the salaried member's services to others in circumstances that amount to disguised employment. It is therefore provided that, in the calculation of the deemed 'attributable earnings' of the worker under *Social Security Contributions (Intermediaries) Regulations 2000, SI 2000/727, reg 7*, any amounts deemed to be a personal salary payment or benefit in kind by *SI 2014/3159* are to be excluded from the income of the intermediary that is the starting point (step 1) for the IR35 calculation. Credit is then given in step 7 for payments on which Class 1 or Class 1A contributions have been paid pursuant to *SI 2014/3159*. [*SI 2014/3159, reg 6*].

Note that the income tax provisions on partnerships with mixed membership needed no particular changes to the *Contributions Regulations* (other than the provisions on AIFM firms outlined below) because the Class 4 liability generally automatically follows the identification of profits chargeable under *ITTOIA 2005, Part 2, Chapter 2*.

The decision of the Supreme Court in *Clyde & Co LLP v Bates van Winkelhof* [2014] UKSC 32 is also worthy of mention, because the court held that members of a LLP are classed as 'workers' under *s 230(3)* of the *Employment Rights Act 1996*. Although not directly relevant to NIC liability, there is a potential side-effect to the decision. The case centred on whether a member of a LLP could benefit from 'whistleblower' protection afforded by *ss 43A to 43L* of that Act, inserted by the *Public Interest Disclosure Act 1998*, but the ramifications of the decision are potentially much wider. The Pensions Regulator subsequently announced, for example, that LLP members were, as a result of the decision, potentially subject to the auto-enrolment rules under *Pensions Act 2008*, although without explaining how a member's profit share might fall within the definition of earnings used in that Act. The definition of 'worker' is replicated across various pieces of employment protection legislation, so a LLP member is apparently now also potentially entitled to be paid the National Minimum Wage (under *NMWA 1998*) and to claim paid holiday (under the *Working Time Regulations 1998, SI 1998/1833*), neither of which is compatible with self-employed profit-sharing arrangements. It is not unknown for an employment tribunal to award arrears of holiday pay to a person who is self-employed for income tax and NIC purposes and gross up the award for PAYE and NIC because the cross-over between the different regulations can be confusing. 'Worker' can mean either a person working under a contract of service (who would be within Class 1 NIC and PAYE) or a self-employed person who is obliged to provide personal service to the other contracting party who is not thereunder a customer of the self-employed person's business (who would not be within Class 1 and PAYE).

Salaried partners

[52.5] The term 'salaried partner' is generally used to denote a person who is held out to the world as being a partner with his name appearing on a firm's notepaper etc but who, instead of receiving a share of profits, receives a salary as remuneration and, possibly, some profit-related bonus. Whether or not such a person is truly a partner for NIC purposes in a general or limited partnership will depend on the facts, and the substance of the relationship between the person and the other parties must be examined. As noted above, the term 'salaried member' was introduced from 6 April 2014 to encompass such persons who, while commonly referred to as partners, are members of a

LLP and fulfil the conditions set out above. If there is clearly a contract of service only qualified by the fact that the servant is being held out as a partner of a partnership or LLP, he is no true partner. If, however, though paid a fixed salary not dependent on profits, the person is party to a full partnership deed and is entitled to share in the profits on a winding-up, he may well be a true partner. (*Stekel v Ellice* [1973] 1 All ER 465, [1973] 1 WLR 191). If such a person is a true partner, in a general partnership, his share of profits or gains for Class 4 purposes will be his salary. If he meets the conditions to be classed as a salaried member of a LLP, his share of profits will be subject to Class 1 primary and secondary liability (see above).

Partners as secondary contributors

[52.6] Although a partnership is not, in English law, a separate legal entity, it (rather than the individual partners) will be treated as the secondary contributor in relation to earnings paid to its employees. If the partnership defaults in the payment of contributions, therefore, it is submitted that there is only one offence, but that HM Revenue and Customs may proceed against one or more of the partners who may be separately fined and ordered to pay an amount equal to the unpaid contributions (see **12.6** ARREARS OF CONTRIBUTIONS), or against all the partners who are jointly and severally liable. Before the DSS's enforcement regime was transferred to HMRC, the partners might have been prosecuted under the powers in *Social Security Administration Act 1992* and then jointly convicted and ordered to pay the sum in question.

Partners may also become liable as secondary contributors where one of their number is supplied by the partnership to work for someone else within the terms of *Categorisation Regulations, Reg 5 and Sch 3 para 2(a)* (see **4.13** agency workers) or within terms such that the 'IR35' provisions apply (see **40.8**). The rules for 'salaried members' of LLPs from 6 April 2014 provide for the LLP to be liable as the secondary contributor in respect of payments of earnings and the provision of benefits in kind to any such members (see above). Note that these 'salaried member' rules do not apply to general or limited (ie, 1907 Act) partnerships.

Class 4 contributions

[52.7] Where a trade or profession is carried on in partnership, the liability of any partner in respect of Class 4 contributions is to arise in respect of his share of the profits or gains of that trade or profession; and, for this purpose, his share is to be *aggregated* with his share of the profits or gains of any other trade, profession or vocation (see **5.17** AGGREGATION OF EARNINGS). [*SSCBA 1992, Sch 2 para 4(1)*].

Under self-assessment the share of profits is determined on the basis of the profit sharing arrangements *in the basis period*. As Class 4 contributions are payable in respect of profits chargeable to tax, a partner's share of profits must be arrived at on this basis for Class 4 purposes also.

Example

Alder, Birch and Cypress are in partnership as arboriculturists. Their profit for the year ended 30 June 2016 is £34,000 and during that year C is a salaried partner while A and B share the remaining profit in equal shares. The tax assessment for 2016–17 is £34,000. Although A and B continue to share profits on the same basis, however, C's salary for the year ended 30 June 2016 is £12,000 and for the year ended 30 June 2017 is £14,000. For Class 4 purposes the 2016–17 assessment is to be:

			£
C		=	12,000
A	½ × (£34,000 – £12,000)	=	11,000
B	½ × (£34,000 – £12,000)	=	11,000
			£34,000

Under self-assessment Class 4 contributions are, like income tax, self-assessed individually with each partner having been notified by the partnership of his/her share of assessable profit.

Example

Diamond and Emerald are in partnership as jewellers sharing profits in the ratio of 1:1 until 30 September 2014 and in the ratio of 1:2 after that date. Diamond also runs a nightclub. The partnership profits for the years to 30 September 2014, 30 September 2015 and 30 September 2016 are £36,000, £38,000 and £34,000. D's profits from his nightclub are £28,000 for 2013–14, £24,000 for 2014–15 and £32,000 for 2015–16.

D and E will each separately self-assess their tax and Class 4 National Insurance liabilities. In the case of D, this will be based on the total income from both sources of self-employment income.

D's Class 4 liability for 2014–15 is:

		£
£36,000 × ½		18,000
Nightclub		28,000
		46,000
Less: Excess over upper annual limit (£42,385)		3,615
		42,385
Less: Lower annual limit		7,956
Class 4 contributions due:		£34,429
£34,429 @ 9% =	£3,098.61	
£3,615 @ 2%	72.30	
	£3,170.91	

E's Class 4 liability for 2014–15 is:

		£
£36,000 × ½		18,000
Less: Lower annual limit		7,965
Class 4 contributions due:		£10,035
£10,035 @ 9% =	£903.15	

D's Class 4 liability for 2015–16 is:

		£
£38,000 × ⅓		12,666
Nightclub		24,000
		36,666
Less: Lower annual limit		8,060
Chargeable at main rate		£28,606
Class 4 contributions due:		
£28,606 @ 9% =	£2,574.54	

E's Class 4 liability for 2015–16 is:

		£
£38,000 × ⅔		25,333
Less: Lower annual limit		8,060
Class 4 contributions due:		17,273
£17,273 @ 9% =	£1,554.57	

D's Class 4 liability for 2016–17 is:

		£
£34,000 × ⅓		11,333
Nightclub		32,000
		43,333
Less: Excess over upper annual limit (£43,000)		333
		43,000
Less: Lower annual limit		8,060
Class 4 contributions due on:		£34,940
£34,940 @ 9% =	£3,144.60	
£333 @ 2% =	£6.66	
	£3,151.26	

E's Class 4 liability for 2016–17 is:

		£
£34,000 × ⅔		22,666
Less: Lower annual limit		8,060
Class 4 contributions due on:		£14,606
£14,606 @ 9% =	£1,314.54	

D and E's Class 4 liabilities for 2014–15 were payable in two equal interim instalments on 31 January 2015 and 31 July 2015 based on the 2013–14 assessments, with the balance payable on 31 January 2016. Similarly, their Class 4 liability for 2015–16 is payable in two equal instalments on 31 January 2016 and 31 July 2016 based on the 2014–15 assessment, with the balance payable on 31 January 2017 (together with, for the first time, the Class 2 liability for the year of assessment) and so on.

AIFM firms

[52.8] Partners in alternative investment fund management firms ('AIFM firms') are subject to regulatory requirements in connection with the *Alternative Investment Fund Managers Directive* (2011/61/EU) that require them to retain certain profits, in effect deferring their remuneration. This is normally arranged by having a special purpose corporate partner to which the restricted profits are allocated until the rules allow their distribution to the actual partners. This structure became problematic when anti-avoidance provisions were introduced by *FA 2014, s 74* and *Sch 17* to deem profits allocated to corporate members of LLPs to belong to the humans who controlled them: the human partners in the AIFM firms could be taxable on income that they were unable to access.

FA 2014, Sch 17, para 15 therefore inserted new tax rules as *ITTOIA 2005, ss 863H-863L* allowing an AIFM firm (as defined in *s 863H*) to elect to allocate all or part of the relevant restricted profit to the AIFM firm itself without that share being then deemed to belong to the human members.

The partner whose relevant restricted profit is allocated to the firm is not taxed personally on the amount so allocated. Instead, the firm is chargeable to tax under *ITTOIA 2005, Part 2, Ch 2* for the tax year in which the period of account ends, and the tax is charged at the additional rate. The profits to which this provision applies are variable remuneration, either deferred remuneration or upfront remuneration vesting in the form of instruments with a retention period of at least six months, and the remuneration must be awarded in accordance with AIFMD remuneration guidelines issued by the European Securities And Markets Authority on 3 July 2013 (ESMA/2013/232).

When the remuneration eventually vests in the human partner, it is treated as his remuneration in the year of vesting, so long as he is still carrying on the AIFM trade, although not necessarily as a partner in the AIFM firm. The vested amount is then treated as allocated profit net of tax, with a credit for the tax that has been paid on those profits by the AIFM firm.

If vesting does not occur until the individual is no longer carrying on the AIFM trade, the former partner is treated as receiving non-trading income equal to the amount of profit allocated and the relevant tax credit.

If vesting never occurs, perhaps because the relevant performance targets are not met, HMRC guidance is that no further income tax is payable by the firm, nothing is repayable, and no Class 4 NICs are due.

The NIC implications of the tax rules are fairly straightforward. A corporate member of an AIFM firm can never be liable to Class 4 contributions as it can never be a self-employed earner. Any profit share allocated to the corporate member cannot therefore create a Class 4 liability. The *Social Security (Contributions) (Amendment No 5) Regulations 2014, SI 2014/3196*, in force from 3 December 2014 but taking effect for the tax year 2014–15 onwards, introduced a new exception from Class 4 liability for amounts allocated to the corporate member of an AIFM firm rather than to the relevant human member.

Under *The Social Security (Contributions) Regulations 2001, SI 2001/1004, reg 94B*, where an AIFM firm elects into the special provisions under *ITTOIA 2005, s 863H*, no Class 4 contributions are payable in respect of that allocated profit. [*SI 2001/1004, reg 94B(2)*]. In other words, the *FA 2014* anti-avoidance rules on artificial allocation of profit to corporate members are disapplied.

As is the case with income tax, that is not the end of the story. If all or part of the allocated profit vests in the individual at a time when he is still carrying on the AIFM trade (whether as a partner in the AIFM firm or otherwise), the amount treated as his profit under *ITTOIA 2005, s 863J(2),(5)* is deemed to be earnings for Class 4 purposes in the year in which the profit is chargeable to income tax under *ITTOIA 2005, Pt 2, Ch 2*. [*SI 2001/1004, reg 94B(3)(4)*].

If vesting occurs at a time when he is not carrying on the AIFM trade, no Class 4 liability can arise, despite there being an amount of deemed taxable income.

member cannot, therefore, create a Class 4 liability. The *Social Security (Contributions) (Amendment No 7) Regulations 2014, SI 2014/3159*, in force from 31 December 2014 and taking effect for the tax year 2014–15 onwards, introduced a new exception from Class 4 liability on amounts allocated to the corporate member of an AIFM firm rather than to the relevant human member.

Under *The Social Security (Contributions) Regulations 2001, SI 2001/1004, reg 94B*, where an AIFM firm elects into the special provisions under *ITTOIA 2005, s 863H*, no Class 4 contributions are payable in respect of that allocated profit (*SI 2001/1004, reg 94B(2)*). In other words, the FA 2014 anti-avoidance rules on artificial allocation of profit to corporate members are disapplied.

As is the case with income tax, that is not the end of the story if all or part of the allocated profit vests in the individual at a time when he is still carrying on the AIFM trade (whether as a partner in the AIFM firm or otherwise), the amount treated as his profit under *ITTOIA 2005, s 863J(3)(5)* is deemed to be earnings for Class 4 purposes in the year in which the profit is chargeable to income tax under *ITTOIA 2005, Pt 2, Ch 2* (*SI 2001/1004, reg 94B(3)(4)*).

If vesting occurs at a time when he is not carrying on the AIFM trade, no Class 4 liability can arise, despite there being an amount of deemed taxable income.

53

Rates and Limits

Cross-references. See ADMINISTRATION 2; ANNUAL MAXIMUM 7; CLASS 1 CONTRIBUTIONS 15; CLASS 1A CONTRIBUTIONS 16; CLASS 1B CONTRIBUTIONS 17; CLASS 2 CONTRIBUTIONS 18; CLASS 3 CONTRIBUTIONS 19; CLASS 4 CONTRIBUTIONS 20; COLLECTION 21; CONTRACTED-OUT EMPLOYMENT 23; EARNINGS LIMITS AND THRESHOLDS 33; MARINERS 45; REDUCED LIABILITY ELECTIONS 54; SHARE FISHERMEN 56; VOLUNTEER DEVELOPMENT WORKERS 59.

Other Sources. Former leaflet E12(2013).

Introduction to rates and limits relating to NICs

[53.1] As explained in the various chapters to which cross-references are given above, the power to change the rates, limits and brackets which govern contribution liability is, provided the changes lie within defined parameters, in the hands of the Treasury. Normally, the majority of such changes are announced in November or December's Autumn Statement and take effect from the beginning of the following tax year, but mid-year changes are possible. It is expected that these changes will be announced in the Autumn Budget following the Chancellor's statement in March 2017 that the 2017 Spring Budget would be 'the last Spring Budget'. This was in fact the case with the Autumn Budget 2017. Where changes lie outside the powers of the Treasury they are achieved by an Act of Parliament, for example, those with regard to the changes that took effect from 6 April 2003. [*National Insurance Contributions Act 2002*]. The same approach took place with respect to the second 1% increase in all Class 1 and Class 4 rates with effect from 6 April 2011 [*National Insurance Contributions Act 2011*] and the introduction of the nil rate of secondary contribution for under-21s from 6 April 2015 [*National Insurance Contributions Act 2014*.] The *NIC (Rate Ceilings) Act 2015* took the unusual step of 'locking' the rates of Class 1, Class 1A and Class 1B contributions at their current levels, and tying the upper earnings limit to the 40% income tax threshold, for the remainder of the current parliament, ie, until 5 April 2020 (but now April 2018 following the June 2017 general election). Given the Government's plan to abolish Class 2 contributions and merge it into Class 4, at some point in the next few years, it was unsurprising that Classes 2 and 4 were not 'locked' in a similar way. Since the abolition of Class 2 will also have an inevitable impact on how voluntary contributions are calculated, the omission of Class 3 from the Act is also understandable.

The lower earnings limit is linked very loosely to the single person's rate of retirement pension under the pre-2016 regime. At one time, the LEL was statutorily required to be set always within £1 per week of the full basic state pension, but that link was broken when the government introduced the 'triple lock' indexation mechanism for the basic pension (ie, guaranteeing a minimum 2½% annual increase even if inflation of prices and wages is lower), because indexation of the LEL above the rate of earnings inflation could have been seriously detrimental to the NI Fund's income over a period of years. The basic pension for 2015–16 was set at £115.95 pw, compared with the LEL of £112 pw. The former similar direct link whereby the employee upper earnings limit was a multiple of the LEL also no longer exists: the UEL is now capped by reference to the higher rate income tax threshold [*NICRCA 2015, s 3*] and is likely to remain linked for the foreseeable future. Any change to the pre-2016 pension rate and thus to the LEL became largely meaningless in NIC terms when contribution liabilities ceased to arise until the earnings exceeded the employee and employer thresholds. There is now an even more important disconnect: under the post-2016 state pension scheme, entitlement is earned by having Class 1 earnings at the LEL for the year, but the value of the weekly single-tier pension earned now bears no relation whatsoever to the weekly LEL, and the UEL is wholly irrelevant, with the transition of Class 1 NICs from social insurance premium to earned income tax. The only time the LEL comes into play is where a qualifying year comprises earnings subject to NIC of at least *n* times the LEL (see **13.6** and **13.7** for the possible values of *n*), or where earners claiming SSP, SMP, etc need to have earned at the LEL for a certain number of weeks in order to qualify for the statutory payment.

Class 1 contributions

Earnings limits

[53.2] See **33.3** EARNINGS LIMITS AND THRESHOLDS for the factors affecting the level at which these limits may be set and **33.4** EARNINGS LIMITS AND THRESHOLDS for the formulae whereby earnings limits for periods of other than one week are to be calculated.

Earnings limits (see below for Earnings Thresholds)

Tax year	*Weekly*	*Monthly*	*Annual*
	£	£	£
Lower earnings limits			
2018–19	116.00	503.00	6,032.00
2017–18	113.00	490.00	5,876.00
2016–17	112.00	486.00	5,824.00
2015–16	112.00	486.00	5,824.00
2014–15	111.00	481.00	5,772.00
2013–14	109.00	473.00	5,668.00
2012–13	107.00	464.00	5,564.00
2011–12	102.00	442.00	5,304.00
2010–11	97.00	421.00	5,044.00
2009–10	95.00	412.00	4,940.00

Upper earnings limits

Tax year	*Weekly*	*Monthly*	*Annual*
	£	£	£
2018–19	892.00	3,863.00	46,350.00
2017–18	866.00	3,750.00	45,000.00
2016–17	827.00	3,583.00	43,000.00
2015–16	815.00	3,532.00	42,385.00
2014–15	805.00	3,489.00	41,865.00
2013–14	797.00	3,454.00	41,450.00
2012–13	817.00	3,540.00	42,475.00
2011–12	817.00	3,540.00	42,475.00
2010–11	844.00	3,656.00	43,875.00
2009–10	844.00	3,656.00	43,875.00

Upper secondary threshold for 0% rate for under-21s and under-25 apprentices

Tax year	*Weekly*	*Monthly*	*Annual*
	£	£	£
2018–19	892.00	3,863.00	46,350.00
2017–18	866.00	3,750.00	45,000.00
2016–17	827.00	3,583.00	43,000.00
2015–16 (under-21s only)	815.00	3,532.00	42,385.00

Earnings thresholds

[53.3] The following tables set out employee's and employer's earnings thresholds:

Employee's (Primary) Earnings Threshold

Tax year	*Weekly* £	*Monthly* £	*Annual* £
2018–19	162.00	702.00	8,424.00
2017–18	157.00	680.00	8,164.00
2016–17	155.00	672.00	8,060.00
2015–16	155.00	672.00	8,060.00
2014–15	153.00	663.00	7,956.00
2013–14	149.00	646.00	7,755.00
2012–13	146.00	634.00	7,605.00
2011–12	139.00	602.00	7,225.00
2010–11	110.00	476.00	5,715.00
2009–10	110.00	476.00	5,715.00

Employer's (Secondary) Earnings Threshold

Tax Year	*Weekly* £	*Monthly* £	*Annual* £
2018–19	162.00	702.00	8,424.00
2017–18	157.00	680.00	8,164.00
2016–17	156.00	676.00	8,112.00
2015–16	156.00	676.00	8,112.00
2014–15	153.00	663.00	7,956.00
2013–14	148.00	641.00	7,696.00
2012–13	144.00	624.00	7,488.00
2011–12	136.00	589.00	7,072.00
2010–11	110.00	476.00	5,715.00
2009–10	110.00	476.00	5,715.00

Upper accrual point

[53.4] The upper accrual point applied from 6 April 2009 to 5 April 2016 and remained (as designed from the outset) fixed at its introductory level of £770 per week, £3,337 per calendar month and £40,040 per annum. The contracted-out rebate applied only up to this amount; from April 2009 full rate contributions were due from this amount up to the Upper Earnings Limit with the additional rate applying only above the Upper Earnings Limit. From April 2012 the UAP was relevant only to members of contracted-out salary-related pension schemes.

[*SSCBA 1992, s 122(1)*, inserted by *National Insurance Contributions Act 2008, s 3; Social Security (Contributions) Regulations 2001, SI 2001/1004, Reg 11(1A)* as inserted by *Social Security (Contributions) (Amendment) Regulations 2009, SI 2009/111, Reg 3(3)*; repealed by *Pensions Act 2014, s 24, Sch 13, para 29* and *Social Security (Contributions) (Amendment) (No 2) Regulations 2016, SI 2016/352, Reg 10(b)*].

Earnings brackets before 5.4.99

[53.5] From 1992 to 1999, Class 1 secondary contributions were calculated at different rates dependent on the earnings bracket into which the period's earnings fell. Earnings brackets were intended to lighten the burden of employer NICs in respect of low earners, but were complex to administer and they were abolished in April 1999, to be replaced by a single employer rate. See earlier editions of this work for details if necessary.

Class 1 contribution rates after 6.4.99

[53.6] The table below sets out the contribution rates for normal employed earners and their secondary contributors which apply to all earnings from the appropriate Earnings Threshold.

Employees pay primary contributions at the standard rate (SR) and, above the UEL, the additional rate (AR). A small number of married women and widows who made an election before 11 May 1977 and are still below state pension age pay a married women's reduced rate (MWRR). Employers have only one standard rate since the abolition of contracting out, plus a nil% rate for certain young earners. Where earners were in contracted-out employment before 6 April 2016, either contracted-out salary related (COSR) or (before 6 April 2012) contracted-out money purchase (COMP), a rebated rate of contributions was payable as shown in the table and further explained below.

The rates as stated are reduced in the case of certain MARINERS (see **45.11** to **45.13**). From 6 April 2015, the employer's secondary rate was reduced to nil% for employees aged under 21 on the date of payment of the earnings, and the same treatment was extended to the employers of qualifying apprentices under the age of 25 with effect from 6 April 2016.

Where an employee was in contracted-out employment before 6 April 2016, primary contributions were payable at the 'rebated' contracted-out rate on earnings from the Employee's Primary Threshold (PT) up to the Upper Accrual Point (UAP). Before 6 April 2009, the rebate applied on earnings up to the Upper Earnings Limit (UEL). Since 6 April 2003, the additional rate (AR) has been payable on the excess of earnings over the UEL. Earnings between the UAP and the UEL (in the period 6 April 2009 to 5 April 2016) were subject to the standard main rate of primary contributions.

Secondary contributions were payable at the rebated contracted-out rate on earnings between the Employer's Secondary Threshold (ST) and the UAP (the UEL prior to 6 April 2009) and at the not contracted-out rate on any balance of earnings above those amounts. The rebate for COSR and COMP schemes was the same for employees but differed for employers, as shown below.

In addition, a rebate of contributions applied in respect of the slice of earnings from the Lower Earnings Limit (LEL) to the PT (from 6 April 2000) and ST (from 6 April 1999), at the appropriate rate. The primary rebate was treated as set out in **23.5** CONTRACTED-OUT EMPLOYMENT.

Under the NICA 2014 and NICA 2015 rules for age-related secondary contributions (for under-21s and under-25 apprentices respectively), the employer benefits from a nil% rate in respect of earnings from the secondary threshold up to the Upper Secondary Threshold (UST) and Apprentice Upper Secondary Threshold (AUST), both set initially at the same level as the UEL. Where the under-21 employee was a member of a COSR pension scheme during 2015–16, the employer had no liability for secondary contributions but was still entitled to reclaim the contracting out secondary rebate of 3.4% on earnings from the LEL to the UAP (see Table I in booklet CA39 (2015)). This anomaly does not arise with under-25 apprentices, as their nil% rate was introduced at the same time as contracting out was abolished.

From 6 April 2001 up to and including 5 April 2011, the PT and ST were the same. They then diverged but were re-harmonised from 6 April 2014, only to diverge again from 6 April 2015. From 6 April 2017 following a recommendation from the OTS, the thresholds were again aligned. [OTS: 'The closer alignment of income tax and national insurance', March 2016, page 51.]

Where a married woman or widow has a valid reduced rate election in force, her primary contributions are payable at the reduced rate on earnings between the PT and UEL and, from 6 April 2003, the additional rate is payable on the excess above the UEL. The primary rate was not reduced further by a contracting out rebate before the abolition of contracting out. The secondary contributions are calculated as set out above, whether not contracted-out or, before 6 April 2016, contracted-out.

Secondary contributions only are payable in respect of earnings paid to an earner over pensionable age and neither primary nor secondary contributions are payable in respect of earnings paid to an earner who is under the age of 16 (see **3.1** and **3.7** AGE EXCEPTION).

	Primary				*Secondary*		
	MWRR	*SR*	*AR above UEL*	*COR up to UAP*	*SR*	*COSR up to UAP*	*COMP*
	%	%	%	%	%	%	%
2018–19	5.85	12.0	2.0	n/a	13.8	n/a	–
2018–19 U-21 & U-25A	n/a	12.0	2.0	n/a	0 †	n/a	–
2017–18	5.85	12.0	2.0	n/a	13.8	n/a	–
2017–18 U-21 & U-25A	n/a	12.0	2.0	n/a	0 †	n/a	–
2016–17	5.85	12.0	2.0	n/a	13.8	n/a	–
2016–17 U-21 & U-25A	n/a	12.0	2.0	n/a	0 †	n/a	–
2015–16	5.85	12.0	2.0	10.6	13.8	10.4	–
2015–16 U-21	n/a	12.0	2.0	10.6	0 †	–3.4	–
2014–15	5.85	12.0	2.0	10.6	13.8	10.4	–
2013–14	5.85	12.0	2.0	10.6	13.8	10.4	–
2012–13	5.85	12.0	2.0	10.6	13.8	10.4	–
2011–12	5.85	12.0	2.0	10.4	13.8	10.1	12.4
2010–11	4.85	11.0	1.0	9.4	12.8	9.1	11.4
2009–10	4.85	11.0	1.0	9.4	12.8	9.1	11.4

† *0% up to UST or AUST, 13.8% on excess over UST or AUST.*

Note that a U-21 apprentice is subject to the apprentice rate in priority to the U-21 rate, which may differ in future.

	Primary rebate on LEL to ET (COSR. COMP same before 6.4.2012)	*Secondary rebate on LEL to ET*	
		COSR	*COMP*
2016–17	n/a	n/a	n/a
2015–16	(1.40)	(3.4)	–
2014–15	(1.40)	(3.4)	–
2013–14	(1.40)	(3.4)	–
2012–13	(1.40)	(3.4)	–
2011–12	(1.60)	(3.7)	(1.4)
2010–11	(1.60)	(3.7)	(1.4)
2009–10	(1.60)	(3.7)	(1.4)

Class 1 contribution rates from 6.4.92 to 5.4.99

[53.7] For contribution rates during the years when earnings brackets were used to determine the level of liability for employers, please refer to earlier editions of this work.

Class 1A contribution rates

[53.8] The Class 1A contribution rate is the standard secondary Class 1 rate (the Class 1 rate appropriate for the highest secondary earnings bracket until 5 April 1999) for the tax year in which the benefits (car and fuel only until 6 April 2000) were provided, with *no* reduction where the employment was contracted-out or where the employee is under 21 or an apprentice under 25.

2018–19	13.8
2017–18	13.8
2016–17	13.8
2015–16	13.8
2014–15	13.8
2013–14	13.8
2012–13	13.8
2011–12	13.8
2010–11	12.8
2009–10	12.8

[*SSCBA 1992, s 10(5)*].

Class 1B contribution rates

[53.9] The Class 1B contribution rate is the standard secondary Class 1 rate (the Class 1 rate appropriate for the highest secondary earnings bracket until 5 April 1999) for the tax year in which the benefits (car and fuel only until 6 April 2000) were provided, with *no* reduction where the employment was contracted-out or where the employee is under 21 or an apprentice under 25.

	%
2018–19	13.8
2017–18	13.8
2016–17	13.8
2015–16	13.8
2014–15	13.8
2013–14	13.8
2012–13	13.8
2011–12	13.8
2010–11	12.8
2009–10	12.8

[*SSCBA 1992, s 10A(6)* as inserted by *SSA 1998, s 53* and amended by *Welfare Reform and Pensions Act 1999, s 77*].

Class 2 rates and small profits threshold/small earnings exception limits

[53.10] See **56.4** SHARE FISHERMEN for reason for increased contribution rate, **59.3** VOLUNTEER DEVELOPMENT WORKERS for reason for reduced contribution rate, and **18.4** CLASS 2 CONTRIBUTIONS for circumstances in which exception on the grounds of small earnings could be claimed for years up to 5 April 2015.

Tax year	*Normal weekly rate*	*Share fisherman's special rate*	*Volunteer development worker's special rate*	*Small profits threshold/small earnings exception limit*
	£	£	£	£
2018–19	2.95	3.60	5.80	6,205 SPT
2017–18	2.85	3.50	5.65	6,025 SPT
2016–17	2.80	3.45	5.60	5,965 SPT
2015–16	2.80	3.45	5.60	5,965 SPT
2014–15	2.75	3.40	5.55	5,885 SEE
2013–14	2.70	3.35	5.45	5,725 SEE
2012–13	2.65	3.30	5.35	5,595 SEE
2011–12	2.50	3.15	5.10	5,315 SEE
2010–11	2.40	3.05	4.85	5,075 SEE
2009–10	2.40	3.05	4.75	5,075 SEE

[*SSCBA 1992, ss 11(1), 11(4), Social Security (Contributions) Regulations 2001, SI 2001/1004, Regs 125(c), 152(b)*].

Voluntary contribution rates

[53.11] Class 3 contribution rates are as follows.

Tax year	*Weekly rate (£)*
2018–19	14.65
2017–18	14.25
2016–17	14.10
2015–16	14.10
2014–15	13.90
2013–14	13.55
2012–13	13.25
2011–12	12.60
2010–11	12.05
2009–10	12.05
2008–09	8.10
2007–08	7.80
2006–07	7.55

[*SSCBA 1992, s 13*].

Class 3A contribution rates

[53.12] Class 3A contribution rates vary according to the age of the state pensioner at the date of payment between 12 October 2015 and 5 April 2017. A single payment buys an extra 'unit' of pension, adding £1 per week to the contributor's state pension, and rates per unit are as follows. A maximum of 25 units may be purchased in total, but it is not necessary for all units to be bought in a single transaction.

Age at contribution date	Amount (£) for each additional pension unit of £1 per week
62 (women only)	956
63 (women only)	934
64 (women only)	913
65	890
66	871
67	847
68	827
69	801
70	779
71	761

72	738
73	719
74	694
75	674
76	646
77	625
78	596
79	574
80	544
81	514
82	484
83	454
84	424
85	394
86	366
87	339
88	314
89	291
90	270
91	251
92	232
93	216
94	200
95	185
96	172
97	159
98	148
99	137
100	127

Class 4 contribution rates and annual profit limits

[53.13] Class 4 rates and profits limits are as follows.

Tax year	*Rate (Lower limit to upper limit)*	*Rate (on profits above upper limit)*	*Lower limit*	*Upper limit*
	%	%	£	£
2018–19	9.00	2.00	8,424	46,350
2017–18	9.00	2.00	8,164	45,000
2016–17	9.00	2.00	8,060	43,000
2015–16	9.00	2.00	8,060	42,385
2014–15	9.00	2.00	7,956	41,865
2013–14	9.00	2.00	7,755	41,450
2012–13	9.00	2.00	7,605	42,475
2011–12	9.00	2.00	7,225	42,475

Tax year	*Rate (Lower limit to upper limit)*	*Rate (on profits above upper limit)*	*Lower limit*	*Upper limit*
2010–11	8.00	1.00	5,715	43,875
2009–10	8.00	1.00	5,715	43,875

[*SSCBA 1992, s 15(3), s 15(3ZA)*].

Annual maxima

Overall annual maximum

[53.14] Subject to what is said at 7.1 ANNUAL MAXIMUM, no individual earner is required to pay total contributions at standard rates (of Class 1) in excess of the figures stated below (in not contracted-out values for years before 6 April 2016) (see 7.4 ANNUAL MAXIMUM).

The figures stated are to be used with great caution, however, as adjustment is necessary to take into account Class 1 liability at the additional rate of 1% or 2% on earnings above the UEL.

Tax year	*Maximum contributions payable at the main 12% rate* £
2018–19	4,642.80
2017–18	4,509.24
2016–17	4,273.92
2015–16	4,197.60
2013–14	4,121.28
2012–13	4,267.56
2011–12	4,312.08
2010–11	4,279.22
2009–10	4,279.22

Class 4 limiting maximum

[53.15] If an individual's Class 1 contributions at the main rate and Class 2 contributions in a tax year total less than the figure stated below, any Class 4 liability which would arise at the main rate is to be limited to the difference between the Class 1 (main rate) and Class 2 contributions paid and the figure stated below (see 7.5 ANNUAL MAXIMUM).

The figures stated are to be used with great caution, however, as adjustment is also necessary to take into account Class 1 and Class 4 liability at 1% or 2% on earnings above the UEL/upper profits limit (see 7.5 ANNUAL MAXIMUM).

Tax year	*Maximum payable at main rates*
	£
2018–19	3,413.34
2017–18	3,315.24
2016–17	3,144.60
2015–16	3,089.25
2013–14	3,175.65
2012–13	3,278.75
2011–12	3,305.00
2010–11	3,180.00
2009–10	3,180.00

Interest

[53.16] Interest became due on overdue contributions (except Class 2 and Class 3) from 19 April 1993. Interest on overpayments of secondary Class 1 contributions arises from the same date but on repayments of Class 4 contributions only from 6 April 1995. See www.hmrc.gov.uk/rates/interest.htm

From	*Overdue contributions*	*Overpaid contributions*
	%	%
21 November 2017	3.00	0.50
23 August 2016	2.75	0.50
29 September 2009	3.0	0.50
24 March 2009	2.5	Zero
27 January 2009	3.5	Zero
6 January 2009	4.5	0.75
6 December 2008	5.5	1.50
6 November 2008	6.5	2.25
6 January 2008	7.5	3.00

State Second Pension accrual thresholds

[53.17] Set out below, for information purposes, are the low earnings thresholds for additional state pension from 6 April 2002 to 5 April 2016, which accrued S2P entitlement at the highest rate (the flat rate since April 2012), together with the upper limit of the second tier of earnings, the top of the band on which S2P accrued at only 10% (see **13.11**). These figures were quite distinct from the 'Earnings Threshold' for contributions purposes and had no application to the calculation, or recording by employers, of NICs. As S2P was replaced by the single-tier state pension from 6 April 2016, there is no equivalent for later years.

Tax year	*Low earnings threshold / Tier 1 limit (£)*	*Tier 2 limit (£)*
2015–16	15,300	40,040

Tax year	*Low earnings threshold / Tier 1 limit (£)*	*Tier 2 limit (£)*
2014–15	15,100	40,040
2013–14	15,001	40,040
2012–13	14,700	33,000
2011–12	14,400	32,600
2010–11	14,100	32,200
2009–10	13,900	31,800
2008–09	13,500	31,100
2007–08	13,000	30,000
2006–07	12,500	28,000
2005–06	12,100	27,800
2004–05	11,600	26,600
2003–04	11,200	25,600
2002–03	10,800	24,600

54

Reduced Liability Elections

Cross-references. See CLASS 1 CONTRIBUTIONS 15; CLASS 2 CONTRIBUTIONS 18; CREDITS 24; HUSBAND AND WIFE, AND CIVIL PARTNERS 39; 53.7 RATES AND LIMITS.

Other Sources. Tolley's Payroll Handbook; Tolley's Practical NIC Newsletter, June 2002, page 46; Leaflet CWG2 (2017) and HM Revenue and Customs National Insurance Manual NIM30001–NIM30028.

Introduction to reduced liability elections

[54.1] The position of a married woman or widow under contribution law is now, in general, no different from that of any other person but, until 11 May 1977 (and for a transitional period thereafter in the case of certain widows and married women within a year of retirement age), a married woman or widow had the right to elect not to participate in the contribution scheme and a relatively small number of such elections continue in force at the present day. In effect, the woman elected to pay a reduced rate of Class 1 contribution and to forfeit any right to state benefit based on her own contributions, relying instead on derived rights and a 60% uplift to her husband's pension instead (or inheriting her husband's pension if he was deceased when she reached state pension age). See HM Revenue and Customs National Insurance Manual NIM30019 onwards. [*Social Security (Contributions) Regulations 2001, SI 2001/1004, Regs 127, 138 and 139.*]

The women to whom the making of such an election was open were those who, on 10 April 1977, were married or were widowed and entitled to either widow's benefits under the State scheme or industrial or war widow's pensions at a rate equivalent to or greater than the standard rate of basic (ie, pre-2016) widow's pension (£119.30 per week from April 2016 for those who reached state pension age before 6 April 2016). [*Social Security (Contributions) Regulations 2001, SI 2001/1004, Reg 127.*]

At its peak, an election was in force for between three million to four million women (Pensions Bill Debates, 2 July 2013, c 191), but the number of valid elections in place is understood to have been something less than 13,000 by

2010–11 according to government guidance on the planned single-tier state pension to be introduced in April 2016. Parliamentary briefing note SN 6525 updated in the House of Commons library in March 2015 put the number at around 10,000 and falling, although HMRC had refused to supply the information in response to a Freedom of Information Act request (Ref No 2600/09) made in 2009 because the exercise would have been too costly. The Pensions Minister, Steve Webb, stated during the same debate on the single-tier pension proposals that some 80,000 women would reach state pension age under the new post-2016 regime having paid the 'married woman's stamp' at some point in their past, although some '60,000-odd' were not at risk of losing any pension because of that fact. The rest would need special protection, having expected for many years that their husbands' contributions would provide for them, which is otherwise not the case under the post-2016 scheme.

Certificates of election

[54.2] Before 6 April 1975, when the 'stamp' was flat-rate and state pensions were not generally earnings-related (except for a small amount of graduated retirement benefit), employed married women had to pay a 'stamp', but self-employed married women were exempt, with the option to pay a full 'stamp'. Whilst an election of the kind described at **54.1** above for married women in employment to opt out had to be made in writing to the Secretary of State for Social Security on a form CF9 supported by a marriage certificate and other relevant documentation, in the case of a woman who, before 6 April 1975 was married and *self*-employed but who had *not* elected to pay Class 2 contributions, a reduced rate election was deemed to have been made on 6 April 1975. This deemed election will have continued in force until a terminating event occurred, see **54.8** below. [*Social Security (Contributions) Regulations 2001, SI 2001/1004, Regs 135, 136, 137*]. Where a married woman was employed before 6 April 1975 and had elected to *not* pay the flat-rate Class 1 contributions due up to that point, she was also deemed to have made a reduced rate election at a later date. [*National Insurance Act 1965, s 10(1), National Insurance (Married Women) Regs 1973, Reg 3(1)(a), Social Security (Contributions) Regulations 2001, SI 2001/1004, Reg 127, Reg 135*].

If a married woman was employed by her husband before 1975, that employment was disregarded *unless* the employment was in a trade or business in which she was ordinarily engaged for 24 hours or more in a contribution week. Where she was so engaged, she was, under *National Insurance Act 1965, s 1(3)* and *National Insurance (Classification) Regs 1972, Sch 1 Part II para 17* treated as *self-employed* provided her weekly earnings from the activity were ordinarily £4 or more [*National Insurance (Classification) Regs 1972, Sch 1 Part II para 22*] (increased to £8 from August 1974). A woman deemed to be self-employed in this way would have been deemed to have made a reduced rate election on 6 April 1975 if she had not elected to pay Class 2 contributions. See HM Revenue and Customs National Insurance Manual NIM30019 to 30028.

Earlier elections made under *Contributions Regs 1975, Reg 91, Reg 94* and in force at 6 April 1977, or under *Married Women Regs 1973, Regs 2(1)(a), 3(1)(a)* or *Contributions Regs 1969, Reg 9(3)(4A)* and in force at 6 April 1975, were continued under new regulations. [*Social Security (Contributions) Regulations 2001, SI 2001/1004, Reg 129, Reg 135*].

There are still a very small number of women who were either employed by their husband or self-employed before 6 April 1975 and, because their circumstances have not changed or changed little since then, do not actually possess a certificate of reduced liability. *Social Security (Contributions) Regulations 2001, SI 2001/1004, Reg 135*, a regulation giving transitional relief, provides that they are entitled to one (unless they have subsequently ceased to qualify to continue to pay the reduced rate (see **54.8** below)). This transitional provision is not widely known by NIC&EO and other HM Revenue and Customs staff, and individuals may be able to readily fend off an approach for arrears if their circumstances enable them to send the following letter:

National Insurance Contributions Office

. . . .

. . . .

Dear Sirs,

Either I have remained in continuous self-employment since before 6 April 1975.

Or I was employed by my husband until 5 April 1975 (and therefore not allowed to pay contributions) and have been continuously self-employed since 6 April 1975.

I am therefore covered by the transitional regulation 135 of the Social Security (Contributions) Regulations 2001 and request that you now issue me with a 'Certificate of Election' (CA4139).

Yours faithfully,

. . . .

Note to the letter

Limited gaps after 6 April 1978 and/or a cessation of self-employment replaced by employment with earnings at or above the LEL may also result in an individual retaining entitlement (see below). In suitable cases, the first sentence in the above letter should be adapted accordingly.

An election, latterly, has resulted in the issue of a certificate of election, CA4139. If its holder is an employed earner, it has to be handed to the secondary contributor in relation to her employment as authority for primary Class 1 contributions to be paid in respect of her earnings at a reduced rate (see **54.8** below). (The rate of secondary contributions is unaffected.) Where a woman has more than one employed earner's employment, certificates are required for each. [*Social Security (Contributions) Regulations 2001, SI 2001/1004, Reg 133(1)(3)(6)*].

Validity of elections

[54.3] Where a reduced rate election was renewed after 5 April 1987 a new form of certificate was issued but an unexpired old-type certificate, CF383, remains valid until replaced. The validity of a new or old type of certificate CF383 may be checked by reference to the contents of boxes A and B thereon. Earlier evidence of a reduced rate election consisted of either a certificate CF380, a tear-off form CF2AR(TO) from a 1974–75 special national insurance card or a CF380A (printed in green). The first two of these should have been exchanged for current certificates by 5 April 1980 and are *no longer valid*. They must not, therefore, be accepted as proof that an election is currently in force. The CF380A remains valid only if the holder has continued in the employment of the employer by whom she was employed on 5 April 1980 at a level of earnings equal to or exceeding the lower earnings limit (see EARNINGS LIMITS AND THRESHOLDS 33). (Leaflet CWG2 (2017) para 3.7.1.)

Secondary contributor liability

[54.4] The person who is the secondary contributor in relation to earnings paid to a woman is responsible for any underpayment of contributions which arises as a result of giving effect to an invalid reduced rate election certificate. In practice, HM Revenue and Customs will hold a secondary contributor responsible if a properly organised payroll system *would* have alerted the secondary contributor to the fact that a woman's election must have been brought to an end, eg where a woman has reverted to using her maiden name or has told a member of the personnel department that she has become divorced. (Leaflet CWG2 (2017), para 3.7.3). This is clearly of concern to an employer when a married woman gets divorced and omits to tell him; the consequence of this is that a considerable amount of contributions can go unpaid and it is the current practice to demand the underpaid contributions from the employer. If the employer refuses to pay because he or she was not aware that the employee was divorcing then the NIC&EO will usually come to some mediated agreement with both the parties to resolve the situation. (CA Specialist Conference 11 October 1994). As the idea of the divorce courts being required to notify the authorities direct has been discounted in the past, the onus is probably on the employer to educate his or her employees as to the importance of an early disclosure of a change of their personal circumstances. Some employers require an annual declaration to be signed by any woman who claims to hold a reduced rate election to the effect that it is still valid and that she has not divorced during the year.

Return of certificates

[54.5] Each certificate remains the property of HM Revenue and Customs and, if it ceases to be of effect, the woman is to notify the secondary contributor, retrieve the certificate from him and return it to HM Revenue and Customs, which in practice means the NIC&EO Individuals Group. [*Social Security (Contributions) Regulations 2001, SI 2001/1004, Reg 133(1)(c),(4)*].

The secondary contributor should return a woman's certificate to her if:

- the woman leaves his employment, or
- the woman tells him that her marriage has ended in divorce or annulment, or
- the woman reaches state pension age (see 3.7), or
- the expiry date shown on the certificate has passed, or
- the woman has not been liable to pay contributions (including deemed contributions on earnings between the LEL and the employee's earnings threshold from 6 April 2000) for two consecutive tax years because her earnings have not, during that time, reached or exceeded the lower earnings limit, or
- the woman has changed her name, or
- she remarries, or
- she asks for it back (in which case, standard rate contributions must be deducted from any subsequent payment of earnings).

If the certificate cannot be returned to a person who has left, it should be sent with a note of explanation to HM Revenue and Customs NIC&EO, Individuals Group, Lindisfarne House, Longbenton, Newcastle upon Tyne NE98 1ZZ.

(Leaflet CWG2 (2016), para 82).

Example

Sickly Ltd has a number of married women and widows on its payroll and holds apparently valid forms CF383 and CA4139. Sickly Ltd notes that such employees must have their reduced rate certificate returned under the circumstances above.

However, Sickly Ltd was not aware until now that it will be liable for any NICs underpaid where an employee is paying reduced rate contributions unless the employee was at fault or that the underpayment was not due to negligence on Sickly's behalf, and this includes having inadequate arrangements in place for the employee to say that they are no longer entitled to pay NICs at the reduced rate. Sickly Ltd therefore immediately issues the following letter to the relevant female employees:

To:. . . . .
From: Sickly Ltd, Payroll Department
Dated:
Dear . . . .

Married women's and widow's reduced rate elections

Your reduced rate election certificate to pay lower national insurance contributions was lodged with this department on . . . . [Date] . . . .

As you may be aware you are required by law to tell us if you are no longer entitled to pay National Insurance contributions at the reduced rate and return the certificate, which we currently hold, to the National Insurance Contributions & Employer Office.

There are a number of reasons why a reduced rate certificate may no longer be valid and these include

(a) divorce or annulment of your marriage
(b) you becoming widowed but not being entitled to Widow's Benefit after an initial period
(c) you losing your right to Bereavement Benefit for a reason other than marriage

> If any of the above applies in your case will you sign Part A of the slip below stating the reason and return it to the Payroll Department immediately. If none of the above applies please sign Part B stating that this is the case and then return Part B immediately to the Payroll Department. All the information you supply on this form is confidential and protected under the Data Protection Act 1998.

Despite all that is said above, certain employers of Crown servants, such as the civil service and HM Forces, do not actually have to hold certificates of election for married women employees who, since before 6 April 1975, have had a reduced rate election and also been continuously employed by the same employer. (HM Revenue and Customs National Insurance Manual NIM30016.) Such circumstances will now be extremely rare.

Effect of an election

[54.6] Where a woman has made such an election as is described at **54.1** above and that election is currently in force:

- any main primary Class 1 contributions payable in respect of earnings paid to her or for her benefit that fall between the primary earnings threshold and the upper earnings limit are to be at a reduced rate which was the same (5.85% from 6 April 2011, 4.85% from 6 April 2003 and 3.85% previously) whether or not the employment was contracted-out;
- she is to be under *no* liability to pay any Class 2 contribution;
- she is to be precluded from paying Class 3 contributions for any year in respect of the whole of which the election has effect;
- she is not to be entitled to credited contributions (see CREDITS **24**);
- she was not entitled to home responsibility protection prior to 6 April 2010 in relation to retirement pension for any year in respect of which the election has effect (home responsibility protection ceased after 5 April 2010 – see **24.24**);
- she is to derive no earnings factor (see EARNINGS FACTORS **28**) from any contributions paid at a reduced rate (ie, she accrues no benefit entitlements).

[*SSPA 1975, s 27(5); Social Security (Contributions) Regulations 2001, SI 2001/1004, Reg 127(3), 131, 132 as amended by Social Security (Contributions) (Amendment No 2) Regulations 2003, SI 2003/964, Regs 5, 6; Home Responsibilities Regs 1978, Reg 2(4)(a); SSCBA 1992, s 22(4).*]

The 5.85% rate is reflected in separate ready-reckoner contribution tables. Whereas standard rate contributions are paid under Table A, the contributions for a woman with a reduced rate election are set out in Table B. In 2015–16 and earlier years, rebated contributions payable by members of COSR pension schemes would have been under Table D, while those for married women would have been under Table E. The primary contributions under Table E would have been the same as in Table B, but the secondary contributions would have attracted the contracting-out rebate.

Liability for Class 1 contributions at the additional rate from 6 April 2003 (currently 2%), Class 1 secondary contributions for the employer, and Class 4 contributions are entirely unaffected by such an election. Further, such women are capable of receiving Statutory Sick Pay, Statutory Maternity Pay, Statutory Adoption Pay and, in the appropriate circumstances, Statutory Shared Parental Pay if all the other qualifying conditions are met.

In a reported case, a woman (W) began paying Class 1 NICs in 1960. She married in 1965 and stopped paying Class 1 in 1968, when the then DHSS received an election, purporting to be from her, to pay the reduced rate of contributions applicable to married women. In 2005 W claimed that she should have been credited with payment of Class 1 NICs for 1968–69 to 2004–05. HMRC rejected her claim and she appealed to the Special Commissioners. The Commissioner dismissed her appeal, finding that in July 1968 W had 'made a married woman's election not to pay Class 1 National Insurance Contributions'. (*Whittaker v HMRC* [2006] STC SCD 271 Sp C 528. See also *Morgan v HMRC* [2009] STC SCD 93 Sp C 722.)

The Commissioners and Tribunals have generally accepted the accuracy of the information held on the Newcastle records system and there has been a series of decisions where it was accepted that the relevant elections not to pay full rate NIC had been made. In the case of *Franks v HMRC* [2012] UKFTT 438 (TC) HMRC contended that Mrs Franks made elections on 13 May 1970 and 6 April 1977. There was no valid reason for an election being made in May 1970 as Mrs Franks was then at home looking after a child and had no intention of working. The Tribunal accepted she did not make this election and that the HMRC records were incorrect. The Tribunal did consider, however, that Mrs Franks made the latter of the two elections. Whether this decision, which casts some doubt on the accuracy of the HMRC records, will allow future appeals to succeed remains to be seen.

Revocation of election

[54.7] An election may, by notice in writing on Form CF9 (or CF9A if a widow), be *revoked* by the woman who made it and any such revocation may be cancelled by notice in writing to HM Revenue and Customs before the date on which the notice of revocation is to have effect. Revocation will take effect from the Sunday following the date of the notice or such later Sunday as may be specified in that notice. A revocation can be cancelled in writing at any time before it is due to come into effect. The form once completed should be sent to HMRC, NIC&EO, Individuals Group, Lindisfarne House, Benton Park View, Newcastle upon Tyne, NE98 1ZZ. [*Social Security (Contributions) Regulations 2001, SI 2001/1004, Regs 127(5)(6), 137.*] See Leaflet CWG2 (2017), para 3.7.2 and HM Revenue and Customs National Insurance Manual NIM 30010.

Cessation of elections

[54.8] An election will continue in force until one or other of the following terminating events occurs.

- The woman ceases to be married other than by reason of her husband dying, eg by divorce or annulment. In the case of divorce, the relevant date will be that of the decree absolute.

- The ending of the tax year in which a woman ceases to be a widow who fulfils the conditions as regards entitlement to bereavement/widow's benefits etc (see **54.1** above), unless she remarries or again becomes a qualifying widow before the end of the tax year concerned. The tax year in question is the one in which the husband died if the death was between 6 April and 30 September. Where the husband died between 1 October and 5 April it is the end of the following tax year.
- The ending of two consecutive tax years which begin on or after 6 April 1978 and in which the woman has no earnings in respect of which any primary Class 1 contributions are payable (or would be payable but for the fact that, from 6 April 2000, they fall between the lower earnings limit and the employee's earnings threshold) and in which she is at no time a self-employed earner. This is known as the two-year test. Earnings from an employed earner's employment during the two years will not prevent the election being terminated if those earnings at no time reach the lower earnings limit. Whilst the certificate may be withdrawn by HM Revenue and Customs when its computer checks show that there are two consecutive blank years, it is almost certain that such action will take place well into the third year. Employers should therefore keep a check on this matter because they will be liable to pay any arrears.
- The ending of the week in which the woman gives notice to HM Revenue and Customs of revocation of her election or, if the woman wishes and so specifies in her notice, the ending of any subsequent week in the same tax year, unless the woman cancels her revocation before such a week ends (see **54.7** above).
- The ending of a tax year in which an erroneous payment on account of primary Class 1 contributions at the contracted-out rate is made by or on behalf of the woman, provided that the woman wishes to pay contributions at the standard rate from the beginning of the next tax year.
- The date (not being earlier than 6 April 1982) on which an erroneous payment (or, if there is more than one such payment, the date on which the first erroneous payment) on account of primary Class 1 contributions at the not contracted-out rate is made by or on behalf of the woman, provided:
  - (a) she wishes to pay contributions at the standard rate from that date; and
  - (b) after 5 April 1983 and on or before 31 December in the next complete calendar year following the end of the tax year in which the erroneous payment was made she notifies HM Revenue and Customs of that wish; and
  - (c) from the time of the erroneous payment to the time she notifies HM Revenue and Customs of that wish, no contributions have been paid by her or on her behalf at the reduced rate and no contributions have been payable by her or on her behalf in respect of any contracted-out employment; and
  - (d) she has not procured a refund in respect of any erroneous payment (see **55.3** REPAYMENT AND RE-ALLOCATION).

In the case of (*a*) above, the election can continue in force for a specified period after the certificate holder becomes a widow. [*Social Security (Contributions) Regulations 2001, SI 2001/1004, Reg 130*].

[*Social Security (Contributions) Regulations 2001, SI 2001/1004, Reg 128(1)(a)–(f), (2)*].

State Pension

[54.9] *Pensions Act 2014*, ss 11–12 and Schs 6–7 make special provision for women who have had a reduced rate election but do not reach state pension age until after 5 April 2016. Under the pre-April 2016 rules, women with an election had chosen to rely on their husband's contribution record, with the expectation of entitlement to a Category B state retirement pension of 60% of the single state pension, giving a maximum joint pension for a married couple of £190.80 per week (ie, the single person's Category A basic pension of £119.30, plus the Category B pension of £71.50).

Under the single-tier state pension from 6 April 2016, each individual reaching state retirement age will receive a pension based on his or her own contribution record, with no inherited or shared entitlements, except for certain women with a long history of reduced rate contributions. *Pensions Act 2014* generally removed the option for the woman to rely on her spouse's or civil partner's record on reaching state pension age on or after 6 April 2016. Had this new rule been applied consistently, married women who had no earnings factor on their record as a result of having made a reduced rate election would have been entitled to no state pension in respect of years before April 2016.

To protect such women, if they had a reduced rate election in force at the start of the final 35 tax years before the tax year in which they reach state pension age, their state pension will be calculated in an alternative way if this is more beneficial than the transitional rate pension to which they would otherwise be entitled. The alternative calculation provides a transitional rate of state pension at least equivalent to the combination of any additional pension based on her own NI record and the equivalent of the old basic pension. This will be either the 60% rate applicable for a spouse payable when both she and her husband have reached pensionable age, or the equivalent of the full basic pension if she is widowed or divorced. As a simplification measure, it was decided that the full standard rate would be used, so the amounts will not be dependent on the spouses' National Insurance record.

It was not possible for a woman with a reduced rate election to cancel her election in 2015–16 and pay full contributions for any period before that tax year with a view to increasing her future single-tier pension entitlement.

Key Points regarding reduced liability elections

[54.10] Points to consider are as follows.

- As no new reduced liability elections have been possible since 1977 there are few 'optants' under state pension age now. Recent HMRC estimates are that there are now fewer than 10,000 and possibly as few as 2,500 actively paying Table B contributions.
- Employers need to have a system in place to remind employees to advise changes in personal circumstances. Otherwise HM Revenue and Customs will look to them alone for the payment of the employee's arrears.
- A holder of a reduced rate election may revoke it at any time with effect from a current or future time, although the change to the state pension regime in 2016 means that any such revocation is too late to make a material difference to the woman's retirement benefits.

55

Repayment and Reallocation

Cross-references. See ANNUAL MAXIMUM 7; MULTIPLE EMPLOYMENTS 47; RATES AND LIMITS 53.

Other Sources. Simon's Taxes, Volume 2, para A8.266 onwards; Tolley's Practical Tax, Vol 8 No 12; HM Revenue and Customs National Insurance Manual NIM37000, NIM37500, NIM38000, NIM38500.

Introduction to repayment and reallocation of NICs

[55.1] The fact that a person has paid contributions which he was not liable to pay does not, of itself, entitle that person to a repayment of the contributions in question. See 55.2 below. Subject to that, Class 1, Class 1A, Class 1B or Class 2 contributions paid in error are to be returned by HM Revenue and Customs to the person or secondary contributor who paid them subject to a number of provisos. See 55.3 below.

Reallocation of contributions

[55.2] Where contributions are paid which are of the wrong class, or at the wrong rate, or of the wrong amount, HM Revenue and Customs is entitled (and may be expected) to treat them as paid on account of contributions properly payable under contribution law. [*SSCBA 1992, Sch 1 para 8(1)(g); Social Security (Contributions) Regulations 2001, SI 2001/1004, Reg 51(1), Reg 101, Reg 109*]. Where Class 1A or Class 1B contributions fall to be repaid, they may be reallocated as a payment on account only of secondary Class 1 or Class 2 contributions properly payable. [*Social Security (Contributions) Regulations 2001, SI 2001/1004, Reg 51(2)*]. Such adjustments will be made before, and are to be reflected in, any calculation relating to a repayment. [*Social Security (Contributions) Regulations 2001, SI 2001/1004, Reg 57(1)(a), Reg 102, Reg 110*].

Repayments

Repayment of contributions paid in error

[55.3] Subject to the rule stated at **55.2** above, Class 1, Class 1A, Class 1B or Class 2 contributions paid in error are to be returned by HM Revenue and Customs to the person or secondary contributor who paid them, provided:

(a) the error was made at the time of payment and related to some then-present or then-past matter; *and*

(b) the amount of the contributions (other than Class 1A or Class 1B contributions) to be returned exceeds one-fifteenth of a standard rate contribution payable on earnings at the Upper Earnings Limit in respect of primary Class 1 contributions prescribed for the last or only tax year in respect of which the contributions were paid, ie £5.84, 2018–19; £5.67, 2017–18; £5.38, 2016–17; £5.28, 2015–16; £5.22, 2014–15; £5.19, 2013–14; £5.37, 2012–13; £5.42, 2011–12; £5.38, 2010–11; and

(c) in the case of Class 1A or Class 1B contributions, the net amount to be returned is more than 50p.

[*SSCBA 1992, Sch 1 para 8(1)(m); Social Security (Contributions) Regulations 2001, SI 2001/1004, Regs 52, 102(1), 110*].

A mistaken belief that income would be treated as arising from self-employment when, in fact, HM Revenue and Customs treated it as arising for tax purposes from employment, in consequence of which Class 2 contributions were paid and no claim for small earnings exception from Class 2 liability was made, was an error within the terms of *Social Security (Contributions) Regulations 2001, SI 2001/1004, Reg 52* and the Class 2 contributions paid were repayable. Payment of Class 2 contributions in circumstances where losses (not quantified until later) from a self-employed activity would, if they had been quantified at the time when Class 2 liability arose, have enabled a claim for small earnings exception to succeed was, however, not an error within the terms of *Reg 52*. (*Morecombe v Secretary of State for Social Services*, The Times, 12 December 1987). The effects of this judgment have now been remedied by regulation as described at **55.10** below.

Contributions paid by a secondary contributor in respect of an earner whom HM Revenue and Customs had already categorised as self-employed would be covered by this regulation, but contributions paid in respect of an earner who was later categorised as self-employed would not.

Repayment of overpaid Class 1A contributions is governed by *Social Security (Contributions) Regulations 2001, SI 2001/1004, Reg 55* (see HM Revenue and Customs National Insurance Manual NIM17080 and **21.43** COLLECTION) and other Classes by *Reg 52*.

Primary contributions paid by a secondary contributor in error will normally be returned to the secondary contributor provided he has not already recovered them from the primary contributor (eg by deduction from earnings paid). Where such contributions have already been recovered from the primary contributor they will be returned to the primary contributor unless he consents in writing to their return to the secondary contributor. [*Social Security (Contributions) Regulations 2001, SI 2001/1004, Reg 52(7)*, as amended by *Social Security (Contributions, Categorisation of Earners and Intermediaries) (Amendment) Regulations 2004, SI 2004/770, Reg 12*]. Although from 8 October 2002, *Social Security (Contributions) (Amendment No 3) Regulations 2002, SI 2002/2366, Reg 8* enables such consent to be given by whatever electronic means the Board may allow, there is still no capability for electronic communication at present.

Accelerated payment notices

[55.4] The introduction of accelerated payment notices by *NICA 2015* added an element of uncertainty to the question of repayment. As outlined above, repayments of contributions may be requested under *Reg 52* where those contributions were paid in error, but *NICA 2015, Sch 2 para 17* deems an accelerated payment to be a payment of the understated contributions, and not a payment on account of those contributions, which is how any accelerated payment would be treated for tax purposes under *FA 2014, s 223(3)*. If it is later determined that no contributions were due because HMRC's interpretation was wrong (ie, it is HMRC that was in error, rather than the contributor), it is difficult to see how the overpayment could legally be repaid, as the provisions of *para 17* mean that there will have been no error made at the time of payment, so *Reg 52* can be of no application.

HMRC believes that it does indeed have the power (and the obligation) to return contributions paid under an APN that are subsequently found not to have been due. In correspondence with the CIOT about the possible need for explicit refund provisions in the NIC Bill in September 2014, it provided the following explanation:

> 'Our view is that where
>
> - liability to pay NICs is finally and conclusively determined in a particular appeal,
> - a ruling will be relevant in determining other appeals,
>
> then HMRC does not have to rely on *regulation 52* of the *Social Security (Contributions) Regulations 2001* ("the Contributions Regulations") in order to repay NICs.
>
> In the circumstances, authority for the repayment comes from the binding nature of the final determination, as between the parties, and also *regulations 10 to 12* of the *Social Security Contributions (Decisions and Appeals) Regulations 1999 (SI 1999 No 1027)*, which make provision in respect of appeals including
>
> - the effect of the tribunal determination on the decision under appeal,
> - the settling the appeal before it has been determined by the tribunal,
> - paying or repaying contributions in line with determinations (even if there is a further appeal).
>
> The accelerated payment provisions in the *Finance Act 2014* ("FA 2014") do not make any express provision for the repayment of tax when the underlying liability dispute is determined in the taxpayer's favour. The provisions do not interfere with the general binding nature of the courts' decisions and the existing administrative provisions that apply to final determinations or settled appeals. The amendments

made to *section 56* of the *Taxes Management Act 1970* by [*FA 2014*] *section 225* affect the payment or repayment of NICs during the course of the litigation but not the obligation to repay NICs that are overpaid as a result of the final determination.

Nothing in FA 2014 or the NICs Bill alters HMRC's obligation to repay tax and NICs which have been found on the final determination to have been overpaid. Neither do they restrict the ability of HMRC to settle an appeal before it is determined by the tribunal, in light of a ruling on a point of law in a related appeal, or to repay NICs as if the matter had been determined by the tribunal.

Outside of an open appeal situation, where HMRC

- is engaged in a relevant NICs dispute, see *paragraphs 5 to 8 of Schedule 2 to the NICs Bill*, and
- concedes that liability is not in dispute

then HMRC would not have the authority to hold onto the accelerated NICs. In the circumstances, the principles of public law would require HMRC to repay the NICs collected in advance of the resolution of the dispute.

We do not think that express provision in the *NICs Bill* is necessary because there is sufficient authority for HMRC to make a repayment. HMRC is committed to ensuring that where accelerated NICs are found not to be due or are overpaid, that [*sic*] repayments are made.

As we do not have to rely on *regulation 52* of the *Contributions Regulations [2001]* to repay accelerated NICs, there will be no requirement for those who have paid the NICs to make an application before repayment can be made.'

While the outcome is clearly as it should be, it is not clear that the legislation does indeed give HMRC the authority to make the refund. The provisions of the Social Security *Contributions (Decisions & Appeals) Regulations 1999* are plainly designed to deal with situations where the liability is in dispute and remains under appeal and unpaid because the liability has been postponed; they do not obviously provide authority for repayment of disputed contributions that have been paid under a statutory duty such as that imposed by *para 17*.

Application for repayment

[55.5] An application for repayment of contributions made in error must be made (in such form and manner as HM Revenue and Customs directs) within six years from the end of the year in which the contributions were paid, or, if HM Revenue and Customs is satisfied that there has been good reason ('reasonable excuse' from 8 October 2002) for delay, within such longer period as it may allow. It is understood that the phrase 'in such form and manner' as HM Revenue and Customs directs has led to requests having to be made in individual cases for a written application which once accepted by NIC&EO will be acknowledged by the issue of an official claim form depending on the validity of the claim.

Overpayments are handled by various teams at NIC&EO in Newcastle and at the Accounts Office.

- Class 1 individuals: Payment Reconciliation team (0300 200 3500)
- Class 1 employers: Customer Operations Employer Office (0300 200 3401)

- Class 1A: the relevant Accounts Office (ie, Shipley or Cumbernauld)
- Class 2: Payment Reconciliation/Self-Employment Services (0300 200 3505, but 0300 200 3500 for refunds of voluntary Class 2)
- Class 3 paid unnecessarily: Payment Reconciliation (0300 200 3500)
- Class 2 or 3 paid unnecessarily by those overseas: International Caseworker (0300 200 3506 or +44 191 203 7010)
- Class 4: Deferment Services (0300 056 0631)

[*Social Security (Contributions) Regulations 2001, SI 2001/1004, Reg 52(3)(8)(9)*, as amended by *Social Security (Contributions) (Amendment No 3) Regulations 2002, SI 2002/2366, Reg 8* and *Social Security (Contributions, Categorisation of Earners and Intermediaries) (Amendment) Regulations 2004, SI 2004/770, Reg 12*].

The *Social Security Act 1998* provided for Class 1, 1A or 1B contributions which are paid by or for an earner in error because the earner is not an employed earner to be treated as if the earner was nonetheless actually employed in employed earners employment throughout the period. In certain prescribed circumstances such contributions are not treated as those of an employed earner in cases of contributions paid in error. [*SSCBA 1992, s 19A* inserted by *Social Security Act 1998, s 54*]. This onerous provision is, however, overridden if, by the end of the second year, either:

- an application had been made for a determination by the Secretary of State for Social Security (ie under the pre-1 April 1999 quasi-appeals procedure);
- a question of law arising in connection with the above has been referred to a Court under *SSAA 1992, s 18*;
- a written request has been made to an officer of the Board of HM Revenue and Customs for a decision under *SSC(TF)A 1999, s 8(1)(a)* or for such a decision to be varied;
- a tax appeal is under way in respect of any associated Class 1B liability;

and the question, reference, request or appeal has not been finally settled by the end of the second year. [*Social Security (Contributions) Regulations 2001, SI 2001/1004, Reg 59*].

In calculating the amount to be returned, any amount of contributory benefit paid because of, and attributable to, the contributions paid in error is to be deducted after being abated by any income support, etc which would have been paid had the contributory benefit in question not been received. [*Social Security (Contributions) Regulations 2001, SI 2001/1004, Reg 57(1)(b)(2)*]. Any minimum contributions paid by HM Revenue and Customs on behalf of the Secretary of State for Work and Pensions to a personal pension scheme under *Pension Schemes Act 1993, s 42A(3), s 43*, are also to be deducted. [*Social Security (Contributions) Regulations 2001, SI 2001/1004, Reg 57(1)(d)(f)*]. Between 1986 and 1993, schemes that became contracted out were entitled under SSA 1986, s 7 to a 2% incentive payment in addition to the normal contracting out rebates, as the government tried to persuade employers and contributors to opt out of SERPS to reduce the long-term cost of the state pension scheme. Such incentive payments were also to be deducted in calculating the amount of any return of contributions. [Social Security *(Contributions) Regulations 2001, SI 2001/1004, Reg 57(1)(e)*].

Class 4 contributions paid in error are also returnable to the person who paid them but, if the error is one which affects both tax and contributions (eg an error in the financial accounts on which the assessment to both tax and Class 4 contributions was made), recovery must be sought from the business's tax office under *Taxes Management Act 1970, s 33* instead of from the NIC&EO. [*Social Security (Contributions) Regulations 2001, SI 2001/1004, Reg 101(b), Reg 102(1), Reg 110(1)* as amended by *Social Security Contributions (Amendment No 3) Regulations 2002, SI 2002/2366, Regs 14, 15, 16*].

There is no time limit on applications for refunds of Class 3 contributions that do not count for benefit purposes (ie, there was no reason to pay them when payment was made, with the result that they could not validly have been paid), or for refunds of Class 2 or Class 4 contributions in excess of the annual maximum (see **55.12**).

The time limit within which application for repayment of *ordinary* Class 4 contributions paid in error must be made is 'five years after the 31 January next following the year of assessment' or, if later, two years from the end of the tax year in which the payment was actually made. Note however that amendments to Class 4 profits that depend on amendments to ITTOIA profits will only be possible if the self-assessment for the relevant year is itself open to amendment, which may mean that HMRC argues that the four-year ITSA time limit applies.

In the case of Class 2 contributions and special Class 4 contributions paid in error in excess of the liability, the limit is 'six years after the end of the year of assessment' in which the contribution was due to be paid. [*Social Security (Contributions) Regulations 2001, SI 2001/1004, Reg 102(2)(3), Reg 110(2)(3)*].

Refund applications made after the relevant time limit has expired may still be allowed if there was a reasonable excuse for not making the application within the time limit and the application is made without unreasonable delay after the excuse has ceased.

See HM Revenue and Customs National Insurance Manual NIM38504.

Repayment of not contracted-out element in contributions

[55.6] Where a secondary contributor has paid in respect of 2015–16 or earlier years an amount on account of Class 1 contributions at the not contracted-out rate but the employment concerned was, or had become, a contracted-out employment, HM Revenue and Customs will, on the secondary contributor's application, return the amount so paid after deducting the amount of Class 1 contributions payable at the contracted-out rate. [*Social Security (Contributions) Regulations 2001, SI 2001/1004, Reg 54(1)*].

The primary element of the repayment will be repaid to the primary contributor unless he consents in writing or by electronic format as approved to its return to the secondary contributor. [*Social Security (Contributions) Regulations 2001, SI 2001/1004, Reg 54(2)*].

Application for a repayment in these circumstances must be made in an approved form and manner within six years from the end of the year in which the contracting-out certificate in respect of the employment was issued or, if

HM Revenue and Customs is satisfied that there has been good reason for the delay, within such longer period as the officer of the Board may allow. [*Social Security (Contributions) Regulations 2001, SI 2001/1004, Reg 54(3)*]. From 8 October 2002, *Social Security (Contributions) (Amendment No 3) Regulations 2002, SI 2002/2366, Reg 9* ensured that such decisions are to made by officers of the Board of HM Revenue and Customs and can also therefore be the subject of an appeal (see **9** APPEALS). However, the delay must now be by reason of a 'reasonable excuse'. 'Reasonable excuse' has a narrower meaning than 'good reason' (which applied until October 2002) which was defined as 'some fact which, having regard to all the circumstances (including the claimant's state of health and the information which he had received and that which he might have obtained), would probably have caused a reasonable person of his age to act as he did'. It aligns more with 'just cause' which has been held to require consideration of the interests of the general body of contributors as well as the claimant.

Repayment of precluded Class 3 contributions

[55.7] Where a Class 3 contributor has paid a Class 3 contribution which he was not entitled to pay, HM Revenue and Customs will, on written application being made to him in an approved manner (including electronic means), return that contribution to the contributor. [*Social Security (Contributions) Regulations 2001, SI 2001/1004, Reg 56*]. Alternatively, the contribution may, with the consent of the contributor, be appropriated to the earnings factor of another year if there is an entitlement to pay Class 3 contributions in that other year (see **19.7** CLASS 3 CONTRIBUTIONS). There is no time limit for the making of such refunds (see HM Revenue and Customs National Insurance Manual NIM38504).

Repayment of contributions exceeding the annual maximum

[55.8] Where contributions are paid in excess of the ANNUAL MAXIMUM 7 they are to be repaid by HM Revenue and Customs provided written application is made to it. No amount will be returned unless it exceeds, in the case of Class 1 or 2 contributions, one-fifteenth of a standard rate contribution payable on earnings at the Upper Earnings Limit in respect of primary Class 1 contributions prescribed for the last or only tax year in respect of which the contributions were paid (see **55.3** above for yearly figures), and, in the case of Class 1A, Class 1B or Class 4 contributions, fifty pence. [*SSCBA 1992, s 19(2)(b); Social Security (Contributions) Regulations 2001, SI 2001/1004, Reg 52A* as inserted by *Social Security (Contributions, Categorisation of Earners and Intermediaries) (Amendment) Regulations 2004, SI 2004/770, Reg 12* and amended by *Social Security (Contributions) (Amendment No 3) Regulations 2010, SI 2010/646, Reg 2; Security (Contributions) Regulations 2001, SI 2001/1004, Reg 102(1), Reg 110(1)* (2003–04 onwards)].

Class 1, 2 and 4 repayment priority

[55.9] Contributions are returned to the earner in a strictly prescribed order of priority. This is to ensure that where contracted-out employments are involved in the refund claim (and, before April 2012, there was no 'appropriate personal pension'), the annual maximum amount of contributions which is retained for any year before 2016–17 contains the maximum amount of contributions at the contracted-out rate. Unless notice had been given to HM Revenue and Customs under *Pension Schemes Act 1993, s 44(1)* that the contributor concerned was or intended to become a member of a personal pension scheme, the order of priority before the abolition of money purchase contracting out in April 2012, was:

(a) ordinary and special Class 4 contributions [*Social Security (Contributions) Regulations 2001, SI 2001/1004, Reg 100(1), Reg 110(1)*];
(b) primary Class 1 contributions at the reduced rate [*Social Security (Contributions) Regulations 2001, SI 2001/1004, Reg 52A(5)(a)*, as amended by *Social Security (Contributions, Categorisation of Earners and Intermediaries) (Amendment) Regulations 2004, SI 2004/770, Reg 12*];
(c) Class 2 contributions [*Social Security (Contributions) Regulations 2001, SI 2001/1004, Reg 52A(5)(b)*, as amended by *Social Security (Contributions, Categorisation of Earners and Intermediaries) (Amendment) Regulations 2004, SI 2004/770, Reg 12*];
(d) primary Class 1 contributions at the main primary percentage [*Social Security (Contributions) Regulations 2001, SI 2001/1004, Reg 52A(5)(c)*, as amended by *Social Security (Contributions, Categorisation of Earners and Intermediaries) (Amendment) Regulations 2004, SI 2004/770, Reg 12*];
(e) primary Class 1 contributions in respect of contracted-out salary related scheme (COSRS) employments [*Social Security (Contributions) Regulations 2001, SI 2001/1004, Reg 52A(5)(d)*, as amended by *Social Security (Contributions, Categorisation of Earners and Intermediaries) (Amendment) Regulations 2004, SI 2004/770, Reg 12*];
(f) primary Class 1 contributions in respect of contracted-out money purchase scheme (COMPS) employments [*Social Security (Contributions) Regulations 2001, SI 2001/1004, Reg 52A(5)(e)*, as amended by *Social Security (Contributions, Categorisation of Earners and Intermediaries) (Amendment) Regulations 2004, SI 2004/770, Reg 12*]. Such contributions have not been payable from 2012–13 onwards following the withdrawal of contracted out rebates for COMPS arrangements (although rebates for earlier years may still be claimed where appropriate).

Where notice of membership of, or intention to join, an appropriate personal pension scheme had been given under *Pension Schemes Act 1993, s 44(1)*, paragraph (*d*) would have come after (*e*) and (*f*) in the above priority listing. [*Social Security (Contributions) Regulations 2001, SI 2001/1004, Reg 52A(5)(8)*, as amended by *Social Security (Contributions, Categorisation of Earners and Intermediaries) (Amendment) Regulations 2004, SI 2004/770, Reg 12*]. This did not apply from 2012–13 onwards as contracted out rebates were withdrawn for personal pension arrangements (although HMRC may still currently be checking and paying rebates for earlier years).

It should be noted, as regards contracted-out contributions from 6 April 1997 to 5 April 2012, that COSR contributions were generally repaid before COMP contributions. However, only the secondary contributor's payroll rebate rate differed under the two contracted-out regimes. Since the rate of primary contributions was identical this elaboration could, in practice, be disregarded since secondary contributions were payable without any maximum limit.

The amount returnable in respect of contributions falling within (e) above is dependent on the amount of contributions paid at contracted-out rates. The same was true until 5 April 2012 for contributions falling within (f) above. If the amount paid at contracted-out rates is:

- not less than 53 times the amount payable at the contracted-out rate on earnings at the Upper Earnings Limit for the year (ie earnings between the Earnings Threshold and the Upper Earnings Limit (prior to 6 April 2009) or Upper Accrual Point (after 5 April 2009), there is to be returned (to the extent that a repayment remains due) any amount paid at contracted-out rates;
- nil or less than 53 times the amount payable at the contracted-out rate on earnings at the Upper Earnings Limit for that year, there is to be returned (to the extent that a repayment remains due) the amount paid at standard rates.

On the introduction of the UAP of £770 per week in April 2009 the proportion of an individual's earnings which attracted contracted-out rebates was reduced from the UEL, then £817 per week, to the UAP of £770 per week. This means that the refund calculations in this respect now take into account the UAP figure rather than the higher UEL figure used in the refund calculations prior to 6 April 2009. Therefore the Rules 2 and 3 within *Social Security (Contributions) Regulations 2001, SI 2001/1004, Reg 52A(6)* were amended to ensure that the rebates do not exceed the UAP threshold.

[*Social Security (Contributions) Regulations 2001, SI 2001/1004, Reg 52A(6)*, as amended by *Social Security (Contributions, Categorisation of Earners and Intermediaries) (Amendment) Regulations 2004, SI 2004/770, Reg 12* and *Social Security (Contributions) (Amendment No 3) Regulations 2010, SI 2010/646, Reg 2*].

In the case of primary Class 1 contributions within (b), (d), (e) or, before 6 April 2012, (f) above, the order of priority is:

(i) contributions at the special armed forces rate (**11.6**);
(ii) contributions at the special mariners rate (**45.12**);
(iii) other primary Class 1 contributions as specified.

The position for contributions overpaid since 6 April 2016, when contracting out ceased to be available, is now much simpler, since no account need be taken of rebated contributions for such periods, and there is no place for contracted-out employments in the order of priority applied to repayment calculations. The example below explains the more complex calculations needed for periods before 6 April 2016.

Example

Throughout 2015–16 Auk was employed by Bunting Ltd, Curlew Ltd and Dipper Ltd. Until 4 October 2015 he was also self-employed. His employments with C and D were contracted-out through membership of a COSR scheme. His assessable profits for 2015–16 were £10,000 and earnings from B, C and D were £10,000, £16,500 and £41,000 respectively. Each employer paid weekly. He paid contributions as follows:

	Class 2	*Class 4*	*Class 1* Not contracted-out employment (n-c-o)	*Class 1* COSR employment (c-o)
	£	£	£	£
S/employment	72.80	174.60		
B (n-c-o)			232.80	
C (c-o)				863.34
D (c-o to UAP)				3,358.58
D (n-c-o above UAP)			115.20	
	£72.80	£174.60	£348.00	£4,221.92

The basic annual maximum for 2015–16 was £4,197.60 (see Step 2 below) but this had to be adjusted to the personalised maximum to allow for the 2% charge (see 7 ANNUAL MAXIMUM and 53.14 RATES AND LIMITS). The calculation of the personalised annual maximum was as follows:

Step		
1. Calculate 53 × (UEL – PT), ie 53 × (£815 – 155)		£34,980.00
2. 12% thereof		£4,197.60
3. Earnings from each employment that fell between PT and UEL: 10,000 – 8,060 = 1,940 16,500 – 8,060 = 8,440 41,000 – 8,060 = 32,940	43,320	
4. Deduct figure in step 1 (34,980)	8,340	
5. As the line above gives a positive figure, multiply by 2%		166.80
6. Earnings from each employment which exceeds UEL	Nil	
7. Multiply step 6 result by 2%		Nil
8. Add steps 2, 5, 7 – this gave the personalised annual maximum		£4,364.40

It is clear that this was exceeded, but in order to ascertain by how much it had been exceeded it was necessary to convert to standard rate any Class 1 contributions paid at other rates (see **7.4** ANNUAL MAXIMUM).

	£
Class 1 (Not contracted-out rate)	348.00
Class 1 (Contracted-out rate £4,221.92 × 12/10.6)	4,779.53
Class 2	72.80
Class 4	174.60
	5,374.93
Personalised annual maximum	4,364.40
Excessive *notional* contributions	£1,010.53

It is on this *notional* figure of £1,010.53 that the repayment calculation was based.

	£		*Repayment due* £
Excessive notional contributions	1,010.53		
Repay: Class 4	174.60		174.60
	835.93		
Repay: Class 2	72.80		72.80
	763.13		
Repay: Class 1 (not contracted out)	348.00		348.00
	415.13	× 10.6/12	366.70
Total repayment due			£962.10

The above example includes the effect of the employee's contracted–out rebate on earnings from the Lower Earnings Limit to the primary threshold.

Until 2015–16, when Class 2 collection was moved into the ITSA regime and became assessable in arrears on the basis of known profits, a contributor who over-contributed as regarded Class 1 or Class 2 contributions (eg by being concurrently in employed earner's employment and self-employment or in two or more employed earner's employments and failing, or not being permitted, to defer a sufficient amount of his liability to prevent contributions in excess of the annual maximum being paid) would be informed of the fact by NIC&EO and invited to apply for repayment provided the excess payment was at least equal to half the current LEL. The position will, for 2015–16 and later years, generally only arise where a contributor has more than one employed earner's employment. Smaller amounts are left to individual contributors to claim. Any delay may be avoided by applying directly, without awaiting notification of overpayment, to the HM Revenue and Customs, Payment Reconciliation, NIC&EO, Benton Park View, Longbenton, Newcastle upon Tyne, NE98 1ZZ. Repayment will be expedited if the application is supported by evidence of contribution payments (ie forms P60 or detailed statements from the secondary contributors concerned).

Where over-contribution extends to Class 4 contributions, positive action on the part of the contributor is not only desirable but essential. This is because records may not be kept by NIC&EO of Class 4 contributions as they currently do not count for benefit purposes and are generally collected by HMRC Accounts Offices dealing with self-assessment payments. Any over-contribution will, therefore, remain undetected and un-repaid unless and until it is claimed. It should be noted that the NIC&EO has no statutory duty to check for over-payments and that the onus of obtaining repayment is placed on the contributor. Most tax software used by agents ignores the annual maximum calculation, as does HMRC's self-assessment system, so overpayments may go undetected without manual intervention.

An application for a refund of Class 4 contributions should be made online using the contributor's government gateway ID (www.gov.uk/government/publications/national-insurance-application-for-refund-of-class-4-national-insurance-contributions-ca5610) or on form CA5610 to HM Revenue and Customs, Deferment Services, Benton Park View, Longbenton, Newcastle upon Tyne, NE98 1ZZ.

A pro-forma which incorporates all the rules of repayment calculation (other than those involving volunteer development workers, mariners and members of the armed forces) is given at the end of this chapter. The pro-forma is not suitable for years before 2012–13 where a notice of membership of a personal pension scheme might have been given (see above).

Class 2 repayment for low earners

[55.10] Any self-employed earner who discovers that he has paid Class 2 contributions in respect of a period before 6 April 2015 which is, or falls within, a tax year when exception from Class 2 liability could have been obtained had it been applied for in time (see **18.4** CLASS 2 CONTRIBUTIONS), may, under certain conditions, obtain repayment of the Class 2 contributions paid.

The conditions are that the application:

- must be in writing to HM Revenue and Customs;
- must be supported by evidence of the earnings (ie profits) of the tax year in respect of which a repayment of Class 2 contributions is sought;
- must not be made before the beginning of the following tax year;
- must be made by 31 January in that following tax year if the repayment claim is in respect of 2002–03 or a subsequent year (previously, the time limit was 31 December in that following tax year).

[*Social Security (Contributions) Regulations 2001, SI 2001/1004, Reg 47(1)(2)*, as amended by *Social Security (Contributions) (Amendment No 7) Regulations 2003, SI 2003/2958 Reg 3*, subsequently revoked from 6 April 2015 by *Social Security (Miscellaneous Amendments No 2) Regulations 2015), SI 2015/478, Reg 24(1)(b)*].

In a note from the then DSS to the ICAEW, the DSS justified the relatively short time limit for refund applications on the grounds that difficulties could otherwise arise in connection with a subsequent claim to a contributions-related benefit. Appreciating the practical problems involved in producing formal accounts within such a short time scale the DSS said that it will accept evidence other than formal accounts as long as it covers the period for which a refund has been sought, but that it had no plans to extend the time limit. (ICAEW Technical Release 12/92, Annex G). Nonetheless, despite the interaction with benefit entitlement which could have arisen from the first Sunday in January, the then Inland Revenue introduced, in 2003, a further month in which to claim by the change noted above, in order to harmonise with the self-assessment tax return time limit. Any contributory benefit paid on the basis of contributions reclaimed would be refundable. It would be expected, however, that anyone claiming benefits in the first month of the calendar year would not seek a refund of the contributions.

NICA 2015, s 1, Sch 1 made this procedure obsolete for years from 6 April 2015, as Class 2 contributions are now assessed and collected via the income tax self-assessment tax return, with the small earnings exception converted into a 'small profits threshold'. If profits do not exceed the SPT, no contributions will be payable other than voluntarily, and it may be expected that Class 2 contribution exception may be claimed in the return based on known income and Class 1 contributions figures, just as Class 4 contribution exemption may be claimed via boxes 100–102 in the SA103F ITSA return pages.

Retrospective Class 2 exception

[55.11] Where, upon submission of an application within the time limits laid down, HM Revenue and Customs finds that exception from Class 2 liability on the grounds of small earnings would have been available to the contributor for years before 6 April 2015 had he applied for it, he would be granted exception retrospectively and the Class 2 contributions would be repaid, less any amount paid by way of contributory benefits specified in *SSCBA 1992, s 20(1)* which would not have been paid but for the Class 2 contributions which were being repaid. [Social Security (Contributions) Regulations 2001, SI 2001/1004, *Reg 47(3)(4)(5)*, revoked by *Social Security (Miscellaneous Amendments No 2) Regulations 2015, SI 2015/478, Reg 24(1)(b)*].

> *Example*
>
> Ernest is a self-employed joiner. His accounts for the years ended 31 May 2013 and 31 May 2014 were prepared on 31 October 2014 and showed net profits of £2,000 and £2,400 respectively. The actual profit for the tax year 2013–14 was, on the time apportionment basis which had to be used for those years, £2,333 (ie $^{2}/_{12}$ × £2,000 + $^{10}/_{12}$ × £2,400) and, because those profits were below the small earnings exception limit for that year (£5,885), Ernest could, at any time before 31 January 2015, have applied for retrospective exception and repayment of Class 2 contributions paid during 2013–14. In practice, Ernest would also have been well advised to also claim small earnings exception for 2014–15 and suspend further Class 2 payments for the rest of the tax year with effect from October 2014, if similar levels of profit were still being made.
>
> Exception and repayment prevent the year from being a qualifying year for benefit purposes on the basis of Class 2 contributions (see **13.5** BENEFITS: CONTRIBUTION REQUIREMENTS and **28.6** EARNINGS FACTORS).

Interest on Class 1, Class 1A, Class 1B and Class 4 repayments

[55.12] Repayments of Class 1 contributions for 1992–93 onwards, Class 1A for 1991–92 onwards and Class 1B for 1999–2000 onwards have carried interest at the same rate as income tax refunds (see **42.11** LATE-PAID CONTRIBUTIONS) from the relevant date until the repayment is issued. The relevant date in respect of 1999–2000 onwards is 14 days after the end of the year in respect of which the contribution was paid. [*SSCBA 1992, Sch 1 para 6(3), Social Security (Contributions) Regulations 2001, SI 2001/1004, Reg 77, Sch 4 para 18*]. For rates of interest see **53.16** RATES AND LIMITS.

With the advent of in-year interest charges for Class 1 under the RTI regime (see **21.36** LATE-PAYMENT INTEREST), employers who overpay and correct the payroll reports by the submission of a correction FPS or EYU might also expect to see repayment interest credited to their tax account, but they will be disappointed. The system has been set up so as to deprive employers of any true interest recompense for any such overpayment corrected in-year by FPS, although an EYU may result in some interest being credited.

From 6 May 2014, the *Social Security (Contributions) (Amendment No 3) Regulations 2014, SI 2014/1016* inserted into the collection machinery in *Social Security (Contributions) Regulations 2001, SI 2001/1004, Schedule 4* new *paras 10(4)* and *11(3A)*. The overpayment corrected by the return is deemed to have been paid to HMRC on the payment date for the tax month or quarter in which the correction is made (ie, by the 19th or 22nd of the following month, depending on whether payment is made by cheque or electronically. Where an EYU is submitted to correct the values for an earlier RTI year, new *para 11ZA(3)* deems the overpayment to have been made on the payment date for the deductions due for the last period in the year covered by the return.

Interest is paid on all Class 4 repayments however they arise. [*ITTOIA 2005, s 749*; *SSCBA 1992, Sch 2 para 6*.] See **53.16** for rates payable. See **55.13** below as regards interest on repayments of Class 1 and Class 1A contributions. Also, see **42.11** LATE-PAID CONTRIBUTIONS for interest supplement paid on disputed NICs liability subsequently repaid.

Refunded interest

[55.13] Interest will be refunded if charged incorrectly [*Social Security (Contributions) Regulations 2001, SI 2001/1004, Reg 78, Sch 4 para 19*] and will be remitted if the contribution in respect of which it is charged was paid late as a result of an error by an HM Revenue and Customs official. In this context an error is a mistake or omission which neither the employer nor any person acting on his behalf has caused or materially contributed towards. [*Social Security (Contributions) Regulations 2001, SI 2001/1004, Reg 79, Sch 4 para 20*]. The remission is for the period from the normal reckonable date (see **42.11** LATE-PAID CONTRIBUTIONS) or the date of the error if that is later, until fourteen days after the employer is advised in writing that the error has been rectified.

De minimis limit for repayment

[55.14] Whilst there are no *de minimis* limits specified below which interest payable or receivable will be disregarded, there are lower limits on the amount of contributions which will be repaid (see 55.3 above).

PRO FORMA REPAYMENT CALCULATOR FOR YEARS UP TO 6 APRIL 2015			
Key:	smr = standard main primary rate rr = reduced rate comr = contracted-out main primary rate c-o = contracted-out n-c-o = not contracted-out		
		NOTIONALLY PAID	
Class 1 primary at:			
Reduced rate	× smr ÷ rr	. . . (*a*)	
Standard/main rates (n-c-o employment & c-o employment above UAP)		. . . (*b*)	
Contracted-out/main rates (c-o-employment) . . .	× smr ÷ cor	. . . (*c*)	
Class 2		. . . (*d*)	
	Sub-total (a)+(b)+(c)+(d)	. . . (*e*)	
Class 4		. . . (*f*)	
	Sub-total (e)+(f)	. . . (*g*)	
ANNUAL MAXIMUM	(*w*, if *e* exceeds *w*; *x*, if any Class 4 contributions payable and *x* exceeds *e* but does not exceed *g*; *g*, if any Class 4 contributions payable and *x* exceeds both *e* and *g*; otherwise *e*)	. . . (*h*)	
EXCESS NOTIONAL CONTRIBUTIONS (g-h)		(*i*)	
NOTIONAL REPAYMENT		NOTIONAL REPAYMENT £	ACTUAL REPAYMENT £
Class 4 (lesser of *f* and *i*)		. . .	. . .
	Sub-total	(*j*)	
Class 1 at rr (lesser of *a* and *j*)		. . .	× rr ÷ smr = . . .
	Sub-total	. . . (*k*)	
Class 2 (lesser of *d* and *k*)		. . .	. . .
	Sub-total	. . . (*l*)	
Class 1 at smr in n-c-o employment and on earnings in c-o employment above UAP up to UEL (lesser of *b* and *l*) (lesser of *b* and *m*)		. . .	. . .
	Sub-total	. . . (*m*)	

Class 1 at main rates in c-o employment (if *c* greater than *y*, lesser of (*c*–*y*) and *m*; if *c* is equal to or less than *y*, lesser of *c* and *m*)	. . .	× comr ÷ smr = . . .
REPAYMENT DUE		. . .

Notes

w = personalised annual maximum (see 7.4 ANNUAL MAXIMUM)

x = personalised Class 4 limiting maximum (see 7.5 ANNUAL MAXIMUM)

y = 53 × weekly primary contributions on earnings at the UEL [(comr × (UAP–ET)) + (smr × (UEL–UAP)) – (primary rebate rate × (ET–LEL))]

2015–16

The above proforma should still be usable, with the omission of references to Class 2 contributions, which are to be paid only by 31 January 2017 with the self-assessment balancing payment for the year, by which time the correct liability ought to have been established.

2016–17

No contributor will pay contracted-out Class 1 contributions after 5 April 2016, as the rebates were abolished by *Pensions Act 2014* and consequential amendments were made to the *Contributions Regulations 2001* by *Social Security (Contributions) (Amendment) (No 2) Regulations 2016, SI 2016/352, Parts 2 and 3*, the former removing references to contracted-out rates for the future and the latter preserving the rules for periods up to 5 April 2016.

56

Share Fishermen

Cross-references. See CATEGORISATION **14**; CLASS 2 CONTRIBUTIONS **18**; MARINERS **45**.

Other Sources. Tolley's National Insurance Brief, November 1996, page 84; HM Revenue and Customs National Insurance Manual NIM35001–NIM35007.

Introduction to share fishermen and NICs

[56.1] Share fishermen are (unlike other self-employed earners) liable to pay an increased rate of Class 2 contribution in order that they may acquire a contribution record which will entitle them to contribution-based jobseeker's allowance (JSA(C) – unemployment benefit prior to October 1996). [*Social Security (Contributions) Regulations 2001, SI 2001/1004, Reg 125*(c)].

Definitions regarding share fishermen

[56.2] A share fisherman is:

- any person who is ordinarily employed in the fishing industry otherwise than under a contract of service (see **14.5** CATEGORISATION) as a master or member of the crew of any UK fishing vessel within *Merchant Shipping Act 1995, s 1(3)* manned by more than one person, and remunerated in respect of that employment in whole or in part by a share of the profits or gross earnings of the fishing vessel (ie a sea-going share fisherman for benefit regulation purposes); or
- any person who has been ordinarily so employed but who by reason of age or infirmity permanently ceases to be so employed and becomes ordinarily engaged in employment ashore in the UK otherwise than under a contract of service making or mending any gear appurtenant to a UK fishing vessel or performing other services ancillary to or in

connection with that vessel and is remunerated in respect of that employment in whole or in part by a share of the profit or gross earnings of that boat (ie an on-shore share fisherman).

[*Social Security (Contributions) Regulations 2001, SI 2001/1004, Reg 115*].

See also HM Revenue and Customs National Insurance Manual NIM35001.

A fisherman employed under a contract of service is to be treated as a mariner.

For the meaning of 'ordinarily employed' see **14.21** CATEGORISATION.

The National Insurance Commissioners have held that ordinary employment as a share fisherman ceases when a person otherwise within the above definition is stood-down from the crew of a boat of which he is not an owner or when the boat of which he is an owner and for which he works is offered for sale. (Decisions *R(U) 29/58*, *R(U) 6/63* in the unemployment benefit series).

A 'British ship' is a vessel belonging to Her Majesty or whose port of registry is in the UK or a hovercraft. [*Merchant Shipping Act 1995, s 1(3)*].

Where an EU national or resident share fisherman works on an EU-registered ship, he is subject to the same EC legislation as mariners, under which the flag of the vessel determines which member state is 'competent' (ie, entitled to charge contributions and liable to provide benefits). This means that, eg, a Polish fisherman working on a UK-flagged trawler will ordinarily be subject to UK social security legislation, unless a form A1 has been issued to make him subject to the legislation of a different state. (See HMRC Revenue and Customs National Insurance Manual NIM35007.)

Categorisation of share fishermen

[56.3] Under the normal rules of categorisation, a person must be gainfully employed in the UK if he is to be categorised as an employed earner or as a self-employed earner. [*SSCBA 1992, s 2(1)*]. He must also fulfil certain conditions of residence or presence here if he is then to be liable to pay contributions (see **51.4** and **51.5** OVERSEAS MATTERS). A share fisherman, however, though he might not meet these conditions because of the intrinsic nature of his activity outside the 12-mile limit, is nonetheless to be categorised as a self-employed earner and is to be subject to the same conditions of domicile and residence as are mariners (see **45.5**) so far as actual liability to contributions is concerned. [*SSCBA 1992, s 117; Social Security (Contributions) Regulations 2001, SI 2001/1004, Reg 125*]. See HM Revenue and Customs National Insurance Manual NIM35003.

Rate of contribution

[56.4] From 6 April 2018, the rate of a share fisherman's Class 2 contribution is £3.60 per week. [*Social Security (Contributions) Regulations 2001, SI 2001/1004, Reg 125(c)* as amended by *National Insurance Contributions Act 2015 (NICA 2015), Sch 1, para 33(1)*].

Rates for earlier years are stated at **53.10** RATES AND LIMITS.

A share fisherman unable to go fishing but who takes on alternative self-employment unconnected with the boat is only liable to pay the *ordinary* Class 2 contribution for the weeks in question. See HM Revenue and Customs National Insurance Manual NIM35004.

Where Class 2 contributions are paid late, the normal rules about the appropriate rate are applied (see **42.8**). [*Social Security (Contributions) Regulations 2001, SI 2001/1004, Reg 125(g)* as amended by *Social Security (Miscellaneous Amendments No 2) Regulations 2015, SI 2015/478, Reg 16*.] Before 6 April 2015, the provision referred to the year in which liability for Class 2 contributions arose. Since the reform by *NICA 2015, Sch 1*, the hook on which the rate hangs is the year for which the contributor is eligible to pay a Class 2 contribution. This deals with the introduction of the small profits threshold and the option to pay Class 2 contributions for those whose profits do not exceed it: they may still wish to pay Class 2 voluntarily now to protect their entitlement to JSA(C).

Annual maximum

[56.5] The special Class 2 rate referred to at **56.4** above is to be substituted for the normal rate in any calculations connected with the ANNUAL MAXIMUM 7 contributions of a share fisherman. [*Social Security (Contributions) Regulations 2001, SI 2001/1004, Reg 125(d)*].

Class 2 exception

[56.6] The circumstances under which a self-employed earner might be excepted from liability to pay a Class 2 contribution are to be extended, in the case of a share fisherman, so as to include any week in which he is entitled to contribution-based jobseeker's allowance (unemployment benefit) or would be so entitled were his contribution record adequate (see **18.6** CLASS 2 CONTRIBUTIONS). [*Social Security (Contributions) Regulations 2001, SI 2001/1004, Reg 125(e)*].

Collection

[56.7] Although due at different rates, collection is by the same method as for other Class 2 payments (see **18.8** CLASS 2 CONTRIBUTIONS). This means that share fishermen will pay through their income tax self-assessment for 2015–16 onwards. EEA residents who are liable to UK NICs by virtue of working on a UK-flagged fishing vessel are unlikely to have an obligation to file an SA return – see **56.10** below.

Class 4 contributions

[56.8] Insofar as Class 4 contributions in respect of a share fisherman's profits or gains are not collected through self-assessment, the special direct collection procedure described at **21.51** COLLECTION is to apply. [*Social Security*

(Contributions) Regulations 2001, SI 2001/1004, Reg 125(f)]. See HM Revenue and Customs National Insurance Manual NIM24000 and NIM35006.

HMRC Fishing Units

[56.9] HM Revenue and Customs Fishing Units are at Caledonian House, Greenmarket, Dundee DD1 4QX (Tel 0300 056 8680) for Scotland, otherwise Longbrook House, New North Road, Exeter, EX4 4UD (Tel 0300 056 7134). They operate two voluntary schemes to help share fishermen ensure that they put aside enough money to pay their tax every six months. The Scottish Share Fisherman (SSF) scheme operates a savings account with the Bank of Scotland, the Share fishermen's Voluntary Tax Saving Scheme (SVTSS) for England, Wales and Northern Ireland operates a savings account with Barclays Bank.

A pre-agreed percentage (minimum 20%, rising in 5% increments) is deducted by settling agents, under an agreement made with each share fisherman, from the income received from share fishing, which is paid to the relevant bank. Each January and July, HMRC Debt Management & Banking take money by direct debit from the relevant accounts to settle their tax and Class 4 liabilities. The background is explained at SAM80080 and the banking arrangements at DMBM220000. Share fishermen have no right to make withdrawals from the savings accounts until after 31 January following the end of the tax year, and they have filed all returns and settled all taxes due for that and earlier years.

Following the reform of Class 2 by *NICA 2015*, the arrangement extends to the Class 2 contributions for 2015–16 included in the SA liability for the year and due by 31 January 2017.

EEA residents

[56.10] Share fishermen who are EEA nationals and resident outside the UK but working on a British-registered vessel are subject to the same *EC Reg 883/04* rules as other mariners. As non-residents, they are unlikely to have an SA filing obligation, so they must make alternative arrangements with HMRC to pay Class 2 contributions, which will usually involve HMRC sending a bill by 31 October (see www.gov.uk/pay-class-2-national-insurance).

HMRC guidance refers to NIM29003, but this merely and unhelpfully states that the 'text has been withheld because of exemptions in the Freedom of Information Act 2000'. This usually indicates that there is an avoidance opportunity that HMRC chooses not to publicise. See **45.6** MARINERS.

57

Subpostmasters

Cross-references. See ANNUAL MAXIMUM **7**; CATEGORISATION **14**; **20.6** CLASS 4 CONTRIBUTIONS for exception of Class 1 contributors in respect of earnings chargeable to tax under *Income Tax (Trading and Other Income) Act 2005 (ITTOIA 2005), Part 2 Chapter 2*; DEFERMENT OF PAYMENT **27**; REPAYMENT AND REALLOCATION **55**.

Other Sources. Simon's Taxes, Volume 2, para A8.294; Tolley's National Insurance Brief, February 1995, page 14; Tolley's Practical NIC, June 1999, page 44, November 2003, page 81, December 2003, page 89; Taxation, 20 December 2007, page 670; HM Revenue and Customs National Insurance Manual NIM21019, NIM24625 and NIM24640; HM Revenue and Customs Business Income Manual BIM66301.

Introduction to subpostmasters and NICs

[57.1] A true subpostmaster (see 57.4) almost invariably enjoys a dual employment status for contribution purposes. He is an *employed earner* by reason of the 'office holder' relationship he enjoys with Post Office Ltd (a subsidiary of Post Office Group plc) and he is a *self-employed earner* by reason of the fact that he is gainfully employed other than as an employed earner in running an ancillary business (eg a newsagency) from the premises in which he performs his duties as a subpostmaster (see **14.18** CATEGORISATION). Only if the business is carried on through the medium of a limited company will this not be the case (see **57.9** below).

Until the *Post Office Act 1969* transformed the Post Office into a statutory corporation, a subpostmaster was a CROWN SERVANT **25** who held an appointment which was terminable at the Crown's pleasure. Since 1969, however, that has no longer been the case. (*Malins v The Post Office* [1975] ICR 60). Now a subpostmaster is under a contract for services (*Hitchcock v Post Office* [1980] ICR 100) but that does not mean that he is a self-employed earner. A subpostmaster continues to occupy an office by Post Office appointment and, as that office is an office with earnings chargeable to tax as employment income (formerly under Schedule E), it takes precedence over his contract for services and takes him into the category of *employed earner*.

[Social Security Contributions and Benefits Act 1992 (SSCBA 1992), s 2(1)(a)]. (See **14.4** and **14.17** CATEGORISATION.)

Categorisation

[57.2] As an employed earner, a subpostmaster is liable to pay CLASS **1** CONTRIBUTIONS **15** (and such contributions are, in fact, deducted from his earnings by the Post Office), while, as a self-employed earner running another business in the sub-post office alongside the employment, a subpostmaster is liable to pay CLASS **2** CONTRIBUTIONS **18** and profit-related CLASS **4** CONTRIBUTIONS **20**.

The anomalies to which dual status can give rise have twice led to investigations by the Parliamentary Commissioner, but the position of a subpostmaster remains unchanged for the present. (See *C43/J, HC Paper 49, Session 1974–75, p 81; 3A/624/77, HC Paper 246, Session 1977–78, p 156*). A determination in 1984 by the Secretary of State for Social Security did, however, bring about one revision of practice by the former DSS which partly relieved a subpostmaster's contribution burdens in certain instances (see **57.9** below) and at least one case was heard by the General Commissioners early in the century.

The privatisation of the Royal Mail in 2014 was preceded by a separation of the mail delivery service (now majority-owned by the private sector and the staff through Royal Mail plc) and the post office network, which is wholly state-owned through Post Office Ltd and has undertaken a 'Network Transformation' project which is changing the model under which sub-post offices operate. This may change the NIC position significantly in due course as contracts are updated, as offices become franchised businesses.

Categories of Post Offices

[57.3] There are three categories of Post Office, numbering in all around 11,500 offices, including around 1,100 'outreaches'. The first category is Crown Post Offices or 'directly-managed' offices run by POL, of which there were 350 in 2014. The second is classed by POL as 'agency types' of which there were 10,255 in 2014, consisting of a number of types (see below). The third was the 1,100 'outreach' sub-post offices which are categorised as 'satellite', 'mobile' and 'hosted partner offices'.

The majority of the agency offices are governed by a 'Subpostmaster's Contract'.

Under the 2014 reorganisation plans, there were to be three new sub-post office models: local, main and community. The first two are based on retail businesses and carry no fixed element of subpostmaster pay, whereas the third is designed for post offices where there is no other retail outlet nearby and still attracts a fixed element of subpostmaster pay. Some 500 former subpostmasters had left the network by July 2014 and taken compensation, and another 500 to 600 of those classed as 'local' might be forced to leave if they do not have or develop a large enough retail business alongside the Post Office business, according to the National Federation of Subpostmasters. Post Office Ltd was asking all subpostmasters except in community offices to move onto new contracts, but they will remain on the traditional contracts for the next few years if they so choose. The new contracts are not employment contracts but contracts for subpostmasters to provide services to Post Office Ltd using their own premises and staff. Since the post-office network has been kept in public ownership despite the privatisation of Royal Mail, HMRC will presumably not alter its view that traders acting as subpostmasters hold an office (keeping them within Class 1 NIC) or whether they will be regarded as self-employed traders, or as directors of companies, running retail outlets from which a sub-post office is operated. In January 2014, the Certification Officer under the *Trade Union and Labour Relations (Consolidation) Act 1992 (TULR(C)A 1992)* announced his decision to derecognise the National Federation of Subpostmasters as a trade union on the basis that the 7,100 subpostmasters who made up the membership of the NFSP were neither employees of, nor 'workers' for, the Post Office, but *TULR(C)A 1992* does not recognise the classification in tax and NIC legislation of 'office holder'.

It is understood the Post Office has entered into some agreements direct with limited companies without it requiring a named individual to be 'the subpostmaster'. These cases are generally those where a Post Office is situated within, for example, a large multi-branch supermarket – see also 57.9. The two tax districts of HM Revenue and Customs that deal primarily with the subpostmaster issues and Post Office are: South Yorkshire area (based in Sheffield) liaison for all staff of Post Office Ltd including subpostmasters but not staff employed by them); and Glasgow Blythswood (Royal Mail, Parcelforce, Post Office Headquarters' staff and other schemes). See HM Revenue and Customs Employment Income Manual EIM68200 ff.

Subpostmasters as sole traders or in partnership

[57.4] It is common practice for a subpostmaster who is in business on his own account or in partnership, to include in his accounts as trading income not only the receipts he obtains from retail sales but also the gross amount of the remuneration he receives from the Post Office. (This practice has always been encouraged and facilitated by HM Revenue and Customs which will issue a 'no-tax' code NT to the Post Office so as to ensure that earnings are paid gross.) Against that total income he will set the cost of goods sold and the establishment and running expenses of the business. The resulting net profit (after any adjustments required under the Taxes Acts) would then provide the basis for the calculation of Class 4 contributions. The orthodox view for many years was that a subpostmaster who follows the procedure described above may claim exception from Class 4 contributions for a year of assessment on profits equal to an amount of earnings calculated by reference to the Class 1 primary contributions which he has (or, but for deferment, would have) paid in that year of assessment. The effect of this would frequently have been to reduce the Class 4 assessment to nil.

Although this practical and fair approach was applied for many years, the CA took a different view from the mid-1990s and this view was perpetuated by the Inland Revenue subsequently. In practice, the position as it was originally widely understood (and applied by the authorities) was restored from 2003–04 onwards (see below) – although the authorities' interpretation of the new legislation may be questionable. [*Social Security (Contributions) Regulations 2001, Reg 94A*, inserted by *Social Security (Contributions) (Amendment No 7) Regulations 2003, SI 2003/2958, Reg 4*].

The authorities took a different view for a time because as explained at **20.2–20.6** CLASS **4** CONTRIBUTIONS, the rules applied above are strictly applicable only where profits *chargeable* to income tax under what was Schedule D include earnings which attract a liability for Class 1 contributions. [*SSCBA 1992, s 15(1); Social Security (Contributions) Regulations 2001, SI 2001/1004, Reg 94(1)*]. 'Chargeable' means 'chargeable in law' yet a subpostmaster's remuneration from the Post Office is not, in law, chargeable to tax under what is now *ITTOIA 2005, Part 2 Chapter 2*. It is, as the CA rightly pointed out when levying Class 1 contributions on that remuneration, *chargeable* (though not actually *charged*) to tax under *Income Tax (Earnings and Pensions) Act 2003 (ITEPA 2003)*, not *ITTOIA 2005*. The charge to tax under *ITTOIA 2005* is a mere expediency.

In other words, because the precise terms of *SSCBA 1992, s 15(1)* are not sufficiently wide to bring the Post Office remuneration into charge, the Class 4 profits should, in law, be determined by merely eliminating from the profits on which the *ITTOIA 2005, Part 2 Chapter 2* assessment is based the remuneration from the Post Office which has been included in those profits, and *Social Security (Contributions) Regulations 2001, SI 2001/1004, Reg 94* should be ignored as irrelevant in this particular context. There will be a multiplicity of circumstances in which such an approach will greatly benefit a subpostmaster yet it seems that the Secretary of State for Social Security was never challenged as to the validity of the seemingly incorrect approach to these matters which was taken by his Department.

It is understood that a number of cases were due to be heard before the General Commissioners and that in at least one case, the decision was given in favour of the subpostmaster. The then Inland Revenue's response to this development was, however, not to change its previous guidance.

The position of the former Inland Revenue changed, however, in December 2003 when a note appeared on its internet site indicating that the traditional method of calculation (ie true deferment) would be restored with effect from 2003–04. The HMRC Employment Status Manual at ESM4400 currently states:

> The practice of treating the remuneration of a sub-postmaster/sub-postmistress as a trade receipt of an individual or a company applies for income tax purposes only. The Post Office is liable to pay secondary Class I NICs and the sub-postmaster/sub-

> postmistress primary Class 1 NICs on his/her salary. Where the remuneration is introduced into the business the amount to be included in computing the trading profits is the gross remuneration before deduction of NICs. National Insurance contributions are not an allowable deduction either from Schedule E emoluments/employment income or from the receipts of the trade. However, with effect from the 2003/2004 tax year onwards, regulation 94A of the Social Security (Contributions) Regulations 2001 excepts from liability for Class 4 NICs all earnings which an earner derives from employed earners employment but which are included in the calculation of trade profits.

Without this, the same income would have been subject to (at least) a double charge at the (at the time) new 1% 'additional' rate, ie now 2% as Class 1 when paid by the Post Office and a further 2% as Class 4 (applying the Contributions Agency mid-1990s interpretation). The legislation was in the *Social Security (Contributions) (Amendment No 7) Regulations 2003, SI 2003/2958* and added new *Reg 94A* into the 2001 regulations. However, whilst *Reg 94A* refers to cases where 'an amount representing those earnings is included in the calculation of profits' it immediately adds the words 'chargeable to income tax under Schedule D' (terminology has not yet been updated for the change in the income tax law). Thus arguably the 2003 legislation did not actually change anything in law. Given the announcement on its own website, however, HMRC will find it difficult not to apply this 2003 provision on the interpretation that it itself set out when introducing it. Thus it may be possible to argue before the tribunals that if HM Revenue and Customs' interpretation of the current law is correct, then the old law – referring to 'chargeable to Schedule D' as it and the new legislation both do – must always have meant the same as the current interpretation of the current law. See IR Press Release, 19 November 2003.

Though HMRC continued to hold the line about the treatment of pre-April 2003 Class 4 contributions, it is known that, in a case that was scheduled to be heard by the Special Commissioners in the first part of 2007, with 18 hours left to the hearing, the authorities declined to argue their case. HMRC agreed to repay Class 4 contributions reclaimed for some earlier years and agreed not to pursue payments for years that had remained unpaid. Affected subpostmasters – those whose Class 1 earnings are below the Upper Earnings Limit, where the effect of the annual maximum does not therefore solve the problem – could have claimed repayment under *Reg 102*. The authorities should not have been able to claim the lack of any error due to accepted practice being followed, given the fundamental doubt expressed in this book in many previous years' editions, in Tolley's Practical NIC Newsletter and in other publications. See Taxation, 20 December 2007, page 670.

Where, for 2003–04 onwards, the earnings are strictly taxable as 'general earnings' (as is the case with subpostmasters) but included in the accounts for convenience, no deferment application is legally required. [*Social Security (Contributions) Regulations 2001, SI 2001/1004, Reg 94A*]. The Class 4 entries on the self-employed tax return are now therefore simply adjusted to take account of this using Box 102 on the SA103 Self-assessment (full) page SEF 5. Note that Box 101 (37 on the Self-assessment short pages) should not be ticked as there should be no deferment certificate.

Example

Pat is an urban subpostmaster in business on his own account. His accounting year ends on 5 April and his trading accounts for the years ended 5 April 2013, 2014, 2015 and 2016 have been, in summary, as follows:

	2013	*2014*	*2015*	*2016*
Post Office fees	41,000	46,000	50,000	52,000
Sales etc	26,000	27,000	29,000	30,000
	67,000	73,000	79,000	82,000
Expenses	18,500	19,500	21,500	22,500
Net profit	£48,500	£53,500	57,500	59,500

Class 1 primary contributions deducted from the Post Office fees in each year were for the year ended

5 April 2013	*5 April 2014*	*5 April 2015*	*5 April 2016*
£4,007.40	£4,134.40	£4,231.78	£4,311.30
(no 2% charge – below UEL)	(including 2% charge on £4,550)	(including 2% charge on £8,135)	(including 2% charge on £9,615)

In practice a portion of the Post Office fees is, in any event, not subjected to Class 1 as it relates to the payment of staff wages, and a substitution allowance to pay a deputy during absences, which are themselves subject to Class 1 in their own right, so the Post Office has agreed with HMRC to treat that element as a reimbursed business expense in calculating the liability for the subpostmaster; however, this treatment is – for ease of illustration – not addressed in the example.

Class 4 profits and the amounts of those profits which will have been excepted from Class 4 liability on the view permitted by *Reg 94A* were as follows:

Tax year	*Profits* £	*Excepted* £	*Balance* £
2012–13	48,500	41,000	7,500
2013–14	53,500	46,000	7,500
2014–15	57,500	50,000	7,500
2015–16	59,500	52,000	7,500

Class 2 liability could have been deferred for 2013–14 and 2014–15 (since the fees liable to Class 1 contributions in those years exceeded the Upper Earnings Limit). See **27.8** DEFERMENT OF PAYMENT. Had the Post Office fees not exceeded the Upper Earnings Limit for any year up to 5 April 2015, Class 2 contributions would have had to be paid. After 6 April 2015, even if the Class 4 profits are likely to exceed the small profits threshold, no deferment of Class 2 is necessary as Class 2 contributions are now assessed in arrears when the SA tax return is completed.

If the profits for the year ended 5 April 2012 had been the same as those for 2012–13, the 2011–12 NIC liability would have arisen – reflecting the authorities' more recent view following the introduction of *Reg 94A* referred to above – as follows:

Class 1 primary		£4,053.00
Class 2	52 × £2.50 =	130.00
Class 4*		5.50
*(limited so that total NIC paid at the main rates when Class 4 added did not exceed the Class 4 limiting amount – Class 1 and Class 2 exceeded £3,305.00 so Class 4 at the main rate was Nil; potential Class 4 liability of £7,500 – 7,225 × 9% = £24.75). However, the additional rate of 2% was due on £275.		
Total NIC due for 2011–12		£4,488.50

These same principles apply equally when computing the liabilities of a subpostmaster who carries on business in partnership (see PARTNERS 52).

Case law

[57.5] A 1999 case that came before the Employment Tribunal is also of interest. A subpostmistress in the Highlands of Scotland claimed that she was entitled to have her pay from Post Office Counters (as the company was then known) raised from £2.22 per hour to £3.60 per hour (the National Minimum Wage at the time) as an employee. Post Office Counters stated that the subpostmistress was self-employed and as a consequence they were not liable to pay the amount of (then) £3.60 per hour. The argument put forward by Post Office Counters was that she was not contracted to provide personal services. The Post Office Counters agency development manager also stressed that subpostmasters were agents and not employees. However, the industrial tribunal in Inverness ruled that the purpose of the *National Minimum Wage Act 1998* was to ensure that adult workers were paid at least the minimum amount unless they were genuinely 'self-employed' and they concluded that the subpostmistress was an employee for this purpose. The Post Office impliedly recognised the worker status of subpostmasters by making a top-up payment to 800 post offices so that the remuneration of those subpostmasters was brought up to that of the national minimum wage.

It is now generally accepted that subpostmasters are not employees of the Post Office Ltd, but whether or not they are 'workers' for National Minimum Wage (and *Working Time Regulations*, auto-enrolment and whistleblowing protection, etc) purposes is a highly contentious issue. The employment tribunal cases of *Bain v Post Office Counters Ltd* and *Hayward v Post Office Counters Ltd* considered this very point. Under the *Employment Rights Act 1996* an individual is a worker if he has entered into or works under a contract 'whereby the individual undertakes to do or perform personally any work or service for another party to the contract whose status is not by virtue of the contract that of a client or customer'. The *Bain* employment tribunal case considered whether Mrs Bain was a 'worker' for the purposes of the *National Minimum Wage Act 1998* and therefore eligible to receive the National

Minimum Wage. The tribunal held that she was a 'worker' for this purpose. The fact that subpostmasters' contracts do not require them to carry out the services required personally was considered irrelevant given the extent of responsibility imposed to ensure that the significant rules, requirements and responsibilities are complied with. The degree of control exercised by the Post Office Ltd and the numerous detailed instructions contained in Mrs Bain's contract were in the tribunal's view inconsistent with the relationship being with someone who was self-employed. Also, Mrs Bain was obliged to attend training sessions which it was considered would be pointless if she was expected to assume little or no personal role in the running of the post office.

In the more recent *Hayward* case the employment tribunal held that Mr Hayward was not a worker. The tribunal's view was that it was clear from his contract with Post Office Ltd that he was not required to undertake the work personally and the fact that he chose to do so was irrelevant. The tribunal held that the legal obligations under the contract must be looked at in order to determine Mr Hayward's legal status. The tribunal found that the principal purpose of the contract was the efficient delivery of post office services which could be delegated by Mr Hayward. Personal service was not a pre-requisite under the terms of the contract and therefore he was not a worker. This is entirely consistent with the fact that Post Office Ltd, in agreement with HMRC, accounts for Class 1 contributions on only part of the subpostmaster's Post Office remuneration because the payment includes an allowance for employing staff to work on the counter, which indicates that personal service is not required. This point might not have been relevant in *Bain* or the Inverness case on the facts.

The *Hayward* decision was upheld by the EAT ([2002] UKEAT 0442_01_1812), a higher tribunal, so the principle is now a precedent. The case, whilst not directly related to NICs, does highlight the problems faced when trying to determine the actual status of subpostmasters — this seems to be determined by the Post Office, NIC&EO and HM Revenue and Customs according to the result that produces the least financial burden to, or greatest tax/NICs gain for the respective bodies. The divergence of treatment in this latest case only serves to underline the confusion in the area of subpostmasters. When *Hayward* reached the EAT, it was heard together with three other cases, in one of which HMRC was pursuing Post Office Ltd over an alleged minimum wage underpayment to a subpostmistress. The EAT decided in all cases that the subpostmasters/mistresses were neither employees nor 'workers', and that Post Office Ltd was a client of each of the claimants, not their employer.

The only recent case involving the tax position of subpostmasters is *Devaraj* [2014] UKFTT 713 (TCC) TC03834, which concerned the treatment of a payment of compensation on the closure of the sub-post office run by the taxpayer. Post Office Ltd taxed the payment under *ITEPA 2003, s 401*, allowing for £30,000 to be tax-free. In deciding that the payment constituted employment income payable to an officeholder, the judges simply accepted the decisions in *Bimson* [2012] UKFTT 216 (TC) and *Uppal* [2010] UKFTT 215 as precedents, despite the fact that they were heard only at First-tier, without looking critically at the contracts under which Mr Devaraj had been working and deciding whether he was, in fact, an office holder or merely a self-employed agent. Since the tax charge arose under *s 401* as compensation, the payment should have generated no NICs charges, as it would not have constituted earnings.

Small earnings exception

[57.6] The practice of including Post Office fees in the general accounts of the business as described at 57.5 above also used to give rise to problems in connection with a claim for Class 2 exception on the grounds of small earnings. (See **32.2** EARNINGS FROM SELF-EMPLOYMENT) However, with effect from 6 July 1994 *Social Security (Contributions) Regulations 2001, SI 2001/1004, Reg 45* was amended to ensure that where a person with a business also had earnings from employed earner's employment, and those earnings were shown in the accounts of the business as a receipt, that amount was to be disregarded in assessing earnings for the purposes of the small earnings exception. (CA National Insurance News, Issue 2, page 6). [*Social Security (Contributions) Regulations 2001, SI 2001/1004, Reg 45*]. The provision was revoked from 6 April 2015 by the *Social Security (Miscellaneous Amendments No 2) Regulations 2015, SI 2015/478, Reg 24* because Class 2 earnings are now measured by reference to profits in respect of which Class 4 contributions are payable (*SSCBA 1992, s 11(3) as substituted by National Insurance Contributions Act 2015, Sch 1, para 12*) so, as described at 57.4 above, the payrolled earnings should be automatically excluded.

Subpostmaster trading in partnership with spouse or civil partner

[57.7] One situation which can give rise to difficulties is that in which a subpostmaster and his or her spouse or civil partner trade in partnership (see PARTNERS 52). An appointment to the office of subpostmaster is an *individual* appointment and the remuneration paid by the Post Office is the remuneration of the person holding the appointment only. Accordingly, if Class 4 liability is ascertained by reference to profits *charged* to tax under *ITTOIA 2005, Part 2 Chapter 2* and relief is claimed under *Social Security (Contributions) Regulations 2001, SI 2001/1004, Reg 94* as amended by *Social Security (Contributions) (Amendment) Regulations 2003, SI 2003/193* or *Reg 94A*, relief will be available only to the member of the partnership who holds the Post Office appointment.

> ***Example***
>
> George is subpostmaster of Hopefuleigh and runs the business in partnership with his wife, Iris. They share profits equally. For the year 2016–17 their profits were £35,000. Those profits required no adjustment for tax purposes and reflect G's remuneration from the Post Office of £27,000 in the year to 5 April 2017. The Class 4 profit for 2016–17 is £35,000, divided between G and I in accordance with their profit-sharing arrangement for 2016–17, ie G: £17,500, I: £17,500. The lower annual profit limit for Class 4 contributions in 2016–17 is £8,060 so that G and I each have a liability of 9% on £9,440. Relief amounting

to £27,000 may, however, be claimed under *Social Security (Contributions) Regulations 2001, SI 2001/1004, Reg 94A* by G only, thus eliminating his Class 4 liability entirely. But I's liability remains, and G's unused relief of £17,560 (£27,000 – (£17,500 – £8,060)) is lost.

G could request that the statutory basis apply to his earnings and they be taken out of the profits, leaving a profit of £8,000 under *ITTOIA 2005, Part 2 Chapter 2* shared between G and I of £4,000 each. This income for 2016–17 would be covered by the Class 4 lower annual profit limit and the Class 2 small profits threshold would also be applicable. The tax, accounting and pension contribution implications of such action are beyond the scope of this book but should also be considered.

It will be seen that George and Iris would be well-advised to have an agreement that George receives a partner's salary equivalent to his Post Office remuneration for the ensuing year and that only the remaining profits are then shared equally. Given such an agreement for 2016–17, George's profit share for Class 4 purposes will be £27,000 + ($^1/_2$ × £8,000) = £31,000 while Iriss share will be $^1/_2$ × £8,000 = £4,000. After deducting the lower annual limit, Iris would have had no Class 2 or Class 4 liability and George's liability would have been 9% on £22,940. George will then claim *Social Security (Contributions) Regulations 2001, SI 2001/1004, Reg 94A* relief of £27,000 and his liability will also be extinguished. Following *Social Security (Contributions) (Amendment No 7) Regulations 2003, SI 2003/2958* adding new *Reg 94A*, the problem arguably disappears without the need for any variation to the equal-share agreement. George's and Iris's Class 4 profits become $^1/_2$ × (£35,000 – £27,000) = £4,000 each and any Class 4 liability is eliminated by the lower annual profit limit of £8,060.

The 2010 case of *Uppal* highlights the absurdity of the treatment of subpostmasters as office holders rather than traders working under a contract for services with the Post Office. Mr and Mrs Uppal traded as partners in a retail business that housed the sub-post office, and Mrs Uppal ran the post office side of the business, but Mr Uppal was the named subpostmaster. When the Post Office closed the sub-post office, it paid £74,647 in compensation, which the partners shared equally. However, HMRC treated the whole payment as compensation for the termination of the office, allowed one £30,000 exemption and argued that the Post office had correctly taxed the balance under PAYE because it fell within *ITEPA 2003, s 401*. The FTT accepted that the whole of the payment was partnership property, and that half had been correctly received by Mrs Patel, but held nevertheless that the payment to her was by reason of the termination of her husband's office, so her half was taxable on him. NICs were not in point, since the whole amount was compensation rather than earnings, but the result was arguably wholly unfair.

Remuneration no longer treated as a trade receipt

[57.8] The concession (see HMRC Business Income Manual BIM66301) whereby the subpostmaster's income could be treated as a trade receipt, but only for income tax purposes, was withdrawn from 6 April 2017. As a consequence, the complications arising in computing profits subject to Class 4

NICs, described in preceding and subsequent paragraphs, should largely disappear since the subpostmaster's income will now be consistently treated as employment income and taxed at source.

On 21 April 2017, in an announcement published on its website, HMRC stated that the concession would be subject to a one-year 'grandfathering' provision until 5 April 2018 for those currently using the concession. No new users can take advantage of the concession.

The concession has been withdrawn owing to the new contracts being issued by the Post Office to subpostmaster's (see 57.3). HMRC expected that the new contracts would render the concession largely obsolete by April 2017.

Subpostmaster trading through a limited company

[57.9] Where a sub-post office is operated through the medium of a limited company, great difficulties may be encountered. At one time, a limited company could not itself be appointed by the Post Office as subpostmaster, so the normal procedure was (and continues to be in many cases still) for the company to nominate one of its directors or senior employees for the office. That individual is then appointed subpostmaster but holds the office as a nominee for the limited company. Although this procedure may not always apply nowadays where the sub-post office is operated by large multiples (see 57.5), the historical position still applies to smaller, local concerns and Post Office Ltd will still insist that a director be nominated to hold the office of subpostmaster. The rest of this section is concerned with such smaller companies only and does not apply in the case of large multiples (typically quoted companies) where no one has been appointed to hold that office.

Remuneration forming part of company profits

[57.10] Provided a subpostmaster is required by the company of which he is a director to hand over his Post Office remuneration to the company, and does in fact do so, the concessionary treatment accorded to subpostmasters who carry on trades will be extended to such nominee subpostmasters also. In practice, the Post Office will agree to pay the salary to the company as nominee for the individual and the company will request the issue of a NT PAYE code. Publication of this extended concession (which, it will be noted, does for nominee subpostmasters what Extra-Statutory Concession A37 does for nominee directors who are required to hand over their fees to a company — see **29.68** EARNINGS FROM EMPLOYMENT: GENERAL) was under consideration by the Inland Revenue as long ago as February 1986 but has not yet taken place.

The present position, then, is that a subpostmaster who is a director of a company to which he hands over his Post Office remuneration (or to which the Post Office pays the salary with a NT code) receives that remuneration without deduction of tax, and the remuneration forms part of the profits of the company for corporation tax purposes. That is unobjectionable from a taxation point of view but is a disastrous arrangement from a contribution point of view – see EIM68205.

The problem arises out of the requirement in law that primary and secondary Class 1 contributions must be accounted for on the Post Office remuneration paid to a subpostmaster, whether he is a nominee subpostmaster or not. (The legislation referred to at **29.68** EARNINGS FROM EMPLOYMENT: GENERAL which extinguishes Class 1 liabilities on fees handed over to a company by a nominee director, thus giving legal effect in the contribution field to HM Revenue and Customs Extra-Statutory Concession A37 (see also CA 28 Supplement April 1996) does not extend to nominee subpostmasters who hand over their Post Office remuneration to a company.) In consequence, Post Office remuneration taken into a company's trading account will already have suffered a charge to Class 1 contributions yet that remuneration will then, effectively, in whole or in part, be paid out by the company in the form of wages, salaries or directors' remuneration, all of which again attract primary and secondary Class 1 liabilities. Thus, the charge for both primary and secondary Class 1 contributions will frequently be wholly or partly duplicated unless the subpostmaster is a shareholder and can take dividends instead of salary.

Example

Jane is subpostmistress of Kwietspot but runs her business through Letterbox Ltd, a company in which J owns all the shares except for one which is owned by her mother. L's accounts for the year ended 31 March 2017 reveal profits of £40,000, which include J's Post Office remuneration of £30,000 but take no director's remuneration into account. Remuneration of £30,000 is then voted to J for the year, and the company profit is reduced to £10,000. In other words, J and L are, on the face of it, restored to the same positions they would each have occupied had J never brought her Post Office remuneration into the company. Yet that is far from the result. The £30,000 director's remuneration voted to J attracts a primary Class 1 contribution of £2,632.80, which J must suffer, and a secondary Class 1 contribution of £3,020.54, which L must suffer. J has, however, already suffered a primary Class 1 deduction of £2,632.80 at the hands of the Post Office when her Post Office remuneration was paid to her, and the Post Office has already suffered a secondary Class 1 contribution charge of £3,020.54 on that same remuneration. It is, of course, true that J will be able to recover primary Class 1 contributions which she has paid in excess of her personalised ANNUAL MAXIMUM 7 (in this case £4,613.92) for 2016 –17, but, even after recovery of £651.68, HM Revenue and Customs will, because of double counting, have obtained primary Class 1 contributions of £4,613.92 on earnings of £30,000 (a levy of 15.4%) and secondary Class 1 contributions of £6,041.08 on the same earnings (a 20.14% levy)! In other words, J will have paid £1,981.12 of unnecessary contributions and her company will have paid £3,020.54 of unnecessary contributions.

One apparent solution to the problem illustrated is to treat the Post Office remuneration introduced into the company as what, in law, it is: a loan to the company by the subpostmaster. Then, the 'director's remuneration' which would otherwise have been voted should be reduced by the amount of that loan with only the remainder (if any) being voted, the balance being treated as what, in law, it truly is: a repayment of the loan. But if that were to be done, the Post Office remuneration would escape the tax net (because Post Office Ltd is given a PAYE code of NT). Accordingly, in a case such as Jane's, the best solution to the problem might simply be for the subpostmaster to advise HM Revenue and Customs that he should be assessed to tax on his Post Office remuneration under *ITEPA 2003* and to keep his Post Office remuneration out of the company, although there may then be discussions about the fact that Post Office Ltd has paid a part of that sum free of NICs because it represents business expenses.

In the case of a large company with a number of sub-post offices and but a single nominee subpostmaster there *is* no solution, simple or otherwise. The only remedy in such a case — which, whilst technically correct, may be quite impracticable — is to re-arrange matters so that a different director is appointed subpostmaster of each sub-post office run by the company and for each such director to be selected on a basis which ensures that he becomes subpostmaster of a sub-post office which yields remuneration of a lesser amount than the director's remuneration he might be expected to receive. Post Office remuneration would then be left out of the company's account; each director/ subpostmaster would, by arrangement with HM Revenue and Customs, be assessed to tax on his Post Office remuneration under *ITEPA 2003*; and director's remuneration would be voted by the company only on a 'top-up' basis. HMRC states in ESM4400:

> Where a retail trade or business is carried on by a company from the same premises as a sub-post office, the Post Office salary is the income of the office holder and not of the company. In practice, however, no objection should be raised to a request to treat the Post Office salary as income of the company provided that the office holder is required to, and does, hand over this remuneration to the company.

It is understood that, following a determination by the Secretary of State for Social Security (reported in *National Federation of Self Employed and Small Businesses Press Release, 10 December 1984*), the then DSS permitted 'remuneration' paid to a subpostmaster by his company to be regarded (to the extent that it did not exceed Post Office fees introduced to the company by the subpostmaster) as a loan repayment and not as earnings liable to either primary or secondary Class 1 contributions, but only where the 'remuneration' had not been voted by the company in general meeting. Once voting had taken place, the amount voted would have acquired the quality of true remuneration (see **15.4** CLASS **1** CONTRIBUTIONS) and would have become earnings for contribution purposes, irrespective of the fact that its source might have been earnings already subjected to Class 1 contributions. However, this approach would appear to be prejudicial for income tax and corporation tax purposes.

Relief subpostmasters

[57.11] A relief subpostmaster will normally be regarded as an employee of the subpostmaster unless, by reference to the tests of employment status (see CATEGORISATION **14**), he is found to be a person who is in business on his own account as a relief subpostmaster. Those tests might generally be regarded as satisfied if the relief subpostmaster charges fees for providing relief cover for a number of sub-post offices and their associated businesses and for looking after the related property and contents, although HMRC has been known to argue that a relief subpostmaster is always acting under the close control of the subpostmaster and must follow Post Office procedures to the letter if he is to be accepted as a substitute by Post Office Ltd, which vets all such candidates for security purposes.

Key Points regarding subpostmasters and NICs

[57.12] Points to consider are as follows.

- Whilst the authorities in previous incarnations have proved difficult in the past, the Class 1 income can these days simply be deducted from profits measured for both Class 2 and Class 4 purposes.
- Withdrawal of ESC BIM66301 whereby a subpostmaster's employment income could be treated as a trading receipt.
- No deferment or other application is required; Class 2 and Class 4 reliefs are now claimed on the self-assessment tax return.
- Subject to overriding commercial concerns, from a purely National Insurance point of view the carrying on of a sub-Post Office through a limited company should be avoided unless the Post Office will appoint the company itself, rather than a shareholder/director, as the subpostmaster. In practice, the Post Office will only do this if the company is a large multiple, although this may change with the reforms following privatisation of the delivery service, and the restructuring under which all but community offices are expected to have a substantial retail operation onto which the sub-post office can simply be bolted. It makes little sense for the Post Office's franchise operations to be treated as if they were run by an employee of the Post Office, when the commercial reality is that the subpostmaster is an independent businessman who may incur losses on the Post Office business because of the way in which 'remuneration' has been restructured under the latest contracts.

58
Underwriters at Lloyd's

Cross-references. See ANNUAL MAXIMUM 7; CLASS 2 CONTRIBUTIONS 18; CLASS 4 CONTRIBUTIONS 20; DEFERMENT OF PAYMENT 27.

Other Sources. Simon's Taxes Volume 2, Para A8.310; HM Revenue and Customs Manuals — Lloyd's Underwriters and Lloyd's Market Bulletins.

Introduction to underwriters at Lloyd's

[58.1] At the start of 1997 the DSS Contributions Agency (now in HMRC's domain) confirmed their view that individuals who were external members of Lloyd's, ie non-working Names, are subject to Class 4 and Class 2 contributions on their Lloyd's profits where they exceed the appropriate thresholds. The NICs position for external individual Names is that Class 4 contributions have been due from the year 1997–98 onwards (when self-assessment commenced) and will be collected through the usual channels. Since most Names are now corporate entities, the policy is of limited application, since they can have no liability under Class 2 or Class 4. The remainder of this chapter refers to individuals who maintain their Lloyd's membership as individuals or members of a LLP.

Class 2

[58.2] Class 2 contributions have been due since 1 January 1997 unless the non-working Name:

- is abroad (by which HMRC presumably means ordinarily resident abroad – see below);
- is over pension age;
- has been granted the small earnings exception (pre-6 April 2015) or has profits below the small profits threshold (from 6 April 2015);
- is a married woman/widow with a reduced rate liability; or
- until 6 April 2015, had a deferment on account of other earnings.

The office to contact in connection with registration is: HM Revenue and Customs, NIC&EO Contact Centre, Customer Account Section, Longbenton, NE98 1ZZ. Tel 0300 200 3310. HMRC prefers 'customers' to register online and has closed its dedicated helplines for the newly self-employed. See **18.1** CLASS 2 CONTRIBUTIONS: SELF-EMPLOYED EARNERS.

Non-working Names

[58.3] The view adopted by the then CA is perhaps questionable but was never challenged. Most non-working Names might not consider that they are 'gainfully' employed as *Social Security Contributions and Benefits Act 1992, s 2(1)(b)* requires but, rather, making a passive investment.

HMRC indicated that from 6 April 2013 all sleeping partners would be liable to pay Class 2 and 4 NIC. This would appear consistent with their view that Names fell within the Class 2/4 regime before the *National Insurance Contributions Act 2015 (NICA 2015)* reform of Class 2, since non-working Names are members of one or more trading syndicates.

However the Class 2 liability has now been codified (if not exactly clarified) by the *NICA 2015* reform. Names, whether working or non-working, are clearly in business: *Social Security Contributions and Benefits Act 1992 (SSCBA 1992, s 122)* defines 'employment' (which encompasses any gainful work, rather than just work under a contract of employment) as including any 'trade, business, profession, office or vocation'.

Names are therefore self-employed earners for the purposes of the Act. *Social Security Contributions and Benefits Act 1992, s 11* as recast from 6 April 2015 applies to any person in employment as a self-employed earner in the tax year, and provides for compulsory Class 2 liability only if the earner has relevant profits (defined as Class 4 trading profits) above the small profits threshold (SPT). Eligibility to pay Class 2 contributions voluntarily arises if the self-employed earner has no such profits (be that because he has made a loss in his business or is merely in business without trading), or has trading profits below the SPT. A non-working Name will now at the very least be eligible to pay Class 2 contributions by virtue merely of being in business and, if profits exceed the SPT *and fall within Class 4 liability*, the Name will be liable to pay such contributions.

Assuming the Agency's view on the old provisions to be correct, their statement that Class 2 need not be paid if the Name was 'abroad' was equally highly questionable. If there was any 'gainful employment' as regards Lloyd's of London then it no less continued to take place in the UK irrespective of the fact that the Name was abroad on an extended holiday or working for some employer completely unconnected with underwriting activities. The residence and presence conditions for liability to Class 2 are set out in *Reg 145(1)(d)* and they dictate that liability will arise only if the earner is ordinarily resident in the UK or, if he is not so ordinarily resident, that before the period in respect of which any such contributions are to be paid he has been resident in the UK for a period of at least 26 out of the immediately preceding 52 contribution weeks. Class 4 liability arises only if the earner is resident in the UK at any time during the tax year. [*Regulation 91(b)*.] It is far from certain however that there is any Class 4 liability for any non-working Name.

At a joint Lloyd's and Inland Revenue seminar for Lloyd's Names in May 1997 the imposition of Class 4 NICs on Names was explained by the then Inland Revenue even though this was at that time within the ambit of the CA. It was stated that the CA had looked at the role of the managing agent in the *Gooda Walker* case and much store had been placed in Gibson LJ's comment that 'On general principles a principal who employs an agent to carry on a trade nevertheless owns and carries on that trade, even though the income received by the principal from it is not immediately derived from the carrying on by him of the trade'. See *Deeny and others v Gooda Walker Ltd (in voluntary liquidation) and others (IRC third party)* [1996] STC 39. The *obiter dictum* of Gibson LJ in this case was viewed by the CA as a peg on which to hang their Class 4 hat. See also *McBride v Blackburn* [2003] STC SCD 139 Sp C 356.

Interestingly, HMRC's Lloyd's manual has simply stated for many years that Class 4 liability is 'under review' (LLM 5430). It has always been open to question why the Lloyd's income of non-working names has to be *deemed* for 'all purposes of the Income Tax acts' (under FA 1993, s 180) to be immediately derived by him from carrying on that business if it is already earnings on basic principles, as HMRC claims in the context of NICs.

Tax return

[58.4] The SA103L (2016) Notes to the tax return (page LUN 8) give information on Class 4 NICs and says that for all Names (working or non-working Names), Class 4 must be paid unless the Name is 'excepted', ie, they are exempt or deferment applies, or the earner is over state pension age at the start of the year, or is not resident throughout the year. They used to also state that sometimes, where both Class 1 and Class 4 contributions are payable, the latter may be due only at the 2% additional rate because a deferment (see DEFERMENT OF PAYMENT 27) can operate until such time as the overall contributions may be determined. Only HM Revenue and Customs NIC&EO Deferment Services can agree to the deferment and for this application form CA 72B should be used. Where deferment of contributions is granted via the issue of certificate CA2703, box 64 should be marked with an 'X'. The notes now refer to the possibility of a reduced Class 2 liability where the Name is both employed and self-employed (ie, because of the annual maximum rules), but curiously no reference is made to the same rules potentially limiting or eliminating any Class 4 liability at the main rate. In the past, a Name might also have had Class 2 deferment if he or she already had UK employment income, but the *NICA 2015* reform of Class 2, which has moved Class 2 collection onto a retrospective basis, has removed the need for Class 2 deferment. Instead, the Box 63 tickbox now provides the route to opt to pay Class 2 voluntarily where the Name is not liable to pay (eg, because of losses).

In the case where the Name has incurred losses in previous years that have not been utilised against trading profits and are carried forward to the current year, the Class 4 NICs liability can be reduced by the amount of the loss that has been set off. Sideways loss relief for income tax purposes, against non-trading income, is disregarded for Class 4 purposes, and such losses are carried forward, for NIC purposes only, against future trading profits. See loss relief in **32.9** EARNINGS FROM SELF-EMPLOYMENT.

59

Volunteer Development Workers

Cross-references. See ANNUAL MAXIMUM **7**; CLASS 2 CONTRIBUTIONS **18**; LATE-PAID CONTRIBUTIONS **42**; OVERSEAS MATTERS **51**.

Other Sources. Simon's Taxes, Volume 2, para A8.315; former Leaflet NI 38; HM Revenue and Customs National Insurance Manual NIM34001–NIM34060.

Introduction on volunteer development workers and NICs

[59.1] At a meeting held on 25 and 26 June 1984, the EC Council called on EC Member States to take steps to encourage young people to participate in development projects organised by the EC beyond its frontiers, to bring together young Europeans who wish to work in developing countries, to support the creation of national committees of European volunteers for such development work, and to provide social protection for such volunteer development workers. (Council Recommendation 85/308 13 July 1985). One response of the UK Parliament was to bring into force the legislation described in this chapter. See HM Revenue and Customs National Insurance Manual NIM34001.

[*Social Security (Contributions) Regulations 2001, SI 2001/1004, Regs 149–154*].

Categorisation

[59.2] Any person who:

(a) is certified by HM Revenue and Customs as being a volunteer development worker, and

(b) is ordinarily resident in the United Kingdom (see **51.5** OVERSEAS MATTERS), and

(c) is employed outside the United Kingdom in circumstances under which no liability for Class 1 contributions arises in respect of his earnings,

is to be included in the category of self-employed earner for contribution purposes.

[*Social Security (Contributions) Regulations 2001, SI 2001/1004, Regs 149–150* as amended by *Social Security Contributions (Amendment No 3) Regulations 2002, SI 2002/2366, Reg 17, Reg 150*].

The effect of (c) above and *Social Security (Contributions) Regulations 2001, SI 2001/1004, Reg 146(1)(2)* is to exclude from this self-employed categorisation provision, for the first 52 weeks of his employment abroad, anyone who, though ordinarily resident in United Kingdom or Northern Ireland and certified as an overseas development worker, is gainfully employed overseas by an employer who has a place of business in the United Kingdom (see **51.8** OVERSEAS MATTERS).

HM Revenue and Customs National Insurance Manual NIM34015 used to list approved organisations, but the list has been 'under review' for several years. NIM34020 shows around 150 developing countries, although the list seems not entirely reliable, as the 'Federal Republic of Yugoslavia' was apparently added to it in January 2002, ten years after it was formed by Serbia and Montenegro, and it is still there, 12 years after it ceased to exist because Montenegro declared its independence.

Contribution liabilities and options

[59.3] Once a person is categorised as a self-employed earner, a liability to pay Class 2 contributions will arise, subject to the person fulfilling conditions of residence and presence in the United Kingdom (see **18.2** CLASS **2** CONTRIBUTIONS and **51.5** OVERSEAS MATTERS). A volunteer development worker who is so categorised is, however, excepted from normal Class 2 liability but is entitled to pay a Class 2 contribution, known as 'VDW Class 2', free from the normal constraints of residence and presence requirements, at a special rate for any contribution week during which he is ordinarily employed as a volunteer development worker (see **51.9** OVERSEAS MATTERS). See HM Revenue and Customs National Insurance Manual NIM34030. Before the reform of Class 2 on 6 April 2015, any self-employed earner would have had a liability to pay Class 2 contributions subject to making a small earnings exception claim. However, the legislation recognised that volunteer development workers should have an option rather than a liability to pay contributions, so a specific exception from liability to pay a Class 2 contribution was included in *Regulation 151(a)*. Following the reform, Class 2 *liability* (see *Social Security Contributions and Benefits Act 1992 (SSCBA 1992), s 11(2)*) arises only in respect of income that would be subject to Class 4 liability, ie, income from a trade or profession, and those deemed self-employed without trading income have been given the option of paying voluntarily (see *SSCBA 1992, s 11(6)*), so the specific exception was repealed as it had become otiose.

[*Social Security (Contributions) Regulations 2001, SI 2001/1004, Reg 151, Reg 152*].

The special weekly rate of the optional Class 2 contribution is calculated by applying a rate of 5% to the Lower Earnings Limit for the week concerned, ie in 2018–19, 5% × £116 = £5.80. [*Social Security (Contributions) Regulations 2001, SI 2001/1004, Regs 152(b)*.] Class 2 contributions paid at this special rate will, as in the case of SHARE FISHERMEN **56**, enable the contributor to acquire or maintain a contribution record on the basis of which he will be entitled to contributions-based jobseeker's allowance (unemployment benefit) and, in certain cases, industrial injuries benefit. See HM Revenue and Customs National Insurance Manual NIM34040.

[*Benefit Persons Abroad Regulations 1975, Reg 13B* as inserted by *Benefit Persons Abroad Amendment Regulations 1986, Reg 2*.]

The normal rules concerning method of, and time for, payment of Class 2 contributions and Class 3 contributions (see **21.47–21.48**) do not apply to volunteer development workers who wish to pay special Class 2 contributions. [*Social Security (Contributions) Regulations 2001, SI 2001/1004, Reg 152(d)*.] Instead, a volunteer development worker should complete a form CF 83 (now contained in online 'leaflet' NI 38) indicating that he wishes to pay special Class 2 contributions and he should give the completed form to the organisation through whom he has been recruited for work overseas. That organisation will then submit the form to the HM Revenue and Customs and will act as agent in paying special Class 2 contributions. Oddly, the application form asks for information about the monthly salary or weekly wage being paid to the worker, because HMRC allegedly 'needs' to know this, even though the wage is wholly irrelevant to the amount of contributions payable.

It should be noted that these special provisions are of no application to a volunteer development worker who is under a contract of service to an employer who has a place of business in the United Kingdom. Such a VDW will be an employed earner in accordance with the normal rules and, when he is sent overseas, his contribution liability (if any) will be determined in accordance with the rules set out at **51.9** OVERSEAS MATTERS. It is possible, however, to pay special Class 2 contributions after the expiry of any period during which there is a Class 1 liability.

Late-paid contributions

[59.4] The normal rules relating to the late payment of Class 2 contributions do not apply in the case of volunteer development workers [*Social Security (Contributions) Regulations 2001, SI 2001/1004, Reg 153(2)*]. Instead, a special Class 2 contribution paid by a volunteer development worker after the end of the tax year immediately following the tax year in which there falls the week to which the contribution relates is to be paid at the highest of all special Class 2 rates which have applied in the period from the week to which the contribution relates to the date of payment, unless the rate at the beginning and end of that period is the same.

[*Social Security (Contributions) Regulations 2001, SI 2001/1004, Reg 153(4)*].

A late paid contribution paid in the tax year in which there falls the week to which the contribution relates, or paid in the tax year immediately following, is payable at the special rate which applied for the week in question.

[*Social Security (Contributions) Regulations 2001, SI 2001/1004, Reg 153(1)(3)*].

Annual maximum

[59.5] In the case of a volunteer development worker, the ANNUAL MAXIMUM 7 which serves to limit the total amount of contributions payable for a year is reduced by the amount of any special Class 2 contributions which are paid in respect of that year. [*Social Security (Contributions) Regulations 2001, SI 2001/1004, Reg 152(c)*].

The effect of this is to ensure that, where contributions are paid in excess of the maximum, any return of contributions to him will consist entirely of contributions *other than* special Class 2 contributions, thus preserving any entitlement to contributions-based jobseeker's allowance (unemployment benefit) which those special Class 2 contributions have created.

Key Points regarding volunteer development workers

[59.6] Points to consider are as follows.

- Only those not liable to Class 1 contributions on basic principles can be considered for the special volunteer development worker treatment.
- Someone employed to work in a recognised developing country can be treated as self-employed and eligible for the volunteer development worker special Class 2 rate.
- The special Class 2 rate, unlike ordinary Class 2, also buys the right to contributions-based jobseeker's allowance.
- A NIC helpline is available for volunteer development workers: 0300 200 3500, or +44 191 203 7010 from abroad.

Table of Statutes

Paragraph references printed in **bold** type indicate where the Statute is set out in part or in full.

G

H

I

R

S

Table of Statutory Instruments

Paragraph references printed in **bold** type indicate where the Statutory Instruments is set out in part or in full

T

U

V

W

Table of Cases

A

B

C

D

E

F

G

H

I

J

K

M

N

O

P

Q

R

S

T

Y

Decisions of the European Court of Justice are listed below numerically. These decisions are also included in the preceding alphabetical list.

Table of Published Decisions

Index

C

F

G

H

M

O

U

V

Twelve-year Summary of Rates and Limits

The table on the following pages shows the twelve-year summary of NIC rates and limits.

The paragraph numbers in the table correspond to paragraphs in the text. See those paragraphs for further details.

2007–08	2008–09	2009–10	2010–11	2011–12	2012–13	2013–14	2014–15	2015–16	2016–17	2017–18	2018–19
CLASS 2 CONTRIBUTION RATES AND LIMITS: Normal weekly rate (see **18.6**)											
£2.20	£2.30	£2.40	£2.40	£2.50	£2.65	£2.70	£2.75	£2.80	£2.80	£2.85	£2.95
Share fisherman's special rate (see **56.4**)											
£2.85	£2.95	£3.05	£3.05	£3.15	£3.30	£3.35	£3.40	£3.45	£3.45	£3.50	£3.60
Volunteer development worker's special rate (see **59.3**)											
£4.35	£4.50	£4.75	£4.85	£5.10	£5.35	£5.45	£5.55	£5.60	£5.60	£5.65	£5.80
Small earnings exception limit/small profits threshold (see **18.4**)											
£4,635	£4,825	£5,075	£5,075	£5,315	£5,595	£5,725	£5,885	£5,965	£5,965	£6,025	£6,205
CLASS 3 CONTRIBUTION RATES: Normal rate (see 19.8)											
£7.80	£8.10	£12.05	£12.05	£12.60	£13.25	£13.55	£13.90	£14.10	£14.10	£14.25	£14.65
CLASS 4 CONTRIBUTION RATES AND LIMITS											
Lower annual limit (see **20.9**)											
£5,225	£5,435	£5,715	£5,715	£7,225	£7,605	£7,755	£7,956	£8,060	£8,060	£8,164	£8,424
Upper annual limit (see **20.9**)											
£34,840	£40,040	£43,875	£43,875	£42,475	£42,475	£41,450	£41,865	£42,385	£43,000	£45,000	£46,350
Rate up to the upper annual limit (see **20.9**)											
8.00%	8.00%	8.00%	8.00%	9.00%	9.00%	9.00%	9.00%	9.00%	9.00%	9.00%	9.00%
Rate above the upper annual limit (see **20.9**)											
1.00%	1.00%	1.00%	1.00%	2.00%	2.00%	2.00%	2.00%	2.00%	2.00%	2.00%	2.00%
Limiting amount♯ (see **7.5**)											
£2,485.80	£2,890.30	£3,180.00	£3,180.00	£3,305.00	£3,278.75	£3,175.65	£3,197.56	£3,237.65	£3,293.00	£3,466.29	£3,569.69
Share fisherman's limiting amount♯ (see **7.4**)											
£2,520.25	£2,924.75	£3,214.45	£3,214.45	£3,339.45	£3,313.20	£3,201.10	£3,232.01	£3,272.10	£3,327.45	£3,500.74	£3,604.14
CLASS 1, 2, AND 4 LIMITING AMOUNT											
Annual maximum♯ (see **7.1**)											
£3,323.10	£3,876.95	£4,279.22	£4,279.22	£4,312.08	£4,267.56	£4,121.28	£4,146.72	£4,197.60	£4,273.92	£4,509.24	£4,642.80
SSP, SMP, SPP and SAP RECOVERY											
Statutory Sick Pay (see **15.13**)											
*	*	*	*	*	*	*	*	*	0%	0%	0%

2007–08	2008–09	2009–10	2010–11	2011–12	2012–13	2013–14	2014–15	2015–16	2016–17	2017–18	2018–19
Statutory Maternity Pay etc (see **15.14**)											
92%	92%	92%	92%	92%	92%	92%	92%	92%	92%	92%	92%
Higher Rate§											
104.50%	104.50%	104.50%	104.50%	103.00%	103.00%	103.00%	103.00%	103.00%	103.00%	103.00%	103.000%

♯ THESE FIGURES SHOULD BE USED WITH EXTREME CARE AS FURTHER ADJUSTMENT IS REQUIRED FOR THE ADDITIONAL RATE (1% FROM 2003–04, 2% FROM 2011–12 – see 7 ANNUAL MAXIMUM)

* Recovery determined by the Percentage Threshold Scheme until 5 April 2014

§ **Only** if small employer's relief applies, otherwise 92%

SPT replaced SEE from 6 April 2015